INVESTMENTS

Second Edition

Keith Cuthbertson
and
Dirk Nitzsche

JOHN WILEY & SONS, LTD

Copyright © 2008   John Wiley & Sons, Ltd
                    The Atrium, Southern Gate, Chichester,
                    West Sussex PO19 8SQ, England
                    Telephone +44 (0) 1243 779777

First edition published 2001 © John Wiley & Sons, Ltd.

Email (for orders and customer service enquiries): cs-books@wiley.co.uk
Visit our Home Page on www.wiley.com

Reprinted November 2011

Other Wiley Editorial Offices

John Wiley & Sons Inc., 111 River Street, Hoboken, NJ 07030, USA

Jossey-Bass, 989 Market Street, San Francisco, CA 94103-1741, USA

Wiley-VCH Verlag GmbH, Boschstr. 12, D-69469 Weinheim, Germany

John Wiley & Sons Australia Ltd, 42 McDougall Street, Milton, Queensland 4064, Australia

John Wiley & Sons (Asia) Pte Ltd, 2 Clementi Loop #02-01, Jin Xing Distripark, Singapore 129809

John Wiley & Sons Canada Ltd, 6045 Freemont Blvd, Mississauga, ONT, L5R 4J3

Wiley also publishes its books in a variety of electronic formats. Some content that appears in print may not be
available in electronic books.

Library of Congress Cataloging-in-Publication Data

Cuthbertson, Keith.
    Investments / Keith Cuthbertson and Dirk
Nitzsche. — 2nd ed.
        p. cm.
    Includes bibliographical references and index.
    ISBN 978-0-470-51956-1 (pbk. : alk. paper)
  1. Derivative securities. 2. Investment analysis. I. Nitzsche, Dirk.
  II. Title.
    HG6024.A3C883 2008
    332.64'57—dc22
                                                    2008002731

A catalogue record for this book is available from the British Library

ISBN: 9780470519561 (P/B)
Typeset by Thomson Digital, India
Printed and bound in Great Britain by Scotprint, Haddington, East Lothian

This book is printed on acid-free paper.

Contents

PART 3: ASSET RETURNS AND PORTFOLIO THEORY

PART 4: EQUITY MARKETS

PART 5: FOREIGN EXCHANGE MARKET

PART 6: FIXED-INCOME MARKETS

Preface

You may remember the rookie football player in the movie *Jerry Maguire* screaming 'Show me the money! Show me the money!' at his eponymous agent (played by Tom Cruise). Well this phrase certainly sums up a key motivation for this book, although as the reader will discover, the methods needed to make money and then protect its value can involve quite subtle strategies. Sure, you can make and lose (usually other people's) money in financial centres such as London, New York, Tokyo and Hong Kong without having much technical knowledge. But the majority of well-paid jobs today in banking and finance, particularly as you rise up the corporate ladder, require a clear understanding of basic theoretical ideas and how these translate into real world decisions.

Some financial decisions are rather complex and may involve risking vast sums of money. One only has to think of the losses of Orange County, Metallgesellschaft, Nick Leeson of Barings, Professors Scholes and Merton at Long Term Capital Management, John Rusnak at Allied Irish Bank and Jérôme Kerviel at Société Générale – and there are others we could cite.

The material in the second edition of this book has been tried and tested primarily on students taking MBA and MSc finance courses at Tanaka Business School (Imperial College), CASS Business School in the City of London and professional courses in the City at banks, mutual funds, actuaries and legal firms. Our 'consumers' pay 'serious money' and for the most part are not interested in theories solely for their elegance but for their applicability to real world issues. Keat's dictum in *Ode on a Grecian Urn* that "Beauty is Truth, Truth Beauty – that is all ye know on earth and all ye need to know", has not been embraced 100% by the people we have met.

This book is aimed at final year undergraduates in finance and business studies, and core courses for MBA and MSc finance students, as well as those undertaking professional qualifications in the finance sector. No prior knowledge of math or stats is assumed beyond that in a first-year undergraduate 'quants for business studies' course and basic material in math and stats is provided on the web site for the book.

After completing a one- or two-semester course based on this text, the student can then deepen their knowledge of financial markets by reading our companion text *Financial Engineering: Derivatives and Risk Management*, also published by John Wiley & Sons, Ltd.

OVERVIEW

A key aim of the book is to take basic concepts from finance and to demonstrate how these can be used to understand real world practical issues facing investors, firms and regulators. The book covers the following broad themes:

- **Behaviour in financial markets**, including the pricing of risky assets and alternative investment strategies practised by proprietary trading desks of investment banks, mutual and hedge funds and private equity. The use of derivatives in speculation, hedging and in providing insurance for corporates and banks is also analysed in detail.
- **Decisions in corporate finance** such as raising capital, the valuation of firms and investment projects, creating shareholder value and hedging business and financial risk.
- **Non-traditional approaches.** Here we include 'behavioural finance', chaos theory, anomalies, volatility and bubbles. We also examine the behaviour of chartists and momentum traders and the use of technical analysis, candlestick charts and more technical methods such as artificial neutral networks for predicting asset prices.
- **Practical aspects used 'On the Street'**, these include activities such as short selling, 'haircuts' and margins, bid-ask spreads, price quotes and interpreting information in the financial press such as the *Financial Times* and *Wall Street Journal*. We emphasise the limitations of some 'textbook models' (e.g. mean-variance portfolio allocation) and therefore include a discussion of the home bias problem, hedging foreign currency receipts, model error and sensitivity analysis. Speculative strategies in stock, bond and spot-FX markets are also examined including momentum, value-growth and P-E ratio analysis. Hedging corporate risk using recently established energy and weather derivative contracts is also analysed.
- **Accessible style.** Given the heterogeneous academic backgrounds of students on many MBA and MSc finance courses we do not shy away from occasionally using contemporary analogies to reinforce theoretical ideas. Take for example, Mr Vincent Vega in the opening shot of the film *Pulp Fiction,* where he is talking to his partner Jules about his recent trip to Amsterdam. Are you aware that in discussing the relative merits of a Big Mac in L.A. and a Big Mac in Amsterdam, Vincent was imparting important information on the difficulties in testing purchasing power parity? Although the primary aim of Vincent's visit seems to have been a mixture of international portfolio diversification and risky arbitrage with illegal substances. You will meet more of these analogies in the text (and even more if you attend our lectures).

CHANGES TO SECOND EDITION

We have re-written and re-organised nearly all the chapters to emphasise practical issues, particularly on valuation and risk analyses. Part 1 (Chapters 1–5) provides an overview of markets, players and financial instruments. Part 2 (Chapters 6–8) covers valuation techniques applied to the firm and the choice of discount rates. Part 3 (Chapters 9–13) introduces the concepts required to understand international portfolio allocation, including strategic and tactical allocation and the practical limitations of standard textbook approaches. This section also covers asset pricing models such as the CAPM and APT. Part 4 (Chapters 14–17) covers all aspects of equity market investment including stock valuation and the EMH, as well as behavioural finance and technical trading. Part 5 (Chapter 18) covers the foreign exchange market, including covered and uncovered interest parity as well as purchasing power parity. Part 6 (Chapters 19–22) discusses fixed income markets including money and bond markets, the term structure of interest rates and bond market strategies. Part 7 (Chapters 23–27) covers forwards, futures, swaps and options, including energy and weather derivatives. Part 8 (Chapters 28–31) provides an analysis of portfolio management as practised by mutual funds, hedge funds and private equity and also discusses methods of measuring the risk of the assets held by banks and investment companies.

ACKNOWLEDGEMENTS

Thanks go to many people, particularly our ex-colleagues at Tanaka Business School (Imperial Collage) and our current colleagues at CASS Business School in the City. Our thanks also go to our current and past MBA and MSc students and finance practitioners on Executive Education courses and the friendly people at John Wiley.

STUDENT LEARNING

The text includes aims and a summary for each chapter, worked examples, end-of-chapter questions, technical appendices and glossary of terms, and a list of symbols and abbreviations used. Separate case study 'boxes' highlight the following three broad objectives:

- **Linking theoretical ideas to 'real world' issues using case studies** – such as Collateralised Debt Obligations (CDOs), Islamic bonds (*Sukuk*), immunisation of pension liabilities, strategic and tactical asset allocation, momentum and value-growth strategies, valuation of Internet stocks, the Yen carry trade and weather derivatives such as the spark spread swap.
- **Public policy issues** – the sub-prime crisis, Nick Leeson and the collapse of Barings Bank, the losses at Orange County on bond derivatives, hedge funds and the collapse of Long Term Capital Management, the losses by the trader Jérôme Kerviel at Société Générale, carbon trading and the growth of private equity.
- **Finance can be Fun** – this includes a mini 'soap opera' of the amorous relationship between Barbie and Ken and how derivatives can help the course of true love. The 'Big Mac index', 'Bowie Bonds', 'Ying and Yen', 'Are Casinos a Risky Business?', 'Private Equity People', 'Superman and Hedge Funds', 'Options Я Us' and 'Noble Pursuits' also fall under this heading.

---

114   COST OF CAPITAL

CASE STUDY 7.2   DIFFERENT LINES OF BUSINESS

The market return is supposed to represent all the systematic economic risk factors (e.g. due to changes in interest rates, exchange rates and the economic cycle) that affect the business risk of *all* firms and the firm's beta represents that firm's sensitivity to changes in these economic fundamentals. So far we have assumed that the project or the firm itself is involved in one fairly homogeneous type of business (e.g. restaurants, retail goods, car manufacturing). But how can we calculate beta for a multiproduct firm? Suppose a firm has 25% of its sales revenue from retail goods and 75% from running hotels. Then the firm's overall beta would be calculated as:

$$\beta_{firm} = 0.25\beta_{retail} + 0.75\beta_{hotel}$$

and we would have to obtain the two betas either based on our own time series data from comparable firms in these two sectors, or we could 'purchase' the beta estimates from a specialist firm (e.g. investment bank or broker). Here we used weights based on sales because it is sensible and easy to determine, but other possibilities include weights based on the firm's operating assets used in these two business sectors.

However, there is not a great deal of advantage to be had here. If the firm has a relatively stable payout ratio *and* earnings yield, then this implies that the dividend yield will also be fairly stable – so you may as well go straight to the data for the dividend yield. If either the earnings yield or the payout ratio is highly variable, then you are no further forward: taking an average of either ratio is likely to highly imprecise and therefore so will be your estimate of the long-run dividend–price ratio. If things move around a lot then estimates of averages will always be imprecise; of course more data helps, but you may require an awful lot of data to get an accurate estimate. Sure, some things in life are free, but mostly they are uncertain.

Estimating the constant growth rate of cash flows to use in [3] can be based on historical average growth rates of cash flows (profits) for the firm or for the industry, but estimates obtained by different methods might vary widely (e.g. an average of the last five years or the last ten years), so our forecast of R_g using the above equation is also subject to error.

In addition, it is worth mentioning that an estimate of the *equity premium* can be obtained using equation [3], where the dividend yield is for all the firms in the S&P 500 and the growth rate g used will probably be taken to be the historical long-run growth rate for the whole economy. This forecast for $R_m = Div/P + g$ can then be used in the CAPM equation [2] to give an estimate of the cost of equity finance for the firm, R_S.

As you can see, estimating the cost of equity capital is as much a science as an art, but clearly the cost of equity for the firm should exceed the risk-free rate. Use of the CAPM – possibly in conjunction with equation [3] to forecast the equity premium – at least provides a useful starting point to pin down this elusive number.

---

336   BEHAVIOURAL FINANCE AND ANOMALIES

SUMMARY

- Some behavioural finance ideas are consistent with the 'no free lunch' proposition; that is, returns are not easy to predict and you cannot make money from repeated gambles after taking account of risk and transaction costs. However, 'no free lunch' does not necessarily imply that 'the price is right' (i.e. that price equals fair value).
- Evidence from psychological studies is used in the behavioural finance approach to explain anomalies such as value-growth and momentum strategies and the behaviour of the discount on closed-end funds.
- The anomalies literature has unearthed many potential cases where abnormal profits may be made. In many cases, strategies for beating the market (e.g. weekend and January effects, value-growth and momentum strategies) require the investor to hold risky positions, and it is still much debated whether such profits would survive transaction costs and adjustments for perceived risks by investors.
- Other anomalies (e.g. ADRs, twin shares, index effect, closed-end funds) seem to persist and involve little risk, so here the empirical evidence gives stronger support to the behavioural finance view.
- There do appear to be some anomalies that are genuinely exploitable by well-informed traders, but they are difficult to detect and may disappear once enough traders recognise the anomaly and try to exploit it.

EXERCISES

Q1   How would you define a 'noise trader' and a 'smart-money' (or 'rational') trader?

Q2   Can noise traders outperform smart-money traders and hence survive in the market?

Q3   How might the interactions of noise traders and smart-money traders lead to mispriced shares?

Q4   Name one stock-market anomaly that you believe provides a profitable trading strategy.

Q5   At the end of 1999 and in the first three months of 2000, certain dot-com companies were being floated for hundreds of millions of dollars even though they had only been trading for a few years, had very small turnover (e.g. $1m p.a.) and had not yet shown a profit. Is this rational or a classic example of noise traders causing a stock-market bubble?

Q6   Can noise-trader behaviour explain the discounts found on closed-end funds (investment trusts in the UK)?

Q7   What is loss aversion?

WEB SITE

Accompanying resources can be found on the book's web site, indicated by icons in the margin. **www.wileyeurope.com/college/cuthbertson.**

The **Student** web site hosts the following resources:

 Download Excel 'hands-on' software reproducing the tables in the text. These Excel files are 'cell based' so the student can clearly see the methods used and directly relate these to material in the text (e.g. pricing a bond using spot rates, calculating the yield to maturity, forward rates, etc.). Interactive user inputs and graphical results also aid comprehension (e.g. price yield relationship for bonds, Black–Scholes equation for the option price-stock price relationship).

 Useful linked web sites for further financial information on a wide variety of topic areas (e.g. futures and options exchanges, central banks, financial regulators, Internet share dealers and general investment information services).

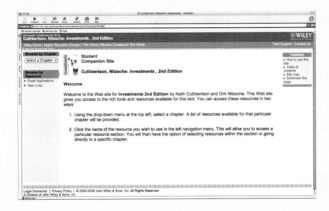

The web site hosts for **Lecturers** hosts the following resources:

- All figures and tables in the text (for use in WORD or Powerpoint).
- A set of Powerpoint slides for complete lectures, which can then be customised.
- Answers to end-of-chapter questions from the text.

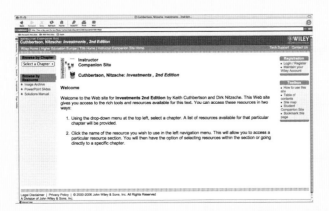

List of Symbols and Abbreviations

$f(.)$	Function (of a set of variables)
a	Number of days in the year (for day count convention of money market instruments)
Aaa, Aa, A, Baa, etc.	Moody's Corporate Bond Ratings
AAA, AA, A, BBB, etc.	Standard & Poor's Corporate Bond Ratings
AR	Abnormal return (on a stock) or appraisal ratio
AAR	Annual abnormal returns
ADR	American depository receipts
AI	Accrued interest
AIM	Alternative investment market (UK)
AMEX	American Stock Exchange
ANN	Artificial neural network
APT	Arbitrage pricing theory
APV	Adjusted present value
ARCH	Autoregressive conditional heteroscedasticity
AV	Abandonment value
B	$-value of debt of a firm
BBA	British Bankers Association
BDT	Black–Derman–Toy model for pricing interest rate derivatives
BF	Value of a floating rate bond (as one leg of an interest rate swap contract)
BIS	Bank for International Settlements
BOPM	Binomial option pricing model
BMV	Ratio of the book value of asset to the market value of assets
B–S	Black–Scholes option pricing model
BX	Value of a fixed rate bond (as in the fixed leg of a swap contract)
C	Price of call (call premium) or coupon (interest) payment on a bond
$C(S, T, K, r, \sigma)$	Price of call option given the spot price of the underlying asset S, time to maturity T, strike price K, risk-free rate r and volatility (standard deviation), σ of the underlying asset return
C	Correlation matrix (for value at risk calculations)
CAL	Capital Allocation Line

CAPM	Capital Asset Pricing Model
CAR	Cumulative abnormal return (on a stock)
CBOT	Chicago Board of Trade
CC	Cost of carry (for futures contract)
CD	Certificate of deposit
CDD	Cooling Degree Days (on a weather derivative)
CDO	Collateralised Debt Obligation
CF	Conversion factor used for T-bond futures
CF_i (FCF_i)	Cash flows (Free cash flows) in period i
CFTC	Commodity futures trading commission
CIP	Covered Interest Parity
CME	Chicago Mercantile Exchange
CML	Capital market line
CMR	Cumulative mortality rate
CP	Commercial paper
cp_T	(Coupon) swap rate at maturity of a swaption
CTD	Cheapest to deliver (bond)
CV	'Continuing value' of a firm
C-VaR	Credit value at risk
D	Duration of a bond or 'dollar discount' for money market assets or dividends paid (on a stock)
DCF	Discounted cash flow
DDM	Dividend discount model
DPV	Discounted present value
dz	Standard Wiener process
E	Shareholder equity capital or company earnings per share
E^*	Expected value in a risk neutral world
EAR	Equity (total) assets ratio
EBITDA	Earnings before interest, tax and depreciation and amortisation
EDF	Expected default frequency
EFP	Exchange of futures for physicals (on a commodity derivative)
EH	Expectations hypothesis of the term structure of interest rates
EMH	Efficient markets hypothesis
ERM	Exchange Rate Mechanism
ECB	European Central Bank
Er_{12}	Expected interest rate between the end of year-1 and the end of year-2
ETF	Exchange traded funds
EWMA	Exponentially weighted moving average forecasting scheme
ER	Expected value of the return R, on an asset
F	Futures/forward price (e.g. forward rate for foreign exchange)
f	Logarithm of the forward rate for foreign exchange ($f = \ln(F)$)
f_{12}	Forward interest rate which applies to an investment between the end of year-1 and the end of year-2
f_c	Continuously compounded forward rate of interest
FDIC	Federal Deposit Insurance Corporation
FRA	Forward rate agreement

FRN	Floating rate note
FRU	Forward rate unbiasedness
FSA	Financial Services Authority
FT	*Financial Times*
FV	Face value (e.g. of a bond or T-bill)
FVF	Face value of one futures contract
TVS	Total value of spot position in an asset
FX	Foreign exchange
g	Growth rate of dividends or earnings
GARCH	Generalised ARCH model
GBM	Geometric Brownian motion
GDR	Global depository receipts
h	Hedge ratio
HDD	Heating degree days (on a weather derivative)
HML	High minus low. The return on stocks of companies with high book-to-market value BMV minus the return on stocks of companies with low BMV
HPR	Holding period return
ICE	International Commodities Exchange (London)
IMF	International Monetary Fund
IMM	International Money Market of the Chicago Mercantile Exchange, CME
IO	Interest only strips (on MBS)
IPO	Initial public offering
IR	Information ratio (for performance of a portfolio)
IRR	Internal rate of return
J	Size of the jump, in a jump diffusion process
K	Strike price of an option
k	Number of 'up' movements in BOPM
KC	Capital cost (of a physical investment project)
LBO	Leveraged buyout
LIBID	London Interbank Bid Rate
LIBOR	London Interbank Offer Rate
LIFFE	London International Financial Futures Exchange (now superseded by NYSE-EURONEXT)
M	Maturity value (of a bond or T-bill)
m	Number of days until an investment matures (for day count convention of money market instruments) or number of payments per year in a swap.
MA	Moving average
MBO	Management buyout
MBS	Mortgage-backed security
MCS	Monte Carlo simulation
MD	Modified duration
MMR	Marginal mortality rate
MPC	Monetary Policy Committee
MSD	Marginal standard deviation
M^2	The 'M-squared' measure of performance of a portfolio

NASDAQ	National Association of Securities Dealers Automated Quotation System
NAV	Net asset value (of the assets of a mutual fund)
$N(\mu, \sigma)$	'Normal' probability distribution with population mean μ and standard deviation σ
N_f	Number of futures contracts
NPV	Net present value
NYMEX	New York Mercantile Exchange
NYSE	New York Stock Exchange
OBS	Off balance sheet
OCC	Options Clearing Corporation
OTC	Over-the-counter
P	Price of an asset (e.g. stock or bond), price of put option (put premium) or price index of goods and services
$P(S, T, K, r, \sigma)$	Price of put option (put premium), given the spot price of the underlying asset S, time to maturity T, strike price K, risk-free rate r and volatility (standard deviation), σ of the underlying asset return
P&L	Profit and loss figures
PDE	Partial differential equation
P-E, P/E	Price to earnings ratio (of a stock/firm)
PI	Profitability index
p_i	Probability of outcome i
PO	Principal only strips (in a MBS)
PPP	Purchasing power parity
PSBR	Public sector borrowing requirement
PV	Present value
q	Risk neutral probability (in the BOPM)
Q	Notional principal value (e.g. par value in a swap agreement)
Q_f	Quoted index price of futures contract
R_t	Return (%) on an asset (i.e. capital gain + per period cash flow) or the rate of interest (yield) on a long-term government bond
$\overline{R}$	Arithmetic mean return on an asset
R&D	Research and development
Repo	A sale and repurchase agreement. A means of collateralised borrowing. The sale of securities with an agreement to purchase the securities back at a slightly higher price – this results in a known fixed interest rate for borrowing funds. The counterparty is said to undertake a *reverse repo*
r_t	Nominal (risk-free) spot rate of interest between today ($t = 0$) and time t
RAR	Risk adjusted asset ratio
R_c	Continuously compounded return on an asset
r_{corp}	Interest rate charged by a bank to a corporation
RE	Rational expectations or retained earnings (per share)
REITS	Real Estate Investment Trust
R_m	Return on the market portfolio of assets

RMSE	Root mean squared error
RNV	Risk neutral valuation
ROC	Return on (total) capital employed
ROE	Return on equity capital
rp	risk premium (on a stock)
rr	Real return on an asset (i.e. the nominal return less the rate of price inflation)
RSI	Relative strength index
Er_{12}	Forecast (or expected value) of the 'short-term' interest rate between the end of year-1 and the end of year-2
S	Current (spot) price of an asset (e.g. stock price, exchange rate) or the total value of the equity (of a firm)
S&L	Savings and Loans: financial institutions in the USA who lend mainly mortgages
$s^2, \hat{\sigma}^2$	Sample variance
S_{BE}	Breakeven share price
SEC	Securities and Exchange Commission
SMB	Small minus big (the return on small company stocks less the return on stocks of large companies)
SR	Sharpe ratio for a portfolio. It is the expected excess return divided by the standard deviation of portfolio returns
SIM	Single index model
SIO	Stock index option
SML	Security market line
Sp	Interest rate credit spread
T_n	Term premium on an government bond with n-years to maturity
T	Time to expiration/maturity of a derivatives contract or total tax payments
t	Marginal tax rate
TR	Treynor ratio. The ratio of expected excess return to the asset's beta
TV	Terminal value of a stream of cash flows
U	Utility
UIP	Uncovered interest parity
USD	US dollars (Swift code)
UU, UD, DD, etc.	Movements in a decision tree or lattice, where U indicates an 'up' move and D refers to a 'down' move
V	Value of an asset/portfolio/firm
VAR	Vector autoregressive system of equations
VaR	Value at risk
WACC	Weighted average cost of capital
WC	Working capital
WCS	Worse case scenario
w_i	Weight of asset-i in a portfolio of many assets
YTM	Yield to maturity (on a bond)
y	Yield, yield to maturity (i.e. the internal rate of return on a bond) or the convenience yield on a commodity

y_f	Settlement yield on futures contract
z	\$-value of one index point (on a derivatives contract)
Δ	Delta of an option (or discrete change in a variable)
Γ	Gamma of an option
Λ	Vega of an option
θ	Theta of an option
α	'Alpha'. The intercept in a linear regression model of (excess) asset returns on a set of 'factors'. Alpha measures the abnormal return (i.e. return adjusted for risk) on the asset/portfolio. If the single factor used is the excess market return then it is known as 'Jensen's alpha'
β	The slope in a linear regression model. Beta of asset i, beta of futures, beta of portfolio
d_i	Discount rate $d_i = (1 + r)^{-i}$
ε_{it}	Specific risk of asset-i at time t
χ	Convexity of a bond or the dollar cost-of-carry for a futures contract
μ	Expected value of a variable (e.g. the true or population mean return on a stock)
π	Rate of inflation (of goods and services)
ρ	Correlation coefficient or the 'rho' which measures the change in value of an option per unit of time (to maturity)
$\sigma, \sigma(R)$	(Population) standard deviation or volatility in asset returns (σ^2 = variance)
$\sigma_{ij}, \sigma(R_i, R_j), \text{cov}(R_i, R_j)$	Covariance between the return on asset-i and the return on asset-j

PART 1

FINANCIAL MARKETS

Markets and Players

AIMS

- To discuss the key players in financial markets.
- To introduce the concept of fair value and the efficient markets hypothesis.
- To examine the role played by arbitrageurs, speculators and hedgers.
- To introduce market risk and credit risk.

INTRODUCTION

The real wealth of the economy is in tangible assets such as land, buildings and machinery and the human capital that can help produce goods and services in the future. Financial markets and institutions channel funds to where they are likely to be most productive – they facilitate the process of real investment by moving funds between surplus and deficit units, which may be individuals, firms or the government.

Finance is the antithesis of Polonius's advice to his son, in Shakespeare's *Hamlet*, of 'neither a borrower or lender be'. Individuals benefit from consuming goods and services, which are primarily produced by firms but also by the government sector (e.g. education, health and transport facilities in many countries). To produce 'goods', firms and the government often have to finance additional capital investment expenditures by borrowing funds. In general, individuals (as a group) are net savers and are in a position to lend funds, while firms are net borrowers; the government may either be a net borrower or a net lender.

Just as there are a wide variety of goods to purchase, there are also a wide variety of methods of borrowing and lending money, to suit the preferences of different individuals and institutions. When you 'walk around' alternative supermarkets, department stores and the Internet, you face a bewildering array of merchandise. Some sellers try as far as possible to cater for the 'mass market' (e.g. Wal-Mart, Marks & Spencer), others cater for more idiosyncratic tastes and styles (e.g. Jean-Paul Gaultier, Versace), while some sell rather shoddy goods. (There are no examples we can name here, because of possible litigation – but you will have your favourites.) Similarly, the markets for funds cater both for the relatively homogeneous 'mass market' but also try to tailor 'products' to individual requirements.

Brand names and reputation effect can be important, when selling goods and also when providing financial services and trading assets. 'Brand names', like the London Stock Exchange, the New York Stock Exchange (NYSE) and the Chicago Board of Trade, as well as financial intermediaries such as Merrill Lynch, Morgan Stanley, Citigroup, Salomon Brothers, Goldman Sachs and so on, are key institutions in transferring funds between different 'players' in the financial marketplace. The financial services of some providers have a good reputation, while some other financial products are on a par with 'shoddy goods' – junk bonds or bonds of certain emerging economies come to mind here. But that's not to say that these do not provide 'value for money' – they may be 'high risk', but they may also provide high returns to compensate for such risk.

All of the issues discussed in this opening chapter will be considered in greater depth in subsequent chapters. Nevertheless, we think it is useful to try to take in some of the 'big picture' before getting immersed in the finer details of the plethora of financial instruments and players in today's modern economies.

1.1 MARKETS

Financial markets facilitate the exchange of financial instruments such as stocks, bills and bonds, foreign exchange, futures, options and swaps. These assets are the means by which 'claims' are transferred from one party to another. Frequently, financial assets involve delayed receipts or payments and they therefore also transfer funds across time (e.g. if you purchase a bond you hand over cash today, but the payouts from the bond occur over many future periods).

Financial instruments are generally referred to as securities. Securities differ in the timing of payments, whether they can be readily sold prior to maturity in a secondary liquid market (e.g. via the stock exchange) and in the legal obligations associated with each security (e.g. bondholders must be paid before equityholders). Many securities are ***readily negotiable claims***. *Readily negotiable* means that the owner of the security may sell it quickly and with low transaction costs; then the market is said to be ***liquid***.

Some financial instruments (e.g. stocks and bonds) derive their value purely on the basis of the future performance of the issuer (e.g. the firm). A financial instrument has no intrinsic value – it is usually a piece of paper or an entry in a register. In an extreme case, if the issuer ceases to make payments on the instrument (i.e. the issuer *defaults*), the instrument may become worthless.

Other financial instruments known as **derivatives** (i.e. forwards, futures, options, swaps) have value because their payoff depends on the price of other financial assets (e.g. stocks, bonds) or real assets (e.g. oil, silver, agricultural products).

Trading in financial instruments may take place face to face, for example pit trading on the NYSE and trading in futures contracts on the Chicago Mercantile Exchange (CME). Trading in some markets takes place via telephone with the aid of computers to track prices (e.g. the foreign exchange or FX market). There is also a general move towards settling transactions using only computers (i.e. non-paper transactions).

A 'non-marketable instrument' is one that is not traded in a secondary market like the NYSE. It is usually a financial agreement between two (or more) parties with the arrangement being held to maturity of the contract (e.g. a term loan or deposit in a bank) – these are **over-the-counter** (OTC) agreements. A bank term loan to a firm is a non-marketable OTC instrument, since neither the bank nor the firm can (in general) *easily* shift this specific contract to other parties. Clearly, this 'non-marketability' is a matter of degree. In fact there is a secondary market in 'bundles' of bank loans in the US and bank loans can also be securitised, but these possibilities are quite costly (see Case Study 1.1). Other large OTC markets include the Eurobond market, spot and forward markets in foreign exchange, swaps markets and options' contracts.

CASE STUDY 1.1   LOAN SALES

In some well-developed financial systems there is a secondary market in buying and selling bank loans. Note that this is different from securitisation, since the loans are directly sold by a bank to another counterparty (e.g. another bank, an insurance company or hedge fund); no new 'securities' are created and sold. The loan sales market is most active in the US and grew tremendously in the 1980s as leveraged buyouts (LBOs) financed mergers and acquisitions.

If a bank finances an LBO, for example when a private equity group takes over a large firm, the bank will have a large concentrated loan on its balance sheet. Similarly, banks sometimes lend in specific geographical areas and sectors (e.g. oil loans in Texas). Since the regulatory changes of 1988 (i.e. the 'Basle Accord'), banks have to hold capital (i.e. broadly share capital plus retained profits) equal to 8% of their loan value outstanding, which they consider an expensive form of finance. However, if these loans are sold *without recourse* to a counterparty, then the default risk is transferred to the counterparty and the capital charge on the bank is removed. This encourages loan sales.

These bank loans may be classified as non-distressed (i.e. bid price exceeds 80 cents per $1 of loans) or distressed (i.e. bid price is less than 80 cents per $1 of loans or the borrower is in default). The main sellers of these 'bundles' of bank loans are large investment banks (e.g. Merrill Lynch, Goldman Sachs) whose corporate finance departments may have originated the LBO loans in the first place. After selling the loans the original bank may continue to collect the interest payments on the loans (for a fee) and may also earn an origination fee for setting up the initial loan agreements.

The buyers of loan sales are large banks and hedge funds who speculate on the change in market value of such loans, as the credit default risk of the constituent companies alters over time. They hope to influence the outcome of any restructuring deal in their favour. These 'loan sales' can be traded in the secondary market, but are rather like trading in *illiquid* junk bonds. The illiquidity arises because it can often take up to three months to complete a loan sale and many deals fall through before completion because of legal problems (or because the market price moves below the initial offered price in the loan sale deal). Clearly, this market is less liquid than if the loans were fully securitised (see later in the chapter).

1.2 PLAYERS

Funds are channelled from individuals to the corporate sector and between individuals via financial intermediaries such as banks, savings and loan associations (building societies in the UK), pension funds and insurance companies. Why have financial intermediaries taken up this role in preference to direct lending from people to companies (and the government)? The main reasons involve transactions, search and information costs and risk spreading.

Banks take mainly short-term deposits from individuals and firms and on-lend them as bank loans. They can assess the creditworthiness of borrowers and a diversified loan portfolio reduces credit (default) risk. Also, by taking advantage of 'the law of large numbers' banks can hold fewer low-yield 'cash balances' and pass on this cost saving in the form of lower interest rates to borrowers or higher interest rates to depositors. For example, the daily *net* flow of cash out of a large commercial bank is much less than the 'over-the-counter' *gross* flow because a large number of surplus and deficit units use the same branch on any one day. In contrast, a small operator would have to hold a high level of 'cash reserves'. This is part of the reason financial intermediaries can engage in **asset transformation**. That is, they borrow 'short' and lend 'long'. There are *economies of scale* for banks in terms of providing the infrastructure to administer accounts, to advertise and monitor their borrowers and lenders.

Individuals often want to hold deposits that pay variable interest rates while borrowers often prefer to borrow at fixed interest rates. If a financial intermediary is a floating rate payer (on its deposits) and receives fixed payments on its loans, then it is subject to interest rate risk as it will lose income if deposit rates rise (since it cannot alter its fixed loan rate). However, it can use the derivatives market to remove (hedge) this risk by using interest rate swaps.

Investment banks such as Goldman Sachs or Merrill Lynch also advise corporations on raising finance via bond issues and stock issues. If it is the first time the firm has gone to the capital market then the new issue is known as **an initial public offering (IPO)**. The optimal mix of debt and equity finance may be important in the overall cost of capital for the firm. Investment banks also provide legal and financial expertise in mergers and acquisitions – in principle this is how inefficient managers are replaced by more efficient managers and is the **market for corporate control**.

Governments borrow short-term money by issuing Treasury bills (T-bills) and obtain long-term finance by issuing Treasury bonds (T-bonds) with maturities up to about 30 years. The rate of interest for different maturities is known as the yield curve. Central banks influence short-term interest rates by purchasing or selling T-bills in the market; short-term interest rates then influence long-term rates. The graph of the relationship between short-term and long-term rates of interest is known as the **yield curve** and is usually upward sloping – for example, the annual interest rate you receive on money lent for 10 years is usually higher than the annual rate of interest on money lent for 1 year. Theories of why the yield curve takes on particular shapes are known as the **term structure of interest rates**.

Portfolio diversification means that if you invest in a large number of 'risky' assets (e.g. stocks) then the 'risk' on the whole portfolio is much less than if you hold just a few stocks. So financial intermediaries 'pool' the funds of many individuals and purchase a diversified portfolio of financial assets, which is held on behalf of the individual investors.

Mutual funds (unit trusts in the UK) are financial intermediaries who take in funds from investors. They purchase a portfolio of financial assets (e.g. stocks and bonds) on behalf of the investors and the mutual fund then issues its own shares (units) against this portfolio. Since each share *in the fund* is a claim on income from a number of different securities, mutual funds allow investors to hold a diversified portfolio at low (administrative) cost. Mutual funds are **open-end** funds – the managers of the fund agree to repurchase an investor's shareholding in the fund, at a price equal to the market value of the underlying securities (called the *Net Asset Value*, NAV). When investors 'cash in' their shares in the fund, its managers will sell off some of the underlying assets in the fund at their market value (NAV) and use the proceeds to redeem the investors' shares in the fund. Any accrued dividend income from the underlying shares in the fund is either paid out (distributed) to the investor or can be reinvested in other stocks by the managers – and the investor will then hold more shares (units) of the fund.

In contrast, **closed-end** funds (i.e. investment trusts in the UK, but not in the US) have no obligation to repurchase an investor's shares in the fund. Shares of closed-end funds are quoted on a stock exchange and are traded in the open market just like the shares of a company.

If an investor in a closed-end fund wants to 'cash in' her holdings, then she must sell the shares of the fund on the stock market for whatever price she can obtain – she cannot sell her shares back to the managers of the closed-end fund. The NAV of a closed-end fund is the market value of all the shares held by the fund. But the *market price* of shares of the fund can differ from the net asset value of the underlying shares. Often closed-end funds sell for much less than their net asset value. This 'discount' cannot be accounted for by management fees, bid-ask spreads and so on, and is therefore referred to as a 'puzzle' or 'anomaly'.

Mutual funds provide diversified funds of many different asset classes. There are money market mutual funds that invest in T-bills and commercial bills, equity and bond funds and real estate investment trusts (REITS). Mutual funds are often subsidiaries of large banks and insurance companies (e.g. Morgan Stanley, Citigroup, Merrill Lynch, Legal and General). The investment decisions of a mutual fund are taken by a group of investment managers. Most mutual funds have 'active' investment policies; that is, they try to 'beat the market', either by buying underpriced shares (**security selection**) or by increasing their exposure to the market when they expect it to rise substantially (**market timing**). There are relatively few mutual funds that have a passive investment strategy and track a broad market index (e.g. the S&P 500 index).

Hedge funds are also pooled investments, but they have far more freedom than mutual funds in the types of asset in which they can invest and the types of trades they can undertake.

Insurance companies take funds from the personal sector in the form of life assurance, pension payments and other insurance policies, while pension funds collect payments from defined benefit (salary) and defined contribution pension schemes. Future payments of pensions are long-term liabilities and pension funds invest in a mixture of government T-bonds, corporate bonds, equities and property, in both domestic and overseas markets. The precise mix of these assets that a pension fund should hold is a source of controversy – particularly after large stock market crashes that can rapidly erode the assets of the fund and may threaten its solvency.

Net inflows into pension funds and insurance companies are often given to the same investment managers who run mutual funds. However, in many countries the proportion of funds one can invest in certain asset classes (e.g. foreign stocks and bonds) is set by law, although such restrictions are gradually being eased in Europe, the US and even in Japan. Recently pension funds, particularly UK funds, have started investing in hedge funds and private equity funds.

Securitisation

Securitisation is the term used for the practice of issuing marketable securities backed by non-marketable cash flows – it has become a very large market in recent years. For example, suppose that a bank has made a series of long-term loans, so the bank has taken on a large amount of credit exposure. One way of reducing this exposure would be to create a separate legal entity known as a *special purpose vehicle* (SPV), into which the loans are placed and therefore are 'off balance sheet' for the bank. If the bank gets into financial difficulties with its other activities, the loans in the SPV cannot be claimed by the bank's creditors. The SPV then issues securities to investors entitling them to the stream of income paid out of the interest payments on the loan – this is **securitisation**. The default (credit) risk on the loans is now

spread among a number of investors, rather than just applying to the bank. The bank contin-
ues to collect the interest payments and repayments of principal on the loans (for a fee) but
passes these on to the owners of the securities – hence the term *pass-through securities*. For
example, if they are home loans to individuals, these securities would be **mortgage-backed
securities (MBS)**. In the US, the Government National Mortgage Association (GNMA or
Ginnie Mae) bundles up home mortgages into relatively homogeneous 'pools', for example
$100m of 6%, 20-year conventional mortgages. GNMA then issues, say, 10,000 MBS, so
each purchaser of an MBS has a claim to $10,000 of these mortgages and is entitled to receive
1/10,000 of all the payments of interest and principal. MBS are marketable and highly liquid.
From the investors' point of view, purchasing such securities provides them with a higher
yield than government bonds and allows them to take on exposure to the (mortgage) sector.
But they can at any time sell the MBS in the secondary market (at whatever the current market
price happens to be).

Other **asset-backed securities** include marketable securities whose cash flows depend on
corporate loans by banks, car loans (e.g. VW, General Motors), credit card receivables (most
large banks), music royalties (e.g. Bowie and Rod Stewart), telephone call charges (e.g.
Telemex in Mexico) and football season tickets (e.g. Lazio, Real Madrid).

Investors in asset-backed securities share in the default risk that arises if the underlying borrowers default on their payments. If you hold a diversified portfolio of asset-backed, securities then
the default risk depends on the correlations between the default risk for the different categories
of asset-backed securities (e.g. whether lots of people who owe credit card debt default on some
of their payments at the same time as people who owe money on car loans). A slightly different way of 'bundling up' the default risk is to issue securities where the investor can decide
whether she is willing to take the 'first hit' from any defaults or, being rather less risk tolerant,
is only willing to take the hit on the last few debtors who default. This type packaging of
credit risk is known as a collateralised debt obligation (CDO); see Case Study 1.2.

CASE STUDY 1.2   COLLATERALISED DEBT OBLIGATION (CDO)

CDOs are a way of 'repackaging' credit risk and creating 'tranches' of debt that have
different payments on default. In this way, debt of average risk can be split into bundles of high- to low-quality debt. A pool of bank loans or corporate bonds, each with
a different default risk, are placed in a portfolio, where the assets have (say) an average promised yield of 8.5%. This portfolio of assets is placed in a special purpose vehicle (SPV), an entity independent of the issuers of the bonds or loans.

The credit risk on these assets is then split into (say) four *tranches*. The first tranche
will be liable for the first 5% of any losses due to defaults or ratings downgrades. This
is a very risky tranche, since if only 2.5% of the initial loan portfolio defaults this
amounts to a 50% loss on the first tranche – it is 'toxic waste'. The first tranche is often
retained by the originator of the CDO, since it is difficult to sell to investors. The second

and third tranches might be liable for the next 10% and 15% of losses, respectively, leaving the forth tranche liable for any losses greater than 30% on the initial portfolio of securities. Tranches 2–4 will be sold to investors. Representative promised yields on tranches 4 (least risky) to 1 might be 6%, 8%, 16% and 32% – these are yields before any allowance for expected defaults.

Tranche 4 might be rated AAA by S&P rating agency since it will not be affected by credit events until the original portfolio has fallen in value by more than 30%. The ratings for the other tranches will depend on their perceived risk, which depends on the default risk for each of the bonds in the portfolio and the default correlations between the issuers of the bonds. Hence CDO are a means of creating some high-quality debt from average (or low-quality) debt in the original portfolio. This of course assumes that each tranche of the debt is correctly rated and gives the correct 'signals' to buyers of the CDOs about the risk.

In the 2007 US *sub-prime mortgage crisis,* many home owners had been given huge loans of 100% or more of the value of the house. Some could not meet their repayments and house prices in the US also fell, so the collateral underlying these loans was suspect – hence some major banks such as Merrill Lynch, Citigroup and UBS took large losses on their CDOs.

Regulation

Trading between different players requires rules – these are sometimes self-imposed and sometimes imposed by law. There are a myriad of regulatory rules in developed financial markets. In the US the Securities and Exchange Commission (SEC) has broad oversight over the trading of securities, but some markets are regulated by other bodies (e.g. the futures market is regulated by the Commodity Futures Trading Commission, CFTC). However, there is a great deal of self-regulation, so the National Association of Securities Dealers (NASD) oversees players in the NASDAQ stock market and the NYSE has its own regulatory body. Professional institutions such as the Chartered Financial Analyst (CFA) Institute also ensure standards of professional expertise and conduct. The Federal Reserve Board has broad responsibility for the overall financial system, regulating bank lending to security market traders and also setting margin requirements on stocks and stock options.

Where there is lots of money to be made, some people are inclined to cheat or bend the rules, as they might say. Sometimes the law has a direct impact such as the legal cases brought against certain traders (e.g. Henry Blodgett of Merrill Lynch) and institutions (e.g. mutual fund market timing scandal by Elliot Spitzer, the New York Attorney General).

In the UK, the Financial Services Authority (FSA) is a key regulator for most financial institutions and has the power to impose fines on institutions, but the Bank of England has responsibility for issues relating to systemic risk.

Financial institutions are subject to market (price) risk and risk of counterparties' default (credit) risk. The Basle Committee of Central Bankers has devised a common set of rules so that banks' capital provisions are based on their market and credit risk exposure.

1.3 ISSUES AND IDEAS

It is not difficult to think of issues that face companies, financial intermediaries and individual investors. We want to raise some of these and at the same time mention some concepts that might be useful in answering these questions – which are then dealt with in the rest of the book.

Companies have to decide whether to undertake investment in new plant or equipment, or to buy a potential takeover target. Investors have to decide if it is worth paying the market price for a stock or bond. This involves **valuation**. The investment project for the firm or the takeover of another firm involves assessing what the future cash flows from these investments will be. But we should not treat all future cash flows equally. It seems intuitively obvious that first, cash flows that accrue further in the future should be valued less than cash flows that 'arrive' early; and secondly, if cash flows are highly uncertain then these should have a lower value than cash flows that are more certain. These two facts are dealt with by using **discounting and present value** techniques. Cash flows that you receive from holding a government bond (known as coupons) are more certain than cash flows (dividends) from holding equity, so the latter cash flows will be discounted more heavily when calculating the present value. Put another way, the discount rate used for dividend payments on a stock will be higher than the discount rate used for coupon payments on a government bond.

Your estimate today of the intrinsic value of the future cash flows from an asset is known as the **fair value (V)** of the asset, also called the 'true' or 'theoretical' value. The fair value should be determined by 'fundamentals'; that is, economic variables that influence, for example, the future dividend prospects of a firm based on its published accounts and company strategy. To decide whether to purchase the asset (i.e. new factory, takeover target, stocks or bonds) you compare the fair value of the asset with the market price P (i.e. cost of the asset). If $P < V$ you buy the asset and if $P > V$ you sell the asset.

How do we decide exactly how much to discount future cash flows when valuing an asset? The way we approach this question is to see what determines the average return investors require in order to be willing to hold a risky asset like a stock. The higher the perceived risk of a stock, we would expect that investors require a higher average return and hence the discount rate should be higher. The difficulty is in determining what exactly constitutes risk and how to measure it. The **Capital Asset Pricing Model** and other multifactor models are of key importance here.

Let's now turn to investors. We assume that they like return but dislike risk. A key issue is how to combine several assets (e.g. stocks, bonds, cash) in order to obtain the right combination of risk and expected return for the investor – this is dealt with in **portfolio theory** (asset allocation). Portfolio theory demonstrates that even if, blindfolded, you throw around 35 darts at the stock price pages of the *Wall Street Journal* and put equal amounts in each stock you hit, this random portfolio of stocks will have much less risk than any of the stocks taken individually. This *naïve diversification* is about the only 'free lunch' in finance. It arises because each of the 35 firms is affected by random events that are largely independent of each other – for example, one firm may be badly affected by a rejection of its patent application while another may find it has an early breakthrough in its biotechnology R&D project. These random **firm-specific** events cancel out in a large portfolio, hence reducing overall risk.

However, you can't get rid of all risk by a *random choice* of stocks. Your diversified portfolio will still experience 'ups and downs' because of the **market risk** that affects the returns on all firms to a greater or less extent. For example, changes in interest rates by the Central Bank can affect the returns of many firms – however, not all by the same quantitative amount (e.g. bank stocks may be more affected by interest rate changes than the stocks of media firms). Portfolio theory tells you how to combine stocks, not in a naïve or random way, but on the contribution they make to the return and risk of your *overall portfolio.* You can trade off higher risk against a higher return to obtain the best or optimal combination of risky assets in your portfolio – this is *efficient* diversification and leads to a concept called the *efficient frontier.* So far we have just discussed the choice *among* a set of risky assets. But portfolio theory also addresses the *asset allocation* question; that is, whether you should put most of your own funds in your 'best' portfolio of risky assets and only a little in a risk-free asset such as a bank deposit (or vice versa). This depends on how risk averse or risk tolerant you are.

Hedging

Suppose you run a mutual fund and by July you have already made considerable gains since the beginning of the year. However, you think that over the next six months the market will be more volatile than usual and as your performance will be assessed in six months' time you want to 'lock in' the value of your portfolio at its current level – this is hedging.

To keep things simple, suppose you hold 10,000 shares of AT&T – this is highly risky, since AT&T's share price on the NYSE can move up or down by a large amount. However, suppose you can find another (mystery) asset F that is traded in Chicago, whose price is also risky. Now, suppose the return on AT&T shares and the return held on your position in asset F are *perfectly negatively correlated* and also move dollar for dollar. This means that every time the AT&T share price goes up by $1 in New York the value of your position in asset F goes down by $1 in Chicago. Hence if you hold *both* risky assets, the gain on one is offset by the loss on the other and you have reduced the riskiness of your overall portfolio – that is, AT&T shares plus your position in asset F – to zero. Your initial position in AT&T shares has been perfectly **hedged** with your position in asset F. As we shall see, the mystery 'asset F' that is used to hedge an existing position in some other (underlying) asset (e.g. AT&T stocks) is a (short) position in a futures contract (on AT&T stock) – this is discussed in Chapter 24.

Another simple example of hedging is if you are a UK resident who holds shares in the US company AT&T, which you intend to sell in a year's time. You are subject to two sources of risk: the dollar value of the AT&T shares, and the risk that the dollar–sterling exchange rate will move against you. Today you can (partially) hedge the foreign exchange risk by agreeing to sell the US dollars you expect to obtain in a year's time from selling your AT&T shares, in exchange for sterling at the agreed one-year forward rate of exchange; see Chapter 18.

Another way of changing the risk profile of your portfolio is to ensure that your initial portfolio of 10,000 AT&T shares does not fall below a certain minimum value, but also allowing yourself to benefit from any increase in the value of the shares on the NYSE. This is a form of **insurance**. So-called call and put options can be used to provide insurance – not surprisingly, this branch of finance is often referred to as **financial engineering**.

Speculation

While portfolio theory suggests that you hold a diversified stock portfolio, you might think you have superior information on certain stocks and can use this information to 'beat the market'. This is **active management** (or more commonly 'stock picking' or speculation). This suggests that you are able to identify underpriced or overpriced stocks; that is, stocks where the market price is above or below the 'true' or 'fair' value for the stock.

For example, suppose you have a method for determining the fair value of a particular stock based on your forecasts of future cash flows for the firm and after careful scrutiny of the company's accounts and future plans (i.e. based on the 'fundamentals' of the firm). Suppose the market price, P = $90, is less than your estimate of the fair value, V = $100. If you believe your forecast is superior to that of other market participants, you should purchase this underpriced stock and wait. If your view about future prospects for this firm are correct, then the rest of the market should eventually recognise this, revise its view of fundamental value to be V = $100 and also purchase the stock. As many traders step in to purchase the stock its market price will rise, until the market price P = $100, which equals its fair value. You personally can then sell the stock at a $10 profit. You have done this because you traded on superior information *to the market* – valuable information is differential (and correct) information.

This speculative strategy is a form of **risky arbitrage**, since a moment's thought will alert you to the potential uncertainties in the strategy – although we will ignore these here. Generally, speculators do not like risk (i.e. they are **risk averse**), but providing the potential rewards from speculation are sufficient to cover the risks in the trade (and transaction costs of buying and selling shares), speculation is perfectly rational. On the other hand, *gamblers* will bet on events that are risky just for the love of gambling, even though it can be shown that the expected returns from their repeated bets will leave them worse off (e.g. roulette, where the 'house' wins if the ball lands on 0 or 00 and there are numbers 1 to 36 on the wheel, see chapter 10).

Assume that your fundamental analysis has been successful: the market recognised the mispricing and corrected it, bringing the market price into line with the fundamental value. If this happens quickly the market is said to be 'efficient' – or put another way, 'the price is right'. If at the outset the market had the same information as you and processed it in the same way, then the price would always have been equal to fair value – the market would have incorporated this information in its price quotes and you would never have found a trader who was quoting P = $90.

The **efficient markets hypothesis (EMH)** suggests that it is hardly ever possible to make money by stock selection – after taking account of transaction cost and the riskiness of the strategy. This is because there are so many informed traders in the market that the price of the stock is always kept arbitrarily close to the fair value. So the EMH implies P = V at all times – in other words, 'the price is right'. The EMH recognises that there may sometimes be a small discrepancy between P and V, but this is not large enough for a speculator to make enough profit to cover her transaction costs in the trade and to compensate her for the fact that the trade is highly risky. If the EMH is true, then economic welfare may well be enhanced if we (metaphorically) shoot nearly all the 'Masters of the Universe' (e.g. 'King Henry' Blodgett of Merrill Lynch, Nick Leeson of Barings etc.) and close down nearly all active mutual and hedge funds. So you can see that this is a big question and many 'big guns' in finance have tried to address it.

Why might profitable opportunities occasionally be available to well-informed investors? One reason might be that not all traders base their decisions about the fair price of a share on economic fundamentals. Speculation can be based on a forecast of 'fundamentals' (as described above with AT&T shares) and these speculators, if they are correct on average, help to bring prices in line with fundamental value. However, some speculators might not forecast returns based on fundamentals but merely on 'rules of thumb', which they see (or think they see) in the data. For example, some speculators might base their analysis of future returns based purely on the past behaviour of returns. A speculator might have a rule that says 'buy a stock after a rise of more than 2% on any one day and then sell it if it subsequently falls more than 2% in a day' – these speculators are known as **noise traders**, since they do not use any information about the economic fundamentals of the company (e.g. costs and revenues) in making their 'bets'.

If there are a substantial number of noise traders in the market, then they might push the quoted price of a share away from its fair value and therefore 'the price may not be right'. Not only that, but 'fundamental traders' (i.e. 'rational speculators' or 'risky arbitrageurs') may be able to take advantage of the 'irrational behaviour' of noise traders and hence make a profit from stock trading at the expense of the noise traders.

The idea that there are strategies whereby you can 'beat the market' has spawned many investment techniques such as chartism, candlesticks, neural networks and so on, and alternative strategies such as value growth and momentum. When it appears that we can 'beat the market' we say there are pricing anomalies – rational explanations for such anomalies are to be found in the **behavioural finance** literature.

Any marketable financial asset can provide a vehicle for speculation, including bonds, foreign currency, futures and options. Although speculative activity is often frowned on by outsiders, nevertheless, as we shall see, speculators provide funds to enable hedging activity to take place (which is usually applauded by outsiders).

There are two very good rules of thumb to apply to financial markets, which you ignore at your peril.

- If you see the prospect of a high average return from repeated 'bets', this will usually imply a high level of risk 'hiding' somewhere in the background.
- There are few (if any) 'free lunches' in financial markets – the market is efficient most of the time and you pay 'fair value' for most 'meals' (i.e. assets) you purchase.

Arbitrage

We have already noted that some asset prices (e.g. stocks) are determined by **risky arbitrage**; that is, setting the price of an asset equal to its fair value based on economic fundamentals.

However, the term **arbitrage** is usually reserved for transactions that are (in principle) risk-free. For example, arbitrage implies that two identical assets (e.g. shares of AT&T) cannot simultaneously sell for two different prices on two different stock exchanges.

For instance, if oil is being quoted by one trader at $70 per barrel and by a trader on another exchange at $75 a barrel, then you can get on the phone (or computer network) and purchase at $70 and *simultaneously* sell to the other trader at $75 per barrel. You never see the oil but you make $5 on the deal (excluding transaction costs) – which is virtually risk free, as the two trades are undertaken simultaneously. So, if this were to happen even for an instant, traders would buy at the low price and simultaneously sell in the other market at a high price. The large number of buy trades would raise the price in one market while the large number of sell trades would lower it in the other, bringing the prices quickly into equality. This is the process of (risk-free) arbitrage.

We noted above that **derivatives** (forwards, futures, options, swaps) have value because their payoff depends on the price of the spot asset 'underlying' derivative contract (e.g. stocks, bonds, oil, silver etc.). Arbitrage is an important concept in the pricing of derivative securities, since it ensures that by trading in two markets (e.g. the futures market in Chicago and the spot market for shares in New York), the price of the derivatives contracts (e.g. futures contract on a stock) is closely linked to the price of the underlying asset in the spot market (shares in New York). The reason two prices in two different geographical locations may move dollar for dollar is due to arbitrage. Arbitrage was also the insight that allowed Black, Scholes and Merton to produce the famous Black–Scholes–Merton options pricing formula in 1973, which later won them the Nobel prize in economics (Black did not receive the prize as it cannot be awarded posthumously).

Figure 1.1 summarises the role of arbitrageurs, hedgers and speculators – all these players are needed so that financial markets function correctly.

Market risk and credit risk

The final issue we want to comment on is how we measure the overall risk of financial institutions such as a large investment bank, which holds a wide variety of marketable assets such as stocks, bonds, foreign assets and derivative securities. Two key risks are market risk, due to fluctuations in asset prices, and credit risk, due to default or credit downgrades of the counterparties with which the bank deals. For example, the hedge fund Long Term Capital Management (LTCM) lost around $4bn in 1997 and was rescued by a consortium of banks

• Arbitrageurs:
  Ensure that quoted price = 'fair value' (risky arbitrage)
  Equalise prices of identical securities (risk-free arbitrage)

• Hedgers:
  Offset risks that they currently face

• Speculators:
  Take risky 'open' positions to exploit profitable opportunities
  May be based on 'fundamentals' - equivalent to 'risky arbitrage'
  May involve 'rules of thumb' - and hence noise traders

FIGURE 1.1: Traders

at the request of the Federal Reserve Board under Alan Greenspan. LTCM failed to assess its risk correctly. There are various methods used to measure the changing market risk of a diverse portfolio of assets and this is generally referred to as **Value at Risk** – pioneered by J. P. Morgan's risk management group.

The reason for the rescue of LTCM was that a number of banks had lent it considerable sums of money and it was thought that if LTCM went into liquidation, this would also impair the solvency of some banks. The banks were counterparties to loans they had supplied to LTCM and this gave rise to **credit risk**. There are many other forms of risk. **Liquidity risk** is the risk that you can only sell off a substantial amount of your assets within a reasonable period by pushing the price well below its current price. This is because in times of crisis there may be only a few traders who will take the opposite side of the trade (i.e. buy the assets from you). In the case of banks, liquidity risk sometimes refers to the difficulty they might have in raising short-term wholesale deposits (e.g. large three-month deposits from other banks). If the bank cannot obtain funds from the wholesale markets then it will not be able to finance its loan portfolio. The bank is not bankrupt because (we assume) the value of its assets (i.e. loans) exceeds that of its deposit liabilities, but it may have a short-term liquidity crisis. Central Banks can lend 'cash' on a short-term basis to such banks (in exchange for banks providing the Central Bank with 'collateral' in the form of 'high-grade' assets such as T-bills and government T-bonds; this is known as the lender of last resort facility). For example, this is operated via the 'discount window' at the US Federal Reserve Bank. Other risks include **operational risk** (i.e. failure of computer systems), **legal risk** (enforceability of contracts) and outright fraud.

When banks face a liquidity crisis and they cannot borrow from other banks in the interbank market, there may be a 'run' on the bank (i.e. depositors queuing up outside to get their money out). Then Central Banks must step in to provide liquidity (to solvent banks) as a lender of last resort. The decision of whether to provide liquidity to a bank that is also likely to be insolvent often finally rests with the government (Treasury), since ultimately any losses are paid by taxpayers – this may involve a redistribution of wealth from taxpayers (who are not depositors in the failed bank) to those with deposits in the bank.

If the market or credit risk of a bank's assets is thought to be too high, then either the positions in risky assets must be reduced or the bank must offset the risk it currently holds by hedging some of its risky positions (e.g. by using derivatives). Note that commercial firms can also use derivatives markets to reduce some of their business risks – for example an airline can use derivatives markets to hedge risks due to fuel prices.

SUMMARY

- The key players in financial markets are individuals, firms and investment companies such as banks, pension funds and insurance companies, mutual funds and hedge funds.
- Firms obtain external finance for investment projects and for mergers and takeovers by issuing bonds and stocks.

- Central banks can influence short-term interest rates that then feed through to long-term rates – this is the term structure.
- Portfolio theory is used to determine the best combination of risky assets to include in your diversified portfolio – it addresses the asset allocation problem. It also considers the question of how you should divide your own wealth between risky assets (such as stocks) and a risk-free asset (such as a bank deposit).
- The fair value of an asset is the value today of the future cash flows from the asset. Present value techniques are used to estimate fair value.
- The efficient markets hypothesis (EMH) implies that the market price always equals the fair value of the asset – so 'the price is right' and active investors can't 'beat the market'.
- The behavioural finance literature tries to explain why some prices may not equal fair value and hence it may be possible to 'beat the market' by using techniques such as chartism, candlestick, neural networks and so on, or using strategies such as value, growth or momentum.
- Derivatives are priced by arbitrage and they are useful for hedging and speculation.
- Value at Risk refers to the risk of banks' assets due to price changes and credit risk is the risk of default from counterparties.

EXERCISES

Q1   If the government has a persistent budget deficit of, say, $30bn (assume this is equivalent to 5% of the total output of the economy; that is, of GDP), then how can it finance the deficit and what might be the consequences for the economy in general?

Q2   Why have financial intermediaries become so important in the economy? Do you think they will survive in their present form?

Q3   What is the yield curve and what does it tell you?

Q4   What is an asset-backed security (ABS)?

Q5   How might a large bank seek to reduce the riskiness of its overall holdings of bank loans?

Q6   If you hold around 35 stocks chosen randomly from the pages of the *Wall Street Journal*, why is the riskiness of this portfolio much less than the average risk of holding one stock chosen at random?

Q7   A bank's source of funds consists of deposits on which it pays a variable (floating) interest rate (LIBOR–1%), but its assets consist mainly of long-term loans that pay a fixed interest rate of 8%. LIBOR is currently 7%. What is the interest rate risk the bank faces? Assume that the liabilities and assets of the bank are $100m.

CHAPTER 2

Raising Finance

AIMS

- To analyse the main forms of ownership and the role of debtholders, shareholders, directors and managers.
- To examine mergers and takeovers and the market for corporate control.
- To examine debt and equity instruments used by firms to raise long-term capital.

2.1 OWNERSHIP AND CONTROL

The purpose of setting up a firm is the creation of value. By this we mean that the owners raise 'cash' by various means and use this to buy materials, capital equipment and labour. The aim is to use these inputs to produce *future* cash flows that exceed the cash used to finance the firm. The suppliers of capital to the firm are debtholders (bank loans and bonds) and equityholders, each of which has a claim on the future cash flows of the firm.

Debtholders must be paid before equityholders, they have a legal right to be repaid and can place the firm into liquidation (bankruptcy/receivership in the UK) if any debt interest payments are not forthcoming. However, in practice if a firm cannot pay its debt interest the debtholders will not immediately put the firm into liquidation. Instead they often undertake complex legal negotiations with the firm to find a way out of the problem – this may involve a complex restructuring of the debt, for example deferred interest payments or swapping some of the debt for equity. So in times of financial distress the debtholders can have a substantial influence on the strategy of the firm, but in 'normal' times the debtholders are 'passive' and merely receive their interest payments. In part this is because legally, debtholders do not have voting rights on company policy.

Equityholders are owners of the firm and have voting rights to change the board of directors, although in practice this happens rather infrequently, so this aspect of the 'market for corporate control' is rather weak. Equityholders are 'last in the queue' for payment – but any cash flow remaining from the operating activities of the firm and after paying debtholders legally belongs to the equityholders.

Firms have both assets and liabilities. Total assets are divided into current and fixed assets. In the accounts, current assets usually have a life of less than one year (e.g. cash and short-term bank deposits, inventories of finished goods) while fixed assets have a longer life. Fixed assets include *tangible assets* such as buildings and machinery (see Figure 2.1) as well as financial

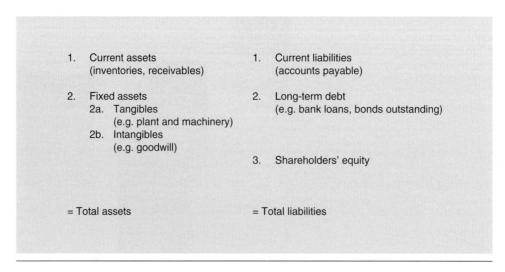

FIGURE 2.1: Balance sheet

assets (e.g. shares of other companies) and *intangible assets* such as patents, goodwill and the quality of management. The firm also has liabilities in the form of *short-term debt* (usually repayable within the year), such as bank loans and commercial bills. *Long-term debt* may be marketable (e.g. corporate bonds) or non-marketable (e.g. long-term bank loans). Shareholder equity represents the residual claim on the firm's assets.

$$\text{Shareholder Equity} = \text{Total Assets} - (\text{Current Liabilities} + \text{Long-Term Debt}) \quad [1]$$

The Chief Financial Officer (CFO) is responsible for all aspects of finance for the firm. Some key issues for the CFO discussed in this book are:

- How to raise funds to finance new investment activities of the firm.
- How to decide on the best capital investment projects.
- How to choose the appropriate debt – equity mix to maximise the value of the firm.
- Merger, takeover and disinvestment decisions.
- How to hedge risks faced by the firm (e.g. commodity price rises, foreign currency receipts/payments, variable rate loans); hedging usually involves the use of derivatives such as futures, options and swaps.

We now turn to the issue of how control of the firm is divided between managers, directors, bondholders and shareholders. Answers to these questions depend in part on the legal structure of the firm and we consider the three main forms of ownership below. The three main forms of ownership are *sole proprietor, partnership and limited company (or corporation),* with the latter form accounting for most of the output (GDP) produced in developed industrial economies.

Sole proprietor

The owner of the firm is a single individual who has unlimited liability for the firm's debts. The firm is not subject to corporation tax, but the individual owner is subject to income tax. The ability to raise finance is limited to the owner's initial wealth, the future profits she can plough back into the business and any (bank) loans she can obtain.

Partnership

The most commonly known partnerships involve the professions such as lawyers, architects and accountants. Whenever two or more people combine for the purpose of conducting business, a partnership is created. The profits of the partnership are subject to income tax and both profits and tax are usually 'shared' on a pro-rata basis. Some partners may be designated as having limited liability (i.e. limited partnership) but there is always a sub-set of the partners who must have unlimited liability (i.e. general partnership). New partners are allowed to enter and old partners leave. The agreement usually includes terms and conditions for the distribution of assets on dissolution of the partnership. The limited partners generally do not participate in managing the business. Equity contributions are limited to the funds provided by the partners.

Limited company (corporation)

A limited company (or corporation) is owned by the shareholders. If the company goes bankrupt, personal assets of the 'share-owners' may not be taken to payoff any of the company's residual debts. The corporation therefore has limited liability and is subject to corporation tax.

In principle the shareholders control the management, although in practice this direct link is usually rather weak, being exercised by voting (at the AGM) on specific issues, including the election of directors, who then appoint managers to run the day-to-day affairs of the company.

The shareholders can also indirectly influence the managers' behaviour, since if managers are thought to be underperforming, the shareholders can sell their shares which will depress the share price and encourage a takeover bid. After the takeover, the incumbent management may find themselves out of a job. Hence the managers have an 'indirect' incentive to maximise the value of the firm and this works in the interests of existing stockholders. The management–shareholder relationship comes under the heading of *corporate governance,* while the takeover literature is often referred to as the ***market for corporate control***. In the corporation there is a separation of ownership and control. The shareholders act as principals and appoint the directors, who then appoint managers as their agents. This can give rise to conflicts of interest known as **principal–agent (or agency) problems**. The control mechanism may be enhanced if the managers also hold shares (or deferred share options) in the company, since their remuneration then depends directly on the value of the firm's shares. We say 'may' because managers' share holdings may also lead them to undertake manipulation of the company accounts to artificially inflate the share price.

In the UK, setting up a limited company is usually done via the Company Formation Agency. A certificate of incorporation is issued by the Registrar of Companies based at Companies House. The 'Memorandum and Articles of Association' set out the rights and obligations of the firm and corporations must file accounts annually with Companies House (which are publicly available). In the US the procedure is similar. A **registration statement** by the corporation must be lodged with the Securities and Exchange Commission (SEC) and a prospectus issued to potential new shareholders. For an IPO, an advertisement known as a **tombstone** will appear in the press with basic details of the new share offer and the institutions involved. In the US each state has its own laws that must be adhered to (e.g. Nevada has relatively lax laws on setting up corporations to provide 'gambling services').

In the UK a ***public limited company*** (**plc**) is a corporation whose shares have a listing on the stock exchange. The requirements for listing are detailed and rigorous, but then shares in the company can be freely traded. A ***private liability company*** is a corporation whose shares are not freely transferable.

To set up a company start-up capital is needed, and for a limited liability company this initially consists of a mixture of (bank) loans and an equity issue (sometimes limited to the firm's directors). The funds raised are then used to provide plant and machinery, and pay wages and other costs. Once profits (earnings) accrue these are initially distributed to debtholders (interest income) and the remainder are either retained or distributed to shareholders as dividends. Debtholders have a legal right to be repaid and can place the firm into liquidation (receivership in the UK) if debt interest payments are not forthcoming. However, debtholders (usually) do not have voting rights on company policy.

A 'plc' or corporation is owned by the shareholders who have limited liability. The latter makes it easier to raise equity finance in large amounts by issuing shares to investors, because the most the investor can lose is her initial investment (and not her other personal assets). Hence limited liability plus an active secondary market in shares facilitates the raising of large amounts of cash. This is the major advantage of a corporation over a partnership. However, not every entrepreneur thinks that a publicly quoted company is necessarily the best form of legal organisation for a successful company; see Case Study 2.1.

CASE STUDY 2.1   FLOAT AND SINK?

Several well-known firms have floated on the stock market only to become disillusioned by the behaviour of stockholders, whom they believe undervalue the company's shares. These firms initially floated to gain access to finance for expansion. Richard Branson floated his Virgin group in 1986 and bought it back in 1988. Andrew Lloyd Webber, a theatrical (musical) entrepreneur who wrote the music for shows such as *Cats* and *Phantom of the Opera,* floated his company, known as *The Really Useful Theatre Group,* in 1986 and bought it back in 1990. In fact, both Branson and Lloyd Webber did rather well in the buy-back. Branson bought back in 1988 at the same share price as at flotation and then sold off the music division (to EMI for £510m) for more than the buy-back cost for the *whole* group. Lloyd Webber floated for £36m, bought back in 1990 for £77.5m, but then sold 30% of the group to recording company Polygram for around £78m one year later.

Another 'high-profile' company that became disillusioned with the City was The Body Shop, a 'green' cosmetics group then owned by Anita and Gordon Roddick, which floated for £4.6m in 1984. The Roddicks criticised the 'pinstripe dinosaurs' and 'short-termist' attitudes in the City. In 1992, the share price fell 40% in a day after a profit warning. The Roddicks complained that institutional investors did not understand the culture and long-term goals of the firm, which involved expanding into foreign markets (e.g. USA, Asia) where large profits would only accrue after substantial investment in marketing and retail outlets.

In 1995 the Roddicks tried to convert their plc into a charitable trust so that they could rid themselves of the short-termism of the City's institutional investors. This would have involved buying out the institutional shareholders and an original founder, Ian McGlinn, who owned 28% of the shares (the Roddicks owned 24% of the shares). In November 1995 Body Shop shares traded at around 156p and the City view was that a buy-back would require an offer of around 175p per share, valuing the company at £330m. However, the buy-back would have required substantial mezzanine finance (i.e. mainly bank loans), with the concomitant risk of high gearing and interference from creditors had interest payments not been met. For those reasons, in March 1996 the Roddicks abandoned their buy-back plans. (In 2006 they agreed to a takeover of The Body Shop by cosmetics firm L'Oréal for £652m.)

The above shows that some entrepreneurs, perhaps in somewhat unconventional industries and with 'unconventional' management styles, do believe that shareholders persistently underprice their shares and are 'short-termist'. Clearly, if you 'go public' you incur an obligation that a private company does not, namely to communicate your business strategy effectively to the shareholders and to maximise shareholder value. These entrepreneurs became disillusioned because, despite their efforts at communication, they believed that the City undervalued their companies.

The question is whether this anecdotal evidence holds true for a large number of companies. Is it the case that some shares are persistently undervalued while others may also be overvalued? (The latter's CEOs, presumably, do not complain). Put another way, do stock prices correctly reflect the intrinsic or fair value of a company's stock given its future investment plans and prospects? To answer this question we require a more formal analysis, as discussed in subsequent chapters.

Market for corporate control

Another mechanism to align the interests of managers and shareholders is via mergers and takeovers. The idea here is that efficient 'new' managers replace 'inefficient' incumbent managers – this is the market for corporate control. How does this take place and why is this process often subject to some form of regulation?

Merger activity is usually financed either by 'cash acquisitions' or from shareholders in the target firm receiving shares in the acquiring firm (i.e. effectively the 'new' merged firm). The acquirer must gain over 50% of the target's shares and in doing so the share price of the target will be bid up (i.e. the bid premium).

The funds in a cash acquisition come from retained earnings, rights issues (by the acquirer) or new debt finance (e.g. bank loans, bond issues – including sometimes junk bonds). A 'cash offer' provides certainty to the shareholders of the target firm and does not dilute the equity base of the acquirer in the new merged firm (i.e. the acquirer will own 100% of the merged firm). The disadvantage for the target shareholders is that because the price is bid up in the merger process (by 30–40% on average), they are subject to capital gains tax (since the gains are realised).

What happens when the acquirer offers its shares to the target? Suppose at the end of the bid process, the acquiring firm is worth $100m and the target firm $50m on the stock market. The acquirer might then offer one 'new' share for two of the target's shares. Because the capital gain (i.e. the bid premium) on the target's shares is not realised, there is no capital gains tax liability (at the time of the merger). Also, the acquiring firm does not have to deplete its cash resources (or increase its debt level), although its original shareholders will see their equity stake diluted because the target shareholders now own part of the merged firm.

In the UK at the end of the 1990s, about 60% of the value of merger activity comprised 'cash acquisitions', 33% were by offering shares in the acquirer (to the target shareholders) and about 2% by the issue of preference shares and loan stock (i.e. bonds) to the target shareholders. In the US, particularly in the 1980s, the proportion of mergers financed by junk bonds was very much higher than in the UK.

The details of the merger process are different in different countries, but the broad procedures are similar. We will illustrate the issues using the UK system based on the *City Code on Takeovers and Mergers,* which is administered by the **Takeover Panel**. The UK system is 'self-regulatory' rather than statutory and has as its aim 'the fair and equal treatment for all shareholders'. This implies (inter alia):

- Information must be given to all shareholders on the terms of any merger offer.
- The acquirer must present any claims about the benefits of the merger with 'due care and consideration' and the financial aspects must be certified by independent accountants.
- The target management must act in the best interest of the shareholders (and not in their own interest).
- The acquirer must not artificially inflate its own share price by getting 'friendly parties' to buy its shares (and hence having to swap fewer of its now 'higher priced' shares for each share in the target firm). This was a big issue in Guinness's hostile takeover of Distillers, for which Ernest Saunders, the Chief Executive of Guinness, was prosecuted.
- The bid process should not be unduly dragged out.

To facilitate an orderly merger process, the Takeover Panel requires that a 3% holding in any company is disclosed (whether or not a merger is in the offering) so that a potential target can prepare a defence. If an acquirer has more than a 30% stake in a company, then the Takeover Panel usually insists that the acquirer makes a formal bid for all the shares in the target firm (the 30% also includes so-called 'concert parties', where a group of firms each buys a stake in the target firm with a view to one of them instigating a takeover in the future). The acquirer (whether friendly or hostile) has to provide a formal bid document to the target's board, who then must immediately inform their shareholders and send the bid document to them within 28 days. The target's board has 14 days to respond to the offer document. They may suggest that their shareholders reject the offer (e.g. 'derisory offer', 'totally unacceptable'). The bid then becomes a hostile one rather than a friendly one. There are then attacks and counter-attacks and revised offers are likely to be made by the acquirer (e.g. offering a higher share price to the target shareholders). If no other bidders enter the race, then there is a maximum of 60 days from the initial offer document for the target shareholders to vote on the revised offer. If the offer is rejected, then the acquirer cannot launch another bid for a year. If a second bidder emerges during the process, then it has a maximum of 60 days to present its offer and then both firms' offers must be voted on by this date.

There are many 'game theory' elements in the bid process of a hostile takeover and the public relations machine is used by both sides (usually at great expense) to present their respective cases. Other defensive tactics used in a hostile takeover include:

- **White Knight** – get a friendly company to make a bid.
- **Pac Man** – make a counterbid for the bidder.
- **Poison Pills** – increase the acquirer's costs should the bid be successful (e.g. target shareholders are given bonus cash payments if the bid is successful).
- **Crown Jewels defence** – target sells off most profitable parts of the business.

The 'market for corporate control' is about 90% of the time via friendly mergers and only about 10% are hostile takeovers. Of course, mergers are not the only way in which a firm can

grow. Most firms grow organically by investment in their own profitable projects or sometimes by strategic alliances (e.g. among airlines in the late 1990s) that allow firms to tap new
markets. Also, do not forget that firms sometimes divest themselves of assets (i.e. their subsidiary firms) in order to concentrate on their 'core business' (e.g. UK banks and building
societies in the 1980s purchased estate agency businesses, but these were not successful and
the banks sold them off in the 1990s). 'Small' can also be profitable!

2.2 RAISING FINANCE

Individuals, governments and firms need to raise finance in order to invest. In this section we
concentrate on various methods of raising finance by firms – both start-ups and established
firms.

Business angels are wealthy individuals who come together to provide start-up finance for
small companies (e.g. 'dot-com' companies, spin-outs from scientific inventions). They will
often provide a mixture of debt (i.e. loans) and equity finance. When the company is ready
to come to market or wishes to expand its operations, then **venture capital** firms may
become involved. These are usually independent organisations that obtain funds from a variety of sources (banks, life assurance and pension funds and wealthy private investors, some
of whom are 'dumb dentists', who join the bandwagon). These funds are then used to
finance unquoted companies, which promise high returns but with concomitant high risks
(e.g. biotechnology, computer software and Internet firms – the 'dot-coms'). Large banks
such as Citigroup, J.P. Morgan and Goldman Sachs will often set up venture capital subsidiaries. Generally there will be some equity participation (or an option to convert debt to
equity) by the venture capital company. The finance is usually medium term (5–7 years) and
there is generally direct and active involvement by the venture capitalists with the strategic
management decisions of the company. Initially any share capital will be largely illiquid
(i.e. held privately and not quoted on an exchange), but when the 'new' company becomes
established the original venture capital investors will 'cash in' their equity by either selling
the firm on to another company or offering shares in the firm to the public in an initial public
offering.

Private equity partnerships are very similar to venture capital firms in their organisation,
involvement and financing, but they tend to engage in larger deals with established companies.
They generally use a large amount of debt finance in the takeover of established publicly quoted
firms and any equity stake is then held privately by the partners in the partnership. They hope
to 'turn around' the firm and then either sell it directly to other parties or to refloat it in an IPO.
Private equity is mainly concerned with the market for corporate control via takeovers; they
deal primarily in leveraged buy-outs (LBOs) and management buy-outs (MBOs), but this may
involve an injection of additional capital once the takeover has taken place.

Corporate securities

A corporation can raise long-term funds from three main sources: retained earnings; non-
marketable debt (e.g. bank loans) and marketable debt (e.g. corporate bonds); and equity capital (e.g. ordinary shares).

A firm can expand its activities by raising finance by stock or debt issues, but in doing so it opens itself to scrutiny by potential investors (e.g. pension funds, banks, venture capitalists etc.). It can also use retained earnings to finance its expansion, which involves far less scrutiny of the managers by the incumbent shareholders.

A limited company is a firm owned by two or more shareholders who have limited liability (i.e. their responsibility for covering the firm's losses does not reach beyond the capital they have invested in the firm). In return for their capital investment, shareholders are entitled to a portion of the company's earnings, in accordance with their proportionate shareholding. Firms issue equity and debt (corporate bonds) to raise finance for investment projects.

Primary (new issues) and secondary markets

The initial sale of securities (equities and bonds) takes place in the **primary market** and there are two main vehicles: initial public offerings and private placements. Most **initial public offerings (IPOs)** or **unseasoned new issues** are *underwritten* by a syndicate of merchant banks (for a fee of around 1.5–2% of the value underwritten). In a **firm commitment**, the underwriter buys the securities from the corporation at an agreed price and then hopes to sell them on to other investors at a higher price (thus earning a 'spread' on the deal). The advantage to the corporation is the guaranteed fixed price, with the underwriter taking the risk that other investors may be willing to pay less for the shares.

IPOs have been a feature of the sell-off of publicly owned industries in many industrial countries and emerging market economies, for example in the UK the privatisation of British Telecom, British Airways, British Gas and Railtrack. In some large public offerings by government the lead banks will run 'roadshows' where they inform institutional investors of prospects for the industry. In the case of the sale of the UK government's remaining 40% stake of £4bn in the UK's large power generators, National Power and PowerGen, in 1995, the lead banks were Barclays DeZoete Wedd (BZW) and Kleinwort Benson, who acted as 'bookrunners'. They obtained bids from institutional investors worldwide, who were asked to state how much they would purchase at particular prices and whether the bids were firm or indicative. (Retail investors were also allocated a proportion of the shares on a tapering scale if they were oversubscribed; that is, if someone bid for 10,000 shares and another person for 500 at the offer price, then the latter might receive his bid in full and the former might only receive 2000 shares, or even none at all.) For institutional bids computers are used to 'construct' a demand curve for the offer and display other information such as the geographical distribution of potential sales and demand by type of customer (e.g. banks, corporates, pension funds, hedge funds etc.). In contrast, the Czech Republic in the 1990s used a voucher scheme to enable individuals to obtain shares in newly privatised industries. In many developing countries the privatisation of banks and power generators has involved IPOs. Of course, many companies whose shares are not initially traded eventually come to market via an IPO, such as Richard Branson's Virgin, Anita Roddick's The Body Shop and recently dot-com companies such as Google.

The alternative to a firm commitment is for the underwriter to agree to act as an agent and merely try to sell the shares at the offer price in a *best efforts* deal. Here the underwriter does not buy the shares outright and hence incurs no underwriting risk. Usually, if the shares cannot be sold at the offer price they are withdrawn.

Sometimes the underwriter has a *green-shoe provision* whereby she can purchase additional shares from the company (say up to 15% of the initial issue) at the offer price, over a fixed period of time (e.g. for 30 days after the flotation). If the issue is oversubscribed and the post-issue market price goes above the offer price, the underwriter can make additional profits by buying shares from the company and selling them in the open market.

Because of the relatively high transaction costs of public offerings (and evidence of economies of scale), they are used only for large flotations. For smaller firms 'going public' **private placements** are often used. Here, debt or equity is sold to large institutions such as pension funds, insurance companies and mutual funds, on the basis of private negotiations. Sometimes a new issue is a mix of IPO and private placement.

It is rather difficult to set a 'fair price' for a new issue. If the offer price is too high, then the issue will be unsuccessful and may be withdrawn, while if the offer price is too low, this will hurt the existing shareholders, since less funds will be raised (than otherwise) and their equity stake has been diluted (i.e. a given level of future earnings is now 'spread over' more share-holders). Empirical work in the US shows that on average, IPOs are oversubscribed and the initial rise in the price of shares immediately after an IPO is in excess of 15%.

So IPOs are underpriced, on average. Why is this? It may be because of the *winner's curse*. If Mr Average decides to 'blindly' apply for 1000 shares in every IPO, the underpricing does not in fact imply that he will earn the average return of over 15%. This is because the 'smart money' will apply for (say) twice as many shares as Mr Average, if they believe the share is genuinely underpriced. Then the 'smart money' will be allocated twice as many shares as Mr Average, if they are allocated on a pro-rata basis. If the 'smart money' thinks that an IPO is overpriced, then they will apply for no shares and Mr Average will receive his full allotment of 1000 'duff' shares, on which he will lose money. This is the winner's curse. To counteract the winner's curse and attract the average investor, underwriters will tend to underprice IPO's on average.

After securities are originally sold they are said to trade in the **secondary market**, either in an auction market or a dealer market. An **auction market** provides continuously updated prices to all participants either on the floor of an exchange or via computers. Most stocks of large corporations are bought and sold in auction markets. **Dealer markets** involve dealers getting in touch with each other on a bilateral basis, usually over the telephone (or 'wires').

The largest equity market in Europe is the London Stock Exchange (LSE) and the largest in the US is the New York Stock Exchange (NYSE). A firm that wishes its equity to be traded on these markets must apply to be listed, and must satisfy certain criteria (e.g. minimum bounds are placed on market capitalisation, yearly turnover, pre-tax profits and the propor-tion of shares in public hands).

Stock exchange listing

If a company wishes to widen its share ownership and raise additional finance, then it may seek a listing on a stock exchange. The broad requirements for a listing are:

- A minimum amount of the firm's shares must be available for purchase/sale on the exchange (e.g. on the London Stock Exchange the figure is 25%, and on the Alternative Investment Market (AIM) it is 10%).

- The company must provide detailed financial information (e.g. company assets, profits etc.), both past data (e.g. over the last three years) and then on a periodic basis (e.g. annually).

The US stock exchange has particularly onerous reporting disclosures, and hence an alternative for UK firms wishing to attract US investors is the issue of **American Depository Receipts (ADRs)**. Here a US bank (e.g. Morgan Trust Guarantee) acts as an intermediary and purchases and holds UK company sterling denominated shares (listed on the London Stock Exchange). The bank then sells US investors, *dollar-denominated* 'receipts' each of which is 'backed' by a fixed number of UK company shares. These 'receipts' or ADRs are traded (in US dollars), rather than the UK shares themselves. The US investor has the same rights as a UK investor (but not the rights of an owner of US listed shares) and the sponsoring bank collects the sterling dividends, converts them into US dollars and passes them on to the holder of the ADRs. There are about 2000 ADR programmes outstanding, worth around $400bn. This idea has been extended to **Global Depository Receipts (GDRs)**, which allow shares to be traded on exchanges outside the US, and has been particularly useful in allowing 'emerging markets shares' to trade on developed exchanges (e.g. in London and Paris).

It has become more common in recent years for multinational firms to be listed on more than one exchange, in order to attract a wider investment market.

In general, two types of shares are issued: ordinary and preference shares. **Ordinary shareholders** (in the US, '**common stock**') are the owners of the firm with a residual claim on 'earnings' (i.e. profits, after tax and payment of interest on debt). Such 'earnings' are either retained or distributed as dividends to shareholders. Ordinary shares carry voting rights at the AGM of the company. In the UK, **preference shares** (or preferred stock in the US and participation certificates in the rest of Europe) have some characteristics of ordinary shares and some characteristics of debt instruments. In particular, holders have a claim on dividends that takes 'preference' over ordinary shareholders, but they usually do not carry voting rights. A corporation can raise additional capital by selling additional shares on the open market or by selling more shares to its *existing shareholders* – the latter is known as a **rights issue**.

In recent years in the UK and US, the supply of corporate equity has been reduced by **share** *repurchases*, whereby the company buys back a proportion of shares from each shareholder. Repurchases are often used when the company has accumulated a large amount of retained earnings (capital) but has no investment projects that it thinks can earn more than the market return. Assuming that the repurchase does not affect expectations of the firm's future profits, repurchases raise earnings per share and the share price (for the same reason that a split reduces the price), so that investors receive a return in the form of a capital gain rather than dividend income. Other countries tend to have legal limits on the amount of its own shares that a company can buy back, but these restrictions are gradually being eased.

Because a full listing is expensive, some companies are listed on a '**second market**' where the listing requirements are less onerous. In the UK the second market is called the Alternative Investment Market (AIM) and there are around 1600 firms listed. In all countries the differences between the listed and second market are to be found in the required levels of disclosure of company information, the amount of capital raised by public stockholding and the membership costs. For example, on the London and Paris second markets the amount of shares required to be held in 'outside hands' is 10% rather than the 25% for a full listing. Thus these 'second markets' impose less stringent regulations on companies wishing to have their shares traded, and are often viewed as a starting point for new firms aiming eventually for a full listing. Secondary market shares are regarded as being more risky than fully listed shares.

2.3 CORPORATE DEBT

Firms borrow for the short term (less than one year) from banks via an ordinary bank loan. A *financial letter of credit* from a bank to a firm allows the firm to borrow (up to a certain limit) from the bank at times determined by the firm. Similarly, a firm may have an arrangement to draw down further funds from an existing bank loan–this is known as a *loan commitment*. Both the letter of credit and the loan commitment are known as *off balance sheet items* because they do not appear on the bank's balance sheet until they are activated at some time in the future.

Firms can also borrow short term from the capital market by issuing commercial bills – this is a popular method of raising finance in the US.

Borrowing at horizons longer than a year can be via term loans from banks (in either the domestic or foreign currency). The loan can either be at a fixed rate or at a floating rate (where the periodic interest payments depend on the level of interest rates in the future). The floating rate on the loan will be at LIBOR plus a spread. LIBOR is the rate at which highly credit-rated banks lend funds to each other and the firm will pay a premium over this rate depending on its own credit rating. These loans if large may be syndicated – a lead bank will have other banks in a consortium and the loan will be 'spread' among these banks thus spreading any credit risk across banks in the consortium.

An alternative to an OTC bank loan is for the firm to issue corporate bonds, either in the domestic or in a foreign currency. Just as with a bank term loan, by issuing bonds a corporate obtains a large amount of cash 'up front' (e.g. to spend on real investment projects) in return for a promise to pay a stream of cash flows (the 'coupons') in the future, until the maturity date of the bond (when the principal will also be repaid). The coupon payments can either be fixed or vary with some reference interest rate (i.e. 'floating'). Bonds therefore allow a transfer of cash (and hence purchasing power) between two parties and allows the borrower to pay back the loan (plus interest) over time. Without this mechanism the investment project might not be possible. Corporate bond issues are mainly undertaken by large multinationals in their respective domestic markets (and currencies), but smaller 'firms' are now tapping into these markets (see Case Study 2.2). The US has by far the most active corporate bond market, whereas firms in Europe and Japan tend mainly to use bank term loans as a source of long-term debt finance.

CASE STUDY 2.2   BOWIE BONDS

Would you like to own a piece of David Bowie or even Rod Stewart? This may not be literally possible, but you can certainly own a claim on the royalties of their back catalogue of songs. Towards the end of the 1990s you could purchase a 'Bowie Bond' (and hence hand over cash to Bowie) in return for a promise to receive a portion of his future song royalties. These bonds carry credit counterparty or default risk, because David or Rod's old hits may go out of fashion and future sales revenues might not cover the promised future coupon payments on the bond.

Merrill Lynch has recently been involved in extending this idea and trying to get funding via bond issues for collectives of artists, people having intellectual property rights (e.g. inventors of computer games) or other media assets (e.g. book publishers). For example, Italian film company Cecci Gori (which made *Il Postino*) acquired the rights to show a back catalogue of Hollywood films in Italy. Merrill Lynch separated the credit risk on future film revenues from the credit risk of the overall company and hence was able to sell these 'movie bonds' at a high price (low yield).

So, if you have a good idea you need to develop (e.g. for a new computer game or film), don't sell the intellectual property rights to a large company, find someone who will issue bonds against a proportion of the future revenues.

All bonds have specific legal clauses that restrict the behaviour of the issuer (e.g. they must keep a minimum ratio of profits to interest payments – so called 'interest cover') and determine the order in which the debtors will be paid in the event of bankruptcy. These conditions are often referred to as **bond covenants** or **bond indentures**. Often the bond indenture will be made out to a corporate trustee whose job it is to act on behalf of the bondholders and see that promises in the indentures are kept by the company.

The payment on some bonds are specifically 'backed' by specific tangible assets of the firm (e.g. mortgage bonds in the US are backed by specific real estate), so if the firm goes bankrupt, these 'secured' bondholders can sell off these assets for cash. (Such bonds are generically referred to as 'senior secured debt'.) However, most bonds are only payable out of the 'general assets' of the firm and in the US these bonds are called **debentures**. So a debenture in the US is really unsecured debt (i.e. not tied to specific assets of the company). The terminology here differs between countries and in the UK debentures are a little different from the US. In the UK, a *debenture or secured loan stock* is simply the legal document that indicates a right to receive coupon payments and repayment of principal. A **fixed-charge debenture** is backed by specific assets (e.g. buildings and fixed assets like the rolling stock of railroad companies), while a **floating-charge debenture** is only secured on the general assets of the firm. So in the UK a debenture could be either secured or unsecured. **Unsecured loan stock** is a bond where the holder will only receive payment after the debenture holders.

Subordinated debt is the lowest form of debt in terms of repayment if the firm goes bankrupt (i.e. it is junior debt). It ranks below bond/(US) debenture holders and often after some general creditors, but above equityholders' claims. It is therefore close to being equity, but the subordinated debtholders do not have voting rights.

Rather than concentrating on the name given to the bond, the key issues are:

- whether the payments on the bond are secured on specific assets or not
- the order in which the different bondholders will be paid, if default occurs

The order in which bondholders receive payment in default is usually very difficult to ascertain ex ante. When a firm enters bankruptcy proceedings it can take many years to work out who will receive what and in what order the creditors will be paid. It is usually a messy business involving expensive corporate insolvency lawyers and practitioners.

International bonds

Some bond issues involve foreign currencies. **Eurobonds** or **international bonds** are bonds denominated in a different currency from the countries in which they are issued. They are often issued simultaneously in the bond markets of several different countries and most have maturities between 3 and 25 years. For example, a US firm issuing bonds in London, Paris and Singapore, denominated either in Yen or in US dollars, would both be classified as Eurobond (or international bond) issues. Eurobonds are also issued by governments and international organisations like the International Bank for Reconstruction and Development, the finance arm of the World Bank in Washington DC.

Eurobonds pay interest gross and are bearer instruments (and therefore are attractive to thieves, as anyone who has seen the opening scenes of the film *Heat* with Al Pacino and Robert De Niro will know). Tax is not deducted at source and they are unsecured. The issuer may face exchange rate risk, since a home currency depreciation means that more home currency is required to pay back one unit of foreign interest payments. However, if the firm's products are sold for foreign currency (e.g. oil, which is priced in US dollars) then the exchange rate risk of a Eurobond issue in US dollars is reduced. However, some major financial disasters have been partly the result of defaults on Eurobond issues, for example the Latin American debt crises of the 1980s and the Russian 'melt-down' of 1998 (see Case Study 2.3). Although most Eurobonds are 'floaters' they can also be issued with fixed coupons, and as zeros, convertibles and mortgage-backed bonds. Clearly, some companies borrow in foreign currency because they have subsidiaries in these foreign countries.

CASE STUDY 2.3   RUSSIAN EUROBOND ISSUES

In 1996, it looked as if the Russian economy was over the worst. 'The worst' had been extremely bad, as output had fallen dramatically after the move from communist central planning to privatisation and a more market-oriented economy. The distribution of income became much more unequal, as only relatively few benefited from the market economy while others (e.g. pensioners, ordinary workers and government employees) saw their savings rendered worthless by rampant inflation and devaluation and many became unemployed.

Nevertheless, in 1996 the Russian government made its first Eurodollar bond issue since the revolution of 1917. About 45% of the $1bn issue was taken up by US investors, 30% in Asia and about 25% in Europe. The yield was about 340–350 bp (basis points) above US Treasuries (to reflect the higher credit risk involved in lending to Boris Yeltsin's government rather than to Bill Clinton's). Hence, in 1996 investors had faith in Russia's ability to use this finance wisely. Foreign investors were attracted by the risk premium of around 350 bp above US Treasuries.

Municipalities in Russia (e.g. the cities of Moscow and St Petersburg) and large Russian oil (e.g. Lukoil) and gas (e.g. Gasprom) companies also considered raising funds via Eurobond issues. Unfortunately, all did not go well for the Russian economy, as in 1998 the Russian government defaulted on its *rouble-denominated* debt and froze Western investors' accounts in which these bonds were held. The value of these bonds fell sharply. (Note that Russia did not default on its debt denominated in foreign currency.) There were therefore worries that the Russian bond default could lead to financial difficulties for Western banks that had invested heavily in Russian bonds (and would receive less foreign currency given the rouble devaluation) and that this might lead to a systemic crisis.

However, by 2000 things were looking up a little. After the crisis of 1998, oil prices rose sharply from their $10 a barrel low point (Russia is a large oil exporter) and the devaluation of the rouble of over 80% against the US dollar led to a rise in exports and tax receipts. Russia negotiated a write-off of more than a third of its $32 billion debt with the 'London Club' (of banks) and swapped the rest for long-dated, low-interest Eurobonds. It was also looking for a similar deal from its other European creditors who are owed in the region of $40 billion.

Foreign bonds are bonds issued by foreign borrowers in a particular country's domestic market. For example, if a UK company issues bonds denominated in US dollars in New York then these are foreign bonds, known as **Yankee bonds** (and must be registered with the SEC under the 1933 Securities Act), and would probably be listed on the NYSE. If the UK company issued Yen-denominated bonds in Tokyo, they would be known as **Samurai bonds**. There are also **Bulldogs** in the UK, **Matadors** in Spain and **Kangaroos** in Australia. The bonds are domestic bonds in the local currency and it is only the issuer who is foreign. Foreign bonds are registered, which makes them less attractive to people trying to delay or avoid tax payments on coupon receipts.

New issues of bonds (unlike shares) are usually sold via a syndicate of banks (minimum about $100m) to institutional investors, large corporations and other banks, but some are issued by private placement. New issues are usually underwritten on a firm commitment basis. Most Eurobonds are listed on the London (and Luxembourg) stock exchange and there is a secondary market operated mainly OTC between banks by telephone and computers (rather than on an exchange) under the auspices of the International Securities Markets Association (ISMA). Eurobonds are credit rated and nearly all new issues always have a high credit rating (i.e. there is not a large 'Euro' junk bond market).

Hybrid debt instruments

There are many variants on the 'plain vanilla' corporate bonds discussed above and we briefly mention these below; more details are provided in Chapter 20. **Debt convertibles (convertible bonds** or **convertible loan stock)** are bonds that are 'convertible' into ordinary shares of the same firm, at the choice of the bondholder, after a period of time. The shares are 'paid for' by surrendering the bonds. They are therefore useful in financing new high-risk, high-growth firms, since they give the bondholder a valuable 'option' to share in the future profits of the company, if the bonds are converted to equity. Convertibles will usually carry a lower coupon because of the benefit to the bondholder of the in-built option to convert to ordinary shares (i.e. the convertible bondholder has a call option on the stock). **Exchangeable bonds** are like convertibles except the bonds are exchanged for the shares of another company.

A **callable bond** is one where the issuer (i.e. the company) has the option to redeem the bond at a known fixed value (usually its par value) at certain times in the future, prior to the maturity date. The company may wish to call the bond if the market price rises above the call price and if it does, the holder of the bond is deprived of this capital gain. Clearly, call provisions provide a disincentive for investors to buy the bonds, consequently callable bonds offer higher yields when issued than those on conventional bonds. Usually, there is a specific period of time (e.g. the first three years after issue) within which the company cannot call the bond and sometimes there may be a set of prices at which the bond can be called at specific times in the future.

A **floating-rate note (FRN)** is a bond on which the coupon payments \$C are linked to a short-term interest rate such as three or six-month LIBOR. FRNs are particularly popular in the Euromarkets.

Some companies also raise finance by issuing **deep-discount bonds**. These are zero-coupon bonds and they are attractive to institutions such as pension funds, which have a known *nominal* payment (e.g. a pension lump sum) at a specific date in the future. A 'zero' then provides a perfect hedge.

Mezzanine finance is a catch-all term for hybrid debt instruments that rank for payment below 'conventional' debt but above equity – these are also often referred to as **subordinated, high-yield, low-grade** or **junk bonds**.

European firms tend to obtain a large proportion of finance from retained earnings and bank loans, so the corporate bond market in Europe is much smaller than in the US. The biggest market is in plain vanilla corporate bonds with either fixed- or floating-rate coupons. But clearly, there are many specialist debt securities that can be tailored to meet the requirements of specific investors. There are also 'investment boutiques' that will combine existing securities (including equity, bonds and options) to provide the investor with a particular desired risk–return trade-off. This is often referred to as **structured finance**.

Bond ratings and spreads

Bond rating agencies study the quality (in terms of default risk) of corporate, municipal and government bonds and give them a rating. The ratings classifications used by Moody's and the equivalent ratings by Standard and Poor's are shown in Table 2.1. The description of the ratings are Moody's (but Standard and Poor's and Fitch have similar classifications). The lower the credit rating, the higher will be the firm's cost of borrowing in debt markets.

TABLE 2.1: Bond ratings

Moody's (S&Poor's)	Description (Moody's)
	Investment Grade Debt
Aaa **(AAA)**	Judged to be of the best quality. They carry the smallest degree of investment risk and are generally referred to as 'gilt edge'. Interest payments are protected by a large or an exceptionally stable margin and principal is secure. While the various protective elements are likely to change, such changes as can be visualised are most unlikely to impair the fundamentally strong position of such issues.
Aa **(AA)**	Judged to be of high quality by all standards. Together with the Aaa group they comprise what are generally known as high-grade bonds. They are rated lower than the best bonds because margins of protection may not be as large as in Aaa securities, fluctuation of protective elements may be of greater amplitude or there may be other elements present that make the long-term risks appear somewhat larger than in Aaa securities.
A **(A)**	Possess many favourable investment attributes and are to be considered as upper-medium-grade obligations. Factors giving security to principal and interest are considered adequate, but elements may be present that suggest a susceptibility to impairment some time in the future.
Baa **(BBB)**	Are considered as medium-grade obligations, i.e. they are neither highly protected nor poorly secured. Interest payments and principal security appear adequate for the present, but certain protective elements may be lacking or may be characteristically unreliable over any great length of time. Such bonds lack outstanding investment characteristics and in fact have speculative characteristics as well.

continued overleaf

Speculative Bonds

Ba **(BB)**	Judged to have speculative elements; their future cannot be considered as well assured. Often the protection of interest and principal payments may be very moderate and thereby not well safeguarded during other good and bad times over the future. Uncertainty of position characterises bonds in this class.
B **(B)**	Generally lack characteristics of the desired investment. Assurance of interest and principal payments or of maintenance of other terms of the contract over any long period of time may be small.
Caa **(CCC)**	Are of poor standing. Such issues may be in default or there may be present elements of danger with respect to principal or interest.
Ca **(CC)**	Are speculative to a high degree. Such issues are often in default or have other marked shortcomings.
C **(C,D)**	Lowest-rated class of bonds and issues so rated can be regarded as having extremely poor prospects of ever attaining any real investment standing.

Source: Copyright Moody's Bond Record, June 1992, p. 3. www.moodys.com

In Figure 2.2 the starting point for AAA rated at 6.07% is purely arbitrary, since all rates move up and down with changes in inflation so it is the spreads (e.g. the difference between yields on BBB and AAA bonds) that measure the relative riskiness of two corporate bonds with the same maturity. The spreads over US Treasuries for 20-year corporate bonds is around 50 bp on average. For various ratings the average spreads are AAA (7bp), AA (23 bp), A (25 bp), BBB (120 bp), while for junk bonds the spread varies enormously over the business cycle from around 300 bp to over 850 bp, with an average over the last 20 years of around 400 bp. The positive relation between risk and return is clear to see in Figure 2.2, with yields rising from a baseline 6.07% on the highest investment-grade bonds to a level above 12% on speculative (junk) bonds.

Finally, note that there are three ways in which the supply of corporate bonds may be reduced, if *the firm wishes* to reduce its leverage (i.e. its debt-to-equity ratio):

- repayment on maturity without a corresponding new issue
- repurchasing by the company in the open market
- under a call provision or when the bond is converted

Of course, the firm can always recapitalise by buying its bonds in the open market and reissuing different types of bonds (or equity). Also, if holders of convertible bonds choose to convert to equity, this will change the debt–equity ratio.

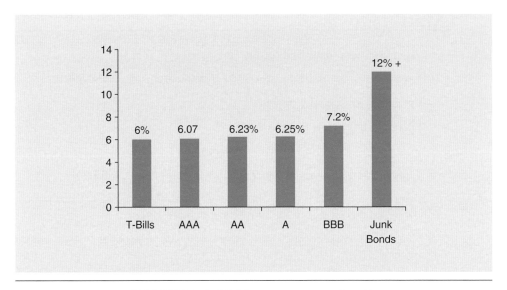

FIGURE 2.2: Yields on corporate bonds

SUMMARY

- Firms can be organised with a sole proprietor, as a partnership or as a corporation with limited liability.
- Business angels and venture capital firms provide start-up funds for new high-risk firms and the equity stake is usually held privately.
- The market for corporate control largely takes place via mergers and takeovers, although some firms also take a strategic decision to divest themselves of part of their business.
- Domestic and foreign firms issue a wide variety of equity and debt instruments to finance new capital projects or to finance mergers and takeovers.
- Large corporations raise long-term finance from internal funds (retained profits) and from external sources such as corporate debt (e.g. bank loans, corporate bonds) and by making new equity issues via IPOs and rights issues (to existing shareholders).
- Companies can apply for listing on a 'second market' where the listing requirements are less onerous than a full listing on a stock exchange such as the London or New York exchanges.
- All bonds have specific legal clauses (bond covenants or indentures) that restrict the behaviour of the issuer and determine the order in which the debtors will be paid, in the event of bankruptcy.
- Convertible bonds give the holder the opportunity to obtain an equity stake in the firm, at some time in the future, at a fixed known price.
- Callable bonds give the firm the opportunity to redeem its bonds at par value at certain times in the future – this allows the firm the possibility of refinancing its debt at a lower interest cost.

EXERCISES

Q1   What constitutes 'debt' and 'equity'?

Q2   How do the rights of debtholders differ from the rights of equityholders?

Q3   Is preferred stock equity or debt?

Q4   What is an IPO? How does it take place?

Q5   What is a Eurobond (or international bond)?

Q6   What are the main types of bond issued by governments and firms?

Q7   If you start a high-tech firm, what are the initial likely sources of finance and how would this change as the firm becomes successful?

Q8   What are the possible risks for a private equity firm undertaking a leveraged buy-out (LBO)?

CHAPTER 3

Financial Instruments

AIMS

- To examine money market assets such as term deposits and loans, the Euromarkets, Treasury bills, commercial bills, certificates of deposit and repos.
- To examine government bonds.
- To see how companies borrow long-term debt via bank loans and the bond market.
- To examine different corporate bonds: fixed- and floating-coupon bonds, junk bonds, callable and convertible bonds.
- To examine equity finance via ordinary shares, preference shares and rights issues.
- To outline the main types of derivative contracts – forwards, futures, options and swaps.

INTRODUCTION

The **fixed-income market** comprises assets whose future payments are either fixed or determined according to a prearranged formula (e.g. the cash payout paid at the end of year 2 will be determined by the six-month interest rate beginning in eighteen months time). The money market is a subset of the fixed-income market dealing in short-term assets, while the bond market deals in long-term fixed-income securities.

3.1 MONEY MARKETS

The money market refers to a loosely connected set of institutions that deal in short-term lending and borrowing either over the counter (OTC), for example bank deposits and loans (under one year maturity), or by issuing marketable securities (usually with a maturity of less than one year). These money market instruments include those issued by the public sector (e.g. Treasury bills, local authority bills) and by the private sector (e.g. commercial bills/paper, trade bills, certificates of deposit (CDs)).

Eurocurrency market and LIBOR rates

Deposits and loans in your own currency can be obtained from your correspondent bank located in your own country (e.g. a dollar deposit by a US resident in a New York bank). But you can also obtain dollar loans/deposits from a bank outside the US. For example, Eurodollars are US dollars deposited in a bank outside the US, for example in Barclays in London or in Credit Agricole in Paris. These time deposits can be on-lent by the banks in the form of US dollar term loans to companies. These are the **Eurocurrency markets** and are direct competitors with the domestic loan markets. Euromarket interest rates are usually floating; that is, they are reset every three or six months and the interest rate you pay depends on the rates prevailing in the future.

The rates of interest paid are based on quoted **LIBOR** rates set by the London interbank market. For example, a corporate might be able to borrow funds at LIBOR+0.5% and would receive LIBOR−0.3% on its term deposits – hence the bank makes a spread of 0.8%. LIBOR rates will be quoted for all major currencies, so there is a USD-LIBOR rate and a Swiss Franc-LIBOR rate (Figure 3.1). For the Euro there is a Euro-LIBOR rate quoted by a consortium of banks in London and a 'Euro-Euribor' rate quoted by a consortium of European banks – needless to say both rates are very similar (this is arbitrage again). For US$-LIBOR, Euro-LIBOR and £-LIBOR the one-year rates are slightly below the six-month rates, probably indicating that the market thinks annual price inflation will fall slightly relative to inflation over the next six months. (EURONIA and SONIA stand for Euro and Sterling overnight index average rates of interest, respectively.)

Brokers can borrow from banks agreeing to repay the bank immediately if the bank requests it – these are **call loans**. The broker uses these call loans to on-lend to his clients who wish to purchase stocks on margin.

The **Federal Funds rate** is the rate at which large US banks (which are members of the Federal Reserve System, the 'Fed') lend and borrow from each other. It is mainly an overnight market.

MARKET RATES

Oct 2	Over night	Day	Change Week	Month	One month	Three months	Six months	One year
US$ Libor*	5.03813	+0.017	+0.186	-0.313	5.12625	5.24000	5.16250	4.97563
Euro Libor*	3.92250	-0.005	-0.325	+0.080	4.38250	4.79188	4.75563	4.71750
£ Libor*	5.81000	+0.010	+0.079	+0.481	6.14625	6.25875	6.25500	6.14750
Swiss Fr Libor*	2.36500	+0.015	+0.065	+0.245	2.54167	2.79000	2.88000	2.99500
Yen Libor*	0.65750	-0.016	+0.029	+0.011	0.78250	1.02563	1.09625	1.15500
Canada Libor*	4.94167	+0.050	+0.192	+0.692	4.90333	4.92167	4.90000	4.85000
Euro Euribor	-	-	-	-	4.38	4.60	4.75	4.72
Sterling CDs	-	-	-	-	6.00	6.21	6.17	6.07
US$ CDs	-	-	-	-	4.87	5.00	4.92	4.72
Euro CDs	-	-	-	-	4.350	4.770	4.720	4.660
US o'night repo	4.76	+0.050	-0.140	-0.510				
Fed Funds eff	4.92	+0.340	+0.180	-0.380				
US 3m Bills	3.83	+0.025	+0.140	-1.085				
SDR int rate	3.82	-	+0.030	-0.270				
EONIA	3.83	-0.029	-0.389	-0.001				
EURONIA	3.8013	-0.1787	-0.4107	-0.0253				
SONIA	5.7604	+0.0122	+0.1429	+0.4761				
LA 7 Day Notice	6.00-5.90							

	Over night	One Week	One month	Three months	Six months	One year
Interbank £	5.85-5.60	5.88-5.80	6.12-6.04	6.20-6.10	6.23-6.13	6.10-6.00

*Libor rates come from BBA (see www.bba.org.uk) and are fixed at 11am UK time. Other data sources: US $, Euro & Cds: dealers; SDR int rate: IMF; EONIA: ECB; EURONIA & SONIA: WMBA. LA 7 days notice: Tradition (UK).

FIGURE 3.1:
Source: Financial Times, reproduced by permission.

Bills

Bills are marketable 'paper' and are usually **discount instruments**. This means that the holder of the bill does not receive any interest payments: the bill derives its value wholly from the fact that it is redeemed at maturity for an amount greater than its selling price. For example, if a firm or government issues a six-month bill today at a price of $980 and with a face value of $1000, then the market quotes the **discount rate**, which is 2% (= $20/$1000) over six months or 4% p.a. However, the cost of borrowing is actually the **yield** on the bill, which is 2.041% (= $20/$980) over six months (or 4.082% at a simple annual rate).

Short-term *Treasury bills* are issued to cover temporary shortfalls in the government's net receipts. For example, a government purchasing department may have to pay its suppliers of stationery next week, but in this particular week tax receipts may be unusually low. It may therefore obtain the finance required by issuing Treasury bills.

Newly issued UK T-bills normally have a maturity of 91 or 182 days, and are pure discount bearer instruments. In the US T-bills are issued with maturities of 13 weeks, 26 weeks and 1 year. Again, they are pure discount bearer instruments. The 13-week and 26-week T-bills are issued by auction every Monday, with the securities allotted on the basis of the highest prices in the (sealed) bids.

The commercial paper market is very large in the US, as corporates often borrow short-term money by issuing **commercial bills** rather than using bank loans.

A **banker's acceptance** is created when a firm gets a bank to issue a security stating that the bank will pay money to one of the firm's creditors at a fixed time in the future – it is like a post-dated check. But once the bank has 'accepted' responsibility for ultimate payment to the holder of the acceptance, it can be traded in the secondary market (at a discount to its face value) and is effectively a debt of the bank. Banker's acceptances are used to finance foreign trade where the initial borrower of the funds may have a relatively low credit rating. But by being 'accepted' the security has the high credit rating of the bank.

If a corporate or financial institution has a short-term cash surplus it can place it in a bank six-month term deposit – but the money is tied up for six months. An alternative is for the corporate to place the funds on deposit at the bank by using a certificate of deposit. A **certificate of deposit (CD)** is a 'piece of paper' giving the terms (i.e. amount, interest rate and time to maturity) on which a corporate has placed funds on deposit. In this respect it is like a (fixed) term deposit. However, with a CD, if the corporate finds itself in need of cash (before the six months are up) it can sell the CD to a third party and hence obtain cash immediately. CD rates are quoted on a yield basis (rather than as a discount on the face value).

Market makers hold an inventory of bills and CDs and stand ready to buy and sell them (usually over the phone) at prices that are continuously quoted and updated on the dealers' screens. At the core of the market in the US are the 'money market banks' (i.e. large banks in New York), government securities dealers, commercial paper dealers and money brokers (who specialise in finding short-term money for borrowers and placing it with lenders).

Most of the above assets have very little default risk and therefore most would qualify as risk-free assets, earning a risk-free interest rate. Clearly, rates of interest on bank term deposits are known with certainty, but how about the yield on T-bills? If you intend to hold the T-bill to maturity, then today you know exactly the return you will get and in this sense the T-bill yield is a **risk-free rate**. However, if you intend to sell the T-bill prior to maturity, the future selling price and hence the return are not known with certainty and in this sense the T-bill is not risk free.

Repurchase agreements, repos

A widely used method of borrowing short-term cash (used particularly by market makers and dealers in government securities) is to undertake a **repurchase agreement** or **repo**. A repo, or more accurately a 'sale and repurchase agreement', is a form of collateralised borrowing. Suppose you own a government bond but wish to borrow cash over the next seven days – this is a 'term repo'. You can enter an agreement to sell the bond to Ms A for $100 today and *simultaneously agree* to buy it back in seven days' time for $100.10. You receive $100 cash (now) and the counterparty Ms A receives $100.10 (in seven days) – an interest rate of 0.1% over seven days (or $5.21\% = 0.1 \times 365/7$, expressed as a simple annual rate). Ms A has provided a collateratised loan, since she holds the bond and could sell it if you default on the repo. In fact because you might default on the loan, if you provide bonds worth $100 today, Ms A will actually lend you slightly less than $100 cash (say $99) – this is known as a 'haircut'.

Central banks often use repos in their open market operations, rather than outright purchases/ sales of bonds, when trying to influence interest rates. Repos can be as short as over one day and there are very active markets in maturities up to three months. Note that if you undertake a repo, the counterparty is said to undertake a **reverse repo** and the counterparty will there- fore be *lending* money. Further details of assets traded in the money market and the methods used to determine their prices and yields are the subject of Chapter 19.

Repo = borrowing money (by selling a security to a counterparty).
Reverse repo = lending money (by purchasing a security from a counterparty).

3.2 BOND MARKETS

Government bonds

Medium- and long-term bonds are issued to raise funds to cover any excess of long-term planned government spending over forecasted tax revenue (i.e. the government's budget deficit, or public sector borrowing requirement, PSBR).

Government securities have several common characteristics. First, they are generally regard- ed as being free from default risk. This makes them a safer investment than most other instru- ments, and so allows governments to offer lower yields, reducing the cost of debt finance to the taxpayer. There is usually a very active secondary market in these instruments (in indus- trialised nations).

- Medium- and long-term bonds pay out fixed amounts known as *coupon* payments, usual- ly paid semi-annually, as well as a lump sum at redemption. Government bonds may be **bearer securities**, in which case whoever currently holds the security is deemed to be the owner, or there may be a **central register** of owners to whom interest payments (and even- tually the redemption value) are made.
- Bonds issued by the UK government (through the Debt Management Office) are called gilt-edged stock, or just gilts. They are issued usually on a monthly basis, for maturities of up to 30 years. **Eurobonds** are issued by governments in London, denominated in curren- cies other than sterling.
- Bonds issued by the US government (through the Federal Reserve Bank) are **Treasury notes** that have a maturity of between 1 and 10 years and **Treasury bonds** at maturities between 10 and 30 years (and sometimes longer). Coupon payments are usually made semi-annually.

Some governments (e.g. UK and US) also issue index-linked bonds where the coupon pay- ments and redemption value are adjusted for changes in inflation. For investors, index-linked bonds provide a hedge against inflation and therefore give a (near) guaranteed real return. Case Study 3.1 outlines the introduction of Islamic bonds, which may expand quite rapidly over the next few years.

CASE STUDY 3.1   ISLAMIC BONDS

Many Muslims believe that the Koran prohibits the payment of interest (*riba*) and all financial speculation (*gharar*). This clearly inhibits Muslims using many products familiar in Western banking. However, recently Islamic bonds (*sukuk*) have been introduced that circumvent these problems. These Islamic bonds make regular payments just like the coupons on Western bonds, but the payments must be generated by some form of business activity owned by the issuer and not by interest earned on cash. For example, Pakistan issues Islamic bonds and uses receipts from state toll-roads with which to pay the regular coupon payments.

In 2007 the UK Treasury began the legal processes required to issue UK government bonds that are Sharia compliant. These will allow Muslims worldwide to invest in UK government bonds, but also other savings products such as National Savings. This will widen the consumer base for financing the UK government deficit and also helps the City to be a key player in the provision of financial instruments to Muslims. These Islamic bonds may be more expensive to issue than standard bonds, partly because religious advice will be required so that they are Sharia compliant. However, London seems to be ahead of its rivals in New York, Tokyo and Frankfurt in attempting to attract Islamic finance business, so it may gain first-mover advantage in the Western financial system. The UK government hopes that a large primary market as well as a secondary market in Islamic bonds will develop rapidly in London. This will include sovereign bonds as well as corporate bonds issued by firms in Islamic areas such as Turkey, North Africa, the Middle East, Malaysia and the Philippines. Once again, the UK government and the City are combining forces to provide innovative ways to attract more financial business to the City of London.

Other public-sector securities

In the UK, local authorities and public corporations (companies) also issue debt, denominated in both sterling and foreign currencies. In the US, bonds issued by states, counties, cities and towns are called **municipal bonds**. These public-sector securities are not perceived as being free from default risk, nor are the markets for them as deep or as liquid as those for central government debt. Consequently they tend to offer higher yields than central government debt.

For longer-term borrowing, some local governments (municipalities) and central governments use the syndicated bank loan market (i.e. an OTC transaction involving several banks) or the Eurobond market.

The technical details of the relationship between bond prices and yields on government bonds and further details of these important markets are discussed in Chapter 20. In Chapter 21 we look at a related issue, namely the relationship between yields on bonds of different maturities (yield curve) and explanations for the shape of the yield curve, which is referred to as the *term structure of interest rates*.

Corporate bonds

A corporate can raise long-term debt finance through bank loans or an issue of corporate bonds. We discussed the former in Chapter 2 and here we elaborate on raising finance through marketable debt, such as corporate bonds.

A public issue of bonds follows a similar procedure to that for stocks. In general, the issue must be approved by the board of directors (and sometimes by a vote of the stockholders) and often a registration statement has to be issued to the regulatory authorities (e.g. the Securities & Exchange Commission (SEC) in the US). The registration statement includes an *indenture* or *deed of trust*, which is a written agreement between the bond issuer and a trust company. The trust company is appointed by the issuing company to represent the bondholders' interests and the bond indenture will cover the following issues:

- the 'cash' terms in the bond (e.g. amount of issue, par value of each bond, coupon rate, maturity date, etc.)
- collateral protecting the bondholder
- sinking fund arrangements
- protective covenants
- convertible and call elements

Let's consider each of these elements in turn. The bond issue might be for $100m total value, with each bond having a face value of $1000. A coupon of 10% p.a. payable every six months would imply dollar payments of $100 p.a. (10% of $1000), in two equal instalments of $50 every six months. The maturity date might be in 20 years time. The selling price of the bonds might be 99, which implies 99% of $1000 or $990 per bond. The bonds may be either registered or bearer bonds.

Collateral

The collateral protecting the bondholder can be of several types. For example, in the US a **collateral trust bond** has as collateral shares owned by the company issuing the bonds. So if the bond issuer owns shares in another company – XYZ, say – then the latter can be sold and the proceeds used to pay the bondholders their coupon payments and repayment of the principal. **Mortgage-backed securities** are bonds that are secured on specific assets (e.g. railroad bonds are often secured on the company's rolling stock, which could be sold to other railroad companies to payoff the bondholders).

The term **debenture** is a tricky concept, since its meaning can vary in different countries. In the US a debenture is an unsecured bond. If the firm defaults, a debenture holder in the US will only receive payment after payments have been made to mortgage and collateral trust bondholders. Most industrial and finance company bonds in the US are debentures, while the exceptions here are bonds issued by US utilities and railroads, which are secured on specific assets. Another key factor in a bond issue is whether the bonds are senior debt or junior debt, since this determines the order in which debtors will be paid in the event of bankruptcy.

Sinking fund

Although the face (par) value of all bonds issued could be paid at maturity, a sinking fund to pay off the bond's par value gradually over a period of time is more usual. Typically, the company makes equal annual payments to the trust company after a 'grace period' of several years (e.g. 7 years on a 20-year bond). These payments are sufficient to redeem at par, say, 80% of the outstanding bonds (with the remaining 20% 'balloon' paid at maturity). The trust company uses these sinking fund payments to redeem the outstanding bonds either by purchasing them at market prices or by selecting bonds randomly (by lottery) and purchasing them at face (par) value.

The existence of a sinking fund allows bondholders an 'early warning' if the company is getting into financial distress, since it will then not be able to meet its sinking fund provision. But there are also advantages to the issuer. The company may have the option either to repurchase its bonds in the open market (when the market price is below par value) or to repurchase at par (when the market price is above par value). Hence the company may gain a valuable option from the sinking fund provisions.

Protective covenants

These are either restrictions on things the company may want to do that would harm the bondholders (i.e. *restrictive covenants*) or actions that the company must undertake to enhance the position of bondholders (i.e. *positive covenants*). Restrictive covenants might include:

- restrictions on the amount of dividends that can be paid to shareholders
- restrictions on sales of company assets (e.g. of subsidiary companies)
- restrictions on issues of more long-term debt

Positive covenants might include:

- forcing the company to hedge some of its interest rate risk
- maintaining a minimum level of liquid assets to pay creditors

The US corporate bond market is the largest in the world and Figure 3.2 (from the *Financial Times*) shows the (bid) yield, (bid) price and credit ratings by Standard & Poor's (S&P), Moody's and Fitch. The yield and credit rating are (usually) inversely related. For example, retailer Wal-Mart with an S&P rating of AA has a yield of 4.93% (for bonds maturing in August 09) while DaimlerChrysler with a BBB+ rating has a yield of 5.38% (for bonds maturing in September 09). In the last column of Figure 3.2 is the yield spread over government bonds (T-bonds) of the same maturity. Generally, the yield spreads widen as the credit rating falls – as one would expect.

As we see below, these spreads are a measure of the 'risk premium' on the bond. Also, in the next chapter we see how the yields on corporate bonds can be used to calculate a market-based measure of the probability of default of the corporate. These probabilities are used by banks in determining the probability of default of their *whole portfolio* of corporate bonds and corporate loans, which determines the amount of 'capital' they hold as a 'cushion' against these possible 'bad debts'. This whole area is known as credit risk assessment and is currently the

GLOBAL INVESTMENT GRADE

Oct 3	Red date	Coupon	Ratings S*	Ratings M*	Ratings F*	Bid price	Bid yield	Day's chge yield	Mth's chge yield	Spread vs Govts
■ US $										
KFW Int Fin	03/10	1.75	AAA	Aaa	AAA	101.91	0.97	+0.02	+0.01	+0.09
CIT Group	02/08	3.50	AA	Aa1	AA+	99.36	5.54	-0.02	-0.38	+1.57
GE Capital	06/07	5.00	AAA	Aaa	n/a	99.96	5.48	-0.03	–	+0.59
Depfa Pfandrbnk	10/07	3.38	AAA	Aaa	n/a	99.26	5.38	-0.15	–	+0.48
Goldman Sachs	01/08	4.13	AA-	Aa3	AA-	99.60	5.54	-0.06	-0.42	+1.56
Citigroup	02/08	3.50	AA	Aa1	AA+	99.36	5.54	-0.02	-0.38	+1.57
Canada	11/08	5.25	n/a	Aaa	AAA	100.69	4.56	+0.03	-0.18	+0.41
DaimlerChrysler	09/09	7.20	BBB+	A3	A-	103.23	5.38	+0.06	+0.07	+1.36
Wal Mart	08/09	6.88	AA	Aa2	AA	103.39	4.93	-0.05	-0.17	+0.95
Du Pont	10/09	6.88	A	A2	A	104.01	4.78	+0.01	-0.14	+0.80
Philipps Petr	05/10	8.75	A-	A1	A-	110.32	4.55	+0.03	-0.15	+0.56
Unilever	11/10	7.13	A+	A1	A+	105.87	5.03	+0.03	-0.05	+1.01
Bank America	01/11	7.40	AA-	Aa2	AA-	107.13	5.01	+0.01	+0.12	+1.02
JP Morgan	02/11	6.75	A+	Aa3	A+	105.07	5.07	-0.02	-0.06	+1.07
France Telecom	03/11	7.75	A-	A3	A-	109.02	4.84	-0.02	-0.14	+0.84
Petronas	05/12	7.00	A-	A1	A	107.76	5.10	-0.03	-0.12	+0.89
Goldman Sachs	11/14	5.50	AA-	Aa3	AA-	98.59	5.74	-0.02	-0.22	+1.54
Italy	09/23	6.88	A+	Aa2	AA-	115.10	5.45	+0.03	–	+0.90
Pacific Bell	03/26	7.13	A	A2	A	105.70	6.59	-0.03	+0.06	+1.78
Deutsche Tel	07/13	5.25	A-	A3	A-	98.53	5.55	+0.02	+0.05	+1.32
DaimlerChrysler	01/31	8.50	BBB+	A3	A-	124.52	6.45	-0.09	-0.09	+1.68
FHLMC	03/31	6.75	AAA	Aaa	AAA	120.81	5.20	+0.02	+0.04	+0.41
GE Capital	03/32	6.75	AAA	Aaa	AAA	110.96	5.90	-0.02	-0.09	+1.13
Gen Motors	11/31	8.00	BB+	Ba1	BB+	106.00	7.46	–	–	+2.23
■ Euro										
Dresdner Fin	01/07	4.00	MATD	MATD	MATD	100.00	–	–	–	–
Eurohypo	02/07	4.00	AAA	Aaa	AAA	100.00	4.14	–	–	+0.65
BNG	05/07	2.88	MATD	MATD	MATD	99.97	–	–	–	–
ING Bank	07/07	5.63	AA	Aa1	AA	100.20	3.71	-0.03	–	-0.20
TPSA Eurofin	12/08	7.75	BBB+	Baa1	BBB+	103.35	4.79	+0.01	-0.20	+0.63
BAT Int Fin	02/09	4.88	BBB+	Baa1	A-	99.84	4.98	+0.22	+0.40	+0.93
VW Int Fin	05/09	4.13	A-	A3	A-	99.14	4.67	+0.12	+0.19	+0.64
SMBC Int Fin	06/09	8.50	A	Aa3	BBB+	105.14	5.28	+0.01	+0.23	+1.30
Depfa Pfandrbnk	01/09	3.75	AAA	Aaa	AAA	99.15	4.44	+0.01	+0.07	+0.38
Mannesman Fin	05/09	4.75	A-	Baa1	A-	99.90	4.80	+0.25	+0.25	-0.77
Deutsche Fin	07/09	4.25	AA	Aa1	AA-	99.95	4.27	-0.26	-0.26	+0.24
Repsol Int Fin	05/10	6.00	BBB	Baa1	BBB+	102.81	4.80	+0.21	+0.24	+0.69
Elec de France	10/10	5.75	AA-	Aa1	AA	103.41	4.53	+0.02	+0.06	+0.41
HVB	09/11	5.00	AAA	Aa1	AAA	101.89	4.46	+0.02	+0.01	+0.28
■ YEN										
Tokyo Elec	11/06	2.80	MATD	MATD	MATD	100.00	2.80	–	–	–
Nippon Teleg	07/07	2.50	MATD	MATD	n/a	100.00	2.44	–	–	–
Toyota Motor	06/08	0.75	AAA	Aaa		99.85	0.97	–	+0.05	+0.40
KFW Int Fin	03/10	1.75	AAA	Aaa	AAA	101.91	0.97	+0.02	+0.01	+0.09
Chubu Elec	07/15	3.40	NR	Aa2	AA-	112.70	1.57	–	+0.04	–
■ £										
DaimlerChrysler	12/06	7.50	BBB	Baa1	BBB+	100.00	–	–	–	–
HBOS	04/08	6.38	AA	Aa1	AA+	99.79	6.60	-0.04	+0.47	+1.26
Network Rail	03/09	4.88	AAA	Aaa	AAA	99.27	5.33	-0.01	-0.36	+0.30
Boots	05/09	5.50	BB-	B2	BBB	94.62	8.94	-0.03	+0.34	+3.91
France Telecom	03/11	7.50	A-	A3	n/a	104.56	6.01	+0.01	-0.29	+0.98

US $ denominated bonds NY close; all other London close. *S - Standard & Poor's, M - Moody's, F - Fitch.

Source: Reuters

FIGURE 3.2:

Source: Financial Times, reproduced by permission.

subject of revised regulatory rules, which are being implemented under the auspices of the Bank for International Settlements (BIS) in Basle (see Cuthbertson and Nitzsche, 2001b).

Callable bonds

In the US almost all debentures are callable. A **call provision** allows the company to *call* (i.e. repurchase) the bond at a known fixed value (the call price) at specific times in the future. Generally the call price is set above the face value. So for example, a call price of 105, with a par value of $1000, implies that the bond can be called for $1050 – a *call premium* of $50. Often the call premium is initially set equal to the (dollar) coupon and then declines to zero over the life of the bond.

The call provision on a bond is an embedded option that benefits the company rather than the bondholders. Consider the following. If interest rates fall then the market price of the bond may rise to, say, $1100 above the call price of $1050. If so, the company may be able to call the bond at, say, $1050, whereas the market price is currently at $1100. After calling each bond and paying $1050, the company can reissue bonds *with the same coupon and maturity* at the higher market price of $1100 (or equivalently at a lower yield to maturity). The company therefore needs to issue fewer bonds to refinance the existing bonds outstanding. (We ignore the transaction costs of refinancing here.)

A company aiming to maximise shareholder wealth should 'extract' any advantage it can get from bondholders. So a firm should call its bonds (and refund its debt) as soon as the market price of the bond exceeds the call price. In practice, firms often do not call their bonds even when the market price is at a substantial premium to the call price, but the reasons for this are far from clear.

Perhaps the firm does not call the bond because it is trying to maximise *future* receipts from bond sales and therefore does not seek to expropriate all of its advantage from the current bondholders. Clearly, a call provision is a disincentive to purchasing the bonds, since bondholders may be deprived of capital gains when interest rates fall sharply. Consequently, callable bonds offer higher coupons (and yields) compared to conventional (non-callable) bonds. Note also that the call provision is not usually operative in the first few years (e.g. for the first 7 years on a 20-year bond).

If the company has to pay a higher coupon (or yield), why would it issue callable bonds rather than conventional bonds? One reason might be for tax purposes. The higher coupons are tax deductible for the company but taxable for the bondholder. If the bondholder is in a lower tax bracket than the company, the company will gain more than the bondholder will lose in taxes. The company may use this tax saving to pass on in the form of higher coupons. Second, because the callable bond has a higher coupon, it has a lower duration and is therefore less sensitive to changes in interest rates, which *may* also benefit shareholders by reducing their risk. Perhaps the most cogent reason for issuing callable bonds is that the call provision gives the company the option to 'get rid of' any restrictive covenants in the bond indenture, prior to maturity of the bonds. For example, if the company sees a profitable acquisition target, but the bond covenants prohibit a takeover or merger, the company can go ahead with the acquisition by first calling the bonds.

Convertible bonds

Debt convertibles (convertible bonds or convertible loan stock) are bonds that are 'convertible' into ordinary shares of the same firm, at the choice of the bondholder, after a period of time. The shares are 'paid for' by surrendering the bonds. The pros and cons of convertibles are summarised in Case Study 3.2.

CASE STUDY 3.2   CONVERTIBLE BONDS

A convertible bond gives the holder the right (but not the obligation) to purchase a given number of shares at a fixed price at some time in the future. Convertible bonds will usually carry a yield below that on similar conventional bonds, because the convertible has a valuable 'embedded call option'. They are usually unsecured and subordinated (i.e. junior debt). From the investor's point of view, convertibles allow a periodic coupon payment, but if the firm is successful the investor can share in higher profits by converting the bond into equities at a later date. Hence, the investor does not have to be so worried about the firm issuing extra senior debt, which would rank over the convertible. Also, if the company invests in high-risk projects then at least the holder of the convertible will share in the gains if these are successful (whereas an ordinary bondholder would only receive the fixed-coupon payments). Convertibles are therefore useful to protect the bondholder against a wrong assessment of the risk of the firm and are often issued by smaller and more risky firms.

Convertibles also usually have a provision whereby the issuer can *buy back (or 'call')* the convertible bond at a fixed price. This call provision is a way of forcing conversion and the issuer will undertake this option if the current market value of the bond is greater than the current value of the shares the issuer has to 'give up', at conversion.

Clearly, convertibles if converted alter the *debt–equity ratio* of the company. If they are converted then they also 'dilute' the holdings of the existing shareholders, since the profits of the company are now spread over a larger number of shareholders (of course the company does save on the interest payments and the repayment of principal). In their financial statements companies must show how their earnings per share would be affected by conversion.

It should be obvious that if the stock price rises sufficiently, then the convertibles will be exchanged by their holders for stocks at a fixed price. This works as follows. Suppose the convertible is a 20-year bond with an 8% coupon and is issued at par (= $100) in 2005. The current share price is $2, the *conversion price* is $2.50 and the latter 'option' can be exercised at any time after 2008. The *conversion ratio* is:

$$\text{Conversion Ratio} = \frac{\text{Nominal value of bond}}{\text{conversion price}} = \frac{\$100}{\$2.50} = 40$$

So each bond can be converted into 40 shares. Convertibles are protected against stock splits and stock dividends. For example, if in the above case there was a 2 for 1 stock split, the conversion ratio would be increased to 80 and the conversion price would drop to $1.25. Often the conversion price is stepped up over time to reflect the potential growth in the firm's profits.

The bondholder will only be tempted to exercise this option if the stock price after 2008 rises above the conversion price of $2.50 (the latter is equivalent to the strike price K in a conventional option). The *conversion premium* is:

$$\text{Conversion Premium} = \frac{K - S}{S} = \frac{\$2.50 - \$2}{\$2} = 25\%$$

If the stock price does not rise above $K = \$2.50$, then the bondholder will not exercise the 'embedded option' and will continue to receive the 8% coupon.

The *advantages to the issuer* of the convertible are:

- It can issue convertibles at a lower yield than a conventional bond.
- If the firm believes its current stock price is artificially low, it can raise funds by issuing convertibles. If the stock price subsequently rises, the firm issues more shares when the bonds are 'converted' but it then does not have to use its cash flow to pay further coupons and principal (e.g. issuing convertibles can be useful for governments who wish to privatise state firms that have no track record in the market).
- The covenants on hybrid 'debt–equity' such as a convertible are usually less than on conventional bonds (e.g. often unsecured and the holders do not impose restrictions on interest cover, etc.).
- Interest payments are tax deductible against profits.

The *advantages to the holder* of a convertible are:

- Periodic fixed-coupon payments.
- Payment before any ordinary shareholders.
- Option to switch from debt to equity.
- They can share in higher profits if the firm does well since the bonds will then be converted to shares. Hence they are useful when the risk of a company is difficult to assess and when the scale of its future senior debt issues are uncertain.

Who issues convertible bonds? Well in the main, more convertibles are issued by:

- young high growth firms, rather than established firms
- firms with relatively low credit ratings rather than high credit ratings

Convertibles are often unsecured and subordinated debt. In a sense, the payments profile for convertibles matches the expected revenues of firms that issue them. Young firms have low net cash flows in their early years and this is matched by the lower coupon payments of convertibles (relative to conventional bonds). However, later cash flows are expected to be high. While this makes conversion likely, it is at a time when the firm is strong enough to withstand 'dilution' and higher dividend payments. Issuing convertibles also partially solves the problem of accurately assessing the riskiness of young firms or the possibility that they may act in a risky or cavalier fashion, such as taking on high-risk strategies in the future without the consent of bondholders (i.e. an agency problem). Compared with a conventional bond, the holder of a convertible can share in the profits from these 'high-risk' projects if they are successful. Convertibles, like warrants, are 'equity kickers'.

There is one final aspect of convertibles you should be aware of. Most convertibles have a (deferred) call provision. When the convertible bond is called, the holder has the following choices:

- 'sell' the bond to the company and receive the call price in cash (of, say, $K = 105\%$ of $1000)
- convert the bond into shares at the known conversion value (i.e. conversion ratio $\times$ current share price)

Clearly, the bondholder will convert to shares if the conversion value exceeds the call price of $K = \$1050$, otherwise she will take the cash of $1050. This choice clearly affects the cash flow of the firm and its debt–equity ratio.

Unfortunately, establishing the 'fair price' for warrants, convertibles and callable bonds is far from straightforward and we cannot deal with it in this book. However the interested reader should consult Cuthbertson and Nitzsche (2001b).

Other marketable debt

There are a number of permutations on the 'conventional' or 'plain vanilla' corporate bond, besides their convertible and callable properties. These are designed to appeal to particular investors and some of these are outlined below.

A **floating-rate note (FRN)** is a bond on which the coupon payments $C are linked to a short-term interest rate such as three- or six-month LIBOR. FRNs are particularly popular in the Euromarkets. Future coupon payments on an FRN are uncertain but somewhat paradoxically, this implies that their market price does not fluctuate as much as that of a conventional 'fixed-coupon' bond. Intuitively, the price of the 'floater' does not alter much because as interest rates change both the numerator (i.e. the floating coupon payment) and the denominator (i.e. the interest rate) move in the same direction, partially cancelling each other out. In contrast, for a fixed-coupon bond a change in interest rates only affects the denominator of the bond price formula and hence the price alters substantially. Since changes in inflation (expectations) are a major source of changes in interest rates, then 'floaters' can be seen as reducing inflation risk, compared with holding a fixed-coupon bond.

> Floaters are often issued with 'floor' or 'floor and ceiling' provisions, which limit the range of coupon adjustments. These floors and ceilings are a form of embedded options, in the floater. For example, if current interest rates are 10%, the FRN might have a floor of 8% and a ceiling of 12%, which limits the lowest and highest coupon rate payable in any period. So if, for example, current interest rates are 14%, the coupon payable will only be 12% (of the par value) in that period.

Some companies also raise finance by issuing **deep-discount bonds**. These are zero-coupon bonds and they are attractive to institutions such as pension funds that have a known *nominal* payment (e.g. a pension lump sum) at a specific date in the future. A 'zero' then provides a perfect hedge. Because coupon bonds can be 'stripped', there are relatively few deep-discount bonds issued. **Income bonds** (in the US) allow the issuer to defer coupon payments if the firm's income is insufficient, and this cannot lead to the company being in default. However, income bonds are not popular, partly because they 'have the smell of death' since they signal an increased probability of financial distress and partly because of the difficulties of measuring the firm's income and hence whether the coupons can be deferred.

Medium-term Notes (MTN) are very popular in the US, where they are issued by a corporate to an agent who then *offers them continuously* to investors in different amounts and maturities (e.g. 9 months to 1 year, 1 to 2 years and so on, up to 30 years). They fill the funding gap between commercial paper and long-term bonds. They can be fixed- or floating-rate debt, with coupons in domestic or foreign currency, or with coupons linked to an equity index. The more complex MTNs are known as *structured notes* since they are often tailored by the agent based on a specific request by an investor.

Mezzanine finance is a catch-all term for hybrid debt instruments that rank for payment below 'conventional' debt but above equity – they are often also referred to as **subordinated**, **high-yield**, **low-grade** or **junk bonds**. Since the early 1980s, it has become common for firms to make initial offerings of bonds graded below investment grade (i.e. usually those ranked below BBB by S&P and below Baa for Moody's). These were often issued in the 1980s in the US as a source of finance for management buy-outs MBOs (for example the $25bn takeover of RJR Nabisco) or raising cash for takeovers (i.e. leveraged buy-outs, LBOs). Interest payments on such debt are either fixed or floating (e.g. linked to LIBOR). These bonds have a high risk of default and hence carry a high yield. They have come to be known as **junk bonds**.

There is a contentious debate over whether a portfolio of junk bonds does earn a return that compensates for the risks involved. There have been surprisingly few actual defaults on junk bonds, although if default were unlikely they would, of course, not offer such a high yield. They appear to be useful speculative instruments for investors who wish to increase their risk exposure, and for companies who wish to avoid the ownership and control implications of issuing equity. Some junk bonds arise from 'fallen angels'. If a company starts out with a high credit rating, performs poorly and then experiences a downgrade in its rating to below triple-B, this would be referred to as a **fallen angel**.

> **CASE STUDY 3.3   JUNK BOND KING**
>
> The junk bond 'king' of the 1980s was Michael Milken, who worked for the invest-ment bank Drexel Burnham Lambert and who was able to persuade large institutional investors to purchase junk bonds, which were then used for MBOs or takeovers. The debt-to-equity ratio of such financial deals could be higher than 10 to 1, so the firms were very highly geared and some inevitably failed. Once a year Drexel held a lavish party that colloquially became known as the 'Predator's Ball'. Milken was in fact sent to jail for fraud (and paid about $600m in fines) and Drexel went bankrupt in 1990.

Because high-coupon bonds are risky, in some LBOs they are issued with **deferred-coupon payments** (e.g. for three to seven years) or are **step-up bonds**, where the coupon starts low and increases over time, or **extendable reset bonds**, where the coupon is periodically reset so the bond trades at a pre-determined price (e.g. if the credit spread over Treasuries increas-es the yield, then the coupon will be raised to reflect this, so that the bond will still trade near par).

3.3 EQUITY MARKETS

Firms can raise debt finance from bank loans and this does not affect the ownership of the firm, which may be in the hands of a small number of 'initial investors' whose shares are not traded. (These may be 'family firms' or firms with a minority shareholder interest from busi-ness angels or venture capitalists.) However, at some point the firm may wish to raise addi-tional equity finance by an initial public offering (IPO) of shares. The ownership of the firm will then pass to the 'new' shareholders (as a group). In this section we begin by discussing the difference between ordinary and preference shares. In addition, a 'mature' publicly quot-ed firm may wish to raise additional equity finance and one method for doing so is a 'rights issue' and this is discussed below. We also consider the use of scrip issues and stock splits.

Ordinary shares

In general, there are two types of shares issued: ordinary and preference shares.

Essentially, ordinary shareholders are the owners of the firm, with a residual claim on prof-its (after tax and payment of interest on debt). Such 'earnings' are either retained or distrib-uted as dividends to shareholders. For example, **ordinary shares** (of UK companies) have the following characteristics:

- Voting rights (usually one vote per share) are set down in the Memorandum of Association, which include the right to appoint the board of directors and the auditors.

- Shares are normally non-redeemable with a par value (i.e. fully paid-up value), but they can be issued 'partly paid' and then paid for in instalments.
- Shareholders are the residual claimants on the firm's profits and therefore may not receive dividends if current (or previous retained) earnings are low.

'Preferred ordinary' and **'deferred ordinary'** shares rank behind **'ordinary shares'** for receipt of payment. 'Deferred' are second in the 'pecking order' for dividend payments. Some firms also have non-voting shares.

Preference shares

Preference shares have some characteristics of ordinary shares and some characteristics of debt instruments. The characteristics of **preference shares** are:

- Holders have a claim on dividends that takes 'preference' over ordinary shareholders. Dividends are often paid at a pre-defined rate (either fixed or floating) and are often 'cumulative' rather than 'non-cumulative' (i.e. if 'cumulative' then any shortfall in dividend payments is made up in future years, before any further payments to ordinary shareholders).
- They are usually non-voting but they are often granted voting rights if preferred dividends have not been paid for some time. Preferred stockholders cannot put the firm into liquidation.
- If the firm goes into liquidation, payments to preference shareholders are paid after those to debtholders but before any payments to ordinary shareholders.
- In the US preferred stock dividends cannot be deducted as an 'interest expense' when calculating the issuer's corporate tax payments. (So US companies with losses have an incentive to issue preferred stock.) For ordinary US investors preferred dividends are taxed as income, but for US corporates who hold preferred stock of other companies, 80% of the dividends are tax deductible. Hence if the corporate tax rate were, say, 35% on bond income received, the effective tax rate on preferred dividends received would only be 7% ($= 0.2 \times 0.35$). Not surprisingly, most preferred stock in the US is held by corporates and because of the low effective tax rate, its pre-tax yield can often be below that on T-bonds.

Some preference shares are convertible into ordinary shares at a predetermined rate on specific dates, at the choice of the holder. These **convertible preference shares** are often issued as 'mezzanine finance' to venture capitalists. Hence investors get a fixed return and they can convert to ordinary shares if the firm is ultimately successful.

Rights issue

When a company initially 'goes public' (i.e. becomes a corporation), it usually obtains finance by issuing **ordinary shares** in an IPO or private placement, and it can also raise additional finance from debt (e.g. additional bank loans or corporate bond issues) or from preference shares. However, after some years, the board of directors may decide that additional ordinary share capital is required to finance fixed investment or to repay existing debt.

TABLE 3.1: Rights issue, Longevity.com

Data:	Existing equity	= 1m shares (at $25 par value)
	Current share price	= $100
	Current market cap.	= $100m (=1m × $100)
	Extra funds required	= $26.666m
	Offer price for new shares	= $80
Question:	What is the value of the shares after the rights issue (i.e. the 'ex-rights' price)? What could you sell your 'rights' for?	
Answer:	Number of new shares issued = $26.666 m/$80 = 333,333 shares. Hence, we have to issue 1 new share for every 3 existing shares. This is a 'one-for-three rights issue'.	
	3 old shares @ $100	= $300
	1 new share @ $80	= $80
	Hence, 4 shares are worth	= $380
	Value of 1 share (ex-rights)	= $95
	Hence, value of 1 right	= $15 (=$95 − $80)

Suppose a public company has been in existence for some time and it initially obtained finance via an IPO (i.e. unseasoned new issue). It now wants to raise additional equity finance. It could simply sell additional shares in the open market, which would constitute a **seasoned new issue**. However, since the *new* shareholders will receive dividends, the funds available for *existing* shareholders are likely to be reduced: their holding has become **diluted**. Because of the latter adverse effect, it is customary (or a legal requirement) to offer the new shares to *existing* shareholders in proportion to their existing holdings; this is a ***pre-emptive rights issue***. (Another reason for a rights issue is to fund a takeover by issuing the new shares to the shareholders of the company to be taken over, but here no cash is raised.) The cost of a rights issue (for cash), usually amounts to about 2 to 5% of total receipts from the issue.

However, countries differ over pre-emptive rights. In the US and Germany some companies can issue additional shares by auction (i.e. an unseasoned new issue) and do not have to offer them first to existing shareholders. If the directors sell some of 'the rights' to financial institutions by prior arrangement, this is known as a ***private placement***. An example of a 'one for three' rights issue is given in Table 3.1.

Existing equity for Longevity.com is 1m shares, at a current price of $100 per share, and hence the market value is $100m. To ensure that the rights are taken up, the offer price in the rights issue must be less than $100. Suppose Longevity.com chooses a share offer price of $80 (allowing for a contingency of a 20% fall in the share price before the rights issue would not be taken up). It wants to raise $26,666m to expand its range of funeral parlours, hence (ignoring rounding):

$$\text{Number of new shares} = \frac{\text{Funds Required}}{\text{Subscription Price}} = \frac{\$26.666m}{\$80} = 333,333$$

Shareholders (by convention) always get one right for each share they own and hence 1m rights are issued. However, the crucial point is how many 'rights' must be exercised to receive one new share:

$$\frac{\text{Number of 'rights' needed}}{\text{to buy one new share}} = \frac{\text{Number of 'old' shares}}{\text{Number of 'new' shares}} = \frac{1\text{m}}{333,333} = 3\,\text{rights}$$

This is a 'one for three' rights issue (Table 3.1). The rights clearly have value to existing shareholders since they have the option to purchase 'new' shares at $80, when the existing shares are currently worth $100. However, it is not quite as simple as this. If we assume that future earnings per share are unchanged by the rights issue, then these earnings are now spread over more shares, so the price of the shares should fall after the rights issue. What will the ex-rights share price be? Suppose the investor initially held three shares, then after the offer:

3 old shares @ $100	= $300
1 new share @ $80	= $80
Hence, 4 shares are worth	= $380
Value of 1 share (ex-rights)	= $95

Hence:

$$\text{Value of 1 right} = \text{new price} - \text{subscription price}$$
$$= \$95 - \$80 \quad = \quad \mathbf{\$15}$$

The ex-rights price will be $95 if the market price of the old shares remains at $100. The shareholder is no better off after taking up the rights, since she now holds four shares worth $95 per share (= $380), whereas before she owned three shares worth $100 per share, but she has also paid an extra $80 for the one share in the rights issue.

If a shareholder did *not* take up her rights issue then the value of her shareholding would fall by $15, since she now has three shares at $95 (= $285), whereas she started off with three shares at $100 (= $300). However, the shareholder receives an allotment letter for the new shares and if she doesn't wish to take up the rights, she can sell the allotment letter, for a premium. Given the 1 for 3 rights issue she could sell the rights for $15 per share, since she holds the allotment letter. The 'old' shareholder then ends up with three shares at $95 plus $15 in cash, a total of $300, which equals the pre-rights value of her initial three shares. The person who purchases the rights for $15 per share pays the subscription price of $80 and hence a total payment of $95 per share. The latter of course equals the ex-rights price she would pay by buying the share in the open market at $95.

It is always possible that the share price falls below $80, say to $70 before the rights are taken up. In this case none of the existing shareholders would take up the rights at a price of $80. Hence the rights issue has to be underwritten, for which the underwriter gets a small 'stand-by fee'. However, in practice the subscription price is set relatively low so that it is rare that rights issues are not fully taken up.

The directors decide the ratio of 'new to old' shares depending on whether they think the current price is too high. If they wish to lower the ex-rights price substantially (for a given amount of funds to raise) they will issue many more new shares (e.g. 1 for 2 rights issue). For example, if the subscription price for Longevity.com is set at $53.33 (i.e. 2/3 of $80) then:

$$\text{Number of new shares} = \frac{\$26.666\text{m}}{\$53.33} = 500,000$$

Given that the initial number of shares is 1 million, this implies that $26.666m can be raised with a subscription price of $53.33 and a 1 for 2 rights issue.

Script issues and splits

Script issues and stock splits are rather peculiar 'animals', since they do not raise additional finance and merely result in a 'cosmetic' change to the share price, but no overall change in share value. Their main *raison d'être* is that investors psychologically seem to like low quoted prices – although what constitutes 'low' varies from country to country.

In a **script issue**, new shares are *given* to existing shareholders. A script issue may ensue if the directors feel the quoted share price is too high. In a 1 for 1 script issue, one new share is given free for each existing share held by an investor. In a 1 for 2 **stock split**, each share held by an investor with par value $1 is replaced by two shares with par value of $0.50. In both of these cases the market price of each share held falls by one-half (but of course the total value of the shares held is the same). To give another example, if the share price was currently $100 then a 4 for 1 script issue would result in a market price of $20.

A **script dividend** (or **stock dividend**) is an issue of shares in lieu of a cash dividend and is usually an option given to shareholders. The firm does not have to pay out any cash, there is some share dilution and the shareholder gains additional shares (which may be taxed at a lower effective rate than the cash dividend).

In the UK the 'acceptable' range of market prices is around £1–15, whereas in the US prices up to $100 seem 'acceptable' and in Switzerland quoted prices equivalent to over $1000 are not uncommon. Of course, one possible advantage of a low quoted price is that 'small' investors can purchase at least one stock! But given the transaction cost of buying one share, this is hardly a compelling reason for stock splits and script issues to lower the quoted price. Note that a **reverse split or conversion** sometimes takes place when the stock price is at a very low level. So replacing 4 old shares with 1 new share will quadruple the quoted price.

3.4 DERIVATIVE SECURITIES

Under this heading we have forwards, futures, options and swaps. Forwards, futures and options are 'contracts' whose value depends on the value of some other underlying asset. The **forward market** in foreign currency is the most active forward market. In a forward contract you fix the price for delivery at a specific time in the future. For example, you might have a forward contract for delivery of US dollars (for sterling) in six months time on a principal of

£1m, at a six-month forward rate of F = 1.9 dollars per pound sterling. In a forward contract, the forward rate is fixed today but no money changes hands today. However, in six months time, one party to the deal will receive $1.9m dollars in exchange for paying £1m. Today, the forward contract 'locks in' a delivery price for a future date and as such, the forward contract removes any exchange risk. Forward contracts usually result in delivery of the underlying asset (in this case foreign currency) and are OTC instruments – deals are done over the telephone.

A futures contract is very similar to a forward contract except that futures contracts are traded on an exchange and you can 'close out' or 'reverse' your initial deal and hence get out of the contract very easily whenever you want (all it takes is a telephone call). Futures contracts are written on a wide variety of 'assets', for example on agricultural products (such as corn, live hogs), on commodities (such as oil, gold and silver) and on financial assets (such as foreign exchange, stock indices, T-bonds and interest rates). A key feature of futures prices is that they are closely linked to the price of the underlying asset. For example, if the spot price of gold in New York (on NYMEX) moves up (down) by $1 then the futures price of gold in Chicago (on the CBOT) will also move up (down) by around $1.

It is easy to see how futures contracts can be used for speculation. For example, if you buy (go long on) a futures contract on gold in Chicago at a quoted price of $660 (per troy ounce) and the spot price of gold rises, then so will the futures price. The holder of the futures contract can then sell the contract at a higher price (in Chicago), say at $670, and she receives the difference, $10, in cash (from the person who took the opposite side of the deal) via the futures clearing house in Chicago. (Each futures contract on gold traded in Chicago is for 100 troy ounces, so the actual profit on one contract would be $1000.) Similarly, if a speculator thinks that the gold price will fall in the future, she can sell a futures contract today and if she is correct she can close out the deal later by buying back the futures at a lower price. The two trades are done in Chicago and the futures clearing house notes that you sold at, say, $660 and bought back the contract at $640 and you will be 'sent' a profit of $20 (per troy ounce).

One of the advantages of futures contracts (for hedging or speculation) is that when a futures contract is entered into, the buyer only has to place a small amount of collateral with the futures exchange (e.g. 5% of the value of the gold underlying the futures contract) as a 'good faith' deposit so that she does not renege on the terms of the contract. (This is known as a **margin payment**.) Hence the investor gains leverage, since she only uses a small amount of her own funds, yet she will reap substantial financial gains if the spot price (and hence the futures price) rises.

Futures contracts can also be used for hedging a position you already hold in the spot asset. For example, suppose you have to purchase heating oil in six months time and you fear a rise in the spot price of heating oil (at New York harbour) over the next six months. If you do nothing and heating oil rises in price your costs will soar. However, if you buy a futures contract on heating oil (in Chicago) today, then the futures price will rise (approximately) dollar for dollar with the spot price. So in six months time if heating oil in the spot market at New York harbour has risen by $1, so will the futures price, which you can now close out (i.e. sell) in Chicago at a profit of $1. The profit on the futures offsets the higher cost of the heating oil in New York.

A slightly more complex futures contract is a sterling interest rate futures contract on three-month LIBOR, where the futures contract matures in two months time. This gives the owner of the futures contract the right to 'lock in' a fixed borrowing rate, beginning in two months time, and lasting for a further three months.

A **call option** on AT&T shares gives the owner of the option the right (but not the obligation) *to buy* a fixed number of AT&T shares for a fixed price, at a designated time in the future. The value of the option contract depends on the movement of the underlying stock price of AT&T – hence the term *derivative*. To purchase an option you have to pay an option premium, but this is a small fraction of the value of the assets (e.g. stocks) underlying the option contract. Therefore the investor again obtains 'leverage'. One of the key differences between futures and options is that with options you can 'walk away from the contract'. So, if the option increases in value you can benefit from the upside, but if it falls in value the most you can lose is the option premium. Hence, the option provides **insurance** and the 'insurance premium' is the option premium you pay at the outset.

Share warrants are not 'shares' but a call option – usually issued by the company on its own shares. It is therefore an option to buy a stated number of the company's shares over a certain period in the future, at a price fixed today. In fact, warrants are often initially 'attached' to ordinary *bonds* that are issued by private placement and sometimes warrants are attached to bonds issued in an IPO. Because bonds with warrants attached have an embedded long-term option to purchase the company's shares, these bonds can be issued at lower yields than conventional bonds. A bond issued with warrants attached allows the investor to 'get a piece of the action' should the company do well and its profits and hence share price increase, while also allowing the investor to receive the coupon payments on the bond. In addition, the bondholder can 'detach' the warrant and sell it in the open market at any time she wishes. (Occasionally, companies also issue warrants *on bonds* – the warrant can be used in the future to purchase a particular bond of the company at a fixed price.) Sometimes, warrants are issued on their own (i.e. not attached to a bond issue) and these were a very popular form of raising finance for Japanese firms in the 1980s.

Warrants are also given to managers to encourage them to raise the profits and hence the share price – they are then referred to as **executive share options**. A share option given to managers might have a strike price set at 10% above the current share price and may not be 'cashed in' (exercised) until, say, two years hence. This gives managers the incentive to stay with the firm and raise its profits and share price. The interests of the managers are then aligned with those of the shareholders (who also want to see a rise in the share price) and managers are more focused on profits rather than pure 'empire building'. Managers will usually be given a series of share options with different dates on which they can be exercised and with different strike prices – then the managers have an incentive package over many years.

You will exercise a warrant when the share price $S = \$110$, say, is above the strike price $K = \$100$, at which point you hand over cash of, say, $100 and receive the company's shares worth $110. Warrants issued by a firm, which are subsequently exercised, therefore involve 'share dilution' for existing shareholders as there are now more shares outstanding.

Sometimes an institution will issue warrants on another company, such as Salomon Bros issuing warrants on Eurotunnel shares. This is often called the *covered warrants* market, because Salomon's must cover its position by being ready to purchase Eurotunnel shares in the open market. Warrants are also sometimes offered by institutions on a 'basket' of different shares.

If you hold a **put option** this gives you the right *to sell* the underlying asset in the future, at a price fixed today. If you buy a put option today (in Chicago, say) then you have to pay the quoted put premium. The put (like the call) can be used to provide insurance. For example, if you currently own a stock worth $100 and you fear a fall in prices over the next three months, you can buy a put option today that will guarantee that you can sell your stock in Chicago for $100 (even if the price of the stock in New York is, say, $30).

However, the interesting feature of the put option is that if the share price on the New York stock exchange rises to $120, then you can 'throw away' your put option and sell your shares on the NYSE for $120. So by holding the AT&T shares and then buying a put option on these shares, you can not only set a floor price for the shares but you can also benefit from any increase in the value of the shares. This sounds too good to be true – but it is true. The put option provides you with a form of insurance (like the insurance policy on the value of your house) and for this you have to pay for the put – this is the cost of your insurance premium. So, call and put options can be used to 'engineer' different forms of pay-offs or 'insurance'; not surprisingly this branch of finance is often referred to as **financial engineering**.

A **swap** is an agreement between two parties (e.g. a corporate and a swap dealer) to exchange a series of cash flows in the future. Large investment banks such as Merrill Lynch, Morgan Stanley and Goldman Sachs act as swap dealers. For example, a firm can negotiate an interest rate swap with Merrill's whereby it agrees to pay Merrill's interest at a floating rate in return for receiving fixed rate payments from Merrill's every six months for the next five years. Or it might agree to pay a fixed amount of US dollars in return for receiving a fixed amount of Euros – this is a currency swap. Swaps are like a series of forward contracts and are extremely useful to corporates in hedging interest rate and exchange rate risk for a series of periodic cash flows, over a long horizon.

Forwards, futures, options and swaps are extremely useful instruments for hedging (i.e. reducing the risk of an existing portfolio position) as well as for speculation. Futures and options are traded in auction markets, but there is also a large over-the-counter (OTC) market in options, while the forward market for foreign exchange and swaps consists purely of OTC transactions.

SUMMARY

- The money markets deal in lending and borrowing at short horizons (less than one year).
- Some money market instruments are OTC (e.g. term loans and deposits) and others are marketable assets, such as T-bills, commercial bills, banker's acceptances and certificates of deposit.
- The London interbank rate is the rate at which large banks in London lend and borrow from each other. Banks lend at the offer rate, LIBOR, and pay the bid rate, LIBID, to funds deposited with it. The spread between LIBOR and LIBID is the bank's profit margin on the transaction.

- Large corporations raise long-term external finance from corporate debt (e.g. bank loans and from issuing corporate bonds) and from new equity issues.
- When corporates raise finance by an *initial sale* of shares to the public this is an initial public offering (IPO). Subsequent issues of shares are seasoned issues and right issues.
- Corporate bonds can be 'plain vanilla' with either fixed or floating coupons as well as convertibles and callable bonds.
- A callable bond gives *the issuer* the option to buy back the bonds at a predetermined price over a certain time period. This gives the issuer the possibility of refinancing the debt at lower cost in the future.
- A convertible bond can be exchanged for a certain number of stocks of the firm, at a predetermined price, at certain times in the future. It allows *the holder* an option of obtaining an 'equity stake' in the firm if it is subsequently successful.
- The value of derivative securities such as forwards, futures and options depends on the value of the underlying asset (e.g. stocks, foreign exchange) in the derivative contract.
- Forward contracts (e.g. on foreign exchange) 'lock in' a price for future delivery and usually forward contracts are held to maturity and 'delivery' takes place.
- Futures contracts can be used for hedging and speculation. They can be used to 'lock in' a known buying or selling price for the underlying asset in the futures contract (e.g. corn). But because they can be easily 'closed out', they can be used for speculation.
- Options provide 'insurance' in the form of a maximum purchase price (call) or minimum selling price (put) that you can obtain in the future for the underlying asset. But options also allow the holder to 'walk away' from the contract, if it is more advantageous to buy or sell the underlying asset in the spot market.
- *Warrants* are call options issued by a company – they give the holder the right to purchase a fixed number of shares in the future at a fixed price. Warrants are often initially 'attached' to bonds but can be sold separately in the secondary market.
- Swaps are an agreement (with a swap dealer) to exchange cash flows in future periods according to a pre-arranged formula. For example, a corporate might agree to pay a fixed amount of US dollars to the swap dealer in exchange for receipt of a fixed amount of Euros, at specific times in the future – this is a currency swap.

EXERCISES

Q1   What is the federal funds rate?

Q2   Why is a T-bill called a 'discount instrument' and what is the discount rate? If a three-month T-bill has a maturity value of $1000 and is issued at a price of $990, what are the discount rate and yield on the T-bill, on the day it is issued?

Q3   Why is a repo like going to a pawnbroker?

Q4   What are the advantages to holding a convertible bond rather than a conventional bond? Why would a firm issue such bonds?

Q5 A firm is undertaking a '1 for 4' rights issue. The current share price is $3 and you hold 100 shares. The ex-rights price is $2.80. How much could you obtain for the 'rights' you have acquired?

Q6 As an active equity investor who already holds stocks, why might you consider buying/selling futures or options?

Q7 You need to purchase heating oil in six months time. You decide to hedge your future purchase using heating oil futures with one year to maturity, available on NYMEX. What happens if the spot price of heating oil falls by $1 over the next six months?

Trading Securities

AIMS

- To describe over-the-counter (OTC) and auction markets.
- To discuss the role of brokers and market makers (dealers) and to explain the bid–ask spread.
- To explain how margin accounts provide leverage and how to execute a short sale.
- To outline various types of buy–sell orders that can be executed via your broker.

4.1 TYPES OF MARKET

Over-the-counter (OTC)

Rather than taking place on an organised exchange where prices are continuously quoted (e.g. the New York Stock Exchange), some financial deals are instead negotiated directly between two (or more) parties – these are **dealer markets**. For example, this applies to the market for bank loans and deposits and the market for spot and forward foreign exchange. Actual trades usually take place over the telephone between the two counterparties, with screen quotes providing the initial basis on which to trade. If you have a particularly 'large' deal then you may not be able to deal at the screen quotes, but at quotes agreed over the phone. These transactions are said to take place in **over-the-counter (OTC) markets**.

OTC markets often give rise to 'non-marketable instruments'; that is, financial assets that are not traded in the secondary market but are usually held to maturity. A bank term loan to a firm is a non-marketable (OTC) instrument, since neither the bank nor the firm can (in general) *easily* shift this specific contract to other parties. Clearly, this 'non-marketability' is a matter of degree. In fact there is a secondary market in 'bundles' of bank loans in the US and bank loans can also be securitised, but these possibilities are quite costly and cannot be accomplished quickly.

Auction markets

Trading may take place in markets where prices are continually quoted in 'one place' either physically at a specific geographic location (e.g. NYSE) or electronically (e.g. Archipelago in the US). In some auction markets, notably the NYSE and the futures and option markets in Chicago, trading takes place face to face in a 'pit'. Physical auction markets often also have platforms that allow electronic trading. Challenges to traditional markets have appeared from dealing systems on the Internet such as Charles Schwab and E*Trade.

There is also competition between *order-driven* dealing systems (i.e. where buyers and sellers are matched electronically), which predominate in a number of European centres, and the NYSE and NASDAQ, which have *quote-driven* systems (i.e. market makers/dealers quote firm bid and ask prices for particular sizes of trades).

NYSE and AMEX

The NYSE provides pit trading in around 3000 shares with daily trading of around 1.5 billion shares. The conditions for listing are that a firm has a large number of shares publicly held, with market value in excess of around $100 million and with annual pre-tax income in excess of around $2 million. The American Stock Exchange (AMEX) focuses on smaller firms and in exchange-traded funds (these are securities that are claims on portfolios of specific stocks). In 2006 the NYSE merged with the electronic trading platform Archipelago.

The NYSE uses *specialists* who trade only in a specific stock and brokers who wish to sell a stock have to bring the trade to the *specialist's post* on the floor of the exchange. Specialist belong to a 'specialist firm', who provide trades across a wide range of stocks via each of their specialists. They can also trade on their own account.

Block transactions (technically this is any trade of over 10,000 shares, but is often in the millions) can be executed on the NYSE via specialists, but if the trade is very large it is channelled through 'block houses' who try to match buyers and sellers and who may buy some of the shares on their own account and later resell them to the public. However, the vast majority of trades on the NYSE are executed electronically on 'SuperDot'.

NASDAQ

This consists of a large number of broker-dealers and is an OTC market in stocks of 'small' companies. Many (but not all) of these 'small' stocks are quoted on the National Association of Security Dealers Automated Quotation System. There are various levels of membership of NASDAQ depending on whether you wish to act as a market maker/dealer, or just a broker or just receive information on *inside quotes*. Most trades are now undertaken on electronic trading platforms.

London stock exchange

In London shares are traded on the quote-driven SEAQ (Stock Exchange Automated Quotations) and these tend to be larger trades. On SEAQ the **touch** is the difference between the highest bid and lowest offer price and on SEAQ these are displayed in a 'yellow strip' on the screen. But there is also an order-driven system (SETS, Stock Exchange Electronic Trading Service), which also incorporates an electronic clearing system. Most trading is now via SETS. Any buy or sell orders that can be crossed are executed automatically. Stocks of smaller companies are traded on the Alternative Investment Market, AIM.

Market makers (dealers)

Market makers (or dealers) hold an inventory of securities that they stand ready to buy or sell at quoted prices – this is known as a **book**. Most dealers are located in large investment banks. A dealers will execute trades on her own behalf and also for 'clients' (usually brokers).

Market makers (dealers) *buy at the bid price* and *sell at the ask price*
therefore
the bid price is always lower than the ask price.

Ordinary investors who approach a market maker (probably via their broker) are on the 'other side of the trade' and therefore they *buy (from the dealer) at the ask price* and *sell (to the dealer) at the bid price.* The difference between the two prices is the **bid–ask spread**. The bid–ask spread allows dealers to make a profit, as they buy securities at a lower price than they sell them. If a market is highly competitive, the bid–ask spread will be reduced to a level that just allows dealers to make a profit.

Price quotes differ between dealers. On electronic trading screens the bid and ask prices (and the quantities they are willing to trade at these prices) from all the dealers are presented in a list. At the top of the list are the *best* bid and ask prices from the dealers. So for buy orders from all dealers the best bid price might be $95. For sell orders the best ask price from among all dealers might be $95.05. These 'best' prices are known as the *inside quotes* and here the inside spread is 5 cents. However, the inside quote will usually be valid only for a small trade (e.g. 5000 shares) and if you wish to trade a larger lot, you will have to search through the quotes to get the best deal (which might involve splitting your trade between different dealers).

The **tick size** is the minimum price movement allowed on a particular security. For example, the tick size for government bonds in the US is 1/32 of 1% (of the par value). The **tick value** represents the cash value of 1 tick. Clearly, this depends on the size of the deal being quoted. For example, on $100,000 held in government bonds, the tick value is $31.25[$=\$100,000(1/3200)$].

Changes in interest rates are generally discussed in terms of **basis points**. A rise in interest rates from 5% to 6% is a change of 100 basis points (bp), hence 1 bp is equivalent to 0.01%. Different markets (e.g. for FX, futures and options) have different tick sizes and tick values. These concepts provide a useful shorthand for market participants who might, for example, state that 'bond yields are up by 10 basis points'.

Brokers

Whereas dealers trade on their 'own account' and hold positions in various securities, a **broker** acts as a middleman between two investors (usually referred to as counterparties; see Figure 4.1). The broker brings the buyer and seller together (e.g. this could be two different dealers or a private or institutional investor and a dealer). The broker does not hold a 'book' but charges a commission for transacting the deal between the two counterparties. Sometimes the broker will consolidate the commission in the bid–ask spread. Most large banks provide both a brokerage service and have dealers who run a book.

There are full-service brokers and discount brokers (e.g. Charles Schwab, E*Trade). Both types of broker execute orders (including short sales) often over the Internet, they also hold securities for safekeeping (in 'street name') and provide margin loans. In addition, full-service brokers provide research services and investment advice.

4.2 MARGIN ACCOUNT

Today most investors are able to purchase securities via a broker, either via a cash account or a margin account.

- **Cash account:** This is like a normal deposit account but it is held with the broker. Positive (negative) flows occur when the investor buys (sells) securities. It must always have a positive balance and the investor provides all the funds.
- **Margin account:** This is like a bank account with an overdraft limit. If the overdraft is taken up the broker charges the investor interest. The portfolio of securities owned by the investor are usually held with the broker as collateral (against default). The broker generally borrows the funds 'on call' from banks and this loan is passed on to the investor.

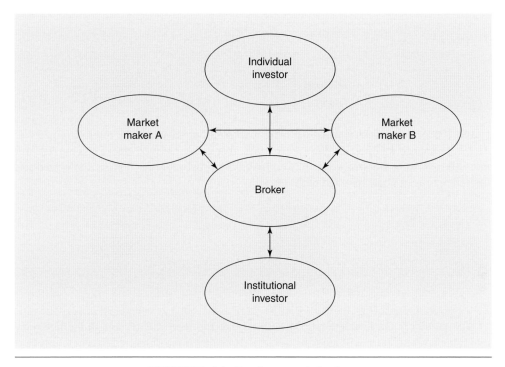

FIGURE 4.1: Brokers and dealers

If you buy shares in the normal way using just your own funds (or 'capital'), then the return is known as the 'unlevered return', R_u. If shares are purchased partly using own funds and partly by borrowing funds (using the margin account), then the return on this investment is known as the 'levered return', R_L. As a speculator, when you 'leverage' your stock purchases it is like a gambler increasing her bet by augmenting her own funds by borrowing from the bank. Consider purchasing 100 shares at $2 per share and selling them at $2.50. This gives an unlevered return of 25%:

$$\text{Unlevered return}, R_u = \frac{\$250 - \$200}{\$200} = 25\% \qquad [1]$$

Using the margin account gives the investor **leverage**; that is, to magnify the return (positive or negative) relative to that obtained when only own funds are used. Let's examine the relationship between the unlevered and levered return.

Suppose the investor now purchases 100 shares at $2 per share, but she now uses an **initial margin** of 70% and borrows 30% of the funds at 10% interest (from the broker). The levered return is calculated as follows:

Own funds ('equity') used, OF	$= 0.7\ (\$200) = \$140$
Borrowed funds, BF	$= 0.3\ (\$200) = \$60$
Total funds, TF $=$ OF $+$ BF	$= \$200$

Sale proceeds $\qquad = 100\,(\$2.50) = \$250$
Interest on loan $\qquad = 0.10\,(\$60) = \$6$

$$\text{Levered return}, R_L = \frac{\text{\$-Profit}}{\text{`Own Funds'}} = \frac{\$250 - (\$140 + \$60 + \$6)}{\$140} = 31.4\% \qquad [2]$$

Hence, the levered purchase using the margin account has increased the return from 25% to 31.4%. In finance we often use the *excess* return, that is the return on stocks less the risk-free rate – this is what we will do here. The relationship between the (excess) unlevered and levered returns can be expressed neatly as follows:

$$\text{Excess unlevered return} = \frac{\text{Total Funds}}{\text{Own Funds}} \times \text{Excess unlevered return}$$

$$(R_L - r) = \frac{\text{TF}}{\text{OF}}(R_U - r) = \frac{\$200}{\$140}(25\% - 10\%) = 21.4\% \qquad [3]$$

So the levered return is $R_L = 21.4 + 10 = 31.4\%$, the same as calculated in [2]. The ratio TF/OF = 1.428 is the leverage ratio: it tells us that for every 1% change in the unlevered return the levered return will move by 1.428%. Note that if the unlevered excess return were to fall by, say, 15%, then the levered excess return would fall by more – that is by 21.42% (= 1.428% × 15%).

Leverage (borrowing) increases your *average* return relative to the (unlevered) return if you only use your own funds – but leverage also increases the volatility of your returns. Case Study 4.1 shows how these two effects interact.

CASE STUDY 4.1   MUTUAL FUNDS AND HEDGE FUNDS: A CAUTIONARY TALE

Equation [3] implies that if stock prices rise or fall by 1%, then the leveraged investment will gain or lose by 1.428%, so the *volatility* of the levered return is 1.428 times the volatility of the unlevered return:

$$\sigma_L = 1.428\sigma_U$$

where σ denotes volatility, which is measured by the standard deviation of the returns on the investment.

Suppose you are an unlevered investor such as a mutual fund and you are not allowed to borrow on margin. Then your return from investing is $R_U = 25\%$ and the riskiness of your investment is given by the standard deviation of stock returns, which we take to be $\sigma_U = 30\%$. You like return but dislike risk, and one simple measure of the (excess) return per unit of risk is the ratio:

$$SR_U = (R_U - r)/\sigma_U = 15/30 = 0.5$$

SR is known as the *Sharpe ratio*. When going by car from A to B you may measure the 'performance' of your car by the miles per gallon it does – you like the miles it does, but are also concerned about the cost of the petrol. The Sharpe ratio is a measure of the performance of your investment – you like the return but are concerned about the 'cost' to you of the riskiness of the stock. The higher the Sharpe ratio from your investment, the better you feel.

Now consider a levered investor, for example a hedge fund, who invests in exactly the same stock as the mutual fund but borrows 30% of the funds invested. The hedge fund can rightly claim that its average return is 34.1%, much higher than the average return of the mutual fund at 25%, and it will splash this fact all over the financial press and ask you to place your money with it – otherwise you are surely a 'dumb investor'. But suppose you are also concerned about risk, so you measure the success of an investment not just by the expected return but also by the standard deviation of the return. What is the Sharpe ratio of the hedge fund? It is:

$$SR_L = (R_L - r)/\sigma_L = 1.428(R_U - r)/1.428\sigma_U = SR_U$$

It is the same as the Sharpe ratio of the (unlevered) mutual fund! The hedge fund does not give you a higher return per unit of risk than does the mutual fund; the higher average return of the hedge fund is offset by its higher risk. You are just as sensible investing in the mutual fund as you are in the hedge fund – you are not 'dumb' if you forgo the seemingly attractive offer of the hedge fund. The hedge fund is here demonstrating no more skill than the mutual fund, since both (by assumption) invest in the same stock. What is more, the above figures are before management charges, so if the hedge fund charges more in management fees (which includes any performance fees) then the mutual fund is a better bet – you would actually be dumb investing in the hedge fund. The moral of the story is always to consider risk as well as expected return – and don't always believe what you see in the adverts you find in the financial press.

Now let us turn to the practical matter of the maintenance margin and margin calls by the broker. The initial margin m_0 (%) is the proportion of the total outlay that is initially provided by the investor's own funds (i.e. the investor's equity).

$$m_0 = \frac{\text{Own Funds}}{\text{Own Funds} + \text{Borrowed Funds}} = \frac{OF}{OF + BF} \tag{4}$$

Clearly, the initial margin is $m_0 = \$140/(\$140 + \$60) = 0.7$ (70%). To minimise default risk, the broker will insist on a *maintenance margin*, whereby the investor pays more 'own funds' into the margin account if the share price falls. For example, if the *maintenance margin, m,* is set at 60%, then from equation [4] we see that when the investor's capital falls to $OF_m = \frac{m.BF}{(1-m)} = \frac{0.6(60)}{1-0.6} = \$90$, a *margin call* for extra funds will be initiated. This represents a fall in the value of investor's equity of $50 (= \$140 - \$90 = OF - OF_m$). Suppose the share price fell from \$2 to \$1.20, which represents a loss in *market value* of \$80 (= \$0.80 × 100). Hence the margin call would be \$30 (= \$80 - \$50). The payment of a maintenance margin is a form of *marking to market* and is also used (in a slightly different way) in futures markets.

As we shall see, there are other ways to obtain leverage, most notably by investing in futures or options. With futures, you can gain exposure to the market (e.g. stock market) of, say, \$100m by paying only a relatively small margin payment of, say, \$5m (i.e. around 5%). A similar effect occurs with options. If you purchase a call option on shares you only pay a relatively small option premium of around 10% of the value of the shares in the option contract. But if share prices rise you reap the whole of the benefit of the increase in value of all the shares in the option contract.

4.3 SHORT SELLING

If an investor purchases a security (e.g. equity) she is said to go long and if she sells a security *she owns*, she is said to **go short**. However, if she sells a security *that she does not own* she makes a **short sale**.

Suppose the investor thinks that a particular share will fall in price in the future but she does not own the share. She may be able to make a profit by short selling. Initially, she borrows the share from her broker for an agreed time period. The broker has to 'locate' the shares – which may be borrowed from a custody bank or fund management company or from an existing client who is long in the shares. Suppose our short seller sells the shares for \$100. If the price actually does fall to say \$90, then she can repurchase it at a lower price and return the share to the broker, thus pocketing the difference of \$10. In this example short selling involves 'infinite leverage', because the investor uses no own funds. If the stock pays dividends over the period of the short sale, then the short seller has to pay an equivalent amount to the broker (which is then passed on to the broker's client who really owns the share). Of course, if the share price rises the investor who has sold short will make a loss (which can increase without limit). In the US you can only short sell on an 'uptick' (i.e. only if the last change in price was positive).

Short selling is risky for the broker as the short seller may not 'replace' the shares. So the broker requires the proceeds from the short sale to be held at the brokerage firm and will also require that you place a margin payment (say, 50%) with the broker. The margin payment usually consists of other securities owned by the short seller (e.g. T-bills) – this is the initial margin. Further margin calls are made if the share price subsequently rises. However, if the price subsequently falls, the short position is worth more and the investor may be able to withdraw cash from her margin account.

The calculation of the rate of return from short selling is usually based on the initial receipts from the sale of the shares. For example, suppose you short sell 100 shares at \$2 per share and buy them back at \$1.50. Assume that the \$200 proceeds from the short sale can be invested to earn interest of 10% (= $20) – but note that it is not necessarily the case that the receipts from the short sale can be used to earn interest. Assume that the dividend yield on the shares is $d = 5\%$ and that these dividends accrue over the period you have short sold the shares. The dividend payments (over the period you borrow the shares) must be paid to the owner (via the broker's account) and are equal to $10 (= 5\% \times $200). The return to short selling would be calculated as:

$$\text{Return} = \frac{\text{Net Profit}}{\text{Proceeds from Short Sale}} = \frac{\$200 - \$150 + \$20 - \$10}{\$200} \tag{5}$$

$$= \frac{\$60}{\$200} = 30\%$$

$$\text{Return} = \% \text{ Price change} + r - d = 25\% + 10\% - 5\% = 30\%$$

The broker usually takes a small (percentage) commission for organising the short sale, which is known as a 'haircut' and should also be deducted from the above return.

4.4 TYPES OF ORDER

There any many different types of buy or sell orders that the investor can give to her broker and some are listed below.

- **Market order:** An instruction to buy immediately at the lowest offer price and sell at the highest bid price.
- **Limit order:** For example, a *buy limit order* is an instruction to purchase 1000 shares of XYZ but only if the price is below (or falls below), say, $5.
- **Stop order:** An instruction to buy or sell as soon as the price passes a particular level. A stop-loss order for 1000 shares at $5 implies that the shares are to be sold as soon as the price drops below $5. A buy stop order is the purchase of 1000 shares if the price rises above $5.
- **Stop limit order:** This might be an instruction to 'sell 1000 shares at $5, stop $4.95 limit'. Hence the order will be executed if the share price falls below $5 but does *not* fall below $4.95.
- **Fill-or-kill order:** This is an instruction that is cancelled if it cannot be executed immediately.
- **Open order (Good till cancelled):** This is an order that remains 'operative' until it is either executed or cancelled.

SUMMARY

- Market makers (dealers) hold an inventory of securities and buy from investors at the *bid price* and sell at the *ask price* (for specific sizes of orders). The difference between the two prices is the *bid–ask spread*. Dealers trade on their own account – they run a 'book'.

- Brokers execute orders for clients but do not trade on their own account.
- Stocks and derivatives are still traded in a 'pit', but more trades are now undertaken on electronic trading platforms.
- Investors can borrow from their brokers and buy stocks on margin. This provides *leverage* – higher average returns but also increased risk. If prices move against the investor she will be asked for additional margin payments.
- If you buy a stock you *go long*, if you sell a stock you already own you *go short* the stock. If you borrow a stock from your broker and sell this stock that you do not own, this is *short selling*. Short sales require margin payments and possible margin calls.
- There are many types of buy and sell orders that investors can arrange with their broker.

EXERCISES

Q1   What are the bid–ask spread, tick size and tick value?

Q2   Do market makers and brokers have different functions?

Q3   What is short selling?

Q4   If your broker contacts a dealer who quotes 95.01–95.04 on a stock, what price will your broker pay to purchase/sell the security?

Q5   When investing in stocks, what is the leverage ratio?

Q6   If you buy stocks 'on margin', does this imply that you have a better investment portfolio than if you just invest your own funds? Assume that you are risk averse.

CHAPTER 5

Investment Companies

AIMS

- To explain closed-end and open-end funds.
- To demonstrate the structure of the mutual fund industry.
- To outline the different types of mutual fund.
- To discuss fees, returns and taxes on mutual funds.
- To present the late trading and market timing scandals.

5.1 INVESTMENT COMPANIES

Investment companies are pooled investments that enable investors to enjoy economies of scale in gaining access to well-diversified portfolios of securities. Each investor has a claim on this pool of securities. Investors buy shares in the investment company and ownership is proportional to the number of shares owned and hence proportional to the amount invested. The value of each share is known as the net asset value (NAV) and is determined as:

$$NAV = \frac{Market\ value\ of\ assets\ -\ liabilities}{number\ of\ shares\ outstanding}$$

The liabilities of the investment company are usually relatively small and might include outstanding rent on buildings and funds to be paid to third parties (e.g. brokers or investment advisers).

We can classify investment companies (e.g. under the US Investment Company Act of 1940) as either *unit investment trusts* or *managed investment companies*.

Unit investment trusts

In the US, 'unit investment trusts' invest in a portfolio of securities (e.g. stocks, corporate or municipal or government bonds) and this portfolio remains unchanged over the life of the fund – so it is referred to as *unmanaged*. The sponsors of the unit investment trust (usually a large bank or brokerage firm) will buy securities that are deposited in a trust and then shares ('units') are sold to the public.

The investor can sell his shares back to the investment trust at their NAV and the trust either sell securities from the portfolio to pay him or will sell his shares to a new investor. The investment trust always sells shares to investors at a premium (of around 2–5%) above NAV and this is how it makes its profits. Unit investment trusts in the US[1] are now quite a small sector, holding only about $40bn in assets.

Managed investment companies

Managed companies are classified as open-end or closed-end and they can and do change the composition of their portfolios. **Open-end companies** are commonly known as mutual funds. In the US both open-end and closed-end funds are run by a board of directors who are elected by shareholders. The sponsors of the fund are often also the managers of the fund (e.g. Fidelity mutual funds are set up and managed by Fidelity), but some funds hire outside portfolio managers. The mutual fund management company is registered with the SEC in the USA and the FSA in the UK.

Investors buy shares (units) in the mutual fund, but the number of shares in issue varies according to demand, hence the term 'open-ended'. The shares of the mutual fund are not traded on an exchange. When the investor 'cashes' in her shares in the fund, she sells them

---

[1] There may be a source of confusion as in the UK, mutual funds are often referred to as Unit Trusts but their correct designation is Open Ended Investment Companies, OEIC.

to the fund itself, at NAV, and the number of 'units' in the fund decreases. But the 'share price' always reflects the underlying net asset value. However, for US mutual funds any sell or buy orders that arrive during the day will be settled at the NAV calculated at 4 p.m. (New York time) that day. This gave rise to the mutual fund 'late trading' and 'market timing' scandals in the US in 2003 – see Case Study 5.1.

CASE STUDY 5.1   BETTER LATE THAN NEVER

Suppose at 4 p.m. New York time the NAV of a fund is announced and equals $100. Some general positive economic news arrives at 4.15 p.m. (for example an increase in the consumer confidence index) and you can purchase the fund at 4.15 p.m., but at the NAV based on the 4 p.m. prices of the underlying shares, then it is likely that when you sell the fund at tomorrow's NAV it will be higher. If bad economic news arrives at 4.15 p.m., then you would sell the fund at its 4 p.m. price. This is *late trading* and is illegal in the US. Late trading does not guarantee a profit on your trade since you cannot reverse your trade in the fund until 4 p.m. the next day – but you do have an informational advantage that you can try to exploit. If you are successful, then the fund has to buy or sell underlying stocks in the fund's portfolio and hence your gains are at the expense of other holders of the fund. It was only large brokers who could engage in late trading as they were allowed to submit 'legitimate' buy–sell orders submitted to them before 4 p.m., as well as some submitted to them after 4 p.m., to the fund for execution after 4 p.m.

Market timing does not violate securities laws and exploits 'stale prices'. When a US investor buys/sells a mutual fund during the day, she does so at the price prevailing at 4 p.m. (NY time). The simplest example of market timing involves a US mutual fund that invests in Japanese stocks. The 4 p.m. prices are based on the last few trades of stocks in the fund and for Japanese stocks this would be the prior 1 a.m. price (NY time), when the NAV of the fund is determined. However, the Nikkei-225 *futures price*, which closely tracks the Nikkei-225 index of stock prices, is quoted over a 24-hour period (via trading on the GLOBEX electronic platform).

So, a US investor who notes that the Nikkei-225 futures price has increased between 1 a.m. and 4 p.m. (because of the arrival of good news about the Japanese economy) knows that the 'true' NAV of the Japanese mutual fund is now higher. She can therefore purchase the Japanese fund online from the fund complex, at zero transaction cost *at its stale price,* just before 4 p.m. New York time. (By purchasing from the fund complex using an existing money market fund, you avoid transaction costs that you would incur through online trading firms such as Charles Schwab & Co and E*Trade.) She can subsequently sell the Japanese mutual fund at any time before 1 a.m. (NY time) *the next day*, when the NAV is determined in Japan. So the trading strategy is to buy the fund when the Nikkei-225 futures is up (at 4 p.m.) and liquidate the position when the futures is down.

There are risks in this strategy. Bad news about the Japanese economy could arrive between 4 p.m. and 1 a.m., pushing the price of Japanese equities down, and hence the

1 a.m. NAV would be lower. Also, the US investor faces exchange rate risk if the Japanese yen depreciates over the 4 p.m. to 1 a.m. period, when the US investor holds the Japanese mutual fund. However, Boudoukh *et al*. (2002) show that between January 1997 and November 2000, a US investor using this market-timing strategy could have earned high returns and a high Sharpe ratio by investing in Pacific/Japanese (no-load) funds. For example, whereas the annual Sharpe ratio for simply holding the funds lies between 0.29 and 0.42, the market-timing strategy gives Sharpe ratios mainly in the range 5–10 – a substantial level for financial markets. The key factor in producing such high Sharpe ratios is that the Nikkei futures predict the sign of the next day's stock returns in Japan over 75% of the time on average (whereas the proportion of times due to 'luck' would be only 50%, Boudoukh *et al*., 2002, Table 3).

Elliot Spitzer, the New York attorney general, helped bring these issues into the public domain. Mutual fund sponsors had to pay around $1.5bn in penalties and new rules were implemented to curb these practices. The rules include:

- A strict 4 p.m. cut-off for the mutual fund to redeem shares at that day's NAV (after 4 p.m. they are executed at the next day's NAV).
- A redemption fee of 2% if mutual fund shares are sold within a week of purchase – and these fees go into the fund, not to the management company.
- Prices of securities in closed markets (like Japan) can be updated to reflect the likely impact on NAVs of any change in the price of the underlying shares in the fund, between the close of the foreign market and 4 p.m. NY time.

Closed-end funds purchase a portfolio of securities, but once the shares of the fund have been issued to investors the fund itself does not redeem or issue further shares. An existing investor in a closed-end fund who wants to cash in her shares must sell them on the open market to another investor, at whatever price she can get. The shares of closed-end funds are traded on stock exchanges just like the shares of any other company. Existing shares of closed-end funds often sell at a discount to their NAV, although when they are initially issued they sell at a premium. The discount is (P–NAV)/NAV, which appears as a negative figure (in the *Wall Street Journal*); a positive figure indicates a premium[2]. The discounts on closed-end funds vary over time and discounts between 1% and 20% for different funds are frequently observed.

These discounts tend to narrow over the life of the fund, so if you purchase a fund at a discount just after it has been issued (i.e. you avoid paying the premium on issue) then you might see the discount narrow over the next few years. This looks like an exploitable 'anomaly' and it has been estimated that buying funds at a discount can earn an average return over 12 months of around 6% higher than on a fund selling at NAV. We discuss this anomaly in Chapter 15.

In the US, **Real-estate investment trusts (REITS)** operate very much like a closed-end fund, issuing shares as a claim on investments by the fund in real estate (*equity trusts*) or in a bundle

---

[2] The *Financial Times* reports discounts and premiums of UK closed-end funds (called 'investment trusts' in the UK) but a positive (negative) number indicates a discount (premium).

of mortgage loans (*mortgage trusts*). They are usually highly leveraged, financing a large portion of their activities by either borrowing from banks or issuing bonds. The sponsors are usually large banks and insurance companies, who also normally manage the portfolio.

Hedge funds and private equity are investment companies, but are usually structured as a limited private partnership. They are very lightly regulated (by the SEC in the US and the FSA in the UK) and many escape any kind of regulation altogether. They have much more freedom in the kinds of actively managed investment strategies they undertake, compared with mutual funds, and they undertake substantial leverage. Hedge funds grew very rapidly after 2000 and by 2008 accounted for about $1 trillion of assets under management. Recently there has been much comment on whether pension funds and insurance companies should invest substantially in hedge funds and private equity. We discuss these two types of investment company in a later chapter.

5.2 MUTUAL FUNDS

The management company of a mutual fund often manages a 'complex' or 'family' of funds with various investment objectives, and often they elect the same individuals to the boards of each of their funds within a fund family (for example Barclays Global Investors, Black Rock Merrill Lynch Investment Managers, Credit Suisse Asset Management Funds, Fidelity International, Goldman Sachs Asset Management, Invesco Perpetual, J. P. Morgan Asset Management, M&G Investments, Schroders, UBS Global Asset Management). New funds are continually introduced, while less successful funds may merge with other funds (often within the same family) or may cease to exist.

The mutual fund industry in the US and UK has increased dramatically over the last 30 years and now accounts for a substantial amount of private-sector saving and substantial new net inflows of saving into risky financial assets. For example, at end 2007 US mutual funds held around $10 trillion in total fund assets (about half of the world's fund assets), which is about 90% of investment company assets. There are a total of around 8500 funds, offered by around 500 fund complexes. Nearly half of US households hold mutual funds, comprising around 20% of their total financial assets (Investment Company Institute, 2006). Most funds are actively managed in that they either try to pick 'winner stocks' or they engage in market timing (i.e. predicting relative returns of broad asset classes). Actively managed funds generally charge higher fees than 'index' or 'tracker' funds (which mimic movements in broad market indexes). In the US and UK about 70% of institutional funds are actively managed and this rises to over 90% for retail funds. Recently there has been an ongoing debate on whether mutual funds should adopt more hedge-fund-like strategies.

Types of fund

Mutual funds can be classified into different categories and most fund families tend to provide funds in all categories.

- **Equity funds.** These funds hold most of their assets in common stock, but around 5% of assets in money market securities for liquidity purposes to meet any net sales of shares by fundholders. Broad categories of funds include growth funds, income funds and sector funds. *Growth* *funds* invest in equities of companies where it is expected that most of the return will come from capital appreciation rather than the dividend yield. The *income-style classification* tends to hold equity that pays out a consistently high dividend yield. Sector funds invest in particular industrial sectors, such as telecommunications, media, utilities, technology stocks and so on.

- **International funds.** Some equity funds also offer funds based on indexes of foreign stocks in different countries (e.g. Japan, Far East) or on a world index. Equity funds also specialise in active investment strategies in different geographical regions, so investors can, for example, choose from European equity, Japanese equity or American small company funds. China, India and emerging market funds are also available.
- **Bond funds.** In the US different bond mutual funds might be offered on government, corporate or municipal bonds or mortgage-backed securities. Bond funds might also differentiate themselves by holding only short-dated or long-dated bonds, bonds of only highly rated corporates or funds based on holdings of low-rated (junk) bonds.
- **Balanced funds.** These hold a mix of stocks and fixed-income assets, often in fairly stable proportions. But there are also *life-cycle funds* where the proportion of stocks and bonds will be fixed to attract particular types of clientele – for example, a fund with 80% stocks and 20% fixed-income assets might be attractive to younger investors and with asset proportions the opposite of these for older investors. Some life-cycle funds will alter the proportions (according to a pre-agreed formula) in each asset class, as the investor gets older.
- **Index funds.** These funds are designed to closely track a particular index such as the S&P 500, the Wiltshire 5000 index or the US Small Cap Index, as well as indices of foreign stocks (e.g. Nikkei 225 index, Pacific Basin index)[3]. There are also index funds based on bond indices and real estate indices. For example, an index mutual fund based on the S&P 500 (e.g. Vanguard 500 index fund) will simply purchase shares in the fund in proportion to the value of each of the 500 companies' shares in the S&P500 index itself. These funds are not actively managed and generally have low expense ratios, some as low as 0.3% and rarely above 1.5% of NAV.

Fee structure and selling

An actively managed fund charges an annual management fee of around 1.5–3% of NAV, depending on the fund chosen. Some funds charge a 'sales fee' called the **front-end load** – this is used to pay direct marketing costs, including compensation to selling brokers (or IFAs). The fund determines the load, but it is retained by the selling broker (or IFA) as compensation for investment advice provided. Front-end loads can be as high as 6%, which means that if you put $1000 in the fund, $60 goes to pay the financial adviser and only $940 is invested. Some funds are no-load funds. Some funds also charge a **back-end load**, which is an 'exit fee'. These might start at 5% or 6% but taper by, say, 1% p.a. and often reduce to zero if you hold the fund for five years or more before selling it.

The **operating expenses** of the fund are the costs incurred in running the fund, such as salaries and administrative expenses, and usually amount to 0.3% to 2% of fund assets. They are deducted from the assets of the fund (so NAV is reduced). In the US, **12b-1 charges** refer to costs incurred in advertising the fund, the production of prospectuses for the fund and,

---

[3] With the recent appearance of Exchange Traded Funds, ETFs, investors may also 'track' a diversified position in a given style category (e.g. small stocks, telecom stocks). ETFs are also redeemable at market value at any time of the trading day (and for example, not just at 4pm New York time as for US mutual funds) and ETFs often have special tax privileges.

most importantly, commissions paid to brokers for selling the fund to clients. These costs are deducted from the NAV of the fund. The total expense ratio (TER) of the fund is the sum of the operating expenses and the 12b-1 fee; the investor in the fund only sees the TER in the prospectus (and not its component parts). The 12b-1 fees are limited to 1% of the average fund's net assets over the year (0.75% for the sale of the fund and an additional 0.25% for the maintenance of shareholders' accounts).

Many funds offer different 'asset classes' – usually designated by letters such as A, B, C and so on. This provides the investor with a choice of fees for a particular fund. For example, one 'class' might involve a zero front-end loan but a high 12b-1 fee. Another class might have no back-end load. Clearly, which class you choose depends in part on how long you intend to hold the fund – if you think this is for a very short period, then you may pick a class that has zero front and back-end loads and a higher 12b-1 fee (paid annually), perhaps purchased directly from the fund rather than through a broker (or IFA in the UK).

Funds can be sold *indirectly* via brokers (IFAs in the UK) or by *direct marketing* of funds via fund offices, newspapers, mail, telephone sales, Internet and so on. There is often no front-end load fee if the fund is sold via direct marketing. Funds can also be sold via 'fund supermarkets' such as Charles Schwab's One Source – there is no load fee but instead, the broker shares the management fee with the mutual fund company. 'Fund supermarkets' offer a menu of 'participating funds' that can be held in a single consolidated account. In the US, directly marketed funds may use the 12b-1 fee to pay for advertising or shelf space at a fund supermarket, which implies that current shareholders bear the cost of attracting new shareholders.

Size, expenses and costs

In 2003 the average US mutual fund had assets of $941m, but the large standard deviation of around $3400m indicates a few large funds: the largest having assets of over $82.2bn, with an interquartile range of $49–565m. There were about 6600 funds and 16,000 share classes, of which 56% charged a load fee, 66% charged a 12b-1 fee and 32% had neither. The SEC requires that all US mutual funds report an annual total expense ratio or TER (as a percentage of total net assets), which comprises operating expenses (i.e. management, legal, accounting and custodial fees) plus the 12b-1 fee, but excludes trading costs associated with purchases/sales of fund assets. In the US the average (NAV-weighted) TER in 2003 was 76 bp, with operating expenses accounting for 80% (61 bp) and 12b-1 fees for 20% (15 bp) of the TER. A few funds (around 100) are index funds with average operating expenses of 42 bp, with a standard deviation of 19 bp and ranging from 8 to 85 bp. Trading costs for funds, that include brokers' commissions and bid–ask spreads, are not included in the management fee and the TER, but are deducted directly from the NAV.

Restrictions or covenants to mutual fund activity vary across funds. But in 2000 about 90% of funds could not buy on margin, around 65% could not short securities and about 25–30% could not trade either index futures or individual options. In addition, around 20% were not allowed to borrow money and about 20% of funds could not hold restricted securities (e.g. those obtained by private sale). But of those funds that are *not* restricted in the above fashion, a maximum of only about 12% of funds actually used any one of the above techniques over the 1996–2000 period, and there are no appreciable trends in this figure over this period (Almazan *et al.*, 2004).

Returns

In the US when a fund sells underlying securities in the fund, the capital gain has to be distributed to the shareholders of the fund along with any dividends received from the underlying shares. The monthly return on a fund is the change in the NAV plus any dividend and capital gains distributions (per share/unit in the fund):

$$\text{Return} = \frac{NAV_1 - NAV_0 + income\ and\ capital\ gains\ distributions}{NAV_0}$$

The measured return excludes any back-end or front-end loads. Any expenses from trading the underlying shares in the fund and the TER are deducted before calculating the NAV – so higher trading costs and TERs reduce NAV (other things being equal). Except for load fees, the 'return' is therefore the return to investors in the fund – often referred to as the 'net return'.

Taxation

In the US, mutual funds are 'pass-through' as far as the tax authorities are concerned – the fund does not pay taxes itself but (as long as it passes virtually all its income to shareholders and any of its capital gains from selling the underlying shares) taxes are paid by individual shareholders. These capital gains and dividends are passed on to shareholders by the fund once or twice a year. This creates a problem for people who purchase the fund just before a distribution, since they will pay tax on the distributions even though the actual transactions in the underlying shares may have taken place one year earlier. Also, if a fund has a high turnover, then capital gains are realised by the fund and the investor in the fund will pay taxes on these realised gains. On the other hand, a fund with a low turnover, which does not sell the underlying shares in the year even though they have increased in value, will not have a realised capital gain and hence there will be no tax to pay (by the shareholders in the fund). So as an investor in the fund, you have no choice about the timing of the sale of securities from the fund and hence no control over your tax planning (unless, that is, the fund is held as part of a tax-deferred retirement account such as an IRA or 401(k) account). Turnover rates[4] on actively managed funds are often in excess of 60% and some can be as high as 120%, whereas for index funds the turnover rate is likely to be as low as 1% to 2%. As we have noted, high turnover rates reduce NAV and this must be more than compensated for by the higher return on the stocks that are purchased relative to those that are sold.

Information on mutual funds

There is now almost 'information overload' on mutual funds – although it is still difficult to obtain long runs of data on funds' returns, costs, trades and asset holdings, without paying large sums to data vendors. Snapshots of a fund's returns and costs can be obtained from the prospectus of the fund and if requested, US funds have to provide investors with the Statement of Additional Information (SAI), which lists the directors of the fund and the amount held in different securities at the end of the fiscal year. The Investment Company

---

[4] If a fund has assets of $100m and it sells $50m of securities and replaces them with another $50m of different securities then the turnover rate would be 50%.

Institute (ICI) in the US and the Association of Investment Managers (AIM) in the UK provide fund information in their annual directories. There are a myriad of Internet sites that provide fund information, of which www.morningstar.com provides very detailed reports on funds (and ETFs) and also provide the Morningstar 'star ratings', which are based on each fund's return score minus its risk score (relative to funds in the same investment style).

5.3 EXCHANGE TRADED FUNDS (ETFS)

Exchange traded funds are similar to index mutual funds in that they track particular indexes, but they are traded like ordinary shares on an exchange. You will see ETFs in the US referred to as 'spiders', 'diamonds' and 'cubes' – these refer to ETFs on the Standard and Poor's Depository Receipt, which is a unit investment trust on a portfolio that tracks the S&P 500 index, the Dow Jones Industrial Average, ticker DIA0, and the NASDAQ 100 Index, ticker QQQ. The sponsors of ETFs are large investment banks (e.g. Merrill Lynch, Barclays Capital) and mutual funds (e.g. Vanguard). There are now over 200 ETFs available on the US market with assets under management of around $350bn. There has been quite phenomenal growth in this asset class in the US since their introduction in 1993 and they are popular in other countries such as the UK.

ETFs can be purchased and sold at any time of the day at their NAV and not just at the 4 p.m. NAV, as is the case with mutual funds. ETFs can also be sold short or purchased on margin. ETFs have a potential tax advantage over mutual funds, since small investors can choose when to sell their ETFs and incur liability to tax, whereas with a mutual fund it is the fund managers who decide when and what shares to sell. Also large investors in ETFs can *exchange* their ETFs for the underlying shares (in proportion to their value in the index) and therefore, as no capital gains are realised, there are no tax implications of selling the ETF. The fact that large investors can supply the underlying shares for a share in the ETF or redeem existing ETFs for the underlying shares means that ETFs trade very close to NAV – otherwise arbitrage opportunities would be possible.

The disadvantage of ETFs for small investors is the commission and any bid–ask spreads paid to the broker, which does not occur if you purchase no-load mutual funds directly from the fund itself.

SUMMARY

- *Open-end companies* are commonly known as mutual funds. Investors buy shares (units) in the mutual fund and when the investor 'cashes' in her shares in the fund, she sells them to the fund itself, at net asset value (NAV).
- *Closed-end funds* purchase a portfolio of securities, but once the shares of the fund have been issued to investors, the fund itself does not redeem or issue further shares. An existing investor who wants to cash her shares in the fund must sell them to another investor, at whatever price she can get.

- In the US, *unit investment trusts* invest in a portfolio of securities (e.g. stocks, corporate or municipal bonds) that are *fixed* for the life of the fund, so they are referred to as *unmanaged.*
- In the US, *real estate investment trusts (REITS)* issue shares as a claim on investments by the fund in real estate or in a bundle of mortgage loans.
- *Hedge funds* and *private equity* are usually structured as a limited private partnership. They are very lightly regulated and their investments involve substantial leverage.
- *Mutual funds* are arranged in 'families' that contain equity funds, international funds, bond funds and balanced funds (which have a mix of stocks and fixed-income assets).
- Mutual funds can be sold indirectly via brokers (IFAs in the UK) or by direct marketing of funds. They can also be sold via 'fund supermarkets'.
- The *net asset value* (NAV) of a mutual fund is the market value of the assets of the fund less the liabilities of the fund divided by the number of shares in the fund.
- *Index funds* are designed to closely track a particular index such as the S&P 500, as well as indexes of foreign stocks (e.g. Nikkei 225 index, Pacific Basin index), bond indices and real estate indices.
- An actively managed fund charges an annual management fee of around 1.5–3% of NAV, depending on the fund chosen. Some funds charge a 'sales fee' called the *front-end load*, while others charge a *back-end load* that is an 'exit fee'.
- The operating expenses of the fund and (in the US) *12b-1 charges* are deducted from the NAV of the fund. The total expense ratio (TER) of the fund is the sum of the operating expenses and the 12b-1 fee.
- Many funds offer different 'asset classes', which provides the investor with a choice of fees for a particular fund.
- *Exchange traded funds* (ETFs) are diversified portfolios of stocks that track a particular index and, unlike mutual funds, can be traded at any time of day, and can be sold short and purchased on margin. They are traded like ordinary shares and hence you incur bid–ask spreads and brokers' commissions on purchases/sales.

EXERCISES

Q1 What is the difference between an *open-end* and a *closed-end* investment company?

Q2 What problems do 'stale' prices cause when the assets of US mutual funds are marked to market, using these out-of-date prices?

Q3 What are 12b-1 fees and what are they used for?

Q4 How do we measure the return on a US mutual fund?

Q5 How do exchange-traded funds (ETFs) differ from mutual funds?

Q6 What are load fees?

PART 2

VALUATION

Valuation Techniques

AIMS

- To understand compound interest and its 'mirror image', discounting.
- To learn why and how we evaluate capital investment projects using either discounted present value (DPV) or the internal rate of return (IRR) criterion.
- To examine the relative merits of DPV, IRR and other decision criteria (e.g. payback period, discounted payback, profitability index) for choosing between alternative investment projects.
- To show how decision trees and scenario analysis can be used in DPV calculations when there is uncertainty about future cash flows.
- To discuss a number of practical issues in applying the DPV technique, such as mutually exclusive projects, capital rationing and real versus nominal cash flows.
- To show how DPV techniques can be used to value bonds and stocks.

INTRODUCTION

In this chapter we illustrate the use of compounding, discounted present value (DPV) and the internal rate of return (IRR). Using simple arithmetic examples, we consider the correct method of valuing a physical investment project and the decision to go ahead with specific investment projects. The same techniques can also be used to value the firm as a whole – this is used by stock analysts to pick under- or over-valued companies and to spot potential takeover targets (e.g. by private equity companies).

We show that when the discounted present value of a prospective investment just equals the capital cost of the project (DPV = KC), or equivalently the NPV = 0 or the IRR of the project just equals the cost of borrowing, then this implies the commonsense notion that 'the investment project earns just enough profits to cover the repayment of interest and principal on the borrowed funds'. When evaluating an investment project the latter statement is the most intuitive, but in finance theory it is most conveniently analysed and expressed in terms of the concepts of DPV and IRR. In calculating present value (PV) in practice, the key factors are how to forecast future cash flows from the project and what discount rate to use to reflect the uncertainty surrounding these cash flows. We deal with these issues in Chapters 7 and 8. We also note that PV techniques can be used to estimate the fair value of bonds and stocks.

6.1 COMPOUNDING AND DISCOUNTING

Suppose the annual interest rate is 10% (equivalent to $r = 0.10$) *and is expected to remain constant*. You have $A = \$1000$ to invest, today. What is the terminal value (TV) of $1000 in two years time? *At the end of the first year we have:*

$$TV_1 = A + rA = (1 + r)A = (1.10)\$1000 = \$1100 \qquad [1]$$

Now reinvest both the $1000 initial capital **and** the first year's interest receipts (of $rA = \$100$) for a further year, then *at the end of the second year we have:*

$$TV_2 = [(1 + r)A(1 + r) = (1 + r)^2A]$$
$$= \$1100(1.1) = (1.1)^2\$1000 = \$1210 \qquad [2]$$

Compounding takes account of interest on interest – the $100 interest from the first year is reinvested in the second year and earns additional interest. In general, the **terminal value after *n* years** of an initial investment of $A is:

$$TV_n = A(1 + r)^n \qquad [3]$$

Discounting

Discounting is the exact opposite of compounding. Suppose someone offers you the prospect of $1210 payable with certainty, after two years. How much are you prepared to give her as a loan today if the interest rate is 10% p.a.? The answer of course is $1000, since if you had

$1000 today you could invest it and have $1210 in two years time. We then say that the **discounted present value (DPV)** of $1210 (payable in two years time) is $1000 (today). The term *discounted cash flow* (DCF) is also used and in general the method is known as *the present value (PV) technique*. The amount payable in two years is reduced (discounted) to an equivalent amount today. Hence, if $V_2 = \$1210$ then the DPV is:

$$DPV = \frac{V_2}{(1 + r)^2} = \frac{\$1210}{(1.1)^2} = \$1000 \qquad [4]$$

Put another way, $1000 today (i.e. the DPV) is equivalent to $1210 in two years time. In the capital markets, if you can promise certain delivery of $1210 in two years time, someone will lend you $1000 today. Now, suppose I offer to pay you $1100 $(=V_1)$ in one year's time and $1210 $(=V_2)$ in two years time. How much are you prepared to give me as a loan *today* in exchange for these *two* certain future payments? The answer is that you will give me $2000 today, because:

$$DPV = \frac{V_1}{(1 + r)} + \frac{V_2}{(1 + r)^2} = \frac{\$1100}{(1.1)} + \frac{\$1210}{(1.1)^2} = \$2000 \qquad [5]$$

The important principle here is that if the interest rate (i.e. the opportunity cost of the money) is positive, then amounts of money that accrue at different points of time must be measured/compared *at one specific point in time*. The PV concept takes this 'specific point' as *today*, but in principle it could be any *one* specific point in time, for example the terminal date at the end of the second year or any other year.

6.2 INVESTMENT APPRAISAL: 'VITO'S DELI'

As we shall see, the concept of DPV is widely used to evaluate all types of investment decisions, such as physical investment in plant and machinery (capital investment/capital budgeting), investment in stocks and bonds and in the pricing of futures and options.

Net present value

PV is probably the most widely used concept in finance. Suppose we consider a physical investment project, namely buying a New York delicatessen called Vito's Deli. Also suppose that forecast sales revenues less operating costs (e.g. wages and materials), known as free (or net) cash flows, are $CF_1 = \$1100$ *at the end* of year 1 and $CF_2 = \$1210$ at the end of year 2. At the end of year 2 you know with certainty that your deli will be 'torched' by a rival (the Bucconi brothers) and as you have no insurance, it will then have zero value (see Figure 6.1). Note that the cash flows CF_1 and CF_2 are the same as used above. Suppose that the capital (or 'investment') cost of purchasing the deli today is KC = $2100 and the interest rate is 10% $(r = 0.1)$. The interest rate is the 'opportunity cost' of the use of your own funds, since we assume the best alternative use of your own funds is to invest them in a bank account at the rate r. (Equally, we could also have assumed that the $2100 was a loan from the bank and the same analysis as below would apply.) Is the deli business the correct investment decision (i.e. the one that maximises your return)?

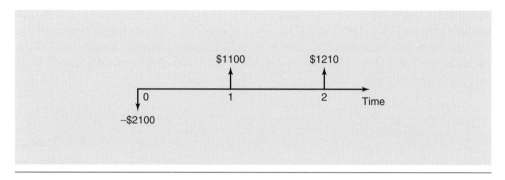

FIGURE 6.1: Cash flows for Vito's deli

Calculation A:

Total cash flows (undiscounted) = $2310
Capital cost (today)   = $2100
Crude profit   = $210

This crude calculation suggests we should invest in the deli business since the profit is positive.

Calculation B:

DPV (cash flows)   = $2000
Capital cost (today) = $2100
Net profit (on DPV basis) = −$100

Here, using the DPV formula (calculation B), we have DPV = $2000 and with a capital cost KC = $2100, the net present value, NPV = DPV − KC = −$100. Hence in this case:

DPV (cash flows) < Capital cost, KC [6]

or

Net present value, NPV = DPV − KC < 0 [7]

It looks as though we should **not** invest in the project, which is the correct answer. The reason the PV approach (Equation [6]) is correct is most easily seen by compounding to the terminal date, two years hence, and taking account of the *opportunity cost* of the funds used to invest in the deli. The next best (here, the only) alternative use for your initial funds of KC = $2100 is placing them on deposit at the bank, which pays an annual rate of interest r. This yields a terminal value (TV) of:

End of Year 2 (Bank)

$$\textbf{TV(bank)} = \$2100(1 + r)^2 = \$2100(1.1)^2 = \$2541$$ [8]

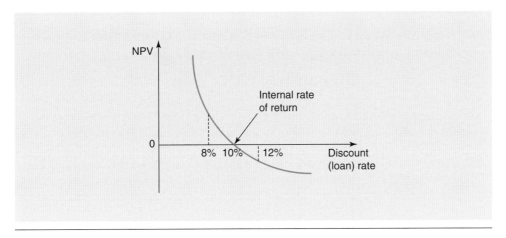

FIGURE 6.2: NPV and the discount rate

If you invest in Vito's Deli, your $1100 revenues received at the end of year 1 can be invested at r to give $\$1100(1 + r) = \$1100(1.1) = \$1210$ at the end of year 2. This can be (directly) added to your cash flow at the end of year 2 ($= \$1210$) since both are measured *at the same time period*. Hence investing in Vito's Deli gives a terminal value of:

End of Year 2 (Vito's)

$$\text{TV(Vito's)} = \$1210 + \$1210 = \$2420 \tag{9}$$

Clearly, the terminal value of Vito's Deli ($2420) is less than the terminal value of investing in the bank ($2541). Hence you should *not* invest in Vito's Deli. The DPV or NPV rules are equivalent to comparing terminal values; that is, if DPV (Vito's cash flows) < KC then this implies that TV (Vito's cash flows) < TV (bank loan). The above also stresses the fact that even if you are given your initial outlay of $2100 (by Uncle Paulie) the money is not 'free'. It has an *opportunity cost* and the relevant calculation is Calculation B not Calculation A. It is clear from the DPV formula that the higher the cost of borrowing r the lower will be the DPV and the NPV and this is depicted in Figure 6.2.

NOTE: TERMINAL VALUE AND DPV

To show the equivalence of comparing all cash flows either by terminal value or PV, let's examine the above figures a little further. After investing the first year's cash flows from Vito's in Bank A at $r = 10\%$ for one year and adding them to the cash flows in year 2, we would have:

$$\text{TV (Vito's)} = \$1210 + \$1210 = \$2420$$

But if today we offered to give another Bank B $2,420 in two years time, how much would Bank B give us today (as a loan)? It would give us today:

$$DPV = \$2420/(1.1)^2 = \$2000$$

So once again we find that our profits are worth $2000 today – but this is less than the capital cost of project of KC = $2100, so we would not go ahead with the deli.

As long as you adjust any cash flows to the same point in time and only then compare them, you will always came to the same decision about the viability of an investment.

If the investment expenditures are spread over several years, then the NPV is calculated using cash flows *CF* (i.e. revenues minus operating costs) net of any investment (capital) expenditures in the years in which they occur KC_i, so the NPV is:

$$NPV = \frac{CF_1 - KC_1}{(1 + r)} + \frac{CF_2 - KC_2}{(1 + r)^2} - KC_0$$

The PV concept can be used to rank the viability of several capital investment projects that are independent of each other and where there are no capital constraints on borrowing funds. By independent we mean that each project's cash flows do not depend on or influence the cash flows from any other prospective investment projects (e.g. setting up delis in towns that are geographically far apart). At any point in time, the firm is faced with one discount (loan) rate and can use this to calculate the NPV for each individual project. We can now think of ranking these projects according to their NPVs, from highest to lowest. Hence:

When funds are available, invest in all projects for which the NPV is positive.

However, note that if there is a capital constraint on finance, then the NPV criterion is misleading (see 'performance index' below).

Valuation of the whole firm

The PV approach can be used to value the whole firm. Here we merely aggregate the free cash flows and capital costs from all the firm's current and planned projects and find their total NPV. It can be shown that:

If managers invest in all positive NPV projects, then this maximises the value of the firm and maximises the returns to shareholders.

The PV approach is one way in which stock analysts try to calculate the 'fair value' of the firm to see if it is currently over- or undervalued. Suppose that by summing the NPVs of all the divisions of the firm the analyst finds that the NPV of the firm is $V_{firm} = \$100$m. If this is an all-equity firm and there are $N = 10$m shares outstanding, then the 'fair value' of these shares is $V_s = \$10$ per share ($= 100/10$). If the shares are currently trading at $P = \$9$, then the analyst might recommend purchasing this undervalued share. If an investor moves fast enough and is first to purchase at $9 and this is followed by other investors believing the analyst's calculation of fair value, then as other investors buy the share its price will rise towards its fair value of $10. The investor who was first to purchase the share will make $1 capital gain and other investors who pile in after her will make less than $1. If investors are rational then they will stop buying when the market price reaches its fair value of $10. There are many practical issues to discuss about the above simple example and these are explored in Part 4.

If we assume that the firm in question is 'levered' – that is, financed by a mix of debt and equity – then the debtholders (i.e. banks and bondholders) are also entitled to some of the cash flows (operating profits) of the firm, so the value of the equityholders' stake in the firm is:

LEVERED FIRM

Value of equity = Value of the firm $-$ Value of debt

$V_s = V_{firm} - V_{Debt}$

The value of the firm is calculated using *all* the (operating) cash flows accruing to the firm's activities and finding their PV. These cash flows 'belong to' the equity and debtholders. So to calculate the fair value of just the equity and hence the 'fair' stock price, we need first to deduct the value of the outstanding debt (e.g. bonds, bank loans) from our calculation of V_{firm} to obtain V_s. How we value the firm's debt we discuss in Part 6, but for the moment you can assume that we merely deduct the market value of the firm's outstanding bonds and outstanding bank loans from our calculation of V_{firm}.

Internal rate of return

The internal rate of return (IRR) provides an equivalent way of evaluating physical investment projects, as the DPV criterion. Consider an investment project with a capital cost *today* of KC = $2000 and net operating cash flows accruing in the future of $CF_1 = \$1100$ and $CF_2 = \$1210$. Suppose we discount these cash flows using an 'unknown' discount rate y, then the PV of these future cash flows is:

$$\frac{CF_1}{(1 + y)} + \frac{CF_2}{(1 + y)^2} = \frac{\$1100}{(1 + y)} + \frac{\$1210}{(1 + y)^2} \qquad [10]$$

We now ask the question: 'What is the discount rate that will just make the PV of the cash flows equal to the capital cost of the project?' This 'break-even' rate of return is the solution to:

$$\$2000 = \frac{\$1100}{(1 + y)} + \frac{\$1210}{(1 + y)^2} \tag{11}$$

Here, the break-even return is $y = 0.10$ (or 10% p.a.) and is called the IRR of the investment project (see Figure 6.2). Here 'break-even' means that the DPV (cash flows) = Capital cost. If some capital costs occur immediately but some are spread over several future years, then the internal rate of return is calculated by using cash flows net of investment expenditures $(CF - KC)$, but the IRR is still the break-even discount rate, which makes the NPV equal to zero:

$$NPV = \frac{CF_1 - KC_1}{(1 + y)} + \frac{CF_2 - KC_2}{(1 + y)^2} - KC_0 = 0$$

The value y is the IRR. But note that the calculation of y does not involve any interest payments on the funds borrowed to finance the investment – the latter is taken care of in our investment rule, which is:

Invest in the project if IRR $\geq$ cost of the funds (loan rate = r).

In our simple example, the investment is financed by bank borrowing, but in practice other sources of funds may also be used (e.g. new issues of bonds and equity) and the overall cost of these funds is often known as the **hurdle rate** for the project. In more academic language, the hurdle rate is known as the weighted average cost of capital or the WACC for short.

If the cost of borrowing $r = 10\%$ p.a., then an IRR of $y = 10\%$ suggests it is just worthwhile to invest in the deli. Note also that for $r = 10\%$, the DPV of this project is $2000, which just equals the capital cost of $2000 and hence the NPV = 0. The DPV rule also indicates that the deli investment is just viable for $r = 10\%$. Hence, our two investment rules give equivalent decisions. They are, invest in the project if:

DPV > KC or equivalently NPV > 0 [12a]

or

IRR > r [12b]

If DPV > KC or IRR > r, then this implies that at the end of the investment period (i.e. terminal date) you will have more 'cash' if you invest in a physical investment project such as Vito's Deli rather than investing your own funds in a bank deposit (i.e. the next best alternative use for the funds). Or, if the capital cost is financed by a bank loan, you will be able to payoff the principal and interest and still have some cash remaining in two years time.

Let us examine the DPV and IRR rules and interpret them in the kind of language more frequently used by business people. The 'bottom line' for an investment project from a business perspective is that the cash flows generated at least payoff the initial capital (cash) outlay and any interest on this capital (or opportunity cost of the own funds used). We now demonstrate using a simple example that:

> If DPV = KC or if the IRR just equals the opportunity cost of the funds (e.g. bank lending rate r), then the investment project will just pay back the principal and the interest on the loan.

For example, if KC = \$1528 and $CF_1 = CF_2 = \$1000$, then the IRR using equation [11] is easily found to be IRR = 0.2 (or 20%). If we let the bank loan rate $r = 0.2$, then the DPV equals \$1528, which just equals the capital cost. Given the cash flows CF_1 and CF_2 the sequence of payments is given in Table 6.1.

TABLE 6.1: Cash flow with DPV = 0 or IRR = Cost of borrowing

	End of 1st Year	**End of 2nd Year**
Loan outstanding (including interest)	(1.2) \$1528 = \$1833.6	(1.2) \$833.6 = \$1000
Receipts	−\$1000	−\$1000
Amount Owing	=\$833.6	= 0

At the end of year 1 the initial loan of \$1528 has increased to \$1833.60 (= \$1528(1.2)), part of which is paid off with receipts of \$1000, leaving an outstanding loan of \$833.60. At the end of year 2 this accrues to around \$1000, which can be wholly paid off with the \$1000 received at the end of year 2 (ignoring rounding errors). Note however that the above simple analysis side-steps some of the problems that can arise when using the IRR concept and it is not always the case that DPV and IRR rules give identical decisions in the ranking of investment projects.

6.3 PROBLEMS AND REFINEMENTS

Generally speaking, business people prefer to talk in terms of IRR. Hence they can say that 'project A is expected to earn an IRR of 10%, which is 3% over borrowing costs'. However, the PV method is the one that nearly always gives unambiguously correct investment decisions. As we see below, in certain circumstances the IRR investment rule given above has to be amended, otherwise it may indicate the wrong project choice.

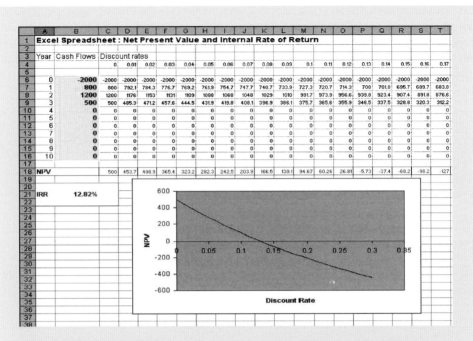

This spreadsheet produces the NPV–discount rate relationship. Cash flows up to 10 years are input in column B. Columns C, D . . . calculate the present value, PV, of the cash flows using the discount rate in row 4. The NPV is the sum of the PV of cash flows and is reported in row 18. The graph plots the NPV of row 18 against the discount rates in row 4.

The Internal Rate of Return can be calculated using the Excel function, ' = IRR'.

Different cash flow profiles

Consider the cash flows from the three projects A, B and C shown in Table 6.2. Project A has 'normal' or 'regular' pattern of cash flows, namely an initial investment outlay of −$100 and receipts (in one year) of $150.

The NPV is negatively related to the bank loan rate (i.e. the discount rate) and the IRR is 50% (Figure 6.3). The NPV rule indicates that the project should be implemented for any discount

---

TABLE 6.2: Different cash flow profiles

Projects	Cash flows
Project A (normal)	(−100, 150)
Project B (Rolling Stones concert)	(100, −150)
Project C (open cast mining)	(−100, 245, −150)

Note: NPV gives correct decision for A, B, C, but IRR gives wrong decision for B and C.

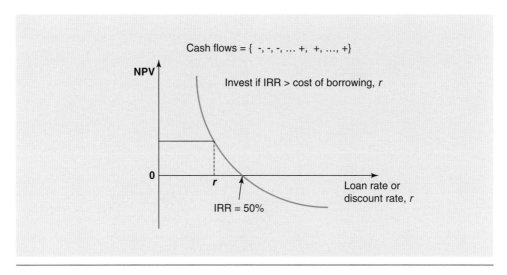

FIGURE 6.3: Project A, normal cash flows

rate r below 50% and the IRR rule gives the same investment decision rule (i.e. invest in the project if IRR (= 50%) > r, the cost of borrowing).

Consider the cash flows for project B, a Rolling Stones concert. Here, ticket sales before the concert result in an inflow of $100 and the cash outflow of equipment and salaries of $150 takes place after one year. The graph of the NPV against the discount rate is positive as in Figure 6.4 and the IRR is again $y = 50\%$.

The NPV becomes more positive as the loan rate increases (above 50%). Hence the NPV rule indicates that a loan rate *greater than 50%* implies that project B should be implemented,

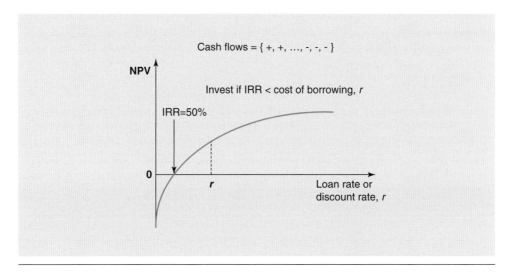

FIGURE 6.4: Project B, Rolling Stones concert

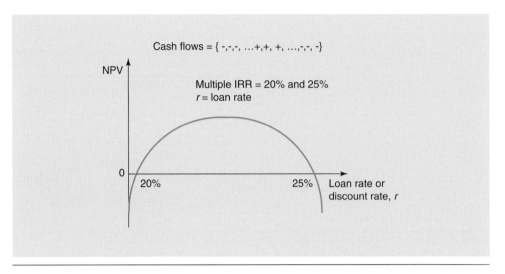

FIGURE 6.5: Project C, open-cast mining

since then the NPV > 0. However, somewhat paradoxically, the latter implies a reversal of the usual IRR rule: for this project to go ahead we require IRR $<$ discount (loan) rate, r. The paradox is resolved by noting that the cash inflow (at $t = 0$) from project B of \$100 is equivalent to borrowing \$100 with an implicit cost equal to the IRR of 50%. If the *actual cost* of borrowing from the bank is greater than 50%, then it pays to get your \$100 today, by undertaking project B. Hence you invest in project B if IRR $< r$.

Cash flows from project C could be due to an investment in open cast mining, where there are large initial capital costs, followed by positive receipts from the sale of the minerals and a final negative cash flow due to the cost of returning the site back to its original state. The NPV–discount rate relationship is shown in Figure 6.5, with a positive NPV for discount rates between 20 and 25%, and therefore on the basis of the NPV rule, project C should be undertaken for $20\% < r < 25\%$. This profile of cash flows, namely $\{-, +, -\}$, gives multiple values for the IRR $= 20\%$ or 25%. Clearly, if the bank loan rate equals 22% one value of the IRR indicates we go ahead with the project (IRR $= 25\%$) and the other (IRR $= 20\%$) that we do not.

The above problems apply whenever the cash flows have the same *qualitative* form as in projects A, B and C. For example, if a project initially has a *series* of negative cash flows followed by a *series* of cash flows that are always positive (like project A), then the NPV and the usual IRR rule both give the same investment decisions. Similarly, a *series* of cash flows that are all initially negative, then some are positive, and then some are negative again may give multiple values for the IRR. A summary of the above might be:

Use NPV and not IRR when cash flows are irregular.

Mutually exclusive projects

Mutually exclusive projects are those for which you can either accept project A or accept project B or reject both – but you cannot *accept* both of them. For example, you might only be able to build either an apartment building or a movie theatre on a particular piece of land (but not both). For mutually exclusive projects the usual IRR criterion can give incorrect investment decisions in two specific cases known as the **scale problem** and the **timing problem**. It is still possible to use the IRR criterion in a modified form, but it is worth noting that the usual NPV criterion poses no problems for mutually exclusive projects.

TABLE 6.3: Scale problem

	Cash flow at $t = 0$ ($)	Cash flow at $t + 1$ ($)	NPV ($) ($r = 10\%$)	IRR (%)
Project A	−10	15	3.64	50
Project B	−80	110	20	37.5

Scale problem

To illustrate this issue, consider the NPV and IRR from the two projects in Table 6.3. For project A, the businesswoman pays out $10 now and receives $15 at $t + 1$. The NPV for $r = 10\%$ is $3.64 and the IRR is 50%. Project B involves an outlay of $80 and a payout at $t + 1$ of $110, giving an NPV of $20 but an IRR of only 37.5%. The projects are mutually exclusive, so you can choose only one of them. Intuition (and the NPV criterion) would suggest you choose project B, since it has a larger NPV of $20, which exceeds that of project A of $3.64. However, the IRR criterion indicates you should choose project A with an IRR of 50% rather than project B with an IRR of only 37.5%. Which is correct?

It turns out that the NPV criterion gives the correct investment choice, primarily because the IRR ignores the issue of the scale of the two projects. After all, 50% of almost nothing is nearly nothing while 37.5% of a lot is quite a lot. In these circumstances the problem is in part caused by the mutually exclusive nature of the projects (i.e. only one at best can be implemented). The IRR rule (i.e. invest if IRR > cost of borrowing) can be shown to give a similar investment decision to the NPV rule providing we consider the **incremental IRR** relative to the cost of borrowing. The incremental cash flows are those in moving from the smaller (S) to the larger (L) project (see Table 6.4).

> Incremental cash flows = cash flow of B − cash flow of A

TABLE 6.4: Incremental cash flows

	Cash flow at $t = 0$	Cash flow at $t + 1$
Incremental cash flow	L − S = −80 − (−10) = **−70**	L − S = 110 − 15 = **95**

The incremental IRR is calculated using:

$$0 = -70 + \frac{95}{(1 + IRR)} \qquad [13]$$

The *incremental* IRR in moving from the smaller to the larger project is 35.7%, which exceeds the discount (loan) rate $r = 10\%$, hence the incremental IRR rule gives the same investment decision as the standard NPV criterion. Notice also that the *incremental* NPV using $r = 10\%$ equals $-70 + 95/(1.1) = 16.36 > 0$, which also indicates that you should move from project A to project B. In summary, mutually exclusive projects can be handled by either of the following equivalent decision rules:

- Choose the project with the largest NPV.
- Choose the 'larger' project if the *incremental* IRR exceeds the discount (loan) rate.
- Choose the 'larger' project if the *incremental* NPV is positive.

Timing problem

Suppose a firm can use a plot of land either to build a warehouse that earns considerable revenue in the early years (project E, Table 6.5) or to build a deli that earns most of its revenues in later years (project L, Table 6.5). The timing problem for these mutually exclusive projects can be illustrated by considering project E, whose positive cash flows in the early years of the project are larger than those of project L, while in later years the relative size of the cash flows is reversed (see Table 6.5). The NPV of the two projects are shown in Figure 6.6.

For a discount rate less than 8.71%, $NPV_L > NPV_E$, but project E has a higher IRR (33.15%) than project L (18.36%). Hence the two criteria give conflicting investment decisions. Once

TABLE 6.5: Timing problem with mutually exclusive projects

	Time period				NPV			
Year	**0**	**1**	**2**	**3**	**0%**	**10%**	**15%**	**IRR**
Project E	−10,000	12,000	1000	1000	4000	2486.85	1848.44	33.15%
Project L	−10,000	1000	1000	14,000	6000	2253.94	830.94	18.37%

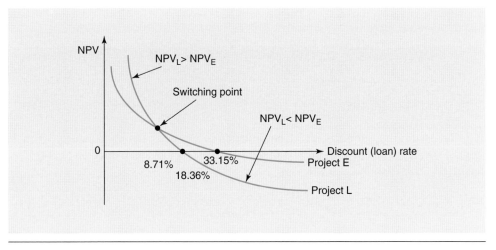

FIGURE 6.6: Mutually exclusive projects

again, the usual NPV criterion turns out to be correct, although calculation of the incremental IRR (or the incremental NPV) will also result in 'correct' investment decisions (as outlined above).

NPV and IRR

Overall, then, our conclusions on investment decision rules are:

- NPV and IRR give identical decisions for independent projects with 'normal cash flows' (i.e. ones of the form $\{-, -, \ldots, +, +\}$, with only one sign change).
- For cash flows that change sign more than once, for example $\{-, -, +, +, -, -\}$, the IRR gives multiple solutions and cannot be used. Use NPV.
- For mutually exclusive projects use the standard NPV criterion or the incremental IRR criterion.

Real versus nominal

Cash flows and discount rates can be measured either in nominal terms or in real terms. In the DPV formula the rule is very straightforward, namely:

> The same value for the DPV ensues if:
> Nominal cash flows are discounted at the nominal rate,
> or
> Real cash flows are discounted at the real interest rate.

Suppose the inflation rate is $\pi = 5\%$ p.a. and the real rate $rr = 3\%$ p.a. Then the nominal rate of interest is given by:

$$(1 + \text{nominal rate}) = (1 + \text{real rate})\,(1 + \text{inflation rate})$$

$$(1 + r) = (1 + rr)\,(1 + \pi)$$

$$1.0815 = (1.03)\,(1.05) \tag{14}$$

If \$1 invested for a year earns 8.15% but inflation is 5%, you can only purchase 3% more 'goods' (i.e. Sak's hampers) at the end of the year. Note that an approximation to [14] if we ignore the '$rr.\pi$' term is:

$$r = rr + \pi \tag{15}$$

To show that each method gives identical results, consider a nominal cash flow in one year's time of CF = \$100, discounted at a nominal rate r = 8.15%. The DPV using *nominal variables* is:

$$\text{DPV}_N = \frac{CF}{(1 + r)} = \frac{\$100}{1.0815} = \$92.464 \tag{16}$$

If inflation $\pi = 5\%$ p.a. the real value of CF dollars payable in $t = 1$ year's time is:

$$CF_r = \frac{CF_t}{(1 + \pi)^t} = \frac{\$100}{(1.05)^1} = \$95.238 \tag{17}$$

The DPV using *real variables* is:

$$\text{DPV}_r = \frac{CF_r}{(1 + rr)} = \frac{\$95.238}{1.03} = \$92.464 \tag{18}$$

As can be seen, the DPV is the same in both cases. This is easy to see algebraically by substituting for CF_r and rr in [18], using equations [17] and [14].

Timing of capital expenditures

In practice, the capital costs of an investment project may take place over several years. But this provides no additional problems because we either discount 'net cash flows' ($CF_i - KC_i$) in each year or discount CF_i and the capital costs KC_i in each year separately.

A very different issue arises when we consider the possibility that the investment project could be started at any time in the next five years. (For simplicity, and without loss, we assume the project is worthless if not started within five years.) By delaying the start of the project, you forgo the revenues you would otherwise earn in the early years. On the other hand, you also delay the capital costs. What is the optimal start date for the project (assuming it has a positive NPV at $t = 0$)?

When net cash flow and investment costs are known with certainty, this is a simple problem. We merely work out the NPV for each 'start period', $t = 0, 1, 2, 3$ etc. For example, assuming we start the project in year 3, this has a NPV *in year 3* of NPV_3. Hence for each start date for the project we have a set of NPVs labelled NPV_t (for $t = 0, 1, 2, 3, 4, 5$). These NPVs at t can be discounted back to $t = 0$, to give a set of values $NPV_{0,t}$, which stands for 'NPV at $t = 0$, assuming the project is started at t', hence:

$$NPV_{0,t} = NPV_t/(1 + r)^t$$

We then choose the year ($= t$) to commence the project that gives the highest $NPV_{0,t}$. Let's see what is really happening with the above procedure. Intuitively, we start the project 'later' if the growth rate of NPV_t, − that is, $g_t = (NPV_t / NPV_{t-1}) - 1$, is higher than the discount rate r. By delaying, the percentage increase in the NPV of the cash flows exceeds the cost of borrowing. So, if the increase in NPV_t in years 1, 2, 3, 4, 5 is $g_t = 11\%$, 12%, 11%, 12%, 9% and the (risk-adjusted) discount rate is 10%, then the optimal investment date is to start in year 4, since after that date the increase in NPV of 9% by waiting a further year does not exceed the cost of borrowing. In this case, it will be found that $NPV_{0,4}$ takes the largest value.

Uncertainty and risk

There may be a great deal of uncertainty concerning the future cash flows from a capital investment project. One way of dealing with this is the use of **decision trees**. For example, consider the following simple one-period case. Suppose there is a 75% chance of a cash inflow of $V_U = \$100$ (i.e. the economy is 'up') and a 25% chance that $V_D = \$40$ cash inflow (i.e. the economy is 'down') at the end of year 1. We could use the expected cash flow V^e in the DPV calculation where:

$$V^e = 0.75\,V_U + 0.25\,V_D = \$85 \quad \text{and hence} \quad NPV = -KC + V^e/(1 + r).$$

The problem with decision trees is that they can quickly become very complicated. For example, if we have only two possible states of the economy at the end of the year of U or D, then by the second year we have 4 ($= 2^2$) possible outcomes (i.e. UU, UD, DU and DD). After 10 years we have 1024 ($= 2^{10}$) possible outcomes, for which we need estimates of probabilities and cash flows! Not only that, suppose at $t = 1$ we have the possibility of selling the factory for a known abandonment value $AV_1 = \$50$ (Figure 6.7). To find the NPV of the project when abandonment is possible, we have to work back through the tree, starting at $t = 2$, since our decision of whether to invest today depends on whether we abandon at $t = 1$ or not. Suppose on the U branch we use the expected present value approach above to calculate the NPV *at $t = 1$* of the expected cash flows for the outcomes UU and UD using the conditional probabilities p_{ulu}, p_{dlu}. Suppose we find *NPV (not abandon)*$_1^U = \$150 > AV_1 (= \$50)$. We then take NPV $= \$150$ as our value at $t = 1$ on the U path. It is more likely that we would abandon on the D-path, since the expected values at $t = 1$ of the cash flows at $t = 2$ on the DU and DD nodes are likely to be low. If *NPV (not abandon)*$_1^D = \$40 < AV_1 (= \$50)$, then we abandon the project and take $AV_1 = \$50$ as

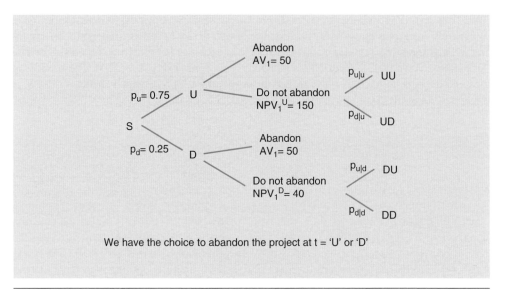

We have the choice to abandon the project at t = 'U' or 'D'

FIGURE 6.7: Decision tree

our value for the D-path. Hence the NPV at $t = 0$, when we take account of the abandonment option, is:

$$NPV = -KC + [0.75\,(\$150) + 0.25\,(\$50)]/(1 + r)$$

and if this were greater than zero we would go ahead with the project at $t = 0$ (see Kellogg and Chames, 2000, for a user-friendly account of the valuation of a biotechnology company using decision trees). Because decision trees quickly become very complex, another method of valuing investment projects where outcomes are very uncertain and there are possibilities for expansion or abandonment of the project is **real options theory** (see Cuthbertson and Nitzsche, 2001b).

There are other methods we could use to get a feel for the impact of uncertainty on the NPV of the project. For example, we could use **sensitivity analysis**. Here we calculate several different values for the NPV based on a variety of *independent* assumptions, taken one at a time. We have our central NPV calculation ($NPV_c = \$10m$, say) and we then alter one forecast (e.g. assume lower sales volume) while keeping all other factors the same. If our new NPV is very different from the central NPV (e.g. $NPV_n = -\$1m$), then we may wish to go back and do more market research and refine our analysis of this crucial assumption. The difficulty here is that in reality, the assumption of a lower sales volume in a recession is likely to be accompanied both by lower output prices and lower input costs (e.g. wages). That is, these three variables are positively correlated. The variables in the sensitivity analysis are not really independent and hence the latter technique may give highly misleading results. We really therefore need to consider these interdependencies in any simulation we undertake: the technique is then often referred to as **scenario analysis**. Clearly, getting these 'correlations' right is rather difficult, although past data on the variables can be used to get 'ball-park' estimates. Also, there is a limit to how many 'scenarios' one might undertake.

An advanced form of scenario analysis is *Monte Carlo Simulation (MCS)*, where we can quickly and (relatively) easily undertake many simulations of the variables, while still maintaining the interrelationships between them. However, this technique is not widely applied in business investment decisions. But recently it has been used to try and value investments in biotechnology and Internet companies, where possible 'central' cash flow forecasts are clearly difficult to ascertain. This is **real options theory** again (see Cuthbertson and Nitzsche 2001b).

6.4 OTHER DECISION RULES

Payback period

The **payback period** is the number of years it takes for the (undiscounted) future receipts to exceed the initial capital outlay, which for the cash flows in Table 6.6 is two years. A judgement is then made as to whether this period is reasonable given the uncertainty attached to future cash flows. The payback period is quite often used in conjunction with a full NPV calculation, since it provides a useful simple yardstick with which to compare the NPV figure (which is likely to have a larger degree of uncertainty than the payback period). Sometimes the cash flows are discounted before the payback period is calculated. For example, in Table 6.6 the discounted cash flows are $435, $378 and $348 for years 1 to 3 respectively. Hence the **discounted payback period**, given a capital cost of $1000, is between two and three years.

The problem with the payback methods are that they ignore the contribution of 'distant' cash flows that accrue after the payback period, to the value of the investment project. If the payback method had been used, the Channel Tunnel between England and France would no doubt never have been built. (Some would also argue that even on a NPV calculation the project was not viable.)

Return on capital employed

The **return on capital ROC**, (also referred to as the return on assets ROA) is:

$$\text{ROC} = \text{Profits} / \text{Total Assets} = \text{EBIT}\,(1-t) / \text{Total Assets}$$

TABLE 6.6: Investment appraisal – other methods

		Year 0	Year 1	Year 2	Year 3	Year 4
1.	CF	−1000	500	500	700	0
2.	Discount factor, d	1	0.8696	0.7561	0.4972	–
3.	PV	−1000	435	378	348	–
4.	**NPV = 161**					
5.	**Payback period = 2 years**					
6.	**Discounted payback = 2−3 years**					

The ROC can be applied to a particular project or division of a (non-financial) firm or to the firm as a whole. The difficulty lies in the measurement of 'profits' and 'total assets'. First, profits can be measured in many different ways (see below) and there is then the question of whether we use current profits, an average of past profits or an estimate of forecast profits over the next few years. Total assets is usually taken as the book value of equity plus debt. Although widely quoted as a 'rule of thumb' figure and as a point of comparison between firms in a particular sector or for a single firm over time, the ROC ignores the time value of money and should not be used in preference to PV techniques.

Profitability index (PI)

If we take discounting into account, the PV approach may be reinterpreted in terms of a rate of return on capital, which is known as the *profitability index (PI)*.

$$\textbf{Profitability Index} = \frac{PV\,(Cash\,Flows)}{PV\,(Capital\,Cost)} = \frac{PV\,(Cash\,Flows)}{KC}$$

For example, suppose that PV = \$120m and the initial capital outlay for the project is KC = \$100m at $t = 0$. The NPV = \$20m, which implies that we proceed with the project. The value of PI = \$120m/\$100m = 1.20, which is interpreted as a 20% return. It is easy to see that NPV = PV(CF) − KC > 0 is equivalent to PI > 1. Indeed, both criteria give identical investment decisions when ranking *independent* projects. If capital costs accrue over several years, then the denominator is the PV of the capital costs. For mutually exclusive projects the PI index may give the wrong investment decision because of the scale problem, but this can be corrected by seeing if the incremental PI index exceeds unity.

Capital rationing

There is one area where the NPV rule gives incorrect results and this is when a firm does not have enough funds to undertake all projects with a NPV > 0. When the firm is subject to *capital rationing*, independent projects must be ranked by the PI index and implemented from the highest to lowest (but with all PI > 1) until the capital constraint is reached. Intuitively, the PI index works in this case because it measures 'bang per buck', since the present value of receipts is scaled by the capital cost of the project. The NPV rule breaks down because the NPV of one large project using all the capital funds available may be exceeded by the sum of the NPVs of two other projects (each of which used half the capital available), even though each taken separately has a lower NPV than the large project.

6.5 VALUING STOCKS AND BONDS

Bonds

Can we apply the PV method to value other assets such as stocks and bonds? Yes we can, since the fair value of these assets depends on their future cash flows discounted at a rate that reflects the riskiness of these cash flows. The higher the variability in future cash flows, the higher the discount rate. Let's take bonds first. If you buy a government bond (e.g. Treasury bond), then the future cash flows each year, $C = \$60$ say (called coupons), are known with certainty, as is the maturity value $M = \$1000$ that you will receive when the bond matures in n years time. So the appropriate discount rate to use is the observed risk-free rate (yield), r, and the fair value of the bond that matures in n years time is:

$$V_{bond} = \frac{C}{(1 + r)} + \frac{C}{(1 + r)^2} + \cdots + \frac{C + M}{(1 + r)^n}$$

Because the coupon payments are known and everyone agrees that the appropriate discount rate is the risk-free rate, then all market participants will agree that this is the correct value for the bond and the market price will equal this value $P_{bond} = V_{bond} = 990$, say. This is because if the market price of some of these bonds were quoted by some dealers at a price $P_{bond} = \$980$ below their fair value $V_{bond} = \$990$ then many speculators would step in and offer to buy these bonds – the additional demand for these bonds would quickly push their price up to the fair value of \$990. This is a form of arbitrage and the fact that this ensures that the observed bond price equals its fair value is an example of the **efficient markets hypothesis**. Although corporate bonds are not quite the same as government bonds (since the coupon payments are not certain as the firm might go into liquidation), nevertheless we can consider the fair value of the outstanding bonds as equal to their market values.

NOTE: BANK LOANS

How would you obtain the current *market* value of the firm's outstanding bank loans? Well, you could assume that this is equal to their historic (book) value in the bank's accounts and this is what we usually do in practice. But if the firm has entered business areas that have become more risky since the loans were granted, then the true market value of these loans is lower, because this increased risk should be reflected in a higher discount rate.

Stocks

The cash flows that accrue to stockholders are dividends (D), but today we do not know what these future dividend payments will be – we can only try to forecast them. The cash flows to stocks are uncertain and therefore the discount rate will be higher than the risk-free rate – the discount rate will consist of the risk-free rate plus an extra amount known as the risk premium. For the moment assume we know the discount rate to use for each year, R_t, which is usually called the 'required return on equity' or the 'cost of equity finance'. How it is determined is the subject of later chapters. The fair value of the stock is:

$$V_{stock} = \frac{D_1}{(1 + R_1)} + \frac{D_2}{(1 + R_2)^2} + \frac{D_3}{(1 + R_3)^3} + \cdots \tag{19}$$

where the number of terms goes on for ever. To calculate fair value we often simplify matters by assuming that the discount rate is constant in each year ($= R$) and that dividends grow at a constant rate $g = 0.03$ (3% p.a., say), for ever. With these two assumptions, the stock-valuation model is known as the **dividend discount model** DDM (or **Gordon growth model**) and the above formula simplifies to:

$$V_{stock} = \frac{D_1}{(R - g)} \qquad [20]$$

where $D_1 = (1 + g)D_0$ is the forecast of next year's dividends. We can now calculate the fair value of the stock based on our estimates of the (constant) required return on the firm's equity and the forecast growth rate in dividends. Clearly, these assumptions are quite strong and may be incorrect – issues discussed in future chapters.

Let us push this model a little further. If most people trading in the market have broadly the same views about R and g, then arbitrage will ensure that the market price of the stock equals its fair value, so $P_{stock} = D_1/(R - g)$. We can rearrange this equation to give:

$$R = \frac{D_1}{P} + g \qquad [21]$$

This equation assumes that the DDM is the correct valuation model for stocks (i.e. the market price is the 'correct' price) and a consequence of this is that the return on a stock should equal the dividend–price ratio plus the growth rate of dividends. As we shall see, this equation provides one method of calculating the discount rate we should use when valuing a firm that is financed (in part) by equity finance. To calculate the cost of equity finance R, we simply have to *forecast* the long-run dividend–price ratio and the long-run growth rate of the firm's dividends.

SUMMARY

- Cash flows that accrue at different points in time cannot be directly compared: they must first be discounted. Cash flows are worth less today the further into the future at which they are received. This is the concept of *discounted present value* (DPV).
- Capital investment projects can be compared using either the net present value (NPV) concept or the *internal rate of return (IRR)*. These two methods give identical decision rules when we consider independent projects, there are no capital constraints and cash flows are 'normal'.
- In general, the NPV approach is more straightforward than the IRR approach when cash flows are uneven or for mutually exclusive projects.
- Uncertainty can be dealt with by using expected values and decision trees. However, in practice this is not always easy to apply. Here *scenario analysis* is a useful complementary approach. Even then, the degree of uncertainty may still be very large because of measurement problems, but NPV provides a useful framework for analysing alternative possible outcomes.

- The PV technique can be used to find the fair value of other assets such as stocks and bonds.
- The *dividend discount model DDM* (or Gordon Growth model) is a special case of the PV method where we assume a constant discount rate and a constant growth rate of cash flows, for ever.

EXERCISES

Q1   What is the relationship between 'compounding' and 'discounting'?

Q2   Intuitively, why should you invest in a project if its NPV is positive?

Q3   What is the internal rate of return (IRR) of an investment project? Can you discover what assumptions IRR makes about the *reinvestment* rate for cash flows from the project? (Hint: use a two-period investment project.)

Q4   What are the 'payback period' and the discounted 'payback period'? Why are they a poor guide to investment decisions?

Q5   You have won the National Lottery. Lottery officials offer you the choice of the following alternative pay-outs:

a) Alternative 1: £160,000 one year from now
b) Alternative 2: £200,000 five years from now

Which should you choose if the discount rate is:
0%?
5%?
10%?

Q6   Suppose you are considering an investment in which you pay £5000 one year from today and receive an annual income of £1500, £2000 and £2500 in the three years that follow. Assume that the discount rate is 10% p.a. What is the net present Value (NPV)?

Assume now that the first payment of £5000 is due today and you will receive £1500 in one years time, £2000 in two years time and £2500 in three years time. The discount rate is still 10%. How would this change your answer?

Q7   An investment project earns £110m at the end of the first year and £121m at the end of the second year. The capital cost (today) is £200m. What is the internal rate of return (IRR) of the project?

If the cost of capital (i.e. cost of borrowing or hurdle rate for the project) is 12%, should you invest in the project? Briefly explain the intuition behind your answer.

Q8   Your own personal pension fund has a capital value of £50,000 on your retirement day and the fund is offering you the following deal. You receive a pension of £5000 at the end of every year for the next 25 years, *if you live that long*. (This is your guaranteed annuity, expressed in £s p.a.) The current interest rate on

25-year money is 8% p.a. (This would be the yield on 25-year government bonds.) Your pension must be in the form of an annuity payment and the pension fund cannot invest your £50,000 in the stock market.

a) Is your pension fund offering you a good deal, if you live for 25 years?
b) Assume that your £5,000 p.a. guaranteed pension will just cover the £50,000 you have in your pension fund today, and therefore the pension fund will just break even. Show that if your pension fund is to remain viable it expects you to die after about 21 years.
c) If the yield (to maturity) on government bonds is 8%, what would be the price of a government bond today, which pays out £5000 p.a. in each of the next 21 years (starting in one year's time)? In practice, how does your pension fund guarantee it will be able to pay you £5000 p.a. for the next 21 years?

CHAPTER 7

Cost of Capital

AIMS

- To show how the CAPM can be used to calculate the required return on equity.
- To examine the *after-tax weighted average cost of capital* (WACC) for a firm financed by a mix of debt and equity – that is, a levered firm.
- To show how the WACC changes as the firm finances its activities by using more debt and less equity.

7.1 VALUE OF THE FIRM

In this chapter we use PV techniques to value the firm as a whole – often referred to as the **fair value** or **enterprise value** of the firm. In principle, using PV techniques to value any asset (investment project, the firm itself, equities, bonds) is easy – you just work out the future cash flows that accrue to the owners of the asset and discount these at an appropriate discount rate. The more (less) risky the cash flows the higher (lower) is the discount rate used. But in practice things are much more difficult, as we shall see.

To undertake a PV calculation to find the enterprise value of a particular firm, we need to forecast the future cash flows that accrue to both debtholders and equityholders, and then choose an appropriate discount rate to use. In reality, there are many alternative sources of finance (e.g. banks, bonds, debentures, preference shares, ordinary shares), each of which has a different cost. We can think of the 'overall cost of finance' as a weighted average of all of the costs of these different sources of finance (with the weights in proportion to the different types of funds used). This is known as the **weighted average cost of capital (WACC)** and is the denominator used in the PV calculation. By using the WACC we are explicitly taking account of both the cost of equity and the cost of debt to the firm and their relative contribution to the overall cost of capital. We can also incorporate any tax implications of interest on the debt in our calculation of the WACC – more of this later. A firm that uses a mix of debt and equity finance is known as a **levered firm** and the method we are using to find the enterprise value of the firm is sometimes referred to as the 'cost of capital' approach.

Debt finance involves a cash inflow at $t = 0$ (e.g. from a bank loan or bond issue) and a series of interest payments (and repayment of principal) giving rise to periodic cash outflows. However, we ignore these cash outflows when we value the *whole* firm and we only consider *free cash flows* (*FCF*). Loosely speaking, free cash flows are *after-tax operating cash flows* (i.e. sales revenues less costs of production such as materials costs, administrative and sales costs, less tax payments) minus investment expenditures on capital equipment. These FCFs are available for distribution to both kinds of stakeholders (i.e. bondholders and equityholders) and this is what makes the firm worth something today. There is also another cash flow issue to consider. Interest payments on debt are (usually) tax deductible, but surprisingly we do not consider these 'debt tax savings' when calculating our FCFs – instead, as we shall see, the tax benefits of debt finance are taken care of by using the *after-tax* cost of debt in our calculation of the WACC. These rather subtle issues in the calculation of FCF are fully considered in the next chapter.

> In calculating the value of the firm (or an individual investment project) we ignore any cash outflows arising from debt financing, including debt interest payments to bondholders and any tax savings to the firm from using debt finance. Instead, any benefits from tax deductibility of debt interest are taken care of by using the after-tax cost of debt finance.

This approach enables us to keep cash flows from the business operations of the firm separate from any cash flows due to financing of the firm. The value of the firm (to debt- and equityholders), sometimes called the 'enterprise value', is therefore the PV of these *operating* free cash flows:

CASE STUDY 7.1   VALUE OF EQUITY

The issue of how the firm's total value is split between its stakeholders – that is, the debt- and equityholders – is left until a later chapter. Of course, it is only when we are able to undertake this split that we can find the value of the firm that 'belongs to' the equityholders and see whether the shares of the firm are under- or overvalued. The debtholders have first claim on the FCF and the equityholders have a residual claim. Hence as we shall see, one way to value the equityholders' claims is to take our calculation of the fair value of the whole firm and deduct the market value of the bonds and bank loans issued by the firm:

$$V_{equity} = V_{firm} - V_{debt}$$

$$V_{firm} = \sum_{i=0}^{n} \frac{FCF_i}{(1 + WACC)^i} \qquad [1]$$

where n years is the assumed life of the firm and WACC uses the after-tax cost of debt. The value of the firm calculated using equation [1] is often referred to as the 'fair value', since it is your best estimate of what the firm is actually worth. (Of course, the market value of the firm formed by the views of many market participants may be different from your personal estimate of 'fair value' – but the implications of that need not concern us here, at the moment we just want to calculate 'fair value'.) Note that if we can lower the WACC by changing the proportions of debt and equity finance, then this will increase the value of the firm. This is the 'capital structure' question of Modigliani-Miller, which we discuss below. Although we are mainly concerned with valuing the whole firm, the issues discussed can also be applied to valuing a specific investment project of the firm (e.g. expanding your chain of pizza parlours) – here we merely use the cash flows that accrue to a specific investment project and discount them using the WACC.

In this chapter we concentrate on how we choose an appropriate discount rate when valuing the whole firm, which has been financed by a mix of debt and equity – that is, a levered firm. To keep things simple, we consider debt finance to consist of bank loans and bonds issued by the firm, while equity finance is in the form of common stock.

Cost of equity

The cost of *new* equity finance is the return that has to be paid to (existing and new) stockholders. There are numerous models of what determines the (equilibrium) return on equity and here we use the Capital Asset Pricing Model (CAPM):

Return on stock = risk-free rate + risk premium + random component   [2a]

$$R_S = r + \beta_S(R_m - r) + \varepsilon \qquad [2b]$$

where R_S is the stock return for a particular firm, r is the risk-free rate, $R_m - r$ is the excess return on the market portfolio, such as the S&P 500 index, β_S is the firm's estimated beta and ε is a random error. One way to think about the CAPM is to consider the return on a stock being made up of three elements. First, the risk-free rate. Second, a risk premium that depends on *systematic* economic (or fundamental) factors that influence *all* stocks to a certain extent (e.g. changes in interest rates, exchange rates, state of the business cycle) and the impact of these factors on our particular firm depends on its own specific beta (i.e. the betas of different stocks, such as those for a car manufacturer or a high street retailer, are different). Finally, a firm's performance depends on random events that are specific to that firm, such as an unexpected jump in sales, competitors going bankrupt, strikes, patent disputes, computer malfunctions (e.g. in banks), breakdowns (e.g. leakage at nuclear installations), legal, environmental and other regulatory complications (e.g. outcome of drug trials in a pharmaceutical firm, employment tribunal cases, fraud that damages reputation, particularly for financial institutions). These *specific (or idiosyncratic) risks* are represented by ε and we assume that they have zero effect on average over time (although in any particular year they can be large). Because of the latter assumption and because by definition random events are not predictable (they are like the outcome of a coin toss), the *expected (or forecast)* return on a stock is:

$$ER_S = r + \beta_S(ER_m - r) = 3 + 8\beta_S \qquad [2c]$$

where ER_S is the expected (or forecast) stock return for our firm, $(ER_m - r)$ is the *expected* excess return on the market portfolio, such as the S&P 500 index (= 8%, say), β_S is the firm's estimated beta and we have assumed the risk-free rate ($r = 3\%$). There is a more rigorous way of deriving the CAPM, but we deal with this in a later chapter and it does not conflict with the intuitive exposition above.

The use of 'expected' can be taken to mean a forecast and often this is obtained by taking some kind of average of past data and assuming that the future will be much like the past. The beta for the firm can be estimated from, say, monthly data over the last 60 months, with the dependent variable being $(R_s - r)$ and the independent variable $(R_m - r)$. 'Beta' is then the slope of this regression line. Suppose $\beta_S = 1.5$, then this implies a cost of equity capital of $ER_s = 15\%$. (You can refine this calculation a little by using the security market line SML, but we ignore that here.) Because regression estimates of beta for a *specific firm* are often measured with considerable error (i.e. low R-squared in the regression), sometimes the return on a *portfolio* of firms (in the same sector as our firm under consideration) is used as the dependent variable and the industry beta that results is then used as the best estimate for the beta of our specific firm. The regression might be run over a rolling 60-month data window, which results in different estimates of beta as we move through the data – this gives us an indication of how beta varies over time, whether there is a trend up or down for example. A broker or other specialist research firm may be able to supply estimates of firm and industry betas, usually for a fee. The CAPM is known as a single-factor model as it only has one independent variable – if other variables help to explain the systematic movements over time in our firm's stock return these can also be included in the regression, and then we have a so-called multifactor model.

As cash flows accrue in the future, the risk-free rate and excess return on the market $R_m - r$ should represent a *forecast* over the life of the cash flows. For example, we might take r to be the rate on 10-year Treasury bonds, as these are virtually free of default risk and sell in highly liquid markets (so their interest rate is a true reflection of all market participants views). In practice, the choice of exactly what maturity Treasury bond we choose is usually of secondary importance (but usually rates on different maturities around the 10-year mark will be fairly similar).

Trying to put a figure on the future excess market return (often referred to as the *equity premium*) is difficult and generally much judgement is required. For example, in the US we could use the average return on a broad market index like the S&P 500. On the one hand, using more data (say, over the last 100 years) to calculate the average usually implies a more accurate measure. However, using data from a long way in the past may not accurately reflect what might happen over, say, the next 20 years, which might be the duration of the cash flows from the investment project. Usually we look at a 60-month (or 120-month) rolling average of $R_m - r$ to see how it varies over time and use this as a basis to forecast ahead, probably adding adjustments to take account of any data deficiencies or our 'hunch about the future'. For example, the average based on the S&P 500 does not include all stocks that have existed over time – many small-cap stocks are not represented in the index. Sometimes firms that used to be in an index are removed entirely from the index if they go bankrupt, so there may be survivorship bias in the actual data that gives an upward bias to the historical figures. We may also feel that recent data is 'abnormal', perhaps because we consider that it contains elements of a 'bubble' caused by unrealistic views (e.g. prices of Internet and media stocks in the late 1990s). So for example, it would have been a good idea when making a forecast of the 'equity premium' in 2000 to heed the advice of Robert Shiller in his book *Irrational Exuberance* (2000) and to 'shade down' any forecast of the equity premium based an average of recent data.

There is also an issue of whether we use an arithmetic or geometric average to measure the average market return – the geometric average is always less than the arithmetic average (unless all returns are equal in each period). If stock returns are independent over time (i.e. like a coin flip), then it can be shown that the arithmetic average provides the best forecast, but often practitioners look at both averages and often take a view that the best forecast lies somewhere between these two estimates.

There is another method to estimate the return on equity for a *particular firm* that does not employ the CAPM and that is to use the following equation:

$$R_S = Div/P + g \qquad\qquad [3]$$

which says that the return is made up of the dividend yield plus the growth rate of cash flows g. (This equation is based on the Gordon growth model/dividend discount model.) The estimate of the dividend yield will be an average of past dividend yields for this particular firm; or you might use the industry average if your firm is reasonably similar to the industry as a whole. If dividends are rather volatile (or not paid at all) then you might use the earnings yield (which includes retained profits) in place of the dividend yield. Another option is to calculate the dividend yield using the earnings yield multiplied by the payout ratio, (Div/E):

$$Div/P = (E/P) \times (Div/E) \qquad\qquad [4]$$

> ## CASE STUDY 7.2   DIFFERENT LINES OF BUSINESS
>
> The market return is supposed to represent all the systematic economic risk factors (e.g. due to changes in interest rates, exchange rates and the economic cycle) that affect the business risk of *all* firms and the firm's beta represents that firm's sensitivity to changes in these economic fundamentals. So far we have assumed that the project or the firm itself is involved in one fairly homogeneous type of business (e.g. restaurants, retail goods, car manufacturing). But how can we calculate beta for a multiproduct firm? Suppose a firm has 25% of its sales revenue from retail goods and 75% from running hotels. Then the firm's overall beta would be calculated as:
>
> $$\beta_{firm} = 0.25\beta_{retail} + 0.75\beta_{hotel}$$
>
> and we would have to obtain the two betas either based on our own time series data from comparable firms in these two sectors, or we could 'purchase' the beta estimates from a specialist firm (e.g. investment bank or broker). Here we used weights based on sales because it is sensible and easy to determine, but other possibilities include weights based on the firm's operating assets used in these two business sectors.

However, there is not a great deal of advantage to be had here. If the firm has a relatively stable payout ratio *and* earnings yield, then this implies that the dividend yield will also be fairly stable – so you may as well go straight to the data for the dividend yield. If either the earnings yield or the payout ratio is highly variable, then you are no further forward: taking an average of either ratio is likely to highly imprecise and therefore so will be your estimate of the long-run dividend–price ratio. If things move around a lot then estimates of averages will always be imprecise; of course more data helps, but you may require an awful lot of data to get an accurate estimate. Sure, some things in life are free, but mostly they are uncertain.

Estimating the constant growth rate of cash flows to use in [3] can be based on historical average growth rates of cash flows (profits) for the firm or for the industry, but estimates obtained by different methods might vary widely (e.g. an average of the last five years or the last ten years), so our forecast of R_S using the above equation is also subject to error.

In addition, it is worth mentioning that an estimate of the *equity premium* can be obtained using equation [3], where the dividend yield is for all the firms in the S&P 500 and the growth rate g used will probably be taken to be the historical long-run growth rate for the whole economy. This forecast of $R_m = Div/P + g$ can then be used in the CAPM equation [2] to give an estimate of the cost of equity finance for the firm, R_S.

As you can see, estimating the cost of equity capital is as much a science as an art, but clearly the cost of equity for the firm should exceed the risk-free rate. Use of the CAPM – possibly in conjunction with equation [3] to forecast the equity premium – at least provides a useful starting point to pin down this elusive number.

Cost of debt

The cost of *existing* debt we take to be the observed interest rate (yield to maturity) on debt R_B given the credit rating of our particular firm (e.g. using Standard and Poors, Moody's or Fitch rating services will give a higher cost of debt for a BBB relative to a AAA-rated firm). The yield will also vary with maturity and usually long-term yields (e.g. on 15–20-year bonds) are used to reflect the life of an investment project. Clearly, when valuing the firm we might consider its life to be infinite (assuming no bankruptcy), but as the yield curve is usually flat at long horizons, using the liquid 10–15-year yields is usually fine. As corporations can deduct interest payments from their debt payments, the after-tax cost of debt is:

$$R_B^* = R_B(1 - t) \tag{5}$$

where t is the marginal corporate tax rate. Any probability and costs of bankruptcy from existing debt should already be factored into the market yield (interest rate) by market participants. However, as the firm issues new debt there may be an *increased risk* of bankruptcy (with consequent loss of sales), as well as any additional costs should the firm actually go bankrupt (e.g. fire sale of assets, etc.). Hence the *expected* cost of new debt should reflect these factors. If you believe that additional debt finance will lower the credit rating of your firm (perhaps because the interest cover – that is, profits over debt interest payments – will deteriorate) then the current yield should be adjusted upwards.

Retained earnings

At this point it is worth briefly discussing one other importance source of finance that is widely used in funding physical investment projects: retained earnings. Even though these funds are held by the firm, their cost is not zero. Retained earnings are owned by the shareholders. In

---

CASE STUDY 7.3   CAPM AND BONDS

The monthly return on a bond is the percentage change in price plus any coupon payments (expressed as a percentage of the price). So bond returns can be considered just like stock returns and if the CAPM is applied to bonds:

$$ER_B = r + \beta_B(ER_m - r)$$

The beta for a bond can be obtained in the same way as for a stock using a time series regression on monthly bond return data. The beta should capture the riskiness of corporate bonds and bond betas are generally quite small (say, 0.1–0.2) relative to stock betas, as we might expect. The bond CAPM equation can then be used to calculate the cost of debt finance and in principle, as the bond beta should reflect all the systematic risks assessed by credit ratings companies, it should give a similar answer to our first method. However, the CAPM method is not used very much for bonds, since observed bond yields are thought to provide a more accurate starting point for an analysis of the cost of debt in the future.

principle, all of the retained earnings could be distributed to existing shareholders, who could then invest the funds in other comparable firms and hence earn a positive rate of return. If the firm paid out retained earnings in dividends then it would have to issue more shares to obtain funds for its investment project. Hence broadly speaking, the opportunity cost of retained earnings is equal to the cost of raising *equity finance*. The only true cost advantage of retained earnings over other sources of external finance is the saving in flotation costs of issuing new shares.

Weighted average cost of capital

Having calculated the cost of equity and the cost of debt, we can now determine the after-tax weighted average cost of capital (WACC). Assume that equity and bonds are the only sources of finance. The total annual expected cost of issuing $B of debt and $S of equity (stocks) finance is:

$$C = R_s S + R_B (1 - t) B$$

The total value of the firm's capital (i.e. debt plus equity) is:

$$V = S + B \tag{6}$$

and hence the after-tax WACC, namely the dollar amount the firm expects to pay out to the bond and stockholders per unit of capital raised, is:

$$\text{WACC} = \frac{\text{Total Cost}}{\text{Total Value}} = \left(\frac{S}{S+B}\right) R_S + \left(\frac{B}{S+B}\right) R_B (1 - t) \tag{7}$$

$$= (1 - z) R_S + z R_B (1 - t)$$

where $z = B/(B + S)$ is the proportion of debt finance in total finance and represents the amount of leverage. (Note that 'leverage' is also often used for the 'debt–equity ratio', B/S.) The term $(1 - z) = S/(S + B)$ is the proportion of equity finance. With no corporate taxes we simply set t = 0 in the above equation.

An example of the calculation of the WACC is given in Table 7.1. Where possible, the value of debt B and equity S are measured using *market values*. So $S = N_s P_S$ is simply the number of shares outstanding multiplied by the current share price and similarly for bonds, $B = N_B P_B$. If market values are difficult to obtain, then book values from the published accounts are used. The after-tax WACC should be used as the discount rate in the NPV formula to discount the free cash flows from the firm's operational activities.

There are many subtle academic issues in the appropriate use of the WACC that we are side-stepping here. One problem is that there is an element of circularity in what we are trying to do. To estimate the fair value of the whole firm (sometimes called 'enterprise value') we need to know the WACC, but to calculate the 'weights' (e.g. $B/(S + B) = B/V$) in the WACC we need to know the market value of the firm! In fact this circularity problem can be solved using

TABLE 7.1: Calculating the weighted average cost of capital

Data: Market value of debt B = $40m   Number of outstanding shares = 4m
            Share price = $15   Yield on existing debt = 10%
            Corporate tax rate t = 30%   Excess market return $R_m - r$ = 8.5%
            Risk free rate r = 5%   Firm's beta = 1.2

Question: Calculate the WACC.

Answer: <u>Cost of equity</u>
            R_s = 5% + 1.2 (8.5%) = **15.2%**
            <u>Cost of debt (after tax)</u>
            R_b^* = (1 − 0.3)10% = **7%**
            <u>Cost of Capital</u>
            Value of equity S = $60m   Value of debt B = $40m
            WACC = 0.6(15.2%) + 0.4(7%)
                 = **11.92%**

Note that this calculation of the WACC assumes that the debt–equity ratio remains constant so that we can use the firm's current cost of equity capital of 15.2%. (If the debt–equity ratio increases substantially, then according to Modigliani-Miller I, the cost of equity would increase with increasing leverage.)

an iterative process, but we will ignore this, as it is hardly ever used in practice. Another issue is why use *current* market values to determine the weights given to equity and debt in the WACC formula when these might change over the life of a particular investment project or over the life of the firm as a whole. These are legitimate questions, some of which are raised below. But they are largely overshadowed by the uncertainty in measuring the basic inputs that go into calculating the WACC, so practitioners often tend to ignore the finer points of the academic scribbling in this area and take some practical short cuts – we do the same.

The rather straightforward WACC calculation as described above is pretty much the best you can do if the following conditions hold.

USING THE WACC

WACC can be used to discount cash flows if:

i) Future cash flows have the same degree of business risk as existing cash flows; that is, future projects are 'scale enhancing' (e.g. when expanding your chain of hamburger outlets).
ii) Future projects do not lead to a (large) change in the firm's debt ratio.

The business risk of a firm is the volatility in profits caused by changes in revenues and costs due to general economic conditions (i.e. the business cycle). So to give an extreme example, the business risk of a company involved in retail food outlets is likely to remain the same if it expands its chain of restaurants, but not if it decides to set up a large biotech company. Strictly speaking, the above WACC calculation assumes that the amount of debt outstanding is rebalanced every period to maintain a constant B/V ratio for the firm as a whole. So in other words, the WACC works for the 'average' project.

As we noted above, the FCFs are not adjusted for any interest payments on debt finance because we are valuing the whole firm and want a measure of FCF that accrues to both debt and equityholders. Somewhat paradoxically, lower tax payments due to the tax deductibility of debt interest are also not included in our measure of FCF, because the tax benefits of debt finance are picked up by using the lower *after-tax* cost of debt and hence a lower WACC – more on this rather subtle point later.

When an investment project radically alters the degree of leverage, then the above WACC formula needs rather complex ad hoc adjustments that we touch on below, but in a practical rather than a theoretical way. This whole issue is known as the 'capital structure question' and is closely connected with the so-called Modigliani-Miller theorems on the value of levered firms (i.e. firms that use debt finance as well as equity finance) and unlevered firms (i.e. those that raise finance only through equity issues).

7.2 LEVERAGE AND THE WACC

First, let's examine the WACC simply as a weighted average formula rather than from a finance perspective. How do weighted averages behave when R_S is larger than R_B and we alter leverage z? Suppose $R_B = 10\%$ p.a. The required return to shareholders R_s will exceed R_B because shareholders receive earnings only *after* the bondholders have received their interest payments. (This is also true if the firm goes into liquidation.) Hence shares are more risky than bonds. To start the ball rolling, if leverage $z = 20\%$, let us assume that shareholders require $R_s = 15\%$ p.a. and the corporate tax rate $t = 0$. Hence:

$$\text{WACC} = (1 - z)\,R_S + z\,.\,R_B = 0.8(15\%) + 0.2(10\%) = 14\% \tag{8}$$

If we increase leverage to $z = 50\%$ and R_S and R_B *remain unchanged* at 15% and 10%, then

$$\text{WACC} = 0.5(15\%) + 0.5(10\%) = 12.5\% \tag{9}$$

Hence the WACC has fallen simply because we have put greater 'weight' on the lower figure R_B. Below we see that as leverage increases we expect shareholders to demand a higher return on their equity holdings so R_S will rise, which tends to increase WACC. It may be the case that as leverage z increases from $z = 0.2$ to $z = 0.5$ then R_S will rise to 18% p.a. If so, the WACC remains unchanged at 14%: WACC = 0.5(18%) + 0.5 (10%) = 14%. Clearly, if R_S increases above 18% or if bondholders also demand higher returns (because of increased risk of bankruptcy), then the WACC will increase as the proportion of debt finance increases. Hence, *as a matter of arithmetic,* as leverage increases it is possible for the WACC to increase, decrease or remain the same – what happens to the WACC depends on what finance theory says will happen to R_S and R_B. (The latter is what Modigliani and Miller worked out in their Nobel prize-winning papers.) If the WACC first falls and then rises as we increase the proportion of debt finance, then there will be an 'optimum' debt level where the WACC is at its smallest value possible and hence the value of the firm is at its highest level (if we make the reasonable assumption that an increased use of debt finance does not affect the firm's operating profit). Clearly, a corporate treasurer will try to implement this optimal debt–equity ratio, although as we shall see it is not an easy task in practice and is subject to wide margins of error.

Leverage/financial risk

Let's try to get more ideas from finance theory on how the WACC will change for a firm financed via a large debt issue (and hence relatively small amounts of equity). Consider two firms with the same business risk. By that we mean that their operating profits can take one of three values, $Y = \{80, 100, 120\}$, depending on whether the state of the economy is {bad, as expected, good}. If the firm is all equity financed (unlevered), then all profits go to the shareholders and the variability in profits around their expected value of 100 is plus or minus 20 (i.e. 20%).

Now suppose the firm is partly financed by debt and the interest payments on the debt are 30, no matter what the outcome for profits. (We assume that there are always enough profits to pay the interest, so there is no risk of bankruptcy in this example.) Since bondholders are paid before shareholders, the cash flow available to shareholders is now $(Y - 30) = \{50, 70, 90\}$. The expected payout to shareholders is 70 with variability of 20, but the latter implies a volatility of 28.6% ($= 20/70$). In a sense, the use of debt has meant that the variability in operating profits of 20% has been 'levered up' to give a volatility of 28.6% in cash flows to *equityholders* (around the expected value of 70). Although you can't truly show it in this simple example, the increased volatility arises because the equity base of the firm is reduced as debt replaces equity, so any volatility in profits is spread over less equity – magnifying changes to the *return* on equity. This additional volatility in equityholders' cash flows is solely due to the increased leverage and is known as *financial risk*. It arises in part because equityholders are paid after bondholders and when profits fall the equityholders suffer disproportionately: for example if profits fall to 30 then equityholders get nothing. Presumably equityholders will want compensation in the form of higher average returns, the more the firm resorts to debt finance. Note that when we refer to 'more debt finance', what we mean is that the investment plans of the firm are fixed and the firm decides to finance this investment by issuing more debt and using the funds raised to reduce its outstanding equity (by buying back some of its shares in the open market).

An all-equity-financed firm will have a cost of equity capital determined solely by the business risk of the firm. For the moment, assume that we know this return and call it R_S^U, the unlevered return on equity. How high will the equityholders want the average return on their equity to rise so that they will be willing to hold the firm's shares, even though the proportion of debt finance is increasing (i.e. increasing financial or leverage risk)? We still have the same business risk, but we increase 'financial risk' as the debt–equity ratio B/S increases. It turns out that as we switch to more debt finance, the return equityholders require in this levered firm R_S^L is given by the following (rather messy) equation:

$$R_S^L = R_S^U + (1 - t)(R_S^U - R_B)\frac{B_L}{S_L} \qquad [10]$$

where t = marginal corporate tax rate. Equations dealing with the relationship between levered and unlevered returns also apply to betas. So the following equation also holds:

$$\beta_S^L = \beta_S^U + (1 - t)(\beta_S^U - \beta_B)\frac{B_L}{S_L} \qquad [11]$$

The required return by equityholders is higher than that for bondholders, so $R_S^U - R_B$ is positive, hence:

> There is a positive relationship between the required return on equity in a levered firm R_S^L and the debt–equity ratio B_L / S_L.

Now let's see what happens to the required return on equity and hence the WACC if a firm is considering moving to a target debt–equity ratio in the future that is much higher than the average for the past – as would be the case for example with an LBO via a private equity takeover of a firm. What WACC should we use to discount future cash flows after the takeover?

First, we consider the weights of debt and equity in the WACC formula. We might use the long-run *target proportions* of debt and equity to calculate z, which will then be fixed in all future years. An alternative method is to estimate how the weights z change as the proportion of debt to equity changes *each year*. Then the discount factor for, say, year 2 would be $1/[(1 + WACC_1)(1 + WACC_2)]$ where $WACC_1$ and $WACC_2$ have different weights $z = B/(B + S)$ each year, as the firm slowly moves from its present debt–equity ratio towards its long-run target ratio. But in what follows we assume a fixed target debt–equity ratio, so z is fixed.

The next question is how to adjust the return on equity. In principle this is straightforward: we simply plug in the *target* debt–equity ratio B_L / S_L in equation [10] and calculate R_S^L. But you may have spotted a problem here: do we know R_S^U? Maybe we could use the CAPM, estimate β_S^U on past data and hence calculate $R_S^U = r + \beta_S^U(R_m - r)$. If we could find a firm with identical business risk to our firm *but one that is entirely equity financed*, then its observed returns would be unlevered returns and we could estimate its unlevered beta on past data. But this situation is unlikely in practice, since nearly all firms are levered. So here's a way out, which is not too difficult.

First, we assume that the bond beta is small relative to the equity beta, so we set $\beta_B = 0$ in [11] and rearrange the equation to give:

$$\beta_S^U = \frac{\beta_S^L}{(1 + (1 - t)B_L/S_L)} \qquad [12]$$

We now estimate the levered beta β_S^L using the CAPM equation and *historical* data on the firm's equity returns – which are levered returns. We now 'plug in' the *historical average* for the debt–equity ratio in [12] to derive an estimate of the *historical* unlevered beta, $\tilde{\beta}_S^U$. Now we turn equation [12] on its head and use our estimate of the *historical* $\tilde{\beta}_S^U$, together with the higher *target values* of the debt–equity ratio $(B_L/S_L)_{target}$ to calculate our new forward-looking levered beta:

$$\tilde{\beta}_{S,new}^L = \tilde{\beta}_S^U[1 + (1 - t)(B_L/B_S)_{target}] \tag{13}$$

Because our target debt–equity ratio is higher than our historical debt–equity ratio, then $\tilde{\beta}_{S,new}^L$ will be higher than the unlevered beta and hence $\tilde{R}_S^L = r + \tilde{\beta}_S^L(R_m - r)$ will be higher than its historical value.

The estimated levered cost of equity capital $\tilde{R}_S^L$ is now used in the WACC formula together with estimates of the cost of debt finance R_B based on observed bond yields.

So far we have assumed that the increase in the debt–equity ratio has not affected the cost of debt. But as debt levels rise, there are increasing risks that in some years the level of profits might not be sufficient to cover the annual payments on the bonds (or bank loans), which could trigger actions by the debtholders. Also, suppliers might be less willing to extend trade credit, while customers of the firm might be less willing to purchase goods because the firm has a higher probability of ending up in poor financial health or going into liquidation. Hence new and existing bondholders may require an increased return. It is difficult to estimate the impact of higher leverage on bond yields, but one method is to take comparable firms with leverage equal to your target leverage and see if their credit rating is lower. If they do have a lower credit rating, this will be reflected in a higher quoted bond yield. For example, if your

---

TABLE 7.2: Levered and unlevered returns

RU = 8% Return on unlevered (100%) equity
RB = 3% Return on debt (at very low levels of debt)
t = 0.3 Corporate tax rate

Debt, $B	Equity, $S	Debt Ratio B/S	Leverage Ratio B/(B + S)	Levered Return on equity	Levered Return on Debt	WACC(t > 0) with taxes	WACC (t = 0) Zero tax rate
0	1000	0	0.00	8.00	3.00	8.00	8.00
100	1000	0.1	0.09	8.35	3.10	7.79	7.87
200	1000	0.2	0.17	8.70	3.20	7.62	7.78
300	1000	0.3	0.23	9.05	3.35	7.50	7.73
400	1000	0.4	0.29	9.40	3.55	7.42	7.73
500	1000	0.5	0.33	9.75	3.80	7.39	7.77
600	1000	0.6	0.38	10.10	4.10	7.39	7.85
700	1000	0.7	0.41	10.45	4.45	7.43	7.98
800	1000	0.8	0.44	10.80	4.90	7.52	8.18
900	1000	0.9	0.47	11.15	5.40	7.66	8.43

firm is currently rated BBB but you think that when it increases its debt–equity ratio to its new target level it will be given a BB rating, then you will use the average yield on BB-rated debt in the WACC formula.

In practice, what happens to the WACC as you move more towards debt finance depends on many factors and an illustrative calculation is given in Table 7.2. The estimated unlevered return on equity is 8% and at low levels of debt this firm can raise debt finance at 3%. The levered return on equity (calculated using the above method) rises from 8% with zero debt to just over 11% with 90% debt finance. The cost of debt also rises with the debt–equity ratio, as the risk of insolvency increases at higher debt levels. The overall WACC (assuming a tax rate of 30%) first falls and then rises as the debt–equity ratio rises. The optimal debt–equity ratio is around 50–60% when the WACC is at its minimum value of 7.4%. If a debt–equity ratio at this level did not adversely affect the operating cash flows of the firm (due to suppliers and customers worrying about the ability of the firm to meet its debt payments), then this optimal debt ratio would also maximise the value of the firm.

That's about as far as we wish to go in adjusting the WACC when the firm is contemplating a major change in its debt–equity ratio in the future, either because of an LBO or simply because a new large investment project will be financed with a very different debt–equity mix. Notice that apart from some leveraged takeovers, the debt–equity ratio for the firm as a whole might not change very much when we are considering a small set of new investment projects, even though the latter may have a very different debt–equity mix. This is because the debt–equity weights in the WACC apply to the *firm as a whole* (i.e. existing and new projects) and this overall average might not change much if the scale of the new projects is relatively small, even though they have very different debt–equity ratios to existing projects.

SUMMARY

- In the cost-of-capital approach to firm valuation, the effects of leverage and financial risk are taken care of by adjusting upwards the cost of equity, any increased risk of bankruptcy is reflected in a higher cost of debt finance and, finally, the tax benefits of debt are taken care of by using the after-tax cost of debt in the WACC formula.
- The CAPM provides a method of estimating a firm's beta and the cost of equity finance.
- The market return (or equity premium) can be forecast using $R_m = Div/P + g$ where the dividend–price ratio and the growth rate of cash flows reflect those for the economy as a whole.
- The cost of debt R_B is usually taken to be the rate on long-term corporate bonds for firms with the same credit rating.
- Free cash flows do not contain any adjustments arising from the fact that the firm is partly debt financed – somewhat paradoxically, in calculating cashflows we treat the (levered) firm as if it were 100% equity financed.
- In the WACC, use of the after-tax cost of debt, $R_B(1 - t)$ captures the tax benefits of debt finance.
- In calculating the WACC we distinguish two cases.

Case A: CONSTANT DEBT–EQUITY RATIO

If the firm's debt–equity ratio has not changed much in the past and will not change much in the future then:

- Use the average *historical* debt–equity ratio as the 'weights' in the WACC formula.
- Use the firm's *historical* stock returns to estimate historical (levered) beta and calculate $R_S = r + \beta(R_m - r)$ with forecasts for r and $(R_m - r)$.
- For the cost of debt finance use the current quoted yield on bonds with the same credit rating as your firm.

Case B: CHANGING DEBT–EQUITY RATIO

If the firm's target debt–equity ratio will change dramatically in the future then:

- Use the *target debt–equity ratio* as the 'weights' in the WACC formula.
- Use the regression CAPM with the firm's *historical* stock returns (or industry stock returns) to estimate the historical *levered* beta and then derive the historical unlevered beta using:

$$\tilde{\beta}_S^U = \frac{\beta_S^L}{(1 + (1 - t)B_L/S_L)}$$

- Use $\tilde{\beta}_S^U$ together with *target values* of the debt–equity ratio $(B_L/S_L)_{target}$ to calculate the new levered beta:

$$\tilde{\beta}_{S,new}^L = \tilde{\beta}_S^U[1 + (1 - t)(B_L/B_S)_{target}]$$

- Use the CAPM relationship to calculate the levered cost of equity: $\tilde{R}_S^l = r + \tilde{\beta}_S^L(R_m - r)$
- Use R_S^l in the WACC formula together with any adjustments to R_B required by the higher target debt levels.

EXERCISES

Q1   Broadly speaking, what determines the 'fair value' or 'enterprise value' of a firm?

Q2   The cost of *equity finance* to the firm is often measured using the CAPM. What is the intuition behind this?

Q3   Under what conditions does the WACC fall continuously as the debt–equity ratio (i.e. leverage) increases? Assume that the corporate tax rate is zero. Initially assume the debt to total asset ratio (i.e. $B/(S + B)$ is $z = 20\%$, and assume that

shareholders require a return on equity of $R_s = 15\%$ p.a. and $R_B = 10\%$ p.a. Calculate the WACC. Then increase z to 50%, keep $R_B = 10\%$ and $R_s = 15\%$

Q4 Why can we consider the value of the firm to be equal to i) the PV of future cash flows to debt and equityholders and ii) the market value of equity S plus the market value of debt B? Is this not contradictory?

Q5 Is it reasonable to assume that the future earnings of a company are independent of the method of financing the company?

Q6 Two firms have identical free cash flows in the future – they rise and fall together. The firms have the same business risk. But firm A is all-equity financed while firm B is highly leveraged, since it is financed with 90% debt and 10% equity. Why would the equityholders of firm B want a higher expected/required return than the equityholders of firm A?

Q7 Why might there be a particular debt–equity ratio that will maximise the value of the firm?

Q8 Show that the equation for the WACC (denoted R_w):

$$R_w = (1 - z) R_s + z.R_b \qquad \text{where } z = B/(B + S) \qquad [1]$$

can be rearranged to give:

$$R_s = R_w + (R_w - R_b)\frac{B}{S} \qquad [2]$$

Hence demonstrate under what conditions the cost of equity capital rises with the debt–equity ratio.

Q9 In a Modigliani-Miller world, without corporate taxes the value of the firm is independent of the debt–equity ratio, but if we include corporate taxes in the model then the value of the firm is maximised with 100% debt. Intuitively, what is the cause of this dramatic change in outcomes?

Valuing Firms

INTRODUCTION

Having discussed some complexities with respect to the WACC in the previous chapter, we now consider practical problems when trying to measure and forecast free cash flows of the firm as a whole (or for a specific investment project, when valuation is often referred to as **capital budgeting**). Conceptually, free cash flows (FCF) to the firm are cash flows that are available for distribution to debt and equityholders, after deduction of all expenditures required for the firm's business operations, so:

$$FCF = (\text{Revenues} - \text{Input costs}) - \text{changes in working capital} - \text{taxes}$$
$$- \text{capital expenditures, Capex} + \text{other non-operating cash flows} \qquad [1]$$

We need to extract these figures from the published accounts – not always an easy task – and then to provide forecasts that can be used with the after-tax WACC to give the 'fair value' or '**enterprise value**' for the whole firm. We also discuss an alternative method of valuing the firm known as **adjusted present value (APV)**. First, we treat the levered firm as if it were an all-equity firm and discount cash flows using the return on equity (not the WACC). Next, we make adjustments by adding any tax advantages from depreciation and interest payments on debt, to give a value for the levered firm.

It may be the case that by altering the proportion of debt (to equity) finance the value of the firm will change because of the tax advantages of debt finance. This is the so-called capital structure question, and we discuss what might influence the capacity of firms to take on extra debt and hence determine their optimal debt–equity ratio. Finally, we discuss the *equity value* of the firm and how this may be used in deciding on merger and takeover targets.

8.1 FORECASTING CASH FLOWS

In valuing the whole firm we want to obtain forecasts of actual 'free cash flows' that will accrue to the bond and stockholders. It turns out that this is not as straightforward as it might appear at first sight. First, we have to decide what methods of forecasting cash flows to use and there will undoubtedly be difficulties in obtaining accurate forecasts. Secondly, accounting conventions used in the published accounts mean that the latter do not give actual cash flows for all items in the profit and loss account. There are also complications to do with tax payments, since depreciation and debt interest payments are both tax-deductible items.

Taxes, depreciation and working capital

In principle, what constitutes sales revenues R and input costs C – such as labour and materials, lighting, heating, apportionment of overheads, selling and administrative costs – is relatively straightforward. **Earnings before interest, tax and depreciation (EBITD)** are defined as:

$$EBITD = \text{Sales Revenues} - \text{Operating Input Costs} = R - C \qquad [2]$$

Operating input costs are often broken down in the published accounts into cost of goods sold (COGS) and selling, general and administrative costs. **Depreciation (D)**, in principle, represents the wearing out of (fixed) capital equipment, but in published accounts it is not an actual cash expenditure – it is a figure derived by accountants (using rules in the tax code) to determine the amount of tax the firm has to pay.

The simplest form of depreciation is **straight-line depreciation**. For example, if the capital cost at $t = 0$ is $KC = \$1000$, the life of the project is taken to be $n = 5$ years and scrap value is estimated as $SV = \$0$, then the *constant* (dollar) depreciation per annum is:

$$D = \frac{KC - SV}{n} = \frac{1000}{5} = \$200 \text{ p.a.} \qquad [3]$$

In the income and expenditure (or profit and loss) accounts of a firm it is customary to report earnings after deduction of depreciation (this would be reported as EBIT). This is thought to give a clearer picture of contribution of profits/earnings to the value of the firm than would deducting *actual expenditure* on fixed capital (investments), since the latter are 'lumpy'. For example, above we have total expenditure of $1000 but depreciation spreads this figure out over a five-year period, giving a smoother series for reported annual profits in any single year. We return to this issue below.

In determining free cash flow, we require *actual* expenditures on fixed investment, whether this is for new equipment or replacement equipment. Therefore as we shall see, the accountant's figures for 'depreciation' are irrelevant, since they do not involve actual cash flows and they are *only important to the extent that they reduce taxable income*. The tax authorities in most countries allow depreciation to be deducted from earnings before calculating corporate tax liabilities. We are going to calculate tax payments allowing for depreciation but ignoring any tax deductibility of interest payments on debt; that is, as if our (levered) firm were 100% equity financed. We deal with this subtle problem in more detail later, but for the moment note that tax has been calculated as if our firm were unlevered (i.e.100% equity financed).

$$\text{Tax payments (unlevered) } T_U = t(R - C - D) = t\,(\text{EBIT}) \qquad [4]$$

where t = corporate tax rate (e.g. $t = 0.35$) and EBIT is earnings before interest and tax (but net of depreciation), as usually defined in published accounts. The way we have chosen to calculate tax payments implies that after-tax cash flows can be referred to as unlevered net income:

$$\text{Unlevered net income} = R - C - T_U = (R - C)(1 - t) + tD \qquad [5]$$

$$\text{Unlevered net income} = \text{After-tax operating earnings} + \text{Depreciation tax shield}$$
$$= \text{EBITD}(1 - t) + tD$$

Hence an addition to (after-tax) operating cash flow is provided by the **depreciation tax shield**, tD. The higher is depreciation, the higher are after-tax cash flows and the higher the value of the firm to debt and equityholders. In effect, the government, by allowing tax deductibility for depreciation, provides a subsidy to the stakeholders of the firm (i.e. debt and equityholders). What the government loses in tax payments the stakeholders gain. In practice, the rate at which machines, land and buildings are assumed to depreciate for tax purposes is set by the tax authorities (i.e. there is a difference between 'economic depreciation' and depreciation as expressed in the tax code). The tax authorities usually allow **accelerated depreciation** and set a schedule showing how a particular piece of capital equipment (e.g. buildings) can be written down. For example in the US, an asset deemed to have a life of $n = 5$ years can be written down in each year according to the following percentages: $w_i = 20\%, 32\%, 19.2\%, 11.52\%, 11.52\%$ and 5.76%.(There are six values here because the IRS in the US assumes that you purchase mid-year.) The annual dollar depreciation and unlevered taxes each year would be:

$$D_i = w_i (KC), \quad T_{U,i} = t(R_i - C_i - D_i) \tag{6}$$

and

$$\text{Unlevered net income} = R_i - C_i - T_{U,i} \equiv EBITD_i - T_{U,i} \tag{7}$$

Often in practice, to calculate enterprise value we discount unlevered net income using the WACC and therefore assume that cash flows from the depreciation tax shield are as uncertain as the operating cash flows[1]. However, if we assume that the tax code is unlikely to change and the firm can carry forward losses (i.e. if taxable profits are negative in any year, it can still obtain the benefit of the tax shield in later years), taxes should be discounted at the risk-free rate r, while the operating cash flows $R - C$ are discounted using the WACC. Which discount rates to use for different cash flows is a controversial issue in corporate finance – for now assume that all cash flows are discounted using the WACC.

Working capital is rather a slippery concept for non-accountants. It provides a correction for the fact that revenues and costs in the published accounts are 'smoothed' figures and may not

---

[1] If we separate out operating cash flows $EBITD$ from the depreciation tax shield we can use a different discount rate for each. We have $D_i = w_i (KC)$, and the annual depreciation tax shield (year i) $= t (w_i KC)$, therefore:

$$\text{Unlevered net income} = R - C - T_U \equiv EBITD(1 - t) + (Deprn \; tax \; shield)$$

The PV of the depreciation tax shield over the next 5 years is:

$$PV (Deprn \; tax \; shield) = t \sum_{i=1}^{5} w_i(KC)/(1 + R)^i = t (KC)\left[\sum_{i=1}^{5} w_i/(1 + R)^i\right]$$

where R is the chosen discount rate for the depreciation tax shield which could be the riskfree rate r or the WACC. As operating cash flows $EBITD(1 - t)$ are treated separately, these can now have a different discount rate to that used for the tax shield. If $R = WACC$ then this method is the same as using equation [5] and discounting with the WACC. Note that the term in square brackets can be found in 'tax tables', giving for example a value of 0.7733 for the present value (per \$ of capital cost) for $n = 5$ and WACC $= 10\%$. Hence, the PV of the tax shield for $KC = \$10,000$ is: PV(tax shield) $= 0.35 (10,000) 0.7733 = \$2,706$.

represent actual cash flows. This is because there can be leads and lags in actually receiving or paying out cash amounts. For example, if customers delay payment for goods received then the accountants' forecast for sales revenue in a particular year will overstate the actual cash inflow. It is the *change* in working capital Δ(WC) that is important in accurately calculating future cash flows. Working capital is:

Working Capital (WC) = Inventory level + Accounts receivable − Accounts payable
Increase in WC = Increase in inventories + Increase in accounts receivable
− Increase in accounts payable

The actual cash flows accruing to the project (or whole firm) will not equal the forecast of revenues and costs prepared by the various divisions (e.g. marketing, production, engineering) and a better estimate of future operating cash flows to use in our PV calculations is:

$$\text{Operating CF (after tax)} = (R - C - T_U) - \Delta WC \qquad [8]$$

where ΔWC = *increase* in working capital. Changes in WC (from year to year, say) arise because:

1. If customers are slow to pay for goods, then **accounts receivable** (i.e. uncollected bills) will increase and so will ΔWC. Hence the actual cash inflow will be less than the *forecast* revenues. For example, accounts receivable in year 1 will increase if we assume that $100 of expected sales of $1000 (in year 1) will be sold on credit. Hence actual cash flows in year 1 will be $900 (= Sales − ΔWC = $1000 − $100). Note that if this $100 cash is subsequently received in year 2, then accounts receivable will fall by $100 in year 2 and actual cash flow in year 2 will show an increase.
2. If the firm undertaking an investment project expects to get credit from its suppliers of $100, then this is an increase in **accounts payable** (i.e. what you owe). So ΔWC will fall and cash flow will increase, because actual cash payments are less than the forecast value for input costs, C.
3. If it is thought prudent in the planning process for some output to be added to inventory to avoid a stockout (e.g. unsold cars held at the factory), then this will be entered as an **increase in inventories**. Hence, ΔWC is positive and this leads to a reduction in measured cash inflow.

In general, the change in working capital is positive in the early years of a project (as customers are allowed goods on credit and planned inventories rise) and hence reduces measured cash inflows. But in later years, as inventories are sold off and customers' debts are paid off, then ΔWC is negative, thus adding to cash flows. Over a long period of time we might expect the *cumulative* effect of changes in working capital on operating profits to be zero, as ΔWC is basically a correction of leads and lags in receipts and expenditures.

We now bring all of the above elements together to calculate the free cash flow for an investment project (or for the firm as a whole).

8.2 STYLISED ACCOUNTS FOR FREE CASH FLOW

Tables 8.1–4 give a stylised example of how to determine free cash flows from an individual investment project or the value of the firm as a whole (i.e. assuming that the cash flow figures are aggregated across all projects currently being undertaken or planned by the firm). We assume a five-year horizon for simplicity.

Sales revenues

To forecast sales revenues we can adopt a number of alternatives. The simplest is just to use past data on sales revenues to give some indication of future sales revenues. In our stylised example, we have used growth rates of 50%, 33%, 25% and 20% in years 2–5 respectively, so we assume that sales growth declines in future years (and in our stylised example, sales are zero after year 5; clearly an unrealistic assumption that is 'corrected' below when we discuss continuing value). Alternatively, to obtain forecast revenue figures for our particular firm, we might form a view about the future market share (based on past data and future competitive pressures), together with an estimate of the future growth of the *total* market for the industry sector as a whole (e.g. in sportswear if that is the line of business we are in) so,

$$g_{firm} = market\ share \times g_{industry}$$

TABLE 8.1: Capital account

		Year 0	Year 1	Year 2	Year 3	Year 4	Year 5
1.	Capital cost, KC	1000	0	0	0	0	0
2.	**Depreciation**[1] $(= KC - SV)/n$		200	200	200	200	200
3.	Accumulated depreciation ($=$ sum of depreciation)	0	200	400	600	800	1000
4.	Year-end book value	1000	800	600	400	200	0
5.	Working capital, WC	0	400	500	600	500	200
6.	**Total book value** $(= 4 + 5)$	1000	1200	1100	1000	700	200
7.	**Change in Working Capital, ΔWC**[2]		400	100	100	(100)	(300)

Notes: 1. Total capital cost is KC = $1000. Scrap value SV = 0 at $n = 5$ years.
   Hence D = (KC − SV)/5 = 200 per year (straight-line depreciation).
2. () indicates a negative number

**CASE STUDY 8.1   AUTOREGRESSIVE AND EWMA
MODELS**

An *autoregressive model* can be used to forecast (industry) earnings growth g in future years:

$$g_t = 0.6 + 0.8g_{t-1} + 0.1g_{t-2}$$

where the weights (0.8, 0.1) might be imposed (then it would be called an exponentially weighted moving average model or EWMA) or estimated from past data (autoregressive model). If last year's earnings growth is $g_1 = 4\%$ and the previous year's was $g_0 = 3\%$, then next year's forecast is:

$$g_2 = 0.6 + 0.8(4) + 0.1(3) = 4.1\%$$

and the forecast for the year after is:

$$g_3 = 0.6 + 0.8(4.1) + 0.1(4) = 4.28\%.$$

This is a recursive forecast. The forecast values for earnings growth rise slowly each year until they reach the equilibrium level, $g = 0.6 / (1 - 0.8 - 0.1) = 6\%$ p.a. In fact this is also an *error correction model*: if we start off below the equilibrium level and have been growing at 3% and 4% in earlier years, then the equation predicts that this 'deviation/error' from the equilibrium level of $g = 6\%$ will be slowly eradicated in future years.

Additional variables (e.g. output growth in the whole economy, interest rates and so on) might also be included in the above equation to improve its predictability. However, purely statistical forecasts are rarely used on their own and the corporate strategy or marketing department might also have a view of future market potential and competitive pressures in which the firm operates, which would lead to adjustments to the figures produced by a statistical forecast.

Instead of forecasting revenues directly, we might forecast the growth in sales *volume* for different sectors of the business (e.g. the percentage growth in the number of trainers, sports shirts and so on sold by a firm like Nike or the sportswear sector as a whole) and the price at which they will be sold, to get an estimate of future revenues. Of course you can always provide historical data on revenues (or its components) to a statistician, who will produce a purely statistical forecast for you based on any number of models.

Overseas sales and costs

Foreign sales revenue presents additional problems, since it has to be converted into the domestic currency but it is difficult to know what the level of the exchange rate will be in the future. However, you can always sell your foreign exchange revenues in the forward exchange market and then you know today exactly how much domestic currency you will receive in the future. For example, if you are a UK-based firm and the current quoted dollar–sterling two-year forward rate is 0.51 £/$ (1.95 $/£), then $100m sales revenues forecast for two years ahead will result in sterling receipts of £51m delivered in the forward contract and you would enter the latter in your calculation of FCFs in year 2. In a currency swap you can agree today to exchange future annual dollar amounts for a *known* amount of annual sterling receipts for many years into the future. So a currency swap is like a set of forward (foreign exchange) contracts – one for each year – which are 'bundled up' (by a financial intermediary such as Morgan Stanley) and then sold to you as a 'swap'. (Other types of derivative contracts such as futures and options can also be used, but we do not discuss these here.) However, active forward (futures and options) markets, even for the currencies of developed economies, may not be available for horizons longer than two or three years. Currency swaps are available for up to 10 years for the currencies of developed economies. Any firm has to take a view as to whether it will choose to 'lock in' the exchange rate it will receive in future years by entering into a swap contract, or whether it will choose simply to exchange any foreign currency receipts from overseas sales at whatever the (spot) exchange rate turns out to be in the future. The above problem also applies to any operating costs that are denominated in foreign currencies (e.g. oil, which is priced in US dollars on world markets).

At longer horizons, forecasts of exchange rates are notoriously difficult and often the assumption is used that the exchange rate from, say, year 3 onwards will be equal to the current quoted (spot) exchange rate. Of course, the actual exchange rate in all future years will not equal the current exchange rate, but if it is sometimes above and sometimes below the current level (with equal probabilities), then on average over many years your sales receipts (or operating costs) in the home currency may be reasonably accurate.

Input costs

You can use similar methods to forecast costs of production, sales and marketing as described above to forecast sales revenues – broadly speaking, forecasts will be partly based on extrapolations from past data (e.g. growth rates) together with assessments of new information that might take effect in the future (e.g. slower growth in energy prices). An alternative method which is frequently used, is to base your estimates of input costs on the 'cost–revenue' ratio. In the past it may be the case that the ratio of cost to revenues has been fairly constant (e.g. 60%) and you may assume this will continue in the future. If so, then given a forecast for sales revenues $R = 1000$ in year 1, say, then your forecast input costs are $C = 0.6R = 600$ and EBITD $= R - C = 0.4R = 400$. This is consistent with the figures in Table 8.2, where we have assumed that the cost–revenue ratio is constant at 60% in years 1 to 5. A similar 'ratio approach' can be used with taxes. If the ratio $T/EBITD$ has been fairly constant in the past (at, say, 25%) and you think it will remain constant in the future, then forecast tax receipts in any year will be given by $T = 0.25(EBITD)$, where $EBITD$ is your forecast of annual earnings. However, note that if your future capital expenditure plans are going to be very different from those in the past, then the 'tax shield' provided by depreciation may be very different – in which case you will have to explicitly calculate depreciation for each year as in Table 8.2 (which naturally results in a $T/EBITD$ ratio that is not constant).

TABLE 8.2: Depreciation and tax

		Year 1	Year 2	Year 3	Year 4	Year 5
1.	Sales, R	1000	1500	2000	2500	3000
2.	Labour + Materials Cost, C	600	900	1200	1500	1800
3.	EBITD[1] ($= 1 - 2$)	400	600	800	1000	1200
4.	Depreciation, D	200	200	200	200	200
5.	**EBIT (i.e. after Depreciation)** $= R - C - D (= 3 - 4)$	200	400	600	800	1000
6.	**Tax**[2] $= 0.30(R - C - D)$	60	120	180	240	300

Notes: 1. EBITD = earnings before interest, tax and depreciation. Profits (before tax) reported in the income and expenditure (or profit and loss) account would be EBIT = (EBITD − D). Corporate tax rate is assumed to be $t = 0.30$ (30%).

Other cash flows

Table 8.1 shows the capital account *as set out by the firm's accountants*. The firm is planning to invest, KC = $1000. The accountant uses straight-line depreciation over five years, with zero scrap value, giving depreciation of $200 per year (row 2). Hence the year-end book value of fixed assets (row 4) declines to zero by year 5. *The level of* working capital is shown in row 5 and the total book value of capital in row 6. The *change in* working capital from year to year is shown in row 7. Therefore the forecast levels of corporate tax $T = t(R - C - D)$ are given in row 6 of Table 8.2.

Having transferred our tax figures to Table 8.3 (row 4) and our figures for the increase in working capital (WC) to row 6, we are in a position to calculate the free cash flow (FCF) to use in our PV calculation. Earnings before interest, tax and depreciation EBITD $= R - C$ are shown in row 3. Unlevered net income is shown in row 5, from which we deduct the increase in working capital (row 6) and the *actual* cash expenditures on fixed investment. Note that in Table 8.1 the accountant assumed that total fixed investment of $1000 took place in year 0 and then she used straight-line depreciation (of $200 p.a.) to obtain the 'book value' of investment. In Table 8.3 we are interested in *actual* cash flows in each year, so it is the projected *expenditures* on fixed investment that are relevant (i.e. $600 in year 1 and $400 in year 2). To correctly calculate FCF these figures should represent 'gross' expenditure on plant and equipment; that is, the sum of expenditure on new ('net' investment') on plant and equipment plus any cash expenditures on replacing old equipment that has 'worn out' (so-called economic depreciation or, more simply, replacement investment).

The **cash flow from non-operating assets** (Table 8.3, row 9) might, for example, include receipts from the sale of a subsidiary or factory, which occurs when large companies decide to concentrate on their 'core competences' (to use the business strategy jargon). Firms often hold shares in other companies or government and corporate bonds and any sales (purchases) of these shares would be a cash inflow (outflow)– row 11. Table 8.3 also contains net interest income from any fixed-income assets the firm owns, such as bank

TABLE 8.3: Calculating free cash flow

		Year 1	Year 2	Year 3	Year 4	Year 5
1.	Sales[1], R	1000	1500	2000	2500	3000
2.	Labour + Material cost[1]	600	900	1200	1500	1800
3.	**Earnings before interest, tax and depreciation, EBITD** $(= 1 - 2)$	400	600	800	1000	1200
4.	Tax[1], T	60	120	180	240	300
5.	**Unlevered net income** $(= 3 - 4)$	**340**	**480**	**620**	**760**	**900**
6.	Increase in Working capital[2]	400	100	100	(100)	(300)[5]
7.	Capital cost, KC (Investment expenditure)[3]	600	400	0	0	0
8.	**Operating Cash flow (after tax)** $(= 5 - 6 - 7)$	**(660)**	**(20)**	**520**	**860**	**1200**
9.	Cash flow from non-operating assets[6]	50	0	0	100	0
10.	Net interest income from assets	10	15	20	15	10
11.	Decrease (Increase) in marketable securities	0	(10)	20	15	(10)
12.	**Free Cash flow[4], FCF** $(= 8 + 9 + 10 + 11)$	**(600)**	**(15)**	**560**	**990**	**1200**

Notes: 1. Figures are from Table 8.2 and include the tax benefit from depreciation (but not from debt interest payments).
2. An increase in working capital is a cash outflow. Figures are from Table 8.1 (row 7).
3. These are the actual cash expenditures in investment in each year and they sum to the total capital cost KC (in Table 8.1).
4. Cash flow available to investors (i.e. debtholders and equityholders).
5. () indicates a negative number.
6. For example sale of a subsidiary, warehouse, office block, etc.

deposits, government bonds or bonds issued by another firm (row 10). So we have calculated FCF to the firm using:

$$\text{FCF} = (\text{Revenues} - \text{Input costs}) - \text{changes in working capital} - (\text{unlevered}) \text{ taxes} - \text{investment expenditures} + \text{other non-operating cash flows} \qquad [9]$$

FCF is shown in row 12 and these are the figures that would be discounted using the after-tax WACC, to give the fair value of the firm as a whole (or the NPV of a capital investment project).

WACC and tax payments on debt interest

Note that in our calculation of FCF we do not deduct any interest payments on the debt issued by the firm – this is because we want to value the firm from the point of view of all the stakeholders, bondholders *and* stockholders, so it would be incorrect to deduct the cash flow that eventually goes to bondholders.

There is an even more subtle point to be made. The interest paid on debt $R_B B$ is tax deductible, so the taxes *actually paid* by a levered firm will be $T = t(EBITD - D - R_B B)$ where the amount $t R_B B$ is known as the tax shield on debt (interest). But in calculating FCFs we assumed that taxes paid were $T_U = t(EBITD - D)$, so our calculation of taxes looks to be too high and hence our measure of FCFs is too low. Have we made a mistake? It turns out we have not – although to fully appreciate this you need to do a course in corporate finance. In the meantime here's a short explanation.

Above when calculating the value of the (levered) firm we used cash flows that ignored all cash flows to do with debt – both the interest payments on the debt and any tax shield from the debt. Somewhat paradoxically, we calculated cash flows *as if* our levered firm were an all-equity-financed firm (i.e. an unlevered firm). But the tax shield clearly provides a cash advantage to our levered firm in the form of lower tax payments. How is this reflected in our PV calculation? Well, we use $T_U = t(EBITD - D)$ to calculate tax payments, but the value of the debt tax shield is reflected in our use of the *after-tax* cost of debt $R_B(1 - t)$, which gives us a lower value for the WACC (and a higher value for the firm) than if we had just used R_B in the WACC formula. Thus the value of the tax shield to the firm is reflected in a lower value for the denominator (i.e. the WACC) of the PV calculation, rather than a lower figure for tax payments due to tax relief on the debt interest. This is all a bit tricky, so Case Study 8.2 is a summary of how we estimate the value of a levered firm (for which debt interest payments are tax deductible).

As far as valuing the firm is concerned, we are now home and dry. But accountants often have their own little foibles and ways of doing things and it may be worth mentioning a few of these. First, accountants like to note how free cash flows are used. An illustration is given in Table 8.4. Basically, any free cash flow can be used either to pay dividends to shareholders and interest income to debtholders or to retire (i.e. buy back) outstanding shares or pay back the principal on debt (i.e. bondholders, bank loans and so on). A negative free cash flow requires some kind of external finance, such as the increase net debt (e.g. short-term bank loans) shown for year 1 in row 5 of Table 8.4.

It is also perhaps worth noting that the published income and expenditure account would be different from the entries in Table 8.4 and would probably contain the following:

CASE STUDY 8.2   VALUING A LEVERED FIRM

- Estimate cash flows as if the firm is all equity financed – so ignore *any* cash flows due to debt interest in the numerator of the PV formula.
- Calculate tax payments including any tax savings from depreciation (but not tax savings from debt interest).
- Use the *after-tax* cost of debt together with the levered cost of equity in the calculation of the WACC.

TABLE 8.4: Use of the free cash flow of the firm

		Year 1	Year 2	Year 3	Year 4	Year 5
1.	Free cash flow (Table 8.3, row 12)	−600	−15	560	990	1200
FINANCING (USE OF FREE CASH FLOWS)						
2.	Interest paid to debtholders	30	30	30	30	30
3.	Dividends paid	100	105	110	115	120
4.	Change in share capital + = repurchases () = new issues	100	100	100	100	100
5.	Change in net debt outstanding + = decrease () = increase	(830)	(250)	320	745	950
	Total financing (= 2 + 3 + 4 + 5)	−600	−15	560	990	1200

- Gross profit = Sales revenue − Cost of goods sold COGS
- Operating income = Gross profit − Selling, administrative costs
  − R&D expenditures − Depreciation
- EBIT = Operating income − other income
- Pretax income = EBIT − Interest income (expense)
- Net Income = Pre-tax income − Taxes paid

'Other income' is income from activities that are not the firm's core operations (e.g. receipts of dividends from shares in other companies), whereas 'Interest income (expense)' is actual payments of debt interest to bondholders. Given that published accounts have figures for EBIT and depreciation D, then it is easy to get figures for EBITD = EBIT + D and to calculate T_U. Note that 'taxes paid' are *actual* taxes paid and therefore include tax savings from depreciation *and* from interest payments on debt – we should therefore not use the published 'taxes paid' figures in calculating FCFs (unless we add back taxes paid on debt interest).

Note that actual capital expenditures (Table 8.3, row 7) would not appear in the income and expenditure accounts but in some version of the reported, capital account.

A couple of final points. If we are dealing with the PV of an investment project, then only the ***incremental* costs** should be included in the calculation of FCF. Hence, if the project uses no resources from head office (e.g. marketing, sales, legal expertise, R&D) then these should not be included in the costs of this project (of course, they should be included in the costs attributable to the *whole firm's* cash flow). Only incremental overhead costs (e.g. extra administrative staff) should be included.

Costs should be measured in terms of what economists call **opportunity costs**. For example, if the investment project uses a factory building that is already owned by the firm, then its cost is not zero but the income the building could earn 'in its next best alternative use'. This might be the rental income obtainable from another firm, if the building could be leased in the open market.

If the project reduces the firm's cash flow from other areas (e.g. introducing a new soft drink reduces sales of the firm's existing soft drinks range), then this lost revenue must be deducted from the sales figures for the project.

Finally, genuinely **sunk costs** must not be deducted from the cash flows of the project. Sunk costs are those that remain unchanged whether or not we go ahead with the project. For example, if we are at the point of deciding whether to start building our pizza parlour, then *past expenditures* on market research with customers is irrelevant to the decision of whether to start building *now* – bygones are bygones. Of course, such costs were relevant in deciding *a few years ago* whether to initiate the project at all, but now they are sunk costs and not relevant to the next stage of the project.

Adjusted present value (APV)

At this point it is worth mentioning an alternative way of working out the value of a levered firm known as *adjusted present value* (APV). In principle (if you make consistent assumptions) this gets you the same answer as the above method using the after-tax WACC. To use the APV method you again work out the cash flows *as if the firm were all equity financed*, so your cash flows are $EBITD - T = EBITD - t(EBITD - D) = EBITD(1 - t) + tD$. Now here's the switch: you discount these cash flows at the unlevered cost of equity R_S^U (not the WACC). Next, to obtain the value of the levered firm (to equity and debtholders) you add on the value of the tax shield from the debt, so using APV:

Value of levered firm, V_L

$= $ Value of unlevered firm, V_U + Present value of debt tax shield   [10]

$= [EBITD(1 - t) + tD]/R_S^U + PV(t.R_B.B)$

If the debt level in all future years is known with certainty, then the annual cash flows $t.R_B.B$ from the debt tax shield can be discounted at the appropriate corporate bond rate. In textbooks it is often assumed for expositional purposes that the cash flow from the tax shield is a perpetuity hence, $PV(t.R_B.B) = t.R_B.B/R_B = tB$ and the above relationship can be represented as:

$V_L = V_U + tB$ [11]

So the value of a levered firm is equal to the value of an unlevered firm (with the same business risk) plus the present value of the tax shield. This relationship implies that the value of a levered firm (which pays taxes) increases as the proportion of debt finance increases – this is one of the famous Modigliani-Miller propositions and suggests that you can maximise firm value by having 100% debt finance. However, this analysis ignores the *expected costs* of debt finance such as the increased risk of bankruptcy and costs of financial distress – so in practice, as we noted above, the optimal debt level for a firm is likely to be less than 100%. The APV method does not appear to be used much in practice (although it is much discussed in corporate finance texts) and this is why we have concentrated on the approach that uses the after-tax WACC.

8.3 OPTIMAL DEBT LEVELS

In practice the optimal level of debt for a firm depends on the value of the debt tax shield relative to the costs of financial distress. The ability of a firm to take on more debt without appreciably raising the return required by debt and equityholders is known as the firm's 'debt capacity' and will depend on such factors as the following:

1. The greater the variability in earnings, the higher the risk of liquidation or 'distress' and the lower will be the firm's ability to take on more debt at current yields (e.g. compare the earnings volatility of a high-fashion retailer with those of a large department store).
2. The ability to take on extra debt will be higher, the greater are the liquidity and marketability of the firm's assets. If a firm owns a large proportion of tangible assets (e.g. property, plant and equipment) relative to intangible assets (e.g. the web site of a dot-com company or the expertise of biotechnologists who can easy find a job with another firm), the higher will be the firm's debt capacity.
3. The debt capacity of the firm will be higher the higher the proportion of variable to fixed costs (e.g. if you can quickly reduce staffing costs, you may lower the probability and cost of default).

So firms with less volatile earnings, with highly marketable assets and flexible labour (e.g. workers on short-term contracts) might be able to have higher leverage, without the interest cost on their marginal debt increasing.

It is also worth noting that although debt levels are likely to influence the cost of debt and equity finance, the degree of leverage may also affect cash flows. So, the optimal debt level may be even more difficult to work out in practice, because debt levels influence both the numerator and the denominator of the PV formula.

For example, debt levels might influence future cash flows if they affect managerial incentives. Firms with high leverage have to meet high interest payments every year or the firm fails and managers lose their jobs. This may provide strong incentives for managers (and other workers) to increase productivity, cut costs and concentrate on their 'core competencies'. Also, highly leveraged firms may not have a high level of earnings after paying debt interest. This means that they cannot 'empire build' since there is little or no 'free cash flow'. They can only empire build by subjecting themselves to outside scrutiny by 'going to market' for additional funds and this they may be reluctant to do. Hence, high leverage might increase profits by discouraging 'empire building'.

It is also the case that highly concentrated shareholdings (e.g. family-held shares) rather than a highly diffuse shareholder base (i.e. millions of shareholders) might improve efficiency.

Therefore moving to a smaller shareholder base by buying back equity with funds obtained from additional debt finance might improve efficiency and the cash flows of the firm. The counter-argument is that 'diffuse shareholders' are not really diffuse, since effectively voting at the AGM is dominated by a few large institutional shareholders (e.g. insurance companies, pension funds and hedge funds).

Signalling and pecking order

Rather than using the concepts of debt capacity and tax shields to estimate the optimal level of debt, we can use the idea of a pecking order in the use of different sources of finance. Given the investment plans and dividend payouts of the firm (which tend to be 'sticky'), any fluctuations in earnings may require changes in the degree of external finance. In terms of hassle for managers, it is clearly easiest to finance projects from retained earnings, followed by debt issues and finally by issuing equity. This is called the 'pecking order' and arises because the justification and information managers have to provide increase as one moves from internal finance, to debt, to equity.

With a pecking order, each firm's observed debt ratio could simply reflect its past cumulative requirements for external finance. Indeed, if it is generally accepted that highly profitable firms use mostly internal finance, then a firm issuing a large amount of debt or (*a fortiori*) equity finance is giving a signal to the market that its current and future profitability is in doubt. This is likely to raise the cost of such finance. Also, if the firm does issue equity (e.g. a rights issue), investors might see this as a signal that the firm thinks its shares are overvalued and it is trying to obtain funds now, since rough times are ahead. They will therefore only supply new finance at a much lower market price (i.e. they require a higher future return on equity). The pecking order theory appears to explain *intra*-industry debt patterns among mature firms quite well, since within an established industry (e.g. chemicals) those firms with lower profits also have higher debt ratios. However, the theory does not do so well at an *inter*-industry level and for 'young' companies. Here we see some rapidly growing firms (e.g. in biotechnology) with relatively low earnings, yet with very low debt ratios and much of their external finance coming from equity (e.g. via venture capitalists and new issues).

Where does this leave us?

Well, it leaves us without a well-defined theory of the optimal debt–equity mix that actually fits the facts. This is why we regularly read in the financial press that some firms in an industry are either issuing more debt and using the funds to buy back equity, or are using retained earnings to buy back equity – both of which increase leverage. Meanwhile, other firms in the same sector might have unchanged leverage. Buy-backs such as the Virgin Group (Richard Branson) and the Really Useful Group (Andrew Lloyd Webber) increase leverage. Also, junk bonds were used extensively in the 1980s in management buy-outs and takeovers, again increasing leverage in those firms (sometimes to extremely high levels). Meanwhile, other firms (e.g. Carphone Warehouse, the JCB group that produces mechanical diggers of that name and Barbour, who produce waxed jackets) have near zero debt.

Certainly, some executives do believe that there is an optimal debt–equity ratio for their firms. However, precisely what the optimal leveraged position is (e.g. is it 50% or 60%?)

requires a careful assessment of many factors and we do not have one single 'complete' theory that can provide the answer.

8.4 CONTINUING VALUE

We now return to the problem of forecasting cash flows. Suppose we are using PV techniques and the after-tax WACC to value the whole firm – how can we deal with cash-flow forecasts after year 5? First, we could simply try to forecast cash flows in *every single* future year. Note that we will presumably be more uncertain about cash-flow forecasts for many years ahead than for just a few years ahead. The PV technique quite rightly discounts cash flows in the distant future more heavily than those in the near future. However, even though the distant cash flows are each relatively heavily discounted, they can as *a group* contribute substantially to the overall calculation of our central estimate of firm value, since there are so many of them. (Adding up a lot of small numbers can give you quite a large total.)

While we might feel able to forecast annual free cash flows *separately* for each year over the next five years, say, this becomes extremely difficult as we extend the time horizon. One commonly used approach is to split the analysis into two periods. We undertake a detailed year-by-year cash-flow analysis for, say, the first five years and then use some simplifying assumptions to estimate the value of all the cash flows after year 5. The latter is often called the **continuing value** (CV) of the firm. Hence the value of the firm is then given by:

$$
\begin{aligned}
V_{firm} &(at\ t = 0) \\
&= NPV(FCF\ in\ years\ 1\ to\ 5) \\
&\quad + CV(at\ t = 0, for\ cash\ flows\ from\ year\ 6\ onwards)
\end{aligned}
\qquad [12]
$$

We can measure continuing value in a variety of ways, but useful simplifying assumptions are:

- The WACC is constant in all future years.
- After year 5 cash flows will grow at a constant rate (e.g. $g = 0.03$ or 3% p.a.) *in all future years.*

Then the value at the end of year 5 of all cash flows from year 6 onwards that grow at the rate g forever (known as a growing perpetuity) is:

$$
V_5(at\ t = 5) = \frac{FCF_6}{WACC - g} = \frac{(1 + g)FCF_5}{WACC - g}
\qquad [13]
$$

and these cash flows at $t = 0$ (today) are worth

$$
CV\ (at\ t = 0) = \frac{V_5}{(1 + WACC)^5}
\qquad [14]
$$

where CV is the value today of all future cash flows from year 6 onwards. Note that the formula only works if $WACC > g$. A special case is if you assume that cash flows after year

5 are constant (i.e. $g = 0$), known as a perpetuity, then equation [13] simplifies to:

$$V_5(\text{at } t = 5) = \frac{FCF_5}{WACC} \qquad [15]$$

Note that CV depends on a forecast for the constant growth rate of cash flows g from year 5 onwards. How can we obtain a reliable estimate of g? The usual method concentrates on the life cycle of the firm and the strategic opportunities open to it (so those lectures on corporate strategy may be of some use here). A starting point might be to look at the growth rate of *mature* firms in the industry, since this is likely to be the outcome for this particular firm after a five-year period. This figure can be adjusted up or down depending on your view of the potential success of this firm's strategy relative to comparable firms – again, it's an art rather than a science. Another possibility is to assume that the growth rate of the firm's cash flows will eventually equal the growth rate of the whole economy – say 3–4% p.a. for a developed Western economy.

Note that the use of five years in the above example is purely arbitrary – you can choose whatever period you think is reasonable to apply cash-flow forecasts for *individual* years and then apply the CV method after that.

The practical problems with continuing value are that it tends to be very sensitive to small changes in the forecast value for g and that usually CV turns out to be a large figure, relative to that for the NPV of the first five years' cash flows – not surprisingly given that CV is the present value of *all* cash flows from year 5 onwards, which are expected to grow at the rate g for ever. It is useful to explore this problem area by calculating alternative values for CV depending on alternative assumptions about growth rates. This is a type of sensitivity analysis.

It is useful now to consider the formula for V_5 assuming a constant growth rate g_2, which applies after year 5 *but only for the next 10 years,* say (after which the firm is closed down with zero liquidation value – to keep things simple). This is known as a growing annuity (over 10 years) and the formula for the present value at $t = 5$ turns out to be a bit messy:

$$V_5(\text{at } t = 5) = \frac{FCF_6}{WACC - g_2}[1 - v^{10}] \qquad [16]$$

where $v = [(1 + g_2)/(1 + WACC)]$, $FCF_6 = (1 + g_2)FCF_5$ and again we require $WACC > g_2$. The above are 'two-period' models. But we can also divide up the time period of the firm's existence into several time periods, with different growth assumptions for each time period. This is more realistic, but the equations become more messy (not difficult, just messy). By way of illustration, suppose we assume that after year 5 the growth rate is $g_2 = 0.06$ for the next 10 years (taking us up to year 15), then $g_3 = 0.03$ for all years after that. How do we calculate the value of the firm? We just apply equation [8] for the third period, which begins in year 15 and lasts for ever, so:

$$V_{15} = \frac{(1 + g_3)CF_{15}}{WACC - g_3} \qquad [17]$$

The 'fair value' of the firm at time $t = 0$ is then

$$V_{firm}(t = 0) = \text{NPV (FCF, years 1–5)} + \frac{V_5}{(1 + WACC)^5} + \frac{V_{15}}{(1 + WACC)^{15}} \qquad [18]$$

The above is obviously a 'three-period model'. It is also easy to incorporate the assumption that the growth rate is zero in any period by using the above formulae but simply entering $g = 0$ where appropriate. In effect, we now have two elements to the CV, the value of the cash flows between years 6 and 15 and the value of the cash flows from year 15 onwards. We hope you can see that you can split up the whole time period into as many 'slices' as you like, assuming a different growth rate for each slice. It is also still worth doing a sensitivity analysis for different assumptions about growth rates (or even the WACC too) in order to get some idea of the margins of error for your calculations.

We cannot overemphasise the fact that valuing the firm (or an investment project of the firm) is a necessary but hazardous task, requiring inputs from finance, accountancy, statistics and economic forecasting and strategy.

8.5 VALUE OF EQUITY

Above, the firm in question is 'levered'; that is, financed by a mix of debt and equity. The value of the whole firm (to debt and equityholders) is calculated using *all* the (operating) cash flows accruing to the firm's activities (with no deduction of interest payments on debt). These cash flows 'belong to' the equity and debtholders. So, to calculate the fair value of just the equity V_s (and hence the 'fair' stock price), we need to deduct the value of the outstanding debt (e.g. bonds, bank loans) from our calculation of V_{firm}

LEVERED FIRM

Value of equity = Enterprise value of the firm − Value of debt

$$V_s = V_{firm} - V_{Debt} \qquad [19]$$

How we value the firm's debt we discuss in a later chapter. Once we have calculated V_s then our estimate of the fair value of the firm's stock is V_s/N_s, where N_s is the number of shares outstanding. If the market's view of the fair value of the stock coincides with your calculations, then the quoted market price P_s should equal (or at least be close to) V_s/N_s.

Free cash flows to equity

An alternative way of finding the value of the firm's *equity* is to discount only those cash flows that directly accrue to the equityholders.

$$V_{equity} = \sum_{t=1}^{\infty} \frac{FCFE_t}{(1 + R_{S,t}^L)^t} \qquad [20]$$

The cash flows are discounted at the (levered) cost of equity R_S^l (not the WACC) and broadly speaking the FCF to equity is:

> FCFE = (Net income + Depreciation) − change in working capital
> − Capex + Net borrowing [21]

and

> Net borrowing = (New debt issued − Debt repayments).

'Net income' is from published accounts and includes *tax savings* from both depreciation and debt payments – as the latter is no longer reflected in the discount rate, R_S^l. Depreciation is added back to net income since it is not an actual expenditure. The FCFE figures can then be discounted to directly give the value of the firm that 'belongs to' the equityholders, V_S. If applied on a consistent basis this gives the same value for equity as the enterprise value approach. This is because if the debt is correctly priced (see Chapter 20) the PV of net borrowing (i.e. new debt issued less debt interest paid less repayments of debt) over the life of the debt is zero. Hence, the only advantage of debt in the FCFE approach is the tax savings on interest payments – just as in the enterprise value approach, when using the after-tax cost of debt in the WACC.

However, there are several difficulties with the FCFE approach. First, using a constant cost of equity capital assumes a constant debt–equity ratio, otherwise we have to adjust R_S^l depending on our estimate of a firm's debt capacity over time and this is difficult. Also, interest payments on the debt may have different risk characteristics to the ordinary operating cash flows of the firm and therefore the choice of an appropriate discount rate in [20] is problematic. Therefore in practice, 'enterprise value less the value of the debt' is more often used to obtain the fair value of equity, rather than the above approach.

8.6 MERGERS AND ACQUISITIONS

Let us suppose you are an entrepreneur and have managed to attract funds from insurance companies, pension and hedge funds and maybe some of your own funds, with the aim of finding and purchasing 'underpriced' companies. The equity stake is provided by all the above investors, who will be issued with new shares once the target company is taken over, but they also know that you will finance part of the acquisition by taking on debt (e.g. issuing bonds and taking out bank loans). Let us assume that you intend to undertake 70/30, debt–equity financing. Again to keep things simple, assume that the target firm is currently 100% equity financed. (This assumption is not very restrictive, since if the target firm is partly debt financed you would still effectively have to payoff its existing debt with the new debt you raise.) This example is like a **private equity** firm purchasing a publicly quoted company (so the newly issued shares would not be publicly traded), or it could simply be a purchase by firm A of a target firm, where the two firms are in separate lines of business and are to be operated independently of each other.

In principle, the way to go about this should now be pretty clear. You hire a consulting company or the corporate finance arm of a large bank (or do it in-house if you are a large private equity firm) to estimate the fair value of your target firm. As you are moving from 100% equity finance to 70/30 debt–equity finance, you will have to make those complicated adjustments to the levered return on equity, the cost of debt finance and the WACC, based on your target debt–equity ratio of 70/30. You also have to estimate future cash flows, which will incorporate any cost savings you intend to make after the acquisition, any additional investment costs of developing new product lines, any redundancy costs, shortfalls in the company pension scheme and so on, together with any additional expected sales revenues.

Suppose your central estimate of fair value turns out to be $V = \$100m$ and there are currently $N = 10m$ shares outstanding, so the estimated fair value per share is $10. If the current share price is $P = \$7$ the shares are undervalued (i.e. $P < V$) and you can afford to pay a bid premium of up to $3 or 43% ($= 3/7$) of the current market price, in order to purchase a controlling interest in the target firm. As news of your takeover reaches the market, the share price of the target will rise. (It may rise a few days before the initial announcement of your bid if the information leaks out.) You might initially offer, say, $8 per share, but if this offer is not recommended by the board of the target company you might raise your offer to $8.50. If the board of the target company still does not recommend your offer to its shareholders, then you may have to enter a hostile bid, purchasing more shares on the open market and pushing the price up further. You might eventually gain control of over 50% of the shares at a price of, say, $9 (and this price must then be offered to the remaining shareholders), so your expected gain from the takeover is $100m fair value less the $90m paid to acquire the firm.

If you purchased the firm using all your own funds (i.e. 100% equity finance), then you would have made $10m on $90m capital – an 11% return. But if you use 70/30 debt–equity finance, then the debtholders will provide $63m and your own equity capital will provide $27m. If the bid goes through and your calculations are correct, your return on equity is 37% ($10m/$27m), much higher than the 11% return for a 100% equity takeover – this is leverage. It is part of the reason leveraged buyouts and private equity are currently so much in the news. (If all of the equity return is in the form of capital gains and the private equity buyers eventually sell the firm, they may also be taxed at a lower rates of capital gains tax, rather than at higher income tax rates – but that's another issue.)

Sometimes the application of PV comes up against severe measurement problems. This occurs when the project is unique or one-off, as occurs for example when valuing Internet (dot-com companies) or biotechnology and other new 'high-tech' firms, which have a limited track record (see Cuthbertson and Nitzsche, 2001b). Similar difficult valuation problems arise when applying the PV approach to value mergers, as we see next.

Instead of a takeover of a stand-alone firm, consider the application of NPV techniques to a merger of two firms. Mergers occur when two (or more) firms join together to form a single unit. Merger activity often comes in waves, so for example in the UK there were high levels of merger activity in 1986–89, in 1995–98 and 2005–07. The big deals usually take up many column inches in the financial press, for example the pharmaceutical merger between Glaxo and Wellcome, the takeover of Forte by Granada (at about $60bn) in the leisure industry and the media merger of AOL–Time Warner (over $200bn), as well as the many mergers taking place in the financial sector at the turn of the millennium. Mergers are an example of the 'market for corporate control', the idea being that the merger should 'add value'. In principle, the gains from a merger are given by:

$$\text{Gain} = \text{NPV}_{A+B} - (\text{NPV}_A + \text{NPV}_B) - \text{transaction costs}$$

The merger adds value if the NPV of the *joint firm*, A + B, has greater value than the individual firms taken as separate entities (after taking account of transaction costs due to investment bankers', underwriters' and lawyers' fees). Why might the value of the joint firm be greater than the sum of the parts and can we use NPV to measure these gains? Another key issue is who acquires the gains: society in general, the acquiring firm or the target firm? We discuss these issues below.

Cash flows (profits) of a merged firm might be higher because of additional revenues or lower costs. These might arise because of economies of scale resulting in lower marketing and distribution costs, lower costs in the provision of central services and lower labour costs. The merger might open up a new customer base (e.g. in a merger between two banks) or result in the acquisition of technical skills (e.g. the R&D knowledge base of Glaxo and Wellcome, the Internet knowledge of AOL gained by Time Warner). Genuine real resource gains (i.e. producing or selling goods and services at a lower unit cost) are what are important for society in general. However, a merger might also result in financial gains that are important to the companies concerned, such as a lower tax bill (e.g. if one firm has high investment grants or tax breaks on investment expenditure). Note that a (conglomerate) merger that produces a less *variable* earnings stream is an inefficient way of reducing shareholder risk, since it is much easier for shareholders to change the composition of their own stock portfolios.

Assume for simplicity of exposition that all firms are 100% equity financed. We often measure NPV_A and NPV_B of A and B *separately* by using the current market value of the shares of A and B prior to the *announcement* of the merger. However, calculating the NPV of the merged firm involves a wide range of very uncertain calculations, and this becomes even more difficult if much of the value of the combined firm comes from an increased 'knowledge base' (e.g. in biotechnology or Internet firms); from reputation or brand names (e.g. in advertising or media firms); or from integration of management 'cultures' or 'synergies' – two key buzzwords in the management speak used in this area. It is fairly obvious that scenario analysis will have to be used in conjunction with any NPV calculations, given the wide range of possible assumptions one could make.

Another practical problem is what discount factor to use when calculating the NPV_{A+B}. If the merger involves **horizontal integration** (i.e. when firms A and B are in the same industry), as with the pharmaceutical companies Glaxo and Wellcome, then one could reasonably assume that the merger was scale enhancing and use the WACC for the combined company (taking account of the target debt–equity ratio of the merged firm). However, for a merger involving **vertical integration** (i.e. a merger between firms in different stages of the production process), say between an oil producer and a refinery industry, the business risk and hence the cost of equity capital for the two firms are likely to be very different and the appropriate cost of capital for the merged company will depend on how these two disparate businesses are expected to grow within the merged firm. The appropriate choice of discount rate for a conglomerate merger (i.e. a merger of two very disparate firms) is even more acute.

Empirical evidence on whether particular mergers have been successful is very mixed. This is primarily because although we know what happens to the NPV of the profits of the merged firm (and other measures such as the rate of return on capital and so on), we cannot say precisely what would have happened *if it had not* merged. The only handle we can get on the latter is to look at the performance of a 'control group' of firms in that sector that did not merge (but the latter is clearly not *identical* to what would have happened to A and B had they not merged). What evidence there is suggests that *on average* the real resource gains to society from mergers are probably positive (but not very positive and subject to large margins of error). However, there are clear financial gains made by the directors of the acquiring firm (e.g. higher salaries, stock options and status) and by the shareholders of the target firm (since they receive a bid premium of, on average, a 30–50% increase in the value of their shares, immediately after a successful takeover). The directors of the acquired firm usually lose out (e.g. they are sacked but sometimes given a 'golden parachute' payout), as do the shareholders of the acquiring firm (whose share price tends to rise less than or at best at the same rate as similar non-merged firms in the sector). Often the ordinary employees of both firms suffer, since many mergers are undertaken to achieve lower costs through economies of scale (e.g. in bank mergers and retail mergers where the number of outlets or branches is reduced).

In practice, acquiring firms often do undertake some kind of scenario analysis using NPV to work out the value of the merged firm, but they are fully aware that the analysis is subject to a wide margin of error. However, the latter is better than a wild guess or hunch about the advantages of a merger. Nevertheless, it is probably true that some mergers take place to achieve specific managerial goals, rather than being undertaken solely in the interests of the shareholders (this is the so-called principal–agent problem). One of the key ideas here comes from Jensen (1986), who argues that 'free cash flow' is the immediate trigger for merger activity. If a firm has undertaken all projects with NPV > 0, yet it still has positive cash flows, this surplus should be distributed (in dividend payments) to shareholders. This maximises shareholder wealth, because the latter can now purchase shares in companies that still have not exhausted projects with NPV > 0. However, it is Jensen's view that instead, managers use this free cash flow for merger acquisitions. This is because the managers want to empire build and earn higher salaries as well as enjoying the 'thrill of the chase' in the merger process. Indeed, they may have a genuine yet misguided view that they have superior managerial qualities that can add value in the target firm. In the words of Tom Wolfe's 1980s novel *Bonfire of the Vanities*, such people believe that they are 'Masters of the Universe'; or maybe they are Gordon Gekko types (as played by Michael Douglas in *Wall Street*), who believe that 'lunch is for wimps'.

One of the most difficult attributes to value in a merger is the extra flexibility that the merged firm might have to exploit future opportunities. This is even more acute in industries that are subject to rapid technological innovation. For example, in 1997 Cable and Wireless Communications, formed from a merger of Nynex CableComms, Bell Cablemedia, Videotron and Mercury Communications, was to be floated, with most City estimates of the PV of the merged group ranging from £4.5bn to £6bn. The merged group would have access to a national network of cable customers. However, the difficulties lay in estimating the future customer base. The latter involves a careful analysis of such factors as 'penetration rates' relative to the number of homes 'passed' (i.e. the number of homes paying to take the service compared with the number that could potentially take it). Also important is the 'churn rate'; that is, the number of customers who fail to renew their subscriptions, which can be around 30% in the UK. The latter was an issue in 2000 for ONdigital, a digital TV venture owned by Carlton Communications and Granada Media that had provided free set-top boxes if the subscriber took out a 12-month subscription. It was relying on subscribers setting up high-speed Internet access via the television to reduce the churn rate.

Another interesting example is the AOL–Time Warner merger. AOL, an Internet service provider, merged with Time Warner, which produces and distributes movies, cable television and magazines. Both companies presumably see that together, they have an option to expand into the new media technologies. In the merger AOL provides additional customers plus its Internet technology and expertise, while Time Warner has currently an operable (broadband) delivery system (i.e. cable). Time Warner can also offer AOL extensive high-quality, tried-and-tested media products (e.g. the Batman movies, television series, toys and so on). Each firm could have grown organically (e.g. by AOL manufacturing its own media content and Time Warner its own Internet technology), but they believed that the merger would accomplish this at lower cost and risk; see Case Study 8.3.

CASE STUDY 8.3   TIME WARNER AND AOL: BIG SONG AND DANCE?

In 2000, Time Warner was viewed as an 'old media' company involved in cable television, movies and magazines, while America OnLine (AOL) was 'new media', working via the Internet. The sales of Time Warner at around $26bn were about five times larger than those of AOL at $5bn. So how could Time Warner hand over 55% of the merged company to AOL? Surely the NPV of Time Warner was far greater than that of AOL, even if the discount rate for AOL was much lower than that for Time Warner (which is unlikely given the high risk attached to AOL's revenues). The answer must lie in the NPV of the merged company. Both AOL and Time Warner must believe that the NPV_{A+B} is greater than each NPV taken separately.

The market capitalisation of AOL (in 2000) was around $160bn, while that of Time Warner was about $80bn. Hence the combined company was then currently worth $240bn, of which AOL's shareholders owned 55%, equal to $132bn. So it looks as if AOL's shareholdings were worth $160bn before the merger and only $132bn immediately after the merger, a loss of $28bn in value, implying that AOL was offering its shares at about a 17% discount. This is fine as long as the merged company is expected to have higher returns in the future than AOL would have had if it did not merge. What are the possible synergies in this merger that will enable higher future revenues (or lower costs) for the merged firm?

First, Time Warner can provide advertising via its cable television and print media for the output of AOL and the Internet services it provides. This is not uncommon, for example CBS paid for its investment in Sportsline with 'free' advertising. Time Warner can also offer AOL immediate access to its new cable facilities (which take digital signals) so that high-quality videos can be delivered via the Internet. Finally, Time Warner has an inventory of high-quality media products (e.g. feature films and news service CNN) that AOL can market via the Internet. Almost 75% of AOL's Internet customers stay within the company's 'walled garden' of content and AOL also has 40% of the total US Web market. This market is large and has the potential to develop into a 'world market' as more countries embrace the Internet.

Of course, Time Warner could itself have tried to exploit the Internet and indeed it did, but the strategy was a failure. Also, AOL could have tried to produce quality media content, but this is a time-consuming and expensive process and requires expertise that AOL did not have. So in the fast-moving media market the two companies believe that their marriage of technologies and expertise will generate additional revenues via a wider market for their complementary products. In short, they hope to establish a quality 'Internet media brand' that can respond flexibly to future developments. However, while NPV is a useful way of thinking about the key issues involved, it definitely does not provide a definitive solution.

Another major issue in some mergers is regulatory concern about the possible reduction of competition. The US regulatory body, the Federal Trade Commission (FTC), expressed concern that Time Warner might refuse its popular content to other cable networks unless they favoured AOL as their Internet service provider (ISP). (This is a similar issue to the Paramount Pictures case of 1948, when the Supreme Court forced the film studios to divest themselves of the movie theatres they also owned.) The FTC is pushing for open access to other ISPs. Regulatory uncertainties such as these make the NPV calculation of a merger exceptionally difficult.

As noted above, there is a branch of finance called **real options theory**, which suggests that the PV of a merger is not just the discounted cash flows from the 'best guess' of what the merged firm's future profits will be. Instead, the merger is also seen as giving the merged firm greater opportunities to take advantage of *possible* future developments (e.g. to expand quickly should a particular new technology provide rapid and efficient access to a worldwide consumer base). These possible future developments of the merged firm have a value today, even though you do not know for certain today that any particular course of action in the future will be worthwhile. According to real options theory, these strategic possibilities provide an added 'option value' that should be added to the conventional NPV to give the 'true' NPV of the proposed merger (see Cuthbertson and Nitzsche, 2001b).

SUMMARY

- In practice, calculation of free cash flows requires forecasts of sales revenues, operating costs, depreciation and taxation, changes in working capital and cash flows from other non-operating assets.

- Forecasts of sales revenues and operating costs are usually based on extrapolations of past data (e.g. growth rates) together with adjustments based on the firm's strategic plans.
- When valuing the firm, different cash-flow assumptions are often used for different time periods. Explicit annual forecasts are often used for the first five to ten years, followed by constant growth-rate assumptions for future periods. This gives rise to the calculation of 'continuing value' using two- or three-period models for cash flows.
- A change in capital structure occurs when additional debt finance is raised and used to buy back some of the equity (and there are no changes in operating cash flows).
- The impact of increased leverage on the WACC depends on how much the required return on equity and the required return on debt rise as the proportion of debt finance is increased – at the end of the day this is an empirical matter.
- When calculating the value of a levered firm, FCFs do not include any payments due to debt. Instead, the impact of the tax shield from debt finance on the value of the firm is taken care of in the denominator of the PV formula by using the *after-tax* cost of debt in the WACC.
- An alternative method of valuing the firm, known as the APV, uses the (unlevered) return on equity to discount operational cash flows and then explicitly adjusts for the value of any tax shields from depreciation and interest payments on debt.
- The value of equity can be calculated using either
  a) enterprise value (using the after-tax WACC) minus the value of the outstanding debt or
  b) directly calculating the free cash flow to equityholders (FCFE) and discounting using the levered cost of equity.

EXERCISES

Q1   What is the depreciation tax shield and how does it arise?

Q2   When calculating the fair (enterprise) value of the firm we include the tax savings from any depreciation allowances, but we do not include the tax savings from interest payments on debt, even though the latter are tax deductible. So we must therefore underestimate the 'true' net income available to the firm and hence underestimate the fair value of the firm. Is this true?

Q3   Suppose we want to calculate the fair value of the firm to *equityholders* (only). How can we do this?

Q4   What is the 'pecking order' theory of capital structure?

Q5   What is the continuing value of the firm?

Q6   Calculate the continuing value of a firm if it has free cash flows $FCF_5 = \$100m$ at the end of year 5 and these cash flows are expected to grow at $g = 3\%$ thereafter and the WACC $= 15\%$ p.a.

PART 3

ASSET RETURNS AND PORTFOLIO THEORY

CHAPTER 9

Measuring Asset Returns

AIMS

- To discuss alternative methods of calculating asset returns, including the arithmetic mean return, the geometric mean return and the continuously compounded return.
- To examine the risk and return on stocks, bonds and T-bills over the last century.
- To calculate *sample statistics*, such as the mean, variance, standard deviation, covariance and correlation coefficient.
- To explain the concepts of a *random variable* and the *probability distribution* for discrete and continuous random variables.
- To show how 'population statistics' such as the expected value and variance are related to their sample counterparts.
- To analyse the *normal distribution*.
- To explain the usefulness of the *central limit theorem*.

INTRODUCTION

Finance is the study of asset prices and these prices are stochastic or random; that is, we cannot predict with certainty what their values will be tomorrow. We can only make probabilistic statements. In this chapter we introduce the basic ideas of random variables, probability distributions and some elementary statistics used in finance.

Broadly speaking, in statistics we generally assume that a random variable like a stock return has certain features that are constant over time. These are referred to as the 'true' or *population parameters*, such as the mean return μ and the standard deviation σ of the return. In addition, we often assume that the returns occur with specific probabilities and hence come from a specific probability distribution (e.g. the normal distribution). We cannot observe the population parameters (μ,σ) since we do not have access to *all* possible data. Therefore we take a *sample* of data (e.g. monthly stock returns between January 1997 and January 2007) and use a formula to estimate some sample statistics. For example, the arithmetic mean $\bar{R} = \sum_{i=1}^{T} R_i / T$ might be used as an *estimator* of the true population mean, μ. We then see if these *sample statistics* provide a reasonable estimate of the underlying true population parameters and if not, how close our sample statistics are likely to be to the true population parameters. In this way we can assess our degree of ignorance or, equivalently, our degree of knowledge about important financial concepts, such as the mean return on a stock and its risk, as measured for example by our *estimator* of the (true) population standard deviation. The link between the unobservable true population parameters and their sample estimates requires statistical proofs and we merely present these results, rather than formally deriving them. However, we begin by looking at the different ways in which we can measure returns and interest rates.

9.1 MEASURING ASSET RETURNS

As we shall see, there are many alternative ways of measuring the 'return' on different assets. Consider the return on a one-year Treasury Bill *if you hold it to maturity*. Suppose you purchase the T-bill today for $95 and it has a face (or par or maturity) value of $100. A T-bill is a liability of the government and is therefore free of default (credit) risk. If the T-bill has exactly one year to maturity, there is no market (or 'price') risk for the investor, since she knows that she will receive $100 in a years time. The **nominal risk-free return** on this investment is:

$$r = [(\$100 - \$95)/\$95]100 = 5.26\% \, \text{p.a.} \tag{1}$$

This return is the risk-free annual rate of interest (or yield) on your investment. It is also the internal rate of return on your investment, since r is the solution to $95 = 100/(1 + r)$.

We can decompose the nominal return r into a real return rr and the expected rate of inflation π. Suppose that all (risk-free) rates of interest are 5.26% p.a. If you initially have $100, a nominal return of $r = 5.26\%$ p.a. implies that you will receive $105.26 in one years time. But suppose price inflation is 2% p.a. over the coming year; how much extra consumer goods could you buy at the end of the year, compared with the beginning of the year? You could approximately purchase 3.26% more consumer goods at the end of the year when you cash in your investment – this implies that the **real rate of interest** is 3.26% p.a.

Real return (rate of interest) $\approx$ nominal return (rate of interest) $-$ inflation rate

$$rr \approx r - \pi \qquad\qquad [2]$$

To see why this is the case, suppose that your consumer goods consist of a Saks hamper that initially cost \$50 (and contains an assortment of goodies)[1]. At the beginning of the year your initial wealth of \$100 could purchase two Saks hampers. If you do not purchase the hamper (i.e. defer your consumption) and invest the \$100, then at the end of the year you have \$105.26. However, the Saks hamper now costs 2% more at \$51, so you can only purchase 2.064 ($=$ 105.26/51) Saks hampers. The percentage increase in the number of Saks hampers you can purchase after investing your money for a year is 3.2% $= [(2.064 - 2)/2] \times 100$. The percentage increase in the number of Saks hampers you can purchase at the end of the year is known as the real return on your investment, which here is 3.2% p.a. (which is close to the 3.26% approximate value calculated above). The real rate of interest is a 'real reward' for postponing consumption of the Saks hamper for one year. The exact figure for the real return is given by:

$$\text{Real return} = \frac{(1 + \text{nominal return})}{(1 + \text{inflation rate})} - 1$$

$$rr = \frac{(1 + r)}{(1 + \pi)} - 1 = \frac{(1.0526)}{(1.02)} - 1 = 0.032 \ (3.2\%) \qquad\qquad [3]$$

This is how we calculate the ex-post (or *after the event*) real return from last year's observed nominal return and last year's inflation rate. But we can also use this relationship to think about what determines the risk-free interest rate over the coming year, since:

Nominal (risk-free) return $\approx$ expected real return $+$ expected inflation

$$r \approx rr + \pi \qquad\qquad [4]$$

This is sometimes referred to as the *Fisher equation*. The real return is usually assumed to be equal to the real growth rate of the economy, so for Western economies it would be a figure of around 3.2% p.a. and would be expected to be fairly constant year to year. So, the main influence on interest rates *over the coming year* is what the market thinks next year's inflation rate will be. If the market thinks that next year's inflation rate will be 3%, then today's one-year nominal interest rate will be $r_1 = 6.2\%$. Similarly, today's five-year nominal interest rate will be largely determined by the market's view of the expected inflation rate *over the next five years*. If inflation over the next five years is expected to average 4% p.a., then we would observe the current five-year interest rate to be $r_5 = 7.2\%$ p.a. As we see in later chapters, if interest rates increase as the time horizon of the investment increases, this is described as an upward-sloping yield curve – and implies that the market expects inflation to rise over the next five years. But at these nominal interest rates, investors over both one year and five years expect to receive a real return (in terms of extra Saks hampers) of 3.2% p.a.

---

[1] A 'hamper' contains a variety of food items which are put inside a wicker basket and the hamper is then used for picnics. A hamper from Saks may contain champagne, caviar, pate etc. which is our 'representative' basket of goods.

Holding period return

Often bonds and stocks are held for a specific period of time and then sold. How do we measure the return over a specific time horizon? Suppose you purchase a stock today for $P_0 = \$100$ and sell it one period later for $P_1 = \$102$, and you also receive a dividend payment $D_1 = \$1$ at the end of the period (just before selling the stock). The holding period return HPR is:

$$\text{HPR} = \frac{(\text{Sale Price} + \text{Dividends Received}) - \text{Purchase Price}}{\text{Purchase Price}} \qquad [5]$$

$$= \frac{(P_1 + D_1) - P_0}{P_0} = \frac{(P_1 - P_0)}{P_0} + \frac{D_1}{P_0} = 0.02 + 0.01 = 0.03\ (3\%)$$

So the HPR can also be expressed as:

$$\text{HPR} = \text{Capital gain} + \text{Dividend yield}$$

The capital gain is 2% and the dividend yield is 1%. If dividends are not paid exactly at the end of the period, the same formula is usually used and therefore the HPR ignores any reinvestment income between the dividend receipt and the end of the holding period.

Returns over several periods

To simplify the following calculations, assume that all dividend payments are zero. Suppose that your stock has prices $P_0 = \$100$, $P_1 = \$110$ and $P_2 = \$105$ in successive years. The 'standard' annual returns (HPRs) would be calculated as $R_1 = [(\$110 - \$100)/\$100] = 0.1\ (10\%)$ and $R_2 = [(\$105 - \$110)/\$110] = -0.045454\ (-4.5454\%)$. You might want to say that your return over two years is $R(0, 2) = 5.4546\% = 10\% - 4.5454\%$ and the average annual return is $\bar{R} = 2.7273\%$ p.a. – this is known as the **arithmetic mean return**. But it would be incorrect to calculate your final wealth as $\$100(1 + \bar{R})^2 = \$105.52$, since is it obvious that you only end up with \$105 at the end of the second year. The arithmetic average gives a misleading measure of the cumulative return over two years. The 'average compound return' over the two years is given by $100(1 + g)^2 = 105$, which gives $g = \sqrt{105/100} - 1 = 0.02469\ (2.47\%\text{ p.a.})$ and is known as the *geometric mean return*. Note that to calculate the geometric return we only require the initial and final price (and not the intermediate price P_1). However, we can relate the geometric return to the returns in each time period. The correct way to use our 'standard' returns to obtain final wealth after two periods is:

$$W_2 = \$100(1 + R_1)(1 + R_2) = \$100(1.10)(0.9545) = \$105 \qquad [6]$$

If we now define the **geometric average return** as:

$$(1 + g)^2 = (1 + R_1)(1 + R_2)$$

$$g = \sqrt{(1.1)(0.9545)} - 1 = 0.02469\ (2.47\%\text{ p.a.}) \qquad [7]$$

then final wealth can be correctly determined as:

$$W_2 = \$100(1 + g)^2 = \$100(1.02469)^2 = \$105 \tag{8}$$

So once you know the geometric average return over a particular horizon, you can use the above equation to calculate final wealth. The geometric average return is also referred to as the *time-weighted average return*, since equation [7] gives equal weight to each of the individual returns when calculating g.

Note that as a summary of the 'average return' we could quote the arithmetic average $\overline{R} = 2.7273\%$ p.a. or the geometric average $g = 2.47\%$ p.a. But if we are interested in an average figure that, when compounded, gives the correct (historical) value of terminal wealth, then it is the geometric average we would use. The geometric average is always less than the arithmetic average (unless we have the unlikely case where returns are constant in each period, and then the arithmetic and geometric averages are the same).

It can also sometimes be useful to define 'returns' in terms of the **continuously compounded return**. This is the (natural) logarithm of the value of your assets at the end of the period divided by the initial investment. For the above stock prices, the continuously compounded returns would be:

$$R_{cc,1} = \ln(110/100) = 0.09531 \, (9.53\%)$$
$$R_{cc,2} = \ln(105/110) = -0.04652 \, (4.652\%)$$

For small changes, the continuously compounded return is quite close to the standard return. For example, if the stock price moves from 100 to 100.2, the standard return is 0.002 (0.2%) and $\ln(100.2/100) = 0.001998$ (0.1998%), which is very close to 0.2%. However, for large changes in price, the standard measure of the return (i.e. HPR) and the continuously compounded return do differ.

What are the advantages of using continuously compounded returns? First, it is easy to calculate the final value of your wealth when you invest over several periods, since you can simply 'add' the individual returns:

Total return over two periods:	$R_{cc}(0, 2) = R_{cc,1} + R_{cc,2} = 0.04879 \, (4.879\%)$
Final wealth	$W_2 = \$100 \, e^{R_{cc,1}+R_{cc,2}} = \$105$

The *average* continuously compounded return is $\mu_{cc} = \frac{1}{2}(R_{cc,1} + R_{cc,2}) = 0.02439 \, (2.439\%)$, so final wealth can also be calculated as:

$$W_2 = \$100 \, e^{\mu_{cc}(2)} = \$105 \tag{9}$$

So once you know the *average* continuously compounded rate μ_{cc} and the time horizon $T = 2$ years, you can easily calculate final wealth.

If the *continuously compounded* rate of return on an asset (e.g. stock return or interest rate) is assumed to be constant – which is often an assumption used in derivatives pricing – then we can easily move between terminal values and present values. Suppose you lend $100 today and receive $105 in one years time, then the interest rate (or 'standard' method of calculating the return) is $r = 5\%$ p.a. The continuously compounded interest rate would be $r_{cc} = \ln(105/100) = 0.04879\,(4.879\%\,\text{p.a.})$. If you invest $100 today at a constant interest rate $r_{cc} = 4.879\%$ p.a., then in 10 years it will be worth:

$$V_{10} = \$100e^{r_{cc}T} = 100e^{0.04879(10)} = \$162.89 \tag{10}$$

Similarly, it is easy to find the present value. Suppose you are offered $162.89 to be paid in 10 years time and today the constant value for the continuously compounded interest rate is $r_{cc} = 4.879\%$ p.a. What is the $162.89 worth today? The present value is:

$$P_0 = \$162.89e^{-0.04879(10)} = \$100 \tag{11}$$

So, if you promise to give the bank $162.89 in ten years time (with certainty), the bank will give you $100 today. This is equivalent to pricing a bond. For a bond that pays $162.89 in 10 years time, it is worth paying $100 today. You must always get the same answer for the price of the bond whether you use $r = 0.05$ in the formula $P_0 = \$162.89/(1 + r)^{10}$ or $r_{cc} = 0.04879$ in the formula $P_0 = \$162.89e^{-r_{cc}(10)}$, so there must be a relationship between the annual rate of interest r and the equivalent continuously compounded rate. This is:

$$\ln(1 + r) = r_{cc} \tag{12}$$

You can check this, since $\ln(1.05) = 0.04879$. So the above formula can be used to switch from continuously compounded rates r_{cc} to 'standard' rates r or vice versa. We use continuously compounded rates when this is the most useful way of proceeding[2].

Conceptually, what does earning a continuously compounded rate mean? Well, it is as if you are being paid interest-on-interest every second – although the approximation is a good one if you think of 'continuously compounded' as being paid interest daily. To see this, suppose that the annual interest rate is $r = 10\%$ p.a. but that interest is paid quarterly (i.e. $q = 4$ times per year), then the terminal value at TV at the end of the year of a $100 investment is:

$$TV = \$100(1 + 0.1/4)^4 = \$110.38 \tag{13}$$

Suppose we imagine the frequency of compounding increases so that q increases from 4 to 5, 6, . . . to, say, 365 times *per year.* The terminal value at the end of the year, for different values of q, is:

$$TV = \$100(1 + r/q)^q \tag{14}$$

---

[2] It is also the case that $\ln(1 + g) = \mu_{cc}$, since above we used $\ln(1 + 0.02469) = 0.02439$, and the latter is the value we obtained for μ_{cc}. With continuously compounded rates the relationship between variables can often be expressed more simply (i.e. in linear form). For example, from equation [3] we see that $\ln(1 + rr) = \ln(1 + r) - \ln(1 + \pi)$, so it follows that $rr_{cc} = r_{cc} - \pi_{cc}$ and therefore the relationship is linear, when variables are expressed in terms of continuously compounded rates.

TABLE 9.1: Compounding frequency

Compounding frequency	Value of $100 at end of year ($r = 10\%$ p.a.)
Annually ($q = 1$)	110
Quarterly ($q = 4$)	110.38
Weekly ($q = 52$)	110.51
Daily ($q = 365$)	110.5155
Continuously compounded	110.5171
TV $= 100\,e^{0.10(1)}$ (where $n = 1$)	

For practical purposes daily compounding (i.e. $q = 365$) gives a result very close to continuous compounding (see the last two entries in Table 9.1).

Further details on the relationship between different ways of measuring returns (and interest rates) can be found on the web site.

Root-T rule

Before we get into discussions of statistical issues, it is worth noting that the so-called root-T rule can be used to 'scale up' or 'scale down' figures for volatility. To use the root-T rule, stock returns must be random or, more precisely, be identically and independently distributed (*iid*). Broadly speaking, 'identically' means that stock returns must have been generated randomly from a probability distribution that has a constant (population) mean μ and variance σ^2. 'Independent' means that picking any one return has no influence on the size (or sign) of any other returns. If returns are *iid* then the return and variance scale with the time horizon T and the standard deviation scales with $\sqrt{T}$:

$$\mu_T = T\mu \tag{15}$$

$$\sigma_T^2 = T\sigma^2 \quad \text{and} \quad \sigma_T = \sqrt{T}\sigma \tag{16}$$

If you are told that monthly returns on a stock (which are *iid*) have a mean return $\mu = 1\%$ p.m. and standard deviation $\sigma = 2\%$ p.m., then you can immediately infer that the *annual* mean return is 12% p.a. and the annual standard deviation is $\sigma_T = \sqrt{12}(2\%) = 6.93\%$ p.a[3].

There is one further implication of the root-T rule to bear in mind and that is when scaling the Sharpe ratio. Suppose that $\mu = 1\%$ p.m. (12% p.a.), the standard deviation of stock

---

[3] Note that this 'root-T rule' is conceptually different from the formula for the 'sample estimate of the mean return $\sigma_{\bar{X}} = \sigma/\sqrt{n}$,' which we discuss below.

returns is $\sigma = 2\%$ p.m. (6.93% p.a.) and the risk-free rate equals 0.4% p.m. (4.8% p.a.). The Sharpe ratio using *monthly* returns is $SR_{mth} = (1 - 0.4)/2 = 0.3$ and the Sharpe ratio using *annual* figures is $SR_a = (12 - 4.8)/6.93 = 1.039$, so the annual figure seems to imply a much better performance than does the monthly figure. Clearly, this cannot be the case – scaling should not alter performance statistics. So you must not compare the Sharpe ratios of two investment funds where the Sharpe ratio is measured using monthly data for one fund and annual data for the other fund. You must put them on the same basis. For example, if you are told that the *monthly* Sharpe ratio of fund A is 0.3, you must first scale it up to an annual figure using $SR_a = \sqrt{12}\, SR_{mth} = 1.039$ before comparing it with the annual Sharpe ratio of another fund, B. Again, this is a consequence of the root-T rule.

9.2 A CENTURY OF RETURNS

Figure 9.1 shows the US monthly *real* S&P500 index from January 1915 to April 2004. It shows the changing purchasing power (over goods) of holding a diversified portfolio of stocks that mimics the S&P 500 index. The 1930s crash and the recent crash of 2000–03 are clearly visible, as well as the major long-run rise in the index in the 1990s.

The monthly real return on the S&P500 (Figure 9.2) represents the monthly percentage changes in Sak's hampers you could consume if you had held some of your wealth in the stocks that form the S&P index. The monthly return on the index (which excludes dividend payments on

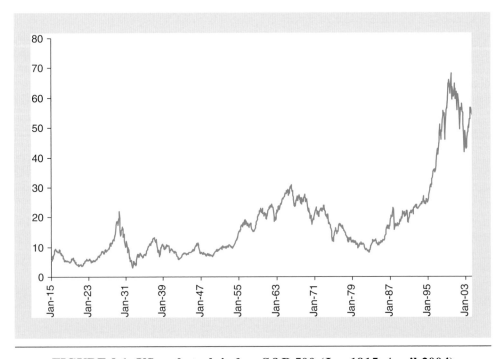

FIGURE 9.1: US real stock index, S&P 500 (Jan 1915–April 2004)

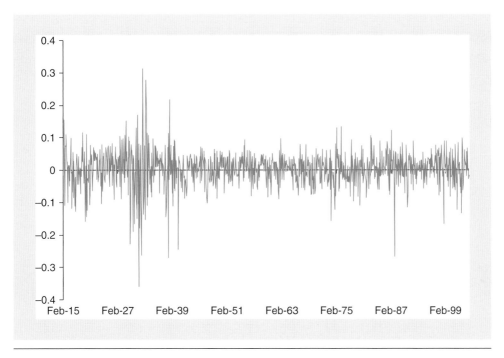

FIGURE 9.2: US real return S&P 500 (Monthly, Feb 1915–April 2004)

the stocks) appears to have a reasonably *constant* long-run mean return, frequently crosses its mean value, and hence it is said to be *mean reverting*. But the variability (variance) in the monthly return is clearly visible. The relatively large proportion of 'outliers' in Figure 9.2 (i.e. very large or very small returns) probably implies that the (unconditional) returns distribution has 'fatter tails' than the normal distribution. There also appear to be more large negative returns than there are large positive returns (i.e. negative skewness), which also indicates that returns are probably not normally distributed. This is confirmed in the histogram of returns where the fat tails and the negative skew are clearly visible (Figure 9.3).

Returning to Figure 9.2, it is evident that the *volatility* in the monthly returns goes through periods of calm (e.g. the 1950s and 1960s) and turbulence (e.g. 1930s, 1970s and at the end of the 20th century). Once returns become highly volatile they tend to stay volatile for some time; similarly, when the absolute value of returns (i.e. either positive or negative, disregarding the sign) is relatively small, it tends to stay small for some time. Hence volatility is persistent over time, which is called *conditionally* autoregressive. As volatility in econometrics is known as heteroscedasticity, the behaviour of volatility in Figures 9.1 and 9.2 is said to follow an autoregressive conditional heteroscedasticity (ARCH) process.

Now let us take a look at *average annual* returns and volatility for stocks, T-bonds and T-bills using a long data series for the period 1900–2000 (Table 9.2). The arithmetic mean returns $\bar{R}$ (in real terms) for stocks in the UK, US and for a world index (including the US) are between 7.2% and 8.7% p.a. (Table 9.2A) – the geometric means are about 2% below the arithmetic means. The return per unit of risk (Sharpe ratio) for US stocks 0.43 = 8.7/20.2. Note that the

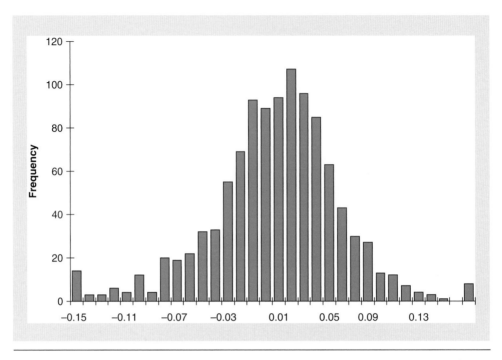

FIGURE 9.3: US real return S&P 500 (Monthly, Feb 1915–April 2004)

standard deviation of stock returns is not quite the measure of risk that we want, since we expect stock returns to vary with the risk-free rate and so it is really the standard deviation of *excess* returns that is important. But to the extent that stock returns are much more volatile than risk-free rates, we do not lose much by looking at the volatility of returns. The standard deviation of these returns is around 20% p.a., indicating the high risk attached to holding stocks *in any particular year*[4].

The average (real) return on government long-term bonds (Table 9.2B) is around 2% p.a., with lower volatility than stocks of around 10–14% p.a., which gives a return per unit of risk (Sharpe ratio) for the US of 0.21, much lower than for stocks.

T-bills (Table 9.2C) have a lower average (real) return than bonds of around 1% p.a., with an even lower volatility than bonds of $\sigma \approx 5$ *to* 6% p.a. The *relative* returns on equities, bonds and bills and their volatilities in the 14 other countries studied by Dimson *et al.* (2001) follow the above patterns noted for the US and UK.

The historical **equity premium** is the *excess* return of stocks over bonds or bills (Table 9.3) and is the average *additional* return (over bills or bonds) that investors in stocks require. For the US, the (arithmetic) average equity premium over bills (7.7%) is higher than over bonds (7%). We

---

[4] It can be shown that if returns are normally distributed with mean μ and standard deviation $\sigma = 0.20$, then $\bar{R} - g = (1/2)\sigma^2$ (all variables measured as decimals). For the UK, $\bar{R} - g = 1.8$ and $(1/2)\sigma^2 = 2\%$, which is quite close, indicating that annual continuously compounded returns are approximately normal – and it is only the extreme tails of the actual distribution of returns where we observe some deviation from normality.

TABLE 9.2A: Real returns, 1900–2000, % p.a.[5]

	Inflation		Real return					
	Arith.	Geom.	Arithmetic mean	Std. dev.	Std. error	Geometric mean	Minimum return	Maximum return
UK	4.3	4.1	7.6	20.0	2.0	5.8	−57 (in 1974)	+97 (in 1975)
US	3.3	3.2	8.7	20.2	2.0	6.7	−38 (in 1931)	+57 (in 1933)
World (incl. US)	n.a.	n.a.	7.2	17.0	1.7	6.8	n.a.	n.a.

TABLE 9.2B: Real bond returns (% p.a.)

	Inflation		Real return			
	Arith.	Geom.	Arithmetic mean	Standard deviation	Standard error	Geometric mean
UK	4.3	4.1	2.3	14.5	1.4	n.a.
US	3.3	3.2	2.1	10.0	1.0	1.6
World (incl. US)	n.a.	n.a.	1.7	10.3	1.0	1.2

TABLE 9.2C: Real returns on bills (% p.a.)

	Inflation		Real return		
	Arith.	Geom.	Arithmetic mean	Standard deviation	Standard error
UK	4.3	4.1	1.2	6.6	0.7
US	n.a.	n.a.	1.0	4.7	0.5

[5] Annual averages taken over 1900–2000. 'World' comprises 16 developed countries including USA, Canada, South Africa, Australia, Japan and European countries. The real return where $= (R - \pi)/(1 + \pi)$ where R = nominal return and π = inflation rate and therefore the average real return does not equal the average nominal return minus the average inflation rate (the latter is an approximation, valid only for low inflation rates). The standard error has been calculated as $\sigma/\sqrt{T}$. Figures are extracted from Dimson, *et al.* (2001).

TABLE 9.3: Equity premium (% p.a.), 1900–2000

	Over bills			Over bonds	
	Arith.	**Geom.**	**Standard error**	**Arith.**	**Geom.**
UK	6.5	4.8	2.0	5.6	4.4
US	7.7	5.8	2.0	7.0	5.0
World (incl. US)	6.2	4.9	1.6	5.6	4.6

have used 101 observations to estimate the sample mean, so the error in measuring the equity premium is given by its 'standard error' $\sigma_{\bar{R}} = \sigma/\sqrt{101} = 2\%$ p.a. (see below). A 95% confidence interval for the (arithmetic) *mean* US equity premium is approximately $(\bar{R} - \bar{r}) \pm 2\sigma_{\bar{R}} = 7.7\% \pm 4\%$ (see below), which covers quite a wide range, so we cannot be very certain about the true (population) value of the equity premium. This is because even with a large amount of data, the mean equity premium is measured with substantial error because of the high volatility of the underlying stock returns themselves (of around $\sigma = 20\%$ p.a.).

The average equity risk premiums calculated above (see Dimson *et al.*, 2001) are about $1\frac{1}{2}\%$ higher than in some earlier studies (Barclays Capital, 2005; Ibbotson Associates, 2001; and Jorion and Goetzmann, 1999). This is due to different time periods and country coverage and different computational methods (e.g. whether dividends as well as price changes are included in measured returns for all countries).

Sharpe ratio

Clearly, if your private or state pension contributions are to be invested in risky assets such as stocks, you need to carefully assess the return you might obtain and the risk you are taking on. High average stock returns in the US cannot be merely due to the high productivity of the US economy or impatience (time preference) on the part of consumers, otherwise real returns on bonds would also be high. The reward to saving in government *index-linked* bonds is not high (at around 3% p.a. in real terms), so what high stock returns imply is a high reward for bearing *stock market risk*. As we have seen above, this risk is substantial, and the *mean* US equity premium of 7.7% (over bills) is the reward for holding this stock market risk.

Using the CRSP database, Figure 9.4 demonstrates the *first law of finance*, namely that a high average return implies a high level of risk (i.e. standard deviation)[6]. The ex-post Sharpe ratio

---

[6] We must be a little careful here. With some types of investment such as pension contributions you might only be concerned with the uncertainty about the *cash flows* from your investments – hence the low average return on government bonds might be because they provide a vehicle which delivers *certain* cash flows in the future. The standard deviation of annual returns on the bond may therefore not be a useful measure of risk, for long term investors who are concerned with cash flows rather than the HPR.

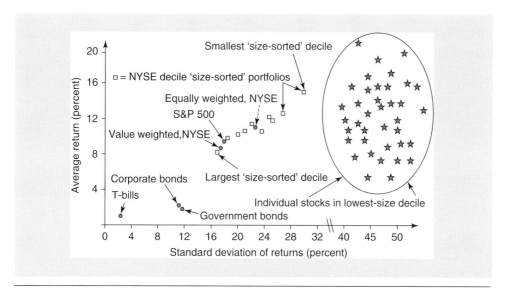

FIGURE 9.4: Mean and standard deviation: annual averages, US real returns (post-1947)

$= (\bar{R} - \bar{r})/\sigma$ measures the (excess) return per unit of risk[7]. Figure 9.4 shows that the Sharpe ratio in the post-Second World War period for US government and corporate *bonds* is very low, at around 0.1. But the Sharpe ratio for the stocks that trade on the NYSE is around 0.5, with that for portfolios containing small-capitalisation stocks about the same. Clearly, it is relatively easy to obtain high *average returns* – you simply take on more risk by moving from, say, a portfolio of T-bills or bonds to a stock portfolio. You also obtain higher average returns if you move from a well-diversified portfolio such as the S&P 500 to a less-diversified portfolio such as the lowest size-decile portfolio of stocks – but this may not result in a higher reward-to-variability (Sharpe) ratio.

There appears to be a relationship between average returns and risk (standard deviation) for very large asset classes, such as T-bills and the S&P 500; or a 'small stock' portfolio (consisting of 10% of stocks that have the lowest market capitalisation) versus a 'large stock' portfolio. Does this average return–standard deviation relationship apply to individual stocks? If we plot average returns on *individual* small stocks (which are all taken from the lowest size decile), we see that there is no relationship between average returns on individual small stocks and the standard deviation of their returns; see Figure 9.4[8]. (The relationship between the average returns on individual 'large market-cap stocks' and their standard deviations would give a similar 'scatter' picture to that in Figure 9.4, but all the points would lie to the left, as *individual*

---

[7] Note that the riskiness of stock returns is given by the standard deviation of returns $\sigma = 20\%$, which must not be confused with the *error* in measuring the *average return*, which is $\sigma_{\bar{R}} = \sigma/\sqrt{n}$ where n is the number of observations used in measuring $\bar{R}$.

[8] We update the 'identity' of Nth 'smallest stock' each quarter and then calculate the average return over a long time horizon. For example, firm-A might be the smallest market cap stock in quarter-1, but stock-B might be the 'smallest size' stock in quarter-2. The identity of the 'smallest stock' will change over time, as market capitalisation values change over time. So the average 'return' for the 'smallest stock' is in reality an average of the returns for different stocks, which happen to be the 'smallest size' in each quarter.

stocks of large companies tend to have lower returns and standard deviations than for individual small stocks.) Hence, at present we do not know what determines the average return on individual stocks – as we shall see, it is not the variance of the individual stock's return, but the stock's return covariance (correlation) with the market return, which determines the average return on *individual* stocks. Figure 9.4 clearly shows that if we combine individual stocks into a single portfolio we may be able to reduce risk, as the standard deviation of returns for the S&P 500 portfolio is less than the standard deviation on individual stocks – this is partly because in the S&P 500 portfolio we get rid of firm-specific risk and we can also take advantage of any low correlations between individual stock returns.

Our overall conclusions are that for very large asset classes, the average return on these portfolios is higher, the higher is the volatility (standard deviation) of returns; but the average return on *individual* stocks does not appear to be related to the volatility of *individual* stock returns.

Importance of the equity premium

For investors, the forward-looking equity premium is important because it provides an estimate of the future value of any funds invested in the stock market, relative to the risk-free return. This is particularly important for pension funds that invest (a proportion) of their assets in equities. For defined-contribution pension schemes, the individual saver receives at retirement a 'pot of money' that she usually then invests (all or part) in an annuity. The equity part of this pot of money is extremely sensitive to the mean return on stocks. For example, for the US using $g = 6.7\%$ p.a., \$100 invested at $t = 0$ accumulates to $\$100 \ (1.067)^{30} = \$700$ after 30 years, whereas if the (geometric) mean equity return is one standard deviation lower (i.e. $g = 4.7\%$ p.a.), the \$100 accumulates to about \$400 after 30 years. These are real returns, so the higher equity return increases wealth by a factor of 7 but the lower return by a factor of only 4. For a defined-benefit pension scheme (i.e. pension is based on final salary), the forward-looking equity return is important for the solvency of the pension scheme.

The historic real (geometric) return on equities of 6.8% for the world index demonstrates that over the last 100 years a world index (*tracker) fund* (or even a US or UK fund) would have performed very well (even after deduction of annual fees of around 1% p.a.). An actively managed fund would involve management fees of around 2–3% and so historically it too would have done reasonably well, even if it had only performed as well as a tracker (which the average active fund seems just about to manage to do). However, if you believe that the forward-looking real equity return is closer to, say, 4% (see below), then the active fund looks much less attractive, with its high management fees. You might then be better off with index-linked bonds, with a real return of around 3% p.a. (e.g. John Ralfe switched all of UK chemist Boots' pension fund into bonds in 2001).

As we have seen in earlier chapters, a key input for companies in calculating their cost of equity capital is a forward-looking measure of the equity premium (adjusted by the company's beta). Historically, the US/UK equity premium has been high at around 7% p.a. (arithmetic mean), which with a beta of unity and an average real interest rate of 3% p.a. (say) gives a (real) cost of equity capital for the firm of 10% p.a. With inflation projected to be around 2%, this would give a nominal cost of equity capital of 12%, which would be used in a NPV calculation for investment projects and takeover decisions. This would also be the hurdle rate used by the firm (i.e. the internal rate of return of the investment project must exceed 12% p.a.). If the forward-looking required return on equity is really lower than 12%, then clearly the firm should lower its hurdle rate, otherwise value-enhancing investment projects may be rejected.

Because of their market power, state or privatised utilities are often subject to price caps (e.g. prices can rise no faster than the consumer price index less x%) or 'rate of return regulation' (i.e. the rate of return on capital cannot exceed y% p.a.). In the case of the latter, a forward-looking return on the firm's equity is required and for this we need a forecast of the equity premium. Hence the forecast equity premium is important for institutional investors such as pension funds, for individuals' investments in active or passive mutual funds and for the hurdle rate for corporate investment projects.

Forecasting the equity risk premium

Needless to say, forecasts of the equity premium are subject to wide margins of error. Welch (2000, 2001) asked 226 financial economists to forecast the average equity premium over the next 30 years for the US and the (arithmetic) mean was 7.1%, with a standard deviation of around 2%. This forecast is a little lower than the 101-year historical US equity premium of 7.7% (Table 9.3), but the standard error of respondents' replies is about the same as the historical standard error of 2% (Table 9.3). Respondents seem fairly closely 'anchored' to the historical premium when forming their view of the future premium (see the psychological biases noted in Chapter 15).

Dimson *et al.* (2001) adjust the ex-post historical risk premium for the impact of unanticipated higher earnings at the end of the 1990s, to take account of the fact that increased international diversification may have lowered the required return, as might diminished investment risk (e.g. because of the ending of the Cold War, progress in multilateral trade talks and so on) and because of reduced risk aversion of the marginal investor. They suggest a *forecast equity premium* of 5.4% for the US, 3.7% for the UK and 4% for the world index (arithmetic averages, with geometric averages about 1% lower). Campbell (2001), using a variety of methods, suggests a forecast US equity real return of 6.5% to 7% (arithmetic) and 5% to 5.5% (geometric), with a forecast real interest rate of 3% to 3.5%. This implies a forecast range for the equity premium of 3% to 4% (arithmetic) for the US. As we have noted, Table 9.3 shows *historical* equity premiums, which are much higher than the above *forecasts*.

While the geometric mean is the best way to report historical average returns, it is not clear what method we should use to forecast future average returns over a long horizon. Statisticians will provide numerous 'best' methods for forecasting returns. If stock returns are random with a 'true' mean return μ that is constant, then it can be shown that the best forecast of future returns is to use the arithmetic (sample) average return, $\overline{R}$. But we know that $\overline{R}$ is measured with error (i.e. we cannot be sure that $\overline{R}$ equals the true mean, μ) and any errors will be compounded the further we project into the future. There is no consensus view about how to forecast the average return, but Jacqier, Kane and Marcus (2003) suggest a useful rule, which is to use a weighted average of the arithmetic and geometric means when we want to forecast over long horizons. For example, if you have used 100 years of data to calculate $\overline{R}$ but you want to forecast 25 years ahead, they show that an unbiased forecast over the next 25 years would be to compound at a rate μ_{new} where:

$$\mu_{new} = (25/100)g + [(100 - 25)/100]\overline{R} \tag{17}$$

TABLE 9.4: Long-horizon risk and return, 1920–96

	Probability of loss			Value at risk (5% left tail)		
	1 year	5 years	10 years	1 year	5 years	10 years
US (Price change)	36.6	34.3	33.7	−27.8	−45.5	−51.2
US (Total return)	30.8	20.7	15.5	−24.5	−33.7	−22.3
UK (Price change)	40.3	32.5	45.2	−24.5	−54.8	−50.8
UK (Total return)	30.1	22.1	30.8	−24.9	−47.8	−45.1
Median (Price change) −30 countries	48.2	46.8	48.2	−31.0	−60.3	−65.4
Median (Total return) −15 countries	36.1	26.9	19.9	−24.7	−39.9	−34.8
Global index (Price change)	37.8	35.4	35.2	−20.8	−40.4	−41.1
Global index (Total return)	30.2	18.2	12.0	−16.7	−19.8	−11.2

Notes: 1. The global index uses GDP weights.
2. Total return is the % price change plus the % dividend yield.
3. Statistics are calculated from the empirical distribution of returns.
4. The median price change using total returns has less coverage, as data is only available on dividends for 15 countries.

The 'weight' placed on the (historical) geometric mean (0.25) is determined by the forecast horizon (25) you require, relative to the number of years used to estimate the arithmetic mean (100).

Table 9.4 reports some loss probabilities using data from the last century. As you can see, the investment period is almost irrelevant when it comes to the probability of encountering losses on the US market when we use price changes (i.e. exclude dividend payments when calculating returns) – the probability of a loss from holding stocks drops from 36.6% (over one year) to 33.7% over 10 years. But when we use total returns (i.e. including dividend payments in returns), the probability of a loss falls from 30.8% over one year to 15.5% over 10 years – this demonstrates the importance of using *total* returns rather than price changes when looking at returns over longer horizons. This 'probability of a loss' is the concept of risk the press has in mind, when it claims in the financial pages that 'stocks are less risky in the long run'.

The probability of a loss takes no account of how much you might lose if you do incur a loss and clearly the latter is of paramount importance. If the probability of a loss over, say, 20 years is 1%, this initially sounds fine, but if you do incur a loss and this results in a loss of all your wealth, this presents quite a different picture of 'risk'. The value at risk (VaR) is the *maximum* percentage loss in the value of your wealth that could occur with a probability of 95%. It follows that if the VaR over one year is −24.5%, then there is a 95% chance that you could lose *less than* 24.5% of your wealth but a 5% chance that you could lose *more than* 24.5% of your wealth, over the next year. As you can see from Table 9.4, the maximum percentage of your wealth you might lose (with 95% probability) does vary over different holding periods and generally (using total returns) the maximum amount you could lose *increases* the longer you hold stocks. With this definition of risk, stocks certainly appear to be more risky over longer horizons – contrary to what you often hear in the press. We deal with VaR in greater detail in Chapter 31.

There is another measure of risk closely related to VaR known as *conditional* VaR (or the conditional tail expectation). This measure asks the question: 'If I do end up in the bottom 5% of possible outcomes, what is the average loss I will incur?' If we could add up all the possible losses in the bottom 5% of outcomes and take the average of these figures, then this would be the conditional VaR. Clearly, the conditional VaR will be a larger (absolute) figure than the VaR itself, which is on the upper boundary of the worst 5% of outcomes. The conditional VaR is an expected value that accounts for the whole lower 5% worst-case outcomes.

What exactly constitutes risk, how we measure it and how we interpret it are not as clear cut as you might think, and much of the rest of the book is concerned with how we can clarify these issues.

9.3 DESCRIBING DATA

Every day, analysts access a vast amount of financial data. To handle data effectively, it is important to summarise the data without losing too many of its individual characteristics. The simplest way to obtain an overview of the data is to plot it (i.e. time-series graphs, scatter plots, bar chart). Another way to summarise a large data series is to group the individual observations (e.g. daily stock returns) into a frequency distribution. Another commonly used technique is the calculation of summary statistics (e.g. mean, standard deviation, skewness, kurtosis, correlation). Summary statistics can be calculated for grouped data (e.g. returns for the largest 10% of firms quoted on the NYSE) as well as ungrouped data (i.e. individual firms).

Frequency distribution and percentiles

A useful way of analysing data sets is to construct an empirical frequency distribution. We can then see whether this empirical distribution is similar to any of the standard distributions (e.g. the normal distribution). Sometimes, in order to summarise a large data set, we can group the observations into similar bands (e.g. number of company defaults per year between 0 and 10, 10 and 20 and so on). The *frequency distribution* is then a graph of the frequency with which the data falls into these bands. Table 9.5 shows the (absolute) frequency with which particular returns are observed for the 393 monthly returns of General Motors' stocks from January 1975 to September 2007. From Table 9.5 we see that 97 monthly returns were between 0% and 5%, but only 5 of the monthly returns were less than −20%. The relative frequencies are simply:

$$\text{Relative frequency} = \frac{\text{absolute frequency}}{\text{total number of observations}}$$

The total number of returns in all the bands is 393. Hence for example, the relative frequency for returns between 0% and 5% is 24.68% ($= 97/393$). The *cumulative frequency*, as the name suggests, gives the frequency with which returns lie in a particular *range,* starting from the smallest. For example (Table 9.5, column 4), the relative frequency with which returns fall between 'less than 20%' and '0% to 5%' is:

Cumulative frequency ('less than 20%' to '0% to 5%')

$$= 0.0127 + 0.0305 + 0.0433 + 0.1450 + 0.2545 + 0.2468 = \textbf{0.7328}$$

TABLE 9.5: Frequencies and frequencies distributions

Range	Frequencies	Cum. frequencies	Relative frequencies	Cum. rel. frequencies
up to −20%	5	5	1.27%	1.27%
−20% to −15%	12	17	3.05%	4.33%
−15% to −10%	17	34	4.33%	8.65%
−10% to −5%	57	91	14.50%	23.16%
−5% to 0%	100	191	25.45%	48.60%
0% to 5%	97	288	24.68%	73.28%
5% to 10%	67	355	17.05%	90.33%
10% to 15%	22	377	5.60%	95.93%
15% to 20%	10	37	2.54%	98.47%
more than 20%	6	393	1.53%	100%

Of course, the cumulative frequency for *all* the returns, from their most negative value to their largest positive value, must be unity. An empirical frequency distribution is also usually referred to as a **histogram**, where the area of a bar represents the relative frequency for the returns that lie within the bar.

Percentiles determine the value of returns at various cut-off points of a data series. All return observations are ordered in ascending order and if q% of the returns are below, say, a return of −15%, then the qth percentile return is said to be −15%. The **median** (i.e. the middle value from all the ordered returns) is a special percentile, namely the 50th percentile. For example, from the final column of Table 9.5 we see that 0.0433 (i.e. 4.43%) of all returns are less than *minus* 15%. Hence the 5th percentile for returns is said to be equal to (here, close to) *minus* 15%. The 99th percentile is a return of 21.63%, which means that only 1% of all the returns in our data set has values that exceed 21.63%. Other percentiles for monthly stock returns on General Motors are reported in Table 9.6.

If we include all returns that lie in the bottom 10th, then this set of returns is known as the 'bottom **decile**' of returns− and we could if we wished calculate summary statistics such as the mean return and the standard deviation of returns in this bottom decile. We could of course repeat this for the other nine deciles. Then we could make statements about the difference in mean returns (or standard deviation) of the 'top' and 'bottom' deciles of returns.

Sample statistics

Sample statistics try to capture the general properties of the shape of a frequency distribution of data. Generally, these summary statistics are referred to as 'moments'. The mean or expected

TABLE 9.6: Percentiles: monthly returns, General Motors' shares

Percentile	Value
1st	−23.86%
5th	−14.59%
10th	−9.16%
50th	0.34%
95th	13.35%
99th	21.63%

value is the 1st moment and measures the central tendency of a data set. The variance (or standard deviation) is the 2nd moment and measures the dispersion of the data points around the mean. A measure of the symmetry (or non-symmetry) of the distribution is known as skewness, which is the 3rd moment. Finally, the degree of 'peakness' of the distribution and the presence of 'fat tails' is measured by the kurtosis (i.e. 4th moment). In addition to these summary statistics for *individual* random variables (e.g. the return on AT&T stocks), we are also interested in co-movements between two (or more) variables. For example, do the monthly returns of AT&T stocks tend to rise or fall with the monthly returns of Microsoft's stock? The strength of this co-movement can be measured by the covariance or correlation coefficient between the two stock returns. As a first approximation, random variables such as stock returns are usually assumed to have *population* means, variances, skewness and so on that are constant (over time) and their correlation is also often assumed to be constant over time. Sample statistics using real data (e.g. arithmetic mean) are then used to provide *estimates* of these 'population parameters'.

The arithmetic mean is the most widely used statistical measure of central tendency of a data series. (Other measures of central tendency include the median – the middle value – and the mode – the value that occurs the most times.) Suppose we have a data series consisting of n stock returns $R_t (t = 1, 2, \ldots, n)$, then the **sample (arithmetic) mean** is:

$$\overline{R} = \frac{\sum_{t=1}^{n} R_t}{n} \qquad [18]$$

The **geometric mean return** is:

$$g = \sqrt[n]{(1 + R_1)(1 + R_2) \cdots (1 + R_n)} - 1 \qquad [19]$$

Table 9.7 reports the FTSE100 stock price index at the end of June for the last six years, together with the annual (holding period) returns (e.g. return for 2007 is 13.28% = (6607.9/5833.42 − 1) ×100%). Using equations [18] and [19] the mean returns are:

TABLE 9.7: UK stock market index and returns (2002–07)

Year (June)	FTSE100	Returns
2002	4656.36	
2003	4031.17	−13.43%
2004	4464.07	10.74%
2005	5113.16	14.54%
2006	5833.42	14.86%
2007	6607.90	13.28%

Arithmetic mean: $\bar{R} = (1/5)(-13.43\% + 10.74\% + 14.54\% + 14.86\% + 13.28\%)$

$$= 39.99/5 = 7.998\%$$

Geometric mean: $g = \sqrt[5]{(1 - 0.1343)(1 + 0.1074)\cdots(1 + 0.1328)} - 1$

$$= 1.4287^{(0.2)} - 1 = 7.396\%$$

The **median** is that return that lies in the middle position when the returns are ordered by size from lowest to highest. In our example, given the returns $\{-13.43\%, 10.74\%, 13.28\%, 14.54\%, 14.86\%\}$ the median is 13.28%. The **mode** is the observation that occurs most often – with our limitation of only six data points this would be 15% (to the nearest per cent).

The **standard deviation** measures the spread around the mean:

$$\hat{\sigma} = \sqrt{\frac{\sum_{t=1}^{n}(R_t - \bar{R})^2}{n - 1}} \qquad [20]$$

In equation [20] we divide by $n - 1$ rather than n, in order to get an unbiased estimate of the true population parameter σ. (In mathematical terms, unbiasedness means that our values of $\hat{\sigma}$ are centred around the 'true' population value, σ.) The standard deviation has the same units as $\bar{R}$ (e.g. per cent or proportion) and is therefore a more useful measure than the sample variance, $\hat{\sigma}^2$. Because the units are the same, the standard deviation can be directly compared to the arithmetic mean, as when using the Sharpe ratio.

Skewness is a measure of the deviation from symmetry of the distribution of the data. It is the 3rd moment of the (frequency) distribution and is calculated as:

$$\text{Skew} = \frac{E(R_t - \mu)^3}{\sigma^3} = \frac{n}{(n - 1)(n - 2)}\sum_{t=1}^{n}\left(\frac{R_t - \bar{R}}{\hat{\sigma}}\right)^3 \qquad [21]$$

(where 'E' stands for the 'expected value'). If stock returns are normally distributed, then skew would be zero. If skew is positive (negative), then the frequency distribution of returns has a long right tail (left tail), compared with the normal distribution. If a distribution is skewed to the left and hence has many more large values that are below the mean than above the mean, then the standard deviation will be a misleading measure of risk – since we normally think of risk as the possibility and size of potential losses. The *lower partial standard deviation* (LPSD) attempts to get round this problem by using equation [20], but we only include returns that are below the mean (i.e. we only consider one side of the distribution). However, the LPSD is not used very often as a measure of risk, because for diversified portfolios of stocks its value does not differ very much from the standard deviation. (This is because both measures give quite a high weighting to small deviations from the mean, since this is where most returns lie– while it is true that returns in the extreme tails are a long way from the mean there are usually not many of them, so they don't necessarily contribute a great deal in the formula for the standard deviation or LPSD.) Another measure of risk would be only to include those returns that are more than m% below the mean (and ignore all other returns) when using the formula for the standard deviation, but again this approach is not often used. The standard deviation, for all its problems, is the most common measure of risk.

The 4th moment, **kurtosis**, measures the degree of 'peakness' and the presence of 'fat tails' and is given by:

$$\text{Kurt} = \frac{E(R_t - \mu)^4}{\sigma^4} - 3$$

$$= \left(\frac{n(n+1)}{(n-1)(n-2)(n-3)} \sum_{t=1}^{n} \left(\frac{r_t - \bar{R}}{\hat{\sigma}}\right)^4\right) - \frac{3(n-1)^2}{(n-2)(n-3)} \qquad [22]$$

The normal distribution has a kurtosis value of 3 and hence a Kurt value or excess kurtosis of zero. If the data is more peaked than in the normal distribution, then Kurt > 0 (known as leptokurtic), whereas a lower peak has Kurt < 0 and is known as platykurtic. As well as the above, there are other statistics that also summarize the data set (i.e. range, modified range, absolute deviation and so on), but these need not concern us.

Using our five annual returns on the FTSE100, the sample variance, standard deviation, skewness and kurtosis are:

Sample variance:

$$\hat{\sigma}^2 = (1/4)[(-13.43 - 7.998)^2 + (10.74 - 7.998)^2 + \ldots + (13.28 - 7.998)^2]$$

$$= 584.46/4 = 146.12$$

Sample standard deviation: $\hat{\sigma} = \sqrt{146.12} = 12.09$

Skewness:

$$\text{Skew} = \frac{5}{(4)(3)}\left[\left(\frac{-13.43-7.998}{12.09}\right)^3 + \left(\frac{10.74-7.998}{12.09}\right)^3 + \cdots + \left(\frac{13.28-7.998}{12.09}\right)^3\right]$$

$$= -2.1375$$

Kurtosis:

$$\left(\frac{5(4)}{(4)(3)(2)}\left[\left(\frac{-13.43-7.998}{12.09}\right)^4 + \left(\frac{10.74-7.998}{12.09}\right)^4 + \cdots + \left(\frac{13.28-7.998}{12.09}\right)^4\right]\right)$$

$$-\frac{3(4)^2}{(3)(2)} = 0.8333(10.10) - 8 = 0.4166$$

Ignoring the fact that we have used only five observations, the skewness and kurtsosis figures indicate that our returns are not normally distributed.

Sample covariance and correlation

The degree of association between the return on two stocks, A and B, can be measured using the sample **correlation coefficient**:

$$\hat{\rho} = \hat{\sigma}(R_A, R_B)/\hat{\sigma}(R_A) \cdot \hat{\sigma}(R_B) \qquad [23]$$

where $\quad \hat{\sigma}(R_A, R_B) = \dfrac{\displaystyle\sum_{t=1}^{n}(R_{A,t} - \overline{R}_A)(R_{B,t} - \overline{R}_B)}{n-1}$

and $\hat{\sigma}(R_A)$ and $\hat{\sigma}(R_B)$ are the sample standard deviations for our two assets. $\hat{\rho}$ is the sample estimate of the 'true' population correlation coefficient ρ. The statistic $\hat{\sigma}(R_A, R_B)$ is known as the *covariance* between the returns on the two assets. The correlation coefficient and the covariance can be positive, negative or zero. Unfortunately, the value of $\hat{\sigma}(R_A, R_B)$ depends on the units used to measure returns (e.g. percentages or proportions). This is why we often use the correlation coefficient $\hat{\rho}$, which lies between -1 and $+1$ so that:

$\hat{\rho} = +1$	Returns on asset A and asset B are perfectly positively related.
$\hat{\rho} = -1$	Returns on asset A and asset B are perfectly negatively related.
$\hat{\rho} = 0$	Returns on asset A and asset B are not (linearly) related.

For example, if $\hat{\rho} = +0.70$ between the monthly returns on British Airways (BA) and easyJet's stock, this implies that a positive return on BA stocks is accompanied about 70% of the time by a positive return on easyJet stocks. Note that there is no causation implied by the correlation coefficient. It is not necessarily the case that changes in the business practices of BA (more flexible working arrangements) have a direct effect in causing easyJet also to immediately look for cost savings in the business (or vice versa). The correlation could be due to the fact that both firms are influenced in the same direction by an extraneous variable (e.g. a fall in oil prices might cause both BA and easyJet stock returns to increase). Statistics can never

TABLE 9.8: Summary statistics

	Boeing	RETURNS General Electric	S&P 500
Mean	0.0135	0.0104	0.0079
Standard deviation	0.0879	0.0612	0.0411
Variance	0.0077	0.0037	0.0017
Maximum value	0.3212	0.1895	0.1324
Minimum value	−0.4576	−0.2784	−0.2468
	Correlation matrix		
Boeing	1		
General Electric	0.3896	1	
S&P 500	0.4986	0.7467	1
	Covariance matrix		
Boeing	0.0077		
General Electric	0.0021	0.0037	
S&P 500	0.0018	0.0019	0.0017

Note: Returns are monthly and measured as decimals over the period January 1975 to September 2007.

establish causality, only associations between variables. Causality requires an interpretation based on some kind of model of the industry – which may or may not be correct. For example, if we know that easyJet hedges its fuel costs but BA does not, then the change in oil prices is unlikely to be the *cause* of the high correlation between the returns.

Table 9.8 shows summary statistics for the rate of return on Boeing and General Electric stock, as well as the return on the S&P 500 over the sample period of January 1975 to September 2007. General Electric has a lower mean return than Boeing, but the latter has a higher standard deviation. Boeing and General Electric's returns have a relatively low correlation of 0.39, but both are quite highly correlated with the S&P 500. The correlation of Boeing's shares with the market is 0.50, whereas General Electric's correlation with the market is 0.75.

9.4 THEORETICAL PROBABILITY DISTRIBUTIONS

Many investment decisions have to be made under uncertainty. In order to quantify this uncertainty, we can use probabilities and probability distributions. This enables us to say whether a particular event will or will not occur with a certain frequency (likelihood or probability).

The idea of random events and probabilities is fairly well understood for simple problems. For example, a single toss of a six-sided die[9] has the same probability, 1/6 (0.1666), of yielding a single integer from the set $X_i = \{1, 2, 3, 4, 5, 6\}$ – this is a **uniform probability distribution**. There are only six possible outcomes (also known as 'events') and hence it is a discrete probability distribution and the variable X_i is a *discrete random variable.* In contrast, we can also have *continuous random variables.* Continuous random variables can take *any* value (over a specific range). Most financial time series are continuous random variables. The best-known continuous probability distribution is the normal distribution, which is symmetric and bell-shaped– and this is usually our 'baseline' distribution against which we compare other distributions. Theoretically, what is good about the normal distribution is that once we know the mean μ and standard deviation σ, we know everything about the whole of the distribution (and if a computer is given values for μ and σ, we can obtain a graph of the 'bell shape'). Other continuous probability distributions are the Students' t-distribution, which is symmetric but has slightly fatter tails than the normal distribution, so is useful for modelling stock returns that you think have a relatively large probability of 'outliers' in either direction. The lognormal distribution is useful for representing the distribution of stock prices. In fact, if (continuously compounded) stock *returns* are normally distributed, then the stock *price* will be lognormally distributed– the lognormal distribution cannot have negative values, so prices cannot be negative and it has a long right tail, so very large prices are not ruled out although they do not occur very often. The F-distribution and the 'chi-squared' χ^2 distribution are useful for testing hypotheses about statistical parameters, such as whether the standard deviations of the returns on two stocks are statistically different from each other.

The uniform distribution gives an equal probability of drawing any number, over a specified range. Figure 9.5 shows a uniform distribution for a discrete random variable that takes values $\{1, 2, 3, 4, 5, 6\}$ with probability of 1/6th for each outcome (e.g. outcomes from the roll of a die). Other examples of discrete probability distributions are the binomial and Poisson distributions. The binomial distribution is used in option pricing theory, whereas the Poisson distribution finds applications in the insurance industry (e.g. probability of car accidents or property damage by fire), as well as in determining the number of defaults (bankruptcies) in a group of firms. The uniform distribution for a *continuous* random variable over the range a to b has a probability density function $f(x) = 1/(b - a)$ and is shown in Figure 9.5.

Population parameters

When we look at actual data, we try to infer properties of the 'true' distribution by looking at sample statistics such as the *sample* mean and *sample* standard deviation. The latter are supposed to be useful measures of the 'true' mean and standard deviation, which we cannot usually observe because we do not have all of the possible outcomes for the random variable (e.g. stock returns) in our sample of data. But we can investigate the properties of some purely theoretical probability distributions for which we do know all the possible outcomes. Useful summary statistics for these theoretical probability distributions are the expected value and the variance (or standard deviation), which we can calculate exactly. These are

---

[9] 'Die' is the singular of 'dice'. Perhaps the most famous phrase involving this word is when Gaius Julius Caesar marched from Gaul towards Rome with the 13th legion and the border of Italy was then taken to be a small river called the Rubicon. Caesar hesitated as 'crossing the Rubicon' would have signalled civil war. After he had crossed he is reputed to have said (in Greek not Latin) the 'The die is cast' meaning his future lay partly in the hands of 'lady luck' – although I think he thought the probability of success was greater than the probability of throwing a '6'.

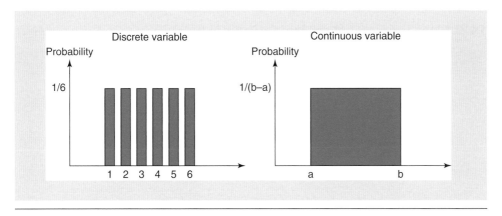

FIGURE 9.5: Uniform distribution: discrete and continuous

known as 'population statistics', to differentiate them from their 'sample statistics', which are estimated using a limited set of data.

Suppose you throw a die a large number of times and receive X_i dollars depending on what number comes up – if you throw a six you receive $6 and so on. The number {1, 2, 3, 4, 5, 6} on the die is a discrete random variable. The amount you *expect* to win if you throw the die a large number of times is given by the (theoretical) expected value (or *EX*) or 'population mean':

$$\mu \equiv EX = \sum_{i=1}^{6} p_i X_i = (1/6)(1 + 2 + 3 + 4 + 5 + 6) = 3.5 \qquad [24]$$

where p_i denotes the probability for a particular outcome or 'event' (here 1/6)

   X_i denotes the possible payoffs from these 'events' (here 1, 2, 3, 4, 5 or 6 dollars)

We can also measure the dispersion of our winnings. Each throw gives a deviation from the mean of $X_i - \mu$ with probability p_i (= 1/6). A measure of the average dispersion is given by the (population) *standard deviation*:

$$\sigma = \sqrt{\sum_{i=1}^{6} p_i (X_i - \mu)^2} = 1.71 \qquad [25]$$

and σ^2 is known as the (population) *variance*. You can see that the formulae for the expected value and the population standard deviation are very similar to their *sample estimators* (i.e. sample mean, sample standard deviation) introduced above – the latter assume that each data point has equal probability, whereas the population statistics use actual probabilities (which may not always be equal). Table 9.9 shows some properties of discrete and continuous random variables.

The return on a stock is a random variable, but unlike the above outcomes, which are discrete (i.e. X_i can only take integer values 1 to 6), the return on a stock can in principle take many values. The stock return is a *continuous* random variable. The probability of observing any particular value for the return, for example $X = 1.0120\%$, is zero. We can only think in terms

TABLE 9.9: Properties of random variables

	Discrete	**Continuous**
	$p_i \geq 0$	
	$\sum_i p_i = 1$	$\int_{-\infty}^{\infty} f(x)\,dx = 1$
Mean (1st moment)	$\mu = \sum_i p_i X_i = 1$	$\mu = EX = \int_{-\infty}^{\infty} x f(x)\,dx$
Variance (2nd moment)	$\sigma^2 = \sum_i p_i(X_i - \mu)^2$	$\sigma^2 \equiv Var(X) = \int_{-\infty}^{\infty} (x - \mu)^2 f(x)\,dx$

of the probability of obtaining a value between, say, $X_1 = 1.0119\%$ and $X_2 = 1.0121\%$, and to calculate this we have to integrate over the continuous *probability density function (PDF)*. Note that the range X_1 to X_2 for which we want to calculate the probability could be very small or very large.

Two or more random variables

So far we have only looked at the population parameters for a single random variable. However, in the real world we have many random variables that may be related to each other. Therefore, it is useful to look at some additional population summary statistics that describe the relationship between two or more random variables. If the return on one stock goes up does the return on the other stock go up as well, does it go down or is it unaffected? The true degree of (linear) association between the returns on the two stocks (in the whole population) is known as the population *covariance* or *correlation coefficient*. The formula for the population covariance is:

$$\text{cov}(x, y) \equiv \sigma_{x,y} = \sum_i \sum_j p_{i,j}(X_i - \mu_X)(Y_j - \mu_Y) \qquad [26]$$

where $p_{i,j}$ denotes the joint probability that outcomes X_i and Y_j occur simultaneously. The *population correlation coefficient* is calculated as:

$$\rho_{x,y} = \sigma_{x,y}/(\sigma_x \cdot \sigma_y) \qquad [27]$$

If the true correlation between two stock returns is positive, then if the return on X is positive in, say, 1000 observations, the return on Y will also be positive more than 500 times. The strength and frequency of this association is measured by the covariance or the correlation coefficient,

TABLE 9.10: Three scenarios for the economy

State k	Probability of state k, p_k	Return on Stock A	Return on Stock B
1. Good	0.3	17%	−3%
2. Normal	0.6	10%	8%
3. Bad	0.1	−7%	15%

but the latter has the advantage that its value always lies between −1 and +1 (whereas the covariance depends on the units used to measure X and Y, for example X could be weight in kilogrammes or pounds and Y could represent height in either inches or centimetres and the units chosen would determine the size of the covariance). Clearly, these definitions are similar to their sample counterparts, but they use the true or population parameters $p_{i,j}$, μ_X, μ_Y.

In the previous section we calculated the (sample) mean return for the FTSE and S&P returns. The formula for the sample mean $\overline{R}$, weights each observation equally. If stock returns really do have a constant population mean μ, then the sample mean $\overline{R}$ is an unbiased estimate of this true mean, μ. However, sometimes we want to consider the *expected outcome* of different possible scenarios. Table 9.10 shows three possible scenarios or states that the economy might take over the next year – good, normal and bad– and the probability of each scenario occurring. For each of the three scenarios, denoted k, there are three possible outcomes for the stock returns of two firms, A and B.

Given these three scenarios with probabilities 0.3, 0.6 and 0.1, the expected return, variance and standard deviation are:

$$\mu_A = p_1 R_{A,1} + p_2 R_{A,2} + p_3 R_{A,3} = 0.3(17\%) + 0.6(10\%) + 0.1(-7\%) = 10.4\%$$

$$\sigma^2(R_A) = p_1(R_{A,1} - \mu_A)^2 + p_2(R_{A,2} - \mu_A)^2 + p_3(R_{A,3} - \mu_A)^2$$
$$= 0.3(17 - 10.4)^2 + 0.6(10 - 10.4)^2 + 0.1(-7 - 10.4)^2 = 43.44$$

$$\sigma(R_A) = 6.59$$

For stock B the expected return $\mu_B = 5.4$, the variance $\sigma^2(R_B) = 34.44$ and the standard deviation $\sigma(R_B) = 5.87$. The covariance of the two stock returns is:

$$\sigma(R_A, R_B) = p_1(R_{A,1} - \mu_A)(R_{B,1} - \mu_B) + p_2(R_{A,2} - \mu_A)(R_{B,2} - \mu_B)$$
$$+ p_3(R_{A,3} - \mu_A)(R_{B,3} - \mu_B)$$
$$= 0.3(17 - 10.4)(-3 - 5.4) + 0.6(10 - 10.4)(8 - 5.4)$$
$$+ 0.1(-7 - 10.4)(15 - 5.4)$$
$$= -33.96$$

and the correlation coefficient is $\rho = -33.96/(6.59)(5.87) = -0.88$.

9.5 NORMAL DISTRIBUTION

The normal distribution is a theoretical (mathematical) distribution for a random variable, which is bell-shaped and symmetric around the mean. It is extremely useful in representing asset returns such as stock and bond returns (over a short horizon) in calculating market risk (Value at Risk), and in pricing options (as we see in later chapters). A random variable is one where each return is independent of previous returns, hence the probability of a positive stock return in this period is unrelated to whether previous returns were positive or negative or zero. The complete shape of the normal distribution is known once we have its mean and standard deviation. If X is a normally distributed random variable, then the equation representing this bell shape is:

$$f(x) = \frac{1}{\sigma\sqrt{2\pi}}e^{\frac{1}{2}\left[\frac{x-\mu}{\sigma}\right]^2} \quad \text{for} \quad -\infty < x < \infty \tag{28}$$

Suppose a random variable (such as stock returns) is normally distributed, with mean $\mu = 10\%$ p.a. and standard deviation $\sigma = 20\%$ p.a. This implies that if we observe 100 years of returns, about 68 of them should be in the range $\mu \pm \sigma$, which is a range of -10% p.a. to $+30\%$ p.a. (Figure 9.6). It follows that in about 32 years out of 100 we should expect to observe returns that are either below -10% or above $+30\%$. Because the normal distribution is symmetric, we can go a little further than this and state that in 16 ($= 32/2$) of the years we expect to observe returns greater than 30% p.a. and in a further 16 years (out of the 100 years) we expect to observe returns less than -10% p.a. Incidentally, for the normal distribution it can be shown that you will observe returns that are more than 1.65 standard deviations below the mean, about 5 times in every 100 occurrences (i.e. 5% of the time). Hence the (percentage) Value at Risk for a stock that has normally distributed returns is $\mu - 1.65\sigma$; see Chapter 31.

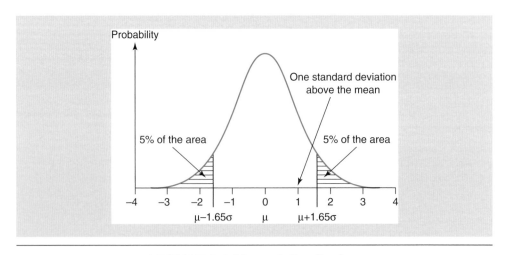

FIGURE 9.6: Normal distribution

The probability that a continuous random variable X takes any single specific value is zero. But (as above) we can calculate the probability that X lies between two particular values, say $x_1 = -1\%$ and $x_2 = +0.5\%$. This is given by the area under the normal density function between x_1 and x_2, which mathematically is (rather cumbersomely) written as:

$$P(x_1 \leq X \leq x_2) = \int_{x_1}^{x_2} f(x)dx = F(x_2) - F(x_1) \tag{29}$$

$F(x_1)$ is known as the *cumulative density function* for a value x_1. It is the *area* under the normal curve from the far left (i.e. $-\infty$) to point x_1. This gives the probability that the random variable X lies in range $-\infty$ to x_1.

Often we assume that asset returns (e.g. monthly stock returns) follow a normal distribution (though this is not quite true). The normal distribution for a random variable with $\mu = 0$ and $\sigma = 1$ is shown in Figure 9.6 and this is known as the **standard normal distribution**. For the standard normal distribution we can calculate areas under the curve. For example, the area between $x = -\infty$ and $x = -1.96$ (i.e. the cumulative density) is denoted $\Phi(-1.96) = 2.5\%$ and $\Phi(0) = 50\%$ (see Appendix, Table 9.A1).

The values for the cumulative standard normal distribution, $\Phi(-1.96)$ say, can be obtained by using the Excel function NORMSDIST (-1.96), which returns 0.025, implying that 2.5% of the area of the standard normal bell-shaped curve lies below the value of -1.96 on the x-axis.

The distribution is symmetric, so the area between $x = 0$ and $x = +1.96$ of the standard normal distribution contains 47.5% of the area and between $x = -1.96$ and $x = +1.96$ the area is 95%[10].

The beauty of the normal distribution is that we can easily work out the probability that our stock return will lie in a particular range. For example, we can be 95% confident that the stock return R will lie in the range:

$$R_i = \mu \pm 1.96\sigma \tag{30}$$

since 95% of the area of the standard normal distribution lies within ± 1.96 standard deviations of the mean. Using Table 9.A1 allows us to read off probabilities when $\mu = 0$ and $\sigma = 1$ without having to solve equation [29]. However, for a normally distributed random variable X_i with mean μ and standard deviation σ we first need to transform X_i into a *standard normal variable*, which can be done with the following transformation:

$$z_i = \frac{(X_i - \mu)}{\sigma} \tag{31}$$

---

[10] For the normal distribution denoted $N(\mu,\sigma)$ the cumulative density is denoted $F(X)$ whereas for the *standard normal* distribution $N(0,1)$ the cumulative density is usually written $\Phi(X)$ in statistics texts, but in finance texts as $N(x)$.

It is easy to show that $z_i \sim N(0,1)$; that is, z_i is normally distributed with mean zero and standard deviation of unity[11]. For example, the probability that our stock return X with $\mu = 3.5\%$ and $\sigma = 8.25\%$ will take a value between 0% and 10% and can be easily obtained. $X_1 = 0\%$ implies $z_1 = -0.4242$ and $X_2 = 10\%$ implies $z_2 = 0.7879$. We require the area between $z_1 = -0.4242$ and $z_2 = 0.7879$. (Since the normal distribution is symmetric, this is also the area between 0.4242 and -0.7879.) From Table 9.A1 (or using Excel) we can calculate:

$$P(0\% < X < 10\%) = P(-0.4242 < z < 0.7879) = 0.448 \text{ (or } 44.8\%)$$

The *Students' t-distribution* is similar to the normal distribution as it is symmetric around a mean of zero. However, the t-distribution has a flatter peak (i.e. platykurtic) and also fatter tails (see Figure 9.7, which compares the normal distribution and the t-distribution).

Asset *prices* (e.g. stock prices) follow a *lognormal distribution*. Suppose that the current stock price is P_0 and we assume that the *continuously compounded* return $R_{cc} = \ln(P_1/P_0)$ is normally distributed with mean μ and standard deviation σ. The stock price is then given by $P_1 = P_0 e^{R_{cc}}$ and is said to be lognormally distributed. What does the distribution for the stock *price* look like? The lognormal is a bit like the normal distribution but with a 'thin' and very elongated right tail, and the left tail is truncated at $P = 0$ since the lognormal distribution does not allow negative values (prices). Hence the lognormal distribution is highly positively skewed. You can see how this happens by assuming that $P_0 = 100$ and the continuously compounded return is normally distributed with a mean of $\mu = 0$ and a standard deviation $\sigma = 10\%$. Given the normality assumption, equal positive and negative (continuously compounded) returns around the mean of zero are equally likely. Suppose that the returns could be $+10\%$ or -10% in each successive period. What are the outcomes for the price *level*, P? For positive values these are given by $P_1 = 100e^{0.1} = 110.52$, $P_2 = 110.52e^{0.1} = 122.14$ and so on, and for negative values they are $P_2 = 100e^{-0.1} = 90.48$, $P_2 = 90.48e^{-0.1} = 81.87$ and so on. The gaps between the 'up' prices get successively larger, starting at 10.52 followed by 11.62, while the (absolute values of the) gaps between successive 'down' prices get

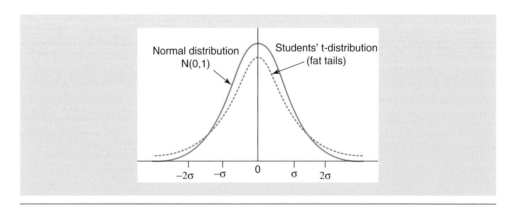

FIGURE 9.7: 'Students' t' and normal distribution

---

[11] The equation for this probability density function is equation [28] with $\sigma = 1$, that is, $f(z) = (1/\sqrt{2\pi})e^{-z^2/2}$.

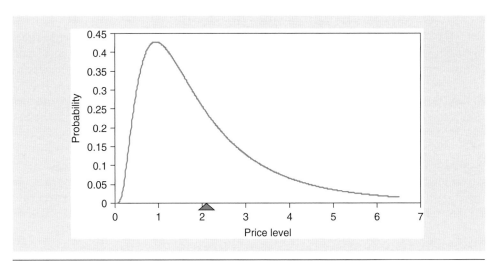

FIGURE 9.8: Lognormal distribution, $\mu = 0.5$, $\sigma = 0.75$

successively smaller, starting at (minus) 9.52 followed by (minus) 8.61. Hence the right tail of the distribution for prices gets elongated and the left tail is truncated and never falls below zero. This is what we mean by prices being lognormally distributed.

The mean (expected value) of the price level obtained from the lognormal distribution is higher than e^{μ} because of the elongated right tail, and in fact the mean price level is given by:

$$EP_1 = P_0 e^{\mu + \frac{1}{2}\sigma^2} = 100\, e^{0 + (1/2)(0.1)^2} = 100.5 \qquad [32]$$

So even though the continuously compounded mean *return* is $\mu = 0$, this results in a mean price *level* that is above \$100 and is equal to \$100.5. Take another example. If we start with $P_0 = \$1$ and the mean (continuously compounded) return $\mu = 0.5$ (50%) with standard deviation $\sigma = 0.75$ (75%), then the distribution of outcomes for the price level after one year is given in Figure 9.8. The expected (average) price level in one years time is $EP_1 = P_0 e^{\mu + \frac{1}{2}\sigma^2} = \$1e^{0.5 + (1/2)(0.75)^2} = \$2.18$ and in Figure 9.8 is the point at which the lognormal distribution just 'balances' on the triangle. For completeness, we note that the 'width' of the lognormal distribution is given by the standard deviation of the end-of-year price level:

$$stdv(P_1) = P_0 \sqrt{e^{2\mu T}(e^{\sigma^2 T} - 1)} \quad \text{and } T = 1 \qquad [33]$$

9.6 CENTRAL LIMIT THEOREM

An important statistical concept regarding the behaviour of the sample mean $\overline{X}$ is the central limit theorem (CLT). The CLT states that the *sampling distribution of the mean* of a random variable becomes more like the normal distribution as the sample size increases. The latter result applies no matter what the shape of the underlying distribution for the individual values for X_i (which is often not known in 'real-world' practical applications). To demonstrate the implications of the CLT, consider an experiment where we *do know* the 'true' population distribution of possible outcomes. For example, the possible outcomes you get from repeatedly throwing a six-sided die is a uniform distribution, with each outcome $\{1, 2, 3, 4, 5, 6\}$ equally likely with a probability of 1/6th. This probability distribution could not be further from the bell-shaped normal distribution. However, suppose you throw the die $n = 30$ times and on each throw you receive $\{1, 2, 3, 4, 5, 6\}$ dollars depending on what number comes up. After 30 throws you calculate the mean (average) payoff from these 30 throws, which we denote by $\overline{X}(30 \ throws)$. The 30 throws constitute 'one game' and after $m = 1$ game the mean payoff might be \$3.7. Now repeat the 30 throws, say 1000 times (i.e. you play the '$n = 30$ die-throwing game', $m = 1000$ times). For each of the 1000 games, record your *average* payoff. These 1000 average payoffs might be $\overline{X}(30 \ throws) = \{\$3.7, \$4.2, \$2.2, \$4.2, \ldots, \$2.8, \$3.1\}$, where the mean payoff from your 1000th game is \$3.1. Notice that the mean return $\overline{X}(30 \ throws)$ from each game, which comprises 30 throws of the die, is itself a random variable, since it differs in each of your 1000 games. Suppose you now plot these 1000 values for $\overline{X}(30 \ throws)$ in a histogram. You will find that the histogram looks remarkably like the normal distribution and it will be centred on the true population mean $\mu = (1/6)(1 + 2 + 3 + 4 + 5 + 6) = 3.5$. Hence, as long as the sample size 'n' is large enough, any analysis of the sample mean can be conducted using the normal distribution, *even though the 'parent' (population) distribution is not normal (e.g. uniform)*. This is a very powerful and useful result.[12]

A second property of the central limit theorem is that the error in our estimate of the population mean μ when we use the sample mean $\overline{X}$ as an estimator gets smaller the larger is n, the number of observations use to calculate $\overline{X}$. The error in estimating μ is given by the standard error of the sample mean $\sigma\left(\overline{X}\right)$:

$$\sigma\left(\overline{X}\right) = \frac{\sigma}{\sqrt{n}} \qquad [34]$$

where σ is the standard deviation of the individual outcomes X_i in the population probability distribution and n is the sample size used to calculate the mean[13].

What this implies is shown in Figure 9.9 for two random variables X and Y, which have radically different *population* distributions. But the means $\overline{X}$ and $\overline{Y}$ both have distributions that approach the normal distribution as n increases.

To summarise, if we have a random variable X_i following *any* probability distribution (e.g. uniform, binomial or any other shape), with population mean μ and standard deviation σ, then

---

[12] Note that it is the sample size n which is important, not the number of repetitions m of the game (here fixed at 1,000). As n, the number of observations used to calculate the mean $\overline{X}$ increases, the closer the distribution of $\overline{X}$ values gets to the 'bell shaped' normal curve.

[13] When throwing the 6-sided die the population standard deviation is $\sigma = \sqrt{\sum_{i=1}^{6}(X_i - 3.5)^2/6} = 1.71$, hence when using $n = 30$ observations in calculating the mean return $\overline{R}$, the error in our estimate around the true population mean is $\sigma\left(\overline{R}\right) = \sigma/\sqrt{n} = 0.31$.

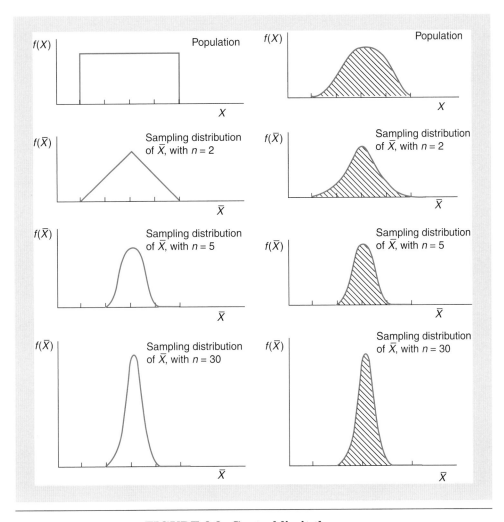

FIGURE 9.9: Central limit theorem

the sample mean $\overline{X}$ will have a probability distribution that approaches the normal distribution with mean μ and standard deviation $\sigma(\overline{X}) = \sigma/\sqrt{n}$. We can therefore estimate the population mean μ with increasing accuracy by using the sample mean $\overline{X}$ and increasing the size n of our sample. This sounds too good to be true – and it is, a little. What we have said is true providing that the population mean and population standard deviation are *constant*. But suppose that in the real world the 'true' (population) mean $\mu_1 = 10$ in the first half of our data set and $\mu_2 = 20$ in the second half of our data set. Clearly, it is no use using all the data to calculate a value for the sample mean $\overline{X}$, since this single number could not represent an estimate of two different population means– using more data here is just plain silly. We would be better off splitting our data set into two halves and using half the data to calculate $\overline{X}_1$ and the other half to calculate $\overline{X}_2$. However, in real-world situations we do not know how the 'true' mean is changing, so we tend to use just the more recent data to calculate the sample mean. This implies a more imprecise statistical estimate, but one that may be closer to today's true mean $\mu_1 = 10$ (rather than yesterday's true mean, $\mu_2 = 20$) and hence more useful as a forecast for the true mean in the near future. The alternative (which we do not pursue in this book) is to use so-called regime-switching models (see Cuthbertson and Nitzsche, 2004).

SUMMARY

- The average return on a stock (or other asset) can be measured by the *arithmetic mean return* or *geometric mean return*. The geometric mean return is used to compare the *historical performance* of different assets, since a higher geometric return implies a higher final value of wealth (for the same initial investment).
- The *continuously compounded return* is defined as the logarithm of the ratio of the value of your investment at time t = 1 to its initial value at time t = 0. Continuously compounded returns also simplify the calculation of future value and present value. For example, if you are to receive $100 in three years time (from a bond you hold) and the annual continuously compounded return (interest rate) is $r_{cc} = 3\%$ p.a., then the present value is $P_0 = \$100\,e^{-(0.03)(3)} = 91.39$. Therefore a bond that pays $100 in three years time could be sold today for $91.39.
- To summarise historical data on asset returns we can construct a frequency distribution (or histogram). Summary *sample statistics* that inform us about the shape of the histogram include the sample mean, standard deviation, skewness and kurtosis (i.e. the four 'moments').
- The degree of (linear) association between two returns is given by the correlation coefficient. A correlation coefficient of $+0.7$ implies that when the returns on one stock increase on 100 days, those of another stock will also tend to rise on around 70 of these 100 days (and on the remaining 30 days there will be no association between the returns). A correlation coefficient of $+0.7$ does *not* imply that when the return on stock A goes up by 1%, the return on stock B rises by 0.7% on average – the correlation coefficient is best viewed as a 'frequency count', not a 'quantitative relationship' between two variables.
- We often assume that stock returns follow a particular *probability distribution* such as the *normal distribution*. This implies that there are constant population ('true') parameters such as the population mean μ and standard deviation σ (which are unobservable), which determine the possible outcome for stock returns. We then take a set of data and calculate *sample estimates* of these population parameters. For example, the sample mean $\overline{R}$ and sample standard deviation $\hat{\sigma}$ are *estimators* of the 'true' population parameters μ and σ, respectively.
- The *central limit theorem* states that if a set of random outcomes X are independent over time (i.e. like a coin flip) and are drawn from the same distribution (e.g. the uniform distribution), then the sample mean $\overline{X}$ has a distribution that becomes closer to the normal distribution as the number of observations used to calculate $\overline{X}$ increases.
- The *normal distribution* is widely used in finance to represent the distribution of stock and bond returns and the return from holding foreign currency (i.e. the percentage change in the exchange rate). If a variable (such as stock returns) is normally distributed, then 68% of returns lie within the range $\mu \pm \sigma$ and 95% of returns lie in the range $\mu \pm 1.96\sigma$.

APPENDIX

TABLE 9.A1: Standard normal distribution

This table gives the area under the standard normal curve between zero and a point z standard deviations above zero. For example, the area between $z = 0$ and $z = +1.96$ is 47.5%, implying that the area to the right of $z = +1.96$ is 2.5% ($= 50\% - 47.5\%$).

z	0	0.01	0.02	0.03	0.04	0.05	0.06	0.07	0.08	0.09
0	0.0000	0.0040	0.0080	0.0120	0.0160	0.0199	0.0239	0.0279	0.0319	0.0359
0.1	0.0398	0.0438	0.0478	0.0517	0.0557	0.0596	0.0636	0.0675	0.0714	0.0753
0.2	0.0793	0.0832	0.0871	0.0910	0.0948	0.0987	0.1026	0.1064	0.1103	0.1141
0.3	0.1179	0.1217	0.1255	0.1293	0.1331	0.1368	0.1406	0.1443	0.1480	0.1517
0.4	0.1554	0.1591	0.1628	0.1664	0.1700	0.1736	0.1772	0.1808	0.1844	0.1879
0.5	0.1915	0.1950	0.1985	0.2019	0.2054	0.2088	0.2123	0.2157	0.2190	0.2224
0.6	0.2257	0.2291	0.2324	0.2357	0.2389	0.2422	0.2454	0.2486	0.2517	0.2549
0.7	0.2580	0.2611	0.2642	0.2673	0.2704	0.2734	0.2764	0.2794	0.2823	0.2852
0.8	0.2881	0.2910	0.2939	0.2967	0.2995	0.3023	0.3051	0.3078	0.3106	0.3133
0.9	0.3159	0.3186	0.3212	0.3238	0.3264	0.3289	0.3315	0.3340	0.3365	0.3389
1	0.3413	0.3438	0.3461	0.3485	0.3508	0.3531	0.3554	0.3577	0.3599	0.3621
1.1	0.3643	0.3665	0.3686	0.3708	0.3729	0.3749	0.3770	0.3790	0.3810	0.3830
1.2	0.3849	0.3869	0.3888	0.3907	0.3925	0.3944	0.3962	0.3980	0.3997	0.4015
1.3	0.4032	0.4049	0.4066	0.4082	0.4099	0.4115	0.4131	0.4147	0.4162	0.4177
1.4	0.4192	0.4207	0.4222	0.4236	0.4251	0.4265	0.4279	0.4292	0.4306	0.4319
1.5	0.4332	0.4345	0.4357	0.4370	0.4382	0.4394	0.4406	0.4418	0.4429	0.4441
1.6	0.4452	0.4463	0.4474	0.4484	0.4495	0.4505	0.4515	0.4525	0.4535	0.4545
1.7	0.4554	0.4564	0.4573	0.4582	0.4591	0.4599	0.4608	0.4616	0.4625	0.4633
1.8	0.4641	0.4649	0.4656	0.4664	0.4671	0.4678	0.4686	0.4693	0.4699	0.4706
1.9	0.4713	0.4719	0.4726	0.4732	0.4738	0.4744	0.4750	0.4756	0.4761	0.4767
2	0.4772	0.4778	0.4783	0.4788	0.4793	0.4798	0.4803	0.4808	0.4812	0.4817
2.1	0.4821	0.4826	0.4830	0.4834	0.4838	0.4842	0.4846	0.4850	0.4854	0.4857
2.2	0.4861	0.4864	0.4868	0.4871	0.4875	0.4878	0.4881	0.4884	0.4887	0.4890
2.3	0.4893	0.4896	0.4898	0.4901	0.4904	0.4906	0.4909	0.4911	0.4913	0.4916
2.4	0.4918	0.4920	0.4922	0.4925	0.4927	0.4929	0.4931	0.4932	0.4934	0.4936
2.5	0.4938	0.4940	0.4941	0.4943	0.4945	0.4946	0.4948	0.4949	0.4951	0.4952
2.6	0.4953	0.4955	0.4956	0.4957	0.4959	0.4960	0.4961	0.4962	0.4963	0.4964
2.7	0.4965	0.4966	0.4967	0.4968	0.4969	0.4970	0.4971	0.4972	0.4973	0.4974
2.8	0.4974	0.4975	0.4976	0.4977	0.4977	0.4978	0.4979	0.4979	0.4980	0.4981
2.9	0.4981	0.4982	0.4982	0.4983	0.4984	0.4984	0.4985	0.4985	0.4986	0.4986
3	0.4987	0.4987	0.4987	0.4988	0.4988	0.4989	0.4989	0.4989	0.4990	0.4990
3.1	0.4990	0.4991	0.4991	0.4991	0.4992	0.4992	0.4992	0.4992	0.4993	0.4993

EXERCISES

Q1   What are the key features of the normal distribution?

Q2   Assume that *monthly* returns on the dollar–pound sterling exchange rate are normally distributed with a mean of 1% and a standard deviation of 8%. What is the probability that monthly returns are (i) more than 1.5%; (ii) less than 3%; and (iii) between −2% and 4%?

Q3   What does the central limit theorem say about the sample means as an estimate of the population mean?

Q4   The (simple) interest rate is 8% p.a. If you take out a loan of £100,000, what would be the amount owed at the end of the year if the compounding frequency is (i) semi-annual; (ii) quarterly; (iii) monthly; or (iv) daily? How would you calculate the continuously compounded rate of interest?

Q5   Two stock price indices have the following values:

Time period	S&P 500	Dow Jones Industrial
2001	1139.45	9851.56
2002	936.31	8896.09
2003	1058.20	9782.46
2004	1173.82	10428.02
2005	1249.48	10805.87
2006	1400.63	12221.93
2007	1481.14	13371.72

   (a) Calculate the annual returns, the arithmetic average and geometric average returns.

   (b) Calculate the first four moments for the two stock returns.

   (c) Calculate the correlation coefficient between the two stock returns.

Q6   Would an investor prefer investments with positive or negative skew?

10

Portfolio Theory

AIMS

- To show how the risk of a portfolio of stocks depends on the variance (standard deviation) of individual stock returns and the covariances (correlations) between stock returns.
- To demonstrate why *specific risk* is low in a well-diversified portfolio and the only major risk that remains is *market risk*, which is reflected in the covariances between stock returns.
- To show how portfolio risk and the expected return on a portfolio of *risky assets* are related via the *efficient frontier* – this is *diversification*. Expected returns, variances and covariances of returns are inputs to portfolio analysis.
- To show that a combination of a risk-free asset (e.g. bank deposit or loan) and a risky portfolio of stocks gives rise to a 'new' portfolio with a *linear* relationship between the expected return and risk – this is the *capital allocation line*.
- To show how an investor who can borrow or lend at the risk-free rate obtains an optimal diversified portfolio of stocks by maximising the *reward-to-variability* or *Sharpe ratio*. This analysis uses the *capital market line* (*CML*) and the efficient frontier – it provides the solution for the optimal risky asset proportions to hold in stocks in the *mean-variance model* of portfolio choice.
- To demonstrate how the risk tolerance of different investors influences how much of the risk-free asset and the risky portfolio of stocks they will hold.

INTRODUCTION

In this chapter we analyse the mean-variance model of portfolio choice, which forms the basis for the (one-period) capital asset pricing model (CAPM). The CAPM can be interpreted as a model of equilibrium asset returns, is widely used in the finance literature and is formally introduced in Chapter 13. In the next chapter, we use portfolio theory to analyse how far we should diversify internationally.

Throughout this chapter we will consider that the only risky securities are equities (stocks), although strictly portfolio theory and the mean-variance model apply to choices among *all* risky assets (i.e. stocks, bonds, real estate and so on). Portfolio theory is concerned with two major issues. First, in what proportions you should hold risky assets like stocks – this is the *optimal diversification problem*. The second issue is the *asset-allocation problem* – that is, how much should the investor place in risky assets (stocks) and how much in a risk-free asset such as a bank deposit. For example, she might wish to put some of her own funds in a bank deposit with the remainder placed in stocks. Alternatively, if she is not too worried about risk but likes a high return, she may be willing to borrow money (e.g. a bank loan) at the risk-free rate of interest, add this to her own funds and invest all these funds in the stock market – this is a *leveraged portfolio*. The asset-allocation problem depends on the preferences of the investor – that is, whether she is risk averse or risk tolerant – and gives rise to the concept of the *capital allocation line*.

The concepts used in mean-variance portfolio theory are quite numerous and somewhat complex. We begin with a discussion of what determines the risk of a portfolio comprising many risky assets, like stocks – this involves concepts such as diversification and the efficient frontier. Having analysed the choice *among* a set of risky assets, we then address the *asset-allocation* question – that is, whether you should put most of your own funds in your 'best' portfolio of risky assets and only a little in a risk-free asset such as a bank deposit (or vice versa). This depends on how risk averse or risk tolerant you are. Throughout the chapter we assume that transaction costs and taxes on investment income and capital gains are zero.

10.1 PORTFOLIO RISK AND RETURN

The expected return on an *individual* security is denoted ER_i and we assume the risk on an *individual* security can be adequately measured by the variance σ_i^2 or standard deviation σ_i of its return. Throughout this chapter we shall use the following equivalent ways of expressing expected returns, variances and covariances:

- **Expected stock return** $\equiv \mu_i \equiv ER_i$
- **Variance of stock return** $\equiv \sigma_i^2 \equiv \mathrm{var}(R_i)$
- **Covariance of returns** $\equiv \sigma_{ij} \equiv \mathrm{cov}(R_i, R_j)$

The expected return on a *risky portfolio* of two stocks held in proportions w_1 and w_2 is:

$$ER_p = w_1 ER_1 + w_2 ER_2 \qquad [1]$$

If you have $300 invested in the stock market, with $100 in stock 1 and $200 in stock 2, then $w_1 = 100/300 = 1/3$ and $w_2 = 200/300 = 2/3$ – the weights sum to unity. The risk of a portfolio of stocks is measured by *portfolio* variance, which depends on the variances of individual stock returns and the covariance σ_{12} (or correlation ρ) between the returns:

$$\sigma_p^2 = w_1^2\sigma_1^2 + w_2^2\sigma_2^2 + 2w_1w_2(\sigma_{12}) = w_1^2\sigma_1^2 + w_2^2\sigma_2^2 + 2w_1w_2(\rho\sigma_1\sigma_2) \qquad [2]$$

The standard deviation of returns is denoted σ_p and is measured in the same units as the expected return (e.g. per cent), hence the standard deviation is usually taken as our measure of risk. The covariance of returns σ_{12} is related to the correlation coefficient:

$$\rho = \sigma_{ij}/\sigma_i\sigma_j \qquad [3]$$

For the special case where the two stocks have the same standard deviation σ, then $\sigma_{12} = \rho\sigma^2$. The covariance and correlation coefficient both have the same sign, but the covariance has the annoying property that it depends on the units used to measure returns (e.g. proportions or percentages), whereas the correlation coefficient is 'dimensionless' and must always lie between $+1$ and -1. If $\rho = +1$ the two asset returns are perfectly positively (linearly) related and the asset returns *always* move in the same *direction* (but not necessarily by the same amount). For $\rho = -1$ asset returns always move in opposite directions. If $\rho = 0$ the asset returns are not (linearly) related – hence a positive return for stock 1 could be accompanied by a positive, negative or zero return for stock 2. Put another way, when $\rho = 0$ observing that stock 1 has a positive return tells you nothing about the current return on stock 2.

The covariance between two stock returns is a measure of the strength of their co-movement. But you are probably more familiar with the correlation coefficient between two stock returns. Suppose we observe that the return on stock A increased on 1000 specific days and the return on stock B also increased on 700 of these same days, while on the remaining 300 days there was no relationship between the two stock returns (i.e. when stock A's return increased, stock B's return may have either increased, decreased or stayed the same, with equal probability). Put simply, we would then say that the correlation coefficient between the two stock returns is $+0.7$. The correlation coefficient is essentially a 'frequency count' of the direction of movement of the two returns and the covariance is a similar measure of association between co-movements in the two stock returns.

As we shall see, the 'riskiness' of a portfolio, consisting of both risky assets (stock 1 and stock 2), depends crucially on the sign and size of the covariance or correlation coefficient, ρ. If $\rho = -1$, risk can be completely eliminated by holding a specific proportion of initial wealth in each asset. Even if ρ is positive (but less than $+1$), the riskiness of the overall portfolio is reduced (although not to zero) – this is diversification.

The power of diversification

Assume for the moment that funds allocated to the safe asset have already been fixed and we are focusing only on the amount of money an investor wants to invest in a set of risky assets. Consider the reason for holding a diversified portfolio. Putting all your wealth in stock 1, you incur an expected return ER_1 and risk of σ_1^2. Similarly, holding just stock 2 you expect to earn

ER_2 and incur risk σ_2^2. If there is a negative covariance (negative correlation) between the two returns, then when the return on asset 1 rises, that on asset 2 tends to fall. Hence, if you diversify and *hold both assets,* this would reduce the variance of the *risky* portfolio consisting of stock 1 and stock 2.

To simplify even further, suppose that $ER_1 = ER_2 = 5\%$, $\sigma_1 = \sigma_2 = \sigma = 20\%$ and $\rho = -1$. The assumption that $\rho = -1$ and that the variances are equal implies that the returns always move by equal and opposite amounts – so, when the return on asset 1 increases by 1%, that on asset 2 falls by 1%. Now suppose you put half your initial wealth in each of the risky assets, $w_1 = w_2 = 1/2$, to form your risky portfolio. Diversification has reduced the risk on this portfolio to zero: an above-average return on asset 1 is always matched by an equal below-average return on asset 2. You can see this by putting the above figures $\sigma_1 = \sigma_2 = \sigma = 20\%$ and $\rho = -1$ in [2] and you find $\sigma_p = 0$[1]. Our example here is undoubtedly a special case, but this result is the basis for hedging using futures contracts (see later chapters and Cuthbertson and Nitzsche, 2001b). However in general, even if the covariance is zero or positive (but returns are not perfectly positively correlated, $\rho \neq +1$), it still pays to diversify and hold a combination of both assets – as we see below.

The key inputs in mean-variance portfolio theory that determine optimal diversification decisions are expected returns, variances and correlations between risky asset returns. We can derive a 'theoretical' optimum that depends on these 'inputs', but we also have to estimate them. Table 10.1 gives historical sample averages for these statistics based on monthly stock returns for different US industrial sectors (over the period January 1995 to July 2007). The average monthly return on the Diversified Financials sector at 1.45% exceeds that for the Movie and Entertainment sector at 0.37%, and what is more the Diversified Financials sector has a lower standard deviation at 6.00% than the Movie and Entertainment sector at 7.19%. If these historical figures are good estimates of the (constant) population parameters, then why would anyone hold shares in the Movie and Entertainment sector, rather than putting all their money in the Diversified Financials sector? The reason given above for having some of *both* assets as part of your portfolio is that if the correlation between returns is less than +1, then there may be some diversification benefit to be had from including Diversified Financials along with Movie and Entertainment shares. Indeed, the historical correlation coefficient between the returns in these two sectors is 0.6382 (Table 10.1), so there will be some diversification benefits in holding stocks in both sectors. It is also clear from Table 10.1 that you might also include the Integrated Oil and Gas sector in your portfolio, because not only did it have a high average return of 1.29% p.m., it has relatively low correlations with some of the other sectors.

We noted in an earlier chapter that even if, blindfolded, you throw 35 darts at the stock price pages of the *Wall Street Journal* and put equal amounts in each stock, this random portfolio of stocks would have much less risk than any of the stocks taken individually. This *naïve diversification* is about the only 'free lunch' in finance. It arises because each of the 35 firms is

---

[1] The expected return on the risky portfolio is $ER_p = (1/2)5\% + (1/2)5\% = 5\%$ and since the risk of this portfolio is zero, the *excess* return must be zero – hence the risk-free rate in this stylised example would have to be $r = 5\%$. This demonstrates the 'first law of finance' which is 'no risk implies your portfolio earns the risk-free rate' – otherwise, as we see in later chapters a risk-free arbitrage possibility would be possible.

TABLE 10.1: Monthly stock market returns (January 1995 to July 2007)

	Chemical	Movie and Entertainment	Diversified Financial	Automobiles	Integrated Oil and Gas
Mean return	0.90	0.37	1.45	0.39	1.29
Standard deviation	5.23	7.19	6.00	7.59	5.04
Correlation matrix					
Chemical	1				
Entertainment	0.3361	1			
Financial	0.5207	0.6382	1		
Automobiles	0.4388	0.4950	0.5356	1	
Oil	0.5009	0.2328	0.3715	0.2662	1

affected by random events that are largely independent of each other (i.e. uncorrelated)–for example, one firm may be badly affected by a rejection of its patent application, while another may find it has an early breakthrough in its biotechnology R&D project. These random **firm-specific** events cancel out in a large portfolio, hence reducing overall risk (Figure 10.1).

We can demonstrate this effect by setting $\rho = 0$, in equation [2], which becomes:

$$\sigma_p^2 = (w_1)^2\sigma_1^2 + (w_2)^2\sigma_2^2 \text{ and } \sigma_p = \sqrt{(w_1)^2\sigma_1^2 + (w_2)^2\sigma_2^2} \qquad [4]$$

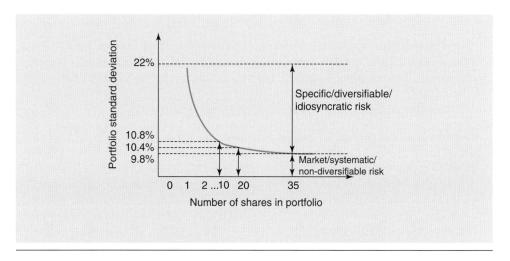

FIGURE 10.1: Random selection of stocks

For illustrative purposes, assume that $\sigma_1 = \sigma_2 = \sigma$ and $w_1 = 1/2$, then $\sigma_p = \sigma/\sqrt{2}$ and in general, as we see below, if we have n stocks with *uncorrelated returns* then $\sigma_p = \sigma/\sqrt{n}$. A large number of uncorrelated ($\rho = 0$) returns, results in a portfolio standard deviation that is very small. This is the 'law of large numbers' – the uncertainty surrounding the expected (average) return on a large number of independent 'bets', is very small – see Case Study 10.1.

CASE STUDY 10.1   ARE CASINOS RISKY?

We are not talking here about the risk that Moe Greene got into while running a casino in Vegas for Michael Corleone in *The Godfather* trilogy, or the risk that Robert DeNiro (playing Sam 'Ace' Rothstein) found himself in while running another Vegas casino in the film of the same name. We deal with outcomes that only involve spins of the roulette wheel, where we know the probability distribution of outcomes – unlike Moe Greene, who miscalculated his probability of survival. The roulette wheel has numbers 1 to 36 plus 0 and 00, giving a total of 38 equally likely possible outcomes, each of which has a probability of 1/38. You are not allowed to place bets on 0 or 00, so your odds of winning on the numbers 1 to 36 is 35:1.

If you place a $1 bet on a single number and your number comes up then you win $36 (your original bet plus $35) and if you lose you end up with zero. The *casino's* profit is therefore −$35 if you win and +$1 if you lose, so the casino's expected profit is:

$$E\pi = (1/38)(-\$35) + (37/38)(\$1) = \$0.0526$$

The standard deviation of outcomes of each $1 bet for the casino is:

$$\sigma = \sqrt{(1/38)(-35 - 0.0526)^2 + (37/38)(1 - 0.0526)^2} = \$5.76$$

This is quite a high standard deviation given the small expected profit of $0.0526 for the casino for each $1 bet. But now suppose there are $n = 10m$ of these $1 bets placed each month, then the standard deviation of the casino's average revenues per dollar is:

$$\sigma(\text{average revenues per \$}) = \$5.76/\sqrt{10,000,000} = \$0.0018215$$

A 95% confidence interval for average revenues is therefore $0.0526 \pm 2(0.0018215)$, which gives a range of 0.048957 to 0.056243. Hence given $10m worth of $1 bets placed, a casino's monthly profits will be between $489,570 and $562,430 in 95 out of 100 months – this amounts to very little risk. Casino owners have definitely weighed up the odds; this is the effect of diversification caused by many independent bets of equal size. Of course, if the casino allowed one huge bet of $10m, then it would face possible large losses of $35 \times \$10m = \$350m$, so casinos put an upper limit on the amount of any individual bet.

In practice, portfolio variance (standard deviation) falls very quickly as you increase the number of stocks held from 1 to 35 and thereafter the reduction in portfolio variance is quite small (Figure 10.1).

The benefits of diversification in reducing risk depend on returns having less than perfect (positive) correlation, for example:

$$\text{if } \rho = +1: \qquad \sigma_p = (w_1\sigma_1 + w_2\sigma_2)$$

Hence σ_p is a (linear) weighted average of σ_1 and σ_2, so there is no diversification effect. However:

$$\text{if } \rho < +1: \qquad \sigma_p < (w_1\sigma_1 + w_2\sigma_2)$$

and σ_p *must be less than* the weighted average of σ_1 and σ_2, so there is some risk reduction due to diversification.

In practice, you can't get rid of all risk by *randomly* adding stocks to your portfolio, because even in a well-diversified portfolio, the returns on different stocks will all experience ups and downs at the same time, because of the **market (systematic) risk** that affects all firms to some extent. For example, changes in interest rates by the Central Bank can affect investors' expectations of future profits and hence the stock returns of many firms – although the stock returns of different firms will not move by the same *quantitative* amount (e.g. the returns on bank stocks may be more affected by interest rate changes than will the stock returns of media firms).

Portfolio theory tells you how to combine stocks, not in a naïve or random way, but on the contribution they make to the return and risk of your overall portfolio – so you can trade off higher risk against a higher expected return in order to obtain the best or optimal combination of risky assets in your portfolio. This is *efficient* diversification and leads to a concept called the *efficient frontier.*

The **market risk** of a portfolio is defined as risk that cannot be diversified away by adding extra stocks to the portfolio. It is also referred to as **non-diversifiable or systematic risk**; see Figure 10.1. There is always some non-zero risk even in a well-diversified portfolio and this is because of the effect of (non-zero) covariances (or correlation coefficients) between asset returns caused by market wide effects on all stocks. To see this, note that the variance of a portfolio of n assets held in proportions $w_i (0 < w_i < 1)$ is:

$$\sigma_p^2 = \sum_{i=1}^{n} w_i^2\sigma_i^2 + \sum_{i=1}^{n}\sum_{\substack{j=1 \\ \text{for } i \neq j}}^{n} w_i\, w_j\, \sigma_{ij} \qquad [5]$$

With n stocks there are n variance terms σ_i^2 and $n(n-1)/2$ distinct covariance terms σ_{ij} that contribute to portfolio variance – there are many more covariance terms than variance terms in [5] and if n is large then portfolio variance depends not so much on the n variance terms but much more on the many covariances. To illustrate the dependence of portfolio variance on the covariance terms, consider a simplified portfolio where all assets are held in the same proportions ($w_i = 1/n$). This is an *equally weighted* portfolio. Then:

$$\sigma_p^2 = \frac{1}{n}\overline{\sigma}^2 + \frac{n-1}{n}\overline{Cov} \qquad [6]$$

where $\overline{\sigma}^2$ is the *average variance* of individual stock returns and $\overline{Cov}$ is the *average covariance* between all the stock returns:

$$\overline{\sigma}^2 = \frac{1}{n}\sum_{i=1}^{n}\sigma_i^2 \quad and \quad \overline{Cov} = \frac{1}{n(n-1)}\sum_{\substack{i=1 \\ }}^{n}\sum_{\substack{j=1 \\ \text{for } i \neq j}}^{n}\sigma_{ij} \qquad [7]$$

If all firms are only subject to specific risk and the risk due to economy-wide factors is zero, then the covariances σ_{ij} between all stock returns would be zero. Hence, portfolio variance (equation [6]) would quickly go to zero as you add additional stocks to the portfolio—this is the 'free lunch' provided by naïve diversification.

In practice, most stock returns are influenced by market-wide factors (such as changes in interest rates), hence the average covariance $\overline{Cov}$ is non-zero. So, although the impact of the 'average variance' of stock returns approaches zero in a well-diversified portfolio, the average covariance term cannot be reduced to zero by adding extra stocks to the portfolio. The covariance terms represent systematic or market risk, which affects all stock returns at the same time. To simplify further, assume that all *individual* variances (standard deviations) and covariances are constant (i.e. $\sigma_i^2 = \sigma^2$ and $\sigma_{ij} = Cov$). Then equation [6] becomes:

$$\sigma_p^2 = \frac{\sigma^2}{n} + \frac{n-1}{n}Cov \qquad [8]$$

If $Cov = 0$ (and hence $\rho = 0$), then as $n \to \infty$, portfolio variance approaches zero. Even if $\rho \neq 0$, then the variance term σ^2/n becomes relatively small as n increases, so the variance of *individual* securities makes hardly any contribution to portfolio risk. But the importance of the covariances in determining portfolio variance is easily seen since as $n \to \infty$, then $\sigma_p^2 = (1 - 1/n)Cov = Cov$. Hence, in a well-diversified portfolio only the *covariances of stock returns* make a contribution to portfolio variance – the impact of the variance of *individual* stock returns on *portfolio variance* has been diversified away[2]. However, 'covariance risk' cannot be diversified away no matter how many stocks you include in your portfolio. It is the covariance terms that (in a loose sense) give rise to the market (non-diversifiable or systematic) risk of your portfolio. This covariance risk, as we shall see in Chapter 13, is represented by the beta of the stock.

---

[2] In the special case where the variance of the returns on all stocks are equal then $\sigma_p^2 = Cov = \rho\sigma^2$, so it looks as if portfolio variance depends on the *individual* variances of each stock. But this is somewhat misleading since portfolio risk is *fully determined* by the *covariances* between all of the stock returns.

We can use equation [8] to see how quickly specific risk can be eliminated by using just a small number of stocks, even if there is a small positive correlation between returns. For example, suppose the standard deviation of all stock returns is $\sigma = 22\%$ and the correlation between any two returns is $\rho = 0.2$, so that $Cov = 0.2(22)(22) = 96.8$. If you form an equally weighted portfolio consisting of $n = 10$ assets, your portfolio risk using [8] is $\sigma_p = 11.64\%$, which is 47% smaller than the risk of an individual stock of 22%. If the number of stocks is increased from 10 to 20, the portfolio standard deviation drops to $\sigma_p = 10.78$, which is a further reduction of only 7.4%. If n = 35 the portfolio standard deviation is $\sigma_p = 10.39$, but this is not much greater than the risk of a portfolio when $n \to \infty$, since the portfolio standard deviation then converges to $\sigma_p = \sqrt{Cov} = 9.84\%$.

Separation principle

In portfolio theory the investor has two key decisions to make. First, how to determine the proportion of funds at the investor's disposal to put in each stock – this is the **optimal diversification problem**. A quite remarkable result is that the optimal proportions w_i^* to invest in each stock are *independent of the individual's level of risk tolerance or risk aversion.* A very

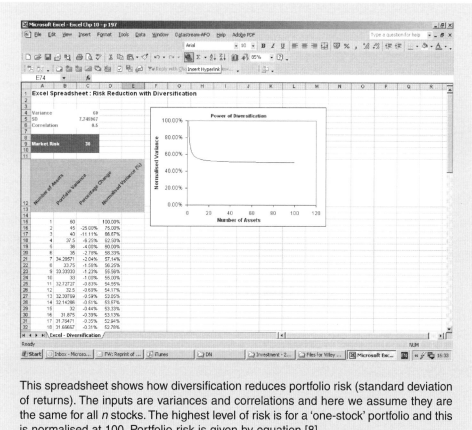

This spreadsheet shows how diversification reduces portfolio risk (standard deviation of returns). The inputs are variances and correlations and here we assume they are the same for all *n* stocks. The highest level of risk is for a 'one-stock' portfolio and this is normalised at 100. Portfolio risk is given by equation [8].

risk-averse investor and an investor who has a high tolerance for risk will both hold the same *proportions* in each stock. The optimal proportions only depend on the individual's forecasts of the objective market variables, namely expected returns, variances and covariances.

The second key decision involves the **asset-allocation problem**. The investor has to decide how much to borrow (or lend) in order to augment (or reduce the amount of) her own wealth invested (in fixed proportions) in the market portfolio of risky assets. Suppose you have a *very* risk-averse investor. Such an investor, faced with the choice between (i) a certain payment of $5 or (ii) paying $5 to enter a game with a 50–50 chance of winning either nothing or $10,000, would choose option '(i)'. Most people are not this risk averse, but a very risk-averse investor will put most of her own wealth into the risk-free asset (which pays an interest rate r) and will only invest a small amount of her own wealth in the risky assets, in the fixed proportions w_i^*. The converse applies to a much less risk-averse person, who will *borrow* at the risk-free rate and use these proceeds (as well as her own initial wealth) to invest in the fixed bundle of risky stocks – again in the optimal proportions w_i^*. This two-stage decision process is known as the *separation principle*.

10.2 PORTFOLIO THEORY

Our main aim in this section is to introduce the key concepts in portfolio theory and show how these are used in determining:

- The optimal proportions w_i^* to invest in each stock – this is the optimal diversification problem.
- How much to borrow or lend in the risk-free asset in order to increase or reduce the investor's exposure to the stock market – this is the asset-allocation problem.

Mean-variance criterion

We assume that the investor would prefer a higher expected portfolio return ER_p rather than a lower expected return, but that she dislikes risk (i.e. is risk averse). Thus, if the agent is presented with a portfolio A (of n securities) and a portfolio B (of a different set of n securities), then according to the mean-variance criterion, portfolio A is preferred to portfolio B if:

$$E(R_A) > E(R_B) \tag{9a}$$

and

$$\sigma^2(R_A) \leq \sigma^2(R_B) \quad \text{or} \quad \sigma(R_A) \leq \sigma(R_B) \tag{9b}$$

where σ is the standard deviation of the return of the portfolio.

Of course if, for example, $E(R_A) > E(R_B)$ but $\sigma(R_A) > \sigma(R_B)$, then we cannot say what portfolio the investor prefers using the mean-variance criterion. Portfolios that satisfy the

TABLE 10.2: **Individual stock returns**

				Return	
State	**Interest**	**Growth**	**Probability**	**Stock 1**	**Stock 2**
1	high	low	0.25	−5	45
2	high	high	0.25	5	35
3	low	low	0.25	10	10
4	low	high	0.25	25	−5

mean-variance criterion are known as the set of **efficient portfolios**. If portfolio A has a lower expected return *and* a higher variance than another portfolio, B, then portfolio A is 'inefficient' and an individual would (in principle) never hold portfolio A if portfolio B is available (i.e. portfolio A is 'dominated' by portfolio B).

Stock returns and variances

To simplify matters we assume there are only four possible scenarios (see Table 10.2) that might influence stock returns. A 'high' level of interest rates is detrimental to equity returns, but high (real) growth in the economy leads to high expected returns. This is because high interest rates (i.e. tight monetary policy) generally imply lower profits, while high growth implies high profits. Some of these profits will then be distributed as dividends and may also lead to capital gains on the stock – both affect the return on the stock. The four possible scenarios have an equal probability of occurrence (of 1/4 each). The expected return on each stock (given the four scenarios) is:

$$ER_1 = \frac{1}{4}(-5\%) + \frac{1}{4}(5\%) + \frac{1}{4}(10\%) + \frac{1}{4}(25\%) = 8.75\% \qquad [10a]$$

and similarly:

$$ER_2 = 21.25\% \qquad [10b]$$

Note that the expected return, using probabilities, is the same as the *sample average* of the return if we had observed $R_1 = (-5\%, 5\%, 10\%, 25\%)$ over a four-year period. The variance and standard deviation of the returns on the two stocks are (see Table 10.3):

$$\sigma_1^2 = \frac{1}{4}(-5\% - 8.75\%)^2 + \frac{1}{4}(5\% - 8.75\%)^2 + \frac{1}{4}(10\% - 8.75\%)^2$$

$$+ \frac{1}{4}(25\% - 8.75\%)^2 = 117.28$$

$$\sigma_1 = \sqrt{117.28} = 10.83 \qquad [11a]$$

TABLE 10.3: **Summary statistics**

	Stocks	
	Stock 1	**Stock 2**
Mean, ER_1	8.75%	21.25%
Std. dev., σ_1	10.83%	19.80%
Correlation (Stock 1, Stock 2)	−0.9549	
Covariance (Stock 1, Stock 2)	−204.688	

and similarly:

$$\sigma_2^2 = 392 \qquad\qquad \sigma_2 = \sqrt{392} = 19.80 \qquad\qquad [11b]$$

Again, this is also the *sample* variance and the standard deviation one would calculate, given the observed values of R_1 and R_2 over a four-year period[3]. The covariance and correlation coefficient between the two stock returns are:

$$\sigma_{12} = \frac{1}{4}(-5\% - 8.75\%)(45\% - 21.25\%) + \frac{1}{4}(5\% - 8.75\%)(35\% - 21.25\%)$$

$$+ \frac{1}{4}(10\% - 8.75\%)(10\% - 21.25\%) + \frac{1}{4}(25\% - 8.75\%)(-5\% - 21.25\%)$$

$$= -204.68 \qquad\qquad\qquad [12]$$

$$\rho = \frac{\sigma_{12}}{\sigma_1\sigma_2} = \frac{-204.68}{(10.83)(19.80)} = -0.9549 \qquad\qquad\qquad [13]$$

The returns on the two assets are negatively correlated. When the return on asset 1 is high, then that on asset 2 tends to be low. At this point, the investor is not allowed to borrow or lend money and she can only use her own wealth to invest in the two stocks. What opportunities are open to her when faced with stocks 1 and 2, given their variances and correlation coefficient ρ?

Efficient frontier

As we alter the proportion of *own* wealth held in the two stocks, both the expected return and standard deviation of the portfolio will change. If the investor chooses to hold a proportion

---

[3] The statistically observant amongst you will know that in calculating the *sample* variance you would divide by $(n - 1) = 3$, rather than '4', as above. But above, we implicitly assume we know the population mean return – that is why we divide by 4. For the *sample* variance you have to *estimate* the mean return and that is why you divided by '3' – you 'lose one degree of freedom', in the statistically jargon. Anyway in a realistic setting with many scenarios or observations it does not make much difference whether you divide by n or $(n - 1)$.

w_1 of her wealth in stock 1 and a proportion $w_2 = (1 - w_1)$ in stock 2, the *actual* return on this risky portfolio (which will not be revealed until one period later) is:

$$R_p = w_1 R_1 + w_2 R_2 \qquad [14]$$

The *expected* return on the risky portfolio is:

$$ER_p = w_1 ER_1 + w_2 ER_2 \qquad [15]$$

and the *variance* of the portfolio return is:

$$\sigma_p^2 = E(R_p - ER_p)^2 = E[w_1(R_1 - ER_1) + w_2(R_2 - ER_2)]^2 \qquad [16]$$
$$= w_1^2 \sigma_1^2 + w_2^2 \sigma_2^2 + 2w_1 w_2 (\rho \sigma_1 \sigma_2)$$

where we have used $\sigma_{12} = \rho \sigma_1 \sigma_2$. How do ER_p and σ_p change, relative to each other, as the investor alters the proportion of her own wealth held in each of the risky stocks? This gives us the *opportunity set* available to the investor.

Remember that the inputs ER_1, ER_2, σ_1, σ_2, σ_{12} (or ρ) to the portfolio problem are fixed and known and we simply alter the proportions w_1 in asset 1 and $w_2 = (1 - w_1)$ in asset 2. Note that there is no maximisation/minimisation problem here – it is a purely *arithmetic* calculation given the definitions of ER_p and σ_p. A numerical example is given in Table 10.4.

For example, for portfolio G (Figure 10.2) we have $w_1 = 0.75$, $w_2 = 0.25$ and:

$$ER_p = 0.75(8.75\%) + 0.25(21.25\%) = 11.88\% \qquad [17]$$

and

$$\sigma^2 = (0.75)^2(10.83)^2 + (0.25)^2(19.80)^2 + 2(0.75)(0.25)[-0.95(10.83)(19.80)]$$
$$= 13.70 \qquad [18]$$
$$\sigma_p = 3.70$$

TABLE 10.4: **Risky portfolio**

| Alternative risky portfolios | Share of | | Portfolio | |
	Equity 1 w_1	Equity 2 w_2	ER_p	σ_p
A	1	0	8.75%	10.83%
G	0.75	0.25	11.88%	3.70%
P	0.5	0.5	15%	5%
Z	0	1	21.25%	19.80%

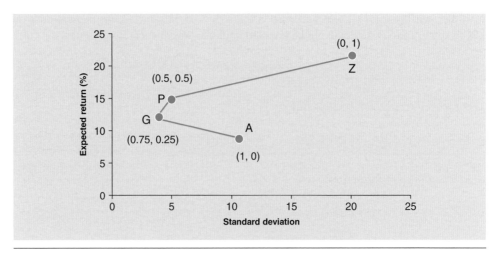

FIGURE 10.2: Efficient frontier

The risk–return combinations in Figure 10.2 represent a feasible set or **opportunity set** for every investor. However, the investor would never choose points along the lower portion of the curve, because points along the upper portion have a higher expected return but involve no more risk, hence:

> The locus of points above and to the right of G = (0.75, 0.25) is known as the efficient frontier.

The efficient frontier is a *non-linear* locus of points in (ER_p, σ_p) space, each point representing different proportions (w_1 and w_2) held in the two stocks. It is clear that combining the two stocks into a portfolio gives the investor a wide set of risk–return combinations – this is the principle of diversification.

If the investor wanted to minimise portfolio risk, she should hold stocks in the proportions (0.75, 0.25) – this is the **global minimum variance portfolio** (see G in Figure 10.2), with $\sigma_p = 3.7\%$ and also results in an expected return of 11.88%. On the other hand, if the investor indicates that she is willing to tolerate risk of $\sigma_p = 5\%$, then the highest return she could *expect* to obtain is 15%, and this would require an asset allocation of (0.5, 0.5). The investor can also infer that if she wants to achieve an expected return of, say, 20%, then she would have to be willing to hold an amount of risk $\sigma_p = 19.80\%$ and the proportions held in each risky asset would be (0, 1). Therefore, a higher expected return is accompanied by higher portfolio risk.

Note that at all points along the efficient frontier there is no borrowing or lending (by construction) but we only invest our own wealth. Where an investor ends up on the efficient frontier depends on her objective. Below we assume that the investor does not want to minimise the riskiness of her portfolio but chooses the proportion to hold in each risky stock in order to maximise the reward-to-variability (or Sharpe) ratio – she is willing to hold more of a risky stock if she thinks there is a higher expected return to be achieved on the whole portfolio. The Sharpe ratio is:

$$SR = (ER_p - r)/\sigma_p \qquad [19]$$

where both the numerator and denominator in the expression depend on the unknown 'weights' w_1 and w_2. But substituting $w_2 = (1 - w_1)$ there is only one unknown variable in [19], which is w_1. An optimiser such as Excel's Solver can be used to find the optimal w_1^* and then we obtain $w_2^* = (1 - w_1^*)$ directly. The optimiser in Solver simply chooses alternative trial values for w_1, works out SR for each of these trial values and then chooses the value for w_1 that gives the largest numerical result for SR when plugged into equation [19]. However, we will first present the solution using the efficient frontier and the capital allocation line.

Capital allocation line (CAL)

Before we show graphically how to maximise the Sharpe ratio, we have to consider the investor's choice between the risk-free asset and the risky portfolio. Consider *one risky portfolio* containing two stocks held in *fixed* proportions, w_i. We arbitrarily take $w_1 = 50\%$, $w_2 = 50\%$, where in Table 10.4 we see that the expected return on this fixed risky portfolio is $ER_p = 15\%$, with standard deviation $\sigma_p = 5\%$. (This is portfolio P in Figure 10.2.) We now combine this risky portfolio with the risk-free asset (e.g. bank account) paying an interest rate $r = 7\%$. The expected return on this new portfolio, consisting of a proportion y held in the risky portfolio and $(1 - y)$ held in the risk-free asset, is:

$$ER_N = (1 - y)r + yER_p = r + y(ER_p - r) \qquad [20]$$

The expected return on our new portfolio is equal to the risk-free rate plus the risk premium of the risky portfolio $(ER_p - r) = 8\%$, times the proportion held in the risky portfolio, y. What is the risk of this new portfolio? The risk-free asset has zero variance and zero covariance with the risky asset portfolio, hence the new portfolio has a standard deviation:

$$\sigma_N = y\sigma_p = y.5\% \qquad [21]$$

What is the relationship between the expected return on our new portfolio and its standard deviation? When $y = 1$, all wealth is invested in the risky asset and $ER_N = ER_p = 15\%$ and $\sigma_N = \sigma_p = 5\%$ – this is point P in Figure 10.3. This is the 'no borrow/no lend' portfolio, where the investor uses all her own funds to invest solely in the risky portfolio of stocks? When $y = 0$ the investor only holds the risk-free asset and $ER_N = r = 7\%$ and $\sigma_N = 0$, which gives the risk-free portfolio F – all the investor's own funds are invested in the risk-free asset.

Suppose we now allow the investor to borrow or lend at the risk-free rate of interest. Thus, the investor can:

- Invest less than her total wealth in the risky portfolio and use the remainder to lend at the risk-free rate.

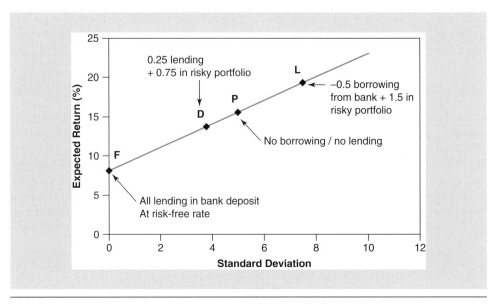

FIGURE 10.3: Capital allocation line

- Invest more than her total wealth in the risky portfolio by borrowing additional funds at the risk-free rate and also investing these funds in the risky portfolio. In this case she is said to hold a *levered portfolio*.

Substituting [21] in [20] for y:

$$ER_N = r + \frac{[ER_p - r]}{\sigma_p}\sigma_N = 7 + \frac{8}{5}\sigma_N \qquad [22]$$

The CAL has an intercept equal to the risk-free rate ($r = 7\%$) and slope $S = (ER_p - r)/\sigma_p = 1.6$. The slope of the CAL is the reward-to-variability or **Sharpe ratio** of the *risky portfolio* – it is the expected (excess) return on the stock portfolio per unit of risk (as measured by the standard deviation of the risky portfolio[4]).

If the investor has own funds $OF = \$100,000$ and she puts a proportion $y = 3/4$ into the risky portfolio P, then she will hold $75,000 in the risky portfolio and $25,000 in the risk-free asset and using [20] the new portfolio has:

$$ER_N = 7\% + (3/4)8\% = 13\% \qquad [23]$$

$$\sigma_N = (3/4)5\% = 3.75$$

$$SR = (ER_N - r)/\sigma_N = (6/3.75) = 1.6$$

---

[4] Note that in practice you are unlikely to find an (unlevered) stock portfolio which has a Sharpe ratio this large – the Sharpe ratio for most diversified stock portfolios is around 0.4–0.6.

This new portfolio is represented by point D (Figure 10.3), which also lies on the CAL (three-quarters of the way along between F and P).

Leverage

We discussed leverage in Chapter 4. Assume that the investor borrows $BF = \$50,000$ from the bank, investing this and her own funds, $OF = \$100,000$, in the risky portfolio, making the total funds in the risky portfolio $TF = \$150,000$. In this case $y = TF/OF = 150,000/100,000 = 1.5$ and hence $(1 - y) = -0.5$, representing a short position in the risk-free asset – that is, borrowing from the bank at $r = 7\%$. The expected return, standard deviation and Sharpe ratio for the levered portfolio are:

$$ER_N = 7\% + 1.5(8\%) = 19\% \tag{24}$$

$$\sigma_N = 1.5(5\%) = 7.5\%$$

$$SR = (ER_N - r)/\sigma_N = (12/7.5) = 1.6$$

These combinations of expected return and risk for the new portfolio are shown in Figure 10.3 as point L. Note that in all of the above cases the risky portfolio P consists of the *fixed bundle* of two stocks in the proportions (50%, 50%). However, although the *proportions* in each risky asset are fixed at every point on the CAL, the *absolute amounts* held in each risky stock vary along the CAL. For example, for the levered portfolio you hold $75,000 (= 50\% \times TF = 50\% \times 150,000)$ in each of stocks 1 and 2, while for the portfolio P you hold $50,000 (= 50\% \times TF = 50\% \times 100,000)$ in each stock. It is not surprising, therefore, that the expected return and risk of the levered portfolio L are higher than the expected return and risk of the 'no-borrow, no-lend' portfolio P.

In our example, all the points (except the intercept) on the capital allocation line represent a *fixed combination* of $w_1 = 50\%$, $w_2 = 50\%$ held in the risky portfolio (of stocks 1 and 2). The only 'quantity' that varies along the capital allocation line is the proportion y of total funds held in the risky portfolio. The risky portfolio P represents the 'no-borrow, no-lend' portfolio. Points to the left of P represent some investment of own funds in the risk-free asset and the remainder in the risky assets, while points to the right of P represent a levered portfolio where the investor borrows from the bank and uses these funds and her own funds to invest in the risky portfolio.

> The *capital allocation line* gives a *linear* risk–return relationship for *any* portfolio consisting of a combination of an investment in the risk-free asset *and* a risky portfolio (which comprises a 'fixed bundle' of stocks). Each point on a given CAL represents different combinations of risk and return as you alter the proportion of funds in the risky portfolio. But all points on the CAL have the same *reward-to-variability* or *Sharpe ratio*.

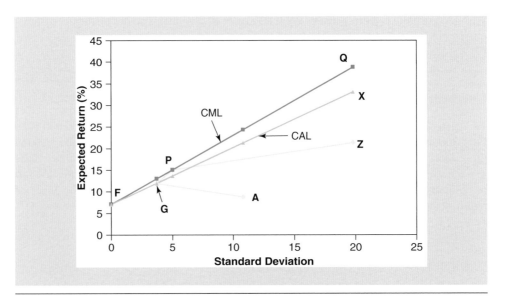

FIGURE 10.4: Efficient frontier and CML

In the above analysis we could equally well have chosen to start with a risky portfolio consisting of *fixed* proportions of 75% in stock 1 and 25% in stock 2, with $ER_p = 11.88\%$ and $\sigma_p = 3.7\%$ (risky portfolio G in Table 10.4). When we combine portfolio G with the risk-free asset, we obtain a new CAL, which goes through F and G (see Figure 10.4). Hence each risky portfolio on the efficient frontier (each with different fixed weights w_i in the two stocks) has its own CAL. All of these CALs are available to any investor who can borrow or lend at the risk-free rate.

When a portfolio consists *only of risky assets,* then as we have seen the efficient frontier in (ER_p, σ_p) space is curved – ER_p and σ_p vary as the w_i *are changed.* But for *any* portfolio consisting of stocks held in *fixed proportions (i.e. a single fixed* risky portfolio), combined with borrowing or lending at the risk-free asset, the relationship between the expected return on this new portfolio ER_N and its standard deviation σ_N *is linear.* This is the CAL, with intercept $= r$ and slope equal to the Sharpe ratio of the risky portfolio. This should not be unduly confusing, since the portfolios considered in the two cases are very different.

10.3 MARKET PORTFOLIO AND THE CAPITAL MARKET LINE (CML)

Although an investor can attain any point along F–G–X in Figure 10.4, *any* investor (regardless of her risk tolerance) would prefer to be on the capital allocation line F–P–Q. This is because at any point on F–P–Q the investor has a greater expected return for any given level of risk, compared with points on F–G–X. The highest CAL attainable is F–P–Q, which is tangent to the efficient frontier and it provides the investor with the highest possible return per unit of risk (Sharpe ratio) and is known as the **Capital Market Line (CML)**.

> The *capital market line (CML)* is the CAL that is tangent
> to the efficient frontier. It is the highest attainable CAL and has the highest
> Sharpe ratio.

Point P in Figure 10.4 represents the highest CAL and the *optimal* proportions at P are $w_1^* = 0.5$ and $w_2^* = 0.5$. This optimal diversified portfolio of risky assets is known as the **market portfolio**. We have now solved the optimal diversification problem. Using both the efficient frontier and the CAL, we know how to distribute our funds between two stocks to maximise the reward-to-variability (Sharpe) ratio. We have done so without assuming anything about the degree of risk tolerance (risk preferences) of the individual investor.

Now if we are willing to assume (and it's a big 'if') that expectations about variances and so on are the same for all investors, then we find that *all* investors hold the same proportions in the risky assets (e.g. all investors hold 1/20 of stock 1, 1/80 of stock 2, etc.) irrespective of their preferences. Hence aggregating, all individuals will hold the risky assets in the same proportions as in the (aggregate) market portfolio (e.g. if the share of AT&T in the total stock market index is 1/20 by value, then all investors hold 1/20 of their *own* risky portfolio in AT&T shares). Note that even if all investors do not have the same view about variances, expected return and so on, then portfolio theory can still be used to calculate a *particular investor's* optimal diversified portfolio in the risky assets. So all is not lost! However, we should not really call the resulting portfolio the 'market portfolio', but merely this investor's optimal diversified portfolio.

Mean-variance portfolio theory is a **passive strategy** because the investor does not look for underpriced or overpriced stocks – the latter would be an **active strategy**. The MV approach, although passive, still requires some action – you need to forecast the 'inputs' – that is variances, covariances and expected returns – and then do the optimisation problem. If the inputs

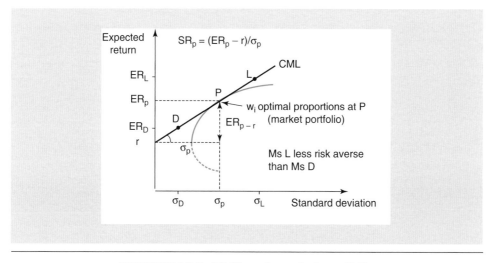

FIGURE 10.5: CML and market portfolio

change over time then you have to find the new optimum proportions and rebalance your portfolio – there is a trade-off here since frequent rebalancing implies higher transaction costs (e.g. broker' commissions, bid–ask spreads).

When there are many risky assets we can still determine the efficient frontier, which is the smooth curve in Figure 10.5 with the optimal diversified (market) portfolio given by point P. At P the investor does not borrow or lend and P represents that point on the efficient frontier that maximises:

$$ SR = \frac{ER_p - r}{\sigma_p} \qquad \text{subject to } \sum_{i=1}^{n} w_i = 1 \qquad [25] $$

This provides us with a useful way of calculating the optimal proportions w_i^*, especially when we have more than two assets. The expected return and the standard deviation of the portfolio both depend on the *known* inputs, expected returns, variances and covariances of *all* the stock returns. The only unknows in [25] are the $w_i (i = 1, 2, 3 \ldots n)$ and using Excel we can

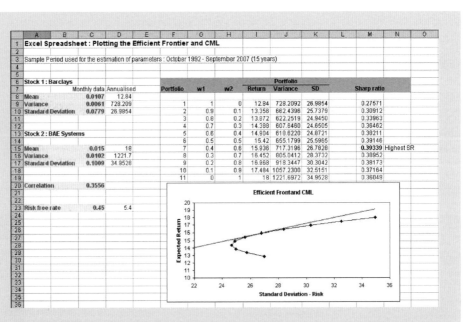

This spreadsheet constructs the efficient frontier and the capital market line for a portfolio of two stocks: Barclays and BAE Systems. The mean, variance, SD and correlation of the two stock returns need to be provided, together with the risk-free rate. Monthly data is used but the monthly figures are annualised. Portfolio variance and portfolio expected returns are calculated as the portfolio weights change between 0 and 1. The optimal portfolio weights (0.4, 0.6) correspond to the 'market portfolio' and give the highest Sharpe ratio of 0.39339. The efficient frontier is graphed. The CML is the equation $r + (SR_{max}) \sigma_p = 5.4 + 0.39339\sigma_p$.

maximise SR subject to the restriction that the proportions held in the risky assets sum to one $\left(\sum_{i=1}^{n} w_i = 1 \right)$[5].

Asset allocation

If we now allow investors to borrow or lend, they will 'mix' the risk-free asset with the optimal risky bundle of stocks represented by P, to get to their preferred position along the CML. Hence investors' preferences determine at which point along the CML each *individual* investor ends up. For example, an investor who has a low risk tolerance (high risk aversion) would end up at a point like D (Figure 10.5) where she puts some of her own funds in the risk-free asset (i.e. a bank deposit earning interest of r) and puts the remainder of her own funds in the risky portfolio of stocks (in the optimal proportions w_i^*). On the other hand, an investor with little or no risk aversion would end up with a levered portfolio at a point like L – she borrows money (at a cost of r) to augment her own wealth and she then invests all these funds in the risky stock portfolio represented by P (but she still holds *all* her n risky assets in the fixed proportions w_i^*). Notice that the risk-tolerant (leveraged) and the risk-averse investor's final positions are both on the same CML, therefore they have the same Sharpe ratio as the investor who neither borrows nor lends but simply puts all her own funds in the market portfolio P. The leveraged investor L has a higher expected excess return $(ER_L - r)$ and higher portfolio risk σ_L than does the risk-averse investor D, but the reward-to-variability ratio is the same for all investors (at D, P or L in Figure 10.5). For example, investor D might be an ordinary retail investor (in a mutual fund, say) whereas investor L might be a leveraged hedge fund. The higher expected return for the hedge fund comes at a cost of higher portfolio volatility, yet this results in exactly the same Sharpe ratio as the mutual fund investor. Of course in practice, the hedge fund would not be a passive investor as assumed here, but would look for underpriced and overpriced securities and undertake an active investment strategy – more of this in Chapter 30.

Separation principle

In determining her overall optimal portfolio, the investor makes two separate decisions. The first is a purely technical decision and the second depends on the risk tolerance of the individual investor.

1. Forecasts of expected returns, variances and covariances of risky assets determine the efficient frontier. The investor then determines the optimal risky portfolio as the *point of tangency* of highest CAL with the efficient frontier. This is a purely technical calculation and requires no knowledge of the individual's preferences (i.e. degree of risk aversion or risk tolerance). *All* investors, regardless of their preferences (but with the same view about expected returns etc.), will 'home in' on the optimal portfolio proportions w_i^* to hold in the risky stocks, represented by P – the *market portfolio*.
2. The investor now determines how she will combine the optimal portfolio P with the risk-free asset. This decision *does* depend on her subjective risk tolerance. At a point such as D (Figure 10.5) the *individual* investor is reasonably risk averse and holds most

---

[5] Since, $\sum_{i=1}^{n} w_i = 1$ then $r = \sum_{i=1}^{n} w_i r$, so the numerator in the Sharpe ratio can also be written $\sum_{i=1}^{n} w_i (ER_i - r)$. We can incorporate the constraint in the maximand by substituting $w_1 = 1 - (w_2 + w_3 + \cdots + w_{n-1})$.

of her own wealth in the risk-free asset and puts only a little into the risky market portfolio P (in the optimal proportions w_i^*). In contrast, Ms L is less risk averse (more risk tolerant) than Ms D and ends up at point L (to the right of P). This is a levered portfolio – she borrows at the risk-free rate to increase her holdings in the market portfolio. An investor who ends up at P is moderately risk averse and puts all of her own wealth into the market portfolio and neither borrows or lends at the risk-free rate.

10.4 FURTHER ISSUES

Different values for the correlation coefficient

At any point in time there will be only one value for each correlation coefficient ρ, estimated from the past behaviour of any two returns. However, it is interesting to see what happens to the efficient frontier when ρ moves from $+1$ to -1, since in the real world ρ may change over time – so in practice the efficient frontier changes and therefore the optimal risky portfolio proportions then need to be recalculated. In Table 10.5 we alter the proportions held in each asset and construct the mean-variance combinations for different values of ρ. In general, as ρ approaches -1 the (ER_p, σ_p) locus moves closer to the vertical axis, indicating that a reduction in portfolio risk is possible for any given level of expected return (Figure 10.6). For $\rho = -1$ the curve hits the vertical axis, indicating that there is some value for the proportions (w_1, w_2) held in the two assets that reduces risk to zero. For $\rho = +1$ the risk–return locus is a straight line between the (ER_i, σ_i) points for each individual security.

Efficient frontier: many assets

We now consider the case of n stocks. When we vary the proportions w_i ($i = 1, 2, \ldots, n$) to form portfolios, it is obvious that there is potentially a large number of such portfolios. We can form asset portfolios consisting of two or three or n assets, each in different proportions. All of these possible portfolios are represented by the points on and inside the convex 'egg'

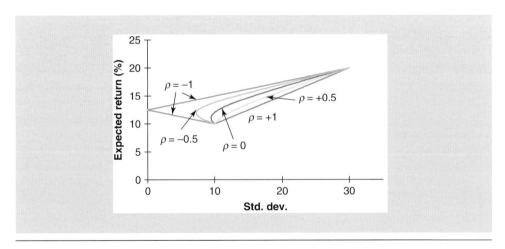

FIGURE 10.6: Efficient frontier and correlation

TABLE 10.5: Efficient frontier – different correlation coefficients

	Summary statistics							
	Asset 1	Asset 2						
Mean	10	20						
std. dev.	10	30						

| | | | Portfolio Std. dev. (two assets) | | | | |
w_1	w_2	Return	$\rho = -1$	$\rho = -0.5$	$\rho = 0$	$\rho = 0.5$	$\rho = 1$
1	0	20	30	30	30	30	30
0.9	0.1	19	26	26.51	27.02	27.51	28
0.8	0.2	18	22	23.07	24.08	25.06	26
0.7	0.3	17	18	19.67	21.21	22.65	24
0.6	0.4	16	14	16.37	18.44	20.30	22
0.5	0.5	15	10	13.23	15.81	18.03	20
0.4	0.6	14	6	10.39	13.42	15.87	18
0.3	0.7	13	2	8.19	11.40	13.89	16
0.2	0.8	12	2	7.21	10	12.17	14
0.1	0.9	11	6	7.94	9.49	10.82	12
0	1	10	10	10	10	10	10

(Figure 10.7) – the points represent the opportunity set available to the investor by combining the risky assets in different proportions.

If we apply the mean-variance criterion, then all of the points in the interior of the portfolio **opportunity set** (e.g. P_1, P_2 in Figure 10.7) are (mean-variance) dominated by those on the curve ABC, since the points on ABC have a lower variance for any level of expected return compared with points like P_1 and P_2[6]. Points on the curve AB also dominate those on BC, so the curve AB represents the *efficient set* of portfolios and is the **efficient frontier**:

- Each point on the efficient frontier represents one 'bundle' of stocks.

- Each bundle comprises n risky assets, held in specific proportions w_i.

---

[6] Suppose you have constructed an efficient frontier for n-risky assets. If you now add an additional risky asset to your portfolio and recalculate the new efficient frontier (for all $n+1$ assets) then the new frontier will be an improvement on your original frontier – that is, it will lie to the left of the original frontier of n-assets. Hence, if you ignore transactions costs (and computational problems) it is always better 'in theory' to have more assets in your portfolio – but in practice there are additional issues to consider which we discuss in later chapters.

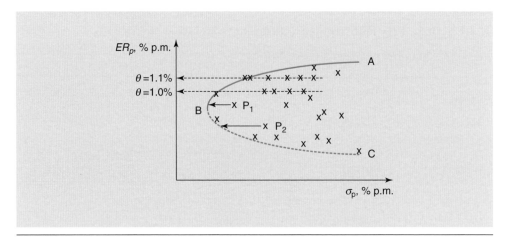

FIGURE 10.7: Efficient frontier, many stocks

Once you have determined the efficient frontier using Excel, it is useful to see how the frontier changes when you:

1. Estimate correlation coefficients and variances over different historical time periods to see how the efficient frontier has changed over time.

2. Input different values for expected returns (based on different historical data periods), so again you see how sensitive the position of the efficient frontier is to changes in these key inputs.

3. Include different assets in your portfolio, with their associated inputs, to see how the efficient frontier changes (e.g. include a hedge fund in your set of risky assets).

Note that when the number of assets is large, calculating the variance of the portfolio requires statistical estimates of n variances and $n(n-1)/2$ separate covariances. So for $n = 25$ stocks the inputs for the portfolio problem amount to 350 separate estimates (namely 25 expected returns, 25 variances, 300 covariances). However, there are shortcuts available to reduce the number of statistical estimates required, a popular one being the *single index model (SIM)*, which we discuss in a later chapter.

Optimal risky portfolio

Note that even when you have mapped out the efficient frontier for n stocks, this does not enable you to determine the optimal proportions to hold in risky assets. As noted earlier, this requires a different optimisation using Excel's Solver. You have to set up the Sharpe ratio (see equation [25]) as the maximand and get Solver to calculate the optimal asset proportions, w_i^*.

CASE STUDY 10.2   EFFICIENT FRONTIER

To 'map out' the efficient frontier for an n-asset portfolio (for $n > 2$ risky assets) we use an optimisation technique that minimises portfolio variance (or standard deviation) for any given level of expected portfolio return. Hence, we undertake the following constrained optimisation:

$$\underset{w_i}{Min} \; \sigma_p^2 = \sum_{i=1}^{n} w_i^2 \sigma_i^2 + \sum_{i=1}^{n} \sum_{\substack{j=1 \\ \text{for } i \neq j}}^{n} w_i w_j \sigma_{ij} = w' \Omega w$$

subject to: $ER_p = \sum_{i=1}^{n} w_i ER_i = w' ER = \text{constant, } \theta$

and $\sum_{i=1}^{n} w_i = w'e = 1$

where $w = n \times 1$ vector of portfolio weights
    $\Omega = n \times n$ variance-covariance matrix
    $ER = n \times 1$ vector of individual expected returns
    $e = n \times 1$ unit vector.

This optimisation can be done in Excel using Solver. You need to input the constant θ, for example $\theta = 1\%$ (per month), which is the trial expected return, ER_p (Figure 10.7). Solver then gives you the appropriate *point* on the efficient frontier, with weights $w_i^{(1)}$ ($i = 1, 2, 3, \ldots n.$). These weights $w_i^{(1)}$ are used to calculate the standard deviation for the portfolio (using the above equation), which corresponds to the chosen $ER_p = \theta = 1\%$. The optimisation problem discards all the points to the right of the chosen point on the efficient frontier along the horizontal line at $\theta = 1\%$. This gives you one point on the efficient frontier. You then choose another value for $\theta = 1.1\%$, say, and redo the optimisation problem to give you the second point on the efficient frontier. This is repeated so that you 'map out' the whole of the efficient frontier. There are quicker methods to calculate the efficient frontier than outlined above – see Cuthbertson and Nitzsche, 2004).

If you want to constrain the portfolio weights so that short selling is not allowed, then you need to add the constraint $w_i > 0$ in the optimisation problem – this can also be done using Excel Solver.

Asset allocation and preferences

Above we demonstrated how to maximise the Sharpe ratio to obtain numerical results for the optimal proportions to hold in each risky asset (stocks). Suppose the result of this gives optimal weights $w_1^* = 0.6$, $w_2^* = 0.4$, which when used to calculate the expected return and risk on the risky portfolio of stocks gives $ER_p = 15\%$, $\sigma_p = 20\%$. How do you now decide on

Excel Spreadsheet : The Efficient Frontier, using Solver

Time	Asset 1		Asset 2		Asset 3	
Period	Index	Return	Index	Return	Index	Return
1	259.34		362.07		476.2	
2	274.18	0.05564	379.01	0.04573	512.34	0.07315
3	261.08	-0.049	381.33	0.0061	507.22	-0.01
4	260.64	-0.0017	393.19	0.03063	539.14	0.06103
5	262.75	0.00806	408.01	0.037	545.69	0.01208
6	261.52	-0.0047	400.19	-0.0194	552.09	0.01166
7	259.65	-0.0072	402.98	0.00695	535.85	-0.0299
8	272.83	0.04951	404.76	0.00441	580.47	0.07998
9	261.52	-0.0423	395.44	-0.0233	545.9	-0.0614
10	264.05	0.00963	385.29	-0.026	541.86	-0.0074
11	266.3	0.00849	386.22	0.00241	512.82	-0.0551
12	279.66	0.04895	411.11	0.06245	573.21	0.11133
13	283.78	0.01462	411.37	0.00063	582.01	0.01524

Solver Parameters [? X]

Set Target Cell: $H$28
Equal To: ○ Max ● Min ○ Value of: 0
By Changing Cells: $C$34:$E$34   [Guess]
Subject to the Constraints:
$C$34:$E$34 >= 0
$F$34 = 1
$H$27 = $L$29
[Add] [Change] [Delete]
[Solve] [Close] [Options] [Reset All] [Help]

	Germany	UK	USA			
ER	0.0075	0.01064	0.01672	Average	5.194	0.00433
Var	0.001	0.00072	0.00274	int. rate		(The monthly interest rate is reported in decimals figure.)
SD	0.03159	0.02684	0.05234			(The annual interest rate is reported as a percentage.)

Data used for Plotting Efficient Frontier and CML

Variance Covariance Matrix				Portfolio		Portfolio			
	Germany	UK	USA				SD	ER	Sharpe Ratio
				ER	0.0085	1	0.0316	0.0075	0.10037
Germany	0.001	0.00047	0.00124	Var	0.00074	2	0.0292	0.008	0.12574
UK	0.00047	0.00072	0.00099	SD	0.02721	3	0.0272	0.0085	0.15337
USA	0.00124	0.00099	0.00274			4	0.0259	0.009	0.18037
						5	0.0253	0.0095	0.20441
						6	0.0255	0.01	0.22242
ER	0.0075	0.01064	0.01672	Sum of w		7	0.0264	0.0105	0.23378
weights	0.68272	0.31728	0	1		8	0.0275	0.011	0.24261
						9	0.0287	0.0115	0.24988
						10	0.0302	0.012	0.25403
						11	0.0322	0.0125	0.25378
						12	0.0339	0.013	0.2558

This spreadsheet uses matrix notation and the Excel optimiser Solver to calculate the efficient frontier for a portfolio consisting of *n* stocks. To obtain a point on the efficient frontier, we have to minimise portfolio variance for a chosen expected return (e.g. 1%). We minimise portfolio variance by allowing the portfolio weights to change. Another required constraint is to ensure that the sum of the weights equals 1 (Cell F34). Also if we do not allow short selling, then all the individual weights need to be constrained to be positive. To draw the CML we first find the optimal portfolio weights (the market portfolio) by maximising the Sharpe ratio, $SR = (ER_p - r_f)/\sigma_p$. Having obtained a numerical value for SR_{max} and knowing the risk-free rate r, the CML is the graph $ER = r + (SR_{max})\,\sigma$ where we vary σ, and calculate the corresponding values for *ER*.

the allocation of your own $100,000 between the risky portfolio and investment in the risk-free asset? This can be demonstrated as follows, where we noted above that this requires knowledge of your preferences concerning risk versus return. This information can be represented in equation [26]:

$$U = ER_N - 0.005(A)\sigma_N^2 \tag{26}$$

U is an index of your expected satisfaction ("happiness") from your investment – or 'expected utility', in the economics jargon. A higher level of expected portfolio return or a lower level of portfolio risk implies more satisfaction. The constant A represents the risk tolerance of the individual investor. The larger is A, the less risk tolerant (i.e. the more risk averse) you are – since given any increase in portfolio risk, the larger is A, the lower is the value for U, your index of satisfaction. A reasonable value is A = 3 and the 0.005 is a scaling factor, so that the expected return and standard deviation can be entered as percentages and the way you trade off risk against return is reasonable in quantitative terms – see below. We now add information about the CAL using our previous equations [20] and [21] (assume $r = 7\%$):

$$ER_N = r + y(ER_p - r) \qquad \text{and} \qquad \sigma_N = y.\sigma_p \qquad\qquad [27]$$

Substituting [27] in [26]:

$$U = r + y(ER_p - r) - 0.005(A)y^2\sigma_p^2 \qquad\qquad [28]$$

In order to obtain the optimal amount y^* to hold in the risky portfolio of stocks, we differentiate [28] with respect to y, set the resulting expression to zero and rearrange to give:

$$y^* = \frac{(ER_p - r)}{0.01(A)\sigma_p^2} = \frac{8}{0.01(3)20^2} = 0.66666 \qquad\qquad [29]$$

The optimal allocation shows that this particular investor holds less in the risky asset – and hence more in the risk-free asset, $(1 - y^*)$ – the lower is the expected return and the higher is the risk of her optimal stock portfolio and the lower her personal level of risk tolerance. These are very intuitive results. With our inputs to the portfolio problem, the proportion of own funds of $100,000 that should be placed in the risky portfolio of stocks is 0.666 (= \$66,666), with \$33,334 in the risk-free asset (e.g. bank deposit). The actual optimal *dollar* amounts in the two risky stocks are then \$40,000 (= 0.6 × 66,666) and \$26,666 (= 0.4 × 66,666). Given the investor's asset-allocation decision, the expected return and risk (on the new portfolio) are:

$$ER_N = r + y(ER_p - r) = 7 + 0.666(8) = 12.33\% \qquad\qquad [30]$$

$$\sigma_N = y.\sigma_p = 0.666(20\%) = 13.33\% \qquad\qquad [31]$$

The expected return and risk for the new portfolio are less than for the risky portfolio ($ER_p = 15\%$, $\sigma_p = 20\%$) because the investor puts some of her own funds in the risk-free asset (i.e. in Figure 10.5 she ends up at a point like D rather than at P).

One final point. How do we know that A = 3, together with the scaling factor 0.005 in [26], are reasonable? One way to think of this is that the average stock market investor holds about two-thirds of their (financial) wealth in risky assets and about one-third in the risk-free asset. The average return on the risky portfolio comprising all stocks in the S&P 500 is around $ER_{S\&P} = 15\%$ p.a., with $\sigma_{S\&P} = 20\%$ p.a. With $r = 7\%$, our utility model for the representative investor implies that the optimal proportion held in the S&P 500 should be:

$$\bar{y} = 0.666 = \frac{(ER_p - r)}{0.01(A)\sigma_p^2} = \frac{8}{0.01(A)20^2} \qquad\qquad [32]$$

Solving this equation gives A = 3, which is therefore consistent with historical market data from investors who hold the S&P 500 as their risky portfolio.

Sharpe ratio as a performance measure

Suppose you have two diversified portfolios of risky assets to choose from, say two different mutual funds, and you want to invest all your available wealth in just one of these funds. How do you know which fund has performed the best? One possibility is to use the Sharpe ratio as a measure of past performance. You would collect monthly returns on each fund over, say, the last 10 years and for each fund estimate the mean return, $\bar{R}$, and its standard deviation, $\hat{\sigma}$. Then you take the average risk-free rate $\bar{r}$ (e.g. bank deposit rate or T-bill rate) and calculate the historic Sharpe ratio for each mutual fund:

$$SR = (\bar{R} - \bar{r})/\hat{\sigma} \quad \text{where} \quad \bar{R} = \sum_{t=1}^{T} R_t/T \quad \text{and} \quad \hat{\sigma} = \sqrt{\sum_{t=1}^{T} (R_t - \bar{R})^2/(T-1)}$$

Thus for two mutual funds, the one with the higher Sharpe ratio may be deemed the more successful since it gives a higher excess return per unit of risk. The Sharpe ratio is therefore a *performance measure* that can be used to rank the relative performance of two different mutual funds, where you are going to take only one of them as your 'best' *single* risky portfolio. We will have much more to say about performance measures in later chapters.

SUMMARY

- Naïve diversification can be accomplished by holding around 35 stocks chosen *randomly* – this results in a reduction in the riskiness of the stock portfolio because the specific risk of the individual stocks tends to cancel out. However, a randomly selected portfolio will still have *systematic (market) risk* due to economy-wide factors that affect all stocks to some extent.
- The *efficient frontier* represents different proportions of your *own wealth* held in stocks – this produces a curved relationship between the expected portfolio return and the riskiness of the portfolio return (as measured by portfolio standard deviation). The shape of the efficient frontier is determined by the correlations (covariances) between all the stock returns and by the variances of the individual stocks. Stocks with relatively low (or even negative) correlations with other stocks reduce portfolio risk and the efficient frontier moves to the 'north west' – this is the benefit from *diversification*.
- The capital allocation line (CAL) shows that the expected return and risk of a portfolio consisting of the risk-free asset and any risky portfolio (e.g. of stocks) are linearly related. The slope of the CAL is given by the Sharpe (reward-to-variability) ratio of the *risky* portfolio, $[(ER_p - r)/\sigma_p]$.

- Mean-variance (MV) portfolio theory assumes that investors choose the optimal proportions w_i^* to hold in the risky portfolio of n stocks by maximising the Sharpe ratio. In a *diversified efficient portfolio* the contribution of the variances of *individual* stocks to overall portfolio variance is relatively small and portfolio variance is mainly determined by the *covariances* between all the individual stock returns.
- MV portfolio theory predicts that:
  - If all investors make the same forecasts for the inputs to the portfolio problem (i.e. expected returns, variances and covariances), then they will all hold the *same optimal proportions* in stocks, regardless of their different levels of risk tolerance. These optimal proportions constitute the *market portfolio*, which is a fixed bundle of risky stocks.
  - Investors' preferences enter in the second stage of the decision process, namely the choice between the optimal fixed bundle of risky securities and the risk-free asset. A *risk-averse* investor will put part of her own wealth in the risk-free asset (e.g. bank deposit) and part will be placed in the fixed bundle of risky assets. A *risk-tolerant* investor will borrow the risk-free asset (e.g. take out a bank loan) and use these funds as well as her own wealth to invest in stocks (in the optimal fixed proportions) – this is *leverage.*

These two stages are known as the *separation principle.* The optimal proportions held in the risky stocks are independent of an investor's preferences, but the choice between the risky bundle of stocks and the risk-free asset does depend on the individual investor's risk tolerance.

EXERCISES

Q1   If you have one risky asset and one risk-free (safe) asset, what is the capital allocation line (CAL)?

Q2   If you have two risky assets, what is meant by the opportunity set?

Q3   What is the Sharpe ratio and, intuitively, why would an investor choose the proportion of risky asset to hold in order to maximise the Sharpe ratio?

Q4   The returns on a Treasury bill (i.e. a risk-free asset) and on equity (i.e. a risky asset) are given below (for four states of the economy):

State of the economy	Prob. of state of economy occurring	Return (% p.a.)	
		T-bill	**Equity**
1	0.25	4	−10
2	0.25	4	0
3	0.25	4	15
4	0.25	4	50

The maturity of the T-bill equals the holding period of one year and hence is the risk-free asset.

a) Calculate the expected return (*ER*) and the standard deviation (*SD*) of the returns on (i) the Treasury bill and (ii) the equity. (Use $n = 4$ rather than $n - 1 = 3$ when calculating *SD*.)

b) Calculate the expected return (*ER*) and the standard deviation (*SD*) of *a portfolio* consisting of the risk-free asset and the risky asset (equity), corresponding to the following proportions y held in each asset.

Share of

T-bill (1–y)	Equity (y)
1	0
0.5	0.5
0	1
−0.5	1.5

c) Plot a graph of the expected return against the standard deviation for each value of y and indicate on the graph the proportions of each asset held.

d) What is meant by 'leverage' in the context of this graph? Why do you obtain leverage when $1 - y = -0.5$ and $(y) = 1.5$, if you have own funds of $100?

Q5 The return from equity 1 (risky asset) and equity 2 (risky asset) depends on the state of the economy:

| State of the economy | Probability p_i | Rate of return (%) | |
		Equity 1	Equity 2
1	0.25	0	35
2	0.25	0	15
3	0.25	7.5	10
4	0.25	15	10

a) Calculate the expected return (*ER*) and the standard deviation (σ_i) of the returns on equity 1 and equity 2, and the correlation coefficient between the two returns.

b) Calculate the expected return (ER_p) and the standard deviation (σ_p) *on a portfolio* of equity 1 and equity 2 (i.e. two risky assets) corresponding to the following proportions w_i held in each asset.

(Note: $ER_p = w_1 ER_1 + w_2 ER_2$ and $\sigma_p^2 = w_1^2 \sigma_1^2 + w_2^2 \sigma_2^2 + 2 w_1 w_2 \rho \sigma_1 \sigma_2$)

Share of

Equity 1: w_1	**Equity 2: $w_2 = (1 - w_1)$**
1	0
0.75	0.25
0.5	0.5
0	1

c) For each portfolio (i.e. combination of w_1, w_2) plot a graph of the expected return (ER_p) against the standard deviation ($SD = \sigma_p$) and indicate on the graph the proportions of each asset held. What are the opportunity set and the efficient frontier?

d) What is the proportion of each risky asset held in the minimum variance (SD) portfolio?

e) Suppose there is a risk-free asset (e.g. a T-bill) that has a return of 4%. What are the optimal proportions of the two risky assets (equity 1 and equity 2) that any investor would hold? What is meant by 'optimal' here?

f) How would your answer to (e) change if the return on the risk-free asset is 10% rather than 4%?

Q6 According to mean-variance portfolio theory, how would the portfolio held by an extremely risk-averse investor and risk tolerant investor differ? For example, would one of them hold 70% of a 'high-risk' share and 30% of a 'low risk' share, while the other held exactly the opposite *proportions* of these two risky assets?

Q7 What, if any, is the relationship between the CML and the Sharpe ratio?

11

International Portfolio Diversification

AIMS

- To show that even if stocks are selected *randomly*, the level of *systematic risk* can be reduced by holding foreign as well as domestic stocks.
- By adding foreign assets to our existing domestic assets, we move the efficient frontier 'to the left', thus giving a better risk–return trade-off.
- To analyse whether international investors should hedge the currency receipts from their foreign asset holdings.
- To discuss the issue of industrial versus geographic diversification.
- To determine the sensitivity of optimal portfolio weights to changes in estimates of mean returns, variances and covariances.
- To suggest some practical solutions to implement international portfolio diversification.

INTRODUCTION

In an earlier chapter we introduced the ideas behind portfolio theory and the benefits of diversification considering only domestic assets. In this chapter we want to see if investors can benefit even more by investing internationally and what role the exchange rate plays.

First, let us briefly review some results of portfolio diversification and consider the additional issues when adding foreign assets. We know that if you *randomly* select stocks from a large market (e.g. NYSE or the London Stock Exchange) the risk of the portfolio, measured by the standard deviation of portfolio returns, quickly falls to a near minimum value when only about 35 stocks are included. Nevertheless, some risk remains – this is known as systematic or market risk. A question arises as to whether this minimum level of systematic risk can be reduced by widening the choice of stocks in the portfolio, to include foreign stocks (and other foreign assets).

Secondly, can we do better than a *random* selection of stocks? In general, we are interested in trading off risk against return. The efficient frontier gives this trade-off for a given set of assets once we know the variances and covariances (correlations) of returns (and we have a forecast of expected returns). If we can widen the set of assets (e.g. include foreign as well as domestic assets), then it may be possible to move the efficient frontier substantially 'to the left', giving a better risk–return trade-off to the investor.

Thirdly, if we include foreign assets in our portfolio, the investor will usually be interested in the return (and risk) measured in terms of her home currency. If the investor does not hedge these risks, then we need estimates of variances and correlations for bilateral exchange rates. If the investor hedges these risks, then broadly speaking we need only consider returns (variances and covariances) measured in local currency and we can ignore exchange-rate risk. However, there is still the issue of what financial instruments to use for the hedge. Should we use forwards, futures, options or swaps?

Fourthly, suppose we base our international portfolio decisions on the efficient frontier using variances and correlations *between broad market indices* (e.g. S&P 500, Nikkei 225, FTSE 100, CAC, DAX). If we then *mechanically* allocate across industries in each country according to existing market capitalisation weights in each index, we will obtain a particular industry weighting in each country. Alternatively, we could base our initial efficient frontier on the variances and correlations between returns across *all* the major *industries* in the world. This would result in a different set of optimal industry weights and we can then examine which efficient frontier gives the best risk–return trade-off.

Fifthly, if we allow the investor to borrow and lend at a risk-free rate, and we have the investor's forecasts of expected returns and covariances, we can determine the optimal portfolio weights for this particular investor. We can then compare the performance of alternative international investment strategies (e.g. holding an equally weighted world portfolio) using performance measures such as the Sharpe ratio.

Finally, optimal portfolio weights clearly depend on estimates of the future values of the expected returns and their variances and covariances. We need to know how sensitive our optimal weights are to minor changes in these crucial inputs (since they are invariably measured with error) and whether constraining these weights (e.g. no short sales) can improve matters.

In 2006, the five largest stock markets accounted for nearly 75% of world stock market capitalisation. The US at 48% accounted for the largest percentage, followed by Japan (10%), the UK (9.6%), France (4.2%) and Germany (3%). Emerging markets, including China and India, played a very minor role having relatively small market capitalisations, usually below 0.25% for any of these countries.

Table 11.1 shows the mean monthly return, standard deviation, maximum and minimum returns and correlations of the main indices of the five largest stock markets over the period January 1988 to August 2007. The mean monthly returns differ substantially, being *minus* 0.113% p.m. (−1.36% p.a.) for the Nikkei 225 and 0.757% p.m. (9.08% p.a.) for the S&P 500. The Nikkei has a standard deviation of 6.24% p.m. (21.6% p.a.), which is slightly higher than 6.03% p.m. (20.9% p.a.) for the German market index, the DAX. The US had a low standard deviation of 3.74% p.m. (13% p.a.), as did the UK at 4.16% p.m. (14.4% p.a.).

Some of the correlations between international markets are quite low, particularly between the Nikkei and the other indices. The highest correlation coefficient of 0.8278 is between the German and French stock markets. A key issue for the benefits of international diversification is whether these *historical* low correlations will persist in the future and whether the estimates of the volatilities and (particularly) the average returns are constant over time. Figure 11.1 shows a graph of the standard deviation of the S&P 500, which is calculated using a rolling five-year window. There are long periods when volatility is both above and below the long-term average level of volatility – this is the well-known phenomenon of persistence in volatility. Clearly, volatility is time varying and it would be dangerous to use a measure of long-term volatility (estimated using the last 20 years of data) to forecast future volatility, particularly over short horizons.

TABLE 11.1: Monthly returns (January 1988 to August 2007)

	S&P 500	Nikkei 225	FTSE all share	CAC 40	DAX
Mean return	0.7568%	−0.1128%	0.5607%	0.7338%	0.6822%
Std. deviation	3.74	6.24	4.16	5.79	6.02
Max	11.95%	18.35%	12.52%	19.54%	17.39%
Min	−11.23%	−22.88%	−14.68%	−18.45%	−23.08%
Correlation Matrix					
S&P 500	1				
Nikkei 225	0.4137	1			
FTSE all	0.7341	0.3993	1		
CAC 40	0.6790	0.3815	0.7243	1	
DAX	0.6789	0.3609	0.7016	0.8278	1

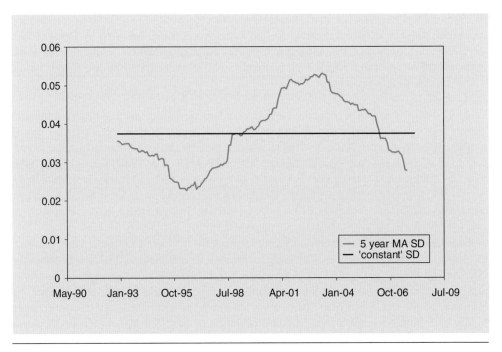

FIGURE 11.1: Volatility of the S&P 500

11.1 THE BASICS

The benefits of portfolio diversification depend on finding new assets that have a low correlation with existing assets in the portfolio. For n assets the expected return and portfolio variance are:

$$ER_p = \sum_{i=1}^{n} w_i ER_i \qquad\qquad [1]$$

$$\sigma_p^2 = \sum_{i=1}^{n} w_i^2 \sigma_i^2 + \sum_{i}^{n} \sum_{j\, i \neq j}^{n} w_i w_j \rho_{ij} \sigma_i \sigma_j \qquad\qquad [2]$$

In an early study of international diversification, Solnik (1974) concentrated on the possible *risk-reducing benefits* of international diversification (and ignored the expected returns from the portfolio). He asked the questions:

- How many *domestic* securities must be held to ensure a reasonable level of diversification?
- Does *international* diversification lead to less risk?

He used an equally weighted portfolio ($w_i = 1/n$) and estimates of the σ_{ij} were based on simple (arithmetic) sample averages (using weekly returns from 1966–71). The steps in the analysis were:

1. Portfolios are generated by randomly choosing from a large set of possible stocks.
2. Form a portfolio of $n = 1$ stocks and repeat this m times. Calculate the average standard deviation $\sigma_p(1)$ for a '1-stock portfolio' (i.e. $\sigma_p(n = 1)$ is averaged over all of the m, 'one-asset' portfolios). This averaging prevents the calculation being dominated by one particular stock with a very large standard deviation.
3. Repeat (2) for $n = 2$, then $n = 3, \ldots$, etc. size portfolios to obtain a sequence of average values for $\sigma_p(n)$ for each size portfolio.
4. Scale each of the estimated 'size-based' standard deviations using $\sigma_p^{(1)}$:

$$V(n) = [\sigma_p(n) / \sigma_p(1)]^2$$

Plot $V(n)$ against n, the number of securities in the portfolio (note that $V(1) = 100\%$).
5. Repeat steps 1 to 4 for different countries.

Solnik's key results were that having about 20 randomly selected domestic securities achieves the minimum level of systematic (market) risk within any one country. For example, for the US and Germany the minimum values of $V(n)$ are 27% and 44% respectively, implying that Germany has a higher level of systematic risk.

How effective was international diversification in reducing risk? Solnik assumes perfect hedging of foreign currency returns (at zero cost of forward cover), so that any prospective foreign currency receipts from the foreign asset are sold in the forward market (or you borrow foreign currency to purchase the shares). Note that in practice the above does not guarantee that you are fully hedged, since you do not know *exactly* what the shares will be worth in, say, one month's time. For example, for a US resident investing in the German all-share index (the DAX), the dollar-hedged return is:

Hedged Return	=	Return on the DAX	+	Forward premium on the Euro
R_{us}^h	=	R_{DAX}	+	$(F - S)/S$

(In the above we have used the Euro as the foreign currency, although when Solnik's study was done this would have been the Deutsche Mark.) For a US-based investor an *unhedged portfolio* in German securities provides a return in dollar terms of

Unhedged return	=	Return on the DAX	+	Appreciation of the Euro
R_{us}^u	=	R_{DAX}	+	R_S

where R_{DAX} = return on DAX (proportionate)

R_S = return on \$/€ (i.e. proportionate change in the \$/€ spot rate)

$(F - S)/S$ = forward premium on the Euro (exchange rates measured as \$/€)

Solnik (1974) then takes nine countries and randomly selects stocks from these countries, forming different-size *international* portfolios. For the unhedged portfolio the standard deviation of returns and the correlation coefficients are derived using the *unhedged* return. For the hedged returns, the forward premium is assumed to be small relative to R_{DAX} and is set to zero. Therefore, hedged returns are equal to local currency returns. Solnik then calculates the statistic $V_p^{(n)}$ for the hedged and unhedged portfolios.

The hedged international diversification strategy will reduce portfolio risk σ_p, if correlations between returns in different local currencies are low, relative to those within a single country. Solnik finds that for a US-based investor the statistic $V(n)$ falls to about 11% for the internationally diversified portfolio (whether hedged or unhedged), which is well below that for the domestic US portfolio of about 27%. The reason the unhedged portfolio does nearly as well as the hedged portfolio is that in the former, movements in the set of bilateral exchange rates (against the dollar) will tend to be offsetting. Also, changes in most exchange rates against the dollar were not large up to 1974 (when Solnik's study ends) because the quasi-fixed exchange rate regime of Bretton Woods was in existence until about 1973. The Solnik study was pioneering in this area but has obvious limitations, namely:

- Historical averages are used in estimating covariances and variances.
- It takes no account of the expected returns from the portfolios.
- It assumes perfect hedging of foreign currency receipts.

Industry-based international diversification

Cavaglia *et al.* (1994, 1995) extend the Solnik analysis in a number of ways—in particular, their analysis considers both risk and return. The aim is to see if one can obtain a better risk–return trade-off from international diversification using one of the following scenarios:

- Diversify by optimal allocation *across countries* based on aggregate 'broad market' indices (e.g. FTSE 100, DAX, S&P 500, etc.) and then use index tracking for the industrial allocation. The latter implies allocating industry stocks based on their existing weights in the broad market index. Call this the *broad indexing market portfolio*.
- Diversify by choosing the optimal weights w_i across *all* industry sectors in *all* the countries (in the study). Call this the *cross-industry portfolio*.

The above scenarios assume:

- All prospective foreign currency receipts are 100% hedged in the forward market at cost equal to the known forward premium (so only the variation in local currency returns determines the variation in the total return to foreign investment).
- Expected returns, variances and covariances are based on historical (monthly) sample averages.
- The optimal weights for each scenario are based on maximising the Sharpe ratio ($S = R_p/\sigma_p$ where R_p and σ_p have their usual definitions) with no short sales (i.e. all $w_i > 0$) in their base case.

The intuition behind this approach is as follows. The 'cross-industry portfolio' will tend to have a lower variance than the 'broad market indexing portfolio' if the correlation between *industry returns in different countries* is lower than the correlation between the returns on the *broad market indexes* (e.g. FTSE 100, DAX, S&P 500). For example, for UK and US broad market return indices and the industry correlations we have:

$$\rho \text{ (FTSE, S\&P)} \approx 0.35 - 0.7$$

$$\rho \text{ (UK industry-}i\text{, US industry -}j) \approx 0.1 - 0.4 \text{ (on average)}$$

Not surprisingly perhaps, the 'cross-industry strategy' is found to give a better risk–return efficient frontier than simply allocating funds based on the broad market indexes, the respective Sharpe ratios being 1.12 and 1.94 (see Table 11.4, Cavaglia *et al.*, 1994). Of course, if one adopts the cross-industry strategy, the final allocation of funds across different countries (i.e. the sum of the optimal industry weights in each country) will in general be very different to the optimal country weights obtained with the broad market indexing strategy. For example, the US allocation of funds in the cross-industry strategy is $w_{us} = 27\%$, whereas for the broad market strategy 62% of the total portfolio is held in US-denominated assets (see Table 11.5, Cavaglia *et al.* 1994).

Cavaglia and Cuthbertson (1995) extend the above analysis to include *rolling forecasts* of the expected returns and variances and covariances as inputs to the portfolio problem and uses these to calculate optimal portfolio weights. The results are qualitatively similar to those reported above.

Key factors in international portfolio allocation

One important question an investor has to address is whether *always to fully hedge* the expected future foreign currency receipts. The answer lies in the correlations between returns on domestic and foreign stock markets and their correlation with the return on the spot currencies. An unhedged position adds an extra element of risk, namely the variance of the spot FX rate, and often exchange-rate volatility can be quite substantial, sometimes even exceeding the volatility in the stock market. However, an unhedged portfolio also gives rise to the possibility of low (or negative) correlations between the spot FX rate and either the domestic stock market or the foreign stock market, or both. These correlations may offset the impact of the high variance of the spot FX rates and hence reduce the overall portfolio variance of the *unhedged portfolio*.

However, there are many more factors to consider in evaluating international diversification. These include:

- How many countries to include in the study and how many assets within each country (e.g. only stocks, or bonds or property, or some combination of each).
- What the numeraire currency (i.e. home country) in which we measure returns and risk will be. Results are not invariant to the choice of home currency or the time horizon (e.g. one month or one year) over which returns are measured.
- We must consider expected returns as well as risk and provide a measure of portfolio performance that includes both (e.g. the Sharpe ratio).

- It may be just as beneficial in practice if we use some simple method of international portfolio diversification (e.g. an equally weighted allocation between alternative countries or an allocation based on a set of existing weights, as in Morgan Stanley's Capital International World Index).
- Whether to hedge or not hedge prospective foreign currency receipts. The practical and important detail is that any foreign currency receipts may be uncertain (e.g. the next dividend payment is not known with certainty and neither is the selling price) and hence it may be worth hedging using options or futures/forwards.
- Alternative forecasts of changes in exchange rates (e.g. historical arithmetic averages, random walk model, use of the forward rate as a predictor of next period's spot rate) give rise to different unhedged optimal portfolio weights, as do different forecasts of variances and covariances (correlations).
- The different optimal portfolio weights using different forecasting schemes may not be statistically different from each other, if the alternative forecasting schemes have wide margins of error.

We can only briefly deal with these issues in this chapter, but it is worth noting the results in Eun and Resnick (1997), who consider a number of these crucial issues. They consider the home country as the US, use a monthly return horizon and six foreign-country stock indices (Canada, France, Germany, Japan, Switzerland and the UK). They use simple historical arithmetic averages to measure the variances and covariances of returns, but because the optimal portfolio weights are rather sensitive to changes in expected returns, they consider a number of alternative forecasting schemes. They measure these variables using in-sample data and calculate the optimal portfolio weights. But they then compare the outcome for the portfolio return and standard deviation for ex-ante portfolios, over a 12-month 'out of sample' period (using a 'bootstrapping' method). They use the Sharpe ratio to determine the optimal portfolio weights. In broad terms they find that for a US-based investor:

- For an unhedged portfolio, investing in an internationally diversified portfolio gives results that are superior (in terms of the Sharpe ratio or 'stochastic dominance analysis') to investing solely in US stocks. This result applies irrespective of whether the international portfolio comprises an equally weighted portfolio or weights equal to those in Morgan Stanley's Capital International World Index or the optimal weights given by mean-variance analysis. However, the gains to an unhedged internationally diversified strategy are only *marginally better* than a solely domestic investment, at least for a US investor. (Clearly this result may not hold for an investor based in a small country where international diversification, even if unhedged, may be a substantial improvement on a purely domestic strategy).
- When considering the hedging decision, fully hedging using forward contracts nearly always produces superior results than not hedging (e.g. this applies whether one uses the optimal portfolio weights, the equally weighted portfolio or the weights in Morgan Stanley's Capital International World Index). Also, the use of the forward market is usually superior to using a protective put to hedge foreign currency receipts. Hence there is reasonably strong evidence that for the US investor, if she diversifies internationally it pays to fully hedge the foreign currency receipts in some way.
- They also find that using this month's spot rate as the best forecast of next month's spot rate (i.e. the random walk model) provides a better forecast than using the current quote forward rate to predict next period's spot rate. (This probably implies that the forward rate is a biased predictor of next period's spot FX rate.)

It appears from the above evidence that there are gains to be had by investing internationally, even for a US resident, whose domestic market makes up nearly half of world stock market capitalisation. It is therefore something of a puzzle why, in practice, there is so little international diversification. This 'home bias puzzle' is outlined in Case Study 11.1.

CASE STUDY 11.1   HOME BIAS PUZZLE

Porfolio theory suggests possible gains from international diversification when domestic and foreign returns have lower correlations than those between purely domestic securities, or if exchange-rate movements lower these correlations. It has been estimated that a US resident would have been 10–50% better off investing internationally (in the G7 counties) than purely domestically. However, somewhat paradoxically, US residents keep over 85% of their assets in the US. This also applies to investors in other countries, although the figure for other countries is usually less than this 90% in domestic assets – for example, UK pension funds currently have about a 30:70 home: foreign country split. The problem is so pervasive that it is known as the *home bias puzzle*. It appears as if neither the risk of imposition of capital controls nor high taxes on foreign investments can explain why these apparent gains to holding foreign equity are not exploited.

One reason for this home bias may be a perceived lack of information about the detailed performance of many foreign-based companies (e.g. small foreign firms). Also, sometimes there are legal restrictions on foreign investments. For example, some pension funds are restricted in the range of assets in which they can invest and this may include foreign assets. Another reason for home bias is that a 'proven gain' using past data does not necessarily imply a gain in the (uncertain) future. Yet another reason investors might not diversify internationally is that they wish to consume mainly *home-country* goods and services with the proceeds from their investments. Deviations from *purchasing power parity* can be large (e.g. plus or minus 20%) over, say, a 5–10-year horizon and this introduces uncertainty, since you may wish to cash in your foreign investments just when the exchange rate is least favourable to you when switching funds to purchase home goods. With increasing globalisation, equity returns across different countries have become more positively correlated, althought in principle they still allow for mean-variance gains (at least ex-ante). With the cost of information flows becoming lower (e.g. the prospect of increased information on foreign companies and real-time stock-price quotes and dealing over the Internet), it is always possible that the home bias problem may attenuate and investors may become more willing to diversify internationally.

On the other hand, some argue that the home bias problem is illusory once one takes into account the fact that the inputs to the mean-variance optimisation problem are measured with huge uncertainty. Although a US investor holding her stocks in the same proportions as in the S&P 500 may not hold precisely the mean-variance optimum proportions, nevertheless her S&P 500-indexed portfolio may be within a 95% confidence band of this optimum position. This argument may apply with even greater force if we recognise that in the real world, we need to make a genuine forecast of the inputs (i.e. forecasts of expected returns and the variance–covariance matrix) to the mean-variance optimisation problem. If we take account of uncertainty in our forecasts of foreign markets, the S&P 500-indexed portfolio may actually do as well as or even outperform the optimum mean-variance international portfolio.

There is also the technical issue addressed in the text, that an 'industry allocation' rather than a 'country allocation' is the correct focus for the application of mean-variance analysis and there is no reason the former may not give a higher weight to domestic assets. So there are plenty of practical reasons why the 'theoretical optimum' from applying mean-variance portfolio theory to international diversification may not be the best outcome in practice.

11.2 MEAN-VARIANCE OPTIMISATION IN PRACTICE

It is probably true to say that a large proportion of investment funds are not allocated on the basis of mean-variance optimisation. Usually, a wide variety of criteria such as political risk, business risk and the state of the economic cycle are used in a relatively informal way by the investment policy committee (of a large investment company) to determine asset allocation across different countries. What are the problems associated with the pure application of mean-variance optimisation as espoused in the textbooks that make it difficult to apply in practice? Most obviously, it only deals with risk as measured by the variance–covariance matrix and not other forms of risk (e.g. political risk) and (in its simplest form) it only covers one specific time horizon (e.g. one month or one year etc.). However, the main reason it is not widely used is that it is somewhat of a 'black box' and the results are subject to potentially large estimation errors.

Estimation errors

For 11 developed stock markets (including the largest five markets), Britten-Jones (1999) estimated the optimum mean-variance portfolio weights and their standard errors – which turned out to be very large. Using monthly data over a 20-year horizon, from 1977 to 1996, the optimal weights varied tremendously, for example from −45.2% for Canada (indicating short selling Canada on a massive scale) to 59.3% for the US. When testing to see if these *estimates* of the optimal weights are statistically significantly different from zero, Britten-Jones finds that very often they are not. For example, the t-statistics for the weights for the US are 1.26 and for Canada *minus* 1.16 – both indicate that the standard errors of the point estimates are so large that their true values could just as easily be zero. Hence on statistical grounds it is difficult to argue with an investor if she only invests in shares of her own country or forms an equally weighted portfolio that is not based on any form of mean-variance optimisation.

Let us consider possible estimation errors in a little more detail. Suppose that (continuously compounded) monthly returns are random (strictly, they are identically and independently distributed), with a constant true population mean $\mu = 1\%$ p.m. (12% p.a.) and true population standard deviation $\sigma = 4\%$ p.m. (13.86% p.a.). Then it can be shown that the best *estimates* of these 'true' parameters are:

$$\overline{R} = \frac{\sum_{i=1}^{n} R_i}{n} \tag{3a}$$

$$\hat{\sigma} = \sqrt{\frac{\sum_{i=1}^{n} (R_i - \overline{R})^2}{n - 1}} \tag{3b}$$

The above formulae can be applied to the appropriate mean return and standard deviation for any particular horizon (e.g. daily, weekly, monthly returns) – we ignore complexities due to the use of overlapping data. Suppose we make the heroic assumption that these *estimates* from our fixed set of data happen to be equal to the true values, so $\overline{R} = 1\%$ p.m. and $\hat{\sigma} = 4\%$ p.m[1]. It can be shown that the error in estimating the true mean μ, when using the arithmetic mean $\overline{R}$, is given by:

$$\sigma(\overline{R}) = \frac{\sigma}{\sqrt{n}} \tag{4}$$

Suppose we wanted to obtain an estimate of the 'true' mean return of $\mu = 1\%$ p.m. that was accurate to $\pm 0.1\%$[2]. Given that $\sigma = 4\%$ p.m., this would require n $= 4^2/(0.1)^2 = 1600$ monthly observations; that is, 133 years of monthly data! If we had 1600 monthly observations (assuming monthly returns are normally distributed), we could then be 95% certain that the true mean return was somewhere between 0.8% and 1.2% p.m. ($\approx 1 \pm 2\,(0.1)$). Clearly, the accuracy of our estimate of the mean return obtained from a moderate sample of, say, 60 monthly observations (i.e. five years) will be very poor. For example, for n $= 60, \sigma(\overline{R}) = \sigma/\sqrt{n} = 0.52\%$, so the error is more than half the true mean of $\mu = 1\%$ p.m. Here we can be 95% certain that the true mean lies between 0.04 and 2.04% p.m. ($\approx 1 \pm 2\,(0.52)$), but this is a very large error band.

There is an additional problem. If the population mean is not constant over time, then even using a lot of past data will not provide an accurate estimate, as data from the beginning of the period will not provide an accurate representation of the changing population mean. Hence, analysts tend to use other methods to estimate expected returns. They might use an estimate of expected returns from the SIM or the security market line (SML), or even use predictions from the APT and other multifactor models of expected returns. They will also combine these estimates with ancillary information on the firm or sector's company reports – this is a form of Bayesian estimation.

What about the accuracy of our estimate of the sample standard deviation $\hat{\sigma} = 4\%$ p.m.? Of course, above we assumed that this is the same as the 'true' standard deviation – but in reality we cannot know this, we can only obtain an estimate of its true value. If we assume that returns are random (strictly, that they are identical and independently distributed), then the error in using the estimator $\hat{\sigma}$ to measure the true standard deviation σ is given by:

---

[1] Remember that because of estimation error, it is rather unlikely that your *estimates* will turn out to be (exactly) equal to their 'true' values – so we are presenting the most 'rosy' outcome here.

[2] To be precise, so that we are 68% certain that the true mean is in the range $\overline{R} \pm 0.1\%$. Here we also assume that monthly returns are normally distributed.

$$\text{stdv}(\hat{\sigma}) = \frac{\sqrt{2}\,\sigma^2}{\sqrt{n-1}} \tag{5}$$

Suppose we used 5 years (n = 60 monthly observations) of data to estimate the standard deviation of returns, $\hat{\sigma} = 4\%$ p.m. The error in this estimate is $\text{stdv}(\hat{\sigma}) = \dfrac{\sqrt{2}\,(4^2)}{\sqrt{60-1}} = 0.38\%$ p.m. Hence the accuracy of our estimate $\hat{\sigma} = 4\%$ p.m. is pretty good, since the error is relatively small at 0.38% p.m. (i.e. 9.5% of its estimated value). We can be 95% certain that the 'true' population standard deviation σ (which is unobservable) lies between 3.24 and 4.76 (= $4 \pm 2(0.38)$), which is quite a small error band[3]. Hence, it just happens to be the case that with a given set of data, estimates of variances (and covariances) are subject to much less error (relatively speaking) than are estimates of expected returns.

Black box?

The 'black-box' element in mean-variance portfolio analysis arises because the optimal weights w_i^* simply 'pop out' of the maximisation procedure and it is often difficult (especially with many assets) to undertake a sensitivity analysis that is tractable and easy to understand. Estimation error arises because the inputs – that is, the forecast of returns (*ER*) and of the elements of the variance–covariance matrix $\{\sigma_{ij}\}$ – may provide poor predictions of what actually happens in the future. The 'optimiser' will significantly overweight (underweight) those securities that have large (small) forecast returns; negative (positive) estimated covariances and small (large) variances. Generally, it is the bias in forecasts of expected returns that is the major source of error; by comparison, forecasts of the σ_{ij} are reasonably good.

Generally, historical averages of past returns (e.g. the sample mean return over a given window of recent data) are used to measure future expected returns. These methods can be improved on, for example by using more sophisticated recursive multivariate regressions, time-varying parameter models or pure time series models (e.g. ARIMA and the stochastic trend model), Bayesian estimators and most recently, predictions based on neural networks.

Forecasts of the variances and covariances can be based on exponentially weighted moving averages (EWMA) or even simple ARCH and GARCH models (see Cuthbertson and Nitzsche, 2004 for a survey). Essentially, these methods assume that the variance (or covariance) is a weighted average of past *squared* returns. Of course, they involve increased computing costs and more importantly costs in interpeting the results for higher management who may be somewhat sceptical and lack technical expertise. However, we have little or no evidence on how these more sophisticated alternatives might reduce the 'estimation error' in the mean-variance optimisation problem. But Simmons (2000) provides a simple yet revealing sensitivity analysis. She uses historical sample averages for ER and the variance–covariances

---

[3] Again we are assuming normally distributed returns or that we have a large number of observations so that the central limit theorem applies.

and calculates the optimal weights (from a US perspective). She assumes no short sales, and includes US equities, US bonds, US money-market assets, European stocks and Pacific stocks as the set of portfolio assets. She then repeats the exercise using EWMA forecasts for variances and covariances and finds a dramatic change in the optimal weights. This demonstates the extreme sensitivity of mean-variance analysis to seemingly innocuous changes in the inputs.

What evidence we do have (e.g. Frost and Savarino, 1988; Jobson and Korkie, 1980, 1981) on the estimation error from mean-variance optimisation uses simple historical sample averages for forecasts of R_i and σ_{ij}. As we shall see, in general these studies suggest that the best strategy is to constrain the weight attached to any single security to a relatively small value, possibly in the range 2–5% of portfolio value, and one should also disallow short sales or buying on margin.

A technique known as *Monte Carlo simulation* allows you to measure the estimation error implicit in using the M-V optimiser. Monte Carlo simulation allows repeated samples of asset returns and the variance–covariance matrix to be generated. For each run of simulated data, we can calculate the estimated optimal portfolio return R_p, its standard deviation σ_p and hence the Sharpe ratio $((R_p - r)/\sigma_p)$. We then compare these simulated outcomes with the known 'true' values given from the underlying known distribution. The procedure involves the following steps where:

n = number of assets in the chosen portfolio (e.g. 20)

m = number of simulation runs in the Monte Carlo analysis

q = length of data sample used in calculating mean returns and the variances and covariances

1. Assume that returns are multivariate normal with true mean returns μ_i and variance–covariance matrix $\Sigma = \{\sigma_{ij}\}$. In the two-asset case the 'true values' of $\mu_1, \mu_2, \sigma_1, \sigma_2$ and σ_{12} will be based on historical sample averages using $q = 60$ data points (say). But from this point on we assume that these values are known *constants*. We know the true 'population parameters' $\mu_i, \{\sigma_{ij}\}$ and can therefore calculate the true optimal weights w_i^* and the true optimal portfolio returns $R_p^* = \sum_{i=1}^{n} w_i^* \mu_i$ and standard deviation σ_p^* that maximise the Sharpe ratio, $SR = (ER_p^* - r)/\sigma_p^*$.

2. Assume asset returns are generated from a multivariate normal distribution, which encapsulates the correlation structure between the asset returns:

$$R_i = \mu_i + \varepsilon_i$$

where ε_i is drawn from a multivariate normal distribution, with known variance–covariance matrix Σ, as noted above. Now generate $q = 60$ simulated returns R_i for each of the $i = 1, 2, \ldots, n$ assets. This is our first Monte Carlo run (i.e. $m = 1$).

3. With the $q = 60$ data points for each return series, calculate the sample average returns $E\hat{R}_i^{(1)} = \sum_{i=1}^{q} \frac{R_i^{(1)}}{q}$ and variance–covariance matrix $\Sigma^{(1)}$. Then use these as inputs to solve the portfolio-maximisation problem to give our 'first-run' values for the *simulated* optimal portfolio weights $\hat{w}_i$, portfolio return and its variance $(\hat{R}_p, \hat{\sigma}_p)^{(1)}$.

4. Repeat steps (2) and (3) m times and use the m-generated values of $(\hat{R}_p, \hat{\sigma}_p)$ to obtain their average values (over m runs), which we denote $(\overline{R}_p, \overline{\sigma}_p)$ together with the average Sharpe ratio $\hat{S} = \dfrac{(\overline{R}_p - r)}{\overline{\sigma}_p}$. We can compare these averages from the Monte Carlo simulation with the known true values $(R_p^*, \sigma_p^*$ and $\sigma^*)$ to provide a measure of the bias produced by our estimation method for expected returns and covariances.

Some empirical results from Jobson and Korkie (1980) for monthly returns on 20 stocks generated from a known multivariate distribution show that the Sharpe ratios for the simulated data $(\overline{R}_p, \overline{\sigma}_p)$, the known population parameters (R_p^*, σ_p^*) and an equally weighted portfolio were vastly different at 0.08, 0.34 and 0.27 respectively. Hence, estimation error can be substantial and radically alters the risk–return trade-off.

Frost and Savarino (1988), in a similar experiment, found that the biases $\overline{R}_p - R_p^*$ and $\overline{\sigma}_p - \sigma_p^*$ (particularly the former) fell dramatically as the portfolio weights in any one asset are restricted to a small positive value and if no short sales are allowed. In addition, for investors who are either twice or half as risk averse as the market investor, the best outcome (in terms of certainty-equivalent returns) occurs if the M-V optimisation is undertaken under the restriction that no more than about 3–5% is held in any one security. Also, note that either short selling or buying on margin considerably worsens performance. Thus it appears that mean-variance optimisation can provide some improvement (albeit not large) in portfolio performance as long as some restrictions are placed on the optimisation problem.

Index tracking in equity markets using market value weights (w_{im}) is fairly commonplace. One constrained optimisation strategy is to maximise the Sharpe ratio subject to the optimal weights (w_i^*) not being more than, say, 2% from the current market weights for that stock (i.e. $\hat{w}_i^* = w_{im} \pm 0.02 w_{im}$). Cavaglia et al. (1994) find that the Sharpe ratio can be improved for an international equity portfolio (i.e. one that includes equity held in a large number of countries) as one moves a small 'distance' away from the current market value weights. It is also the case in practice that no investment manager would believe the optimal weights if these are not close to her intuitive notions of what is 'reasonable'. Indeed, UK pension funds rarely invest more than 5% of their equity portfolio in a single stock (even though an indexing strategy on the FTSE 100 would involve holding about 15% in Vodafone and a Finnish pension fund would have to hold over 50% in Nokia!).

Some constraints need to be placed on the weights obtained from the M-V optimiser if unrestricted optimisation means that the investor holds a significant percentage of any one firm or industry sector (e.g. as might be the case when holding 90% of your wealth in small-cap stocks or a large proportion of stocks in emerging markets). Unconstrained optimisation, which allows short selling, often results in weights implying that you should short sell large amounts of one stock and use the proceeds to invest long in another stock. Practitioners would simply not believe that such strategy would be successful, ex-post (i.e. after the event).

There have been attempts to see if a given portfolio is close to, in a statistical sense, the M-V optimal portfolio (e.g. Jobson and Korkie, 1980). However, such tests appear to have low power (i.e. they tend not to reject mean-variance efficiency when it is false) and do not allow for inequality constraints (e.g. no short selling), so this approach is not often used in practice.

It is also worth noting that there are some technical problems in calculating the optimal weights. If the covariance matrix is large, there may be problems in inverting it and then the optimal weights may be very sensitive to slight changes in the estimated covariances.

It remains the case that, for all its elegance, mean-variance optimisation is in practice merely one method of deciding on portfolio allocation. Other judgmental factors such as an assessment of political risk and the state of the economic cycle in different countries or industries play as important a role as 'pure' mean-variance analysis. Current market-value proportions as embodied in the S&P index (for example) would not be the same as those given by an unconstrained mean-variance analysis (e.g. one that uses sample averages as forecasts of the mean return and the covariance matrix). Therefore in practice, mean-variance analysis tends to be used to see if new forecasts of R_i and σ_{ij} provide some improvement in the Sharpe ratio. Sensitivity analysis is also usually conducted with 'user-imposed' changes in key returns and covariances (rather than basing them on historical averages) and then seeing how much this might improve the Sharpe ratio. As the scenarios change, if the optimal weights w_i^* vary greatly in the unconstrained optimisation problem, then some constraints will be placed on the w_i^* (e.g. that the new optimal proportions do not vary greatly from the current market value 'index-tracking' weights and also perhaps that no short selling is allowed). In summary, our overall conclusions might be that mean-variance optimisation is useful if:

- Portfolio weights are constrained to a certain extent (e.g. hold less than 5% of value in any one asset, do not move more than 2% away from the market index weight or do not allow short sales).
- Better forecasts of returns R_i and covariances $\{\sigma_{ij}\}$ are used in place of historical averages.
- A small number of assets are used (e.g. using mean-variance optimisation for allocation between, say, 20 country indexes) so that transparency and sensitivity analysis are possible.

11.3 PORTFOLIO ALLOCATION: KEY QUESTIONS

There are billions of funds under management in investment companies around the world. These funds are often managed by independent advisers such as Vanguard and Fidelity Investments or Aberdeen Asset Management, or 'in house' by large pension funds or insurance companies. How do they decide on their optimal asset allocation and changes in this allocation? First, they will have an existing position which they, along with their clients (e.g. the trustees of a pension fund), are broadly happy with. This initial allocation will almost certainly not be the result of unconstrained mean-variance analysis as outlined in the textbooks. It will involve the following key considerations:

- Can we get most of our diversification benefits from purely domestic investment? Clearly, the answer will be broadly 'yes' if the domestic economy is large as in the US or in the countries covered by the Euro. The answer may be 'no' for small open economies: those in the Far East (Singapore, Thailand, Malaysia, etc.), in Eastern Europe (Czech Republic, Hungary, Poland, etc.) and even for the economies of South America.

- How far should we diversify internationally, given the domestic currency base of our investors? (At present the bulk of pension recipients usually want to spend most of their pension in the domestic economy.) If we do invest abroad, should we hedge or not hedge the foreign currency receipts?

It is likely that of the funds allocated domestically and internationally, some will be 'index trackers' – that is the proportions will mimic those of some broad market index (e.g. FTSE 100, S&P 500). The domestic/international allocation will probably be decided largely on ad hoc grounds, with most allocated to domestic currency assets. Allocation to specific foreign countries may mimic the proportions in some world indices (e.g. Morgan Stanley's World Index excluding the domestic economy) or tempered by perceptions of political risk and perhaps a general 'gut feeling' about the future performance of these economies. A large proportion of funds will be invested in actively managed mutual funds – recently alternative investments such as hedge funds and private equity have attracted more funds.

Probably many active mutual funds are 'covert trackers' and use only a proportion of their assets to try to 'pick winners'. Tracking a chosen benchmark is transparent – pension fund trustees are clear about the benchmark adopted. Index tracking is a **passive asset-allocation strategy**. This does not mean that no effort is required! The investment manager still has to decide on the subset of assets in the broad market index (e.g. S&P 500) that will best track the index.

Often the optimal mean-variance asset allocation will be judged against this baseline index tracker position. Hence, the optimal mean-variance weights might be calculated (based on forecasts of expected returns and covariances), but these would be highly constrained so that the final weights produced by the optimiser do not move more than 10% from their current index tracker values (e.g. from 20% to 22%).

Most mutual funds claim to be **'active' funds**, looking for 'winner stocks'. The possible variants here are numerous. If the asset manager 'places bets' on the direction of, say, stock and bond prices and switches between these two assets and a safe asset (e.g. bank deposit or T-bill) based on her view of the future state of the macro-economy, this is generally known as **market timing**. Gambling on the *longer-term* behaviour of economies (e.g. the Asian economies, the emerging markets of Eastern Europe and countries in South America) is often referred to as **strategic asset allocation**. Switching funds between countries based on short-run views about the state of the economic cycle (e.g. the US is entering an expansionary phase and Japan a contractionary one) is often referred to as **tactical asset allocation**. Clearly, the use of these terms is far from precise. *Hedge funds* use active portfolio management techniques and usually have highly leveraged positions, either by buying on margin or using derivatives. Because of this leverage, hedge funds can often produce high returns on own capital invested, but they can also be extremely risky investments.

We do not have enough space here to explain fully the basis of fundamental models of forecasting expected returns for use in active portfolio management, and indeed different analysts will have different models. These often consist of regressions of stock returns on fundamental variables such as the price–earnings ratio, book-to-market ratio or term structure variables such as the spread between high-grade and low-grade corporate bonds. They hope that these 'signals' will help predict tomorrow's returns in a repeated gamble, after correcting for risk and transaction costs. Often the 'model' will not be explicit (even within the management company) and may remain in the analyst's head. This is useful, since the accuracy of the model cannot be verified and she can change her 'story' (i.e. the model in her head) to accommodate any new facts that do not fit in with her previous investment pronouncements. Of course, it may be that stock returns cannot be modelled in a formal way, although this does not excuse active portfolio managers whose investment decisions result in a Sharpe ratio below that given by a broad market index. Since the latter outcome appears to occur with remarkable frequency (see for example Timmermann and Blake, 1999), we can most charitably view these active portfolio managers as satisfying the human craving for a story to explain recent events, even though the stories lack coherence and consistency and are no help whatsoever in predicting what will actually happen in the future – soothsayers are alive and well and earning good money in the major financial centres around the world!

SUMMARY

- There are gains to diversification using only a small number of assets (about 35). Greater risk reduction can be obtained if we diversify internationally, even if we *randomly* choose the diversified set of stocks.
- When we consider expected return and risk, international diversification generally improves the risk–return trade-off (i.e. pushes the efficient frontier to the left), particularly if the foreign returns are hedged with forwards, futures or options. The improvement from international diversification is more debatable when returns are unhedged and must be examined on a case-by-case basis for a particular home-currency investor.
- Diversification can proceed on the basis of a random selection of stocks, or an equally weighted portfolio, or tracking a broad market index (e.g. Morgan Stanley World Index) or using a mean-variance optimiser.
- The main problem in accepting the results from a totally unconstrained mean-variance analysis is that the optimal proportions (weights) are very sensitive to forecasts of expected returns and to stock returns that have either very high or very low forecast variances. In practice, therefore, the optimal proportions are constrained in some way (e.g. that they must not differ from the current proportions by more than 2%).
- There are many asset-allocation strategies. Indexing is a passive strategy. Some portfolio managers try to time the market while others look for 'winner stocks' or 'winner countries' – these are active strategies.

EXERCISES

Q1   Why might portfolio variance fall as we add foreign assets to our domestic portfolio?

Q2   What does 'hedging foreign currency receipts' mean? Is it possible to perfectly hedge receipts from a portfolio of foreign stocks?

Q3   What is market timing?

Q4   Why might an (unhedged) internationally diversified portfolio have a lower standard deviation than a purely domestic portfolio even though exchange rates are themselves highly volatile?

Q5   What is the 'home bias problem' and why is it difficult to ascertain whether this really is a genuine puzzle (or anomaly)?

Show how the (uncovered) return in US dollars to a US investor from investing in the DAX (i.e. the German stock index) is given by

$$R_{us} = R_{DAX} + R_{\$/E}$$

where $R_{\$/E}$ is the annual return on the USD/EURO exchange rate.

Q6   Let S_0 = current spot rate (US dollars per Euro). Suppose a US investor has \$A and she wants to invest in the DAX. First, she switches the \$A into Euros and obtains A/S_0 Euros. Investing A/S_0 Euros in the DAX results in a payout of $A/S_0 (1 + R_{DAX})$ in Euros after one year (where R_{DAX} is the annual return on the DAX). These Euros are then converted back to US dollars at the rate S_1, the spot rate in one year's time. The appreciation (return) on the Euro $R_{\$/E} = S_1/S_0 - 1$. Show that the percentage return to the US investor *in US dollars* is:

$$\% \text{ Return in } \$ = \frac{A(1 + R_{\$/E})(1 + R_{DAX})}{A} - 1 \qquad [1]$$

If we assume ($R_{\$/E} \times R_{DAX}$) is small relative to $R_{\$/E}$ or R_{DAX}, then show that [1] approximates to:

Return in $ = R_{DAX} + R_{\$/E}$

Q7   What are the key issues in deciding whether to hedge an internationally diversified portfolio using the forward currency markets?

12

Single-Index Model

AIMS

- To show how the stock return for a specific company is influenced by two sources of risk. The first arises from systematic economy-wide (macroeconomic) factors such as interest rates, oil prices and so on. The second is the firm-specific (micro-economic) component of risk due to random factors such as strikes, technological breakdowns, patent applications, legal cases and so on.
- To show how to estimate the single-index model (SIM), which uses the return on a broad-based stock-market index as the chosen 'systematic factor'.
- To show how the market model can be used to simplify the inputs required to calculate the optimal portfolio weights (i.e. the 'tangent' portfolio) for the risky assets held in your portfolio.
- To show how the SIM and multifactor models can be used to provide a measure of risk-adjusted portfolio performance based on 'alpha'.
- To demonstrate how the SIM can be used in 'event studies' to calculate the impact on stock returns (and hence the equity value of the firm) of an event such as an announcement of a takeover bid or higher than expected earnings.

12.1 FACTOR MODELS

We know from the chapter on portfolio theory that stock returns for a particular firm are influenced by specific (or microeconomic) risks of that firm such as strikes, patent applications and so on. Clearly, changes in macroeconomic variables, such as interest rates, economic growth, inflation or oil prices, are also likely to have an effect on the stock returns of *many different* companies, but the quantitative impact of these systematic (macro) factors on each company will be different. For example, one might expect that the return on the shares in an airline would move more in response to changes in oil prices than would the share price of a telecommunications company. Instead of assuming that movements in a company's stock returns are explained by several different factors, we could simplify matters and choose one variable (factor) that we thought explained movements in most stock returns reasonably well. This would be a **single-factor model**:

$$R_i = \alpha_i + \beta_i F + \varepsilon_i \qquad [1]$$

It is unlikely that any *single* macroeconomic factor will explain movements in a specific company's stock return very accurately. Therefore, practitioners argue that as several macroeconomic variables are likely to affect almost all stocks (to some extent), the best single factor to explain the *individual* returns of most companies is a broad-market stock-return index, such as the S&P 500 (for US firms) or the FTSE All-share index (for UK firms). When the single factor chosen is a market index, the single factor model is known as the **single-index model (SIM)**:

$$\tilde{R}_i = \alpha_i + \beta_i \tilde{R}_m + \varepsilon_i \qquad [2]$$

where a tilde over a variable indicates an *excess* return, for example, $\tilde{R}_i = R_i - r$. When using the market model practitioners are not always consistent in their use of excess returns $\tilde{R}_i = R_i - r$ versus returns R_i. Often in practice this does not matter too much, as changes in the risk-free rate are small relative to changes in stock returns, so practitioners use the form for the SIM that is most convenient. The SIM is not really a 'model' in the sense that it embodies any specific ideas about the behaviour of investors in the market, but is best viewed as a *statistical model,* which assumes that the return on *any* stock R_i may be partly explained by movements in the market return. The SIM implies that a stock has two sources of risk, a systematic or market component (which affects all stocks to some extent) and a firm-specific component represented by ε_i. There is no correlation between the market return R_m and the firm-specific risk ε_i, simply because strikes, patent applications and so on occur independently of the state of the overall stock market. It follows that the variability in any individual stock return depends on the variability of the market factor and the variability in the firm-specific component:

$$\text{Total risk of stock } i = \text{Systematic risk} + \text{Firm-specific risk} \qquad [3]$$

$$\sigma_i^2 = \beta_i^2 \sigma_m^2 + \sigma^2(\varepsilon_i)$$

You can also write σ_i^2 as $\sigma^2(\tilde{R}_i)$ and σ_m^2 as $\sigma^2(\tilde{R}_m)$ if this makes the notation clearer. The systematic (market) risk of the individual stock is caused by movements in the overall stock market, which are then transmitted to the *individual* stock return, depending on the size of each firm's beta. So the systematic risk of the stock is crucially dependent on the stock's beta β_i (as well as the volatility of the overall market return, σ_m).

As we shall see, the variability in the firm's specific risk can often contribute as much to the overall variability in the stock return as does the variability in the systematic (market) risk. This should not be too surprising, as individual firms are subject to large firm-specific events that can affect the volatility of their share price. Firm-specific risk is sometimes positive $\varepsilon_i > 0$, causing a rise in the stock return (above normal), and sometimes negative $\varepsilon_i < 0$, having an adverse impact on the stock return. Although these specific risks average out to zero over time, they nevertheless are a major cause of volatility in the firm's stock return.

Let's look at an example. Figure 12.1 shows the excess return of British Airways stock together with the return on the market (i.e. FTSE All-share index). We can see that the BA stock return is more volatile than the market return. Regression estimates (see this chapter's Appendix and the web site) of the market model using 20 years of monthly data from September 1987 to August 2007 give:

$$\tilde{R}_{BA} = 0.0002 + 1.6066\,\tilde{R}_{FTSE} + \varepsilon_{BA} \qquad R^2 = 44.4\% \qquad\qquad [4]$$

$$(0.0055) \quad (0.1165)$$

The numbers in brackets are the standard errors of the estimated coefficients. The R-squared of the regression indicates that the market return explains 44.4% of the variation in the

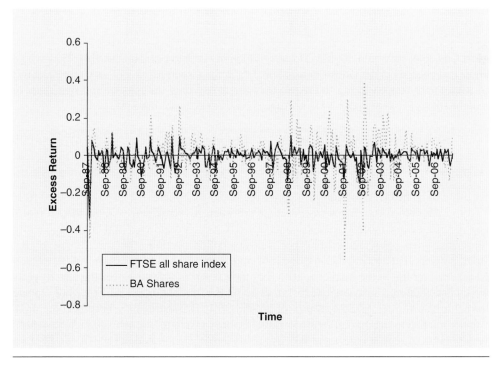

FIGURE 12.1: Excess returns (BA, FTSE All-share index)

(excess) return of BA stock. If the R-squared is unity, then all the points would line up exactly on the straight line. So an R-squared of 44% indicates that there will be a relatively large number of times that the actual returns are either above or below those predicted by the regression line – this represents the specific risk of BA's stock. The total risk for BA stocks and the contribution of market and specific risk are:

$$\text{Total risk of stock } i = \text{Systematic risk} + \text{Firm-specific risk} \qquad [5]$$

$$\sigma_i^2 = \beta_i^2 \sigma_m^2 + \sigma^2(\varepsilon_i)$$

The total risk of BA stocks is $\sigma_i^2 = 0.0131\%$ p.m. – market risk accounts for $\beta_i^2 \sigma_m^2 = 0.0058\%$ and specific risk for $\sigma^2(\varepsilon_i) = 0.0073\%$, so specific risk is a relatively large element of the total risk. Market risk for BA might arise from unexpected changes in oil prices or interest rates (which we hope are picked up by changes in the market return), while specific risk might include strikes, lost luggage, abnormal weather conditions and unforeseen maintenance costs).

The R-squared measures the ratio of systematic (market) risk to the total risk of BA's shares, which using [5] can be expressed:

$$\text{R-squared} = \beta_i^2 \sigma_m^2 / \sigma_i^2 = 1 - \sigma^2(\varepsilon_i)/\sigma_i^2 \qquad [6]$$

$$= 0.0058/0.0131 = 1 - (0.0073/0.0131) = 44.3\%$$

Given an R-squared of 44%, this means that around 56% of the variability in BA's observed stock return is due to firm-specific risks.

Most City analysts would not use 20 years of monthly data to estimate the SIM. They would argue that changes in the industry mean that data in the distant past is not very representative of what might happen in the future. So they might use only the most recent five years of monthly data (i.e. September 2002 to August 2007) to estimate the SIM, giving:

$$\tilde{R}_{BA} = 0.0038 + 2.5543 \, \tilde{R}_{FTSE} + \varepsilon_{BA} \qquad \text{R-sqrd} = 45.81\% \qquad [7]$$

$$(0.0116) \quad (0.3648)$$

By using only the last five years of data we see that the estimate of beta has increased from 1.61 to 2.55. Hence BA shares have become more sensitive to changes in the market return and therefore carry more systematic (market) risk, which requires a higher average return for shareholders. (Remember that in a well-diversified portfolio the specific risk of BA stock is diversified away and hence does not contribute to the average return.) If the expected (excess) return on the market is 10% p.a., then whereas investors over the last 20 years would have required an average (excess) return on BA of around 16% p.a., they now appear to require an average (excess) return of around 25%. BA shares may have become more volatile relative to the market return because of its exposure to oil prices (which have been very volatile in recent years) and because of its large pension deficit, which would make its profits more exposed to both the overall performance of the stock market and also to interest rates.

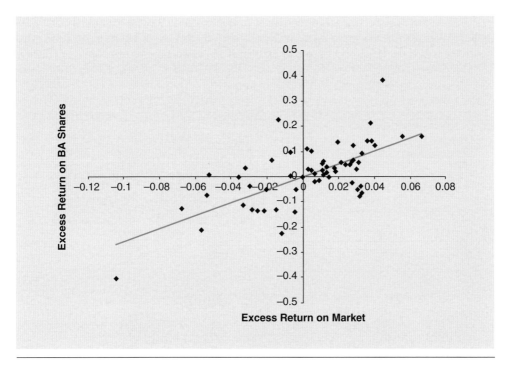

FIGURE 12.2: Excess returns – BA vs market returns

Figure 12.2 shows the scatter diagram of the (excess) returns of BA shares against the (excess) market return using only 60 observations. We can see that there is a positive relationship between BA returns and the market return with a beta value equal to 2.55.

On the London Stock Exchange, BA shares belong to the Travel and Leisure sector, which contains over 30 shares, including EasyJet, Thomas Cook, Intercontinental Hotels, National Express and Ladbrokes. The Travel and Leisure (T&L) index comprises all 30 shares and therefore is a more diversified portfolio than any of the firms taken in isolation. The SIM applied to the Travel and Leisure sector gives for the sample period September 1987 – August 2007:

$$\tilde{R}_{\text{Sector}} = 0.0009 + 1.0800\, \tilde{R}_{FTSE} + \varepsilon_{\text{Sector}} \qquad \text{R-sqrd} = 82.33\% \qquad [8]$$
$$\phantom{\tilde{R}_{\text{Sector}} = } (0.0023) \quad (0.0483)$$

and for the sample period September 2002–August 2007:

$$\tilde{R}_{\text{Sector}} = 0.0065 + 0.9978\, \tilde{R}_{FTSE} + \varepsilon_{\text{Sector}} \qquad \text{R-sqrd} = 77.32\% \qquad [9]$$
$$\phantom{\tilde{R}_{\text{Sector}} = } (0.0034) \quad (0.1075)$$

We might not be too surprised that the beta of the Travel and Leisure sector is close to unity and its firm-specific risk, $\sigma(\varepsilon_i) = 0.0354\%$ p.m., is less than the firm-specific risk for BA alone,

$\sigma(\varepsilon_{BA}) = 0.0854\%$ p.m., when using our 20-year sample. This is because the firm-specific risks of the individual firms that make up the index cancel each other out in a portfolio of firms. This is also the reason the R-squared values for the Travel and Leisure sector regressions are higher.

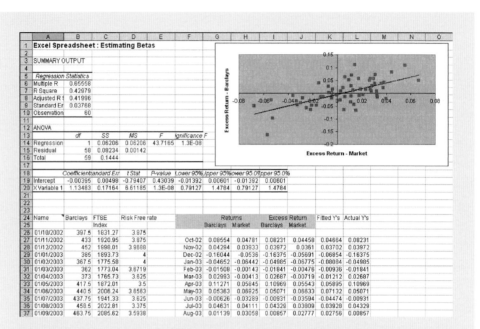

This spreadsheet uses the Regression Function in Excel's Data Analysis Tool. We calculate the OLS coefficients together with standard errors and other descriptive statistics, such as R^2 and the ANOVA test. The Excel function = LINEST might be useful if the regressions are being repeated many times (i.e. recursive estimation, estimating betas of many companies). From the estimated coefficients it is possible to calculate the 'fitted' y-values for the stock return, which are on the line given by OLS. The graph shows the excess return on Barclays' stock against the excess market return (FTSE index).

Various data providers (i.e. Bloomberg, Reuters, Datastream) calculate betas for their clients and Table 12.1 shows these betas for some UK companies. According to these estimates, British Airways and Rolls-Royce have betas near 2, which means that their stock returns move twice as much as any change in the market return. Marks & Spencer, a UK retailer, and British Petroleum stocks fluctuate less than the market return, as they have betas less than 1. The returns of GlaxoSmithKline, a leading UK pharmaceutical company, are not very highly correlated with the market return and have a beta of only 0.21. Of course, the overall volatility of each of these stock returns also depends on the individual firm's specific risk.

As you can see, estimates of betas can vary widely depending on the data period used in estimation or on which data provider you obtain your betas from. Because of the uncertainty

TABLE 12.1: Company betas, September 2007

Company	Beta
British Airways	1.896
BP	0.769
Rolls Royce	1.986
Marks and Spencer	0.637
Barclays	1.103
Glaxo Smith Klein	0.210

surrounding estimates of beta for individual firms, a weighting scheme is often used to obtain an 'adjusted beta' or 'smoothed beta' for the firm, which is a weighted average of the estimated beta and the market beta. If the 'weight' chosen is 2/3, our adjusted beta for BA is:

$$adj-\beta = (2/3)\beta_{\text{est}} + (1/3)\beta_m$$
$$= (2/3)[\beta_{\text{est}} - \beta_m] + \beta_m = (2/3)[2.55 - 1] + 1 = 2.03 \qquad [10]$$

where the market beta $\beta_m = 1$. Hence if the estimated beta is above 1 the adjusted beta is lower than the estimated beta – the formula pulls the estimated beta closer to 1. (This also applies if the estimated beta is below 1, say 0.5, since then the adjusted beta will be higher at 0.666 and closer to 1 than the estimated value.) The idea behind the adjustment is that statistically, it can be shown that the betas of many firms move towards 1 over time and we want our estimate of beta to be forward looking. The reason that betas of firms move towards 1 seems to be that as they grow, firms themselves become less specialised and hence become more like the 'average firm' in the market. The above equation also has an intuitive statistical rationale. When we are uncertain about a measured quantity like beta, our best estimate should combine our prior beliefs with our estimate based on the data. Our prior belief about any firm picked at random is that it is on average like the market as a whole and hence has a beta of 1 – we then combine this with our estimated beta to get the best estimate of the true beta. (This is a type of Bayesian estimator, where the weights depend on the uncertainty (standard error) attached to your estimate of the firm's beta relative to the uncertainty attached to your estimate of the market beta.)

Where do we get the 'weight' of 2/3 from? This is obtained by observing how quickly the betas of existing firms move towards 1, which can be obtained by regression techniques. Alternatively we can choose a value based on our implicit views about how quickly the particular firm we are examining will become like the average firm in the economy (or the average firm in its sector, since the sector beta, as we saw above, is usually close to one).

Alpha as a performance measure

It can be shown that 'alpha', the constant term in the SIM, is given by:

$$\alpha_i = (\bar{R}_i - \bar{r}) - \beta_i(\bar{R}_m - \bar{r}) \qquad [11]$$

where we have explicitly used excess returns in the SIM equation. According to the CAPM, the required return to compensate for market risk is $\beta_i(\bar{R}_m - \bar{r})$; see the next chapter. So alpha measures the actual average return minus the required return and is therefore a measure of the *abnormal return* on the stock. A positive alpha implies that the firm's stock has an average (excess) return, that is more than required to compensate for the (beta/systematic) risk of the stock. The alpha from a regression based on the SIM is a widely used measure of risk-adjusted performance, known as **Jensen's alpha**. The higher is alpha, the greater is the outperformance of the stock after correcting for risk.

Presumably, finding stocks with positive alphas is difficult, since this implies that they earn a return in excess of their systematic (market) risk premium. In our earlier example (using 20 years of monthly data) the alpha for BA is 0.0002% p.m., and 0.0038% p.m. when the sample period covers the last five years. Given the large standard errors on these coefficients, neither intercept is statistically significantly different from zero, so BA earns a return that just compensates for its beta risk. Similar results are obtained for the return on the portfolio of stocks in the Travel and Leisure sector.

The reason alpha is important as a **performance criterion** can most easily be seen in the following simple example. Suppose you have two risky diversified portfolios. The first has an expected return of 25%, a beta of one and a zero alpha. The second has an expected return of 17%, a beta of 0.5 but an alpha of 2%. Should you choose portfolio-1 as the best portfolio because it has the highest expected return? No, you should not if you are considering which portfolio will provide more return, *given its beta risk*. The market risk premium is 20%, so the following represents our initial situation:

$$ER_1 = r + \beta_1(ER_m - r) = 5 + (1)\,20 = 25\% \tag{12a}$$

$$ER_2 = \alpha_2 + r + \beta_2(ER_m - r) = 2 + 5 + (0.5)\,20 = 17\% \tag{12b}$$

Now consider combining each portfolio with the risk-free asset so that the two new portfolios have the same betas. If we put a proportion y_1 in risky portfolio-1 (and $1 - y_1$ in the risk-free asset) and y_2 in risky portfolio-2 (and $1 - y_2$ in the risk-free asset), the two betas in the two new portfolios will be $y_1\beta_1$ and $y_2\beta_2$ and for these to be equal:

$$y_1 = y_2(\beta_2/\beta_1) \tag{13}$$

Hence, if we arbitrarily let $y_2 = 50\%$ then $y_1 = 25\%$ and the expected returns on the two new portfolios are:

$$ER_{N1} = y_1[r + \beta_1(ER_m - r)] + (1 - y_1)r = 10\% \tag{14a}$$

$$ER_{N2} = y_2[r + \beta_2(ER_m - r)] + (1 - y_2)r + \alpha_2 y_2 = 12\% \tag{14b}$$

The betas on these two new portfolios, $y_1\beta_1$ and $y_2\beta_2$, are the same (by construction), so both new portfolios have the same systematic (market) risk. But the new portfolio-2, which combines the risky portfolio with positive alpha and the risk-free asset, has a higher expected return[1]. So a positive alpha security (or portfolio) will always give you a higher expected

---

[1] Portfolio-2 also has a higher Treynor ratio.

return once you have taken account of beta risk – and this is one reason security analysts talk in terms of finding 'high-alpha' securities. Of course, a high-alpha security is a violation of the CAPM/SML (see next chapter), but that's what stock analysts look for. The above suggests that if you find a security with a positive alpha and you add this to your already existing risky portfolio, then there could be some overall gain. This is because you can add this positive alpha security and increase expected portfolio return without adding any more systematic/beta risk – the latter is the incremental risk you add to overall portfolio variance, when adding the positive alpha security. Below, we discuss adding positive alpha securities to an existing portfolio and we find that this can lead to an increase in the Sharpe ratio.

Multifactor models

For some stocks or portfolios of stocks, it may be the case that we can improve on the SIM. There may be other systematic risk factors that influence stock returns of particular companies. A multifactor model may also improve the explanatory power and 'fit' of our equation. Above we noted that the R-squared of the SIM for BA is about 45%, although for some stocks it can be as high as 65%. However, there is still a substantial amount of variation in stock returns that is not explained by the market factor. Fama and French (1988) suggest using a three-factor model. They use the excess return on the market, but they also include a factor that accounts for the fact that small stocks are more risky than large stocks; and a factor to capture the idea that firms with high book-to-market value also tend to have high average returns. Those two additional factors are found to be important in the US and UK markets.

Carhart (1997) adds a variable that picks up the fact that stocks that have recently experienced high returns continue to have high returns over the next 3–12 months – this is the momentum factor. It has been shown to be important in accounting for the high average returns in the US, although in the UK the momentum factor is generally not statistically significant for well-diversified portfolios. The important thing is that even if we have extra factors in our regression, the intercept (alpha) still provides a valid measure of the *abnormal* return on a stock (or portfolio of stocks) and is therefore still a valid risk-adjusted performance measure. We discuss these multifactor models later in the book when we investigate the performance of active mutual funds.

12.2 PORTFOLIO INPUTS AND THE SIM

The SIM can be used to reduce the number of estimated parameters we require to determine our optimal portfolio of risky assets. For a portfolio of n securities we have:

$$ER_p = \sum_{i=1}^{n} w_i ER_i \tag{15}$$

$$\sigma_p^2 = \sum_{i=1}^{n} w_i \sigma_i^2 + \sum_{i=1}^{n} \sum_{j=1, i \neq j}^{n} w_i w_j \sigma_{ij} \tag{16}$$

If we directly estimate the variances and covariances using the usual textbook formulae, then we need to undertake a large number of calculations. In general, to calculate the optimal proportions to hold in the risky portfolio, we require forecasts of n expected returns ER_i, n

TABLE 12.2: SIM Regression – three stocks, monthly returns data

		alpha	beta	$\sigma(\varepsilon_i)$
Stock 1	BA	0.0038	2.5542	0.0879
Stock 2	M&S	0.0044	0.4425	0.0659
Stock 3	Barclays	−0.0030	1.1744	0.0356
Market return				
ER_m		0.0094		
σ_m		0.0316		

variances and $n(n - 1)/2$ separate covariances, to use as our inputs. It is the large number of covariances that is the main problem. If the SIM is a good statistical description of stock returns we know that[2]:

$$ER_i = \alpha_i + \beta_i ER_m \qquad [17]$$

$$\sigma_i^2 = \beta_i^2 \sigma_m^2 + \sigma^2(\varepsilon_i) \qquad [18]$$

So for each stock i we can calculate the n expected returns and n variances once we have estimated the SIM for each stock (and made our forecast for the expected market return). What about the covariances? The SIM makes an additional assumption, namely that the firm-specific risk between any two firms is zero (on average). What this means, for example, is that if you observe a strike at one particular firm in a certain week, then most other firms will probably not have a strike. Clearly, this may not always be true of firms in the same industrial sector, but it is likely to be true for the many other firms outside this specific sector. Mathematically this implies that for any two firms, ε_i and ε_j are independent (i.e. not correlated). In the SIM the covariance between any two stock returns is then:

$$cov(R_i,R_j) = cov(\alpha_i + \beta_i R_m + \varepsilon_i, \alpha_j + \beta_j R_m + \varepsilon_j) = \beta_i \beta_j \sigma_m^2 \qquad [19]$$

The only source of common variation in the returns of any two stocks is the variation in the market return, which affects each stock return via each stock's beta. Hence, the only additional input we need to calculate *all* the covariances is the variance of the market return, which can be obtained using the usual textbook formula. In all, we need $(3n + 2)$ estimates – n betas, alphas and estimates of each stock's specific risk $\sigma^2(\varepsilon_i)$, plus estimates of the expected market return and its volatility[3]. Had we used direct estimates we would have required n estimates of expected returns, n estimates of variances but $n(n - 1)/2$ covariance estimates. For $n = 50$ stocks the SIM requires 152 inputs, but the standard direct approach requires a staggering 1325 inputs.

---

[2] If we use the excess returns version of the SIM then the expected return of the stock would be calculated as $ER_i = r + \alpha_i + \beta_i(ER_m - r)$ where $ER_m - r$ is the forecast equity risk premium over the chosen investment horizon.

[3] Instead of obtaining estimates of $\sigma^2(\varepsilon_i)$, and then calculating the volatility of stock returns using [18], an analyst is likely to provide estimates of the volatility of stock retuns σ_i^2 directly – this still implies we need 3n + 2 estimates in total.

TABLE 12.3: SIM calculation of portfolio inputs

| | | Expected return | Variance–covariance matrix (VCV) | | |
			Stock 1	Stock 2	Stock 3
Stock 1	BA	0.0278	0.142	0.0011	0.0030
Stock 2	M&S	0.0086	0.0011	0.0045	0.0005
Stock 3	Barclays	0.0080	0.0030	0.0005	0.0026

As an illustration, Table 12.2 shows the results for the SIM applied separately to three stocks and Table 12.3 shows the resulting expected returns, variances and covariances obtained using the above formulae, which would then form the inputs for the portfolio-optimisation problem.

Are firm-specific risks uncorrelated?

We have shown how the SIM can be used to reduce the number of inputs when trying to determine the optimal risky portfolio weights w_i^* by maximising the Sharpe ratio. In the SIM we calculate the expected returns on each stock as $ER_i = \alpha_i + \beta_i \overline{R}_m$ and hence include the stock's alpha in this calculation. However, the main reason for the reduction in the number of inputs is that instead of *directly estimating* $n(n - 1)/2$ separate covariances using the standard formula, the SIM implies that the covariance between any two stock returns is $cov(R_i, R_j) = \beta_i \beta_j \sigma_m^2$, so we only need to estimate n betas. The latter result follows from our *assumption* that the specific risk between any two stock returns is zero.

But in practice, the specific risk between any two stocks may not be zero – this is measured by the correlation between the residuals from the two SIM equations. One question is how much the optimal proportions differ when we use the SIM assumption of zero correlation between the specific risk of any two stocks, compared with using the full set of directly estimated covariances between all the stock returns. The answer is very little – as the efficient frontiers in the two cases are very close to each other, so the optimal tangent point P is also very similar. This is for two reasons. First, the optimal weights are heavily influenced by the inputs for expected returns, rather than differences between estimates of the covariances[4]. Second, in practice the correlation between the residuals (specific risk) of different stock returns is not too large (and is offsetting in a large portfolio – some are positive and others negative). We see in a later chapter how the mean-variance optimisation can be very sensitive to changes in certain inputs but not for others. All inputs are measured with error and it seems that using the SIM expression $cov(R_i, R_j) = \beta_i \beta_j \sigma_m^2$ to calculate stock return covariances does not lead to *statistically different* optimal risky portfolio weights w_i^*. (But note that the point estimates of the optimal weights might be quite different, although the large standard

---

[4] But the two efficient frontiers differ around the global minimum variance point, as this is determined without reference to the inputs for expected returns, so covariances then play a more dominant role in determining the efficient frontier around this point.

errors on these estimates mean that you can bring the estimates 'closer together' without violating what the statistical results are telling you.)

Portfolio Variance

When we want to measure the riskiness of a *portfolio* of stocks, the SIM can again be very useful since it reduces the number of calculations needed to produce estimates of all the covariance terms. It can be shown that our equation [3] above also applies to the *portfolio* variance:

$$\sigma_p^2 = \beta_p^2 \sigma_m^2 + \sigma^2(\varepsilon_p) \qquad [20]$$

But we know that in a well-diversified portfolio, specific risk approaches zero so the above equation can be simplified to:

$$\sigma_p = \beta_p \sigma_m \quad \text{where } \beta_p = \sum_{i=1}^{n} w_i \beta_i \qquad [21]$$

Hence to calculate the risk of a well-diversified portfolio we only require the portfolio beta and an estimate of the standard deviation of the market return. This result is useful when we calculate the Value at Risk for a large portfolio of stocks in a single country; see Chapter 31.

If we have a multifactor model, then this too can be used to reduce considerably the number of calculations required to obtain the inputs for any portfolio problem involving portfolio variance. For example, if you have a two-factor model then all the variances and covariances between all of your n stocks needed to calculate *portfolio* variance only require the two beta estimates for each stock (i.e. $2n$ betas in all) – this involves less computation than directly estimating $n(n - 1)/2$ covariances and n-variances, but we do not pursue this further here.

12.3 COMBINING ACTIVE AND PASSIVE PORTFOLIOS

Even when we use the SIM, it is still a huge task, since the number of different stocks can be very large in the portfolio of a mutual fund, for example. Suppose you are managing a diversified US mutual fund. What usually happens in practice is you first choose a stock portfolio to mimic a broad-market index such as the S&P 500 (by holding all 500 stocks or a subset that tracks the index reasonably accurately). This is your *passive portfolio*. This is not the 'market portfolio' of mean-variance portfolio theory (since we have not done any optimisation), but it is reasonable to assume that it is statistically close to the 'true' market portfolio in terms of expected return and risk (standard deviation). Hence, the passive market portfolio has a 'true' beta of one, specific (residual) risk of zero and an alpha of zero[5]. Not unreasonably, we assume that the S&P 500 is also the benchmark portfolio in the fund's prospectus. Now you put your stock analysts to work on the active part of your strategy: to find stocks that can be mixed with your existing passive market portfolio to improve the

---

[5] This would also be true of any *estimates* of these parameters, since if you regress this 'passive' portfolio return R_m on the 'market return', which is also R_m you obtain just this result, in your sample of data – the regression fits perfectly with a beta of unity, and with residual risk and alpha of zero.

risk–return trade-off and hence eventually put you on an even higher CAL than you are currently.

The first question is how to identify these 'active stocks'. Next, you want to know what proportion of available funds you should put in the (risky) passive portfolio relative to the risky active stocks – this is your 'active plus passive' risky portfolio, which we call your *Big portfolio B*. It turns out that the alpha of your active portfolio helps determine the optimal proportions to hold. To keep things simple for the moment, suppose that your security analyst has found a *single* hedge fund that has an alpha α_A[6]. It can be shown that:

$$SR_B = SR_m + [IR_A]^2 = SR_m + [\alpha_A/\sigma_A(e)]^2 \qquad [22]$$

where $IR_A = \alpha_A/\sigma(e)$ is known as the **information ratio** (of the active portfolio). So the Sharpe ratio of the 'big' (risky) portfolio will be larger than that for the passive (market) portfolio as long as the active portfolio (the hedge fund) has a non-zero alpha. The Sharpe ratio SR_B will increase, the larger is the information ratio; that is, the larger is the active portfolio alpha ('abnormal return'), relative to its specific (residual) risk $\sigma_A(e)$. By adding the active portfolio to your existing passive market portfolio you are adding specific risk, but this is worth it if the active portfolio has a large enough abnormal return to compensate.

If we have more than one fund or stock with a non-zero alpha, then it can be shown that the SIM implies that the information ratio for an *active portfolio* of stocks depends directly on the information ratio for each actively picked stock:

$$(IR_A)^2 = [\alpha_A/\sigma(e)]^2 = \sum_{i=1}^{k} [\alpha_i/\sigma(e_i)]^2 \qquad [23]$$

So a stock analyst will be looking for a subset of, say, k stocks that she thinks have large non-zero alphas and hopefully large information ratios. It turns out that she will overweight positive alpha (and hence positive IR) stocks and underweight (or short sell) negative alpha (IR) stocks. But it is really the IR rather than alpha that in this particular analysis is the key performance criterion.

Not surprisingly, both the alpha and specific risk of the active portfolio have an impact on the proportion of funds you hold in the active *relative to* the passive (market) portfolio. These optimal weights can be determined in the usual way by maximising the Sharpe ratio of the 'big portfolio':

$$SR_B = \frac{ER_B - r}{\sigma_B} \qquad \text{subject to } w_m + w_A = 1 \qquad [24]$$

However, if we are willing to apply the SIM to the active portfolio (i.e. assume that the correlation between the specific or residual risk of the active and passive portfolios is zero), then it can be shown that the optimal weight in the active portfolio is:

---

[6] We are assuming hedge fund returns are normally distributed with constant 'conventional' betas – as we see in the chapter on hedge funds, neither of these assumptions may be true in the real world. But this 'active fund' need not necessarily be a hedge fund, it could be any security or portfolio with a non-zero alpha.

$$w_A^* = \frac{w_A^0}{1 + (1 - \beta_A)w_A^0} \quad \text{where } w_A^0 = \frac{\alpha_A/\sigma^2(e_A)}{ER_m/\sigma^2(R_m)} \qquad [25]$$

where

$$AR_A = \alpha_A/\sigma^2(e_A) \qquad [26]$$

is known as the **appraisal ratio**. The optimal weight in the passive (market) portfolio is then $w_m^* = 1 - w_A^*$. The optimal weight in the active portfolio can be either positive or negative depending, in part, on the sign of α_A. If α_A is negative, the active portfolio should be short sold. If your security analyst had uncovered two hedge funds, both with positive alpha, *and you were restricted to investing in only one of them* to optimally combine with your passive portfolio, then you would choose the one that had the highest information ratio.

But why not combine *both* hedge funds with the passive market portfolio to make up your 'big portfolio'? This results in an even larger Sharpe ratio than if you include only one of the hedge funds – and this new Sharpe ratio is given by equation [22], where now α_A is the alpha of the active portfolio of two hedge funds $\alpha_A = w_1^*\alpha_1 + w_2^*\alpha_2$ held in optimal proportions (w_1^*, w_2^*). But how do we determine the *optimal* values (w_1^*, w_2^*) *and* $w_m^* = 1 - w_1^* - w_2^*$? This is discussed in Appendix 12.2[7].

If the optimal weight for any active fund is negative but short positions are prohibited, then that active portfolio weight would be set to zero (i.e. you do not hold this active fund). The greater the number of active stocks (i.e. those with non-zero alphas) that are uncovered by stock analysts, the more diversified the active portfolio will be and its weight in the 'big portfolio' will increase relative to the passive portfolio.

Sometimes the optimisation can lead to crazy results, for example shorting the whole of the funds in the passive/market portfolio and using all the proceeds to invest in the active portfolio. Clearly, this result can be overruled by putting into the optimisation procedure a constraint that all the weights should be positive. But this will produce an expected Sharpe ratio for the 'big portfolio' that is smaller than the unconstrained case – although how much smaller we don't know until we actually do the calculation. Another way of trying to avoid crazy results is to add the constraint that the **tracking error** of the chosen active portfolio should not exceed a particular tolerance level, say 5% p.a. The tracking error is defined as the difference between the return on our active portfolio (denoted A) and the benchmark return, which we take to be the market portfolio:

$$TE = R_p - R_m = (R_A - r) - (R_m - r) = \alpha_A + (\beta_A - 1)(R_m - r) + e_A \qquad [27]$$

---

[7] You may remember from the chapter on portfolio theory that it is possible to 'improve' the efficient frontier (i.e. 'move it to the left') if you add additional risky assets to your existing portfolio of risky assets. But if you 'improve' the efficient frontier and are then allowed to borrow and lend at the risk-free rate, you will end up on a higher capital allocation line, CAL. The new 'tangent portfolio' will then have a higher Sharpe ratio than that obtained with the original efficient frontier. All we are doing here is finding the optimal portfolio weights for this 'new' set of risky assets consisting of combinations of the active and passive risky portfolios.

where

$$\alpha_A = \sum_{i=1}^{k} w_i \alpha_i, \qquad \beta_A = \sum_{i=1}^{k} w_i \beta_i, \qquad e_A = \sum_{i=1}^{k} w_i e_i \qquad [28]$$

and there are k securities in the active portfolio. To constrain the standard deviation of the tracking error to 5%:

$$\sigma(TE) = \sqrt{(\beta_A - 1)^2 \text{var}(R_m) + \sigma^2(e_A)} = 5\% \qquad [29]$$

As $\sigma(TE)$ depends on the portfolio weights, this becomes another constraint to include when we maximise the Sharpe ratio of the 'big' risky portfolio. It is generally found that this tends to prevent crazy solutions for the optimal proportions (but at the cost of a lower *expected* Sharpe ratio, compared with the unconstrained case).

Whether portfolio managers use the above optimal procedures is a fairly open question. The whole analysis requires a mean-variance approach, so that factors such as skewness are assumed not to matter to investors – but this is not an unreasonable assumption if the portfolio is rebalanced frequently, since higher moments are likely to be relatively unimportant. However, it is likely that active portfolio managers look for active stocks with either non-zero alphas or non-zero t-alphas or non-zero information ratios, and add these to the existing passive portfolio *in a rather informal, judgemental way,* rather than using an optimisation procedure. Choosing to include stocks on the basis of the above three criteria is not equivalent, but using the *IR* and the t-statistic of alpha are reasonably similar[8].

Even after noting our simplifying assumptions (e.g. use of the SIM), you can see the formidable practical problems we still face. By arbitrarily taking the S&P 500 as our market/benchmark portfolio, we have saved ourselves a lot of computations compared to doing a full optimisation with these 500 stocks to get the 'true' optimal proportions in our passive portfolio. But now our security analysts have to find stocks (or funds) with non-zero alphas – not an easy task. Then in order to improve the expected Sharpe ratio we have to combine these optimally with the passive (market) portfolio, to get the final optimal proportions to hold in these two risky portfolios[9]. An important point is that even if we hold the optimal proportions, we still do not know what will happen in the future and what the out-turn Sharpe ratio will be. This is because although we have chosen optimal weights, these are only optimal *given our input forecasts* – if these are wrong then it's a case of 'garbage in, garbage out'. Maybe this is another reason why in practice the investment committee of a fund combines the analysts' stocks with positive alphas with its passive/benchmark portfolio of assets in a rather informal, judgemental way – the ex-post errors (i.e. after the event) of this method may be no worse than the ex-post errors when using the optimal procedure.

---

[8] $IR_A = \alpha_A/\sigma(e)$, whereas $t_\alpha = \alpha/[\sigma(e)/\sqrt{T}]$ so if two funds are estimated with the same number of observations, both of these metrics give similar qualitative results.

[9] The individual investor will then combine this 'big risky portfolio' with the risk-free asset, depending on her risk tolerance.

Black–Litterman

To make the optimal portfolio weights less sensitive to slight changes in the *estimated* inputs, Black and Litterman (1992) suggest that the inputs for expected returns should be a weighted average of historical estimated values (and their estimated standard errors) and your own prior views (and the subjective uncertainty surrounding these prior views). So to implement this approach, the investor must state her prior views about returns and the uncertainty surrounding them – at least for a subset of the total assets considered. This method has much to commend it, although putting a precise figure on your own uncertainty about your forecast for returns on, say, 50 stocks can be difficult. Maybe this is why, for all its academic merits, this method does not appear to be that widely used, although it is certainly worth looking at if you are thinking of a career in active portfolio management.

12.4 EVENT STUDIES

Event studies have been used to measure the quantitative impact of an event (or events) on the value of a firm (or firms). The event might be the announcement of a takeover bid, quarterly earnings announcements, the announcement of new share issues or an initial public offering (IPO) of shares. In the US, event studies can be used in evidence in legal cases of insider dealing, which require a measure of abnormal share-price movements. If the market is efficient it should very quickly reflect the expected impact of the event on all future cash flows, which should then be speedily compounded in stock prices, so that there should be no *abnormal* returns in the post-event period. For example, suppose firm A with a current market value of $100m has a cumulative *abnormal* return of 3% after the discovery and announcement that its accounting firm has been negligent – then the accounting firm is liable to pay firm A $3m in damages.

In principle, the event study methodology is relatively straightforward. Assume we have an event at time τ (Figure 12.3), which we take to be an announcement of a takeover bid. The

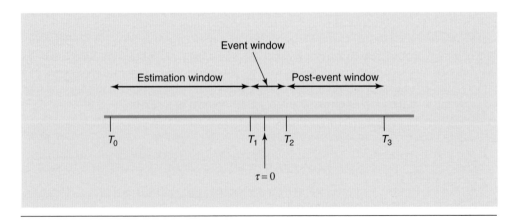

FIGURE 12.3: Event study

estimation window (T_0 to T_1) is used to measure the 'normal' or 'required' return on the target firm's stock (prior to the event happening) and the most commonly used statistical model is the SIM (or *market model*)[10]:

$$R_{it} = \alpha_i + \beta_i R_{mt} + \varepsilon_{it} \quad t = T_0, \ldots T_1 \tag{30}$$

The *abnormal return* (AR) over the event window $T_1 + 1$ to T_2 is then the actual return minus the required return based on the SIM parameter estimates:

$$AR_{it} = R_{it} - \hat{R}_{it} = R_{it} - (\hat{\alpha}_i + \hat{\beta}_i R_{mt}) \quad (t = T_1 + 1 \, to \, T_2) \tag{31}$$

Note that the SIM parameters are estimated with data prior to the event window, but the stock return and the market return data apply over the period of the event window. We can then add up these individual abnormal returns over the event window to obtain the *total impact* of the event as measured by the cumulative abnormal return (CAR):

$$CAR_{it} = \sum_{t=T_1+1}^{T_2} AR_{it} \tag{32}$$

The event day may be one single day $\tau = 0$, but if the news of the event leaks (e.g. a merger announcement) then the event window can be extended backwards towards T_1 and this prevents the estimation of the 'normal' return being contaminated by the impact of the event. For example, in event studies of merger and acquisitions (M&A), T_1 may be 10 days before the actual official announcement.

Figure 12.4 gives a stylised example of the results for the abnormal return for, say, the top decile of firms that have the largest positive abnormal earnings announcements ('good news') and for the bottom decile of firms whose abnormal earnings announcement are the worst ('bad news'). Prior to the announcement of the event, there may be some leakage of information about the upcoming event, so there are some relatively small abnormal returns for around 10–15 days before the event. Most of the abnormal return occurs on the event announcement day, but for some events there is **post-event drift** as the abnormal return persists for some time. The EMH predicts that there should not be any post-event drift in returns since information should be immediately compounded in stock prices. Whether the presence of post-event drift leads to profitable investment opportunities depends on the transaction costs incurred when implementing the strategy. For example, one strategy is to buy those firms in the top decile that have the largest positive earnings announcement surprises ('good news firms') and short sell those in the bottom earnings decile ('bad news firms'). You would then earn the cumulative abnormal return that takes place after the earnings announcement in

---

[10] In practice when using *daily data*, imposing $\beta_i = 0$ (i.e. constant mean return model) makes little difference to the results, since R_{mt} adds little to the explanatory power of the equation when using daily returns. The so-called **market model** is also used. This is the same as the SIM but the estimation technique takes account of the fact that the error terms (i.e. specific risk) across different firms may be correlated. Note therefore that when calculating inputs to the optimal portfolio problem you would not use the market model, since it does not reduce the number of calculations required to estimate all the covariances you need. But the market model creates little or no additional problems to the SIM, where estimation of alpha and beta is concerned.

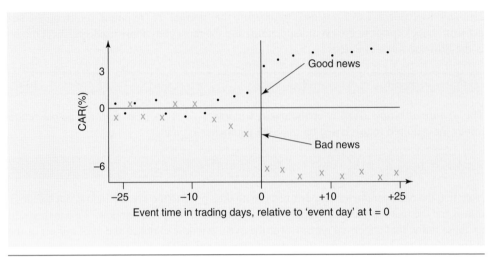

FIGURE 12.4: Cumulative abnormal returns

Figure 12.4. Presumably, a realistic interpretation of the EMH would allow for the possibility of some leakage of information prior to the event (e.g. investors might notice large purchases by a small group of investors prior to the official announcement of a takeover or might obtain better information on the firm's future earnings as the announcement day gets closer).

Event studies of M&A announcements tend to find that target firms' shares exhibit a cumulative abnormal return of around 20% on average, with some pre-announcement drift but little post-announcement drift. The share price effects on the acquirers are very close to zero, on average. This suggests that M&A on average do not reduce competition (else we would see both targets' and acquirers' shares rising), but the acquirers do pay a substantial bid premium in the market for corporate control. Case Study 12.1 uses the event study approach to analyse the possibility of detecting insider trading and to assess the market's view of takeovers.

CASE STUDY 12.1   INSIDER TRADING AND M&A

When there is a rumour of a takeover, the share price of the target company will tend to rise sharply. This often happens a few days before any official announcement of the takeover, as the information begins to dissipate into the market. Clearly, a takeover bid is a somewhat abnormal event and produces an abnormal change in price. Given the normal day-to-day activities of the firm we might expect that daily returns are normally distributed. However, if on any day there is some exceptionally good news (e.g. a takeover bid) or bad news (e.g. failure of a patent application), this may cause extremely large rises or falls in the stock price, which may be incompatible with the normal distribution. In practice, this tends to make daily stock returns have fatter tails than those given by the normal distribution. It is also the case that for some firms, bad news occurs more frequently than good news, so the distribution of daily returns is skewed to the left.

Let us look at what happens to some stock returns around the announcement date of a takeover bid. We will measure daily price changes relative to those for the sector as a whole, so our return is really the abnormal return – crudely speaking, the latter amounts to using the CAPM and assuming a beta of one with respect to the sector index. We measure the standard deviation using the previous year's daily returns.

Abnormal daily price changes prior to M&A announcements

Company	Date	% Price change relative to sector (1-day)	Standard deviation	Probability*
Amec	8 Nov 2006	3.0	1.9	0.028
Countrywide	5 Feb 2007	4.3	2.3	0.010
Reg Vardy	29 Nov 2005	8.1	4.9	0.000
Viridian	5 Oct 2006	11.5	9	0.000

* This is the probability of observing a rise in price equal to or above that actually observed (assuming that daily returns are normally distributed).

Remember that the normal distribution implies that the daily change in price will lie within two standard deviations of the mean, on 95 out of 100 days. Therefore there is only a 2.5% probability that the stock price will move more than two standard deviations in either direction. For example, on 8 November 2006 Amec's share price moved 3% in one day, a few days ahead of a takeover bid from a private equity group. This amounts to about two standard deviations and the probability of this occurring is around 2.5%. Similarly, Countrywide, a chain of UK estate agents, had a daily price rise of 4.3% in February 2007, 18 days before a takeover bid. This is a move of 2.3 standard deviations, which would occur only 1% of the time if returns were truly normally distributed. The car dealership Reg Vardy saw a share price rise of 8.2% in November 2005 (relative to its sector), four days before there was a takeover offer. This is a move of around five standard deviations with a probability of just one in 3.5 million. Finally, Viridian (an Irish energy utility) had a share price increase in October 2006 of 11.5%, equivalent to nine standard deviations. After the price rise Viridian issued a statement announcing that it was considering a bid from Bahrain's Arcapita.

In principle, information about a takeover is not supposed to leak to the market, because it provides an opportunity for insiders who are in possession of this information to tell others, who can profit from it by trading ahead of the announcement. If you are a statistician who truly believes that daily returns are normally distributed, then if you appear as an expert witness, you would be likely to conclude that there is a prima facie case for investigating the possibility of insider trading in the shares of Reg Vardy and Viridian. Because the daily returns around an event like a takeover are not normally distributed, this makes testing for abnormal returns less than straightforward (see Cuthbertson and Nitzsche, 2004 for further details). However, if the statistics suggest some kind of insider trading, you would then go and look at all trades in these particular shares to see if those people who had traded prior to the announcement day had any connection with either company.

As a financial economist, you may also be interested to know how the market views the future prospects of the takeover target, should the takeover succeed. Once the information about the takeover leaks to the market and the market believes that the takeover is a good thing, then traders will immediately 'factor in' the improved prospects for the target company into its current share price. So, we expect to see successive price rises (above those for the sector) as the information leaks into the market, and when the bid is formally announced we expect to see a further jump in the price. After lengthy negotiations the bid may succeed and if the market thinks this is a good thing for the target, its price will immediately rise even more. These *cumulative* (abnormal) price rises measure the market's view of the prospects (profits) for the target firm in the future. So, if the cumulative price rise after the M&A announcement is, say, 35%, then the market believes that the merger will add 35% additional value to the target. Of course, this is also the bid premium that the acquirer will have to pay to take over the target firm.

In takeovers it is often the case that the acquirer's share price stays the same or even falls slightly, whereas the target's share price increases substantially. The gains to the takeover therefore appear to accrue to the target shareholders. Obviously, this is the market's view at the time the takeover is implemented and the market is not always correct. Therefore it is often the case that after a merger, the combined firm may well do worse than the two firms would have done if they had continued as separate entities.

Event studies are also used to examine the effect on a firm's market value, of announcements that the firm will raise new funds by equity or bond (debt) issues. These studies generally find an (abnormal) price fall of around 2.5–3.5% for equity issues and a fall of around 0.2% for bond issues. This makes equity issues more costly than bond issues and is consistent with the Myers-Majluf (1984) 'pecking order' view of capital structure.

It is worth noting at this point that for event studies involving *several* firms, one might split the sample of firms *before* working out AR_i and CAR_i. For example, when measuring the impact of, say, earnings news on a sample of n firms, one might split the firms into three different 'event samples': those experiencing 'good', 'bad' and 'no news'. The 'good', 'bad' or 'no news' firms might be those with earnings news 'greater than 2.5%', 'less than *minus* 2.5%' and 'between *minus* 2.5% and 2.5%' respectively. Or, as described above, we could put the firms into deciles based on the size of the abnormal earnings announcements for each firm. The 'news' in each case is the actual earnings announcement minus the *expected* earnings, where the latter is obtained either from survey evidence of analysts' forecasts or some simple time-series extrapolation of past earnings.

There is now a large body of evidence that conditional on observable *public* events, stocks experience **post-event drift** in the same direction as the initial event impact. These events include earnings announcements, of which Figure 12.4 is a stylised example (Bernard and Thomas, 1989, 1990). For example, Bernard and Thomas (1989) sort all stocks on the NYSE and AMEX based on the size of their unexpected earnings (where the expected change in earnings is assumed to be constant). They find 'post-earnings announcement drift' or 'under-reaction' over the 60 days after the event. The decile with largest positive earnings surprises outperforms the decile with poor earnings surprises in 46 out of 50 quarters studied, with an average return for 'good minus bad' deciles of about 4%, which is not explained by differences in CAPM betas. Post-event drift also applies to dividend initiations and omissions (Michaely *et al.*, 1995), as well as stock issues and repurchases (Ikenberry *et al.*, 1995; Loughran and Ritter, 1995) and analyst recommendations (Womack, 1996).

SUMMARY

- The single-index model (SIM) assumes that an individual stock is subject to two types of risk-systematic (market) risk and firm-specific risk. The SIM explains the (excess) return on a stock by systematic changes in the market index and the size of this effect is measured by the stock's beta. The remaining volatility in a firm's stock return is due to microeconomic, firm-specific risk caused by random events like strikes, unanticipated cost increases, legal and environmental regulatory issues etc.
- The intercept (alpha) and the beta for a stock can be estimated with the SIM, using time-series data on excess stock returns and the excess returns on a market index.
- The estimated alpha can be interpreted as a performance measure, since it measures the average return on the stock less the required return to compensate for the systematic/beta risk of the stock.
- A positive alpha indicates that the stock has outperformed its market benchmark and has earned a positive risk-adjusted (abnormal) return. The alpha of a stock (or portfolio of stocks) can also be estimated for a multifactor model and this multifactor alpha can also be interpreted as a risk-adjusted (abnormal) return.
- The specific risk of the stock is unimportant if the stock is held as part of a well-diversified portfolio.
- The SIM is widely used by practitioners to considerably reduce the number of calculations required for the inputs used in determining optimal portfolio weights for a risky asset portfolio. The SIM can also be used to simplify the calculation of portfolio variance, which is itself a measure of risk, in the Value at Risk approach.
- In practice, it is probably the case that portfolio managers start with a passive portfolio and then look for securities (or funds) with non-zero alphas (i.e. their 'active portfolio'). The passive and active portfolios are then combined in such a way as to maximise the Sharpe ratio of the composite 'big portfolio'. This 'big portfolio' results in an improvement in the Sharpe ratio (compared with just holding the passive portfolio).
- Event studies often use data prior to the announcement of the event to estimate the parameters of the SIM. These are then used in the post-event period to calculate the 'normal' or required return on a stock, and hence the 'abnormal' return due to the event under investigation.
- Several studies using announcements of mergers and acquisitions, earnings and stock and bond issues show that prices do not always react immediately to publicly announced events. This would be a refutation of the EMH only if dealers could make profits from post-event drift, after correction for transaction costs and the risks in implementing the strategy.

APPENDIX 12.1: SIM AND PORTFOLIO VARIANCE

In this analysis the 'returns' can be either stock returns or *excess* returns[11]. If each stock return can be represented by the SIM, then the return on a *portfolio* of n stocks is:

$$R_p = \sum_{i=1}^{n} w_i R_i = \sum_{i=1}^{n} (w_i \alpha_i + w_i \beta_i R_m + w_i \varepsilon_i) \tag{A1}$$

$$R_p = \alpha_p + \beta_p R_m + \varepsilon_p \tag{A2}$$

$$\text{where} \quad \beta_p = \sum_{i=1}^{n} w_i \beta_i, \quad \alpha_p = \sum_{i=1}^{n} w_i \alpha_i, \quad \varepsilon_p = \sum_{i=1}^{n} w_i \varepsilon_i \tag{A3}$$

Since the market return is independent of specific risk, then portfolio variance is:

$$\sigma_p^2 = \beta_p^2 \sigma_m^2 + \sigma^2(\varepsilon_p) \tag{A4}$$

Suppose we invest equally in each of our n assets, so that $w_i = 1/n$. If we now assume that specific risk is uncorrelated across firms, then:

$$\sigma^2(\varepsilon_p) = \frac{1}{n} \sum_{i=1}^{n} \frac{\sigma^2(\varepsilon_i)}{n} \tag{A5}$$

as all the covariances between the individual error terms are zero, $\text{cov}(\varepsilon_i, \varepsilon_j) = 0$. As $n \to \infty$ then the specific risk of the portfolio of stocks approaches zero, $\sigma^2(\varepsilon_p) \to 0$. This is the same result that we derived earlier, demonstrating that in a well-diversified portfolio the only risk that matters is covariance risk. For the SIM this covariance risk is represented by the term $\beta_p^2 \sigma_m^2$, with all the systematic covariance terms represented by the $\beta_i \beta_j$ terms that are subsumed in the β_p^2 term.

APPENDIX 12.2: OPTIMAL WEIGHTS FOR ACTIVE FUNDS AND THE PASSIVE FUND

The passive market portfolio has expected return ER_m, an alpha of zero, beta = 1 and no specific risk, $\sigma^2(e_m) = 0$. The active portfolio consists of stocks (or funds) with non-zero alphas. The 'big portfolio' consists of a combination of the active and passive portfolios:

$$R_B - r = \alpha_A w_A + (w_A \beta_A + w_m(1))[R_m - r] + w_A e_A \tag{A1}$$

$$\sigma_B^2 = (w_m(1) + w_A \beta_A)^2 \sigma_m^2 + [w_A \sigma(e_A)]^2 \tag{A2}$$

---

[11] Here it is more convenient to represent the SIM in terms of returns R_i rather than excess returns $R_i - r$, since we are explicitly interested in the volatility of R_i rather than the volatility of $R_i - r$. In practice, both the 'returns' version and the 'excess returns' version of the SIM give similar results for portfolio volatility because variations in the risk-free rate are relatively small.

where α_A is the alpha of the active portfolio of two hedge funds $\alpha_A = w_1\alpha_1 + w_2\alpha_2$ and therefore $w_m = 1 - w_1 - w_2$. We can use Excel to maximise the Sharpe ratio of this 'big portfolio', now containing three risky assets – the passive portfolio and two hedge funds:

$$SR_B = \frac{ER_B - r}{\sigma_B} \qquad \text{subject to } w_m + w_A = 1 \qquad [A3]$$

Alternatively, we can assume that the SIM holds for each hedge fund, then the optimal weights (w_1^*, w_2^*) in the two hedge funds $(i = 1, 2)$ can be determined *analytically* as follows:

1. Calculate the *appraisal ratio* for the two hedge funds: $AR_i = \alpha_i/\sigma^2(e_i)$
2. The *initial* weights in the two hedge funds are $w_i = AR_i/\sum_{i=1}^{2}AR_i$ – so the weights sum to one.
3. Now calculate

$$\alpha_A = \sum_{i=1}^{2}w_i\alpha_i \quad \text{and} \quad \sigma^2(e_A) = \sum_{i=1}^{2}w_i\sigma^2(e_i) \quad \text{and} \quad \beta_A = \sum_{i=1}^{2}w_i\beta_i \qquad [A4]$$

4. Next calculate w_A^* using;

$$w_A^* = \frac{w_A^0}{1 + (1 - \beta_A)w_A^0} \qquad \text{where } w_A^0 = \frac{\alpha_A/\sigma^2(e_A)}{ER_m/\sigma^2(R_m)} \qquad [A5]$$

The *optimal* risky 'big portfolio' now has weights $w_m^* = 1 - w_A^*$ in the passive (market) portfolio and proportions $w_i^* = w_A^* w_i$ in each of the two 'active' hedge funds. We can now use the above *optimal* proportions to calculate the expected return and risk for the 'big' portfolio:

$$ER_B - r = \alpha_A w_A^* + (w_A^*\beta_A + w_m^*(1))[ER_m - r] \qquad [A6]$$

$$\sigma_B^2 = (w_m^*(1) + w_A^*\beta_A)^2\sigma_m^2 + [w_A^*\sigma(e_A)]^2 \qquad [A7]$$

The above is quite a complex procedure, even though we have used the SIM to simplify the calculation of some of the inputs. But for the Sharpe ratio to increase when we combine the risky active portfolio with the existing risky (market) portfolio, we have to use the above *optimal* weights and not just combine the two portfolios using arbitrary weights.

APPENDIX 12.3: REGRESSION ANALYSIS

The correlation coefficient can be used to measure the 'degree of association' between any two variables. Regression analysis is used to measure the quantitative impact of one variable X on another variable Y, but regression also tells us the margin of error attached to our estimate of this effect. Multiple regression models have several 'independent' (X) variables that influence the dependent variable, Y (e.g. Fama French 3-factor model). In the single-index model we regress the monthly (excess) return on BA shares on the monthly (excess) return of the market (i.e. the FTSE All-share index):

$$Y_t = \alpha + \beta X_t + \varepsilon_t \tag{A1}$$

where ε_t is a random error term. ε_t represents the specific risk of BA shares and it represents the movements in Y_t that are *not explained* by variations in the return on the FTSE All-share index, X_t. This can be seen by noting that $\varepsilon_t = Y_t - (\alpha + \beta X_t) =$ 'actual value of Y – value of Y predicted by X_t'. The random error ε_t is *assumed* to have a zero mean (specific risk averages to zero over time) and a constant variance, $\sigma^2(\varepsilon_t)$. If changes in X_t closely track changes in Y_t, $\sigma^2(\varepsilon_t)$ will be small. Using ordinary least squares (OLS) to obtain estimates $(\hat{\alpha}, \hat{\beta})$ of the 'true' parameters α and β, for the sample period September 2002 to August 2007 (60 monthly observations) we obtain:

$$Y_t = 0.0038 + 2.5543\ X_t \qquad \text{Rsqd} = 0.4581 \tag{A2}$$

$$(0.0116)\quad(0.3648)$$

$$[0.3276]\quad[7.00]$$

where (.) = standard error of the coefficient and [.] = t-statistic of the coefficient. Note that equation [A2] represents a straight line with an intercept $\hat{\alpha} = 0.0038$ and a slope coefficient, $\hat{\beta} = +2.5543$. Using OLS gives values for $\hat{\alpha}$ and $\hat{\beta}$ that minimise the deviations of the actual observations from those on the regression line. Hence, the regression line that is described by equation [A2] is also called the 'line of best fit'. The regression results can be interpreted as follows. When the excess return on the FTSE increases by 1% then *on average*, the excess return on BA shares increases by 2.5543%. The values in parentheses below the parameter estimates are the standard errors[12] of the estimated coefficients and can be used to calculate confidence intervals or used in hypothesis testing. The ratio $t(\hat{\beta}) = \hat{\beta}/[se(\hat{\beta})]$ reported in equation [A2] allows us to test the hypothesis that the 'true' value of beta is equal to zero, and therefore that no (linear) relationship exists between Y_t and X_t. The smaller is the value of $se(\hat{\beta})$ relative to $\hat{\beta}$ itself, the higher is this t-ratio and the more confident we can be about the precision of our estimate of beta. The ratio $t(\hat{\beta})$ can be shown to have a Students' t-distribution, and if the absolute value of t is greater than 2 (this depends on the sample size) we can be 95% certain that the 'true' beta β is *statistically* significantly different from zero.

The 'R-squared' (Rsqd) of the regression indicates how much of the actual variability in Y_t is explained by the independent variable X_t. The *predicted values* of Y_t are given by the following expression: $\hat{Y}_t = \hat{\alpha} + \hat{\beta} X_t = 0.0038 + 2.5543\ X_t$, which is our

---

[12] For the record, the standard error of $\hat{\beta}$ is calculated as $se(\hat{\beta}) = [1/(n-1)][\sigma(\varepsilon_t)/\text{var}(R_{BA})]$, so the standard error is smaller, the smaller is the 'residual standard deviation' $\sigma(\varepsilon_t)$, relative to the variance of the return on BA shares. The standard error of 'alpha', $se(\hat{\alpha}) = \sigma(\varepsilon_t)\sqrt{\dfrac{1}{n} + \dfrac{(R_{FTSE})^2}{\text{var}(R_{FTSE}).(n-1)}}$

$\approx \dfrac{\sigma(\varepsilon_t)}{\sqrt{n}}$, so the standard error of the intercept $\hat{\alpha}$ is smaller, the smaller is the standard deciation of the residuals. Note also that both standard errors are smaller the more data points n we have used in the estimation (ceteris paribus).

linear regression line. Figure 12.2 shows the scatter diagram of the excess returns on BA shares and the return on the FTSE index and the regression line (equation [A2]). You can see from this figure that as X_t moves so does the predicted value $\hat{Y}_t$. However, $\hat{Y}_t$ will not always coincide with the actual data series Y_t, at all points in time: there is a **prediction error** or '**residual**' that is calculated as:

$$e_t = \text{actual value of } Y_t - \text{predicted value of } Y_t \text{ from the regression}$$

$$= Y_t - \hat{Y}_t = Y_t - (\hat{\alpha} + \hat{\beta} X_t) \tag{A3}$$

e_t, the 'residual' is actually an estimate of the 'true' error term $\varepsilon_t = Y_t - (\alpha + \beta X_t)$ where (α, β) are the 'true' unobservable parameters. If we have a 'good equation' then we expect that $Y_t \approx \hat{Y}_t$ most of the time and hence e_t will be small. The OLS estimation technique actually 'chooses' $\hat{\alpha}$ and $\hat{\beta}$ to make this prediction error as small as possible, but in practice it will not be zero for each data point in the sample. The Rsqrd ('R^2') of the regression measures the proportion of the variation in the actual Y-series, accounted for by the variation in $\hat{Y}_t$. R^2 is calculated as:

$$R^2 = \frac{\sum_{t=1}^{n}(Y_t - \bar{Y})^2}{\sum_{t=1}^{n}(\hat{Y}_t - \bar{Y})^2} \tag{A4}$$

An R^2 of, say, 0.3 implies that on average only 30% of the variation in Y_t is accounted for by variation in the independent variable X_t (and hence 70% is left unexplained). This implies that (since $\hat{\beta} > 0$) whenever X_t increases, only about 30% of the time will Y_t also increase.

Using OLS it is easy to include many independent variables on the right-hand side of the equation, to try to improve our explanation of movements in Y_t. Possible X variables, apart from the market return, that could influence stock returns include the dividend-price ratio of the firm, the book-to-market value of the firm, interest rates, exchange rates, inflation and, in the case of BA, the oil price.

Here, we can only scratch the surface of the complexities involved in regression analysis, but there are a number of issues that need to be addressed if your equation is to be a success, including:

- Do the empirical results conform with your theoretical ideas or even just your gut instinct (e.g. do you really believe that stock prices should rise after a rise in interest rates, even though that is what your 'negative' regression coefficient is telling you)?
- Are the key parameters $(\hat{\alpha}, \hat{\beta})$ statistically significant and of the expected sign (i.e. positive or negative)?
- Are the regression residuals e_t 'well behaved'? Usually we require the residuals to have a constant variance (i.e. homoscedastic), to be unrelated to each other over

time (i.e. not autocorrelated) and not to 'explode' (i.e. to be stationary). One can test the residuals $e_t = Y_t - \hat{Y}_t$ for all of these desirable properties.

- If we estimate the equation using n data points, are the coefficients $(\hat{\alpha}, \hat{\beta})$ stable and does the equation forecast well when we add additional data points $n + 1, n + 2$ etc.? Again, there are numerous procedures to test these propositions, one of the simplest being recursive least squares. Recursive OLS simply repeatedly re-estimates $(\hat{\alpha}, \hat{\beta})$ as we add extra data. We can then plot a graph of $\hat{\beta}$ (or $\hat{\alpha}$) as we move through our sample of data and observe whether $\hat{\beta}$ remains reasonably stable as we add more data points. There are formal tests for the stability of these estimated coefficients (e.g. Chow test).

The above procedures are now standard features in many software regression packages such as Eviews and PCGive, and some of the statistical output is produced by Excel.

EXERCISES

Q1   What does the single-index model (SIM) assume about the sources of risk for an individual stock?

Q2   What does the single-index model (SIM) imply for (i) the determinants of the volatility of individual stock returns; (ii) the correlation (or covariance) between any two stock returns?

Q3   How many inputs do you have to calculate to find the optimal risky asset proportions (the tangent portfolio) and how does the SIM reduce the number of calculations you have to perform to obtain these inputs? Assume you have n stocks to incorporate in your optimal portfolio.

Q4   If you already hold a diversified market portfolio and your stock analysts find some new stocks that have positive alphas and others with negative alphas, what would you do and why?

Q5   In an event study, how do you measure the impact on the value of the target firm of the announcement of a takeover?

Q6   Intuitively, what does the R-squared of a regression represent? Does a high R^2 indicate that the equation will provide accurate forecasts?

CAPM and APT

AIMS

- To explain the link between the CAPM and mean-variance portfolio theory.
- To demonstrate why beta represents the risk of a stock when the stock is held as part of a diversified portfolio. It is beta that determines the average return on a stock.
- To show the linear relationship between the expected (average) return on a set of individual stocks and their respective betas – this is the security market line (SML).
- To demonstrate the uses of the CAPM in constructing stock portfolios, in measuring the risk of a stock portfolio, in estimating the discount rate for project appraisal and in implementing market timing strategies.
- To show how the arbitrage pricing theory (APT) provides a multifactor model to determine the expected (average) returns on individual stocks (and portfolios of stocks).

INTRODUCTION

In Chapter 10 we analysed how mean-variance optimisation by investors leads them to hold risky assets in specific proportions, which gives them the highest reward-to-variability (Sharpe) ratio. In a well-diversified portfolio, firm-specific risk can be diversified away and what matters is only the non-diversifiable or 'covariance risk'. It would therefore seem that a stock should not earn a high average return just because its return volatility is high, but that its average return should be determined by the risk that the investor cannot diversify away; that is, covariance or market risk. The CAPM uses these ideas to show that the average return on individual stocks should depend on covariance risk, and the latter is reflected in the size of the stock's beta.

We also present an alternative model of the required return on a stock known as the APT. The APT also produces an equation to determine the expected or average return on individual stocks and relates this to the stock's beta exposure to particular systematic risks – these risk variables are called 'factors', which could include variables like the change in interest rate, inflation or output and so on. However, the theoretical basis of the APT is very different from that of the CAPM, and as the name suggests, it is based on the idea that in equilibrium there must be no risk-free arbitrage opportunities in the stock market.

13.1 THE CAPM

The capital asset pricing model (CAPM) provides an equation for determining the return on a stock, such as that of AT&T. It states that the expected (average) *excess* return on a stock $(ER - r)$ depends on the expected (average) *excess* market return according to the following relationship:

$$(ER - r)_t = \beta(ER_m - r) \tag{1}$$

In the previous chapters we noted that an estimate of beta can be obtained from a time-series regression of the stock's excess return on the excess market return. Here, we want to concentrate on the interpretation of beta as a risk measure, rather than dwelling on how it is estimated.

Suppose that the average excess market return is $(ER_m - r) = 10\%$ p.a. and the beta of Microsoft is 1.4, then according to the CAPM, the average excess return on Microsoft stocks should be 14% p.a. If the beta of AT&T is 0.7, then the CAPM implies that the average excess return on AT&T should be 7% p.a. Hence the *relative excess* return on the two stocks should be:

$$\frac{\text{Excess return on Microsoft}}{\text{Excess return on AT\&T}} = \frac{(ER_{Micro} - r)}{(ER_{AT\&T} - r)} = \frac{\beta_{Micro}}{\beta_{AT\&T}} = \frac{1.4}{0.7} = 2 \tag{2}$$

The ratio of the average excess returns on the two stocks is 2, which just equals the ratios of their betas. If the average return is a reward for investors holding stocks, then it looks as if the relative size of the two betas measures the *relative* riskiness of the two stocks. We immediately have a paradox here. Surely, the risk of a stock and hence the average return on that stock should depend on the *volatility* of its return and not on this peculiar variable beta – the higher the stock's own volatility, the higher should be the average return on the stock. So the *relative* average returns on two stocks should depend on the ratios of their return volatilities and not the ratio of their betas. As we shall see, the reason that beta is the key variable for determining the average return on a stock, rather than each stock's own return volatility, is because of mean-variance portfolio theory and covariance risk.

From previous chapters you will recall that in a well-diversified portfolio the volatility of *individual* stock returns does not have a large impact on the overall volatility of the *portfolio*. Therefore, if Microsoft and AT&T are held as part of a portfolio with many other stocks, their individual volatilities make little contribution to portfolio variance – the individual return variances are largely diversified away. Hence their individual variances should not influence the *average return* earned by holding these stocks, since individual variances do not add much to *portfolio* risk.

We also learned that the key factors in determining portfolio variance are the covariances (or 'co-movement') between all of the stock returns in the portfolio – the higher the average covariance of stock returns in the portfolio, the higher is portfolio variance. Hence for any *individual* stock, its main contribution to *portfolio* variance actually depends on its return covariance with all other stocks in the portfolio. In the mean-variance portfolio model, 'all stocks' are referred to as the market portfolio. Therefore, if we could show that the beta of, say, Microsoft is related to the covariance between Microsoft's return and the return on all other stocks, we could see why the beta of Microsoft measures its *contribution* to overall portfolio risk and hence why beta determines the average return on Microsoft. The overall risk of the market portfolio is its variance σ_m^2 and beta can be shown to be given by the expression:

$$\beta_{Micro} = \frac{\text{cov}(R_{Micro}, R_m)}{\sigma_m^2} \tag{3}$$

Hence beta represents the 'contribution of Microsoft to portfolio risk' scaled by the *total* risk of the portfolio of all stocks – it measures the *relative* contribution of Microsoft to overall portfolio variance. Remember also that the market return in mean-variance portfolio theory depends on the optimal portfolio weights w_i chosen by investors and is given by:

$$R_m = w_1 R_1 + w_2 R_2 + \cdots + w_n R_n \tag{4}$$

Hence, from [3] and [4] we can see that the beta of Microsoft does depend on the covariances between Microsoft's return R_{Micro} and the returns on *all* other stocks in the portfolio.

You may have gathered by now that the CAPM and mean-variance portfolio theory are inextricably linked. The CAPM assumes that all investors hold the market portfolio and then seeks to determine what the expected (average) return should be on each of these individual stocks, in order that investors as a group are willing to hold these stocks. As we have seen, a key determinant of the return required by investors is the covariance between an individual stock's return and the market return – which is measured by the stock's beta. The stock's own return variance plays little or no part in determining the average return on the stock, as this risk can be diversified away.

In principle, the market portfolio of mean-variance portfolio theory consists of *all* assets (not just stocks) and the risk of this 'total portfolio' is given by the variance of the market return σ_m^2, as there are no other risky assets for the market return to co-vary with[1]. The beta of the market return $\beta_m = 1$, as can be seen from equation [3], with R_{Micro} replaced with R_m, is:

$$\beta_m = \frac{\text{cov}(R_m, R_m)}{\sigma_m^2} = \frac{\sigma_m^2}{\sigma_m^2} = 1 \qquad [5]$$

This just implies that the market return must always move in the same direction and by the same amount as itself, as you can see from equation [1] (since if we set $ER = ER_m$ then this implies $\beta_m = 1$).

Because the CAPM is a logical outcome of mean-variance portfolio theory, it must be subject to the same restrictive assumptions of that approach, which include:

- All investors maximise the return-to-variability or Sharpe ratio.
- All investors make the same forecasts of expected returns, variances and covariances, over the same horizon, and therefore all choose to hold the same market portfolio 'weights' for the risky assets – this is called 'homogeneous expectations' or beliefs.
- There are no taxes or transaction costs.
- Investors can borrow and lend unlimited amounts at the risk-free rate.
- Investment takes place in all publicly traded financial assets (e.g. stocks, bonds, foreign exchange, futures), but the model rules out investments in non-tradable assets such as education and assets provided by the government (e.g. publicly owned power generation, healthcare in some countries).
- Investors may have different endowments of wealth (but no small group of investors dominates the market). Investors can have different degrees of risk aversion (risk tolerance).
- All investors are price takers and they believe that their trades do not have an impact on market prices.

Although some of these assumptions are unrealistic, they are required in order to obtain the CAPM relationship. All models have simplifying assumptions – the CAPM does not claim to be a perfect description of the real world, but what we hope is that it provides a reasonable description and one that results in predictions that match the empirical data better than any other competing theories. In practice we do find that we can improve on the CAPM, by using more than the market return to explain movements in individual stock returns, but we come to this later. Even though the CAPM has deficiencies, this does not mean that it is completely useless – it may be useful in certain circumstances (e.g. in providing a measure of the required return on equity for a large firm, which is then used in PV calculations of cash flows) but not so useful in others (e.g in explaining the spread of average returns on portfolios of small stocks).

We can also express the CAPM as:

---

[1] Throughout this chapter we assume that the only marketable assets available to investors are stocks. In principle mean-variance portfolio theory and the CAPM apply to all available marketable assets (e.g. stocks, bonds, foreign exchange, futures, etc.) and the 'market portfolio' consists of all these assets. In practice, the number of assets considered is always smaller than this 'universe'.

$$ER = r + \beta(ER_m - r) \qquad\qquad\qquad\qquad [6]$$

so that the return on any stock can be viewed as being equal to the risk-free rate plus a risk premium, where the risk premium is given by $\beta(ER_m - r)$ – that is, by the beta of the stock and the expected excess return on the market (i.e. the equity risk premium).

Loosely speaking, if actual returns on a stock when averaged over time approximate the expected (or forecast) return made by investors, ER, then we can think of the CAPM as explaining the average historical return on an individual stock. What does the CAPM tell us about equilibrium average returns on individual stocks? First, note that the *expected* excess return on the market $(ER_m - r) > 0$, otherwise no risk-averse investor would hold the market portfolio of risky assets when she could earn more, *for certain,* by investing all her wealth in the risk-free asset.

The CAPM predicts that stocks that have zero covariance (correlation) with the market return will be willingly held as long as they have an expected return equal to the risk-free rate – put $\beta = 0$ in equation [6]. This is because a stock that is uncorrelated with the market return, when included in a well-diversified portfolio, does not add any additional 'covariance risk' to your portfolio – hence it only needs to earn the risk-free rate. In the real world, the returns on individual stocks often tend to move in the same direction and, in general, $\mathrm{cov}(R, R_m) \geq 0$ and $\beta \geq 0$ for most stocks. According to the CAPM, stocks that have a large positive covariance with the market return (i.e. $\beta > 0$) will have to earn a relatively high expected return in order that investors will willingly hold the stock. This is because the addition of such a stock to an already diversified portfolio adds considerably to *overall portfolio* variance.

It is often the case that the beta of a stock is used to describe the risk this particular stock adds to the portfolio. Hence, stocks for which $\beta_i = 1$ have a return that is expected to move one for one with the market portfolio (i.e. $ER_i = ER_m$) and are termed **neutral stocks**. If $\beta > 1$ the stock is said to be an **aggressive stock**, since it moves *more* than changes in the expected market return (either up or down); conversely, **defensive stocks** have $\beta < 1$. Therefore, investors can use betas to rank the relative riskiness of various stocks and their relative contribution to portfolio risk. But because this covariance risk is rewarded with a higher average return, the above should not detract from the key prediction of mean-variance portfolio theory that *all* investors willingly hold the stocks in the same optimal proportions w_i^*, given by maximising the Sharpe ratio. Hence the 'market portfolio' held by all investors will include neutral, aggressive and defensive stocks held in the *optimal proportions* w_i^*.

We hope you can now see that the CAPM is just another consequence of investors choosing the optimal portfolio of stocks by trading off risk against expected return – that is, mean-variance portfolio theory. If a stock has a high covariance with the market return – a high beta – then it adds considerably to the overall risk of the portfolio and hence investors (according to the CAPM) require a high average return on the stock to compensate for this high *incremental* risk. Then the expected (excess) return on the stock, per unit of additional (covariance or beta) risk it adds to the portfolio, will be the same for all stocks. Hence the average returns on individual stocks predicted by the CAPM are *equilibrium* returns – that is, returns that just compensate investors, so they willingly hold all stocks in their portfolio (in the optimal proportions w_i^*).

CAPM and SIM

The SIM is a purely statistical relationship between the excess return on a stock and the excess return on the market portfolio and implies that the average return on a stock is given by:

$$(\bar{R} - \bar{r}) = \alpha + \beta(\bar{R}_m - \bar{r}) \qquad [7]$$

The CAPM is an asset pricing equation that says that when all stocks are willingly held by (mean-variance) investors, their equilibrium expected return should be given by:

$$(ER - r) = \beta(ER_m - r) \qquad [8]$$

If we assume that average returns are a good (i.e. unbiased) estimate of expected returns, then the key difference between the SIM and the CAPM is that the SIM allows a non-zero value for alpha. We also learned from the SIM that Jensen's alpha can be interpreted as the *abnormal* return on the stock:

'Historical' alpha = average return on stock − return required by investors to compensate for 'covariance risk'

$$\alpha_i = (\bar{R}_i - \bar{r}) - \beta_i(\bar{R}_m - \bar{r}) \qquad [9]$$

But we now know why the term $\beta_i(\bar{R}_m - \bar{r})$ represents the return required by investors to willingly hold stock-i as part of their diversified portfolio. It follows from the above that in the real world, if the CAPM (and therefore mean-variance portfolio theory) applies to all stocks, then all stock-alphas should be zero. A non-zero alpha is therefore both a violation of the CAPM and an indication that stock-i earns an abnormal return after correcting for its contribution to portfolio risk.

There are some investors and portfolio managers who think they can 'beat the market'; that is, pick stocks that earn an average rate of return exceeding that given by the CAPM, or in other words, find stocks with non-zero alphas. 'Active stock-picking' strategies are the subject of later chapters.

13.2 SECURITY MARKET LINE

The CAPM can be rearranged and expressed in terms of the security market line (SML). You can think of the SML as follows. Take 100 stocks and calculate their average monthly return over the last 10 years, $\bar{R}_i$. These averages are taken to be a good measure of the expected return on the stocks. Then either estimate each stock's beta from a time-series regression of 10 years of its monthly stock returns on the excess market return, or take an estimate of beta from a data vendor. If the CAPM is correct, the graph of the average return on each stock against that stock's beta should lie along a straight line (Figure 13.1) – this is the *security market line (SML)*.

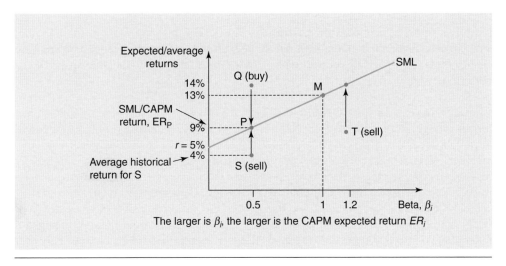

FIGURE 13.1: Security market line (SML)

We can see that the CAPM implies a linear relationship between expected returns and betas. By taking the historical average value of the market return $ER_m = 13\%$ p.a. (say) and the average risk-free rate to be 5%, then the CAPM can we written:

$$ER_i = r + 8\beta_i \qquad [10]$$

where $ER_m - r = 8\%$ p.a. is the excess return on the market (equity risk premium). This relationship between the *cross-section* of expected returns ER_i on each stock and the stock's β_i (Figure 13.1) is *linear* and is known as the *security market line (SML)* . If the CAPM is correct then the average return on *all* stocks should lie on the SML. The beta of the market portfolio is 1, so the corresponding expected return is $ER_m = 13\%$ p.a. (Figure 13.1). Any combination of stocks and borrowing/lending at the risk-free rate will also lie on the SML.

The SML can be used to try to pick underpriced and overpriced stocks and, as we shall see, this is the same as choosing stocks with positive or negative alphas. To see this, consider stock S (Figure 13.1) with $\beta_S = 0.5$ and a historical average return of 4%. You could replicate the beta of stock S by a portfolio with 50% in the safe asset ($\beta_r = 0$) and 50% in the market portfolio (index tracker) with a beta of unity, so that $\beta_p = 0.5(0) + 0.5(1) = 0.5$ But this 'synthetic portfolio' would lie on the SML (at P) and have an expected return of $ER_p = 0.5(5) + 0.5(13) = 9\%$, which is higher than the historical average return on S, even though both have the same beta of 0.5 and hence the same exposure to changes in the market return. Hence stock S earns less than portfolio P with the same beta – therefore stock S would be (short) sold, since its actual return is less than its equilibrium return given by the CAPM. If stock S is sold by investors, its *current* price will fall and this will raise its *expected* return, so that market forces tend to push the expected return on stock S back towards the SML at P. If we ignore the specific risk of stock S for the moment, a (risky) arbitrage strategy would involve, say, a $100,000 short sale of stock S, then using the funds from the short sale to invest \$50,000 in the risk-free rate and \$50,000 in the market portfolio. This is a **zero investment strategy**. The beta of this long–short position is zero, so there is no market risk in the arbitrage strategy. If S really is mispriced (and there is no change in its specific risk), you will make a (risky) arbitrage profit when the mispricing is corrected by the market[2].

Alternatively, consider stock Q, which has $\beta_Q = 0.5$ (Figure 13.1) but currently a higher historical average return than indicated by the SML/CAPM at P. An investor should purchase Q. Securities like Q and S are currently mispriced (i.e. they are not on the SML) and a speculator might short sell S and use the funds to purchase Q. If the mispricing is subsequently recognised and corrected by the market, the price of Q will rise as everyone seeks to purchase it, because of its current high 'abnormal' average return. Conversely, everyone seeks to short sell S, so its market price falls. If you had spotted this mispricing first and executed your trades before everyone else, you would earn a handsome profit from this mispricing. An interesting point is that if the market return $(R_m - r)$ either rises or falls unexpectedly over this period, you still make a profit from the mispricing – since S and Q both have the same beta and you are long S and have short sold Q.

If a stock does not lie on the SML, then it has a non-zero alpha. For example, stock Q according to the CAPM/SML should have a required (average) return of $\bar{r} + \beta(\bar{R}_m - \bar{r}) = 5 + 0.5(8) = 9\%$ p.a., but its historical average return is $\bar{R} = 14\%$. Its alpha is therefore:

$$\alpha_Q = \bar{R}_Q - [\bar{r} + \beta_Q(\bar{R}_m - \bar{r})] = 5\% \text{ p.a.} \qquad [11]$$

Stock Q has earned a 5% p.a. return over and above the required return to compensate for its contribution to portfolio risk. It is a 'positive alpha' stock and would be considered by stock pickers as a possible 'buy recommendation'.

Note, however, that a 'buy recommendation' or a 'long–short' recommendation is not a risk-free strategy – far from it. To implement this active long–short strategy one has to graph the average historical return for a set of securities $\bar{R}_i$ (say, monthly returns averaged over the past five years) against their β-estimates and look for big outlier securities like Q and S – or equivalently (and more directly) find stocks with non-zero alphas. However, remember that in practice this investment strategy is risky, since it assumes that the CAPM is true, that the βs are measured correctly and that any mispricing will be corrected over the time horizon desired by the trader (which is usually fairly short). Also, each of the stocks is subject to specific risk, which can influence the return on the stock, independently of the mispricing. If you have speculative positions in many stocks, the specific risk of your speculative *portfolio* will be reduced, although it is unlikely to be zero. Note that if you have a 'long bias' (i.e. positive portfolio alpha) or a short bias (i.e. negative portfolio alpha), then you will also usually be subject to market risk on your speculative portfolio of stocks (i.e. $\beta_p \neq 0$).

---

[2] Note that we can undertake a similar risky arbitrage with stock-T. We can replicate the beta of stock-T with $\beta_T = 1.2$, by borrowing 20% of your wealth at the risk-free rate and using your own funds plus borrowed funds to invest in the market portfolio with $\beta = 1$.

We also have to be a bit careful applying the concept of the CAPM/SML to identify individual stocks that are mispriced, since *historical* average returns on individual stocks may not be a good indicator of investors' *expected* returns over this historical period. When we take our historical average, the firm may have experienced an *unusual* run of either positive or negative specific risks, so these do not average out to zero, giving a misleading measure of expected returns. Hence one might observe a stock located below the SML, but this may be due to abnormally high negative specific risk rather than a genuinely mispriced stock. This suggest that stock pickers should form *portfolios* of mispriced stocks so that 'abnormal' runs of positive or negative specific risks are more likely to cancel out, and the historical average return is then a better measure of the expected return. (This type of measurement error is reflected in the standard error in the estimate of alpha – ideally we require large non-zero alphas with small standard errors, but not surprisingly these are hard to find.) However, a *portfolio* of mispriced stocks will have a lower specific risk than individual mispriced stocks – which reduces the possibility of future changes in specific risk leading to large changes in returns that are unanticipated by the stock picker.

CAPM as a price equation

So far we have described the CAPM in terms of expected excess *returns*, although the acronym mentions 'pricing'. However, there is a link between the CAPM equation [6] and the stock price. Let EP_{t+1} be the price expected next period (including any dividends) and P_t the price today. The expected rate of return is defined as:

$$ER = (EP_{t+1} - P_t)/P_t \qquad [12]$$

But according to the CAPM:

$$ER = r + \beta(ER_m - r) \qquad [13]$$

Solving the above equations for the current price P gives us:

$$P_t = \frac{EP_{t+1}}{(1 + d)} \quad \text{where } d = r + \beta(ER_m - r) \qquad [14]$$

Thus the CAPM implies that today's stock price equals the PV of tomorrow's expected stock price, where the 'discount rate', d, depends on the beta of the stock. The higher is the stock's beta, the larger the discount rate and the lower the current price of the stock (given the stock's expected future price). This seems very intuitive, as we know that the higher is beta the higher is the contribution of this stock to the overall risk of the (representative) investor's portfolio – it is this risk that determines investors' views of the riskiness of the firm's future cash flows. As we shall see in later chapters, equation [14] implies that the current stock price equals the PV of *all* future cash flows to equityholders, but the key element here is that these cash flows should be discounted using the CAPM required rate of return.

13.3 APPLICATIONS OF THE CAPM

The CAPM is widely used in many areas of finance. We have already noted above that it is used to determine the discount rate in PV calculations of a firm's future cash flows from a physical investment project, or in determining the PV of the future cash flows of a takeover target. Stock pickers use the CAPM to determine the discount rate to apply to future earnings or dividends of the firm, when they are trying to estimate the 'fair value' of the stock. Some other uses are noted below.

Market timing

Assuming that betas are correctly estimated and likely to stay constant in the future, then a speculator would move out of low-beta stocks and into high-beta stocks if she expects a bull market (i.e. a general rise in the stock market). If she expects a bear market (i.e. a general fall in all stock prices), she may tilt her portfolio towards low-beta stocks, or short sell high-beta stocks. (There are other ways to take advantage of timing the market using derivatives, which we explore later.)

Portfolio construction

Suppose an investor would like to hold a diversified portfolio but one that has a specific beta chosen by the investor. For example, the investor might like to hold a portfolio that moves one-for-one with the market return. Noting that $\beta_p = \sum_{i=1}^{n} w_i \beta_i$, she can easily construct such a portfolio. For example, a portfolio beta of $\beta_p = 1$ could be obtained by investing in two stocks with $\beta_1 = 1.2$ and $\beta_2 = 0.7$ holding proportions (of total wealth) of $w_1 = 3/5$ and $w_2 = 2/5$. In practice, many more stocks would be included in the portfolio to eliminate specific risk, and this is exactly what the mutual fund industry does when it provides 'index tracker' funds.

Value at risk

We will see in the chapter on market risk, how the betas of stocks and the portfolio beta can be used to simplify the calculation of the amount of risk held by a bank or other financial institution, that holds many domestic and foreign stocks.

Performance measures

We have already noted that if the investor is comparing two mutually exclusive portfolios in which to hold all of her marketable assets (e.g. stocks and bonds), then the Sharpe ratio is a useful performance measure. The Sharpe ratio is defined as the expected excess return per unit of risk (where the risk is measured as the standard deviation of portfolio returns) and hence is also known as the reward-to-variability ratio. But the Sharpe ratio can be *interpreted* in another way, involving only the difference in expected returns, and this equivalent measure is known as the 'M-squared' measure of performance; see Case Study 13.1.

CASE STUDY 13.1   THE M² PERFORMANCE MEASURE

Another way of looking at the Sharpe ratio as a measure of the performance of an active portfolio is to consider what additional return you could get from the active portfolio, if you make it have the same volatility as the market portfolio. This gives rise to the $M^{2'}$ (M-squared) performance measure.

For example, suppose that your active portfolio has an expected (excess) return of $ER_A - r = 9\%$, with a standard deviation of $\sigma_A = 15\%$, and therefore has a Sharpe ratio of $SR_A = 0.6$. Suppose that the market portfolio has $ER_m - r = 10\%, \sigma_m = 20\%$, giving a Sharpe ratio of $SR_m = 0.5$. The active portfolio therefore outperforms the market portfolio on the basis of the reward-to-variability ratio. We can interpret this performance result in a different and perhaps more intuitive way. Suppose that we combine the active portfolio with the risk-free asset so that this new portfolio N has the same risk (standard deviation) as the market portfolio. If we put a proportion w_A in the active portfolio, we know that $ER_N - r = w_A(ER_A - r)$ and $\sigma_N = w_A\sigma_A$, so if the new portfolio is constructed to have the same volatility as the market portfolio, we require $w_A = \sigma_m/\sigma_A = 20/15 = 1.3333$. So we would borrow 1.3333 of our own wealth from the bank and use this to purchase more of the active portfolio – we leverage up our active portfolio so that it has the same risk as the market porfolio. What is the resulting return on this levered active portfolio? The new portfolio will then have an expected return of $R_N = (1 - w_A)r + w_A ER_A$, so the excess return $R_N - r = w_A(ER_A - r) = 1.3333(9\%) = 12\%$. The excess return on the new portfolio is 2% more than on the market portfolio ($= 10\%$). Hence the higher Sharpe ratio of the active portfolio (0.6) compared with the market portfolio (0.5) is equivalent to a 2% higher return on the new portfolio than the market return – but the new portfolio has been constructed to have the same volatility as the market portfolio. This 2% is known as the *M-squared* (M^2) measure of performance (after Franco Modigliani and his granddaughter Leah, who popularised this approach). Note that the M^2 measure of performance contains no more information than the Sharpe ratio of the active and market portfolio – it is just a different way of presenting the implications of the two Sharpe ratios, in terms of a difference in expected returns, given the same volatility[3].

The Sharpe ratio only applies to the choice between two mutually exclusive portfolios. A more realistic scenario is where the investor is looking for mispriced stocks to add to her existing (passive) diversified portfolio. Then Jensen's alpha provides an appropriate measure of performance, since it uses beta, which measures the *incremental* risk of the stock, when we are considering adding it to our existing well-diversified passive portfolio. Jensen's alpha is often referred to as the 'abnormal return' on the stock. If these 'non-zero alpha stocks' are added to the passive portfolio in an 'optimal way' (as described in previous chapters), then the active stock picker should hold positive-alpha stocks and short sell negative-alpha stocks.

---

[3] This is easy to show: $M^2 = (R_N - r) - (ER_m - r) = w_A(ER_A - r) - (ER_m - r)$. Using $w_A = \sigma_m/\sigma_A$, then $M^2 = (SR_A - SR_m)\sigma_m$.

Generally speaking, the larger is alpha relative to the specific risk of the stock, the greater its contribution to improving the Sharpe ratio. So alpha and the Sharpe ratio as performance criteria are not unrelated – the former applies to the performance of individual stocks and the latter to performance of the overall portfolio of passive plus active stocks.

A further performance measure is the Treynor ratio (TR):

$$TR_i = \frac{ER_i - r}{\beta_i} \tag{15}$$

The Treynor ratio is used to rank stocks or portfolios of stocks. A high performer is a stock that has a high expected (average) excess return relative to its risk, as measured by its beta. (This is similar to the Sharpe ratio, except the latter applies to the whole portfolio so 'risk' is measured by the standard deviation of portfolio returns, whereas the TR applies to individual stocks and so risk is the stock's beta.) If the CAPM applies to all stocks, then the Traynor ratio for all stocks would be the same[4].

However, if some stocks have non-zero alphas then there is a link between TR and Jensen's alpha:

$$TR_i = \alpha/\beta_i + (ER_m - r) \tag{16}$$

Note that a stock with the highest Jensen's alpha need not have the highest TR value, so these two performance criteria can rank stocks differently. As we shall see in later chapters, the 'abnormal return' or alpha of a stock is easily generalised to the case where there is more than one factor that is thought to influence stock returns, hence alpha is a much more common measure of the abnormal performance of a stock (or portfolio of stocks) than is the TR.

13.4 ARBITRAGE PRICING THEORY (APT)

The APT first appeared in 1976 (Ross, 1976), yet for many students it is a little difficult to grasp, as its derivation is not as intuitively appealing as the CAPM. The APT is a multifactor model that allows a number of potential variables (factors) to influence the expected return on any stock, whereas the CAPM allows only one factor, namely market return. At the end of the day, the APT allows the expected (average) return on any firm's stock to be determined by the firm's exposure to different sources of systematic risk or 'factors'. Its exposure to these sources of risk is measured by the beta with respect to each factor. The average required return on the firm's stock then depends on the size of the different betas, which measure its exposure to each risk factor. The APT is a multifactor model of equilibrium (required) returns, but the ideas behind the APT are very different to those behind the CAPM. The CAPM is based on the behaviour of optimising mean-variance investors (all of whom have homogeneous expectations or beliefs), whereas in the APT the determinants of

---

[4] The CAPM states that $(ER_i - r) = \beta_i(ER_m - r)$ and therefore $TR_i = (ER_i - r)/\beta_i = ER_m - r$. So the Treynor ratio is the same for all stocks, if the CAPM holds for all stock returns.

expected stock returns are the result of investors eliminating any (risk-free) arbitrage profits in the market.

Broadly speaking, the APT allows the *actual return* on any stock to be influenced by a number of market-wide variables or 'factors', such as interest rates, the exchange rate and so on. The sensitivity of the return on any stock to each of these factors are the 'factor betas'. So the APT implies that the return on stock A is given by:

$$R_A = a_A + \sum_{j=1}^{k} b_{A,j} F_j + \varepsilon_A \tag{17}$$

where F_j are the factors (variables) that influence the return on stock A and $b_{A,j}$ measure the exposure of firm A to these factors. ε_A represents firm-specific risk. Equation [17] is similar to the CAPM, if we assume that there is only a single factor, which is the excess return on the market portfolio.

Using a relatively sophisticated proof based on risk-free arbitrage, it is possible to show that equation [17] gives an expression for the *equilibrium-expected return* on stock A (when it is held as part of a diversified portfolio):

$$ER_A = \lambda_0 + \lambda_1 b_{A,1} + \lambda_2 b_{A,2} + \cdots \lambda_k b_{A,k} \tag{18}$$

Equation [18] is the APT equivalent of the SML, since it shows that the equilibrium-expected return on stock A depends on a *set of* (factor) betas. If a factor does not influence equilibrium returns, the factor is said to be 'not priced'. Assume that we have two factors, inflation and interest rates:

$$R_A = a_A + b_{A,1} F_1 + b_{A,2} F_2 + \varepsilon_A \tag{19}$$

$$ER_A = \lambda_0 + \lambda_1 b_{A,1} + \lambda_2 b_{A,2} \tag{20}$$

where R_A is the actual return on stock A
$\quad b_{A,j}$ are 'risk factor' exposures
$\quad F_1$ = the change in inflation
$\quad F_2$ = the change in interest rates
$\quad ER_A$ = the equilibrium return on stock A

Strictly, the factors F are *unexpected* events or 'news'. In practice, the change in a variable is often deemed to be unforecastable and is taken as a measure of an unexpected event. Notice that the APT implies that the λs are the same for all stocks (but the betas differ). The theory therefore implies that stocks A and B, with the same sensitivity to economic factors (e.g. $b_{A,1} = b_{B,1}$ etc.), will offer the same equilibrium return. This is because the factors that are 'priced' give rise to 'factor risk' that cannot be diversified away and therefore must influence the risk-adjusted (required) return on the stock.

As with the CAPM and SIM, we can estimate the betas using multiple regression analysis with time-series data on the stock return and the factors. One of the drawbacks of the APT is that it does not tell us exactly what the factors are, or how many factors should be used in

TABLE 13.1: Equilibrium excess returns, APT

Factors	Impact of betas on expected returns λ	Factor betas Firm A b_A	Factor betas Firm B b_B	Contribution to expected excess returns by the individual factors = $\lambda.b_A$ Firm A	Contribution to expected excess returns by the individual factors = $\lambda.b_B$ Firm B
Industrial production	2.75	0.3	0.5	0.825	1.375
Inflation	−4.25	−0.2	−0.1	0.85	0.425
Term structure	1.50	1.8	0	2.7	0
Market return	3.85	1.3	1.0	5.005	3.85
Expected excess return				9.38	5.65

explaining stock returns. But common risk factors used include the growth rate of industrial production, inflation, a credit spread and the (long-short) term spread.

Let's look at an example of how the results from the APT can be interpreted in a four-factor APT model (Table 13.1), where the intercept λ_0 is taken to be the risk-free rate, so the equation explains equilibrium *excess* returns. The λs represent the impact of 'beta risk' on expected returns and each λ is the same for all stocks. What is different between the two stocks is their *exposures* to the different factors, represented by their beta values. We can see that firm A is more exposed to movements in the market return, since its b_{MKT} is higher than that of firm B. Hence changes in the market return make a larger contribution to firm A's expected return than to firm B's expected return. Firm B's return is not influenced by changes in the term structure factor, as it has a beta of zero with respect to this factor. Firm B might be a media or IT firm whose stock return is not affected by changes in interest rates, whereas firm A, which might be a bank, has a beta exposure to this variable of 1.8. Both firms' stock returns are influenced by changes in industrial production and in inflation, and therefore the betas with respect to both of these variables influence both stocks' expected returns.

Heuristic derivation of the APT

Broadly speaking, the APT implies that the return on a stock can be broken down into an expected return and an unexpected or surprise component. For any individual stock, this surprise or news component can be further broken down into 'general economic news' that affects all stocks and 'specific news' that affects only this particular stock. For example, news that affects all stocks might be an unexpected announcement of a change in interest rates by the central bank or an unexpected rise in oil prices. The APT predicts that 'general news' will affect the rate of return on *all* stocks but by different amounts. For example, a 1% unexpected rise in interest rates might affect the return on stocks of a company that was highly levered more than that for a company that was less levered, whereas an unexpected rise in oil prices might affect the stock returns on manufacturing companies more than the stocks of banks. The APT for any stock A may be represented:

$$R_A = ER_A + u_A \qquad [21]$$

where R_A is the actual rate of return on stock A, ER_A is the expected return on stock A and u_A is the unexpected or news element. We can further subdivide the news element u_A into *systematic (or market) risk m_t* – that is, risk that affects a large number of stocks each to a greater or lesser degree; and *specific risk (unsystematic or idiosyncratic risk) ε_A*, that specifically affects a single firm or small group of firms:

$$u_A = m_t + \varepsilon_A \qquad [22]$$

As in the case of the CAPM, we shall find that systematic risk cannot be diversified away because this element of news or new information affects *all* companies. However, we noted in earlier chapters that specific risk can be diversified away. In order to make the APT operational, we need some idea of what causes systematic risk. News about economy-wide variables may be, for example, a government announcement that GDP is higher than expected or a sudden increase in interest rates by the Central Bank. These economy-wide **factors** F may have different effects on different stocks and this is reflected in the different values for the factor betas:

$$m_t = b_{A,1}(F_1 - EF_1) + b_{A,2}(F_2 - EF_2) + \cdots \qquad [23]$$

where E represents expectations of the variable, so that $F - EF$ is the 'surprise' in the factor (i.e. the news). For example, if the market consensus forecast for interest rates is 4% p.a. but interest rates actually turn out to be 5% p.a., then the news or surprise is $F - EF = +1\%$. If a particular stock's interest rate beta equals 0.5, then for every 1% that the interest rate is above its expected level, this would increase the actual return on the stock by 1/2%. Note that the betas here do not have the same interpretation as the CAPM betas and hence are denoted b rather than β.

Portfolio returns

A crucial assumption of the APT is that specific risk ε_i is uncorrelated across different firms, so for any two stocks $Cov(\varepsilon_i, \varepsilon_j) = 0$ and therefore specific risk can be diversified away by holding a large number of securities. For simplicity, suppose that there is only one systematic risk factor, F, and $i = 1,2,3,\ldots n$ securities in the portfolio (held in proportions x_i), hence:

$$R_p = \sum_{i=1}^{n} x_i R_i = \sum_{i=1}^{n} x_i (ER_i + b_i F + \varepsilon_i) = ER_p + b_p F + \varepsilon_p \qquad [24]$$

where $ER_p = \sum_{i=1}^{n} x_i ER_i$ is the expected return on the portfolio, $b_p = \sum_{i=1}^{n} x_i b_i$ is the beta of the portfolio of stocks and $\varepsilon_p = \sum_{i=1}^{n} x_i \varepsilon_i$ is the specific risk of the portfolio. If the specific risk is uncorrelated across securities, then some of the ε_i will be positive and some negative, but their weighted sum is likely to be close to zero. In fact, as the number of securities increases, specific risk is diversified away and $\varepsilon_p \to 0$. Hence in general the APT predicts that:

> The return on a *diversified portfolio* is made up of the *expected* returns on the individual securities plus the systematic risk exposures represented by the factor betas and the level of the economy-wide news factors, F. Specific risk is diversified away and hence does not influence the return on a well-diversified *portfolio*.

It is the possibility of diversifying away the systematic risk that allows one to construct a 'zero-risk arbitrage portfolio', which then results in the key equation (for a two-factor model);

$$ER_i = \lambda_0 + \lambda_1 b_{1,i} + \lambda_2 b_{2,i} \qquad [25]$$

This equation is equivalent to the SML in the CAPM, except here we have two factor betas. The betas are estimated from a time-series regression of stock returns on the (two) factors (e.g. changes in output, changes in interest rates). We then repeat this for 100 different stocks (say) and obtain two betas for each stock. If we assume that the expected return is accurately measured by the historical average return $\overline{R}_i$, then we can perform a cross-section regression of the 100 values of $\overline{R}_i$ (one for each firm's stock) on the two betas for each of these stocks and hence obtain estimates of the λ coefficients. We can use equation [25] in the same way as we used the SML to obtain the required return on any individual stock – this required return can then be used as a discount rate to calculate the PV of the firm's future cash flows (to equity). On the other hand, if we are a stock picker and we find stocks with an average return $\overline{R}_i$ that does not equal our estimate of the required return ($\lambda_0 + \lambda_1 b_{1,i} + \lambda_2 b_{2,i}$), then this stock is potentially under- or overpriced and should be purchased or sold short.

For stocks that do not lie on the SML, we demonstrated above how you could construct a replication portfolio P using the risk-free rate and the market portfolio, which has the same beta as the mispriced stock S but has an expected return that lies on the SML (Figure 13.1). It followed that you could take a 'long–short' position in S and P and earn arbitrage profits. As the betas of S and P are equal, the only risk is the specific risk of stock S. In the APT we can perform a similar arbitrage strategy with mispriced securities, but as the APT assumes that we can form well-diversified portfolios, any specific risk is diversified away and the arbitrage can be shown to be (virtually) risk-free. It is this risk-free arbitrage that keeps the expected return on any stock equal to ($\lambda_0 + \lambda_1 b_{1,i} + \lambda_2 b_{2,i}$) – this is the APT equivalent of the SML.

The APT is not used in practical situations as much as the CAPM, but the idea that more than one variable can influence stock returns is one that has been widely used in many areas of finance. Anywhere you can use the CAPM, you can in principle use the APT if you think that stock returns (or portfolios of stocks) are influenced by more than one factor. In Chapter 29, you will see that the abnormal performance of fund managers is not measured by Jensen's alpha but by an alpha based on a multifactor model similar to the APT.

13.5 TESTING THE CAPM AND MULTIFACTOR MODELS

There has been substantial testing of the CAPM and the evidence is rather mixed. A simple test is to see if the alpha in a time-series regression of excess stock returns on the market return is statistically zero. In general, it is difficult to find individual stocks with non-zero alphas, so this evidence tends to support the CAPM.

Another type of test is first to estimate the betas of, say, 100 stocks using monthly data over the last 10 years – we tend not to use more than 10 years of data because we may not expect betas to be constant over a very long horizon. This is the *first-pass regression.* We then perform a *second-pass regression* by taking the mean returns (calculated using the last 10 years of monthly returns) $\bar{R}_i$ on our $i = 1,2,3,\ldots 100$ stocks and, regressing this on the 100 different betas of our stocks – we are estimating the SML. This regression is:

$$\bar{R}_i - \bar{r} = \gamma_0 + \gamma_1\beta_i$$

If the CAPM is correct then $\gamma_0 = 0$ and $\gamma_1 = \bar{R}_m - \bar{r}$, the average excess return on the market portfolio over the last 10 years. It is found that γ_1 is less than the historical average of $\bar{R}_m - \bar{r}$, so the estimated SML is flatter than the SML given by the CAPM. Also, γ_0 is found to be positive and statistically significant. When other variables such as the specific risk of each stock $\sigma^2(\varepsilon_i)$ are added to the above equation, it is found to be statistically insignificant.

We can improve the power of our statistical tests by using *portfolios* of stocks in the second-pass regression. For example, we could take our 100 stocks and *randomly* divide them into 10 portfolios, each containing 10 stocks. We then use time-series data on the 10 portfolios to estimate the 10 portfolio betas. As the specific risk of the stocks in each portfolio is likely to be uncorrelated across stocks, the specific risk of each portfolio will be small and our estimates of the 10 portfolio betas will be more precise. But there is a big drawback here. We now only have 10 betas (rather than 100 betas) with which to estimate the second-pass regression, so γ_0 and γ_1 will be less precisely estimated. There is another way in which we can try to get round the last problem. After the first-pass regression, where we obtain 100 estimates of beta, instead of *randomly* allocating stocks to the 10 portfolios we can allocate them on the basis of the size of their betas. Hence portfolio 1 will contain the 10 stocks with the highest betas, portfolio 2 the 10 stocks with the next highest betas and so on, until portfolio 10 has the 10 stocks with the lowest betas. The aim here is to get the largest *spread* in the betas, between the lowest-beta portfolio and the highest-beta portfolio. It is well known that estimates of γ_1 are more precise (i.e. have lower standard errors), the more 'spread out' are the values of the independent variables (the $\beta_i's, i = 1,2,\ldots 10$) in the regression.

Above there is some good news for the CAPM – specific risk is not priced and the average return has a positive relationship with stocks' betas. However, the bad news is that the slope of the empirical SML is too flat. So the CAPM is qualitatively correct but fails some of the *quantitative* predictions of the theory.

When theories fail to pass some empirical tests, there are always some 'get-out' clauses – the theory could have failed because various subsidiary conditions are not met. For example, these include:

- Betas are measured with error and this may bias estimates of γ_0 and γ_1 in the second-pass regression.
- Betas may not be constant over time and use of a short data set may imply that statistical tests are inconclusive or, again, biased.
- Roll (1977) and Ross and Roll (1995) have shown that the only really testable implication of the CAPM is that the market portfolio held by all investors is mean-variance efficient – that is, it is on the efficient frontier. So the CAPM is not testable until we know the true portfolio weights in the optimal market portfolio – but we can never know this since we do not know investors' true expectations of individual stock returns, their variances and covariances – we can only estimate them.
- It has also been shown that if you use a market proxy (e.g. S&P 500) that is only slightly different from the true (mean-variance efficient) market portfolio, then you may find no statistical relationship between the average return on stocks and the stocks' *estimated* betas, even though the CAPM is true, when you use the 'true' market portfolio to estimate beta[5].

Moving on to tests of multifactor models, we can always include in the first-pass time-series regression any variable that we think might influence the time series of stock returns. Then we can see if the beta of this factor is statistically significant in the second-pass regression. There are hundreds of studies that use this approach. Some have found that a 'risk premium beta' (based on a factor that is the difference between the yield on high-grade and low-grade bond yields) or a 'labour income beta' (based on a 'growth in labour income' factor) or a 'private business wealth beta' (based on the idea that changes in private business wealth are a risk factor for small businesses), are statistically significant determinants of average stock returns.

Other studies have used macroeconomic factors such as the unexpected growth in industrial production, unexpected inflation or unexpected changes in the term premium (i.e. the spread between the yields on long-term government bonds and short-term government bonds), as well as the 'risk premium beta' noted above. Liquidity is clearly a risk factor–if you cannot sell some stocks without moving their price substantially, then you would want compensation for such liquidity risk. When multifactor models are considered, it is generally the case that evidence in favour of the CAPM is weaker than when we simply look at the expected return–market beta relationship of the SML, but there is little consensus about whether additional factors are really important and whether their effects might only apply in specific historical periods.

Perhaps the most widely accepted multifactor model is the Fama-French three-factor model. This model is based on the empirical fact that the returns on (portfolios of) small stocks earn a higher average return than given by their CAPM betas (i.e. average returns on small stocks lie above the SML). It is also found that stocks with high book-to-market values[6] have high

---

[5] Some of you will recognise that the reason we know the 'true' market portfolio is that we can simulate data on returns and then uses this simulated data to obtain the optimal portfolio weights given by mean-variance portfolio theory – this is Monte Carlo simulation.

[6] The book value of the assets of a company are those 'written in the accounts'. The market value is the price of the stocks multiplied by the number of stocks outstanding in the market.

average returns, which exceed those predicted by the SML. In a first-pass regression Fama-French use a 'size factor', SMB ('small minus big'), in their regression – SMB is a measure of the difference between the returns on small versus big stocks. The economic rational underpinning the specification of a 'size beta' is related to relative prospects. The earnings prospects of small firms may be more sensitive to economic conditions, with a resulting higher probability of distress during economic downturns, hence stocks of small firms are more risky than stocks of large firms.

The book-to-market factor, known as 'high minus low' (HML), is a measure of the difference between the returns on stocks whose firms have a high book-to-market value and those firms that have a low book-to-market value. Firms with high book-to-market ratios represent firms whose prices have 'overshot' on the downside, are 'fallen angels' and therefore are more likely to fail in the future, and hence are more risky.

There is a continuing debate as to whether the above factors really measure systematic economic risks of particular types of firms. But the *betas* on the HML and SMB factors help explain the spread of average returns on many different stock portfolios. For example, if all stocks (e.g. on the NYSE, NASDAQ and AMEX) are divided into portfolios based on three different levels of market capitalisation – small, S; medium, M; and big, B – and then each is further divided into three different levels by book-to-market value – high, H; medium, D; and low, L – then we have nine portfolios (S/H, S/D, S/L, M/H, M/D, M/L, B/H, B/D, B/L) and nine portfolio returns series. The excess market return, SMB and HML factors all explain the time-series movements in these nine portfolio returns with R-squareds in excess of 0.9. When we investigate the second-pass regressions, the average returns on these nine portfolios depend strongly on the SMB factor-beta and the HML factor-beta, indicating that these factors are priced, whereas the CAPM market betas are around unity for all nine portfolios, and hence they do little in explaining the spread of *average* returns across the portfolios. We explore this type of multifactor model further in Chapter 29.

SUMMARY

- The CAPM is a logical outcome of (mean-variance) investors holding stocks in order to maximise the reward-to-variability (Sharpe) ratio.
- The CAPM implies that the expected (average) excess return on any stock depends on the stock's beta. The beta of a stock represents the relative *contribution* of the stock's return to the risk of the overall portfolio – the higher a stock's beta, the higher its covariance risk with other stocks in the portfolio, and hence the higher expected (average) return it must earn, in order that investors will hold the stock as part of their diversified portfolio.
- The SML is a logical consequence of the CAPM and implies that the average return on stocks increase (linearly) with the stock's beta – higher betas imply higher expected (average) returns.
- If a stock does not lie on the SML, this implies that it has a non-zero alpha and speculators should either buy the stock (positive alpha) or short sell the stock (negative alpha).

- The CAPM/SML can be used in a variety of applications, such as determining appropriate discount rates for a firm's cost of equity capital, forming portfolios with specific exposures to the market return and in stock-picking strategies.
- Empirical evidence in favour of the CAPM/SML is mixed. It is difficult to find stocks with non-zero alphas and specific risk does not influence average returns on stocks – these results support the CAPM/SML. However, the average returns on some portfolios of stocks (e.g. average returns on stocks with high book-to-market values relative to average returns on stocks with low book-to-market values) are not explained by the difference in market betas – so some portfolios require several betas to explain average returns, which leads to multifactor models.
- The APT implies that if risk-free arbitrage opportunities are eliminated, the expected (average) return on any stock should depend on that stock's exposure (i.e. betas) with respect to a set of systematic risk factors (e.g. interest rates, inflation). A stock's exposure to each of these systematic risk factors is measured by the betas of the stock's return with respect to the separate factors.

APPENDIX 13.1: DERIVATION OF THE CAPM

A simplified derivation of the CAPM that incorporates some intuition can be derived as follows. The variance of the optimal market portfolio is:

$$
\begin{aligned}
\sigma_m^2 = \; & w_1(w_1\sigma_{11} + w_2\sigma_{12} + w_3\sigma_{13} + \cdots + w_n\sigma_{1n}) \\
& + w_2(w_1\sigma_{21} + w_2\sigma_{22} + w_3\sigma_{23} + \cdots + w_n\sigma_{2n}) + \cdots \\
& + w_n(w_1\sigma_{n1} + w_2\sigma_{n2} + w_3\sigma_{n3} + \cdots + w_n\sigma_{nn})
\end{aligned}
\tag{A1}
$$

where the ws are the optimal weights held in each stock and the $\sigma_{i,j}$ are the return covariances $\sigma(R_i, R_j)$[7]. If the second stock in the portfolio is Ford, then the contribution of Ford's stock return to the variance of the market portfolio is:

$$
w_F[w_1\mathrm{cov}(R_F, R_1) + w_F\mathrm{cov}(R_F, R_F) + w_3\mathrm{cov}(R_F,R_3) + \cdots + w_n\mathrm{cov}(R_F, R_n)]
\tag{A2}
$$

Hence in a well-diversified portfolio, the contribution of Ford's stock to the portfolio variance is dominated by all the covariance terms rather than the single variance term $\mathrm{cov}(R_F, R_F)$. The market return is given by:

$$
R_m = w_1R_1 + w_2R_2 + \cdots + w_nR_n
\tag{A3}
$$

Hence it is easy to see that the term in square brackets is Ford's covariance with the market return:

$$
\text{Ford's contribution to portfolio variance} = w_F\mathrm{cov}(R_F, R_m)
\tag{A4}
$$

---

[7] We have re-written σ_1^2 as '$\sigma_{1,1}$' etc., since the variance of a stock return is simply its covariance with itself.

The *contribution* of Ford to the risk premium of the market portfolio is $w_F(ER_m - r)$, hence the reward-to-risk ratio of Ford is:

$$\frac{Ford's\ contribution\ to\ market\ risk\ premium}{Ford's\ contribution\ to\ market\ variance} = \frac{w_F(ER_F - r)}{w_F cov(R_F, R_m)} = \frac{(ER_F - r)}{cov(R_F, R_m)}$$

[A5]

For the market (tangency) portfolio the reward-to-risk ratio is:

$$\frac{market\ risk\ premium}{market\ variance} = \frac{(ER_m - r)}{\sigma_m^2}$$

[A6]

This ratio is known as the **market price of risk**. If all stocks are to be willingly held by investors, then they must have the same reward-to-risk ratio and this must be the same as the reward-to-risk ratio for the market portfolio itself, otherwise the latter would not be optimal for investors. If two stocks did not have the same reward-to-risk ratios, investors would buy the stock with the higher reward-to-risk ratio, pushing up its current price and hence reducing its future expected return (given unchanged company profits and dividends). Investors would also sell the stock with the lower reward-to-risk ratio, thus lowering its price and raising its expected future return. Hence market forces would tend to bring the two reward-to-variability ratios into equality. At that point there would be no incentive to buy or sell particular stocks – we would have 'market equilibrium'. If we equate the *contribution* of the reward-to-risk ratio of Ford to the reward-to-risk ratio for the market portfolio, we obtain:

$$\frac{(ER_F - r)}{cov(R_F, R_m)} = \frac{(ER_m - r)}{\sigma_m^2}$$

[A7]

Rearranging the above equation we obtain the CAPM for Ford:

$$(ER_F - r) = \frac{cov(R_F, R_m)}{\sigma_m^2}(ER_m - r) = \beta_F(ER_m - r)$$

[A8]

The CAPM states that when Ford stock's are held by mean-variance investors as part of a diversified portfolio, the expected excess return on Ford's stocks will equal Ford's beta multiplied by the expected return on the market portfolio (i.e. the equity risk premium). Finally note that:

$$\sigma_m^2 = \left[w_1 cov(R_1, R_m) + w_2 cov(R_2, R_m) + w_3 cov(R_3, R_m) + \cdots + w_n cov(R_n, R_m)\right]$$

[A9]

Rearranging the equation for β_i:

$$cov(R_i, R_m) = \beta_i \sigma_m^2$$

[A10]

and substituting equation [A10] in [A9] we have:

$$\sum_{i=1}^{n} w_i \beta_i = 1$$

[A11]

So for the market portfolio, the weighted sum of betas equals 1– this is another way of saying that the beta of the market portfolio is 1. A stock with $\beta_i = 0$ when added to the portfolio has zero *additional* effect on portfolio variance, whereas a stock with $\beta_i < 0$ when added to the portfolio tends to reduce portfolio variance. Of course, the greater the amount of stock-i held (i.e. the larger is the absolute value of w_i), the greater is the impact of β_i on total portfolio variance. Since a stock with a small value of β_i considerably reduces the overall variance of a risky portfolio, it will be willing-ly held even though this stock has a relatively low expected return. All investors are trading off risk, which they dislike, against expected return, which they do like. Stocks that reduce overall portfolio risk therefore command relatively low returns, but are nevertheless willingly held as part of a well-diversified portfolio.

EXERCISES

Q1 The CAPM predicts that the required rate of return on any risky asset-i is given by:

$$ER_i = r + \beta_i(ER_m - r)$$

where $ER_m =$ expected market return, $r =$ risk-free rate.

a) Explain the intuitive logic behind the CAPM relationship. How would you measure beta?

b) Intuitively, when a risky asset earns less than the risk free return r, why would you continue to hold this risky asset?

Q2 The security market line (SML) is a rearrangement of the CAPM equation. It is a graph of ER_i against β_i and has the form

$$ER_i = r + (ER_m - r)\beta_i$$

where ER_i, ER_m and r are usually measured by average historical values (using past data).

a) Draw the SML for a case where the (average) excess return on the market is $(ER_m - r) = 5\%$ and the risk-free rate is $r = 3\%$.

b) Suppose that a stock Z has a beta of – 1 and an average historical return of 4%. Plot this on the graph. Is there a risky arbitrage opportunity? If so, what would you do, buy or sell Z?

c) Does a risky arbitrage opportunity exist if a stock has a beta of 3 and an aver-age historical return of 20%?

Q3 What are the practical uses for the CAPM/beta relationship? Show that the SML can be rearranged to give a (one-period) model of the fair price of equity.

Q4 What are the key differences between the APT and the CAPM? What are the problems in testing the APT empirically?

Q5 Suppose the price of risk for five factors are as follows:

Factor		Price of factor risk
1	Industrial production	2.5
2	Inflation	−4
3	Excess market return	3.5
4	Term structure	1
5	Oil	1.5

If two portfolios have the following factor sensitivities (factor betas), what would be the expected equilibrium excess returns for the two portfolios?

Factor		Factor sensitivities	
		Portfolio A	Portfolio B
1	Industrial production	1.5	1.2
2	Inflation	1.5	−0.5
3	Excess market return	1.5	0.9
4	Term structure	2	0
5	Oil	5	0.8

PART 4

EQUITY MARKETS

Stock Valuation and the EMH

AIMS

- To estimate the fair value of a stock using PV techniques and discount rates based on either the capital asset pricing model/security market line (CAPM/SML) or the arbitrage pricing theory (APT).
- To calculate the fair value of a stock using the dividend discount model.
- To calculate fair value using 'relative valuation' and comparables.
- To discuss the efficient markets hypothesis (EMH) and 'stock-picking' strategies.

INTRODUCTION

Portfolio theory suggests that if all investors have the same expectations about returns, variances and correlations and they wish to 'trade off' risk against return, then they will all hold the market portfolio – they are 'passive' investors. However, some investors might feel that they have superior information about the performance of some stocks and will want to tilt their portfolio towards stocks they expect to do abnormally well and away from stocks they expect to do relatively poorly – in short, they wish to speculate with part of the portfolio. If speculators think they can accurately calculate fair value (V) and this differs from the market price (P), then they could earn profits by buying underpriced shares (i.e. where P < V) and short selling overpriced shares (i.e. where P > V). To undertake such a speculative strategy the investor has to be able to calculate the 'fair value' of the stock and the various methods to do this are outlined in this chapter.

Is there an optimal time for a firm to issue new shares? If the firm knows that its current share price P is above its true or fair value V, then it should issue shares today since it will have to issue fewer shares for any *given amount of finance it wishes to raise*. However, in an 'efficient market' the firm does not have such a timing advantage since the market price always equals fair value.

In earlier chapters we noted that the fair value of an asset is determined by the PV of future cash flows. For equity (stocks) there are two major problems. First, future cash flows are uncertain and we need some forecasting method to predict them. Second, the discount rate should reflect the riskiness of these cash flows. Broadly speaking, the greater the risk, the greater the discount factor. We have already noted the 'mirror image' relationship between PV and the internal rate of return (IRR). This also applies to stock picking, where we can classify under- (over-) valued shares using either the PV or IRR approach.

14.1 FAIR VALUE AND EMH

In previous chapters we have calculated the fair value of the firm to equityholders V_S by:

a) Estimating enterprise value (using the WACC) and deducting the value of outstanding debt,
   or
b) Estimating the FCF to equityholders only and discounting using the cost of equity capital.

The fair value of a single stock is then $V_{equity} = V_S/N_S$, where N_S is the number of stocks outstanding. A method very similar to the FCF-to-equity approach is simply to calculate fair value by considering dividends *per share* as the best measure of payments to stockholders. Because future dividends are uncertain (Figure 14.1), the discount rate R should reflect the riskiness of these *future* dividend payments.

$$V_{equity} = \frac{D_1}{(1 + R_1)} + \frac{D_2}{(1 + R_2)^2} + \ldots \ldots$$

[1]

where D_i = *forecast* dividend payments per share and R_i = expected (levered) cost of equity capital in each future year. Note that forecasting FCF to equityholders is very similar to

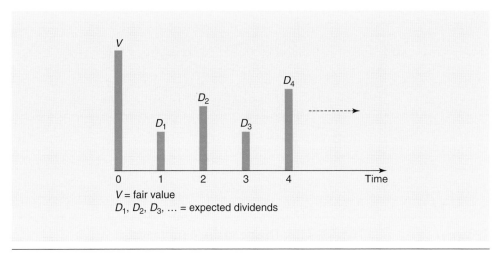

FIGURE 14.1: Equities cash flow

forecasting dividends, since the latter are basically the FCFs to equityholders that are actually *distributed* to shareholders.

Sometimes analysts think they can produce good estimates of dividends over, say, the next four years, but are prepared to assume that dividends will grow at a constant rate from then on. This gives rise to the *two-period model* (i.e. years 1–4 followed by all other years):

$$V_{equity} = \frac{D_1}{(1 + R_1)} + \frac{D_2}{(1 + R_2)^2} + \frac{D_3}{(1 + R_3)^3} + \frac{D_4}{(1 + R_4)^4} + \frac{CV_4}{(1 + R_4)^4} \qquad [2]$$

where $CV_4 = D_5/(R - g)$ is the 'continuing value' (at time $t = 4$) of *all* future dividends after year 4 – assuming constant dividend growth, and R is the (constant) discount rate applicable after year 4. Because of the uncertainty surrounding estimates of the discount rate, $R_i (i = 1, 2, 3, 4)$ are often assumed to be constant in years 1 to 4. Forecasting future dividends is similar to forecasting the FCF to equity (per share) and then multiplying by the payout ratio (i.e. the proportion of earnings paid out in dividends); the latter tends to be fairly constant for mature firms. Hence all the techniques we have talked about for forecasting cash flows from published accounts and other information (e.g. industry prospects) can be used to help forecast dividends.

Dividend discount model: DDM

If we assume that dividends will grow at a constant rate g *from today* (see Figure 14.2) and that the cost of equity capital R is expected to remain constant (over time) then:

$$V_{equity} = \frac{D_0(1 + g)}{(1 + R)} + \frac{D_0(1 + g)^2}{(1 + R)^2} + \cdots \qquad [3]$$

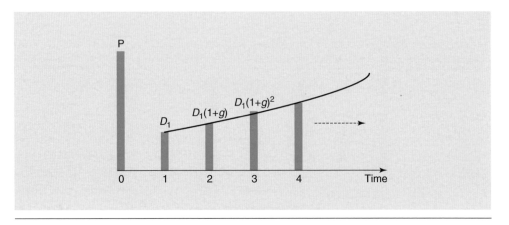

FIGURE 14.2: Dividend discount model

This formula simplifies to:

$$V_{equity} = \frac{D_1}{(R - g)} \qquad [4]$$

where D_1 = forecast dividends at the end of the current year so that $D_1 = D_0(1 + g)$. This is known as the dividend discount (or Gordon growth) model. The discount rate is the cost of equity capital for the firm, which is determined by the 'required return on equity' that investors expect to earn, in order that they will willingly hold the stock (as part of a diversified portfolio of stocks). The CAPM provides one method of estimating R.

The DDM is a rather simple model of valuation, but it may be quite useful in obtaining at least a ball-park estimate of the value of equity; and with alternative scenarios it can provide some idea of how sensitive your valuation calculation is to changes in your assumptions about growth rates and the discount rate.

Stock price volatility

The DDM can be used to illustrate why stock prices may be highly volatile even though investors act in a perfectly rational way and the market always prices stocks correctly (i.e. P = V). Suppose that in January investors think that dividends next year will be D_1 = $10, they will grow at 3% p.a. (i.e. g = 0.03) and the cost of equity capital is R = 0.10. The price of the stock in an efficient market will be P = $D_1/(R - g)$ = $142.8. Now suppose that one month later investors revise the growth rate of dividends down to g = 0.02. Then the new price will be set at P = $125. This is a capital loss of over 12% in one month for anyone who holds the stock. Hence, it is not surprising that changes in stock prices are highly volatile as new information (or news) about future dividend growth (or changes in perceptions of risk that affect the required return on equity) lead to large changes in price, even when traders are acting in a rational way. However, it has been argued (e.g. see Cuthbertson and Nitzsche, 2004) that the stock market is *excessively* volatile, as the observed volatility in actual prices is greater than would occur if investors were always rational and the market were efficient.

Efficient markets hypothesis

Suppose that some active investors use all available information to forecast future dividends and the discount rate and they use equation [4] to calculate the fair price of the stock, which we assume is $V = \$10$. If the actual quoted price $P = \$8$, then speculators would buy the stock, since it is currently underpriced and in the future they would expect the actual price to move towards the fair value, as other investors recognise that it is underpriced. When other investors recognise that the stock is underpriced they purchase the stock and its price begins to rise. When the market price reaches $10, there is no incentive for anyone to purchase the stock (for speculative purposes) because its price now equals its fundamental value (i.e. $P = V$). If you had reacted quickly to the underpricing and purchased at $8, you would sell at $10 and make a capital gain of $2. As all informed investors quickly execute this strategy, the market price will rise very quickly to equal the fair value of $10.

As new information becomes available, this will quickly be reflected in the market price. Suppose that today $P = V = \$10$. However, after the announcement of a successful new drugs trial that would result in higher future profits and dividends for a pharmaceutical firm, one might expect this to lead to a reappraisal of the fair value to, say, $V = \$12$ and for the actual price to rise immediately to $12. Any new information (or news) is quickly reflected in the market price. The ideas discussed above are the basis for what financial economists call the *efficient markets hypothesis* (EMH; see Case Study 14.1).

CASE STUDY 14.1   EFFICIENT MARKETS HYPOTHESIS

- Investors use all available (relevant) information to calculate the fair value of a stock. This is sometimes referred to as *informational efficiency* or rational expectations.
- Stock prices immediately move to reflect fair value, so that $P = V$ at all times.
- Prices only move when new information or news about fundamental variables like future dividends occurs – but as news is unpredictable, so are stock returns.
- It is impossible to trade stocks and make 'abnormal' returns (i.e. returns in excess of the risks in holding stocks) after accounting for the transaction costs of the trade – you cannot 'pick winners'.

It is important to adjust any speculative profits for the risks undertaken and it is this that makes the EMH difficult to test. In the above example, the potential capital gain of $2 as the price moves up from $P = \$8$ to equal $V = \$10$ might involve substantial risk and hence, although a profit on the trade might be made, this may not warrant the risks involved.

If the EMH always held, then P would always be equal to V – there would never be any speculative profits to be made. This is similar to the apocryphal story of a student who joyfully explained to his finance professor that when walking down the street he spotted a $100 bill on the pavement (sidewalk) in the town's marketplace (mall). The professor replied, 'I don't believe you, the market is efficient so someone would have already picked it up.' Well, not quite correct perhaps, but you don't see many $100 bills (or even $1 bills) on the sidewalk, do you? Hence faced with the EMH, it follows that a successful speculative strategy at a minimum requires:

- Some investors who have superior information about future fundamentals (e.g. dividends) and act on it.
- Some stock prices do not immediately adjust to their fair value.

The EMH comes in three variants, depending on what we assume about the information available to market participants. The **weak form** asserts that stock prices already reflect all information that can be obtained from past trading data, such as past prices, trading volumes and so on. The weak form implies that abnormal returns cannot be made by speculators trading on past price signals, so chartism and trend-chasing activity are useless. The **semi-strong form** states that *all publicly available* information is already reflected in the current price. So as well as past prices, fundamental data on the firm's strategy, investment plans, published accounts, earnings forecasts, P–E ratios, book-to-market ratio and so on are useless in predicting future returns. Finally, the **strong form** states that current prices reflect *all relevant information*, including information available only to company 'insiders' (e.g. corporate directors or traders in an investment bank). This is indeed a little strong, since few of us would deny that it is possible for company directors to have useful advance information about company prospects and this could be passed on to others, who could then profitably trade on the information (incidentally, this would be illegal in most countries and is often a criminal offence). When we use the term 'efficient markets' we consider only the weak and semi-strong forms.

A speculative strategy based on fundamentals involves:

$$\begin{aligned} P < V \quad & \text{purchase the stock} \\ P > V \quad & \text{short (or short sell) the stock} \end{aligned}$$

The basic idea here is similar to the PV concept applied to a physical investment decision. The fair value V is the PV of future cash flows (i.e. dividends) and the market price of the stock P is the capital cost of your investment. The key areas of uncertainty in this strategy are:

- Fair value may be calculated using an incorrect model (model risk), e.g. the DDM may be incorrect.
- Fair value may be calculated using incorrect (biased) forecasts of D and R.
- Actual values of D and R may not change in line with your forecasts (fundamentals risk).

Fundamentals risk refers to the fact that *after* purchasing a stock for which $P = 8 < V = 10$, bad news arrives so that the market reappraises its view about V and hence P. For example, bad news about a patent application might cause P to fall to 6 (and V to 10) and if the specu-lator has to close out the position immediately she will lose money.

In practice, analysts who are trying to pick mispriced stocks often trade on the basis of their short-term forecasts of earnings. In the very short term they will be concerned with any announcements about earnings made by the company. Analysts take a view of future earn-ings and their average views are then reflected in the *current* market price of the share. However, if the company announces higher earnings *than the market had expected* , this will probably imply higher dividends than expected and an increase in fair value. Analysts then rush to inform their traders and clients to buy the stock quickly before the price rises. If investors act quickly they may purchase the stock before the price rises substantially and they may make a capital gain. In other words, 'the quick get rich' (and if the financial incentives are right, maybe 'the rich stay quick'). This is why analysts continually watch the news serv-ices on their Reuters and Bloomberg screens: they are looking for price sensitive information that signals a change in fair value and hence price.

Internal rate of return (IRR)

In just the same way as we examine the feasibility of a physical investment project by using either NPV or IRR, we can also do this for investment in stocks. The internal rate of return (IRR) on a stock is the (constant) rate of return that equates the *observed market price* P with the PV of (expected) dividends:

$$P = E\left[\frac{D_1}{(1 + y)} + \frac{D_2}{(1 + y)^2} + \frac{D_3}{(1 + y)^3} + \cdots\right] \qquad [5]$$

where y represents the IRR. Once we have a forecast of dividends we can solve [5] for y. However, if dividend growth is assumed to be constant (e.g. as in the DDM), the calculation of the IRR of the stock is straightforward, since:

$$P = D_1/(y - g) \qquad [6]$$

therefore:

$$y = D_1/P + g \qquad [7]$$

IRR = dividend yield + growth rate of dividends

Our earlier investment strategy was to buy (short sell) the stock if P < V (P > V), where V is calculated using the required rate of return, R. An equivalent strategy, based on the IRR is:

Buy stock if	IRR > required rate of return, R
Sell stock if	IRR < required rate of return, R

TABLE 14.1: IRR and DPV

Data	CAPM required rate of return R $= 13.5\%$ p.a.
	Dividends at end year $= 10$p
	Expected dividend growth $= 5\%$ p.a.
	Current stock price $= 110$p
Questions	1. Calculate the fair value and state your investment decision.
	2. Calculate the IRR on the stock and state your investment decision.
Answers	1. V $= 10$p$/(0.135 - 0.05) = 117.65$p
	P $= 110$p < 117.65p Hence purchase the stock.
	2. y $= $ D/P $+ $ g $= (10$p$/110$p$) + 0.05 = 0.1409\,(14.09\%)$
	y $= 14.09\% > $ R $= 13.5\%$ Hence purchase the stock.

The two investment rules give the same investment decision.

Thus one purchases the stock if the IRR, based on the current market price, exceeds the required (or risk-adjusted) rate of return. An example showing the equivalence of the IRR and PV criterion is given in Table 14.1.

14.2 CALCULATING THE DISCOUNT RATE

In this section we want to demonstrate how the CAPM/SML and arbitrage pricing theory can be employed to calculate the discount rate to use in the PV formula to calculate the fair value of a share. In general the required rate of return on a stock i may be written:

$$R_i = \text{Risk-free rate} + \text{Risk premium for stock } i = r + rp_i \qquad [8]$$

Case A: using the CAPM

The risk premium is different for different stocks and we can use the CAPM/SML to provide an estimate of the discount rate to use in the DDM:

$$R_i = r + \beta_i(ER_m - r) \qquad [9]$$

The risk-free rate is usually taken to be constant and equal to its recent historical average value (e.g. on 5–10-year government bonds). An estimate of the firm's beta is usually obtained from a time-series regression using about the last five years of (monthly returns) data or obtained directly from a risk-measurement service (see below). The forecast excess return on the market $R_m - r$ (i.e. the 'equity premium') is also usually based on its long-run

TABLE 14.2: CAPM and stock valuation

Data   Risk-free rate, r = 3% pa   Stock XYZ, has β = 1.5

Dividend expected end year on XYZ, D_1 = 10p

Average market return R_m = 10% pa   Expected dividend growth = 5% pa

Questions   1. What is the required rate of return R_i on XYZ assuming the CAPM holds?

2. What is the fair price V of XYZ?

3. If the current market price of XYZ is 120p, should you purchase the stock?

4. What are the risks attached to your investment strategy?

Answers   1. $R = r + \beta(ER_m - r)$ = 3% + 1.5(10% − 3%) = 13.5%

2. $V = D_1/(R - g)$ = 10p/(0.135 − 0.05) = 117.65p

3. Do not purchase the stock. Sell or short sell the stock since $P(=120) > V(=117.65)$.

4. After (short) selling the stock, the price may not fall within the invest-ment horizon of the speculator. Unexpected good company news may be released that would lead to a rise in price and hence you would make a loss if you had to close out immediately. The CAPM model used to calculate R may not hold in the future (model error). 'Noise traders' can move P independently of V and this may cause a rise in P.

historical average (e.g. using the S&P 500 for the US market). An example of the use of the DDM is given in Table 14.2.

Case B: using the SML

The problem with using an estimate of beta based solely on the returns of the firm is that it may not be statistically well determined (i.e. the estimate of beta has a high standard error, low t-statistic and the R-squared of the CAPM equation is low). One way to try to overcome this problem is to use the SML, which averages out the relationship between mean returns and the betas of stocks for many different firms. The SML requires a two-step approach. First, we use five years of monthly data (time series) on each firm's (excess) stock return and regress this on the monthly (excess) return on the market. We repeat this for, say, 100 differ-ent firms. This gives us 100 estimates of beta, one for each firm. Secondly, we take the *aver-age* monthly return $\overline{R}_i$ (over, say, the previous five years) for each firm's stock and regress these on 100 *estimated* betas β_i for each firm (Figure 14.3). Suppose that this 'cross-section' regression of $\overline{R}_i$ on the betas for these 100 stocks gives estimates of 5 for the intercept and 8 for the slope, then the SML is:

$\overline{R}_i = 5 + 8\beta_i$

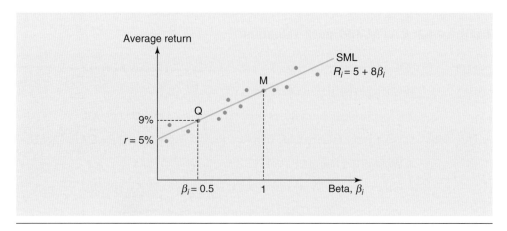

FIGURE 14.3: Security market line

For firm Q with $\beta_i = 0.5$, its historical required return is $R_i = 9\%$ and this could be used as the discount rate in the DDM.

Arbitrage pricing theory (APT)

As we have seen, arbitrage pricing theory (APT) provides an alternative model to the CAPM for determining the required equilibrium return on a stock. Hence APT can be used to determine the discount rate in the PV formula, in order to calculate the fair value, V. Let us examine the practical aspects of using APT in stock selection. Remember that APT is a multifactor model of equilibrium returns and the key elements are:

- The unexpected return on a stock responds to unexpected events (factors) in the economy (e.g. unexpected increases or decreases in inflation).
- Each factor can have a different impact on actual stock returns (i.e. the factor sensitivities or factor betas are different for different firms).
- Some of the factors will influence the required (average) return on the stock.

With two factors (e.g. change in inflation and interest rates):

$$R_A = \alpha_A + b_{A,1}F_1 + b_{A,2}F_2 + \varepsilon_A \qquad [10]$$

$$ER_A = \lambda_0 + \lambda_1 b_{A,1} + \lambda_2 b_{A,2} \qquad [11]$$

where R_A is the actual return on stock A, $ER_A =$ expected return on stock A, $b_{A,i}$ are 'risk-factor' exposures, F_1 is the change in inflation and F_2 is the change in interest rates.

Strictly, the factors F are unexpected events or news. In practice, the *change* in a macro-economic variable is often deemed to be unforecastable and is taken as a measure of an unexpected event. The $b_{A,1}$ and $b_{A,2}$ can be estimated from a *time-series* regression of the return on stock A on the factors F_1, F_2. Once we have the two-factor betas for each stock, the estimates of λ_1, λ_2 can be obtained from the second-pass cross-section regression. The expected return on each of, say, 100 stocks is measured by the average monthly return $\overline{R}_i$ over the last five (or ten) years. Suppose that the estimated λs from the cross-section regression of $\overline{R}_i$ (for i = 100 stocks) on their (100×2) estimated betas, $b_{i,1}, b_{i,2}$ take the values 2 and 0.8 respectively. If the estimated intercept is 6, then the expected return on stock A is given by:

$$ER_A = 6 + 2b_{A,1} + 0.8b_{A,2} \tag{12}$$

For the stocks of AT&T, suppose that the time-series estimates of the risk-factor weightings are $b_{A,1} = 4$ and $b_{A,2} = 2$. Then the required return for investors to willingly hold AT&T stocks is:

$$\overline{R}_{AT\&T} = 6 + 2(4) + 0.8(2) = 15.6 \tag{13}$$

This average return can be used as the discount rate to calculate the fair value V of AT&T stocks. If the market price P < V then you would purchase AT&T as it is underpriced and if P > V then you would short (or short sell) AT&T. Alternatively, you could use the IRR approach; if the IRR of AT&T stocks was greater than (less than) the APT required return $\overline{R}_{AT\&T}$ you would purchase (short sell) AT&T stocks.

Note that the CAPM is an equation similar to [10] but with only one factor, namely the excess market return, so $F_1 = R_m - r$ and all other factors are ignored. Similarly, equation [11] is the multivariate equivalent of the SML. The SML is a relationship between the average returns on many different stocks $\overline{R}_i$ and their *market* betas β_i, whereas [11] allows several factor betas to influence the average return.

Key issues that any practical application of the APT depends on are:

- Isolating the factors F that have a systematic effect on stock returns over time.
- Finding out which factors are priced (i.e. which λs are statistically significant).
- Assessing whether the λs remain constant over different time periods and hence can be used to forecast the *future* return required by investors to compensate them for the various sources of risk.

Although in practice the CAPM is widely used in project appraisal and in calculating the fair value of a stock, the APT or multifactor approach is also used by some practitioners. (There is a voluminous literature on the APT and multifactor models, which is summarised in Cuthbertson and Nitzsche, 2004.)

14.3 COMPANY DATA

Detailed statistical data on company performance and equity betas is provided by large banks, brokerage firms and a number of specialist data vendors such as Bloomberg, Reuters, Thompson Financial and Compustat (Standard and Poor's). Case Study 14.2 explains the various uses for beta.

CASE STUDY 14.2   USES FOR BETA

- *Market timing* – for example, move into high-beta stocks if you expect the market to rise.
- *Performance measures* – if a stock (or portfolio of stocks) earns a higher return than given by the CAPM/SML required return, then it has performed abnormally well and has a positive alpha.
- Betas are used to calculate the cost of equity capital and hence the weighted average cost of capital, which are inputs to PV calculations of *physical* capital projects and in calculating the fair value of a stock.
- Betas can be used to construct customised portfolios with a specific value of beta chosen by the investor. The portfolio beta is simply a weighted average of the firms' betas $\beta_p = \sum_i w_i \beta_i$, where w_i are the value-weighted proportions held in each stock. For example, a client who is highly risk averse may either only hold stocks that have betas less than 1 (i.e. defensive stocks); or if she includes stocks with $\beta > 1$, these will be offset by short selling positive beta stocks ($w_i < 0$), so that the overall portfolio beta is small.
- Betas can be used to simplify the calculation of the market risk (value at risk) of a stock portfolio and hence the overall *position risk* of equity traders and investment managers (see later chapters and Cuthbertson and Nitzsche, 2001b).

Data vendors will often provide lists of high- and low-beta companies so that portfolio managers can easily form portfolios with a desired portfolio beta. If you hold a portfolio with, say, a high beta of 1.5, then the returns on your portfolio will be more volatile than those for the market as a whole, but you will be compensated for this extra risk with a higher *average* return. For example, if the market return averages, say, 1% per month over a five-year period, then your portfolio should have an average return of around 1.5% per month. The high average return simply compensates for the higher market (non-diversifiable or systematic) risk of your chosen portfolio. An illustrative set of information provided by data vendors is given in Table 14.3.

The usefulness of most of the above statistics is fairly self-explanatory. Trading frequency and velocity (columns 2 and 3, Table 14.3) are broad indicators of the liquidity or thinness of the market in these shares. Relatively small-capitalisation stocks (e.g. row 4, Table 14.3) often have low trading frequency and velocity. The 'variability' (column 7) is the volatility of the stock return and can be quite high. However, naïve diversification can reduce the

TABLE 14.3: Data on stocks

Company (sector)	(1) Market cap. (£m)	(2) Trading Freq.	(3) Velocity (% p.a.)	(4) Beta	(5) S. error beta	(6) R^2(%)	(7) Variability (% p.a.)	(8) Specific risk (% p.a.)	(9) Annual abn. ret. (%)	(10) Annual act. ret (%)
1. STOCK A	913	0	83	1.64	0.26	26	53	46	8	40
2. STOCK B	1924	0	72	1.45	0.16	54	33	22	−9	21
3. STOCK C	73	2	2.4	0.29	0.19	3	28	28	−8	6
4. STOCK D	22	3	112	0.11	0.28	0.1	47	47	18	141

Notes: The definitions used are as follows:
    Market capitalisation: This is the market value of the company's ordinary shares outstanding.
    Trading frequency: Average number of days from the previous recorded trade for the share (e.g. 0 = less than one day, 2 = 2 or more days).
    Trading velocity: Value of shares recently traded as a percentage of market capitalisation.
    R-squared (R^2): The proportion of the variability in the company return explained by the market return. This is a measure of how accurately the CAPM explains the movements in the return on a stock. An R-squared of 0.3 indicates that 30% of past movements in the stock return are explained by movements in the market return.
    Standard error of beta: Broadly speaking, we can be 95% certain that the true value of beta lies in the range $\hat{\beta} \pm 2\,se(\hat{\beta})$ where $se(\hat{\beta})$ = estimated standard error of $\hat{\beta}$.
    Variability: Standard deviation of the annual percentage return on the share. If returns are normally distributed, then the return on a share will lie within the range $\bar{R} \pm \sigma$ about 68% of the time. Hence the return will be larger than $\bar{R} + \sigma$ and lower than $\bar{R} - \sigma$ about 16% (= (100 − 68)/2) of the time (i.e. about one year in 6).
    Specific risk: This is the size of the specific (idiosyncratic) risk of the firm's return due to events that only tend to affect this firm. Even with an unchanged market return, the annual return on the stock could move up or down by this amount, on average. Most of this specific risk is eliminated in a diversified portfolio.
    Annual abnormal return (AAR): This is the performance of the share relative to its required return– here it is applied to returns rather than *excess* returns (i.e. stock return minus the risk-free rate). The required return is measured by $\beta_i R_m$ and the *AAR* is:

$$AAR_i = R_i - \beta_i R_m \qquad [14]$$

where R_i is the actual return on the share, β_i is the beta of the share and R_m is the market return (% p.a.). If we take an average of *AAR* over several years, this would give Jensen's alpha. Because changes in the risk-free rate are relatively small, the *AAR* and Jensen's alpha give very similar results.
    Annual return (holding period return): This is the percentage price change plus the dividend yield over the past year. (Gross dividends are assumed to be reinvested in the share at the end of the month in which they are paid.)

volatility of a *portfolio* of stocks (relative to that for any single stock) and of course specific risk (column 8) can be reduced to near zero in a well-diversified portfolio.

If we hold a portfolio of stocks, the above information for individual stocks can be used to calculate the **annual abnormal return** for the portfolio as a whole:

$$AAR_p = R_p - \beta_p R_m \qquad [15]$$

where $R_p = \sum_{i=1}^{n} w_i R_i$ is the portfolio return, $\beta_p = \sum_{i=1}^{n} w_i \beta_i$ is the portfolio beta and w_i is the value-weighted proportion of the portfolio held in stock i. The *average AAR_p* over a number of years can be used as a performance measure for fund managers and is similar to Jensen's alpha.

14.4 RELATIVE VALUATION AND COMPARABLES

A quoted **price–earnings ratio** (or P–E ratio) of 20 simply represents the fact that the market currently values the share at 20 times annual earnings. The P–E ratio of a particular firm can vary substantially from year to year and P–E ratios vary across firms in a particular sector. For example, some P–E ratios of banks are:

Standard Chartered	15.3
Barclays	10.7
HSBC	10.3
Lloyds TSB	11.8

We now want to discuss another method of calculating the fair value of the equity of a particular firm by using the method of comparables. The idea is very simple and is best illustrated using the price–earnings ratio as our measure of value. For example, suppose the whole of the banking sector has an average P–E ratio of 20 and you forecast that Bank X *with its current strategy* will have a long-run level of earnings (per share) of $10 p.a. Using comparables, the fair value for one share in Bank X would be

$$\text{Fair value of one share of Bank X} = (P/E)_{\text{industry}} \times \text{Earnings per share for Bank X}$$

$$= 20 \times \$10 = \$200$$

If there are 1m shares outstanding, then the fair value of the total equity of Bank X is $200m. When using PV techniques to determine enterprise value or the equity value of the firm, we directly estimate the dollar value of the firm based on forecasts of cash flows. When using relative valuation, we assume that the market *correctly prices* the equity (relative to earnings) of a set of comparable firms and this ratio is then used to value Bank X. We assume that Bank X will in the long run have the same P–E ratio as other firms in the industry. In principle, comparable firms have the same business risk, growth prospects and financial leverage as the firms we are trying to value.

How might market participants make use of the valuation of a firm based on comparables? First, consider an IPO. Suppose that Bank X is not a publicly quoted firm (it might be owned by a private equity company) and we are trying to determine the flotation price for an IPO. If the P–E ratio for the comparables is 20, we assume that the market has correctly priced these firms, so the P–E ratio for Bank X should also be 20. Given that the estimate of long-run earnings per share for Bank X is $10 p.a., then the offer price in the IPO would be set around $200 per share.

Now consider Bank X as a takeover target. Suppose that Shark Bank is looking for a prospective takeover target and thinks that if it swallows up Bank X it will be able to cut its branch network, consolidate its retail products and increase the earnings of Bank X by 10% to $11 per share. It therefore values Bank X at $V_{new} = PE \times E_{new} \times N = \$220m$ and this is the maximum it is willing to offer for Bank X. (We assume that the acquisition of Bank X does not affect the rest of Shark Bank's earnings.) As it bids for Bank X it will push up the market value of Bank X's shares and it will cease bidding if the cost of acquiring Bank X's shares exceeds $220m.

P–E analysis of comparables may also be used by speculators to provide an initial ball-park estimate of underpriced (or overpriced) shares. Suppose that you examine the shares of Bank Y and find that its current P–E ratio is 14, whereas the average P–E ratio for comparable banks is 20. Then you might think that Bank Y is underpriced and you would purchase these undervalued shares. You hope that the market has temporarily mispriced Bank Y's shares and that when the market recognises and acts on this mispricing, the price of Bank Y's shares will rise until its P–E ratio equals that for the sector as a whole. Then you will be able to sell your Bank Y shares at a profit. Note that here we do not use the method of comparables to determine the fair value of Bank Y. Instead, we assume that banks as a whole are correctly priced (so the observed P–E ratio for the comparables of 20 is correct), but also assume that the *observed* P–E ratio for Bank Y may be incorrect because the market as a whole has overlooked some (positive) special feature of Bank Y and is therefore setting its price too low (relative to its comparators). However, there is a bit of a conceptual problem here, since Bank Y cannot be *exactly* the same as its comparators, otherwise it would have an observed P–E ratio of 20, like all the other banks.

Of course the above is a very risky strategy, since the observed lower P–E ratio of 14 for Bank Y may simply be due to the fact that the market has correctly noted that Bank Y has less growth potential than its comparators and therefore its true earnings growth only justifies a price equal to 14 times its earnings. To put this issue more bluntly, note that if Bank Y has *abnormally high* current earnings this will produce an abnormally low P–E ratio – but this does not imply that *in the future* its earnings will grow and its shares will perform well. It is therefore a risky strategy to buy shares with low P–E ratios relative to comparables (and short sell those with relatively high P–E ratios). You have to ask some searching questions about whether Bank Y really is undervalued and whether its low P–E ratio does not simply reflect the market's *correct view* that it has relatively poor prospects for earnings growth or has higher risk than its comparator firms (which would be reflected in a higher value for R, the cost of equity capital). Whether the above strategy works over a succession of repeated gambles is an open question and only detailed statistical analysis can determine whether *in the past* this would have been a successful speculative strategy; see Chapter 15 on 'value-growth' strategies for further details.

Other valuation ratios

Stock analysts use a number of alternative valuation ratios when using comparators and some of these are described below.

- **Price-to-book:** This is the price per share divided by the book value per share. There are difficulties in comparing this ratio across firms if accounting conventions differ when calculating book value.

- **Price-to-cash-flow:** If earnings are subject to different accounting conventions, some analysts use a measure of cash flow in the denominator of their comparables ratio. This might be operating cash flow, EBITD or some measure of free cash flow (i.e. net of investment expenditures).
- **Price-to-sales:** Start-up firms may not have any earnings and their tangible capital assets (book value) may be small, but their human capital (i.e. creative people) may be high. In this case some analysts use annual sales (per share) – although remember that sales are not profits and the latter will be influenced by differences in profit margins across firms. Some start-up Internet firms in the late 1990s had no sales and little financial data was available, so analysts used figures on web site 'hits' and forecast sales per hit to try and get some idea of value of the firm – this approach turned out to be very 'hit and miss'.

A sensible analyst will use a number of valuation ratios when assessing a firm against its comparators, but it is not always the case that all valuation ratios imply the same decision. Valuation using comparables is subject to many pitfalls.

What determines valuation ratios?

Using P–E ratios of comparables is an indirect way of using PV techniques, since the market price (in the numerator) must be determined by fundamentals such as future earnings and the discount rate. For presentational ease, assume that the DDM is the correct model of valuation.

Suppose the firm has total earnings (per share) of \$10 but decides to retain a proportion of these earnings to invest in new investment projects (e.g. to expand its retail outlets). If the ploughback (retentions) ratio (i.e. the fraction of earnings reinvested in the firm) is $b = 60\%$, then the firm will reinvest \$6 (per share). It follows that the payout ratio $(1 - b) = 40\%$, hence the firm distributes \$4 in dividends (per share).

$$
\text{Total earnings (per share)} = \text{Retained earnings} + \text{Dividend payments}
$$
$$
E = RE \qquad\qquad + D \qquad\qquad\qquad [16]
$$

with $D = (1 - b)E$ and $RE = b.E$

Since $D = (1 - b)E$, it follows that the *growth* in dividends equals the growth in earnings. For the special case of the DDM, the fair value V and (in an efficient market) the quoted share price is:

$$
P = V = \frac{(1 - b)E_1}{(R - g)} \qquad\qquad [17a]
$$

The long run price–earnings ratio is therefore:

$$\frac{P}{E_1} = \frac{(1 - b)}{(R - g)} \qquad\qquad [17b]$$

It is now clear that the quoted P–E ratio for a firm is determined by the fundamentals that lie behind the PV approach– there is nothing new about the P–E ratio.

A firm will have a higher P–E ratio:
- The higher is the pay-out ratio, $(1 - b)$
- The lower is the cost of capital, R
- The higher is the growth rate of earnings, g

However, the above statements must be interpreted carefully and can be misleading, if we ignore the economics that lies behind [17]. For example, if we increase the pay-out ratio, this implies a higher P–E ratio (other things being equal). But the higher pay-out ratio means lower retained earnings. If, as is often the case, the firm does not wish to obtain external finance, lower retained earnings could result in a lower level of fixed investment in highly profitable projects and hence lower earnings growth, g. Lower earnings growth implies a lower P–E ratio (other things being equal). So, the net effect on the P–E ratio of an increase in the pay-out ratio requires a careful economic analysis of these interactions. Let's try to find out what is likely to happen to the firm's stock price when it uses retained earnings to invest in new projects.

Zero-growth firm

First, consider a firm with a book value of assets in place of BV = $100 m, with N = 3m shares outstanding and total earnings (per share) of $5 p.a., so it has total earnings of TE = $15m p.a. The firm's return on equity from its existing assets (assets in place) is:

$$ROE = TE/BV = 15\% \qquad\qquad [18]$$

Suppose its equityholders require an average return of R = 12.5%, given the riskiness of the firm's business. If the firm distributes all its earnings in dividends, the ploughback rate $b = 0$. Because the firm does not invest any of its earnings in new investment projects, the growth rate in earnings (and dividends) is $g = 0$, the firm accumulates no extra physical capital, so its book value remains at $100m. The fair value of this zero-growth firm and its market price are:

$$P(no\ growth) = E_1/R = \$40 \qquad\qquad [19]$$

Growth firm

Suppose the firm's managers now come up with some innovative investment projects with a return on equity, ROE = 15% p.a., which is a return in excess of the firm's cost of equity capital of R = 12.5%. If they use some of their total earnings to finance these projects, will this increase the value of the firm and the firm's stock price? Well, if you can invest and get a ROE of 15% but the cost of borrowing is R = 12.5%, it looks as if this should boost the share price. But notice that because some earnings will be spent on investment, there will be less available to distribute in dividends, so dividends will fall – which looks as if it might depress the stock price. In fact, as long as ROE > R, the stock price will rise if the firm invests some of its retained earnings.

If the ploughback ratio b = 60%, dividends paid fall from $5 per share to D_1^* = $2 per share, but the firm can now plough back $9m p.a. into new investment (= $b \times$ TE = 0.6 × $15). The percentage increase in the firm's capital stock is 9% (= $9m/BV) and *with an unchanged ROE* this should produce a growth in earnings (and hence dividends) of g = 9%. The growth in earnings is therefore given by:[1]

$$g = \text{ROE} \times b = 0.15 \times 0.6 = 0.09 \qquad [20]$$

Our growth firm is distributing less in dividends ($2 rather than $5), but because of the high ROE this has resulted in a higher growth in earnings (and dividends in the future). The new value for the firm's equity is:

$$P^*(growth) = \frac{D_1^*}{R - g} = \frac{\$2}{0.125 - 0.09} = \$57.14 \qquad [21]$$

So the firm's stock price does increase if it uses retained earnings to finance extra investment – providing the ROE is greater than the cost of equity capital, R.

To see this, suppose that the ROE = 12.5% is the same as the cost of equity capital R = 12.5% and the firm increased its ploughback ratio from 0% to 60% as above. Then g = ROE × b = 0.125 × 0.6 = 0.075 and

$$P^* = \frac{D_1^*}{R - g} = \frac{\$2}{0.125 - 0.075} = \$40 \qquad [22]$$

This gives the same price as for the 'zero-growth' firm – the extra investment by the firm raises earnings (and dividend) growth but not enough to offset the lower initial level of dividends paid out.

The P/E ratio for the growth firm is:

$$P/E_1 = \frac{(1 - b)}{R - \text{ROE} \times b} = 11.4 \qquad [23]$$

---

[1] We have TE = BV × ROE. For unchanged ROE, we have g = (ΔTE)/TE = (ΔBV)/BV = b(TE/BV) = $b \times$ ROE.

It is immediately apparent that a firm with a high ROE will have a high P/E ratio, as one might expect[2]. If the firm has a higher ploughback ratio b, this implies higher earnings growth ($g = $ ROE $\times$ b), but this does not necessarily imply a higher P–E ratio. For example, it is easy to see that if we set ROE $= R$ in the above equation then $P^*/E_1 = 1/R$, which is the same as the P–E ratio for a 'zero-growth' firm. Hence, investment projects that have a ROE $= R$ are 'break-even' investment projects. However, if ROE $> R$ then a higher plough-back ratio does lead to a higher P–E ratio. Of course, if the firm invests retained earnings in projects where the ROE is less than the return required by investors, then growth destroys value. Hence, high earnings growth is only a good thing when funds are used for investments with a ROE that exceeds the cost of equity capital.

In the above analysis, increasing the ploughback rate b leads to a higher share price and P–E ratio if ROE $> R$. However, this result assumes that any retained earnings used to finance the new investment projects do not lower the ROE – but at some point expansion may lead to lower earnings growth than given by the equation $g = $ ROE $\times$ b because of a fall in ROE as marginal projects earn less profits. Also as the firm expands, the market may change its view about the business risk of the firm's activities and this may lead to a change in R (from the constant 12.5% assumed above), which will have a direct impact on the share price. Put another way, the above approach is a *simplification* of a full PV approach and the latter, in principle, should take account of these two points.

From the above analysis, it is clear that when determining the fair value for firm X using comparators, the comparators should have the same fundamentals (business risk, earnings growth prospects, etc.) as firm X – but it may not be the case that firms in the same *industrial sector* have the same business prospects. This is the difficulty when choosing comparator firms.

The above analysis of the DDM highlights the fact that the value of a firm (and its P–E ratio) depends on the ROE, relative to the cost of equity capital R and on the growth rate in earnings. Firms can have low levels of current earnings and dividends yet still command high prices because of their growth potential; the latter may apply to some technology and Internet stocks, which we discuss next.

14.5 REAL OPTIONS APPROACH TO VALUATION

The stock market valuation of Internet and biotechnology companies can sometimes appear excessively high, given that many of these companies have relatively low revenues and often negative operating profit (i.e. EBITDA, earnings before interest, taxes, depreciation and amortisation). Certainly, their stock prices are often highly volatile. Are these stock prices justified or are these stocks excessively overvalued and if so, by how much might we expect the price to fall, if underlying market conditions changed? A stock analyst using convention-al PV techniques to value this type of company has a major problem both in projecting future cash flows (from very limited data) and in setting the appropriate discount rate. There is a new area of research that tries an alternative way of valuing this type of company based on ideas from options theory. We will discuss options further in later chapters, but Case Study 14.3 gives a flavour of this approach.

---

[2] Since the DDM only holds for $R > g$, then we also require $R > $ ROE $\times$ b.

CASE STUDY 14.3   VALUATION OF INTERNET AND BIOTECHNOLOGY STOCKS

Before we illustrate the theory, some examples will provide an intuitive overview of real options. A good example to begin with is a young biotechnology company that is considering stage I of a research project to discover 'blockbuster' drugs, such as a cure for certain types of cancer or AIDS. The share price P for an all-equity firm is:

P = Value of firm's investment projects / Number of shares outstanding

So we need to value the firm in order to determine the fair price for its shares. Suppose that the research projects will proceed in stages, the early stages providing possible breakthroughs for later developments and spin-off drugs. Further suppose that there are only two stages. When using a conventional NPV calculation the stock analyst will assess the *expected* present value of the net revenues over the life (say five years) of stage I, including the probabilities of a 'low', 'medium' or 'major' breakthrough. This can then be compared with the (present value) of the capital costs of the research equipment for stage I. The cash flows will be discounted using the company's risk-adjusted discount rate. Suppose that the conventional NPV for stage I equals *minus* $10m. Should the analyst advise clients not to invest in stage I or has she missed some vital advantages of the project?

Suppose the research being considered in stage I will allow a more informed assessment of the prospects for a further breakthrough drug being discovered at a later date. If so, the biotechnology company would exploit this new knowledge in stage II, given the know-how acquired in stage I. Hence, the stage I project has an embedded option, namely the possible expansion into stage II in, say, five years time. The value of the stage I investment is not only its own cash flows but also the option to exploit stage II. This *embedded option to expand* has value, which should be added to the NPV calculation for stage I. Of course, one cannot know at $t = 0$ whether this option to exploit stage II will be undertaken in five years time. This depends on future research progress, which we cannot know today. However, the option to expand still has a value at t = 0. Indeed, if the value of the option to expand is greater than $10m, then we should go ahead with stage I even though it has a conventional negative NPV.

Surely there is a downside to the above 'fiddling of the figures'? Well, there is, since if there is no breakthrough in five years time, the option to expand will be worth zero (i.e. we will not exploit stage II). But note that the downside is limited to zero. In fact, the embedded option to expand is a *call option* with a strike price equal to the additional investment required (at $t = 5$) to exploit stage II of the research project.

The potential upside is very large, while the downside is truncated at zero (costs and revenues) if we do not go ahead – the typical *asymmetric payoff* from an option. The larger is the variance σ of possible outcomes in stage II the larger the possible upside, while the downside payoff remains at zero. Hence it should not be surprising that this call option (like all options) is worth more, the greater the degree of uncertainty σ in future revenues. (This is taken up in Chapter 26.) So, other things being equal, we have the somewhat paradoxical result that stage I, including its embedded option, is worth more today, the *greater is uncertainty* about future revenues in stage II. Because the conventional NPV calculation concentrates on *expected outcomes*, it does not correctly value these embedded options.

One can easily see that the above analysis could apply to Internet or dot-com companies. Many of these companies had very high share prices in the late 1990s, even though they had relatively low revenues, very often had negative profits and hence negative conventional NPVs. But their share price may have reflected the possibility of expansion into other similar Internet business areas, given the knowledge gained in the current business. This embedded *option to expand* is reflected in their *current* share price.

To value an Internet or biotechnology company using options theory we need to model the stochastic behaviour of the key economic variables faced by these firms, such as revenues and costs. Schwartz and Moon (2000) did this for the Internet company Amazon.com at the end of 1999. Their model has two sources of uncertainty: one is the actual change in revenues, *Rev*, and the other is the *expected* (or mean) growth in revenues, μ.

The *actual growth* in revenues is assumed to equal a 'trend value' plus a random element, which initially has a very large volatility ($\sigma_0 = 20\%$ p.a.), which slowly falls to a long-run level ($\overline{\sigma} = 10\%$ p.a.) as the whole Internet sector becomes more established. Also the *expected growth* rate μ_t changes over time, beginning at its end-1999 high value ($\mu_0 = 44\%$ p.a.) and slowly falling to a lower long-run value ($\overline{\mu} = 6\%$ p.a.) as more competitors enter the Internet business. Not only this, but the expected growth rate is itself uncertain, beginning with an initial standard deviation of $\sigma_0 = 60\%$ p.a., which then slowly falls to zero. Costs are assumed to be equal to 94% of revenues (on average) and hence there is a 6% profit margin over sales. The cash flow of the firm is:

$$Y_t = Rev_t - C_t$$

In practice the cash flow Y is 'earnings before interest, tax, depreciation and amortisation' (EBITDA), but we ignore these complications here. We assume that all cash is retained and earns the risk-free rate, r. If cash balances fall to zero, the firm is assumed to go bankrupt (i.e. we ignore the possibility of raising additional financing or of a merger in future years).

Although the above model is highly simplified, we do have the basic ingredients to value the firm. Schwartz and Moon assume that the value of Amazon is equal to 10 times EBITDA (i.e. at Y_T) at $T = 25$ years (they use Monte Carlo Simulation (MCS) to obtain a representative or average value for the firm). Schwartz and Moon (2000) used a more complex model than the above, and they show that as of December 1999, the model gave a value for Amazon.com of $5.5bn, in their 'baseline' case. Hence, it is possible for Internet companies to have a high valuation if the embedded options for future expansion are factored into the calculation.

The model outlined in Case Study 14.3 is rather simplified and we have to input estimates of its parameters in order to price an Internet stock. Hence the model may be somewhat inaccurate, but it does allow one to evaluate whether quoted market prices of such stocks are 'beyond belief' and also assess the sensitivity of the price to changing circumstances (e.g. different assumptions about the mean growth rate of revenues). The model also shows that one can expect Internet stocks to be highly volatile as investors' views about key parameter estimates change by relatively small amounts, for example investors' views about the volatility of revenues σ_0 changes. The use of options theory in investment decisions and the valuation of the firm are discussed in greater depth in Cuthbertson and Nitzsche, 2001b.

SUMMARY

- The *fair value* of a stock is given by the PV of expected future dividends where the discount rate used reflects the systematic risk of the stock.
- The discount rate R used in calculating fair value can be estimated from either the CAPM/SML or APT.
- An *efficient market* is one in which price reflects all available relevant information and therefore it is impossible to earn abnormal profits (corrected for risk and transaction costs) by active stock picking.
- The efficient markets hypothesis implies that active portfolio management (stock picking) and trying to 'time the market' are futile – such strategies are costly (in terms of managerial effort and the costs of trading) and investors would be better off investing in a passive portfolio that tracks some chosen broad market index.
- The beta of a stock has a wide variety of uses, including calculating the cost of equity capital and forming portfolios with desired beta values.
- If we assume the discount rate is constant and dividends grow at a constant rate, then the dividend discount model DDM (or Gordon growth model) implies that the stock price is given by:

$$P = \frac{D_1}{(R - g)}$$

- Key influences on a stock's price–earnings ratio are the cost of equity capital (R), the return on equity (ROE) and the ploughback rate for retained earnings.
- The value of a stock can be estimated by looking at valuation ratios of comparable firms. Popular valuation ratios include the price–earnings ratio, the price-to-book ratio, and the price-to-sales ratio. The difficulty is in choosing firms that are really similar in terms of business and financial risk to the firm you are trying to value.
- Real options theory is used to value firms that have high potential to expand in the future or may have flexibility to alter their strategy in the future. Options theory tries to put a value on this flexibility.

APPENDIX 14.1: PV AND STOCK PRICES

If an investor only wanted to hold a stock for a short period (e.g. one year), would this invalidate the PV formula for stock prices? Would it still be correct to assume that the stock price equals the present value of dividends *in all future periods*? The answer is yes, provided that investors calculate the expected selling price for their stock in a rational way. We simplify the algebra by omitting expectations signs.

If you are thinking of holding a stock for just one year, then the amount you are willing to pay for the stock today depends on the PV of the cash flows you expect to receive next year; that is, the dividends and the expected selling price for the stock in a years time:

$$P_0 = \frac{D_1 + P_1}{(1 + R)} \tag{A1}$$

where $1/(1 + R)$ is the constant discount factor. Clearly, equation [A1] explicitly incorporates the capital gain on the stock. If we *choose* to use a discount rate of, say, $R = 10\%$ in the PV formula, then equation [A1] also implies that the *return* we expect over the next year, if we purchased the stock today for P_0 and sold it a year later for P_1 (and collected the dividend), is also 10% – this is what using a discount rate of 10% means. Algebraically this can be seen by rearranging [A1]:

$$R = \frac{P_1 - P_0}{P_0} + \frac{D_1}{P_0} \tag{A2}$$

So R is both the discount rate and the *expected* return on the stock over one year:

Return $\equiv$ Expected Capital gain $+$ Expected dividend yield

If investors are rational, then the price you could sell the stock at the end of the year P_1 must be given by a similar equation to [A2], since the next holder of the stock also wants to earn a return of R, hence:

$$P_1 = \frac{D_2 + P_2}{(1 + R)} \tag{A3}$$

Substituting [A3] in [A1]:

$$P_0 = \frac{D_1}{(1 + R)} + \frac{D_2 + P_2}{(1 + R)^2} \tag{A4}$$

So not surprisingly, the price today depends on the expected selling price at the end of year 2 and the dividends you expect to be paid in the first two years. We can replace P_2 by $(D_3 + P_3)/(1 + R)$ and so on, so that:

$$P_0 = \frac{D_1}{(1 + R)} + \frac{D_2}{(1 + R)^2} + \cdots + \frac{D_H + P_H}{(1 + R)^H} \tag{A5}$$

If $P_H/(1 + R)^H$ eventually approaches zero as the time horizon H increases, then:

$$P_0 = \frac{D_1}{(1 + R)} + \frac{D_2}{(1 + R)^2} + \frac{D_3}{(1 + R)^3} + \cdots$$

and the stock price equals the PV of all future dividends. Even if some investors only wish to hold the stock for one year, they have to calculate the selling price P_1. The only way they can do this is to calculate all future prices $P_2, P_3 \ldots$ etc. Hence although they have a 'short horizon', as long as they are 'rational' and base P_2 on expected future dividends, then the 'infinite sum' PV formula for stock prices will hold. Hence the DPV formula does not imply that all investors want to hold the stock for ever, merely that they calculate the future selling price based on future expected dividends.

Speculative bubbles

It is also worth noting that the rather innocuous assumption that $P_H/(1 + R)^H$ eventually approaches zero as the time horizon H increases rules out the possibility of 'bubbles'. If this condition does not hold, then the solution for P_0 in [A5] has an additional 'bubble term' that arises because people *believe* that the stock price will rise even though future dividends are expected to remain constant. If there is a 'bubble', then the market price does not equal its 'fair value' but (for a positive bubble) is higher than its fair value. Investors are prepared to pay a higher market price than the fair value because they think that the next person will be willing to pay an even higher price. Such speculative bubbles could be the cause of large rapid price increases, as for example in the tulip mania in the 16th century, the South Sea Bubble and even the stock-market boom of 1995–2000. For further analysis of speculative bubbles, see Cuthbertson and Nitzsche (2004).

EXERCISES

Q1   Does the dividend discount model ignore the mass of investors who have bought their shares with the intention of selling them in, say, three years time?

Q2   What practical use is there in knowing the beta of your stock portfolio?

Q3   Why might stock prices be highly volatile even though all investors act in a perfectly rational way?

Q4   Why is it better to short sell an overvalued stock and simultaneously buy a different undervalued stock, rather than simply just buying the undervalued stock?

Q5   The dividends of company X are expected to grow at a constant rate of 5% p.a. The last dividend pay-out was $1.80 per share. The risk-adjusted (required) rate of return is R = 11% p.a. The current market price of the share is $35. Should you purchase the share?

Q6   The past performance of BubbleStock is:

Cents	2008	2009	2010
EPS (earnings per share)	10	12	15
Dividends per share	4	4.8	6

BubbleStock is expected to produce earnings per share in 2011 of 20 cents and in 2012 of 26 cents. Earnings growth thereafter is expected to be 10%.

a) What is the pay-out ratio? If the rate of return on BubbleStock required by investors is 14%, what is the fair price for the share at the end of 2010?

b) In the past five years BubbleStock shares have provided a 10%, 12%, 3%, 6% and 8% return. Estimate the expected return and standard deviation of BubbleStock.

c) The expected return on the market portfolio is 7%, the standard deviation of the market portfolio is 6%, correlation of BubbleStock with the market return is 0.7 and the risk-free rate is 5%. If the current market price of BubbleStock is P = 235, is it a good buy (or should we just say 'goodbye' to the stock)?

Q7   A firm is expected to pay dividends of 20p at the end of the year t = 1. Dividends are then expected to grow at 5%. The (risk-adjusted) required rate of return for this firm is 11%. What would you expect its current market price to be? If the dividend pay-out ratio is 60% what would you expect the price earnings ratio to be?

Q8   The dividends of company X are expected to grow at a constant rate of 5% p.a. from now on. The last dividend has just been paid and was $1.80 per share.

a) Given the business risk of company X, investors require an average rate of return on the stock of ER = 11% p.a. Show that the fair value of this share is $31.5. The current market price of the share is $28. As a speculator, should you buy or sell this share? What are the risks involved in your strategy?

b) What would you have done if the market price had been $36 (rather than $28)?

c) Suppose share A has a market price of $28 and another share B (of a firm in the same industry sector) has a market price of $36 and both have the same fair value calculated in (a). They are both mispriced because other traders have not yet correctly recognised the 'true' profit potential of each of these firms. How can you speculate on these two shares while largely insulating your strategy from any general fall in all shares (i.e. the whole market – or 'market risk')?

d) To simplify the calculations, assume that general economic conditions deteriorate (because of a rise in interest rates by the Central Bank) and the market prices of both A and B fall by $1, which simply reflects the fall in 'fair value' (by $1) of both shares (i.e. the rise in interest rates has raised the discount factor for both firms and hence the fair value falls by $1). What happens if you have to 'close out' your positions in A and B *immediately after* this general fall in prices (and hence cannot wait for any mispricing to be corrected)?

CHAPTER 15

Behavioural Finance and Anomalies

AIMS

- To show how behavioural finance differs from the standard efficient markets approach.
- To show how behavioural concepts such as overconfidence, mental accounting, loss aversion and anchoring can account for key aspects of behaviour in financial markets.
- To demonstrate how risk aversion, finite investment horizons and noise trader risk can lead to mispricing.
- To outline the main anomalies found in stock markets and how behavioural finance might explain why such potential profitable strategies might persist. Documented anomalies include the small-firm effect, calendar effects, the price of closed-end funds and the home bias problem in portfolio investment decisions.
- To explain the popular stock-picking strategies of value growth and momentum.

15.1 KEY IDEAS

The efficient markets hypothesis (EMH) asserts that rational behaviour based on fundamentals such as future dividend forecasts should explain the movement in stock prices. The observed market price should equal the fair value based on calculations by rational individuals, who operate in well-informed markets with few or no restrictions on trading stocks – so the EMH can be summed up as 'the price is right'. Since fair value depends on forecasts of future variables such as dividends, then the current stock price should incorporate all the available information about the future prospects for a company. It follows that *changes* in the stock price only take place after new information (or news) about the company's prospects becomes available to the market. As news is by definition unpredictable, then as a first approximation stock returns should be largely unpredictable.

Clearly, the EMH involves a model of how prices are determined and how investors react with each other. Like all models, it is not supposed to give a 100% accurate description of the world but a useful set of assumptions that we hope can explain a wide range of phenomena (and explain them better than rival theories).

There are some quite strong assumptions behind the EMH. In an efficient market all active investors have access to the same information, they process the information in broadly the same rational way and they all have equal opportunities for borrowing and lending. In the real world these conditions are unlikely to be met. For example, different investors may form different probability assessments about future outcomes or use different economic models in determining expected returns. They may also face differences in transaction costs (e.g. insurance companies versus individuals when purchasing shares) or different tax rates, and of course they will each devote a different amount of resources (i.e. time and money) to collecting and processing information. Of course, if these heterogeneous elements play a rather minor role, then asset prices and stock returns will be determined solely by economic fundamentals and rational behaviour. But if not, prices may deviate substantially and persistently from their fair values. As we see below, it is often the assumption of *heterogeneity* in behaviour that allows us to analyse why markets may not be fully efficient.

Behavioural finance adherents take the view that many important phenomena in financial markets (e.g. the very high volatility in stock prices that does not seem to be caused by news) cannot be adequately explained by well-informed rational individuals participating in a relatively frictionless market environment. They claim that there may be some systematic biases in the behaviour of a substantial number of investors in the market – some investors may be over-optimistic or 'chase trends' and thus cause stock prices to move when there are no changes in news about fundamental variables such as future dividends – and this might cause stock prices to be excessively volatile. These 'irrational' traders are often referred to as 'noise traders', since they do not use economic fundamentals to determine the fair value of a stock. It follows that believers in behavioural finance think that very often and for long periods, 'the price might not be right'.

The debate between proponents of the EMH and the behavioural finance lobby has often centred on so-called anomalies – movements in asset prices for which the models used by the EMH group do not seem adequate and there is scope for alternative explanations based on ideas from behavioural finance. So there is a vigorous debate on how far either the rational fundamentals approach (with incorporation of transaction costs) or the alternative behavioural approach can 'explain' the empirical facts, using assumptions that can be generally accepted as reasonable.

Let's parody the debate by considering the performance of a soccer player, David Beckham, who until recently played for Real Madrid (and is currently with L.A. Galaxy). The EMH-fundamentals supporters might say, 'Well he didn't score quite as many goals as predicted by my individual profit-maximising model, because the playing field is not *perfectly* smooth.' The behavioural modeller might say, 'He didn't score many goals because he is not just con-cerned about goals scored and hence his own future earnings. He experiences a much greater loss in self-esteem when the other side scores than when he himself scores, so he tends to spend a lot of time in defensive positions because his satisfaction from playing depends on how he is viewed by other players, not only on his own income.' Alternatively, the behav-ioural modeller might say that those in the opposition teams are irrational (e.g. jealous of his celebrity glamour status off the field) and hence act as 'noise footballers' and want to unfairly disfigure Beckham, so he 'goes forward' less than in a completely rational world where all teams 'play by the rules'. This approach recognises that the outcome of a soccer match depends on the interaction between 'rational' (i.e. profit-maximising) soccer players and the irrational 'noise footballers' and whether the former then begin to imitate the latter. (You may have noticed a certain amount of 'tit-for-tat' behaviour on the soccer field in that when one side begins to commit offences the other side gets rattled and also commits crazy offences directly in front of the referee, such as when Beckham was sent off in the 1998 England–Argentina World Cup game and Ronaldo helped get Rooney sent off in the 2006 World Cup.)

As we noted above, much of the evidence against the EMH is based on so-called anomalies. One element of the literature looks for situations where there are price anomalies between very close substitutes (e.g. twin shares, ADRs, closed-end funds) that should have been arbi-traged away. Another part of the anomalies literature looks for trading rules that earn money after taking account of risk and transaction costs – this requires statistical measures of risk, which can be contentious. Two key questions that behavioural models need to answer are:

- Why does mispricing persist in the market?
- How do noise traders survive in the market?

In behavioural models there are 'no free lunches' (i.e. excess profits corrected for risk and transaction costs). But this does not imply that 'the price is right' (i.e. price equals discounted expected cash flows/dividends). Essentially, 'the price is right' is shorthand for the EMH. But in some behavioural models, prices do not equal fundamental value because the rational traders are inhibited in some way from arbitraging away any mispricing caused by the noise traders.

Note that the EMH does not require that *all* participants in the market are 'efficient' and well informed. There can be a set of irrational or noise traders in the market who do not quote prices equal to fundamental value. All the EMH requires is that there are *sufficient* 'smart-money' traders around (with sufficient funds at their disposal), who recognise that the mar-ket price P_t differs from the fair value V_t and are willing to act quickly on this information. So, if some irrational traders quote $P_t < V_t$, the smart money will move in fast and purchase stocks from the irrational traders, thus pushing P_t swiftly towards V_t and the early movers among the smart money then earn profits from these trades.

Take a simple case where all soccer clubs are financed by share issues (readers who are interested in other sports can substitute their own teams and players). Assume that noise traders initially purchase Real Madrid shares at a fair price of €25. Now assume that after a few hours consuming alcohol in numerous bars, the noise traders as a group *irrationally* feel unduly pessimistic about the ability of Real Madrid's manager. Hence, they sell shares and push down the price of Real Madrid, with the final price settling at P = €20, below the unchanged fundamental value of V = €25. The noise traders have sold at below €25 and hence lose money. Fully informed rational traders (e.g. Victoria Beckham?) should now step in and buy Real's shares while simultaneously hedging their bets by *short* selling a (correctly priced) close substitute security that has similar cash flows to Real Madrid, in future states of the world. Let this substitute security be shares in Barcelona FC (Real Madrid's historic rival). If the general market for soccer shares falls (e.g. due to a loss of lucrative television deals), the 'long–short' rational trader still makes a profit when the mispricing is corrected. The *general market* fall implies a loss on Real Madrid of, say, €1 but a gain of around €1 on the short position in Barcelona. But when the *mispricing* of Real Madrid is corrected, the 'long–short' trader will gain her €5 per share. This is because if rational traders enter the market and buy at €20, they begin to push the price up towards the fair value of V = €25 and in the process make a profit. (This profit is at the expense of the noise traders.) The noise traders initially purchased at a fair price of €25, but sold at below €25 (to the rational traders) and hence they should be forced out of the market by the rational guys (i.e. Darwinian survival of the fittest). The price of Real Madrid will rise to its fundamental value very quickly if there are enough rational traders with sufficient funds willing to enter the market. However, the above scenario may not ensue for the following reasons.

Fundamental risk

Short selling of the substitute security may protect the rational trader from most of the (football) industry (systematic) risk, but specific risk still remains (e.g. news that Beckham, while playing for Real Madrid, has broken his leg). So the arbitrage is not risk-free.

Noise trader risk

Even if Barcelona FC is a *perfect* substitute for Real Madrid, it is still possible for noise traders to become *even more pessimistic* about the abilities of Real Madrid's manager and hence for Real's price to fall further (below €20). This is the *noise-trader risk* faced by the rational traders. If rational traders have long horizons *and* prices eventually do converge to fundamental value, then they will not worry about noise-trader risk, they just have to wait longer for their arbitrage profits and ride out any short-term losses. But professional portfolio managers generally have relatively short horizons and manage other people's money, so there is a separation of 'brains and capital' and hence arbitrage opportunities may not be eliminated.

Short selling

Most pension and some mutual fund managers are not allowed to short sell. Hedge funds can short sell but they would need access to a plentiful supply of (Barcelona) shares from their broker. Also, they need to be able to borrow Barcelona shares for as long as it takes the mispricing to be corrected. If not, they may have to repurchase Barcelona shares in the market at an unfavourable price – known as being 'bought in'. Also, if foreign shares are involved, shorting these (e.g. shares in Inter Milan) can be difficult and brokerage fees and bid–ask spreads need to be factored in to the arbitrage calculation. (As well as the possibility that the Italian football 'market' is not a close substitute for the market risk of Real Madrid shares.)

Model risk

Rational traders cannot be sure that Real Madrid is underpriced at €20, because their estimate of the fundamentals price of €25 (e.g. using the Gordon growth model) may be incorrect. This 'model risk' may limit the positions taken by the rational arbitrageurs.

Learning costs

If there are learning costs in finding the true model or in obtaining all the information for rational traders, then this may limit the *number* of traders who are in a position to spot and hence eliminate the mispricing of Real Madrid shares. It may be that there are enough arbitrageurs, with sufficient funds in the aggregate, so that even over a finite horizon risky profitable opportunities are arbitraged away. The force of the latter argument is weakened if we recognise that any single arbitrageur is unlikely to know either the fundamental value of a security or to realise when observed price changes are due to deviations from the fundamental's price. Arbitrageurs as a group are also likely to disagree among themselves about fundamental value (i.e. they have heterogeneous expectations) and this could increase the general uncertainty they perceive about profitable opportunities, even in the long term. The smart money may therefore have difficulty in *identifying* any mispricing in the market. Hence if funds are limited (i.e. there is a less than perfectly elastic demand for the underpriced securities by arbitrageurs) or horizons are finite, it is possible that profitable *risky* arbitrage opportunities can persist in the market for some time.

If one recognises that 'information costs' (e.g. man-hours, machines, buildings) may be substantial and that marginal costs rise with the breadth and quantity of trading, then this also might provide some limit on arbitrage activity in some areas of the market. For example, to take an extreme case, if information costs are so high that dealers either concentrate solely on bonds or solely on stocks (i.e. complete market segmentation), then differences in expected returns between bonds and stocks (corrected for risk) might not be immediately arbitraged away.

Necessary and sufficient conditions

A great deal of the analysis of financial markets relies on the principle of arbitrage (e.g. see Shleifer and Summers, 1990). Arbitrageurs (or smart money or rational speculators) continually watch the market and quickly eliminate any divergence between the actual price and fundamental value, and hence immediately eliminate any profitable opportunities. If a security has a perfect substitute then arbitrage is risk-free. Risk-free arbitrage ensures that *relative* prices are equalised. However, if there are no close substitutes so that arbitrage is risky, arbitrage may not pin down the *absolute* price levels of stocks (or bonds) *as a whole*.

The risk in taking an arbitrage position only occurs if the smart money has a *finite* horizon. The smart money may believe that prices will *ultimately* move to their fundamental value and hence, in the long term, profits will be made. However, if arbitrageurs have to either borrow cash or securities (for short sales) to implement their trades and hence pay *per period fees* or report their profit position on their 'book' to their superiors at frequent intervals (e.g. monthly, quarterly), an infinite horizon certainly cannot apply to all or even most trades undertaken by the smart money.

First consider the case where there is *no* close substitute security and hence the arbitrageur is exposed to fundamental risk (e.g. unforeseen changes in dividends). Then mispricing can persist if (see Barberis and Thaler, 2003):

i. arbitrageurs are risk averse *and*
ii. fundamental risk is systematic

Condition (i) ensures that no *one* arbitrageur will be willing to eliminate the mispricing by taking a large position and (ii) ensures that mispricing is not eliminated by a large number of investors each taking a *small* position in the mispriced security.

If a perfect substitute security exists (i.e. identical cash flows in all states of the world) and the two securities have different prices, then there is no fundamental or model risk, but only noise-trader risk. The arbitrageur can be completely sure of the mispricing. For this mispricing to persist we require that:

i. arbitrageurs are risk averse and *have short horizons*
ii. noise trader risk is systematic

In (i), we require a 'short horizon' to prevent a single (wealthy!) arbitrageur from waiting for the *certain* mispricing to be corrected. Again, condition (ii) is required so that lots of small investors cannot diversify away the risk of the mispriced security.

15.2 BELIEFS AND PREFERENCES

Above, we have explained why risky arbitrage may be limited and insufficient to keep actual prices of stocks in line with their fundamental value. We now discuss the experimental evidence on individuals' beliefs and preferences (see Barberis and Thaler, 2003; Shiller, 1989; and Shleifer and Summers, 1990 for a summary). Psychological experiments tend to show that individuals make systematic (i.e. non-random) mistakes. Subjects are found to overreact to new information (news) and they tend to extrapolate past price trends. They are *overconfident*, which makes them take on excessive risk.

Behavioural psychology provides experimental evidence that people are not rational in forming their forecasts. A Bayesian approach where the individual weights her prior beliefs and recent information to produce a best forecast is often optimal. But in practice, individuals seem to attach too much weight to recent data and can be *overconfident* about their forecasting ability.

Agents often believe that small samples reflect the 'population' (i.e. the 'law of small numbers' or *sample size neglect*). For example, if David Beckham scores in three consecutive soccer matches, he is on a 'hot streak' and people erroneously increase their subjective probability that he will score in the next game. But this estimate may not be at all representative of his average scoring rate for the whole of the previous season, and in reality there may be no serial correlation in his scoring pattern. Even when people *know* the true data generation process (e.g. a coin toss), then after five heads in a row, they might place a probability greater than $\frac{1}{2}$ that the next play will result in tails (e.g. see the opening scene of Tom Stoppard's play *Rosencrantz and Guildenstern Are Dead*). This is referred to as the 'gambler's fallacy'.

People also *anchor* too much on an initial position. When asked to estimate the percentage of African countries in the United Nations, people's responses were influenced by the initial random number x (where $0 < x < 100$) that they were given. Those who were asked to compare their estimate to $x = 10\%$ replied 25%, while those who were asked to compare with $x = 60\%$, estimated 45% (on average). There are also *memory biases*, whereby a more recent or more salient event will influence people's views on probable outcomes. For example, people who have recently experienced a car theft will overestimate the probability of car theft in their city (compared to someone who has not experienced a car theft).

Mental accounting

How do people assess the outcome of a 'bet' on the stock market? Do they consider what the bet will do to the level of their total wealth (including, for example, their housing wealth, existing investments and bank accounts); or do they assess the outcome of a stock-market investment in isolation to their other assets? Do they consider how the bet will affect their consumption possibilities (e.g. one more or one less holiday) over the next few years; or are they perhaps only concerned about their terminal wealth at a particular target date in the future (e.g. at retirement, say), in which case they are not worried about short-term losses over the next few months but focus on the long term? Another possibility is that the investor is concerned only about *gains* and *losses* from a subset of her stock market investments (even though her well-being depends on gains and losses across all of her investments). Considering only gains and losses in isolation is often referred to as a particular form of *mental accounting* known as *narrow framing*.

We can also consider the possibility that losses are weighted *much more* heavily than gains (of an equal dollar value) – this is *loss aversion*. The impact of loss aversion on your well-being (economists call the latter 'utility') depends on the frequency with which investors monitor their portfolios – if you evaluate your portfolio frequently (e.g. once a month) you will note more periods of negative stock returns than if you evaluate your portfolio every five years. The above discussion should alert you to the many possible ways in which individuals might assess the possible consequences of their decision to invest in stocks and hence how they interpret stock movements and the riskiness of the stock market.

15.3 ANOMALIES

We mentioned at the beginning of this chapter that there have arisen a number of empirical anomalies that the EMH, which relies on rational behaviour by well-informed traders, finds difficult to explain. Below, we discuss the major anomalies that have arisen in the literature. Each anomaly suggests that it is possible to devise rules so that the anomaly can be exploited to earn an abnormal profit, after taking account of the risk of the strategy and the transaction costs in executing it. In short, it is possible to refute the EMH. The debate between the proponents of the EMH and the behavioural finance adherents then centres on whether such anomalies provide possible profitable trading opportunities or are really just a reward for risks that we cannot precisely measure, or that the profits disappear after taking account of transaction costs.

Calendar effects

The weekend effect refers to the fact that there appears to be a systematic fall in stock prices between the Friday closing and Monday opening of the stock market. One explanation of the weekend effect is that firms and governments release good news between Monday and Friday but wait until the weekend to release bad news. The bad news is then reflected in low stock prices on Monday. However, in an efficient market some agents should recognise this and should (short) sell on Friday (the price is high) and buy on Monday (the price is low), assuming that the expected profit more than covers transaction costs and a payment for risk. This action should lead to a removal of the anomaly.

The so-called January effect is a similar phenomenon. The daily rate of return on common stocks appears to be unusually high during the early days of the month of January. For the US one explanation is due to year-end selling of stock in order to generate capital losses, which can then be offset against capital gains to reduce tax liability. (This is known as 'bed and breakfasting' in the UK.) In January, investors purchase stock to return to their original portfolio holdings. Again, if the EMH holds, this predictable pattern of price changes should lead to purchases by non-tax payers (e.g. pension funds) in December when the price is low and selling in January when the price is high, thus eliminating the profitable arbitrage opportunity. The January effect seems to take place in the first five trading days of January (Keen, 1983) and also appears to be concentrated in the stocks of small firms (Reinganum, 1983). There are numerous other calendar effects in the anomalies literature (e.g. turn-of-the-year, holiday and week-of-the-month effects). The question is whether these statistically significant effects, when taken in isolation, remain when dependencies operating across different calendar effects are accounted for.

Data-snooping bias

In a salutary paper, Sullivan *et al.* (2001) note the vast number of studies that find calendar effects in stock returns and address the problem of whether this is due to chance (data mining). They use over 100 years of daily returns data (on the S&P 500 and its futures index) to examine a huge set of up to 9500 possible calendar rules, including some that were not reported in the literature. (Those reported in the literature tend to be only the 'successful' ones and hence bias the results.) The basic idea is to take account of the problem that if you search hard enough on a given data set, you will eventually find a trading rule that appears to work even though this is just due to luck. Once these effects of data mining have been accounted for, Sullivan *et al.* find that the best calendar rule does not yield a statistically significant outcome for the predictability of daily stock returns.

They also find that performance of the best 'in-sample' calendar rule gives an inferior out-of-sample performance. Hence, after accounting for data snooping they find no significant calendar effects. Broadly speaking, the data-snooping idea is an attempt to get round a type of survivorship bias problem, because researchers who fail to find predictability may not get published (or even submit their research). So in the journals we may see a disproportionate number of articles that demonstrate predictability – all having used the same (or nearly the same) data set.

Small firm effect

Between 1960 and the middle of the 1980s, small-capitalised companies earned on average a higher rate of return than the overall stock-market index in many industrialised countries (Dimson *et al.*, 2001). Of course, according to the CAPM this could be due to the higher risks attached to these small firms, which should be reflected in their higher CAPM-beta values. However, the average returns on small firm stocks are higher than their required return as given by the CAPM. Put another more technical way, the average returns of small firms lie above the security market line, which plots the average return of stocks from firms of different sizes against their betas (Cochrane, 2001; Reinganum, 1982, 1983). However, the small firm effect seemed to disappear in the late 1980s after the anomaly had been documented in the academic and professional literature – so eventually the market removed this anomaly (Cochrane, 2001; Dimson *et al.*, 2001).

Winner's curse: 'buy the dogs, sell the stars'

We have noted that there is *mean reversion* in stock returns over long horizons (three to five years). A key issue for the validity of the EMH is whether such predictability can lead to excess profits net of transaction costs and risk. A seminal example of this approach is DeBondt and Thaler (1985). They take 35 of the most extreme 'winners' and 35 of the most extreme 'losers' over the five years from January 1928 to December 1932 (based on monthly return data from the universe of stocks on the NYSE) and form two distinct portfolios of these companies' shares. They follow these companies for the next five years, which constitutes the test period. They repeat the exercise 46 times by advancing the start date by one year each time. Finally, they calculate the average test-period performance (in excess of the return on the *whole* NYSE index), giving equal weight (rather than value weights) to each of the 35 companies. They find (Figure 15.1):

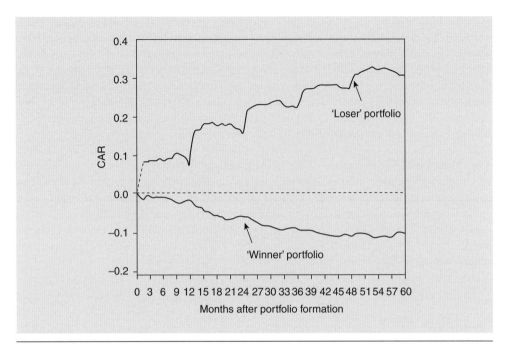

FIGURE 15.1: Cumulative excess returns for 'Winners' and 'Losers' portfolios

- Five-year returns for the loser portfolio are about 30% while losses for the winner portfolio are around 10%.
- Excess returns on the loser portfolio tend to occur in January (i.e. January effect).
- There is long-horizon mean reversion (i.e. a price fall is followed by a price rise and vice versa).

It is worth emphasising that the so-called loser portfolio (i.e. one where prices have fallen dramatically *in the past*) is in fact the one that makes high returns *in the future*: a somewhat paradoxical definition of 'loser'. An arbitrage strategy of buying the loser portfolio and short selling the 'winner portfolio' (i.e. 'buy the dogs' and 'sell the stars') beats the passive strategy of holding the S&P 500 (see DeBondt and Thaler, 1987).

Bremer and Sweeney (1991) find that the above results also hold for very short time periods. For example, for a loser portfolio comprising stocks where the *one-day* price fall has been greater than 10%, the subsequent returns are 3.95% *after five days*. Bremer and Sweeney use stocks of *large firms only*. Therefore they have no problem that the bid−ask spread is a large percentage of the price (which could distort the results). Also, they avoid problems with the 'small-firm effect' (i.e. smaller firms are more risky and hence require a greater than average equilibrium excess return). Hence Bremer and Sweeney also seem to find evidence of abnormal profits. Other studies that demonstrate profits to 'contrarian strategies' over long horizons include Chopra *et al.* (1992) for the US, Richards (1995, 1997) who uses national stock-market *indexes* and Lakonishok *et al.* (1994).

One explanation of the above results is that the perceived risk of the loser portfolio is judged to be high, hence requiring a high average excess return in the future, if one is to hold these stocks. The measurement of risk in early studies is sometimes relatively crude or non-existent.

Twin shares

Froot and Dabora (1999) analyse the case of Royal Dutch and Shell, who agreed to merge cash flows on a 60:40 basis but remained as separate companies. If price equals fundamental value, then the price ratio of these two shares should be Royal Dutch/Shell = 1.5. But underpricing and overpricing are found to have been as large as 35% and 15% respectively and the mispricing is persistent. Here there is little or no fundamental risk and short selling is not difficult. Of course, noise-trader risk remains and this (plus the short horizon of rational traders) could be the cause of the persistent mispricing. Hence there is 'no free lunch' but 'prices are not right'. However, they finally became 'right' in 2001 when the shares sold at a ratio of 1.5, so the mispricing did eventually disappear.

ADRs

ADRs are *foreign* shares held in trust by US financial institutions and traded in New York. The shares also trade in their home stock market, where their price often differs from the New York price. Here the two markets provide a near perfect substitute, so if the ADR in New York is at a premium to the actual share price in the home stock market, then arbitrageurs should short sell the ADR and purchase in the domestic stock market. But persistent price deviations are observed even where there are no restrictions to US ownership of the shares on the home market. Presumably this anomaly is due to noise-trader risk, limiting such arbitrage.

Index effect

When stocks are included (excluded) from the S&P 500 index, there is often a large increase (decrease) in their price. Here, there is a price change that is *independent* of any (observed) change in fundamental value. In other words, 'no news moves prices', which violates the EMH.

Closed-end funds

Closed-end funds issue a *fixed number* of shares and trading in the shares of the closed-end fund then takes place between investors. The cash raised by the closed-end funds is used to purchase a 'basket' of investments, usually comprising stocks and bonds. The shares that comprise the basket in the closed-end fund are generally also traded openly on the stock market. The value of the fund, the net asset value (NAV), ought therefore to equal the market value of the individual shares in the fund. But this is often not the case.

Closed-end fund share prices often differ from the NAV. When initially created, closed-end funds sell at above NAV, when they are terminated they sell at NAV and during their life they usually trade at a discount to NAV, which on average is about 10% but varies over time. This violates the EMH, because investors could buy the closed-end fund's shares at the discount price and at the same time short sell a portfolio of stocks that are identical to that held by the fund. The investor would thereby ensure that she eventually earned a risk-free profit equal to the discount.

Also, the discounts on very different types of closed-end funds that invest in widely different sectors (e.g. banking and manufacturing) tend to move together even though the industry stocks held by the funds are very different – this suggests that 'fads and fashion' for closed-end funds as a whole cause movements in the price of the closed-end funds independently of the economic fundamentals that affect the different industries and hence the NAV of the fund.

Several reasons have been offered for such closed-end fund discounts. First, closed-end fund members face a tax liability (in the form of capital gains tax) if the fund should sell securities after they have appreciated. This potential tax liability justifies paying a lower price than the market value of the underlying securities. Secondly, some of the assets in the closed-end fund are less marketable (i.e. they trade in 'thin' markets). Thirdly, agency costs in the form of management fees might also explain the discounts. However, Malkiel (1977) found that the discounts were substantially in excess of what could be explained by the above reasons, while Lee *et al.* (1990) considered that the discounts on closed-end funds are primarily determined by the stocks of small firms.

There is a further anomaly. At the initial public offering, closed-end fund shares are priced at a premium over the value of the shares that the closed-end fund holds. The value of the closed-end fund then generally moves to a discount within six months. The anomaly is why any investors purchase the initial public offering and thereby pay the underwriting costs via the future capital loss. Why don't investors just wait six months before purchasing the fund at the lower price?

Ideas from behavioural finance are consistent with many of these facts. If noise-trader risk is systematic, then such sentiment could push the closed-end fund price below the NAV of the shares in the fund for sustained periods (see De Long *et al.*, 1990). At liquidation of the fund any noise-trader risk will disappear and hence price will equal NAV. Initial overpricing of the funds may be due to entrepreneurs creating additional funds when noise traders 'favour' this type of investment. The strong co-movement of the discount across diverse closed-end funds (given that the funds' underlying cash-flow fundamentals are not highly correlated) may be due to general movements in noise-trader sentiment about all such funds. Bodurtha *et al.* (1993) find that closed-end funds containing German equities but traded in the US co-move more with the US than the German stock market, again demonstrating a de-linking of cash flows and value that tells against the EMH.

Lee *et al.* (1991) also show that closed-end funds and small stocks are both largely held by individual (US) investors and that the closed-end fund discount and the returns on small stocks are strongly positively correlated, which is suggestive of systematic noise-trader behaviour.

Co-movement

In the efficient markets approach, co-movement in returns is due to co-movement in cash flows, caused by a common factor influencing news about future earnings (e.g. sale of television rights for Spanish league soccer, causing a higher expectation of cash flows for both Real Madrid and Barcelona soccer clubs and hence a rise in both clubs' shares). However, as we have seen with returns on Royal Dutch and Shell, according to the EMH these two share prices should be perfectly positively correlated, but they are not.

To counter the efficient markets view, Barberis and Shleifer (2003) note that 'noise-trader' investors may have 'preferred habitats' of stocks such as small-cap, banking and so on, and that the cash flows (profits) to these different sectors have relatively low correlations. However, if noise-trader sentiment is systematic, the returns on shares in these different sectors should exhibit high co-movement of returns. In addition, any new stocks included in these sectors should begin to move more with that sector than before. Barberis *et al.* (2001) show that this is the case when stocks are added to the S&P 500, since their beta with the S&P 500 increases while their beta with stocks *outside* the S&P 500 falls. These observed changes seem to have little to do with a change in cash-flow co-movement, since inclusion in the S&P 500 signifies no information about correlation between cash flows (profits).

Optimal diversification?

Assuming that mean-variance portfolio theory is the 'correct' method (or model) for investors' portfolio choices, it is found that US and Japanese investors place too great a proportion (usually in excess of 90%) in domestic assets and not enough in foreign assets. This is the home-bias problem. Grinblatt and Keloharju (2001) and Huberman (2001) also find that there is a home-bias problem *within* countries, whereby investors place too much of their stock-market wealth in firms that are located close to them geographically. Grinblatt and Keloharju (2001) claims that Finnish investors hold and trade mainly Finnish stocks, while Huberman (2001) notes that investors hold many more shares in their *local* Regional Bell Operating Company (RBOC) than in *out-of-state* RBOC shares.

It has been found that 401(K) pension plans have a strong bias towards holding *own-company* stock (Benartzi, 2001) even though own-company returns are highly correlated with the individual's own employment prospects. This became widespread knowledge when it was revealed after the collapse of Enron that a large number of its employees held their defined-contribution pension plans mainly in Enron shares and unfortunately lost substantial amounts of money.

Benartzi and Thaler (2001) find that diversification by individuals often follows a simple 1/n rule. Individuals allocate 1/n of their savings to each investment choice offered and appear to disregard the different effective allocations to stocks and bonds that this entails. An example will clarify this process. Suppose you are offered any split you like between a stock fund and a bond fund. Using the 1/n rule you would allocate 50:50 to the stock and bond funds, obviously ending up with a stock–bond allocation of (S, B) = (50%, 50%). Now suppose you are offered any split you like between a stock fund and a balanced fund (where the latter has 50% stocks and 50% bonds). Using the 1/n rule you put 50% in the stock fund and 50% in the balanced fund, but this gives an effective stock–bond allocation (S, B) = (67%, 33%). Finally, suppose you are offered any split between a bond fund and balanced fund. The 1/n rule now gives an effective allocation (S, B) = (33%, 67%). When different cohorts of participants are actually offered one of these three choices, each cohort follows the 50:50 rule fairly closely, resulting in an average allocation to stocks for each cohort of participants of 54%, 73% and 35% respectively.

It follows from the 1/n rule that for 401(K) funds that predominantly offer stock funds, individuals will end up mechanically allocating more to stocks. Benartzi and Thaler (2001) examined 170 retirement savings plans, which are divided into three groups, 'low', 'medium' and 'high' categories, depending on the *fraction* of funds that are stock funds. For example, if the 1/n rule is used then we expect to see the 'low' category, which contains funds with relatively few stock funds (and a large number of bond funds), resulting in an effective allocation to stocks that is rather low. In the 'low', 'medium' and 'high' categories Benartzi and Thaler find that the actual allocation to stocks is 36%, 65% and 85% respectively, which broadly follows the 1/n rule (i.e. the more stock funds relative to bond funds in your plan the more you end up holding stocks, even though in principle any allocation to stocks is possible).

In terms of rational behaviour with full information, the above is difficult to explain. From psychological experiments we know that people do not like situations in which they feel they do not know the objective probability distribution of possible outcomes, and they may therefore feel more familiar with domestic stocks or stocks of the company in which they work. This is an example of *'ambiguity aversion'* – you avoid situations where you have little confidence in the probability distribution of outcomes.

Buying and selling

One direct way of assessing the EMH is to see if active investors do make good investment decisions, over repeated trades. Odean (1999) and Barber and Odean (2001) find that the average return of investors (of a large brokerage firm) underperforms a set of standard benchmarks. In addition, across all investors the average *annual* return on stocks that they buy is worse than those they sell. Also investors are more likely to sell stocks that have risen rather than those that have fallen, relative to their initial purchase price (whereas the latter should be more prevalent given tax offsets for losses). Also, those who trade often (relatively more men than women) earn lower average returns. In short, investors trade too often and are bad stock pickers – they would be better holding a diversified passive benchmark portfolio. It may be that active stock pickers and frequent traders are simply overconfident and that a cohort of new overconfident people continually enters the market. Their reluctance to sell 'losers' (sometimes called the 'disposition effect') may be due to the fact that people do not like to admit to having made an error. (This can be rationalised in terms of *loss aversion* noted above.)

This disposition effect has also been observed in the housing market, where people in a 'bear market' who are selling at a loss relative to their purchase price set their price about 30% higher than vendors of similar properties who are not selling at a loss (since they purchased some time ago). What is more, the loss-averse sellers actually do obtain higher prices than the other vendors (Genesove and Mayer, 2001).

Investment styles

There are many investment styles advocated by gurus in the financial press and by investment houses. Two of the most popular styles over the past 10 years have been 'value stocks' (also referred to as a 'value-growth' strategy) and a 'momentum strategy'. How are these defined?

A crucial difference between these two strategies lies in the time period over which you decide to form your portfolio and the length of time you hold it for. A value-growth invest-ment scenario buys *long-term* losers ('dogs') and short-sells *long-term* winners ('stars') – it is therefore a contrarian or reversal strategy and relies for its success on long-horizon mean reversion in stock returns (i.e. in buying the 'dogs' you hope they do not suffer from 'dead cat bounce' – if you can sort out the language on that one).

Value-growth strategy

DeBondt and Thaler's (1985) 'buy the dogs' strategy, where 'the dogs' are (say) the decile portfolio of stocks that have fallen the most over the last four years, and then selling then after *at least* one year, is an example of a 'value strategy'. Fama and French (1996) and Jegadeesh and Titman (1993) also provide similar examples but with different definitions of 'value stocks'. For example, an alternative definition of 'dogs' is stocks with high book-to-market value (BMV): since book value is relatively stable, firms with high BMV will tend to have low prices (remember that market value is simply the number of shares outstanding multi-plied by the market price of the shares). Fama and French (1996) show that going long 'the dogs' and short selling 'the stars' gives an average *monthly* return of 0.75–1.6% and buying 'the dogs' also yields higher Sharpe ratios than holding the market portfolio – although the extra 'bang' per unit of risk varies over different years.

Ali *et al.* (2003) and Lakonishok *et al.* (1994) find that short selling the bottom quintile of US stocks sorted by BMV (after correcting for size) in July of each year and buying the top quintile (and rebalancing each year) gives average returns of around 8%, 21% and 30% over the subsequent one-, two- and three-year horizons. To implement this strategy you have to have funds or credit lines to sustain losses and also the ability to short sell. It remains a risky strategy. One explanation of the book-to-market effect is that it is due to mispricing caused by market participants underestimating future earnings for high BMV stocks and overesti-mating earnings for low BMV stocks (La Porta *et al.*, 1997; Skinner and Sloan, 2002). But why don't arbitrageurs move in to exploit this opportunity and eliminate the mispricing?

Risk and mispricing

So, are the predictable long-horizon returns from the BMV effect due to the high ex-ante risk of the strategy or due to mispricing over long horizons? This is a difficult question to answer as it requires an acceptable model of risk and an assessment of transaction costs (which should not be high, as this is a long-horizon investment strategy). Ali *et al.* (2003) seek to throw some light on this question by looking at the correlation between BMVs of different stocks and the inherent riskiness of these stocks. (The latter is measured by the variance of residuals from the market model estimated using daily returns over the previous 250 days – this is a measure of the stock's specific risk.) The idea here is that stocks with relatively high specific risk are unlikely to be correctly priced because arbitrageurs general-ly have poorly diversified portfolios, since they follow only a small number of stocks. Hence specific risk is important to arbitrageurs as arbitrageurs with finite investment horizons, they are less likely to take positions in stocks with high specific risk and hence remove any pricing anomalies in these stocks. The 'variance variable' is found to be correlated with the BMV of the stock. Put slightly differently, Ali *et al.* (2003) find that when they isolate the 10% of stocks with the greatest specific risk and then form a portfolio that is long in the highest BMV quintile and short in the lowest BMV quintile of these stocks, this produces a subsequent three-year return of 51.3%. The corresponding return for the lowest-volatility group of stocks is only 1.7% and this pattern appears in 20 of the 22 separate years of the study. So the BMV of a stock may capture some element of the riskiness of a stock and hence the high return from a value-growth strategy may in part be a reward for holding risk that is difficult to diversify away.

Short-selling costs (i.e. the possibility of a 'short squeeze' if brokers request immediate return of stocks) might also constitute a risk of the value-growth strategy. The less a stock is held by institutional investors, the less likely it is that a short squeeze can be met from alternative lenders of the stocks and the higher the perceived cost of arbitrage.

The composition of any portfolio of value stocks will overlap considerably for most definitions of value. For example, for low price, low P–E ratios, high BMV and low market value ('size'), the set of firms might substantially overlap in each decile portfolio you form (particularly the lowest and highest), since it is mainly price that drives movements in *all* these variables. In other words, the *additional explanatory* power or extra predictability in using one rather than another definition of value may be quite small, although book-to-market does particularly well across a wide range of studies.

What is certain is that trying to 'beat the market' over a long horizon seems highly risky. With value stocks you probably have to buy firms whose price has been falling for some years and many of these firms are 'distressed' and close to bankruptcy. At the same time, you have to short sell stocks that have been increasing in price over several years and are the current paragons of corporate virtue and virility. In addition, you may be 'buying the dogs' in a recession period and you will have to hold your position for between, say, one and four years and in the intervening period your position might make losses. This strategy takes a very brave individual and if that individual is employed by an investment bank, he may get fired before the strategy yields positive returns (e.g. after the bursting of the 'dot-com bubble' in 2000 some analysts who had sold stock in 1998 or 1999 were vindicated but by then they had lost their jobs). Maybe in such circumstances there is more *perceived* risk around than is picked up by our ex-post measures (i.e. betas), so that in reality the excess return to value investing is just reward for the additional risk taken, not to mention transaction costs and possible high costs associated with short selling.

Bull run

To underscore the possibility of limited arbitrage, ask yourself what you might have done in 1999 after observing the bull run in the US and UK from 1995. Suppose your analysis of fundamentals implied that the S&P 500 was currently overpriced. You would need to short the S&P 500 and buy a similar correctly priced index (e.g. the Russell 2000 of small stocks) and wait. (If the Russell index of small stocks has, say, a beta of 2 and the S&P 500 has a beta of 1, then you would short $z/2 for every $z you are long the S&P500.)

But even with this long–short (hedge fund) strategy you would face fundamental risk, if any news about large companies in the S&P 500 was not highly correlated with news about small companies. You also face noise-trader risk (i.e. the S&P 500 could rise even more) and model risk (i.e. are you really sure that the S&P 500 is overpriced relative to fundamentals?). If you had held your position for six months or even a year, its value may have fallen dramatically. Of course, if you had been able to hang on until 2002/3, your strategy would probably have been vindicated, but by that time you may have had a nervous breakdown or lost your job, or both! Of course, had you merely purchased the S&P 500 (and not also short sold) the risks would have been even greater – mutual funds are not allowed to short sell, so this is the position they would have found themselves in. Alternatively, you could have taken the bold decision of John Ralfe, manager of the pension fund of Boots, a UK drug store/chemists, who between 1998 and 2000 moved all funds out of equities into bonds – which ex post can be viewed as possibly the best one-off market-timing call of the last 50 years. (In fact the move into long-term bonds, including index-linked bonds, may have been more a desire to match the timing of pension liabilities with the fund's assets and to preserve the purchasing power of the fund.)

Momentum strategy

Another very popular strategy or style is momentum. Here the portfolio-formation time period is small, usually based on the return over the previous year (or less), and the holding period is also short, usually one year. The momentum strategy is to buy short-term 'winners' and sell (short) the short-term 'losers'. You buy the top decile of stocks that have risen the most over the past year and finance your purchases by (short) selling the bottom decile that have risen the least. (This is also called a 'relative strength' strategy.) The strategy is repeated each month and each portfolio is held for the subsequent year. Fama and French (1996) report the average monthly US returns from this momentum strategy of 1.3% p.m. (15.6% p.a.) for the July 1963 to December 1993 period and 0.38% p.m. (4.56% p.a.) over the January 1931 to February 1963 period. Clearly, a successful momentum strategy in beating the market return only occurred in the 1963–93 period, perhaps demonstrating some fragility in this strategy.

Jegadeesh and Titman (2001) re-examined the momentum strategy. They used all stocks from the NYSE/AMEX but excluded NASDAQ stocks (and stocks priced below $5). At the end of each month, stocks were ranked into decile portfolios based on their returns over the previous six months and these portfolios were then equally weighted. Each portfolio was held for six months following the ranking month. The momentum portfolio was self-financing, since the loser portfolio P10 (i.e. lowest returns over the past six months) was sold and the winner portfolio P1 was purchased. The portfolios were rebalanced every month and held for one year. The future average return of the past winners P1 for 1965–97 was 1.67% p.m. and of the past losers P10 was 0.58% p.m., hence the winners outperformed the losers by 1.09% p.m. (a hefty 13.1% p.a.) – and this result also applied over the sub-periods 1965–89 and 1990–97.

To assess the performance of the actual momentum returns relative to their required return (i.e. accounting for market and other risks), Jegadeesh and Titman measured the CAPM/Jensen's alpha and found that the alpha for the top-momentum portfolio P1 = 0.54% p.m. and for the bottom momentum portfolio P10 = −0.57 p.m.; the difference in alphas at

1.1% p.m. (13.2% p.a.) was statistically significant. Similarly, for the Fama-French 3-factor model, the difference in alphas was 1.29% p.m. ($t = 7.8$) – an annual alpha for the long–short portfolio of 15.5% p.a. Hence the long–short 'P1–P10' momentum strategy appeared to generate statistically significant abnormal returns. Note that the highest–decile momentum portfolio had typically increased in price by about 80% in the previous year and the loser portfolio declined by 60%. It therefore only takes a small amount of momentum in stock returns for this to result in a 1% *monthly average* return over the *next* year, after forming your long–short momentum portfolio.

Jegadeesh and Titman (2001) also examined the returns to the momentum portfolios over longer horizons than the one-year holding period used above. They found that the *cumulative* momentum returns for all P1 to P10 portfolios peaked at around 12% p.a. after one year (i.e. an average of 1% p.m.), but that subsequent returns were nearly always negative, so that cumulative returns after month 60 were only about 1% per annum. This demonstrates that a successful momentum strategy requires a relatively short holding period of one year (or less) and that over the long run stock prices are mean reverting (i.e. they return to their long-run trend growth rate).

The above empirical results are consistent with the behavioural phenomenon of 'conservatism bias', where individuals underweight new information when updating their views about the future, so prices adjust slowly to new information. However, once the new information is fully incorporated, stock returns no longer exhibit momentum. The evidence is also consistent with models incorporating 'self-attribution bias' (Daniel *et al.,* 1997), where informed traders attribute their short-term 'winner' stocks to superior skill and their 'loser' stocks to bad luck. This overconfidence means that they purchase more 'winners' and slowly push prices above fundamental value, creating a short-run momentum effect. Rational traders then eventually step in and the gains of the winner portfolio are eventually reversed.

Overall, the fact that the successful momentum strategy outlined in Jegadeesh and Titman (1993) is found to hold on new data from the 1990–97 period weakens the argument that the original 1993 results are due to data-snooping biases. Whether these profits continued in the 2000–02 stock-market meltdown and after remains to be seen.

Transaction costs

On investigating US momentum stocks, it is found that the gains primarily come from shorting small illiquid stocks between November and December (i.e. tax-loss selling) and transaction costs are therefore likely to be high, which may outweigh the gains noted. The Jagadeesh and Titman (1993) profits from momentum trading do adjust for *average* trading costs due to mean commission rates and market impact effects. But this average does not take account of the cross-section differences in transaction costs (e.g. small stocks have higher transaction costs) and their time variation. The figures used also exclude bid–ask spreads, taxes and short-sale costs. The momentum strategy is trading intensive and if rebalancing is every six months, this requires four trades (buy–sell and sell–buy) every six months, so with average abnormal returns (i.e. alpha estimate) over six months of around 6%, this profit could be wiped out if costs per trade exceeded 1.5%.

Lesmond *et al.* (2004) undertake a detailed assessment of the trading costs (including the fact that not all of the momentum portfolio is 'turned over' every six months) and find that momentum strategies on US stocks do not earn profits after correcting for all transaction costs. They investigate the performance of Jagadeesh and Titman's (1993, 2001) P1 (best performers) and P3 (worst performers) portfolios – the best (worst) performers are the top (bottom) 30% of stocks with the highest (lowest) past returns. Transaction costs for the P1 (best performers) and P3 (worst performers) portfolios are found to be around 4.5% and 5% respectively (every six months), whereas the average figure used by Jagadeesh and Titman (1993, 2001) was 0.5%. These 'new' transaction costs imply that the average six-month momentum abnormal returns for the P1–P3 strategy of about 6% (per six months) barely cover transaction costs (and returns net of transaction costs are usually not statistically significant). It remains to be seen whether a more detailed look at transaction costs for other documented successful momentum strategies (e.g. in non-US markets, bond markets and industrial sectors) also imply near zero (net) momentum returns.

The empirical anomalies that have been documented certainly cast doubt on the EMH: it may be possible to make abnormal profits because of some predictability in stock returns. However, it must be noted that many of the above anomalies are most prominent among small and 'distressed' firms (e.g. January and size effects, value-growth and momentum strategies, discounts on closed-end funds). It may be that ex-ante perceived risk is higher than that measured ex post, so these anomalies may not yield excess returns corrected for *perceived* risk. While some anomalies do persist, others disappear (e.g. the small-firm effect). Certainly, the anomalies literature has given the EMH a bit of a hard time. If you look closely and are willing to take on substantial risk over repeated gambles (i.e. lose some cash on the way to your financial nirvana), it is possible to find profitable opportunities in the stock market over specific time periods. This may result in excess profits even after correction for risk (and transaction costs), but there still appear to be no blindingly obvious 'free lunches' around. It is difficult to 'beat the market' by stock picking and although our MBA students did not believe this in the bull run of the 1990s, they have tended to believe it a little more since 2000.

Of course, there is a glaring anomaly in all of this. If it is the case that the EMH is true, why is there a huge industry out there (in London, New York and other major cities) that claims it can 'beat the market' and earn positive returns after accounting for risk and transaction costs? Well, some investment managers may have the 'alchemist's secret' and it is certainly the case that if they did, they would not tell you. This is called trading on 'proprietary information' – in other words, give me your money and I will not tell you in very much detail how I am going to invest it, just trust me! Academics (or anyone else for that matter) can never know with 100% certainty that there are not some traders out there using their own investment strategies to make some of their clients abnormal profits due to their trading skill rather than luck. Academics can only mimic what these traders might be doing and test a set of investment strategies on historical data. Overall, the evidence in favour of the view that 'you can't beat the market' is quite strong, from the wide range of academic studies undertaken. What behavioural finance and the anomalies approach have demonstrated is that there are some strategies that might succeed, but these are difficult to unearth. In addition, what the behavioural finance approach has demonstrated is that even though you may not be able to make abnormal returns, nevertheless stock prices may diverge substantially from their fundamental (fair) value for fairly long periods of time – but to take advantage of exactly when the mispricing is corrected is difficult and hence there may be 'no free lunches' out there.

SUMMARY

- Some behavioural finance ideas are consistent with the 'no free lunch' proposition; that is, returns are not easy to predict and you cannot make money from repeated gambles after taking account of risk and transaction costs. However, 'no free lunch' does not necessarily imply that 'the price is right' (i.e. that price equals fair value).
- Evidence from psychological studies is used in the behavioural finance approach to explain anomalies such as value-growth and momentum strategies and the behaviour of the discount on closed-end funds.
- The anomalies literature has unearthed many potential cases where abnormal profits may be made. In many cases, strategies for beating the market (e.g. weekend and January effects, value-growth and momentum strategies) require the investor to hold risky positions, and it is still much debated whether such profits would survive transaction costs and adjustments for perceived risks by investors.
- Other anomalies (e.g. ADRs, twin shares, index effect, closed-end funds) seem to persist and involve little risk, so here the empirical evidence gives stronger support to the behavioural finance view.
- There do appear to be some anomalies that are genuinely exploitable by well-informed traders, but they are difficult to detect and may disappear once enough traders recognise the anomaly and try to exploit it.

EXERCISES

Q1   How would you define a 'noise trader' and a 'smart-money' (or 'rational') trader?

Q2   Can noise traders outperform smart-money traders and hence survive in the market?

Q3   How might the interactions of noise traders and smart-money traders lead to mispriced shares?

Q4   Name one stock-market anomaly that you believe provides a profitable trading strategy.

Q5   At the end of 1999 and in the first three months of 2000, certain dot-com companies were being floated for hundreds of millions of dollars even though they had only been trading for a few years, had very small turnover (e.g. $1m p.a.) and had not yet shown a profit. Is this rational or a classic example of noise traders causing a stock-market bubble?

Q6   Can noise-trader behaviour explain the discounts found on closed-end funds (investment trusts in the UK)?

Q7   What is loss aversion?

16

Predicting Stock Returns

AIMS

- To explain the practical implications of the efficient markets hypothesis (EMH) for investment strategy, corporate finance issues and the regulation of financial markets.
- To examine tests of the predictability of stock returns.
- To examine whether it is possible to earn *abnormal returns* (i.e. returns after adjustment for risk and transaction costs) by using active investment strategies.

INTRODUCTION

The efficient markets hypothesis (EMH) may be expressed in a number of alternative ways and the differences between these representations can easily become rather esoteric, technical and subtle. We try to avoid such technical issues and present the ideas in intuitive terms. The concepts behind the EMH can be applied to all speculative asset returns (e.g. stocks, bonds, derivatives), but we restrict our discussion to the equity market.

When economists speak of capital markets as being *efficient*, they mean that asset prices and returns are determined as the outcome of trading between rational informed agents in a competitive market. As we saw in Chapter 15, the EMH states that rational traders rapidly assimilate any relevant information on fundamentals to determine the fair value of a stock and then actively buy or sell stocks to instantaneously move market prices so they are equal to fair value. It follows that there should be no opportunities for making a return on a stock that is in excess of a fair payment for the riskiness of that stock (and any transaction costs in buying and selling). In short, *abnormal returns* from trading should be zero. If current and past information is immediately incorporated into current prices, then only new information or news should cause changes in prices. Since news is by definition unforecastable, then price changes should be unforecastable – no information known today or earlier can be used to earn abnormal returns in the future.

16.1 IMPLICATIONS OF THE EMH

What are the implications of the EMH for investment strategy and corporate finance decisions? Under the EMH the current share price incorporates all relevant publicly available information. Hence, investment analysts cannot use publicly available information to devise successful trading rules. The EMH implies that the investor should adopt a 'buy and hold' policy. She should spread her risks by diversifying and should hold the 'market portfolio' (or the 35 or so shares that mimic the market portfolio). Advice such as 'put all your eggs in one basket and monitor the basket closely' should be avoided – active investment strategies are futile and will only involve high transaction costs and lower net returns compared to a passive strategy. You should not try to pick undervalued or overvalued stocks or try to time the market (i.e. move into high-beta stocks today when you are forecasting the market return to be higher than average tomorrow).

The role for investment analysts if the EMH is correct is rather limited and would, for example, include:

- Advising on the choice of the 35 or so shares that mimic the market portfolio or advising on low cost index-tracker mutual funds to hold.
- Advising on altering the proportion of wealth held in each mutual fund as the optimal market proportions change, as you update your estimates of expected returns, variances and covariances as new data becomes available.
- Choosing appropriate investments to maximise *after-tax* returns. For example, if dividends are more highly taxed than capital gains, then for high-rate income-tax payers it may be better to hold shares that have low dividend payouts but high expected capital gains. Also

certain retirement accounts (401(K) and IRA funds in the US and pension contributions in the UK) may have favourable tax status.

- Taking account of the investors' other assets when deciding on stock-market investments. To take an extreme example, many employees of the energy firm Enron invested heavily in the company's shares and had purchased houses in the vicinity of the firm – they were therefore very undiversified. A less extreme example is to hold less in stocks and more in bonds as the individual gets older. The main reason for this is not that stocks are less risky the longer you hold them, but the older you are, the less time you have to recoup any losses from stocks by working longer hours. Finally, if you own a large house then this must be considered part of your risky assets when determining your allocation to stocks[1].

Once you have determined your optimal portfolio of risky assets, you still need advice on the allocation between the risk-free and your risky asset portfolio – this requires knowledge of your own risk tolerance, which is often assessed through questionnaires.

It is worth noting that most individuals do not hold anything like the market portfolio of all marketable assets. Except for residents of the US, this would require most investors to hold predominantly *foreign securities*. But people tend to hold mostly domestic securities – this is the *home-bias puzzle*. Also, individuals and institutions (like pension funds and insurance companies) do not seem to believe the EMH, since only about 10% of mutual funds are index trackers and around 90% of funds under management are 'active funds'.

Let us turn now to some public policy issues. The stock market is supposed to provide the 'correct' signals for the allocation of real resources (i.e. fixed investment). Only a small proportion of corporate investment is financed from new issues (e.g. about 4% on a gross basis in the UK). Nevertheless, the rate of return of a quoted company on the stock market provides a measure of cost of equity finance or the 'hurdle rate' to use in the PV formula for physical investment projects. Other things being equal, if profits from a firm's proposed new investment projects are expected to be high (e.g. the return on equity exceeds the cost of equity capital), then according to the EMH this will be reflected in a high current share price. Hence, the firm can obtain its required funds by issuing fewer shares or it can justify using its retained profits as a source of project finance. However, if the current share price does not reflect future *fundamentals* (e.g. expected future cash flows) but is influenced by whim or fads of 'irrational' investors, this link is broken. For example, an abnormally low share price that reflects ill-informed extraneous factors (e.g. irrational market prejudice) will inhibit the firm from embarking on what (on a rational calculation) is a viable investment project.

The above analysis also applies to takeovers. If the stock market is myopic – that is, it only considers profits and dividends that accrue in the *near* future – then managers fearful of a takeover may distribute more in current dividends rather than using the retained profits to undertake profitable real investment on, for example, R&D expenditure. This strategy will boost the share price and this is generally known as *short-termism*. This could also be a problem if managers are issued with share options but they believe the market is myopic – they then have an incentive to boost the share price in the short run and not pursue long-term profitable investment projects.

---

[1] These issues are by no means straightforward and unfortunately cannot be adequately dealt with using the one-period mean-variance framework we have analysed – see Cuthbertson and Nitzsche 2004.

The view that hostile takeovers are welfare enhancing (i.e. in terms of the output and profits of the firm) requires the assumption that markets are efficient and that takeovers enable 'bad' incumbent managers to be replaced. In this scenario, the hostile bidder recognises that the incumbent bad management has led rational shareholders to mark down the firm's share price. The hostile bidder then pays a price in excess of the existing share price. After replacing the bad managers and reorganising the firm, the ensuing higher future profits are just sufficient to compensate for the higher price the bidder paid for the shares.

Note that if share prices do reflect fundamentals (i.e. future dividends) but news occurs frequently and is expected to make a substantial impact on a firm's future performance, then one would still expect to observe *highly volatile* asset prices, even if the market is efficient. But there is still a prima facie case for insisting that financial institutions have enough resources (reserves) to weather temporary losses due to market volatility. This provides an argument for *capital adequacy rules* such as the Basle Accord on capital adequacy for market risk (value at risk), discussed in a later chapter. Also, if there are systemic risks whereby the failure of one financial institution can lead to failures of many others (i.e. a form of externality), then in principle government action is required to ensure that the level of capital reflects the marginal social costs of the systematic risk, rather than the marginal private costs (for any individual financial institution).

What are the implications of the EMH for issues in corporate finance? If the market is efficient there is no point in delaying a physical investment project in the hope that financing conditions will improve (i.e. that the share price will be higher): under the EMH the current price reflects the fair value given the company's future prospects. Also, in an efficient market, the Modigliani-Miller theorem (in the absence of taxes and bankruptcy) suggests that the cost of capital is independent of the capital mix (i.e. debt–equity ratio). So you cannot increase the value of the firm by altering the mix of finance. The issue of capital mix can also be applied to the maturity (term) structure of debt. Since in an efficient market, yields on long- and short-term corporate bonds fully reflect available information, the proportion of long-term debt to short-term debt will also not alter the overall cost of capital (WACC) to the firm.

It follows from the above arguments that under the EMH, the choice of the appropriate mix of finance or analysing the optimum time to float new stock or bond issues is futile. Of course, if the market is not efficient, the chief financial officer may attempt to 'beat the market' by issuing more bonds or stocks when she thinks the market is irrationally overvaluing these assets, and she can also seek to alter the stock-market valuation of the firm by altering dividend policy or by share-repurchase schemes and so on.

Abnormal returns

As a first approximation, the EMH suggests that stock prices over a short horizon of, say, one day, one week or one month are unpredictable. Stock prices are like a coin flip: what happened to stock prices in the past is of no use in predicting what they might be tomorrow. This is often referred to as the *random walk* behaviour of stock prices – price *changes* are random and unforecastable[2]. You can see why. Stock prices are predictable using public information and you (and everyone else) are predicting a 2% rise over the *next 24 hours*, then according to the EMH everyone would buy the stock now, thus immediately pushing its price up by 2%, so any predictability over the next 24 hours is eliminated. Under the EMH, a prediction of favourable *future* performance leads to favourable current performance and any daily predictability is removed. Stock prices in an efficient market immediately 'jump' to their new fair value. Empirically, daily stock-price changes do closely follow a random walk and hence are unpredictable.

When we move to longer-horizon stock returns we have to interpret the EMH a little more carefully. First, it is stock returns (i.e. capital gains plus dividends) rather than just changes in the stock *price* that are the focus of the EMH. Second, the EMH recognises that there has to be a positive return to stocks, on average, which exceeds the risk-free rate, as stocks are risky assets. To explore these issues further, suppose that investors' required (expected) return on a stock between 'today' ($= t$) and 'tomorrow' ($= t + 1$), denoted ER_{t+1}, depends on the risk-free rate r_t and a *constant* risk premium $rp = 8\%$ p.a.[3]:

$$ER_{t+1} = r_t + rp = r_t + 8\% \qquad\qquad [1]$$

You can think of ER_{t+1} as the expected monthly return on the stock. Since r_t is known today, then the stock return R_{t+1} over the next month is in part predictable – *even under the EMH*. It is easy to see why. In periods when the risk-free rate r_t is relatively high (low) then *on average*, we should observe larger (smaller) positive returns in subsequent periods – this implies that returns are predictable[4].

The EMH does allow you to do better than a 'coin flip'; that is, better than a 50–50 chance of getting the prediction right. So, the EMH does *not* imply that stock returns are unpredictable. Confused? What does the EMH imply? The EMH actually implies that *abnormal*

---

[2] Strictly speaking the correct terminology is that stock prices are a submartingale – the abnormal return on the stock is unpredictable. The random walk is more restrictive and assumes successive price changes are independent and identically distributed, but we ignore these subtleties here.

[3] If we write this as $ER_{t+1} = r + 8\% = k$ where k is now the constant required return, we can use the definition $ER_{t+1} = \frac{EP_{t+1} - P_t}{P_t} + \frac{ED_{t+1}}{P_t} = k$ which after re-arrangement can be shown to imply the PV formula for the stock *price*:

$P_t = \sum_{i=1}^{\infty} ED_{t+i}/(1 + k)^i$. Hence assuming expected returns are constant, is the same as assuming the stock price equals the expected PV of future dividends – see Appendix to chapter 14.

[4] Behind this equation is the assumption that investors are 'rational'. This implies that after making several forecasts, it is equally likely that the outturns for stock returns are above or below their forecast values. Hence the (ex-post) forecast errors ε_{t+1} that is, the difference between the actual and forecast return $\varepsilon_{t+1} \equiv R_{t+1} - ER_{t+1}$ average out to zero (and these errors are random over successive forecasts) – these assumptions are known as 'rational expectations'. Using the above assumption our equation becomes: $R_{t+1} - r_t = 8 + \varepsilon_{t+1}$, so if we run a regression of the actual return on any economic variables know at time t (e.g. the dividend-price ratio) then these additional variables should not be statistically significant – only the constant term should be statistically significant and here should be estimated to be around 8%. Note that the uncertainty surrounding your past forecasts is measured by the standard error of the residual in the regression – and this could be very large (because of specific risk). Rational expectations does not rule out the possibility that in the past you made large forecast errors, only that your past forecast errors are random around zero.

returns are unpredictable. What are abnormal returns in our example? The abnormal return is the stock return *less* the risk-free rate *and* after adjusting the return to compensate for the inherent riskiness of the stock (i.e. the risk premium), which here is $rp = 8\%$.

> Under the EMH:
> Abnormal returns are unpredictable.
> Abnormal return = stock return minus the risk-free rate and after compensation for risk

Mathematically, the EMH implies that abnormal returns $AR_{t+1} = (R_{t+1} - r_t - rp)$ are unpredictable. If we assume that the CAPM is the correct way of adjusting for risk, then the abnormal return each period is $AR_{t+1} = (R_{t+1} - r_t) - \beta_i(R_{m,t+1} - r_t)$ and hence the *average* abnormal return is just the alpha of the stock. Clearly, the difficulty in testing the EMH is knowing whether you have correctly adjusted the actual return for the riskiness of the stock. Rejection of the EMH can always be attributed to having the wrong model for the risk premium.

So, if stock returns are predictable (i.e. better than a coin flip), then on average you can make money from repeated 'bets' – but this does *not* refute the EMH. However, if you can predict stock returns and make enough money to *more than* compensate for the risks and transaction costs involved, this does violate the EMH. It follows that if you find a result in the literature that concludes that stock returns are predictable, don't get too excited – the positive average return you get from repeatedly using this trading rule may just be an adequate compensation for the risky gambles you are taking. The predictor variable (e.g. the price–earnings ratio) may just be a proxy for the changing risk attached to your gambles. You must always adjust your average returns for risk and transaction costs before you can proclaim yourself a 'Master of the Universe'.

Trying to find out whether there really is money to be made from active strategies is very difficult. In order for the market to be efficient there have to be enough 'big players' around to continually assess prospects for future stock returns and act on any mispricing. This information gathering and analysis requires finance. If you are running a $10bn portfolio and you can add, say, 1/10th of 1% to your *annual* return, this is worth $10m. So you can spend up to $10m per year on company research, if you think it will add 1/10th of 1% to your portfolio return. For $10m you can 'buy' a reasonable set of analysts and as there are thousands of investment funds with assets greater than $10bn, it would appear as if there should be no shortage of analysts pouring over company reports. Of course, for the market to be efficient not *everyone* in the market has to be scrutinising company accounts – just sufficient people to spot mispricing and with enough funds (and risk appetite) to eliminate it.

However, this realistic scenario poses a problem for testing the EMH – an abnormal return of 1/10th of 1% is going to be almost impossible to verify statistically, given that the volatility in a diversified stock portfolio is likely to be in excess of 20%. Also, while academics can apply many statistical tests based on *publicly available* investment strategies, we can never be sure that there are not a few guys around with the alchemist's secret. After all, if you have discovered a 'money-making machine' you are hardly likely to tell the world – although given average publication lags in academia, you might be a billionaire by the time your profitable trading rule appears in a journal.

Another thing to look out for is 'cold calling' by someone with a superlative track record. To see what might happen here, suppose you (illegally) sent out 5000 newsletters via the Internet, saying that team A will beat team B in next Sunday's football game, and also sent 5000 letters to different addresses saying that team B will beat team A. (We exclude the possibility of a draw, to keep things simple, but this is easy to incorporate.) Well, you will have 5000 'customers' at the end of the week who know that you picked this week's winning team. Next week you split these 5000 into two groups of 2500 and repeat the exercise (i.e. scam) for team D and team F, who are playing each other. You can see where this is going. After four weeks you will have predicted four winners in a row for 625 of your 'customers'. Now, you give these 'punters' a telephone call offering to predict the outcome of a particular game, next Sunday, if they take out a yearly subscription to your forecasting service. Beware the cold caller: she may have no skill, yet she may take your money in exchange for her 'expert advice' and 100% track record to date. If you have a large number of stock analysts issuing newsletters, then just due to luck a few of them will pick the top funds in successive periods – these are the guys who are interviewed in the *Financial Times* and *Wall Street Journal*. The ones who had just the same level of skill (i.e. none), you won't hear about. This is a form of selection bias. Case Study 16.1 presents another scenario to illustrate this point.

CASE STUDY 16.1   KNOCK-KNOCK WHO'S THERE?

Another way of looking at the issue of 'luck' and possible outcomes is to consider how you might correctly predict whether a particular stock price (e.g. AT&T) will go up (U) or down (D) over the next three years (relative to the S&P 500 if you like), even though you have no skill. You could send out three consecutive annual newsletters to person-1 with the prediction UUU. To person-2 you send three newsletters that predict UUD, to person-3 you send the prediction UDD and so on. There are in fact $8 = 2^3$ possible outcomes for the stock return over the next three years: UUU, UUD, UDD, DDD, DDU, DUU, UDU, DUD[5]. So if you send out eight newsletters in each of the three years, one person will receive a newsletter with 100% correct predictions in each of the next three years. You can then advertise your success of three correct predictions in a row and get the person to whom you sent this newsletter to endorse your excellent forecasting skills. If you wanted to cover all the possibilities for predictions over five years, you would need to send out $2^5 = 32$ newsletters each year. There are a large number of stock analysts covering many different stocks, so there are many more than

---

[5] This is the binomial model in action; see Chapter 26. With only a U or D for each outcome there are 8 possible paths after 3 'steps' in the binomial tree. The number of ways you can get k-'ups' is $C_k^n = n!/(n-k)!k!$, so for example, the number of ways you can get $k = 1$ 'ups' in $n = 3$ three time periods is $C_k^n = 3!/(3-1)!1! = 1$ which is the single path UUU, whereas you can get 'two ups' in three different ways $C_2^3 = 3!/(3-2)!2! = 3$, corresponding to UUD, DUU, UDU.

32 different newsletters published in any given year. Some of these analysts will have a five- or even ten-year record of 100% success in predicting the direction of change in a particular stock price – but this may just be due to luck, and the postman knocking on your door with just the sequence of newsletters that (randomly) contains the last five years' correct predictions for at least one stock the analyst is covering.

16.2 PREDICTABILITY

We have already investigated predictability when discussing the anomalies literature and in this chapter we concentrate on statistically based tests (e.g. using correlation and regression to forecast returns)[6]. But the sources of predictability (e.g. momentum, value, growth) found in the anomalies literature will also manifest themselves in some of our statistical tests.

There are a wide variety of alternative statistical tests of stock return predictability, including correlation, regression and various types of variance ratio statistics. The most frequently used approach is to regress 'tomorrow's' stock returns (or returns in excess of the risk-free rate) on a set of variables known today, which we designate as Ω_t:

$$R_{t+1} = \alpha + \beta' \Omega_t + \varepsilon_{t+1} \tag{2}$$

ε_{t+1} is a zero mean random error (the residual). These regression tests vary, depending on the information assumed, which is usually of the following type:

- Data on past returns (i.e. weak-form tests).
- Data on 'fundamental variables' such as the dividend–price ratio, the earnings–price ratio and book-to-market value (i.e. strong-form tests).

Using past returns as independent variables in equation [2] is similar to examining the correlation coefficient between current returns and lagged returns. (The latter are the autocorrelation and partial autocorrelation coefficients and are summarised in the correlogram.) The above tests can be done for alternative holding periods of a day, a week, a month, a year or for returns over several years. It is possible that we may find predictability at some horizons but not at others.

Short-horizon returns

For *individual* stock returns (on the NYSE) there is weak positive correlation over a weekly horizon. Higher than average returns one week tend to be followed by higher than average returns the next week – this is short-term momentum. But these correlation coefficients are fairly small (for liquid stocks), so the outcome is only very slightly better than a coin flip. However, if you place repeated bets on heads using a biased coin with a heads/tails outcome of 51/49 you can make money, *on average*. For a $1000 bet the expected outcome is

---

[6] The distinction between these two approaches is not absolutely clear-cut since an 'anomaly' usually involves some form of statistical analysis.

$20 (= 0.49(-1000) +0.51(+1000)). So if you place 10,000 bets on heads each for $1000, you expect to end up with $200,000 profit (= $20 × 10,000), from your total stake of $10m (i.e. an expected return of 2%). But there is considerable risk in these repeated gambles – you could have a run of losses (even though the coin flip is random) that might mean periods of cumulative loss. If this example represents a stock-market gamble, then there is also consider-able risk because of the high volatility of stock returns, not to mention transaction costs. Studies show that it is very unlikely you can make profits corrected for risk, over a weekly horizon.

We noted in Chapter 15 that for horizons between three and six months, if you form (decile) *portfolios* of past winners, they have more momentum than the past losers – again, this is pos-itive autocorrelation. At this intermediate horizon we have seen that returns can be substan-tial, but probably not enough to cover transaction costs and compensate for the riskiness of the portfolios held.

Long-horizon returns

Are stock returns over long horizons *mean reverting*; that is, higher than average returns are followed by lower returns in the future? Fama and French (1988) find evidence of mean reversion in stock returns over long horizons (i.e. in excess of two years). They estimate a regression where the return over the interval $t - n$ to t (e.g. over the last $n = 2$ years) deter-mines future returns (e.g. over the upcoming two years):

$$R(t,t + n) = \alpha + \beta R(t - n,t) + \varepsilon_t \qquad [3]$$

Fama and French consider return horizons from 1 to 10 years. They found little or no pre-dictability, except for horizons of between $n = 2$ and $n = 7$ years for which β is negative, indi-cating mean reversion. There was a peak at the five-year horizon when $\beta = -0.5$, indicating that a 10% negative return over five years is, on average, followed by a 5% positive return over the next five years. But the R-squared in the regressions for the three-to-five-year horizons are about 35%, so there is considerable risk in the strategy. Such mean reversion ($\beta < 0$) is con-sistent with evidence from the anomalies literature on contrarian investment strategies, such as that due to De Bondt and Thaler (1985). Note, however, that the Fama-French results appear to be mainly due to the inclusion of the 1930s sample period (Fama and French, 1988, p. 4).

Poterba and Summers (1988) investigate mean reversion by looking at the variance of returns over different horizons. If (continuously compounded) stock returns are unpredictable (strictly speaking, independent and identically distributed over time, like a coin flip), then it can be shown that the standard deviation of returns over T periods is given by the $\sqrt{T}$-rule:

$$\sigma_T = \sqrt{T}\sigma \quad \text{and} \quad \sigma_T^2 = T\sigma^2 \qquad [4]$$

where σ_T is the standard deviation over T periods and σ is the standard deviation over one peri-od. For example, if $\sigma = 20\%$ is the standard deviation annual stock returns, then if stock returns are random the standard deviation over four years should be $\sigma_T = 40\% (= \sqrt{4}.20\%)$. Poterba and Summers (1988) find that the variance of returns increases at a rate that is less than in proportion to T and hence returns are mean reverting for horizons of T between three and eight years – broadly consistent with the Fama-French regression results. This conclusion is generally upheld when using a number of alternative stock-price indexes. However, later work noting that the distribution of stock returns is non-normal and hence that standard tests are inappropriate finds little evidence of mean reversion for stock *indices* for many different countries (Jorion and Goetzmann, 1999; Jorion 2003). So the evidence is not clear-cut, but tends to favour independence over time for (country) stock indices, thus future long-horizon returns are not predictable from past returns.

Multivariate tests

The above tests only examine 'weak-form' predictability – that is, whether past returns help predict future returns – they are univariate tests. However, a number of variables other than past returns have been found to help predict current returns. For example, Keim and Stambaugh (1986) use monthly excess returns on US common stocks (over the T-bill rate) for the period 1930 to 1978. For a number of stock portfolios (based on firm size), they find that the difference in the yield between high- and low-grade corporate bonds helps predict future returns – but for monthly return data, the regressions only explain about 0.6–2.0% of the variability in excess returns.

Fama and French (1988) examine the relationship between stock returns (over different horizons n) and the dividend yield, D/P:

$$R(t,t + n) = \alpha + \beta(D/P)_t + \varepsilon_t \qquad [5]$$

The equation is run for monthly and quarterly returns and for annual returns from one to four years using the NYSE index. Fama and French also test the robustness of the equation by running it over various sub-periods. For monthly and quarterly data the dividend yield is often statistically significant and $\beta > 0$, so a relatively high dividend–price ratio today implies higher future returns. However, the equation only explains about 5% of the variability in actual returns. For longer horizons the explanatory power increases. For example, for returns over the 1941–86 period the explanatory power for one-, two-, three- and four-year return horizons are 12, 17, 29 and 49%[7]. The longer-return horizon regressions are also useful in forecasting 'out of sample'. Campbell and Shiller (1988) use the above regression but with the price–earnings ratio as the dependent variable and find similar results – there is some predictability. (These results are broadly similar to the anomalies literature where you form decile portfolios based on a stock's current price-earnings ratio.)

However, Ang and Bekaert (2001), in a study of stock markets across the world, find that the dividend–price ratio has little or no forecasting power for stock returns when data for the late 1990s is included in the sample; the risk-free rate is then found to be the most robust predictor

---

[7] Nevertheless, this is not as impressive as it looks. You should be wary of statistics indicating 'strong predictability' at long horizons which could be misleading for two reasons. First, 'β' is biased (Stamburgh 1999). Secondly, where the forecasting variable (D/P) is persistent, then as a matter of logic, if short-horizon returns are *very slightly* predictable with a 'small' β coefficient, then longer horizon return regressions will have increasing values of 'β' and increasing R-squareds as the investment horizon increases – see Cuthbertson and Nitzsche 2004.

of stock returns (also see Goyal and Welch, 1999). All in all, this evidence should alert you to the fact that trying to exploit market timing is a hazardous and risky occupation.

Note that none of the above results necessarily violates market efficiency, since any predictability found in the data would have to produce average returns from your repeated 'bets' which more than compensated for risk and transaction costs – and the above studies do not address the latter questions. Indeed, it is possible (although not necessarily true) to interpret these predictability results in terms of a changing risk premium. For example, suppose you have two firms with the same *expected* earnings (or dividends), but firm A has more business risk than firm B. Hence firm A will have a higher discount rate, lower price and lower price–earnings ratio than firm B. Firm A has a lower price so that it earns a higher return in the future to compensate for its higher business risk. Hence a low price–earnings ratio leads to higher future returns, but the latter are a compensation for risk. If the CAPM is correct, then the low P–E ratio firms should have high betas, but as beta is measured with considerable error, the P–E ratio may be picking up some of the 'true' underlying business risk. This is the type of argument used by proponents of the EMH to 'explain' stock-return predictability in terms of compensation for a time-varying risk premium.

16.3 PROFITABLE TRADING STRATEGIES?

When looking at regression equations that attempt to explain returns, an econometrician would be interested in general diagnostic tests (e.g. whether the error term is well behaved), the outside sample forecasting performance of the equations and the temporal stability of the estimated coefficients. In many of the above studies this useful statistical information is not always fully presented, so it becomes difficult to ascertain whether the results are as robust as they seem. However, Pesaran and Timmermann (1994) address these issues. They run regressions of excess stock returns on variables known at time t or earlier. They are, however, very careful about the dating of the information used to predict returns. For example, in explaining annual returns from end January to end January (i.e. the last trading day of the month), they use interest rates up to the last trading day as one predictor variable, but use industrial output data only up to December of the previous year (since it is published with a lag of around one month).

They looked at excess returns on the S&P 500 index and the Dow Jones index measured over one year, one quarter and one month for the period 1954–71 and sub-periods. For annual excess returns a small set of independent variables, including the dividend yield, annual inflation, the change in the three-month interest rate and the term premium (i.e. the spread between yield on long- and short-term government bonds), explain about 60% of the variability in next year's stock returns. For quarterly and monthly data, broadly similar variables explain about 20% and 10% of excess returns, respectively. Interestingly, for monthly and quarterly regressions Pesaran and Timmermann find a non-linear effect of previous excess returns on current returns. For example, squared previous excess returns are often statistically significant, while past positive returns have a different impact than past negative returns on future returns[8].

---

[8] The authors also provide diagnostic tests for serial correlation, heteroscedasticity, normality and 'correct' functional form and these test statistics indicate no misspecification in the equations.

To test the predictive power of these equations, Pesaran and Timmermann use recursive estimation (OLS) and predict the *sign* of the next period's excess return (i.e. at $t + 1$) based on estimated coefficients that only use data up to period t. For annual returns, 70–80% of the predicted returns have the correct sign, while for quarterly excess returns the regressions still yield a (healthy) 65% correct prediction of the sign of returns. Thus these authors reinforce the earlier results that excess returns are predictable and can be explained quite well by a relatively small number of independent variables.

Transaction costs arise from the bid–ask spread (i.e. dealers buy stock at a low price and sell to the investor at a high price) and brokerage commissions. Pesaran and Timmermann use 'closing prices', which may be either bid or ask prices. They therefore assume that all trading costs are adequately represented by a fixed transaction cost per dollar of sales/purchases. They assume that costs are higher for stocks c_s than for bonds c_b. They consider a simple trading rule, namely:

> If the predicted excess return (from the recursive regression) is positive then hold the market portfolio of stocks, otherwise hold government bonds with a maturity equal to the length of the trading horizon (i.e. annual, quarterly, monthly).

Note that it is the 'sign' of the return prediction that is important for this strategy and not the overall (within-sample) 'fit' of the equation (i.e. its R-squared). The above 'switching strategy' avoids potential bankruptcy, since assets are not sold short and there is no gearing (borrowing). The passive benchmark strategy these authors choose is to hold the market portfolio at all times. They assess the profitability of the switching strategy over the passive strategy for transaction costs that are 'low', 'medium' or 'high'. (The values of c_s are 0, 0.5 and 1% for stocks and for bonds c_b equals 0 and 0.1%.)

In general terms Pesaran and Timmermann find that the returns from the switching strategy are higher than those from the passive strategy when using annual returns (i.e. switching once per year in January), even when transactions costs are 'high' (Table 16.1). However, it pays to trade at quarterly or monthly intervals only if transaction costs are less than ½% for stocks. In addition, these authors find that the standard deviation of annual returns for the switching portfolio (Table 16.1) is below that for the passive portfolio (even under a high-transaction-cost scenario). Hence the switching portfolio dominates the passive portfolio on the mean-variance criterion over the data period 1960–90.

The above results are found to be robust with respect to different sets of regressors in the excess return equations and over sub-periods 1960–70, 1970–80 and 1980–90. In Table 16.1 we report the Sharpe ratio, the Treynor ratio and Jensen's alpha for the switching and passive portfolios for the one-year horizon. For any portfolio p these are given by:

$$SR_p = (\bar{R}_p - \bar{r})/\sigma_p \qquad TR_p = (\bar{R}_p - \bar{r})/\beta_p$$

$$\alpha_p = (\bar{R}_p - \bar{r}) - \beta_p(\bar{R}_m - \bar{r})$$

These three performance statistics are alternative measures of 'return corrected for risk': the larger is SR_p or TR_p or α_p, the more successful the investment strategy. In general, except for

TABLE 16.1: Performance measures of the S&P 500 switching portfolio relative to the market portfolio and T-bills (annual returns 1960–90)

	Portfolios							
	Market[1]			Switching[2]			T-bills[3]	
Transaction costs (%)								
For stocks	0.0	0.5	1.0	0.0	0.5	1.0	–	–
For T-bills	–	–	–	0.0	0.1	0.1	0.0	0.1
Returns and performance								
Arithmetic mean return (%)	10.780	10.720	10.670	12.700	13.430	12.210	6.750	6.640
SD of return (%)	13.090	13.090	13.090	7.240	7.200	7.160	2.820	2.820
Sharpe ratio	0.310	0.300	0.300	0.820	0.790	0.760	–	–
Treynor ratio	0.040	0.040	0.039	0.089	0.085	0.081	–	–
Jensen's alpha	–	–	–	0.045	0.043	0.041	–	–
	–	–	–	(4.63)	(4.42)	(4.25)	–	–
Wealth at end of period[4]	1,913	1,884	1,855	3,833	3,559	3,346	749	726

Notes: 1. The market portfolio denotes a buy-and-hold strategy in the S&P 500 index.
2. The switching portfolio is based on recursive regressions of excess returns on the change in the three-month interest rate, the term premium, the inflation rate and the dividend yield. The switching rule assumes that portfolio selection takes place once per year on the last trading day of January.
3. 'T-bills' denotes a roll-over strategy in 12-month T-bills.
4. Starting with $100 in January 1960.

Source: Pesaran and Timmermann, *Journal of Forecasting* 1994, reproduced with permission from John Wiley & Sons Ltd.

the monthly trading strategy under the high-cost scenario, Persaran and Timmermann find that these performance indices imply that the switching portfolio 'beats' the passive market portfolio. It is this type of analysis that quant analysts undertake and they would describe it as trying to find a 'signal' that helps predict future returns. What they usually mean by this is some readily available variable, such as interest rates, price–earnings ratios and so on.

Model uncertainty

Pesaran and Timmermann (1995, 2000) extend the above analysis to include model uncertainty. Unlike the 1994 study, they allow the investor to choose the 'best' model at each point in time. Using recursive estimation on monthly data over 1960(11)–1992(2) for the US and 1965(1)–1993(12) for the UK, the switching strategies give higher Sharpe ratios than holding the passive market portfolio. For example, for the UK (1970–93) the passive market portfolio has a mean return of 20.8% p.a. and standard deviation of 36.5%, giving a Sharpe ratio of 0.33. The monthly switching portfolios (based on high transaction costs) give a mean return of 15.5% p.a. and standard deviation 10.5% p.a., implying a Sharpe ratio of 0.64 (Pesaran and Timmermann, 2000, Table 5). Jensen's alpha for the switching portfolio is 0.058% p.m. (0.7% p.a.), with a t-statistic of 2.58. In the 1980s, when markets were less volatile than the 1970s, the switching portfolios gave lower performance results, but still beat the passive market portfolio. (The results are also very similar when the active strategy uses index futures rather than actual purchase of stocks.) It is noteworthy that the switching portfolios did not 'lose' in the UK bear market of 1974, but neither did they 'win' in the sharp upturn of January–February 1975, since the model indicated that the investor should have been in T-bills in these periods. This may account for some of the overall success of the switching strategy.

Using US data, Pesaran and Timmermann find that there is no single model that performs adequately over the whole 1960–92 period and that genuine outperformance (e.g. Sharpe ratio) based on an active (monthly) switching strategy after taking account of transaction costs is difficult to find.

Keen gamblers might like to note that the above results imply that 'you have to earn your free lunch'. In some years the switching strategy loses money and you would have had to get the crucial 1974 predictions correct. In years when you lose money, you would have to have enough capital (or borrowing facilities) to 'take the hit' and survive to trade another day. And of course, every month you have to perform a large number of regressions and hope that any predictability you find is genuine.

SUMMARY

- The EMH requires some informed active traders with sufficient resources and risk tolerance to ensure that prices equal their fair value. But if the EMH is correct, it implies that most active portfolio management is futile and cannot outperform a passive strategy. Most investors should therefore hold an index fund.

- The EMH does not imply that stock returns are unpredictable. It implies that if you try to exploit any observed predictability, the average return you get from your repeated 'bets' will do no more than compensate you for the riskiness of your positions and any transaction cost you incur. In short, *abnormal* returns to active strategies are zero on average.
- There is short-run momentum in individual stock returns for daily, weekly and monthly horizons. Although higher than average past returns do help to predict future returns, this strategy is unlikely to yield positive *abnormal* returns. At horizons of three months to one year, predictability is stronger for *portfolios* of past winner stocks, but is unlikely to yield positive abnormal returns. At long horizons (e.g. 5–10 years) it is difficult to measure predictability since we have fewer observations, but it seems likely that returns on country stock-market indices over long horizons are random.
- Variables such as the dividend–price ratio, the earnings–price ratio and interest rates have been found to help predict future returns. These relationships do not seem to be stable over different sample periods, but it may be possible to update the coefficients to improve forecasting performance – this is what quant analysts try and do.
- The key question for the validity of the EMH and the success or otherwise of active portfolio management is whether the profits from trading strategies fully compensate for the risk exposure undertaken. There is certainly some evidence that this might well be the case, although it can always be argued that methods used to correct for the risk of the portfolio (e.g. Sharpe ratio, Jensen's alpha) are inadequate and that observed returns do no more than compensate for the risks in the strategy.
- Where the balance of the evidence lies for the EMH is very difficult to judge given the plethora of somewhat conflicting results and the acute problems of statistical inference involved. To us, it appears as if the equity market is pretty efficient. Few, if any, free lunches 'remain on the table' for long – but if you should see one, check out its quality and freshness and look for any costs hidden away in the small print on the menu.

EXERCISES

Q1   Does the EMH imply that you should never change the proportions in which you hold stocks in your portfolio?

Q2   If the EMH were true, would there ever be any takeovers?

Q3   What is a random walk for stock prices? What does this imply for stock returns? Is a random walk a useful statistical representation of stock-price movements?

Q4   How can you test whether stock prices are mean reverting?

Q5   Where does the balance of the evidence lie on whether you can successfully pick winners using regression equations?

CHAPTER 17

Technical Trading Rules

AIMS

- To analyse various *technical trading* methods.
- To analyse *chartist methods* of forecasting prices and the use of *support and resistance* levels. Chartist forecasting methods include high–low extremes, moving-average cross-over methods, filter rules and momentum indices.
- To examine the use of *candlestick patterns* for forecasting.
- To examine whether chartists have a systematic effect on asset prices by producing 'band-wagon' or herding effects.
- To consider the application of *neural networks* and *chaos models* in predicting financial variables.

INTRODUCTION

Technical trading methods are often applied in practice to predict stock prices and spot-FX rates, usually over very short horizons. The popular press certainly presents foreign-exchange dealers and stock traders (of hedge funds) as speculators, par excellence. Often you see young men in striped shirts, wearing primary-coloured braces on television, facing banks of computer screens shouting simultaneously into two telephones in order to execute buy and sell orders quickly. The obvious question that arises is, are these individuals purchasing and selling FX and stocks on the basis of news about fundamentals or do they in fact 'chase trends'? If the latter is true, the question then arises as to whether they can have a pervasive influence on prices and introduce 'excess volatility' into the markets.

As we have seen, it is possible to speculate based on assessing fair value (for a stock) using economic fundamentals (e.g. interest rates, company prospects and so on). In contrast, so-called **technical traders** study only past price movements in the market and base their view of the future solely on past price changes. For example, chartists believe that they can isolate patterns in past price movements that can be used to predict future movements and hence generate profitable trading strategies, even after correcting for transaction costs and the risk-iness of the positions taken. If so, this would be contrary to the 'weak form' of the EMH. Chartists therefore believe that stock prices are not random and they do not immediately jump to their fundamental value when new information arrives in the market. They believe that the market reacts sluggishly to new information (i.e. there is some autocorrelation in asset returns) and their charts and other methods allow them to detect the direction of this sluggish response.

Chartists often use graphs based on very high-frequency data (e.g. tick by tick) and make very short-term trades (e.g. intra-day or over a few days at most). **Technical analysis** is a generic term that includes chartists (graphs), candlesticks (bar charts), filter rules, moving averages and momentum indices. We also discuss **neural networks** and **chaotic models**, which involve non-linear forecasting equations and loosely come under the heading of technical trading rules.

17.1 CHARTISTS

Over short horizons (e.g. intra-day, overnight, weekly), FX traders use forecasts based on some form of technical trading rules, rather than on fundamentals (see Taylor and Allen, 1990). In fact, about 80% of FX spot trades are between broker/dealers and are closed out within the day. With trillions of US dollars per day traded on the spot FX market, one might think that the market is efficient and there are no unexploitable profit opportunities to be made. However, if technical analysts chase trends then they might make money, particularly if the 'fundamentals traders' do not bet against them.

Trading on the basis of economic fundamentals in the spot FX market could be relatively weak because the link between changes in the exchange rate and economic fundamentals such as changes in interest rates (or the money supply) is very imprecise. Fundamentals traders may also have a limited impact on the spot FX rate because they face liquidity con-straints and may have to close out all (or most of) their positions by the end of the trading day (because otherwise, they would incur overnight interest payments as well as risky overnight positions). Similarly, any estimate of the fair value of a stock is likely to be very imprecise, which might limit fundamentals traders from taking risky arbitrage positions in order to exploit noise traders. Hence, there may be scope for chartists to influence prices.

To illustrate some aspects of this approach, consider the idealised pattern given in Figure 17.1, which is known as the **head and shoulders reversal pattern**. On this graph is drawn a horizontal line called the shoulder. Points A and B are the top of the shoulders and B is the head. Once the pattern reaches point D – that is, a peak below the shoulder – the chartist would assume that this signals a full trend reversal. She would then sell the currency, believing that it would fall in the future and she could buy it back at a lower price. As another example, consider Figure 17.2, the so-called **symmetric triangle**, indicated by the oscillations converging on the point at A. To some chartists this pattern would signal a future upward movement as the upward trend in the price series 'breaks out' of its restrictive (narrowing) triangle. Clearly, the interpretation of such graphs is subjective.

It is well known that some chartists also complement their graphical approach with the use of survey data on 'market sentiment'. For example, if sentiment is reported to be optimistic about the UK economy, then chartists may well try to step in early and buy sterling. For chartists as a group to influence the market, most chartists must interpret the charts in roughly the same way, otherwise all they do is to introduce some random noise into prices but no trends.

Support and resistance levels

Another variant on chartism is to use support-resistance levels. These ideas are particularly prevalent in the spot FX market, but can also apply to aggregate stock-market indices. For

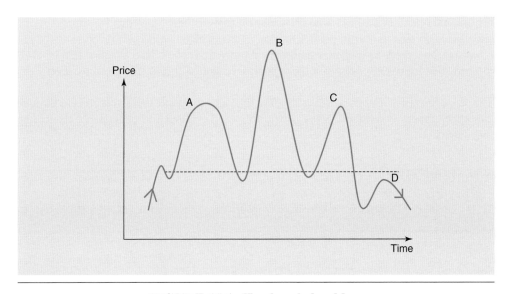

FIGURE 17.1: Head and shoulders

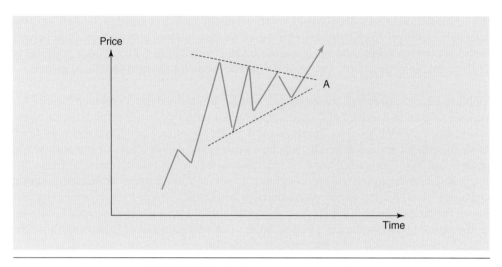

FIGURE 17.2: Symmetric triangle

example, if in the past the spot rate had repeatedly hit an upper level without breaking through it, this is designated as the current **resistance level** (R – R in Figure 17.3). Similarly, the lower limit is known as the **support level**, S – S. These support-resistance levels can change daily and, for example, Reuters' FX screens give these levels at the beginning of the trading day, based on a sample of FX dealers' views of the trading range expected over the coming day.

One way of interpreting these support-resistance levels is to assume they impart information about possible breaks in trend. So if the exchange rate hits the support level (from above) or the resistance level (from below), we can expect a 'bounce' back off these levels (i.e. a form of intra-day mean reversion). Osler (2000) uses intra-day spot FX data on (US) dollar–yen, dollar–(German) mark and dollar–sterling over January 1996 to March 1998 and support-resistance levels from six firms who use technical analysis. She found that the support-resistance levels do have power to predict turning points, which can persist for up to five days. However, she did not investigate whether these predictions could lead to actual trading profits (corrected for risk) by buying at the support level and selling at the resistance level.

The support-resistance approach also assumes that once the price 'decisively' breaks through either the support or resistance levels, it will follow an extrapolative path. Hence the trading rule here is:

> Buy spot FX when the FX rate decisively crosses the resistance level from below.
> Sell spot FX when the FX rate decisively crosses the support level from above.

After a buy decision, the trader is assumed to close out her position either when the spot rate falls back to the R level (making no profit over this period) or at the close of trading (e.g. by midnight if we assume that traders are not allowed to hold an open position overnight). In

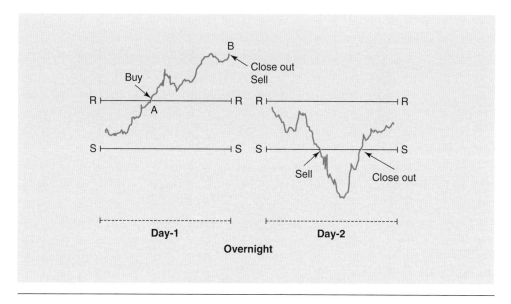

FIGURE 17.3: Resistance and support levels

Figure 17.3 the trader makes a profit on day 1 but not on day 2. It is also possible to lose money. For example, buying on day 1 at A would cause a loss if the spot rate subsequently *fell* throughout the day, being closed out at the lower closing price.

Using tick data and hourly checks on whether to trade, Curcio *et al.* (1996) find that for the Deutsche mark (as it then was), yen and sterling against the US dollar, intra-day trading leads to some small positive returns (relative to buy and hold), but only when exchange rates are trending (up or down). The support-resistance levels were those supplied daily by Reuters, and they adjusted the returns for the bid–ask spread. However, Curcio *et al.* (1996) do not correct returns for risk and transaction costs. Brock *et al.* (1992) and Levich and Thomas (1993), using other types of technical rules, find that profits can be made on *inter*-day trading in the FX market, although these 'profits' do not take account of transaction costs and the profitable trading horizons were much longer than over one day.

Overall, these results suggest that it is very difficult to make profits (net of transaction costs) in the spot FX market by using chartist methods. However, this does not appear to prevent traders from making continued use of these techniques.

Candle charts

These are Japanese in origin and are used to indicate buy or sell decisions largely based on the direction of movement between the opening and closing prices (relative to the degree of underlying volatility in the market over the trading day). To get the ball rolling, consider the 'candles' in Figure 17.4. Any price falls between open and close are designated by black bars and price rises by grey bars. The maximum and minimum intra-day prices are indicated by a

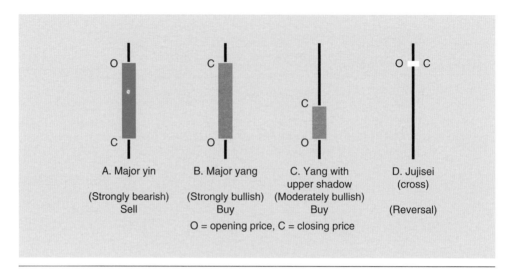

FIGURE 17.4: Candle patterns

thin black line. Thus each day's high–low and open–close prices resemble a candle with a wick at both ends.

Candle A indicates that the market fell considerably between open and close and is known as a *major yin*. The latter is usually taken to indicate that a further fall (bearish) is expected and hence is a strong signal to sell. Candle B is the opposite (i.e. a *major yang*) and is a strongly bullish signal (i.e. buy). Candle C is a *yang with upper shadow*, showing a small rise from open to close but a much larger rise during the day's trading: the signal here is mildly bullish. Candle D is a *Jujisei* (cross), where the market opened and closed at the same price but there was substantial movement during the day. This indicates that a reversal of the recent trend (either up or down) is likely. Clearly, a large amount of judgement is required when interpreting candle patterns and this subjective element means that there are no formal tests of their effectiveness in predicting changes in spot FX rates.

17.2 OTHER CHARTIST FORECASTING METHODS

Some other trading strategies based on past price behaviour but not explicitly on charts include 'high-low extremes', 'filter rules', 'momentum indices' and 'cross-over methods', and we now discuss these methods.

High–low (HL) extremes

In an HL strategy, buy and sell decisions are determined by a movement outside recent highs or lows. Suppose that the highest and lowest closing prices for dollar–sterling over the last $T = 10$ trading days are 1.95($/£) and 1.90($/£) respectively. If on the next trading day (i.e. $T + 1$) the closing price is 2.0($/£) ($> 1.95($/£)), then we buy sterling at the opening of trading on the next day (i.e. $T + 2$). Similarly, if the closing price on day $T + 1$ had been 1.85($/£) ($< 1.90($/£)), then we would sell sterling. This trading rule is based on a break-out from a previous high or low. If the break-out is in the upward direction we buy, believing that the upward movement will continue (the upper break-out is like a moving 'resistance level'). This is a trend-extrapolation strategy. Only one position is signalled each day and we are either long or short, we are never 'square'. When a new buy/sell signal arrives we just close out the old position. If the high and low prices on day $T + 1$ are equal, then the market is 'locked limit' and nothing is done on that day.

Filter rules

This approach is also a trend-following strategy. Suppose we have an $x\%$ filter rule, then the strategy is:

> Buy, if the currency has risen $x\%$ from its most recent low point.
> Sell, if the currency has fallen $x\%$ from its most recent high point.

If $x = 2\%$, then we buy if the price increases by 2%, hoping for a further price rise. The position is then held until the currency moves down $x\%$ from the next highest level reached, since the position was taken. Then the original position is closed out and the investor also goes short. For example, with $x = 2\%$, the investor would buy at A (Figure 17.5), close out at a profit at B and go short. At C the investor would close out the short position (unfortunately at a loss) and go long.

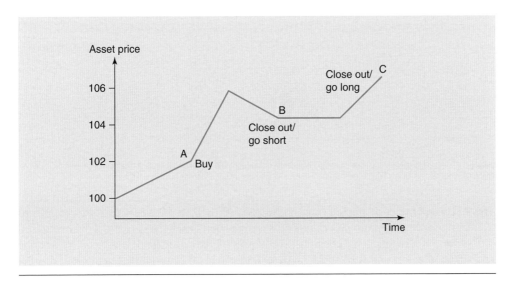

FIGURE 17.5: Filter rule, $x = 2\%$

Momentum methods

These models provide a measure of the relative strength or 'momentum' of up and down *movements* in the spot FX rate. The relative change in direction of the spot rate is measured by the momentum:

$$M_{t+1} = \frac{(1/n)\sum_{i=1}^{n} u_{it}}{(1/n)\sum_{i=1}^{n} d_{it}} = \frac{Average\ of\ 'ups'}{Average\ of\ 'downs'} \tag{1}$$

where $u_{it} = S_{t-i+1} - S_{t-i}$ if $S_{t-i+1} > S_{t-i}$

   $d_{it} = |S_{t-i+1} - S_{t-i}|$ if $S_{t-i+1} < S_{t-i}$

So u_{it} is the 'up' change and d_{it} is the (absolute) 'down' change in the spot rate, each of which is measured over the previous n periods in calculating M. The index can be normalised to lie between 0 and 100 and is known as the **relative strength index, RSI**:

$$RSI_t = 100 - \frac{100}{(1 + M_t)} \tag{2}$$

As can be seen from Table 17.1, for 'average ups' equal to 'average downs', $M_t = 1$ and $RSI_t = 50$, which is a neutral position. If 'average ups' have been twice the size of 'average downs', $M_t = 2$ and $RSI = 66.6$, indicating a substantial recent upward momentum.

TABLE 17.1: Calculation of relative strength index

Average ups	Average downs	M_t	RSI_t
z	z	1	50
$2z$	z	2	66.6
z	$2z$	1/2	33.3
z	$1000z$	1/1000	0
$1000z$	z	1000	100

Note: z = the absolute value of our chosen illustrative 'up' and 'down' movements. This allows us to calculate the corresponding values for the momentum index M and the relative strength index RSI.

The RSI index might be implemented as follows. An $RSI_t = 70$ would indicate recent substantial upward momentum that cannot be sustained and hence the decision would be to sell (i.e. close out existing long positions). Similarly, if the 'average downs' = 2 × 'average ups', then $M_t = 0.5$ and $RSI_t = 33.3$. An RSI_t less than 30 is usually taken to mean that the recent downward momentum is at an end and should be reversed in the future, hence the signal is to buy (or keep the existing position). In summary:

$$RSI_t > 70 \text{ then sell}$$
$$RSI_t < 30 \text{ then buy}$$

Thus the RSI index assumes some mean reversion in the spot rate: rapid rises are expected to be followed by a fall in the future (and vice versa).

Cross-over (moving average methods)

This method is based on the relationship between a 'short' and 'long' moving average of the *level* of the exchange rate. A moving average (MA) is a weighted average of past values of the exchange rate, S, which can either use equal weights or declining weights (i.e. more recent values of S are given greater weight than more distant values of S).

Equally weighted moving average (MA):

$$MA_{t+1} = \frac{1}{n}(S_t + S_{t-1} + \ldots + S_{t-n+1}) \tag{3a}$$

Exponentially weighted moving average (EWMA):

$$EWMA_{t+1} = (1 - \alpha)\sum_{i=0}^{\infty} \alpha^i S_{t-i} \tag{3b}$$

In the EWMA scheme [3b], the weights decline over time. If $\alpha = 0.9$ then successive weights α^i decline as follows: 0.9, 0.81, 0.73 etc. If we just wish to use n past observations in calculating $EWMA_t$ the formula is:

$$EWMA_{t+1} = k\sum_{i=0}^{n-1} \alpha^i S_{t-i} \tag{4}$$

where $k = (1 - \alpha)/(1 - \alpha^n)$. The adjustment k is required because the α^i terms sum to $[(1 - \alpha^n)/(1 - \alpha)]$ and hence k ensures that if all n past levels of S_{t-i} were constant $(= S)$, the moving average EWMA would also be equal to S. Alternatively, it can be shown that (if n is reasonably large):

$$EWMA_{t+1} = \alpha EWMA_t + (1 - \alpha) S_t \tag{5}$$

so that given an arbitrary starting value for $EWMA_1 (= S_1)$, equation [5] can be used to continually update the calculation of EWMA, as each successive value of S_t becomes available. The forecast value of $EWMA_{t+1}$ is independent of the starting value chosen for S_1 after about 70 data points have been used. So if S_1 is the *first* data point in your sample, as long as your first true forecast starts at $t = 70$ the above recursive equation is valid. Hence equation [5] provides a useful recursive computational device for calculating the EWMA forecast (which can be easily programmed in Excel; see Chapter 31).

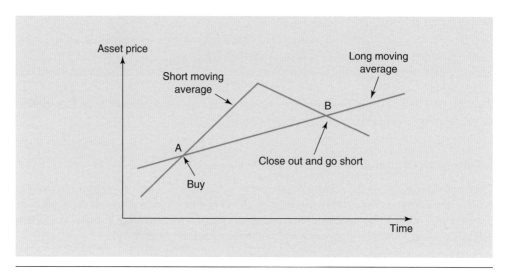

FIGURE 17.6: Cross-over strategy

The cross-over method works like this. First construct a 'short' EWMA from n_1 past data points and a 'long' EWMA from n_2 data points, based on closing prices (with $n_2 > n_1$). For example, $n_1 = 5$ days and $n_2 = 15$ days or $n_1 = 15$ and $n_2 = 20$ days are frequently used. The trading rule is based on the **cross-over point** in the trend in the short EWMA relative to the long EWMA, hence (see Figure 17.6):

> Buy, if short MA crosses the long MA from below.
> Sell, if short MA crosses the long MA from above.

Hence at point A (Figure 17.6) you would buy at the opening of the next trading day and at B you would close out the old position and sell (or go short).

17.3 EVIDENCE ON CHARTISTS

Allen and Taylor (1989) conducted a study on the behaviour of a panel of chartists (between 10 and 20 responded every week) over the period June 1988–March 1989, although the sample of data on which the study is based is rather small. They were telephoned every Thursday and asked for their expectations with respect to the sterling–dollar, dollar–mark (as it was then) and dollar–yen exchange rates for one and four weeks ahead, yielding about 36 observations per chartist per currency. The survey also asked the chartists about the kind of information they used in making their forecasts and who the information was passed on to (e.g. actual traders).

It was found that at short horizons (say, intra-day to one week), as many as 90% of the respondents used some chartist input in forming their exchange-rate expectations. As the time horizon lengthens to three months, six months or one year, the weight given to fundamentals increases and 85% of the respondents judged that over these longer horizons fundamentals were more important than chart analysis. However, chart analysis was always seen as complementary to the analysis based on fundamentals and therefore it is possible that chart analysis influences exchange rates even at these longer horizons.

If one looks ex-post at the accuracy of the chartists' forecasts (taken as a group) for the dollar–mark spot rate, the four-week-ahead forecasts are fairly typical of the results for other currencies. In general, Allen and Taylor find:

- There is a tendency for the forecasts to miss turning points. On a rising or falling market, the chartists' expectations underestimate the extent of the rise or fall.
- Prediction errors are noticeably greater at the four-week horizon than at the one-week horizon. Individual chartists' forecasts for four-week-ahead predictions are generally unbiased, but they are biased for the one-week-ahead predictions.
- For all the chartists taken as a whole, they correctly predict the change in the exchange rate over one-week and four-week horizons approximately 50% of the time. This is what one would expect if their forecasts were purely due to chance.

The above result for all chartists neglects the possibility that individual chartists might in fact do well and do consistently well over time. In fact, there are differences in forecast accuracy among the chartists and there are some chartists who are systematically 'good'. However, one cannot read too much into the last result, since the time period of the survey is fairly short and in a random sample of individuals one would always expect that a certain percentage would do better than average. In fact, if the mean daily FX return is zero and the daily standard deviation of exchange-rate changes is 1% (and normally distributed), then we expect that out of 1000 chartists, 25 (2.5%) will experience a daily return of 2% or more, *purely due to luck*.

Again taking chartists as a whole, Allen and Taylor assess whether they outperform alternative methods of forecasting. For example, some alternatives examined are forecasts based on a 'no-change' random walk model, others based on past changes in exchange rates (e.g. ARIMA models) and forecasts using a system of equations that contain fundamentals such as past changes in exchange rates, the interest-rate differential and relative stock-market performance in the two countries. The results here are mixed. In most cases the chartists did not beat these 'mechanical' statistical equations in forecasting exchange-rate changes. However, overall there is not much in it. All of the statistical forecasting methods and the chartists' forecasts had approximately the same root mean squared errors for one-week- and four-week-ahead forecasts, with, on balance, the random walk probably doing best.

Since Allen and Taylor collected data on expectations (forecasts) of the exchange rate from their survey of chartists, they can correlate changes in chartists' forecasts with changes in the actual exchange rate. We are particularly interested in whether chartists have band-wagon or extrapolative expectations. That is to say, when the exchange rate increases today, does this lead all chartists to revise their forecasts upwards? Allen and Taylor tested this hypothesis, but found that for all chartists as a group, band-wagon expectations did not apply.

Thus chartists' advice does not appear to be intrinsically destabilising, in that they do not overreact to recent changes in the exchange rate. In fact, Allen and Taylor find that chartists tend to have either 'adaptive' or 'regressive' expectations. These two types of expectation formation are essentially *mean reverting*, which means that if expectations of the spot rate are currently above some long-run level, chartists believe that the spot rate will in subsequent time periods tend to fall back towards this long-run level. Overall, the results seem to suggest that there are agents in the market who make systematic forecasting errors, but there appears to be no band-wagon or explosive effect from this behaviour, and at most chartists might influence short-run deviations of the exchange rate from fundamentals.

The Allen and Taylor study did not examine whether chartists' forecasts actually resulted in profitable trades. They merely looked at the accuracy of chartists' forecasts. However, a number of studies have been done (Bilson, 1981; Goodman, 1979, 1980; and Levich, 1980) that have looked at ex-post evaluations of exchange-rate forecasting services, some of which were provided by technical analysts (e.g. chartists). A general finding of these studies is that very few foreign-exchange advisory services outperform the forward rate as a predictor of the future spot rate.

17.4 NEURAL NETWORKS

Neural networks are a purely statistical way of discovering patterns in data and representing these relationships mathematically. A key feature of neural networks is that they use highly non-linear relationships to predict variables such as stock prices and exchange rates over very short horizons – usually intra-day. A neural network is a 'black-box' forecasting system. Given inputs X_i ($i = 1, 2, \ldots, n$), the neural network gives the best method of predicting the outputs Y_j, but it is impossible to put an interpretation or 'story' on how particular values of the X_i give rise to a particular forecast of Y_j. The term **artificial neural network (ANN)** arises because the 'neural net' mimics the behaviour of the neurons in the brain as it 'learns about' the patterns in the data and then represents this pattern mathematically.

There are many situations in finance where an accurate forecast would be useful. For example, suppose we are trying to predict whether or not an individual, financial institution or country will default on a debt obligation. Then the output of our model Y might be dichotomous; that is, $Y = 1$ implies 'default' and $Y = 0$ implies 'no default'. The neural network uses a set of input variables X_i such as income level, age and marital status of the individual and will 'train itself' to yield the best forecast. Take chartism as another example. Maybe a neural network can be trained to recognise chartist patterns and hence produce a forecast of the stock price (or the FX rate) based on a highly non-linear relationship between current stock prices, past movements in the stock price and other asset prices. Because ANNs are non-linear models, they are clearly consistent with the non-linearities found in some empirical studies of financial asset returns. Key features of this approach are:

- The functional form used is highly non-linear and is primarily based on past movements in the asset price and not on any particular economic model based on fundamentals.
- The network is 'trained' on past data from which it 'learns' about the past behaviour of the asset price and updates the parameters of the model in an attempt to minimise forecast errors.

Note that conceptually, this is not an entirely novel approach. Indeed, as a first approximation, a neural network can be considered as a normal *non-linear* regression equation, with time-varying parameters that are updated as new information about the spot rate arises. Neural nets are popular for short-run predictions (e.g. predicting tick-by-tick data) and may also be used as an independent check on a trader's 'gut feelings'.

Alternatively, the method can be used relatively mechanically to trigger buy and sell orders. For example, the neural net would be trained on data up to time t (the training period), which would also provide 'error bands' for any forecast. This model would then be used to give a series of predictions for each of the next 15 minutes (the 'testing period'). If these 'outside sample' predictions lay outside the error band for the existing model, this would lead to the parameters of the ANN being updated. The best model parameters are those that minimise the 'outside sample' prediction errors in the testing period. Having obtained the best equation, it would then be used in a genuine forecast. If the ANN forecasts a rise in the asset price that lies above the upper error band, this would be a 'buy signal'. After, say, 15 minutes, any new data would be added and the parameters re-estimated. The updated equation is then used to provide a further prediction for the next 15 minutes (along with the new error bands).

There are now quite a number of software companies that provide neural net programs that are easy to use (e.g. are menu driven) yet allow the user some flexibility in how she chooses to train the network (e.g. see the Palisade Corporation). More sophisticated systems are used by banks and securities houses and Olsen and Associates in Zurich were early advocates of using this approach to forecast very short-run changes in the spot FX rate. The method is used among a relatively small number of 'quant jocks' for predicting financial time series (see Trippi and Turban, 1996). The method is clearly useful – it is a highly sophisticated statistical technique for fitting non-linear functions to time-series data.

A slightly different way of looking at neural networks is that it is a method that can be used to explain statistically the movement in financial asset returns that is *not* explained by conventional models. For example, if the risk premium on a stock is related not only to beta and the market return but also to other economic variables (e.g. book-to-market value) in a highly non-linear way, then this could be statistically modelled using a neural network while still allowing the change in the spot rate to be partly influenced by interest differentials.

Building blocks

The key elements in a neural network are the inputs X_i, the outputs Y_j and the weights w_i that represent the relative strength of each of the X_is in its effect on the Y_j. Suppose we have three inputs X_i and one output Y (Figure 17.7). If the w_i are the weights, then the *summation function* is:

$$Y = w_1 X_1 + w_2 X_2 + w_3 X_3 \qquad [6]$$

Based on the level of Y from the above equation, the ANN may or may not 'trigger' an output (i.e. the neuron may or may not be activated). For example, a **threshold detector** might give an output y as follows:

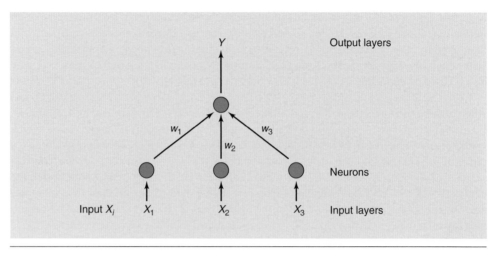

FIGURE 17.7: Neural network (no hidden layers)

$Y > 0.5$ then $y = 1$

$Y < 0.5$ then $y = 0$

This is the kind of output from the ANN that we would use in predicting a default/no-default outcome on outstanding debt contracts. Alternatively, the output y might be a non-linear *transfer function* of Y, a popular one being the sigmoid function:

$$y = \frac{1}{1 + e^{-Y}} \qquad\qquad [7]$$

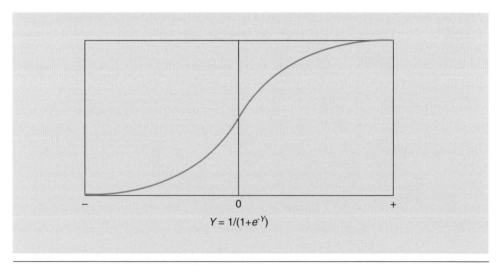

$$Y = 1/(1 + e^{-Y})$$

FIGURE 17.8: Sigmoid transfer function

No matter how large or small Y turns out to be, the output y always lies between 0 and 1 (Figure 17.8). For example, if $X_1 = 6, X_2 = 2, X_3 = 3$ and $w_1 = 0.2, w_2 = 0.3$ and $w_3 = 0.1$, then $Y = 2.1$ and:

$$y = \frac{1}{1 + e^{-2.1}} = 0.89 \qquad [8]$$

The so-called hyperbolic tangent (transformation) allows somewhat greater variability, since the output y then lies between -1 and $+1$. (This would be useful for a model of stock picking where 'good stock return' $= +1$ and 'bad stock return' $= -1$.)

How does the ANN determine the values for w_i? An ANN cannot be fitted to *all* of the available data because in principle it can fit the data with 100% accuracy (because of the flexible non-linear relationship between X_i and Y). This is known as **overfitting** and is illustrated in Figure 17.9. Suppose for simplicity that the true model is linear but we have only three data points $\{A, B, C\}$. A quadratic equation (i.e. one containing terms in X_i and X_i^2) can fit these three points exactly, whereas a linear relationship does not fit so well. An ANN based on a within-sample 'best-fit' criterion (e.g. minimising the residual sum of squares) would search over many non-linear (and linear) relationships and would end up fitting a quadratic function exactly. The forecast with the ANN equation from data point C gives a forecast at D* which is clearly worse than the forecast D** when using the linear equation (point D is the actual outturn data).

Remember that an equation that is *designed* to fit well 'in sample' may not necessarily forecast well out of sample. The choice of the non-linear functional form has to be reasonably flexible, since the relationship under study may be extremely non-linear. It also follows that one will need a large amount of data if the method is to be of practical use, since it is well known that the parameters of non-linear models are very sensitive to alternative small samples of data (and the estimation algorithm may not converge).

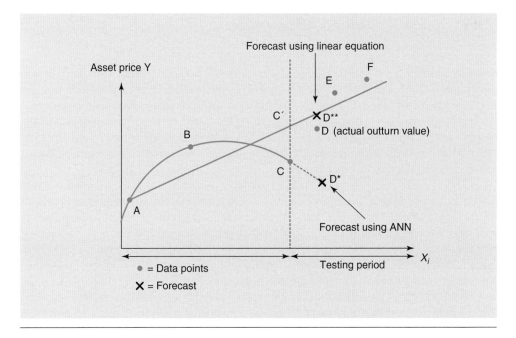

FIGURE 17.9: ANN and overfitting

The overfitting problem can be mitigated by splitting the data into two sets: a *training set* and a *testing set*. (In econometrics these are usually referred to as 'within-sample' and 'out-of-sample' data sets.) We then choose the weights w_i to minimise the forecast errors in the testing set of data. Thus with A, B and C in the training set the ANN 'fits' a quadratic, but this leads to a poor forecast of points D, E and F (Figure 17.9). Hence, the ANN recalculates the weights w_i on the X_i to minimise these forecast errors and hence will learn that the best weights are given by the linear relationship. This is known as **training the network** and is how the network learns and adjusts the weights as new data is incorporated.

Let us extend this overfitting example to the prediction of the spot FX rate where the criteria used in choosing the appropriate neural network is minimising the out-of-sample forecast error. So Ms Neural Network proceeds as follows. She takes the last $T = 1$ year of 15-minute (or even tick-by-tick) data on the spot FX rate. Initially she uses only the first nine months of data to fit her neural network. She then uses this model to predict the next 50 data points (i.e. 50 of the next 15-minute data points) and clearly the existing neural net will make forecast errors. The parameter estimates are then altered to minimise these out-of-sample prediction errors (e.g. minimising the root mean square forecast error). This process is repeated after adding the next 50 data points to the training set and the parameters of the neural net are again updated. In this way the neural net is trained on the existing data, on the basis of the prediction errors (rather than using all the data at one go, to 'fit' one single best model). Apart from the non-linear aspect, however, it is worth noting that this emphasis on model design, based on the out-of-sample prediction, is now common in standard econometric modelling (see Hendry, 1995). Of course, for any model the only 'true forecast' is when the model is used to predict *beyond* the existing complete data set.

There are many different objective functions (or learning algorithms) that we could put forward for choosing the optimal values for w_i (e.g. minimising the sum of squared errors, the sum of absolute errors, the proportion of correct up or down predictions and so on) and each arbitrary choice will give different optimal weights.

The flexibility and highly non-linear relationships that can be produced by an ANN is facilitated by adding *hidden layers* (Figure 17.10). From each 'input neuron' X_i there is an output Y_j that is then linked to all the other neurons in the 'hidden layer' and these in turn are linked to the output layer. (In Figure 17.10 we show only one output layer.) At each neuron the transfer function is operational, making the relationship between the inputs X_i and the output Y potentially highly non-linear. The *network configuration* in Figure 17.10 is an example of what is called a ***multilayer perceptron***. In principle you can have many hidden layers, although in practice one or two are usual.

From the standpoint of a financial economists (or market analysts), the biggest drawback of neural networks is that they are a 'black box'. The inputs (e.g. current and past values for the spot rate) are popped into the box, the algorithm whurrs around and out pops the optimal forecast at the other end, but without any explanation whatsoever. If the neural network is given to another technician who chooses to train it in a slightly different way, then a different forecast will be produced. Quite rightly, managers of the FX trading desk do like to be able to 'tell a story' to justify their actions (particularly if they have to justify why they lost a lot of money). Hence in practice, neural networks are only ever likely to provide a

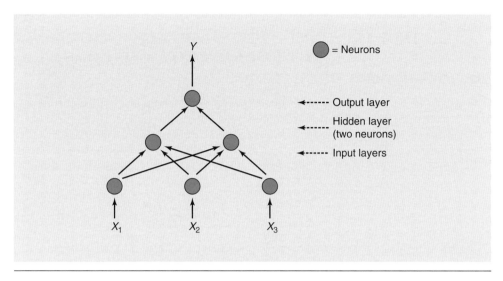

FIGURE 17.10: ANN (one hidden layer)

complementary technique to the traders' gut feelings. On an academic level, neural networks are a way of modelling our ignorance of the behavioural mechanisms behind decisions in the FX market. Neural networks may, at the margin, improve the forecasts from theory or fundamentals-based models and their strengths and weaknesses are summarised in Case Study 17.1.

At this point it is worth briefly mentioning another artificial intelligence-based forecasting system known as an **expert system**. To calibrate an expert system, a fund manager will respond to a set of questions that are then programmed into a computer. For example, she may be asked: 'If GDP rises by 1% p.a. and interest rates also rise by 50 bp, would you buy or sell the S&P 500?' Having programmed the responses to a whole host of scenarios, we check to see if these decisions were correct or incorrect in the past and hence fine-tune our expert system. Then when one of these thousands of scenarios occur in the future, the computer can produce a buy or sell decision based on the expert's past decisions. Clearly, an expert system requires detailed structured interviewing techniques and a tremendous number of scenarios, which need to be coded into a program. It is very labour and computer intensive and for this reason is not widely used.

In summary, we note that ANNs are being used in all areas of financial forecasting, but their success over rival methods has yet to be clearly demonstrated (see Trippi and Turban, 1996). It seems most likely that they will be used extensively in credit scoring where there is plentiful data on which to train the system and test the genuine forecast outturns. Another possible fruitful area is in modelling 'tick-by-tick' data on asset prices such as FX rates and stock prices. Forecasts can then be produced over, say, each successive 10-minute horizon, together with error bands and buy and sell decisions if the forecasts lie outside the error bands. However, probably the greatest weakness of an ANN is that it is a black box and hence you cannot tell a plausible story of why a particular combination of inputs will lead to a particular forecast value.

CASE STUDY 17.1   ARTIFICIAL NEURAL NETWORKS, PROS AND CONS

- ANNs are a useful method of obtaining 'pattern recognition' that can then be used in forecasting, particularly where our theoretical or intuitive knowledge is very weak and the underlying relationships are highly non-linear (and possibly with time-varying parameters). However, it remains a 'black box' (and unlike the black box on an aircraft we usually cannot look inside). In contrast, models based on economic fundamentals (e.g. interest rates for the FX spot rate, dividends for stocks) usually allow some kind of reasonable behavioural assumptions and this helps in explaining the working of the economy and gives credence to the model (assuming that it performs reasonably well on statistical grounds).
- ANNs require considerable judgement in choosing the inputs X_i, the transfer function, the number of hidden layers and the objective function, in order to determine the optimal weights. But fundamentals models also require judgement, for example which variables are most important, which functional form to use (linear or non-linear), which statistical tests are crucial and so on.
- For some situations (e.g. forecasting bankruptcies) ANNs do not necessarily provide significantly better forecasts than simpler or more conventional methods (e.g. non-linear time-series regressions based on fundamentals such as accounting ratios, discriminant analysis, logit and probit models, etc.), yet it has a significantly higher cost in terms of complexity, data requirements and implementation.
- ANNs may prove useful in explaining (in a statistical sense) movements in a variable that remain after using a more conventional model. For example, a great deal of the behaviour of monthly spot FX or stock-return *volatility* may be explained using a simple EWMA or GARCH model. However, there may be some unexplained regularities (e.g. skewness, fat tails) that can then be modelled by applying an ANN in addition to the GARCH model. (Strictly speaking, the ANN is applied to the residuals from the GARCH model.)

17.5 TECHNICAL TRADING IN SPOT FOREIGN EXCHANGE

Various technical trading rules are used by speculators to try to predict changes in spot exchange rates – usually over short horizons. For example, a simple filter rule is to buy the currency when it rises k% above its most recent trough and sell whenever the currency falls k% below its most recent peak. If the market is efficient and UIP holds (see Chapter 18), the interest cost of implementing this strategy should just equal any profits made on changes in the spot rate. Early studies (e.g. Dooley and Shafer, 1983; Levich and Thomas, 1993) do indicate profitable trades, using filter rules over days or weeks–and Engel and Hamilton (1990) have shown that the US dollar over the 1970s and 1980s exhibited long trend-like swings that could be exploited using 'trend-following' filter rules. Of course, substantial losses could be incurred in various sub-periods, so these profits are not risk-free. Using daily or weekly data, there is evidence that technical trading rules can be profitable in the spot FX market even after transaction costs (e.g. Levich and Thomas 1993; Neely *et al.,* 1997). However, the trading frequency in these studies is around 3–26 trades *per annum*. Survey evidence (Allen and Taylor, 1990; Cheung and Chinn 2000) indicates that technical analysis is widely used over very short horizons, namely over a few days, and mainly for intra-day trades (where technical traders aim to have a net open position of zero at the end of the day). So is it possible to make profits (corrected for risk) over very short horizons?

Goodhart and Curcio (1992) use analysts' support and resistance levels published by Reuters, while Curcio *et al.* (1999) examine filter rules using intra-day data but do not find profitable opportunities. Olsen & Associates of Zurich claim that their proprietary (unpublished) trading models using five-minute data do earn profits.

A study by Neely and Weller (2003) uses spot FX bid–ask data sampled at half-hourly intervals (to avoid microstructural problems such as bid–ask bounce) for four currencies against the dollar (i.e. the British pound sterling, Deutsche mark, Japanese yen and Swiss franc). One forecasting model uses a genetic algorithm based on the following signals (i) $S_t/\bar{S}_t$ where $\bar{S}$ = moving average over previous two weeks (ii) difference in nearby futures prices (US minus foreign contract) and (iii)time of day – although the last two are found to be uninformative.

The genetic algorithm is estimated (i.e. trained) and selected over two data periods (ending at 31 May 1996) to yield the highest value for cumulative daily returns net of transaction costs (bid–ask spreads and commissions). The outside-sample forecasting period used to test the model is 1 June 1996–31 December 1996. If the genetic algorithm is trained assuming *zero* transaction costs, then the outside-sample predictions generate significant returns of over 100% per annum. But this involves trading about every hour and implies a *break-even* transaction cost of around 1bp for a one-way trade – the actual cost is around 2–2.5bp for large FX trades, hence the forecasting algorithm does not make profits after transaction costs. When the genetic algorithm is trained using transaction costs of 1 or 2bp, then trading frequency in the out-of-sample period falls sharply and again trading is not profitable after transaction costs. The evidence above therefore points to there being 'no free lunches' to FX trading when using technical trading rules over short horizons.

17.6 CHAOS THEORY

Chaos theory attempts to explain the random patterns we see in asset prices and returns by using deterministic non-linear models. Before commencing our analysis of chaotic systems, it is useful to review briefly the nature of the solutions to a dynamic *linear deterministic* system such as

$$y_t = a + by_{t-1} + cy_{t-2} \tag{9}$$

Equation [9] is a second-order difference equation. Given starting values y_0 and y_1 and the parameters (a, b and c), we can determine all future values of y to any degree of accuracy by repeated substitution in [9]. The problem of deterministic equations like [9] is that in the 'real world' we do not observe deterministic paths for economic variables.

So far, our models to explain the random nature of stock-price (returns) data have involved introducing explicit 'stochastic processes' somewhere into the model. For example, stock prices only move in response to *news* about dividends and news is, by definition, random (i.e. cannot be predicted). In contrast to the above:

> In *chaotic models*, apparent random patterns that we observe in real-world data can be generated by a *non-linear* system that is purely *deterministic*.

There is no commonly agreed definition of chaos, but loosely speaking chaotic systems are deterministic, yet exhibit seemingly random and irregular time-series patterns. The time series produced by chaotic systems are highly sensitive to the initial conditions (i.e. the starting point y_0 of the system) and to slight changes in the parameter values. However, this sensitivity to initial conditions and parameter values does not rule out the possibility of producing reasonably accurate forecasts over *short* horizons. This is because the time series from a chaotic system will be broadly repetitive in the early part of the time series, even if the initial conditions differ slightly.

The sensitivity of chaotic systems is such that if the same chaotic system is simulated on two 'identical' computers (which estimate each data point to a precision of 10^{-8}, say) then after a certain time, the path of the two series will differ substantially because of the minute rounding errors reacting with the highly non-linear system. This kind of result is the source of the observation that if the weather can be represented as a chaotic system, a butterfly flapping its wings in China may result in a hurricane in the Caribbean.

As one might imagine, it can be very difficult to ascertain whether a particular 'random-looking' time series has been generated from a deterministic chaotic system or from a genuinely stochastic system. The latter becomes even more difficult if the chaotic system is *occasionally* hit by 'small' random shocks; this is known as 'noisy chaos'. Tests for chaotic systems require a large amount of data if inferences are to be reliable (e.g. in excess of 20,000 data points) and hence with the 'length' of most economic data this becomes an acute problem.

Most people would agree that human behaviour is not deterministic and therefore the analysis of chaotic models only provides a starting point in explaining movements in asset prices. In essence, chaos theory suggests that financial economists take greater note of the possibility of non-linearities in relationships. Having obtained a model that is non-linear in the variables, one can always 'add on' stochastic elements to represent the randomness in human behaviour. Hence as a first step we need to examine the dynamics produced by non-linear systems. If asset prices appear random and returns are largely unpredictable, we must at least entertain the possibility that these results might be generated in chaotic systems. We have, so far, spoken in rather general terms about chaos. We now briefly discuss a simple chaotic system.

Logistic equation

About the simplest representation of a system capable of chaotic behaviour is the (non-linear) logistic equation:

$$P_{t+1} = \lambda P_t (1 - P_t) \qquad\qquad [10]$$

The steady state P^* is given when $P_{t+1} = P_t = P^*$:

$$P^* = \lambda P^* (1 - P^*) \qquad\qquad [11]$$

and the two solutions are:

$$P^* = 0 \qquad\qquad [12a]$$

and

$$P^* = 1 - (1/\lambda) \qquad\qquad [12b]$$

Not all non-linear systems give rise to chaotic behaviour: it depends on the parameter values and initial conditions. For some values of λ the system is globally stable and given *any* starting value P_0 the system will converge to one of the steady state solutions P^*. For other values of λ the solution is a *limit cycle* whereby the time series eventually oscillates (for ever) between *two* values P_1^* and P_2^*. This is known as a two-cycle (Figure 17.11). This solution is

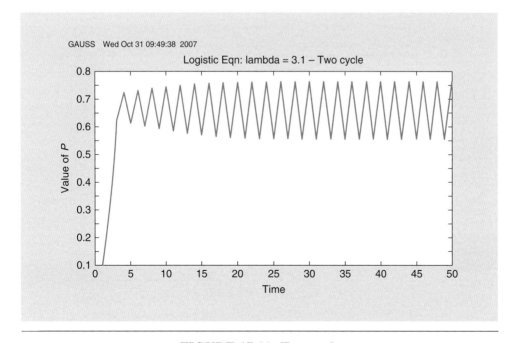

FIGURE 17.11: Two-cycle

known as a *bifurcation*. Again, for different values of λ the series can alter from a two-cycle to a 4, 8, or 16 cyclic pattern.

Finally, for a range of values of λ, the time series of P appears random – this is chaotic behaviour (Figure 17.12). In this case, if the starting value is altered from $P_0 = 0.3$ to 0.300000001, the 'random' time path differs after about 20 time periods, demonstrating the sensitivity to very slight changes in the starting value. This is the butterfly flapping its wings in China causing a hurricane in the Caribbean–but if the initially conditions are slightly different the hurricane will appear in Japan.

The dynamics of the non-linear logistic system in the single variable P, has to be solved by simulation rather than analytically. The latter usually applies a fortiori to more complex single-variable non-linear equations and to a system of non-linear equations where variables X, Y, Z, say, interact with one another. A wide variety of very diverse patterns that are seemingly random or irregular can arise in such models.

A simple model that yields a logistic equation is to assume a long-run equilibrium level for prices P^*, determined by future dividends that we assume are constant (so that $P^* = D/R$ where R = a constant discount rate). Now assume that the change in price is proportional to the gap between P^* and today's actual value P_t:

$$\Delta P_{t+1} = \theta(P^* - P_t) \qquad \theta > 0 \tag{13}$$

This is a form of *error-correction model*. If P_t is below its long-run equilibrium P^*, then prices increase next period; this then reduces the gap or 'error' $(P^* - P_t)$, next period. The

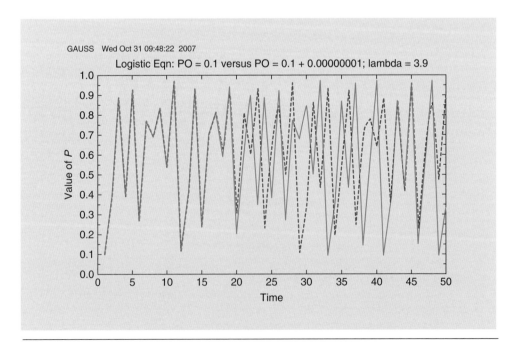

FIGURE 17.12: Chaos, sensitivity to starting values

model in [13] also represents mean reversion, since if P_t is below P^* it moves back towards P^* next period. Let us now assume (rather arbitrarily, it must be admitted) that:

$$\theta = \lambda P^* \qquad \lambda > 0 \tag{14}$$

Hence, if the stock price is high, the adjustment speed (i.e. the value of θ) will be faster. (This is a *non-linear error-correction model*.) Substituting equation [14] in [13]:

$$\Delta P_{t+1} = \lambda P_t(P^* - P_t)$$
$$P_{t+1} = (1 + \lambda P^*)P_t - \lambda P_t^2 \tag{15}$$

Since P^* is a constant (by assumption) we can arbitrarily set:

$$P^* = -(1 - \lambda)/\lambda \tag{16}$$

and [15] then becomes the logistic equation:

$$P_{t+1} = \lambda P_t(1 - P_t) \tag{17}$$

which is capable of generating chaotic behaviour. The above model is very simple (and a little contrived). However, if we can introduce non-linearities into a more realistic deterministic model, it may also yield chaotic behaviour.

In recent years there has been much empirical work on non-linear models in many areas of economics and indeed the non-linearities are often also assumed to be asymmetric (see Cuthbertson and Nitzsche, 2004, and Granger and Terasvirta, 1993, for an overview). The basic idea is similar to that set out above, but in [13] the adjustment parameter λ is assumed to be a non-linear function (often a logistic function) of the 'distance' from equilibrium (i.e. λ is a function of $(P_t^* - P_t)$). Hence the speed of adjustment λ is faster, the further you are from equilibrium. The danger with such models is that the *estimated* non-linearity is due to some single large 'one-off' rise or fall in P (e.g. currency crisis) and the non-linear effect is therefore a rather sophisticated way of taking account of an 'outlier' in the data. However, careful tests of the stability of the key non-linear parameters to changes in the data set can usually distinguish between these competing explanations.

The key conclusions from chaotic models are:

- A purely non-linear yet deterministic process can produce random patterns that do not repeat themselves. These random patterns need not necessarily be highly variable (although they might be) and they have a finite variance.
- The forecasts produced by chaotic systems are highly sensitive to the *initial conditions* and to slight changes in the *parameter values*.
- Sensitivity to initial conditions and parameter values does not rule out the possibility of producing reasonably accurate forecasts *over short* horizons. This is because the time series from a chaotic system will be broadly repetitive in the early part of the time series, even if the initial conditions differ slightly (e.g. weather forecasts one to five days ahead are pretty accurate, but they are not particularly accurate one month ahead).

SUMMARY

- There are a large number of alternative methods used to forecast short-term movements in the spot FX rate and stock prices, most of which rely on predictions based on past movements in these prices. These are *technical trading* methods.
- *Chartists* base their forecasts on time-series graphs. Either they recognise patterns in the data that they think will repeat themselves or they use simple quantitative rules. Other forms of technical trading include the use of high–low extremes, moving-average cross-over points, support-resistance levels and momentum indices.
- Candlesticks are based on the pattern of prices *during the day*, namely the opening and closing prices and the high and low during the day. Again, specific candlestick patterns signal buy or sell decisions.
- *Artificial neural networks* (ANNs) link asset prices to other variables (e.g. past prices, interest rates, etc.) in a highly non-linear relationship. The network is first fitted to a training data set and then tested on additional data. The parameters of the ANN are updated to minimise out-of-sample forecast errors. ANNs are mainly used for forecasting over very short horizons (e.g. tick-by-tick data).
- *Chaos theory* demonstrates how a *non-linear* deterministic system can generate apparently random behaviour. What is perhaps most important is that it alerts us to the possibility of non-linearities explaining asset prices.
- A major difficulty in trying to analyse chaotic models is the very large amount of data required to detect a chaotic (as opposed to a stochastic) process.

EXERCISES

Q1 What are the key features of chaos theory and why are the results counter-intuitive?

Q2 Broadly speaking, how do technical traders differ from fundamentals' traders?

Q3 What is a support level (for spot FX or stock prices) and how is it used by traders?

Q4 What is an exponentially weighted moving average (EWMA) forecast? If the current asset price (e.g. stock price or spot FX rate) is $S_0 = 100$, the previous day's EWMA *forecast* had been 90 and the 'weight' is $\alpha = 0.9$, what would your forecast be for the asset price tomorrow? Briefly comment.

Q5 Does the presence of noise traders automatically imply that asset prices will exhibit trends?

Q6 What is the purpose of a transfer function in an artificial neural network (ANN)?

Q7 What is overfitting applied to artificial neural networks (ANN)? Why is it a problem?

Q8 What is a momentum strategy when applied to technical analysis?

PART 5

FOREIGN EXCHANGE MARKET

CHAPTER 18

Spot and Forward Markets

AIMS

- To provide a brief overview of the evolution of the international monetary system (e.g. fixed but adjustable rates, freely floating rates, currency bands and common currency areas).
- To explain the mechanics of spot FX deals, bid–ask spreads and cross-rates.
- To show how the forward rate is determined by risk-free arbitrage (covered interest parity).
- To demonstrate how speculation in the spot FX market is influenced by domestic and foreign interest rates and expectations of future spot rates – this is uncovered interest parity (UIP).
- To explain the concept of price competitiveness and purchasing power parity (PPP).
- To show the relationship between today's quoted forward rate and the *future* spot rate – the forward rate unbiasedness proposition (FRU).

INTRODUCTION

The FX market is the largest and most active financial market with trillions of dollars changing hands daily. The spot FX rate is also a 'price' that attracts much media and government attention, because changes in the exchange rate can have far-reaching implications for the rest of the economy. In this chapter we cover all the main issues concerning spot and forward FX markets.

We set the scene with a brief history of the international monetary system, emphasising the importance to 'small open economies' (i.e. those with a large export/import sector) of the exchange rate system adopted. We then move on to the more detailed working of the spot market, including bid, offer and cross-rates, and show how these are used by market participants. The next section deals with the forward market, including price quotes by dealers. We then deal with hedging in the forward market and the evidence in favour of covered interest parity. The next section covers speculation in the spot market (i.e. uncovered interest parity) and this is followed by a discussion of price competitiveness and purchasing power parity. In the final sections we show how these basic concepts are interlinked.

18.1 INTERNATIONAL MONETARY SYSTEM

The spot exchange rate is the rate at which you can immediately exchange one currency for another. If you are an importer or exporter of goods, changes in the spot rate can affect the amount you pay out or receive in domestic currency and hence the profitability of your business. If you are an investor and hold foreign assets as part of your portfolio, fluctuations in the spot exchange rate will affect the value of those investments in terms of your domestic currency. Put another way, if you are a UK investor with US assets, when you come to sell your investments their value in terms of sterling receipts will depend crucially on the sterling–US dollar exchange rate prevailing at the time you sell your US assets. Therefore volatility in the spot exchange rate creates uncertainty for importers and exporters and also for investors. One response to this uncertainty is for governments and central banks to try to control the exchange rate. Trying to maintain a fixed exchange rate against a major currency like the US dollar has often been the aim of governments in the past. This was mainly to reduce the impact of fluctuations in the spot rate on the volume of imports and exports, and therefore on fluctuations in domestic output. Another response to such uncertainty is to use and develop financial instruments that can be used to hedge fluctuations in the spot rate such as forward contracts, futures and options contracts, and swaps.

The behaviour of the exchange rate, particularly for small open economies that undertake a substantial amount of international trade, has been at the centre of macroeconomic policy debates for many years. There is no doubt that economists' views about the best exchange rate system to adopt have changed over the years, partly because new evidence has accumulated as the system has moved through various exchange rate regimes. It is worthwhile briefly outlining the main issues.

After the Second World War the **Bretton Woods arrangement** of 'fixed but adjustable exchange rates' applied to most major currencies. As capital flows were small and often subject to government restrictions, the emphasis was on price competitiveness. Countries that had faster rates of inflation than their trading partners were initially allowed to borrow from the **International Monetary Fund (IMF)** to finance their trade deficit. If a 'fundamental disequilibrium' in the trade account developed, then after consultation the deficit country was allowed to fix its exchange rate at a new lower parity (against the US dollar). After a devaluation, the IMF would also usually insist on a set of austerity measures, such as cuts in public expenditure, to ensure that real resources (i.e. labour and capital) were available to switch into export growth and import substitution. The system worked relatively well for a number of years and succeeded in avoiding the re-emergence of the use of tariffs and quotas that had been a feature of 1930s protectionism.

The US dollar was the *anchor currency* of the Bretton Woods system and the dollar was linked to gold at a fixed price of $35 per ounce. The system began to come under strain in the mid-1960s. Deficit countries could not persuade surplus countries to mitigate the competitiveness problem, by a revaluation of the surplus country's currency. There was an *asymmetric adjustment process* that invariably meant that the deficit country had to devalue. The possibility of a large step devaluation allowed speculators a 'one-way bet' and encouraged speculative attacks on those countries that were perceived to have poor current-account imbalances, even if it could be reasonably argued that these imbalances were temporary.

The US ran large current-account deficits that increased the amount of dollars held by foreigners (either as private-sector foreign assets or as official foreign exchange reserves).

Hence, the US government was able to exchange US dollars (which could be produced at near zero cost in terms of real resources) in return for valuable 'real resources' (e.g. oil, rubber, coal). This is known as *seniorage* and is a benefit obtained if your currency becomes a *vehicle currency* (i.e. is used to settle foreign trade between third countries) or is used as part of another country's foreign exchange reserves. Eventually, the amount of these externally held dollars exceeded the value of gold in Fort Knox, when valued at the official price of $35 an ounce. At the official price, free convertibility of dollars into gold became impossible. A two-tier gold market developed (with the free-market price of gold very much higher than the official price) and eventually convertibility of the dollar into gold was suspended by the US authorities. By the early 1970s, pressures on the system were increasing. International capital became more mobile and differential inflation rates between countries widened and caused large deficits or surpluses on the current accounts of different countries. By 1972–73 most major industrial countries had de facto left the Bretton Woods system and floated their currencies.

In part, the switch to a floating exchange rate regime had been influenced by monetary economists. They argued that control of the domestic money supply would ensure a desired inflation and exchange rate path. In addition, stabilising speculation by rational agents would ensure that large persistent swings in the *real* exchange rate (i.e. price competitiveness) could be avoided by an announced credible monetary policy (often in the form of money-supply targets).

Towards the end of the 1970s, a seminal paper by Dornbusch (1976) showed that if FX dealers are rational yet goods prices are 'sticky', then *exchange rate overshooting* could occur. Hence, a contractionary monetary policy (e.g. a cut in the money supply or a rise in domestic interest rates) could result in a major loss in price competitiveness over a substantial period, with obvious deflationary consequences for real trade, output and employment. Although in long-run equilibrium the economy would move towards full employment and lower inflation, the loss of output in the transition period could be more substantial in the Dornbusch model than in earlier monetary models, which assumed that prices were 'flexible'.

The volatile movement in nominal and real exchange rates in the 1970s led Europeans to consider a move back towards more managed exchange rates, which was eventually reflected in the workings of the **Exchange Rate Mechanism (ERM)** from the early 1980s. European countries that joined the ERM agreed to try to keep their bilateral exchange rates within announced bands around a central parity. The bands could be either wide ($\pm 6\%$) or narrow ($\pm 2.25\%$). The Deutsche mark became (de facto) the anchor currency. In part the ERM was a device to replace national monetary targets with German monetary policy, as a means to combat inflation. Faced with a fixed exchange rate against the Deutsche mark, a high-inflation country had a clear signal that it must quickly reduce its rate of inflation to that pertaining in Germany. Otherwise, unemployment would ensue in the high-inflation country, which would then provide a painful mechanism for reducing inflation. The ERM had a facility for countries to realign their (central) exchange rates in the case of a fundamental misalignment. However, when a currency hits the bottom of its band because of a speculative attack, all the European Central Banks in the ERM system agreed to support the weak currency by coordinated intervention in the FX market.

The perceived success of the ERM in reducing inflation and exchange rate volatility in the 1980s led the G10 countries to consider a policy of coordinated intervention (e.g. the Plaza and Louvre accords) to mitigate persistent and large under- and overvaluations of their own currencies. The latter was epitomised by the inexorable rise of the US dollar in 1983–85 and its subsequent fall, which seemed to be totally unrelated to changes in economic fundamentals (e.g. changes in interest rates, or the current account deficit). Recently, some economists have suggested a more formal arrangement for *currency zones* and *currency bands* for the major world currencies (e.g. US dollar, yen, euro) along the lines of rules used for the ERM.

In the early 1990s, the ERM came under considerable strain. Increasing capital mobility and the removal of all exchange controls in the ERM countries facilitated a speculative attack on the pound sterling, Italian lira and the French franc around 16 September 1992 (known as Black Wednesday). Sterling left the ERM and allowed its currency to float. About a year later, faced with further currency turmoil, most ERM bands were widened to $\pm 15\%$, making it almost a flexible exchange rate regime. The move to a single European currency and a currency union (i.e. Economic and Monetary Union, EMU) was thrown into some confusion by the events of Black Wednesday. The economic reasons for a move to monetary union in Europe are complex, but one is undoubtedly the desire to remove the problem of floating or quasi-managed exchange rates. The move to monetary union was formally started at a meeting of EU leaders on 10 December 1991 at Maastricht in the Netherlands before the turmoil on the FX market in 1992.

In January 1999, 11 EU countries formed an **Economic and Monetary Union (EMU)** and irrevocably locked their exchange rates against the Euro, with a view to full implementation of Euro notes and coins in retail transactions beginning in January 2002. The EU countries that entered 'Euroland' were Austria, Belgium, Finland, France, Germany, Ireland, Italy, Luxembourg, Netherlands, Portugal and Spain. The EU countries that initially stayed out were the UK, Denmark, Greece and Sweden. The Euro is now a rival to the US dollar and is an important vehicle and reserve currency.

The interest rate policy in Euroland is determined by the European System of Central Banks (ESCB) with the primary objective of maintaining price stability. The ESCB also conducts the foreign exchange operations (e.g. intervention) and manages the foreign exchange reserves. Somewhat more nebulous is its objective of supporting the general economic policies of the EU. The decisions of the **European Central Bank (ECB)** in Frankfurt are supposed to be made independently of governments of member states and EU institutions. The Governing Council of the ESCB, which consists of the Executive Board of the ECB and the governors of the national Central Banks of the members, determines EU interest rates at its monthly meetings. Day-to-day operations are under the auspices of the governor of the ECB.

The years 1997–99 saw great currency turmoil in the Far East where banking crises in Thailand, Indonesia, Malaysia and Japan resulted in depreciations of some of these currencies against the US dollar of around 30–40%. The immediate reason for the withdrawal of foreign capital was the excess foreign currency borrowing by domestic banks. This foreign currency was then switched into local-currency loans (many of which were used in property speculation) and these became 'non-performing'. Hence, it was (correctly) thought that banks that were unhedged could not pay back the interest and capital on the foreign-currency loans and this triggered a general capital outflow.

Also, in 1998 the Russian rouble depreciated sharply against the US dollar, again because bank loans to Russia denominated in foreign currency seemed to be liable to default. Growth in the Russian economy was virtually non-existent, there were massive falls in tax receipts (and a disintegration of the tax-collecting system) and hence many public-sector workers had wage arrears in excess of six months. The Brazilian 'real' became the next victim in 1999 when Brazil too had to devalue in the face of speculative pressure, which the IMF and the granting of loans from the US were unable to stem. This set of events led for calls in the G10 for a 'new economic order' or a *'new financial architecture'* that involves a more proactive role for the IMF in trying to avert currency crises (or at least mitigate their adverse impact on countries).

Having dealt with the broad issues surrounding alternative exchange rate regimes, we now turn to the detailed workings of the spot and forward FX markets.

18.2 SPOT FX DEALS

When a bank purchases foreign currency in the spot market, it does not receive the funds that day. The foreign exchange (FX) is delivered in two working days' time on what is known as the *spot value date*. Hence a spot deal done on Wednesday will be settled on Friday (the spot value date). A deal done on Thursday will normally be settled on Monday (unless this is also a holiday).

Settlement actually takes place in the two separate countries, even though the deal may be done in a third country. Trading the Euro against Swiss francs would be EURO for CHF in terms of the currencies' SWIFT codes, or 'Euro-Swissy' over the phone. If the trade is with a bank in London, the funds are not transferred in London. Instead, the accounts of the two parties to the deal will be held in their (correspondent) banks in the settlement countries, namely France and Switzerland, and there will be a payment of Euros in France against Swiss francs in Switzerland. Generally, currencies are almost always quoted against the US dollar. Other SWIFT codes and shorthands for these FX trades are:

Currencies	SWIFT codes	Shorthand
Swiss franc – US dollar	USD/CHF	Swissy
Euro – US dollar	USD/EURO	Euros
Japanese yen – US dollar	USD/JPY	Bill and Ben
Pound sterling – US dollar	USD/GBP	Cable

'Cable' refers to the telephone cable under the Atlantic that connects the US and the UK. The use of 'Bill and Ben' for the Japanese yen is Cockney rhyming slang and is used in the London market. Note that the 'slash' (/) here does not mean 'divide by', it is merely a convention used to separate 'base' (the currency on the left) from 'quoted' (the currency on the right). Settlement will be on the same working day in both countries, but because of time-zone differences, settlement will take place earlier in the Far East, followed by Europe and then in the USA.

Base/quoted currency

Dealing with exchange rate quotes can be difficult to grasp at first, since two currencies are always involved (e.g. EURO and USD), and the quote could in principle be either EURO per USD or USD per EURO. There are various conventions, which we now illustrate with specific examples:

If the quote is written	'EURO 1 = USD 0.85' (or in words '0.85 dollars per euro') then
Base currency	is the EURO = 'fixed number' = 'one'
Quoted currency	is the USD = 'variable number' = 0.85 (in this case)

If the quote is written as 'base/quoted', then the above would be denoted 'USD 0.85'. A change from USD 0.8500 to 0.8501 is an increase of 0.0001 or 1 tick or 1 point or 1 pip.

Direct (normal) and indirect (reciprocal) quotes

> Direct quote is: domestic per unit of foreign currency.
> Indirect quote is: foreign per unit of domestic currency.

Most international markets (e.g. US, Australia, Japan) use direct quotes for most currencies, while London uses indirect quotes. For example, a quote by a Swiss bank would be a direct quote such as CHF 160 per EURO 100. Dealers normally trade the base currency (here the euro) in round amounts (e.g. € 5m) and make money from the **bid–ask spread**, the difference between the buying price and selling price of a currency. The 'bid price' is the 'buying price', but we need to make it clear which currency is being bought and which sold by the market maker. The quote by the dealer (market maker) might be as follows:

Bid–ask spread: Quote is USD 1 = EURO 0.8550/60

In the above quote 0.85 is the *big figure,* and the bid–ask spread = 10 points. The rule of thumb to obtain the correct buy or sell outcome is the 'three Bs rule', namely:

> The market maker Buys the Base currency at the Bid price which is the low figure (usually the figure that comes first in the quote).

Hence the market maker:

> Buys $1 and pays out (low) EURO 0.8550 − bid rate
>
> Sells $1 and receives (high) EURO 0.8560 − offer rate

making a net profit on the round trip of EURO 0.0010 (= 10 points). This rule retains the 'buy low, sell high' convention. Note that it is the dealer 'making' the quote who buys $1 at EURO 0.8550, the counterparty must therefore be selling $1 and receiving EURO 0.8550. There are two sides to every deal.

Telephone deals

In the above quote 0.85 is the *big figure* and the quote over the telephone at 0.8550/0.8560 (EURO per $) where bank M is the market maker would go something like this (on Monday 1 March):

Bank A: 'Hi guys. Spot dollar–euro please.'

Bank M: '50/60.'

Bank A: 'OK, at 50 I sell 10 dollars.'

Bank M: 'Done. I buy $10m dollars at 0.8550 for 3rd March and sell you euro 8.55m. My dollars to Merrill's, New York.'

Bank A: 'OK, my euros to Deutsche Bank, Frankfurt. Thanks and bye.'

Note that it is bank M that *gives* the quote and hence is the market maker. Therefore bank M buys the base currency (USD) at the bid (low) rate of 50, so that bank A, the counterparty, is selling $10m and receiving EURO 8.55m.

Market makers

If you are a market maker you can use the bid–ask spread to help achieve your desired holdings of currencies. For example, suppose the big figure is 0.85 EURO per $ and the average *market spread* is 06/16. Suppose you are '**square**'; that is, happy with the dollar and Euro inventory you are holding. You now receive a (telephone) call for a price, but you don't know whether it's a buy or sell order. What do you do? You don't really want to deal, so you need to discourage both buyers and sellers. You do this by widening your spread to 04/18. If you are given dollars at 04 you might be able to immediately sell them in the market at 06 (Euro per $), making 2 points profit and squaring your position. Alternatively, if you sell dollars at 18 (Euro per $) you might be able to buy them back at 16, again locking in a 2-point profit. However, trying to reverse such deals is dangerous, since you may not be able to act quickly enough before rates change against you. This is particularly relevant in thin markets where sufficient liquidity may not be available to absorb your reverse trade (at going rates). The greater your fears on these two counts, the wider your spread will be.

Consider a different scenario where you would rather be long than short dollars and the current market spread is 06/16. You don't know if the caller wants to buy or sell dollar. To increase the chances of getting a deal where you receive dollars, you would *shade the rate upwards* to 10/18. You will therefore pay 10 (Euro per $) to buy dollars, which is better than the market rate of 06. But if the caller is actually trying to buy dollars from you, she faces having to pay 18 (Euro per $) to you, rather than the market's 16. Hence, overall, she will be less inclined to buy dollars from you but more inclined to sell dollars to you.

Cross-rates

Calculation of cross-rates depends on the way the two currencies are quoted against the dollar. The best way to proceed is to use a simple example.

CASE A: BASE (UNIT) CURRENCY DIFFERS

Quotes are written base/quoted and are GBP/USD and USD/CHF. Note again that the slash here merely separates base from quoted and 'GBP/USD' would be a quote in terms of 'USD per GBP' (Table 18.1). Suppose we require quotes for the cross-rate CHF per GBP:

$$\text{Cross-rate} = \frac{\text{CHF}}{\text{GBP}} = \left(\frac{\text{USD}}{\text{GBP}}\right)\left(\frac{\text{CHF}}{\text{USD}}\right) \qquad [1]$$

> Rule for cross-rates when the base currency is different is 'bid $\times$ bid' and 'offer $\times$ offer'. You 'multiply down' the columns.

TABLE 18.1: Cross-rate, base (unit) currency differs

Spot	Bid	Offer
GBP/USD	1.9720	1.9730 ($/£)
USD/CHF	1.5110	1.5115 (SFr/$)
Cross-rate		
GBP/CHF	2.9797	2.9822 (SFr/£)

The market maker quoting the above cross-rates therefore effectively buys the base currency at the bid rate. The big figure is 2.9 and therefore the market maker:

- Buys £1 and pays out 797 Swiss francs.
- Sells £1 and receives 822 Swiss francs.
- Makes a profit of 25 points (in Swiss francs) on the bid–ask spread.

CASE B: BASE (UNIT) CURRENCY THE SAME

Here both quotes are written base/quoted and we take the Swiss franc and the South African Rand as our required *cross-rates* (Table 18.2). The dollar quotes are SFr per $ and Rand per $.

$$\text{Cross-rate} = \frac{\text{CHF}}{\text{Rand}} = \left(\frac{\text{CHF}}{\text{USD}}\right)\bigg/\left(\frac{\text{Rand}}{\text{USD}}\right) \qquad [2a]$$

TABLE 18.2: Cross-rate, base (unit) currency the same

Spot	Bid	Offer
USD/CHF	1.5110	1.5115 (SFr/$)
USD/Rand	5.7050	5.7065 (Rand/$)
Cross-rate		
CHF/Rand	3.7744	3.7766 (Rand/SFr)
Rand/CHF	0.2648	0.2649 (SFr/Rand)

$$\text{Cross-rate} = \frac{\text{Rand}}{\text{CHF}} = \left(\frac{\text{Rand}}{\text{USD}}\right) \bigg/ \left(\frac{\text{CHF}}{\text{USD}}\right) \qquad [2b]$$

Consider the cross-rate 0.2648 SFr per rand (**bid**) in Table 18.2. How is this figure calculated? If market maker A is quoting this cross-rate to a corporate, then the base currency is the rand. Hence, as a market maker bank A is buying rand and selling SFr. To fulfil the cross-rate deal, bank A has to go via the USD, hence:

Bank A must first buy SFr for USDs from market maker bank B

Bank A must also sell rand for USDs to market maker bank B

It is convenient here to assume that B is the counterparty on both sides of the deal, although in practice it would normally be two *different* market makers. It follows from the above that:

Market maker bank B must buy the base currency (USD) and sell SFrs at 1.5110 (bid) and market maker bank B must sell the base currency (USD) and buy rand at 5.7065 (offer)

Hence the cross-rate is:

1.5110 (bid)/5.7065 (offer) = 0.2648 SFr per rand (bid)

(CHF/USD)/(Rand/USD) = (SFr per rand)

Therefore the figure of 0.2648 SFr per rand (**bid**) is obtained from:

$$\left(\frac{\text{CHF}}{\text{Rand}}\right)_b = \left(\frac{\text{CHF}}{\text{USD}}\right)_b \bigg/ \left(\frac{\text{Rand}}{\text{USD}}\right)_o \quad \text{(i.e. 'cross' bid rate} = \text{bid/offer)} \qquad [3a]$$

Similarly, the figure 0.2649 SFr per rand (**offer**) in Table 18.2 is obtained from:

$$\left(\frac{\text{CHF}}{\text{Rand}}\right)_o = \left(\frac{\text{CHF}}{\text{USD}}\right)_o \bigg/ \left(\frac{\text{Rand}}{\text{USD}}\right)_b \quad \text{(i.e. 'cross' offer rate} = \text{offer/bid)} \qquad [3b]$$

Hence:

0.2649(SFr per rand offer) = 1.5115 (offer)/5.7050 (bid)

Rule for cross-rates when base currency is the same is therefore 'divide across' either: (a) bid cross-rate = bid/offer or (b) offer cross-rate = offer/bid

Faced with the cross-rate 0.2648/0.2649 SFr/rand (bid/offer), market maker bank A:

- Buys the base currency of 1 rand and pays out 0.2648 Swiss francs.
- Sells the base currency of 1 rand and receives 0.2649 Swiss francs.
- Makes a spread on the round trip of 1 point.

18.3 FORWARD RATE

The purpose of this section is to explain the detailed workings of the forward market and its relationship to the spot market. There are two main types of deal on the FX market. The first is the spot rate, as outlined in the previous section; the second is the forward rate, which is the guaranteed price agreed today at which the buyer will take delivery of the currency on a specific future date. For most major currencies, the most liquid forward contracts are in the one- to six-month maturities, although forward deals in some currencies are available for three to five years ahead. Use of the forward market eliminates risk from possible future changes in the spot exchange rate as the forward rate is agreed today, even though the cash transaction takes place in (say) one years time. The market makers in the FX market are mainly the large banks (e.g. Merrill Lynch, Barclays).

The pricing of a forward contract involves a relationship between the forward rate and three other variables, the spot rate and the money-market interest rates in the two countries, and is known as **covered interest parity (CIP)**. We shall see that in an efficient market, the quoted forward rate ensures that no risk-free arbitrage profits can be made by transacting between the spot currency market, the two money markets and the forward market.

The relationship between spot and forward rates can be derived as follows. Assume that a UK corporate treasurer has a sum of money £A, which he can invest in the UK or the US for one year. We assume that the transaction must have zero market risk and we also assume zero credit/default risk. For the UK treasurer to be indifferent as to where the money is invested, it has to be the case that the risk-free return from investing in the UK equals the return *in sterling* from investing in the US. Assume that the quoted interest rates in the domestic (sterling) money market, the foreign (US) money market and the exchange rates are:

$$r_d = 0.11 \ (11\%) \qquad r_f = 0.10 \ (10\%)$$
$$S = 0.6666 \ £/\$ \qquad \text{(equivalent to 1.5 \$/£)}$$
$$F = 0.6727 \ £/\$ \qquad \text{(equivalent to 1.4865 \$/£)}$$

Note that the forward rate F and the spot rate S are measured as 'domestic per unit of foreign currency'; that is, £s per \$. We can show that the above figures give equal returns to investing in either the UK or the US. Also, the two investments involve no (market) risk and therefore the corporate treasurer will be indifferent to placing his funds in either the US or the UK – this is *covered interest parity*.

Investment Strategy 1: Invest in UK

In one year receive (terminal value): $\mathbf{TV_{UK}} = \pounds A\,(1 + r_d) = \pounds 100(1.11) = \pmb{\pounds 111}$

Investment Strategy 2: Invest in US

(a) Convert £100 to $150 (= 100/0.6666) in the spot market today *and* invest them in dollar deposits
(b) Dollar receipts at end year are:

$\$150(1.10) = \$(A/S)(1 + r_f) = \$165$

(c) Enter into a forward contract today at $F = 0.6727$ (£/$) to sell $165 for delivery of sterling in one years time Sterling receipts in one year from the US investment are:

$\mathbf{TV_{US}} = \$165\,F = \pmb{\pounds 111} = \pounds[(A/S)(1 + r_f)]F$

All of the above transactions (a)–(c) are undertaken today at known prices, hence there is no (market) risk. Since both investment strategies are risk-free, arbitrage will ensure that they give the same terminal value:

$$\mathrm{TV_{UK}} = \mathrm{TV_{US}}$$
$$\pounds A(1 + r_d) = \pounds[(A/S)(1 + r_f)]F \qquad [4]$$

Hence, covered interest parity can be expressed as:

$$F/S = (1 + r_d)/(1 + r_f) \qquad [5]$$

Subtract 1 from each side of equation [5]:

$$(F - S)/S = (r_d - r_f)/(1 + r_f) \qquad [6]$$

The above CIP formulae are exact, but if r_f is small (e.g. 0.03) then $(1 + r_f)$ is approximately equal to 1 and we have:

$$\text{Forward premium/discount} \approx \text{interest rate differential}$$
$$(F - S)/S \qquad \approx \qquad (r_d - r_f) \qquad [7]$$

Forward points

In the market, outright forward rates are not quoted, but instead the convention is that the *difference* between the forward rate and spot rate $F - S$, or the *forward points* or *forward margins*, is quoted, where:

$$\text{Forward points} = F - S = S\left[\frac{(r_{\mathrm{d}} - r_{\mathrm{f}})}{(1 + r_{\mathrm{f}})}\right]$$

$$\text{Forward points} = F - S = 0.6727 - 0.6667 = 0.0060 \, (+60 \text{ points})$$

Given the forward points of $+60$ from the dealer's screen, he would quote:

$$\text{'Outright' forward rate } F = S + \text{'forward points'}$$

$$= 0.6667 + 0.0060 = 0.6727 \, (\text{£}/\text{\$})$$

The forward points would usually be quoted on FX screens for 1, 2, 3, 6 and 12 months and the value dates for the forward contract would coincide with maturity dates for Eurocurrency deposits and loans. The forward points equal $F - S$, but by covered arbitrage this is the same as an interest differential (multiplied by the spot rate). For example, if $r_{\mathrm{d}} = 5\%$ and $r_{\mathrm{f}} = 6\%$ then if you transfer from the domestic to the foreign currency you will earn 1% more interest. Whatever the spot rate, the only way you *do not* earn a risk-free profit is if the forward domestic currency you receive after one year is 1% less than the spot domestic currency you gave up at $t = 0$; that is, if $(F - S)/S$ equals -1%.

Since we assume CIP holds at all times then the 'forward points' can be calculated from the RHS of equation [6] using $S, r_{\mathrm{d}}, r_{\mathrm{f}}$ and the forward points could be positive or negative (depending on whether r_{d} is greater or less than r_{f}). A further practical complication is that the forward rate calculated from the money market rates will have a bid–ask spread (as noted above) depending on which currency is being borrowed or placed on deposit in the money markets – we ignore this problem here.

Two other rearrangements of the CIP condition are worth mentioning, which are:

$$F = S(1 + CC) \qquad \text{where} \qquad CC = (r_{\mathrm{d}} - r_{\mathrm{f}})/(1 + r_{\mathrm{f}})$$

and

$$F = S + X \qquad \text{where} \qquad X = S(r_{\mathrm{d}} - r_{\mathrm{f}})/(1 + r_{\mathrm{f}})$$

CC is known as the *percentage cost of forward cover* and X is the *dollar* cost of forward cover (both terms are also frequently used in the discussion of FX *futures* contracts; see Cuthbertson and Nitzsche, 2001b). The cost of forward cover clearly depends on the interest differential between the two countries. It is easy to check that the above data are consistent with the (exact) algebraic CIP condition of equation [6]:

$$\text{Interest differential} = (r_{\mathrm{d}} - r_{\mathrm{f}})/(1 + r_{\mathrm{f}}) = (0.11 - 0.10)/1.10 = 0.0091 \quad (0.91\%) \quad [8a]$$

and

$$\text{Forward discount on sterling} = (F - S)/S = 0.0091 \quad (0.91\%) \qquad\qquad [8b]$$

One further 'trick' to note is that the CIP formula [5] looks slightly different if S and F are measured as 'foreign per unit of domestic currency'. However, the following 'rule of thumb' always holds:

> If S and F are measured as 'currency X per unit of currency Y' then in equation [5] the interest rates are r_x in the numerator and r_y in the denominator

For example, if S and F are measured as Swiss francs per US dollar then the CIP condition is:

$$F/S = (1 + r_{SF})/(1 + r_{\$}) \qquad [9]$$

where r_{SF} and $r_{\$}$ are the Swiss and US dollar interest rates, respectively. If the forward rate is quoted for delivery in less than one year, the CIP formula must reflect the interest rate conventions used in both the domestic and foreign markets. For example, if the forward rate is for delivery in 90 days and the Swiss interest rate convention is 'actual/365' and the US convention is 'actual/360', the three-month forward rate would be calculated as:

$$F/S = [1 + r_{SF}(90/365)]/[1 + r_{\$}(90/360)]$$

What forward rate to quote?

Below we show why the bank's quoted forward rate is always given by the CIP equation. This is because a corporate treasurer can create a 'synthetic forward' and if the *quoted* forward rate does not equal this 'synthetic forward' rate then the bank will be giving a corporate treasurer (say) a *risk-free* profit opportunity. Such risk-free arbitrage profits are quickly eliminated (in an efficient market), this is why the CIP equation holds at all times. We demonstrate this proposition by first considering the cash flows in an **actual** forward contract. We then reproduce these cash flows using 'other assets'; that is, the money markets in each country and the spot exchange rate – this is the synthetic forward contract. Since the two sets of cash flows are identical, the *actual* forward contract must have a 'value' or 'price' equal to the *synthetic* forward contract. Otherwise risk-free arbitrage profits can be made.

For example, if you are a UK resident, then you can create a 'synthetic forward' by:

- Borrowing sterling at a cost of r_{UK}.
- Switching the sterling funds into US dollars in the spot market.
- Placing the US dollars on deposit for one year in a US account at r_{US}.

In the synthetic forward, you have therefore promised to pay out sterling from your UK bank loan, but you will also receive dollars from the US bank, both at *the end of the year*. This is a *synthetic* forward contract to receive dollars in exchange for sterling in one years time. Let us look at this in more detail.

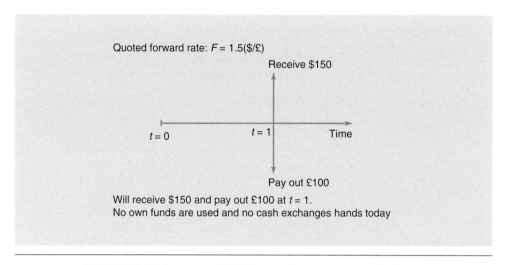

FIGURE 18.1: Actual FX forward contract: cash flows

Cash flows in actual and synthetic forward contracts

If the quoted forward rate is $F = 1.50$ ($/£), then the cash flows in the actual forward contract are as shown in Figure 18.1. Note that no cash changes hands today. Now let us deal with the 'synthetic'. Suppose that money-market interest rates and the spot rate are:

$$r_{UK} = 11\%   r_{US} = 10\%   S = 1.513636 \, (\$/£)$$

Now we create cash flows equivalent to those in the actual forward contract. First, 'create' the cash outflow of £100 at $t = 1$, by borrowing $£100/(1 + r_{UK})$ at $t = 0$, and convert this to US dollars in the spot FX market. Place these dollars on deposit in the US at $t = 0$, from which you will receive dollars at $t = 1$. By investing all the borrowed sterling funds in the US, we reproduce a zero net cash flow at $t = 0$, which mimics that of the actual forward contract. The cash flows for the synthetic forward contract are:

- Borrow $£100/(1 + r_{UK})$ = £90.09   at $t = 0$
- Pay out £100   at $t = 1$
- Convert £90.09 to USD at spot rate   = $136.36   at $t = 1$
                                         = $[100/(1 + r_{UK})]S$
- Lend $136.36 in the US and receive   = $150   at $t = 1$
                                         = $[100/(1 + r_{UK})]S(1 + r_{US})$

Synthetic forward rate, *SF*:

$$SF(\$/£) = \frac{\text{receive USD at } t = 1}{\text{pay out GBP at } t = 1} = \frac{\$150}{£100}$$

$$= \frac{\$100}{1 + r_{UK}} \times \frac{S(1 + r_{US})}{£100} = \frac{S(1 + r_{US})}{(1 + r_{UK})}$$

[10]

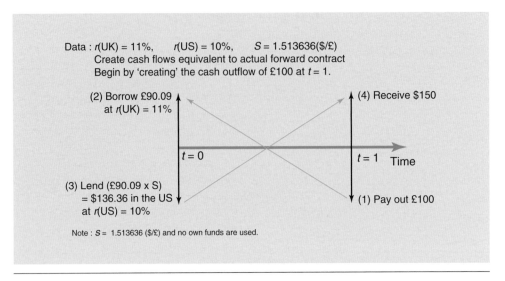

Data : r(UK) = 11%,   r(US) = 10%,   S = 1.513636($/£)
Create cash flows equivalent to actual forward contract
Begin by 'creating' the cash outflow of £100 at t = 1.

(2) Borrow £90.09
    at r(UK) = 11%

(4) Receive $150

t = 0

t = 1   Time

(3) Lend (£90.09 x S)
    = $136.36 in the US
    at r(US) = 10%

(1) Pay out £100

Note : S = 1.513636 ($/£) and no own funds are used.

FIGURE 18.2: Synthetic FX forward contract

The actual forward rate F must equal this synthetic forward rate SF or risk-free arbitrage profits can be made. So, FOREX dealers will calculate and *quote* a forward rate that is equal to $S(1 + r_{US})/(1 + r_{UK})$ to eliminate any arbitrage opportunities.

Arbitrage profits

If the actual forward quote F by bank M does not equal the synthetic forward rate SF, then a corporate treasurer can make risk-free arbitrage profits. To demonstrate this possibility, suppose the treasurer is faced with the following data:

Actual forward quote (from bank M):

$F = \mathbf{1.40}\ (\$/£)$

This implies that the treasurer can *pay* $140 and *receive* £100 at $t = 1$.

Synthetic forward (money market):

Data: $r_{UK} = 11\%$, $r_{US} = 10\%$, $S = 1.513636\ (\$/£)$

Hence, the synthetic forward rate (see above) is $SF = \mathbf{1.50}\ (\$/£)$

This implies that the treasurer can *receive* $150 and has to *pay out* £100 (both at $t = 1$).

Since $SF > F$ (i.e. 1.50 > 1.40 ($/£)), the Treasurer wants to receive sterling from bank M in the actual forward market and will have to pay out $1.40 per pound in one years time, but via the synthetic money market route she can borrow sterling today, invest in the US and will receive $1.50 per pound sterling. The details are as follows.

Arbitrage strategy for corporate treasurer:

- Enter a *forward contract* to receive £100 at $t = 1$ and pay out $140 to bank M.
- Create a synthetic forward by:
  - Borrowing £90.09 in the UK money market at $t = 0$ (i.e. *owe £100 at t = 1*).
  - Convert £90.09 into $136.36 at the spot rate at $t = 0$.
  - Lend $136.36 in the US money market and *receive $150 at t = 1*.

Hence:

  Risk-free profit for corporate treasurer = $150 − $140 = $10

As we shall see below, this also means that bank M, which quoted $F = 1.40 (\$/£)$, will be losing $10 on the deal and would go bankrupt pretty quickly (since the illustrative $10 profit for the corporate treasurer is risk-free and could easily be $1bn and emulated by other corporate treasurers). Given this risk-free profit opportunity, everyone (except bank M) would try to implement this strategy, but this would result in:

- Borrowing in the sterling money market which raises r_{UK} while lending dollars causes downward pressure on r_{US}.
- Buying dollars spot and the dollar appreciates (i.e. S ($/£$) and *SF falls*).
- Selling forward dollars and buying sterling, so forward sterling appreciates (i.e. F ($\$/£$) rises).

The above scenario tends to increase F and lower SF, hence bringing them into equality. If this happens quickly because the transactions involved are all simultaneous, CIP will hold at all times. Later in this chapter we examine whether such arbitrage opportunities exist in the real world, when we also take into account bid–ask spreads and other transaction costs of creating the synthetic forward.

It is sometimes useful to express the CIP condition in linear form by taking logarithms of equation [5]:

$$f - s = r_d - r_f \tag{11}$$

where $f = \ln F$, the logarithm of the forward *price,* and similarly $s = \ln S$ and we have used the approximation $\ln(1 + r) = r$, where r is measured as a decimal. (Alternatively, equation [11] is exact if we use continuously compounded interest rates.)

18.4 HEDGING AND SPECULATION

Long hedge

Suppose a US importer on 1 April will, in six months' time (on 1 October), have *to pay* SFr 500,000 (Swiss francs) for imports from Switzerland. She has a liability in Swiss francs and hence is short Swiss francs. The US importer fears a strengthening of the Swiss franc against the US dollar. If the Swiss franc appreciates (i.e. the dollar depreciates) over the next six months then she *will have to pay out more dollars* (than at the current spot rate). To hedge this position she takes a long position in a Swiss franc forward contract. If the quoted forward rate for delivery on 1 October is $F_0 = 0.6620$ ($/SFr) then she knows today that she will have to pay $331,000 on that day. She has removed the uncertainty. The same principle would apply for a US investor who had other types of Swiss franc liabilities (e.g. had issued SFr bonds or had a bank loan denominated in Swiss francs) and was facing coupon (or bank interest) payments in the future.

Short hedge

An example of a short hedge using a forward contract requires the US resident to have a long position in the cash market. The latter might arise if on 1 April a US multinational expects *to receive* Swiss franc payments on 1 October either from sales of goods in Switzerland or from Swiss investments. Hence the US multinational is long Swiss francs in the cash market and may fear a fall in the Swiss franc, thus receiving fewer US dollars in the future. The US exporter or investor would hedge by selling Swiss francs in the forward market.

Ex post, whether it was better to hedge or not depends on the spot rate on 1 October relative to the forward rate $F_0 = 0.6620$ ($/SFr) that she has locked into on 1 April. Suppose the Swiss franc depreciates (i.e. the US dollar appreciates), so the spot rate in October is $S_T = 0.6600$ ($/SFr). With hindsight, for the US importer it would have been better not to have hedged, since she can obtain more Swiss francs per US dollar in the spot market S_T (relative to the forward market F_0). But the crucial point here is that the spot rate for October is not known in April. If you choose to hedge then you remove risk, so you forgo any potential gains or losses that might accrue if you do not hedge.

Speculation

Now consider the US dollar–pound sterling exchange rate. Suppose the current (1 April) quoted forward rate is $F_0 = 1.50$ ($/£) for delivery on 1 October. Suppose on 1 April you believe that the spot rate on 1 October will be $S_T = 1.52$ ($/£). Hence, you believe that sterling will be worth more in the spot market in October than indicated by the current forward rate. You therefore want to sell sterling in the spot market in October and buy sterling in the forward market. If your guess about S_T turns out to be correct then you can make a speculative profit.

Today 1 April

- *Agree* to receive £1 forward and to supply (sell) $1.50 on 1 October then:

1 October

- In the spot market, pay out £1 and receive $S_T = 1.52$ US dollars and also
- Receive £1 from the forward deal and pay out $F_0 = 1.50$ US dollars.
- Profit $= \$1.52 - \$1.50 = \$0.02$ per £1.

If the principal amount in the transaction is $Q = £100,000$ then:

$$\text{Total \$ profit} = \$(S_T - F_0)Q = \$2000 \qquad [12]$$

Note that this is a highly risky transaction, since if the spot rate on 1 October is below 1.50 (\$/£), the speculator will make a loss (which could be very large). This is also a levered transaction, since the speculator uses none of her own funds on 1 April or on the round-trip transaction on 1 October.

Testing covered interest parity

Let us consider whether it is possible, in practice, to earn risk-free profits via covered interest arbitrage. In the real world the distinction between bid and offer rates for interest rates and forward and spot rates is important when assessing potential profit opportunities. In the strictest definition, an arbitrage transaction requires no capital: the agent borrows the funds. Consider a UK investor who borrows £A in the Eurosterling market at an offer rate $r_{£,o}$. At the end of the period the cost in sterling, C will be:

$$\text{Cost} \quad C = A\left[1 + r_{£,o}\left(\frac{D}{365}\right)\right] \qquad [13]$$

where A = amount borrowed (£s), C = amount owed at the end of the period (£s), $r_{£,o}$ = offer rate on a Eurosterling loan, D = number of days for which the funds are borrowed and the UK day count convention is to use 365 days for 1 year. Now consider the following set of transactions. The investor takes his £A and buys US dollars from the market maker at the offer rate, S_o (£/\$). He invests these dollars in a Eurodollar deposit that pays the bid rate, $r_{\$b}$. He simultaneously sells the US dollars forward at a rate F_b (on the bid side). All these transactions take place instantaneously. The amount of sterling he will receive with certainty at the end of D days is given by:

$$\text{Sterling receipts} \quad SR = \frac{AF_b\left[1 + r_{\$,b}\left(\dfrac{D}{360}\right)\right]}{S_o} \qquad [14]$$

Note that day count convention in the US is to define 1 year as 360 days. The *percentage excess return* (*ER*) to investing £A in US assets and switching them back into sterling using the forward market is therefore given by:

$$ER(£ \rightarrow \$) = 100(SR - C)/A \qquad [15]$$

$$= \left[\frac{F_b}{S_o}(1 + \$r_bD/360) - (1 + £r_oD/365)\right] \times 100\%$$

Now look at the covered arbitrage transaction from the point of view of a US resident. She moves out of dollars into sterling assets at the spot rate, invests in the UK and switches the sterling back into dollars at the current forward rate. This must be compared with the rate of return she can obtain by investing in dollar-denominated assets in the US. A similar formula to that given above ensues and is given by:

$$ ER(\$ \rightarrow \pounds) \left[\frac{S_b}{F_o} \left(1 + r_{\$,b} \left(\frac{D}{365} \right) \right) - \left(1 + r_{\$,o} \left(\frac{D}{360} \right) \right) \right] \times 100\% \qquad [16] $$

Given risk-free arbitrage, one would expect $ER(\pounds \rightarrow \$)$ and $ER(\$ \rightarrow \pounds)$ to both equal zero. Covered arbitrage involves no 'price risk', the only risk is credit risk due to failure of the counterparty to provide either the interest income or deliver the forward currency. If we are to test the CIP hypothesis adequately we need to obtain absolutely simultaneous dealing quotes on the spot and forward rates and the two interest rates. There have been many studies looking at possible profitable opportunities due to covered interest arbitrage, but not all use simultaneous dealing rates. However, Taylor (1987, 1989) has looked at the CIP relationship in periods of 'tranquillity' and 'turbulence' in the foreign exchange market and he uses simultaneous quotes provided by foreign exchange and money-market brokers. We will therefore focus on these studies. The rates used by Taylor represent firm offers to buy and sell and as such they ought to represent the best rates (highest bid, lowest offer) available in the market, at any point in time. In contrast, rates quoted on the Reuters screen are normally 'for information only' and may not be actual trading rates. Taylor uses Eurocurrency rates and these have very little credit counterparty risk and therefore differ only in respect of their currency of denomination.

Taylor also considers brokerage fees and recalculates the above returns under the assumption that brokerage fees on Eurocurrency transactions represent about 1/50 of 1%. For example, the percent interest cost in borrowing Eurodollars taking account of brokerage charges is $r_{\$,o} + (1/50)$, while the rate earned on any Eurodollar deposits is reduced by a similar amount $r_{\$,b} - (1/50)$. Taylor estimates that brokerage fees on spot and forward transactions are so small that they can be ignored.

In his 1987 study, Taylor looked at data collected every 10 minutes on the trading days of 11, 12 and 13 November 1985. This yielded 3500 potential arbitrage opportunities and he found that after allowing for brokerage costs there were no profitable covered arbitrage opportunities. The results therefore strongly support covered interest parity. In his second study, Taylor (1989) re-examined the same covered interest arbitrage relationships, but this time in periods of turbulence in the FOREX market. The historical periods chosen were the November 1967 devaluation of sterling, the June 1972 flotation of sterling, as well as some periods around the General Elections in both the UK and the US in the 1980s. The covered interest arbitrage returns were calculated for maturities of 1, 2, 3, 6 and 12 months. The general thrust of the results is as follows:

- In periods of turbulence there were some profitable opportunities to be made.
- The size of the profits tends to be smaller in the floating-rate period than in the fixed-rate period of the 1960s, and became smaller as participants gained experience of floating rates, post-1972.

- The frequency, size and persistence over successive time periods of profitable arbitrage opportunities increase as the time to maturity of the contract is lengthened. That is to say, there tends to be larger and more frequent profit opportunities when considering a 12-month covered arbitrage transaction than when considering a 1-month transaction.

Let us take a specific example. In November 1967, £1m arbitraged into dollars would have produced only £473 profit. However, just after the devaluation of sterling (i.e. a period of turbulence) there were sizeable risk-free returns of about £4000 and £8000 on risk-free arbitrage at the 3-month and 6-month maturities, respectively. Capital controls (on UK sterling outflows) that were in force in the 1960s cannot account for these results, since Eurosterling deposits/loans were not subject to such controls. Clearly, the market is not always perfectly efficient, in that risk-free profitable opportunities are not immediately arbitraged away. In periods of turbulence, returns are relatively large and sometimes persist over a number of days at the long end of the maturity spectrum, while at the short end of the maturity spectrum profits are much smaller.

The reason for small yet persistent returns over a one-month horizon may well be due to the fact that the opportunity cost of traders' time is positive. There may not be enough traders in the market who think it is worth their time and effort to take advantage of very small profit opportunities. Given the constraint of how much time they can devote to one particular segment of the market, they may prefer to investigate and execute trades with larger expected returns, even if the latter are risky (e.g. speculation on the future spot rate by taking positions in specific currencies).

The risk-free returns available at the longer end of the market are quite large and represent a clear violation of market efficiency. Taylor puts forward several hypotheses as to why this may occur, all of which are basically due to limitations on the credit positions that dealers can take in the foreign exchange market. Market makers are generally not free to deal in any amount with any counterparty they choose. Usually the management of a bank will stipulate which other banks it is willing to trade with (i.e. engage in credit risk), together with the maximum size of liabilities that the management of the bank consider it is prudent to have outstanding with any other bank, at any point in time. Hence there is a kind of liquidity constraint on covered arbitrage. Once the credit limit is 'full', no further business can be conducted with that bank (until outstanding liabilities have been unwound). This tends to create a preference for covered arbitrage at the short end of the market, since funds are 'freed up' relatively frequently.

Banks are also often unwilling to allow their foreign exchange dealers to borrow substantial amounts from other banks at long maturities (e.g. one year). For example, consider a UK foreign exchange dealer who borrows a large amount of dollars from a New York bank for covered arbitrage transactions over an annual period. If the UK bank wants dollar loans from this same New York bank for its business customers, it may be thwarted from doing so because it has reached its credit limits with the New York bank. If so, foreign-exchange dealers will retain a certain degree of slackness in their credit limits with other banks, and this may limit covered arbitrage at the longer end of the maturity spectrum.

Taylor also notes that some of the larger banks are willing to pay up to 1/16 of 1% above the market rate for Eurodollar deposits as long as these are in blocks of over $100m. They do so

TABLE 18.3: Covered arbitrage (% excess returns)

Test date	1 month		6 months		1 year	
	($£ \rightarrow \$$)	($\$ \rightarrow £$)	($£ \rightarrow \$$)	($\$ \rightarrow £$)	($£ \rightarrow \$$)	($\$ \rightarrow £$)
Monday 8/6/87 (12 noon)	−0.043	−0.016	−0.097	−0.035	−0.117	−0.162
Tuesday 9/6/87 (12 noon)	−0.075	−0.064	−0.247	0.032	−0.192	0.15

Source: Taylor, *Economic Journal* 1989, copyright Blackwell Publishing.

largely in order to save on the 'transaction costs' of the time and effort of bank staff. Hence, Taylor recognises that there may be some mismeasurement in the Eurodollar rates he uses, and thus profitable opportunities may be more or less than those found in his study.

Taylor finds relatively large covered arbitrage returns in the fixed exchange rate period of the 1960s; however, in the floating exchange rate period these were far less frequent and much smaller. For example, in Table 18.3 we see that in 1987 there were effectively no profitable opportunities in the 1-month maturities from sterling to dollars. However, at the 1-year maturity there are risk-free arbitrage opportunities from dollars into sterling on both the Monday and Tuesday. Here $1m would yield a profit of around $1,500 at the 1-year maturity.

Taylor's study does not take account of any differential taxation on interest receipts from domestic and foreign investments, and this may also account for the existence of persistent profitable covered arbitrage at maturities of 1 year. It is unlikely that market participants are influenced by the perceived relative risks of default between, say, Eurosterling and Eurodollar investments, and hence this is unlikely to account for arbitrage profits even at the 1-year maturities. Note that one cannot adequately test CIP between assets with different risk characteristics (either 'market price risk' or 'credit risk'). For example, studies that compare covered transactions between Eurosterling deposits and US corporate bonds are unlikely to be very informative about market efficiency in the forward market. Hence our overall conclusion is:

> Risk-free arbitrage opportunities in the FOREX market sometimes do appear at relatively long horizons (1 year), but for the most part there are no large persistent profitable opportunities and covered interest parity holds.

18.5 UNCOVERED INTEREST PARITY

Uncovered interest parity (UIP) is another arbitrage relationship – but this time *risky* arbitrage is involved (or speculation based on fundamentals, if you prefer). To see what is involved here, return to our analysis of the UK corporate treasurer (the 'domestic' investor) who is considering whether it is more profitable to invest in the UK or in the US for one year. But this time assume that the UK investor (rather than using the forward market) is willing to make a forecast today (at time *t*) of what she thinks the spot rate will be in one years time,

E_tS_1. (S is measured in domestic per unit of foreign currency, £/$.) The UK investor is therefore acting as a *speculator* since she does not know what the exchange rate will be in one years time – so investing in the US involves exchange-rate risk. However, UIP assumes that although the UK investor knows there is exchange-rate risk, she ignores this risk when making her investment decisions – she is said to be **risk neutral** and is only concerned with the *forecast (or expected)* return from the US investment.

UIP asks the question: 'What is the relationship between the spot rate and *interest rates* in the two countries (today) and the *forecast* spot rate (for the end of the year) that will just make a UK investor indifferent as to which country she invests her money in?' The simplest way to present the UIP result is:

Interest rate in the UK = Interest rate in US + Expected % appreciation of USD

For a UK investor, the return to investing in a bank deposit in the US is made up of two elements: the interest rate in the US bank (which is known with certainty), plus the return from any *appreciation* in the US dollar over the year. Appreciation of the US dollar implies that the UK investor can obtain more pounds when she cashes in her dollar deposit at the end of the year. If UK interest rates are 12% and US interest rates are 10%, a UK investor would have to expect the US dollar to appreciate by 2% against sterling in order to be indifferent between investing in a UK or US bank deposit. Note that an appreciation of the US dollar by 2% is equivalent to a depreciation of sterling by 2% and then we can express the above relationship in an equivalent way:

Expected depreciation of UK (domestic) currency

= interest rate in UK (domestic) − interest rate in US (foreign)

Another interpretation of UIP is therefore that countries with high current interest rates (relative to another country) should, *on average,* experience a depreciating exchange rate. The difference in interest rates is the *interest differential.* The interest differential in favour of the UK is 2% p.a. and, according to UIP, the *expected* depreciation of sterling should also be 2% over the coming year.

Let us examine the UIP condition in a little more detail. Suppose interest rates in the UK and US are both currently 10%. Assume now that the Bank of England announces an *unexpected* 2% rise in UK interest rates. There is now a 2% interest differential in favour of the UK. Assume for the moment that FX dealers believe that the spot rate for sterling will remain constant over the next year (i.e. zero expected depreciation of sterling). Then US investors would all want to invest in the UK. This is because they get a 2% higher interest rate in the UK than in the US and because they do not expect the exchange rate to change, this translates into an *expected* 2% higher return *in dollars* when they switch their funds back to the US at the end of the year. Hence UIP does not at present hold, and there would be many US investors switching out of US bank deposits and into UK bank deposits.

What has to happen so that US investors will no longer wish to switch funds into the UK? To cut to the chase, suppose (for whatever reason) that US investors now expect a depreciation of sterling over the next year of 2% (this just equals the interest differential in favour of sterling bank deposits). Now the 2% extra interest they get from UK banks (relative to US banks) at the end of the year will just be offset by the 2% less dollars they *expect to get* at the end of the year because of their forecast of a 2% depreciation of sterling. They now have no incentive to switch from US bank deposits to UK bank deposits and this is because UIP has been restored.

We can push this story a little further. What will happen to the spot exchange rate *today,* after an unanticipated increase in UK interest rates by 2%, if UIP holds? If US investors initially think that the exchange rate will remain unchanged, they will wish to invest in UK bank deposits. To do so they will sell US dollars and purchase spot sterling and this would cause sterling to appreciate *today.* How high will spot sterling rise? Well, the only thing that will stop US dealers buying spot sterling today is if they think they lose out when they convert their sterling into US dollars at *the end of the year.* If spot sterling *today* rises so high that FX dealers believe that *over the next year* it can only fall, they will not invest in the UK today, since when their sterling is converted back into dollars at the *end-year* spot rate, they will receive less dollars. If spot sterling *today* rises so high that US investors expect that *over the coming year* sterling will fall by 2%, this will just wipe out their extra 2% sterling interest payments and they will stop switching funds into the UK.

Note the paradox here. For UIP to hold spot sterling *today* must *rise,* so that dealers *expect a fall* (depreciation) of sterling in the future. So UIP predicts that an *unexpected* rise in UK interest rates will lead to an immediate *appreciation* of sterling.

Looked at another way, UIP infers that if there is currently a 2% interest rate differential in favour of the UK, this implies that (risk-neutral) FX dealers believe that sterling will depreciate by 2% over the coming year. Of course, this is nothing more than FX dealers' 'best guess' of what will happen. The interest differential may give the *best forecast* for the future path of the exchange rate, but it still may be a very inaccurate forecast (although less inaccurate than any other possible forecast). What will actually happen to the spot FX rate over the coming year will depend on a whole host of economic 'shocks' in the two countries over the year ahead (e.g. fiscal policy changes, inflation etc.), so actual exchange rate changes will be far more volatile and uncertain than the *forecast* given by UIP and the interest differential.

You can see that the 'big assumption' behind UIP is that most FX dealers (and investors) are risk neutral. If you are gambling with other people's money (as is the case with most FX speculation), then the assumption that you 'play to win the highest return' and pay no attention to the very high risks involved may be fairly close to the truth and UIP might hold in practice. Also remember that we have assumed a one-year horizon, but in principle UIP applies to any investment horizon and at short horizons (e.g. one-day investments) UIP may certainly hold.

Let's now have a quick look at some equations. UIP is about investing in two different countries where the return is uncertain because you have to forecast the spot rate $E_t S_1$ in one year's time, whereas with CIP you 'lock in' the exchange rate by using today's (one-year) forward rate, F. It should therefore come as no surprise that the only algebraic difference between the UIP and CIP conditions is that for UIP $E_t S_1$ replaces the forward rate F used in the CIP relationships – hence UIP can be expressed in the following equivalent ways:

$$\frac{E_t S_1}{S_0} = \frac{1 + r_d}{1 + r_f}$$
[17]

or

$$\frac{E_t S_1 - S_0}{S_0} = \frac{r_d - r_f}{1 + r_f}$$
[18a]

or

$$\frac{E_t S_1 - S_0}{S_0} \approx r_d - r_f$$
[18b]

Equation [18b] holds as an approximation if r_f is small and hence $1/(1 + r_f) \approx 1$, and is the algebraic representation of 'expected depreciation of the domestic currency equals the interest differential'.

Note that the UIP condition assumes that the market is *dominated* (at the margin) by risk-neutral speculators. Put another way, it is assumed that neither *risk-averse* 'rational speculators' nor 'irrational' *noise traders* (who follow 'trends' and may induce herding behaviour) influence movements in the spot rate. We certainly cannot rule out that at certain times noise traders may have an influence on the spot rate; see Chapters 15 and 17.

Yen carry trade

It's about time you became a novice FX trader. In 2007 one of the major plays in the FX market was the yen 'carry trade'. This trade is based on UIP *not being true!* But let's first remind ourselves of what UIP implies. If Japanese interest rates are very low, say around 1% p.a., while US rates are high at around 5%, then at first sight it looks as if it is worth borrowing today from Japanese banks at 1%, immediately selling yen in the spot market in exchange for US dollars, and investing for a year in US bank deposits. If there is no change in the yen–US dollar spot rate over the year, then at the end of the year you will end up with a profit (in yen, which also implies a profit in US dollars) of 4%. For example, if you borrowed ¥121 today at the Japanese interest rate of 1% p.a. and then switched into US dollars at the spot rate 121¥/$, you obtain $1. You immediately invest $1 in a US bank deposit at 5%, giving you $1.05 at the end of the year, which when switched back to yen at the *unchanged* exchange rate of 121¥/$ gives you ¥127.05 at the end of the year. However, you owe the Japanese bank ¥122.21 (= 121 × 1.01), so your overall profit is ¥4.84 (= 127.05 − 122.21), which, if you wish, you can switch into US dollars, giving you 4 cents profit. The return on your investment is of course equal to the interest differential of 4% between the US and Japan (= 4.84/121). Here UIP is violated, as the interest differential does not equal the (expected) change in the exchange rate. If the US dollar had *appreciated* over the year (again violating UIP), you would have made even more money from your carry trade. However, if there had been a *depreciation* of the US dollar of 4% (i.e. 4% appreciation of the yen), UIP would hold and you would have made nothing from the carry trade. The exchange rate at the end of the year would then have been 116.16¥/$ (= 121 × 0.96). So, your $105 from the US bank would now only get you ¥121.96 (= 105 × 116.16), which is just about what you owe the Japanese bank (= ¥122.21) on your loan at the end of the year. (The slight discrepancy between the figures is because we have used the *approximation* for UIP; had we used equation [18a] then the two figures would be the same.)

Note that UIP does not say that in a *particular year* you cannot make (or lose) some money in the carry trade; what it says is that over a run of bets you will not make money *on average*. What are the risks in the carry trade? There is no risk (of default or 'price risk') from lending and borrowing, since this is done with large banks and at known Euroyen and Eurodollar rates – of course you will have to use the correct bid or ask rates. The risk is solely due to exchange-rate changes (volatility).

The above example demonstrates the key points, but no self-respecting carry trade speculator will tie up her lines of credit or hold a position for a whole year. But remember, there are one-day, one-week, one-month etc. interest rates on which you can borrow or lend and you will then be speculating over short horizons. Let's assume that you 'place your bets' over a one-week horizon but you do this every (working) day, so over one year you can place around 252 bets on any particular carry trade, each of which will be closed out after one week. You could also bet on any two currencies, so every day you could place a (one-week) carry trade on yen–US dollar, yen–pound sterling, yen–Australian dollar and so on – as long as there are liquid eurocurrency markets and spot FX markets then you are in business. Using carry trades on many currencies also provides you with a *portfolio of bets* at any one time, so you get some diversification benefits from reduced risk; when the yen–US dollar carry trade loses, it may be that the yen–Australian dollar carry trade shows a profit. (Note that the latter is an important *practical point*, but UIP actually assumes that risk does not influence what bets you place – you are only concerned about the expected returns on your bets.)

It is worth noting that you could 'get lucky' with your carry trades. UIP does not rule out you making profits on the trade over several consecutive weeks – 'randomness' does not rule out a run of positive movements in the exchange rate, in the same way that you can get 10 heads in a row even thought the coin flip is fair. You have to place a lot of bets to test whether UIP is violated. Another point to note is that over repeated bets you may make small gains and small losses, but your cumulative gains over, say, 52 weekly bets might be quite substantial, even if exchange-rate changes are random and you have no ability to predict them. The danger then is that the exchange rate experiences what we call a 'jump'; that is, in the case of the yen–dollar carry trade suddenly the dollar depreciates by a very large amount against the yen and you experience very large losses in one or two weeks, losses that completely 'wipe you out'. This is the '1000-year storm', but in financial market such storms are often more frequent than traders realise. Anyway, if all traders lose over this crisis period they may still retain their jobs, because nearly everyone else loses too. Finally, note that the yen–dollar carry trade might be 'self-reinforcing' if enough traders slowly catch on to the trade – this is because they are all selling spot yen and buying spot dollars and that in itself may lead to a rise in the dollar–yen rate, thus increasing profits for those carry traders who got in early. However, any effect of this kind is likely to be small (given the overall transactions in the FX market) and must eventually dissipate as everyone who wants a carry trade will eventually obtain one – then the fun might start as the yen begins to falter and depreciates against the US dollar. To see what actually happened over 2006–07 in the yen carry trade, see Case Study 18.1.

> **CASE STUDY 18.1   YING AND YEN**
>
> In late 2006 and early 2007, numerous hedge funds started borrowing in yen when Japanese interest rates were close to zero (less than 1%). Short-term interest rates in the US in 2006–07 were averaging about 4.8% and reached levels of 5.2% in early 2007, which meant there was an interest-rate differential of well over 4% in favour of the US. UIP would imply that the US dollar was expected to depreciate by about 4–5%. However, with the US dollar almost at an all-time low, many speculators were hoping that the dollar would not depreciate by that much. Many economic factors other than interest rates affect exchange rates and a depreciation over the next 12 months of less than 5% would generate a profit in the yen–dollar carry trade, while profits would be larger if the US dollar appreciated. During 2006–07 the US dollar appreciated by about 1.8%, which made the yen carry trade very profitable – and the volatility of the exchange rate was also low, so that made the trade look not too risky. It was estimated by Japanese officials in early 2007 that borrowing in yen for the carry trade amounted to around $80–160bn. This caused some concern among Central Banks around the world, as an unwinding of these carry trades could lead to a sharp depreciation of the US dollar and a worldwide recession. It could also lead to major volatility in the FOREX markets and this turmoil could easily spill over to other financial markets.
>
> There was some nervousness on financial markets on 1 March 2007 when global stock markets suffered substantial losses following a drop of 9% on the Chinese stock market. Unwinding vast amounts in carry trades was a real possibility after a strengthening of the yen (depreciation of the US dollar) by over 4.5% within a 10-day period at the end of February and beginning of March 2007 – the yen moved from 121.41(Yen/$) on 23 February to 116(Yen/$) on 5 March. Although many carry traders would have lost heavily over this period, it did not cause substantial turmoil in the FX market.
>
> For hedge funds, the number one rule is that 'if the music stops playing you need to have a chair' – that means you have to be the first to unwind your position and bring your funds back to a safe harbour and then work out what is going on, before you place any more 'big bets'.

18.6 PURCHASING POWER PARITY

Purchasing power parity (PPP) can be expressed in a number of equivalent ways. A direct way of stating PPP is to say that over the long term the price of identical items sold in two countries should be the same (when expressed in a common currency). For example, the sterling price of a Harrods' hamper[1] sold in London should equal the price of an equivalent hamper sold by Saks in New York, when the latter is converted to a sterling price. So identical

---

[1] A 'hamper' contains a variety of food items which are put inside a wicker basket and the hamper is then used for picnics in the country or by the sea. A hamper from Harrods and Saks may contain champagne, caviar, pate etc. which is our 'representative' basket of goods. Harrod's motto is 'Everything for everyone everywhere' and as it has also embalmed Sigmund Freud, delivered a baby elephant to Ronald Reagan and has a world renowned food hall, then it should be capable of providing a representative basket of goods.

goods should sell for the same price in different markets – PPP is an arbitrage condition. To keep things even more simple, if applied solely to the US economy it implies that a Lincoln Continental should sell for the same price in New York City as in Washington DC (ignoring transport costs between the two cities). If prices are lower in New York then demand would be relatively high in New York and low in Washington DC. This would cause prices to rise in New York and fall in Washington DC, hence equalising prices. In fact, the threat of a switch in demand would be sufficient for well-informed traders to make sure that prices in the two cities were equal. PPP applies the same arbitrage argument across countries. The only difference is that we must convert prices to a common currency.

If domestic tradeable goods are perfect substitutes for foreign goods and the goods market is 'perfect' (i.e. there are low transaction costs, perfect information, perfectly flexible prices, no artificial or government restrictions on trading etc.), then 'middlemen' or arbitrageurs will act to ensure that the price is equalised in a common currency.

PPP implies:

- The same price in a common currency.
- Price competitiveness (or the 'real exchange rate') is constant.

To show that PPP implies the same price in a common currency, consider the following simple example, where the UK is the domestic country and S is defined as £/$. We take $P_f = \$200$ (e.g. a Saks hamper) and the spot rate $S = 0.5$ (£/$) (or \$2 per £). Hence the UK import price of a Saks hamper (ignoring transport costs) is £100 (= $P_f S =$ \$200 $\times$ 0.5£/$). If PPP holds, then the price of an equivalent hamper in Harrods department store in London will also equal £100, so:

$$P_d = P_f S \qquad\qquad [19]$$

where S = exchange rate (domestic per unit of foreign currency), P_d = domestic price, P_f = foreign price.

How does goods arbitrage restore PPP? For example, if P_d rose to £110 then the equality in [19] would not hold. However, a UK resident would now want to purchase the cheaper Saks hamper. The subsequent purchase of spot dollars would lead to an appreciation of the dollar. Also, the increased demand for Saks hampers and the reduced demand for Harrods hampers would raise P_f and lower P_d. All of these changes would tend to restore price competitiveness and equalise prices in a common currency, thus restoring the equality in [19]. This is the usual perfect competition assumption, here applied to domestic and foreign firms. Absolute equality of prices is known as the **strong form of PPP**.

If goods arbitrage were the only factor influencing the exchange rate, then the exchange rate *should always* obey PPP. Let us define the 'PPP exchange rate' as:

$$S_{ppp} = P_d/P_f \qquad\qquad [20]$$

We can think of the above equation as giving us the value for the exchange rate that will just preserve price competitiveness (i.e. the same price for a Harrods hamper as for a Saks hamper). For example, if a Harrods hamper costs £100 in London and a Saks hamper costs $200 in New York, then S_{ppp} = £100/$200 = 0.5 £/$. The *actual* exchange rate S that would just make you indifferent as to which (identical) hamper you puchased would be $2 per £ (or equivalently S = 0.5(£/$)). If the actual exchange rate S does not equal the PPP exchange rate, one of the currencies will be either over- or undervalued and the price of both of the hampers will be different in a common currency. Again, suppose that P_d = £100 and P_{US} = $200, so that S_{ppp} = £100/$200 = 0.5 £/$. If the actual spot rate is S = 0.55(£/$), then the pound is undervalued since you can get more pounds per dollar than is warranted by the relative prices of 0.5. A US resident can take $200, the price of a Saks hamper, and exchange it for £110 (= $200 × 0.55 $/£), which will enable her to purchase more than one (identical) Harrods hamper.

The *level* of prices in two countries might not be equal because of transport costs or slight mismeasurement of the price and there might be a fixed gap between the sterling import price of US goods (e.g. the Saks hamper) and the UK pound sterling price of an equivalent 'basket' (e.g. the Harrods hamper). When we examine price indices representing a basket of goods in the two countries, differences in composition and measurement problems with the indexes might also mean that the absolute level of prices is not equal. However, if any gap between the two prices (or price indexes) remains fixed over time, then PPP implies that the *inflation rates and the change in the exchange rate in the two countries will be related:*

% depreciation of pound sterling = % inflation rate in the UK − % inflation rate in US

This is the so-called **weak form of PPP**. For example, if the inflation rate in the UK is expected to be 6% p.a. while that in the US is expected to be 4% p.a., to preserve UK price competitiveness the sterling spot rate will have to depreciate by 2% over the coming year (i.e. the US dollar will appreciate by 2%). The 2% higher sterling prices (relative to US prices) at the end of the year would make UK goods (Harrods hamper) too expensive for US citizens if the exchange rate remained unchanged. But if the US dollar appreciates by 2% this means that US citizens can obtain 2% more pounds for every dollar and this effectively lowers the dollar price of UK goods (Harrods hamper), so they are no more expensive than the equivalent US goods (Saks hamper).

There is no causality implied by the PPP relationship per se. Any one of the three variables can be considered as the 'left-hand side' variable. PPP is a relationship that must hold if price competitiveness is to be maintained, but any (or all) of the three variables can change to bring about this equality. Often, however, the PPP condition is used to analyse changes in the exchange rate over the longer term. If PPP holds, the exchange rate should be determined by relative inflation rates:

% depreciation of £ = % UK inflation rate − % US inflation rate

If one country's long-term inflation rate is much higher than that of another country, this is a signal that the high-inflation country is likely to experience a depreciation in its currency (e.g. some Latin American countries in the 1980s, economies in transition in Eastern Europe and Russia in the 1990s). In contrast, one might expect goods arbitrage to work rather imperfectly in moderate inflationary periods in complex industrial economies with a wide variety of heterogeneous tradeable goods. Hence PPP may hold only in the very long run in such economies.

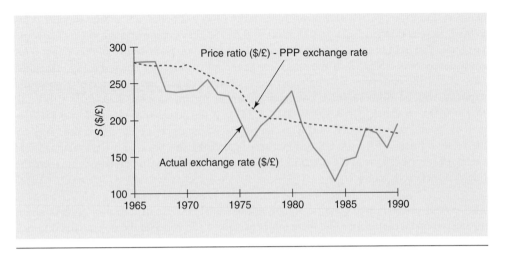

FIGURE 18.3: Actual and PPP exchange rates

There have been a vast number of empirical tests of PPP, but only recent ones use the latest statistical techniques (e.g. cointegration using panel data). We do not have time to examine these studies in detail, but refer the reader to a comprehensive study by Ardeni and Lubian (1991), who examine PPP for a wide range of currencies of industrialised nations (e.g. US, Canada, UK, France, Italy). They find no evidence that relative prices and the exchange rate are linked when using monthly data over the post-1945 period. However, for annual data over the longer time span of 1878–1985 they do find that PPP holds, although deviations from PPP (i.e. changes in price competitiveness) can persist for a considerable time. Hence if we were to plot the PPP exchange rate S_{ppp} against the actual exchange rate S – see equation [20] – then although there is some evidence that S and S_{ppp} move together in the long run (for most currencies), nevertheless they can also deviate substantially from each other over a number of years. It follows that the real exchange rate (i.e. price competitiveness) is far from constant over time spans of several years.

This can clearly be seen in Figure 18.3, where we plot $S_{ppp} = P_{US}/P_{UK}$, the PPP exchange rate against the actual US dollar–sterling spot rate S (USD per £). For example, if we assume (not unreasonably) that just before 1979 the UK was price competitive against the US, $S_{ppp} = S = 2$ ($/£). In 1979 the then Prime Minister, Margaret Thatcher, embarked on a tight monetary policy and raised UK interest rates from 12% to 15%. Over the next few years there was a massive appreciation in the actual exchange rate by over 30%, while the PPP exchange rate (i.e. relative prices) remained largely unchanged. This resulted in a loss of UK competitiveness, a fall in exports and a rise in unemployment. By 1982–83 competitiveness was back at its 1979 level (i.e. $S_{ppp} = S$), but clearly the actual exchange rate can make large and persistent swings away from its PPP level, thus causing persistent changes in competitiveness that are independent of productivity and price changes in the two countries.

The evidence found by Ardeni and Lubian (1991) reflects the difficulties in testing for long-run equilibrium relationships in aggregate economic time series, even with a very long span of data, given measurement problems in forming a representative index of tradeable goods. One's view might therefore be that the forces tending to produce PPP are rather weak, although in the very long term there is a tendency for PPP to hold (see Fisher and Park, 1991; Grilli and Kaminsky 1991). The very long run here could be 5–10 years.

CASE STUDY 18.2 BIGMAC INDEX

A lighthearted suggestion by *The Economist* magazine is that rather than using aggregate price indices (e.g. RPI, CPI), we might examine PPP by looking at the price of a Big Mac burger in different countries. Some of you might remember the minimal research on this topic carried out by Vincent Vega at the beginning of Quentin Tarrantino's film *Pulp Fiction,* where Vincent was explaining to his partner Jules the differences between a Big Mac in the US and in Amsterdam.

Each Big Mac is in a sense a homogeneous basket of goods (e.g. bun, meat, ketchup, gherkin), produced locally in over 100 countries. There are no acute measurement problems here: a Big Mac is a Big Mac wherever you purchase it. In contrast, aggregate price indices cover a whole host of goods and services that may not be perceived as being equivalent in different countries (e.g. a restaurant meal in China, the US and France).

The Economist's BigMac Index demonstrates the strengths and weaknesses of the PPP approach to measuring 'overvalued' and 'undervalued' currencies, which is so vital when choosing an appropriate rate at which to enter a common currency such as the euro or, in the case of China, precisely what level the Renminbi ("people's currency") should be so that Chinese exports are price competitive relative to American goods. How are the figures in Table 18.4 related? If you were a US citizen, where would you visit for an expensive and a cheap Big Mac? Do the figures refute PPP?

Another somewhat lighthearted way of looking at PPP is *The Economist's* BigMac Index (see Case Study 18.2).

Bill Clinton was a well-known devotee of hamburgers and as a result after a gruelling election campaign, he was a little overweight when he became President in 1992. (The American term for a lover of junk food is a 'Bubba'.) So let us find out where 'Bubba Bill' could obtain his lowest-cost hamburger in 2007 – or should he believe that PPP holds at all times so the cost to him is the same wherever he buys his hamburger? First, take the UK relative to the US. Calculate the Big Mac PPP exchange rate and compare it with the actual exchange rate *(S)*:

Big Mac PPP exchange rate $S_{ppp} = \$P/\pounds P = 3.41/1.99 = 1.71$

Actual exchange rate, S $\qquad = 2.01\ (\$/\pounds)$

Percentage difference $= (2.01 - 1.71)/1.71 = +18\%$

In the UK a Big Mac costs £1.99 whereas in the US you would have to pay $3.41. According to PPP, that implies that the exchange rate should be 1.71($/£), but the quoted spot rate is 2.01($/£). If you were Bill Clinton you would not buy your Big Mac in the UK (as it would be cheaper buying them at home in the US). Looked at another way, for a Piccadilly Circus Big Mac, Bill Clinton would have to pay £1.99 $\times$ 2.01($/£) = $4. So instead he will send for a take-out from Georgetown costing $3.41. Actually, if Bill really wants to save money he should go to China, Hong Kong, Russia or Singapore (see Table 18.4) for his Big Mac (ignoring transport costs). In

TABLE 18.4: The BigMac Index 2007

Country	Price in local currency	Implied PPP of the dollar	Actual exchange rate (20.07.07) foreign currency per $	% Over (+) or under (−) valuation of $
Canada	Can $3.88	1.14	1.05	+8
China	Yuan (Renminbi) 11.00	3.23	7.60	−58
Euro Area	€3.06	1.12	1.36	+22
Hong Kong	HK $12.00	3.52	7.82	−55
Russia	Rouble 52	15.2	25.6	−41
Singapore	S $3.95	1.16	1.52	−24
UK	£1.99	1.71	2.01	+18
USA	$3.41	–	–	–

Source: Data taken from 'BigMac Currencies', *The Economist*, 5 July 2007, p. 81. Copyright *The Economist* Newspaper Limited, London.

fact, in 2007 the most expensive Big Macs were to be found in Norway and Iceland, where they were 10% and 123% more expensive than in the US. The cheapest Big Macs could be found in South East Asia, with China being the cheapest place to 'supersize you'.

Of course, there are problems in using the BigMac Index as a measure of competitiveness: transport costs, differences in sales taxes, possible subsidies to cattle farmers and possible differences in profit margins in different countries. Also, one major problem with Table 18.4 is that it is a 'snapshot' at a point in time. Maybe any two Big Mac prices (expressed in a common currency) will move towards equality or at least move up and down together over time. If prices are equalised then PPP would hold and Bill Clinton would pay the same price (in US dollars) for his Big Mac wherever he happens to take his holidays. The reader might like to look at a recent issue of *The Economist* to see whether certain countries in Table 18.4 have come closer to equalising their Big Mac prices.

Forward rate unbiasedness

Does the quoted forward rate have anything to do with the market's view of what the future spot exchange rate will be? It is straightforward to see that if CIP and UIP are both true, this implies that today's forward rate is an unbiased predictor of the *future* spot rate – this is **forward rate unbiasedness (FRU)**. The CIP and UIP relationships are:

$$F/S = (1 + r_d)/(1 + r_f) \quad \text{and} \quad S_{t+1}^e/S_t = (1 + r_d)/(1 + r_f)$$

which implies:

$$F_t = E_t S_{t+1} \tag{21a}$$

or

$$f_t = E_t s_{t+1} \tag{21b}$$

where $f_t = \ln F_t$ and $E_t s_{t+1} = \ln (E_t S_{t+1})$. Tests of the FRU condition usually assume rational expectations (RE), so that the forecast error for the future spot rate ε_{t+1} is zero on average (and independent of any information available at time t):

Forecast error = actual spot rate − forecast of the spot rate

$$\varepsilon_{t+1} = s_{t+1} - E_t s_{t+1} \tag{22}$$

Hence equation [21b] becomes:

$$s_{t+1} = f_t + \varepsilon_{t+1} \tag{23}$$

Initial tests of the FRU condition consisted of a regression of s_{t+1} on f_t where we expect the intercept in this regression to be zero and the slope coefficient to be unity. Unfortunately, even though these tests appeared to support FRU, it was later found that there were statistical problems with the test (because the spot and forward rates are random walks and hence have a 'unit root'; see Cuthbertson and Nitzsche, 2004). To get round this statistical problem we subtract s_t from both sides of equation [23] so an equivalent form of the FRU condition is:

$$s_{t+1} - s_t \quad = \quad f_t - s_t \tag{24}$$

Change in the spot rate = forward premium/discount

When this regression is estimated for almost any pair of bilateral exchange rates, it is found that the regression coefficient on the forward premium is closer to *minus one* than the theoretically expected value of *plus one*. This implies that there is something amiss with either the CIP or UIP condition. Given our observation that CIP holds, it is the UIP condition that appears to be at fault. Either all FX market players do not use RE (i.e. they make systematic under- or overpredictions of the future spot rate) or there is a time-varying risk premium that breaks the risk-neutrality assumption implicit in the UIP condition. There has been a lot of academic blood spilled over the FRU issue, and it is still not resolved. (For other reasons why the FRU condition might break down, see Cuthbertson and Nitzsche, 2004.)

Overview

In the real world one would accept that CIP holds, as here arbitrage is risk-free. One might *tentatively* accept that UIP holds in all time periods, since financial capital is highly mobile and speculators (e.g. FX dealers in large banks) may act as if they are risk neutral (after all, it's not their money they are gambling with, but the bank's). Hence one would then also expect FRU to hold in all periods. However, UIP and FRU do not hold empirically and this is probably because investors are concerned about the riskiness due to exchange-rate changes and this invalidates the risk-neutrality assumption of the UIP (and FRU) relationships.

From what has been said above and one's own casual empiricism about the real world, it would seem highly likely that CIP holds at all times. Agents in the FX market are unlikely to miss any *risk-free* arbitrage opportunities. On UIP one might accept that this is the best *approximation* one can get of behaviour in the spot market, but it is not a very good one. We know that FX dealers take quite large open speculative positions, at least in the main currencies, almost minute by minute. Hence, FX dealers who are 'on the margin' and actively making the market may mimic risk-neutral behaviour. However, this assumption may break down in the frequent crisis periods that occur in the spot market and over reasonably short horizons when the riskiness of uncovered transactions involving the spot exchange rate is quite large.

Given relatively high information and adjustment costs in goods markets, one might expect PPP to hold only over a relatively long time period (say, 5–10 years). Indeed, we know that, in the short run, movements in price competitiveness are substantial.

SUMMARY

- In most spot FX transactions the US dollar is the *vehicle currency*. Rates are usually quoted with respect to the US dollar.
- Cross-currency transactions, for example Brazilian real to Swiss franc, involve going from the Brazilian real to US dollars and then to Swiss francs.
- Currency forwards are OTC contracts that can be designed to fit the client's requirements exactly as to amount, delivery dates and currencies. Currency forwards can be used for hedging and speculation.
- The *forward rate* is determined by *covered interest arbitrage*. This ensures that there are no *risk-free* arbitrage profits to be made by switching between risk-free assets (e.g. bank deposits) in two different countries.
- Forward quotes are usually given in terms of the *forward points (or swap points)* rather than as outright forward quotes.
- *Uncovered interest parity (UIP)* ensures that the *speculative* expected return to investing in a foreign currency equals the return to investing in the domestic currency. The UIP relationship assumes that speculators are risk neutral.
- *Forward rate unbiasedness (FRU)* implies that the quoted forward rate is an unbiased forecast of the future spot rate. Evidence suggests that UIP and FRU do not hold in practice and this may be due to investors requiring compensation for the riskiness of their foreign investments.
- *Purchasing power parity (PPP)* implies that similar goods sold in different countries should sell for the same price (in a common currency).
- Purchasing power parity only holds over a relatively long time periods (say, 5–10 years). Hence under freely floating exchange rates there may be substantial swings in price competitiveness, and this will affect imports and exports and hence result in booms and recessions.

EXERCISES

Q1   You are a market maker (dealer) and the spot rates you are quoting are 1.6000/1.6010 ($ per £). Explain how you can make a profit on a 'round-trip' of 'buy–sell'.

Q2   What are the key differences between the spot and forward FX markets? Can you use both for speculation?

Q3   What are forward points?

Q4   Dealers are quoting the following rates for 'cable' (GBP/USD, base/quoted)

Dealer A	1.5205/15
Dealer B	1.5207/17
Dealer C	1.5200/10
Dealer D	1.5202/12

To which dealer would you sell GBP?
From which dealer would you buy GBP?

Q5   Given the following information:

Spot rate of US dollar and pound sterling is 1.65 ($/£).
3-month UK interest rates are 7.5% per annum (actual/365, day-count basis).
3-month US interest rates are 6% per annum (actual/365 day-count basis).
Assume there are 30 days in each month, then:

a. Calculate the 30-day forward rate and the forward margin.
b. Is sterling at a forward discount or a forward premium?

Q6   A UK firm knows that it will receive $10m in one years time from the sale of goods in the US. Current interest rates are $r_{uk} = 10\%$, $r_{us} = 12\%$ and the spot rate is S $= 1.6$ ($/£).

a. Calculate the forward rate.
b. Explain how the UK firm could hedge this inflow of $10m in one years time by *using the money markets and the spot FX market* (i.e. by not using the forward market directly).

Hint: As the firm will receive $10m in one years time, get the firm to borrow the present value of $10m from a US bank at the US interest rate, immediately switch this into sterling at the spot rate and then lend at the sterling interest rate for one year.

Q7   What is the key difference between uncovered interest parity (UIP) and the covered interest parity (CIP) relationship?

Q8   Suppose that the 1-year spot interest rate in Euroland is $r = 8\%$ p.a. and in the US it is $r^* = 5\%$ p.a. and (rather stupidly) FOREX dealers (who are risk neutral) expect the Euro-USD exchange rate over the next year to remain unchanged. Assume that uncovered interest parity holds.

a. What will happen to the spot exchange rate, *today* and why?
b. At what point will the spot exchange rate stop rising or falling?
c. What are the likely consequences for UK exports and imports in the short term and in the longer term?

Q9   Assume that inflation in Euroland is 5% p.a. and in the US it is 2% p.a. If purchasing power parity (PPP) holds, what is the (approximate) expected change in the exchange rate of the euro over the next year?

Q10   Why might the economy take a long time to achieve PPP?

Q11   The current exchange rate is 1.00 (euros per dollar). The price of Californian wine is $10 (per bottle) and the price of Europlonk is €10 (per bottle). The exchange rate now moves to 0.9 euros per dollar, but the local-currency price of the Californian wine and the Europlonk remain the same. What are the likely consequences for the US economy and the Euroland economy?

PART 6

FIXED-INCOME MARKETS

CHAPTER 19

Money Markets

AIMS

- To demonstrate the relationships between quoted rates of return and prices.
- To explain the use of discount rates, the dollar discount and yield to maturity.
- To discuss the main types of money-market instruments, such as T-bills, banker's acceptances, bank deposits and loans (including the Euromarkets), commercial bills, certificates of deposit and repos.
- To provide an overview of the practical operation of these markets, particularly for the UK and the US.

INTRODUCTION

The money markets provide a means of borrowing and lending on a short-term basis, and the most liquid markets comprise maturities of up to six months. The Central Bank uses the bill market to smooth out daily and weekly cash payments or receipts between the government sector and the private sector. For example, if government expenditure (payments) exceeds tax receipts on a particular day, the Central Bank may sell bills in the market to obtain additional cash. The Central Bank also actively undertakes net purchases (or sales) in the bill market in order to inject or withdraw cash from the banking or private sector. These open-market operations are usually an attempt to influence interest rates, and the money supply.

The money market also facilitates borrowing and lending *within* the private sector. For example, a manufacturing firm that has surplus funds for three months may place them in a term deposit at a commercial bank or alternatively may purchase a 'bill' issued by another firm that is short of cash. There is of course both a thriving new issues market for bills and a highly liquid secondary market. Banks lend and borrow funds from each other in the interbank market, while foreign residents are able to purchase domestic money-market assets. In large markets such as London, one can also purchase money-market assets that are denominated in a foreign currency (e.g. US dollar certificates of deposit purchased in London).

Unfortunately for the student (or embryonic market practitioner), there are a wide variety of conventions used in money markets. One key distinction is whether returns are calculated on a discount basis or a yield basis. For example, suppose I purchase a bill at $98 and its face value (i.e. maturity value) three months later is $100, then we could define the 'dollar discount' as $2 and describe the bill as a 'discount instrument'. It would seem sensible to calculate the percentage return based on the $98 paid for the bill; the 'return' (over three months) would be 0.02048 or 2.0408% $[=(\$100 - \$98)/\$98]$. This method of calculation is referred to as being on a *yield basis*. However, this convention does not apply to the Treasury bill market. The Treasury bill market quotes the percentage return based on the *face value* of $100. Hence the quoted rate in the T-bill market would be 0.02 or 2% $[=(\$100 - \$98)/\$100]$ over three months, and this is known as the *discount rate*. Hence T-bill rates are *quoted* on a 'discount basis' rather than a 'yield basis'.

Another issue that arises is the so-called day count convention, in grossing up the return from, say, three months to an annual return. Common sense suggests using the actual days to maturity. Hence if I purchase a bill on a Tuesday and sell it 33 days later, the maturity period should be 33 (days). Also one might think that a (non-leap) year should amount to 365 days. However, day-count conventions differ both between markets (e.g. US and UK Treasury bills) and between different instruments trading in the same market (e.g. US bills and bonds). Some markets assume that there are 30 days in every month and (only) 360 days in a year! Clearly, these day-count conventions need to be made explicit for the different instruments.

We have noted above that some money-market instruments such as T-bills are sold on a discount basis. Other instruments (e.g. certificates of deposit) earn interest in the conventional manner. That is, you lend $A now at a prearranged interest rate and collect the principal plus interest at the end of the investment period. There is also the question of whether one uses simple interest or compound interest when converting from, say, a three-month rate to an annual rate. In the money markets the 'street' uses simple interest, whereas textbooks tend to emphasise compound (or even continuously compounded) rates. For the practitioner, all these calculations are usually done automatically using in-house software. However, it is still important to understand the conventions being used. There are a tremendous variety of money-market assets and we will only consider a subset. Although we will say a little about the organisation of some of these markets, this is not the central theme of this chapter.

19.1 MONEY-MARKET INSTRUMENTS

In this section we outline the main money-market instruments, including bank deposits, interbank borrowing, Treasury bills, commercial bills and banker's acceptances, certificates of deposit (CDs) and repurchase agreements (repos). We begin with an account of these instruments for the UK and then note any major differences in the US market. As one might expect, similarly named instruments (e.g. Treasury bills, CDs) have similar functions in both the UK and US markets. Generally speaking, key differences are in such matters as day-count conventions and market operations (e.g. differences in new issue procedures).

Prices, discount rates and yields

The principle variables of interest in the purchase of financial assets are the price paid, the maturity value, any interest or coupon payments that may accrue and the dates on which money will change hands. For an instrument with a payment at $t = 0$ and a *single* receipt at time $t > 0$, the important factors are what you pay out, what you receive and the time between the two events. The way you calculate the 'return' is then a matter of convenience (or custom and practice). In short, interest rates are of *secondary* importance, but it is these rates that are quoted when a transaction is agreed and only after this will the other details be sorted out. The quoted interest rates are related to the invoice price paid by simple formulae. There is an arbitrariness about the conventions used 'on the street'; for example the use of simple grossing up from quarterly rates to annual rates rather than using *compound* interest. However, since *all* participants use simple grossing up, this does not create any problems. The markets do not all use the same day-count conventions and possibilities here include:

- Actual/actual: actual days to maturity/actual days in the year.
- Actual/360: actual days to maturity/360 days in a year.
- 30/360: months are assumed to have 30 days and a year is assumed to have 360 days.

Euromarket interest rates

The Euromarket is a market in wholesale bank loans and deposits. A large volume of transactions consists of interbank lending and borrowing, although large corporates are also active in the market. Lending and borrowing can take place in all the major currencies. The origin of the term Euromarket is lending and borrowing the 'home currency' from a bank that is located offshore. So a UK company that borrows US dollars from a US bank in London is taking out a Eurodollar loan. The term 'Euro' does not imply that the loan has to originate from a bank situated in Europe.

Eurodollar deposits (and loans) are quoted on a simple yield basis (i.e. they are 'add-on' rather than discount instruments). The conventions used in calculating interest in the Euromarkets can differ depending on the geographical location or currency in which one undertakes the borrowing and lending. The basis can be either 360 or 365 days in a year. For example, a 365-day basis is used for sterling but nearly all other currencies use a 360-day basis. The day-count convention is usually either **actual/360** or **actual/365**. However, by mutual agreement between the two parties, any basis can be used. For example, a quoted interest rate of 10% p.a. using alternative day-count conventions results in payments of:

- **10% over 90 days on US\$1m (360-day basis):** $0.1\left(\dfrac{90}{360}\right)\$1\,m = \$25{,}000$

- **10% over 90 days on US\$1m (365-day basis):** $0.1\left(\dfrac{90}{365}\right)\$1\,m = \$24{,}657$

Hence 10% p.a. simple interest on a 365-day basis is equivalent to simple interest of $10.139\%\,[=0.1(365/360)]$ on a 360-day basis. There is a further method of calculating interest rates that is used in certain European countries for *domestic deposits* and we refer to this as the **continental** or **30/360 method**. Here each month is treated as if it had 30 days (and hence 360 days make 1 year). For example, consider:

A deal from 4 December to 12 May

4 December–4 May	= 5 months = 5 × 30	= 150 days
4 May–12 May		= 8 days
	Total days	= 158 days
Proportion of 1 year	= 0.4388 (= 158/360)	

The actual number of days between 4 December and 12 May is 159, but this is of no consequence. What is important is the amount paid at the outset of the deal (at $t = 0$) and the amount received at the end (at $t = T$). We can then use whatever measure of return is most convenient (e.g. simple interest, compound or continuously compounded rates).

Euromarket rates on deals less than one year (usually) pay the interest at maturity. For deals over one year, interest is paid annually on the anniversary of the deal, with the final payment on, say, a 2.5-year deal being at maturity. So, a 2.5-year deal from 10 December will pay two interest payments in the following two years on 10 December, followed by a final interest payment (plus repayment of principal) on 10 June. If the anniversary is not a business day, then payment will be rolled forward to the next business day, usually a Monday (providing this does not take you into the next month).

LIBOR and LIBID

LIBOR (London Interbank Offer Rate) is the interest rate at which a first-class bank in London lends out (or offers) funds to another high credit-rated bank in London. If a bank has funds deposited with it, then it pays out interest at the bid rate (LIBID; London Interbank Bid Rate). A 'round trip' for the bank would be to borrow funds at LIBID and on-lend them at LIBOR:

> For the bank to make a 'round-trip' profit: LIBOR > LIBID

The usual way to report bid–ask (offer) quotes differs in different geographical locations. For example:

Quotes in USA: bid/offer $\left(\text{e.g. } 8\frac{1}{4} - \frac{1}{2}\right)$

Quotes in London: offer/bid $\left(\text{e.g. } 8\frac{1}{2} - \frac{1}{4}\right)$

Both quotes mean: I lend at $8\frac{1}{2}\%$ and borrow at $8\frac{1}{4}\%$

In essence, LIBID is the bank's funding cost (at the margin) for subsequent on-lending to, say, a commercial customer. In the language of economics, it is the bank's 'marginal cost of funds' (ignoring reserve requirements and any taxation). The LIBOR rate you actually pay will differ depending on the size of the deal. The rate *quoted* will often be an average of LIBOR rates taken from a sample of reference banks, usually at 11 a.m. London time, under the auspices of the British Bankers' Association (BBA). LIBOR rates are applicable to any 'offshore' currency that banks borrow or lend in London. So, for example, there are Swiss franc, US dollar, yen and so on LIBOR rates quoted in London. The equivalent rates elsewhere are NIBOR or NYBOR (New York), PIBOR (Paris), FIBOR (Frankfurt), MIBOR (Madrid), ADIBOR (Abu Dhabi), SIBOR (Saudi or Singapore) and HKIBOR (Hong Kong).

There is a complex little twist that has arisen in Europe due to the adoption of a common currency (the euro) among (now) 15 countries. You can now get a **euro-LIBOR** quote which is the (average) rate for borrowing the 'offshore' Euro (i.e. from beyond the euro zone's frontiers) from banks in London and it is calculated by the BBA. It is also possible to borrow from banks within the euro zone, based mainly on an average rate determined from a set of banks *within* the members who use the euro. This is known as **Euribor**. This is confusing to say the least and can get a little 'liborious'.

Bank deposits

A deposit placed in a bank from tomorrow and maturing the next business day is referred to as 'tomorrow/next' (or *tom/next*). A Euromarket deposit, unless stated otherwise, will begin on the *spot date*, which will be two business days from the day the trade took place (e.g. over the telephone). The *value date* is the maturity date of the deposit, when interest and any principal are normally repaid.

A *call deposit* is one that is repayable 'at call', which, although this sounds like immediate payment, usually involves payment two working days hence, to give time for the required paperwork to be completed.

An *overnight deposit* is a deposit that is repaid on (or rolled over to) the next *business* day. Within a single time zone this poses no problems. Also, for example, Hong Kong can deal overnight in US dollar deposits since New York is about 13 hours behind, giving plenty of time for Hong Kong to complete the paperwork with New York. In contrast, London cannot easily deal overnight with Frankfurt in euros, since deals have to be completed by 8 a.m. in Frankfurt.

Pricing of pure discount instruments

The formulae outlined below are appropriate for pure discount instruments. These include bills of exchange, bank acceptances, commercial bills and Treasury bills. They are traded at a discount: the market price is below the redemption (or face) value of the bill. For a bill with one year to maturity with a discount rate $d\%$ and face value FV = \$100 the price P is (see Figure 19.1):

$$P = (1 - d/100)100 \qquad\qquad [1]$$

Hence the discount rate (d) is:

$$d = \left(\frac{100 - P}{100}\right)100\% \qquad\qquad [2]$$

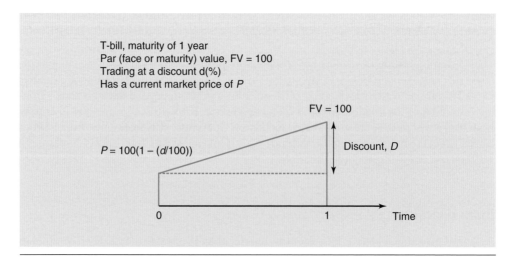

T-bill, maturity of 1 year
Par (face or maturity) value, FV = 100
Trading at a discount d(%)
Has a current market price of P

FV = 100

$P = 100(1 - (d/100))$

Discount, D

0   1   Time

FIGURE 19.1: Discount instruments: 1-year bills

If the bill has less than one year to maturity the *discount rate*, which is the rate quoted 'on the street', is an annualised percentage based on the *face value*:

$$d = \left(\frac{FV - P}{FV}\right)\left(\frac{a}{m}\right)100\%$$ [3]

where d is the discount rate (% per annum), P is the purchase price (per $100 nominal), m is the number of days to maturity, FV is the face value ($100 nominal) and a is the number of days in a year.

If we know the discount rate we can rearrange equation [3] to determine the market price (see Figure 19.2).

$$P = FV\left[1 - \left(\frac{d}{100}\right)\left(\frac{m}{a}\right)\right]$$ [4]

The difference between the face value and the market price paid is referred to as the (dollar or sterling) discount D:

$$D = FV - P$$ [5]

Using equations [4] and [5] we can also express the discount as:

$$D = FV\left(\frac{d}{100}\right)\left(\frac{m}{a}\right)$$ [6]

If we are given the quoted price then it is straightforward to calculate the discount rate and the (sterling) discount (see Table 19.1). 'On the street' market makers quote the discount

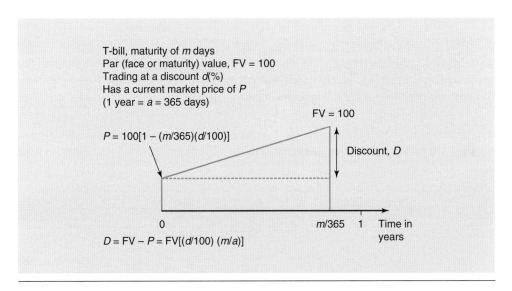

FIGURE 19.2: Discount instruments: bills < 1 year

TABLE 19.1: Discount rate, UK T-bills

Data	UK Treasury bill, day count is actual/365
	91-day bill, face value FV = £1m, market (purchase) price P = £950,000
Questions	Calculate (i) the discount rate d and (ii) the sterling discount D.
Answers	(i) $d = [(£1,000,000 - £950,000)/£1,000,000](365/91)100 = 20.05\%$
	(ii) $D = \text{FV} - P = £1,000,000 - £950,000 = £50,000$

---

rate on T-bills, but using the above formulae one can calculate the current market price (see Table 19.2).

Finally, note that if quotes are discount rates on a 30/360 day count basis, then on 1 April for a maturity date of 1 September, the discount rate (d) is given by:

$$d = [(\text{FV} - P)/\text{FV}](360/150)100 \qquad [7]$$

where 150 is the maturity period based on 30 days per month. The actual number of days to maturity is 153, but this is of no consequence since the participants all use the same convention in this market. Although for T-bills the 'street' quotes discount rates, it is possible to calculate the rate of return on a yield basis for comparison with other instruments.

Yield on a T-bill

The yield y is the sterling discount (FV – P) as an annualised percentage of the *price paid*:

$$y = \left(\frac{\text{FV} - P}{P}\right)\left(\frac{a}{m}\right)100 \qquad [8]$$

So in Table 19.1 the yield on the T-bill is 21.11%, whereas the discount rate is 20.05%. For any discount security the rate on a yield basis always exceeds the rate on a discount basis (because the price paid is always less than the face value).

TABLE 19.2: The discount on UK T-bills

Data	UK Treasury bill, face value £500,000, 80 days to maturity, quoted discount rate 11% p.a.
Questions	Calculate (i) the (sterling) discount D and (ii) the invoice price P.
Answers	(i) $D = (\text{FV} - P) = \text{FV}(d/100)(m/a) = £500,000(11/100)(80/365)$
	$= £12,054.79$
	(ii) $P = (\text{FV} - D) = £487,945.21$

It is easy to manipulate equations [8] and [4] to obtain the relationship between the quoted discount rate d and the return on a yield basis y:

$$y = \left(\frac{d.\text{FV}}{P}\right) = \frac{d}{\left[1 - \left(\dfrac{d}{100}\right)\left(\dfrac{m}{a}\right)\right]} \qquad [9]$$

Yield instruments

For money-market instruments such as a term deposit in a bank (e.g. a Eurodollar deposit or loan) or a certificate of deposit, the 'street quote' is the return on a simple **yield basis**, which is the usual way we think of 'interest'. This is the same formula as equation [8], but we must interpret the final payment as a terminal value (TV). If the initial outlay or principal $P = \$100$, say, is placed on deposit at a yield y *for one year*, then the amount you receive after one year, the terminal value (see Figure 19.3), is:

$$\text{TV} = P\left(1 + \frac{y}{100}\right) \qquad [10]$$

For yield instruments with less than one year to maturity the 'street' uses simple interest to determine the terminal value (see Figure 19.4).

$$\text{TV} = P\left[1 + \left\{\frac{m}{365} \times \frac{y}{100}\right\}\right] \qquad [11]$$

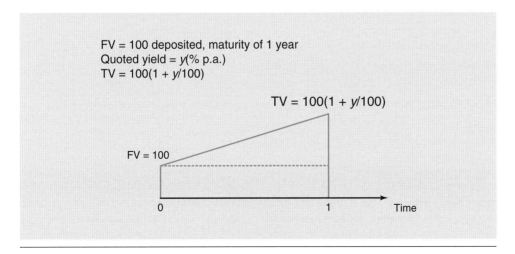

FIGURE 19.3 contents:
FV = 100 deposited, maturity of 1 year
Quoted yield = y(% p.a.)
TV = 100(1 + y/100)

TV = 100(1 + y/100)

FV = 100

0   1   Time

FIGURE 19.3: Yield instruments: 1-year CDs

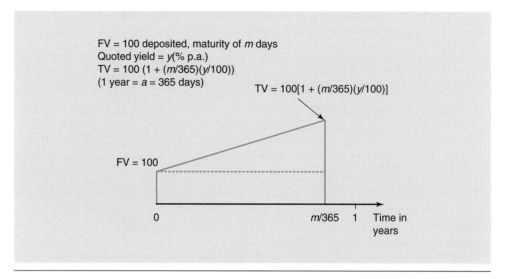

FIGURE 19.4: Yield instruments: deposits < 1 year

Alternatively, if you are promised a payment TV in m days time the amount you would be prepared to pay today (i.e. the current price of the yield instrument) is:

$$P = \frac{TV}{1 + \left(\dfrac{m}{365}\right)\dfrac{y}{100}} \tag{12}$$

It follows that the yield (y) is given by:

$$y = \left(\frac{TV - P}{P}\right)\left(\frac{a}{m}\right)100 \tag{13}$$

which is an equivalent form to equation [8]. Hence the calculated yield on a T-bill and the *quoted yield* (equation [13]) on yield instruments (e.g. bank deposits) are on an equivalent basis.

19.2 UK AND US INSTRUMENTS

UK interbank market

Major banks lend and borrow funds from each other from maturities of one day up to around two years. However, most transactions are for maturities of less than six months. Quotes are on a yield basis and the day-count convention is actual/actual. Banks lend funds at the London Interbank Offer Rate (LIBOR) and pay the London Interbank Bid Rate (LIBID) on funds deposited with them. It follows that in order to make a profit, LIBOR is greater than

LIBID. These two interbank rates provide a reference rate for other (sterling) money-market rates (e.g. for sterling FRNs and for the interest rate applicable on the floating leg of an interest-rate swap).

Sterling floating-rate note, FRN

These are negotiable bearer instruments. A bearer instrument means that the ownership resides with the person who physically holds the asset (in contrast to being on a register, which is held centrally and records changes of ownership). Interest is payable in most cases at three-month intervals and the rate is fixed at a margin over LIBOR for the period concerned.

UK discount instruments

UK Local Authority bills are quoted on a discount basis and issued by local authorities with most maturities for a period of three or six months. Treasury bills are pure discount securities, undertaking to pay a fixed sum on a specified date. In the UK, offers of new T-bills are made on Fridays and may be taken up at any time during the following week. The date of take-up is the *issue date* and most UK bills mature 91 days later. The auction procedure for new issues is very similar to that for US T-bills, which is discussed below.

A **bill of exchange** enables a seller of goods (e.g. a manufacturer) to extend credit to his customer. However, the manufacturer can obtain early payment of the bill by selling it prior to its maturity date. For example, a manufacturer will get his customer to sign the bill saying that he owes the manufacturer £50,000, say. In the UK, bills that have been accepted are also known as 'two-name' paper, since they bear the name of both the drawer (manufacturer) and the acceptor (customer). The manufacturer can then sell (discount) the bill to a bank and obtain funds immediately; in this case the bill of exchange becomes a **bank acceptance**. If the acceptor is not a bank, the bill is a **trade bill**. (When a bill matures, it is normally presented for payment to the acceptor, i.e. the manufacturer's customer.) Calculation of the market price of a bank acceptance, quoted 'on the street' on a discount basis, is given in Table 19.3.

TABLE 19.3: UK bank acceptance

Data	Bank acceptance for £1m face value, with 87 days to maturity, are sold at 12% discount
Questions	Calculate (i) the (sterling) discount and (ii) the price of the security.
Answers	(i) D = discount = £1m(12/100)(87/365) = £28,602.74 (ii) $P = (FV - D)$ = £971,397.26

UK certificates of deposit

Certificates of deposit (CDs) are quoted on a yield basis. A CD is a bearer instrument certifying that a sum of money has been deposited with the bank issuing the certificate, at a fixed yield, and that on the stated maturity date the funds will be repaid by the issuing bank with interest. Interest may accrue on a periodic basis or at maturity. If the CD is negotiable it can be sold in the secondary market, if immediate access to cash is required by the holder of the CD. (Cashing a non-negotiable CD usually involves a withdrawal penalty.) CDs in the UK are often referred to as wholesale deposits because the minimum deposit is large. Other market details for UK CDs are given in Case Study 19.1.

CASE STUDY 19.1   CD MARKET CONVENTIONS

The UK CD market is very liquid and the market conventions are broadly similar to those in other banking centres such as New York, the euro area and the Far East. Key features of the UK market are:

- Units of at least £500,000.
- Minimum/maximum redemption period is 7 days/5 years.
- Interest on 1 year (or less) CDs is paid on maturity.
- Interest on CDs with maturity greater than 1 year is paid annually.
- Quotations ('on the street') are on a yield basis.
- Day-count basis is actual/actual.

The CD is quoted on a simple yield basis, so Figure 19.4 applies when determining the (terminal) value at maturity. The terminal value of a 90-day sterling CD with initial yield y_0 is:

$$TV = FV\left[1 + y_0\left(\frac{90}{365}\right)\right]$$

[14]

However, if the CD was issued some time ago, what is its current price P in the secondary market? This must equal the PV (using simple interest) of the known terminal payment at maturity TV. Suppose the current quoted yield is $y = 11\%$ and the CD has $m = 62$ days to maturity, then the current price can be calculated as in Table 19.4, using the following formula:

$$P_t = \frac{TV}{\left[1 + y_t\left(\frac{m}{365}\right)\right]}$$

TABLE 19.4: Sterling CDs

Data	Quotes are on a (simple) yield basis.
	£1m CD issued at 12.5% for 120 days.
	Now, current yield = 11%.
	Assume CD now has 62 days to maturity.
Question	Calculate the current purchase price of the CD.
Answer	On maturity holder receives $£1m[1 + (12.5/100)(120/365)] = £1,041,095.89$
	Hence price paid 62 days before maturity is the PV at 11%.
	Price paid = $£1,041,095.89/[1 + (11/100)(62/365)] = £1,021,999.99$
Check	Purchase price paid = £1,021,999.89
	Receipt at maturity = £1,041,095.99
	Interest earned = £19,096
	Yield = $(£19,096/£1,021,999.89)(365/62)100 = 11\%$ p.a.

Bid and offer rates

Market makers 'buy low' and 'sell high'. Hence their bid *price* for bills is below the offer *price*. However, in the interbank market banks 'bid' a rate for money (i.e. the *bid rate* is what they pay on money placed on *deposit* with them). Naturally, the banks wish to lend at a higher rate than that at which they borrow, so their offer *rate* (LIBOR) exceeds their bid *rate* (LIBID):

Interbank market:	offer rate, LIBOR > bid rate, LIBID
Bills and CDs:	bid price < offer price
	therefore bid rate > offer rate

US instruments

The quoted rates for US *Treasury bills, bank acceptances and commercial papers* are on a discount basis. The day-count convention is actual/360, so the discount rate–price relationship is given by equation [4] and an example is provided in Table 19.5.

US Treasury bills

US three- and six-month bills are auctioned every Monday, with the amounts to be auctioned usually announced on the previous Tuesday. One-year bills are auctioned in the third week of every month (announced the preceding Friday). When it is temporarily short of cash the

TABLE 19.5: US Treasury bill (price and discount rate)

Data	Price = \$97.912 per \$100 of face value, days to maturity = 182. Day-count convention: actual/360.
Question	Calculate the quoted discount rate.
Answer	$d = [(100 - 97.912)/100](360/182) = 4.13\%$

Treasury issues 'cash-management bills' with maturities to match those of the projected shortfall. The US Treasury auction first involves deducting the total of non-competitive tenders (of up to \$1m for each bid) and non-public purchasers (e.g. the Federal Reserve). Non-competitive tenders are based on quantity (not price) and the price paid is the average price paid by the competitive bidders. The competitive bidders are allocated Treasury bills on the basis of the highest to the lowest bid prices. When the issue is exhausted, allocations are at the 'stop yield' and are in proportion to the quantities tendered. Those bidding at a higher yield (lower price) than the stop yield receive no allocation. The difference between the average yield of all the bids accepted and the stop is called the 'tail'. Note that although bids are submitted on a discount basis, the allocation is based on yields (which can be calculated from the discount rates).

An illustrative result from a Treasury auction is given in Table 19.6. After deducting non-competitive bids and the Fed's allocation, \$7bn is available for competitive bidders. Those who bid at a yield of 6.01% or below (i.e. at a higher price) receive the entire amount for which they bid. This would leave \$0.4bn [\$7bn − \$6.6bn] to be allocated to those who bid

TABLE 19.6: US Treasury auction, T-bills

Total issue	\$10.0bn
Less non-competitive bids	\$0.5bn
Less Federal Reserve	\$2.5bn
Amount for competitive bidders	\$7.0bn

Competitive bids

Amount (\$bn)	Cumulative bids	Bid (yield)
0.5	0.5	5.55
0.7	1.2	5.56
0.8	2	5.57
1	3	5.58
1.1	4.1	5.59
1.2	5.3	6
1.3	6.6	6.01
1.5	8.1	6.02

at 6.02%. Each of these bidders will receive 26.67% [=$0.4bn/$1.5bn] of the amount they bid. The stop yield is therefore 6.02%. The average yield of full-allocation bidders is 5.58% and completely unsuccessful bidders were 'shut out' at higher yields than 6.02%. The tail is therefore 0.44% (=6.02% − 5.58%).

US commercial paper

Commercial paper (CP) is a means of short-term borrowing for large municipalities (i.e. local authorities in the UK) and corporates. It is an alternative to borrowing from banks. In the US commercial paper refers to an unsecured promissory note and differs from a bill of exchange in being a liability of the issuer directly, rather than indirectly via an acceptor. For this reason, US commercial paper is not quite equivalent to the UK commercial bill. CP may be issued on a pure discount basis or may bear interest at maturity (e.g. LIBOR + 1% on a floating-rate basis). Paper of less than 270 days to maturity is a bearer instrument, but for maturity periods of 270 days or more, the paper must be registered (with the Securities and Exchange Commission, SEC). The most common maturity range is 30–50 days or less, since paper with less than 90 days to maturity is eligible collateral for a bank when dealing at the Fed discount window.

Back-up lines of credit are needed to obtain a commercial paper rating. Issuers of commercial paper can increase their rating by using *credit enhancement*; that is finding a highly rated third party who will guarantee repayment if the issuer defaults. This enables smaller, riskier firms to access the commercial paper market by using these enhancements. Firms can also raise their credit ratings by purchasing either *indemnity bonds* from insurance companies or *stand-by letters of credit* from banks. Both of these ensure that the third party will repay the paper if the issuer defaults. The stand-by letter of credit is usually attached to the commercial paper and so the issuer 'rents' the credit rating of the bank. Studies have shown that equity prices respond positively to a commercial paper issue with a stand-by letter of credit attached, but that there is no equity response when the letter of credit is omitted. Hence, the market sees the bank who issues the letter of credit as revealing new information about the creditworthiness of the issuer. The markets therefore have less information than do the banks on credit risk.

CP may be issued to a dealer ('dealer paper') or directly ('direct paper') to the lender. To payoff maturing CP the issuer usually sells a new tranche of CP to other investors. The issuer therefore faces *roll-over risk* and because of this the CP is usually backed by unused lines of bank credit (for which a commitment fee is charged). CP is also rated by the credit-rating agencies. The CP is usually held to maturity, so secondary market activity is relatively small.

US certificates of deposit

As in the UK, CDs are traded on a yield basis, however US CDs use a day count of actual/360. CDs may be negotiable or non-negotiable. For the latter, the funds can only be withdrawn before the maturity date if a withdrawal penalty is paid. Negotiable CDs can be repeatedly sold in the

TABLE 19.7: US certificates of deposit

Data	Notional $1m, 90-day CD with 7% yield.
Question	What are the payments at the end of 90 days?
Answer	Payment = $1m$[1 + (7/100)(90/360)]$ = $1,017,500

open market. Negotiable CDs are usually issued in denominations of $1m or more and have maturities greater than seven days and less than one year. However, some term CDs with maturities greater than one year are also issued. Normal CDs pay interest at maturity, while term CDs pay interest semi-annually. The yield on CDs depends in part on the credit rating of the issuing bank, and their liquidity. CDs that are issued outside the US but denominated in dollars are known as Eurodollar CDs, while Yankee CDs are denominated in dollars but issued by a foreign bank with branches in the US. Table 19.7 shows the calculation of principal plus interest and Table 19.8 demonstrates how the purchase price of a CD in the secondary market is calculated.

Comparing rates

Obviously, in comparing the return on two money-market assets one cannot use a discount rate for one asset and the yield for another. Even when both assets are quoted on a yield basis, one has to ascertain whether they use the same day-count convention. In general, in comparing the rates on assets using different trading rates or day-count bases, you should first convert to prices. The return can then be recalculated on a consistent basis.

To demonstrate how we move from the rates quoted 'on the street' to a measure of return, consider a US T-bill with 90 days to maturity with a quoted *discount rate* of 10% (actual/360) and a 90-day Eurodollar deposit (actual/360) with a quoted *yield* of 10%:

TABLE 19.8: US marketable CDs (purchase price)

Data	Day-count basis: actual/360, quotation is yield basis.
	$5m CD originally issued at 7.25% for 60 days.
	Proposed purchase at 7% yield with 21 days to maturity.
Question	Calculate the purchase price P.
Answer	Except for the day-count basis (and currency), the calculation is the same as for sterling CDs:

$$\text{Price paid} = \$5\,m\frac{[1 + (7.25/100)(60/360)]}{[1 + (7/100)(21/360)]} = \$5,039,837.33$$

In the above calculation we first find the amount payable at the end of 60 days (i.e. principal + interest) and we then discount back to the present using the current yield of 7%.

T-bill

Price of T-bill = \$100 − \$10(90/360)   = **\$97.50** (per \$100 face value)

Dollar interest earned on the T-bill over 90 days   = **\$2.50**

Alternative returns

Simple annual return = $[(\$100/\$97.50) - 1](365/90) = 0.1040$ (**10.40%**)

Compound return = $[(\$100/\$97.50)]^{(365/90)} - 1 = 0.1081$ (**10.81%**)

Continuously compounded return = $(365/90)\ln(\$100/\$97.50) = 0.1027$ (**10.27%**)

Eurodollar deposit

\$97.50 invested in a 90-day Eurodollar deposit gives:

Receipts after 90 days = $\$97.50[1 + 0.10(90/360)]$ = **\$99.94**

Dollar interest earned on the CD over 90 days   = **\$2.44**

Alternative returns

Simple annual return = $[(\$99.94/\$97.50) - 1](365/90) = 0.1015$ (**10.15%**)

Compound return = $[(\$99.94/\$97.50)]^{(365/90)} - 1 = 0.1054$ (**10.54%**)

Continuously compounded return = $(365/90)\ln(\$99.94/\$97.50) = 0.1002$ (**10.02%**)

What is important in the comparison is what you pay, what you receive and the time between receipts and payments. The day-count conventions are merely 'rules' for extracting these three elements. You can then use whatever method of calculating the annual return you feel is most sensible. If we compare each of the alternative returns in turn, we can see that the T-bill always has a higher return (comparing simple, compound or continuously compounded measures). This should be fairly obvious, since the T-bill earns a dollar amount of \$2.50 over 90 days, whereas the CD only earns \$2.44 (both on an initial outlay of \$97.50).

A further question is why the three measures of return give different values. Take for example the Eurodollar deposit. The *simple annual return* assumes that the dollar gains of \$2.44 are not reinvested in subsequent periods, but that only the initial principal of \$97.50 is reinvested each time (if you like, the \$2.44 earned each period is immediately spent). The *(discrete) compound return* assumes that any interest earned (i.e. \$2.44 in the first period) as well as the principal of \$97.50 is reinvested in the second and subsequent periods; that is, one earns interest on interest. In fact both these returns (i.e. simple and compound) are not entirely a realistic measure of what one could actually earn over the year, since when you come to roll over your initial investment, interest rates will have changed. However, they are both a reasonable way of reporting returns on different instruments (on a comparable basis).

The continuously compounded return may be less familiar, but again it gives the right qualitative answer (i.e. the T-bill has a higher return than the Eurodollar deposit). In some respects the continuously compounded return is a little tricky. For example, for the Eurodollar deposit, why is its continuously compounded return of 10.02% less than its discrete compound return of 10.54%? This is because when using the continuously compounded return it is assumed that the interest on interest is earned continuously (e.g. daily) rather than just 4.055 times per year (as with the discrete compound return). Hence, you require a lower continuously compounded return to reach the same end point than you do if interest is only compounded 4.055 times per year.

Repurchase agreement

A repo, or more accurately a 'sale and repurchase agreement', is a form of collateralised borrowing. It is used by market makers (dealers), hedge funds and also by Central Banks when they want to influence the amount of cash (reserves) held by banks. Suppose a market maker wishes to borrow $10m *overnight*. He can agree to sell securities (e.g. T-bills or T-bonds) that he holds to a counterparty (e.g. a broker) for their current market price of $10m, in exchange for $10m cash. He also *simultaneously* agrees to buy back the securities the next day at a price higher than $10m, say ($10m + $1800). This is equivalent to an overnight interest rate of 0.018% or 6.48% p.a. (using an actual/360 day-count convention). In practice, the amount of cash loaned will be *less than* the market value of the securities – this is the 'haircut' demanded by the lender of the funds. If the haircut is 1% then the lender will only supply $9.9m cash when the $10m of bonds are handed over and if the overnight interest rate charged on the $9.9m is 6.48% p.a.; the interest payment is $1782 ($= 0.0648 \times 9.9m/360$). Hence the lender of the funds holds securities that are worth more than the $9.9m. If the borrower defaults, the lender can subsequently sell the securities at their market price one day later and is virtually assured that he will receive from the sales at least $9.9m plus the $1782 interest. Note that in principle any security can be used in a repo, such as a bill, bond or even equities, but the greater the risk of the collateral losing value over the term of the repo loan, the larger will be the haircut. If the borrower of funds is a highly rated credit-worthy institution and provides highly liquid government securities as collateral, then the haircut may be between zero and 0.25% (i.e. $\frac{1}{4}$ of 1%).

When viewed from the perspective of the acquirer of funds, the transaction is a repo. From the point of view of the counterparty, the supplier of funds, it is called a *reverse repo*. Hence:

> Repo = borrowing money by selling a security to a counterparty.
> Reverse repo = lending money by purchasing a security from a counterparty.

Repos provide *leverage*. For example, suppose you wish to purchase $10m worth of T-notes (with five years to maturity). Instead of using your own funds or borrowing money from a bank, you could borrow a proportion of the $10m from your broker, buy the five-year T-notes and deposit these with your broker as collateral for the loan you used to buy the T-notes with in the first place. You then own $10m of T-bonds, but you would have only had to pay, say, $1m of your own cash to your broker as initial margin (i.e. we have assumed that the initial margin is 10% of the total amount borrowed).

One can undertake a reverse repo to cover a short position. For example, if a dealer short sold $20m of T-bills three weeks ago and now has to deliver the T-bills to broker A, he can buy the securities now from broker B and agree to sell them back at a higher (fixed) price at a later date. Broker B is receiving a cash loan (i.e. a repo) from the dealer who is paying for the T-bills and earning interest (i.e. a reverse repo). But the dealer is also obtaining T-bills to replace those from the short position with broker A. Eventually, of course, the dealer would need to buy the T-bills outright in the open market, since the T-bills received in the reverse repo are merely 'on loan'.

There is credit risk in a repo agreement. Even though in the above example the lender of the cash retains the T-bills as collateral, the borrower could fail to repurchase the T-bills at the agreed price. For example, if interest rates have risen overnight, the market value of the T-bills will fall and the borrower might default. Clearly, repos that have a maturity greater than one day have greater credit risk than overnight repos.

The main characteristics of repo agreements in the US are:

- **Maturities:** Short-term, usually overnight to a few days. Some for one, two or three weeks and one, two or three months.
- **Principal:** For short-term maturities (less than one week) usually about $25m or more. Minimum transaction with securities dealers is $1m.
- **Yields:** Typically, sale and repurchase price are equal, with an agreed rate of interest to be paid. The alternative is a repurchase price above the sale price (i.e. an implicit interest rate).

To reduce credit risk exposure in a repo, the seller of T-bills will receive less cash than the market value of the securities. This is called the **initial margin**. The initial margin provides the lender of the cash with a cushion should T-bill prices fall over the term of the repo. Also, the collateral to be paid will be periodically increased if the market value of the T-bills falls below some prearranged level (known as the 'maintenance margin'). This additional 'margin call' is referred to as the 'variation margin' (and is based on 'marking to market' the value of the T-bills or T-bonds). A classic case of a highly leveraged bond position using repos is that of Robert Citron, the Treasurer of Orange County (see Case Study 19.2), who on these and other instruments (known as reverse floating-rate notes, FRNs) lost about $2bn in December 1994 on a notional bond portfolio of about $7bn.

CASE STUDY 19.2 ORANGE COUNTY
(REPOS AND LEVERAGE)

Robert Citron, the Treasurer of Orange County (in California), managed a fund of around $7.7bn but he also borrowed $13bn via the repo market, posting T-bonds as collateral. This gave him considerable leverage and raised his overall exposure to about £20bn (after initial margin calls had been paid). Up to February 1994 all went well, but then US interest rates began to rise and dealers asked for additional margin payments, as the bonds used as collateral in the repos fell in value.

Part of this cash came from a separate $600m bond issue by Orange County, but when its paper losses became known in December 1994, Credit Suisse First Boston refused to roll over $1.25bn of repos. Citron could not meet his margin requirements and Orange County filed for bankruptcy, although many repo brokers had by then sold Citron's bonds held as collateral.

Although it was the *margin calls on the repos* that triggered Citron's collapse, the major losses occurred because of another type of leveraged transaction, known as 'reverse floaters' (i.e. reverse floating-rate notes, FRNs). *Reverse (inverse) floaters* pay out to the holder if interest rates fall. But they also have 'embedded leverage', in that the pay-out formulae involve a multiplier whereby payments or receipts are a multiple of interest-rate changes.

Citron held about $8bn of these leveraged inverse floaters, and with a multiplier of around three this implied an actual exposure of about $24bn. After February 1994 interest rates rose, so Orange County had to pay out on the inverse floaters and this was the major source of its $2bn losses. The purchase of some of these reverse floaters was financed from funds obtained in the repo market.

Ideally, securities in a repo should be delivered to the lender of the funds. However, this can be costly, particularly for short-term repos. Hence, often the borrower is allowed to place the securities (T-bills) in a segregated customer account or custodial account (for the lender) at the borrower's clearing bank. These methods provide some security for the lender, although not as much as actually holding the collateral (i.e. T-bills) himself.

Dealers use the repo market to finance their inventory and to cover short positions. Dealers will also attempt to earn profits by running a matched book, by taking on repos and reverse repos with the same maturity. For example, a dealer may borrow money in a term repo with a money-market fund for five days at a rate of 5.5% and simultaneously enter into a reverse repo with a trader at a (lending) rate of 5.56%. If the collateral in the two deals is the same, then he is locked in a positive spread of 0.06%.

The Federal Reserve can influence interest rates by outright purchases or sales of T-bills. But in general it uses the repo market instead to achieve the same aim. Note that if the Fed sells securities it is not called a repo, but somewhat confusingly a *matched sale*. When it buys securities (i.e. lends funds) it is not referred to as a reverse repo but as a *system repo*.

Federal Funds rate

The Federal Funds rate is not, as the name might suggest, the rate at which banks borrow from the Federal Reserve Board. It is in fact an interbank rate, namely the rate at which US banks borrow and lend from each other.

Depository institutions (i.e. commercial banks and thrifts) have to maintain reserves (which earn no interest) at the Federal Reserve in proportion to their deposits outstanding.

If a commercial bank is short of reserves then it will bid for funds from surplus banks and pay the Federal Funds rate. Most transactions are for overnight funds, but longer-term transactions of up to six months also occur. Commercial banks can also borrow in the repo market and, because the latter is a collateralised loan whereas Federal Funds are not, the Fed Funds rate is usually higher (by about 25 bp) than the repo rate. Usually, as a last resort a bank will borrow from the 'discount window' of the Fed using short-term commercial paper as collateral.

SUMMARY

- There are a wide variety of conventions used in money markets. One key distinction is whether returns are calculated on a *discount basis* (e.g. for T-bills and banker's acceptances) or on a *yield basis* (e.g. bank loans and deposits, commercial bills/paper and CDs).
- The Euromarket is a market in wholesale bank loans and deposits in offshore currencies. A large volume of transactions consists of interbank lending and borrowing, although large corporates are also active in the market. Lending and borrowing can take place in all the major currencies.
- Major banks lend and borrow funds from each other from maturities of one day up to around two years, but most transactions are for maturities of less than six months. Banks in the UK lend funds at the *London Interbank Offer Rate (LIBOR)* and pay the *London Interbank Bid Rate (LIBID)* on funds deposited with them. Hence LIBOR > LIBID.
- A *repo* is a sale and repurchase agreement. It is a form of collateralised borrowing. A repo implies borrowing money by selling a security to a counterparty. A *reverse repo* applies when you are lending money by purchasing a security from a counterparty.
- The *Federal Funds rate* is the rate at which US banks borrow and lend *from each other*. (It is *not* the rate at which banks borrow from the Federal Reserve Board.)

EXERCISES

Q1   Which is higher, LIBOR or LIBID, and why? Which is higher, the bid price or the ask (offer) price on a T-bill?

Q2   What is a repo? Give a simple example of how you calculate the (simple annual) rate of interest (yield) on a 7-day T-bill repo. (Assume the day-count convention is actual/365.)

Q3   A UK T-bill with 60 days to maturity has a face value of FV = £1m and a quoted discount rate of $d = 10\%$ p.a. The day-count convention is actual/365. Calculate:

  (a) The (sterling) discount, D.
  (b) The market price, P.
  (c) The (simple) annual yield, y.

Q4   A 6-month US T-bill was issued some time ago and now has a market price $P = 98 per $100 face value. The number of days left to maturity is now 90. The day-count convention is actual/360. Calculate:

(a) The quoted discount rate, d.
(b) The (simple) annual yield, y.

Q5   A 1-year UK T-bill has a quoted discount rate of 8% p.a. and face value FV = £100. The quoted yield on a 1-year UK CD is 8.5% p.a.

(a) What is the (one-year) holding-period return (HPR) on the T-bill and the CD?
(b) Which gives the highest return (if held to maturity)?

Q6   A UK CD has a *quoted* current yield $y = 10\%$ p.a. and a face value of £1m. It now has 60 days to maturity, but when it was issued it had an original maturity of 120 days and a quoted yield of $y = 12\%$ p.a. The day-count convention is actual/365. Calculate:

(a) The current market price P of the CD.
(b) Whether at this price you will earn 10% over the remaining life of the CD.

Q7   The *continuously compounded* yield on a 180-day CD is 10.3% p.a. On a 180-day T-Bill the yield is 10.4% p.a., but this has been determined using discrete compounding, *every 90 days*. Assuming that both instruments use a day-count convention of actual/360, which one provides the higher return?

Q8   The 7-day repo rate is $r = 6\%$ p.a. (actual/360 day-count convention). What is the interest payable on a 7-day repo for $1m, using bonds as collateral (assume a zero haircut)?

20

Bond Markets

AIMS

- To explain the relationship between various measures of the return on a bond. This includes the definition of *spot rates,* the *yield to maturity* and the *holding period yield*.
- To show that the fair price of a coupon-paying bond is determined by spot rates of interest. Otherwise risk-free arbitrage profits can be made by a strategy known as *coupon stripping*. The yield to maturity is then derived from the price.
- To describe the key features of government bond markets in the UK and US, including price quotes, accrued interest and the *strips and repo markets*.
- To explain the pricing of corporate bonds.

INTRODUCTION

As with money market instruments, there are a wide variety of different types of bond. A conventional government bond usually pays a fixed amount every six months to the holder (known as the coupon) plus the redemption value on a fixed maturity date. However, not all bonds have fixed coupons or fixed maturity dates. For example, some corporate bonds can be redeemed (or 'called') prior to their maturity date, while other corporate bonds (i.e. convertible bonds) can be exchanged for common stock (equity) of the issuer, at some future date. So convertibles have a mixture of payments in terms of coupons and then dividends if converted into equity.

Bonds are usually issued to obtain long-term finance – initial maturities are from 1 year to 30 years (with some being non-redeemable and known as perpetuities or consols). They are issued by governments and their agencies (e.g. Municipal Securities in the US and Local Authority Bonds in the UK) and by the corporate sector. They may be denominated in the home currency of the issuer or in a foreign currency (e.g. a UK corporate issuing dollar-denominated bonds). A key difference between government-issued bonds and those issued by corporates is default risk. Generally speaking, government bonds denominated in the home currency are described as 'risk free', meaning there is no default risk. This is because governments usually have the legal right to print their own currency in order to pay the interest and principal on the bonds. Of course, zero default risk would not necessarily be true for government bonds denominated in a foreign currency, as was the case for countries like Mexico and Argentina, who effectively defaulted on dollar interest payments on their foreign bonds.

In this chapter we first discuss 'risk-free' government bonds, which provides the main analytical concepts for the reader to study the other types of bond mentioned above. We begin with an analysis of the various ways of measuring the return on a bond and the relationship between yields and prices. As with the money market, we shall see that there is a wide range of conventions and terminology. Next, the organisation of the UK and US government bond markets is discussed, including such topics as market makers, settlement procedures, new issues and the use of repos and the strips market. Finally, we present the main types of corporate bond and this is where we discuss convertible and callable bonds.

20.1 PRICES, YIELDS AND RETURN

This section deals with the various definitions of yields and the calculation of bond prices. Unlike the money market, the bond market uses compounding when calculating yields.

After discussing 'zeros', we consider the three main ways in which the return on a coupon-paying bond may be measured: the running (or 'interest') yield, the yield to maturity and the 'total return'. Finally, we demonstrate how we can use risk-free arbitrage to price a coupon-paying bond by considering it as a series of zero-coupon bonds. This allows a consistent methodology for the pricing of bonds and an analysis of the strips market, which concludes this section.

Pure discount/zero-coupon bonds

Bonds that have a single pay-out but have a maturity greater than one year are usually classified as pure discount or zero-coupon bonds. Suppose a pure discount bond has a single payout M in n years time. If we know M and the observed market price P, then we can calculate the current spot rate r using the PV formula:

$$P = \frac{M}{(1 + r)^n} \qquad [1]$$

Hence:

$$r = \left(\frac{M}{P}\right)^{1/n} - 1 \qquad [2]$$

r is known as a spot rate of interest (or spot yield) for maturity date n (see Table 20.1). If we have lots of 'zeros' of different maturities, we can observe their current market prices and calculate spot rates for one year, two years, three years and so on. For example, the spot rates at 10 a.m. today might be 5.0, 5.12, 5.23, . . . 5.51, 5.52, 5.52, 5.52, . . . for years 1, 2, 3, . . . , 15, 16, 17, 18, . . . , respectively. If we plot a graph of the spot rates against time to maturity, then this is known as the (spot) yield curve (at 10 a.m. today) – here the **yield curve** is upward sloping and then flattens out for maturities longer than 16 years. What these spot rates imply is that if you want to borrow, say, $1000 at 10 a.m. today and pay back all the interest and principle in exactly 16 years time, then you will end up paying $1000(1.0552)^{16} = \$2362.42$ in 16 years time. So the 16-year spot rate is the cost of borrowing money today, with one single repayment in exactly 16 years time. As the yield curve is currently upward sloping, it costs more to borrow money the longer the time horizon over which you wish to borrow. Apart from the bid–ask spread (which we ignore), the cost of lending money at 10 a.m. today, with one repayment in either 17 or 18 years time, is also 5.52% p.a.

The price of zeros is determined by the supply of bonds (i.e. borrowers of money) and the demand for bonds (i.e. lenders of money). Usually, governments are borrowers of money and issue bonds, while pension funds, insurance companies and (older) individuals are lenders of money and purchase bonds. The price of a 'zero' will change when the balance of supply and

---

TABLE 20.1: Spot rate on a 'zero'

Data	P = current price = $62,321.30
	M = redemption value = $100,000
	$n = 6$ years
Question	Calculate the six-year spot rate, r.
Answer	$r = (\$100{,}000\ /\ \$62{,}321.30)^{1/6} - 1 = 0.082$ (**8.2% p.a.**)

demand in the market for funds (for a particular maturity date) changes. But note that it is always true of interest-bearing assets like bonds that:

> The bond price falls if any (spot) yield increases.

Generally speaking, interest rates of all maturities tend to move up and down together (although not by exactly the same amount), so by 3 p.m. the yield curve may still be upward sloping but all spot rates may be higher by around 0.1%, say. This would be called an upward shift in the yield curve. Analytically, spot yields are the building blocks for analysing fixed-income assets like coupon-paying bonds.

Coupon-paying bonds

Coupon-paying bonds provide a stream of payments called coupons (C), which are known (in nominal terms) for all future periods, at the time the bond is purchased. On (convention-al) government bonds the coupon payment is constant for all time periods. Most bonds are redeemable at a fixed date in the future for a known price, namely the **par value, redemption price** or **maturity value, *M*** (Figure 20.1). There are some bonds that although they pay coupons, are never redeemed and these are known as **perpetuities** (e.g. 2-1/2% consols issued by the UK government). The price quoted in the financial press and on electronic trading screens is known as the 'clean price'. The pricing formulae below all refer to the clean price. However, the actual price paid by an investor is known as the 'invoice price' and includes either 'accrued' or 'rebate' interest. We deal with this additional complexity below.

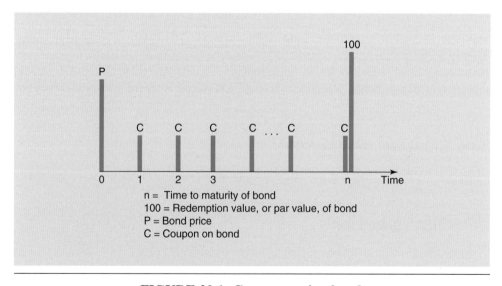

FIGURE 20.1: Coupon-paying bond

Interest yield/coupon rate (current yield in US)

The interest yield on a bond is usually quoted in the financial press and is calculated as:

$$\text{Interest yield} = \frac{Annual\, Coupon}{Current\, Clean\, Price} \cdot 100\% \qquad [3]$$

The interest yield is a very poor measure of the return on a bond, since:

- It ignores any capital gains that occur if the bond is purchased at a discount and held to maturity.
- It ignores 'interest-on-interest' from coupon payments.

Yield to maturity/redemption yield

The yield to maturity (YTM) is the internal rate of return of the bond. Knowing the market price P, the coupon C and the maturity value M, the YTM (y) is the solution to:

$$P = \frac{C_1}{(1 + y)} + \frac{C_2}{(1 + y)^2} + \cdots + \frac{(C_n + M)}{(1 + y)^n} \qquad [4]$$

Using the annuity formula and constant coupons, this simplifies to:

$$P = \frac{C}{y}\left(1 - \frac{1}{(1 + y)^n}\right) + \frac{M}{(1 + y)^n} \qquad [5]$$

The YTM is that constant rate y that equates the PV of future cash flows C_i (and the maturity value M) with the market price. Here, P, C_i and M are known and we (or the *Financial Times*) can calculate y using Excel.

If coupon payments are annual, then $i = 1, 2, 3, \ldots$ refers to years and y is at an annual (compound) rate. However, for government bonds the C_i are usually fixed amounts paid semi-annually. For semi-annual coupons, we replace y in the above formula by $y/2$ and C_i is replaced by the semi-annual coupon payments $C_i/2$ and $i = 1, 2, 3, \ldots$ refers to 6, 12, 18, \ldots months. It follows that $y/2$ is the semi-annual compound rate, and y is the simple annual rate (which in the US is known as the 'bond-equivalent yield') and is quoted 'on the street'. A simple example is given in Table 20.2 where the YTM is 14.2% p.a. The YTM is made up of three elements:

> YTM = coupon rate + interest on the coupons + capital gain (or loss) from the difference between the purchase price P and the maturity value M.

The YTM measures the (annual compound) rate of return on the bond if (i) it is held to maturity and (ii) all the coupon payments can be reinvested (on receipt) at a rate of interest equal

TABLE 20.2: Calculation of YTM

Data	Market price $= \$900$.
	10% coupon bond, par value $= \$1000$.
	Semi-annual coupon payments, three years to maturity (6×6 months).
Question	Calculate the YTM.
Answer	$\$900 = \$50/(1 + y/2) + \$50/(1 + y/2)^2 + \cdots$ $+ \$50/(1 + y/2)^5 + \$1050/(1 + y/2)^6$
	The solution y to the above equation is usually found using a simple algorithm (e.g. the IRR function in Excel). **YTM $=$ 14.2% p.a.**
	This can be verified by working out the PV of the RHS using $y = 0.142$, which is found to be $900.

to the (current) YTM. If these conditions do not hold, then the YTM will not correctly measure the return on the bond even if it is held to maturity. It is the assumption that the *future* coupon payments can be reinvested at the *current* YTM, which creates problems, since we do not know today at what rate of interest we can reinvest these future payments. However, the YTM is the best single figure we can use to approximate the average annual return on the bond if held to maturity, and it is widely used when discussing bond strategies among market participants.

The YTM can be calculated using the 'clean price' or the invoice price. For the UK, when P is the invoice price then y is known as the **gross redemption yield** (and is published daily in the *Financial Times*). Note that the YTM does not determine (in an economic sense) the price of the bond – it is *derived from* the observed market price (which in turn is determined by supply and demand for funds). However, if someone has already calculated the YTM, equation [4] can of course be used to calculate the current price (see Table 20.3). It is clear from

TABLE 20.3: Calculation of bond price (when YTM is given)

Data	20 year, 10% coupon bond, par value of $1000.
	Current YTM is 11% p.a., semi-annual coupon payments.
Question	Calculate the price of the bond.
Answer	$C = 0.5(0.10 \,(\$1000)) = \$50, n = 2(20) = 40, y = 0.11/2 = 0.055$
	The PV of the coupon payments is given by the ordinary annuity formula
	$Z = C[1 - 1/(1 + y)^n]/y = \$50[1 - 1/(1.055)^{40}]/0.055 = \$802.31$
	PV (of M) $= \$1000/(1.055)^{40} = \$117.46$
	Price of bond $= \$802.31 + \$117.46 = $ **$919.77**

equation [4] that the yield and price of a bond are negatively related and the relationship is non-linear (called 'convex'; see below).

YTM and coupon rate

The coupon rate (or coupon yield) is defined as C/M. There are some 'rules of thumb' used by traders when discussing the relationship between the YTM and the coupon rate of a bond. It is easy to show that if the coupon rate equals the YTM, then the bond is currently trading at a price equal to its par value. For example, consider a bond with a 10% coupon (annual), which also has a YTM of 10%, two years to maturity and a par value of £100. We can easily demonstrate that the *market price* of this bond equals its par value of £100, since using equation [4] we get:

$$P = £10/(1.1) + £110/(1.1)^2 = £100 \qquad [6]$$

If the coupon rate (C/M) is below the YTM, the market price will be below the par value (of £100) and the bond currently sells 'at a discount'. Conversely, if the coupon rate C/M is above the YTM the bond is trading 'at a premium' (and will currently sell at a price above its par value). The qualitative relationship between market price, coupon rate and YTM is given in Table 20.4 and they can be deduced from the following rearrangement of equation [4]:

$$\frac{P}{M} = \frac{C}{M}\left(\frac{1 - 1/(1 + y)^n}{y}\right) + \frac{1}{(1 + y)^n} \qquad [7]$$

The coupon rate is C/M and setting this to y, in equation [8], gives $P/M = 1$; that is, the price of the bond equals its par value. Also it follows that if (C/M) is less than y then (P/M) < 1 and the price is below the par value.

Holding period return

We know that the YTM is the (approximate) average annual return if you purchase the bond today and hold it to maturity. Pension funds often hold bonds to maturity, since the coupons on the bond are used to pay pensions. But suppose you are thinking of purchasing the bond today as a speculator and selling it before maturity – how do we calculate your *expected* or forecast return? We know that your expected return is made up of the coupon payments, interest on the coupon payments and any capital gain on the price of the bond – this is known

---

TABLE 20.4: Yield and price relationship

Bond sells at	Relationship
Par	when coupon rate = YTM
Discount	when coupon rate < YTM
Premium	when coupon rate > YTM

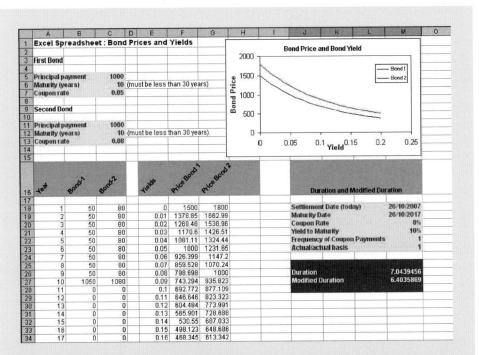

	A	B	C	D	E	F	G	H	I	J	K	L	M	O
1	Excel Spreadsheet : Bond Prices and Yields													
2														
3	First Bond													
4														
5	Principal payment		1000											
6	Maturity (years)		10	(must be less than 30 years)										
7	Coupon rate		0.05											
8														
9	Second Bond													
10														
11	Principal payment		1000											
12	Maturity (years)		10	(must be less than 30 years)										
13	Coupon rate		0.08											
14														
15														
16	Year	Bond-1	Bond-2		Yields	Price Bond 1	Price Bond 2			Duration and Modified Duration				
17														
18	1	50	80		0	1500	1800			Settlement Date (today)			26/10/2007	
19	2	50	80		0.01	1378.85	1862.99			Maturity Date			26/10/2017	
20	3	50	80		0.02	1269.48	1538.96			Coupon Rate			8%	
21	4	50	80		0.03	1170.6	1426.51			Yield to Maturity			10%	
22	5	50	80		0.04	1081.11	1324.44			Frequency of Coupon Payments			1	
23	6	50	80		0.05	1000	1231.65			Actual/actual basis			1	
24	7	50	80		0.06	926.399	1147.2							
25	8	50	80		0.07	859.528	1070.24							
26	9	50	80		0.08	798.698	1000			Duration			7.0439456	
27	10	1050	1080		0.09	743.294	935.823			Modified Duration			6.4035869	
28	11	0	0		0.1	692.772	877.109							
29	12	0	0		0.11	646.646	823.323							
30	13	0	0		0.12	604.484	773.991							
31	14	0	0		0.13	565.901	728.698							
32	15	0	0		0.14	530.55	687.033							
33	16	0	0		0.15	498.123	648.686							
34	17	0	0		0.16	468.345	613.342							

This spreadsheet calculates the prices of two different bonds as we change the YTM and then graphs the 'convex', bond price–yield relationship for each bond. We assume that both bonds have annual coupon payments.

Duration and Modified duration are calculated using the Excel functions ' = DURATION' and ' = MDURATION'. The settlement date, maturity date, coupon rate, current yield, frequency of coupon payments and day-count convention are the inputs required.

as the holding period return HPR; (somewhat confusingly, also referred to as the holding period *yield*).

Suppose the horizon you have in mind is two years and you think that interest rates will fall from their current level of 10% to 9.5% after one year and to 9% after two years (and then remain constant). You decide to purchase a five-year, 10% (annual) coupon bond and close out your position after two years. The calculation of the expected HPR = 11.11% is demonstrated in Figure 20.2 and Table 20.5. The forecast of interest rates will determine both the interest you will receive on the first coupon payment and the expected selling price of the bond in two years time. Lower interest rates imply that you expect the bond price to rise over the next two years. The approximate *annual* return is about 11.7% p.a., made up of 1.26% capital gain and 10.4% from the coupons – so the latter constitutes most of the return.

If you had an extremely short speculative horizon – say, over one week – then you are unlikely to be paid the coupon payment in the next week and your speculative gain is limited to the capital gain on the bond. The concept of duration (see the next chapter) is useful when calculating prospective capital gains on a bond.

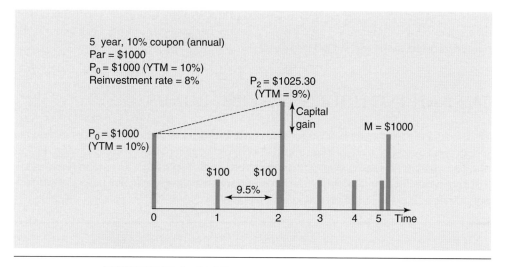

FIGURE 20.2: Holding period return (two years)

TABLE 20.5: Expected HPR

Data	Five-year, 10% (annual) coupon, par value $1000, trading at par (i.e. current YTM = 10%).
Question	Calculate the expected HPR assuming a horizon of two years, a reinvestment rate of 9.5% and a YTM *in two years time* of 9%.
Answer	Two coupons + interest on interest = $100 + $100(1.09) = $209. After two years the bond will have three years to maturity. Expected price after two years:

$$= \frac{\$100}{(1.09)} + \frac{\$100}{(1.09)^2} + \frac{\$100}{(1.09)^3} + \frac{\$1000}{(1.09)^3} = \$1025.3$$

A fall in the YTM produces a capital gain on the bond of $25.3
Terminal Value, TV = $209 + $1025.3 = $1234.3

Approximate return after two years
= (209/1000) + (25.3/1000) = 20.9% + 2.53%

= 23.43% (11.7% p.a.)

Holding period return (geometric return)

$(1 + r^*)^2 = \$1,234.3/\$1000$, therefore $r^* = $ **11.11% p.a.**

In general, the annual compound HPR, r^*, can be calculated from:

$$r^* = \left[\frac{TV}{P}\right]^{1/n} - 1 \qquad [8]$$

where TV is the value of all receipts at the end of the investment horizon (i.e. coupon payments and interest on interest + sale price), P is the purchase price of the bond and n is the number of years in the investment horizon.

20.2 PRICING COUPON-PAYING BONDS

This section discusses why bonds should be priced using spot rates. Bond prices that do *not* reflect prevailing spot rates can be subject to coupon stripping and risk-free arbitrage opportunities, which is the reason market participants ensure that spot rates are used to price bonds. The spot rate is the (annual compound) rate of return on an investment that has a one-off payout at time n. It is the return on a zero-coupon bond.

$$P = \frac{M}{(1 + r_n)^n} \qquad [9]$$

If there were zero-coupon bonds for all maturities, we could observe their prices P_1, P_2, etc. and use equation [9] to calculate r_1, r_2, r_3 etc. These spot rates would be the outcome of the demand and supply for zero-coupon bonds in the market. Any (non-callable) coupon bond can be viewed as a 'bundle' of zero-coupon bonds. Hence the price of a coupon-paying bond should equal the PV of the future coupon payments, where each coupon payment is discounted at the appropriate spot rate:

$$P = \frac{C_1}{(1 + r_1)} + \frac{C_2}{(1 + r_2)^2} + \cdots + \frac{C + M}{(1 + r_n)^n} \qquad [10]$$

Each C_i may be viewed as a one-off payment at times 1, 2, 3, ... (and for most bonds $C_i = C$, a constant). The maturity (redemption) value M is a one-off payment at time n. Each separate coupon (and the redemption) payment may be considered as a zero-coupon bond, discounted at the spot rate applicable to payments at $t = 1, 2, 3, \ldots$ Spot rates are the correct way to price government stock, since all coupons at time t on different bonds are discounted at the *same* rate, r_t. Once we have the spot rates, the price of a coupon-paying bond is easy to calculate, as shown in Table 20.6.

TABLE 20.6: Pricing coupon-paying bonds using spot rates

Data	Bond A: Exchequer Stock $8^{3/4}\%$, annual coupon, two years maturity, par = £100.
	Bond B: Exchequer Stock 12%, annual coupon, two years maturity, par = £100.
	Current spot rates $r_1 = 0.05$ (5%), $r_2 = 0.06$ (6%).
Question	Calculate the market price of the two bonds.
Answer	*Price (Bond A) =* £8.75/(1.05) + £108.75/(1.06)^2 = **£105.12**

Calculation of spot rates

We now turn to the problem of estimating spot rates when they are not directly observed in the market. In the US and UK, T-Bills are risk-free pure discount bonds but are only issued with maturities up to one year. In general, government bonds with maturities greater than one year are issued as coupon-paying securities. However, spot yields can be calculated from coupon-paying bonds in several ways and here we demonstrate the method known as *bootstrapping*. Table 20.7 considers the case where we can directly observe the 6-month and 12-month spot yields (r_1 and r_2) on zero-coupon bonds, but not the 18-month spot yield r_3, since we assume that there are no zero-coupon bonds with maturities longer than one year. However, the 18-month spot yield r_3 can be derived using the observed market price of a *coupon-paying bond* with 18 months left to maturity.

Similarly, if we have coupon-paying bonds for 2 years, 2.5 years and so on, then the bootstrapping procedure can be repeated to calculate spot rates for these years. In this way we can obtain the complete spot-yield curve. Where a coupon-paying bond does not exist for a particular maturity (e.g. for maturity of 7.5 years), the spot rate can be derived as an interpolation of the (derived) seven-year and eight-year spot yields. In fact it's a little more subtle than this, since after deriving the spot yields for those years for which we have coupon-paying bonds, a smooth curve is fitted through all these data points, using rather sophisticated techniques (e.g. cubic splines).

Coupon stripping

In the US zero-coupon securities are created by dealer firms, by selling off the 'ownership' of the coupon payments from coupon-paying bonds. These 'zeros' are therefore 'synthetic' securities. However, observed interest rates on 'stripped' Treasuries can give a misleading

---

TABLE 20.7: Calculation of spot rates by bootstrapping

Data   Bond A: Zero-coupon bonds (six months and one year): $r_1 = 8\%$ p.a., $r_2 = 8.3\%$ p.a.

Bond B: Coupon-paying bond with maturity 1.5 years, coupon rate = 8.5%, coupons paid every six months, market price $P = 99.45$, par value = 100.

Question   Calculate the 18-month spot rate r_3.

Answer   The 'correct' price of the bond is given by:

$$99.45 = \frac{4.25}{(1 + r_1/2)} + \frac{4.25}{(1 + r_2/2)^2} + \frac{104.25}{(1 + r_3/2)^3}$$

Observed spot rates on 6-month and 12-month bills are $r_1 = 0.08$, $r_2 = 0.083$, hence $99.45 = 4.0865 + 3.9180 + 104.25/(1+r_3/2)^3$

The only unknown in the above equation is r_3 and $r_3 = 0.0893$ *(8.93% p.a.)*

measure of risk-free spot rates, because (i) strips are less liquid/marketable, hence their yields reflect a liquidity premium and (ii) there is preferential tax treatment for some holders of strips (e.g. some overseas purchasers) and this 'tax effect' is reflected in observed yields. Even though spot rates are observable in the strips market, it may still be necessary to use bootstrap procedures to obtain good estimates of the true risk-free spot rates.

We now demonstrate why coupon-paying bonds should be priced using spot rates. If coupon bonds are *not* priced using spot rates, there is a potential (risk-free) arbitrage profit to be made from 'coupon stripping' the bond.

The example in Table 20.8 shows that the 'fair price' of a two-year coupon-paying bond, calculated using current spot rates, is $\hat{P} = \$966.48$. Suppose that a dealer has not used spot rates to price the bond and is quoting a price of $P = \$960$ − the bond is underpriced. You can make an arbitrage profit by buying low and selling high. You purchase the bond for $960 from the dealer and simultanously offer to sell the first coupon payment of $90 to a pension fund and the second payment of $1090 to an insurance company. Given current spot rates, the pension fund will be willing to pay you $81.8 *today* to secure the payment of $90 from you in one years time. Similarly, the insurance company will be willing to pay you $884.6 *today,* to secure the payment of $1090 in two years time. So today you receive $966.4 from the pension fund and insurance company and you use this to purchase the two-year coupon bond at $P = \$960$, making a risk-free profit of $6.4 today. We have assumed that you move fast and your trade does not affect current prices (or current spot yields).

However, there are lots of arbitrageurs around to spot this mispricing. So lots of arbitrageurs (like you) buy the two-year coupon bond, which will tend to increase its price. Also, by selling one-year and two-year strips, their prices fall (or equivalently their spot yields rise). Arbitrage will continue until the market price of the two-year coupon bond equals the PV of the sum of the receipts from coupon stripping (using spot rates); that is, until the market price of the coupon bond equals its fair value. Since arbitrage here involves a near risk-free

---

TABLE 20.8: Equilibrium price of coupon-paying bonds

Data	Observed one-year spot rate = 10%.
	Estimated two-year spot rate = 11%.
	Coupon bond is Treasury, two-year, 9% (annual) coupon, maturity value $M = \$1000$, with quoted market price of $P = \mathbf{960}$.
Question	Calculate the 'fair' or 'equilibrum' price of the bond and hence show that there are profits to be made from coupon stripping.
Answer	PV from selling 1st coupon = $90 / (1.10) = $81.8182.
	PV from selling 2nd coupon + redemption value
	$= \$1090 / (1.11)^2 = \$884.6684$.
	Using spot rates, 'fair price' $\hat{P} = \mathbf{\$966.4866}$.
	Buy the bond for $P = \$960$ *today* and simultaneously sell the two coupons for $81.8 and $884.6, making an arbitrage profit of $6.4 today.

transaction, the market price of the bond will quickly reflect its fair value. Our key result is therefore:

> The market price of a coupon bond is determined by the current term structure of spot rates.
> The YTM is then derived from the quoted market price.

20.3 MARKET STRUCTURE: UK AND US

In this section we look at the market structure of the UK and US bond markets, including the key market participants, settlement procedures, new issues and the index-linked, repo and strips markets. The methods used for price quotes and the relationship between price quotes, accrued interest and the invoice price are also examined. We begin with the UK gilts market and then discuss the US Treasury bond market.

British government (gilt-edged) securities

In the UK, long-term government bonds (gilts) are issued to finance the government's budget deficit (or, as it is often referred to in the UK, the Public Sector Borrowing Requirement, PSBR). The main holders of gilts include UK life assurance and pension funds, the personal sector and overseas residents. Conventional stocks (about 87% of the total) are issued with maturities up to about 25 years and index-linked stocks (about 11% of the total), whose return is based on the rate of inflation, are also available (Figure 20.3). Large banks act as

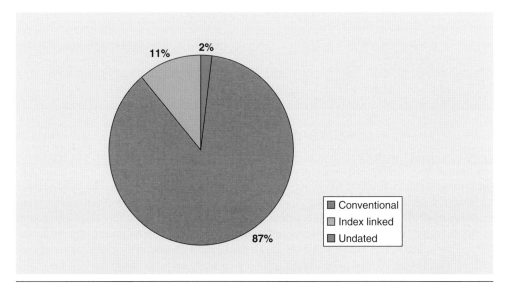

FIGURE 20.3: Gilts outstanding

primary dealers in the gilts market and they must quote firm bid and offer prices. They can deal through brokers, which allows trading on a 'no names basis', and gilts can be short-sold.

On conventional (gilt-edeged) stocks, a fixed rate of interest (the coupon) is paid every six months and there is usually a fixed repayment date and maturity value (normally the par value). For example, consider the Treasury 6%, 2028. The holder of this gilt will receive £6 interest each year (£3 every six months) on each £100 nominal of stock. The gilt will be redeemed at par on a specified date in 2028. Some gilts are undated – they pay coupons for ever but the principal amount is never repaid by the government.

Settlement procedures for the purchase and sale of gilts take place mainly through the Debt Management Office (DMO), which:

- Records the ownership of stock in a central gilts register.
- 'Moves' gilts electronically as ownership changes.
- Arranges for a settlement bank to receive payments/receipts from the purchase/sales of the (gilt-edged) stock and aggregates these daily.
- Organises *new issues* by auction, which are described in Case Study 20.1.

CASE STUDY 20.1   BOND AUCTION

Suppose that £2000m of a new stock is to be sold by public offer. The following bids are received:

at £99.000	for £1000m
at £98.937	for £500m
at £98.875	for £1000m

If the offer is taking place through an auction, the Bank sells:

£1000m at £99.000
£500m at £98.937
£500m at £98.875, so that those bidding £98.875 receive 50% of the stock for which they bid.

Index-linked stocks

Index-linked stocks account for about 11% of the total UK gilts market. The coupon payments and redemption value are adjusted for changes in inflation as measured by the retail price index (RPI). Index-linked gilts provide a hedge against inflation and therefore give a (near) guaranteed *real* return. However, inflation adjustment is based on the change in the RPI eight months before the first coupon payment and the redemption payment is also adjusted by the RPI eight months prior to maturity (any capital gain is not subject to UK tax). The real rates of return on index-linked stock are quoted on the basis of assumed inflation (e.g. 3%, 5%). Because of the lag in calculating the inflation adjustments, the higher the assumed rate of inflation is (e.g. 5% rather than 3%), the lower is the real redemption yield.

Price quotes (per £100 nominal value) and the redemption yield (i.e. yield to maturity) for UK gilts, both conventional and index linked, are shown in Figure 20.4.

UK GILTS – cash market
www.ft.com/gilts

Oct 24	Price £	Day's Chng	W'ks Chng	Int Yield	Red Yield	52 Week High	52 Week Low	Amnt £m	Last xd date	Interest due
Shorts (Lives up to Five Years)										
Tr 7.25pc '07	100.16	-0.01	-0.03	7.24	5.78	102.31	100.17	11,655	29/11	Je7 De7
Tr 5pc '08	99.82	-0.01	+0.08	5.01	5.48	100.06	99.42	14,928	28/02	Se7 Mr7
Tr 5.5pc '08-12...+	100.16	+0.02	+0.16	5.49	5.30	100.76	98.27	1,026	31/08	Mr10 Se10
Tr 9pc '08 ......+	103.36	-0.03	+0.10	8.71	5.38	107.29	103.24	687	3/10	Ap13 Oc13
Tr 4pc '09	98.62	+0.06	+0.31	4.06	5.05	98.63	97.05	16,974	27/02	Se7 Mr7
Tr 8pc '09 ......+	105.29	+0.08	+0.36	7.60	5.07	108.23	104.36	393	17/09	Mr25 Se25
Tr 5.75pc '09	101.50	+0.10	+0.46	5.67	4.99	102.46	99.79	12,006	27/11	Je7 De7
Tr 4.75pc '10	99.59	+0.12	+0.58	4.77	4.92	99.77	97.05	12,774	28/05	De7 Je7
Tr 6.25pc '10	103.73	+0.15	+0.68	6.03	4.93	105.29	101.27	5,205	17/11	My25 Nv25
Tr 4.25pc '11	97.83	+0.17	+0.80	4.34	4.96	98.07	94.78	13,750	25/02	Se7 Mr7
Cn 9pc Ln '11	113.53	+0.20	+0.87	7.93	4.96	117.52	111.14	5,664	4/07	Ja12 Jy12
Five to Ten Years										
Tr 7.75pc '12-15 ..+	110.07	+0.21	+0.95	7.04	5.08	112.97	107.12	804	18/01	Jy26 Ja26
Tr 5pc '12	100.42	+0.21	+0.97	4.98	4.89	101.47	96.93	14,009	28/02	Se7 Mr7
Tr 5.25pc '12	101.33	+0.23	+1.06	5.18	4.92	101.24	97.75	7,750	30/05	De7 Je7
Tr 9pc '12 ......+	116.82	+0.24	+1.06	7.70	5	120.95	113.69	403	27/07	Fe6 Au6
Tr 8pc '13	115.63	+0.28	+1.27	6.92	4.92	119.67	111.64	6,489	19/09	Mr27 Se27
Tr 5pc '14	100.64	+0.30	+1.38	4.97	4.89	102.86	95.99	13,699	29/08	Mr7 Se7
Tr 4.75pc '15	99.34	+0.33	+1.54	4.78	4.85	101.74	94.37	13,647	28/08	Mr7 Se7
Tr 8pc '15	120.51	+0.37	+1.71	6.64	4.91	125.65	115.56	7,744	27/11	Je7 De7
Ten to Fifteen Years										
Tr 4pc '16	94.04	+0.35	+1.66	4.25	4.83	96.35	89.02	13,500	30/08	Mr7 Se7
Tr 8.75pc '17	129.89	+0.44	+2.01	6.74	4.89	136.46	124.47	8,136	17/08	Fe25 Au25
Ex 12pc '13-17 ...+	136.86	+0.31	+1.39	8.77	4.95	144	133.07	57	4/12	Je12 De12
Tr 5pc '18	101.40	+0.40	+1.87	4.93	4.83	101.34	96.01	—	—	—
Tr 4.75pc '20	99.64	+0.45	+2	4.77	4.79	103.60	93.94	10,743	28/02	Se7 Mr7
Tr 8pc '21	131.47	+0.57	+2.49	6.09	4.82	138.28	124.86	17,573	28/05	De7 Je7
Over Fifteen Years										
Tr 5pc '25	103.42	+0.56	+2.07	4.83	4.71	109.17	97.34	16,188	27/02	Se7 Mr7
Tr 4.25pc '27	94.71	+0.55	+2	4.49	4.66	100.86	88.93	4,500	—	—
Tr 6pc '28	117.93	+0.67	+2.39	5.09	4.66	126	111.19	12,340	29/11	Je7 De7
Tr 4.25pc '32	95.68	+0.63	+2.11	4.44	4.54	102.91	89.59	17,326	28/05	De7 Je7
Tr 4.25pc '36	96.35	+0.69	+2.12	4.41	4.48	104.38	90.20	15,668	28/02	Se7 Mr7
Tr 4.75pc '38	104.68	+0.75	+2.27	4.54	4.47	114.06	98.49	14,958	29/11	Je7 De7
Tr 4.5pc '42	100.87	+0.77	+2.19	4.46	4.45	102.18	95.25	6,500	28/11	Je7 De7
Tr 4.25pc '46	97.19	+0.80	+2.19	4.37	4.40	107.74	91.86	13,750	29/11	Je7 De7
Tr 4.25pc '55	98.52	+0.87	+2.29	4.31	4.32	110.87	93.37	11,602	29/11	Je7 De7
Undated										
Cons 4pc ....+	82.17	+0.75	+2.28	4.87	—	89.47	75.56	358	—	—
War Ln 3.5pc....	77.99	+0.77	+2.34	4.49	—	86.41	71.23	1,939	23/05	Je1 De1
Cn 3.5pc '61 Aft...+	76.12	+0.73	+2.22	4.60	—	84.13	69.67	89	—	—
Tr 3pc '66 Aft. ....+	64	+0.61	+1.84	4.69	—	70.58	58.66	53	—	—
Cons 2.5pc ......+	54.73	+0.53	+1.61	4.57	—	60.53	50.06	272	—	—
Tr 2.5pc ....+	55.71	+0.55	+1.67	4.49	—	61.72	50.88	—	—	—
Index-Linked (b)				**(1)**	**(2)**					
2.5pc '09 .....(78.8)	262.13	+0.17	+0.64	1.22	1.93	262.64	252.80	3,304	12/05	Nv20 My20
2.5pc '11 .....(74.6)	279.81	+0.58	+2.17	1.70	2	280.02	267.96	4,631	15/08	Fe23 Au23
2.5pc '13 .....(89.2)	236.07	+0.69	+2.91	1.81	2.01	235.72	225.10	7,347	8/08	Fe16 Au16
2.5pc '16 .....(81.6)	264.86	+1.11	+4.22	1.69	1.84	264.27	249.43	6,956	18/07	Ja26 Jy26
1.25pc '17† (193.725)	96.33	+0.47	+1.67	1.70	1.70	99.15	90.73	8,100	14/11	My22 Nv22
2.5pc '20 .....(83.0)	272.10	+1.45	+5.18	1.53	1.63	273.76	253.24	6,350	8/04	Oc16 Ap16
2.5pc '24 .....(97.7)	242.78	+1.76	+4.02	1.40	1.48	246.67	225.92	6,583	9/07	Ja17 Jy17
1.25pc '27 ..(194.07)	100.02	+0.80	+1.86	1.29	1.29	104.82	92.89	5,950	12/11	My22 Nv22
4(1/8)pc '30 ..(135.1)	237.68	+1.87	+3.49	1.22	1.28	242.44	220.93	5,021	12/07	Ja22 Jy22
2pc '35 ...(173.6)	144.34	+1.42	+2.19	1.04	1.09	145.53	131.25	9,389	18/01	Jy26 Ja26
1.125pc '37 ..(202.2)	103.45	+1.34	+1.48	—	—	104.88	94.43	—	—	—
1.25pc '55† .(192.20000)	118.35	+1.95	+2.33	0.84	0.84	126.50	108.73	5,288	12/11	My22 Nv22

All UK Gilts are Tax free to non-residents on application. xd Ex dividend. +Indicative. Closing mid-prices are shown in pounds per £100 nominal of stock. Weekly percentage changes are calculated on a Friday to Friday basis. Gilt benchmarks and most liquid stocks, are shown in bold type. A full list of Gilts can be found daily on ft.com/bond&rates.

Prospective real redemption rate on projected inflation of (1) 5% and (2) 3%. (b) Figures in parentheses show RPI base for indexing (ie 8 months prior to issue) and have been adjusted to reflect rebasing of RPI to 100 in January 1987. Conversion factor 3.945. RPI for Jan 2007: 201.6 and for Sep 2007 207.3. † I.L. 1 1/4pc 2017 has a base RPI of 193.725, I.L. 1 1/4pc 2055 has a base RPI of 192.2 with a 3 month lag. The 'clean' price shown has no inflation adjustment. The yield is calculated using no inflation assumption.　Source: REUTERS Ltd.

FIGURE 20.4: Gilts prices

Source: Financial Times, reproduced by permission.

Strips in the UK gilts market

A strips market in UK gilts was established in the mid-1990s. The term STRIP stands for Separate Trading of Registered Interest and Principal of Securities. Originally 'stripping' referred to the practice of physically stripping coupons from a bearer bond certificate. In a strips market, an investor can exchange (all or part of) the coupons on a coupon-paying bond for a set of individual coupons (which exactly match the cash flows of the parent bond). These separate coupons can then be sold in the market. Conversely, an investor can exchange a set of strips and 'reconstitute' a coupon-paying bond.

The advantage of a strips market from the investor's point of view is basically to avoid reinvestment risk, by purchasing strips to match a known future outflow of funds (e.g. future pension payments by pension funds). Also, the strips market increases the duration of existing bonds. For example, the duration of the 'principal strip' of the longest conventional bond is more than twice that of the underlying coupon-paying bond (at a yield of around 6%). Hence pension funds that have long duration liabilities can more easily match these liabilities, using strips.

The strips market allows synthetic bond products to be manufactured. For example, 'deferred payment bonds' result from the purchase of a coupon-paying bond and selling off the coupons for the early years in the strips market. An 'annuity bond' involves selling the principal/redemption payment as a strip and retaining the coupon payments.

US Treasury bonds

In broad terms, the US system operates in a similar fashion in terms of dealing and settlement to the UK government bond market. In the US, Treasury securities with a maturity of two years or greater are issued as coupon-paying securities. Maturities of 2, 3, 5, 7, 10 and 30 years are issued. Coupon securities with a maturity between 2 and 10 years are called 'notes' and those over 10 years are called bonds, but we will refer to both as bonds. The bonds are held in book entry form at the Federal Reserve so the investor only receives a receipt of ownership; as in the UK this allows low-cost transfer of ownership. The Fed sells new issues by auction. There is also a large active strips market in the US.

Index-linked bonds in the US are known as TIPS (Treasury Inflation-Protection Securities). They give a risk-free return in terms of purchasing power over the basket of goods that makes up the Consumer Price Index (CPI).

Dealer profits are made from (i) the bid–ask spread; (ii) any capital appreciation on their inventory (or depreciation on any securities held short) and (iii) the 'carry' earned on the difference between the interest earned on bonds and the cost of financing them.

The Treasury strips market has been active in the US since the early 1980s. The mechanism is that firms (e.g. Merrill Lynch, Salomon Brothers) purchase coupon bonds and place them in a custodial account at a bank. The firms then issue receipts representing ownership of each coupon and the principal (called the corpus). These receipts are then sold to investors as Treasury strips.

20.4 PRICE QUOTES AND ACCRUED INTEREST

Price quotes: US bonds

Price quotes on US bonds (and notes) are in units of 1/32 of 1% of par (where par is $100). So 99:30 is a quote of 99-30/32. The minimum price movement (the tick size) is 1/32 (of 1%). An illustrative 'verbal' price quote is:

- '6% Feb 26 at 99:07, 99:09'. This signifies a 6% coupon bond redeemable in February 2026 and with a bid–ask price of 99-7/32(bid) = 99.21875 and 99-9/32(ask) = 99.28125, per $100 nominal.

The 'Ask Yld' for US Treasuries is the yield to maturity (using the ask price). The 'tick value' on a par value of $100,000 is $31.25 = (1/32) (0.01) $100,000.

Price quotes: UK gilts

The quoted price is the clean price (i.e. it excludes accrued or rebate interest). The price is quoted per £100 of nominal stock in decimals (see Figure 20.4). The following key features apply to quotes:

- An illustrative quote might be 105.29, implying a price of £105.29 per £100 nominal.
- Tick size is 0.01.
- Dealers sell bonds at a higher price than they will buy the bond (i.e. offer price > bid price).

Key features from the investor's point of view are the redemption date, the coupon rate, the (clean) price (per £100 nominal) and the increase or decrease in price since the previous day (+ or −). Some stocks are *double dated* (e.g. 'Treasury 12–1/2%, 15–18') and can be redeemed by the government at any time between these two dates. **Index-linked stocks** have their yields calculated for two assumptions (high/low) about future inflation.

The quoted price is the clean price, but the invoice price to be paid requires calculation of accrued/rebate interest. The treatment of accrued interest in the UK and the US bond markets is very similar and therefore we examine this mainly from a UK perspective. However, where the terminology differs between the two markets we point this out. An investor may purchase a bond between coupon payment dates. If the investor is to receive the next coupon payment (i.e. the bond is 'cum dividend'), then he must compensate the seller of the bond for the coupon interest earned from the time of the last coupon payment. This is known as accrued interest and is calculated as follows:

$$\textbf{Accrued interest} = C \times \frac{n_1}{n_2} = \frac{C}{2} \times \frac{Days \ since \ last \ coupon \ payment}{Days \ separating \ coupon \ payments} \qquad [11]$$

where C is the *annual* coupon
n_1 is the number of days from last coupon payment to settlement date
n_2 is the number of days in the 'year'.

TABLE 20.9: UK gilts market (accrued interest)

Data	On 31 March 2008 (for settlement on 1 April), 9% UK Treasury 2030 was quoted at 106.1875 (with £100 par value).
	Most recent coupon payment was 6 February 2008.
Question	Calculate accrued interest.
Answer	22 days from 6 February + 31 days in March + 1 day in April. Hence $n_1 = 54$ days and the accrued interest (AI) is: AI = £9 (54/365) = £1.3315 per £100 nominal of stock

Market conventions determine n_1 and n_2. For UK gilts and US Treasury coupon securities, n_1 and n_2 are on 'actual/365' basis. An example of the calculation of accrued interest is provided in Table 20.9.

Invoice Price

The quoted (clean) price assumes that the owner of the bond will receive the next coupon payment. In the UK, gilts can be sold either cum dividend or ex dividend and this is reflected in the invoice paid per £100 nominal value.

- **Cum dividend:** The purchaser of the bond receives the next coupon payment and the seller does not, even though the seller has held the bond for part of this coupon period. The purchaser therefore compensates the seller and pays an invoice price:

$$\text{Invoice price} = \text{Clean price} + \text{Accrued interest}$$

The invoice price is the total proceeds (per £100 nominal) that the buyer pays the seller of the bond. In our example the invoice price is:

£106.1875 + £1.3315 = £107.52 (per £100 nominal of stock)

- **Ex-dividend:** The purchaser is excluded from receiving the next coupon (but the clean price 'includes' the next coupon payment). Hence the seller of the bond (who *will receive* the next coupon payment) owes the purchaser '**rebate interest**' (see Table 20.10). The invoice price paid by the purchaser (investor) is therefore lower than the clean price.

TABLE 20.10: UK gilt (rebate interest)

Data	On 31 March 2008 (for settlement 1 April):
	9% Treasury 2025 is quoted at £111.156 xd (i.e. clean price, xd = ex-dividend).
	Next coupon payment date is 25 April, 24 days hence.
Question	Calculate the rebate interest and invoice price.
Answer	Rebate interest = 9.0 (24/365) = £0.592 per £100 nominal.
	Invoice price = 111.156 − 0.592 = £110.564 (per £100 nominal)

> Invoice price = Clean (quoted) price − Rebate interest

In the UK gilts market, the recipient of the coupon payment is determined about 37 days before actual payment, after which date the bond goes ex-coupon. In the US the invoice price (paid) by the purchaser, as in the UK, is the clean price with adjustment for accrued or rebate interest.

20.5 PRICING CORPORATE BONDS

The pricing of corporate bonds, especially those with convertible and callable properties, can be rather technical. One difficulty lies in trying to get a measure of the risk and cost of distress/bankruptcy, which should clearly affect the bond price. We can therefore only deal with highly simplified cases below (for futher details see Cuthbertson and Nitzsche, 2001b). We deal with two rather different approaches. The conventional appoach uses the familiar discounting technique, but we also briefly present a more 'modern' approach that employs options-pricing theory.

Pricing a plain vanilla corporate bond can be tackled in a similar fashion to that for government bonds. However, the cash flows (and face value) C on the corporate bond are *expected coupons, E(C)*:

$$E(C) = (1 - p)C + p(\theta C) \qquad [12]$$

where p is the probability of default (in a particular year) and θ is the recovery rate if the corporate goes into default. (The default probability can be calculated from observed yields on corporate bonds.) If the probability of default is unrelated to other events in the economy, then we could discount these cash flows at the risk-free rate to obtain the bond price. However, in reality bonds do have some market risk (i.e. positive betas) and the probability of default depends on the state of the economy (e.g. recession or boom). Therefore one might (rather crudely) take the risk-free spot rate r and add a risk premium *rp* to reflect uncertainty caused by the business cycle. The price of the corporate bond is given by:

$$P = \frac{E(C_1)}{(1 + r_1 + rp_1)} + \frac{E(C_2)}{(1 + r_2 + rp_2)^2} + \cdots + \frac{E(C_n + M)}{(1 + r_n + rp_n)^n} \qquad [13]$$

It is obvious from the above formula that a fixed-income trader can speculate on changes in corporate bond prices based on either forecasts of changes in the risk-free rate or changes in the credit (default) risk of the company. Since each corporate bond is affected in the same way by changes in the risk-free rate, speculators concentrate on predicting relative changes in the risk premium – not surprisingly, this is known as a **relative value trade** (and is discussed futher in the chapter on hedge funds). For example, ideally you would go long in a corporate bond with a duration of 10 that you expect to improve its credit rating and short sell a corporate bond of a firm (also with a duration of 10) that you expect to undergo a rating decline. Since you have equal (dollar) long and short positions (in matched-duration bonds), the value of your speculative bond portfolio will remain unchanged if there are unexpected changes in (risk-free) spot rates (i.e. parallel shifts in the yield curve). You are merely exposed to the relative credit risk of the two corporate bonds. If your guess about credit-rating changes is correct, you will make a speculative profit, having used little of your own funds (since the proceeds from the short sale can be used to finance your long position). In practice, of course, you do not need to find two bonds both with the same duration, since you can combine a number of bonds so that the *portfolio* durations are equal for the long and short positions.

The importance of credit risk came to the fore in the summer of 2007 when the sub-prime mortgage crisis in the US spilled over into other markets, particularly the UK; see Case Study 20.2.

CASE STUDY 20.2   SUB-PRIME CRISIS, 2007

In the summer of 2007 the US was hit by a crisis in sub-prime mortgages. We have already noted that home mortgages can be 'bundled up' into mortgage pools and the banks then sell these collateralised debt obligations (CDOs) to investors – this is *securitisation*. Banks and Savings and Loan Associations no longer 'originate and hold' mortgages but 'originate and distribute' large chunks of them. Sub-prime refers to the fact that some mortgage pools contain mortgages issued to borrowers who have a high credit risk (e.g. based on credit-scoring models) and therefore have a higher probability of default on their payments than do 'normal' credit-worthy borrowers. There is clearly an incentive for financial advisers to sell mortgages and hence gain commission, even if the mortgagees undertake 'self-certification', where their income is not checked by anyone and they may therefore obtain mortgages that are very large in relation to their 'true' income. When the housing market turned down in the US, the underlying value of some houses was less than the amount borrowed and some homeowners defaulted. Investors in these asset-backed sub-prime mortgages suffered losses, as did banks who had issued mortgages to sub-prime borrowers but had not yet managed to sell these mortgages as CDOs.

Also, some clauses in the securitisation documents allowed investors to hand back loan pools that lost value quickly. In effect, no one wanted to purchase CDOs involving sub-prime, because it is difficult to value assets that are not 'transparent' since their ultimate value depends on the economic position of a pool of mortgagees and their ability to repay. Uncertainty about which banks were deeply involved in sub-prime led to a liquidity crisis as banks became wary of lending to each other in the one-month and three-month interbank market. Interbank rates increased, even though the Fed lowered its discount rate to ease the crisis.

In September 2007, fearing a 'fire sale' of mortgage-backed securities and CDOs, Citigroup, Bank of America and JP Morgan met with the US Treasury and came up with the idea of raising between $75bn and $100bn to purchase mortgage-backed securities, repackage them and then sell them on to investors in an orderly fashion at a later date. This became known as the 'Superfund' or 'master liquidity enhancement conduit', M-LEC. The Superfund would only purchase 'high-rated' mortgage backed assets and not sub-prime. It would therefore 'separate out' the high-quality debt from low-quality debt, since there was evidence that the sub-prime crisis had caused abnormally low prices of even high-quality debt. This was because some banks and investment vehicles (e.g. hedge funds) were forced to sell off their high-quality debt as they could not roll over their short-term finance, which mainly consisted of issuing asset-backed three-month commercial paper. The latter source of roll-over funding had virtually dried up as investors (e.g. money-market mutual funds) became worried about the creditworthiness of some banks and hedge funds. If it were successful, the Superfund would also allow banks to avoid the need to take assets back onto their books from special investment vehicles (SIVs), which are off-balance sheet operating companies set up by banks to exploit the difference between low-cost short-term debt and higher-yielding long-term investments in asset-backed securities.

The difficulty with the Superfund idea is establishing a fair price for the assets it purchases, since if it purchases assets at below 'fair value' (and some of these mortgage pools and CDOs based on them are hard to value), then it would be partly bailing out banks who had taken on excessive risks – this creates a moral hazard problem, as a subsidy today merely encourages banks to act less prudently in the future. As Warren Buffett commented about the Superfund, 'Not only can you not turn a toad into a prince by kissing it, but you cannot turn a toad into a prince by repackaging it.' At the time of writing it is not clear if the Superfund idea will go ahead.

November 2007 saw the retirement of Stan O'Neal, the boss of Merrill Lynch, when the firm announced prospective losses on sub-prime of $8bn. This was closely followed by the departure of Chuck Prince, the boss of Citigroup, who announced losses of between $8bn and $11bn on its sub-prime portfolio of around $60bn. UBS head Huw Jenkins also 'stepped down'.

Although banks do 'offload' mortgages from their balance sheets, if they are purchased *on margin* by a hedge fund (say) that also uses the same bank as its prime broker, the bank has not really spread the risks of the mortgage pool very widely. If the pool becomes 'toxic waste', the hedge fund cannot sell the mortgage backed securities at a reasonable price and hence may not be able to pay back its loans to the bank.

Some sub-prime mortgage pools were given a AAA rating by rating agencies and the latter have come under criticism because of their conflicts of interest – they are paid by the issuers to give the rating and hence may tend to give too high a rating to help secure future business. Sometimes AAA-rated asset-backed securities can be nearly as dangerous as Class-A drugs.

The mortgage crisis spread to the UK in September 2007. A mortgage bank, Northern Rock, financed a large proportion of its mortgage loans by borrowing in the three-month and six-month interbank market and rolling over the finance. With the uncertainty casued by the US sub-prime crisis because some of the 'toxic waste' might have been held (or financed) by UK banks, the sterling interbank market experienced a liquidity crisis. As a consequence, Northern Rock had to borrow from the Bank of England's lender of last resort facility (equivalent to the Fed discount window) at a penal rate – an amount estimated at between £20bn and £30bn on a balance sheet of around £100bn. These loans from the Bank of England (ultimately from the taxpayer) are collateralised by Northern Rock's mortgage book, which is thought to be sound.

However, news of this emergency borrowing caused a run on Northern Rock, with its depositors queuing up to withdraw their deposits. The last time there had been a significant run on the UK banking system was at the bank Overend Gurney in 1866 and the Bank of Glasgow in 1878. After a few days, the government (Treasury) agreed to underwrite all deposits in Northern Rock, 'while the crisis persists'. Meanwhile, Northern Rock's board of directors examined alternative bids by companies such as the Virgin Group and some private equity firms to purchase/takeover Northern Rock. Otherwise the bank's branch network, its IT systems and its mortgage book could be sold separately.

The UK Treasury also announced an investigation into the deposit insurance scheme, which in the UK only covers about 90% of deposits in each bank up to £33,000 ($66,000); US deposits are insured up to $100,000. The Treasury is also investigating a change in European law that would allow the Bank of England not to have to disclose its lender of last resort arrangements (for a period), so in the future it could facilitate 'secret negotiations' with potential buyers for a liquidity-constrained bank like Northern Rock. Northern Rock's share price fell by over 80% – and was referred to as 'Northern Wreck'. It has now been 'temporarily' nationalised.

Valuing corporate bonds using options theory

Even with our limited knowledge of options theory, we can gain some insights into the valuation of corporate debt – although after reading the later chapters on options the ideas here should be relatively straightforward. Anyway, a key advantage of this approach is that it directly shows how uncertainty in the form of the volatility of the firm's assets directly affects the bond price.

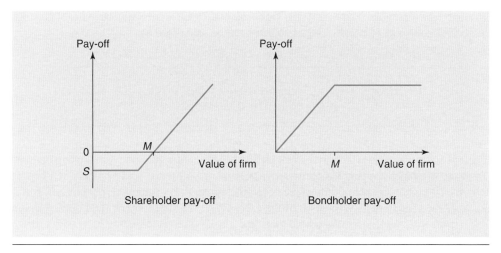

FIGURE 20.5: Shareholder and bondholder payoffs

Suppose for simplicity that all bondholders hold zero-coupon bonds with a maturity of 10 years and maturity (face) value of M. If at the end of 10 years the value of the firm's assets V_T is greater than M, the bondholders will be repaid in full (and any excess $V_T - M$, accrues to the shareholders, not the bondholders). However, if $V_T < M$, the shareholders who have limited liability can 'walk away' from the firm and the bondholders will not be repaid in full. The maturity value M is like the strike price in an option contract. The bondholders receive the minimum of M or V_T and if $M > V_T$ their loss is $M - V_T$. The payoff to the bondholders is shown in Figure 20.5 and mathematically it can be expressed as follows:

$$\text{Payoff to bondholders at } T = M - \max(0, M - V_T) \qquad [14]$$

Figure 20.5 indicates that the bondholders' payoff is like a put option written on the firm's assets, with a strike price of M (plus an amount of cash M).

So far, we have only given the possible payoffs at time T (the maturity of the bond), but what we require is the market value of the corporate bond B_t today. However, once we know the payoff at T, options pricing theory can be used to determine B_t, which is given by a complicated formula (Merton, 1973), here expressed schematically as:

$$B_t = f(M/V_t, \sigma, T - t, r) \qquad [15]$$

where r is the risk-free rate
          σ is the volatility (i.e. standard deviation of the value of the firm)
          $T - t$ is the time to maturity of the bond
          f means 'function of the variables' in parenthesis.

In particular, it is found that the current price of the bond is negatively related to the firm's leverage (i.e. proportion of debt outstanding M/V_t) and to the volatility of the firm's assets σ (e.g. this would probably be higher for an IT firm than for a chain of supermarkets). The model also implies that the corporate–Treasury yield spread will widen, either with increased leverage or with higher volatility of the firm's assets. These are intuitively plausible results. In general, the value of a risky corporate bond can be calculated as:

> Value corporate bond = Value of risk-free bond − Value of implied put option written by the bondholders

There is another way in which we can tackle the valuation of a corporate bond using options. To do so, we somewhat paradoxically first look at the payoff to the equityholders. If $V_T < M$ then the equityholders get nothing, since even the bondholders cannot be paid in full. But if $V_T > M$ the shareholders receive all of the excess $V_T - M$, after paying the bondholders in full. Hence the payoff to the shareholders is like a call option (see Figure 20.5) with a strike price M. The shareholders have paid S, the initial equity investment in the firm, for this embedded call option. This call option is valuable to shareholders since they have limited downside risk but can benefit greatly if the firm is successful (remember that the bondholders only get the fixed amount M, no matter how successful the firm). To value this call option V^c at time t, given the payoffs at time T, is again rather difficult and is taken up in Chapter 26. But once we have calculated V^c then:

> Value corporate bond = Value of the firm V_t − value of the implied call V^c held by the shareholders

In practice, things are even more complicated since most bonds are coupon-paying bonds, not zeros. Hence, for a 10-year annual-coupon bond, the shareholders have 10 sequential call options with strike prices of $C, C, \ldots\ldots$ and $C + M$. In addition, if the shareholders do not exercise one of their call options, the value of their later call options is zero (since ownership of the firm's assets will pass to the bondholders, in liquidation). But these technical problems can be surmounted and options theory provides a useful approach to valuing risky debt.

SUMMARY

- *Spot rates* refer to the cost of lending (and borrowing) money today, with the principal and interest payable at one specific time in the future.
- The *yield to maturity (YTM)* is the return on a bond if it is held to maturity and all the future coupons can be reinvested at the current YTM. The *holding period return (HPR)* is the return on a bond over a fixed horizon and includes the capital gain, any coupon payments and any interest-on-interest.
- The *'fair' or equilibrium price* of a coupon-paying bond is determined by spot rates of interest, otherwise risk-free arbitrage profits can be made by a strategy known as

coupon stripping. Once we have calculated the 'fair' price we can then infere the YTM that is consistent with this price.
- Bond prices and the YTM are inversely related.
- The government bond markets in the UK and the US are very liquid. Most are 'plain vanilla' coupon bonds, although there are also some *index-linked bonds*. There are also active strips and repo markets in bonds.
- Pricing plain vanilla *corporate bonds* is similar to that for government bonds, but with the proviso that the coupon payments are subject to *default risk* and the discount rate may have to be adjusted to include a risk premium. Their price will alter if risk-free rates change or if the risk of financial distress alters (e.g. as reflected in a change in S&P or Moody's bond rating).
- Another approach to pricing corporate bonds is to use options theory. Also, when corporate bonds have embedded options to convert (to ordinary shares) or have call provisions, then clearly options theory is required (see Cuthbertson and Nitzsche, 2001b).

EXERCISES

Q1   What is a Treasury 'strip'?

Q2   What are the key features of a bond that determine the yield to maturity?

Q3   The quoted (clean) price for a UK gilt-edged stock is £105.21875 xd (xd = ex dividend; that is, excluding the next dividend/coupon payment). Will this be the invoice price paid by the purchaser?

Q4   Assume that you require a 10% (compound) return on a zero-coupon bond with a par (face value) of £1000 and five years to maturity. What price would you pay for the bond?

Q5   Consider a 7% coupon US government bond that has a par value of $1000 and matures five years from now. The coupon payments are made annually. The current yield to maturity (YTM; redemption yield) for such bonds is 8%. Calculate the market price of the bond and state whether you expect this bond to sell at par, at a premium (over par), or at a discount.

Q6   Consider the following German government coupon bond (i.e. Bund):

Price = €769.42
Coupon = 7% p.a. (paid every six months)
Par value = €1000
Maturity = 15 years

Show that the semi-annual yield on the bond is $y = 5\%$, so that the yield to maturity on a 'bond-equivalent basis' (i.e. simple annual yield) is 10%.

Q7   Why are coupon bonds priced using spot yields? What then is the significance of the yield to maturity (YTM)?

21

Term Structure of Interest Rates

AIMS

- To demonstrate how *spot rates* for different maturities are related and hence give rise to the *yield curve.*
- To explain the shape of the yield curve using various models of the *term structure* of interest rates.
- To show how *forward rates* can be estimated from spot rates.
- To show how forecasts of inflation can be inferred from observed spot and forward rates.
- To show how the yield curve for corporate bonds can be used to extract the market's view of the *probability of default* for the corporate.

21.1 THE YIELD CURVE

You can borrow (and lend) money over different periods of time. For example, you can borrow money today and pay back the principal and interest in one year – the cost of borrowing might be $r_1 = 9\%$ p.a. If you borrow today and pay back the principal and interest in two years time (i.e. there are no interim payments), the quoted interest rate might be $r_2 = 10\%$ p.a. Because both of these interest rates are quoted for borrowing from today over a fixed horizon (with no interim payments), they are known as **spot rates** (or spot yields).

The (spot) yield curve shows the relationship between these spot rates and the maturity of the loan. We assume that we are dealing with risk-free investments; that is, there is no risk of default. For example, the yield curve at 10 a.m. today might look like that in Figure 21.1. The yield curve in Figure 21.1 is upward sloping, which simply means that if you borrow money at 10 a.m. today, then the longer the maturity of your loan, the higher the (spot) interest you will pay. Note that spot rates apply to a transaction that is conceptually different from a standard loan. In a standard loan, the repayments schedule will include interim payments and therefore the interest rate charged cannot be called a spot rate (although the rate charged on these standard loans is *related to* spot rates and is the yield to maturity of the loan).

Spot rates at any one time are determined in the market by the interplay of the supply of funds by lenders and the demand for funds by borrowers. As the supply and demand for funds change, the spot rates change and the yield curve alters its shape or position. Usually if there is a change in demand and supply of funds at a particular horizon (e.g. lending over two years), this also influences the supply and demand at all other horizons, so for example if r_2 increases then all other spot rates will also tend to increase. The correlation coefficient between changes in any two spot rates of interest is very high, in excess of 0.9. Although spot rates tend to move up and down together, they do not all move by the same absolute amount. In general, 'long rates' tend to move less than 'short rates'. So for example, if the one-year rate increases by 1% (e.g. from 9% to 10%) over the next week, the three-year rate might only increase by 0.95% (see curve B–B in Figure 21.1). However, if all spot rates do happen to move up or down by the same absolute amount, this is called a *parallel shift* in the yield curve.

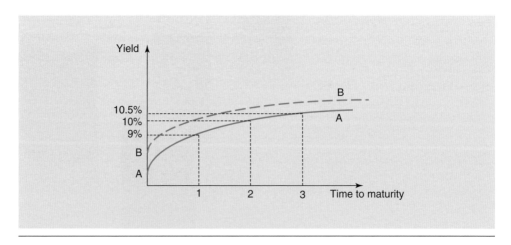

FIGURE 21.1: Yield curve

We have described spot yields in terms of borrowing and lending money over specific horizons. This can be done by buying a zero-coupon bond (i.e. lending money) or issuing (selling) a zero (i.e. borrowing money), so the spot rates can be inferred by observing the market price of zeros. For example, if the market price on a two-year zero is $92 per $100 face value, the two-year spot rate is 4.26% p.a. (calculated from $(1 + r)^2 = 100/92$). Pure discount government bonds for long maturities do not exist, but spot yields can be derived from data on a set of coupon-paying bonds.

> The yield curve is the relationship between interest rates (yields) on zeros and time to maturity.

Usually the (spot) yield curve is upward sloping and flattens out at long maturities, but as we shall see it can also be downward sloping, which implies that it costs less to borrow money over, say, one year than it does over, say, five years.

So far we have merely described what the yield curve is – and it's a very simple concept. It tells you how much it will cost you (per annum) to borrow (or lend) money for a fixed horizon, starting immediately (and with no interim payments). But what determines the shape of the yield curve at any point in time? As we shall see, this analysis is known as the *term structure of interest rates* and broadly speaking the shape of the yield curve is determined by the market's expectations about future price inflation.

21.2 FORWARD RATES

Spot rates all refer to borrowing (or lending) money *starting today*. Suppose instead that you go to a bank today but offer to lend $100, starting in one years time, with repayment one year later – this is known as a forward rate (of interest). For example, if today you offered to lend $100 starting in one years time and the bank quotes a forward rate $f_{12} = 11\%$, you would receive $111 at the end of year 2. How does the bank know what forward rate to quote? The bank calculates forward rates from observed spot rates of interest.

Calculation of forward rates

Figure 21.2 may help here, in terms of a heuristic argument. The 'correct' forward rate is based on the fact that investing $1 over two years at r_2 should give the same dollar amount at the end of year 2 as investing at $r_1 = 9\%$ in the first year, followed an investment at f_{12} between years one and two.

In Figure 21.2, note that the two-year investment earns 10% in *each* of the two years. Also, *in the first year*, the two-year rate is 1% (= 10% − 9%) higher than the one-year rate

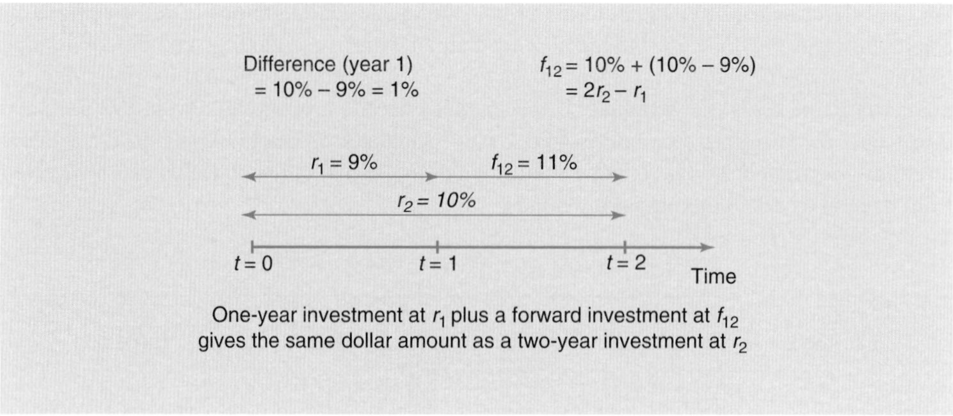

Difference (year 1)
= 10% − 9% = 1%

$f_{12} = 10\% + (10\% - 9\%)$
$= 2r_2 - r_1$

$r_1 = 9\%$ $f_{12} = 11\%$

$r_2 = 10\%$

$t = 0$ $t = 1$ $t = 2$
                                      Time

One-year investment at r_1 plus a forward investment at f_{12}
gives the same dollar amount as a two-year investment at r_2

FIGURE 21.2: Forward rate, f_{12}

($r_1 = 9\%$). Hence between $t = 1$ and $t = 2$ the forward rate must equal 10% plus the amount 'lost' in the first year. Thus the correct forward rate is:

Forward rate: $f_{12} = 10\% + (10\% - 9\%) = 11\% = 2r_2 - r_1$

This calculation ignores interest on interest, which makes the correct forward rate a little higher at 11.009% (see below). More formally, let f_{12} denote the forward rate applicable between years 1 and 2. Consider the following alternative investment strategies:

- **Strategy 1:** A = $100 invested over two years gives $A(1 + r_2)^2 = \$121$ at $t = 2$.
- **Strategy 2:** A = $100 invested at r_1 gives $A(1 + r_1) = \$109$ at the end of year 1.
                At $t = 0$ (today) you phone up a bank for a forward quote to lend $109 at the end of year 1 for a further year.

At $t = 2$ you will know that you will receive from strategy 2:

$$\$109\,(1 + f_{12}) = \$A(1 + r_1)(1 + f_{12}) \tag{1}$$

Since the two investment strategies are risk-free, arbitrage will ensure that the quoted rates are such that either investment strategy will result in the same payout at $t = 2$, hence:

$$A(1 + r_2)^2 = A(1 + r_1)(1 + f_{12}) \tag{2}$$

Rearranging equation [2]:

$$(1 + f_{12}) = \frac{(1 + r_2)^2}{(1 + r_1)} = \frac{(1.10)^2}{(1.09)} = 1.11009 \tag{3}$$

If we use the approximation $\ln(1 + z)^n = z$ (for $-1 < z < 1$), [2] and [3] can be expressed as linear relationships:

$$2r_2 \approx r_1 + f_{12} \qquad\qquad [4a]$$

or

$$f_{12} \approx 2\,r_2 - r_1 \qquad\qquad [4b]$$

(If we use *continuously compounded* rates – that is, $r_{cc} \equiv \ln(1 + r)$ – the above linear relationships are exact.) For the moment, assume that the approximations in equation [4] are accurate. We can repeat the above argument for a three-period horizon to obtain:

$$(1 + r_3)^3 = (1 + r_1)(1 + f_{13})^2 \qquad\qquad [5]$$
$$3r_3 \approx r_1 + 2f_{13} \qquad\qquad [6]$$

where f_{13} is the implicit (annual) forward rate between year 1 and year 3 and hence applies to an investment horizon of $3 - 1 = 2$ years. Note that we can also compare our three-year investment at r_3 with a known two-year investment at r_2 and the forward rate f_{23} between years 2 and 3:

$$(1 + r_3)^3 = (1 + r_2)^2(1 + f_{23}) \qquad\qquad [7]$$
$$3r_3 \approx 2r_2 + f_{23} \qquad\qquad [8]$$

Equations [6] and [8] can be used to calculate the forward rates f_{13} and f_{23} from the known spot rates. Forward rates can be calculated for any horizon by using the appropriate recursive formula and data on spot rates. From the above, the following equation is seen to hold for discrete and continuously compounded rates, respectively:

Discrete
$$f_{m,n} = \left[\frac{(1 + r_n)^n}{(1 + r_m)^m} \right]^{1/(n-m)} - 1 \qquad\qquad [9a]$$

Continuously compounded $\quad f_{m,n} = \left[\frac{n}{n - m} \right] r_n - \left[\frac{m}{n - m} \right] r_m = \left[\frac{nr_n - mr_m}{n - m} \right] \qquad [9b]$

where $n > m$. For example, for $n = 3$, $m = 2$, [9b] gives $f_{23} = 3r_3 - 2r_2$, which is of course the same as equation [8].

On the web site for the book you will find an Excel file that takes data on 10 (continuously compounded) spot rates r_1 to r_{10} and calculates all the one-period forward rates $f_{t,t+k}(k = 1, 2, \ldots)$, for example $f_{1,2}, f_{2,3}, f_{3,4}, \ldots f_{9,10}$. In one case we assume an upward-sloping spot-yield curve and in the other we have a downward-sloping curve. We then plot the spot rates and the corresponding forward rates against time to maturity: these are the *spot and forward yield curves*.

It is a matter of arithmetic (and can be seen in Figure 21.3) that:

> When spot rates increase with time to maturity (i.e. $r_1 < r_2 < \cdots < r_{10}$), the forward rate curve lies above the spot rate curve (and vice versa).

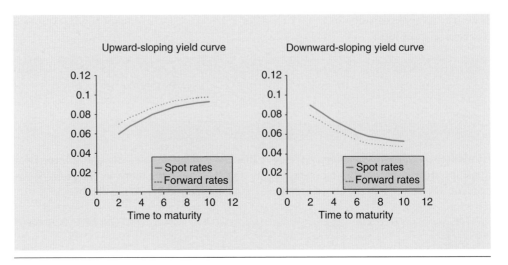

FIGURE 21.3: Yield curves

Besides the obvious fact that forward rates directly tell you at what rates you can borrow (or lend) money over different horizons, *starting some time in the future,* they are also widely used in pricing many different types of fixed-income securities, particularly derivative contracts based on interest-rate products such as T-bill and T-bond futures contracts, options on T-bonds and interest-rate swap contracts.

Estimating yield curves

There are many different types of yield curves, but all of them are a graph of some measure of yield against maturity (e.g. spot yield curve, forward yield curve). There are a wide range of coupon-paying bonds with different coupon-payment dates, different tax treatments and so on. Also some maturities may be traded in illiquid markets so that observed prices may not be representative of actual traded prices. Hence not all spot yields will lie exactly on a smooth curve and some statistical methods are required to fit a smooth curve to actual data on spot yields.

A popular method is the cubic spline technique. Here, separate curves are fitted to various sections of the yield curve (e.g. for rates between one- and five-year maturities, then between five- and ten-year maturities, etc.) and these separate curves are smoothly joined at each of the intersection points of the separate curves (e.g. at five-year maturity, ten-year maturity, etc.), so the whole curve is smooth but has different slopes for each section.

21.3 THEORIES OF THE TERM STRUCTURE

There are various hypotheses as to why rates of interest for longer maturities are usually (but not always) higher than rates for shorter maturities. These ideas come under the general heading of the term structure of interest rates. We begin by discussing these alternative theories before moving on to see how forward rates may be used to predict the future course of interest rates as well as the future rate of inflation.

Theories that attempt to explain possible different shapes of the (spot) yield curve include the expectations hypothesis, the liquidity preference hypothesis, market segmentation and the preferred habitat hypothesis. They differ only in their treatment of the term (risk) premium. We deal with each in turn.

Expectations hypothesis

The *pure expectations hypothesis (PEH)* assumes that investors are risk neutral – they are indifferent to risk. Investors know that there may be risk attached to their particular investment strategy, but they ignore this risk when making their investment decisions. Consequently, they base their investment decisions only on *expected* returns. For example, consider investing $A today (at $t = 0$) for three years (e.g. in a three-year zero-coupon bond) with yield r_3. The terminal value of the investment is:

$$TV_3 = A(1 + r_3)^3 \qquad [10]$$

Here r_3 is the 'long rate', since it applies for a three-year period (expressed at an annual rate). Next consider the alternative strategy of investing $A in three, 'rolled-over', *one-period* investments, over the three-year horizon, and reinvesting any interest earned. Ignoring transaction costs, the *expected* terminal value $E(TV_3)$ of this series of *one-period investments* is:

$$E(TV_3) = A(1 + r_1)(1 + Er_{12})(1 + Er_{23}) \qquad [11]$$

where E implies that expectations (forecasts) are made today. Er_{12} and Er_{23} are forecasts made today about the one-year spot rates beginning in years 2 and 3, respectively – these one-year interest rates are 'expected short rates', since they apply over successive one-year periods.

A single investment over three years gives a known terminal value, since r_3 is known today. Rolling over three one-year investments gives a terminal value that is subject to uncertainty, since the investor must forecast the future values of the one-period yields, Er_{12} and Er_{23}. However, under the PEH we assume that this risk is ignored and hence the terminal values of the above two alternative investment strategies will be equalised:

$$(1 + r_3)^3 = (1 + r_1)(1 + Er_{12})(1 + Er_{23}) \qquad [12]$$

The equality holds because if the terminal value corresponding to three-year investment exceeds the *expected* (forecast) terminal value of that on the sequence of one-year investments, investors would today buy three-year bonds and sell the one-year bond. This would result in a rise in the current market price of the long bond and hence a fall in its yield, r_3. Simultaneously, sales of the one-year bond would cause a fall in its current price and a rise in r_1. Hence the equality in equation [12] would be quickly (instantaneously) restored, if bond traders behave like risk-neutral investors (maybe because they are gambling with other people's money).

Taking logarithms of [12] and using the approximation $\ln(1 + z) \approx z$ for $|z| < 1$ (or using continuously compounded rates), we obtain the linear relationship:

$$r_3 = (1/3)\left[r_1 + Er_{12} + Er_{23}\right] \qquad [13]$$

Note that the PEH compares a risk-free investment over a three-year horizon with a risky 'rolled-over' investment and the above (risky) arbitrage equation only holds if investors really are risk neutral. On the other hand, the equations we used to derive forward rates are based on (risk-free) arbitrage and therefore the forward rates we calculate will be used to give forward quotes by banks.

One way of stating the PEH based on equation [13] is that it implies:

> The 'long rate' is a weighted average of current and 'expected' future
> short rates.

If we had considered a two-period investment horizon, the PEH would have given the two-year rate as:

$$r_2 = (1/2)\left[r_1 + Er_{12}\right] \qquad [14]$$

Shape of the yield curve

The spot yield curve is a graph of spot yields against the maturity of the bond. The PEH provides one way of analysing the shape of the spot yield curve. For example, suppose the one-year spot rate is $r_1 = 4\%$. If future short rates are expected to remain constant so that $r_1 = Er_{12} = Er_{23}$, using equations [13] and [14] the long rates r_2 and r_3 are also seen to equal 4%. Hence when future short rates are forecast to remain unchanged, the yield curve will be flat; that is, one-year, two-year and three-year spot rates will all equal 4%. However, if short rates are *expected* to rise in the future (e.g. $r_1 = 4\%, Er_{12} = 8\%$ and $Er_{23} = 9\%$), from equations [13] and [14] we have $r_2 = 6\%, r_3 = 7\%$ and the spot yield curve will be upward sloping (see Figure 21.4).

Expected future short rates are largely determined by what investors think inflation will be in future years. Hence today's yield curve will be upward sloping if investors think that inflation between years 1 and 2, and years 2 and 3 will be higher than the rate of inflation over the coming year. Hence the shape of the yield curve gives an indication of the market's view of future inflation.

Yield curve		**Inflation**
Flat	$\Rightarrow$	*expected to remain unchanged*
Upward sloping	$\Rightarrow$	*expected to rise in the future*
Downward sloping	$\Rightarrow$	*expected to fall in the future*

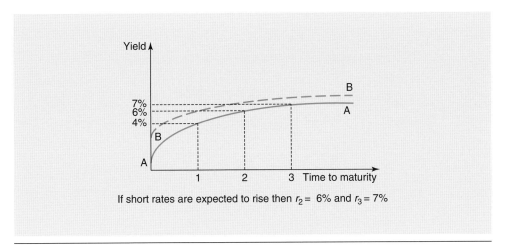

If short rates are expected to rise then $r_2 = 6\%$ and $r_3 = 7\%$

FIGURE 21.4: Yield curve

The PEH ignores risk or the **term premium**. Although the *nominal* return on a long bond is (reasonably) certain, the *real* return is likely to be more risky than on a series of rolled-over one-year investments. The rate paid on future one-year investments is likely to approximately equal the rate of inflation in these future periods. But for the long bond, the interest rate is fixed in nominal terms over the life of the bond and hence is uncertain in real terms (because of uncertainty about future inflation rates). Therefore, the return on the long bonds ought to contain a 'reward for inflation risk'; that is, a term premium T_n. So for example equation [13] now becomes:

$$r_3 = (1/3)\left[r_1 + Er_{12} + Er_{23}\right] + T_3 \tag{15}$$

Different theories of the term structure make different assumptions about the precise nature of the term premium. Indeed, if we assume that the term premium is a (non-zero) constant in each year and does not depend on the maturity of the bond (i.e. $T_n = T$), this constitutes the **expectations hypothesis (EH)**. All this means is that under the EH, interest rates for all maturities will be above those predicted by the PEH by the same amount T ($= 1\%$, say). Hence, the *shape* of the yield curve is the same under the EH as under the PEH but is shifted up, parallel to itself, by 1%.

Liquidity preference

Here, the assumption is that the term premium does *not* vary over time, but it does depend on the maturity of the bond. For example, bonds with longer periods to maturity may be viewed as being more risky than those with a short period to maturity. The increased risk on longer-maturity bonds may be due to increased uncertainty about inflation or because lenders like to lend at short horizons while borrowers prefer a longer horizon. The extra payment that investors require to compensate them for this increased risk is called the **liquidity premium**. If the liquidity premium is higher for bonds with longer maturities, then the basic qualitative shape of the yield curve will remain as described above (for the EH) but it will be steeper (see Figure 21.5).

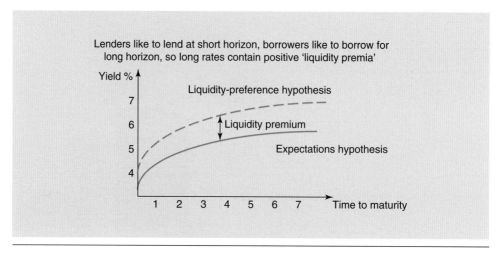

FIGURE 21.5: Liquidity preference

Market segmentation

The market-segmentation hypothesis states that the yield on bonds of different maturities depends on *all* the factors that influence the supply and demand for these bonds (e.g. the proportion of wealth held in each of these assets, the variance of returns, price inflation, etc.). However, in practice the market-segmentation hypothesis usually assumes that the yield on a bond has to rise when the proportion of debt held in bonds of this maturity increases. So the basic shape of the yield curve is still determined by expectations of future inflation, but may be slightly altered by the outstanding proportion of bonds at each maturity.

Preferred habitat

The preferred habitat theory is rather agnostic about the determinants of the term premium. It suggests that yields on bonds for widely differing maturities are largely unrelated, so we cannot infer what the shape of the yield curve will be.

Time-varying risk

Of course, if the term premium varies over time and also varies differently for bonds of different maturities, the shape of the yield curve will not be as clear-cut as in the expectations hypothesis or liquidity-preference hypothesis.

However, the empirical evidence suggests that the expectations hypothesis has a reasonable amount of support for most developed industrial economies (see Cuthbertson and Nitzsche, 2004). While there is some evidence of small yet constant term premia between yields on different maturity bonds, it remains the case that current long rates are primarily determined by forecasts of expected future short rates and the latter are strongly influenced by expectations about future inflation.

21.4 FORWARD RATES AND THE TERM STRUCTURE

The theories of the term structure have been discussed in terms of spot rates. However, as forward rates can be calculated from spot rates, the term structure must also say something about forward rates. To see this we return to the two-period case. If investors are risk neutral and the EH holds:

$$2r_2 = r_1 + Er_{12} + T_2 \qquad\qquad [16]$$

But because of (risk-free) arbitrage, forward and spot rates are related:

$$2r_2 = r_1 + f_{12} \qquad\qquad [17]$$

Comparing equations [16] and [17] we see that:

$$f_{12} = Er_{12} + T_2 \qquad \text{or} \qquad Er_{12} = f_{12} - T_2 \qquad\qquad [18]$$

Hence, under the EH, the quoted one-year forward rate is equal to the *market's forecast* of the one-year interest rate (between the end of year 1 and year 2) plus the term premium. If the term premium T_2 does not change over time, changes in the market's forecast of future short rates will be reflected in changes in the quoted forward rate. The EH assumes $T = 0$ hence:

> The EH implies that the observed forward rate is an unbiased predictor of the expected future spot rate.
> Quoted forward rates can be used to predict future values for nominal interest rates and hence inflation rates.

21.5 YIELD CURVE AND INFLATION

Suppose we have estimated the yield curve for a particular day and it shows one-year spot rates at $r_1 = 6.5\%$ with four-year rates rising to $r_4 = 9\%$ and becoming flat thereafter. The yield curve can be used to provide the market's expectation (forecast) of future inflation over the next four years.

The **Fisher hypothesis** implies that the quoted four-year rate is partly a compensation for expected future inflation and partly a 'real return' in terms of the increased goods and services you can buy if you invest over four years:

Nominal rate = Real rate + Expected inflation

Hence:

$$r_4 = rr_4 + \pi_4^e \qquad \text{or} \qquad \pi_4^e = r_4 - rr_4 \qquad\qquad [19]$$

Assume that the real return is determined by the long-run growth rate of the economy, which we take to be 3% p.a. Then a four-year rate of 9% would reflect the 3% real return plus a 6% return to compensate for future inflation. So, if we simply observe the four-year spot rate we can infer that the market's forecast for the average annual inflation rate over the next four years is 6%.

If there is a market in index-linked (default-free) government bonds, the real rate (ignoring tax effects) is also observable and may change over time (reflecting productivity growth in the economy). Estimates of the real rate from index-linked bonds indicate that in the UK variations in the real rate are usually quite small ($\pm$ 1/2% p.a.), so the assumption of a constant real rate may be reasonable.

Note that although the market's forecast of future inflation as calculated above may provide the best predictor available, nevertheless it may not be very accurate. This is because unforeseen events (e.g. a stock-market collapse or a recession) occurring between the time the forecast is made and the end of the forecast period will influence the actual inflation rate, so that it deviates from the 'best' forecast.

Can we use the EH to infer the market's forecast of inflation in particular years, rather than the average over the four years illustrated above? Yes we can, by using observable forward rates. Assuming that the (pure) expectations hypothesis is correct, the forward rate is the best predictor of future short rates (e.g. $Er_{34} = f_{34}$). So for example, if we want to know what the market's current forecast of inflation is between years 3 and 4, then this is equal to the forward rate f_{34} minus the real rate. So for example, if $f_{34} = 6.2\%$ (and taking $rr = 3\%$), the market's forecast for inflation between the end of year 3 and the end of year 4 is 3.2%. Knowing the forward rate curve, we can calculate the market's view of inflation over any years we care to choose, by calculating the appropriate forward rate.

Does this mean that Central Banks (such as the Bank of England and the Fed) are wasting their time looking at an extensive list of economic indicators and building large models of the economy, when trying to forecast inflation? Should they not simply look at forward rates determined by all market participants and infer future inflation from this market data? Certainly, Central Banks should look at the forward curve as an initial indicator of what the market thinks about future inflation.

But in reality, the relationship between nominal spot (and forward) rates and inflation expectations may be more complex than given by the basic Fisher hypothesis, because investors are concerned not just about expected returns but also about the risk attached to their forecasts of inflation and the real rate (i.e. growth of the economy). A more complex Fisher equation recognises that when you lend money, the rate of interest must contain an added payment to reflect the uncertainty about forecasts, hence:

> Nominal rate of interest = expected inflation + inflation risk premium
> + expected real rate + real rate risk premium

Changes in the above risk premia may distort the information about future inflation contained in quoted spot (and forward) rates. This is why Central Banks also examine many other factors (e.g. cost pressures from a depreciating currency, commodity price forecasts, the projected level of aggregate demand) when trying to forecast future inflation. Although forecasts obtained from market rates often get the direction of change in inflation right (e.g. an upward-sloping yield curve indicates higher expected inflation), nevertheless the quantitative forecast obtained from market rates may not be very accurate because of changes in the above risk premia. It is also the case that Central Banks 'have to tell a story', explaining their inflation forecasts. But forecasts of inflation extracted from the yield curve are just forecasts, with no story attached – they just encapsulate what the market thinks, but do not tell you *why* the market thinks that inflation will be at the level given by forward rates.

21.6 TERM STRUCTURE OF CREDIT RISK

In this section we give a simplified account of how we can extract the probability of default for, say, a BB-rated corporate from information on the yield curve for BB-rated firms. In other words, we are using spot rates to infer what the market thinks is likely to happen to corporate defaults in future years – which may be useful for investors in assessing the risk of corporate bonds and for Central Banks in helping them form a view about the future course of the economy. Extracting default probabilities is currently at the forefront of research, particularly models using options theory, but the approach adopted here will only give us 'ball-park' estimates.

The yield curve for Treasury bonds reflects interest rates required by investors for risk-free investments at specific maturities. The yield curve for an AAA-rated corporate will lie above the T-bond yield curve because at any maturity (e.g. 10 years), an AAA-rated bond has a higher probability of default than the T-bond. There will also be spot yield curves for AA-, A-, BBB-, BB-rated bonds and so on that will all be above each other, with that for CCC-rated bonds being the 'highest'.

To see how to extract default probabilities, suppose that we have spot yields (and hence the implied forward yields) for Treasuries and BBB-rated bonds. (The spot yield curve might have to be estimated from coupon-paying corporate and Treasury bonds.)

Treasuries	$r_1 = 10\%$	$r_2 = 11\%$	$f_{12} = 12\%$
Corporate BBB	$r_{c,1} = 12\%$	$r_{c,2} = 14\%$	$f_{c,12} = 16\%$

Let p_{01} represent the probability that a BBB-rated bond will pay out (survive) at the end of year 1 and hence $1 - p_{01} =$ the probability of default. Then *risk-neutral* investors would be indifferent between investing \$1 in either the corporate or the Treasury bond if:

Expected return on BBB corporate bond = Return on T-bond

$$p_{01}(1 + r_{c1}) = (1 + r_1) \qquad [20a]$$

Hence

$$p_{01} = \frac{(1 + r_1)}{(1 + r_{c1})} = 0.982 \qquad \text{[20b]}$$

So, the probability of default in year $1 = (1 - p_{01}) = 0.018\,(1.8\%)$. A spread of $2\% \,(= 12\% - 10\%)$ therefore implies a 1.8% probability of default in year 1. The analysis can be made more realistic by assuming a recovery rate of $\theta\,(= 0.25$, say) if the corporate defaults. Then risk neutrality implies

Expected return on corporate bond = Return on T-bond

$$(1 - p_{01})[\theta(1 + r_{c1})] + p_{01}(1 + r_{c1}) = 1 + r_1$$

We can easily solve the above equation for p_{01}:

$$p_{01} = \frac{(1 + r_1) - \theta(1 + r_{c1})}{(1 + r_{c1})(1 - \theta)} = 0.976 \qquad \text{[21a]}$$

This approach also gives us the determinants of the credit spread for the BBB-rated corporate:

$$credit\ spread = (r_{c1} - r_1) = \frac{1 + r_1}{(\theta + p_{01} - p_{01}\theta)} - (1 + r_1) \qquad \text{[21b]}$$

This approach therefore predicts that the spread will be lower, the higher is the recovery rate, as we might expect. Let us continue with our simple example for year 2, where p_{12} is the probability that the corporate does *not* default between years 1 and 2 (given that it has not defaulted in year 1). Hence $1 - p_{12}$ is the *marginal probability of default* – the probability of default in year 2, given that there has been no default in year 1. At $t = 0$, the return on \$1 invested *at the end of year 1* in the forward market is $(1 + f_{12})$. The expected return in the second year from investing in the corporate bond is $p_{12}(1 + f_{c,12})$, hence under risk neutrality $p_{12}(1 + f_{c,12}) = (1 + f_{12})$ and:

$$p_{12} = \frac{(1 + f_{12})}{(1 + f_{c,12})} = 0.965$$

The marginal probability of default in year $2 = (1 - p_{12}) = 0.035\,(3.5\%)$. The *cumulative probability* of survival by the end of year 2 is:

$$C_p(survival, 0–2) = p_{01}p_{02} = (0.982)(0.965) = 0.95\,(95\%)$$

Hence, the cumulative probability of default by the end of year 2 is:

$$C_p(default, 0–2) = 1 - p_{01}p_{02} = 0.05\,(5\%)$$

Notice that the cumulative probability of default by the end of year 2 is 5%, which is *not* equal to the sum of the *marginal* probabilities of default $p_{01} = 1.8\%$ and $p_{12} = 3.5\%$. In our example the probability of default in year 1 is 1.8% and in year 2 it is 3.5% (given 'survival' in year 1). The yield curve of the corporate therefore reflects the market's view that there may be a recession in year 2, leading to a higher default rate. If (at $t = 0$) the market believed that year 2 would be a boom year, this would be reflected in the yield curve, which would then imply a fall in the default probability in year 2 compared with year 1. So we have not only derived the default probabilities implicit in the observed term structure, but noted that these probabilities may have predictive power for future recessions or economic booms.

The nice feature of the above methodology is that it is forward looking. However, it is a fairly simple approach and therefore has some drawbacks, including the following:

- The assumption of risk neutrality may be inappropriate.
- Spot yields on corporate bonds are assumed to reflect only the risk-free rate and the default risk premium (i.e. there are no embedded options in the bond).
- Estimating corporate spot yields from the relatively illiquid corporate bond market is difficult because the majority of bonds are coupon paying and many have callable features.

The above drawbacks imply that a more thorough analysis requires the use of option-pricing techniques.

SUMMARY

- The *spot rate* is the rate of interest that applies to money borrowed today and paid back at a single point in the future (with no interim payments).
- Spot rates can be derived from the quoted prices of zero-coupon bonds.
- The *yield curve* is a relationship between interest rates for different maturities.
- The *expectations hypothesis* implies that long rates are a weighted average of current and expected future short rates. The shape of the yield curve therefore depends on the market's expectations about future short rates. An upward- (downward-) sloping yield curve implies that inflation is expected to increase (decrease) in the future.
- A *forward rate* is an interest rate that applies to an investment occurring between two future time periods. Forward rates can be calculated from spot rates.
- The yield curve for corporate bonds can be used to extract an estimate of the *probability of default* for the corporate in future years.

EXERCISES

Q1   What is the (spot) yield curve and why is it useful?

Q2   What are the two key features we require from a fitted yield curve?

Q3 The 1-year spot rate (on US T-bonds) is 9% p.a. The 2-year spot rate is 9.5% p.a. and the 3-year spot rate is 10% p.a.

(a) Calculate the implied one year ahead, 1-year forward rate, f_{12}. Explain why a 1-year forward rate of 9.6% would not be expected to prevail in the market.
(b) Calculate the forward rates f_{23} and f_{13}. Is there any link between f_{12}, f_{23} and f_{13}?
(c) Very briefly, mention one practical use for spot rates and one practical use of forward rates.

Q4 If the expectations hypothesis (EH) holds, why might the yield curve be:

(a) flat
(b) upward sloping
(c) downward sloping

What might cause a parallel shift in the yield curve?

The government implements a credible 'tight' monetary policy by raising short-term (e.g. 3-month) interest rates. Why might this result in a downward-sloping yield curve?

Q5 (a) You can lend $100 to a bank at a forward interest rate $f_{12} = 13\%$ quoted today but applicable to funds lent at the end of year 1 for a further year. The spot rates for 1-year money and 2-year money are currently 10% p.a. and 12% p.a. respectively. Explain whether you would take the bank's offer.
(b) In principle, how can one calculate the forward rate f_{13} (i.e. the rate of interest applicable between the end of year 1 and the end of year 3) and f_{23}?
(c) What are the practical uses of forward rates in finance?

Q6 Quoted spot (interest) rates are as follows:

Year	Spot rate, %
1	$r_1 = 5.00$
2	$r_2 = 5.40$
3	$r_3 = 5.70$
4	$r_4 = 5.90$
5	$r_5 = 6.00$

(a) What are the discount factors for each date; that is, the value today of $1 paid in year t?
(b) Calculate the PV and hence the fair price of the following Treasury notes (i.e. coupon bonds) all of which have a $1000 par value.

    (i) 5% coupon, 2-year note
    (ii) 5% coupon, 5-year note
    (iii) 10% coupon, 5-year note

(c) What are the 1-year forward rates applicable between (i) year 1 and year 2, (ii) year 2 and year 3?

22

Bond Market Strategies

AIMS

- To show how *duration and convexity* can be used to provide an approximation to the change in bond prices.
- To demonstrate how a *single* cash pay-out in the future can be exactly met by choosing a bond portfolio with the same duration as the liability. This is *single-period immunisation.*
- To analyse how a *series* of cash outflows in the future can be met either by 'cash-flow matching' or by 'duration matching' – the latter is known as *multi-period immunisation.*
- To show how a small number of bonds can be held that accurately track the return on a broad market bond index. This is *bond indexing.*
- To discuss *active bond strategies*, which include taking bets on the direction of interest-rate changes, twists in the yield curve and analysing mispriced bonds using the yield curve.

INTRODUCTION

Bond market strategies are often classified as either 'passive' or 'active'. The passive strategies we analyse are immunisation, cash-flow matching and indexing. A pension fund manager is faced with a known liability outflow in the future (i.e. pension payments). A major problem is to ensure that these payments can be met. One method is to try to assemble a portfolio of bonds such that all the cash flows from the bond come as close as possible to meeting these liabilities. However, what bonds should she choose and in what proportions should she hold each bond? The concept of 'duration' plays a key role here. Loosely speaking, if the duration of the bond portfolio equals the duration of the liabilities, then (to a first approximation) she will be hedged against future changes in interest rates. This strategy is known as *duration matching* or *portfolio immunisation*.

But the liabilities of a pension fund consist of a *series* of cash flows. To ensure that the cash outflows can be met, some form of *multi-period immunisation* is required. Two practical solutions are available. First, one can match each individual cash outflow with a portfolio of bonds *dedicated* to that particular cash flow. Alternatively, one can try to ensure that the duration of the whole *portfolio* of bonds equals that of *all* the liabilities – duration matching. An alternative to duration matching is *cash-flow matching*. Here, projected cash outflows are met by purchasing a set of bonds whose coupon and maturity pay-outs at each point in time exactly match those of the liabilities.

Bond indexing provides our final passive strategy. This requires bond portfolio managers to choose a relatively small number of bonds such that they 'track' the performance of a chosen bond index.

Active bond strategies require bond managers to 'take bets' on the future course of interest-rate movements, shifts in the yield curve or on spotting mispriced bonds. The activities of the Central Bank are keenly monitored by bond dealers, since the timing, size and direction of interest-rate movements are partly dependent on the actions of Central Banks.

22.1 DURATION AND CONVEXITY

The duration D of a bond is a 'summary statistic' that tells you how much the bond price will change after a change in the yield to maturity (YTM). For example, suppose that a speculator currently holds a coupon-paying bond with a market value of $1000 and a duration of $D = 5$. If there is a fall (rise) in the YTM of 1/2% (50 bp) over the next week (e.g. the YTM moves from 5% to 4.5%), the price of the bond will rise (fall) by approximately 2.5% over the next week, hence:

$$\% \text{ change in bond price} \approx -D \times \text{absolute change in YTM} \qquad [1]$$

The minus sign in the above formula captures the fact that a fall (rise) in the YTM leads to a rise (fall) in the bond price and note that the duration formula only gives an approximation to the change in price. The actual (or 'true') change in price will differ from that given by the duration formula, but the approximation is quite accurate for small changes in yields. If we require a more accurate measure of the change in price, we can also use a concept known as the convexity of the bond.

According to the duration formula, the change in the value of the bond held by the speculator will be around 2.5% or $25. Clearly, duration is useful for fixed-income traders who speculate on changes in interest rates – the larger the duration of the bond, the greater the percentage change in the bond price and hence the greater the risk of the bond position.

The relationship between the true change in bond price and the change in YTM is shown in Figure 22.1 by the curved or 'convex' line. The approximate change in price, given by the duration formula, is represented by the straight line. The actual price *rise* will exceed that given by the duration equation – and the actual price *fall* will be less than that calculated using duration. For small changes in yield, the actual price change and that given using the duration formula will be very close.

Duration of a portfolio of bonds

The duration of a portfolio of bonds is simply a weighted average of the duration of the constituent bonds in the portfolio, where the weights w_i are determined by the market value of the individual bonds:

$$D_p = \sum_{i=1}^{n} w_i D_i \qquad [2]$$

where $0 < w_i < 1$ (assuming no short selling) and $\sum w_i = 1$. For example, if you hold $200m in bonds with duration $D = 4$ and $400m in bonds with duration of $D = 12$, the duration of the bond portfolio is $(200/600)\,4 + (400/600)\,12 = 9.333$. This implies that if bond yields change by 1%, the *value* of your bond portfolio will change by approximately 9.333%, so:

% change in value of bond portfolio $\approx -\, D_p \times$ absolute change in YTM

So the change in value of your bond portfolio would be $60 ($=$ 9.3333 \times 600).

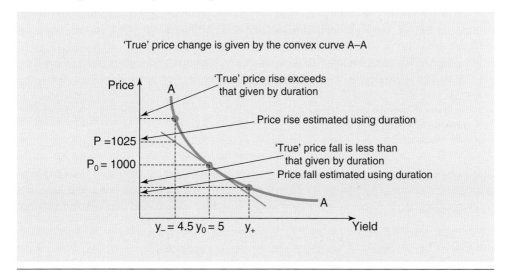

FIGURE 22.1: Duration and price changes

TABLE 22.1: Determinants of price changes

Four bonds priced initially to give YTM = 9%

1) 9% coupon, 5 years to maturity, initial price = 100

2) 9% coupon, 20 years to maturity, initial price = 100

3) 5% coupon, 5 years to maturity, initial price = 84.1746

4) 5% coupon, 20 years to maturity, initial price = 63.1968

Change in yield from 9% to:	Change (bp)	Percentage price change for bonds with different coupons and maturity			
		(1)	(2)	(3)	(4)
		9%, 5 year	9%, 20 year	5%, 5 year	5%, 20 year
6.00	(−300.00)	12.80	34.67	13.73	39.95
8.00	(−100.00)	4.06	9.90	4.35	11.26
8.99	(−1.00)	0.04	0.09	0.04	0.10
9.01	(1.00)	−0.04	−0.09	−0.04	−0.10
10.00	(100.00)	−3.86	−8.58	−4.13	−9.64
12.00	(−300.00)	−11.04	−22.57	−11.89	−25.09

Notes: The initial YTM is 9% and the first two columns indicate the illustrative new yields in per cent and the change in yield in bps. Columns 1–4 show the percentage change in bond price for different coupons and maturities.

The relationship between bond price changes, the coupon rate on the bond and the time to maturity of the bond are summarised below and in Table 22.1.

- Price change is greater the lower the coupon rate (e.g. compare columns 1 and 3 or 2 and 4).
- Price change is greater the longer the term to maturity (e.g. compare columns 1 and 2 or 3 and 4).
- For a given change in yield, the actual price increase is greater than the price decrease (e.g. column 4 for yields of 6 and 12).

The above properties are merely an arithmetic consequence of the PV formula for pricing the bond and the first two properties are encapsulated in the duration of the bond. But now let's be even more precise about how duration is calculated for an n-period coupon-paying bond:

$$D = \sum_{t=1}^{n} v_t t \quad \text{where} \quad v_t = PV(CF_t)/P = \{CF_t/(1+y)^t\}/P \qquad [3]$$

CF_t are the cash flows from the bond (i.e. coupons, maturity value) and P is the market price of the bond. The 'weights' v_t in this formula reflect the importance of each cash flow relative to the price of the bond; that is, $PV(CF_t) = C_t/(1 + y)^t$ is the present value of a *single* coupon payment and $PV(C_n + M) = (C_n + M)/(1 + y)^n$ is the present value of the last coupon payment plus the maturity value. The weights v_t sum to unity, since the *sum* of the PV of all the cash flows from the bond equal the price of the bond. In the duration formula each 'weight' is multiplied by 'time', $t = 1, 2, \ldots, n$. If we write out the formula for D in full it is:

$$D = \sum_{t=1}^{n} v_t t = \frac{\left[PV(C_1)1 + PV(C_2)2 + \cdots + PV(C_n + M)n \right]}{P} \qquad [4]$$

> The duration of a bond is a time-weighted average of the future cash payments.

A *zero-coupon* bond of maturity n has only one payment M at time n, and it can be shown that (see Appendix 22.1):

> The duration of a zero-coupon bond equals its maturity.

Duration is a useful summary statistic for calculating changes in bond prices, but what determines duration? Some useful rules of thumb for duration are:

> The duration of a coupon bond
> 1) generally increases with time to maturity (and always does so for bonds selling at or above par)
> 2) is higher if the coupon rate is lower
> 3) generally increases when the current YTM is lower.

It can be shown (see Appendix 22.1) that for small changes in yields, the *proportionate* price change of the bond is given by:

$$\frac{dP}{P} = -D \frac{dy}{(1 + y)} \qquad [5]$$

This is a little more involved than our original duration equation above because of the inclusion of the term $(1 + y)$ in the denominator. Also note that in using this equation we have to

TABLE 22.2: Calculation of duration

Data	5 years to maturity, 13.52% coupon (annual), $M = \$100$, YTM = 11%.
Question	Calculate duration and the change in price if the YTM increases to 12%.
Answers	Current price, $P = \$13.52/(1.11) + \$13.52/(1.11)^2 + \cdots$ $+ \$113.52/(1.11)^5 = \$12.18 + \$10.97 + \cdots$ $+ \$67.37 = \mathbf{\$109.31}$

$PV(C_1) = \$12.18, PV(C_2) = \$10.97$, etc.

$D = [\$12.18(1) + \$10.97(2) + \cdots + \$67.37(5)]/\$109.31$
$= \mathbf{3.991 \text{ years } (4 \text{ years})}$

Change in price:
$dP/P = -D\,dy/(1+y) = -(3.991)\,0.01/(1.11) = \mathbf{-0.036\,(3.65\%)}$

New price (at YTM = 12%) = $\$109.31\,(1 - 0.036) = \mathbf{\$105.38}$

express y as a proportion – so a yield of 5% would appear in this formula as $y = 0.05$ and an increase in yield of 1% would be $dy = 0.01$, giving a proportionate change in price for $D = 5$ of $dP/P = -5\,(0.01)/(1.05) = -0.0476$; that is, a fall of 4.76% in the price. D is known as the **Macaulay duration**. Duration for a particular coupon bond is calculated in Table 22.2, along with the approximate price change using the duration formula.

> Duration provides a good approximation to the change in price of a
> bond for parallel shifts in the yield curve and for small changes in yields
> (of around 25 bp).

We can rearrange equation [5] in a number of equivalent ways. For example:

$$\frac{dP}{P} = -MD.dy \quad \text{where } MD = \frac{D}{(1 + y)} \qquad [6]$$

% change in bond price $\approx -MD \times$ absolute change in YTM

The term MD is known as **modified duration**. Sometimes a useful shorthand employed by bond traders is to refer to the **dollar duration** (DD) of a bond, which is defined as :

$$dP = -DD.dy \quad \text{where } DD = (MD).P \qquad [7]$$

Knowing DD, one can immediately calculate the (approximate) price change for a given change in yield. Going one step further, for a 1 bp (0.01%) change in yield we have

$dy = 0.0001 (= 1/10,000)$, hence:

$$dP(\text{for } 1 \text{ bp}) = PVBP = \frac{MD \times P}{10,000} \qquad [8]$$

The expression in [8] is known as '**price value of a basis point**' (**PVBP**). To illustrate the use of PVBP, consider a trader who has $P = \$1m$ in a bond with a modified duration $MD = 5$, hence $PVBP = \$500$. Suppose there is now a 1 bp change in the yield – that is, for example, a change from YTM $= 5\%$ to YTM $= 5.01\%$ – then the value of the bond portfolio will change by \$500.

Convexity

Duration only provides a first-order approximation to the change in price of a bond and hence is only accurate for small changes in interest rates (e.g. up to 25 basis points). A more accurate approximation is found by also using the convexity of the bond. Convexity χ (with annual coupon payments) is defined as:

$$\chi = \frac{\left[\sum_{t=1}^{N} t(t+1)CF_t/(1+y)^t \right]}{P(1+y)^2} \qquad [9]$$

Convexity measures the curvature of the the price–yield relationship.

Unfortunately, there is really no intuition behind this rather messy convexity formula – it arises from the mathematics of approximating changes in a non-linear relationship between two variables, the price change and the change in the YTM. However, once we have calculated the bond's convexity (in Excel, say) our improved approximation to the change in price is then given by:

$$\frac{dP}{P} = -MD.(dy) + \frac{1}{2}\chi(dy)^2 \qquad [10]$$

Convexity is a desirable trait in a bond, since if you can find two bonds with the same duration, the bond with the highest convexity (i.e. curvature in the price–yield relationship) will exhibit a larger rise in price when yields fall and a smaller fall in price when yields rise (compared with the low-convexity bond). However, this advantage will be reflected in the higher price you have to pay for the high-convexity bond.

The price changes calculated using duration and 'duration plus convexity' are both approximations to the true price change. The actual (true) price change will differ from that given by the above formulae if either the change in yield is large or there is a non-parallel shift in the yield curve; see Table 22.3.

TABLE 22.3: Duration and convexity

Data	A 5-year zero coupon bond, face value $1000, 5-year spot rate (= YTM) of 10%.
Question	Calculate (i) duration, (ii) convexity, (iii) the approximate price change and (iv) the actual price change, for a 2.0% (200 bp) change in interest rates.
Answers	*Duration*

$$P = \$1000 / (1.10)^5 = \$620.92$$

The duration of a pure discount bond equals its maturity, $D = 5$.

Convexity

$$\chi = [5(6)\,\$1000/(1.10)^5]/\$690.92\,(1.1)^2 = 22.28.$$

Price change: using duration

$$dP/P = -5\,(0.02)/(1.10) = -0.0909\,(-9.091\%).$$

Price change: using duration and convexity

$$dP/P = -0.0909 + (1/2)\,22.28\,(0.02)^2 = -0.08645\,(-8.645\%).$$

Actual price change

Initial price (at 10% yield) = $1000/(1.10)^5 = $620.92.

Price (at 12% yield) = $1000/(1.12)^5 = $567.43.

Actual price change $= -8.615\%$.

Using duration *and* convexity provides a closer approximation to the actual change in price.

EXCEL ⊗ The calculation of duration and convexity and the true change in the bond price can be easily calculated using Excel and an example can be found on the web site.

22.2 PORTFOLIO IMMUNISATION

Another use for duration is to enable you to choose a portfolio of coupon-paying bonds so that you can meet a *known* set of payments accruing in the future – this is known as portfolio immunisation. In effect, immunisation insulates your balance sheet from changes in yields. For example, a pension fund has to make sure it has enough assets to meet its pension payments on particular future dates. Initially, to keep things simple, let us suppose that the pension fund has a known *single* payment of $A payable in four years time – the duration of the pension liability is 4. The pension fund has to choose a bond (or bonds) so that it can be assured of receiving this amount. Which bonds should it choose? Clearly, if zero-coupon bonds are available with a maturity of four years, the pension fund could purchase these bonds today, so that they have a maturity value of $A, in four years time.

But if the pension fund purchased a *coupon-paying bond* it would face the reinvestment risk of the coupons; if the bond had a maturity greater than four years, the pension fund would also face an uncertain selling price in the fourth year. However, it is possible to choose a coupon bond that will meet a fixed 'one-off' liability in four years time, *providing:*

1. We assume that the reinvestment rate for the coupons in all future periods equals the YTM.
2. The bond we choose has a duration of four years.
3. The market value of the bond equals the *present value* of the future liability.

If the above conditions are met, then if the YTM rises or falls by 1% in the future, the pension fund will still receive $A in four years time.

In Table 22.4 we assume a *single* pension liability of $165.95 payable in four years time, so the duration of the liability is $D_L = 4$ and with the current YTM = 11% the present value of the liability is $V_L = 165.95/(1.11)^4 = \$109.31$. We must now choose a bond with a duration of 4 and a current value of $109.31. The 5-year, 13.52% coupon bond, maturity value $M = \$100$, has a current market value of $109.31 and a duration of 4 – so it fulfils all of the above requirements (Table 22.4).

In Table 22.4 we show that if the YTM remains at 11%, the selling price of the bond in year 4 plus the coupon payments and interest-on-interest gives $165.95 at the end of year 4. If there is an immediate change in the YTM to either 12% or 10%, the bond will still give approximately $165.95 at the end of year 4. So the pension liability in year 4 will be met, no matter what happens to the YTM – the pension liability has been immunised by choosing a bond with a duration equal to that of the pension liability. The reason for the slight discrepancy in the final value of the bond and the pension liability in year 4 is because the convexity of the bond and the liability are not the same.

In Table 22.4 it is clear that after a change in yield, any increase (decrease) in interest-on-interest is exactly offset by the decrease (increase) in the price of the bond in year 4. For example, if yields rise to 12% the price of the bond in year 4 falls from $102.27 to $101.36, but this is just offset by a rise in coupon interest payments from $63.68 to $64.62. The bond has 'immunised' the total receipts available in four years time from any changes in the YTM.

We could have chosen a *portfolio* of bonds with which to immunise the liability. The criteria that ensure that a *single* cash outflow will be met by the immunised bond portfolio are (see Appendix 22.2):

Portfolio immunisation

- Present value of the bond portfolio = present value of the liability.
- Duration of the bond portfolio = duration of the single liability.
- Yield curve is flat – so the reinvestment rate for the coupons equals the YTM.
- Small and parallel shifts in the yield curve – so the duration formula applies.

TABLE 22.4: Immunisation (single liability)

Data	Liability in four years time = $165.95. Present value of liability = 109.31, $D_L = 4$. A 5-year, 13.52% (annual) coupon bond, $M = \$100$, YTM = 11%, with price $P = 109.31$ and duration, $D_B = 4$.
Questions	What are the total receipts in four years time assuming: 1) YTM = 11% with coupons reinvested at this rate? 2) YTM of either 12% or 10%?
Answers	**YTM = 11%**

Expected price of bond in year 4 = $113.52/(1.11) = \$102.27$
Coupons + Interest-on-interest =
$\quad$ $\$13.52 \, (1.11)^3 + \$13.52 \, (1.11)^2 + \$13.52 \, (1.11)^1 + \$13.52 = \$63.68$
Total receipts (year 4) = **$165.95**

YTM = 12%

Expected price of bond in year 4 = $113.52/(1.12) = \$101.36$
Coupons + Interest-on-interest =
$\quad$ $\$13.52 \, (1.12)^3 + \$13.52 \, (1.12)^2 + \$13.52 \, (1.12)^1 + \$13.52 = \$64.62$
Total receipts (year 4) = **$165.97**

YTM = 10%

Expected price of bond in year 4 = $113.52 \, (1.10) = \$103.20$
Coupons + Interest-on-interest =
$\quad$ $\$13.52 \, (1.10)^3 + \$13.52 \, (1.10)^2 + \$13.52 \, (1.10)^1 + \$13.52 = \$62.75$
Total receipts (year 4) = **$165.94**

As we have noted already, the duration of a bond portfolio alters merely because of the passage of time and also if the YTM changes. The duration D_L of the single liabiltiy also falls as its life gets shorter. Hence the bond portfolio needs to be periodically rebalanced to ensure that $D_B = D_L$ at all times. The frequency of rebalancing depends on a trade-off between the potential costs of a duration mismatch and the transaction costs of buying and selling bonds. Clearly, immunisation does not involve trying to find mispriced bonds, so it is a passive strategy.

By 'duration matching' using several bonds, we have more flexibility in our choice of bonds and this is likely to be beneficial in terms of greater liquidity and lower bid–ask spreads. For example, a single liability payable in 10 years may be duration matched by many different bond portfolios. A *bullet portfolio* would have bonds with durations close to 10 years, whereas a *barbell portfolio* has bonds with a wider span of durations. For example, if we have a single liability payable in 10 years, then $D_L = 10$. We can duration match this liability with the following bond portfolios.

Barbell portfolio: Equal amounts in 5 and 15-year duration bonds

$$D_p = (1/2)5 + (1/2)15 = 10$$

Bullet portfolio: Equal amounts in 9 and 11-year duration bonds

$$D_p = (1/2)9 + (1/2)11 = 10$$

For non-parallel shifts in the yield curve, spot rates at different maturities alter by different amounts. Duration matching does not ensure immunisation for non-parallel shifts, since it is spot rates that determine the reinvestment rate for coupon payments. For a bullet portfolio, the spot yields are closer to each other than for a barbell portfolio. Hence, the bullet portfolio involves less immunisation risk than the barbell portfolio. However, the barbell allows a wider choice of bonds and hence greater liquidity and lower dealing costs. As well as reducing immunisation risk by choosing a bullet portfolio, one can also take account of non-parallel shifts in the yield curve by using more advanced definitions of duration.

An example of using the duration approach when there are non-parallel shifts in the yield curve can be found on the web site.

Multiperiod immunisation

So far, to keep things reasonably simple, we have only chosen a bond portfolio to match a *single* pension liability at a specific date in the future. But a pension fund has known pension payments over many future years. One method of meeting these multiperiod cash outflows is to take *each* separate liability payment and duration match it with a *dedicated* portfolio of bonds. For example, in Table 22.5 a liability outflow of $1000 in two years time is matched with a portfolio of bonds whose weighted (portfolio) duration is two years (and whose current value is $1000). Similarly, the cash outflow of $2000 at the end of year 4 is matched with a bond portfolio with $D_p = 4$ and current market value of $2000.

A second method is to treat all the future pension payments en masse (rather than individually) and also to 'lump together' all our bonds so that the duration of the portfolio of bonds matches the duration of all these pension cash outflows. Let us assume we use only two bonds (A and B) in our portfolio. What we have to do is:

a) Calculate the duration of the pension liabililities, D_L and their present value, V_L.
b) Match durations: $w_a D_a + w_b D_b = D_L$.

TABLE 22.5: Multiperiod immunisation, dedicated portfolio

	End year 2	**End year 4**
Liabilities (cash flow)	$1000	$2000
Asset portfolio	Portfolio of coupon-paying bonds with $D_p = 2$ and $V = \$1000$	Portfolio of coupon-paying bonds with $D_p = 4$ and $V = \$2000$

c) Make sure that the total in bonds $V_{bonds} = V_a + V_b$ equals the present value of the liabilities V_L, (that is, $V_{bonds} = V_L$) or equivalently $w_a + w_b = 1$.[1]

An illustrative case for calculating how much to hold in each of the two bonds is given in Table 22.6.

TABLE 22.6: Matching portfolio durations

Data	Liabilities: $100 in each of next five years
	Bonds: a) 1-year, 6% coupon bond (annual), par value = $100.
	b) 4-year, 8% coupon bond (annual), par value = $100
	Current YTM is 10% p.a.
Question	Calculate the amounts to invest in each bond to immunise all the cash flows from the liability.
Answers	*Liabilities*

Present value: $V_L = \$100/(1.1) + \$100/(1.1)^2 + \cdots + \$100/(1.1)^5$
$$= \$379.07$$
$PV_1 = \$100/(1.1) = \$90.91, \quad PV_2 = \$100/(1.1)^2 = \$82.64$, etc.
Duration, $D_L = (1\,PV_1 + 2\,PV_2 + \ldots + 5\,PV_5)/PV_L = 2.81$

One-year bond

Price, $P_a = \$106/(1.1) = \$93.36, \quad D_a = 1$ year.

Four-year bond

Price, $P_b = \$8 / (1.1) + \$8/(1.1)^2 + \$8 / (1.1)^3 + \$108/(1.1)^4$
$$= \$7.27 + \$6.61 + \$6.01 + \$73.77 = \$93.66$$

$D_b = [\$7.27\,(1) + \$6.61\,(2) + \$6.01\,(3) + \$73.77\,(4)]/\$93.66 = 3.56$

Duration match: $D_a w_a + D_b w_b = D_L$ hence $1w_a + 3.56w_b = 2.81$
Substititute: $w_a = 1 - w_b$ to obtain $w_a = 0.293$ and $w_b = 1 - w_a = 0.707$
$ amount in one-year bond = 0.293 $(V_L) = \$111.21$
$ amount in four-year bond = 0.707 $(V_L) = \$267.86$

Duration matching ensures that the change in the value of the bond portfolio and the change in the value of the pension liabilities will be approximately equal, after a change in yields. Because we use duration to calculate changes in value and we assume parallel shifts in the yield curve, the above calculations do not ensure exact immunisation. Duration matching is not sufficient to ensure that all individual future pension payments will be met, even for parallel shifts in the yield curve, but the method is quite effective and widely used in practice.

---

[1] $w_a = V_a/V_{bonds}$ and $w_b = V_b/V_{bonds}$ therefore $w_a + w_b = 1$

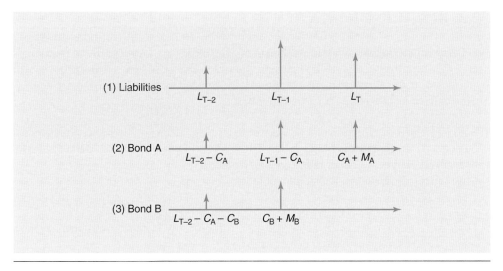

FIGURE 22.2: Cash-flow matching

Cash flow (exact) matching

Multi-period liabilities could in principle be met by purchasing several zero-coupon bonds of different maturities, with face values that match the payment schedule of your liabilities. But there may not be a liquid enough zeros market to achieve this. If this is the case, the series of liability cash flows can be met by a strategy known as cash flow ('exact') matching. The aim is to find the lowest-cost portfolio that generates a pattern of cash flows that exactly matches the stream of liability payments. In this process we begin with the last liability payment L_T and work back to the present, as follows (see Figure 22.2):

- Choose bond A with a maturity date T and final year payout $C_A + M_A$ equal to L_T.
- Coupon payments from bond A at $T-1$ are used to meet part of the liabilities L_{T-1} so that we require additional funds $(L_{T-1} - C_A)$ at $T-1$. We purchase bond B with maturity $T - 1$ and final payment $(C_B + M_B) = (L_{T-1} - C_A)$.
- Repeat the above until the first liability payment is covered, each time purchasing the lowest-cost bond (in terms of transaction costs).

This is a passive strategy, requiring no rebalancing, and the only risk is credit risk. So far, we have ignored interest-on-interest from coupons. A variant on the above would be to assume a low expected reinvestment rate and use this *prospective reinvestment income* to meet part of the future liability payments. Clearly, there is some market risk in this strategy, since actual reinvestment rates might fall below those expected. Cash-flow matching is rather restrictive on the types of bonds you can hold and it is therefore not very popular.

With multi-period liabilities, matching the duration of the *portfolio* of assets to that of the liabilities does not guarantee meeting cash-flow liabilities in all periods. Also, non-parallel shifts in the yield curve that tend to occur at shorter maturities would undermine an immunisation strategy. In **combination matching** these risks are minimised by cash-flow matching for the first few years (say, over five years) and then duration matching the portfolio in later years.

22.3 BOND INDEXING

Bond market indexing is similar to stock market indexing (index tracking). Bond indexing is a strategy where the bond portfolio manager chooses a *sample* of bonds that she hopes will 'replicate' or 'track' a particular bond index – it is classified as a passive investment strategy. There are three main types of bond market index:

- Value-weighted (total return) broad market index (e.g. Lehman Aggregate Bond Index, Salomon Broad Investment Grade Index (BIG), Merrill Lynch US Broad Market Index).
- Specialised market (e.g. high-grade corporate index).
- Customised (e.g. Salomon Pension Fund Index).

A US *broad market index*, as its name suggests, will probably include government, agency, corporate bonds, mortgage-backed and Yankee bonds. A *customised index* such as a pension fund index will, for example, contain bonds of long duration and hence will closely match the duration of the pension fund liabilities. Obviously, the bond manager will not include all the bonds in the chosen market index, as this would involve prohibitive transaction costs.

The monthly performance of a bond portfolio is usually measured by the total return R:

$$(1 + R) = \frac{Coupons \: + \: reinvestment\: income \: + \: end\text{-}of\text{-}period\: value}{Initial\: Portfolio\: Value} \tag{11}$$

Also of interest to bond managers is the variability in R – the variance (or standard deviation) of monthly returns may be used as a measure of the riskiness of the bond portfolio.

Tracking error is the difference between the performance of the bond manager's 'replication portfolio' and the bond index she is trying to mimic. For a bond portfolio manager who is trying to mimic an index, sources of tracking error include:

- Transaction costs in constructing the replication portfolio.
- Difference in composition of the replication portfolio and the index itself.
- Discrepancies between transaction prices (e.g. bid–ask) of the replication index and the prices used in constructing the market index.

In a broad market index there could be as many as 5000 bonds represented and some of these will be very thinly traded. Also, bonds are continually removed from the index (as their maturity falls below one year) and others are added to replace them. So it is not an easy task to replicate the index.

Replicating the index

There are two broad methods of trying to replicate the chosen index: stratified sampling and the optimisation approach. In **stratified sampling** the bonds that comprise the chosen *bond market index* are classified according to particular characteristics. This is illustrated in Table 22.7.

TABLE 22.7: Stratified sampling

1. Duration	a) Less than five years	b) Greater than five years	
2. Sectors	a) Treasury	b) Agency	c) Corporates
3. Rating	a) AAA, AA, A	b) BBB, BB, B	c) Below B

Hence, the number of stratified cells = $2 \times 3 \times 3 = 18$. The percentage market value of these different types of bond in the bond index will then be found. For example, 5% by value of the bond index may comprise 'corporates below B rating'. The bond portfolio manager will then choose a subset of bonds that fall into this cell, to replicate this aspect of the index.

In the **optimisation approach** the fund manager will have an explicit quantitative target. For example, she might try to maximise total return R, over a specific horizon, while still matching the cell breakdown described above. Alternatively, based on historical data she may choose those bonds that minimise the variance of the past tracking errors. So far, we have described what is usually referred to as 'plain vanilla' indexing. In *enhanced indexing* the aim is to exceed the performance of the benchmark index, by pursuing an active strategy with *part* of the available funds (e.g. buying underpriced bonds and selling overpriced bonds).

Some idea of the tracking error of monthly holding-period returns (HPRs) over a two-year period for three types of bond index is given in Table 22.8. The mean (monthly) return tracking error for the broad market bond index and the government bond replication index are both low, at 2 bp (i.e. 0.02 %), with that for corporates being higher at 9 bp. These figures are also reflected in the cumulative tracking error over a two-year period. The standard deviation of the tracking error is large for corporates and this high figure is also reflected in the 54 bp standard deviation of the broad market replication index, which includes corporates.

TABLE 22.8: Tracking error monthly returns (basis points)[1]

Index	Mean return[2]	Std dev.[3]	Cumulative total return[4]
Broad market	2	54	34
Government	2	2	31
Corporate	9	17	156

Notes : 1. Two-year period, for measurement of tracking error.
    2. Difference between monthly return on replication index and actual index, averaged over two years, expressed in basis points.
    3. Standard deviation of monthly tracking error (bp).
    4. Sum of tracking error of monthly returns over two-year period, at an annual rate in basis points.

22.4 ACTIVE BOND STRATEGIES

Active strategies in the bond market are perhaps not as numerous as those in the equity market. In part, this is because plain vanilla bonds are relatively homogeneous assets compared to equities, differing only in their maturity, coupon payments and level of credit (default) risk. However, in recent years with the growth in hedge-fund activity and the increased use of debt finance by private equity companies, there are a wide variety of active bond strategies (which can also be undertaken using other fixed-income derivative products). Note that a fixed-income 'desk' would generally hold a fairly well-diversified set of bonds and would use a subset of the bonds in pursuing active strategies.

In an active strategy you are concerned about the holding-period return, where you close out your positions fairly frequently. The total return is then made up of the bond price change plus any coupons and reinvested income from the coupons. There are two main types of strategy. The first is a **directional bet**, where you forecast the overall level of interest rates – that is, movements up and down in the whole yield curve. If you forecast falling interest rates, you would move into long-duration bonds – if you forecast rising interest rates, you would move into short-duration bonds or sell (short sell) some of your bonds and hold cash. The second type of strategy is a **relative value trade** (or **bond swap**), where you go long an underpriced bond (i.e. one with an abnormally high current yield) and short sell an overpriced bond (i.e. one with an abnormally low yield). If the yield spread narrows, you will make a profit on the trade. In a relative value trade you are automatically protected to some degree from parallel shifts in the yield curve. But if your relative value trade involves a duration mismatch between the long and short positions, this risk can be hedged using interest-rate derivatives, such as bond futures.

If your forecast of interest rates is based on the state of the economy, the directional bet may be classified as a *macro strategy*. Here one tries to predict the direction of changes in interest rates over the business cycle, including possible actions by Central Banks when setting short-term rates. The main impact on interest rates come from expectations about future inflation and whether the economy is thought to be growing too fast, possibly leading to higher inflation in the future. In the long term we expect interest rates to be determined by the real growth of the economy (i.e. the real interest rate), expected inflation and any default risk premium specific to a particular industrial sector:

Interest rate = real rate + expected inflation + default risk premium

For example, near the peak of the business cycle inflationary pressures are likely to build up and one might expect interest rates to rise (either by Central Bank action or because of an increase in inflation expectations) in the near future. Hence, the portfolio manager might switch out of long-duration bonds into short-duration bonds and cash. Eventually, as the economy slows down and inflationary pressures subside, one would expect a fall in interest rates and hence a move back into long-duration bonds.

This market-timing strategy would be undertaken for different countries around the world depending on the state of their respective business cycles, so a trader might be buying UK bonds while at the same time being a net seller of US bonds. However, timing of bond purchases and sales based on forecasts of interest-rate movements is very difficult to accomplish successfully and therefore active macro strategies can be highly risky.

Twists in the yield curve

A macro strategy is generally based on forecasts of equal changes in interest rates at all maturities (i.e. a parallel shift in the yield curve), but some fixed-income traders try to predict twists in the yield curve. For example, if the analyst expects an easing of monetary tightness, she would expect short rates to fall. However, if monetary laxity implied higher rates of inflation in the future, she might expect long rates to rise to reflect the inflation premium. To take advantage of this forecast twist or 'steepening' in the yield curve, she would move out of long-duration bonds and into short-duration bonds.

Regression techniques

Regression techniques can be used to try to predict current interest-rate changes from previous changes in interest rates and from the long–short yield spread. According to the expectations hypothesis, the long–short yield spread should have predictive power for future changes in yields. Consider using weekly data and assume that changes in the three-year rate (over the next week) depend on the 'three-year–one-year' spread ($r_3 - r_1$):

$$\Delta r_{3t} = a_1 \Delta r_{3t-1} - b_1 (r_3 - r_1)_{t-1} + c_1 \qquad [12]$$

where $\Delta r_{3,t} = r_{3,t} - r_{3,t-1}$ is the change over one week in the three-year yield. Estimates of a_1, b_1 and c_1 ($b_1, c_1 > 0$) can be obtained by regression analysis. Equation [12] is a form of error-correction model (ECM). In equilibrium, when all interest rates are assumed to be constant (i.e. $\Delta r_3 = 0$), the equation gives $r_3 = r_1 + c_1 / b_1$, where the term (c_1 / b_1) represents the liquidity premium – that is, the three-year rate exceeds the one-year rate in equilibrium. In addition, the dynamic equation implies that if $r_3 > r_1$ at time $t - 1$, r_3 then will fall in the next period (i.e. $\Delta r_{3t} < 0$) – *ceteris paribus*. Knowing values of the independent variables at $t - 1$, we can predict the change in the three-year rate next period and hence the capital gain on (three-year maturity) bonds (over the next week). If the equation predicts a fall in three-year rates over the next week, then you *buy* three-year bonds today in the hope of making a capital gain over the next week, if your predictions are correct – this is a 'directional bet'. The above equation is merely illustrative and in practice it might also contain other lagged values of the change in interest rates as well as other spreads, for example the six-month–one-month spread (see Cuthbertson and Nitzsche, 2004).

Similar equations for the change in interest rates for other maturities r_i ($i = 2, 4, 5$, etc.) can also be estimated. If we have a set of equations explaining Δr_1, Δr_2, etc., we can predict interest-rate movements along the whole of the yield curve and hence predict bond-price changes for bonds of different maturities. The analyst can then decide on a reallocation of her portfolio across the maturity spectrum to maximise her expected holding-period return from a switching strategy.

Substitution swap

Here the trader looks for two bonds that are nearly identical in terms of their coupon, maturity, duration, credit rating, bond covenants, call provisions and so on, but she believes that bond A is overpriced and bond B is underpriced. So she takes a long position in bond B and short sells bond A. If the yield curve experiences a parallel shift (either up or down), the trader is largely protected because the increase in price on one bond is offset by the loss on the other bond – and the trader would make sure that the durations of her long–short positions were offsetting (or would hedge any parallel shifts in the yield curve using interest-rate futures). Note that after a parallel shift in the yield curve the under/overpricing remains unchanged. What the trader is hoping for is that *other traders* will recognise the mispricing and then buy the underpriced bond B and (short) sell the overpriced bond A, hence raising the market price of B and lowering the price of A. If our trader puts on the trade before the market recognises (and corrects) the mispricing, then she will make a profit after the two bond prices have returned to their 'normal levels' – and she has also been hedged against parallel shift in the yield curve.

For example, suppose a 15-year maturity, 7% coupon bond of the Ford Motor Company is priced to give a YTM of 7.1%, whereas a similar Chrysler 7% coupon bond is trading at a YTM of 7%. If the credit rating of the two firms is the same, there is no apparent reason for the Ford bond to be trading at a higher yield. If you thought yields were going to converge, you would buy the higher yield Ford bond and short sell the Chrysler bond, so if the spread narrowed you would make money by closing out your bond postion. Of course, there are risks in the strategy, since if the credit risk of Ford increased (because of an adverse report on the safety of its vehicles) its yield would increase, the spread would widen and the price of Ford bonds would fall, giving you a loss on your long position if you had to close out immediately.

A variant on the above is an *intermarket spread*, which is a relative-value trade between *two different sectors* of the bond market. For example, suppose that you think the spread between the current yield on a BB-rated corporate bond and T-bonds is unusually wide at 3% and will narrow in the future to its normal historical level of 2%. Then you would go long the corporate bond and short sell the T-bond, hoping to make a capital gain as the spread moved back to its historical level. The future level of the spread largely depends on the market's view on future changes in the risk of default (ratings downgrade) of the corporate, so this is a relative-value trade on changes in default spreads.

The hedge fund Long Term Capital Management (LTCM) lost over $4bn in 1998 when executing spread strategies. In September of that year it was rescued by a consortium of New York Banks (under the direction of the Federal Reserve Board). Ordinary commercial banks had lent money long term to LTCM, which had a debt–equity ratio in excess of 20:1, increasing to around 50:1 during the crisis period. The fund was founded in 1994 by John Meriwether, a former head of Salomon Brothers bond arbitrage division who left after the 1991 Salomon bond scandal. In the latter, Paul Mozer, a bond trader reporting to Meriwether, had tried to corner the primary Treasury auction market by submitting bids in excess of the firm's approved limits. Meriwether was alleged to have failed to supervise traders properly and was subsequently fined $50,000 by the SEC. Two Nobel prize winners in economics, Robert Merton and Myron Scholes (of Black–Scholes–Merton option-pricing fame), also joined LTCM. For an idea of what happened, see Case Study 22.1.

CASE STUDY 22.1   LONG TERM CAPITAL MANAGEMENT (LTCM)

LTCM's positions were *highly leveraged* (often by using derivatives). But a good idea of what occurred can be seen by considering a bet on a narrowing of the yield *differential* between US corporate bonds and US Treasuries, $r_c - r$, so-called *relative value* or *convergence trades*. If you are long corporates and short Treasuries, then if the yield spread narrows you will make profits. The fall in r_c implies a rise in corporate bond prices and hence a gain on your long corporate position. A rise in yields on Treasuries (which also narrows the spread) will lead to a fall in T-bond prices and hence a profit from your short Treasury position. LTCM had also placed such bets on interest rates in emerging markets and on interest rates in Europe, converging towards relatively low rates for Germany as the January 1999 date for the introduction of a common currency (the euro) grew closer. For example, Italian rates were above German rates, so a convergence trade would involve going long Italian government bonds and short selling German government bonds.

These spread positions were largely hedged against a general upward or downward movement in the level of all yields (i.e. a parallel shift). Hence there was no need to worry about largely unpredictable and volatile parallel shifts in the yield curve. However, the spreads were so small that to make large profits for investors in LTCM (and the Nobel prize winners), the trades had to be highly leveraged (i.e. financed by borrowing). Most of this borrowing was by repos. LTCM would sell some of its assets for cash to banks, with the promise to buy them back at a higher price at a fixed date in the future. Normally banks require collateral that is worth slightly more than the cash loaned out, in case the assets held as collateral fall in value. The bank (or broker) will also charge a small commission on the trade – this cost is the 'haircut'. But seemingly LTCM was loaned funds with near zero haircuts (the total haircut for LTCM's £10bn of borrowing was reported to be very small) and it also had a $900m credit line from major US banks.

By the end of 1997 the 16 partners in LTCM had invested about $1.9bn of their own money in the fund. The balance sheet had assets of $125bn, supported by equity of $5bn – a leverage ratio of 25 to 1. To control risk, LTCM stated that its target maximum risk level was equal to the volatility of an unleveraged position in US equities (e.g. the volatility of the S&P 500 index). The firm also charged relatively large annual fees of about 2% of capital plus 25% of profits (whereas many other hedge funds had about a 1% fixed fee and a charge of 20% on profits).

Unfortunately for LTCM, after Russia defaulted on its debt in August 1998 (the 'thousand-year storm'), spreads against Treasuries rose. Also, LTCM was long rouble-denominated debt and short Russia's foreign currency-denominated debt, believing that this gave it a natural hedge, since if Russia defaulted on its rouble-denominated debt it would also default on its foreign currency debt. In fact, Russia only defaulted on its rouble-denominated debt, so the hedge failed. Contagion spread to other emerging markets and faced with falling corporate and emerging market bond prices, LTCM sought to unwind its long positions. But the market in some of these emerging market bonds was very illiquid, so it was difficult to sell without causing prices to plummet (a 'fire sale'). This is 'liquidity risk'. LTCM also faced margin calls on its T-bond futures positions. By the end of September 1998, LTCM had lost $4.4bn (compared with end 1997), of which $1.9bn was the partners' money, about $700m losses were the Union Bank of Switzerland and $1.8bn losses were by other investors in LTCM.

If LTCM's counterparties had to liquidate LTCM's collateral in the repos (with near zero haircuts), this would have meant losses and possible bankruptcy for some banks. Had LTCM gone bust, many banks would have suffered severe losses on their loans to LTCM after any 'fire sale' of collateral provided by LTCM and any sale of LTCM's remaining assets. Therefore the Fed stepped in to organise a rescue operation. The whole episode led to calls for hedge funds to come under some regulatory control.

Those banks that, under the direction of the Fed, pumped money into the rescue (about $3.6bn to give them an 90% equity stake in LTCM) have since made profits as spreads returned to their normal pattern and narrowed in 1999. But the original lenders to LTCM lost substantial amounts. Some of the above spread strategies were actually conducted using futures and options on interest rates (rather than buying or selling the underlying bonds themselves). This allowed large positions to be taken with only relatively small payments for the option premia – that is, LTCM used options to leverage its positions.

Finally, it is worth noting that the fixed-income desk of a large bank will continually monitor its risk position. For example, scenario analysis (or stress testing) is often used to assess the impact of various parallel and non-parallel shifts in the yield curve on the value of a bond portfolio. The scenarios are based on the types of yield-curve shifts observed in the past. Also, Value at Risk (VaR) techniques can be used to assess the riskiness of the fixed-income desk, see Cuthbertson and Nitzsche (2001b).

SUMMARY

- Duration D (or modified duration, MD) and convexity X can be used to provide an *approximation* to the change in price (value) of a bond (portfolio), for a given change in the yield to maturity.

  % change in bond price $= - MD \times$ absolute change in yield, (dy)
  % change in bond price $= - MD \times$ absolute change in yield $+ (1/2)X(dy)^2$

- Matching the duration of a bond with the duration of a single future cash outflow (e.g. a one-off lump-sum pension payment) ensures that the reinvested coupons and

the receipts from the sale of the bond will be sufficient to meet the future cash out-flow of the liability. This is an *immunisation strategy*.
- In practice, immunisation (or duration matching) is not perfect when there are *multi-period liabilities* (i.e. cash pay-outs over many periods) and non-parallel shifts in the yield curve.
- *Cash-flow matching* to meet multi-period liabilities requires the fund manager to find a set of bonds where the timing of coupon payments and the maturity value of the bonds exactly coincide with the timing of the liability payments.
- *Bond indexing* is the construction of a bond portfolio that acccurately tracks the total return on a chosen bond market index.
- *Active bond strategies* involve speculation with part (or all) of the bond portfolio. Directional bets on interest-rate changes are generally known as *macro strategies*. Given a forecast of a general fall in yields, speculators might switch out of cash and into bonds and towards bonds with long durations.
- *Relative-value* (convergence) trades try to take advantage of perceived abnormally high yield spreads. You take a long postion in the bond with the high yield and a short position in the bond with the relatively low yield. If the spread narrows you can close out the position and make a profit. You are largely protected from parallel shifts in the yield curve.

APPENDIX 22.1: DURATION AND CONVEXITY

The price of a coupon-paying bond is a non-linear (convex) function of the yield to maturity, y :

$$P = \frac{C}{(1 + y)} + \frac{C}{(1 + y)^2} + \cdots + \frac{(C + M)}{(1 + y)^n} \qquad [A1]$$

Any non-linear function can be approximated by a Taylor series expansion of which the first two terms are:

$$\frac{dP}{P} = \frac{1}{P}\left[\frac{\partial P}{\partial y}dy + \frac{1}{2} \frac{\partial^2 P}{\partial y^2}(dy)^2 \right] \qquad [A2]$$

Differentiating [A1] with respect to y gives:

$$\frac{dP}{dy} = \frac{-C}{(1 + y)^2} - \frac{2C}{(1 + y)^3} - \cdots - n\frac{(C + M)}{(1 + y)^{n+1}}$$

$$= \frac{-1}{(1 + y)} \times \left[\frac{C}{(1 + y)} + \frac{2C}{(1 + y)^2} + \cdots + n\frac{(C + M)}{(1 + y)^n} \right] \qquad [A3]$$

It follows that:

$$\frac{1}{P}\frac{dP}{dy} = \frac{-D}{(1 + y)} \quad \text{or} \quad \frac{dP}{P} = -MD.(dy) \qquad [A4]$$

$$\text{where} \quad D = \frac{1}{P}\left[\frac{(1)C}{(1 + y)} + \frac{2C}{(1 + y)^2} + \cdots + \frac{n(C + M)}{(1 + y)^n}\right] \qquad [A5]$$

Equation [A4] provides the formula for the price change in terms of duration given the definition of D in [A5]. To calculate an expression for convexity we note from [A2] that we need to differentiate [A3] a second time:

$$\frac{d^2P}{dy^2} = \left[\frac{(1)(2)C}{(1 + y)} + \frac{(2)(3)C}{(1 + y)^2} + \cdots + \frac{n(n + 1)(C + M)}{(1 + y)^n}\right]\frac{1}{(1 + y)^2} \qquad [A6]$$

If we now define convexity X as:

$$X = \frac{1}{(1 + y)^2}\left[\sum_{i=1}^{n}\frac{i(i + 1)}{(1 + y)^i}\right]\frac{1}{P} \qquad [A7]$$

Then equation [A2] becomes:

$$\frac{dP}{P} = -MD \cdot (dy) + \frac{1}{2}X \cdot (dy)^2 \qquad [A8]$$

Zero-coupon bond

It is straightforward to show that the duration of a zero-coupon bond equals its maturity. We have:

$$P = \frac{M}{(1 + y)^n} \qquad [A9]$$

and

$$\frac{dP}{P} = -n\left[\frac{M}{(1 + y)^{n+1}}\right]\frac{dy}{P} \qquad [A10]$$

Substituting for P from [A9] into [A10]:

$$\frac{dP}{P} = \frac{-n}{(1 + y)}dy \qquad [A11]$$

Duration is defined as:

$$\frac{dP}{P} = \frac{-D}{(1 + y)}dy \qquad [A12]$$

Comparing [A11] and [A12] we see that the duration of a zero equals its maturity, n.

APPENDIX 22.2: CONDITIONS FOR SUCCESSFUL IMMUNISATION

Assume that all the cash flows from the liabilities have a present value V_L, where the discount rate used is the yield to maturity (YTM), y. The present value of the liabilities is therefore a function of the future cash outflows and the YTM, hence $PV_L = f(\text{future cash outflows}, y)$.

For ease of exposition, assume that we have a portfolio containing only two bonds with current prices P_1 and P_2. The current value of the bond portfolio is:

$$V_B = N_1 P_1 + N_2 P_2 = V_1 + V_2 \qquad [A1]$$

where N_1, N_2 are the number of bonds held (of each type) and $V_i = N_i P_i$ is the dollar amount held in each bond. Differentiating [A1]:

$$dV_B = N_1 P_1 \left(\frac{dP_1}{P_1}\right) + N_2 P_2 \left(\frac{dP_2}{P_2}\right)$$
$$= V_1 \left(\frac{dP_1}{P_1}\right) + V_2 \left(\frac{dP_2}{P_2}\right) = -(V_1 D_1 + V_2 D_2)dy \qquad [A2]$$

where we have substituted $dP_i/P_i = -D_i\, dy$. (Here we can either assume that we are using continuously compounded yields or you can interpret D as the *modified duration*.) The change in the (present) value of the liabilities is:

$$dV_L = -(D_L dy).V_L \qquad [A3]$$

Immunisation implies that the change in the dollar value of the bond portfolio should equal the change in the dollar value of the liabilities; that is $dV_B = dV_L$. We also need to impose the condition that the initial dollar value of the chosen bond portfolio V_B equals the *present value* of the future liability stream of cash outflows, V_L:

$$V_B = V_L \qquad [A4]$$

Equating [A2] and [A3] and using [A4] we obtain:

$$\frac{(V_1 D_1 + V_2 D_2)}{V_B} = D_L \qquad [A5]$$

But the left-hand side of [A5] is simply the duration of the bond *portfolio* D_p, since:

$$D_p = w_1 D_1 + w_2 D_2 \quad \text{where} \quad w_i = V_i/V_B. \qquad [A6]$$

Hence, successful immunisation requires $dV_B = dV_L$ and [A5] implies that the duration of the bond portfolio D_p must equal the duration of the interest-sensitive liabilities D_L while [A4] implies that we must choose the dollar value of our bond portfolio to equal the present value of the liabilities, $V_B. = V_L$. It is straightforward to show that this leads to two equations in two unknowns w_1, w_2:

$$w_1 D_1 + w_2 D_2 = D_L$$
$$w_1 + w_2 = 1$$

These are easily solved by substituting $w_1 = 1 - w_2$. Having solved for w_1 and w_2 the dollar amounts in the two bonds are $V_1 = w_1 V_L$ and $V_2 = w_2 V_L$. Alternatively, you can solve directly for the dollar values in each bond by representing the above two equations in terms of V_1 and V_2:

$$V_1 D_1 + V_2 D_2 = V_L D_L$$
$$V_1 + V_2 = V_L$$

The only unknowns are V_1 and V_2.

EXERCISES

Q1   Give two reasons the concept of duration is useful.

Q2   What is meant by the convexity of a bond? Why might you be willing to pay more for bond A that has a greater convexity than bond B?

Q3   Why might a pension fund use cash-flow matching? Will it use this technique for the whole of its bond portfolio ?

Q4   Consider a 10% coupon bond (annual coupons) with par value $100, yield to maturity of $y = 10 \%$ and 5 years to maturity. Calculate:

(a) The current market price, P.
(b) The Macaulay duration, D.
(c) The (approximate) price change if the yield to maturity rises to 10.5% or falls to 9.5%.
(d) The 'true' price change for $y = 10.5\%$ and $y = 9.5\%$.

Q5   What conditions are necessary to ensure a successful immunisation strategy? Are these conditions met in practice?

Q6   What are the difficulties implementing a bond-indexing strategy?

Q7   Portfolio A:

   1-year zero coupon bond, face value $= \$2000$.
   10-year zero coupon bond, face value $= \$6000$.

Portfolio B: 5.95 year zero coupon bond, face value $= \$5000$.

Current yield curve is flat and $y = 10\%$ p.a. (continuously compounded).

(a) Show that the duration of portfolio A equals that of portfolio B.
(b) What is the actual percentage change in value of portfolio A for a 10-basis point increase in yield?
(c) Does the duration formula give approximately the same answer?
(d) Repeat (b) for portfolios A and B for an increase in yield of 5% p.a. Which portfolio has the higher convexity?

PART 7

DERIVATIVES

Derivative Securities

AIMS

- To explain *forward and futures* contracts, their similarities and differences.
- To examine the basic concepts behind *call and put options* and how their payoffs at maturity can provide 'insurance'.
- To show how *interest-rate swaps and currency swaps* can be used to alter the cash-flow profile of existing payments or receipts, and hence reduce the risk attached to such cash flows.
- To analyse how derivative securities are used in speculation, hedging and arbitrage.

INTRODUCTION

There are three main types of derivative securities, namely futures, options and swaps. Derivative securities are assets whose value depends on the value of some other (underlying) asset and is *derived* from the value of this underlying asset. For example, a futures contract on a stock such as AT&T would not be traded if AT&T went bankrupt. These derivative securities can be used by hedgers, speculators and arbitrageurs. Derivatives often receive a bad press, partly because there have been some quite spectacular derivatives losses. Perhaps the most famous are the losses of Nick Leeson, who worked for Barings Bank in Singapore and lost $1.4bn when trading futures and options on the Nikkei 225, the Japanese stock index. This led to Barings going bust. More recently in 1998, Long Term Capital Management (LTCM), a hedge fund that levered its trades using derivatives, had to be rescued by a consortium of banks under the imprimator of the Federal Reserve Board (see Chapter 22). This was all the more galling since Myron Scholes and Robert Merton, two academics who received the Nobel prize for their work on derivatives, were key players in LTCM.

The theory of derivatives is a bit like nuclear physics. The derivative products that it has spawned can be used for good, but they can also be dangerous if used incorrectly. Let us see how these products can be used, so that you can make up your own mind on this issue.

23.1 FORWARDS AND FUTURES

Except where explicitly noted, we will use 'forward' and 'futures' interchangeably, since analytically they are very similar, even though the way the contracts are traded differ in some respects. A holder of a long (short) forward contract has an agreement to buy (sell) an asset at a certain time in the future for a certain price that is fixed today.

> The *buyer (seller or short position)* in a *forward/futures contract:*
> - acquires a legal obligation to buy (sell) an asset *(the underlying)*
> - at some specific future date *(maturity/expiry date)*
> - in an amount *(contract size)*
> - and at a price *(the forward/futures price)* that is fixed today.

A **forward contract** is an over-the-counter (OTC) instrument and trades take place directly (usually over the phone) for a specific amount and specific delivery date, as negotiated between the two parties. In contrast, **futures contracts** are standardised (in terms of contract size and delivery dates), trades take place on an organised exchange and the contracts are revalued (marked to market) daily. When you buy or sell a futures contract, on say cocoa, it is the legal right to the terms in the contract that is being purchased or sold, not the cocoa itself (which is actually bought and sold in the spot market for cocoa). As we shall see in the next chapter, there is a close link between the futures price and the spot price (for cocoa), but they are not the same thing!

Futures contracts are traded between market makers in a 'pit' on the floor of the exchange, of which the largest are the Chicago Board of Trade (CBOT), the Chicago Mercantile Exchange (CME), these two merged in August 2006, and the Philadelphia Stock Exchange (PHLX). However, in recent years there has been a move away from trading by 'open out-cry' in a pit towards electronic trading between market makers (and also over the Internet). The largest pit-trading futures exchange in Europe was the London International Financial Futures Exchange (LIFFE), which merged with NYSE-Euronext and became an electronic trading platform. You can also trade 'out-of-hours' in many contracts traded in Chicago using the GLOBEX electronic trading platform. Futures contracts traded on US exchanges are shown in Table 23.1.

Originally, futures markets were introduced to eliminate risk due to changes in the spot price of agricultural commodities. For example, a farmer might know in April that he is to harvest 5000 bushels of wheat in September. A wholesaler who purchases grain for the food industry might know his requirements as early as April. The two participants can eliminate (or hedge) risk by negotiating a contract to supply grain in September at a price agreed in April. This is a type of forward contract and eliminates risk for each side of the bargain. Similar considerations to the above apply to an agent who stores grain that has already been harvested. He can hold on to the grain for a number of months in the hope that the spot price for grain will increase. Alternatively, he can negotiate a price today, for delivery of the grain at some time in the future. Both the merchant who holds the grain and the purchaser are 'locked in' to the forward price quoted today and thereby reduce to zero any risks due to future changes in the *spot* price of wheat.

Market classification

A key feature of futures and options is that the contract calls for *deferred delivery* of the underlying asset (e.g. AT&T shares), whereas spot assets are for *immediate delivery* (although in practice, there is usually a delay of a few days). To distinguish between purchases and sales of derivatives and the underlying (spot) asset, the latter are often referred to as transactions in the **cash** or **spot market**. A primary use of derivative securities is to minimise price uncertainty. Therefore, where the underlying assets (e.g. currencies, shares) are widely traded and yet exhibit great volatility, there is likely to be a large active derivatives market.

Trading in derivative securities can be on a trading floor (or pit) or via an electronic network of traders, within a well-established organised market (e.g. with a clearing house, membership rules, etc.). However, many derivatives contracts – for example, all FX forward contracts and swap contracts – are over-the-counter (OTC) instruments, where the contract details are not standardised but individually negotiated between clients and dealers. Options are traded widely on exchanges, while the OTC market in options (particularly 'complex' or 'exotic' options) is also very large.

Today there are a large number of exchanges dealing in futures contracts. Most can be categorised as agricultural futures contracts (where the underlying asset is, for example, pork bellies, live hogs or wheat), energy futures (e.g. crude oil, natural gas, heating oil), metallurgical futures (e.g. silver, platinum) or financial futures contracts (where the underlying asset could be a portfolio of stocks represented by the S&P 500, currencies, T-bills, T-bonds,

TABLE 23.1: Selected futures contracts

Contract	Exchange	Contract size
1. Grains and oilseed		
Corn	CBOT	5000 bu (bushels)
Soybeans	CBOT	5000 bu
Wheat	CBOT	5000 bu
2. Food		
Cocoa	NYMEX	10 metric tonnes
Orange juice	NYMEX	15,000 lb
3. Metals and petroleum		
Gold	NYMEX	100 troy oz
Crude oil (light sweet)	NYMEX	1000 barrels
Silver	CBOT	5000 troy oz
4. Livestock and meat		
Hogs-lean	CME	40,000 lb
Pork bellies	CME	40,000 lb
5. Foreign currency		
British pound	CME	£62,500
Swiss franc	CME	SFr125,000
Euro	CME	€125,000
Japanese yen	CME	¥12.5m
6. Stock indices		
S&P 500	CBOT	$250 × index
Value Line	KCBT	$25 × index
FTSE 100	NYSE-EURONEXT	£10 × index
Eurotop 100	NYSE-EURONEXT	€20 × index
Nikkei 225	CBOT	$5 × index
7. Interest rates		
Eurodollar, 90 day	IMM	$1,000,000
US T-bills	IMM	$1,000,000
US T-bonds	CBOT	$100,000
UK 3m sterling int rate	NYSE-EURONEXT	£500,000
UK 3m Euribor	NYSE-EURONEXT	€1m
UK long gilt future	NYSE-EURONEXT	£100,000

Notes: CBOT   = Chicago Board of Trade   CME   = Chicago Mercantile Exchange
       NYMEX = New York Mercantile Exchange   IMM   = International Money Market (Chicago)
                                                KCBT   = Kansas City Board of Trade
Correct as of March 2008

Eurodollar deposits, etc.). Agricultural, energy and metallurgical futures are often generically referred to as 'commodity futures'. There are some futures contracts that do not really fit into any of these definitions, such as weather futures, which we meet in a later chapter.

Futures contracts in agricultural commodities have been traded (e.g. on CBOT) for over 100 years. In 1972 the CME began to trade currency futures, while the introduction of interest-rate futures occurred in 1975 and in 1982 stock index futures (colloquially known as 'pin-stripe pork bellies') were introduced. The CBOT introduced a clearing house in 1925, where each party to the contract had to place deposits into a margin account. This provides insurance if one of the parties defaults on the contract. The growth in the volume of futures trading since 1972 has been astounding.

Analytically, forwards and futures can be treated in a similar fashion. However, they differ in some practical details (see Table 23.2). Forward contracts (usually) involve no up-front payment and cash only changes hands at the expiry of the contract. A forward contract is negotiated between two parties and (generally) is not marketable. In contrast, a futures contract is traded in the market and it involves a down-payment known as the **initial margin**. However, the initial margin is primarily a deposit to ensure that neither party to the contract defaults. It is not a payment for the futures contract itself. The margin usually earns a competitive interest rate, so it is not a 'cost'. As the futures price changes then 'payments' (i.e. debits and credits) are made into (or out of) the margin account. Hence a futures contract is a forward contract that is 'marked to market' daily.

Because the futures contract is marketable, the contracts have to be standardised, for example by having a set of fixed expiry (delivery) dates and a fixed contract size (e.g. $100,000 for the US T-bond futures on IMM in Chicago). In contrast, a forward contract can be tailor made between the two parties to the contract, in terms of size and delivery date. Finally,

---

TABLE 23.2: Forward and futures contracts

Forwards	Futures
• Private (non-marketable) contract between two parties	• Traded on an exchange
• (Large) trades are not communicated to other market participants	• Trades are immediately known by other market participants
• Delivery or cash settlement at expiry	• Contract is usually closed out prior to maturity
• Usually one delivery date	• Range of delivery dates
• No cash paid until expiry	• Cash payments into (out of) margin account, daily
• Negotiable choice of delivery dates and size of contract	• Standardised contracts

forward contracts almost invariably involve the delivery of the underlying asset (e.g. currency), whereas futures contracts can be (and usually are) closed out by selling the contract prior to maturity. Hence with futures, delivery of the underlying asset rarely takes place.

A forward or futures contract can be used for speculation, even if the forward contract is held to maturity. A speculator using a forward contract makes her gain or loss *at the time the contract matures*. For example, suppose the forward price on a commodity (e.g. silver) at $t = 0$ is $F_0 = \$100$ per tonne, with maturity date in September. If the spot price in September ($= T$) turns out to be $S_T = \$105$ per tonne, then the holder of the (long) forward contract can accept delivery of the commodity in the forward contract (and pay out $100 at T) and then sell it onwards in the spot market for $S_T = \$105$, giving an overall profit of $5 per tonne ($= S_T - F_0$).

Now consider speculation with futures contracts, which can be closed out at any time. Indeed, most futures contracts are closed out prior to maturity. When they are, the clearing house sends out a cash payment that reflects the change in value of the futures price between your opening trade and closing out the contract (i.e. a buy followed by a sell, or vice versa). Therefore futures contracts can be used for speculation even when they are closed out prior to maturity. Because the price of a futures contract is derived from the price of the underlying asset, the changes in the futures price usually move (nearly) one for one with changes in the price of the underlying spot asset.

Speculation with futures is straightforward. Suppose you purchased a three-month futures contract at a price $F_0 = \$100$ and one month later you closed out the contract by selling it at the market price of $F_1 = \$110$. Then the clearing house effectively sends you a cheque for $10. (It obtains this $10 from the person who initially took the other side of the deal – the institutional details differ from this, as we shall see in the next chapter, but the principle is correct.) It also follows that you would earn a $10 profit if you initially *sold* a contract at $F_0 = \$100$ and later closed out the contract by *buying it back* at $F_1 = \$90$ (i.e. 'sell high, buy low'). The number of possible types of futures contracts that can be traded is almost limitless, but only those that are useful for hedging and speculation will survive. The exchange will remove any futures contract where trading volume is low.

23.2 OPTIONS

Options are a little more difficult to understand than forwards and futures and here we do no more than present a quick overview. While futures markets in commodities have existed since the middle of the 1800s, traded options contracts have been around for a far shorter period of time.

> The holder of an option has the right to buy or sell an 'asset' (the underlying) at some time in the future at a fixed price, but she *does not have to exercise this right*.
> This is a key distinction between options and forward/futures contracts.

Table 23.3 provides a summary of the main types of option contract and the assets underlying these contracts.

TABLE 23.3: Selected options contracts

Contract	Exchange	Contract size
1. Individual stocks	CBOE, NYSE, AMEX, PHLX, NYSE-EURONEXT, SIMEX	Usually for 100 stocks
2. Index options		
S&P 500 index	CBOE	$100 × index
Dow Jones Ind	CBOE	$100 × index
Russell 2000	CBOE	$100 × index
3. Foreign currency options		
Sterling	PHLX	GBP 31,250
Japanese yen	PHLX	JPY 6.25m
Canadian dollar	PHLX	CND 50,000
Swiss franc	PHLX	CHF 62,500
4. Options on futures contracts		
Options on interest-rate futures:		
Eurodollars	IMM	$1m
1-month LIBOR	IMM	$3m
US T-bills	IMM	$1m
US T-bond and 5-year T-note	CBOT	$100,000
3-month Euribor	NYSE-EURONEXT	as for futures
UK long gilt	NYSE-EURONEXT	as for futures
Options on index futures:		
S&P 500 index	CBOE	$500 × premium
NYSE Composite	CBOE	$500 × premium
Nikkei 225	CBOE	$5 × premium
Most commodities (agriculture and metals) on which there are futures contracts (see above).	CBOT, CME, KCBT, NYMEX	The same as in the futures contract (see above)
Options on foreign currency futures		
British pound	IMM	GBP 62,500
Japanese yen	IMM	JPY 12.5m
Swiss franc	IMM	CHF125,000

Notes: CBOT   = Chicago Board of Trade
 NYMEX = New York Mercantile Exchange
 CBOE   = Chicago Board Options Exchange

CME   = Chicago Mercantile Exchange
IMM   = International Money Market(Chicago)
KCBT = Kansas City Board of Trade
PHLX = Philadelphia Stock Exchange

Correct as of March 2008

For the moment we will consider only stock option contracts, so the underlying asset in the option contract is the share of a particular company that is traded on the New York stock exchange. The option contract itself we assume is traded in Chicago.

Above we noted that the holder of a long futures contract commits herself to buy an asset at a certain price at a certain time in the future *and if she does nothing before expiration,* she will have to take delivery of the underlying in the contract, at the agreed delivery price. In contrast, the holder of an option can simply walk away from the contract. She has the choice as to whether or not to exercise the option and hence buy or sell the underlying asset (e.g. stock) at a fixed price, at a certain time in the future in Chicago. As we see below, this right without any obligation to exercise the contract allows the holder of an option to benefit from any 'upside', while also providing insurance. For this privilege, an investor must pay an up-front, non-returnable fee in order to purchase an option contract – that is the option price or premium.

The holder of a so-called **European** option can buy or sell *the underlying asset* (e.g. stock) in Chicago only on the expiry day of the option contract. But the holder of an **American** option can take delivery of the underlying asset in Chicago by presenting (exercising) the option contract in Chicago *on any day* before the expiry date. We will almost exclusively deal with European options. Note, however, that all option contracts you hold (whether American or European, calls or puts) can be *sold* to a third party, at any time prior to expiration – this is known as **closing out** or **reversing** the contract.

There are two basic types of options: calls and puts (which can either be American or European).

Call options

A *European call option* gives the holder (the long) the right (but not an obligation):

- to purchase the underlying asset at a
  - specified future date (the *expiration/expiry/maturity date*)
  - for a certain price (the *exercise or strike price*)
  - and in an amount *(contract size)* that is fixed in advance.
- For this privilege you pay, today, the *call premium/price*.

For the moment think of a call option as a piece of paper that contains the contract details (e.g. strike price, expiry date, etc.) and you can purchase this contract today in the options market in Chicago if you pay the quoted option price. There are always two sides to every trade, a buyer and a seller, but we will just concentrate on your trade as a buyer of the option. Note that all transactions in the option contract are undertaken in Chicago, but the underlying asset, for example a stock, will be traded on another exchange (e.g. NYSE).

How might a speculator use a call option contract? Consider for example the purchase in July of a (European) call option on the shares of XYZ. Suppose that the strike price in the contract is $K = \$80$, the expiry date T is in three months' time in October, and the quoted call premium in July is $C = \$3$ per share in Chicago. If the actual price of the stock in October (on the NYSE) turns out to be $S_T = \$88$, then the holder of the call option can present (i.e. exercise) the option in Chicago on a specific day in October and receive a pay-off of $S_T - K = \$88 - \$80 = \$8$ from the options clearing house in Chicago. (As we see later, this $8 is provided by the other side of the contract – that is, the initial seller of the call option – but don't worry about this at this point.) The speculator's profit after deduction of the call premium, $C = \$3$, is $5 per share. The speculator has made $5 on an outlay of $3 over a three-month period, which is a percentage return of $(5/3 - 1) \times 100\% = 66.6\%$. This large percentage return implies that options provide *leverage* for speculators.

If the spot price in October turns out to be less than the strike price, then the option expires worthless (i.e. its pay-out is zero) and the speculator 'throws it away' (i.e. does not present/exercise the option in Chicago). But the most the speculator can lose is known in advance – it is the put premium, $C = \$3$. So a speculator who is long a call option has some rather nice advantages – she can benefit from any upside in the stock market but can never lose more than the (rather small) option premium she paid.

Closing out

Usually options are not held to expiration. Instead, a speculator holding a long call reaps a prof-it by closing out (or 'reversing') her long position, by selling (shorting) the call option prior to expiration to another trader (the counterparty). As we shall see, if there has been a rise in the price of the underlying stock S since the option was initially purchased then the call premium C will also have increased from, say, $C_0 = \$3$ to $C_1 = \$4$, say between July and August. Hence when the speculator closes out (i.e. sells) her long call option in August in Chicago, she will receive $C_1 = \$4$ from the counterparty to the deal (i.e. the purchaser). She therefore makes a speculative profit of $1 (= \$4 - \$3)$, the difference between the buying and selling price of the call. The buyer will actually receive her cash payment of $4 from the sale of the option (to another counterparty) via the options clearing house in Chicago.

Conversely, if the stock price falls after she purchased the call for $C_0 = \$3$, then the call pre-mium will now be below $3 and when the speculator sells it (i.e. closes out) in Chicago (to another trader) she will make a loss on the deal (but never more than the initial option premi-um paid of $3). Thus a **naked** (or **open**) **position** in a long call held over a short horizon can be risky.

Put options

If you *buy* a European put option (in Chicago) this gives you the right to *sell* the underlying asset (in Chicago) at some time in the future for a price that is fixed in the contract, hence:

> A *European put option* gives the holder the right (but not an obligation):
>
> - to sell the underlying asset at a
>   - specified future date *(expiration/expiry/maturity date)*
>   - for a certain price *(strike/exercise price)*
>   - in an amount *(contract size)* that is fixed in advance.
> - For this privilege you pay, today, the *put premium/price*.

Long put

There are also opportunities for speculation if you buy (i.e. go long) a put option. In contrast to speculation with a long call, a speculator will buy a put option if she expects the stock price *to fall* in the future (and end up below the strike price). Suppose in July you can purchase an 'October put' (i.e. its expiry date is a specific day towards the end of October) with a strike price $K = \$70$ for a price $P = \$2$. If the spot price of shares in New York in three months' time in October is $S_T = \$65$ (i.e. below $K = \$70$), then the payoff to a speculator who is already long the put option is $(K - S_T) = \$5$. This will be paid to you via the options clearing house *in Chicago* when you present (exercise) your put option contract. Your net profit is $3 (i.e. \$5 minus the cost of the put $P = \$2$) on an outlay of own funds of \$2; that is, a return of 150% over three months – again, the option provides leverage for the speculator.

If the spot price of the share in New York in October turns out to be higher than the strike price (e.g. $S_T = \$73, K = \$70$), then the put option expires worthless (its pay-out is zero) and the speculator 'throws it away' (i.e. does not present/exercise the option in Chicago). But again, the most the speculator can lose is known in advance – it is the put premium, $P = \$2$. So a speculator who is long a put option has some rather nice advantages – she can benefit from any *fall* in stock prices but if she guesses wrong and the stock price rises, she can never lose more than the (rather small) put option premium she initially paid.

Options can also be used to provide **insurance**. For example, suppose you are a pension fund and already own shares whose current price in July (in New York) is $S_0 = \$72$, but you are worried about a fall in price of the shares over the next three months. You can 'insure' your shares by buying a put option with a strike price of, say, $K = \$70$, with three months to maturity. If stock prices in New York fall below \$70, then instead of selling your stocks in New York at, say, \$30, you can present (exercise) your put option in Chicago, hand over your shares and receive $K = \$70$ for each share (via the options clearing house). You have guaranteed a minimum price for your shares in three months of $K = \$70$ at a cost of $P = \$2$; the latter is the price of your insurance. True, you will have lost \$2 per share (i.e. the initial price of $S_0 = \$72$ less the price obtained in Chicago of $K = \$70$) and this is the 'deductible' in your insurance contract. Losing \$2 per share because you had the foresight to take out insurance by buying the put option is a lot better than if you had not purchased the insurance, since then your stocks would have fallen in value by $42 (= 72 - 30)$ on the NYSE.

How does this 'options insurance contract' look if prices rise over the next three months? Suppose prices rise on the NYSE from \$72 in July to \$80 in October. Then your long put is worthless (as \$80 exceeds the strike price $K = \$70$) and you 'throw it away'. But you can sell your shares in New York for $80, so you are happy. The insurance policy provided by the put has allowed you to fix a minimum price $K = \$70$ at which you can sell your shares in the future in Chicago (even if they are worthless on the NYSE), but it also allows you also to benefit from any upside if stock prices rise, when you can simply sell your stocks in New York at the high price. There are many types of situation that can be analysed using an options framework and some of these are discussed in Case Study 23.1.

CASE STUDY 23.1   'OPTIONS Я-US'

Although some people may not be aware of it, they probably hold options. Aristotle, in Book I of *Politics,* mentions the Greek philosopher Thales who developed a 'financial device' that was in fact an option. One winter he 'read the stars' and decided that next autumn would result in an exceptionally good olive harvest. He therefore quietly went around the owners of olive presses and paid them a small retainer (i.e. the call option premium) to secure the right to be first to use their olive presses in the autumn, for a fixed price (the strike price), if he so wished. Come autumn, the harvest was good and therefore the demand for the olive presses was high and Thales could charge a high price to the olive growers. Even if Thales had been wrong about the harvest, the most he could have lost was the small option premium.

Now consider rural bus services, whose fares are often subsidised via local government taxes (e.g. rates, sales taxes and community charges). If you live out of town you have the option to take the bus to town by paying the known fixed fare (= the strike price). You will do this if the value to you of your journey by bus exceeds the strike price. Hence, you are holding an implicit call option and the call premium is that part of your local taxes that goes to subsidise the bus company.

Next, suppose that in January you have been offered a place at one of several universities, if you achieve a grade B in your examinations in June. You will make your final choice of a specific university in the following September. The (implicit) option premium is the time and effort you put into studying and you have nine months to decide on your choice of university (i.e. the time to maturity of the option).

If you decide to go to university, you will have to 'pay' the strike price (i.e. tuition and living expenses and earned income forgone during the course). You will choose that university with the largest net payoff $S_T - K$, where S_T is the (present value) of your *additional* earnings after graduating. This is a type of *exotic option*, since you are allowed to choose the university that maximises the possible payoffs $S_T - K$ from the *different* universities who have made you an offer. Because you can choose that university with the highest payoff (i.e. the maximum value of the $S_T - K$), this is also known as a *rainbow option (or min–max option).*

However, suppose that, after nine months (= expiry date), you have found a good job with an excellent training programme. Then you might not exercise your option to go to any university since the additional income from being a graduate S_T might be less than the (opportunity) costs of your degree course K (including the lost income from leaving your job), that is, $S_T < K$. Your exotic option therefore expires 'out of the money'.

Suppose it is January, so you do not yet have your examination results. You are holding a form of exotic option known as a *barrier option*. If your intellectual prowess increases and you achieve the grade B in six months' time, the option 'knocks in' and can be exercised later (i.e. in September) if you wish. So to be even more precise you are holding a *knock-in option*. If you do not achieve the grade B within the next six months, the university offer is void and your implicit option expires worthless. The option you hold is said to be *path dependent,* since the payoff in September depends on how well you did at an earlier date (i.e. in your examinations in June).

Car insurance is like a (put) option, with the strike price set equal to the insured value of your car and usually with maturity of one year. Suppose your car is currently worth $S_0 = \$40,000$ and you decide to insure it for a maximum of $K = \$36,000$, so the 'deductible' (or 'excess') in your insurance contract is \$4000 (i.e. 10% of its market value). You pay an insurance premium up front, which we assume is \$720 (i.e. 2% of the insured value of \$36,000). The insurance premium of \$720 is just like the payment of the put premium. The fact that you choose a deductible of \$4000 means that the strike price in the put $K = \$36,000$ is below the *current* spot price $S_0 = \$40,000$, so you are purchasing a '10%-out-of-the-money' put.

If you do not have an accident (i.e. the underlying value of your car remains largely unchanged), then the put option expires out of the money, since in one years time $S_T \approx \$40,000 > K (= \$36,000)$ – and you 'throw away' your insurance contract – that is, you do not exercise your implicit put option. However, if you have an accident and the market value of your car falls to $S_T = \$5,000$, then it would take \$35,000 $(= S_0 - S_T)$ in repairs to bring it back up to its market value of \$40,000. But the insurance company will only pay you \$31,000, which equals the \$35,000 garage bill less your deductible of \$4000. This \$31,000 is just the payoff to a put option with a strike price of \$36,000, since the payoff is $K - S_T = 36,000 - 5000 = \$31,000$. In total, your payment from the insurance company is $(S_0 - S_T) - (S_0 - K) = 35,000 - 4000$, but this equals $(K - S_T) = \$31,000$.

If you take out a fixed-rate home mortgage with the possibility of early prepayment of all or part of the principal outstanding, then you have also purchased an implicit option from the lender. If interest rates fall you will exercise this option by paying off the interest and principal of the original loan and remortgaging at lower interest rates. This prepayment option can make the value of a mortgage pool very sensitive to changes in interest rates. The value of this implicit option will be reflected in slightly higher interest payments by the borrower.

As an investor, you can purchase a *guaranteed equity bond*, which offers you at least your original investment plus a proportion of any gain in the stock market. This is a structured product. The investment company 'engineers' the outcome by using most of your money to purchase a coupon-paying bond, but using some of your investment to buy a call option on a stock index (e.g. S&P 500, FTSE 100). The call option provides a (leveraged) return should the stock market rise. If the stock market falls, the call options expire worthless, but your original investment is secured from the coupon payments (and principal) on the bonds.

Investment companies offer stock market funds with a guaranteed floor, set at say, 3% below your initial investment. The investment company is able to offer you 'upside potential' by investing most of your money in a diversified stock portfolio (i.e. one that closely tracks a broad market index), but it also uses a small proportion of your funds to *buy put options* on a stock index (with a strike price 3% below the current value of the stock index; that is they are 3% out of the money). The put options guarantee a minimum price (the strike price) at which the shares can be sold, should stock prices fall dramatically. But if stock prices rise, the value of your stock holding will increase. Your net gain is the value of the stocks less the put premia paid to set up this 'structured product'.

So there are many hidden options out there in the world, but sometimes investors are not aware that they are holding these options.

23.3 FRAS AND SWAPS

Forward rate agreements (FRA)

In a forward rate agreement, one party agrees to pay a floating interest rate at some point in the future in exchange for receiving a fixed rate of interest. For example, suppose that today Ms Forward phones up a large investment bank like Merrill Lynch and buys an FRA to start in one year and last for a further year, on a notional principal of $100m. The payoff to this long position in an FRA is[1]:

> Payoff from long FRA $= \$100m\ (LIBOR_T -$ Agreed fixed rate in the FRA$)$

$LIBOR_T$ is the one-year LIBOR rate in one years time. If $LIBOR_T$ turns out to be 8% when the agreed fixed rate in the FRA is 6%, then Merrill Lynch will pay Ms Forward $2m (2% of $100m). On the other hand, if LIBOR turns out to be 5% in one years time then Ms Forward will pay Merrill Lynch $1m (i.e. the payoff to the long FRA is *minus* $1m).

Why would Ms Forward want to enter into an FRA today? Suppose she already has a $100m bank loan with Citibank on which she pays a floating interest rate and assume she pays LIBOR. Normally she would be happy with this floating-rate loan, but suppose that today

---

[1] Because the amounts owing in an interest rate contract occur at the end of the period, the amount paid out in the FRA at time T would be Payoff$/(1 + LIBOR_T) -$ but this is not of crucial importance in our example since this convention also applies to a bank loan/deposit.

she thinks that interest rates in one years time are likely to be very high. She can hedge her next interest payment on her floating-rate loan with Citibank by *today* taking out an FRA with Merrill Lynch. The effective cost to Ms Forward of the loan repayment in one years time is:

$$
\begin{aligned}
\text{Effective cost of loan at } T &= \$100\text{m [LIBOR}_T - \text{payoff in the FRA]} \\
&= \$100\text{m [LIBOR}_T - (\text{LIBOR}_T - \text{fixed rate in the FRA)]} \\
&= \$100\text{m} \times \text{Fixed rate in the FRA}
\end{aligned}
$$

Hence by taking out the FRA, Ms Forward has effectively swapped her floating-rate payments on her original bank loan for fixed-rate payments at the fixed rate negotiated in the FRA. Of course, if LIBOR rates in one years time are lower than the fixed FRA rate (negotiated at $t = 0$), Ms Forward will pay Merrill Lynch the difference. However, the payments on her original bank loan will be at the lower LIBOR rate, so again she effectively ends up with net payments (i.e. the bank loan plus the FRA) equal to the fixed rate in the FRA.

So an FRA is a form of *forward contract* that allows one to 'lock in' or hedge interest-rate risk over a specific period in the future. In the above example, Ms Forward went long an FRA because she was trying to hedge a future floating-rate loan repayment. But suppose that she knows today that she will receive \$100m (e.g. from sales receipts on goods sold by her firm) in one years time and she knows that she will then put this money in a deposit account at whatever the one-year LIBOR rate is in one years time. If you are thinking of lending money in the future, you will lose out if interest rates fall since your deposit will earn less interest. Hence:

$$
\begin{aligned}
&\text{To hedge a fall in future lending rates} \Rightarrow \text{sell (short) an FRA} \\
&\text{Payoff from short FRA} = \$100\text{m (Agreed fixed rate in the FRA} - \text{LIBOR}_T)
\end{aligned}
$$

The effective interest rate earned on your deposit is then the LIBOR rate payable on your deposit at Citibank plus the payoff to the short FRA – that is, $100m [LIBOR_T + (Agreed FRA rate - LIBOR_T)] = Agreed FRA rate.

What is the agreed fixed FRA rate that Merrill Lynch will quote you? This is just the forward rate quoted today, which applies to money borrowed/lent in one years time for a further year – that is, the forward rate, f_{12}.

Banks are the main participants in FRA over-the-counter (OTC) instruments – that is, they are not traded continuously in a standardised format on an exchange, but they can be tailored to suit individual requirements. By taking a long position in the FRA, Ms Forward has effectively 'swapped' her payment on her bank loan at an unknown floating rate in the future (i.e. LIBOR_T) for a known payment based on the fixed rate in the FRA. In fact, as we see below, an *interest-rate swap is* nothing more than a series of FRAs over several interest rate reset periods. For example, a five-year swap with interest payments reset every year is equivalent to four separate FRAs, the first one beginning in one years time, the second in two years time and so on.

Swaps

Swaps are derivative contracts that first appeared in the early 1980s. They are primarily used for hedging interest-rate and exchange-rate risk over many future periods.

> A swap is a negotiated (OTC) agreement between two parties to exchange cash flows at a *series* of pre-specified future dates.

A *plain vanilla interest-rate swap* involves a periodic exchange of interest payments. One set of interest payments are fixed and known for each period in the future, while the other set of interest payments vary, depending on the prevailing level of some 'floating' interest rate (usually LIBOR). The interest-rate swap will be based on a notional principal amount. For example, Ms Average might agree to receive annual interest payments from the swap dealer at whatever the US dollar LIBOR rate turns out to be at the end of each year, in exchange for payments to the swap dealer at a *fixed rate* of 5% p.a., based on a notional principal amount of $100m. Ms Average is a floating-rate receiver and a fixed-rate payer in the swap. The payments are based on a stated notional principal, *but only the interest payments are exchanged.* The payment dates, the fixed rate and exact floating rate (usually LIBOR) to be used in the swap calculations are determined at the outset of the contract.

Suppose that one-year LIBOR rates turn out to be 6% and 3% in one and two years time respectively. At the end of the first year the swap dealer owes Ms Average $6m in interest and Ms Average owes the swap dealer $5m. So the swap dealer will pay Ms Average the net amount of $1m (equivalent to a net payment of 1%); that is $100m ($LIBOR_1$ − fixed rate). In year 2 the swap dealer owes Ms Average $3m and she owes the swap dealer $5m, so at the end of year 2 Ms Average pays the swap dealer $2m (equivalent to a net payment of 2%) – that is, she has a net position of $100m ($LIBOR_2$ − fixed rate) = −$2m. So the swap is just like two FRAs with the same fixed rate applying in each year. One FRA starts in one years time and the other in two years time. An interest-rate swap is a series of forward contracts on interest rates, where one of the interest rates is fixed at the same level in each year.

The intermediaries in a swap transaction are usually large investment banks who act as swap dealers. They are usually members of the International Swaps and Derivatives Association (ISDA), which provides some standardisation in swap agreements via its *master swap agreement,* which can then be adapted where necessary to accommodate most customers' requirements. Dealers make profits via the bid–ask spread (on the fixed leg of the swap) and might also charge a small brokerage fee for setting up the swap. If swap dealers take on one side of a swap but cannot find a counterparty, then they have an open position (i.e. either net payments or receipts at a floating rate). They usually hedge this position using interest-rate futures contracts until they find a suitable counterparty.

Interest-rate swaps

Why might you use an interest-rate swap? One reason is to remove interest-rate risk. Suppose that Microsoft has an existing long-term bank loan with Citibank on which it pays a variable (floating) interest rate, but it is worried about rising interest rates in the future so it wants to switch to a fixed-rate loan. It could go back to Citibank and negotiate to switch from its floating-rate loan to one in which it pays a known fixed interest payment every year. But renegotiating loan contracts for large corporations is a tricky and expensive proposition – think of all those lawyers' fees to change the covenants in the bond, not to mention lengthy registration periods to issue new debt. It is easier and cheaper to keep the existing floating-rate loan with Citibank but undertake a swap. This will result in Microsoft ending up with what it wants – namely, to have fixed, known interest payments. Let's see how this happens (Figure 23.1).

Microsoft currently pays a floating rate of LIBOR + 0.5% to Citibank. Microsoft now enters a swap deal (with Merrill Lynch) to receive LIBOR and pay 6% fixed. Microsoft's LIBOR payments to Citibank are cancelled out by Merrill Lynch's (the swap dealers) payments to Microsoft. It pays a fixed rate to Merrill Lynch of 6% plus the original fixed spread on LIBOR of 0.5% (to Citibank), giving net fixed payments by Microsoft of 6.5%. Microsoft has transformed an initial floating-rate liability to Citibank into fixed-rate payments of 6.5% by using the swap. Microsoft effectively now has the equivalent of a fixed-rate loan. If the maturity of the swap is for the same period as the remaining period for the bank loan and for the same principal, then Microsoft will have known interest payments

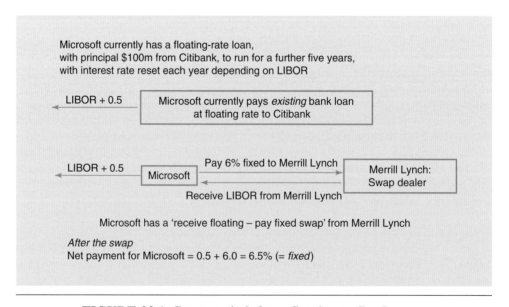

FIGURE 23.1: Swap, switch from floating to fixed payer

over the rest of the life of the loan. In a swap the floating rate is usually LIBOR (without any spread) and the swap dealer will then determine the appropriate fixed rate in the swap. (It is beyond the scope of this book to explain how the fixed rate in an interest-rate swap is determined, but you would be right in thinking it depends on forward interest rates – for this see Cuthbertson and Nitzsche, 2001b.)

Now let us see how a swap can be used to reduce interest-rate risk for a financial intermediary like a bank or Savings and Loan Association (building society in the UK), so that the financial intermediary can lock in a profit over future years. A commercial bank or Savings and Loan (S&L) in the US usually has fixed-rate receipts in the form of loans or housing mortgages, at say 12%, but raises much of its finance in the form of short-term floating rate deposits, at say LIBOR – 1% (Figure 23.2). Income from the deposits varies as market interest rates vary and this is a source of risk for the financial intermediary.

If the deposit rate is LIBOR – 1% and LIBOR currently equals 11%, the bank pays out 10% to depositors. If its fixed-rate mortgages and loans earn 12%, the financial intermediary currently earns a profit (spread) of 2% p.a. However, the danger is that if LIBOR rises by more than 2% the S&L will be making a loss – the source of the risk is future changes in the LIBOR rate. However, the financial intermediary can get rid of this risk if it enters into a swap with Merrill Lynch to receive LIBOR and pay a fixed rate. Suppose that Merrill Lynch sets the fixed-rate payment in the swap at 11%. By entering into the swap the financial intermediary is protected from any future rises in interest rates, since it now effectively has fixed-rate receipts of 2%.

We have seen that one reason for entering into a swap is to remove interest-rate risk over many future years. Another reason for undertaking a swap is that some firms find it cheaper to borrow at floating rates and then use a swap to create the fixed-rate payments that they really want. It is sometimes cheaper to do this than to go and directly obtain a fixed-rate loan from your correspondent (usual) bank. For example, suppose that firm A finds

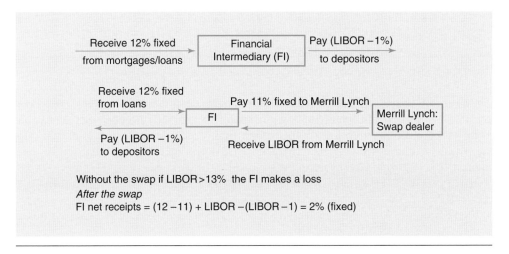

FIGURE 23.2: Remove interest-rate risk

it *relatively cheap* to borrow at a floating rate but would prefer to *ultimately borrow* at a fixed rate. Firm A does not go directly and borrow at a fixed rate from its corresponding bank, say Citibank, because its fixed-rate loans are relatively expensive. Instead, it borrows (cheaply) at a floating rate (from Morgan Stanley) and enters into a swap where it pays floating and receives fixed. If the swap route is cheaper than directly going to Citibank for a fixed-rate loan, the 'cost saving' is known as the *comparative advantage* in the swap. This cost saving provides the financial incentive behind the expansion of the swap business.

Currency swap

A currency swap, in its simplest form, involves two parties exchanging cash flows denominated in different currencies. Nowadays, one reason for undertaking a swap might be that a French firm (Effel), with a subsidiary in the US selling spectacles, might wish to issue $100m in US dollar-denominated debt and eventually payoff the interest and principal with dollar revenues from sales receipts from its US subsidiary. This reduces Effel's foreign exchange exposure.

However, it might be relatively expensive for Effel to raise US dollar finance from its correspondent US bank, as it might not be well established in this foreign loan market. But, if Effel can raise finance (relatively) cheaply in a fixed-rate euro loan, it could do so and then go to a swap dealer and agree to pay (fixed) US dollar interest and receive (fixed) euro interest in the swap. Effectively, Effel now has a US dollar loan that can be paid off from the US dollar receipts earned by its US subsidiary. Note that unlike interest-rate swaps where the principal is 'notional' and is not exchanged either at the beginning or the end of the swap, this is not the case for currency swaps.

> Effel *ultimately* wants to borrow in US dollars but finds it cheap to *initially* borrow in euros and then agree a currency swap to receive US dollars and pay euros.

The swap will enable Effel to achieve its desired outcome at the lowest interest cost. Let's see how this works out in detail. Suppose, for simplicity, that the current spot exchange rate is $1 per euro. Effel's euro loan is for €100m from Crédit Agricole at 9% interest. The swap dealer is Merrill Lynch, which charges 8% US dollar interest in exchange for 9% euro interest. The following takes place in the swap.

At $t = 0$
- Effel borrows €100m from Crédit Agricole, its correspondent bank, at 9% and pays this to the swap dealer, Merrill Lynch.
- Merrill Lynch receives €100m from Effel and pays Effel $100m (Effel uses this to invest in its US subsidiary).

At $t > 0$
- Effel's revenues from its US subsidiary are used to pay Merrill Lynch $8m p.a. (8% of $100m).
- Merrill Lynch pays Effel €9m p.a. in the swap and Effel passes this on to Crédit Agricole.

At maturity of the loan
- Effel pays ($100m + $8m) to Merrill Lynch from revenues earned from its US subsidiary.
- Merrills pays (€100m + €9m) to Effel, which uses it to payoff the loan to Crédit Agricole.

So even though Effel *initially* borrows euros, after the swap it is as if Effel has a US dollar loan. A more light-hearted, but we hope instructive, analogy for a currency swap is given in Case Study 23.2.

CASE STUDY 23.2   SWAPS: KEN AND BARBIE

Consider Sharon and Darren, two 9 year olds from Essex. Darren is genetically predisposed to choose the best (i.e. lowest cost, highest quality) Ken doll around and he purchases one from his local shop. Sharon, on the other hand, is predisposed to choose the best Barbie doll around, which she duly does. Some years pass and Sharon decides that what she would really like is a Ken doll, while Darren decides he would now really like a Barbie doll.

Sharon knows that Darren is good at buying Ken dolls and their accessories and Darren knows that Sharon is good at buying Barbie dolls and their accessories. So at $t = 0$ (today) Sharon and Darren swap dolls. However, they also agree to swap the annual replacement outfits required for each doll so they remain well dressed. Therefore, every year Darren receives from Sharon a replacement outfit for Barbie and Sharon receives a replacement outfit for Ken from Darren. If the maturity of the swap is four years, then at this point they swap dolls back again (since by this time both prefer the 'real thing').

Thus, although Sharon initially purchased a Barbie doll, the swap enables her effectively to have a Ken doll together with his annual update of clothes. Similarly, Darren effectively has a Barbie doll over the life of the swap. Our 'Ken and Barbie' example is therefore like a plain vanilla currency swap.

Indeed, we can push our analogy a little further. Suppose that the swap involves the same replacement outfit for Ken every year (e.g. a John Travolta disco outfit), but the type and cost of Barbie's outfits are uncertain each year (e.g. in some years second-hand retro outfits and in others designer labels). Then Darren's annual receipt of clothes for Barbie would be variable, while his annual payments for Ken's clothes would be fixed. Darren is the 'receive variable–pay fixed' leg of the swap. Sharon's annual clothes parcel would be the mirror image of Darrens'. Sharron is therefore the 'receive fixed–pay variable' leg of the (clothes) swap. The latter scenario is equivalent to one leg of the currency swap being at a variable (or floating) interest rate and the other at a fixed interest rate. Swaps? Just child's play.

Note that if Ken and Barbie were a pure interest-rate swap, Sharon would not exchange Barbie (the principal) at the outset of the swap and Darren would not exchange Ken. But the two sets of clothes would be swapped every year (equivalent to the interest payments in the swap). Thus if we use Ken and Barbie as an example of an interest-rate swap then Ken and Barbie end up as cross-dressers – very post-modern.

Pricing a currency swap

Pricing a standard currency swap is quite straightforward. To keep the figures simple, suppose that the swap payments are in one years time and two years time and then the swap terminates. What is the fixed exchange rate in US dollars per pound (sterling) that should be quoted as the swap rate? If you agree today to pay £1 at the end of the year and £1 at the end of two years, how many US dollars would you receive in each year?

The current quoted one-year and two-year forward FX rates determine the amount of US dollars you can receive. If the spot FX rate is $S = 2.0(\$/£)$, $r_{UK} = 6\%$ p.a. and $r_{US} = 5\%$ p.a. (and the yield curves in both countries are flat), we know that the one-year and two-year forward rates are $F_1 = S(1 + r_{US})/(1 + r_{UK}) = 1.9811$ and $F_2 = S(1 + r_{US})^2/(1 + r_{UK})^2 = 1.9624$. So if you went to the forward market and offered to pay £1 at the end of each of the next two years, you would receive \$1.9811 at the end of the first year and \$1.9624 at the end of the second year. These *two* amounts are worth $F_1/(1 + r_{US}) = \$1.8867$ plus $F_2/(1 + r_{US})^2 = 1.7799$, today, making a total of \$3.6666. But in a swap the amounts exchanged at the end of each year are a *constant* F^* dollars per pound. Because someone interested in a swap could use the two forward markets, the value of the swap today had better equal \$3.6666, hence we require:

$$\frac{F_1}{(1 + r_{US})} + \frac{F_2}{(1 + r_{US})^2} = 3.6666 = \frac{F^*}{(1 + r_{US})} + \frac{F^*}{(1 + r_{US})^2} \qquad [1]$$

Since we know that $r_{US} = 0.05$, the above equation gives $F^* = 1.9721$, which would be the constant swap rate for this two-year currency swap, quoted by the swap dealer. Clearly, a currency swap is a series of forward FX agreements with a constant exchange rate for each period of the swap.

Credit derivatives

There are also derivatives that have a payoff depending on some measure of the creditworthiness of a firm or group of firms. Suppose that you own $1m (face value) in a corporate bond (the 'reference bond'), but you are worried that the corporate might default in the future. You can enter into a **credit default swap** with a financial institution (the swap dealer). You agree to pay the swap dealer a fixed amount of $Q per year (which comes from the coupon receipts from the corporate bond). In return, the swap dealer agrees to buy the bond from you for $1m (the face value of the bond) if the corporate bond is in default – even though it might only be worth $200,000 in the 'distressed debt market'. Alternatively, the credit default swap could be cash settled, whereby you keep the bond (worth $200,000) and the swap dealer pays you $800,000. If the bond does not default, you pay the swap dealer $Q per year and you receive nothing from the swap dealer. The $Q per year is the cost of your insurance premium[2].

Credit default swaps can be used by banks to extend loans to corporates without increasing their credit risk exposure. Suppose that you already hold $100m on your loan book as bank loans to corporate A and you do not wish to increase your exposure. If corporate A asks for a further $1m credit, you would purchase a $1m bond issued by corporate A and immediately enter into a credit default swap with another bank (which has little credit exposure to corporate A). Here the credit default swap is being used to spread the credit risk of corporate A among a wider set of banks.

If you hold a corporate bond and the corporate suffers a credit-rating downgrade (or the market views it as more risky), the yield on the bond will rise and the market price of the bond will fall. Suppose that the normal credit spread over Treasuries for your corporate bond is $sp = 2\%$. You could purchase a **credit spread option** with a strike rate of $K = 2\%$ and a payoff $= D. \max (sp_T - K, 0)$, at maturity of the option. (D is the modified duration of the underlying corporate bond.) If the spread at maturity of the option has widened to $sp_T = 3\%$ because the bond is deemed to be more risky and the duration of the bond is $D = 10$, then the option payoff is 10% of the value of the bond. This payoff should compensate you for the fall in the market price of the bond. If the yield spread falls below 2% then the payoff to the option is zero. The option premium is the cost of this 'credit downgrade insurance'.

There are also options that give you the right (but not the obligation) to enter into a credit default swap in the future, at a payment rate $Q, which is fixed today. This is a credit swaption.

---

[2] If the bond yield (which reflects the default risk of the bond) is say 1% above the risk-free rate, then the payment per year in the swap will be approximately $Q = 0.01 \times \$1m = \$10,000$ p.a. If Q were less than $10,000 then an arbitrageur could buy the reference bond in the market and enter into the swap contract and make a profit (even if the bond defaults). Alternatively if Q is greater than $10,000 an arbitrageur can short-sell the reference bond and enter into the swap contract. This result is approximate as it assumes that at the time of default, the no-default value of the bond is $1m and it also ignores the default risk of the swap dealer (who might default at the same time as the reference bond defaults).

23.4 HEDGERS, SPECULATORS AND ARBITRAGEURS

Part of the reason for the success of both futures and options is that they provide opportunities for hedging, speculation and arbitrage.

Hedgers

Examples of hedging using the forward market in foreign exchange are perhaps most common to the layperson. Using the futures market is, for the hedger, very similar in principle to using the forward market. If an exporter based in the US expects to receive £3000 in three months time, then the corporate treasurer can buy dollars today in the forward market or buy dollar futures contracts. There are of course differences in practice. A futures contract for foreign exchange is for fixed amounts and therefore the hedger has to buy that number of contracts that most closely matches the amount of currency required. However, the key element in both cases is that the US company fixes the price today that it will receive when the money is delivered. Alternatively, the US exporter can 'insure' (i.e. set a lower limit for) her US dollar receipts by buying a put option on sterling at a strike price of $2.0 per £. She is then assured of receiving a minimum of $2.0 per £, but if in three months' time the spot exchange rate is $2.1 per £ she can walk away from the option contract and exchange her £3000 at the higher spot rate. For the privilege of having this option she has to pay an option premium at the outset.

Futures contracts, *if held to maturity*, neutralise risk by fixing the price that the hedger will pay or receive at the maturity of the futures contract. However, it can be shown that even if the futures contract is closed out before maturity, much of the risk can be hedged, although some does remain (this is known as **basis risk**). Options contracts are slightly different in that they provide insurance. Investors in options can protect themselves against adverse price movements in the future, but they still retain the possibility of benefiting from any favourable price movements. For this insurance the 'long' has to pay an option premium.

Speculators and leverage

In our example in the earlier section on call options, the purchaser of the call option on XYZ has the right to one share in three months at a strike price of $K = \$80$. For this she paid $C = \$3$. Alternatively, she could have purchased one share in the spot market at $S_0 = \$78$ and held on to this share for three months. Note that here the amount of capital she has to put up is much larger, at $78, than for the option, which is $3.

By October the stock price has risen to $S_T = \$88$. The dollar amount of profit from holding the shares is larger, at $10, than the net profit from exercising the call of $\$5 = (S_T - K - C)$. However, the long call only costs you the option premium of $3 per share, whereas the transaction in the cash market requires $78 per share. The call option involves far less 'own capital' and hence earns a higher percentage return of 167%, compared with 12.8% on the outright share purchase. Options therefore provide a form of **leverage** (see Figure 23.3).

Leverage also applies to futures contracts, because a speculator does not have to provide any of her own funds. Suppose you ring up Chicago and buy a three-month futures contract (on shares) in January at a price of $F_0 = \$90$, but you do not pay any money to the futures market – we ignore margin requirements, which carry a competitive interest rate so are not a cost.

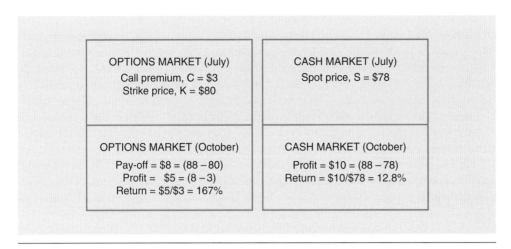

FIGURE 23.3: Leverage from options

Suppose that the spot price of the shares in New York in March is $S_T = \$100$ and you have held your futures contract to maturity. Then the speculator in the futures market can pay $F_0 = \$90$ and take delivery in Chicago of the shares underlying the futures contract. She can then immediately sell the shares at a profit in New York at a spot price $S_T = \$100$. The profit is $S_T - F_0 = \$10$. In principle, she has provided no capital herself and hence the leverage is infinite. If (as is usual) the long futures contract is not held to maturity but closed out, then the speculative profit depends on the increase in the futures price, $F_1 - F_0$, so if the futures price when she closed out in, say, February is $F_1 = \$98$, the profit is $8.

By using futures, speculators can make very large losses as well as very large gains. However, there is a difference between futures and options. In the case of futures the potential loss equals the potential gain (assuming equal probabilities of a fall or rise). But when call or put options are purchased by speculators, the speculator's loss is limited to the option premium but the upside can be very large. For example, a speculator who is long a call option makes a profit if the spot price S_T at expiry is above the strike price K. However, if the spot price falls below the strike price, say even to zero, the speculator's loss is limited to the option premium payment of $3 – her downside risk is limited. Note, however, that *the writer* of a call does have (virtually) unlimited downside risk.

Arbitrageurs

Arbitrage involves locking in a risk-free profit by entering into transactions in two or more markets simultaneously. Usually arbitrage implies that the investor does not use any of his own capital when making the trade. Arbitrage plays a very important role in the determination of both futures and options prices, as we shall discuss later. Arbitrage is often loosely referred to as the 'law of one price' for financial assets. Simply expressed, this implies that identical assets must sell for the same price. Let us consider a very straightforward example of arbitrage.

Suppose that the price of XYZ's shares in New York is $100, while in London they are trading at £120 and the spot exchange rate is £1 for $1. Clearly, there is a risk-free profit to be made here by buying low and selling high. A UK resident buying shares of company XYZ on the New York Stock Exchange (NYSE) for $100 (at a cost of £100) and *simultaneously* selling them on the London Stock Exchange (LSE) for £120 makes a risk-free profit of £20 (or $20) per share. In a fully informed market one would not expect such risk-free arbitrage opportunities to persist for very long. In fact, the forces of supply and demand (or even just the price information on dealers' screens) would bring these two prices quickly into equality. Large purchases in New York would push the dollar price of the shares up, while sales in London would push the sterling share price down – at an unchanged exchange rate this would bring the two prices nearer to equality. In addition, in order to purchase the shares on the NYSE, UK residents would have to purchase dollars and sell sterling and hence the dollar would appreciate relative to sterling – again leading to an equalisation of prices (in a common currency).

Suppose that the exchange rate moved to £1.20 per $1. In this case a UK resident would have to give up £120 in order to purchase $100 spot to buy XYZ on the NYSE. This is exactly the amount he would need to purchase it on the LSE. Of course, in practice how much the two stock prices or the exchange rate move to achieve equality of prices is indeterminate. It is just that all three 'prices' will quickly move to eliminate any (risk-free) arbitrage opportunities. This is the 'law of one price'.

An example of where risk-free arbitrage is used to establish the price of a derivative asset is the determination of the forward foreign exchange rate (see Chapter 18). Covered interest arbitrage implies that risk-free profits can be made, unless the forward rate is determined at all times by:

$$F = S\frac{(1 + r_d)}{(1 + r_f)} \qquad\qquad [2]$$

where S is the spot exchange rate (domestic per unit of foreign currency), F is the forward exchange rate, r_d is the domestic interest rate and r_f is the foreign interest rate. As can be seen from the above equation, arbitrage provides a strong link (or correlation) between the spot price and the forward price. As we see in the next chapter, risk-free arbitrage is the method used to price a futures contract.

By way of an analogy, consider Dolly the sheep. You will remember that Dolly was cloned by scientists at Edinburgh University and was an exact replica of a real sheep. She was a form of genetic engineering or 'synthetic' sheep. Suppose that we could create 'Dolly' in Edinburgh at a cost of £200 per sheep, which was below the current market price of the real sheep (in the Highlands) at, say, £250. Then no one would buy sheep in the Highlands at £250 when they could get Dolly in Edinburgh for £200 and this arbitrage would ensure that the price of the Highland sheep would very quickly fall to £200. Dolly is like a 'synthetic' or 'replication' portfolio in finance – so the real sheep eventually must equal the cost of producing an identical replica. Indeed, Larry Summers, a prominent US economist (and previous US Secretary of the Treasury), has rather impishly characterised the difference between economists and traditional finance specialists with the following analogy. He says that economists are interested in why, for example, the price of a bottle of ketchup moves up and down (e.g. because of changes in incomes, production costs etc.), while finance specialists are only interested in whether an 16 oz bottle of ketchup sells for the same price as two 8 oz bottles. Luckily given the material in this text, we can justifiably call ourselves *financial economists* and avoid this somewhat pejorative analogy.

SUMMARY

- In a *forward contract* a price is agreed today, for delivery of the underlying asset in the contract at a specific date in the future. Forward contracts are usually held to maturity, when delivery takes place.
- *Forward contracts* are over-the-counter (OTC) agreements whose terms (e.g. size, delivery date and price) are negotiated between two counterparties.
- *Futures contracts* if held to maturity are very similar to forward contracts. However, futures contracts are standardised agreements (e.g. size, delivery date) that are traded on exchanges and their price fluctuates continuously.
- Futures contracts involve a 'good faith deposit' that is known as a margin payment and most futures contracts are closed out before maturity.
- Both forwards and futures can be used for hedging. Even if a futures contract is closed out before maturity, you can effectively 'lock in' the futures price quoted at time $t = 0$, when the contract is entered into.
- *Options contracts* can provide insurance in that they can be used to limit 'downside risk' while allowing 'upside capture'. If you *plan* to purchase shares in the future and are worried that their price might rise, you can guarantee the *maximum* price you will have to pay by purchasing a call option today. If you *already own shares* and you are worried that their price might fall in the future, you can buy a put option that will fix the *minimum* price you will receive for your shares.
- Options can be used for speculation without having to put up much capital, since you only pay a small option premium (relative to the spot price of the underlying asset) – so options provide *leverage*.
- Acting as a speculator, if you think that stock prices will rise (fall) in the future you would buy a call (put) option. The most a speculator can lose when buying calls or puts are the respective option premia. But a speculator who sells (writes) a call or put option has almost unlimited risk.
- A *forward rate agreement* FRA is a contract agreed today, to exchange interest payments based on the future LIBOR rate, in exchange for fixed interest payments. A long position in an FRA for a notional principle of \$100m has a payoff $= \$100m$ $(\text{LIBOR}_T - \text{fixed rate in the FRA})$. Only the difference in interest is paid (or received).
- An FRA allows you to hedge future interest payments/receipts for a specific date in the future.
- *An interest-rate swap is a series of FRAs.* Interest-rate swaps allow you to convert floating-rate (variable) interest payments/receipts into fixed-rate payments receipts.
- *Swap dealers* act as intermediaries and try to match those who want to make fixed-rate payments and receive floating-rate payments with a counterparty who wishes to do exactly the opposite. If the swap dealer cannot exactly match two opposite swap deals, she will use interest rate futures contracts to hedge her position.

- *Currency swaps* allow you to swap payments/receipts of principal and interest in one currency for payments/receipts in a different currency. The fixed exchange rate F^* in the currency swap can be calculated from known forward rates of exchange.
- *Risk-free arbitrage* allows one to determine the 'fair price' of derivative securities.

EXERCISES

Q1   Why are futures and options contracts referred to as 'derivatives'?

Q2   In what ways is an agreement to marry Vito Corleone's daughter in one years time a type of futures or forward contract? Which one does it more closely resemble?

Q3   What is the difference between a European and an American option, as far as the buyer and the writer are concerned?

Q4   If $K = 150$ and the put premium is $P = 5$, should you exercise the option if the spot price at expiry is $S_T = 148$? What is your profit?

Q5   The strike price for a put is $K = 100$ and the put premium is $P = 2$. Why is the put payoff (for the long) at expiration equal to 5, when the stock price at expiry is 95?

Q6   Under what circumstances would you make a profit at maturity, from a long position in futures contract on live hogs?

Q7   How does going long a futures contract give you leverage compared with going long in the spot market? Take stocks as an example and use $F_0 = \$101$ and $S_0 = \$100$, with outturn values (three months later) of $F_1 = \$111$ and $S_1 = \$110$.

Q8   You have a (mortgage) loan for $200,000 that has been in existence for two years and has a further 10 years to maturity. Interest on the loan is paid every year, at whatever the (one-year) interest rate is at that time (i.e. it is a floating-rate loan at LIBOR). You took out this loan when interest rates were low, but now you think that interest rates will be permanently higher in the future. How can you use the swaps market to effectively give you a loan with a fixed interest rate?

CHAPTER 24

Futures Markets

AIMS

- To examine trading arrangements when using futures contracts, including margin requirements, closing out positions and newspaper quotes.
- To analyse how *risk-free arbitrage* can be used to determine the fair price for a futures contract.
- To examine how futures can be used for *hedging* a position in the underlying asset (e.g. portfolio of stocks) and in hedging changes in interest rates.
- To show how futures are used for *speculation*.

24.1 TRADING ON FUTURES MARKETS

We have already discussed the basic principles behind forward and futures contracts. Forward contracts are analytically easier to deal with than futures contracts and so we often apply mathematical results from forwards (e.g. pricing forward contracts) to futures contracts. However, there are differences in practice between the two types of contract and we discuss the mechanics of both of these contracts in this section.

Forward contracts are traded over the counter (OTC), whereas most futures are traded on an exchange. The differences between these two approaches are summarised in Figure 24.1.

OVER THE COUNTER	EXCHANGE TRADED
• Supplied by intermediaries (banks)	• Traded on exchanges (e.g. NYSE-EuroNext, CBOT, CME)
• Customised to suit buyer	• Available for restricted set of assets
• Can be done for any amount, any settlement date	
• Credit risk of counterparty and expensive to unwind	• Fixed contract sizes and settlement dates
• Allows anonymity, important for large deals	• Easy to reverse the position
• New contracts do not need approval of regulator	• Credit risk eliminated by clearing house margining system ('marking to market')

FIGURE 24.1: Derivative markets

The range of assets on which futures contracts are written is very wide and they are traded on a large number of exchanges around the world (Figure 24.2). The basic requirements in buying and selling different types of futures contracts and in using them for hedging and speculation are very similar, even though futures contracts are written on a diverse set of underlying assets. The growth in futures and forward contracts is primarily due to the increased volatility of the underlying assets and the need to hedge this risk. Futures contracts are available on a wide variety of underlying assets, whereas only the forward market for foreign exchange rivals trading on futures markets.

A futures exchange is usually a corporate entity whose members elect a board of directors who decide on the terms and conditions under which existing contracts are traded and whether to introduce new contracts (subject usually to the regulatory authority, which in the US is the Commodity Futures Trading Commission, CFTC, and in the UK the Financial Services Authority, FSA).

The market price of the futures contract is known as the futures price and each contract specifies a delivery month. When the contract is first negotiated, the quoted futures price is the *delivery price or contract price* for the underlying asset. The quoted futures price then varies

INSTRUMENTS	EXCHANGES

• Money-market instruments
  3-month Eurodollar deposit,
  90 day US T-bills,
  3 month sterling or euro deposits
• Bonds
  US T-bond, German Bund, UK gilts
 	
• Stock indices
  S&P 500, FTSE 100
 	
• Currencies
  Euro, sterling, yen, etc.
 	
• Mortgage pools (GNMA)
	CBOT
	CME
	NY Mercantile Exchange, NYMEX
	Philadelphia Stock Exchange
	Pacific Stock Exchange
	
	NYSE-Euronext (was LIFFE)
	
	Singapore, Hong Kong,
	
	Tokyo, Osaka
	
	Sydney Futures Exchange

FIGURE 24.2: Financial futures

continuously until the expiry date, when the futures price must equal the spot price (as the underlying asset in the futures contract is then for immediate delivery):

$$F_T = S_T \tag{1}$$

For pedagogic purposes we assume that futures contracts are traded on individual stocks (even though in practice not many of these contracts are traded). Today, the *buyer* of a futures contract at a quoted price $F = \$100$ is said to be *long* and if she holds the contract to maturity she must purchase the **underlying asset** in the futures contract (e.g. AT&T shares) in Chicago (i.e. the delivery point), at a price of $100 at a specific date in the future (the maturity date of the futures contract). At maturity, the long in the futures contract must purchase the stock in Chicago at $100 even if the spot price in New York is then, say, $60 or $120.

The *writer* or *seller* of the futures is said to be *short* and *if she holds the contract to maturity* she must supply the underlying asset at a price of $100 in Chicago. Here we have assumed that Chicago is where the futures contract is traded and where delivery takes place. Since each contract always has a buyer and a seller, then if the contracts are held to maturity there will always be a 'short' ready to deliver the underlying asset to the person holding the long position in the futures contract.

Financial futures are written on financial assets (e.g. stock indices, currencies, T-bills or T-bonds), whereas agricultural or metallurgical futures are written on, say, wheat or silver (respectively). The underlying asset (e.g. AT&T shares) is traded at a spot price in the cash market (which in this case is the NYSE). The futures price is linked to the *current* spot price, hence the generic term **derivative security**.

Futures markets can be used for speculation, hedging or arbitrage. Because there is always a counterparty to a futures contract (i.e. Ms A is long, Ms B is short), any gains by Ms A are met by Ms B – overall it is a zero-sum game (ignoring transaction costs). However, for any individual trader on one side of the market (i.e. either long or short) there are potential cash gains and losses to be made.

Since futures contracts (unlike forward contracts) are traded on an exchange, there needs to be some standardisation of the contracts and price quotes. Also, to minimise default risk, a clearing house and some collateral are required to compensate a trader if another trader defaults (this is taken care of with margin payments).

Standardisation

The futures exchange sets the size of each contract, minimum price fluctuations, the 'quality' and place for delivery, any daily price limits and margin requirements, as well as opening hours for trading. For agricultural commodities, the type or grade is fixed in the futures contract (e.g. wheat of a particular quality or variety). The futures exchange sets the minimum contract size (e.g. 5000 bushels of wheat), delivery dates (e.g. March, May, June, July, September and December for wheat) and delivery arrangements (e.g. only in towns A, B and C).

For futures on financial assets, such standardisation is easier. For example, an FX futures contract on the pound sterling is a rather homogenous product and only delivery dates, settlement price and contract size need to be set by the exchange. Some examples of the contractual arrangements on futures contracts for US T-bonds, the sterling-dollar FX rate and the S&P 500 equity index are shown in Table 24.1. Some contracts have expirations only out to a year or two, but others can be for a much longer period. It depends primarily on the demand for such contracts by hedgers. For example, the Eurodollar futures contract has maturities out to 20 years or more because these contracts are used by swap dealers to hedge their interest-rate swap positions.

The **size of the contract** is important. If it is too small, speculators will not trade the contract because the transaction costs per contract will be relatively high – but if it is too large, hedgers will not be able to hedge relatively small amounts (e.g. the Eurodollar futures has a contract

TABLE 24.1: Futures (Contract specifications)

Commodity	Delivery	Contract	Minimum price change	Daily limit
1. US T-bonds (CBOT)	March, June, Sept., Dec.	$100 000 (8% coupon bond)	$ 31.25 (= 1/32 of 1%)	$2000 (= 2%)
2. £-Sterling (CME-IMM)	Jan, March, April, June, July, Sept.,Oct., Dec.	£ 125,000	$ 6.25 (= ½ tick)	None
3. S&P500 (CBOT)	Next 4 months and March, June, Sept., Dec.	$250 × (S&P500)	10 points (0.1) = $ 25	None

size of $1m and you cannot hedge $500,000 using half a contract). The **tick size** and **tick value** should be easily understood by market participants and yet relatively small for obvious reasons. For example, the US T-bill futures contract has a contract size of $100,000 and a tick size of 1/32 of 1% (of the contract size). Hence the minimum price change (tick value) is $31.25 ($= 0.0003125 (\$100,000)$).

The total number of futures contracts outstanding is called the **open interest**. As each contract has both a long and a short position, this counts as 'one' open interest. Looked at another way, open interest is the number of deals outstanding that could either be closed out before maturity or result in delivery of the underlying.

Futures exchanges and traders

In some futures markets traders meet face-to-face in a pit, such as on the International Money Market (IMM) in Chicago, on the trading floor of the Chicago Board of Trade (CBOT) and until 1999 on the London International Financial Futures Exchange (LIFFE). Traders in the pit indicate prices and deal sizes using hand signals and the system is known as **open outcry**. All exchanges *settle* trades using computers, but now more exchanges are moving away from open outcry and trades are conducted electronically. Some of these systems are 'order driven', whereby the buyers and sellers are 'matched' via the computer, as, for example, on NYSE-Euronext (previously LIFFE). Futures trading is becoming more global. For example, GLOBEX, which is owned by the CBOT and Reuters (UK), provides an *after-hours* electronic futures trading system – 'after-hours' being from a US perspective. Note, however, that GLOBEX does not automatically match buyers and sellers and then automate the trades. It merely provides price information to traders.

Futures trading

Public orders must be placed through a broker, who will then contact a floor broker in the exchange. Trades are monitored by the **Clearing House** (e.g. Chicago Board of Trade Clearing Corporation) and all floor traders must have an account with a member clearing firm. If your floor broker purchases a futures contract on your behalf, you will have to pay the initial margin to the floor broker, who will then pay this into her clearing firm, say ABC. The seller may be a local or a broker acting on behalf of a customer 'off the floor'. The seller of the futures also deposits the initial margin with her clearing firm, XYZ. Both clearing firms ABC and XYZ each aggregate up their net positions from their customers and deposit a margin payment with the CBOT clearing corporation, who then guarantees both sides of the contract.

Margins and marking to market

Margin payments provide financial protection in case one of the counterparties to the futures contract defaults. Suppose that you purchase one US T-bond futures contract at noon on day 1, when the current futures price $F_0 = \$98$ (per $100 nominal), and one contract is for delivery of $100,000 nominal value of US T-bonds (see Table 24.2). To make things easy, let us act as the clearing house and define 'one tick' as a change in F of 1 unit. The **tick value** of a *change* in F of 1 point is therefore $\$1000 = (1/100) \times \$100,000$. (In reality, for the US T-bond futures contract the tick value is $32.50, but forget this for now and use our simpler tick value.)

TABLE 24.2: Marking to market

Day	Settlement (price)	Mark to market	Margin payment	Balance
1	$ 94,000 (94.0)	− $ 4000	$ 5000	$ 1000
2	$ 93,500 (93.5)	− $ 500	$ 4000	$ 4500
3	$ 98,500 (98.5)	+ $ 5000		$ 9500

Buy at $F_0 = \$\,98$ (noon, day 0)
Contract size = $ 100 000
Initial margin = $ 5000
Maintenance margin = $ 4000

The **initial margin** is $5000 and the **maintenance margin** is $4000. The initial margin is not a payment for the futures contract. It is a good-faith deposit to ensure that the terms of the futures contract are honoured. Some large, active traders can in fact post Treasury bills for margin calls. Note that if the balance in the margin account falls below the maintenance margin of $4000, the trader has to deposit extra funds, known as a **variation margin**, to restore the balance to the *initial margin* (of $5000).

When you purchase the contract at $98, you deposit your initial margin of $5000. Suppose that by the end of day 1 the futures price falls dramatically, from $F_0 = \$98$ to $F_1 = \$94$. The investor has a loss of $4000, since at the end of day 1 she can now only sell her futures contract for $94,000. The balance on the margin account is therefore reduced to $1000 (see Table 24.2). This is **marking to market**. The balance at the end of day 1 of $1000 is below the maintenance margin. Hence the next morning, the investor must immediately pay a variation margin of $4000, so that the balance in the margin account at the *beginning* of day 2 is back to $5000. Suppose now that the futures price at *the close* of day 2 falls to $F_2 = \$93.50$, so that there is an additional loss of $500, which brings the balance in the margin account to $4500. On day 3, the investor reverses her position and closes out at $F_3 = \$98.50$ (i.e. an increase of 5 points) and $5000 is added to the margin account, which now stands at $9500, which is paid to the 'long' by the clearing house. Since the long has previously paid in $5000 + $4000, the net profit over the three days is $500. Of course, this equals the change in the futures price $(F_3 - F_0)$ grossed up by the tick value – that is $500 ($= (\$98.50 - \$98.00)\$1000$).

In the case of a price fall, the long pays into the margin account and the exchange credits the margin account of someone who has a short position (i.e. who has previously sold one futures contract). The opposite occurs for a rise in the futures price. The investor can withdraw (if she wishes) any excess in the margin account, over and above her initial margin. But to ensure that the balance in the margin account never becomes negative, a variation margin may be payable. (This is usually about 75% of the initial margin.)

If the balance in the margin account falls below the maintenance margin, the investor must top up her account (i.e. pay the variation margin) so that it equals the *initial margin* by the next day. If the investor does not do this, her broker closes out the position by selling the contract. Clearly, it is possible for the futures price to fall so dramatically during the day that the required margin call may exceed the amount in the margin account. To prevent this happening, the exchange sets daily price limits. If the price falls (or rises) during the day by as much as the 'limit down' ('limit up'), then trading (usually) ceases for that day. These *circuit breakers* limit the daily payments/receipts to and from the margin accounts so that the balance in the margin account does not fall below zero and can be increased before trading begins the next day. Often the initial margin is set equal to the value of the contract's daily price limit and therefore the initial margin can be small relative to the value of the asset underlying the futures contract. So even if margin funds did not earn a competitive interest rate, speculators could still obtain considerable leverage by using futures contracts.

Closing out

In practice, most futures traders (about 99%) close out their positions before the expiration of the futures contract. They therefore make a gain or loss depending on the difference between the initial futures price $F_1 = \$100$ and the futures price at which they close out the contract, say $F_2 = \$110$ (Figure 24.3). If you are long the futures, then when the futures price *increases*, the profit from your futures position also *increases* – this is a positive relationship. Of course, if you are long the futures and F falls, then the value of your futures position also falls (i.e. you make losses) – but this too is a positive relationship.

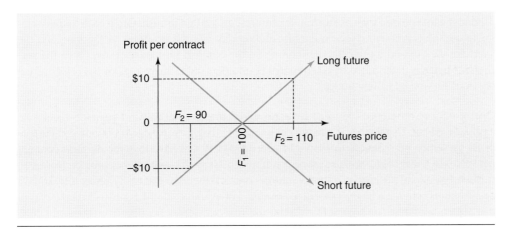

FIGURE 24.3: Speculation with futures

Closing out the contract merely involves **reversing** your initial trade. So if in January you purchased a September futures contract (on stocks) at F_1 and you rang up Chicago in July and sold a September futures contract at F_2, the profit on the trade is equal to $F_2 - F_1$. By buying and then later selling the same September futures contract, any delivery of the underlying to you is nullified.

The profit on the futures position $F_2 - F_1$ can be shown to equal the *cumulative gain* or loss incurred day by day as the contract is marked to market. So in practice, the profit accrues in daily instalments over the life of the futures contract. Although most futures contracts are closed out via reversing the initial trade, it is the possibility of delivery that links the futures price to the underlying spot price via risk-free arbitrage and results in the futures price in Chicago (over short time horizons) moving almost dollar for dollar with the spot price (in New York) – see below.

Now consider an investor who has initially sold (shorted) a futures contract at $F_1 = \$100$ (Figure 24.3). She earns a profit of \$10 if the futures price *falls* to $F_2 = \$90$, since she can then buy back the contract (and hence close out her position) at a lower price then she initially sold it. Conversely, if the futures price *rises* to $F_2 = \$110$, the person who has a short futures position makes a loss.

Delivery and settlement

The seller of the futures has to deliver and usually delivery can take place on any of several days in the delivery month (and sometimes on any day during the delivery month). So the person holding a short September wheat futures might notify the clearing house that she intends to deliver. The clearing house then selects (usually in a random fashion) someone with a long position in September wheat futures and lets them know that they must accept delivery within the next few days. So for commodities, delivery is usually in the form of a warehouse receipt and the precise time and place for delivery are determined by the party with the short position. After delivery the 'long' then responsible for any warehousing costs or, for livestock futures, for the care of the animals.

Some financial futures contracts involve the delivery of the underlying asset (e.g. T-bills, T-bonds) while others, such as stock index futures, are settled in cash. Often cash-settled contracts use the settlement price on the last trading day and the positions of the long and the short are then closed by the clearing house and the contract no longer exists. Often the **settlement price** is determined by a settlement committee and is an average of the prices of the previous session's last few trades.

One of the key differences between forwards and futures is that forward contracts cannot be easily closed out. Usually Ms A can only close out her long *forward contract* (with counterparty B) by selling her contract to Ms C. In general, Ms B will have to agree the new contract between Ms A and Ms C, because of the credit risk to Ms B who is short the contract. However, if Ms A has a long position in a 'hogs' *futures* contract[1] then she can easily offset it by selling a *new* futures contract *with the same delivery date*. For example, if on 1 February you purchased one September futures on hogs at $F_0 = \$100$ and sold one September futures on hogs on 1 June for $F_1 = \$110$, then you make a cash profit of \$10 but there will be no delivery of hogs *to you* in September. As far as you are concerned this contract in now nullified. For a light-hearted view of delivery and settlement of forward and futures contracts, see Case Study 24.1.

CASE STUDY 24.1   HEDGING: KEN AND BARBIE

If you still find forwards and futures a little bewildering, perhaps the following analogy will help. Just think of a forward or futures contract in terms of an engagement or marriage to a partner. A partner here is a homogenous commodity. For example, this might include the market in 'Sloane Rangers' (of a given age range but of either sex) who parade up and down the King's Road in their designer sunglasses and clothes.

---

[1] A hog is a type of pig

Other reasonably homogeneous markets include 'Essex man and woman', royalty, Hollywood celebrities and the occupants of many clubs in big cities and on holiday islands (Ibiza comes to mind). In somewhat disparaging terms, these spot markets are colloquially known as 'cattle markets'. To financial economists, markets are impersonal: 'It's the price that matters, stupid!' We will make our market impersonal but interpersonal. Assume that there is a market in a homogeneous class of men called 'Ken'. The spot price of Kens varies with their earning power and their general demeanour.

Now, Barbie might be quite willing to pay the spot price $S = \$100$ in January to take delivery of a Ken and immediately marry him (e.g. in the 'Elvis suite' in Las Vegas). Using the spot market is all very well if you know that you want a partner immediately. But what if you knew you definitely wanted to be married to a Ken, but not until after you had sown some 'wild oats' over the coming year. The problem you have is that if Kens do very well in the job market over the next year, their spot price will be high and you might not be able to afford one. You currently have a 'naked' position in spot Kens. As a hedger, what you require is a contract that fixes the price of the 'underlying' Ken today, for delivery in one years time. This is a forward contract on a Ken. So a *forward contract* is like a traditional engagement with the price of the dowry fixed at the outset of the contract.

Unfortunately, a forward contract has one major drawback. It is very difficult and expensive to get out of the contract and hence delivery invariably takes place. Do you remember the film *The Godfather* with Marlon Brando as Vito Corleone? Well, in terms of our analogy, a forward contract is like agreeing an engagement with Vito Corleone's daughter, Connie. Since the costs of reneging on such a contract are prohibitively high (e.g. horse's heads in people's beds) the marriage to Connie went ahead. This is the case with forward contracts on financial assets: they nearly all go to delivery.

The key difference between a forward and a futures contract is that the latter is easily 'reversed' or 'closed out' prior to maturity. A futures contract is therefore like an engagement between Hollywood stars. In terms of our analogy, all Barbie has to do to 'close out' her long position in a December Ken futures contract is to phone up the futures exchange (in June, say) and sell one (December) Ken futures contract. Then no delivery (i.e. marriage) will take place at the end of the year. (Of course, Barbie may have made a loss or gain on her futures position if she closes out in June before maturity, but this may be preferable to delivery in December, if she has changed her mind about the desirability of a Ken.)

Newspaper quotes

An example of futures quotes for gold on 10 October is given in Table 24.3. The size of the contract is for 100 troy oz of gold and the price is in US dollars per troy oz. There are various maturity dates.

The opening futures price (for the trade immediately after the opening bell), and the 'high' and 'low' daily futures prices during the trading day are given in columns 2 to 4. The 5th column gives the settlement price, which is an average of prices just before the closing bell, and

TABLE 24.3: Futures quotes (10 Oct)

Gold(CMX), 100 troy oz: $ per troy oz					
Month	Open	High	Low	Settle	Change	Open interest
Oct '07	736.1	736.5	735.5	737.4	4.6	633
Dec '07	739.0	746.5	732.2	743.1	4.4	299,488
Feb '08	744.8	752.3	742.7	749.4	4.4	33,161
April '08	751.3	751.3	749.3	755.5	4.5	18,513
June '08	753.0	762.1	753.0	761.6	4.5	18,037
Aug '08	761.0	767.6	761.0	767.4	4.5	18,244

the 6th column shows the *change* in the settlement price since the previous day. The latter is used to calculate daily changes in margin requirements. Thus between the previous trading days the settlement price for December futures increased by $4.4 and an investor long in one gold futures contract would have his margin account credited by $440 (= 100 × $4.4). The open interest is the number of futures contracts currently outstanding. Futures prices on other commodities are given in Figure 24.4.

Metal & Petroleum Futures

	Open	High	Contract hi lo	Low	Settle	Chg	Open interest
Copper-High (CMX)-25,000 lbs.: cents per lb.							
Oct	361.10	364.90		359.25	**360.10**	0.80	982
Dec	361.90	367.35		358.25	**361.75**	0.45	61,215
Gold (CMX)-100 troy oz.; $ per troy oz.							
Oct	736.10	736.50		735.50	**737.40**	4.60	633
Dec	739.00	746.50		732.20	**743.10**	4.40	299,488
Feb'08	744.80	752.30		742.70	**749.40**	4.40	33,161
April	751.30	751.30		749.30	**755.50**	4.50	18,513
June	753.00	762.10		753.00	**761.60**	4.50	18,037
Aug	761.00	767.60		761.00	**767.40**	4.50	18,244
Platinum (NYM)-50 troy oz. $ per troy oz.							
Oct	1380.00	1380.00		1380.00	**1381.60**	6.40	182
Jan'08	1368.50	1381.00		1362.00	**1379.60**	6.40	14,381
Silver (CMX)-5,000 troy oz.: cnts per troy oz.							
Oct	...	...		...	**1347.5**	22.5	0
Dec	1334.5	1368.5		1325.0	**1358.3**	22.3	77,067
Crude Oil, Light Sweet (NYM)-1,000 bbls.; $ per bbl.							
Nov	79.26	81.10		78.39	**80.26**	1.24	238,589
Dec	78.50	80.23		77.71	**79.54**	1.14	282,586
Jan'08	77.83	79.43		77.09	**78.83**	1.00	106,464
Dec	74.30	75.88		74.10	**75.52**	0.85	157,930
Dec'09	73.10	74.15		72.55	**73.88**	0.81	58,521
Dec'10	72.50	73.55		72.50	**73.33**	0.85	55,773
Heating Oil No. 2 (NYM)-42,000 gal. $ per gal.							
Nov	2.1670	2.2050		2.1415	**2.1853**	.0257	64,746
Dec	2.1833	2.2208		2.1600	**2.2028**	.0247	64,774

FIGURE 24.4: Futures prices

Source: *Wall Street Journal,* Oct 2007, reproduced by permission.

24.2 FORWARD AND FUTURES PRICES

In this section we analyse how forward and futures prices are determined as functions of known variables such as the current market price of the underlying asset and the risk-free interest rate. We will consider a simple case, without entering into the details of contract specifications. Forward contracts are easier to analyse than futures contracts, since the latter have the added complication of daily settlement (i.e. marking to market), whereas for the forward contract there is one payment at the expiry date. However, it can be shown that the futures price of an asset closely follows that of the forward price, for any given maturity. Therefore, in general, we will use forward and futures prices interchangeably. In general we assume:

- zero transaction costs
- zero tax rates
- agents can borrow or lend unlimited amounts at the 'free' rate of interest
- short selling of the underlying asset is possible
- risk-free arbitrage opportunities are instantaneously eliminated

We will in the main use risk-free arbitrage arguments when valuing futures contracts and this method is also referred to as the **carrying-charge** or **cost-of-carry** determination of futures prices. Risk-free arbitrage arises because it is possible to create a 'synthetic forward' contract.

Non-income-paying security

Consider the determination of the futures price on a contract for a non-income-paying security (i.e. a share which pays no dividends). The contract is for the delivery of a single share in three months' time (Figure 24.5). We will set up a situation where initially it is possible to make a risk-free arbitrage profit because the quoted futures price is incorrect. Consider the following prices:

```
Stock price              S = $100
Risk-free rate           r = 4% p.a.
Quoted futures price     F = $102

Strategy today
    Sell futures contract at $102 (receive nothing today)
    Borrow $100, buy stock (= synthetic future)
    Use no 'own funds'

Three months' time (T = 1/4)
    Loan outstanding       = $100 (1+0.04/4)   = $101
    Deliver stock, receipt from futures contract = $102
    Risk-free profit = $1
```

FIGURE 24.5: Arbitrage

$F = \$102$ is the *quoted* futures price in Chicago in July for delivery in September.
$S = \$100$ is the spot price of the share on the NYSE in July.
$r = 0.04$ is the interest rate (4% p.a., simple interest) in July.
$T = 1/4$ is the time to maturity of the futures (as a fraction of a year).

With the above quoted prices it is possible to earn a risk-free profit. Here's how. The arbitrageur borrows $100 today from a bank and purchases the share on the NYSE. She therefore knows for certain that she can deliver the share in three months in September (since it is 'in her pocket' and will stay there). This strategy involves no own capital, since the money is borrowed – it is known as a *zero investment strategy*. The arbitrageur at $t = 0$ also rings up Chicago and sells a futures contract at $F = \$102$ (to another trader, who may be a hedger or a speculator for example – we don't care, we only care about *our* trades). Note that this sell order is noted by the clearing house in Chicago and you do not have to pay any money today in Chicago (we ignore margin payments). But by selling a September futures contract in July *and holding it to maturity,* you are legally obliged to deliver one share in September in Chicago, for which you will receive $102.

You borrowed $100 in July to purchase the share on the NYSE, so that you are certain of having a share in three months time (it's in your pocket) to deliver against your short futures position. What is the cost of providing the share in three months time? You will owe the bank the initial loan of $100 plus the interest, so you will owe $101 [$= \$100(1 + 0.04/4)$] in September. Note that algebraically, the amount you owe in September is $S(1 + rT)$. By purchasing the stock in the spot market in July with borrowed money, you are able (with certainty) to deliver it in three months time in September – you have created a synthetic futures contract at a cost (in September) of $SF = \$101$.

At maturity of the futures contract the arbitrageur receives $F = \$102$ in September and delivers one share. The cost of having the share 'in your pocket' ready for delivery in September is $101, therefore you realise a risk-free profit of $(102 - 101) = \$1$ in September. The strategy is risk-free since the arbitrageur knows S, F and r at $t = 0$. The synthetic future has a cost of $SF = S(1 + rT)$, which is lower than the quoted futures price F.

Many (cross-market) arbitrageurs will take advantage of this risk-free profit opportunity by buying low and selling high. Buying the share in the cash market (NYSE) and borrowing money tends to increase S and r (and hence SF), while selling futures contracts in Chicago will tend to depress the current quoted futures price F – this is just supply and demand. Profitable risk-free arbitrage opportunities across the futures and spot markets will only be eliminated when the quoted futures price equals the price of the synthetic future SF, so the 'no arbitrage' or 'fair' futures price is:

$$F = S(1 + rT) \tag{2}$$

Alternatively we can write the above as:

$$\text{Forward price} = \text{Spot price} + \text{Dollar cost of carry} = \$100 + \$1 \tag{3a}$$
$$F \quad = \quad S \quad + \quad X$$

where the *dollar* cost of carry $X = SrT = \$1$. Equivalently we have:

> Forward price = Spot price $(1 + \text{Percentage cost of carry})$ [3b]
>
> $\qquad F = S\,(1 + CC)$

where the *percentage (proportionate)* cost of carry $CC = rT = 1\%$. Note that the percentage cost of carry (CC) also equals the percentage forward premium $(F - S)/S$. Determining the futures price in this way is known as **cash-and-carry arbitrage.**

While the futures contract is being held, the spot price in New York will change continuously, but because arbitrageurs continually watch their screens their actions will continuously maintain the relationship $F = S\,(1 + rT)$ between the futures price (in Chicago) and the spot price (in New York). It is immediately apparent from equation [2] that the futures price and the stock price will move closely together, if r stays constant. In our case $F = (1.01)S$, so:

> Arbitrageurs ensure that the spot price (in New York) and the
> futures price (in Chicago) move almost dollar for dollar.

If interest rates change then F and S will change by different amounts – this is a source of **basis risk** when hedging with futures contracts.

Futures price at expiry

At expiry of the futures contract (i.e. at T), the futures price must equal the then spot price, $F_T = S_T$. This is because the person with a long futures position can obtain immediate delivery of one stock at a price of $F_T = \$98$, say, paid in Chicago. If the spot price at T (in New York) were, say, $S_T = \$103$, then the person holding the long futures can take delivery of the stock and immediately sell it in the cash market for \$103, making a risk-free profit of \$5. At expiration, unless the *price* of a future contract equals the spot price $(F_T = S_T)$, risk-free arbitrage profits are possible. This can be seen in [2] by setting $S = S_T$ and $F = F_T$ and $T = 0$. (Note that for some contracts where delivery costs are high the basis might not be exactly zero at expiry and F_T would exceed S_T by the amount of delivery costs.)

If r is measured as a discrete compounded rate or as a continuously compounded rate, the above formula becomes:

> $F = S(1 + r)^T$ (discrete compounded rates)   [4a]

or

> $F = S\,e^{rT}$ (continuously compounded rates)   [4b]

In practice, market makers would use equation [2] to determine their quote for F, thus ensuring equality. It is possible for [2] not to hold at absolutely every instant of time and providing a trader can act quickly enough he may make a small arbitrage profit. This is known as **index arbitrage**, if the underlying is a stock index futures contract. To make arbitrage based on a stock index such as the S&P 500 possible, you must be able to submit buy or sell orders on 500 stocks in the index simultaneously. In New York this can be achieved either on the floor of the exchange or electronically via the SuperDot system – hence the term program trading. The futures on the S&P 500 and on S&P index options as well as some options on individual stocks all expire on four specific days of the year. If the positions taken by stock index arbitrageurs on the futures contract have not been unwound by expiration of the contract, there could be either large buy or sell orders on the underlying stocks on these four days – this is known as the **triple-witching hour**. One might expect increased volatility in the stock market on these days, and on average there is an increase in volatility, although it does not appear to be large.

Dividends, storage costs and convenience yield

In practice, futures contracts are not as simple as the one described above. For example, our stock used in index arbitrage might pay out dividends (over the life of the futures contract). The simplest case is to assume a *single* dividend payout after, say, one month of $D = \$1$. If interest rates are $r = 4\%$ p.a., the present value of this future payment is $D_0 = \$1/[(1 + 0.4(1/12)] = \$0.997$. Hence we can borrow \$0.997 today at the one-month interest rate and know that we can pay it back in *one* month when the dividend is paid. Thus we only need to borrow $S - D_0 = \$99.003$ today for *three* months and we will owe $\$99.97 = \$99.003 [1 + 0.04(1/4)]$ at the end of the year. The fair futures price equals the cost of the arbitrage, hence:

$$F = (S - D_0)(1 + rT) = \$99.97 \qquad [5]$$

Notice that all the borrowed funds, \$0.997 plus the \$99.003, are used to purchase the stock for \$100, in order to execute the arbitrage. The \$0.997 you borrow means that you owe $\$1 = 0.997 \times (1 + 0.04/12)$ after one month, but this debt is paid off with the \$1 dividend payout. Hence, the *net* cost of the cash-and-carry arbitrage is the \$99.97 payable after three months, so this is the fair price of the futures contract, quoted today.

If stocks pay out dividends *continuously*, then in the above arbitrage example, when you purchase the stock for \$100 with borrowed money you will earn dividends over the period you hold it and this will reduce the cost of carry. If the rate at which dividends are continuously paid is $d = 2\%$ p.a., then over three months you would receive \$0.5 in dividends ($= S.d.T = \$100 \times 0.02 \times (1/4)$), which would reduce your overall cost of carry. So the fair futures price would be[2]:

$$F = S(1 + r - d)T \qquad [6]$$

---

[2] Strictly speaking this approach only applies when all variables represent *continuously compounded* rates so the correct formula is $F = Se^{(r-d)T}$ however, we use the simpler formula.

Now suppose we consider the fair price of futures contracts on commodities such as grains and oilseed (e.g. wheat, soybeans, sunflower oil), food (e.g. cocoa, orange juice), metals and petroleum (e.g. gold, silver, platinum, heating oil) or livestock and meat (hogs, live cattle, pork bellies). These are actively traded on various exchanges around the world, for example New York Cotton Exchange (NYCE), Kansas City Board of Trade (KCBT), New York Mercantile Exchange (NYMEX) and the International Commodities Exchange (ICE).

These contracts can be priced using cash-and-carry arbitrage, but we have to take account of storage costs and the so-called convenience yield. Dealing with storage costs is straightforward. If, when you undertake cash-and-carry arbitrage, you purchase a barrel of oil in the spot market (using borrowed money again), then you have to store it (and insure it) until the maturity date of the futures contract in your arbitrage deal. So you have a storage cost on top of the existing interest cost of your borrowed money, so the price of a futures contract (on a barrel of oil) is given by[3]:

$$F = S(1 + r + s)T \tag{7}$$

where s = storage cost of oil (expressed as percent per annum). Clearly, this equation indicates that the futures price quoted in Chicago will always be above the spot price for oil quoted (in say Texas). However, in certain periods it is observed that the futures price is below the spot price, (i.e. $F < S$). We then say that commodity futures are in *backwardation*. This outcome is rationalised by considering the *convenience yield y* for oil.

The convenience yield arises because the holder of a spot commodity (e.g. crude oil) has the added advantage that she can supply her local customers if the commodity goes into short supply (e.g. during an abnormally cold winter month) and hence retain customer loyalty. This 'convenient' state of affairs has a value, which is referred to as the convenience yield.

The presence of a convenience yield might therefore prevent cash-and-carry arbitrage operating and this invalidates the above formula. For example, when the current spot price is high (an indication that the commodity is in short supply) and you want to arbitrage by short selling spot oil and simultaneously buying the futures, this may not be possible in practice. You would have to borrow oil today in order to be sure to satisfy delivery when the futures contract matures. But if tanker owners will not deliver the spot oil to the required destination, such arbitrage is impossible. Hence the futures price of the commodity is determined as:

$$F = S(1 + r + s - y)T \tag{8}$$

It is very difficult to assess today what the convenience yield y of holding a spot barrel of oil (over say the next three months) is likely to be. There is therefore not such a close link between changes in spot and futures prices for commodities as there is for contracts on other spot assets (e.g. stock indices, currencies), so F and S may not move $-for-$ because of changes in y and, to a much less extent, changes in storage costs. This makes hedging more difficult. The technical way of saying this is that 'basis risk' is high for commodity futures. We will consider these issues further in Chapter 27.

---

[3] Similarly, when the rates used are continuously compounded the correct formula is $F = Se^{(r+s-y)}$.

Non-storable commodities

How can we price a futures contract on a non-storable commodity like electricity and what about the seasonality in the spot prices of commodities such as agricultural produce like wheat? The spot price of wheat tends to rise just before the harvest, usually around August, and then falls as the wheat comes on to the market. Seasonality in the spot price will be reflected in seasonality in the futures price, because arbitrage is possible within the year, using inventories of wheat. The convenience yield of wheat just before the harvest is likely to be high and just after the harvest, when inventories of wheat are large, the convenience yield would be low. We can use equation [8] to determine the futures price providing we can use some statistical method based on past data to estimate the convenience yield.

Instead of trying to estimate the convenience yield, a different approach to determine today's futures price is to try to forecast the future spot price across the harvest period in August.

Suppose it is May and we wish to determine today's futures price for delivery of wheat in six months time in November. If the expected spot price of wheat (per bushel) for November is ES_T and the riskiness of agricultural produce means that investors require a return of R p.a., then you would be willing to pay $ES_T/(1 + R.T)$ for a bushel of wheat today – where $T = \frac{1}{2}$. If the futures price quoted today for delivery *and payment* of wheat in six months is F_0, then today this amount is worth $F_0/(1 + rT)$ – we discount using the risk-free rate because this payment carries no uncertainty. If we equate the present value of payment for the wheat when delivered in the futures contract with the present value of supplying the spot wheat in six months' time, we have:

$$F_0/(1 + rT) = ES_T/(1 + R.T) \qquad [9a]$$

and

$$F_0 = ES_T\{(1 + rT)/(1 + R.T)\} \qquad [9b]$$

So today's futures quote depends on the expected spot price of wheat, which itself is influenced by expectations of supply and demand for wheat in six months' time. This can lead to seasonality in spot and futures prices. Where possibilities for arbitrage are limited, the close link between spot and futures prices is broken and hedging becomes more difficult. Note also that the above approach implies that the forward price is not an unbiased forecast of the expected future spot price – unless the required return on the spot asset equals the risk-free rate.

24.3 HEDGING USING FUTURES

Futures contracts can be used for hedging an existing position in a spot asset. For example, an oil producer might have a large amount of oil coming on stream in three months time and she may fear a fall in the spot price. Or a US exporter might be receiving sterling from the sale of goods in three months time but fear a fall in the spot rate for sterling (which implies that she will receive fewer dollars). In these cases the investor does not know what the spot price will be in three months time and her future receipts are subject to risk. Hedging can be used to reduce such risk to a minimum. In practice, a perfect hedge is often not possible, hence the phrase: 'The only perfect hedge is in a Japanese garden.'

The basic idea behind hedging is very simple. If you are holding (i.e. long) the underlying asset, you need to take a futures position such that the gain on the futures contract offsets any losses in the spot market. Futures and spot prices tend to rise and fall together because the actions of arbitrageurs ensures that $F = S(1 + rT)$ at all times, so S and F tend to move almost dollar for dollar. Hence, if you are long the underlying asset (i.e. own a share), you need to short (sell) a futures contract today, in order to hedge your spot position. If the spot price falls by $10 in New York over the next month, say, the futures price will fall by about $10 in Chicago. Hence if you initially sold a futures contract for $F = \$101$, one month later it will be priced at $F = \$91$, so you can buy it back and close out your position, making a profit on the futures of $10. The latter just offsets your losses in the spot market in New York (ignoring any basis risk).

Alternatively, if you are thinking of purchasing a share in the future (i.e. you are currently short the underlying) but are worried about a rise in the spot price, you should hedge by purchasing (go long) a futures contract today. If the spot price rises by $10 over the next month, so does the futures price, so you can close out your futures position by selling the futures after one month, making a profit of $10 on the futures. Although your stocks cost you $10 more in the spot market, this is offset by the $10 profit on the futures – so your hedge is successful.

A hedged position is *designed* to result in no change in the value of your position. You therefore forgo the prospect of any big gains (or losses) when you take up your hedged position using futures.

Hedging: stock index futures (SIF)

Suppose that on 15 January a portfolio manager who holds a diversified portfolio of US stocks feels that the stock market is likely to be more volatile than normal over the next two months. This presents opportunities for both large price rises and large price falls. But let us assume that the portfolio manager is very worried about a *general fall* in the stock market over the next two months, between 15 January and 15 March. This may be because the portfolio manager has already achieved her target return and is worried that past gains are more likely to be eroded because of the increased volatility expected over the next two months, which might include the period over which her performance (and bonus) will be evaluated by her superiors. The portfolio manager could sell all her stocks and invest the proceeds in risk-free T-bills over the next two months and then repurchase the stocks in two months time, if she then thought that the stock market had returned to its more normal behaviour with a reduced level of volatility. But this would be expensive in terms of bid–ask spreads and other transaction costs. A cheaper alternative is to use stock index futures to hedge her stock portfolio.

She can hedge on 15 January by using the March futures contract on a stock index (such as the S&P 500). To hedge over two months you require a futures contract that has at least two months to maturity and the closest contract is the March futures – this will be closed out in two months time, before maturity (which is towards the end of March). Stock index futures are cash settled. Each index point ('tick') is assigned a value and for the S&P 500 it is $250 per index point.

Since the trader is long the underlying stock portfolio she takes a **short futures hedge** (i.e. she sells March index futures). An effective hedge position requires a calculation of the number of futures contracts she needs to short. Assume a spot (cash) position of $1.4m in a portfolio of stocks that exactly mirrors the composition of the S&P 500 index – the beta of your stock portfolio $\beta_p = 1$.

For the moment, assume a *perfect correlation* between the underlying market *index S* and the futures *index F* (i.e. correlation coefficient of $+1$) and that both indices move by the same amount. If the S&P 500 index on the New York stock exchange in January is $S_0 = 1400$ and the market falls by 10% over the next two months, the S&P index will be 1260 (i.e. a fall of 140 points). Your stock portfolio will fall in value by $140,000 (= $1.4m \times 10\%$). If we assume that F and S move by the same *absolute* amount, the change in F is also 140 points and the change in value of *one* futures contract is $35,000 (= $140 \times 250). Hence the number of futures contracts to hedge your stock portfolio is:

$$N_f = \frac{\textit{Change in value of spot portfolio}}{\textit{Change in value of one futures contract}} = \frac{140,000}{35,000} = 4 \text{ contracts} \qquad [10]$$

So you would hedge by shorting four contracts. The outcome of the hedged position on 15 March is therefore:

Loss on stock portfolio of $1.4m \times 10\% =$ **$140,000**

Gain on futures $=$ change in futures index $\times$ tick value $\times$ number of contracts

$$= 140 \times \$250 \times 4 = \textbf{\$140,000}$$

The reader can verify for herself that a similar hedged outcome would ensue if the stock price had risen by 10%. The capital gain on the stocks would then be offset by the loss on the short futures position – as F increases, you have to buy back your futures contract at a loss (when you close out your position). In this case, with hindsight it would have been better not to have hedged – but 'hindsight' is not available in January. In any case, the whole idea of a hedge is to remove risk and in doing so, you also forgo any favourable outcomes. You can't have your cake and eat it – you can be a hedger or a speculator in any given deal, but not both.

If the beta of your portfolio of stocks is $\beta_p = 1.5$, then when the market falls by 10% you expect the value of your portfolio to fall by 15% (= $\beta_p R_m$), hence you would need more futures contracts to hedge your stock position – you would in fact need to short six futures contracts. (This is because the change in the *dollar value* of your portfolio is now expected to be $1.4m \times 0.15 = $210,000, so $N_f = (210,000/35,000) = 6$.)

The above example looks a bit too good to be true – a perfect hedge. Yes, it is too optimistic. The reason for this is that we assumed that the *absolute* changes in the two indexes, F and S, were *exactly* the same. In practice this is not the case. First, F and S do not move exactly point for point – they do so only approximately. Secondly, because interest rates might change over the life of the hedge, this alters the relationship between F and S – this is basis risk. Thirdly, because your value for the beta of your portfolio of stocks is estimated with error, when the market moves by 10% the value of your stock portfolio might not move by exactly 15% – this is probably the biggest source of error in the hedge.

Let's return to the case where $\beta_p = 1$ and consider a more realistic scenario where there would be some hedging error. Suppose the initial futures price in January is $F_0 = 1417$. Over the next two months the portfolio manager's worst fears are met and the S&P 500 falls by 10% to $S_1 = 1260$, so the loss on the stock portfolio is $140,000. On 15 March, the March index futures is close to maturity, so it too will have a value close to 1260 and we take this to be $F_1 = 1270$. On 15 March the futures contract is closed out (i.e. sold) and the fall in the futures index price over the two months is $147 (= 1417 - 1270)$ – not quite the same as the fall in the S&P 500 index of 140 points. The outcome of the hedged position is March is therefore:

> Loss on stock portfolio (10%) = **$140,000**
>
> Gain on futures = change in futures index $\times$ tick value $\times$ number of contracts
>
> $= 147 \times \$250 \times 4 = \mathbf{\$147{,}000}$

Hence the hedge position has produced a small profit of $7000, but most importantly it has averted a possible large loss of $140,000 had the position remained unhedged. In practice, hedge positions result in small profits or losses, but these average out to nearly zero for a large number of hedges, implemented over time.

Instead of working out the number of futures contracts you need each time you consider a particular fall (e.g. 10%) in the market index, perhaps the best formula to use (known as the minimum variance hedge ratio) is to calculate the number of futures contracts from:

$$N_f = \frac{\$ - \textit{Value of spot portfolio}}{\$ - \textit{Value of one futures contract}} \times \beta_p = \frac{\$1.4m}{(\$250.1417)} = 3.95 \ (= 4) \qquad [11]$$

where we have used $\beta_p = 1$ (but it also gives you $N_f = 6$ for $\beta_p = 1.5$). The above formula gives an answer very close to our 'simple' method described above[4]. But it also has the advantage that when you are putting on the hedge you can just 'plug in' the known value for the futures (index) price, $F_0 = 1417$, currently quoted on your screen. Notice that in the above we used stock index futures contracts to hedge a *portfolio* of stocks, and this is usually the case in practice. But you might also wish to hedge your holdings in individual stocks (e.g. Microsoft). Here you have an alternative, which is to use individual futures contracts on Microsoft shares. The above formula still applies, but of course the futures contract on Microsoft has a beta of unity with the stock price of Microsoft, so $\beta = 1$, when you hedge using the futures on the stock itself rather than *stock index* futures.

---

[4] If the denominator is instead $250 \times$ S&P 500 index $= \$250 \times 1400$, then $N_f = 4$ and this formula is also sometimes used – both tend to give similar answers.

> **Hedging: Key decisions**
>
> - If you are *long* (i.e. own) the spot asset (e.g. stocks, oil) then *sell (short)* futures contracts today.
> - If you are *planning to purchase* the underlying asset (e.g. stocks, oil) in the future (i.e. you are short in the cash market) then *purchase (go long)* futures contracts today.
> - Hedging works because the actions of arbitrageurs ensure that F and S move together, almost dollar for dollar. Hence a long position in the spot asset (e.g. stocks) and a short position in the futures contract create a (near perfect) negative correlation between the spot and futures prices, so the net change in the value of the hedged position is (close to) zero.
> - Note that any losses on your futures position may involve *margin calls*. Hence a hedger must have lines of credit or other collateral available to meet possible margin calls.

Other uses for SIF

Stock index futures can be used to protect your 'stock picks' from general changes in the market as a whole. Suppose you have just purchased $1.4m of stocks (of say, 10 different companies) that you think are undervalued. You believe that their market prices are below your estimate of fair value and you therefore think that over the next two months prices will rise to fair value – even if the market as a whole remains unchanged. The danger is that the market itself falls and this also affects the undervalued stocks you have just purchased and they too fall in price. In this case, any losses from their fall in price due to the fall in the market could wipe out any price rise from the correction of the underpricing. How can you protect yourself from the impact of the market on these underpriced stocks? You have already solved this problem! If the beta of the portfolio of underpriced stocks is $\beta_p = 1.5$, then if you short six stock index futures contracts you will protect your underpriced stocks from overall changes in the market. If the market falls by 10%, say, then we know that the gain on your short futures will offset any loss on your portfolio of stocks. You are then left with the gains from the underpricing, should these be corrected over the next two months.

Suppose that you hold $1.4m in a portfolio of stocks with $\beta_p = 1.5$. From the above we know that to hedge this spot position, you have to *short* six stock index futures contracts. That is, by shorting six contracts you have made the effective beta of your 'stock portfolio plus short futures' position equal to zero. It follows that if you want to reduce your portfolio's exposure to changes in the market over the next two months so that, for example, the effective beta of your portfolio is 0.75, then you would have to short three futures contracts today (and close out the position in two months time, when the beta of your portfolio would again be 1.5). This is cheaper than reducing beta by selling high beta stocks and buying them back after two months, when you want your portfolio beta to be 1.5 again.

On the other hand, suppose that you thought the market was going to rise (more than average) over the next two months. You could increase the effective beta of your portfolio to say,

$\beta_p = 3$ by *buying* six futures contracts today. Then if you are right and the stock market rises by, say, 10% over the next two months, the value of your stock portfolio plus the profits on your long futures contracts will result in the equivalent of a 30% increase in the value of your wealth, from $1.4m to $1.82m. Hence you have used SIF to *leverage up* the returns on your stock portfolio – this is exactly how some hedge funds leverage their returns (particularly those using macro strategies on domestic and foreign stock markets). Of course, leverage is a 'two-way street': if you guess wrong and the stock market falls by 10% over the next two months, then you lose on your stocks position and you lose on the futures, resulting in an overall loss of 30%, so the value of your assets falls from $1.4m to $980,000.

Hedging: Interest-rate futures

The following illustrates how interest rate futures allow investors to hedge spot positions in money-market assets, such as T-bills and (Eurodollar) deposits and loans. Interest-rate futures are a little more complex than futures on, say, stocks or oil. But the key thing to remember is that the *price* of any interest-bearing asset (e.g. spot T-bills or the price of an interest-rate futures contract) and the *interest rate* move in opposite directions. So when interest rates (or yields) fall, the futures *price* will rise (and vice versa).

Interest-rate futures can be used to lock in an interest rate that will apply in the future or can be used to lock in the price you will pay or receive for a fixed-income asset (such as a T-bill or commercial bill). Consider the following situations:

- It is 1 July and you know that you will receive funds in September that you want to invest in a risk-free T-bill for a further three months. If you do nothing, then three-month spot interest rates in two months time may be very low. So doing nothing is risky. However, you can lock in a known forward rate today, by buying a 'September T-bill futures' at $F_0 = \$98$ (per $100 face value of deliverable T-bills) in July (no money changes hands in July). You hold the futures to maturity, so in September you pay $98 and take delivery of a three-month T-bill with a face (maturity) value of $100. In December, the T-bill matures and you receive $100. The interest rate you have locked in between September and December is $f = 8.2\%$ p.a. $= (100 - 98)/98 \times 4 \times 100\%$ and on 1 July you know that this will be the outcome.
- You hold 91-day T-bills, which you will sell in one months time (i.e. before the bills mature) because you will then need cash to pay your creditors. You fear a rise in interest rates over the next month, which will cause a fall in value of your T-bills. You can hedge your spot position in T-bills by shorting (selling) T-bill futures contracts that mature in one month. If the quoted futures price is $F_0 = \$98$ (per $100 face value of deliverable T-bills), this guarantees that you can sell each of your T-bills for $98 *in one month's time*.
- You will receive $10m in six months time, which you will then want to invest in a Eurodollar bank deposit for 90 days. You fear a fall in interest rates over the next six months, which means that you will earn less interest on your deposits. You can hedge this risk by going long (i.e. buying) Eurodollar futures contracts. If interest rates fall, the price of the Eurodollar futures contract will rise and you can close out your futures position at a cash profit – which can then be used to compensate for the lower interest rate you will receive on your Eurodollar bank deposit.

- You hope to issue $10m of 180-day commercial paper in three months time (i.e. to borrow money). You fear that interest rates will rise over the next three months (i.e. bill prices will fall) so your borrowing costs will increase. You can hedge by shorting (i.e. selling) T-bill futures contracts. If interest rates do rise, the futures price will fall and you can close out your futures at a profit, which will then offset your higher borrowing costs when you issue your commercial bills. This is an example of a cross-hedge, since there is no commercial bill futures contract, you have to use T-bill futures.

So far we have not been precise about what interest rates we are referring to. But to simplify matters, assume that all rates (yields) for all maturities move together and by the same amount.

Interest-rate futures contracts can be used to hedge interest-rate payments/receipts on future cash flows. Suppose that on 15 April an investor is to take out a loan of £1m in two months time (on 15 June) and the loan is for a further three months. The exposure period is two months and the protection period in the futures contract is three months. Suppose that she fears a rise in interest rates over the next two months, so her loan will then cost more. Since futures prices fall when interest rates rise, if she hedges by going short in interest-rate futures, she makes a gain on the futures. The latter offsets the higher interest rate she has to pay on the loan in two months time.

Suppose that the spot three-month interest rate on 15 April is $r_0 = 7\%$ and the quoted three-month forward rate on 15 April (for funds deposited in two months time) is also $f_0 = 7\%$. This means that on 15 April your best forecast of what three-month spot interest rates will be in two months time is 7%, so you expect that between June and September, spot interest rates and the borrowing costs of your loan will be 7%.

$$\text{Expected cost of borrowing, June to September} = \text{£1m} (0.07/4) = \textbf{£17,500} \qquad [12]$$

To illustrate hedging with interest-rate futures, we consider the 'short sterling' interest-rate futures contract, but note that the mechanics of using interest-rate futures is a little more complex than for stock index futures. The contract size for the short sterling contract is £500,000. The futures price F is quoted on an index basis and it is linked to the futures interest rate f_0 by:

$$F_0 = 100 - f_o \qquad [13]$$

f_0 is the contract interest rate, which is fixed today when you buy or sell the futures contract. The next issue to consider is the tick size and tick value. The tick size of the futures is 1/100 of 1% and hence the tick value (over the three-month interest period) is:

$$\text{Tick value} = \text{£500,000} \times (0.01/100) \times (3/12) = \text{£12.50} \qquad [14]$$

Hence traders know that a change in F of 1 unit (i.e. 100 ticks) corresponds to a change in value of £1250. We are now in a position to hedge our future three-month loan (beginning in two months time) with the three-month short-sterling futures contract. On 15 April we fear a rise in interest rates over the next two months, so we *go short* the futures contract. If three-month interest rates do rise over the next two months, the futures *price* will fall and profit from the short futures position will offset some or all of the higher costs of the loan, when the loan is taken out in June. With a contract size of £500,000 and a loan of £1m, the number of June futures contracts *to short* on 15 April is:

$$N_f = £1m/£500,000 = 2 \qquad [15]$$

Suppose that three-month spot interest rates in June rise to $r_1 = 9\%$. Since the June futures contract is now close to maturity, f_1 will also equal 9% and therefore $F_1 = 100 - 9 = 91$. The change in the futures *price* is 200 ticks. The hedged outcome in June is

Cost of borrowing (June–Sept) in spot market $= £1m\,(0.09/4) = £22,500$

Gain on futures $= 200\,\text{ticks} \times £12.50 \times 2\,\text{contracts} = £5000$

Cost of borrowing less gain on futures $= \textbf{£17,500}$

Therefore, even though interest rates rise from 7% to 9% between April and June, which increases borrowing costs on the loan from £17,500 to £22,500, the cash profit on the futures of £5000 just offsets the extra cost, so the net cost of borrowing is £17,500 – the same interest cost that we expected in April when we instituted the hedge. So even though futures contracts are closed out prior to maturity, the hedge is still effective – the futures hedge has locked in a borrowing rate of $f_0 = 7\%$, the forward rate that lies behind the initial futures price F_0.

Hedging using interest-rate futures

- If you are *taking out a loan* in the future and hence you fear a rise in interest rates, *hedge by going short* an interest-rate futures contract.
- If you are going to *place money on deposit* in the future and you fear a fall in interest rates, *hedge by going long* an interest-rate futures contract.

The payoff to an interest-rate futures contract is the difference between the two futures prices:

$$\text{Payoff} = F_T - F_0 = (100 - f_T) - (100 - f_0) = -(LIBOR_T - f_0) \qquad [16]$$

At maturity of the futures contract the contract rate in the futures will equal the spot rate at maturity of the contract – that is, the LIBOR rate. So an interest-rate future has a payoff that depends on the *difference* between the LIBOR rate at expiry of the futures contract and the fixed (known) contract rate f_0, when the future was initially bought or sold. As we have seen, this is the payoff to a floating-rate agreement (FRA) and to a single payment in a swap. Forward contracts on interest rates, FRAs and swaps are different variants on the same idea – that is, where the payoff depends on a difference between two interest rates, one a floating rate (LIBOR) and the other a fixed contract rate.

24.4 SPECULATION

Speculation with futures is relatively straightforward. First, consider stock index futures. The S&P 500 (spot) index S and the futures price F on the index move together, almost dollar for dollar. Hence, if you think that S will rise (fall) in the future (in New York) you will go long (short) in index futures in Chicago. Compared to speculation by purchasing the underlying stocks, the long futures position provides leverage, since you do not have the cost of buying (and later selling) the underlying stocks. You merely have to provide a relatively small good-faith deposit for your margin account. Of course, if the futures price initially falls (before hopefully it ultimately rises) then you have to be prepared to top up your margin account, and you therefore need ready cash or collateral (e.g. T-bills) available.

If you close out a long futures position before maturity, the profit on each futures contract is $F_1 - F_0$. If you hold the contact to maturity ($= T$), the futures and spot price at maturity must be equal (because of arbitrage possibilities) so the speculative profit is $F_T - F_0 = S_T - F_0$.

Speculation with interest-rate futures is also not particularly difficult. If you want to speculate on a future fall in interest rates, you would go long an interest-rate futures contract (e.g. a T-bill futures contract or a 'short sterling' or Eurodollar futures contract). For *any* interest rate futures contract, the key feature is the inverse relationship between interest rates and the futures *price* and it is the latter that determines your profit (or loss). Hence, if interest rates fall the futures price rises and you make a profit from your long position. Clearly, to bet on a future rise in interest rates you would short an interest-rate futures contract. Of course, any naked position in an interest rate futures contract is highly risky, since futures prices can change rapidly in either direction.

SUMMARY

- A futures contract is *marked to market*, so its value changes each day.
- The clearing house keeps track of the margin account and if it falls below the maintenance margin, additional payments have to be made. This minimises counterparty (credit) risk.
- The *clearing house* sets the terms for each futures contract, such as the contract size, tick value, delivery dates, settlement prices and margin requirements.
- Trading is sometimes via *open outcry* in a trading pit (e.g. in Chicago), but recently there has been a move towards electronic trading.
- *Risk-free arbitrage* ensures that the futures price (in Chicago) moves almost dollar for dollar with the spot price (in New York, say) of the underlying asset.
- *Hedging:* If the investor is long the underlying asset (e.g. a portfolio of shares), she should short the futures contract (and vice versa). Any change in value of the spot assets should be offset by the change in the value of the futures position. However, there is always some *basis risk* in the hedge.
- Hedging future changes in interest rates is based on the inverse relationship between the interest rate and the futures price.
- If you are *planning to take out a loan* in the future, you hedge any future rise in the cost of borrowing by going *short an interest-rate futures* contract.

- Conversely, if you are *planning to lend money* in the future, you should hedge by going *long an interest-rate futures contract.*
- *Speculation* in futures allows almost unlimited *leverage* (since any margin payments usually earn interest). A speculator buys (sells) a *stock index futures* contract if she expects the underlying asset price (e.g. the S&P 500 index) to rise (fall) in the future.
- A person who speculates on interest-rate changes would buy (sell) an interest-rate futures contract if she expects interest rates in the future to fall (rise).

EXERCISES

Q1   What are the key differences between forward contracts and futures contracts?

Q2   Explain how a futures contract on a stock can be used for hedging and speculation.

Q3   Briefly explain 'open interest' and 'trading volume' for futures markets. What are the initial margin and variation margin on futures contracts and why are they useful?

Q4   What is basis risk in a hedge and is it ever zero?

Q5   When are a 'long hedge' and a 'short hedge' appropriate? Use the examples of an oil producer and an oil consumer.

Q6   This is a question about margin payments and 'marking to market' the value of the futures contract. It aims to show that even though the Clearing House (in Chicago) has a rather complex procedure, it just ensures that the *change in value* of your futures is simply the number of futures contracts you hold multiplied by the *change* in the futures price.

At the end of day 1 you *purchase* 100 contracts of the September futures at a settlement price of $50,000 per contract.
The initial margin on *any* contracts you *initially* purchase is $2000 per contract. Hence at the end of day 1 you have $200,000 in your margin account.
On day 2 at 11 a.m. you acquire an additional 20 (September) contracts at a price of $51,000 per contract. The *settlement price* at the end of the day is $50,200 per contract.

(a) What is the net gain or loss on the value of *all of your contracts* at the end of day 2? What is the value of *your margin account* at the end of day 2?
(b) What happens if you close out all your contracts at the end of day 2 at the settlement price of $50,200?

Q7   You enter into a futures contract on a (non-dividend-paying) stock with maturity of one year, with $S_0 = \$40$ and $r = 10\%$ p.a.

(a) What is the 'no-arbitrage' (or fair or synthetic) futures price of the contract?
(b) If the *actual* futures price is $F = 46$, how can you make a risk-free arbitrage profit?
(c) If the *actual futures* price is $F = 42$, how can you make a risk-free arbitrage profit?

Q8   Suppose that you hold a diversified portfolio of stocks with a market value of $10m. A futures contract on the S&P 500 has three months to maturity. Each index point on the futures contract (or the S&P 500 index) is worth $250. The current interest rate is $r = 4\%$ p.a. and the current value of the S&P 500 index is $S_0 = 1420$.

You want to hedge your $10m stock portfolio *over the next month*, using stock index futures.

(a) Show that the correct (no arbitrage) fair futures price $F_0 = 1434.2$ (use simple, not compound interest).

(b) How many futures contracts are required to hedge your portfolio of stocks?

(c) What is the outcome of your hedged position if in *one month's* time the S&P 500 has fallen by 8% and the futures index stands at $F_1 = 1315.1$? Compare the hedged and unhedged positions.

Hint: The number of futures contracts for the hedge is given by

$N = -$ (Total value in stock portfolio) / ($250 \times$ level of S&P 500 stock index)

(d) How do we know that the futures index will be $F_1 = 1315.1$ in one months time after the fall in the stock index? Briefly comment on the relationship between the change in the futures and stock indexes.

25

Options Markets

AIMS

- To consider the *payoff profiles at expiry* for long and short positions in calls and puts. To show how options can be used for speculation and for providing *insurance* against adverse outcomes, while allowing the investor to also benefit from any upside.
- To indicate how, prior to expiration, European option premia change as the price of the underlying asset in the option contract changes. (This is the famous *Black–Scholes formula* for the option premium.) This allows speculation over short horizons using options, since you can close out your position (with another trader) and make a profit (or loss) prior to expiry of the option.
- To explain some terminology applied to calls and puts, such as in the money (ITM), at-the-money (ATM) and out-the-money (OTM), as well as *intrinsic value* and *time value*.
- To show how we can use stock index options to 'insure' a stock portfolio against a general fall in stock prices while maintaining upside potential, should stock prices increase.
- To discuss the organisation of options markets, including the role of the clearing house and interpreting newspaper quotes.
- To compare traded options markets and the OTC market.

25.1 OPTIONS

Options contracts are extensively traded on a large number of exchanges, with the underlying assets being individual stocks, stock indices, interest rates, currencies, commodities and futures contracts. There is also a large OTC market in options. The mechanics of trading options and the terminology used are common across a wide range of options contracts.

Call options

A *European call option* gives the holder the right (but not an obligation):

- to purchase the underlying asset at a
- specified future date (*expiration, expiry or maturity date*)
- for a certain price (*exercise or strike price*)
- and in an amount (*contract size*) that is fixed in advance.
- For this privilege you pay today the *call premium/price*.

A European option can only be exercised on the expiry date itself, whereas an **American option** can be *exercised* any time up to the expiry date. Note, however, that European (and American) options can be *sold* to another market participant at any time. Most options traded on exchanges are American, but as European options are easier to analyse we deal mainly with the latter. Note that in this chapter we first concentrate on the pay-off profiles *at expiry*, and later we discuss what causes the change in the price of options from minute to minute.

Long call

Consider for example the purchase in July of a (European) call option on the shares of XYZ. Let us assume that one stock option contract is a contract to buy or sell 100 shares. If the quoted call premium in July is $C = \$3$ per share in Chicago, then the contract will cost $300 to purchase. Let us suppose that the strike price in the contract is $K = \$80$ and that the expiry date T is in three months time in October (Figure 25.1).

First consider how the purchases of a call option can provide insurance. Suppose that a pension fund knows it will receive an inflow of funds in October and knows that it wants to invest in stocks of XYZ with this money. If a pension fund purchases the call option in Chicago in July, it has locked in a *maximum purchase* price of $80, if it decides to exercise the contract in October – this is a form of **insurance**. Clearly, if in October $S_T = \$88 > K = \$80$, the pension fund will exercise the option in Chicago and pay $80 per share, which is cheaper than purchasing them on the NYSE at $88. (The person who initially sold the option contract is legally bound to deliver the share to the pension fund and will receive $80.) On the other hand, if the share price in October is $S_T = \$77$ (i.e. below the strike price of $K = \$80$), the pension fund will not exercise the call option since it can purchase the shares at lower cost in the spot market in New York. Hence, the call option provides insurance in the form of a maximum price payable of $K = \$80$, but also allows the pension fund to walk away from the contract and benefit from lower prices if $S_T < K$. The cost of this insurance is the call premium of $C = \$3$ per share.

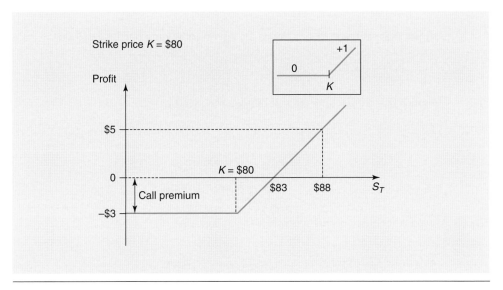

FIGURE 25.1: Buy one European call option

One other thing to note is that the maximum price the pension fund locks in is the strike price in the options contract and not the stock price (on the NYSE) when the pension fund purchases the option contract. For example, suppose that the actual stock price in New York *in July*, (when the pension fund purchased the call option in Chicago), had been $S_0 = \$78$. The price in New York of $78 is *not* the maximum purchase price you lock into, this is the strike price $K = \$80$ in the options contract.

Now consider the **speculative motive** for purchasing the call option (Table 25.1). If the actual price of the stock in October turns out to be $S_T = \$88$, the holder of the call option can take delivery at $K = \$80$ and sell each share in the spot market at $88. The pay-off from the call

TABLE 25.1: Buy (long) call option current

Current share price, $S_0 = \$78$

Traders desk (today, time $t = 0$)
> Contract size = 100 shares
> Strike price, $K = \$80$
> Call premium (price), $C = \$3$
> Premium paid = 100 ($3) = $300

Outcome (3 months later at time T)
> Share price at expiry, $S_T = \$88$
> Payoff at expiry: $(S_T - K)\,100 = (88 - 80)\,100 = $ **$800**
> Profit (net of call price): $(S_T - K - C)\,100 = (8 - 3)\,100 = $ **$500**

is $8 per share (i.e. $S_T - K = \$88 - \$80$) and the profit Π after deduction of the call premium $C = \$3$ is $5 per share (Figure 25.1)[1]. Hence the payoff to holding one long call is:

Payoff $= (+1)$ [Max $(0, S_T - K)$]   if $S_T > K$ exercise the call

The '+1' implies that we are long the call option. The profit is:

$$\Pi = (+1) \text{ [Max } (0, S_T - K) - C] \qquad\qquad\qquad [1]$$
$$= S_T - K - C \qquad\qquad\qquad \text{for } S_T > K \text{ (exercise the call)}$$
$$= -C \qquad\qquad\qquad \text{for } S_T \leq K \text{ (do not exercise)}$$

The break-even stock price occurs when $\Pi = 0$ and hence is:

$$S_{BE} = K + C = \$80 + \$3 = \$83 \qquad\qquad\qquad [2]$$

Since the contract is for 100 shares, if $S_T = \$88$ the speculator makes an overall profit of $500. On the other hand, if at expiry $S_T = \$78$ ($<K$) the speculator would not exercise the option, which expires worthless – but she has only lost the call premium of $300, which was paid when she initially purchased the option.

Thus the speculator who holds (i.e. is long) a call option limits downside risk to the call premium (here $C = \$3$), but can benefit from any upside potential, if the stock price rises above the strike price. Her return is asymmetric and non-linear. So the long call option also provides **insurance** for the speculator, since the most the option speculator can lose is the call premium of $C = \$3$, but holding the long call allows 'upside capture' if stock prices rises (above the strike price).

It is useful to designate the profit profile from options in terms of direction vectors. Hence the pay-off from a long call is $\{0, +1\}$, since the option earns profits that rise one for one with the price of the underlying, once S_T exceeds K (see inset in Figure 25.1).

Write (sell) a call

One simple way to find out what happens to the profit for the writer of a call is to work out the profit for the long call and simply reverse the sign. If the long call makes a profit, the person who wrote (sold) the call makes an equal loss. Let us look at this in more detail.

If $S_T = \$88$, the writer of the call has to purchase the stock in the cash market at $S_T = \$88$, but receives only $K = \$80$ (Figure 25.2). She makes a loss of $8 per share ($= S_T - K$) less the call premium she received $C = \$3$, making a net loss of $5 per share – a mirror image of the gain made by the purchaser of the call. (The writer makes a total loss on one contract of $500.)

Alternatively, if the actual share price in October is (say) $S_T = \$77$ (i.e. below the strike price of $K = \$80$), the *holder* of the call option will not exercise it, since she can purchase the

---

[1] In fact, the net profit *at expiry* will be slightly less, as we have ignored the foregone interest that could have been earned on the initial premium of $300 paid at $t = 0$.

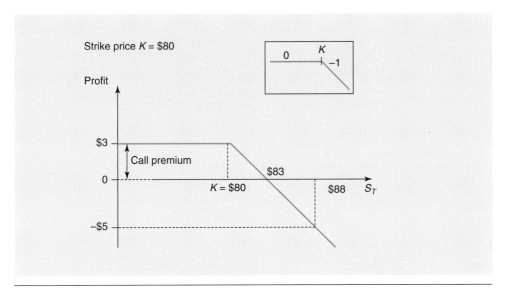

FIGURE 25.2: Sell (write) a European call option

shares at lower cost in the open market. Hence, *the writer* of the call option makes a profit of $3 per share, the option premium received.

The pay-off to holding ***one written call*** (i.e. initially you sold a call) is:

$$\text{Payoff} = (-1)\,[\text{Max}\,(0,\,S_T - K)]$$

The '−1' implies that you initially wrote (sold) a call option. The profit is:

$$\Pi = (-1)\,[\text{Max}\,(0,\,S_T - K) - C] \tag{3}$$
$$= -[(S_T - K) - C] \qquad \text{for } S_T > K$$
$$= +C \qquad\qquad\quad \text{for } S_T \le K$$

Put options

If you *buy* a European put option (in Chicago), this gives you the right *to sell* the underlying asset (in Chicago) at some time in the future for a price that is fixed in the contract, hence:

A European put option gives the holder the right (but not an obligation):

- to sell the underlying asset at a
- specified future date (*the expiration, expiry* or *maturity date*)
- for a certain price *(exercise* or *strike price)*
- in an amount *(contract size)* that is fixed in advance.
- For this privilege you pay the *put premium/price.*

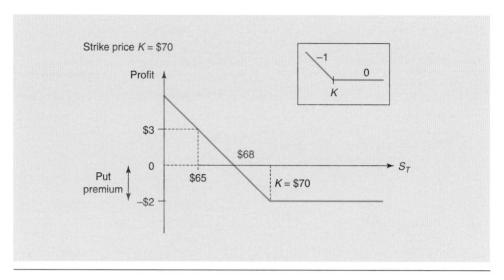

FIGURE 25.3: Buy (long) a European put option

Long put

First, let us see how the purchase of a put option (i.e. you go long the put) can be used to set a *minimum value* that you will receive in the future, *for stocks that you already own*. Suppose that you are a pension fund manager and you hold 100 shares of ABC and the current spot price of these shares is $S_0 = \$72$. You have to pay out someone's lump-sum pension in three months time and you are worried that the stock price will fall *below* $70 over the next three months. You can eliminate this risk by purchasing a put option on 100 shares, with a strike price $K = \$70$ and an expiry date in three months. For this you pay the put premium $P = \$2$ (Figure 25.3).

By purchasing the put, you guarantee that you can, if you wish, sell your shares for $70 each by exercising the put contract in Chicago in three months time – even if the price of the shares on the NYSE is much lower, say $20 per share. The options market in Chicago must honour the trade and the shares you sell in Chicago will be paid for by a person who initially sold a put contract – the counterparty to your initial purchase of the contract. On the other hand, if $S_T = \$75$, which is greater than $K = \$70$, you can walk away from the put contract and sell your shares on the NYSE for $75 per share. This means that whatever happens to the spot price over the next three months, you can either sell the shares at a minimum price of $K = \$70$ (in Chicago), or if the stock price rises above $70, you can throw away the put option (i.e. not exercise it in Chicago) and sell your shares of ABC at the higher spot price in New York. Hence, *if you already own some shares*, buying the put provides **insurance** in the form of a guaranteed minimum price for your shares, while also allowing you to benefit from any upside potential should the share price rise on the NYSE.

There are also opportunities for **speculation** with put options. A speculator will buy a put option if she expects the stock price to fall in the future (and end up below the strike price)

TABLE 25.2: Buy (long) put option

Current share price $S_0 = \$78$

Trader's desk (today, time $t = 0$)
Contract size = 100 shares
Strike price, $K = \$70$
Put premium (price), $P = \$2$
Premium paid = 100 ($2) = $200

Outcome (three months later at time T)
Share price at expiry, $S_T = \$65$
Pay-off at expiry: $(K - S_T) \, 100 = (\$70 - \$65) \, 100 \ = \textbf{\$500}$
Profit (net of put premium): $(K - S_T - P) \, 100 = (\$5 - \$2) \, 100 = \textbf{\$300}$

see Table 25.2. If the spot price of shares in New York in three months time is $S_T = \$65$ (i.e. below $K = \$70$), a speculator who is already long the put option could buy 100 shares in New York for $S_T = \$65$ per share, exercise the put option by delivering the shares in Chicago and receive $K = \$70$ per share from the options clearing house. The speculator will have a pay-off of \$5 $(= K - S_T)$ per share and a net profit of \$3 after paying the put premium of \$2. Hence the pay-off to holding one long put is:

$$\text{Payoff} = (+1) \, [\text{Max} \, (0, \, K - S_T)] \quad \text{if } S_T < K \text{ exercise the put}$$

The profit from the long put is:

$$
\begin{aligned}
\Pi &= (+1) \, [\text{Max} \, (0, \, K - S_T) - P] && [4] \\
&= K - S_T - P && \text{for } S_T < K \\
&= -P && \text{for } S_T \geq K
\end{aligned}
$$

The break-even stock price occurs when $\Pi = 0$ and hence is:

$$S_{BE} = K - P = \$70 - \$2 = \$68 \qquad\qquad [5]$$

If $S_T > K$ then the speculator does not exercise the put (which expires worthless), but the most she loses is the put premium, $P = \$2$. The payoff profile for a long put is $\{-1, 0\}$ because as the stock price *falls* the profits for the holder of the put *rise* – this is a negative relationship.

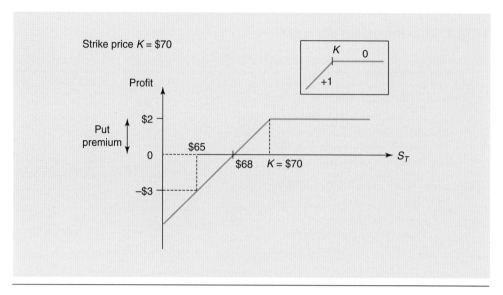

FIGURE 25.4: Sell (write) a European put option

Write (sell) a put

The payoff to the seller of a put is the opposite to that of the buyer of the put. There are two sides to every trade – if one side wins the other loses. Let us look at this in more detail.

The person who initially sold the put (and does not close out) will lose when the put is exercised, if $S_T < K$. For example, if $S_T = \$65$ and $K = \$70$, then at expiry of the put the writer has to purchase the share from the long in Chicago at $K = \$70$, but she can only sell it for $S_T = \$65$ in New York (Figure 25.4). However, this loss is reduced to $3 after allowing for the receipt of the put premium of $2 when the writer initially sold the put, three months ago. Hence the pay-off at maturity to holding one written put (i.e. the initially seller of the put) is:

Payoff $= (-1) [\text{Max} (0, K - S_T)]$

The profit at maturity from holding one written put is:

$$\Pi = (-1) [\text{Max} (0, K - S_T) - P] \qquad [6]$$
$$= -[(K - S_T) - P] \qquad \text{for } S_T < K$$
$$= +P \qquad \text{for } S_T \geq K$$

These payoffs are just the mirror image of the payoffs for a person who is long the put.

Positions in options

It should now be clear that there are two sides of the market in calls and puts. The two parties to each option contract are classified as follows:

Long call = buy a call option
Long put = buy a put option
Short call = sell (or write) a call option
Short put = sell (or write) a put option

For a light-hearted analysis of the payoffs to calls and puts, you can take a look at Case Study 25.1.

CASE STUDY 25.1   OPTIONS: KEN AND BARBIE

Let's return to our analogy with Ken and Barbie. What 'insurance' does Barbie have, if in January she purchases a *December call on Ken*, at a strike price of $K = \$100$, and pays a call premium of $C = \$3$? If, over the next year Kens improve their salaries so that they are worth $S = \$110$, then Barbie will exercise her option. She then turns up at the church in December and marries Ken for a mere payment of $K = \$100$ (to the clergyman officiating), even though a spot Ken would cost her $S = \$110$ at the local 'cattle market' at the club round the corner from her house. (Note that if Barbie holds the call option to maturity and decides to exercise the option, Ken is contractually bound to turn up at the church – he has no choice.) Hence, by purchasing the call option in January Barbie has purchased insurance – she knows the maximum price she will pay for a Ken next December, the strike price in the call option.

On the other hand, if Kens have no pay rises and become heavy drinkers over the next year, their spot price in the local 'cattle market' might fall below $K = \$100$, to, say, $S = \$90$. In this case Barbie *would not exercise her option* and would simply not turn up at the church. Under the terms of the option contract, she does not even have to tell Ken she will not be turning up and this is why Ken received the call premium the previous January – as monetary compensation for his possible subsequent embarrassment at the altar.

If the spot price for Kens in December turns out to be $S = \$90$, then Barbie could, if she wished, purchase a Ken in the spot market at her local club and take immediate delivery. So the option contract ensures that she pays a maximum price of $K = \$100$ for a Ken, yet she can take advantage of the lower spot price for Kens in one years time, if she so wishes.

If you saw the film *Four Weddings and a Funeral*, you will know that Hugh Grant's character Charles did turn up at the church with the intention of marrying 'Duckface'. But he really could have saved himself the trouble and embarrassment by purchasing a long call on Duckface earlier in the year – then he would have had the option of whether to turn up or not (depending on what he thought of Duckface at the maturity of the call option). Those of you who are very familiar with the film will know that Duckface actually had an option of her own. This was a *down-and-out option* on Charles, which she executed with a right hook, once she realised the low spot value she placed on Charles that day and that he had fallen below the barrier of decency expected of an English 'fop'. Down-and-out options do exist. For example, a down-and-out call option on a stock is one that 'dies' (i.e. effectively no longer exists) if the stock price before maturity falls below a pre-specified level (the 'barrier') – even if the stock price at maturity subsequently rises above the strike price, it still remains worthless.

Suppose now that Barbie has been married to Ken for some time but she is getting rather tired of him. Barbie already holds a Ken but is worried he may be worthless in one years time. Should she have a trial separation and then divorce him at the end of the year? The problem is that if she waits a year to divorce him he may turn to drink and his monetary value may fall over the year, thus reducing her pay-out in the divorce settlement. On the other hand, if he does rather well in the jobs market then she may wish to stay married to Ken. How can options help to solve this dilemma? In January Barbie can buy (go long) a *December Ken put contract*. This gives Barbie the right to sell Ken for $K = \$100$ next December, if she wants to. Hence, over the life of the put contract, Barbie has the equivalent of a trial separation.

In December, if Ken's earning power and hence spot price has deteriorated to, say, $S = \$90$, Barbie will deliver him in the put contract (to the solicitors) and get divorced. Under the terms of the put contract she will receive the generous divorce settlement of $K = \$100$, even though Ken is only currently worth $S = \$90$ in the spot market. Of course, if Ken's earning power and spot price rise over the coming year to $S = \$110$, then Barbie will not exercise her put contract to sell Ken for $90 at the solicitors, since he is currently worth $100. So Barbie will throw away her put contract, get back together with Ken and the marriage will continue. (Again, Ken has no choice in the matter, Barbie has purchased the put contract and hence holds 'all the cards' – which is sometimes the case in divorce.) This insurance may have cost Barbie a mere $2, the put premium.

Again, those of you who know the ending of *Four Weddings and a Funeral* will realise that what Charles probably held was an embedded *rainbow call option (or alternative option)*. This type of option has two underlying assets (e.g. two different stocks) and at the maturity of the option, you can take delivery of the underlying asset that has the better pay-off of the two. In *Four Weddings and a Funeral,* Charles was long a rainbow call option based on two underlying assets: first, Duckface and second, the Andie MacDowell character, Carrie. He took the view that the higher pay-off at expiry was Carrie rather than Duckface, so he took delivery of Carrie. Incidentally, a rainbow option is more expensive to buy than a plain vanilla option on either Carrie or Duckface. But you already know that the cost of dating two people simultaneously is generally more expensive than dating either one of them.

We hope the above has whetted your appetite for options contracts, whether applied to financial assets or more light-heartedly about the issues behind your decisions on engagement, marriage and divorce. Who said finance wasn't sexy? Not us. After finishing this text you might want to investigate the practical uses of straddles, straps, condors, butterfly spreads, lookbacks, caps, floors, collars and other 'exotic' derivatives. But if you wait too long to purchase the companion text *Financial Engineering: Derivatives and Risk Management* by Keith Cuthbertson and Dirk Nitzsche, it might have increased in price. So why not hedge by taking out a long futures contract on the book, so you can take delivery in the future at a known fixed price? Alternatively, you could take out a call option on the book that will set an upper limit on the price you will pay for the book in the future (the strike price). But the option also allows you to walk away from the contract, should you hear that the book is not particularly good, so that you would be able to buy it in your local bookstore at a spot price that is below the strike price in your 'KCDN' call option.

Trading strategies: straddles

Suppose you think that the share price of Microsoft is likely to change by a substantial amount after the result of its legal case is announced in three months time, but you are uncertain about the *direction* of movement. If the judgment comes out in favour of Microsoft, the price will rise substantially; if not, the price will fall. Here, you want to be able to make a profit if the share price moves in either direction – this is a **volatility strategy**. How can you use options to take advantage of this strategy? Let's see what happens if you buy a long call *and* a long put on Microsoft, where the strike price and the maturity date (of three months) are the same for both the call and the put – this is called a **long straddle**. We can use our 'direction vectors' to find out what happens.

A long call has a pay-off $\{0, +1\}$ and a long put a pay-off $\{-1, 0\}$. Adding these we get a $\{-1, +1\}$ pay-out, which is the V-shape profile in Figure 25.5. Let us examine the outcome in a little more detail by assuming that the current stock price is $S_0 = 102$ and you buy a call and a put, both with the same strike price $K = 102$. Suppose the put premium is $P = 3$ and the call premium $C = 5$. Both the put and call premiums have to be paid, so the cost of the strategy is $C + P = 8$. You will make a net profit if the stock price moves up or down by more than 8 – that is, ends up below $S_T = 94$ or above $S_T = 110$ – since then the pay-off from either the call $S_T - K$, or the put $K - S_T$, will more than offset the cost of 8.

Your maximum loss will occur when the stock price at expiry of the options in three months time is $S_T = K = 102$, since then both the call and the put will not be exercised and your loss equals the sum of the call and put premia, $C + P = 8$ – but this is your maximum loss, no matter what happens to the stock price in the future. If S_T is *slightly* above or below K, then either the call or the put will be exercised and your losses will be less than 8.

Note that for a straddle to be profitable the investor must have a view about extreme price movements that is different from that held by the 'average' of all market participants. This is because if the market as a whole expects extreme price movements, this would be reflected in a higher value for the underlying volatility of stock prices (σ) and hence higher call and put premia (see below), so the stock price would have to move by more than 8 for you to make a profit.

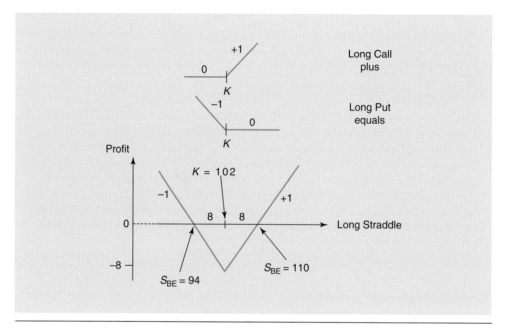

FIGURE 25.5: Long straddle

It is fairly obvious that a ***short straddle*** which involves selling the call and put will have a $(1,-1)$ pay-off at expiry – that is, an inverted V shape. The short straddle has a positive profit equal to the receipt of the call and put premia $C + P = 8$, providing the stock price *at expiry* is close to the strike price. However, the short straddle is subject to potential large losses if there is a large fall or rise in stock prices. Perhaps the most famous losses on short straddle positions are those of Nick Leeson, whose total losses on options and futures positions caused Barings Bank to go bankrupt with derivatives losses of $1.4bn (see Case Study 25.2).

CASE STUDY 25.2 LEESON'S STRADDLE

By the end of 1994, Nick Leeson had sold about 37,000 *Nikkei 225 straddles* – that is, 35,000 puts and 35,000 calls with the same maturity and strike price. He therefore received the call and put premia. These positions were built up over several months and the strike prices were in the range of 18,500–20,000. He did not report these trades to Barings Bank (as he was officially not allowed to sell options), but hid them in his 'error account 88888'. The value of the Nikkei 225 underlying these index options was around $7bn. The Nikkei at the end of 1994 had been trading in the range 19,000–20,000. If the Nikkei remained in its historical range then Leeson's straddle would payoff *at maturity*, since the call and put premia received would be less than fully offset by any pay-outs at maturity to investors holding long positions in these options. This is obvious from the V-shape of the long straddle and the inverted-V pay-off for Leeson, who held the short straddle.

If the options were held to maturity, the potential losses to Leeson could be very high, since either the calls ($S_T > K$) or the puts ($S_T < K$) could be exercised by the 'long'.

On 17 January 1995 the Nikkei was at 19,350, but then the Kobe earthquake struck and by the end of the week the Nikkei had dropped sharply to about 18,950, so the long puts were heavily in the money. Hence Leeson's written puts had made huge losses and this was part of the reason Barings Bank went bust.

25.2 OPTIONS PRICES

Speculation with options will usually not involve holding the option to maturity, but buying and selling (closing out) over a very short period of time. Prior to maturity it can be shown that the option premium varies minute by minute as the stock price, interest rate and the volatility of the stock change.

Let us develop some intuitive arguments that help us to explain the determination of option prices. We consider each factor in turn, holding all the other factors constant. This intuitive approach will help us to understand the mathematical formulae for option prices that we present later. In each case we assume that the investor has a long position (i.e. has purchased a call or a put) and we only consider European stock options (where the stock pays no dividends). The results are summarised in Table 25.3.

Time to expiration, T

- **Calls:** In general, the price today of a European call option, C, is higher the longer the time to maturity of the option. This is because a long maturity option has more time to end up well in-the-money – that is, for S_T to be much higher than K. Of course, S could also fall over the life of the option, but losses are limited to the call premium no matter how far

TABLE 25.3: Factors affecting the value of options

	Long European call option	Long European put option
Time to expiration, T	+	+
Current stock price, S_0	+	–
Strike price, K	–	+
Stock return volatility, σ	+	+
Risk-free rate, r	+	–

Notes: We are only considering options on stocks that pay no dividends.
   '+' indicates a positive relationship between the option price and the variable chosen. That is, a rise (fall) in the variable is accompanied by a rise (fall) in the option premium.
   '–' indicates a negative relationship between the option price and the variable chosen. That is, a rise (fall) in the variable is accompanied by a fall (rise) in the option premium.

stock prices fall. Hence, the longer the time to maturity, the higher the *expected* payoff at maturity and hence you are willing to pay more for the call today.

- **Puts:** The put premium on a European option generally increases with time to maturity, for the same general reasons as given for the call – although there are some rare cases where this can also be a negative relationship, but we shall ignore these.

Strike price, K and current stock price, S

- **Calls:** European call options have a larger payoff the higher is the stock price S_T *at expiry*, relative to the strike price K. However, if stock-price movements are random, then the higher the *current* stock price S_0 relative to the strike price, the more likely it is that the stock price *at expiry* will also be above the strike price. Hence the purchaser of a long European call option will be willing to pay a higher price for the option the higher is (S_0/K).
- **Puts:** It should be obvious that the price of a put option varies with S and K in the opposite direction to that for a call. Hence the value of a long position in a European put option depends negatively on (S_0/K).

Volatility, σ

- **Calls:** The greater the volatility of the return on the stock σ, the greater the possible range of share prices that might occur at the expiry date of the option. But the most the holder of a long call option can lose is the call premium. Hence, high volatility increases the chance of a high share price and hence a high payoff for the call option (at the expiry date), while downside risk is limited. Extremely poor stock-price performance is no worse for the holder of the call option than moderately poor stock-price performance. Therefore the current price of a call option is higher, the higher is the volatility of the underlying stock, since this implies a higher *expected* payoff to the call[2]. This does not imply that holders of call options like risk – it is just that higher volatility of stock prices implies a higher expected payoff (at maturity) to the holder of the call, so the *expected* cash flow to the option holder increases with the volatility of the stock.
- **Puts:** The owner of a long put has a payoff at maturity of $K - S_T$ (if S_T ends up below K). The higher is the volatility of the underlying stock, the larger is the possible payoff at maturity if the stock price ends up below K. However, high volatility also implies that the stock prices could rise well above K, in which case the put is worthless at maturity. But no matter how high the stock price at maturity, the most you can lose is the put premium. Hence the *expected* payoff at maturity to holding the put is higher, the higher is the volatility of the stock. So you are willing to pay a higher price today for a put that has an underlying asset with a high volatility.

---

[2] Consider a call with $K = \$100$ and suppose the initial stock price is also $S_0 = \$100$. Suppose a 'low-volatility' stock can end up at either $98 or $102 with equal probability and a 'high volatility' stock can end up at either $90 or $110. The expected payoff to both *stocks* is the same, namely $100. But the expected payoff for the *call* on the low-volatility stock is $1 = \frac{1}{2}(0) + \frac{1}{2}(2)$ and for the call on the high-volatility stock is higher at $5 = \frac{1}{2}(0) + \frac{1}{2}(10)$. You can easily adapt the above to see why the call premium today is higher, the longer the time to maturity. For any given level of volatility, the stock will have a wider range of outcomes the longer the time to maturity and hence the call will have a higher expected payoff – so you are willing to pay more for it today.

Risk-free rate, r

- **Calls:** The call premium is higher, the higher is the current interest rate, r – although we cannot give a full intuitive interpretation of this result. But try this. At maturity, if you exercise the call option you have to pay the strike price, K. The cost of this payment today (the present value) is Ke^{-rT} (or $K/(1 + r)^T$ if you don't like continuously compounded rates). The higher is the interest rate, the lower is the cost today of paying K in the future[3], hence the more you are prepared to pay for the call option.
- **Put:** Higher interest rates imply a lower put premium. If you exercise the put at expiry, you deliver a stock and receive $K. But K dollars at T are worth less today, the higher is the interest rate, so you are willing to pay less today for the put.

It would be extremely useful if all of the above factors could be included in a single equation to determine the call C or put premium P. This 'closed-form' solution is the **Black–Scholes equation** for option prices and has the general form:

$$C \text{ or } P = f(S_t/K, r, \sigma, T) \qquad\qquad [7]$$

To work out the exact functional form for the Black–Scholes equation is rather difficult, but we discuss this in the next chapter. However, the Black–Scholes equation results in a 'curved' or 'non-linear' relationship between the call (or put) premium and the price of the underlying stock, S. This positive relationship for a long call is shown as the curved line A–B in Figure 25.6. In fact, as the option approaches maturity the 'curved line' moves towards the 'kinked line', which represents the pay-off at maturity. If the current stock price is S_t, then the current call premium would be C_t (point B, Figure 25.6). However, if the stock price remained at S_t the call premium would fall towards point C and the option is said to 'lose time value' as it approaches maturity (see below).

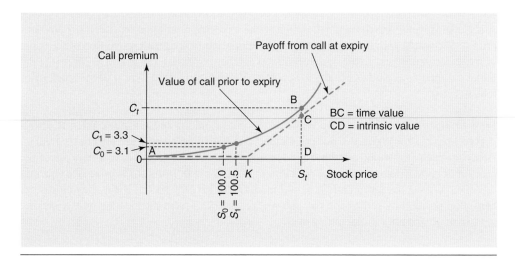

FIGURE 25.6: Black–Scholes

---

[3] The higher is the interest rate today, the less you have to place in a bank account today, to be certain of having $K at maturity of the option. Remember we are also holding the stock price constant in this scenario.

Figure 25.6 shows how we can speculate over short horizons using call options. For example, suppose that immediately after purchasing a call option (on a stock) at a price of $C_0 = \$3.1$ the stock price increases from $100 to $100.5. According to the Black–Scholes formula, the call price will increase to $C_1 = \$3.3$. If the speculator paid the $3.1 to the clearing house at $t = 0$, then at $t = 1$ when she closes out her initial (long) position by selling the call at $3.3 (to another trader), the clearing house in Chicago sends the speculator $3.3. She has made a profit of $0.2, which is a percentage return of $6.45\% = (0.2/3.1) \times 100\%$. Thus there is no need to wait until expiry to earn a speculative profit.

As we see in the next chapter, the ratio of the dollar change in the call premium ($0.2) to the dollar change in the stock price ($0.5) is known as the call **option's delta**, which here is $0.4 = 0.2/0.5$. The delta of a call always lies between 0 and $+1$. But note that although the *dollar* change in the call premium is usually less than the *dollar* change in the stock price, the option still provides leverage compared with speculating with the stock, because leverage refers to *percentage changes*. To see this, note that in the above example the option gives a speculative return (per dollar invested) of 6.67%. Had you invested in the stock you would have earned a considerably smaller percentage return on your capital invested – you would have paid $100 for the stock and sold for $100.5, a return on your own capital of 0.5%[4].

The change in dollar value and the return are two different concepts. In the above example, the percentage return on the stock is 0.5%, but the percentage return from the call is much larger at 6.67%. As a speculator, it is the percentage return (on your own funds) that you are interested in when you compare two investment strategies, betting on the call versus betting on the stock. Another way of looking at this is to note that the percentage change in the call premium for each *1% change* in the stock price would be $13.3\% = 6.67/0.5$. The figure of 13.3% is known as the **option's elasticity** and it clearly indicates that investing in the option provides leverage, compared to investing in the stock.

A speculator would purchase a call option if she expected a bull market (i.e. a rise in stock prices). She would gain leverage (because the call premium is a small proportion of the value of the underlying stocks in the option contract) and her downside loss would be limited to the initial call premium paid (since the lowest price the call can fall to is zero, if the stock price falls to zero).

Prior to maturity the relationship between the put premium and the stock price is also a curved line, but for a put, the put premium P and the stock price S are *negatively related*. Hence, a speculator would purchase a put option if she felt that stock prices would fall in the near future. She would pay the put premium $P_0 = \$2$ at $t = 0$. If the stock price subsequently fell, then at $t = 1$ the put premium would increase to, say, $P_1 = \$2.3$. If she then closes out her initial position by selling the put, she will receive $2.3 from the clearing house, making a profit of 15% on her initial outlay of $2.

We also noted above that the Black–Scholes formula (and our intuition) shows that the price of both calls and puts are positively related to the volatility of the stock – as

---

[4] Clearly here we are considering a 'cash purchase' of the stock and not a levered purchase of the stock using borrowed funds to finance part of the purchase.

perceived by the players in the market. Suppose that the *perceived* volatility of a stock increases (e.g. because the firm has sales overseas in the emerging economies of Asia and economic forecasts for these economies had suddenly become more uncertain). Then both call and put premia would increase and had the speculator been long either calls or puts, she could now close out her position at a profit. Options therefore allow speculators to make a profit (or loss) by predicting changes in volatility. This is sometimes referred to as **trading volatility**.

25.3 INTRINSIC VALUE AND TIME VALUE

Illustrative options price quotes for 1 July for company A's stock and for strike prices of K = 360p (pence) and 390p are shown in Table 25.4. These are American options that can be exercised at any time, so the strike price could be obtained immediately by the long (for either the call or the put). The current share price for company A is $S_0 = 376p$.

TABLE 25.4: Call premia on company A, 1 July

Strike price K	Expiry month		
	October	**January**	**April**
360p	$36\frac{1}{2}$ (16 \ $20\frac{1}{2}$)	50 (16 \ 34)	$57\frac{1}{2}$ (16 \ $41\frac{1}{2}$)
390p	$21\frac{1}{2}$ (0 \ $21\frac{1}{2}$)	$35\frac{1}{2}$ (0 \ $35\frac{1}{2}$)	44 (0 \ 44)
Current share price, $S_0 = 376p$			

Notes: Prices denoted in pence. (.\ .) gives (intrinsic\ time value).

In, out and at the money

For a long position in a call option the above terms apply, depending on the following circumstances:

In the money (ITM):	Current spot price $>$ Strike price ($S > K$)
At the money (ATM):	Current spot price $=$ Strike price ($S = K$)
Out of the money (OTM):	Current spot price $<$ Strike price ($S < K$)

Strictly speaking, an option is in the money if S_T exceeds the *present value* of the strike price (i.e. $S_T > K \exp(-rT)$), but the simpler definitions above are used 'on the street'.

Newspaper quotes

The 360 calls (Table 25.4) must be worth at least 16p because the long has the right to exercise the option and buy company A's stock at $K = 360$p and she could then immediately sell the stocks for $S_0 = 376$p. The possibility of immediate exercise places a minimum intrinsic value (IV) on the option.

> **Intrinsic value** $= S_0 - K = 376$p $- 360$p $= 16$p   [8]

The 360 call for October expiry has a call premium of $36\frac{1}{2}$p, which is greater than the intrinsic value of 16p. The reason for this is that there is a chance that between 1 July and the October expiry date, the share price will increase even further (thus increasing the value of owning the call). This extra amount is known as the time value of the option.

> **Time value** (Oct. call) $=$ **Call premium** $-$ **Intrinsic value**   [9]
>
> $= 36\frac{1}{2}$p $- 16$p $= 20\frac{1}{2}$p

Now consider the 390 call. This has an intrinsic value of zero, since you would not wish to take delivery in the option contract and pay $K = 390$p and then immediately sell the stock in the cash market at $S_0 = 376$p. However, there is a chance that on or before the maturity of the option, the spot price will rise beyond $K = 390$p. For the October 390 call, the long is willing to pay $21\frac{1}{2}$p for that chance. Notice that for either of the calls ($K = 360$p or $K = 390$p), the long is willing to pay a higher call premium, the longer the time to expiry – hence these options have time values that increase with time to maturity (look along the rows). This is because there is a longer time over which the spot price might rise above (or well above) the strike price. In summary, we have:

> For long calls: Intrinsic value, IV $= \max [S_0 - K, 0]$
>
> Time value $= C - IV$

Note that with an American option you can exercise at any time. However, if you exercise the option you only receive the intrinsic value. If you *trade* the option by selling your existing long position then you receive the market price, which is the sum of the intrinsic and time value. Hence, for a plain vanilla American call you will always *trade* the option rather than exercise it. (Note, however, that the latter result does not apply to all types of American options.)

Let us briefly return to Figure 25.6. As the option approaches maturity, the current value of the call, which is represented by the curved line $A-B$, 'collapses' on to the 'kinked line' that shows the pay-off at maturity. The intrinsic value, $\max[S_t - K, 0]$ at stock price S_t, is the distance C–D in Figure 25.6. The quoted call premium is C_t (when the stock price is S_t) and therefore the time value of the option is $(C_t - IV)$ – that is, the distance B–C. The longer the time to maturity of an option the higher the call premium (for any given stock price) and the 'higher' is the curved line. This would also imply a higher *time value* (i.e. the distance B–C would be greater). It is also worth noting at this point that the time value B–C falls rather slowly at first, but very sharply when the option is just a few weeks from expiry.

TABLE 25.5: Put premia on company A, 1 July

	Expiry month		
Strike price K	**October**	**January**	**April**
360p	16 (0 \ 16)	25 (0 \ 25)	$27^1/_2$ (0 \ $27^1/_2$)
390p	31 (14 \ 17)	40 (14 \ 26)	$43^1/_2$ (14 \ $29^1/_2$)
Current share price, $S_0 = 376$p			

Notes: Prices denoted in pence. (.\ .) gives (intrinsic\ time value).

Let us undertake a similar analysis of put options on company A's stocks (Table 25.5). The 390 puts must be worth at least 14p, as the long put could buy the shares spot for $S_0 = 376$p and sell (deliver) them immediately for $K = 390$p by exercising the long put.

Hence, the 390 puts have an intrinsic value of 14p, but the October 390 put premium is 31p. The time value is therefore 17p (= 31p − 14p). This reflects the possibility that between 1 July and the October maturity date of the option, the stock price of company A might fall, thus increasing the pay-off to the put option since you have a right to sell at the strike price of $K = 390$.

> For long puts:
>
> Intrinsic value, IV = max $[K - S_0, 0]$
> Time value = $P - $ IV

Put premia increase as the time to expiry increases (look along the rows in Table 25.5), since over a long horizon there is an increased chance that the spot price will end up below the strike price and the put pay-off will be positive.

In/out of the money

Note that the 360 calls (Table 25.4) are in the money ($S_0 - K > 0$) while the 390 calls are out of the money. Hence the 360 calls have relatively high intrinsic values. The converse applies for the 390 calls, which are out of the money and hence have zero intrinsic value and relatively high time values. Similar considerations apply to the puts.

The price of call and put options on some UK stocks are given in Figure 25.7, where as you can see the two strike prices are usually on either side of the current stock price (which is in parentheses). In traded options markets there would more strikes and further maturity dates available and the OTC market (i.e. mainly large banks) will in principle provide equity options with almost any strike and maturity date.

Option		······Calls······			······Puts······		
		Dec	Mar	Jun	Dec	Mar	Jun
3i Group	1002	75.000	110.000	-	35.000	56.000	-
(*1038.000)	1050	48.500	84.000	-	56.500	78.000	-
Allce & Leics	740	85.500	119.000	-	66.500	89.500	-
(*752.000)	760	72.500	107.500	105.000	73.000	97.500	119.000
ARM	145	11.750	-	-	5.750	-	-
(*149.500)	150	9.000	15.250	18.500	8.000	12.250	14.500
BAE Systems	500	30.750	-	-	18.750	-	-
(*507.000)	520	20.500	36.500	44.750	28.750	37.750	45.500
BG Group	860	61.750	-	-	43.000	-	-
(*870.500)	880	52.000	78.000	96.000	53.250	67.500	77.250
Br Airways	420	28.000	43.250	52.250	23.750	33.250	41.500
(*423.500)	430	23.000	-	-	29.000	-	-
BAT	1750	78.000	-	-	48.500	-	-
(*1763.000)	1800	52.000	93.500	116.500	72.500	117.500	135.000
Cable & Wire	185	10.000	-	-	8.500	-	-
(*186.600)	190	7.500	14.250	18.000	11.000	15.250	19.000
Cadbury Sch	600	36.500	56.500	65.000	18.500	30.000	39.000
(*612.500)	620	26.000	-	-	27.500	-	-

FIGURE 25.7: Prices of call and put options

Source: Financial Times, reproduced by permission.

25.4 ORGANISATION OF OPTIONS MARKETS

Options are traded on individual stocks, stock indices, commodities such as crude oil, foreign currencies, futures contracts and to a much lesser extent on Treasury notes and Treasury bonds. The major exchanges for financial options are the Chicago Board Options Exchange (CBOE), the Philadelphia Stock Exchange (PHLX), the Pacific Stock Exchange (PSE in San Francisco) and NYSE-Euronext. (We discuss futures and options on energy products such as oil and natural gas in Chapter 27.) The CBOE was established in 1973, initially trading stock options. It is the largest organised options market trading standardised contracts and has a deep secondary market.

The **over-the-counter** (OTC) options market tailors the option contract to the buyer's specifications and is now very large, probably over 10 times larger than the traded options market although often the *secondary* OTC market is thin. However, active secondary OTC markets do exist, particularly the interbank market in European options on foreign exchange negotiated for commercial customers. The advantage of OTC markets can be illustrated by considering a portfolio manager who wishes to hedge her particular portfolio of stocks (which we assume does not match any available stock index on which options are available) by buying a put option (often known as a *basket option*).

Advantages of OTC put options

- She can exactly match her portfolio composition with the underlying in the tailor-made OTC put option.
- The expiration date of the put can be tailored to her investment horizon.
- They maintain anonymity, so that the fact she believes the market will fall is not communicated to other traders.
- New options contracts do not need the approval of regulatory authorities.
- Drawbacks to using the OTC market are possibly higher transaction costs and credit counterparty risk.

US stock options

There are about 500 stocks on the CBOE on which options are traded. We will take the example of US stock options to illustrate some of the administrative procedures that operate in this market.

Contract sizes

Options on individual stocks are usually for delivery of 100 stocks. Contract sizes for other options usually involve a contract multiple. For example, for the S&P 500 the multiple is $100 times the index value of the option.

Expiry dates

These are fixed by the exchange and options are traded for expiration up to 4.30 p.m. (Central Time) on the third Friday of the expiry month. Some index options expire on the last day of each quarter.

Expiry dates for options on individual stocks usually extend to about nine months, with some exceptions. For example, *LEAPS (Long Term Equity Anticipation Shares)*, which are primarily options on individual stocks (but some are also on stock indices), have expiration dates of up to three years ahead. Similarly, *FLEX options* on stock indices can have any expiration date up to five years and in addition they permit the purchaser to set any exercise price.

Strike/exercise prices

These might be set at, for example, $2.50 intervals when the underlying stock price is less than $25, $5 intervals when the stock price is between $25 and $200, and $10 intervals for a stock price over $200. Strike prices are set either side of the *current* stock price and as the stock price moves up or down, new strike prices are added.

Trading

An individual who has purchased (or rents) a seat on the CBOE can be either a market maker or a floor broker or both (but not on the same day!). The latter is known as *dual trading*.

The *market maker (dealer)* must stand ready to quote both bid and ask prices on the option. The 'bid' price is the price at which the market maker is prepared to buy and the 'ask' price is the price at which he is prepared to sell. Market makers must stand ready to trade with investors. An investor who has purchased an option can close out her position by selling (writing) the same option (i.e. with the same strike and expiration date). If investors as a whole are not offsetting existing positions, then the number of contracts (i.e. the 'open interest') increases by one.

Floor brokers who have a seat on the exchange merely buy and sell options on behalf of their customers and usually earn a commission on each trade. They do not hold a book and they are not obliged to 'make a market' in the options. There appears to be an accelerating trend away from 'open outcry' in derivatives markets towards screen-based trading, as well as increased use of computers for matching buyers and sellers and in settling trades.

Options clearing corporation (OCC)

For US options markets (except those trading futures options) the Options Clearing Corporation (OCC) standardises contracts and acts as an intermediary, effectively creating two separate contracts. For example, if a trader buys a call option the OCC guarantees that the writer will honour the contract. An option *writer* represents a credit risk to the OCC, since she may not have funds to purchase the underlying in the spot market to effect delivery. The OCC therefore requires the *writer* to post a margin payment (usually in cash and equal to at least 30% of the value of the stocks underlying the option plus the call premium). There is also a maintenance margin, which might be set at a minimum of 15–25% of the value of the stocks underlying the option contract. An option *buyer* has no margin requirement with the OCC, since the most she can lose is the option premium, which is paid in full at the outset of the contract.

Initial margins vary depending on whether one has a naked position (i.e. no offsetting holding in the underlying stocks) or a covered/hedged position. The latter is less risky and involves less initial margin.

Offsetting order

If you originally purchased a call option on a stock at $4.10 at a cost of $410, then you can sell this contract by placing an **offsetting order**. If the option price is now $4.50 and your broker finds a purchaser at this price, $450 will be passed to your clearing firm ABC (and then on to you) and the OCC will cancel your position in this contract. The purchaser will generally not be the person from whom you initially purchased the contract, but if she initially had a short position the open interest will fall by one. About 55% of stock-option contracts are closed out in this manner.

Exercising an option

If the buyer of the call holds the option to maturity and exercises the option, your broker notifies the clearing firm (XYZ) through which the original trade was cleared. XYZ then places an exercise order with the OCC, which '*assigns*' a trader who has previously written a similar contract (i.e. same strike, same maturity, same underlying asset). This may be a random assignment or a first-in, first-out rule may be used. Roughly speaking about 10% of calls and puts on the CBOE are exercised and about 30–40% expire out of the money.

Newspaper quotes

Quotes in the *Wall Street Journal* (see Table 25.6) follow a similar pattern to those in the *Financial Times*. Consider the options on Intel for the CBOT as quoted in the *Wall Street Journal* online edition of Monday 5 November 2007. All prices refer to the previous trading day, Friday 2 November. The current price of the underlying stock is given in the first row, which is $26.80. The strike prices in the second column are set (by the exchange) above and below the current

TABLE 25.6: Intel option, CBOT, *Wall Street Journal* online edition

		Call			Put		
Expiration	Strike	Last	Volume	Open interest	Last	Volume	Open interest
Jan	20.00	6.85	216	136915	0.09	263	146405
Apr	20.00	7.35	412	2259	0.34	10	6422
Nov	22.50	4.29	368	5888	0.03	100	10314
Dec	22.50	4.40	14	3603	0.13	96	3483
Jan	22.50	4.55	484	165421	0.26	260	134777
Apr	22.50	5.04	124	4788	0.69	190	8773
Nov	25.00	1.80	6064	35262	0.12	1127	62772
Dec	25.00	2.25	1901	8490	0.47	883	7619
Jan	25.00	2.61	4048	204784	0.74	508	107419
Apr	25.00	3.45	172	21996	1.39	448	17931
Nov	27.50	0.27	13306	70256	1.07	5859	20912
Dec	27.50	0.81	9834	20000	1.47	1594	6126
Jan	27.50	1.21	8063	160038	1.85	3016	18254
Apr	27.50	2.01	1220	31842	2.51	293	14925
Nov	30.00	0.03	168	8029	3.31	70	1788
Dec	30.00	0.19	2865	6864	. . .	. . .	319
Jan	30.00	0.47	2667	194423	3.70	310	7336
Apr	30.00	1.09	496	24296	4.10	66	2686

Prices at close 2 November 2007 Intel (INTC) Underlying stock price*: 26.80

Underlying stock price represents listed exchange price only. It may not match the composite closing price.

stock price. The expiry dates are in the first column. The columns labelled 'Last' denote the closing price for the call or put option (for the 3 p.m. trade) and these columns are followed by the volume traded as well as the open interest. Note that the quoted option price for the 3 p.m. trade in Chicago might not coincide exactly with the recorded price for the underlying stock (on NYSE/NASDAQ), especially if the option is rather illiquid and hence infrequently traded.

From Table 25.6 you can see that the closing price (on NASDAQ) for Intel is 26.80 and the alternative exercise (strike) prices range from 20.00 to 30.00 (there are other strike prices available that are not reported here). Call prices (premiums) for the $K = 22.50$ strike for expiration months November, December, January and April are 4.29, 4.40, 4.55 and 5.04 respectively, so the call premium increases with the maturity date of the option. The quoted option premium is to buy or sell one share (but 100 shares must be purchased for each contract, so the contract price = '100 $\times$ quoted price').

By looking at the November contracts (Table 25.6) with strike prices $K = 20.00, 22.50, 25.00, 27.50$ and 30.00 you can see that the call premia fall as the strike price increases. The converse applies to the put premia, which are positively related to the strike price. By looking at the $K = 25$-November and $K = 25$-April (of the next year) put contracts, you can see that put premia increase with the time to maturity of the contract. These observations are of course consistent with the Black–Scholes formula for option prices and with our earlier intuitive arguments.

25.5 HEDGING USING STOCK INDEX OPTIONS

Stock index options (SIO) are frequently used to hedge the systematic (market) risk of a *diversified portfolio* of shares. A fund manager using index options is therefore hedging the market risk but leaving the portfolio exposed to specific risk, presumably on the grounds that she is a good 'stock picker' (i.e. she can identify those stocks that will perform well relative to others in the same risk class). To understand the hedging process we need to consider the contract specifications of index options and we focus on the S&P 100 (American-style) contract. The S&P 100 index option is often referred to by its ticker symbol, OEX, and it is the most actively traded option on CBOE.

SIO are settled in cash. If $\$z$ is the value of one index point and the current index level is S, then the face value of (stocks underlying) one index option contract, FVO, is given by FVO = $\$zS$. For the S&P 100 index option, $z = \$100$. Hence, if the index $S_0 = 200$, one SIO contract has a *face value,* $= zS_0 = \$20,000$. Put slightly differently, if FVO = $\$20,000$ then one SIO option contract on the S&P 100 relates to a $\$20,000$ position in an underlying portfolio of shares that mimic the S&P 100. Call and put premia are also quoted in terms of index points.

Suppose you hold a stock portfolio with total value $TVS_0 = \$400,000$, whose composition mirrors the S&P 100 (i.e. your portfolio has a $\beta = 1$) and you fear a price fall in the future. You could limit the downside risk by purchasing puts. This is a **protective put**. If the S&P 100 index currently stands at $S_0 = 200$, then the whole index is worth $\$20,000$ and hence it looks as if you should purchase $N_p = \$400,000/\$20,000 = 20$ put contracts to insure your portfolio. This is correct.

$$N_{\mathrm{p}} = \frac{\text{Total value of (spot) portfolio}}{\text{Value of index point} \times S_0} = \frac{\text{TVS}_0}{zS_0} = 20 \qquad [10]$$

Assume that the strike price chosen is $K = 200$ (i.e. it is an at-the-money put, since the spot price of the stocks is also $S_0 = 200$). If the index falls 20% to $S_T = 160$, then the value of your stock portfolio falls by \$80,000. But if you exercise the put (at expiry) you make a profit of 40 points ($= 200 - 160$) per contract, which with 20 contracts gives you a payoff of \$80,000 ($= 40$ contracts $\times 20$ points $\times \$100$ per point). Here, the loss on the stock portfolio is exactly offset by the gain on the puts. However, there is the put premium to consider. Suppose the put premium paid was $P = 5$ index points. The 20 put contracts would have cost \$10,000 ($= 20 \times \$100 \times 5$ points). Without the puts you would have lost \$80,000. If you are long the puts, you can sell your shares for their original value of \$400,000 (as the strike K is the same as the initial stock level $S_0 = 200$) by exercising the puts (in Chicago) and the cost of this insurance is only \$4000.

Of course, if the S&P index increases the puts would be worthless and you would not exercise them. But the value of your stock portfolio would have risen and the only loss you would have is from the payment of the put premium. In this case your 'insurance' was not needed – but of course insurance does not come 'free', you had to pay for it in the form of the put premium. You are now in a position to understand the 'financial engineering' that lies behind the advertisement in the 'Texas Wall Street Journal' in Case Study 25.3.

CASE STUDY 25.3   'TEXAS WALL STREET JOURNAL'

Invest in our US 'Bush Bonanza Fund'
Steer your way to success in the S&P bull market
Defy gravity, stay ahead if the bears attack.

We *guarantee* you will share in the upside of the S&P index, but if the index should even fall to zero over the next year, you still get your money back*'

'*Administration fee of 7.5% of capital invested.
Send your cheques to Mr D. Rumsfeld, Southfork, Houston, Texas.

What's this all about? If you send in \$1000 what do you think will happen? Well, \$75 will be taken to purchase puts on the S&P 500 index, with a maturity of one year and with a strike price equal to the current value of the S&P 500 index (i.e. an at-the-money put). The remaining \$925 will be used to invest in an index mutual fund that tracks the S&P 500. This is a *structured product* and an example of *financial engineering*.

25.6 OTHER OPTIONS

The underlying asset in an options contract can be individual stocks, stock indices, currencies, futures contracts and T-bonds. There are also options whose pay-off depends on the future value of interest rates (e.g. caps and floors). There is a very large OTC market in options and some options are only available OTC (e.g. caps and floors).

Caps, floors and collars

Simplifying a little, a *caplet* is a call option that pays off $\max[r_T - K_{cap}, 0]$, where r_T is the interest rate at the expiration of the option contract and K_{cap} is the strike (interest) rate. Clearly, a caplet can be used to speculate on a future rise in interest rates – if you expect interest rates to rise in the future (above the strike rate) then you would purchase a caplet. However, let us consider how it can be used to insure you against interest-rate rises.

Suppose that in January interest rates are currently 10%. You decide to purchase a caplet with $K_{cap} = 10\%$ that expires in March. In March if interest rates turn out to be 12%, the caplet pay-off is 2%. The cap contract also includes a notional principal amount of, say, $1m and hence the pay-off would be $20,000. If in January you know you will be taking out a loan of $1m in March and you are worried that interest rates will rise, you could 'lock in' a maximum rate of $K_{cap} = 10\%$ by buying the caplet. In March if $r_T = 12\%$ then your loan costs you 2% more as interest rates have risen, but the caplet provides a cash pay-off of 2% that will compensate you for your higher borrowing costs. But things can get even better. If in March interest rates have fallen to 8%, you can just walk away (i.e. not exercise) the caplet and simply borrow at the current low spot interest rate of 8%. Hence, once again options allow you to insure yourself against adverse outcomes (i.e. high interest rates) but allow you to benefit from any upside (i.e. low interest rates). For this privilege you pay a caplet premium up-front (i.e. in January).

If your loan has a number of reset dates for the interest payable (i.e. it is a floating-rate loan), you can insure your loan costs by buying a series of caplets, each with an expiry date that matches the reset dates on your loan. A *set of caplets* is a *cap*. Financial institutions will design and sell you a cap in the OTC market. (Caps are not traded on an exchange.)

A *floorlet* has a pay-off equal to $\max[K_{fl} - r_T, 0]$ and is therefore a long put on interest rates. Clearly, if you are a speculator and you think that interest rates are going to fall below K_{fl} in three months time, you can make a profit if you are long the floorlet. Alternatively, if you are going to place money on deposit in, say, three months time and you are worried that interest rates will fall, a long floorlet will ensure that the minimum you earn on your deposits will be $K_{fl} = 8\%$, say. For example, if interest rates turn out to be $r_T = 7\%$ in three months time, you exercise the floorlet and earn a profit of 1%, which when added to the interest on your deposit of $r_T = 7\%$ implies that your overall return is 8%. If interest rates turn out to be 9%, you would not exercise the floorlet (since it is out of the money) but simply lend your money at the current high interest rate of 9%. A *floor* is a series of floorlets, with different maturity dates, and can be used to make sure that the *effective* minimum interest rate you will receive from your deposit account (at floating rates) is $K_{fl} = 8\%$ at each reset date (e.g. every six months).

Finally, the combination of a long cap with $K_{cap} = 10\%$ and a long floor with $K_{fl} = 8\%$ is known as a *collar*. This is because if you have a floating-rate loan and you also purchase a collar, the *effective* interest rate payable on the loan cannot go above 10% nor fall below 8%, so the effective interest payable is constrained between an upper and lower level.

Exotics options

There is no end to the types of option that can be offered in the OTC market and those with complex pay-offs are know as *exotic options*. For example, Asian options have a pay-off that is based on the average price over the life of the option. An **Asian (average price) call** option has a pay-off that depends on $\max[S_{av} - K, 0]$, where S_{av} is the average price over the life of the option. So an Asian average-price *currency option* would be useful for a firm that wants to hedge the average level of its future sales in a foreign currency. The firm's foreign currency monthly sales may fluctuate over the year, so an Asian option is a cheap way to hedge, rather than purchasing options for each of the prospective monthly foreign cash flows.

Another type of exotic option is a **barrier option**. This either expires or comes into existence before the expiration date in the options contract. For example, for a **knockout option** the contract may specify that if the stock price rises or falls to the 'barrier level', the option will terminate on that date and hence cannot be exercised. If the option is terminated when the stock price falls to the barrier, it is referred to as a **down-and-out option**, while if it is terminated when the price rises to the barrier, it is an **up-and-out-option**. *Unless they have already been knocked out*, these options have a pay-off at maturity just the same as the pay-off from the 'plain vanilla' calls and puts that we have already discussed at great length.

There are also options that are 'embedded' in other securities. Examples of **embedded options** include callable bonds, convertible bonds, warrants and executive stock options and share underwriting. (The latter involves the underwriter agreeing to purchase any shares that are not taken up by the public, at an agreed minimum price. The agreed minimum price is equivalent to the strike price in a put contract and the underwriting fee is the put premium. The corporate is long the put and the underwriter has written the put.)

In earlier chapters we spent some considerable time discussing real investment decisions using the NPV criterion. The latter usually involved an 'all or nothing' decision based on whether the NPV was positive. However, what that analysis lacked was the ability to incorporate the strategic opportunities that *might arise* in the future from a particular real investment project. For example, if you undertake a NPV calculation as to whether you should enter the 'dot-com' sector, based on a forecast of average growth, you may find that the NPV is negative. However, entering this sector may provide you with golden opportunities, *at some time in the future*, which would not be available if you did not undertake your current negative NPV investment (e.g. eventually capturing part of a global market, as has been done by Google and Amazon). In other words, if you do not invest today, the lost expertise and knowledge may imply that it is too late (and prohibitively costly) to enter this market in, say, five years time. Your initial investment therefore has an *embedded strategic call option* to expand in the future, should the market show rapid growth. Call options are highly valuable when there is great uncertainty about the future. In fact the 'adjusted' NPV of your project is:

$$\text{Adjusted NPV} = \text{Conventional NPV} + \text{Value of the option to expand} \qquad [11]$$

When the premium of the embedded option is added to the conventional NPV, the overall adjusted NPV may be positive, indicating that you should go ahead with the project because of its strategic importance in establishing you in a market that could ultimately be very large. Similarly, a firm could either start its investment in plant and machinery today and face uncertain sales, or it could defer the project for 18 months, by which time the economy may have improved. The manager holds the *option to defer*, which is valuable when uncertainty about future revenues is high.

Real options theory is an application of options pricing to corporate finance and is used to quantify the value of managerial flexibility – the value of being able to commit to or amend a decision. This is a relatively new and complex area of options theory, but one that could aid managers in making strategic investment decisions.

SUMMARY

- A *long call* allows for the possibility of large upside gains to be made as the price of the underlying asset *rises* (above the strike price), but limits downside losses to the call premium. A speculator should buy a call option if she thinks that stock prices *will rise* in the future.
- A *long put* allows for the possibility of large upside gains to be made as the price of the underlying asset price *falls* (below the strike price), but limits downside losses to the put premium. A speculator should buy a put option if she thinks that stock prices *will fall* in the future.
- A *written (short) call* gives unlimited downside risk to the seller should the stock price rise. A *written (short) put* gives substantial downside risk to the seller should the stock price fall. Writers of options therefore have to post margin payments.
- Long calls and long puts can be used to provide insurance.
- A long call implies the *maximum price* you will pay for a stock (at maturity of the option) is the strike price, K. But if the stock price falls in the future you can walk away from the contract (i.e. not exercise the call) and purchase stocks in the spot market at their current low price. Hence a long call provides insurance and the call premium is the price of the insurance.
- If you already hold stocks, a *long put* implies that the *minimum* price at which you can sell your stocks is the strike price, K. But if stock prices rise in the future you can walk away from the contract (i.e. not exercise the put) and sell your stocks in the spot market at their current low price. Hence a long put provides insurance and the put premium is the price of the insurance.

- The call (or put) premium comprises the *intrinsic value* of the option, which is the pay-off to be made on immediate exercise. But option premia also incorporate a *time value*, which reflects the fact that the option may eventually end up in the money at (or before) the expiry date.
- The call premium is positively related to the price of stocks, while the put premium is negatively related to the price of stocks. Both call and put premia increase when the volatility of the share price increases. These relationships are a consequence of the *Black–Scholes formula.*
- A *speculator* who thinks that stock prices will rise (fall) in the near future will buy calls (buy puts). A speculator who thinks that the volatility of stocks will increase will buy either a call or a put or both.
- The options *clearing house* facilitates an active market in traded options by minimising credit (default) risk, as those holding short positions have to post margin payments.
- Newspaper (and screen) quotes are available on calls and puts for several different strike prices and expiry dates. Most traded stock options have expiry dates no longer than one year, but on some stocks traded options are available with expiry dates out to three years. These are know as *LEAPS* – if these longer-term options are written on stock indices, they are know as *FLEX* options.
- The assets underlying an options contract include individual stocks, stock indices, currencies, futures contracts and T-bonds. Some options have pay-offs that depend on the future level of interest rates (e.g. *caps, floors* and *collars*). There is a very large OTC market in options and some options are only available OTC.
- Options with complex pay-offs are know as *exotic options*. Examples include *Asian options and barrier options*, but there are many more.
- Some options may be *embedded* in other securities (e.g. callable bonds, convertible bonds, warrants and executive stock options).
- Decisions to invest in a new business also contain embedded options to expand, to delay production or to abandon the business. These options provide strategic flexibility for the firm and their valuation forms part of *real options theory*.

EXERCISES

Q1   What is the difference between a European and an American option?

Q2   You are a speculator and you think that stock prices will increase. Should you buy a call or a put option?

Q3   If $K = 150$ and the put premium is $P = 5$, should you exercise the option if the spot price at expiry is $S_T = 148$? What is your profit?

Q4   If you exercise a position in a long call option on IBM shares on CBOE, who exactly delivers the shares?

Q5   Would you make a profit on a long call option or a long put option if the stock price was $S = 100$ when you purchased the option and $S = 120$ when you sold the option (assume no change in other factors that influence the option price)?

Q6   If the stock price at maturity of the option contract is $S_T = \$82$, $K = \$80$ and $C = \$3$, would you exercise the option?

Q7   On 1 March the ordinary shares of Branson plc stood at $S = 469p$ (pence). In the traded options market **April 500 puts** have a premium $P = 47p$. You are a speculator and you think S will fall, so you buy a put.

(a) If the share price falls to $S_T = 450p$, how much, if any, (net) profit (in pence) would you make if you held the put to maturity?
(b) What is the % return at maturity if you had purchased the put?
(c) What will the put option be worth at maturity, if the share price moves up to 510p?

Q8   Frank purchased a call option on 100 shares in Gizmo plc one year ago at a call premium of $C = 10p$ per share. The share price at the time was $S = 110p$ and the strike price was $K = 120p$. At expiry, one year later, the share price had risen to $S_T = 135p$.

(a) State whether the option should be exercised.
(b) Calculate the profit or loss on the option.
(c) Would Frank have done better by investing the same amount of cash one year ago in a bank offering 10% p.a.?

CHAPTER 26

Options Pricing

AIMS

- To examine the relationship between European, put and call premia, known as *put–call parity*.
- To demonstrate how the *binomial option pricing model (BOPM)* is used to determine option premia by establishing a risk-free portfolio consisting of a position in the underlying asset and the option. This illustrates the principles of *delta hedging and risk-neutral valuation.*
- To illustrate how the *Black–Scholes formula* is used to provide an explicit equation to determine call and put premia.
- To show how to measure implied volatility and to use it to find mispriced options.
- To outline the linkages between the BOPM and the Black–Scholes approach.

INTRODUCTION

We begin by setting out the put–call parity condition for European options. Next, we present a detailed account of the BOPM, which allows us to introduce the important idea of constructing a risk-free portfolio from two risky assets, namely a call and a stock. This is the principle of delta hedging, whereby changing proportions held in the stock and the option can produce a risk-free portfolio (over small intervals of time), and this enables us to price the option. We generalise the BOPM to many periods. Finally, we turn to the famous (and rather complex) Black–Scholes option-pricing formula and demonstrate how it is related to the BOPM.

26.1 PUT–CALL PARITY: EUROPEAN OPTIONS

In this section we derive the put–call parity relationship. If we know the formula for the price of a call (in terms of fundamental observable variables such as volatility, the underlying stock price, etc.), we can use the put–call parity relationship to determine the price of a put (for options with the same strike price and expiry date).

Put–call parity is an arbitrage relationship between (European) put and call premia, C and P, the share price S, and holding an amount of cash equal to Ke^{-rT} in a risk-free asset (such as a bank deposit or a T-bill that matures at T):

$$\text{(long) share} + \text{(long) put} = \text{(long) call} + \text{cash (equal to } Ke^{-rT}) \tag{1}$$
$$S \quad + \quad P \quad = \quad C \quad + \quad Ke^{-rT}$$

Note that the term Ke^{-rT} uses continuously compounded rates and the equivalent expression using compound rates is $K/(1+r)^T$. We can *nearly* produce the above put–call parity result using our direction vectors to mimic the above equation, namely long stock $\{+1, +1\}$ plus long put $\{-1, 0\}$ equals $\{0, +1\}$, that is the payoff to a long call – but we have 'lost' the 'cash'. The stock plus put portfolio we discussed in Chapter 25 when we considered the case where you already hold shares and then you buy a put. By doing this you establish a minimum value for your stocks (i.e. the strike price in the put), but if stock prices rise (above K) you throw away the put and sell your stocks on the NYSE. The payoffs provided by a 'stock plus put' are the same as if you held a long call – this is financial engineering.

In analysing the above problem we assume that the options cannot be exercised until $t = T$ – that is, put–call parity only holds for European-style options. Note that the signs in [1] indicate whether you are long or short. They are all '+', indicating long stocks, long puts, long calls and long 'cash' (or a T-bill) of $\$Ke^{-rT}$, invested at the risk-free rate, r.

To demonstrate put–call parity we form two portfolios and show that they have the same payoff at time T – hence we conclude that they must be worth the same today. Consider the following two portfolios:

Portfolio A: One *put option* plus one *share* at $t = 0$.
Portfolio B: One *call option* plus an amount of cash equal to Ke^{-rT} at $t = 0$.

TABLE 26.1: Returns from two portfolios, put–call parity

	$S_T > K$	$S_T < K$
Portfolio A[1]	S_T	K
Portfolio B[2]	$(S_T - K) + K = S_T$	K

1. Portfolio A = One put option plus one share at $t = 0$
2. Portfolio B = One call option plus cash of Ke^{-rT} at $t = 0$

Consider the value of portfolio A at expiration (Table 26.1). If the stock price at expiry $S_T > K$ then the put option expires worthless, but the share is worth S_T. Alternatively, if $S_T < K$ the put payoff is $(K - S_T)$ and the long share is worth S_T, hence portfolio A has a payoff = $(K - S_T) + K = K$.

Now consider portfolio B. If $S_T > K$ then the call option's payoff is $(S_T - K)$, while the cash amount Ke^{-rT} held in the risk-free asset has now accrued to $K. Hence the payoff for portfolio B is $(S_T - K + K) = S_T$. Alternatively, if $S_T < K$ then the call option expires worthless, but the amount held in the risk-free asset will have accrued to $K, at T. These payoffs are shown in Table 26.1 and it can be seen that both portfolios yield identical outcomes at the expiry date, T. Since the options are European and cannot be exercised prior to the expiry date, the two portfolios must also have identical values today:

Long call option $+ Ke^{-rT}$ (in risk-free asset) = Long put option $+$ Long share

$$C + Ke^{-rT} = P + S \qquad [2]$$

At time $t = 0$ we know K, r, and S and, given an estimate of σ, we can work out the value of C using the Black–Scholes or binomial model. We can then use equation [2] to deduce the value of P. The put–call parity condition also demonstrates that calls can be converted into puts and vice versa by taking an appropriate position in the share and undertaking borrowing or lending. This is known as *option conversion*. Also we do not need calls, puts, shares and lending/borrowing – given any three, we can always construct a portfolio that has an identical payoff to the omitted asset. This is an example of *financial engineering*.

26.2 BINOMIAL OPTION-PRICING MODEL

To get a handle on the use of delta hedging and risk-neutral valuation in pricing options, we first present a stylised example using an option that only has one period to maturity and where we assume we know the possible outcomes for the stock price (which pays no dividends). The basic idea is to construct a synthetic portfolio, which contains a call option and a share in such a way that this portfolio is risk-free (over a small interval of time). We can then equate the return from this synthetic portfolio to the known risk-free interest rate and solve for the unknown price of the call option. We assume that the stock pays no dividends.

One period BOPM

Consider a one-period problem where there are only two possible outcomes for the share price at $t = 1$, namely 110 and 90:

$S = 100 =$ share price today
$K = 100 =$ strike price of a call option
$C =$ the *unknown* call premium (i.e. price of the call)
$r = 0.05 =$ risk-free rate of interest

We will assume that the 'real world' probability of the stock price moving up or down is $p = 1/2$, so the 'real world' expected stock price at $t = 1$ is $ES_1 = 100 = (1/2)110 + (1/2)90$ and since $S = 100$ the expected stock *return* $\mu = (ES_1/S) - 1 = 0$. As we shall see below, somewhat surprisingly neither the 'real world' probability p of a rise in the stock price nor the 'real world' expected return on the stock μ influences the call premium.

The payoffs to holding *either* one share or *one long* call are given in Figure 26.1. The difference between the two possible payoffs on the share is 20 ($= 110 - 90$). The possible payoffs on the long call are $C_u = 10 (= 110 - 100 = S_u - K)$ and $C_d = 0$. The difference in the two payoffs for holding a long call is $+10$. If we are willing to be a little cavalier with notation, we could write $\Delta S = 20$ and $\Delta C = 10$ and the ratio $h = \Delta C/\Delta S = 1/2$. In

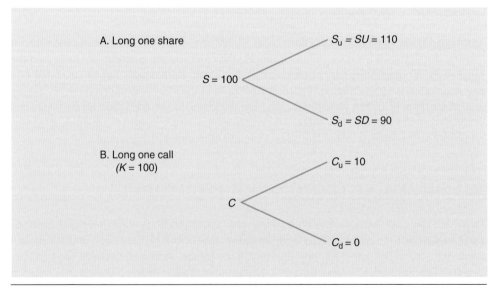

FIGURE 26.1: One-period BOPM

fact, we shall see below that h is the hedge ratio. The difference in the payoff on $\frac{1}{2}$ share, which equals $10\, (= \frac{1}{2} \times 20)$, will just offset the difference in the payoff of $10 on the call.

What we are going to do now, with the help of our hedge ratio, is to construct a portfolio of stocks and the call at $t = 0$ that has a *known payoff* at $t = 1$, no matter what the values of the stock price and call premium are at $t = 1$. This hedge portfolio will involve a cash outlay at time $t = 0$, but because the payoff at $t = 1$ is known, our hedge portfolio must have a return equal to the risk-free rate, or profitable arbitrage opportunities are possible. Consider portfolio A where we are long $\frac{1}{2}$ share and short 1 call.

Payoff to Portfolio A (long 1/2 share, short 1 call):

Payoff for price rise $= (1/2)\,(110) - 10 = 45$
Payoff for price fall $= (1/2)\,(90) - 0\ = 45$

The payoff to portfolio A at $t = 1$ is known with certainty, no matter what the outcome for the stock price (i.e. either 110 or 90). We have created a risk-free portfolio using a hedge ratio of $h = -1/2$. The cost of constructing portfolio A at $t = 0$ is the cost of buying the shares less the receipt from the sale of the call; that is, $(1/2)S - C$. Hence, the payoff of 45, discounted back to today *at the risk-free rate*, must equal the cost of portfolio A:

$$\frac{45}{1.05} = \text{Cost of portfolio today} = (1/2)\,100 - C \qquad [3]$$

Hence $C = 7.1428571$

Equivalently, the payoff from portfolio A is risk-free and therefore must earn the risk-free rate:

$$(1 + \text{risk-free rate}) = \frac{\text{Certain Payout at } t\,=\,1}{\text{Initial Investment at } t\,=\,0} \qquad [4]$$

$$1.05 = \frac{45}{(1/2)100 - C}$$

and therefore $C = 7.1428571$

Arbitrage

The fair price of the option must be $C = 7.14$, otherwise *risk-free* arbitrage profits can be made. To see this, suppose that the quoted option premium is $10, which exceeds the 'fair price' of $C = 7.14$. You are an options trader and you spot this pricing anomaly. As usual, you sell high and buy low. At $t = 0$, you sell (write) the call and receive $10. To guarantee you have the pay-out at $t = 1$, you also purchase half a share. The guaranteed payoff to this hedged portfolio A is $45. With a call premium of $10, the net cost of portfolio A at $t = 0$ is

$40 = (1/2)100 - 10$, and hence the return is 12.5% ($= 45/40$), which is in excess of the risk-free rate of 5%.

Therefore you could borrow $40 from the bank, which with the $10 you get from selling the call enables you to buy half a share. At the end of the period, you owe the bank $40(1.05) = $42, but portfolio A is worth $45 (no matter whether the stock price goes up or down), so you make a risk-free arbitrage profit of $3.

Note that there will be lots of traders who try to implement this risk-free yet profitable strategy. Selling calls would tend to depress C, while borrowing to purchase shares would increase S, thus tending to quickly restore the equality given in equation [3] or [4]. Hence, we expect the quoted call premium to deviate from its fair price only by a small amount and for any discrepancies to be quickly eliminated by the actions of arbitrageurs.

However, let's also consider how you make arbitrage profits if the call is temporarily under-priced at, say, $7. We buy low, sell high. So we *buy the call* and hedge this position by short selling $\frac{1}{2}$ stock, which means we receive $50 ($= \frac{1}{2}$ of $100) at $t = 0$. The net cash inflow at $t = 0$ is $43 ($= 50 - 7$). This can be invested at the risk-free rate to give receipts at $t = 1$ of $45.15 ($= 43 \times 1.05$). Your hedged portfolio will be worth *minus* $45 at $t = 1$, regardless of whether the stock prices rises or falls. Hence you make an overall profit at $t = 1$ of 0.15 ($= 45.15 - 45$).

Formal derivation

Let's now derive the price of the call using algebra. The two outcomes for the stock price are $S_u = SU$ and $S_d = SD$ (where in our example $U = 1.1$ and $D = 0.9$, as shown in Figure 26.1)[1]. Let:

$C_u =$ payoff to the long call if the stock price is S_u
$C_d =$ payoff to the long call if the stock price is S_d

Hence:

$C_u = S_u - K = SU - K$
$C_d = S_d - K = SD - K$ (for $SD > K$ otherwise $C_d = 0$)

Portfolio A (long h shares, short 1 call):

Payoff for price rise at $t = 1$: $V_u = h\,S_u - C_u$
Payoff for price fall at $t = 1$: $V_d = h\,S_d - C_d$

The minus sign indicates that portfolio A consists of one short call. For the two payoffs to be equal at $t = 1$:

$$hS_u - C_u = hS_d - C_d \qquad\qquad [5]$$

---

[1] In fact, the risk-free rate must lie between the rate of return if the stock goes up and its rate of return if the stock goes down, so that $U > R > D$ (with $D > 0$). This ensures that no risk-free arbitrage profits can be made.

$$h = \frac{(C_u - C_d)}{S_u - S_d} = \frac{(C_u - C_d)}{S(U - D)} = \frac{(10 - 0)}{100(0.2)} = \frac{1}{2} \qquad [6]$$

In the above analysis we are *short one* call and [6] indicates that the hedge will then involve going *long h* stocks. The hedge ratio h is also known as the option's 'delta' and this approach is known as **delta hedging**. Having established the hedge ratio to create our risk-free portfolio A, we now determine the call premium C by equating the PV of the known payoff at $t = 1$ with the cost of portfolio A at $t = 0$:

PV of payoff for portfolio−A = Cost of portfolio−A at $t = 0$

$$\frac{hSU - C_u}{(1 + r)} = hS - C \qquad [7]$$

Substituting from equation [6] for h and rearranging, the call premium is:

$$C = \frac{1}{R}[qC_u + (1 - q)C_d] \qquad [8]$$

where $R = (1 + r)$ and $q = (R - D)/(U-D) = 0.75$.

Note that the formula for the call premium does not depend on the 'real world' probability of an up move for the stock price (and hence is independent of the 'real world' expected return on the stock). In the formula for the call premium the weights applied to the two option payoffs C_u and C_d are q and $1 - q$ (and sum to unity) – there is little intuitive insight at present to be gleaned from the expression for q. However, equation [8] is a rather neat formula that says:

> *The call premium C is a weighted average of the payoffs to the call (C_u, C_d), discounted using the risk-free rate.*

Neither the *actual* probability of a fall or rise in the stock price nor the risk preferences of investors enters into the calculation of the price of the call. Hence all investors, regardless of their differing degrees of risk aversion or their different guesses about the 'real world' probability of a rise or fall in future stock prices, can agree on the fair or correct price for a call option. While the *probability* of a rise or fall in the stock price in the future affects the *current* price of the stock, it does not affect the price of the call – because the call is priced *given* the stock price.

The weight q is known as the **risk-neutral probability** of a rise in the stock price, but this must not be confused with the *actual* probability of a rise in the stock price, which does not affect the option premium. The risk-neutral probability is simply a number that lies between 0 and 1 and is derived under the assumption that portfolio A is risk-free and therefore earns the risk-free rate[2]. In some ways the term risk-neutral probability could be misleading, since it appears to imply that we are assuming that investors are risk neutral, which we are not! An alternative is to call q *an equivalent martingale probability* and the latter is used frequently in the continuous time literature. However, we will stick with the more commonly used term, 'risk-neutral probability'. Using equation [8] we can price the option using the risk-neutral probability q. This method of pricing is known as **risk-neutral valuation (RNV)** and plays a major role in the pricing of all types of options.

Why is q known as a risk-neutral probability? We use a scenario or 'what if' argument here. If in the real world the probability of an up move really equalled q, then what would we expect the stock price to be at $t = 1$? This is given by:

$$ES_1 = q(SU) + (1 - q)SD = 0.75(110) + 0.25(90) = 105 \qquad [9]$$

But the initial stock price is $S = 100$, so if we interpret q as the probability of an up move then this implies that the stock price is expected to grow at 5% ($= (105/100) - 1$). But this is also the value of the risk-free rate, $r = 5\%$. Hence, the no-arbitrage mathematical solution in equation [8] is consistent with the assumption that the stock price grows at a rate equal to the risk-free interest rate. Confused? Yes, it's a tricky concept. However, it turns out to be a brilliant insight, since it allows us to price very complex options by simply assuming i) that the stock price grows at the risk-free rate; ii) using the 'pseudo-probabilities' q to weight the option payoffs; and iii) discounting these option payoffs using the risk-free rate (i.e. *not* the CAPM return on the stock). We then obtain the correct 'real world' price of the option using these three 'tricks', even though in the real world the stock price does not grow at the risk-free rate. As long as we use all three tricks, they compensate for each other and enable us to obtain the fair or true option price, in the real world. What do we mean by 'true'? We mean a value for the option price that does not allow any risk-free arbitrage opportunities. Now that does sound sensible and 'real'.

So, somewhat counter-intuitively, it follows from the above analysis that if we have two otherwise identical call options (i.e. same strike price, expiration date and same stock return volatility), but the underlying stock A for one of the options has an *expected growth rate* of zero, while the other stock B has an expected growth rate of 100% p.a., then the two options will have identical call premia. This is because in each case we can create a risk-free hedge portfolio, which by arbitrage arguments can only earn the risk-free rate. Put another way, the call premium is independent of the 'real world' *expected growth rate* of the underlying stock price (and hence independent of the 'real world' probability, p, of a rise in the stock price).

You can show this quite easily with a simple extension of the numerical example given above[3]. Let $S_u = 115$ (so $U = 1.15$) and $S_d = 95$ (so $D = 0.95$), hence the volatility

---

[2] Note that for q to be interpreted as a probability lying between zero and one, we must have $U > R > D$ (and $D > 0$), and these inequalities also ensure no arbitrage opportunities.

[3] We are going to cheat a little here so we get exactly the result we want. We have to do this because it is only if we consider very small changes in the stock price (or equivalently, a very small time interval) that this result 'works out'. If you want to know more consult Cuthbertson and Nitzsche (2001b).

('spread') of stock price outcomes is the same as in our above example, $S_u - S_d = 20$. But the expected stock price $ES_1 = 105 = [0.5(115) + 0.5(95)]$, so the 'real world' expected return $\mu = (ES_1/S) - 1 = 0.05$ (5%), rather than $\mu = 0$ in our initial example above. The payoff to the call is either $C_u = 15$ or $C_d = 0$, we have $q = (1.05 - 0.95)/(1.15 - 0.95) = \frac{1}{2}$, and hence using equation [8] the call premium $C = (1/2)$ $15/1.05 = 7.1428$. This is the same result for the call premium as when we assumed that the expected stock return was zero[4].

Note, however, that we are *not saying* that the call premium is independent of the *volatility* of the underlying stock (represented in the BOPM by $S_u - S_d$ or equivalently '$U-D$', which enters the definition of q). Expected growth and volatility are very different concepts. After all, we can have a stock for which we think the *expected* growth (return) is zero, but we may feel that the range of possible outcomes (around its expected value) is very large. In our simple one-period model the call premium *does* depend on the *range of possible values* for S – in fact, $(U-D)$ indicates the volatility in the stock price in the BOPM, and as we shall see, volatility plays a key role in the Black–Scholes formula.

To show that the call premium depends positively on the volatility of the stock, go back to our original example. Now assume that the outcomes for the two stock prices are $S_u = 120$ ($U = 1.2$) and $S_d = 80(D = 0.8)$, so the volatility (spread) of stock price outcomes has increased to $S_u - S_d = 40$. But the expected stock price $ES_1 = 100 = [(1/2) 120 + (1/2)80]$ and the 'real world' expected return remains at $\mu = (ES_1/S) - 1 = 0\%$. The payoff to the call is either $C_u = 20$ or $C_d = 0$, we have $q = (1.05 - 0.8)/(1.2 - 0.8) = 0.625$, and hence using equation [8] the call premium $C = (0.625)20/1.05 = 11.905$[5]. The latter is higher than the call premium $C = 7.1428$ when we assumed that stock price volatility was smaller, $S_u - S_d = 20$.

Of course, the above example has two key simplifying assumptions, namely that there are only two possible outcomes for the stock price and that the option matures in one period. However, by extending the number of branches in the binomial 'tree', we can obtain a large number of possible outcomes for stock prices. If we consider each 'branch' as representing a short time period, then conceptually we can see how the BOPM approaches a continuous time formulation, which forms the basis of the famous Black–Scholes approach.

---

[4] You could also get the same answer by forming a risk-free portfolio. The hedge ratio $h = (C_u - C_d)/(S_u - S_d) = 15/20 = 3/4$. The cost of the hedge portfolio at $t = 0$ is $(3/4)S - C = 3/4(100) - C$. The payoff at $t = 1$ is either $(3/4)S_u - C_u = 71.25$ or $(3/4)S_d - C_d = 71.25$. Since the outcome at $t = 1$ is the same whether the stock price is 'up' or 'down', then for no risk-free arbitrage opportunities (see equation [4]) we require $71.25 \{3/4(100) - C\} = 1.05$, which we can solve to give $C = 7.1428$.

[5] Again, we can establish the call premium by forming a risk-free portfolio. The hedge ratio $h = (C_u - C_d)/(S_u - S_d) = 20/40 = 1/2$. The cost of the hedge portfolio at $t = 0$ is $(1/2)S - C = 1/2(100) - C$. The payoff at $t = 1$ is either $(1/2)S_u - C_u = 40$ or $(1/2)S_d - C_d = 40$. Since the outcome at $t = 1$ is the same whether the stock price is 'up' or 'down', then for no risk-free arbitrage opportunities (see equation 4) we require $40/\{1/2 (100) - C\} = 1.05$, which we can solve to give $C = 11.905$.

Pricing a put option

We can price a put option by constructing a similar risk-free portfolio of stocks and the put as described above for the call. But this time the risk-free portfolio B is obtained by going *long* some shares and simultaneously going *long* one put. So, if S falls, the loss on the stock will be offset by the gain on the put, making the portfolio of 'stock+put' risk-free. The pay-off to the put is $\max\{0, K-S_T\}$. If $K = 100$ (as before), then for $S_u = 110$ the put payoff is $P_u = 0$ and for $S_d = 90$ we have $P_d = 10$. Let $h_p = 1/2$ be the number of shares to be *purchased*, and we also hold one long put, then:

Payoff to portfolio B (long $\frac{1}{2}$ share + long 1 put):

| Payoff for price rise | $1/2(110) + 0 = 55$ |
| Payoff for price fall | $1/2(90) + 10 = 55$ |

Equating the return on the risk-free hedge portfolio B to the risk-free rate gives:

$$\frac{\text{Certain Payout at } t = 1}{\text{Cost of Investment at } t = 0} = (1 + \text{risk-free rate}) \qquad [10]$$

$$\frac{55}{(1/2)100 + P} = 1.05$$

Hence $P = 2.38$. The formula for P can be shown to be:

$$P = \frac{1}{R}[qP_u + (1 - q)P_d] = \frac{(0.75)0 + (0.25)10}{1.05} = 2.381 \qquad [11]$$

where again $q = (R-D)/(U-D)$. Equation [11] has the same form as that for the call premium, except that we use the put payoffs $P_u = 0$ and $P_d = 10$. The put premium $P = 2.381$ can be checked using put–call parity.

$$P = C - S + K/(1 + r) = 7.143 - 100 + 100/(1.05) = 2.381 \qquad [12]$$

Two-period BOPM

Extending the BOPM to two periods where $U = 1.1$ and $D = 0.9$ gives the stock price outcomes and the possible values of a long call at expiration, as indicated in Figure 26.2.

Because we know that we can create a risk-free hedge portfolio at any node of the binomial tree, we can calculate C using 'backward induction' from the known values of C_{uu}, C_{ud} and C_{dd} in our binomial formula. Here we are implicitly using RNV. For example, considering the two upper branches in Figure 26.2 we have:

$$C_u = \frac{1}{R}[qC_{uu} + (1 - q)C_{ud}] = \frac{0.75(21) + 0.25(0)}{1.05} = 15 \qquad [13]$$

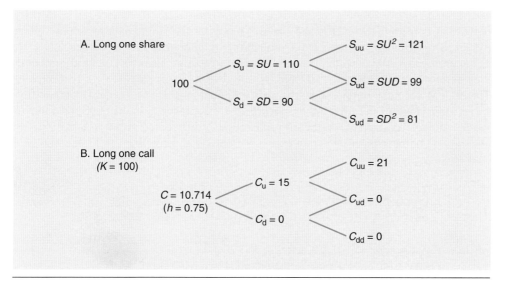

FIGURE 26.2: Two-period BOPM

From the two lower branches we obtain:

$$C_d = \frac{1}{R}[qC_{ud} + (1 - q)C_{dd}] = 0 \qquad [14]$$

We can now solve for C the call premium for this two-period option problem:

$$C = \frac{1}{R}[qC_u + (1 - q)C_d] = \frac{0.75(15) + 0}{1.05} = 10.71423 \qquad [15]$$

Note that the call premium for the option with two periods to maturity has a higher value than our 'identical' option with one period to maturity, where we found $C = 7.143$.

Many periods

Equations [13] and [14] give the values of C_u and C_d in terms of the final payoffs C_{uu}, C_{ud} and C_{dd} and if we substitute in [15] we obtain:

$$C = \frac{1}{R^2}[(1)q^2C_{uu} + 2q(1 - q)C_{ud} + (1)(1 - q)^2C_{dd}] \qquad [16]$$

> The option price is equal to the expected value (using risk-neutral probabilities)
> of the option payoffs at expiry, discounted at the risk-free rate of interest.

The '2' in the above formula represents the two *possible paths* to achieve the stock price SUD (that is, paths UD or DU) and the '1s' represent the single path to achieve either SU^2 or SD^2. We can *interpret q* as the probability of an up move for S and hence $(1 - q)$ as the probability of a down move, in a *risk-neutral world*. Then (risk-neutral) probabilities of out-turns at nodes UU, UD and DD are q^2, $2q(1 - q)$ and $(1 - q)^2$ respectively. The BOPM formula implies that the call premium is the (risk-neutral) probability-weighted average of the final option payoffs at $t = 2$. Hence C is the expected value of the option payoffs (using risk-neutral probabilities), discounted at the risk-free rate. In general, the number of possible paths to any final stock price is given by the binomial coefficients:

$$\binom{n}{k} = \frac{n!}{(n - k)!\,k!} \qquad [17]$$

where $n! = n(n-1)(n-2) \ldots . 1$ and $0! = 1$
n is the number of periods in the binomial tree
k is the number of upward price movements

Lets try it out for $n = 2$:

Number of paths with $k = 2$ ups = $(2!)/(0!\ 2!) = 1$ (i.e. UU)
Number of paths with $k = 1$ ups = $(2!)/(1!\ 1!) = 2$ (i.e. UD and DU)
Number of paths with $k = 0$ ups = $(2!)/(2!\ 0!) = 1$ (i.e. DD)

The formula therefore works for $n = 2$. The reader might like to draw a tree over $n = 3$ periods and verify that the number of possible paths to achieve $k = 1$ up moves is $\binom{n}{k} q^k (1 - q)^{n-k} = (3!)/(2!1!) = 3$ and these are UDD, DUD and DDU. In general, therefore, over n periods the BOPM formula becomes:

$$C = \frac{1}{R^n} \sum_{k=0}^{n} \binom{n}{k} q^k (1 - q)^{n-k} max[SU^k D^{n-k} - K, 0] \qquad [18]$$

The probability of the stock price reaching the value $SU^k D^{n-k}$ after n time periods is $\binom{n}{k} q^k (1 - q)^{n-k}$. Note that the term in square brackets in [18] is just another way of writing the payoff at the nodes. For example, for $n = 2$ these are:

$$C_{uu} = max[0, SU^2 - K] \quad C_{ud} = max[0, SUD - K] \quad C_{dd} = max[0, SD^2 - K] \quad [19]$$

The hedge ratios in the BOPM can be calculated at each node and this is done for $n = 10$ time periods in the Excel file provided.

The price of a put option is also given by equation [18], but with the term max[. . .] replaced by the sequence of put-option payoffs, namely max[0, $K - SU^k D^{n-k}$]. Equation [18] indicates that the price of an option depends on the strike price K, the underlying asset price S, the maturity n, the risk-free rate r and the asset's volatility (U, D), but it does not depend on the risk preferences of individuals or the actual ('real world') probability of a price increase (or decrease).

Where do U and D come from?

At t = 0, r, K and S are known. Above we have shown that if we know U and D, we can price an option by invoking RNV, which is embodied in the BOPM formula. However, since different stocks have different volatilities (heuristically represented by U and D), then different stocks will have different values of U and D and hence different option premia. The size of U and D must be linked to the stock's *actual* measured volatility. It can be shown that one method of achieving this is to set:

$$U = e^{\sigma\sqrt{\Delta t}} \quad \text{and} \quad D = e^{-\sigma\sqrt{\Delta t}} \qquad\qquad \text{[20a,b]}$$

where $\sigma =$ the observed *annual* standard deviation of the (continuously compounded) stock return, T is the time to expiration in years (or fraction of a year), n is the number of steps chosen for the binomial tree and the small time interval is $\Delta t = T/n$.

We divide the T years (or fraction of a year) into n steps, each of which represents a small time period $\Delta t = T/n$. So if the expiry date of the option is in $T = \frac{1}{4}$ year and we decide to have a binomial tree with n = 30 steps, $\Delta t = 0.008333$ of 1 year. So each step in the binomial tree represents about three days. Note that the 'spread' of the lattice (in percentage terms) at any two adjacent points is $\ln(SU) - \ln(SD) = 2\sigma\sqrt{\Delta t}$, so the proportionate gap between SU and SD does depend directly on the 'real world' value of σ, the standard deviation of the stock return. This particular choice for U and D imposes symmetry – that is, U = 1/D – but it can be shown that this is not restrictive if our aim is to construct a risk-neutral lattice. Note also that when U = 1/D then for example the nodes SUD and SDU both equal S, and hence this particular choice of risk-neutral lattice not only recombines but is symmetric. Hence if S (at *t* = 0) is 100, it will also be 100 in the middle node at *t* = 2. Finally, note that U and D do *not* depend on the expected return on the stock and hence neither does the option premium. This is RNV again.

26.3 BLACK–SCHOLES MODEL

The BOPM is a numerical procedure for determining the price of an option. We now turn to an explicit equation to determine the option price. In the 1960s, options were being traded in the US over-the-counter, but rather bizarrely no one knew how to price them correctly. It was easy to work out that for a call option, say, the premium should be higher: the lower the strike price, the longer the time to maturity, the higher the interest cost and the greater the volatility of the underlying stock. But how could all of these be combined to give an explicit equation that could be used quickly to give the correct or fair price for the option? The BOPM had not been invented and the first pricing equation for options was the work of Black, Scholes and Merton. A brief history of the route to the Black–Scholes equation is given in Case Study 26.1.

CASE STUDY 26.1   NOBLE PURSUITS

It was the combined work of Fischer Black, Myron Scholes and Robert Merton that finally solved the option-pricing problem in the early 1970s. Black (after his degree in Physics) initially worked on the pricing of warrants (i.e. options on a company's stocks, issued by the company itself), since these (unlike options) were at this time traded in liquid markets on US exchanges.

Scholes was also working on options pricing in the late 1960s at the Sloan School of Management (at MIT), when he met Black and they began working together. Meanwhile, a young applied mathematician, Robert Merton, joined MIT as a research assistant to Paul Samuelson in the economics faculty. Samuelson, based on his own earlier work, encouraged Merton to explore the theory of warrant pricing.

At this time, Merton developed the use of continuous time finance and Brownian motion. These mathematical ideas were to provide the basis for the Black–Scholes formula.

Merton, Black and Scholes exchanged ideas over several years at MIT. Their path to success might be described as a 'random walk with positive drift'. There were many dead ends encountered, but ultimately the problem was solved.

In 1970, Black and Scholes completed their options-pricing paper. They acknowledged Merton's suggestion of combining the option and the underlying asset to yield a risk-free portfolio. Black and Scholes' paper was initially rejected by the *Journal of Political Economy* (JPE), a publication of the economics faculty of the University of Chicago, because it was too specialised.

The paper was then rejected by Harvard's *Review of Economics and Statistics*, but finally, with the support of Eugene Fama and Merton Miller, it was accepted by the JPE and published in May/June 1973 under the title 'The Pricing of Options and Corporate Liabilities'. Merton, who had collaborated with Black and Scholes, also produced a paper on options pricing in the *Bell Journal* of Spring 1973.

Scholes and Merton both received the Nobel Prize for their work, but unfortunately Fischer Black died before the prize was awarded (it cannot be awarded posthumously). Some of the above academics have also 'put their money where their mind is' and used continuous-time mathematics to try to beat the market, using options to leverage their bets. This was often successful. But not always, as was the case with Long Term Capital Management LTCM, a hedge fund in which both Scholes and Merton were involved, but which effectively went bust in 1998.

Coincidentally, the Chicago Board Options Exchange (CBOE) began trading options (initially in the large smoking room of the Chicago Board of Trade) in April 1973 and the 'new' Black–Scholes formula was soon in use by traders (for more details of this story, see the excellent book by Bernstein 1995). The ivory towers of academia produced something of real practical value (as well as aesthetically pleasing). Whether it be 'Black Holes' or 'Black–Scholes', the power of mathematics to solve problems is impressive, not least in modern finance.

The Black–Scholes (1973) option-price formula applies to European options and it is derived using continuous-time finance and stochastic calculus, which are beyond the scope of this book. But we can still use the resulting Black–Scholes equation to price calls and puts. The assumptions of the Black–Scholes model are:

- All risk-free arbitrage opportunities are eliminated.
- No transaction costs or taxes.
- Investors can borrow and lend unlimited amounts at the risk-free interest rate.
- Stock prices are random, like a coin flip – if your first flip gives 'heads' this does not help you to predict whether the next flip will give you a head or a tail. The technical term for the random stock price process is a 'geometric Brownian motion', which is itself a 'random walk' over a very small time interval.
- Stock prices are continuous and do not experience sudden extreme jumps – such as after the announcement of a takeover or other major firm-specific events (e.g. bankruptcy).
- The stock pays no dividends. The interest rate and volatility of the stock return are constant over the life of the option (or known functions of time – that is, perfectly predictable).

Call option

To work out the exact functional form for the Black–Scholes equation is rather difficult and at first sight the formula certainly looks rather formidable – but that need not worry us, as in practice options premia are calculated on a computer. Here's the formula for the call premium:

$$C = SN(d_1) - N(d_2) \text{ PV} = SN(d_1) - N(d_2) Ke^{-rT} \tag{21}$$

where $$d_1 = \frac{\ln(S/K) + (r + \sigma^2/2)T}{\sigma\sqrt{T}}$$

$$d_2 = d_1 - \sigma\sqrt{T} = \frac{\ln(S/K) + (r - \sigma^2/2)T}{\sigma\sqrt{T}}$$

C = price of call option (call premium)

r = risk-free rate of interest for horizon T (continuously compounded)

S = current stock price

T = time to expiry/maturity (as proportion of a year)

PV = present value of the strike price (= Ke^{-rT})

σ = annual standard deviation of the (continuously compounded) return on the stock

ln = natural logarithm of a variable

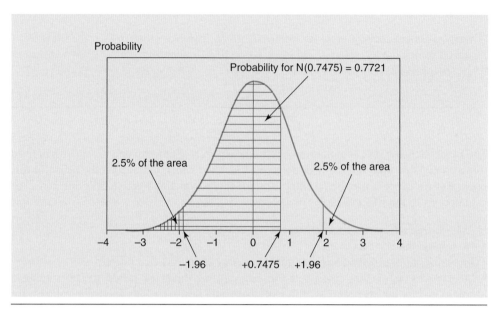

FIGURE 26.3: Standard normal distribution ~N(0,1)

The term e^{-rT} is the exponential function (where $e^1 = 2.718$, so for example $e^{-1} = 1/2.718 = 0.3678$, $e^2 = 2.718 \times 2.718 = 7.389$, etc. You can use the 'exp' function on a calculator, or in Excel.)

You can see that our earlier discussion about the fact that the call premium would depend on the current stock price relative to the strike price (S/K) and the volatility over the life of the option ($\sigma\sqrt{T}$ or $\sigma^2 T$) are clearly visible in the formula. The Black–Scholes 'curve' shows the relationship between the call premium and the stock price: knowing the stock price we can read off the correct price for the call (Figure 26.3). Note that the only input to the Black–Scholes formula that is not known precisely is the volatility of the stock, σ, which has to be estimated before we can calculate the call premium. If two traders have different forecasts for the volatility of the stock (over the life of the option), then even if they both use the Black–Scholes formula they will quote different options prices.

Traders can apply statistical models to forecast volatility[6]. However, they mainly use an estimate of implied volatility from similar options (i.e. traded options with the same underlying

---

[6] The simplest forecast of volatility is to use the sample standard deviation $\hat{\sigma} = \sqrt{\sum_{t=1}^{n}(R_{cc,t} - \bar{R}_{cc})^2/(n-1)}$ where $R_{cc,t} = \ln(P_t/P_{t-1})$ is the continuously compounded return on the stock. When pricing options, daily (continuously compounded) returns are usually used and the annual volatility is then taken to be $\sqrt{252}$ times the estimate of daily volatility. Statistical models used to forecast volatility include so-called ARCH and GARCH models, pioneered by Robert Engle (who won the Nobel prize in economics), and so-called stochastic volatility models both of which assume tomorrow's volatility is related to past volatility – hence the term 'autoregressive conditional heteroscedasticity', ARCH (where 'heteroscedasticity' is the econometricians term for volatility).

stock as the option they wish to price, but with a slightly different strike price). Implied volatility is discussed further below.

What is interesting yet very counterintuitive is that the formula does not contain the expected rate of return on the stock. This means that two investors who have totally different views about the expected stock return (e.g. one thinks the stock price will grow at 5% p.a. and the other that it will grow at 20% p.a.) but agree about its future volatility, σ will still agree on the price for the option. How can this be? It's not easy to explain this counterintuitive result fully, but as we have seen above it is due to the possibility of risk-free arbitrage. So the risk-free rate 'replaces' the expected stock return in the Black–Scholes formula and the option premium turns out to be independent of the expected growth rate of the stock price.

The term $N(d_1)$ is the only new symbol. In fact, $N(d_1)$ is the *cumulative* probability distribution function for a standard normal variable. It gives the probability that a variable with a standard normal distribution $N(0,1)$ will have a value less than d_1. In fact, when $d_1 = -1.96$ then $N(d_1) = 0.025$, which means that there is 2.5% of the total area of the normal curve to the left of the point -1.95. The values of $N(d_1)$ can be found in standard statistical tables or you can use the Excel function 'NORMSDIST(–1.95)', which will 'return' a value of 0.025. So at the end of the day, $N(d_1)$ is just a 'number' (which lies between 0 and $+1$).

Here are some other values of $N(d_1)$ that you might remember from statistics classes:

$$N(-1.65) = 0.05, \ N(0) = 0.5, \ N(+1.65) = 0.95, \ N(+\infty) = 1$$

For negative values of d_1 we can proceed as follows. We know for example that $N(+1.96) = 0.975$ (from tables or Excel). Because the normal distribution is symmetric, $N(-d_1) = 1 - N(d_1)$ and therefore $N(-1.96) = 0.025$. In Table 26.2 we price a call option by hand (rather than using Excel).

Put option

The price, P, of a European put using the Black–Scholes formula is:

$$P = Ke^{-rT} N(-d_2) - S \cdot N(-d_1) \qquad [22]$$

$d_1 = 0.7457$ $\qquad\qquad$ $d_2 = 0.6042$

$N(-d_1) = 1 - N(d_1) = 1 - 0.7721 = 0.2279$

$N(-d_2) = 1 - N(d_2) = 1 - 0.7271 = 0.2729$

Hence: $\quad P = 40.9029 \ (0.2729) - 45(0.2279) = \mathbf{0.9069}$

TABLE 26.2: Pricing a call option

Data	$S = \$45$	$K = \$43$
	$r = 0.1 \ (= 10\% \text{ p.a.})$	$\sigma = 0.2 \ (20\% \text{ p.a.})$
	$T = 0.5 \ (6 \text{ months to maturity})$	

Calculating the Call Premium, C

Present value of excise price: $PV = e^{-rT} = 43 \ e^{-(0.1).(0.5)} = 40.9029$

$$d_1 = \frac{\ln(45/40.9029) + (0.1 + (0.2)^2/2)0.5}{0.2\sqrt{0.5}} = 0.7457$$

$$d_2 = 0.7457 - 0.2(0.5)^{1/2} = 0.6043$$

From tables of the cumulative normal distribution (interpolated) or using Excel function NORMSDIST(0.7457) etc.:

$$N(d_1 = 0.7457) = 0.7721 \qquad\qquad N(d_2 = 0.6042) = 0.7271$$

Hence $C = SN(d_1) - N(d_2) \ PV = 45 \ (0.7721) - 0.7271 \ (40.9029) = \textbf{\$5.00}$

We can check the put premium using put–call parity:

$$P = C + Ke^{-rT} - S = 5 + 43e^{-0.10(0.5)} - 45 = 0.90$$

In practice, of course, traders have all of these calculations programmed using in-house software and only the results appear on trading screens. The calculations can be done in Excel by putting the formula into a cell or using Visual Basic to programme the formula. There are many other pieces of software that can be used, including GAUSS, C++, MATLAB and MATHEMATICA.

> We have moved a long way from the simple payoff diagrams for calls and puts. We now know what causes option prices to change second by second – this is important if you are pricing the option for a large investment bank or speculating over a short horizon.

We can also use Excel to graph the relationship between the underlying stock price S and the call premium C. First, we fix the values of K, r, T (time to maturity) and σ (= volatility). Then we simply create a column of values for S in Excel and use the above formula to obtain the corresponding values of C, the call premium. This is done in Excel on the web site. It is interactive, so you can change the strike price, time to maturity and so on of the option.

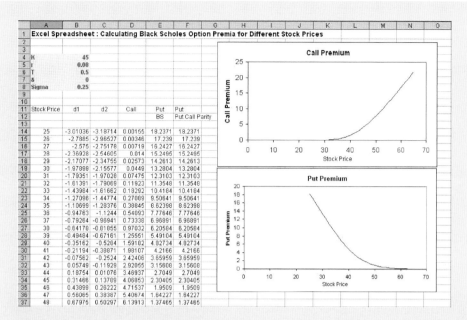

	A	B	C	D	E	F	G	H	I	J	K	L	M	N	O
1	Excel Spreadsheet : Calculating Black Scholes Option Premia for Different Stock Prices														
2															
3															
4	K	45													
5	r	0.08													
6	T	0.5													
7	δ	0													
8	Sigma	0.25													
9															
10															
11	Stock Price	d1	d2	Call	Put BS	Put Put Call Parity									
12															
13															
14	25	-3.01036	-3.18714	0.00155	18.2371	18.2371									
15	26	-2.7885	-2.96527	0.00346	17.239	17.239									
16	27	-2.575	-2.75178	0.00719	16.2427	16.2427									
17	28	-2.36928	-2.54605	0.014	15.2495	15.2495									
18	29	-2.17077	-2.34755	0.02573	14.2613	14.2613									
19	30	-1.97899	-2.15577	0.0449	13.2804	13.2804									
20	31	-1.79351	-1.97028	0.07475	12.3103	12.3103									
21	32	-1.61391	-1.79069	0.11923	11.3548	11.3548									
22	33	-1.43984	-1.61662	0.18292	10.4184	10.4184									
23	34	-1.27096	-1.44774	0.27089	9.50641	9.50641									
24	35	-1.10699	-1.28376	0.38845	8.62398	8.62398									
25	36	-0.94763	-1.1244	0.54093	7.77646	7.77646									
26	37	-0.79264	-0.96941	0.73338	6.96891	6.96891									
27	38	-0.64178	-0.81855	0.97032	6.20584	6.20584									
28	39	-0.49484	-0.67161	1.25551	5.49104	5.49104									
29	40	-0.35162	-0.5284	1.59182	4.82734	4.82734									
30	41	-0.21194	-0.38871	1.98107	4.2166	4.2166									
31	42	-0.07562	-0.2524	2.42406	3.65959	3.65959									
32	43	0.05749	-0.11929	2.92055	3.15608	3.15608									
33	44	0.18754	0.01076	3.46937	2.7049	2.7049									
34	45	0.31466	0.13789	4.06853	2.30405	2.30405									
35	46	0.43899	0.26222	4.71537	1.9509	1.9509									
36	47	0.56065	0.38387	5.40674	1.64227	1.64227									
37	48	0.67975	0.50297	6.13913	1.37465	1.37465									

This spreadsheet uses the Black–Scholes formula to calculate call and put premia for different stock prices. The option premia are graphed against the stock price. Column F recalculates the put premium using the put–call parity relationship.

	A	B	C	D	E	F	G	H
1	Excel Spreadsheet : Calculating the Black Scholes Option Premia							
2								
3	Put-call parity is used here to calculate the **Put premium**.							
4								
5	Only change the values in the yellow shaded area.							
6								
7	S			165				
8	K			158				
9	r			0.05				
10	T			0.02				
11	δ			0				
12	Sigma			0.3				
13								
14								
15		B-S Call Premium		7.680707				
16								
17		B-S Put Premium		0.522786				
18								
19								
20	Auxillary inputs to calculate B-S premia							
21								
22			d1	d2	N -"dash"			
23					(d1)			
24			1.066563	1.024137	0.225888			
25								

This spreadsheet calculates Black–Scholes call and put premia. The inputs are the stock price (S), the strike price (K), interest rate (r), time to maturity (T), dividend rate (d) and volatility (σ).

We are now in a position to answer the question about whether stocks are less risky if you hold them for a long period rather than for a short period. This is discussed in Case Study 26.2.

CASE STUDY 26.2   STOCK MARKETS: PLAY
                       THE LONG GAME?

It is often asserted that stocks are safer in the long run than in the short run – so a young person should hold lots of her wealth in stocks and only a little in a risk-free asset (or government bond) and vice versa for a person nearing retirement. Is this true? Note that this issue concerns a decision made today, looking ahead several periods, so the problem does not really fall within the province of mean-variance portfolio theory, which usually deals with portfolio allocation over a single period.

It is true that if you invest $1m in the stock market today then the *probability of a loss* (i.e. ending up with less than $1m) becomes smaller, the further ahead is the date at which you want to 'cash in your chips'. This is usually referred to as the 'shortfall probability'. A more realistic scenario is to ask what is the probability of ending up with an amount that is less than you would get if you invested in the risk-free asset. For example, suppose the risk-free rate is 5% p.a., the mean return on the stock market is 15% p.a. (so the excess return is 10%), with a standard deviation of 20%, then the Sharpe ratio is 0.5 (= (15 − 5)/20), so these are reasonable 'ball-park' figures[7]. The probability of a shortfall relative to the risk-free investment is the probability that the *excess* return is less than zero. Over a one-year horizon, stocks underperform the risk-free investment if the excess return is more than 0.5 = 10/20 standard deviations *below* its mean. In statistical language this occurs if the standard normal variable $z < -\mu/\sigma = -0.5$, so the shortfall probability is 30.8%. Over 20 years the mean excess return is $\mu \cdot T = 200\%$ and the standard deviation is $\sigma\sqrt{T} = 89.44\%$. So the shortfall probability is the probability that $z < -200/89.44 = -2.236$, which is 1.27%.

This is comforting, but it is not really very comforting, since this low probability tells you nothing about *how much* you would lose, if you did have a loss at the end of your investment horizon. For example, if the stock price can have only two outcomes, +20% and −20%, then at the end of one year the *maximum* you can lose is 20% of your initial investment. After two years the maximum you can lose is 36% (i.e. final wealth W_2 = initial wealth $W_0 \times 0.8 \times 0.8$, which is 64% of initial wealth). But after 20 years, your final wealth could be as low as $W_{20} = W_0(0.8)^{20} = W_0(0.0115)$, so over 99% of your wealth could disappear.

---

[7] We are going to assume continuously compounded returns throughout this example, which allows us to use the result that if the annual mean return and standard deviation are μ and σ, then the mean return over T years is $\mu \cdot T$ and the standard deviation is $\sigma\sqrt{T}$. We will also assume that returns are normally (identically, independently) distributed, the standard deviation of the risk-free rate is zero and it is uncorrelated with the stock return – these are not unreasonable assumptions for this illustrative example.

You are presumably concerned about the likelihood of a loss *and* the severity of the loss, should it occur. How can we get a handle on both? Well, a European put option on a stock (index) protects your portfolio of stocks from downside risk and therefore deals with the severity of a loss. It insures the value of your stocks at a level equal to the strike price in the put. The strike price you might choose could be set equal to your $1m investment, compounded at the risk-free rate until the end of your investment horizon; that is, a put with a strike price $K = Se^{rT} = (\$1m)e^{rT}$. Then your wealth at retirement will end up at least as high as if you had invested your money in the risk-free asset. You have also set the likelihood of a loss (relative to investing your $1m at the risk-free rate) at zero. The put premium you pay today is the cost of the insurance for your stock portfolio. Indeed for each $100 held in stocks the put will cost you today {$24.8, $34.5, $41.43, $61.35, $84.27} for horizons of {10, 20, 30, 75, 200} years.

If you observe the market price of index puts, you will see that their price increases with the time to maturity of the put[8].

On the web site you will find a spreadsheet that demonstrates the increase in put premia as the time to maturity increases.

The put costs you quite a large proportion of your initial investment of $100 and the premium increases with the horizon. As the horizon gets very long, the put premium costs you nearly as much as your initial wealth held in stocks. This is equivalent to you selling off your stocks and investing nearly all your $100 in the T-year risk-free asset. A put with a very long life and a strike price that equals Se^{rT} is equivalent to investing in the risk-free bond itself.

So now you have your answer. Market participants think that stocks are more risky the longer the investment horizon, because today you have to pay a larger put premium the longer the maturity date of the put. That is, you pay a bigger insurance premium the longer the period over which you want to insure your stocks.

This still does not answer the question of how your holdings of risky stocks (relative to holding risk-free assets or government bonds) *should vary* over your life. It turns out that this is by no means an easy question to answer. But if income from your job is fairly predictable (i.e. uncorrelated with stock returns), it is probably a reasonable idea to hold a lot in stocks when you are young and more in the risk-free asset when your 'terminal date' gets closer. On the other hand, if your income is highly variable and positively correlated with stock returns (i.e. with the general state of the economy), you might do the opposite. These ideas are discussed further in Cuthbertson and

---

[8] If you set the strike price $K = Se^{rT}$ in the Black–Scholes formula for a put then you get $d_1 = \sigma\sqrt{T}/2$, $d_2 = -\sigma\sqrt{T}/2$ and $P/S = N(d_1) - N(d_2)$. We take $\sigma = 0.2$ (20% p.a.). It can then be shown that P/S increases as T increases. Also, P/S is independent of the risk-free rate. It is also the case that using put-call parity with $K = Se^{rT}$, gives $P = C$, so the put costs the same as a call. So buying the put, given that you already have the stocks, is equivalent to having the payoff from a European call.

Nitzsche (2004), but there are no absolute clear-cut answers other than the usual one: at any point in your life cycle diversify as much as possible. If you want to buy insurance at some point, then do so. By buying a put you place a floor on your level of final wealth, but you can benefit from any upside in the stock market, since if the market rises you can throw away your put and simply sell your stocks at their high price on the NYSE.

It might be advisable to buy a put when you are nearing retirement, so that you secure a floor price for you stocks but can also benefit from any upside in the stock market.

Delta hedging

In deriving their formula, Black, Scholes and Merton proceed in exactly the same way as in the BOPM. They set up a risk-free portfolio consisting of a position in the option and a position in the underlying stock, so that any gain or loss from the stock is exactly offset by that on the option (over a short period of time) – this is known as *delta hedging*. As with the BOPM, the hedge ratio is given by the change in the option premium divided by the change in the stock price. This is known as the **option's delta** and is denoted Δ_c (for a call). It can be shown that the options delta for a call is $\Delta_c = N(d_1)$, which can be calculated from the Black–Scholes formula, for example:

$$\Delta_c = \frac{\textit{Change in option's price}}{\textit{Change in stock price}} = +0.4$$

The delta of a call is the slope of the Black–Scholes curve (at a particular stock price) – see Figure 26.4.

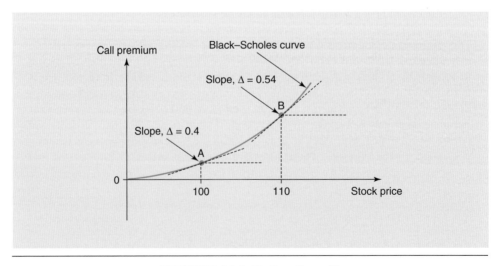

FIGURE 26.4: Delta of a call

For simplicity, suppose that each call is written on one share (in practice the call is written on 100 shares) and the call option's delta is $\Delta_c = 0.4$. The option's delta of 0.4 simply means that when the stock price changes by $1 the call price changes by $0.4 (in the same direction). Suppose that you work for a large investment bank on the options desk and you have just sold 100 call options to a customer; that is, you have written 100 calls. If you do nothing you are subject to market risk, since if the stock price rises, so will the call premium, and if you want to close out your position by buying back the options you will make a loss. To hedge your option position you should:

> Buy 40 shares, for every 100 calls you have sold (written).

If the share price rises by $1, the call premium rises by $0.4, so the investor holding the long call gains $0.4 but the options trader has a loss of $0.4. The options trader has a loss of $40 (= $0.4 × 100 calls) on the 100 *written* calls, but this is offset by the $40 gain on her long position is stocks (= 40 shares × $1). The options trader could close out her short options position by purchasing 100 calls at the new higher price, losing $40, which is just offset by the gain of $40 when she closes out her stock position – she is hedged. There is no loss on portfolio A consisting of $\Delta_c = 0.4$ shares for each single call you have written. Portfolio A is **delta neutral.**

To maintain a delta-neutral position requires continuous *rebalancing*, since Δ_c changes as the stock price changes. At a stock price of $100, $\Delta_c = 0.4$ (say). But given the curvature of the Black–Scholes curve, if the stock price on day 2 is $110, the slope of the curve is higher and could be $\Delta_c = 0.5$ (Figure 26.4). Hence, for a delta-neutral position to be maintained, an extra 0.1 shares (= $0.5 - 0.4$) would have to be purchased for each option trader initially sold. Since the options trader initially sold 100 calls, she will have to purchase an additional $0.1 \times 100 = 10$ stocks (making a total of 50 stocks held), in order to maintain her delta-hedged position over the next day. This is known as *dynamic hedging.*

Delta hedging only provides a hedge against small changes in the stock price and not against large changes, since the option's delta only gives an approximation to the 'true' price change of the call represented by the Black–Scholes curve (Figure 26.4). Also the option's delta does not take account of changes in the call price due to changes in the volatility of the stock return, the risk-free rate or the time to expiration of the option, which all affect the price of the call via the Black–Scholes formula. To hedge your written calls against such changes requires additional hedging strategies (see Cuthbertson and Nitzsche, 2001b).

Mispriced options and delta hedging

Delta hedging can be used to create a risk-free portfolio so that you can profit from mispriced options. Suppose you think that a European call option is currently overpriced at $C = \$10$, because you think the market is inputting a figure for volatility in the Black–Scholes formula that is too high. Taking a naked position and writing (selling), say,

100 options for $10 will result in a profit if the option price falls towards its true (fair) value, as the market recognises that it has used too high a figure for volatility. You will then be able to close out your options position, by buying it back at its new lower price of, say, $9.8. You are *trading volatility*. However, this is a highly risky strategy, since the mispriced option could increase in price if the stock price increases, before the market corrects its forecasts for volatility.

Suppose that the options delta is 0.4. Then you can hedge your options position against changes in the stock price by buying 0.4 shares for every option you have sold – so you buy 40 shares (= 0.4×100). If stock prices rise by $1 you gain $40 on the 40 shares, but the call premium increases by $0.4 and you make a loss of $40 (= 0.40×100 options) on your 100 written options. You are hedged against changes in the stock price and can wait until the call premium falls *due to the market revising downwards its forecast for volatility* – the cause, in your opinion, of why the option was mispriced at the outset. Notice that you only make money if your volatility forecast (which is different from the market's) is correct and the market recognises this fact – you do not make any money from changes in the stock price that result in changes in the call premium, because you have delta hedged this risk.

In practice, there are some risks and costs attached to the above strategy (and to delta hedging):

• When rebalancing the hedged portfolio, you incur transactions costs (e.g. bid–ask spreads).
• Delta hedging only gives a perfect hedge if changes in the stock price are small.

Implied volatility

How can you determine the market's view of the future volatility of stock returns. This can be obtained from observed options prices by inverting the Black–Scholes equation. Let's see how this is done. Data on all the variables $z = \{S, K, r, T\}$ are available, together with the quoted call premium, C. The Black–Scholes equation says that the price is given by an equation of the form $C = f(z, \sigma)$. The only unknown in this equation is the volatility σ, so we invert the Black–Scholes equation $C = f(z, \sigma)$ to obtain the implied volatility σ. The implied volatility is the market's view of what it thinks the volatility of the stock return will be over the life of the option.

In principle, what we do is to choose alternative trial values for σ and calculate the 'theoretical' price, $\hat{C}$, using the Black–Scholes equation. When we find a trial value for σ for which the Black–Scholes theoretical price $\hat{C}$ equals the *quoted market price C*, this value for σ is the market's view of future volatility and is known as **implied volatility**. This is done in Table 26.3 by trial and error and the implied volatility is found to be 0.288 (28.8% p.a.).

Clearly, a more efficient way of proceeding would be to let a computer program choose alternative values for the implied volatility σ to minimise $(\hat{C} - C)^2$. An example of an iterative search procedure to calculate implied volatility can be found in the Excel spreadsheet on the web site, which uses the optimisation function SOLVER.

TABLE 26.3: Implied volatility

S	164
K	165
R	0.0521
T (years)	0.0959
Quoted call premium	5.748

Implied volatility is 0.288(28.8%)

Trial values for sigma, σ	d_1	d_2	N 'dash' (d_1)	Call premium using Black–Scholes
0.282	0.031267	−0.05606	0.398747	5.626545
0.283	0.031466	−0.05617	0.398745	5.646796
0.284	0.031664	−0.05628	0.398742	5.667047
0.285	0.031862	−0.0564	0.39874	5.687298
0.286	0.03206	−0.05651	0.398737	5.707549
0.287	0.032257	−0.05662	0.398735	5.727799
0.288	0.032454	−0.05673	0.398732	**5.74805**
0.289	0.032651	−0.05685	0.39873	5.7683

In the above example, if you thought that the true volatility of the underlying stock was less than the implied volatility of 28.8% p.a., then *you believe* that the true call premium is less than the Black–Scholes quoted price of $5.7. You think that the option is overpriced at $5.7. You would therefore expect the market's view of volatility to fall in the future (to its true value) and hence the quoted call premium also to fall. You could trade volatility by selling the overpriced call today (and delta hedging your position, as described above). If your forecast of volatility is correct and the market recognises this in the future, then you will be able to close out your options position by buying back the option at a lower price, hence making a profit[9].

You can see how the market's view of volatility has changed over time using the implied volatility of the S&P 500 (Figure 26.5); available on the CBOE web site.

---

[9] You can also speculate on changes in volatility using futures contracts. In March 2004 the CBOE futures exchange introduced a futures contract on the 30-day implied volatility of the S&P500 – the ticker symbol of the contract is VIX ('the vix'). The payoff to the futures depends on the implied volatility at the expiration of the contract. If you thought that the volatility of the S&P500 was going to increase in the future, then today you would go long the VIX.

EXCEL ⊗

	A	B	C	D	E	F	G	H	I
1	Excel Spreasheet : Calculating Implied Volatility Using Solver								
2									
3	Only change the values in the yellow shaded area.								
4									
5	S		164		Stock Price				
6	K		165		Strike Price				
7	r		0.0521		Interest rates				
8	T		0.0959		Time to Expiry				
9	δ		0		Dividend rate				
10									
11	Actual Call Premum		5.75		Call premium				
12									
13									
14	B-S Call Premium		5.74998						
15									
16	Cell to be minimised by SOLVER(Actual premium - B-S Premium)^2 =							4.2E-10	
17									
18									
19	Start value (and final value) for Sigma for use in SOLVER =						0.2881		
20									
21									
22	Auxiliary inputs to calculate B-S premier								
23									
24		d1	d2	N -"dash"					
25				(d1)					
26		0.03247	-0.05674	0.39873					
27									
28									

Implied volatility is the volatility estimate that when used in the Black–Scholes formula gives a 'fair price' for the option, equal to the observed (quoted) option price. To obtain implied volatility we set the Black–Scholes formula (which gives the 'theoretical' or fair price) equal to the observed option price (e.g. call premium) and then 'search' across various values for volatility, until the resulting Black–Scholes fair price equals the observed option price. This is done by minimising the squared difference between the Black–Scholes fair price and the quoted price. We use the Excel optimiser Solver, where the target cell is H16 and is found by changing cell G19. The implied volatility for this call option is 28.8% p.a.

26.4 FROM THE BOPM TO BLACK–SCHOLES

We can give some intuitive feel to the Black–Scholes option-pricing formula by considering the BOPM approach, where we increase the number of steps n in the binomial tree. As we increase the number of steps n, then we are also shortening the time interval between each node in the binomial tree $\Delta t = T/n$, so the BOPM becomes more like the Black–Scholes approach, which uses continuous-time mathematics. Suppose that we have:

$$S = 99 \qquad K = 100 \qquad r_c = 0.10 \qquad \sigma = 0.20 \qquad T = 0.3 \text{ (years)}$$

Then the Black–Scholes formula can be used to give the call premium as $C^{BS} = 5.33$. To translate these inputs into the BOPM, we divide the time to expiration into shorter time

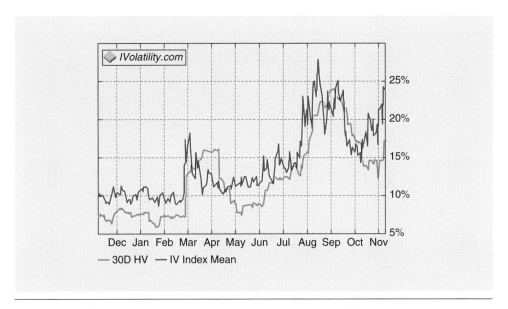

FIGURE 26.5: Implied volatility of the S&P 500 stock index

Source: Reproduced by permission of IVolatility.com

periods $\Delta t = T/n$, where n is the number of steps chosen for the binomial tree, and calculate U and D as follows:

$$U = e^{\sigma\sqrt{\Delta t}} \quad \text{and} \quad D = e^{-\sigma\sqrt{\Delta t}} \qquad [23a,b]$$

We also convert the continuously compounded rate $r_c = 0.10$ used in the Black–Scholes formula into a discrete *periodic* rate r_p to match the time period $\Delta t = T/n$ of our analysis, for the BOPM:

$$R = (1 + r_p) = e^{r_c \cdot \Delta t} \qquad [24]$$

For n = 1:

$$\Delta t = T/n = 0.3/1 = 0.3 \qquad R = (1 + r_p) = e^{r_c \cdot \Delta t} = 1.0304$$

$$U = e^{0.2\sqrt{0.3}} = 1.0618 \qquad D = e^{-0.2\sqrt{0.3}} = 0.9418$$

The call premium for n = 1 is then:

$$C^{(1)} = \frac{qC_u + (1 - q)C_d}{R} = 6.21 \qquad [25]$$

where $q = (R - D)/(U - D)$, $C_u = \max[SU - K, 0]$, $C_d = \max[SD - K, 0]$.

Thus for $n = 1$ the BOPM gives $C^{(1)} = 6.21$, which is not particularly close to the Black–Scholes value of $C^{BS} = 5.33$. However, as we increase n from 1 to 2, 3, . . . , etc., we

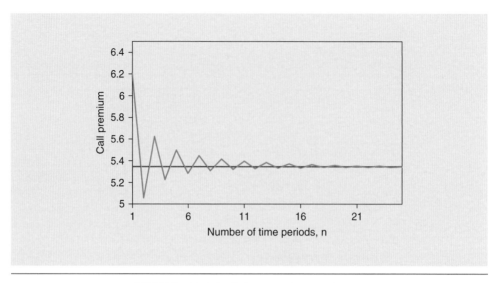

FIGURE 26.6: Call premium, BOPM

see that the BOPM call price for about $n = 30$ is $C^{(30)} = 5.345$ and approaches the Black–Scholes value of $C^{BS} = 5.33$ (and then 'bounces around' this value); see Figure 26.6. In general, for *plain vanilla* options (but not necessarily for complex exotic options), choosing $n = 30$ in the BOPM gives reasonably accurate results.

The Excel file to price options using the BOPM can be found on the web site.

Of course, one of the obvious problems with a numerical method like the BOPM is that it may not converge (at all), it may 'bounce around' the true value for the option premium. This is the price you pay for the flexibility of the binomial approach. The reason the option premium in the BOPM approaches that given by the Black–Scholes formula is that as the number of steps in the binomial tree gets larger (i.e. $n \rightarrow \infty$), the time between each node in the tree is smaller (i.e. $\Delta t = T/n \rightarrow 0$). The 'up–down' lattice of the BOPM then has many possible nodes and there are many possible paths the stock price could take over a small interval of time (e.g. for just three nodes you can have eight possible paths, UUU, UUD, UDD etc.; see below). Hence the lattice of the BOPM begins to look like the random behaviour of the stock price that we see in real data, for example in a graph of *daily* stock prices. This is exactly the random stock price behaviour that Black, Scholes and Merton assumed when deriving their Black–Scholes equation. It is known as a *geometric Brownian motion* and is similar to a random walk for the stock price. (This is explored more in Appendix 26.1.)

Also notice that when the number of nodes in the binomial tree increases, the possible outcomes for stock prices in the final period (T) begin to look more like a 'normal curve'. For example, for only $n = 3$ nodes, a probability of $1/2$ for an 'up' move and U = 1.1, D = 0.9, the outcomes and probabilities are:

Path	Probability	Final stock prices
UUU	1/8	SUUU = 133.1
UUD, DUU, UDU	3/8	SUUD = 108.9
UDD, DDU, DUD	3/8	SUDD = 89.1
DDD	1/8	SDDD = 72.9

If these figures for the probability and the final stock price are plotted in a histogram, it looks (slightly) more like a 'normal curve' than if we just had n = 1 with two outcomes 110 and 90, each with probability of $1/2$. In fact, as the number of nodes n increases (i.e. the time period between each node gets smaller), the histogram for the final stock prices does approach a 'normal curve' – which is the assumption used in deriving the Black–Scholes formula[10].

SUMMARY

- *Put–call parity* is an arbitrage condition that can be used to derive the fair price of a put, given the fair price of a call (or vice versa).
- By constructing a *risk-free portfolio* (from the option and the underlying asset), either the BOPM or the Black–Scholes (continuous time) framework can be used to determine call and put premia. This involves *delta hedging.*
- In the BOPM and the Black–Scholes approach, we can value the option under the assumption that the growth in the stock price equals the risk-free rate. This is the principle of *risk-neutral valuation* and is reflected in the use of the risk-neutral probability, q, in the BOPM.
- The Black–Scholes approach provides an explicit formula to calculate call and put premia. These depend on the current stock price relative to the strike price (S/K), the risk-free rate r, the volatility of the underlying asset σ and the time to expiry T.
- Quoted options premia can be used to 'back-out' the market's current view of the volatility of the underlying stock. If your view of volatility is lower (higher) than the market's, then you can try to take advantage of the perceived mispricing by selling (buying) the option and delta hedging your position (against changes in the option's premia due to changes in the level of the stock price). You are *trading volatility.*
- The option premium in the BOPM approaches that given by the Black–Scholes formula for a European option (as the number of steps n increases or the time period between nodes becomes smaller). However, the BOPM, as a numerical technique, may suffer from convergence problems and may only give an approximation to the true price.

---

[10] To be more accurate, (continuously compounded) stock *returns* are normally distributed but the distribution of the final stock *price* is actually lognormally distributed. This distinction need not concern us here.

APPENDIX 26.1:
BROWNIAN MOTION – PARALLEL UNIVERSE

Suppose we assume that a stock has an annual mean return of $\mu = 0.15$ (15% p.a.) with a standard deviation $\sigma = 0.20$ (20% p.a.). Stock returns are subject to random events, represented by ε_t, a zero-mean random variable, with a standard deviation of unity:

$$R_t = \mu + \sigma.\varepsilon_t \qquad \text{[A1]}$$

Since ε_t has a standard deviation of one, the standard deviation of the stock return will be equal to σ. The random variable ε_t represents 'firm-specific' events such as strikes, environmental issues, breakdown of equipment and so on. We assume that the random error is normally distributed, so $\varepsilon_t \sim N(0,1)$ is a 'standard' normal variable. Since $R_t = (S_t/S_{t-1}) - 1$, it follows that:

$$S_t = (1 + \mu + \sigma.\varepsilon_t)S_{t-1} \qquad \text{[A2]}$$

This equation represents the behaviour of the stock price over annual intervals. But we require a path for stock prices over very small intervals of time. Over a small interval of time, for example $\Delta t = 0.01$ years (i.e. approximately 3.5 days), the mean return is $\mu(\Delta t)$. What about the standard deviation over a small interval of time? It can be shown that if $\sigma = 0.20$ is the annual standard deviation, then over a small interval of time the standard deviation is $\sigma\sqrt{\Delta t}$. Hence, the path for stock prices over a small interval of time can be represented:

$$S_t = (1 + \mu.\Delta t + \sigma\sqrt{\Delta t}.\varepsilon_t)S_{t-1} \qquad \text{[A3]}$$

which is known as a **Geometric Brownian Motion, GBM**. We can use this equation to generate a random series for S. For example, suppose we choose each time interval to be $\Delta t = 0.01$ years (about 3.5 days). By using $\sigma = 0.20$ and $\mu = 0.15$ and setting $S_0 = 100$, we can draw successive values for $\varepsilon_1, \varepsilon_2, \varepsilon_3 \dots$ from $\varepsilon \sim N(0,1)$ distribution (in Excel) and produce a series for the stock price. Note that [A3] is a *recursion*, so if $\varepsilon_1 = 0.49$ then:

$$S_1 = (1 + 0.15(0.01) + 0.20\sqrt{0.01} \cdot 0.49)100 = 101.13 \qquad \text{[A4]}$$

After calculating S_1, this is used to calculate S_2. So, if the next random draw from the normal distribution is $\varepsilon_2 = 0.765$, then:

$$S_2 = (1 + 0.15(0.01) + 0.20\sqrt{0.01} \cdot 0.765)101.13 = 102.83 \qquad \text{[A5]}$$

We can repeat this, say, 100 times, so we generate 100 data points for the stock price, which represents one year in total. This gives us just one possible path that the stock price might have taken over the year. Starting with $S_0 = 100$ again, we can draw another 100 random values for ε_t and get a 'new' path for prices over the year – but one in which the 'true' mean return is still 15% p.a. with annual standard deviation of 20% p.a. We have created a 'parallel universe' where the starting point, mean return and standard deviation for the stock are the same, but we introduce random firm-specific events into our stock price 'universe' (to represent strikes, new innovations, legal problems, etc.). We are replaying history but 'rolling the dice' each time.

Possible paths for the stock price over two years (i.e. we generate 200 stock prices) are shown in Figure 26.A1. For any *single path* for the stock price, it may not grow at 15% p.a. because of the randomness in the price series. For example, if the first random shock is a large negative number, then the stock price after one period will be very low and hence even after two years it may sometimes end up below its initial value of 100 (Figure 26.A1). On average these price series grow at 15% p.a., but there is substantial variation around the mean, because of the annual standard deviation in stock returns, σ. After two years the volatility of stock returns should be $\sigma_{T=2} = \sqrt{2}\sigma_{T=1} = 1.4142\sigma_{T=1}$. In Figure 26.A1 the spread in stock prices at the end of the second year (i.e. observation 200) is approximately 1.4 times the spread of stock prices after one year. This result is very approximate, since we have only used 25 stock price series in Figure 26.A1 and we have cut some corners to keep the exposition as simple as possible. (In fact we have just assumed that the distribution of stock *prices* obeys the 'root-T rule', when in fact it is really the distribution of stock *returns* that follows the 'root-T rule', but we ignore this subtlety here.)

The Excel file to generate a random series for stock prices, given the mean return and standard deviation of returns, can be found on the web site.

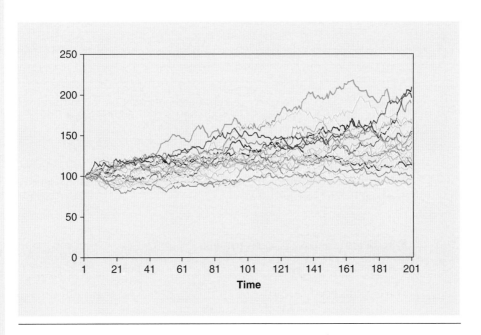

FIGURE 26.A1: Brownian motion

EXERCISES

Q1   Would you pay more for a call option with $K = 100$ and $S = 98$ if it had one day or one month to maturity?

Q2   Would you pay more today for a European put option on a stock with a strike price of $K = 100$ when the current stock price was 98 or when it was 99? Briefly explain.

Q3   Why does the option premium change when the stock price changes?

Q4   Would you pay more today for a call option on a stock that had an annual volatility of 20% p.a. rather than a call on a stock that had an annual volatility of 1% p.a.? (Both calls have the same strike price, initial stock price and time to maturity.) Briefly explain.

Q5   Below are quotes for options on IBM from the *Wall Street Journal*. Explain the key features in the table.

LISTED OPTIONS QUOTATIONS

Monday 3 January

IBM	Strike	Exp	CALL		PUT	
			Vol	**Last**	**Vol**	**Last**
$107^{7/8}$	105	Jan	325	$6^{1/2}$	1679	$3^{1/2}$
$107^{7/8}$	110	Jan	1068	$4^{1/8}$	403	$6^{1/8}$
$107^{7/8}$	115	Jan	928	$2^{1/2}$	21	$9^{1/4}$
$107^{7/8}$	115	Feb	842	$4^{3/4}$	22	$11^{1/4}$
$107^{7/8}$	120	Jan	677	$1^{5/16}$	40	13
$107^{7/8}$	120	Feb	165	$3^{1/4}$	2	$14^{3/4}$

Using the data in the table, calculate and comment on the intrinsic value and time value of the 115-calls that expire in January and February.

Q6   Explain the key items in the following table, which give details of a currency option.

How much would one call option contract cost and what would happen at expiration, if you 'took delivery'?

Philadelphia Exchange: Options quotes, 19 August

31,250 British pounds, cents per unit

BPound	strike	Calls (Sept)	Puts (Sept)
160.60	164	0.48	4.14

Current spot rate on 19 August is 1.6060 US$ per £

Q7 A caplet is a call option that pays out (the maximum of) either $\{r_T - K_C\}$ or zero, at maturity on a notional principal sum of $1000. The current (spot) interest rate is 3%.

$ pay-out from the caplet $= \$1000 \{r_T - K_C\}/100$ for $r_T > K_C$

$r_T =$ market interest rate *at maturity* of the option contract (% p.a.)

$K_C = 3\%$ p.a., the strike (interest) rate of this option.

A floorlet is a put option that pays out (the maximum of) either $\{K_{FL} - r_T\}$ or zero, at maturity on a notional principal sum of $1000.

$r_T =$ market interest rate *at maturity* of the option contract

$K_{FL} = 3\%$ p.a., the strike (interest) rate of this option.

Assume that the maturity date of both options is in one year's time.

(a) You are a speculator and you think that interest rates will rise over the next year. Should you buy the caplet or the floorlet?

(b) You are going to take out a one-year bank loan in one years time for $1000 at a floating interest rate (i.e. you will pay whatever the interest rate happens to be in one year). You are worried that interest rates will rise over the next year, making your bank loan more expensive. Could you use either the caplet or the floorlet to insure yourself against this bad outcome?

(c) How would you feel in one years time if interest rates turned out to be either $r_T = 7\%$ or 1%?

CHAPTER 27

Energy and Weather Derivatives

AIMS

- To outline the main energy and weather derivatives.
- To show how energy derivatives are used for speculation and hedging 'price risk'.
- To show how carbon permits are used to allocate greenhouse gas emissions.
- To show how weather derivatives are used to hedge the 'output risk' of energy producers and users.
- To outline the use of catastrophe bonds by the insurance sector.

INTRODUCTION

We are all aware that there are large oil reserves in a number of countries around the globe, most noticeably those in the Organisation of the Petroleum Exporting Countries (e.g. the Middle East, Venezuela, Nigeria and so on) and Russia, who together control about 60% of the world's oil reserves. (Incidentally, the often much maligned Kazakhstan has the huge Kashagan oil field coming on stream in 2009 at a cost of $30bn – something Borat in the film *Borat: Cultural Leanings of America for make Benefit Glorious Nation of Kazakhstan* failed to mention.) Russia also has huge natural gas reserves and under President Putin it is consolidating its oil and gas holdings in the state-controlled firm Gazprom. Some people fear that this concentration of economic power may lead to more volatile price movements (and possible use of energy supplies as a political weapon – but that's another story).

Energy prices such as those for oil and natural gas are highly volatile and this causes large producers (e.g. oil producers, refiners) and users of energy (e.g. airlines, manufacturing companies) considerable uncertainty about the price they will receive or pay for energy in the future. To mitigate such price risk, consumers and producers can use either over-the-counter (OTC) or exchange-traded energy derivatives such as forwards, futures, options and swaps. These commodity derivatives are widely used by the energy sector, some of which are cash settled and some involving physical delivery. Electricity is a little different to oil and natural gas since it cannot be stored, but its price can vary tremendously on an hourly basis and derivatives contracts on electricity are also available.

The weather in the form of abnormally high or low temperatures affects lots of industries. These include firms in the energy sector (for heating in winter and air conditioning in summer), the leisure sector (hotels, ski resorts) and agriculture (e.g. wine growers, orange growers). Abnormal variations in temperature can affect the output of these industries, which in turn affects their profits, but derivatives contracts on 'temperature' can be used to mitigate these effects. There are also weather derivatives based on the number of frost days in a month or the depth of snowfall at particular locations, which affects the profits of various industries (not least, ski resorts).

In life there is always the possibility of an unusually large natural catastrophe even though this may have a relatively low probability of occurrence, for example very severe hurricanes, floods and earthquakes. Insurance claims against such events could cause a particular insurance company to go bust, so there is a need to offset or spread such risks across many participants. So-called CAT bonds are one way of doing this.

In this chapter we examine how derivatives are used to hedge (or insure) against the price volatility found in spot energy markets and how weather derivatives are used to mitigate changes in profits caused by changes in the weather.

27.1 ENERGY CONTRACTS

We will not give an exhaustive account of energy derivatives, but instead concentrate on the main features of these contracts, so you get a flavour of what's on offer. There has been an active OTC and exchange-traded market in oil products since the early 1980s. OTC forward contracts lock in a price today, for future delivery at specific delivery points.

Futures and options contracts are traded on crude oil and its refined products, gasoline and heating oil, on the New York Mercantile Exchange (NYMEX), the Chicago Mercantile Exchange CME) and the International Commodities Exchange (ICE) in London. (OTC options contracts are also available. Traded options contracts are actually written on the futures price rather than the spot price and are therefore 'futures options' – but we ignore this complication.

One **crude oil futures** contract is for delivery of 1000 barrels, while one gasoline or heating-oil contract is for 42,000 gallons (equivalent to 1000 barrels). That's more than you need to fill the average petrol tank of a '4×4 gas guzzler – known in London as a 'Chelsea tractor'. Some contracts (e.g. light sweet crude oil futures on NYMEX) require physical delivery, while others are cash settled (e.g. Brent crude oil futures on ICE).

There is also the possibility of avoiding the delivery arrangements set by the exchange and instead using 'exchanging futures for physicals' (EFP) arrangements, prior to maturity. This is simply a bilateral agreement on location and price, for delivery between the party with the long futures position and the party with an equal-size short position. The exchange must be notified of the EFP arrangement and the futures positions for both parties are then terminated. EFP might be used when the long wants delivery at a specific location that is different from that stipulated in the futures contract – if it costs more (e.g. transportation costs) to deliver to the long's desired location, she will pay an additional cash amount to the short.

There are also OTC and exchange-traded contracts on **natural gas**. Delivery is 'through the pipe' at a specific geographic location, at a specific uniform rate through the month. The seller of gas (e.g. the short futures position) is responsible for delivery at a specific point, for example at the Henry Hub gas interconnector (in Louisiana) or at Zeebrugge (in Belgium), a key European hub. The supplier of gas might be a separate company to the producer of the gas, particularly in deregulated gas markets such as the US and UK. NYMEX and ICE trade futures (and options) contracts, which (if not closed out) require physical delivery of 10,000 million British thermal units (mbtu) of natural gas. Of course, if you need your gas in Boston then you better make sure you have purchased capacity in the pipe between the Louisiana delivery hub and Boston – because the pipe might be full! Options and swaps on natural gas are also available in the OTC market.

The **electricity market** is a bit different to oil and gas, as electricity cannot be stored. (Technically you can store it in a battery, but it would require a very large battery.) In the US and UK electricity is produced primarily in coal-fired, gas-fired and nuclear plants. The latter provide the base load and extra demand is met by gas and coal stations. The transmission of electricity is costly and there are also transmission energy losses. So electricity in the US is provided first to a specific region and any excess can then be sold in the wholesale market. (As everyone is becoming more 'green' then in the future it may be possible for excess power from your sdar panels to be sold to the national grid.) Spikes in electricity consumption can be triggered by abnormally high temperatures in summer (particularly in the US where air conditioning is widely used) or low temperatures in winter. So there is considerable volatility in electricity prices on a daily basis.

There are active markets in the US and UK in OTC forwards, options and swaps, and NYMEX and ICE trade a futures contract on the price of electricity. The contracts allow one party to receive a specified number of megawatt hours, at a specified price and location, during a particular month. For example, this could be a 5×8 contract, for Monday to Friday only during off-peak hours (11 p.m. to 7 a.m.) within a specified month. There is also a 5×16 contract for peak hours (7 a.m. to 11 p.m.) or a 7×24 contract for delivery over 24 hours.

With an **option contract** on electricity you have precisely that, an option to take delivery at the strike price K or not. If the contract is for daily exercise, then with one day's notice you can choose whether you want to take delivery at a price K for the next day. For an option with monthly exercise, you make a decision at the beginning of the month whether you will take delivery each day at the strike price K.

In electricity and natural gas derivatives markets you can also be a 'swinger'. You can purchase a *swing option* (also called a *take-and-pay option)*. For an 'electric swinger', the option holder sets a maximum and minimum amount of power she will take each day during a specific month and a maximum and minimum for the whole month, with each megawatt taken at the strike price K. You can then swing the amount of power you choose to take each day (within the bounds set), although there is also usually a limit on the number of days on which you can *change* your rate of consumption.

At this point it is also worth mentioning another market that is likely to expand rapidly in the future – carbon trading. This is a market where firms who want to increase their output of greenhouse gases can purchase permits – the supply of permits is provided by firms who have been given an allocation of permits that exceeds their output of greenhouse gases (see Case Study 27.1).

CASE STUDY 27.1   CARBON TRADING

Going 'green' seems to be catching on. On a small scale we have recycling of household rubbish, supermarkets charging for plastic bags or providing their customers with alternatives, houses with wind turbines and holidaymakers paying to offset the carbon emissions of air travel. On a bigger scale we have the Kyoto agreements to reduce greenhouse gas emissions. What methods are available for reducing greenhouse gas emissions from industry? One method is to tax those emissions. The problem here is that you have to set the tax rate at a level you think will achieve your emissions target but, given the technological complexities involved, you could set the tax rate too high or too low, thus undershooting or overshooting your target.

The method that seems to have the most adherents is carbon trading. Currently this affects sectors such as power generation, cement, ceramics, steel and paper industries. However, it is noticeable that the scheme does not cover air transport. The scheme works by setting allocations for emissions for each firm in the scheme. Firms that emit less than their allocation can sell the unused portion of their permits to the extreme polluters, via exchanges in London and Chicago. Although the US did not sign up to Kyoto it has a similar permit scheme limiting carbon dioxide, sulphur and nitrogen oxide emissions. In Europe it has been argued that the initial carbon permit allocation was too generous, so the price of carbon permits in the market was low and this provided little incentive for firms to curb their emissions. The European emissions trading scheme is due to be renegotiated by 2012 and it has been suggested that permits should not be allocated by government decree but should be auctioned. The higher the market price set when trading the permits, the higher the costs of pollution to firms and the greater incentive they have to innovate with clean technology or simply to reduce output. Total carbon dioxide emissions are therefore set by the scheme, but their allocation across firms is set by the market. At the moment, trading environmental permits is solely a spot market activity, but should spot trading increase we can also expect see the development of derivatives markets in this area.

27.2 HEDGING USING ENERGY FUTURES

Running an airline

Suppose you own a medium-size US airline and your marketing manager has told you what ticket prices you will be charging on all your routes, based on maintaining your competitive position in the market. If airline (jet) fuel remains at its current level, it is estimated that you will make a handsome profit over the next three years. But that is a big 'if', in today's volatile oil market. If you do nothing and jet fuel remains at its current level (or falls), you will be a happy CEO and your shareholders will be smiling too. But if jet fuel rises in price, then despite all your efforts on the technical side (reliability, maintenance and staff costs, etc.) you will end up looking pretty bad and may lose your job.

Consider hedging some or all of your projected fuel costs. There is no traded futures contract on jet fuel, the closest being a futures on heating oil (traded on NYMEX). Since you fear a rise in spot fuel costs in the future, you should go long (buy) heating oil futures today. If spot prices do rise over the next year, so will the futures price and you can close out on NYMEX at a profit – the latter offsets the higher cost of your spot jet fuel.

What are the practical complications involved? You have to decide what quantity Q of your fuel to hedge and then calculate the appropriate number of futures contracts for each month:

$$N_f = \frac{Monetary\ value\ to\ be\ hedged\ (= Q \times S)}{Contract\ size\ \times\ S} \times \beta = \frac{Q}{Contract\ size} \times \beta$$

Beta is the slope of the regression line for the change in the spot price of jet fuel on the futures price of heating oil ($\Delta S = \alpha + \beta \Delta F$). Since heating oil and jet fuel prices do not move perfectly together, this is known as a 'cross-hedge' and as you can only estimate the correlation between these two prices, your hedge will be less than perfect – this is *basis risk*. However, over short horizons of, say, a month, the correlation coefficient (and beta) between heating oil and jet fuel is quite high (the beta is around 0.9) and both are reasonably stable over time – so, *on average,* your hedge will work. But basis risk is also affected by changes in the *convenience yield* – that is, the premium that holders of spot heating oil place on having the heating oil available to satisfy their normal customers. This can cause a divergence between changes in the spot and futures prices at particular periods and could lead to large hedging errors.

Suppose in January you decide to hedge 2 million gallons of jet fuel for each of the months of April, May and June. The contract size for heating oil futures is 42,000 gallons (equivalent to 1000 barrels), hence the number of futures contracts for each month is 23.8 (24) – that is, you go long 24 – April, 24 – May and 24 – June contracts. Taken together these are often referred to as a **strip hedge**.

If you close out each contract just before its maturity date, this will provide a reasonably good hedge. Any gains/losses on your futures positions will closely offset any increased/lower costs of the spot fuel in the future. Effectively, you will 'lock in' a known average price of fuel approximately given by the average price of the futures contracts you enter into in January. You will not take delivery in the contracts, because it is jet fuel you require (at various airports) and the futures contract delivers heating oil to New York Harbour. (Also planes don't fly well on heating oil.)

Caps and floors

The futures hedge locks in a known price, but does not allow you to gain from lower fuel prices should they occur. To simplify the exposition, we assume that spot heating oil and jet fuel prices do not differ and move dollar-for-dollar. What if you wanted to set a cap (upper limit) on future fuel costs but also wanted to benefit from lower fuel prices should they occur? Suppose that the current spot price of fuel is $S_0 = \$1.9$ per gallon. We know from our earlier discussions that what we need to do is to purchase a call option (on heating oil) at a specific strike price $K_c = \$2.2$ per gallon (say), and for a maturity that matches the time at which we need to purchase the fuel in the spot market. If spot fuel prices turn out to be high ($S_T > K_c$) and the option is cash settled, we receive $S_T - K_c$ at expiry of the option. Hence, even though the spot price of the oil we purchase is high, the net cost is $S_T - (S_T - K_c) = K_c$, so we effectively end up paying a maximum price of $K_c = \$2.2$ (less the cost of the call option premium). On the other hand, if the spot price of fuel turns out to be low (say, $1.7 per gallon), we throw away the call option (i.e. we do not exercise it) and just buy fuel at the low spot price of $1.7. For the insurance that the option provides you have to pay the call premium at the outset. This use of the call is referred to as a caplet, since it caps your maximum payment for fuel at K_c for a *specific month* in the future. If you want to purchase fuel over several months ahead, then you need a series of calls, all with the same strike but with different maturity dates to match the dates of your future spot purchases of fuel. This requires a strip of caplets, which are collectively known as **A cap** and can be provided OTC by large financial institutions.

It should be fairly obvious that if you are a supplier of jet fuel (and hold large reserves), what you are worried about is a fall in the spot price. You can insure a floor value for your future fuel sales by buying a put option with strike $K_p = \$1.6$, say – this will guarantee you receive at least $1.6 per gallon for your oil in the future. Of course, if spot prices rise, you again throw away the put and simply sell your fuel at the high spot price. In these circumstances the put is (not surprisingly) known as a floorlet and a strip of puts is a **floor**. The advantage of the put is that it gives you the benefit of the upside when spot prices rise, whereas taking a short futures position locks in the price you will pay.

Collar

Let's get really clever now. Go back to the airline that capped its future fuel costs by buying a call at a strike $K_c = \$2.2$, which sets the maximum cost for fuel purchases by the airline. But buying the call could be expensive. The airline could offset some of the cost of the call premium C by selling a put and hence receiving the put premium P. If the airline that is going to purchase fuel in the future undertakes a 'buy call–sell put' trade, this is known as a **collar** (If the call and put premia exactly offset each other it is known as a zero-cost collar). We know what happens if fuel prices rise: the call sets the maximum effective cost of the fuel purchase at K_c.

But what happens if fuel prices fall substantially? If the airline had not sold the put, it would directly benefit from very low spot prices. But the airline has sold a put and if the put is now 'in the money', the airline will have to pay out $(K_p - S_T)$ to the holder (buyer) of the put. If spot prices fall (and $S_T < K$), the *effective cost* of fuel for the airline is equal to the spot price plus the pay-out on the put $= S_T + (K_p - S_T) = K_p$. Hence if $K_p = \$1.6$, the minimum price paid for the fuel by the airline will be $1.6 per gallon (even if spot fuel prices are below $1.6). So if you have to purchase airline fuel in the future but the airline also undertakes a collar trade, it will cap its effective cost at an upper level $K_c = \$2.2$, but also limit the minimum effective price it will pay to $K_p = \$1.6$. (Note that for the above to work as described, the put sold has to have a lower strike price than the strike in the call option; that is, $K_p < K_c$.)

The effective cost (ignoring the cost of the call and the put) of the jet fuel to the airline that undertakes the collar trade is given in Figure 27.1. If the spot price turns out to be between $K_p = \$1.6$ and $K_c = \$2.2$, say $S_T = \$1.8$, then neither of the options is in the money and the airline merely purchases fuel at the spot price of $1.8. But if the spot price turns out to be above $2.2 the effective price paid is capped at $2.2, while spot prices below $1.6 cannot be taken advantage of by the airline, which pays an effective price of $K_p = \$1.6$. A collar trade is therefore quite involved, but the key thing is that it sets a maximum and minimum price paid for fuel by the airline – the maximum price paid is $K_c = 2.2$ and the minimum price paid is $K_p = \$1.6$.

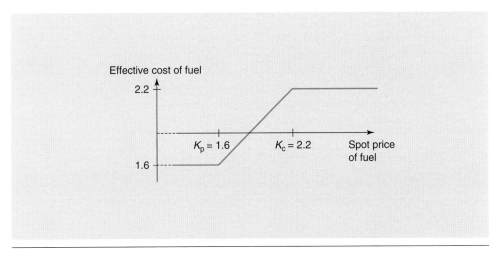

FIGURE 27.1: Collar trade by airline

27.3 ENERGY SWAPS

We have already discussed interest-rate and currency swaps in previous chapters. Now let us see how the energy sector might use swaps to offset any price risks it faces. To get the ball rolling, suppose in January a company such as Centrica in the UK agrees to supply natural gas (NG) to a large industrial customer Z (e.g. a manufacturing firm) at a fixed price S(*fix*), over a six-month period beginning in November. Centrica decides that it will buy the gas in the spot market at whatever price it has to pay at the time (i.e. it pays a 'floating price', S(*float*), to the gas producer, which supplies the gas via the European hub at Zeebrugge (in Belgium). See Figure 27.2.

Clearly, if the spot price rises in the coming month, Centrica's profit margin will be squeezed, and it may even be committed to supplying the gas at a loss if the spot price in Zeebrugge S(*float*) rises dramatically. How can it offset this risk without renegotiating any of its existing contracts with its customers? It can undertake a pay-fixed–receive-floating swap from a swap dealer (see the lefthand side of Figure 27.2 where S(*float*) is the floating price used and X is the agreed fixed price). If the spot price of NG in Zeebrugge increases in the future, Centrica receives more from the swap dealer, which it uses to purchase the NG from its supplier – it has hedged any rising costs of its gas purchase. The net result is that Centrica receives S(*fix*) from its industrial customers and pays the swap dealer X. As long as S(*fix*) is greater than X, Centrica will have locked in a fixed profit margin of S(*fix*) − X on each unit of NG supplied.

There are other important elements to the swap deal. There will be a notional quantity Q of NG in the swap, for example this might be Q = 1 million mbtu *per day* and the 'tenor' of the swap could be every month from November to April. The swap payments to Centrica would then be

> Swap payments each month to Centrica = (1 million) × days × [S(*float*) − X]

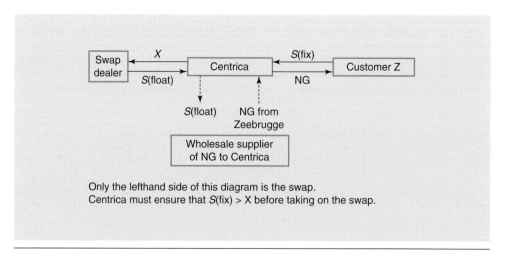

Only the lefthand side of this diagram is the swap.
Centrica must ensure that S(fix) > X before taking on the swap.

FIGURE 27.2: Natural gas, fixed-for-floating swap

where 'days' = number of days in the month. The swap contract may be cash settled each month and it is then a 'contract for differences', as only the net cash payment is made by one of the parties to the swap contract. If in any month:

> $S(float) > X$, then Centrica *receives* cash from the swap dealer.
>
> $S(float) < X$, then Centrica pays cash to the swap dealer.

The floating index $S(float)$ will have to be decided on and this spot price often goes under rather strange names, for example for the Centrica deal it might be the 'front of month inside FERC' index. In fact, the floating payment $S(float)$ you receive from the swap dealer is based on the 'front of month' (FOM) price, but you actually buy your NG at spot prices *throughout* the month, so there is some residual price risk remaining.

The fixed price X quoted in the swap is the 'swap rate' and will vary depending on the maturity of the swap deal, so different swap rates will be quoted for one-year, two-year, . . . etc. swaps. Broadly speaking, the swap rate X is an average of the forward/futures prices for NG over the life of the swap – in terms of jargon, 'the swap is priced off the forward curve' (i.e. forward prices of NG at different maturities).

An OTC swap of the above type can be tailor-made by the swap dealer to suit Centrica. It can begin immediately or can have a delayed start (a 'forward swap') or it can be made to apply only to specific months when Centrica feels that the spot price for NG is likely to be abnormally high. The notional quantity in the swap, which above is 1 million (mbtu) per day, can be preset at different levels on particular days within a month. Alternatively, the notional quantity can be a fixed daily amount within any one month, with different daily levels applying for each separate month. These would then be referred to as 'roller-coaster swaps'. With the swap, Centrica effectively locks in the effective price it pays for NG, regardless of whether the spot price turns out to be high or low in the future.

Suppose that Centrica is happy to receive $S(float) - X$ from the swap dealer when spot prices turn out to be high (and hence has an effective cost of buying NG of X). But when the floating price of NG is less than the fixed price X in the swap, Centrica only wants to *pay* the swap dealer 60% of $S(float) - X$. For example, if $S(float) = 80$ and $X = 100$, then the effective cost of buying NG is $80 + 60\% \times 20 = 92$, whereas with a plain vanilla swap the effective cost would have been $X = 100$. So the 60% swap deal allows Centrica to pay less when prices are low and hence participate in some of the benefit of low prices – not surprisingly, this is known as a **participation swap**.

You may have noticed in Figure 27.2 that the swap dealer has taken on risk, since she is paying $S(float)$ to Centrica each month and receiving X fixed from Centrica, so if NG prices rise in the future the swap dealer will experience losses. How does the swap dealer deal with this problem? Well, she may be lucky and find an offsetting deal with another party who wants to pay the swap dealer a floating price (with the same maturity as the original swap with Centrica). This may happen automatically or the swap dealer can shade her price quotes to encourage such swaps. But let us assume (realistically) that even after these offsetting swaps she still ends up as a net payer at a floating price.

We know that the swap dealer fears a rise in $S(float)$. But if there is a futures contract where the underlying asset is the spot price of NG, she can go long (an appropriate number of) futures contracts. Then if $S(float)$ does rise in the future, she can close out the futures at a profit and use this cash inflow to offset the higher floating payment in her swap deal. So in fact what derivatives markets are very good at providing. is 'risk spreading' across a wide array of participants in these markets. The price risk is still there, but each party only holds a part of it – it is an efficient risk-sharing mechanism. In short, without derivatives markets your gas bill might be even higher. Case Study 27.2 shows how electricity producers can lock in a profit margin on their power generation.

CASE STUDY 27.2 SPARK SPREAD SWAP

We all know that electricity can produce a spark and in the UK an electrician is called a 'sparky'. What can a spark have to do with derivatives and swaps? Suppose that you run a gas-fired power plant that produces electricity. Your profit margin (per unit of electricity) is:

Profit margin of electric power plant $= S(electric) - S(NG)$

where both prices are measured in, say, 'pounds per megawatt hour', £/MWh. (This simplified presentation avoids complications like the 'heat rate', which is the rate at which NG can be converted into electricity.) In fact, Centrica owns gas-fired power plants in the UK, so it provides a good example here. The power plant manager may be willing to take on some price risk due to the spot price of NG rising more than the price of electricity in the future, hence squeezing profit margins. Indeed, if in any future periods $S(NG) > S(electric)$, the manager may actually temporarily shut down the plant and cease to provide electricity to the grid during these periods. (Of course, many other factors may enter into the decision to close down the plant temporarily, not least the ease with which the plant can be up and running again.)

We can view the power plant as earning net receipts of $S(electric) - S(NG)$, which will fluctuate as these two spot prices move up and down over time. Suppose the plant manager thinks that over the next few months electricity or NG prices or both are likely to be more volatile than normal (e.g. due to highly variable weather conditions, which affect electricity prices, or risks in the supply of NG 'through the pipe', which affect spot NG prices). The power plant manager could agree to pay a swap dealer an amount $S(electric) - S(NG)$, in return for receiving a fixed payment X from the swap dealer over the next few months. She will then have fixed the profit margin at X (per unit of electricity sold). The agreed fixed payment X is the *spark spread swap rate*. Once again, swaps allow one party to offset risks from price fluctuations and to lock in known cash receipts over a specific time period.

Crack spread

The 'crack' you have probably heard of is the form of cocaine that celebs allegedly smoke to add zing to their lives (or if you have been to Ireland, 'craic' refers to good times, usually over a Guinness or Murphy's alcoholic beverage). Well, crack appears in energy markets too, in the form of the 'crack spread'. An oil refiner can convert crude oil (CO) into heating oil (HO) and her profit margin (per barrel) depends on the difference between these two prices. (hope you can see the analogy with the spark spread.) Clearly, the oil refiner is worried that in the future We heating oil prices will fall or crude oil prices will rise, or both, since this will hit her profit margins. She could offset this risk by hedging using *separate* futures contracts on crude oil and heating oil – here she would go long crude oil futures and would short heating oil futures. However, to save you the trouble of doing these two transactions, the futures market bundles them together and provides a futures contract on the crack spread – that is, on $S_{CO} - S_{HO}$. Since the oil refiner is worried about a fall in the spot crack spread, she will short crack spread futures, to hedge this possibility. If the spot crack spread rises she makes higher profit margins, but loses an equal amount on the short futures position. On the other hand, if the spot crack spread falls, her profit margins are squeezed but she makes an equal amount when she closes out the short futures position.

There is a 1:1 crack spread futures contract that takes account of the fact that 1 barrel of crude oil can (physically) be refined to produce 1 barrel of heating oil, as outlined above. But it is also possible to take 3 barrels of crude oil and convert this into 2 barrels of gasoline (petrol) and 1 barrel of heating oil. This refiner faces price risk in the ratio 3:2:1 and it may not surprise you that there is a 3:2:1 crack spread futures contract to hedge price risks for this type of refinery. Crack spread contracts are traded on CME and ICE.

27.4 WEATHER DERIVATIVES

Weather derivatives can be used by anyone whose output and hence profits are affected by abnormal movements in the weather. Whereas most futures are used in hedging price movements, broadly speaking weather futures are used to hedge uncertainty about future output (e.g. the number of gallons of heating oil you might sell to consumers). For the moment, let's consider 'temperature' as the only weather variable influencing profits (that is, we ignore such weather factors as the number of days of frost or depth of snowfalls, which clearly affect some firms' output). Energy producers and consumers are affected by temperature, since this influences the amount of energy (heating oil, natural gas, electricity) used for heating in the winter months and (in the US) the amount used for air conditioning. But the volume of agricultural production is also influenced by temperature (e.g. orange production in Florida), as are leisure industries (e.g. holiday companies) and some manufacturers (e.g. of cold drinks or ice cream).

To keep things simple at this point, assume that there are traded futures and options contracts, whose payoff depends on the temperature (at a particular point in time and a particular geographic location), relative to the average daily temperature, which we take to be 65°F. Let us also assume that these derivatives contracts apply to a particular month (and we assume that all months have 30 days). Hence on 15 January, if the market believes that the average *daily* temperature in June will be 70°F, then the current value of the June futures contract is 5°F × 30 days = 150 degree-days. In the jargon, we say that the average cooling degree day (CDD) is 5 and the expected cumulative CDDs in June are 150 – this is because a higher temperature than 65°F, is likely to lead to more energy use for cooling, such as via air conditioning. Traders would say that the June contract is currently trading at 150 CDD. If the contract multiple is $20, the value of the June futures (on 15 January) is $20 × 150 days = $3000.

As you are probably aware, one of the average citizen's main topics of conversation is what the weather is likely to be over the coming months. So, one can only assume that they might like to gamble on the weather. Clearly, this is possible using traded weather futures. On 15 January, assume that the June weather future is trading at 70°F, equivalent to a price of $3000. If you think that the daily temperature in June will be 80°F (and your guess turns out to be correct), then the January futures contract in June will be priced at around (80 − 65) × 30 days × $20 = $9000 and your profit on closing out will be $6000. The latter figure is simply the increase in the average daily temperature of 10°F (= 80 − 70), scaled up by the 30 days and the $20 per index point.

> Profit = Increase in temperature × 30 days × $20

The January price of the futures assumes 150 CDDs in June (i.e. an average daily temperature of 70°F). Hence if you thought that the average temperature in June would be less than 70°F, as a speculator you would sell June futures in January (and hope to close out at a lower price in June).

What would an option on the weather look like? Assume that the average June temperature at a particular location (e.g. Portland, Oregon) is 70°F, so the cumulative CDDs for June are (70 − 65) × 30 = 150. A strike price of K = 150 CDDs for June therefore corresponds to an average temperature of 70°F. Speculation is easy. If in January you think that the average temperature in Portland in June will be higher than 70°F, you might buy an option on CDD with a strike equal to 150. If the average temperature in June turns out to be greater than 70°F, the option will be in the money and can be exercised at a profit. If it is less than 70°F you simply lose your option premium.

Hedging and insurance

Now let's consider hedging with weather derivatives. Suppose that you run a number of large retail outlets in California, which use air conditioning. In January you may be worried that the temperature in July will be abnormally high (due to global warming) so the costs of will rise, cutting into your profits. To offset some or all of this extra energy cost you could buy July weather futures in January. If the temperature turns out to be abnormally high in July, you close out your futures position at a profit – which can be used to offset your higher air-conditioning costs. If the temperature turns out to be lower than average in July, you close out your futures at a loss, but this is offset by lower energy costs. Here the aim of the hedge is to keep overall energy costs in July constant (i.e. so that spot energy costs plus profits/loss on the futures remain constant).

Of course, you have to work out how much profit you will lose for each 1°F rise in temperature. Only then can you decide *how many* weather futures to purchase in order to offset your expected increase in energy costs (and loss in profits). So you need someone to provide you with a business scenario model, which shows how overall profits (in July) vary with temperature.

How would options work? A call option on the weather provides insurance against rising energy costs. If the July temperature turns out to be above its strike level (set in the option contract), then the money you make on exercising the option will just offset the higher air-conditioning costs, so your profits remain at their normal level. However, as the temperature falls (below the strike) your call option is worthless, but your energy costs continue to fall as you use less and less air conditioning. You buy the call option in January and in July you have an asymmetric payoff. You obtain higher than average profits if temperatures are low and normal profits if the temperature is abnormally high – for this you have to pay an insurance premium up front in January, and that is the price of the call option.

So, when hedging with a weather *futures contract* you make average profits, regardless of whether the temperature is high or low. But a *call option* gives you the option of earning high profits if the temperature is low and normal profits if the temperature in July is abnormally high.

Contract details

Now we have sorted out the general principles of speculation and hedging with weather derivatives, let us look at a few of the contractual and institutional details. The first OTC weather derivatives were introduced around 1997 and are based on heating degree days (HDD) and cooling degree days (CDD), defined as:

$$\text{Daily HDD} = \max \{0, 65 - T\}$$
$$\text{Daily CDD} = \max \{0, T - 65\}$$

where T is the average of the highest and lowest temperature (degrees Fahrenheit) during the day at a specific location (e.g. at the Chicago O'Hare Airport weather station calculated by the Earth Satellite Corporation). For example, if $T = 70$ then the daily CDD $= 5$ and the HDD $= 0$. The monthly HDD and CDD are simply the sum of the daily values. For example, if the values of the daily HDD in Chicago in November are 25, 10, 20, 15, 19, 27, 26 (and the rest are 0), then the cumulative HDD for November is 142. (Also note that settlement on CME for weather derivatives is in 0.5 increments.) Note that when temperatures are low (i.e. well below 65°F), HDD is high – a negative correlation. However, CDD increases with temperature (above 65°F) – a positive correlation.

Lots of bespoke weather futures are sold in the OTC market, but some plain vanilla contracts are also available with 24-hour electronic trading (e.g. on the CME Globex trading platform). Both weather futures and European options (on weather futures) are based on monthly HDD or CDD. These products are also available as seasonal products. The winter season is November to March and the summer season May to September – although April can be added to the summer and October to the winter season, so all months can be covered. You can choose from two to six months in a seasonal strip contract, so you might choose, say, three months (December, January and March) from the winter season strip, as these may be the months where your (energy) needs are most volatile and hence need to be hedged. The CME Clearing House guarantees trading on Globex by requiring performance bond (collateral) deposits (i.e. margin payments) at each level in the clearing process – customer to broker, broker to clearing firm and clearing firm to clearing house.

There are also weather derivatives based on the number of *frost days* in the month and on the *depth of snowfall* at particular geographic locations. These work along the same broad principles as weather derivatives based on temperature, described above. Forwards and futures contracts allow you to protect your profits because of volume changes in your business if there are severe frosts in particular months (e.g. for wine growers in Napa and Sonoma Valley in California, who suffer if grapes are harmed by severe frosts) or if there is less or more snowfall than average. The most obvious example of the latter case is a lack of snow at a ski resort, but excessive snowfalls can also severely disrupt transport companies such as road haulage (the trucking business). Options contracts allow you to purchase insurance. For example, a wine grower might buy in November a call option on 'frost days' in March, then the option pays out depending on the number of frost days (above the strike) and this compensates the wine grower for any deterioration in the grape harvest. On the other hand, if there are no frost days in March then there is no loss of grapes to the wine grower but the call expires out of the money. The cost of the insurance is the call premium.

27.5 REINSURANCE AND CAT BONDS

We have seen how weather derivatives can be used to hedge and provide insurance when there are abnormal weather conditions. In general, OTC and exchange-traded weather derivatives are used to hedge changes in temperature (or frost or snowfall) that are slightly different from average. These products are provided in the OTC market by large banks, specialist energy firms and insurance companies. On the other hand, extreme weather conditions such as hurricanes, earthquakes and floods are generally dealt with via some form of explicit insurance contract with an insurance company.

Any single insurance company might hold a large number of catastrophe insurance contracts and may therefore hold lots of risk, from these low-probability but highly costly events. To mitigate some of this risk, an insurance company may reinsure, say, 70% of its risks with other companies, leaving it liable to only 30% of any claim (Lloyd's of London is probably the oldest organisation providing reinsurance). Alternatively, the insurance company can purchase a series of reinsurance contracts for *excess cost layers*. If the insurance company has $100m exposure to hurricane damage in Florida, then it may issue (separate) *excess-of-loss* reinsurance contracts to cover losses between $40m and $50m, $50m and $60m, etc. Between $40m and $50m of losses, the insurance company receives a dollar for dollar payoff from the reinsurer, but receives nothing from this (first) reinsurance contract if losses are outside this range. Hence, for the first reinsurance contract the insurance company has the equivalent of a long bull spread – namely, a long call at a strike of $40m and a short call at a strike of $50m.

Reinsurance contracts are very useful, but the insurance company can also issue bonds to cover catastrophic (CAT) risks. These have a liquid secondary market and can be sold to many investors, thus spreading the catastrophic risk widely. CAT bonds pay a higher than average interest (coupon) but the holders agree to cover the excess-of-loss insurance. For example, by issuing $10m principal of CAT bonds, an insurance company could cover any losses between $40m and $50m by not repaying some or all of the principal on the CAT bonds. Alternatively, it can make a much larger bond issue, with the covenant that any losses between $40m and $50m will be covered by a reduction in interest payments.

Investors' demand for CAT bonds arises from the fact that they pay higher coupons (or yield to maturity) and the returns on CAT bonds have an almost zero correlation with stock-market returns and hence have no systematic market risk. In a diversified portfolio specific risk will be small, so CAT bonds improve the (mean-variance) risk–return trade-off.

SUMMARY

- Forwards, futures, options and swap contracts on the price of energy (oil products, natural gas, electricity) are available OTC and as exchange-traded products.
- Energy derivatives can be used to hedge (forwards, futures and swaps) and to provide insurance (options) against future changes in spot energy prices.
- Some contracts are cash settled and others involve delivery – although alternative delivery arrangements from those stipulated in the contract can be separately negotiated, which is known as 'exchanging futures for physicals' (EFP).
- Weather derivatives can be used to hedge (or provide insurance) against changes in output of energy and other industries, whose profits depend on the weather.
- The value/price of the most actively traded weather derivatives are based on temperature at particular locations at specific times, but others depend on the number of frost days or the depth of snowfalls.
- The key exchanges are the New York Mercantile Exchange (NYMEX) and the International Commodities Exchange (ICE) in London, while the Chicago Mercantile Exchange (CME) trades weather derivatives.

EXERCISES

Q1   It is early January and you have agreed *to sell* 100,000 mbtu of NG at $S(fix) =$ $7.85 mbtu. to a customer in the Boston area in May. This is a 'commercial' forward sale. You will purchase the gas at a later date, probably at the end of February.

The NG futures for May delivery on NYMEX is $F_0(\text{May}) = 7.80$ \$/mbtu (trading terminates three business days prior to the first calendar day of the delivery month). The contract size is 10,000 mbtu and delivery is at Henry Hub (Louisiana).

(a) How can you hedge your price risk between January and the end of February using futures? (Assume that you close out the contract just before maturity.)

(b) If you take the above May futures contract to maturity and accept delivery, what problems might ensue or, put another way, what risks are you taking?

(c) What other alternatives for delivery does the futures exchange allow you?

(d) At the end of *February* you decide to purchase spot gas at Henry Hub and store it. Between the beginning of January and the end of February, the futures and spot prices could have risen or fallen.

> *Prices rise by Feb*
> $F(\text{May contract}) = 7.90$ $S(\text{Feb Henry Hub}) = 7.89$
>
> *Prices fall by Feb*
> $F(\text{May contract}) = 7.70$ $S(\text{Feb Henry Hub}) = 7.69$

Take each case in turn and calculate the effective cost of the gas purchased at Henry Hub in February by using futures contracts at the beginning of January (and closing out in February, before maturity). Compare this with the unhedged outcome and briefly comment.

(e) What is the final 'cash futures basis' (at Henry Hub) and how does this influence the outcome of the hedge? What might cause the final basis to be different from that in the above example?

(f) What is the profit margin on the complete gas deal with your futures hedge, if the cost of transportation between Henry Hub and Boston and the storage cost between Feb and May is 0.02 \$/mbtu?

(g) Here's a more challenging open-ended question. After closing out your futures, you actually buy your spot gas in February at a local distribution point around Boston. What additional risks does this entail? In principle, can you see any simple way of offsetting this risk using a particular type of futures contract? (You can think up your own futures contract to eliminate this risk – you need not search for actual 'real world' contracts.)

Q2   Suppose it is January 08 and you have agreed to sell *100,000 mbtu* of NG at $S(\text{fix}) = \$9.0$ mbtu to customers in the Boston area for *each of the months May–October.*

The contract size is 10,000 mbtu and delivery is at Henry Hub (Louisiana).

Rolling strip hedge (quotes $/mbtu)	
Futures Maturity	$F(t = 0)$ Initial futures Prices in Jan
May 08	7
Jun 08	7.5
Jul 08	8
Aug 08	8.5
Sep 08	9
Oct 08	9.5
Nov 08	10
Dec 08	10.5

Notes:
  To hedge a particular month's spot purchases, use the futures maturing in that month (e.g. to hedge your May spot purchases use the May futures contract, which expires three business days before the first day of the delivery month of May). The 'initial' futures prices on 1 Jan are denoted $F(t = 0)$. So the June futures on 1 Jan has a price $F = 7.5$.

(a) Given the information above, what would be your futures hedge?
(b) Over your hedge period spot prices (S) fall – and fall quite rapidly towards the end of your hedge period. The out-turn spot and futures prices are given below. (For example, just before 1 May the May futures price was 7.1, denoted $F(t = 1)$.)

Date	Spot out-turn	Futures maturity	Futures out-turn $F(t = 1)$
May 08	7.1	May 08	7.1
Jun 08	6.75	Jun 08	6.75
Jul 08	6.5	Jul 08	6.5
Aug 08	6.25	Aug 08	6.25
Sep 08	6	Sep 08	6
Oct 08	5.75	Oct 08	5.75
Nov 08	5.5	Nov 08	5.5

Calculate the effective average price of your gas over the six months and compare this with the unhedged outcome. Briefly comment.

Compared to the 'real world', how have we cheated in this question? So, how might things be different in the real world?

Q3 It is 22 September and you have agreed to sell 10,000 mbtu of NG at $S(fix) =$ 8.40 $/mbtu in January. You do not currently have the NG. The NG futures for Jan delivery on NYMEX is $F_0(Jan) = 8.20$ $/mbtu. The contract size is 10,000 mbtu and delivery is at Henry Hub (Louisiana). You decide to hedge using futures. What is the effective cost of the NG under the following two scenarios?

28 December: Price rise
On 28 December you close out the futures at
$F_1(\text{Jan}) = \$8.70$ and the spot price is also $S_1 = \$8.70$

28 December: Price fall
On 28 December you close out with the futures at
$F_1(\text{Jan}) = \$7.70$ and the spot price is also $S_1 = \$7.70$

Q4 It is 22 September and you have agreed to sell 10,000 mbtu of NG at $S(fix) =$
8.60 \$/mbtu in January. You do not currently have the NG. On 22 September you
decide to hedge your fixed price sale of NG by using an at-the-money (ATM)
option (on NG futures). Assume that the options are cash settled. The payoff to
a call is max $[0, F_T - K]$

An ATM option has a (fixed) strike price equal to the *current* futures price:

Derivatives (22 September)
The NG future for Jan delivery on NYMEX is $F_0(\text{Jan}) = 8.20$ \$/mbtu.
An ATM call costs $C_0 = \$0.15$ (with expiry date of 28 December).
An ATM put would cost you $P_0 = \$0.15$.

28 December: Price rise
On 28 December if you decide to exercise your option you face prices
$F_1(\text{Jan}) = \$8.70$ and the spot price is also $S_1 = \$8.70$.

28 December: Price fall
On 28 December if you decide to exercise your option you face prices
$F_1(\text{Jan}) = \$7.70$ and the spot price is also $S_1 = \$7.70$.

What is the outcome of your hedge in these two cases? Briefly compare this outcome with using futures.

Q5 It is 22 September and you have agreed to buy 10,000 mbtu of NG at $S(fix) =$
7.80 \$/mbtu for delivery in January. You fear a fall in prices between September
and January, when you will be 'selling on' the gas in the January spot market to
your customer.

Derivatives (22 September)
The NG futures for Jan delivery on NYMEX is $F_0(\text{Jan}) = 8.20$ \$/mbtu.
The contract size is 10,000 mbtu and delivery is at Henry Hub (Louisiana).

(a) What are the effective receipts from your NG sales in December under the
following two scenarios?

28 December: Price rise
On 28 December you close out the futures at
$F_1(\text{Jan}) = \$8.70$ and the spot price is also $S_1 = \$8.70$.

28 December: Price fall
On 28 December you close out with the futures at
$F_1(\text{Jan}) = \$7.70$ and the spot price is also $S_1 = \$7.70$.

Now use an option to create a floor
An ATM call costs $C_0 = \$0.15$ (with expiry date of 28 December).
An ATM put would cost you $P_0 = \$0.15$.

Assume that the options are cash settled.

The NG futures for Jan delivery on NYMEX is $F_0(\text{Jan}) = 8.20$ $/mbtu.

(b) What would have been the outcome of your hedge if the two alternative futures prices had been $F_1 = \$7.70$ or $F_1 = \$8.70$? (Assume that the put is cash settled.)

Compare the outcome of your futures hedge with using options.

Q6   In May you have agreed to sell 10,000 mbtu *per day* of NG at $S(fix) = 10.5$ $/mbtu to customers in the Boston area for each of the months in the next year from January–June. You do not currently have the NG. The current swap rate is 10.0 $/mbtu.

(a) How would you hedge your January-June fixed price sales using swaps?
(b) What is the payoff in your swap each month if the spot NG prices turn out to be:

Spot out-turn, S

Jan 09	11.85
Feb 09	11.87
Mar 09	11.65
Apr 09	9.69
May 09	9.49
Jun 09	9.6

(c) What is the effective price you pay for your NG purchases in each month? How might the swap dealer get rid of her risk?

Q7   It is the end of October. A large ski resort called *Its All Downhill* will lose money if there is an unusually warm winter season (e.g. in December to March). How can the ski resort use weather futures (on temperature) to hedge this risk?

Q8   In February, a large water park owned by *DHockney* corporation called *ABiggerSplash* knows that abnormally cool weather over the summer months leads to fewer customers and reduced profits. How can the water park mitigate such losses using weather futures based on temperature?

Q9   You own a ski resort in the northeastern US. In January you may be worried that the snow in March will be much less than usual and hence less people will come to your ski resort and you will make less profit. You think that there will be less snow because you expect higher than average temperatures in March. In principle, how can you work out how many weather futures contracts (based on temperature) you might need to hedge your profits?

Q10   You own a ski resort in the northeastern US. In January you may be worried that the snow in March will be much less than usual and hence less people will come to your ski resort and you will make less profit. There is less snow because of higher than average temperatures. What is the main difference between using a weather futures or a weather option (based on temperature) to mitigate adverse outcomes for your operating profits?

PART 8

PORTFOLIO MANAGEMENT

CHAPTER 28

Private Equity

AIMS

- To outline the business model for private equity.
- To consider the pros and cons of private equity versus publicly quoted companies.
- To discuss risk and returns from private equity.

INTRODUCTION

A private equity firm raises debt and equity capital and invests the funds in different companies. A key feature is that the owner's equity is not freely tradable on a public stock market. The growth in private equity has been very rapid over the last 10 years. There are thousands of private equity firms that invest in a wide range of companies such as start-ups (usually referred to as angel investing or venture capital), firms in the growth phase of their existence (mezzanine capital) and, more recently, in very large, established firms via leveraged buy-outs (LBOs) and management buy-outs (MBOs). Some private equity firms concentrate on particular sectors like IT or biotechnology, whereas others concentrate on particular geographic areas.

28.1 ORGANISATION

How are private equity companies organised? Usually, a group of individuals set up a limited liability partnership, which from the outset might have a limited life of around 10 years. The partners issue a prospectus covering the type of firms in which the company will invest and also provides the track record of the private equity managers. The private equity **general partners** (GP) are usually called the management company, while investors are known as **limited partners** (LP) or 'the fund'. Investors in private equity are generally big players such as pension funds, banks, insurance companies, university endowments, hedge funds and high-net-worth individuals. So private equity has some attributes of a closed-end fund, but the shares of the private equity fund are not listed on an exchange and hence are illiquid. The amount of funds raised varies tremendously from a few million dollars for venture capital funds to well over $10bn for some of the largest private equity companies, such as Blackstone; Kohlberg, Kravis Roberts (KKR); the Carlyle Group; and the Texas Pacific Group in the US; and in the UK, Permira and 3i. Funds are locked up for as long as 10 years and private equity does not have to be as transparent about what it is doing as does a public quoted company.

Private equity groups raise their funds in tranches. Once they have firm commitments from the limited partners, this is called the 'first close' of the fund. These funds will then be 'called' and invested over the next two to five years. But the private equity fund can raise further funds (calls) until what is known as the 'final close'. The private equity fund can then draw down this capital as required, to invest in different ventures. In general, the fund will not invest more than 10% of its assets in one particular venture and will take on between 15 and 30 separate investments over the life of the fund.

A **venture capital** investment will be relatively small, measured in millions, and this will usually involve all-equity finance and seats for the GPs on the board of the invested companies. For large buy-outs the private equity fund will use some of its own equity, but supplement this with four or five times more debt finance from banks and other financial institutions, so buy-outs tend to be **highly leveraged**. Often the assets of the company being acquired, as well as those of the private equity fund, are used as collateral for the loans. It is also possible for the limited partners to invest additional capital in particular deals and these are known as 'co-invest' arrangements. In nearly all deals the private equity group takes control of the companies in which it invests, but occasionally it takes just a minority stake. For example, Blackstone took a minority stake in Deutsche Telekom in 2007, while 3i took a

TABLE 28.1: Large private equity groups

Fund	Closed (year)/open	Size
GS Capital Partners	Open	$19.0bn
Blackstone	Closed (2006)	$15.6bn
Texas Pacific Group	Closed (2006)	$15.0bn
Kolberg Kravis Roberts (KKR)	Open	$16.6bn
Carlyle Partners	Open	$15.0bn
Permira	Closed (2006)	€14.7bn
CVC European Partners	Closed (2005)	€8.0bn

minority stake in the architects Foster + Partners. (The latter is 90% owned by Norman Foster, with a value in the region of £400–500m, and is the firm of architects behind land-mark buildings in London such as the 'Gherkin' (the Swiss-Re tower), the new Wembley sta-dium and the Millennium Bridge; in France, the Millau Viaduct suspension bridge; in Berlin, the new Reichstag building; and in Hong Kong, Chep Lak Kok airport.)

The US is the largest private equity market followed by the UK and some of the larger firms are shown in Table 28.1.

Buy-out deals by private equity were around $50bn in 2000 (95 funds), rising to around $200bn in 2006 (190 funds) and projected to be in excess of $300bn in 2007 (over 200 funds). This deal flow has been partly driven by the relatively low and stable borrowing costs on risky debt over the last 10 years (prior to 2007), which often provides a large part of the finance for private equity investments. The top ten private equity deals in the US were worth between $17bn and $44bn, while in Europe the top five deals amount to around $10–15bn. Most private equity groups are limited partnerships, but a few are publicly quoted companies, for example 3i in the UK and Fortress in the US (see Case Study 28.1).

CASE STUDY 28.1   PRIVATE EQUITY PEOPLE

The key people running private equity funds are generally not well known, even among finance practitioners. For example, Blackstone, one of the largest private equi-ty businesses, was started about 20 years ago by Stephen Schwarzman (former US Commerce Secretary) and Peter Peterson (former head of Lehman Brothers). Initially they were turned down by over 450 potential investors and were finally given funds by the Prudential Insurance Company. In 1987 their first fund had around 30 investors and invested in USX, a US Steel and energy group. Since then Blackstone has invested in a wide range of businesses including asset management companies, hedge funds, a UK pubs group and the Savoy Group in London. Its largest private equity deal in 2006 was the $38bn purchase of Equity Office Properties. Blackstone currently has capital of around $20bn.

In Europe, Permira, a relatively large fund, is headed by Damon Buffini. Starting from humble origins in the UK, he gained a place at Cambridge to read law and also obtained an MBA from Harvard, before being hired by Schroder Ventures UK. He came to prominence in the UK following trade union attacks on Permira after it had taken over Bird's Eye (frozen foods) and closed one of its factories in Hull, with the loss of hundreds of jobs. Partly because of this, there was a trade union-organised protest outside his local church, Holy Trinity in South London, where he was confronted by a mock camel. The point was that it is easier for a camel to pass through the eye of a needle than for a rich man to enter the kingdom of heaven. To a certain extent Mr Buffini then became the public face of private equity in the UK, giving evidence (along with others) to a House of Commons select committee enquiry into private equity.

In 2007, Blackstone unveiled plans for an initial public offering IPO and flotation on the stock market, with initial guesses that the flotation would be worth between $20bn and $60bn. For the GPs an initial public offering means that they can capitalise the future profits of the fund and withdraw their own capital as cash, which may be doubly advantageous if they feel that the stock market is currently at its peak. By going public, the firm will be subject to much more stringent reporting requirements, including having to report and justify the fees and salaries of what will then be the managers of a publicly quoted company.

One of the key ideas behind private equity's success is that it can acquire long-term funds, taking its time about choosing its investments and in deciding the optimum time to liquidate those investments. Thus private equity is not under constant pressure to deliver a steady continuous stream of dividends to satisfy shareholders, as a public company would have to do. By going public, Blackstone effectively has the attributes of a closed-end fund (but with much more illiquid assets), which must report to its common stockholders. This may inhibit its ability to make strategic long-term investments. However, this has not stopped the Chinese government from investing $3bn of its $1200bn foreign exchange reserves in Blackstone, giving it about 10% of the company's equity. The Chinese government has agreed to keep its stake for at least four years and not to invest in rival private equity groups. It is hoping that private equity will enhance the risk–return trade-off of its FX portfolio, much of which is currently invested in low-yield US Treasury bonds.

28.2 MAKING MONEY

How do private equity firms make their money? First, GPs charge management fees that range from 2–4% of committed capital for the first five years (and somewhat smaller after that) and on top of this they also charge for monitoring, legal and other costs. The most important payment for general partners is the share of profits generated from investments, usually set at around 20% of profits (above some target rate, known as the hurdle rate). The profits usually accrue to the fund as a whole rather than to individual deals and are known as 'carried interest'. Roughly speaking, profits are measured after the fund has returned to investors any capital drawn down and after deduction of management and other fees. So investors get 80% and the general partners 20% of the carried interest. However, some funds have deal-by-deal carried interest.

Investors' capital might be recouped by the private equity company floating some of its businesses (IPOs), or by a private sale to corporate buyers or to another private equity firm. Some private equity funds may also return capital to investors via a refinancing deal. A private equity company renegotiates its debt, possibly takes on more debt and pays out to the limited partners some of this new debt in the form of a dividend. There is limited liquidity in the secondary market (i.e. 'private equity secondaries'), whereby existing limited partners can sell their equity stake (and remaining unfunded commitments) to another party – this is facilitated OTC by firms such as Goldman Sachs, Credit Suisse and Landmark Partners.

There is also an issue about when profits can actually be 'booked' in the accounts. In the US a new accounting standard, SFAS 159, allows private equity firms to calculate the option value for the future carried interest and this can be immediately entered into the accounts. The option value can be adjusted through time and a final adjustment comes at the exit point when the investments are realised; such an adjustment to profits at the closing date of the fund could be positive or negative. In principle, this smoothes out the reported earnings of private equity. If profits could only be booked when the investments were actually liquidated (e.g. after an IPO of the fund), this would give rise to very irregular and 'lumpy' profits figures. However, it is possible that the option valuation might not be very transparent and therefore could inflate profits in particular years. But the private equity group cannot be too aggressive in estimating its option value in any particular year, as it may have to take losses later when the fund investments are actually realised.

Are private equity groups good for the economy? On the one hand, people argue that private equity provides efficient management and higher growth in the companies it manages, but others argue that private equity funds are mere 'asset strippers'. Private equity groups take a close interest in the firms they have acquired and often insist that the managers of the firm also have an equity stake. Therefore, it could be said that there are fewer conflicts of interest (agency costs) between managers and owners than there is in the diffuse ownership structure of publicly quoted companies. However, because the general partners take 20% of the carried interest, they may be more interested in the upside than in limiting the downside. This gives them an incentive to go for broke if their fund is doing badly.

When private equity invests in young venture capital funds (usually with 100% equity), direct control and the GPs sitting on the boards of small companies can be invaluable. But such hands-on direct control is probably more difficult with large LBOs. On the other hand, having high levels of debt finance means that the directors and managers have to concentrate on 'core competences', so that future earnings can cover debt interest payments. Note, however, that a high level of debt also means that private equity investments are highly levered and therefore highly risky – they have the usual business risk but also high financial risk. Investors in private equity require a high return on their equity capital to compensate for this 'leverage risk' (i.e. the *levered betas* of firms run by private equity are higher than the unlevered betas of firms with the same business risk, but a lower proportion of debt finance).

In 2006–07 private equity firms were able to obtain debt on rather favourable terms – 'cov-lite' or 'covenant-lite' debt – which had fewer restrictive covenants than previously. Covenants are restrictions that lenders place on borrowers. They can be regular 'maintenance covenants', like having to report interest coverage (i.e. the ratio of EBITDA to interest payments) or leverage (i.e. EBITDA to net debt). (EBITDA stands for earnings before interest, taxes, depreciation and amortisation.) If these ratios drop below target, the suppliers of debt can demand their money back or look for restructuring deals. Covenant-lite loans do not have these maintenance covenants, although they still have 'incurrence-only' covenants, such as not being able to take on new debt or pay out dividends unless they meet a leverage test. Cov-lite loans probably do not give such early warning of firms getting into difficulties as do those with regular covenants.

Because private equity is a relatively new phenomenon, it is difficult to assess whether private equity does better than comparable firms that are publicly owned. One recent US study (Cao and Lerner, 2007) looked at the post-flotation performance of around 500 companies floated by private equity between 1980 and 2002. The study finds that the shares of companies previously managed and restructured by the private equity outperformed both the overall market return and share issues in other comparable initial public offerings. One problem here is comparing like with like; or, put another way, whether the business and leverage risk of the post-flotation private equity firms are the same as the comparator publicly quoted firms used in the study.

How about returns to *investors* from private equity? Kaplan and Schoar (2003) found that between 1980 and 2001, the average of private equity fund returns (net of fees) was approximately equal to the return on the S&P 500. When they isolated those private equity deals that involved LBOs, they found that returns (net of fees) were somewhat lower than those of the S&P 500. On the other hand, Ljungqvist and Richardson (2003) found that mature private equity funds over 1981–2001 generated an internal rate of return of around 20% p.a., which is above the 14% p.a. generated by the S&P 500. So for the private equity industry as a whole, there is still controversy about whether the average dollar invested in private equity earns a return that compensates for the risk of such investments.

What is also noted in these studies is that there are extreme winners and extreme losers in the private equity sector. So the age-old question arises as to whether there are perhaps a small number of successful managers in private equity and how easy it is to spot these managers. Kaplan and Schoar (2003) find substantial *persistence* in leveraged buyout and venture capital fund performance. General partners whose investments in a fund outperform the industry returns are likely to outperform the industry in their next fund, so past winners persist. This persistence appears to be stronger in established funds rather than new entrants. As we have seen, this is very different from the performance of mutual funds where there seems to be little persistence in past winners, although substantial persistence in past losers.

Nevertheless, there is always the question of whether persistence uncovered from past data will continue in the future (that is, whether persistence persists). After all, private equity is relatively new and there may have been genuinely successful private equity mangers in the past who were able to spot undervalued and badly managed firms, which they subsequently turned around. But as more capital pours into the sector, it may become increasingly difficult to find undervalued or badly managed firms.

28.3 PUBLIC POLICY

There is a lack of transparency in private equity compared to publicly quoted companies. But this also means that private equity is not subject to the tyrannies of quarterly reporting and concentration on short-term performance. Private equity may therefore be able more easily to concentrate on longer-term strategic considerations, whereas some publicly quoted companies may be overly concerned about the short term at the expense of long-term strategy. See Case Study 28.2.

CASE STUDY 28.2   A NATION OF SHOPKEEPERS?

Most UK residents would not know that some household names have been taken over by private equity groups, for example Formula One motor racing, music group EMI, car breakdown and insurance company the AA, and Saga, a holiday and insurance company aimed at the over-50s. In 2005–07 there was a rapid growth in private equity deals involving large corporations, and two that caught the eye in the UK were bids for Sainsbury's the supermarket chain and Alliance-Boots the chemists. A consortium of private equity groups comprising CVC, Blackstone Group and KKR made a bid for Sainsbury's of around £10bn in spring 2007. It was thought that the private equity group would use an LBO and then enter into a sale and leaseback agreement on Sainsbury's sizeable property portfolio of around £7.5bn. The company would effectively be split into a property arm and an operating company, which would rent the stores. Sainsbury's stock price rose substantially on news of the bid leaking out, but eventually the bid was withdrawn, so Sainsbury's remains (for the moment at least) a public company. (Note, however, that Sainsbury's has a somewhat concentrated ownership, as the Sainsbury family owns around 15% of the shares – if they did not wish to sell, prospective acquirers would need to purchase shares from other shareholders.)

In spring 2007, Alliance-Boots was being stalked by two private equity groups, KKR and a consortium comprising the private equity group Terra Firma and the Wellcome Trust, a charitable medical research company. Intriguingly, Stefano Pessina, the executive deputy chairman and largest shareholder in Alliance-Boots, was part of the KKR bid, hence KKR had an 'inside track' and the LBO was therefore partly an MBO as well. The final offer was around £11bn. Unlike Sainsbury's, Alliance-Boots has a relatively small property portfolio of around $1.5bn, as it leases most of its shops. On news of the bid, its share price jumped by around 16%, so Pessina's shares went up in value. During the bid procedure KKR upped its original bid by £1bn to £11.1bn ($22.2bn) and this led the Alliance-Boots board to recommend to its shareholders acceptance of the offer. KKR is then allowed to 'look at the books' and undertake due diligence; that is, to see in detail whether the accounts reflect the true worth of the company. Overall, the bid premium was around 40%, by which time KKR had acquired 29.3% of Alliance-Boots shares and with Pessina's 25% stake this gave it a controlling interest, but the bid involves around £8bn of debt finance.

It is thought that the KKR bidders think that Alliance-Boots can increase future profits partly by cost savings, partly by taking advantage of the deregulation of retail pharmacies in Europe and also by strengthening its brand in providing prescriptions, which mostly emanate from the UK's National Health Service. It was the general view at the time that KKR paid a high price for Alliance-Boots and it may struggle to service the debt and expand the business. Alliance-Boot's pension trustees are also be concerned about the group's £3bn pension fund, covering around 67,000 members. It was reported that John Watson, head of the trustees, wanted KKR to commit £1bn to the scheme – a £500m cash injection and an 'appropriate new security' to cover the remaining £500m. The trustees believe that KKR favours a phased 10-year contribution plan, but the pension trustees believe that this is too risky given the scale of the debt finance.

This was the biggest leveraged buy-out in the UK and it was the first time that a FTSE 100 company had been acquired by private equity. The reporting requirements of private equity companies are far less than those for a publicly quoted company, so there were obvious worries for the company's workforce of about 100,000 staff.

Private equity usually involves large amounts of debt finance. As debt interest is tax deductible, this is effectively a subsidy (the 'tax shield' of the debt), which may help lower the overall cost of capital (WACC) for private equity and raise the value of firms in the private equity portfolio. This is part of the famous Modigliani-Miller theorem: that under certain restrictive assumptions the value of the firm increases as the debt-to-equity ratio (leverage) increases, because of the benefit of tax shields. But there is also a potential downside of leverage; namely, the additional risk and costs of financial distress, which may mean that some private equity deals reduce the value of the firms under management. However, the notion that private equity has an advantage over a public company because of its high leverage is not a very strong one, because there is nothing in principle to prevent a publicly quoted company having debt levels just as high.

SUMMARY

- Private equity firms are usually limited partnerships that invest in a range of companies and look for exit strategies over a 5–10-year horizon.
- *Venture capital* is a subgroup of private equity dealing with start-up companies, often in telecoms and biotech, which have a lot of human capital (intangibles) but not much physical capital (tangibles in land, plant and machinery).
- Private equity has increasingly moved towards large leveraged buy-outs followed by restructuring – including restructuring of the board of directors.

- The benefits of private equity to investors are the hands-on approach of the general partners and the long-term strategic approach they are able to take, freed from the continuous scrutiny of publicly owned firms. But there is a lack of transparency concerning their actions.
- Returns to private equity were high in the 1990–2005 period but the risks, given high leverage, are also great. Insurance companies, pension funds and hedge funds are now investing in private equity partnerships.

EXERCISES

Q1   What have been the key drivers in the expansion of private equity firms since 2000?

Q2   Why might some private equity groups consider going public? How is this done?

Q3   What is carried interest?

Q4   Why might pension funds want to become limited partners (i.e. investors) in a private equity fund?

29

Performance of Mutual Funds

AIMS

- To examine how we assess risk-adjusted performance of mutual funds using a fund's *alpha*.
- To examine the historic (ex-post) performance of mutual funds.
- To examine whether it is possible to pick groups of funds that earn positive abnormal returns in the future – this is *persistence*.
- To ascertain whether *money is smart* – that is, whether investors put their money into funds that subsequently do well and withdraw their money from funds that subsequently perform badly.

INTRODUCTION

In this chapter we summarise and evaluate mutual fund performance in the US and UK, concentrating particularly on the literature published over the last 15 years where innovation and data advances have been most marked. The first issue we want to explore is whether actively managed funds taken as a whole or individual funds have a historic (ex-post) performance that gives investors a return that more than compensates for the riskiness of the fund – if so, we say that the fund has a positive *abnormal return* or positive alpha. The next issue is whether investors can today identify a group of funds that will perform well in the future. It may be the case that past winner funds continue to be winners in the future – if so, we say that there is persistence in winner fund performance. Finally, if fund returns persist then it may be possible for investors to reallocate their savings away from 'loser funds' towards 'winner funds' and hence increase their future long-term abnormal returns – in short, 'money may be smart'.

29.1 FACTOR MODELS

One of the major problems in assessing the performance of mutual funds is the need to evaluate the riskiness of the fund's returns. We need to adjust the return on the fund to account for its risk in a tractable, intuitive way. A skilled active manager should be able to pick stocks that earn a positive return after accounting for risk, while still holding a relatively diversified portfolio to minimise specific risk. The CAPM implies that the excess return required to just compensate for a portfolio's risk is given by the portfolio beta times the average (excess) market return:

$$\text{Required return on portfolio due to market risk} = \beta_i(\overline{R}_{mt} - \overline{r}_t)$$

Suppose that the beta of a mutual fund is 0.9 and the average excess return on the market (over, say, the last five years) is 20%, then according to the CAPM a fair return to compensate for the risk of holding this fund is 18%. If the portfolio actually earns an average (excess) return of $\overline{R}_{it} - \overline{r}_t = 22\%$, the historical abnormal return earned by the stock-picking skills of the fund manager is:

$$\text{Abnormal return} = \text{Average return on portfolio} - \text{Average required return on portfolio}$$
$$\alpha_i = \overline{R}_{it} - \overline{r}_t - \beta_i(\overline{R}_{mt} - \overline{r}_t) = 4\% \text{ p.a.}$$

The abnormal return is *Jensen's alpha* for this fund, α_i. If we calculate the (historical) mean return on the portfolio and the mean return on the market and we have an estimate of beta (e.g. provided by a broker or data source such as Morningstar), we can directly calculate alpha. However, an equally simple method of calculating alpha is available using an ordinary least-squares *time-series* regression:

$$R_{it} - r_t = \alpha_i + \beta_i(R_{mt} - r_t) + \varepsilon_{it}$$

Often a monthly value of alpha is estimated by using time-series data on the monthly excess return on the mutual fund portfolio, regressed on the monthly excess return on the market $(R_{mt} - r_t)$. The slope of the regression line gives an estimate of β_i and the intercept in the regression is the estimate of α_i. In practice, an aggregate stock index such as the S&P 500 (for US funds) or the FT All-share index (for UK funds) is used as a measure of the return on the market portfolio, R_m.

Alpha is the return earned by the manager, and has nothing to do with the average level of the market return. If the fund manager has no skill in picking stocks that can 'beat the market', then α_i will be zero. A manager with skill will produce a positive alpha and a manager that underperforms the market will have a negative alpha. Therefore, a positive and statistically significant value of alpha indicates superior risk-adjusted performance or positive stock-picking skills on the part of the fund manager.

3F and 4F alpha

Is the *market* beta the only determinant of the riskiness of a mutual fund portfolio? No. It appears (historically at least) as if portfolios composed of 'small stocks' (i.e. those firms with low market value of equity) earn a higher average return than the market portfolio, but also have higher risk. So if a mutual fund held a large proportion of its assets in small stocks, the market return would underestimate the riskiness of the mutual fund portfolio. Jensen's alpha $\alpha_i = (\bar{R}_{it} - \bar{r}_t) - \beta_i(\bar{R}_{mt} - \bar{r}_t)$, using only the market beta, would be an overestimate of the fund manager's true ability to earn abnormal returns. We therefore need an alpha that takes account of the additional risk in holding small stocks. This is done by also including a 'size factor', SMB ('small minus big'), in our factor regression. The SMB variable is a measure of the difference between the returns on a portfolio comprising small stocks and a portfolio containing large stocks. The economic rationale underpinning the use of a 'size beta' is that the earnings prospects of small firms may be more sensitive to changes in economic conditions, with a resulting higher probability of distress during economic downturns and hence higher systematic risk.

There are also some other factors that are thought to have a separate influence on the riskiness of mutual fund returns. The book-to-market factor, HML ('high minus low'), is a measure of the difference between the returns on stocks whose firms have a high book-to-market value and those firms that have a low book-to-market value. Firms with high book-to-market ratios tend to represent firms whose prices have recently experienced sharp falls; such firms are thought to be in distress and hence more likely to fail in the future. Hence, the returns on stocks whose firms have high book-to-market values are thought to be more risky and investors in such stocks should be compensated with a higher average return.

Carhart (1997) noted that a momentum strategy is easy to implement and studies showed that this 'mechanical strategy' of simply buying stocks that had risen the most over the recent past (e.g. over the last year) led to future returns that were higher than the market return. Since this is an easy strategy to implement requiring little or no skill, we would not wish to reward our fund manager for obtaining a high alpha just by using a mechanical momentum strategy.

Hence, some performance regressions also include a 'momentum factor' (MOM), which is the difference in returns between a portfolio of previously high-performing stocks and previously poor-performing stocks.

There is a continuing debate as to whether the above factors really measure the systematic economic risks of particular types of firms. However, suppose it is true that stock portfolios that include small stocks, stocks with high book-to-market values or stocks that have exhibited momentum do have higher average returns than portfolios of stocks formed from large firms, firms with low book-to-market values or firms whose returns have not increased very much in the recent past. You would not want to say that a portfolio manager who formed portfolios of, say, high book-to-market stocks had stock-picking skill, since almost anybody could undertake this rather mechanical stock-picking strategy. But if you only included the market return in your performance regression, such a portfolio containing high book-to-market stocks would produce a positive (Jensen's) alpha.

Hence, multifactor models of fund returns include factors such as SMB, HML and MOM to account for the higher average returns from these mechanical strategies. It is then thought that the alpha from these *multifactor regressions* more accurately measures the genuine stock-picking skills of fund managers. In other words, to earn an positive abnormal return (alpha) as measured by a multifactor model, the mutual fund manager must use her unique information and insights into future firm performance and not just employ mechanical strategies. If we include all four factors, our regression equation would be:

$$(R_{it} - r_t) = \alpha_i + \beta_{1i}(R_{mt} - r_t) + \beta_{2i} SMB_t + \beta_{3i} HML_t + \beta_{4i} MOM_t + \varepsilon_{it}$$

and the alpha is the abnormal return we are seeking to measure. The above model is referred to as the Carhart four-factor model (4F) and if we *exclude* the momentum factor it is called the (Fama-French) 3F model.

The above regressions are sometimes referred to as *style-attribution models*. The logic is that after considering all systematic (style) influences on fund returns over time, a positive estimated alpha indicates that the fund has an average return from stock-picking skills exceeding that from following mechanical investment strategies (e.g. like holding the market portfolio or investing in small stocks or a mixture of the two styles). A positive (negative) and statistically significant value of alpha indicates superior (inferior) risk-adjusted performance.

The Sharpe ratio is also used to measure performance and to rank funds, but as we have seen this measure is more useful when only one mutual fund will eventually be chosen as the investor's total portfolio, since here the measure of risk used is the standard deviation of the returns of the fund. If the mutual fund is being considered as an *addition* to an already diversified 'passive portfolio' (of stocks and bonds), then factor betas are a more relevant measure of risk and alpha is a more acceptable measure of abnormal performance. Hence, in studies of mutual fund performance it is more usual to see alpha as the reported performance statistic, but sometimes the Sharpe ratio is also reported.

29.2 HISTORICAL PERFORMANCE

Measuring returns

Fund returns can be gross or net of various charges, depending on whether we wish to measure returns to the fund (or fund managers) or returns to the investor/customer. *Net returns* are returns to investors (but before deduction of any load fees or payment of personal taxes).

Net returns are therefore after deduction of all fund expenses and all security-level transaction costs (e.g. brokerage fees and commissions). *Gross fund* returns (*i.e. before expenses but after dealing costs*) R_t^g are usually defined as $R_t^g = R_t^{net} + TER_t$, where *TER* is the total expense ratio. In some studies 'fund return' is the return on the largest share class, while others use the value-weighted return of all individual share classes (see Wermers, 2003a).

Since data on the *identity* of fund managers over time is somewhat sparse, studies that measure returns to specific fund *managers* are much less prevalent than those that measure returns to the fund itself. This is not a major drawback if a fund's style is largely a group decision. However, it is clearly of interest for investors to assess whether performance is at the fund or fund manager level, since this may determine relative fund flows and the question of whether 'money is smart' (see below).

Looking at US actively managed equity mutual funds *as a whole*, their (geometric) average return over the last 25 years has been around 1% below that of a value-weighted broad market index such as the Wiltshire 5000 (where we deduct 0.2% from the return of the Wiltshire 5000 to reflect the expenses of running even the lowest-cost passive index fund). This does not bode well for the actively managed fund industry as a whole. Over long horizons, small differences in returns can lead to large differences in terminal wealth and hence in resources available in retirement. For example, for {10, 20, 30, 40}-year horizons, a 1% p.a. lower return leads to differences in terminal wealth of {10.5%, 22.1%, 35.0%, 49.2%} respectively. The standard deviation of annual returns of actively managed funds and the Wiltshire 5000 are about the same, so actively managed funds have a historical Sharpe ratio that is below that for index funds. These broad results suggest that investors should put most of their investments in stocks into index funds rather than actively managed funds. But they don't – presumably because they believe that they can identify and then buy the 'top' funds and avoid the 'bottom' funds; we discuss this below. However, note that when we look at the distribution of individual alphas for, say, UK funds (Figure 29.1), we see that there are some *potential* winners (and losers), since the spread of alphas across funds is very high. There are a few funds with historical alphas larger than 1.5% per month (18% p.a.), but it still remains to be seen whether the alphas are statistically significant and whether such winner funds can be identified in advance.

For the US, the CRSP (Centre for Research in Security Prices) and Morningstar monthly databases are most frequently used in academic studies, with the latter providing more detail on fund composition. Survivorship bias is the difference between the annual returns of just the surviving funds in the database and the full set of both surviving and dead funds. It has been estimated at around 1% p.a. (for US and UK mutual funds). Given that the average estimated alpha for all actively managed *equity* mutual funds is around *minus* 70 bp per annum, it is important to ensure that a database includes both alive and dead funds, if we are to get an accurate

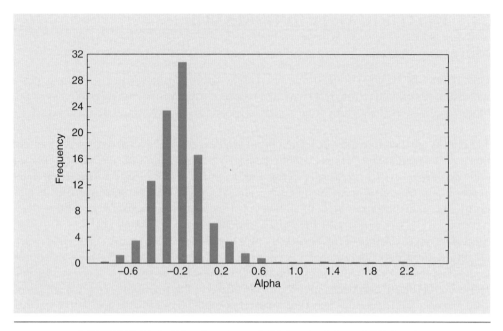

FIGURE 29.1: Distribution of 3F fund alphas, UK funds

picture of performance of the mutual fund industry as a whole. Academic studies post-1995 on US and UK mutual funds tend to use databases that are free of survivorship bias[1].

US and UK results

We now turn to the ex-post performance of US and UK actively managed equity mutual funds. Unless stated otherwise, 'statistically significant' refers to a 5% significance level (or better). How do US active funds perform on average when we consider *abnormal returns* to investors? Over the period January 1975–December 2002 using around 1700 US mutual funds, Kosowski *et al.* (2006) find that the (equally weighted 4F) net return alpha is about minus 0.5% p.a., so the average active fund underperforms its benchmarks. Nevertheless, in an interesting study Kosowski *et al.* (2006) find that the average alpha (depending on the model used) is 3–5% p.a. higher in recessions than in expansions, demonstrating that investment in mutual funds (and particularly growth-oriented funds) may provide added value, in times when consumers are particularly vulnerable to lower incomes and a higher probability of unemployment.

Much less empirical work on performance has been done on UK funds, but the consensus of these results seems to be that between 1975 and 1997, the abnormal average alpha (for 752 funds) using *gross returns* and the 3F model was around *minus* 1% p.a. ($t = 2.3$), so UK funds' stock-picking abilities did not even cover their management fees (Quigley and Sinquefield, 2000).

---

[1] In addition, 'incubation bias' arises if funds only begin to report to a database after a period of successful performance – this problem is more acute for hedge funds than for mutual funds.

The above studies strongly suggest that the average US or UK fund (even within specific sectors) does not earn abnormal positive net returns. Of course, this does not preclude funds in the tails of the distribution having statistically significant alphas, an issue we now discuss.

Luck and fund performance

As we have seen above, there is considerable evidence for the US and the UK that the *average* active equity mutual fund underperforms its benchmark returns. Kosowski *et al.* (2006) examine the performance of *individual* funds and try to measure accurately whether performance is due to luck or skill.

Let's first of all consider how difficult it is to distinguish skill from luck for *individual funds,* when we use standard statistical tests. Suppose we take a mutual fund P that has an R-squared of 0.95, when its monthly (excess) return is regressed on the market return. The single-index model (using excess returns) therefore fits pretty well and the residual risk is relatively small[2]. Suppose the intercept (alpha) in this regression turns out to be 0.08333% per month (1% p.a.), which indicates that the fund has reasonable stock-picking skills, after adjusting for the market risk held by the fund. How much monthly data would we need in order to ensure that this value of alpha is statistically significant? The *t*-statistic of alpha must be greater than 1.96 (assuming normality in large samples) to ensure statistical significance at a 5% significance level. The *t*-statistic of alpha is (approximately) given by:

$$t = \frac{\alpha}{\sigma(e_p)/\sqrt{T}} = \frac{0.08333}{0.9/\sqrt{T}} > 1.96$$

Hence *T* must be greater than 448 months, so we need about 37 years of data to establish (with 95% certainty) that this fund's alpha is statistically different from zero. This is even worse than it looks, since we have assumed that we know the fund's 'true' alpha and residual risk and that the 'true' parameters are constant over the whole data period. Clearly, the larger is the 'true' alpha, the less data we need to establish statistical significance. For example, if we find a really good fund with an alpha of 3% per year, we would only need about 9 years of monthly data to establish statistical significance – this seems more feasible.

There is, however, a further statistical problem, in that funds in the extreme tails of the performance distribution are likely to exhibit non-normality in their specific (residual) risk, hence standard 'critical values' (e.g. the 1.96 used above) may give misleading results. To highlight the importance of skill versus luck, consider whether the stellar performance by some funds even over a run of many years is due to luck or skill. Are these 'stars' just the lucky ones among the cohort of all fund managers? (For example, Peter Lynch of the Magellan fund is cited as a star manager. The US-based Schroder Ultra Fund earned 107% over three years ending in 2001 and was closed to new investors as early as 1998.)

---

[2] Here we have chosen the beta of the fund to be 0.9, the specific (or residual) risk of the fund is $\sigma(e_p) = 0.90\%$ per month (3.1% p.a.) and its total risk $\sigma(R_p) = 4\%$ per month (13.85% p.a.). Remember from the single index model that $\sigma^2(R_p) = \beta^2 \sigma^2(R_m) + \sigma^2(e_p)$ and $Rsqd = [\beta^2 \sigma^2(R_m)] / \sigma^2(R_p)$.

If we are told that a *randomly selected* mutual fund has an abnormal average return of, say, 10% p.a., we might well be impressed. But if we are told that this return of 10% p.a. was achieved by the *best*-performing fund out of, say, 1000 funds, we should be less impressed. This is because in a large universe of 1000 funds there will always be some funds that perform well or badly, simply due to chance. The issue then arises as to how we can separate 'skill' from 'luck' for *individual* funds, particularly when idiosyncratic risks are highly non-normal – as is the case for funds in the extreme tails, in which investors are particularly interested.

Kosowski *et al.* (2006) use a technique known as 'bootstrapping' to try to separate skill from luck. Using around 1700 US funds (January 1975–December 2002), they find that funds ranked above the top 5th percentile (i.e. a maximum of about 90 funds) have a statistically significant 4F alpha, and these funds have α_{4F}^{net} in excess of 4.8% p.a. The proportion of funds with positive alphas is as high as 30–40% in the 1975–89 period, but falls to around 5% in the 1990–2002 period, when there are far more funds and more competition in trying to find mispriced stocks. Using a similar approach on UK data (842 funds, 1975–2002), Cuthbertson, Nitzsche and O'Sullivan (2008) find that only 12 UK funds have genuine skill. If the true alphas of all the funds are set to zero, but we 'replay history' by simulating the errors attached to each fund by randomly choosing from the regression residuals $\tilde{e}_{i,t}$ then we can simulate a time series of returns for each fund using $\tilde{r}_{i,t} = 0 + \hat{\beta}_i' X_t + \tilde{e}_{i,t}$. This procedure is known as bootstrapping. We then use these simulated returns $\tilde{r}_{i,t}$ (where we know alpha = 0) to repeat the regression and *estimate* alpha for each fund. Even though we know that the 'true' alpha is zero, some of the *estimated* alphas could be quite large (or small); for example, if in our random choice of the residuals many happen by chance to be large and positive (negative), we would *estimate* a positive (negative) value for alpha.

In Figure 29.2, the solid line represents the values of alpha that were *estimated* from the simulated data on returns, so we know that the 'true' alphas are zero– this solid line represents the variability in estimated alphas that is solely due to luck. The dashed line represents the estimated alphas using the real data on fund returns. In fact in Figure 29.2 what we show is the *t*-alpha statistic, since this shows the statistical significance of the alpha estimate. You can see that in the right tail of the distribution there are a few funds whose actual 'real world' *t*-alphas exceed the values that would be generated just due to good luck, so it looks as if there are a few top funds that (have *t*-statistics that) indicate genuine skill. There are also many 'real world' funds (in the left tail) that do a lot worse than random bad luck, so these funds seem to have genuinely poor performance. Notice also that in the right tail, to beat good luck the actual *t*-statistic of a top fund would have to be larger than about 2.5, which is bigger than the usual critical value for the *t*-statistic of 1.7–1.96. This is because in the real data, returns are not normally distributed – but the bootstrap takes care of this.

Of course, it is still possible that some of these statistically significance *individual* funds are 'false discoveries', in the same way that among 1000 people who test positive for cancer, some will actually not have cancer. Statistics can never tell us with 100% certainty that something is true. This idea of false positives is a difficult issue in statistics, which Barras *et al.* (2005) address by estimating the 'false discovery rate' (FDR); that is, the proportion of lucky funds among funds with significant (individual) alphas. For all US equity funds (1975–2002), they find a high value for the FDR of around 55% among the 52 top funds, which implies that only about half of these (which constitutes 2% of all funds) have genuine skill. The relatively few skilled equity mutual funds in the US tend to be in either the

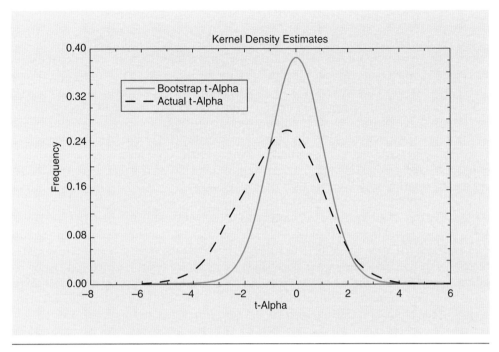

FIGURE 29.2: Estimated and simulated t-alphas

aggressive growth or growth styles, whereas in the UK successful funds tend to be in the 'equity income' style (Cuthbertson, Nitzsche and O'Sullivan, 2008).

At the negative end of the performance scale, UK and US results strongly suggest that between 20% and 40% of funds have a significant negative abnormal performance (Barras *et al.*, 2005; Cuthbertson, Nitzsche and O'Sullivan, 2008; Kosowski *et al.*, 2006).

Overall, what these latest studies demonstrate is the importance of looking at the performance of funds in the tails of the distribution (rather than the average fund) and then making appropriate adjustments for 'luck' before making inferences. The clear message from recent UK and US results is that there are a few top funds that demonstrate skill, but the majority have either no skill and do well because of luck, or perform worse than bad luck and essentially waste investors' time and money.

29.3 PICKING WINNERS: PERSISTENCE

Historical (ex-post) alphas, as described above, tell us about the average abnormal performance of individual funds, usually over the whole period for which we have returns data on the fund. However, it is also important to assess whether there are ex-ante rules that can be used to choose funds today that then go on to earn statistically and economically significant abnormal returns in the future; in short, whether there is *persistence* in fund performance. For investors as a whole to benefit from persistence in returns, we also have to establish that they are smart and allocate additional funds to future winners and withdraw funds from future losers – this is discussed below.

Recursive portfolios

A popular method of testing for the *economic importance* of persistence among winners and losers is the recursive portfolio method. First, a sorting/ranking decision rule is established. For example, using monthly data we might classify funds into deciles at time-*t* (e.g. 1 June 1975), based on *any* fund attribute (e.g. its past turnover, size, previous one-year return or its alpha estimated over the previous 36 months). The 'winner' decile contains the top 10% of funds ranked, for example, by their *past* one-year returns (i.e. from 1 June 1974 to 1 June 1975). Suppose we concentrate for the moment on only the 'past winner' decile of funds (and forget about the other nine decile portfolios of ranked funds). We hope that choosing a past winner fund today will lead to high returns in the future; that is, that past winners will continue to be winners, so winners persist.

At time-*t*, the portfolio (equally weighted or value weighted) of the chosen 10% of mutual funds that are past winners is then tracked each month and its monthly returns over the next year are noted (i.e. over 1 June 1975 to 1 June 1976). The chosen portfolio *holding period* is therefore one year. After one year a new ranking from all the funds is undertaken, based on all funds' returns over the previous year (which is now 1 June 1975 to 1 June 1976). Some funds will drop out of the existing winner decile and new funds will enter. The new past-winner decile of funds is then tracked over the next year and its returns noted. This process is repeated until the end of our data period. This gives rise to a sequence of monthly ex-ante *forward-looking* (or 'post-sort') portfolio returns $R_i^f(t, T)$ for the past-winner decile of funds over the period t ($= 1$ June 1975) to $T = 2007$ (1 June 2007).

We do not know in advance that past winners will give rise to future winners, but the returns $R_i^f(t, T)$ we have constructed allow us to test this proposition. Remember that the composition of the funds that make up the forward-looking returns $R_i^f(t, T)$ will usually consist of a changing portfolio of different mutual funds, although not all funds will necessarily be 'switched' at each rebalancing date. So the composition of the top decile is fixed *for one year,* but the composition can change at each rebalancing date. The forward-looking returns from our past-winner portfolio are normally used in a multifactor regression to see if the estimated (forward-looking) alpha of the past-winner portfolio is positive and statistically significant – if the alpha is positive, then there is persistence in past winners. Note that the sorting rule to form our portfolio can be anything at all (e.g. size of the fund, past returns). What we are really concerned about is whether our chosen sorting rule gives us a portfolio that results in a positive future abnormal performance (i.e. after correcting for risk using a factor model) indicated by the post-sort alpha.

It is important to note that we can sort portfolios into past winners by looking at returns on all funds over the past year, past two years and so on, so the portfolio-formation horizon can differ, and this gives rise to a different set of past winners in your chosen portfolio. In addition, we can hold our past-winner portfolio for one month, one quarter, one year or longer before we rebalance the portfolio – each of these different holding/rebalancing periods can result in a different performance for our forward-looking portfolio. Hence the portfolio-formation period and the portfolio-holding period may be crucial decisions in determining whether past winners become future winners.

In the literature it is usual to refer to holding/rebalancing periods of less than one year as *short horizon* and longer than one year as *long horizon.* Results on whether past winners persist differ depending on the rebalancing period chosen.

Are there sorting rules that allow you to form portfolios of US funds 'in real time' that then 'beat the market'? For US funds it is usually found that short-horizon rebalancing gives rise to winner persistence, but for long-horizon rebalancing periods the evidence for winner persistence is much more contentious. On the other hand, when we examine the past-loser decile (of funds) it is generally found for both short-horizon and long-horizon rebalancing periods that past losers stay just that – losers. A summary of some early studies of persistence of US mutual funds is given in Table 29.1. Below we concentrate on some of the more recent studies.

Long-horizon persistence

Some early US studies using either one-year or three-year rebalancing and with Jensen's alpha (i.e. the market model) or alpha from the 3F model as the performance measure find evidence of a small positive forward-looking alpha of around 0.5% p.a. for the past-winner portfolio and a forward-looking alpha of between -2.4% and -5.4% p.a. for the bottom past-loser decile of funds (e.g. Brown and Goetzmann, 1995; Elton, Gruber and Blake, 1996).

There was something of a watershed when Carhart (1997), using all US equity funds (1963–93), suggested that the persistence found in earlier studies using the CAPM or 3F alpha may be a manifestation of the momentum effect in stocks that are 'accidentally held' by funds, rather than funds being skilled stock pickers. Using the 4F alpha with the momentum factor included, he finds that $\alpha_{4F}^{f,net}$ is negative for all decile portfolios (significantly so for the bottom three deciles), so poor performance persists but good performance does not. This result has been updated and confirmed by Kosowski *et al.* (2006) for the period 1978–2002 using recursive portfolios, ranked on the past 12 or 36 months 4F alpha, with one-year rebalancing periods. The top decile of past winner funds exhibits persistence over one year with a statistically significant alpha of 1% p.a., with growth funds largely responsible for persistence in past-winner funds. At the bottom of the performance distribution (for all funds), deciles 6–10 have significantly negative abnormal performance (of about –1% p.a. for deciles 6–9 and –3.5% for the 10th decile)[3].

Short-horizon persistence

We now turn to evidence of short-run persistence based on monthly or quarterly rebalancing. Studies, particularly for the US, provide prima facie evidence for short-run persistence among past winners when rebalancing of the mutual fund portfolio takes place more than once a year. For example, with *quarterly* rebalancing a positive forward-looking alpha of about 1.3% p.a. is found for the past winners among US funds (Bollen and Busse, 2004).

---

[3] Kosowski *et al.* (2006) when ranking on past 1-year, 4F-alphas and using a 1-year rebalancing period find the top two winner deciles have significant persistence with 4F-alphas of 1.4% p.a. ($p < 0.01$) for the top decile and 0.84% p.a. ($p < 0.01$) for the second best decile fund, and again deciles 6–10 have statistically negative average performance of around -1.8% p.a. Note that Carhart (1997) finds no persistence for the top decile funds and the difference between the two studies may be attributed to the different sample period and more importantly to the non-normality in the specific risk of the top decile funds, which is taken into account in Kosowski *et al.* (2006).

TABLE 29.1: Studies of US mutual fund performance

Study	Period	Type of funds	Risk-adjusted returns	Net of management fees	Control for survivorship bias	Performance persistence
Carhart (1997)	1963–93	All US equity funds	Yes	Yes	Yes	Yes, for loser funds No, for winner funds
Chen, Jegadeesh and Wermers (2000)[a]	1975–95	Mainly US equity funds	Yes	Gross returns	Yes	Yes, but due to momentum rather than selectivity skills
Christopherson, Ferson and Glassman (1998)	1979–90	273 US equity pension funds	Yes	Gross returns	No	Yes, mainly among loser funds
Elton, Gruber and Blake (1996)	1977–93	188 US equity funds	Yes	Yes	Yes	Yes
Fletcher (1999)	1985–96	85 UK American unit trusts	Yes	Yes	Yes	No
Goetzmann and Ibbotson (1994)	1976–88	728 US mutual funds	Yes	No	No	Yes
Grinblatt and Titman (1992)	1975–84	279 US mutual funds	Yes	Yes	No	Yes, mainly for loser funds
Hendricks, Patel and Zeckhauser (1993)	1975–88	Growth-oriented equity funds	Yes	Yes	Yes	Yes, in the short term
Malkiel (1995)	1971–91	All US equity funds	Yes	Yes	Yes	Yes, during the 1970s No, during the 1980s
Volkman and Wohar (1994)	1980–89	332 US mutual funds	Yes	Yes	Yes	Yes

a: This study examines the buys and sells of each fund. It finds that the stockholdings passively carried over (from one period to the next) by winning funds outperform the passively carried-over holdings of losing funds. However, newly bought stocks by winning funds only marginally outperform newly bought stocks of losing funds. This suggests that momentum rather than stock selection skills explains the persistence.

For *monthly* rebalancing, Mamaysky *et al.* (2004) find that the abnormal net return to past winners is between 2.5% and 4.5% p.a.

These results suggest short-run persistence among past-winner funds and an ability to choose funds ex ante (i.e. in real time) that then 'beat the market'. But it is important to remember that to make this an exploitable strategy, we need to know if the forward-looking alpha of the past winner fund more than covers both load fees and rebalancing costs (brokerage fees and any bid–ask spreads on the price of the funds themselves), as investors switch the composition of the past winner fund at each rebalancing date. The more funds you have to buy or sell to rebalance your winner portfolio at each rebalancing date, the higher these costs. Of course, we do not know if more frequent *opportunities* to rank funds will lead to many or just a few funds being rebalanced over the whole life of the strategy – it is conceivable, although highly unlikely, that if you are allowed to rebalance over very short horizons such as *every month,* the composition of the past-winner portfolio will remain unchanged.

Also, if everyone attempted to implement such a strategy, the mutual funds in the past-winner portfolio would have to sell or buy the underlying shares in the fund frequently, and this would have major implications on turnover and trading costs (i.e. the commissions and bid–ask spreads of the underlying shares in the fund). So, with frequent rebalancing, finding sorting rules that give rise to persistence in past-winner funds are promising but as yet are far from definitive, given the unknown impact on returns of fund-rebalancing costs.

There are far fewer studies of persistence on UK data that use the recursive portfolio approach. Generally these use past raw returns or past alphas in order to rank funds into 'winner' and 'loser' portfolios, and the evidence strongly suggests that there is no persistence in past winners (with annual rebalancing) but fairly strong evidence of persistence in past-loser funds (Cuthbertson *et al.*, 2008; Fletcher and Forbes, 2002; Quigley and Sinquefield, 2000); see Table 29.2.

Summary

The evidence on persistence is voluminous, but attempting to give a brief yet balanced summary of performance persistence across US and UK studies is difficult. It seems that there is some persistence among the top decile of US funds ranked by several characteristics, including past raw returns and past 4F alphas. Persistence among past winners does not seem to last longer than one year when we measure future performance using the forward-looking 4F alpha. The past-winner decile of funds earns a future 4F alpha of around 1% p.a. (Kosowski *et al.*, 2006). Unless investors can mimic, with a small number of funds, the performance of the top-decile portfolio (which may currently contain over 180 funds) and avoid load fees to minimise rebalancing costs, it is doubtful that a significant exploitable 'persistence anomaly' exists.

In contrast, there is strong evidence that poor performance persists fairly uniformly across deciles 5–9 with $\alpha_{4F}^{f,net}$ around -1% p.a. and the bottom decile has $\alpha_{4F}^{f,net} = -3.6\%$ p.a. Broadly similar results apply to the relatively few comprehensive UK studies on persistence. Overall, our analysis of persistence provides useful insights for investors about which funds to avoid, but offers much less certainty about which funds to purchase.

TABLE 29.2: Studies of UK mutual fund performance

Study	Period	Type of funds	Risk-adjusted returns	Net of management fees	Control for survivorship bias	Performance persistence
Allen and Tan (1999)	1989–95	131 investment trusts	Yes	No	No	Yes, for both winner and loser portfolios (contingency tables)
Blake and Timmermann (1998)	1972–95	855 equity funds	Yes	No	Yes	Yes
Fletcher (1997)	1980–89	101 funds: growth, income and general	Yes	No	Min. of two years returns	No
Leger (1997)	1974–93	72 investment trusts	Yes	No	No	No
Lunde et al. (1999)	1972–95	As in Blake and Timmermann (1998)	Yes	No	Yes	Yes, contingency tables
Quigley and Sinquefield (1999)	1978–97	752 equity funds: growth, income, general equity and smaller companies	Yes	Yes, estimated	Yes	Loser funds persist, winner funds do not
WM Company (1999)	1979–98	Income and growth funds	No	No	No	No

29.4 FUND CHARACTERISTICS AND PERFORMANCE

First, we examine characteristics that might influence a fund's relative performance, concentrating particularly on differential costs. Then we ask the question: Is money smart? If there is persistence in performance of past-winner or past-loser funds and money is smart, then we expect to observe investors switching from loser to winner funds, with the former ceasing to exist (or changing to a successful strategy) and the latter giving rise to positive abnormal returns – at least over the short run. If performance persists at the fund manager level, rather than at the fund level, then the 'smart money' should follow successful managers; evidence for this is also examined.

Fund characteristics

Do large funds perform better than small funds, or do high-turnover or high-cost funds provide a better return than low-cost or low-turnover funds? In short, what type of fund characteristics influence performance?

There are a large number of US studies in this area seeking to correlate fund performance (e.g. fund alphas) with fund characteristics. The evidence suggests that for funds as a whole, their 4F alphas are strongly and negatively related to costs such as the total expense ratio (TER), load fees and trading costs. As far as load/no-load funds are concerned, the evidence strongly suggests that abnormal returns on load funds do not cover the additional load fees charged. The latter may account for the decline in both the number of funds and cash under management in load funds (in the US), and is also consistent with (no-load) funds trying to recoup charges in higher 12b-1 (advertising) fees (Mahoney, 2004). Here the evidence is clear: investors should choose 'active' no-load funds and funds with low expenses if they wish to increase the probability of positive abnormal returns.

Is money smart?

In a competitive market we might expect active investors to reallocate cash away from past poor performers and towards past winners, in the expectation that this will increase future returns. Key areas for investigation are, first, the relationship between past fund performance and subsequent fund flows; and second, whether fund flows provide an investment signal that can be used to give economically significant future returns – that is, whether money is smart.

Past returns and future fund flows

A strong and significant positive relationship between past performance and subsequent cash flows (after allowing for the influence of other fund characteristics), for a number of alternative performance measures (such as past raw returns or past alpha measures), is reported in Gruber (1996). More recently, Barber *et al.* (2004) re-examine the impact of past returns and different types of fees on future fund flows. They find that (quarterly) flows into individual funds are positively related to past (excess) fund returns, returns squared and 12b-1 (advertising) fees, but are negatively related to front-end loads. They argue that this demonstrates greater sensitivity of flows to advertising and load fees that are 'visible' (see also Del Guercio and Tkac, 2002; Jain and Wu, 2000; Sirri and Tufano 1998; Wilcox, 2003).

Empirical work in the US indicates that fund flows are less sensitive to past performance *when past performance is relatively poor* (Del Guercio and Tkac, 2002; Lynch and Musto, 2003; Sirri and Tufano, 1993). For the UK, data deficiencies imply that the relationship between fund performance and fund flow is comparatively unexplored, but Keswani and Stolin (2008) find evidence that fund flows in the UK respond to past returns.

Flows and future returns

The evidence that investors' cash chases past winners is clear, but we now examine if this 'new money' results in higher future returns. There is some US evidence that funds that receive relatively large cash inflows perform *relatively* better in the future than funds that experience relatively low cash inflows; but this outperformance is relatively short lived (i.e. over one quarter) and 'new money funds' statistically do not beat the market as a whole. So, although 'new money' blindly chases funds with high past (raw) returns, the latter strategy does not earn positive *future* abnormal returns (based on forward-looking 4F alphas).

Due to the paucity of UK data, Keswani and Stolin (2008) is the only study of UK mutual funds that links new cash inflows (and outflows) to future performance as measured by 4F alphas. The data period employed is 1992–2000, using around 500 funds. With monthly portfolio rebalancing they find that 'new money' flows earn higher abnormal returns than 'old money' (i.e. money that stays with a fund), but in each case the 4F alpha is negative.

From the above it can be seen that money is 'smart', but only in the *limited sense* that most cash inflows are into past-winner funds, who subsequently experience higher future returns than past losers. Note that this implies a *relatively* better outcome, but does not imply that smart-money investors can earn positive abnormal returns. We would rather retain the word 'smart' for ex-ante investment strategies that earn *positive* abnormal returns. Investors switching funds to improve their *relative* position, but still earning negative alphas in the future, might be better described as a 'less dumb than average' strategy.

29.5 MUTUAL FUND MANAGERS

Skill and persistence in performance may reside at the fund manager level rather than at the fund level. If so, investors should 'chase' past top-performing managers, not necessarily top funds. Chevalier and Ellison (1999), for a sample of 492 mutual fund managers (1988–1994), find that managers with higher undergraduate SAT scores obtain higher risk-adjusted returns (after controlling for other fund characteristics). They attribute this out-performance to better natural ability, education and professional networks associated with having attended a higher SAT score undergraduate institution. However, Baks (2002), who tracks managers as they move between funds, concludes that the fund typically has a greater influence on future performance than the manager.

So, is money smart? Our overall conclusion from the above studies must be that most (but not all) money is pretty dumb. Investors blindly chase past winners and respond strongly to fund advertising. Past-winner funds do not earn positive risk-adjusted net returns (alphas) in subsequent periods. However, what is also clear is that at the other end of the performance distribution, the absence of large cash outflows from poorly performing funds probably inhibits the competitive process, since most of these funds continue to earn persistently poor abnormal returns (Barras *et al.*, 2005; Kosowski *et al.*, 2006). So it is at the lower end of the performance distribution that money is really dumb.

29.6 BOND FUNDS

Because of space constraints, we only briefly consider the performance of mutual funds that invest primarily in government and corporate bonds. Broadly speaking, persistence in US bond fund performance is similar to that found for domestic equity funds. Blake, Elton and Gruber (1993), using around 300 bond funds, find little evidence of persistence and that expenses are the key determinant of ex-post relative performance. However more recently, Huij and Derwall (2006), using over 3500 US bond funds (1993–2003), find statistically significant negative persistence in forward-looking alphas (of between –1% and –3% p.a.), but no positive persistence when rebalancing *monthly*. But when they use more sophisticated sorting rules, they find forward-looking alphas of 1.27%, 1.13% and 0.53% p.a. for monthly, quarterly and annual rebalancing, respectively; these figures are around 0.5% higher for no-load bond funds. So there is some evidence that before rebalancing costs, the past-winner decile of bond funds exhibit short-run persistence and stronger evidence that loser funds persist.

SUMMARY

- Mutual fund performance is usually measured using time-series multifactor regressions. The intercept, known as alpha, measures abnormal performance.
- The factors can either be interpreted as measuring the risk exposure of the mutual fund or as simple mechanical 'zero-investment' benchmarks (e.g. buy high BMV stocks and sell low BMV stocks). In either case, a *skilled* fund manager should be able to earn an abnormal return after adjusting fund returns for the influence of these factors.
- Ex post, there are around 2–5% of top-performing UK and US equity mutual funds that outperform their benchmarks and 20–40% of funds have poor performance.

- Key drivers of *relative* fund performance are load fees, expenses and turnover.
- Evidence suggests that past-winner funds persist, particularly when rebalancing is frequent (i.e. less than one year), but the transaction costs of switching between funds may imply that abnormal returns to investors from trying to pick future-winner funds may be rather small and uncertain. However, the evidence clearly supports the view that past-loser funds remain losers.
- Studies using manager performance (rather than fund performance) find a statistical relationship between various measures of management skill and future performance, but the effect is not very large or particularly robust.
- Is money smart? It turns out that for investment in US equity mutual funds, a substantial amount of cash flows into past-winner funds and past-winner funds earn future abnormal net returns of around 1% p.a., so some money may be smart. But a key unknown factor is whether these returns exceed the switching costs of the 'persistence strategy'. However, the strong persistence in the performance of poorly performing funds (together with low positive cash inflows rather than large outflows) suggests that a lot of money is dumb.
- Sensible advice for most investors would be to hold low-cost index funds and avoid holding past-loser funds. Only sophisticated investors should pursue an active investment strategy of trying to pick future winners from the universe of mutual funds – and then with much caution.

EXERCISES

Q1   The performance of a mutual fund from the investor's viewpoint depends on the costs incurred by the fund as well as the stock-picking skills of the managers. What are the main costs incurred by a mutual fund, which are ultimately borne by the investor?

Q2   What is a fund family and what advantages does it have?

Q3   What is the difference between the ex-ante performance of a fund and persistence in performance?

Q4   What do we mean when we say that 'money is smart'?

Q5   When ranking the relative performance of individual mutual funds, why do we often use alpha as a measure of performance rather than the Sharpe ratio of each fund?

Q6   The (average) risk-free (safe) rate is $r = 4\%$ p.a. The S&P 500 has a mean average *excess* return (over the safe rate) of $ER - r = 8\%$ p.a. and standard deviation of σ (S&P 500) = 20% p.a. Assume that you care about risk and return and you wish to choose a mutual fund that *maximises the Sharpe ratio,* based on past data. For any portfolio p its Sharpe ratio = $(ER_p - r)/\sigma_p$. The Flaming Ferraris and Madonna Makeover funds have just completed 10 years of investment trading and their excess returns (% p.a.) are:

Excess returns, Flaming Ferraris (FF)	Excess returns, Madonna Makeover (MM)
15	30
7	33
−3	15
20	28
−10	−17
12	33
−10	−21
−2	−16
etc.	etc.

A kindly statistician has calculated that over the 10 years:

- Average (expected) excess returns for FF and MM are **0.4%** and **8.2% p.a.** respectively
- Standard deviation of returns for FF and MM are **14.3%** and **26.5% p.a.** respectively

    variance of returns $= \sum\limits_{i=1}^{n}(R_i - \bar{R})^2/(n - 1)$

(a) If historical performance is a good guide to future performance, who would you get to manage your entire stock-market fund, involving your own wealth of $100,000? Would it be FF or MM, or would you just buy an index tracker on the S&P 500?

(b) Most people are more used to thinking in terms of a *dollar* return and the amount of dollars at risk. So what is the average *(excess) dollar return* from your chosen portfolio (FF or MM or S&P) and what is the range of dollar outcomes? (For example 'mean return = $10,000 p.a. with a one standard deviation of plus or minus $18,000'; this is an example, not the correct answer!) Assume that returns are normally distributed, if you wish.

(c) What is the dollar return per unit of dollar risk (if you invest only your own wealth of $100,000) in the S&P 500?

Suppose you are now faced with a straight choice between MM and an index fund ('tracker') on the S&P 500, and you don't mind holding a relatively high level of risk. You are prepared to *borrow $50,000* from the bank (at cost of $r =$ 4%) to invest a total of $150,000 in either the S&P 500 or with MM. (As a first approximation, don't worry about the interest-cost element when you borrow money, since it is actually taken care of in the Sharpe ratio, which has the *excess* return in the numerator.)

After investing this additional $50,000 in your *chosen portfolio,* are you getting:

(d) a higher expected dollar return (on your $150,000)?

(e) a higher dollar risk (on your $150,000)?

(f) a higher dollar return per unit of dollar risk (i.e. Sharpe ratio, using dollar returns per dollar risk) than you had when you invested just your own $100,000?

30

Hedge Funds[1]

[1] We should like to thank Nick Motson of Cass Business School for comments and discussions in this area.

30.1 MARKET STRUCTURE

Hedge funds, like mutual funds, are pooled investments. At end 2006, *mutual fund* assets in the US amounted to about $9 trillion and although hedge-fund assets grew rapidly between 2000 and 2006, US *hedge-fund* assets in 2006 amounted to around $800bn–$1 trillion – about 10% of mutual-fund assets. It has been reported that hedge funds accounted for nearly half the trading on the New York and London stock exchanges in 2005.

About 90% of hedge-fund managers are based in the US and 9% in Europe, with in excess of 6000 funds worldwide managing around $1 trillion in assets. However, many hedge funds are relatively small and around 80% of funds have less than $100m under management, while one of the largest, managed by Goldman Sachs, had $30bn under management in 2006. By comparison, the largest US mutual fund (Growth Fund of America) has assets under management in excess of $150bn. The number of funds has grown rapidly over the last 15 years (Figure 30.1).

There are many hedge-fund styles, such as long–short, short selling, long-only leveraged, emerging-market funds, distressed securities, global macro and relative-value arbitrage. These strategies are risky, so the term 'hedge fund' is rather misleading.

Hedge funds are usually organised as limited liability partnerships. The 'portfolio managers' are the 'general partners' who make up the 'management company'. The 'investment partnership' then consists of the management company and the investors in the fund, who are known as limited partners (Figure 30.2).

There is always a close operational relationship between the hedge fund and its prime broker. The hedge fund buys and sells securities through the prime broker, obtains finance for leverage

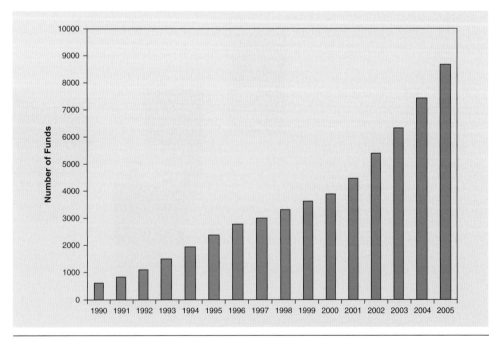

FIGURE 30.1: Number of hedge funds: 1990–2005

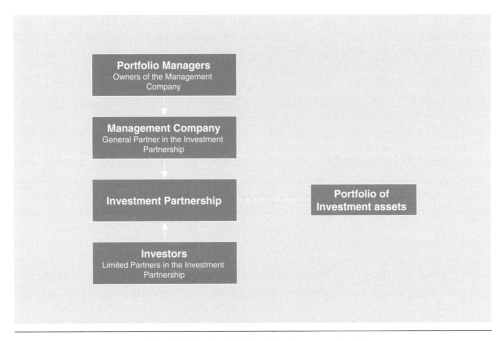

FIGURE 30.2: Hedge fund organisation

and borrows securities for short sales. The prime broker may also provide introductions to new clients as well as offering the usual clearance, settlement and custodial arrangements.

Investing in hedge funds requires a high minimum investment (usually in excess of $1m). Most hedge funds operate a 'lock-up' period of a year or more and you cannot sell your interest in the hedge fund until this period has elapsed. After this period you can liquidate your holdings subject to a minimum advance notice period, usually between one and three months. Hedge-fund managers charge two sets of fees: a fixed management fee of 1–2% of funds under management and a performance fee, usually in the range 15–30% of annual profits. A '2–20' fee structure is not uncommon, which involves an annual fee of 2% and a profit share of 20%. There is also a hurdle rate of return, usually set at zero (or the risk-free rate), above which incentive fees are paid. To prevent excessive risk taking by managers (who themselves may not have a large stake in the fund), the performance fee is subject to a **high watermark provision**, whereby no incentive fee is payable if the net asset value of the fund is lower than in the last accounting period. The limited partners in the hedge fund receive a percentage of profits (proportional to their capital invested in the fund).

The performance fee of hedge funds has made some individuals very rich. In 2005, James Simons of Renaissance Technologies and Boone Pickens earned in excess of $1bn (Stultz, 2007) and the average take-home pay of the top 25 hedge-fund managers in 2004 was over $250m. The high watermark seems to be a very weak device for limiting risk taking. For example, the hedge fund Amaranth lost over $6bn (a 66% fall in value) in September 2006, but the trader who was apparently responsible for these losses had earned around $80m in 2005. As long as there was no malfeasance the trader can retain these profits and there is nothing to stop him trying to open another hedge fund.

In contrast, US *mutual-fund* fees are often exclusively determined as a percentage of funds under management – in part because compensation based on profits is restricted by legislation to be symmetric, so losses would reduce managers' compensation. The Fidelity Magellan mutual fund has a small compensation element of a maximum of 2% (relative to the performance of the S&P 500 benchmark), plus fixed fees of around 1/2% of funds under management. Also, withdrawals of cash from mutual funds are possible on a daily basis, consequently the fund has to hold some low-yielding liquid assets in its portfolio.

Hedge funds are not completely unregulated, but they have far greater freedom in their investment decisions than do mutual funds. In the US, they can gain exemption from some of the restrictions that apply to mutual funds, for example by having fewer than 100 US beneficial owners or by only having investors who are 'qualified' (for example, those with a net worth in excess of a certain amount). In 2006 new rules instituted by the SEC (Securities and Exchange Commission) came into force that require hedge funds to register if they manage more than $25m of assets for 15 or more clients. Their clients must also have a minimum net worth of $1.5 million and a net income of over $750,000. In future, some hedge funds may voluntarily register if they think that this will increase cash inflows to the fund. But if the hedge-fund manager thinks she has profitable investment strategies, she may not be keen to disclose her asset positions when reporting the composition of her portfolio to the SEC, otherwise imitators may use these strategies to set up rival funds. However, because of the lack of transparency of hedge funds, regulators are becoming increasingly concerned about their activities and we may see more stringent reporting requirements in the future.

Fund of funds

To diversify by investing in several hedge funds, you require a substantial amount of capital. This is possible for large institutions such as insurance companies, pension funds and institutional endowments (e.g. the Yale University endowment fund) and very wealthy individuals. Even for these players, the costs of due diligence (i.e. finding out about the fund and its managers) can be high (e.g. around $50,000–100,000). Alternatively, a small investor can invest directly in a fund of hedge funds. However, there will be additional management fees to pay to the fund-of-hedge-fund managers, typically 0.5–1% p.a., and an additional incentive fee, typically 5–10% of net profits, this is on top of fees paid directly to each of the hedge funds in the fund-of-funds portfolio.

However, sometimes hedge funds invested in by the fund-of-funds manager reduce their fees, so that the net performance fees actually paid by the investor are not necessarily increased by much. Using a fund-of-funds allows the investor to spread her capital over several hedge funds, thus obtaining some diversification across the hedge-fund sector. As funds of funds are active funds, you have to believe that your fund-of-funds manager has the skill to pick successful hedge funds and that returns will more than cover any additional fees. The fund-of-funds sector is currently the fastest-growing area of the hedge-fund industry, as institutional investors (e.g. insurance and pension funds and also some mutual funds) and high-net-worth individuals seek hedge-fund returns but with some diversification benefits. At the end of 2006 it was estimated that around 30% of assets held in hedge funds were via funds-of-funds.

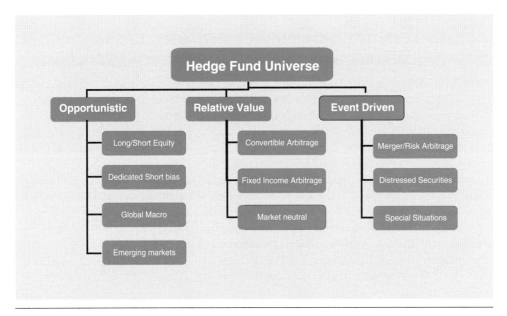

FIGURE 30.3: Hedge fund strategies

30.2 HEDGE-FUND STRATEGIES

Hedge-fund strategies can be loosely classified as opportunistic, relative value and event driven, with many variants possible under these broad headings (Figure 30.3). The four most popular styles are long–short equity 31%, event driven 20%, macro 10% and fixed-income arbitrage 8% (Tremont Asset Flows Report, 2nd quarter, 2007).

Long–short equity

This could be a balanced long–short strategy, whereby receipts from short sales of equity are matched by going long an equal dollar amount. The idea is that the fund manager is a good stock picker of both undervalued and overvalued stocks. The long–short position partly protects the manager from movements in the overall market index – ideally the beta of the long–short portfolio will be around zero, but in practice many long–short funds have positive exposure to the market. Shorting the actual shares involves the possibility of a short squeeze (i.e. having to return the shares to your broker before you have made profits on your trade).

When the long–short position is explicitly designed to have zero exposure to market returns, this is a **market-neutral** strategy. If the manager's overall long–short portfolio is widely diversified, there will be little or no *specific risk* but of course, if the manager picks only a small number of stocks, specific risk could be quite high.

When the long–short hedge fund manager does not have a market-neutral position in stocks, any remaining market risk can be offset, in whole or in part and for specific periods, by using stock-index futures. The key idea is that the manager has stock-picking skill and can make money by short selling overpriced stocks and purchasing underpriced stocks, thus generating

---

CASE STUDY 30.1   DEDICATED SHORT BIAS

In July 2005, after five years on the run and being on the FBI's 'most wanted' list, Michael Berger, former manager of the New York-based Manhattan Investment Fund, was arrested in Austria. Berger had admitted hiding $400m of losses (racked up by shorting Internet stocks), doctoring documents sent to investors and auditors, and was due to be sentenced in the US in 2002. He tried to recant his plea by saying that he had not been of sound mind when he had admitted to the fraud. The investors in the fund included Credit Suisse, Bank Austria and a Kuwait state fund – the initial investment in the fund was around $575m. Investors unsuccessfully sued the auditors, but secured a ruling (still under appeal in 2007) that Bear Stearns, the prime broker of the fund, should pay around $125m to investors. The next issue to be decided is whether Berger *is* an Austrian citizen and thus whether he can be extradited to the US.

---

positive alpha. The manager then hedges any remaining market exposure with stock-index futures – although remember that this involves uncertainties due to margin payments and basis risk (e.g. the beta of the net spot position may not be estimated correctly). Some hedge funds have a **dedicated short bias** and one that did not do too well with this strategy is noted in Case Study 30.1.

Mutual funds cannot short sell securities (until recently, at least) and therefore cannot make money from overpriced stocks. But if an investor already holds mutual funds, adding a hedge fund to her portfolio might involve possible diversification benefits, because if the hedge fund has a dedicated short bias then this 'negative correlation' could move her efficient frontier to the left.

Global macro

This strategy consists mainly of leveraged bets on future changes in a wide variety of asset prices, such as stock prices, interest rates, foreign exchange and commodities. For example, you may have been skilful enough to predict the rapid growth of the Chinese economy at the turn of the millennium and the upward pressure on the natural resource prices that ensued. Hence ideally, a global macro fund would have gone long in primary commodities such as copper, oil and precious metals. You can either use spot markets or more likely derivatives markets such as futures and options contracts on these assets. Perhaps the most famous trade in this area is George Soros selling sterling short and buying Deutsche Marks in September 1992, immediately before sterling was devalued. Over one week, Soros made over $1bn on the trade.

Emerging markets

Some hedge funds specialise in investments in the securities of companies in emerging markets and in the sovereign debt of these countries. Emerging markets include countries in Eastern Europe, Latin America, the former Soviet Union, Africa and parts of Asia (e.g. Indonesia, Vietnam, Thailand and China). Emerging-market hedge funds generally take long positions, as it is usually difficult in such markets to undertake short selling.

Convertible arbitrage

This consists of quite a sophisticated set of strategies and we will only consider a simple case. Suppose you think that a convertible bond is underpriced and therefore you purchase it. Remember that a convertible bond can be viewed as an ordinary plain vanilla bond plus a call option on the company's stock. Let us assume that it is the value of this 'embedded' call option that is underpriced, which in turn makes the convertible bond underpriced. (The 'plain vanilla' bit of the bond is unlikely to be underpriced, because for most bonds the coupons and appropriate spot rates of interest are known and the market prices plain vanilla bonds correctly.) The average credit rating of a bond used in convertible arbitrage will be around BB and ranges from AA to CCC, hence these bonds are quite risky and they also trade in illiquid markets. Most trades will involve leverage ranging from zero to 6:1.

The major risks in this strategy are the possibility of an investment downgrade (i.e. credit risk) and hence a fall in the price of the bond or a liquidity crisis in the market when you come to sell the bond. To hedge the credit risk, the fund manager may short sell the underlying stock of the company and meanwhile wait for the underpricing of the convertible to correct itself in the market. The hedge-fund manager could also, if she wished, hedge the interest-rate risk on the plain vanilla part of the convertible bond by using, for example, interest-rate futures contracts. Another risk in this strategy is in valuing the option part of the bond, which could be quite difficult, involving as it does interest rates, stock prices, possible changes in volatility of the stock price and changes in credit (default) risk. Of course, if a '1000-year storm' should arrive (as was the case with Long Term Capital Management in 1998), credit spreads will rise and liquidity will dry up, both of which push prices down. This could create a large loss on your leveraged long position in the convertible and possibly cause insolvency of the hedge fund.

Fixed-income arbitrage

This is where a fund manager takes both a long and short position in two interest-sensitive assets: for example corporate bonds versus Treasury bonds; or Treasury bonds versus municipal bonds; or arbitrage between the cash market and interest-rate futures contracts. In most trades, the long–short position implies that you are hedged against overall rises or falls in the general level of interest rates (i.e. parallel shifts in the yield curve), but you hope to make profits when the mispricing of the two interest-rate securities is resolved. Usually your spot positions will be highly leveraged or you will use derivatives on fixed-income securities to gain leverage.

Event-driven strategies: merger arbitrage/risk arbitrage

Event-driven strategies include mergers, takeovers, leveraged buy-outs and management buy-outs. In such events the target-company shares generally rise appreciably a few days prior to the formal announcement of any bid (because of leakage of information about the takeover) and then rise rapidly on the announcement date. If the bid is subsequently successful, there is a further rise in the price of the target, until the acquisition is finally confirmed. Information about the timing and possible success of takeover bids is crucial when trying to make a profit from this type of transaction.

The hedge-fund manager can either buy the shares of the prospective target company or could buy a call option on shares of the target (thus gaining leverage). A key danger in this strategy is that the takeover is unsuccessful and there is a fall-back in the share price of the target. The fund manager can hedge against the latter outcome by also purchasing put options on the target company's stock. There is also evidence that the shares of acquiring companies tend to fall slightly on the announcement of the takeover bid, in which case the fund manager could benefit by short selling shares of the acquiring company (or buying a put).

Distressed strategies

A distressed strategy consists in buying securities (either stocks or bonds) of companies that are close to bankruptcy or have even already been declared bankrupt. The hedge fund then becomes a major player in the liquidation or restructuring of the company, after which it hopes that the securities will rise in price. Clearly, these markets are highly illiquid and involve great uncertainties about the reorganisation and financial restructuring of distressed companies (e.g. equity for debt swaps, the recovery rate from debt securities and so on). These strategies carry considerable risk – while some of the risk may be hedged using credit derivatives or put options on the stock, considerable legal and restructuring risk remains.

Special situations

This is a bit of a catch-all strategy and is not clearly defined. It could include merger arbitrage and distressed strategies together with other special situations such as share buy-backs, recapitalisations and seasoned equity offerings. The hedge-fund manager seeks to exploit any perceived mispricing from these situations and will almost certainly undertake leveraged purchases and possibly offset some of the downside risk using put options.

30.3 HEDGE-FUND DATA

Although data sources for the hedge-fund universe are improving, they are generally not as comprehensive and reliable as those for equity mutual funds. Reporting to databases by hedge funds is voluntary and to acquire this data you have to pay a fee to data vendors such as TASS (owned by Reuters), Hedge Fund Research (HFR) or the Barclay's Group. Probably around 60% of funds report to just one database and those that report to all databases may be as low as 25%, so a particular database may exclude many funds from the universe of hedge funds. Because many hedge funds have only short histories, this makes statistical inference all the more difficult. Case Study 30.2 discusses possible biases in hedge-fund databases.

Some hedge funds hold illiquid assets (e.g. emerging market or distressed bonds), which may be difficult to value, so reported returns may be subject to 'smoothing' and may be somewhat inaccurate on a month-to-month basis. This smoothing gives rise to autocorrelation in returns (i.e. high returns in one month have a greater than 50% chance of resulting in high returns the next month), which can create problems when measuring the performance of hedge funds.

In addition, if hedge funds do hold large amounts of illiquid assets and they try to sell these assets in a crisis period (e.g. the Russian bond crisis of 1998), they may put additional

---

CASE STUDY 30.2   BIASES IN HEDGE-FUND DATA

In any database there is the issue of *survivorship bias*. Some databases only report returns for 'live' funds and not those that have 'died' and have been removed from the database. A consensus of academic work provides an estimate of survivorship bias, which unfortunately is quite wide ranging – the difference between the return on 'live' funds and 'live plus dead' funds is estimated at between 1% p.a. and 4% p.a. (Ackermann *et al.*, 1999; Malkiel and Saha, 2006).

There is also a *back-fill bias* (sometimes called 'instant industry bias'). This arises because hedge-fund managers trade with their own funds during an 'incubation period' before reporting to a database. If they are successful, they start reporting their returns and the data vendor then back-fills with the earlier historical returns of the incubation period. Thus if the history of the fund is short, there is an element of bias, since only those funds that are successful in the incubation period report to the data vendor. This bias is often measured by calculating the difference between the return on a portfolio of hedge funds including and excluding the back-fill data. For an equally weighted portfolio this bias is around 1–2% p.a.

There is another type of bias, which we might call *selection bias* and is simply due to the fact that many hedge funds do not report to any database. Some funds that do not report may do so because of poor performance, while funds that have been successful over a relatively short period but are closed to new investors do not have an incentive to report. Not surprisingly, it is impossible to say how selection bias influences average returns for the hedge-fund sector.

---

downward pressure on prices, so the recorded prices they use to value these assets might not reflect the 'true' price they will be able to obtain. Also note that some funds are closed to new investors, but if they are in the database, recorded returns are only attainable by existing investors in the fund (Fung *et al.*, 2005).

The performance of the hedge-fund *industry* is often reported in hedge-fund *indices* provided by data vendors. But the reported returns can differ across the various indices because they contain different funds, are either value weighted or equally weighted, and may or may not contain dead funds or funds that are closed to new investors. The divergence between the different reported indices has narrowed in recent years, although it can still be of the order of 5% p.a. An alternative to constructing 'representative' indices from the raw (but incomplete) data on hedge funds is to use an average of *fund-of-funds returns* to represent the performance of the industry as a whole. This has the advantage of providing a return that investors could actually earn, but coverage is limited to those hedge funds that are part of the fund-of-funds sector.

In recent years **investable hedge-fund indices** have appeared and such funds have seen a rapid growth in inflows of capital – these funds provide investment vehicles that seek to track a particular hedge-fund index. They are rather like 'tracker' fund-of-funds, since the hedge funds in the index are fixed. These investable hedge-fund indices have greater liquidity and transparency and have lower management fees than funds of hedge funds.

30.4 PERFORMANCE

Let's remind ourselves what leverage means. If you have $100m capital and you invest in a hedge fund and make $5m profit after one year, then your *unlevered return* is 5%. Now, suppose you had borrowed $400m to invest in hedge funds, then this will also earn 5% or a profit of $20m. Your own funds of $100m earned $5m, giving you a total gross profit of $25m. If the cost of borrowing is 2%, then you owe the bank $8m (0.02 × $400m), giving you a net profit of $17m. The *levered return* on your $100m own funds is therefore 17%. This result is encapsulated in the expression for the levered return:

$$R_L = r + (500/100)(R_U - r)$$

where 'Total funds/Own funds' = 500/100 is the leverage ratio, $R_U = 5\%$ is the unlevered return and $r = 2\%$ is the risk-free rate. Case Study 30.3 looks at leverage in a light-hearted way.

Let's first consider some results based on the (value-weighted) Credit Suisse/Tremont Hedge Fund *index*. Between 1994 and the middle of 2006, the buy-and-hold return on the hedge-fund index was an average of 10.8% p.a. (net of performance fees and expenses), with a standard deviation of 7.8%. This compares with 10.3% average return for the S&P 500 and standard deviation much higher at 14.5%. So the Sharpe ratio of the hedge fund is around twice that of the S&P 500. However, one immediate question here is whether the standard deviation is a good measure of risk, particularly for hedge funds. It is also notable that the hedge-fund index only overtook the S&P 500 after 2000 – possibly because US hedge funds successfully used short sales (particularly in the bear market of 2000–02). Also note that until very recently you could not implement the above strategy, since you could not directly invest in an index of hedge funds (i.e. there was no index tracker for the universe of hedge funds). The best you

---

CASE STUDY 30.3   SUPERMAN AND HEDGE FUNDS

You may remember that in one of the *Superman* films, the character played by Richard Pryor had the idea of using the bank's computer system to collect all the nickels floating around in cyberspace and crediting them to his account. A partner of LTCM described hedge funds as making money by vacuming up nickels (pennies) since they used arbitrage strategies. Later, less charitable commentators described it as picking up nickels in front of a turbo-charged steam roller – because these arbitrage positions were highly leveraged (in LTCM's case by around 22:1 *on average* over June 1994–August 1997).

could do was invest in fund-of-funds (with higher fees) or in a portfolio of individual hedge funds; we discuss this below.

It is worth noting at the outset that trying to determine whether hedge funds 'beat the market' is much more difficult than for mutual funds (which is not itself devoid of problems). This is because:

- Hedge-fund databases may be incomplete.
- Adjusting returns for the risks inherent in hedge-fund strategies is complex (and controversial), in part due to negative skewness and excess kurtosis in returns.
- Returns from some illiquid strategies are difficult to value correctly.
- We have a relatively short time span of data.

Nevertheless, there is some evidence we can examine. First, using over 3000 hedge funds between January 1999 to March 2004, Ibbotson and Chen (2005) find that the *average* (net return) alpha is 3.7% p.a., much higher than the average for mutual funds, which is negative, between –1% and –3% (depending on the chosen study).

The problem of assessing hedge-fund performance on historical data is the possibility that hedge funds look relatively risk free (in terms of volatility), but are prone to very large losses (and possible insolvency), as with Amaranth's $6bn losses in 2006 and LTCM's $4bn losses in 1997. Hedge funds might be acting very much like an insurance company that sells catastrophe insurance (e.g. insurance against earthquakes). As long as there are no earthquakes, the insurance company looks good. It pockets the premiums, has no claims, its profits are high and not particularly volatile – until, that is, the rare event occurs, by which time it may be too late. Case Study 30.4 explores the issue of assessing the probability of rare events.

CASE STUDY 30.4   MEASURING THE PROBABILITY OF RARE EVENTS

It is difficult to measure the probability of rare events from data – simply because they *are* rare. For example, suppose that the probability of a rare event is p, where the 'indicator function' $I_t = 1$ when the rare event occurs and zero otherwise. An estimate of the probability of the rare event is $\hat{p} = T^{-1}\sum_{t=1}^{T} I_t$ and standard statistical textbooks tell us that the standard error of this estimate of the true value for p is $se(\hat{p}) = \sqrt{p(1 - p)/T}$. Suppose the true probability $p = 5\%$ (i.e. 1 in every 20 years) and we require a standard error of 1%, so we can then be 95% certain that the true probability is $\hat{p} \pm 2\%$. How many years of data do we require? This is given by $T = p(1 - p)/(0.01)^2 = 475$ years of data! Hence, measuring the probability of rare events with any accuracy is extremely difficult, even when we assume that this probability remains constant over time. When rare events have an important impact on a portfolio, then, using the value-at-risk (VaR) methodology, the usual (unconditional) VaR measure may be relatively small, but the VaR *conditional* on a price fall of, say, greater than 5% in any month may be very high.

Lo (2001) points out that a simple strategy of selling 7% out of the money (OTM) puts on the S&P 500 (SPX puts), with maturities less than three months (and rolling over the trade), between 1992 and 1999 would have earned much more than the S&P 500. The put strategy earns 3.7% per month compared with 1.4% per month for the S&P 500 – this amounts to 2721% as opposed to 367% over the whole eight-year period. The short puts resulted in a monthly Sharpe ratio of 1.94 versus 0.98 for the S&P 500, with only six negative monthly returns for SPX puts, compared with 36 for the S&P 500 (out of a total of 96 monthly returns). The reason that selling 7% OTM puts does much better than the S&P 500 is straight-forward. Apart from a few months (e.g. August and September 1998) when returns fell sharply, the put strategy just involves collecting the put premia and there is therefore little volatility over time in the returns to this strategy. However, on the odd occasions that stock prices fall more than 7% and end up below the strike price, the written puts lose money – but this occurs infrequently. This strategy is being 'pitched' to UK mutual and pension fund managers, as they are now allowed to use derivatives for speculation as well as hedging[2].

Selling OTM puts is a very simple strategy and there is no need to pay expensive hedge-fund fees to execute this strategy – you can do it yourself over the Internet. But remember that 1992–99 was a bull market – selling OTM puts might involve a catastrophic outcome for you, if you execute the strategy in a bear market, so beware 'the smell of easy money'. Risk measures used by some hedge-fund managers should include 'tail-risk' measures from extreme value theory, but it would be hard for investors in hedge funds to keep track of such measures – particularly given infrequent reporting and fast-moving markets.

The above demonstrates that a lack of transparency might deceive investors into paying high fees for what is a simple, replicable strategy, which also looks highly profitable, at least over the historical data period considered. Clearly, the hedge fund's strategy of selling OTM puts would be revealed if the dynamic holdings of the hedge fund are disclosed frequently. But if the hedge fund implemented this strategy using delta hedging (e.g. using stock index futures) to replicate the short-put positions, it would look like a contrarian strategy – their stock position would show an increase, just after a stock-price fall. When such a strategy is implemented using many stocks (to mimic the performance of different OTM puts), then even with *position transparency* it might be difficult to detect.

Some hedge funds hold assets (e.g. complex OTC derivatives) that do not have quoted market prices, so valuation requires a theoretical model that may be open to manipulation, for example by manipulating estimates of the forward (yield) curve at long maturities. Hedge funds may also smooth their returns over time, so high valuations (on illiquid assets) are reduced in the current reporting period to provide a cushion for the next reporting period. Such smoothing can reduce reported volatility and hence give rise to increased Sharpe ratios. Smoothing would also produce serial correlation in monthly returns, a phenomenon noted in illiquid hedge-fund styles (Getmansky *et al.*, 2004). There also appear to be patterns in monthly hedge-fund returns, since returns in December are much higher than in other months – Santa Claus is kind to hedge funds (Agarwal *et al.*, 2006).

---

[2] The strategy is pitched to mutual funds as a 'covered call' – but it is basically the same as described above. From put-call parity (for European vanilla options) we know that $S - C = -P + Ke^{-r(T-t)}$. Hence, selling a put (as described above) has a payoff profile equivalent to holding stocks (which mutual funds already do) and then selling a call – a long stock position and then selling a call is known as a 'covered call'.

Individual hedge funds

Until recently there has not been a great deal of work on individual hedge-fund performance because of a lack of reliable data. Early studies show that hedge funds have a high rate of attrition (Brown *et al.*, 1999) and early studies gave conflicting results on both the historical risk-adjusted performance of hedge funds and on the persistence in hedge-fund returns. For example, Fung and Hsieh (1997) find negative historical alphas, while evidence of a positive risk-adjusted performance is noted by Agarwal and Naik (2000). The latter also find some persistence in returns – although the latter is possibly due to the style adopted by the hedge fund rather than genuine managerial skills (Brown *et al.*, 1999, 2001).

Because hedge funds have a wide variety of investment styles, it is difficult to characterise their returns adequately using the *linear* multifactor models that are employed to assess the performance of mutual funds. Usually, many additional return variables are added to the Carhart four-factor model, such as a world stock index, various bond indices (including emerging-market bonds and corporate bond returns) and even a commodity return index. Fung and Hsieh (1997) find that factors measuring the *non-linear* returns to options can help explain hedge-fund returns, indicating that hedge funds earn non-linear payoffs. It follows that the (unconditional) returns of hedge funds may be highly non-normal – this limits the usefulness of (standard) Sharpe ratios as performance measures, as they depend on the assumptions of independence and normality. Also, it is debatable whether the factors used so far in empirical work can explain returns on hedge funds that contain substantial positions in options, since the R-squared from such regression are relatively low (and much lower than those for mutual funds).

The recent study by Kosowski *et al.* (2007) successfully addresses a lot of the data issues noted above and concentrates on the performance of *individual funds*. They find that in a sample of over 2700 funds (January 1994–December 2002), the average fund has an alpha of 5% p.a., but this is not statistically significant. However, if we just consider the individual hedge funds in the top 10% of hedge funds (ranked by *t*-alpha)[3], these have large positive (seven-factor) historical alphas (which are also statistically significant).

All of the 10% of hedge funds in Kosowski *et al.*'s (2007) study which have very low *t*-alphas have negative values for alpha, but these are not statistically significant. Hence historically, the 'best' 10% of hedge funds with high *t*-alphas give genuinely positive abnormal returns, while the 'worst' 10% of hedge funds give negative abnormal returns, but the 'worst' alphas are not statistically different from zero (i.e. bad performance is due to bad luck rather than genuinely bad skill). For example, the 10th best fund has an alpha of 15% p.a., which is highly statistically significant (*p* value <0.001). The better historical performance of hedge funds relative to mutual funds can also be gleaned from the fact that to end 2002, the average (seven-factor) alpha for US hedge funds is 5% p.a., while that for US mutual funds is considerably lower at *minus* 0.5% p.a.

---

[3] Ranking hedge fund performance by *t*-alpha the gives you funds which have highly statistically significant alphas, since *t*-alpha equals the numerical value of alpha divided by the estimated standard error of alpha. A fund with a high value for *t*-alpha has a high alpha value (i.e. high abnormal return) or a precisely estimated alpha, or a combination of both. Note however that a high *t*-alpha could be due to a low value for alpha itself, accompanied by a very small estimation error. Therefore, a high *t*-alpha probably implies a high value for alpha but it does not *guarantee* a high abnormal return on the fund. Having ranked funds by *t*-alpha we still have to look and see if this is due to a high value for alpha, itself.

Styles

What about the performance of particular fund styles? A recent study by Capocci and Hubner (2004) used a multifactor model on a database of over 2700 hedge funds (including 801 'dead funds'), concentrating mainly on the more recent (and accurate) monthly returns over the bull market period of 1994–2000 (for which data on non-survivors is available). Funds are divided into around 20 style categories (e.g. long–short, emerging markets, etc.). Overall, there are around 25–30% of funds within any style category that have positive and statistically significant alphas, with around 5–10% having negative alphas and the majority of funds (i.e. around 60%) having zero alphas. The market betas of the hedge funds are lower than those for mutual funds (at around 0.3–0.6) and for almost all funds, the coefficient on the SMB factor is statistically significant. A subset of the funds also have a significant coefficient on the emerging-market bond return, but only about one third of funds show evidence of a statistically significant HML factor and about 15% of funds have a significant momentum factor. The R-squared for these multifactor regressions is mostly in the range 0.65–0.90. Hence, most hedge funds appear to have exposure to small-cap stocks, while a smaller proportion are also exposed to emerging-market bonds and momentum stocks. Unfortunately, in only a few cases (i.e. long–short, convertible arbitrage, non-classified) do the positive alphas over the whole period 1994–2000 remain positive over sub-periods.

The performance of *funds-of-funds* indicates that the average alpha varies over time and between January 1995 and December 2004 the *average* (net return) alpha was only statistically significant and positive in the October 1998–March 2000 period. But among the top 10–20% of funds, alpha is positive and statistically significant (Kosowski *et al.*, 2007).

Overall, there is evidence that a randomly selected hedge fund will have a negative or zero alpha, but the best hedge funds have positive and statistically significant alphas that exceed those for the top mutual funds. Although here one should not forget the rather acute problems in assessing risk-adjusted hedge-fund performance (which are less severe when looking at mutual funds) and that these alphas are historical average. Also investors do not have the benefit of perfect foresight, so they may not be able to pick future-winner funds in real time. It is to this that we now turn.

Persistence

What about persistence and picking *future* winners from among the universe of hedge funds? There is 'statistical persistence' in hedge fund performance – choosing a hedge fund with an alpha 1% higher than the mean alpha for all funds will, on average, give you an alpha over the next *three years* that is about 1/2% higher than average. But note that this is an average over repeated 'bets' – in some years you will be holding a fund for which next period's alpha is negative, so the strategy may carry considerable risk (Jagannathan *et al.*, 2006).

What happens when we assess persistence by forming explicit portfolios of past winners and tracking their future performance? **Short-term persistence**, at three-month horizons, in hedge-fund *raw returns* has been found in early studies, but such persistence does not occur at longer horizons (e.g. Agarwal and Niak, 2002; Brown *et al.*, 1999; Liang, 2000). Also note that Getmansky *et al.* (2004) argue that short-term persistence may be due to illiquidity in returns, which gives rise to 'return smoothing' and *apparent* persistence in returns.

Capocci and Hubner (2004) rank hedge funds into deciles (i.e. the top 10% of funds) based on their past one-year returns, hold these decile portfolios for one year and then rebalance annually. They find that only two of the decile portfolios have statistically significant alphas – there is no persistence in performance for the top (i.e. past-winner) and bottom (i.e. past-loser) deciles and, surprisingly, it is decile portfolios in the middle (i.e. P7, P9) that show persistence.

Kosowski *et al.* (2007) use the recursive portfolio approach with annual rebalancing and rank hedge funds based on their past '*t*-alpha' (which, as we noted, takes account of both the size and the statistical significance of alpha). In contrast to previous results, they find that *all* decile-sorted portfolios exhibit statistically significant alphas over the future, of between 4% and 6% p.a. for the period January 1994–December 2002. They find that both past-winner and past-loser hedge funds earn positive risk-adjusted returns in the future; this is in sharp contrast to mutual funds, where positive persistence in alphas of past-winner funds is weak and past losers have negative abnormal returns over future periods.

Clearly, 'winner persistence' is much stronger statistically and economically in hedge funds compared with (US or UK) equity mutual funds (see also Agarwal and Naik, 2002) and this in part accounts for the recent interest by pension funds in the hedge-fund industry and for mutual funds' increased interest in the possible use of derivatives (especially in Europe, where the so-called UCITIII rules allow much wider use of derivatives by mutual funds).

There appear to be exploitable strategies based on (annual) persistence in hedge-fund returns (at least before the transaction costs of switching between funds are considered). But research on hedge funds is relatively new and most hedge funds themselves have not been around very long, so statistical results must be interpreted with caution. In the past, the best hedge funds may well have exploited various anomalies in the capital markets, each of which may have existed for some considerable time, thus allowing high and persistent alphas going forward. But as more funds enter the industry to exploit such anomalies, abnormal returns are likely to be smaller and they will persist for less time, so 'making money' becomes more difficult and less frequent. Over a run of years, the balance of probability is that hedge funds will earn less in the future than they have in the past.

30.5 PORTFOLIO THEORY

There is some evidence to show that hedge-fund returns have low correlations with stock and bond returns and that certain hedge-fund *styles* (e.g. dedicated short selling, distressed securities, emerging markets) have even lower correlations. When we take an existing diversified portfolio (of stocks and bonds) and include about 20% by value in a portfolio of hedge funds, the mean-variance efficient frontier improves (i.e. moves northwest to give higher expected portfolio returns or lower portfolio risk, or both). This seems to suggest that hedge funds should be added to conventional portfolios of stocks and bonds, which no doubt accounts for recent investments by pension funds in hedge funds. For example, Fung and Hsieh (1997) find that hedge-fund returns do have relatively low correlations with other securities, hence when around 15–20% of an index tracker is supplemented with a hedge-fund portfolio, this improves the mean-variance, risk-return profile. However, some words of caution are required here.

Note that for most pension funds, holding 20% of their portfolio in hedge funds would be very unusual. Holding up to 5% in hedge funds is more representative, but it is unlikely that this would give a very noticeable improvement in diversification benefits (especially given the margin of error on optimal portfolio weights; Britten Jones, 1999). It is also the case that adding around 20% by value of hedge funds to a conventional stock–bond portfolio may reduce overall portfolio standard deviation, but it also increases negative skewness and excess kurtosis (Kat, 2003).

Remember that measuring the success of an investment strategy using the Sharpe ratio assumes that investors are only interested in the mean portfolio return and its variance. The first problem is that the standard statistical formula for measuring volatility (or standard deviation) is only correct if returns are independent over time – that is, it is like a coin flip, so that today's return, whether high or low, is of no use in predicting tomorrow's return. While this statistical problem can be solved in various ways, it is useful to note that whatever sophisticated estimation method we use to measure volatility, it will involve estimation error. When we measure volatility using the standard statistical formula, we implicitly assume that returns above the mean return make as important a contribution to volatility as do returns below the mean. This would be fine if stock and bond returns follow any *symmetric* distribution such as the 'bell-shaped' normal distribution. When analysing, say, monthly returns for *mutual funds*, this is a fairly good first approximation. But monthly *hedge-fund* returns are not nicely 'bell shaped' and in particular exhibit negative skew and excess kurtosis. Negative skew means that there are more extreme negative returns than there are extreme positive returns, compared with, say, the normal distribution. It is reasonable to assume that investors do not like negative skew and would want a higher return to compensate for this particular source of risk. Harvey and Siddique (2000) show that negative skewness may be an important component of systematic risk, as stocks with high values for negative skewness tend to have high average returns.

Excess kurtosis refers to the fact that hedge-fund returns have both positive and negative returns that are more extreme (compared with the normal distribution). While investors are happy if there are lots of extreme positive returns, they dislike an equal number of extreme negative returns even more. Hence, investors might want higher *average* returns to compensate for this kurtosis risk.

Illiquidity risk is also more prevalent for hedge funds than for mutual funds and again must be factored in to any calculation of risk and return. Finally, although the correlation between hedge-fund returns and the market return may be low when averaged over all historical data, it may be that in crisis periods this correlation is quite high – known co-skewness or 'phase locking'[4]. For example, when we have lots of *large* negative equity returns,

---

[4] Phase locking is also prevalent in biological phenomena such as the automatic synchronisation of the flickering of South East Asian fireflys.

we also tend to have lots of large negative hedge-fund returns too – so there may be much less reduction in diversification risk from adding hedge funds to your portfolio, just at the time when you need it most, in 'crash' periods. Standard statistical estimates use all the data to estimate the correlation coefficient and the large number of small changes in two returns. This may give a low value for the standard correlation coefficient. There may be few large values in the two returns, so even if these two returns *always* move together in crisis periods, this may not affect our standard estimate of the correlation coefficient, since the estimate is dominated by the very many uncorrelated small returns. What we need is a correlation measure that only uses large values for the two returns. There is a further problem: correlation coefficients only pick up *linear* relationships between two variables, but two variables can be related via a non-linear relationship (e.g. $Y = X^2 - (1/X)$ and such an association can only be measured using advanced techniques, which often require substantial amounts of data on the large changes in the variables. (Copulas are used in this branch of statistics.) Hence standard statistics may not pick up any 'phase-locking' effect.

Hedge-fund returns are quite different from mutual-fund returns in that they are further from normal. Hence, mean-variance analysis and the Sharpe ratio might not be the appropriate tools to evaluate the success of any hedge fund strategy. This is why the literature has tended to use alpha as the performance criterion for hedge funds – not that it's perfect by any means, but it is probably the 'least worse' method we have currently available.

30.6 PORTABLE ALPHA

There is much talk of 'portable alpha' among investment professionals. The idea can be applied to any investment fund and refers to the splitting of the fund return into that due to the market return (or some other index) and that due to alpha. Once you have done this, you can hedge away the risk due to the market return and be left only with the return due to alpha – that is, the mispricing. It is as if you want to invest in a successful fund with a positive alpha but you do not wish to take on the market risk that this fund entails. The term is often applied to hedge funds, but the idea is also applicable to mutual funds. Let's see how it works – conceptually it's not very difficult.

Suppose that the return on your fund (portfolio) can be explained by the one-factor model involving the market return (e.g. return on the S&P 500 index) and the beta of your fund is 0.5:

Portfolio return = Alpha + β × Market return = 4% + 0.5 (Market return)

Historically you know that the alpha is 4% p.a. (obtained as the intercept in the above regression), which is what you want to extract. If you simply purchase the fund you will earn an abnormal return of 4% p.a., but you will be carrying market risk given by the fund's beta. However, if you now *sell* index futures contracts, this will offset the market risk. When the market falls by 1% the value of your fund falls by 1/2%, but if your hedge is calculated correctly this can be offset by a 1/2% gain on your short futures position. You are then left with the alpha return of 4%, without any market risk.

You may remember that the correct number of futures contract to short is given by (see Chapter 24):

$$N_f = \frac{\$ - Value\ of\ investment}{\$ - Value\ of\ S\ \&\ P\ index} \times \beta$$

and the dollar value of the S&P 500 index $= S \times \$250$, where S is the current index value and $250 is the value of an index point.

Hence to extract portable alpha we need other assets (e.g. futures contracts) that:

- can be sold short in low-cost liquid markets; and
- have a high correlation with the factors that determine the fund return.

There will still be some systematic risk held by the investor, because the hedge requires an estimate of beta and this estimate may not be an accurate representation of the 'true' beta over the period of the hedge – this is basis risk. By and large, extracting portable alpha from *mutual funds* that mainly hold a diversified portfolio of plain vanilla stocks and bonds is not too difficult in practice. However, don't forget that finding *mutual funds* that are likely to have positive alphas in the future *is* very difficult. Here, it's finding the 'gold mine' that's difficult, not extracting the gold nuggets once you have discovered the mine.

As we have seen, finding hedge funds with positive alphas is by no means easy but is not impossible. However, extracting portable alpha from *hedge funds* is not easy in practice, because it may be difficult to isolate the key factors influencing hedge-fund returns, the factor betas may be measured with considerable error and there may not exist liquid markets that can be used to hedge the (hedge) fund's factor betas. For example, in merger arbitrage the beta of the hedge fund may depend on the beta of a small number of companies in different industrial sectors, and there may not be a liquid futures market on this index or on the stocks of the individual firms. Your alternative is then to use a futures contract on an *aggregate* stock index, which may involve considerable basis risk. So if you think that extracting portable alpha is too complex for you personally, you may consider employing a specialist investment firm to do it for you.

The study by Fung and Hsieh (2004) examined the ability to extract portable alpha from hedge funds that use the relatively simple long–short strategy. Initially they examined the performance of an equity hedge-fund *index*, which represents the performance of many hedge funds with this style (rather than looking at a single hedge fund with this style). Statistically, the hedge-fund index (i.e. our portfolio) is well explained by a two-factor model, based on the return on the S&P 500 and return on a small-cap minus large-cap index (i.e. the SMB factor), giving an R-squared of around 0.85. The betas were estimated with a rolling regression using the last 24 months of data, to pick up changes in betas over time. The factors are hedged by shorting stock-index futures and the number of futures contracts to hedge

TABLE 30.1: HFR long–short equity index, portable alphas (% p.a.)

1996	1997	1998	1999	2000	2001	2002	2003	2004	2005
13.44	13.33	15.48	30.46	8.80	0.79	3.76	8.00	2.01	7.23

the position is recalculated every month as the beta changes. Results for portable alpha over the period 1996–2005 are shown in Table 30.1.

Table 30.1 indicates very high alphas in the boom period up to 2000 and substantially worse performance after that, but still producing positive portable alphas. Although extracting portable alpha works well based on a hedge-fund *index*, Fung and Hsieh (2004) find that results for individual funds are much less robust. For individual hedge funds the R-squared drops to an average of around 0.4, but ranges from virtually zero for some funds up to 0.98 for others. For funds with low R-squareds, this implies that the estimates of betas and alphas are very uncertain. The latter implies that we cannot be sure the fund delivers positive rather than negative alpha, while the former means that the number of futures contracts used in the hedge may turn out to be incorrect, so you may not have a particularly good hedge against changes in the (two) factors.

30.7 FUTURE OF HEDGE FUNDS

As hedge funds attract more institutional investors with fiduciary duties, they will have to become more transparent about their trades and risk positions and perhaps to adopt specific benchmarks (e.g. a specific hedge-fund index). Even now, some funds-of-funds obtain detailed and frequent information (sometimes daily) on hedge fund positions and risk measures. Also, having to stay reasonably close to a benchmark may lead to less investment in highly specialised strategies for fear of tracking error or earning less than the benchmark, as the latter would probably entail substantial outflows of funds. Mutual funds are also gaining more regulatory freedom to invest in derivatives, so there is some convergence between the two sectors. There are also new products on the market that claim successfully to track the behaviour of hedge-fund *indices* (i.e. their average returns, volatility, skewness, etc.) by using mechanical trading strategies (using highly liquid futures and options) that can be programmed with real-time prices. These *replication funds* have much lower fees than funds-of-funds or a portfolio of individual hedge funds, so they may capture some of the investor cash flows that currently go to the traditional hedge-fund sector. After all, why pay high management fees for something you can replicate at lower cost? Goldman Sachs produced one of the first hedge-fund replication portfolios in 2006 (see also Kat and Palaro, 2006). Hence, convergence between mutual and hedge funds in investment approaches seems likely, with a continuum of different types of fund being available to investors.

Precisely which hedge funds to regulate will become more difficult as this convergence takes place. Regulation is likely to be based on rules about disclosure, with hedge funds that do not agree to disclosure requirements remaining in the unregulated sector. Whether this makes the markets more volatile is subject to much debate. Hedge funds may suffer from liquidity risk – they have highly levered positions and their risk strategy often depends on being able to get out of these positions with speed and little price impact. If liquidity is thin and banks begin to call in their loans because they fear a 'meltdown' in parts of the hedge-fund sector, and if there are many banks in this position (due to concentration risk), hedge funds may in part contribute to systemic risk in financial markets. Clearly, this was the view taken by the Federal Reserve in 1998 over LTCM, which had losses exceeding its capital of around $4bn. In addition, banks who are providers of lines of credit (i.e. bank loans for leveraged transactions) may also provide stock lending to funds (for short sales) and may also be counterparties to OTC derivative trades by hedge funds. Of course, these facts are as much an argument for the sensible regulation of the *financial intermediary's* credit risk as they are for the regulation of hedge funds themselves. In contrast to LTCM, the $6bn losses of Amaranth in 2006 seemed to cause minimum impact on markets and financial institutions.

Hedge funds currently widen the area of choice for at least some sophisticated investors, whereas mutual funds widen the set of investments open to somewhat less sophisticated investors. These are two different clienteles and from an investor-protection viewpoint, there is no reason the two cannot co-exist, in the same way that private equity caters to a different investment clientele. However, it is important that investors, particularly retail investors, are informed in an unbiased way about the risk–return profiles of different investments. Given the massive funds available for advertising their funds and maybe an incentive for being 'economical with the truth', there is a prima facie case for government working via truly independent organisations, which have sufficient resources, to provide impartial information on the risk–return profiles of funds. At present, governments have not done much in this area, but the UK regulator the FSA has an investor-education programme that is to be included as part of the school curriculum. In addition, on the precautionary principle, it is probably better that any large–scale savings schemes such as pension funds, which involve marketable assets, have 'default funds' that avoid areas where there is great uncertainty about performance for whatever reason (e.g. lack of data, generally accepted benchmarks, etc.). This would currently exclude hedge funds and private equity from default funds in 401K retirement schemes in the US and the proposed Britsaver scheme in the UK (Cuthbertson *et al.*, 2005; Turner, 2006).

SUMMARY

- Hedge funds are usually organised as limited partnerships.
- There are a wide variety of hedge-fund styles, all with different risk characteristics, but many rely on high levels of leverage and taking long–short positions.
- Funds-of-funds can be used by investors to gain diversification benefits from hedge funds, but such benefits are likely to be small unless 20% of the portfolio consists of hedge funds.

- Because hedge-fund strategies are so diverse, it is difficult to model their returns. Hence, any performance statistics are likely to be subject to large errors of measurement and may omit significant risks (e.g. skewness, liquidity or credit risk).
- The best hedge funds historically have earned statistically significant abnormal returns (alpha) and there is also evidence that past-winner funds persist over horizons of up to one year.
- Given the deficiencies of hedge-fund data and the fact that the industry is now much larger, there is a question mark over whether past performance is a useful guide to the future, as a larger number of funds chase a possibly diminishing set of profitable investment opportunities.
- Hedge funds will continue to exist, but there will be more convergence between mutual funds and hedge funds, particularly if institutional investors such as pension funds and insurance companies seek greater transparency.
- Portable alpha refers to an investment strategy that can pick high-alpha funds and then hedge any systematic (market or factor) risk, normally by using derivatives.

EXERCISES

Q1 How do hedge-fund investment strategies differ from those of mutual funds?

Q2 What data deficiencies are found in most hedge fund databases and what problems does this cause?

Q3 Under what conditions would selling short-dated, out-of-the-money puts on the S&P 500 produce high returns with low volatility, for a hedge fund? What are the risks in such a strategy?

Q4 What is portable alpha and how would you implement this hedge fund strategy?

Q5 Should you be wary when someone suggests investing in hedge funds because they have diversification benefits, if you already hold a well-diversified portfolio of stocks and bonds?

CHAPTER 31

Market Risk and Value at Risk

AIMS

- To explain the concept of value at risk (VaR).
- To measure VaR using the variance–covariance and historical simulation methods.
- To outline methods used in forecasting volatility.
- To assess the accuracy of forecasts of portfolio VaR – this is known as backtesting.
- To look at the 'Basle internal models' approach to setting risk standards.

INTRODUCTION

Financial institutions, particularly large investment banks (and some large industrial and commercial companies), hold net positions in a wide variety of assets such as stocks, bonds, foreign exchange, as well as futures and options contracts. Because the prices of these assets can move very quickly and by quite large amounts, investment banks want to know what risk they are holding over the next 24 hours as well as over the next week or month. Once they know what their risk position is, they can decide to maintain it, hedge it or to simply reduce some of their risk exposure. Risk due to price changes is known as market risk – measuring and monitoring changing market risk is the subject of this chapter.

For their own prudential reasons, financial intermediaries need to measure the overall dollar market risk of their portfolio, which is usually referred to as *value at risk* (VaR). In addition, the regulatory authorities use VaR to set minimum capital adequacy requirements for financial institutions – the shareholders of the bank have to be willing to take a cut in dividend payments and to set up reserves to meet unexpected losses due to unforeseen changes in market prices.

The interaction between investment decisions and risk calculations is now absolutely central in managing mutual funds, hedge funds and pension funds, as well as the proprietary trading positions held by large investment banks. The chief risk officer in a financial institution now has a key role in the management process.

In this chapter we examine the measurement of market risk, mainly using stocks as our example. There are various ways to measure portfolio risk, and we concentrate on the so-called variance–covariance method (sometimes called the delta-normal method), which draws strongly on earlier chapters on portfolio theory. Since market risk varies over time, we examine how to forecast this changing risk and to assess how accurate our forecasts are. In the latter part of this chapter we discuss some alternative methods of measuring risk such as historical simulation and stress testing.

31.1 VALUE AT RISK: VaR

In this section we use concepts from portfolio theory to provide us with a pretty simple yet very useful measure of market risk, value at risk, which is now the industry standard.

Suppose that you hold a portfolio of stocks. The return R_{t+1} *between today and tomorrow* is the capital gain or loss on the stocks (plus any cash payments such as dividends). However, dividend payments are announced in advance, so the source of uncertainty and risk *over the next day* is the fact that you do not know what the price will be tomorrow. For simplicity, we assume that dividend payments are zero, so that the return on the portfolio is:

$$R_{t+1} = \frac{P_{t+1} - P_t}{P_t} \qquad\qquad [1]$$

Measuring returns over one day allows us to determine *daily* VaR for our portfolio. Suppose that you currently hold $3030m in your portfolio of stocks and the chief risk officer reports to the CEO of your bank that over the next 24 hrs (one day) your VaR is $100m, at a 95% confidence level (also referred to as a 5% critical value or 5% 'left tail' value). This implies that:

> If you hold your asset positions fixed, then there is a 95% chance that you will lose *less than* $100m over the next 24hrs.

Note that the risk officer is not saying you *will lose* less than $100m, only that there is a 95 out of 100 chance that you will lose less than $100m. So as a concept, VaR involves a specific probability or confidence level and a specific time horizon over which we measure risk. We cannot predict *exactly* how much we will lose (or gain) over any 24-hour period – since the world is risky – we can only provide a 'best guess' with a certain probability. This is not the only way we can express the VaR concept and an equivalent statement is:

> If you hold your asset positions fixed, then you expect to lose less than $100m in 19 out of the next 20 days.

You can see where the probability bit comes in, since '19 out of 20 days' is equivalent to $5 \times 19 = 95$ out of 100 days; that is, 95% of the time. Expressed in this way, you are saying that if you hold your $3030m position unchanged over the next 20 days, on about 19 of those days you would lose less than $100m. It also follows that:

> If you hold your asset positions fixed, then you expect to lose *more than* $100m in 1 out of the next 20 days.

One day out of 20 is equivalent to 5 days out of 100, so now you can see where the technical term '5% critical value' or '5% left tail' comes from. Note that even though the VaR concept is concerned with potential losses, it is usually reported as a positive number.

Much of the material discussed in this chapter is based on the risk-measurement methodology as set out in *RiskMetrics*^{TM} (1996), which emanates from JP Morgan. Here, use of the term RiskMetrics applies to the general approach found in *RiskMetrics*^{TM}.

Measuring risk

The riskiness of a *single asset* is summarised in the probability distribution of its returns. For stock returns the outcomes can take on many values, and a convenient first approximation is that these outcomes are normally distributed. There is no *single* acceptable measure of the riskiness of a particular distribution, but for the normal distribution the standard deviation (or variance) is widely accepted as a measure of risk. Let's remind ourselves of the simplicity and usefulness of the normal distribution, when we want to specify the probability that certain outcomes might happen.

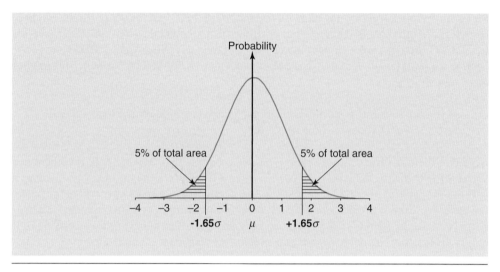

FIGURE 31.1: Normal distribution

For normally distributed returns, we can be 90% certain that the actual return will equal the expected return μ plus or minus 1.65σ (see Figure 31.1), where σ is the standard deviation of the returns. Put another way, we expect the actual return to be *less than* $\mu - 1.65\sigma$ on 5% of occasions or greater than $\mu + 1.65\sigma$, also on 5% of occasions (e.g. 1 time in 20).

The mean daily return on a stock is very small and close to zero. From a statistical point of view, there is a great deal of 'noise' in daily returns (i.e. technically speaking, daily returns have a high standard deviation, relative to the mean return), so:

- When calculating *daily* VaR, we assume that the mean return is zero.
- Hence, 1.65σ is a measure of the (percentage) downside risk (with 5% probability).

If we hold a (net) position of $\$V_0$ in one asset, the (dollar) **value at risk** is:

$$\text{VaR} = \$V_0(1.65\sigma) \tag{2}$$

which is a basic building block for calculating the VaR of more complex portfolios. Calculation of daily VaR is illustrated in Table 31.1.

Are daily returns normally distributed?

It is found that daily *changes* in exchange rates, long-term bond prices and equity prices are all *approximately* normal, but they do deviate somewhat from normality, in the following ways:

- Return distributions often have fatter tails, a higher peak and 'thinner waist' than the normal distribution (i.e. actual returns are leptokurtic).
- Returns are negatively skewed (i.e. there are more observations in the lefthand tail than the righthand tail).

TABLE 31.1: Calculation of daily VaR

Data	Suppose that daily stock returns are normally distributed. The mean daily return on AT&T stocks is $\mu = 0$ and the standard deviation σ of the return on AT&T is 0.005 (0.5% per day). You hold $V_0 = \$115m$ of AT&T stock.
Questions	What is the daily dollar VaR of your position, at 5% left-tail cut-off, and what does this mean?
Answers	If daily returns R are normally distributed, then 1.65 is the cut-off point for 5% of the probability to be in the left tail and 5% in the right tail, leaving 90% of the probability in the centre of the distribution. Hence 90% of daily returns lie between:

$$\mu + 1.65\sigma \quad \text{and} \quad \mu - 1.65\sigma$$

that is, $+0.825\% (= 1.65 \times 0.5\%)$ and -0.825%.

Put another way, only 5% of the daily returns should be more than $+0.825\%$ and 5% should be less than -0.825%. Either of these cases should occur no more than 1 day in every 20 days (i.e. 5% of the time). The dollar VaR of a US investor holding $115m in AT&T stock is:

$$\text{VaR} = V_0(1.65\sigma) = \$115m\,(0.825/100) = \$948,750$$

Hence 95% of the time you should not lose more than $948,750 over the next 24 hours (assuming that you maintain your initial position of $115m).

In Figure 31.2 we show the histogram of daily returns using the S&P 500 index of US stocks. One can see that the mean daily return is very close to zero. The histogram is broadly bell shaped, associated with the normal distribution. But it has a thinner peak than the normal distribution and there are a few more occurrences of extreme negative and positive returns than would be associated with the normal curve (i.e. the empirical histogram has fatter tails in the very extremes than the normal distribution) – this is excess kurtosis. In addition, the empirical distribution is reasonably symmetric, so there is no appreciable negative or positive skew. In fact, for daily returns on most speculative *spot* assets (i.e. not necessarily options prices), it is probably a *reasonable approximation* to assume normality and this is what we have to assume when using the variance–covariance method to measure VaR.

Portfolio risk

How can we measure the dollar VaR of a *portfolio* of assets? Let's take two assets for simplicity – say you hold shares in AT&T and Microsoft, in proportions (or weights) 1/4 and 3/4 respectively. The return on your *portfolio* of assets R_p is:

$$R_p = w_1R_1 + w_2R_2 = (1/4)\,R_1 + (3/4)\,R_2 \qquad [3]$$

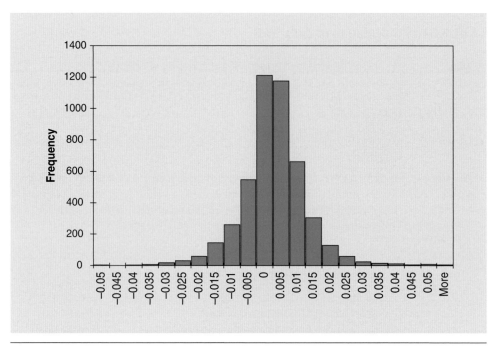

FIGURE 31.2: Daily returns S&P 500 (Jan. 1990–Oct. 2007)

The standard deviation of *returns* on the portfolio is given by the usual formula from portfolio theory:

$$\sigma_p = \sqrt{w_1^2\sigma_1^2 + w_2^2\sigma_2^2 + 2w_1w_2\rho\sigma_1\sigma_2} \qquad [4]$$

where σ_i is the standard deviation of the return on asset i and ρ is the correlation coefficient between the return on asset 1 (AT&T) and the return on asset 2 (Microsoft). So when we have a portfolio of assets (e.g. stocks), consideration must be given to all the correlations between returns when calculating the *portfolio* standard deviation. (Note also that the term $\rho\sigma_1\sigma_2$ is the *covariance* between the two returns, usually written σ_{ij}.)

Consider another problem with [4]. Unfortunately, σ_p is measured as a percentage (if returns are measured as percentages), but the CEO of the bank requires the *dollar* VaR. By analogy with the single asset case it looks like the **dollar value at risk for our portfolio is given by:**

$$\text{VaR}_p = V_{0p}(1.65)\sigma_p = V_{0p}1.65\sqrt{w_1^2\sigma_1^2 + w_2^2\sigma_2^2 + 2w_1w_2\rho\sigma_1\sigma_2} \qquad [5]$$

where V_{0p} is the total amount invested in the portfolio. There is still a slight problem with [5], since it is more convenient if the investor provides the *dollar amount* in each asset. Suppose that the initial dollar amounts held in each asset are $V_1 = \$100$ and $V_2 = \$300$, it follows that the total amount in stocks $V_{0p} = V_1 + V_2 = \$400$ and $w_1 = V_1/V_{0p} = 1/4$ and

$w_2 = V_2/V_{0p} = 3/4$. Substituting for w_1 and w_2 in [5] we get:

$$\text{VaR}_p = \sqrt{(V_1 1.65\sigma_1)^2 + (V_2 1.65\sigma_2)^2 + 2\rho(V_1 1.65\sigma_1)(V_2 1.65\sigma_2)}$$
$$= \sqrt{\text{VaR}_1^2 + \text{VaR}_2^2 + 2\rho(\text{VaR}_1)(\text{VaR}_2)} \qquad [6]$$

This is rather convenient, since we have now related the dollar *portfolio* VaR to the individual VaRs of each asset – this is the first of our building blocks. If the dollar amounts held in each asset (V_1, V_2) are positive, then the smaller the correlation between the two asset returns, the lower the VaR. This is the usual diversification effect in portfolio theory. The smaller is the correlation, the lower the risk of the portfolio and VaR is just the dollar measure of this risk.

Suppose that you have *short sold*, say, $10m of stock 1, then $V_1 = -10$m in the above formula. If stock 2 is held long (say $20m), then the larger is the *positive* correlation between the two stock returns, the smaller is the risk and the VaR.

Worst-case VaR

Let's consider what would make VaR a rather large number, indicating a high-risk portfolio. If asset returns are perfectly positively correlated ($\rho = +1$) and you hold positive amounts of each asset (i.e. V_1, $V_2 > 0$), this is the worst-case scenario, since there are no benefits from diversification by holding two assets. Thus the maximum value that the VaR can take, known as the **worst-case VaR**, is given by setting $\rho = +1$ in [6], which gives:

$$\text{Worst-case VaR}_p = VaR_1 + VaR_2 \qquad [7]$$

Hence, in a worst-case scenario the portfolio VaR is simply the sum of the individual VaRs. In the real world it is unlikely that the correlation between the returns of two stocks like AT&T and Microsoft is +1, so your 'best guess' or 'diversified VaR', as it is correctly called, is given by [6]. In crisis periods, however, it is often the case that correlations increase, and the worst-case VaR provides a high figure that may be representative of these crisis periods (e.g. during the 1987 and 2001 stock-market crashes and the bond-price meltdown of 1997). So, risk managers usually look at both the diversified VaR and the worst-case VaR. This gives them a feel for what would happen if historical correlations did not stay the same but increased due to a crisis.

> Note that there is no diversification effect when $\rho = +1$ (*and* V_1, $V_2 > 0$). However, it is worth noting that if $\rho = 1$ and *one* of the positions is a short position (e.g. $V_1 < 0$ with $V_2 > 0$), there *will be* some risk offset.

Many assets

If we hold n different stocks, the above formulae for the portfolio variance begin to look rather complex. However, by using matrix notation we can simplify the calculation. Using matrix algebra, equation [6] can be written as:

$$\text{VaR}_p = [\mathbf{Z}\ \mathbf{C}\ \mathbf{Z}']^{1/2} \qquad\qquad [8]$$

where $\mathbf{Z} = [VaR_1, VaR_2] = [V_1\ 1.65\sigma_1, V_2\ 1.65\sigma_2]$ is a row vector of the *individual* VaRs for each asset and the correlation matrix is:

$$\mathbf{C} = \begin{bmatrix} 1 & \rho \\ \rho & 1 \end{bmatrix}$$

When we have more than two assets, the VaR for the portfolio can be represented in exactly the same way, but there are more entries in the $\mathbf{Z}$ vector and the correlation matrix, as we have more assets. A statistician (or the RiskMetrics database) provides estimates of the volatilities σ_i and the correlation matrix $\mathbf{C}$, *while the investor can provide the dollar amounts in each asset V_i*. So in practice, to calculate VaR for a portfolio of n stocks we need:

1. The dollar position in each asset.
2. Forecasts of the standard deviation of each asset and the correlations between all of the assets[1].

Note that the $\mathbf{Z}$ vector simply contains the VaRs for the constituent assets.

As mentioned above, when reporting *individual* VaRs these are always taken as positive, even though they represent a loss (which conventionally has a negative sign). In calculating the *portfolio* VaR the *sign* of V_i must be incorporated in $\mathbf{Z}$ – if the stock is held long (i.e. you own it), then $V_i > 0$, but if the stock has been sold short, then $V_i < 0$. A simple example will clarify the issues involved (Table 31.2).

 Let's get a little more adventurous and look at the VaR-Excel Table 31.3 (which you can find on the web site), it calculates the VaR for a portfolio of three stocks using our matrix notation. (You can easily extend it to more assets.)

Each individual VaR is calculated as $VaR_i = V_0 1.65\sigma_i$ – this is in the fourth column. The worst-case VaR is simply the sum of the individual VaRs. The diversified VaR is calculated using the formula $\sqrt{\mathbf{Z}\mathbf{C}\mathbf{Z}'}$. The diversified VaR is much less than the worst-case VaR, because although all the correlation coefficients are positive, stock 2 has been short sold (hence the '−10,000' in the second column) and this 'manufactures' a negative correlation between its return and the returns on stocks 1 and 3. Hence there is a strong diversification effect and the (diversified) VaR at $783 is much less than the worst-case VaR of $1996.

VaR: foreign assets

How do we deal with exchange-rate risk when calculating VaR? Suppose that you are a US-based investor holding €140m in the German stock-market index, the DAX. Here you face risk

---

[1] If the number of assets in our portfolio is n, we have n $-positions, n standard deviations and $n(n - 1)$ correlations. For $n = 5$ that means 20 correlations.

TABLE 31.2: Calculation of portfolio VaR

Data	A US investor holds $10m of AT&T shares and has short sold $5m of IBM shares.
	Daily volatility of AT&T $\sigma_1 = 1.5\%$ and daily volatility of IBM $\sigma_2 = 1.0\%$.
	The correlation between AT&T returns and IBM returns is -0.1.
Questions	1. What is the daily VaR?
	2. What is the worst-case daily VaR?
Answer	Long position: $\text{VaR}_1 = (\$10m)1.65\,(1.5/100) = \$247,500$
	Short position: $\text{VaR}_2 = (\$5m)1.65\,(1.0/100) = \$82,500$

$$\text{VaR}_p = \sqrt{\text{VaR}_1^2 + \text{VaR}_2^2 + 2\rho(\text{VaR}_1)(\text{VaR}_2)}$$

$$= \sqrt{247,500^2 + 82,500^2 + 2(-0.1)(247,500)(-82,500)}$$

$$= \$268,601$$

Note the two negative signs '-0.1' and '$-82,500$', reflecting the negative correlation and the short selling of IBM. These two factors tend to increase portfolio risk and VaR.

Worst-case VaR $= \text{VaR}_1 + \text{VaR}_2 = \$330,000$

TABLE 31.3: VaR, portfolio of three stocks

Assets	Value of asset	Std. dev.	VaR		Correlation matrix (C)		
1	10,000	5.4180%	894		1	0.962	0.403
2	−10,000	3.0424%	502		0.962	1	0.61
3	10,000	3.6363%	600		0.403	0.61	1
				Individual VaRs **Z** $=$	894	−502	600
	Worst-case VaR		$1996	Div. VaR	$783		

due to changes in the DAX and changes in S, the dollar–euro spot rate. In effect, you hold a two-asset portfolio, namely the foreign stock itself and the foreign currency, and the return is:

$$R_p = R_{DAX} + R_S \quad \text{(with equal weights of unity in the two assets)} \quad [9]$$

If the stocks in the DAX go down at the same time as the euro depreciates against the US dollar, a US investor would lose on both counts: a 'double whammy' of losses on the DAX itself plus losses when euros are converted into US dollars. This is because for every euro the US investor has in the DAX, she can obtain fewer US dollars. A positive correlation between the DAX index and the euro exchange rate increases the riskiness of the US investor's portfolio, measured in US dollars. Conversely, a negative correlation between the DAX and the euro exchange rate is better than a positive correlation, when considering the downside risk for a US investor who holds the German stocks.

To measure the dollar VaR for a US investor of a foreign asset, we use the same formula as before – but with some slight modifications. First, because we are interested in the dollar VaR we have to convert the initial position, which is in euros, into US dollars. So if the US investor has €100m invested in the DAX and the *current* dollar–euro spot (exchange) rate is $S = 1.05$ (US dollars per euro), the initial *dollar position* is:

$$V_{0\$} = S(€100m) = \$105m \quad [10]$$

The *dollar VaR* is then given by the usual formula:

$$\text{VaR}_p = \sqrt{\mathbf{ZCZ'}}$$

where $\mathbf{Z} = [\text{VaR}_{DAX}, \text{VaR}_s] = [V_{0\$}1.65\sigma_{DAX}, V_{0\$}1.65\sigma_S]$
   $V_{0\$}$ = the initial dollar value of the position held in shares in the DAX ($105m)
   σ_{DAX} = the volatility of the returns of the DAX index
   σ_S = the volatility of the returns of the dollar–euro spot exchange rate

The $\mathbf{Z}$ vector 'contains' the *same* initial dollar value, $V_{0\$} = \$105m$, for both the DAX and the FX position. This is because for a US investor, holding the DAX in euros is equivalent to holding both $V_{0\$}$ in the DAX plus $V_{0\$}$ in foreign exchange. The correlation matrix $\mathbf{C}$ contains the correlation coefficient between the returns of the DAX and the dollar–euro spot exchange rate. So now we know how to find the dollar VaR for a US bank that holds foreign assets.

31.2 HISTORICAL SIMULATION

When using the variance–covariance method to calculate portfolio VaR, we have assumed that returns are normally distributed – this is why we were able to use the '1.65' scaling factor in our VaR calculations (at a 5% left-tail cut-off). But if returns are actually non-normal, using '1.65' is no longer valid and it would produce biased estimates/forecasts. Historical simulation (HS) directly uses the actual data on returns to calculate VaR, so if actual returns are *not* normally distributed the HS method will take account of this. It is often referred to as

Currently hold $100m in each of 2 assets

Day=	1	2	3.....	700	701	702	703...	...1000
R_1 (%)	+2	+1	+4	−3	−2	−1	−1	+2
R_2 (%)	+1	+2	0	−1	−5	−6	+15	−5
$-Change (m)	+3	+3	+4	−4	−7	−7	+14	−3

Order the 1,000 figures for the $-change in value of the portfolio in ascending order:
−12, −11, −11, −10, −9, −9, −8, −7,−7, −6, −5, −4, −3, ...+8, ...0, +2,.... +10, +10,...... +14

VaR forecast for tomorrow at 1% tail probability (10th most negative) = −$6m

---

FIGURE 31.3: Stylised historic simulation (daily data)

non-parametric. When we used the variance–covariance approach to measuring risk, we have to measure explicitly the variance (standard deviation) of each asset return and the covariances (correlations) between each of the asset returns in our portfolio. These variances and covariances (correlations) are referred to by statisticians as 'parameters'. However, in the HS approach these variances and covariances do not have to be *explicitly* estimated, hence the term 'non-parametric'. Instead, as we shall see, these concepts are encapsulated in the time path of the actual historical returns that we use in the HS approach.

To see how straightforward and intuitive this approach is, consider Figure 31.3, which shows the historical daily returns over the past 1000 days on two stocks, which could be Microsoft and AT&T. In Figure 31.3 there are only a few numbers out of the 1000 total set of numbers, but you can still make an informed guess about what these figures are telling you about volatilities and correlation. For example, *approximately,* what is the mean daily return of stock 1 and stock 2 and their standard deviations – and do the latter look as if they are changing over time? Very approximately, the mean daily return on both stocks could easily be zero. The standard deviation of stock 1 looks to be around 2 and is fairly constant over time. For stock 2 the average volatility is somewhat higher and its volatility clearly varies over time, starting low in the early periods at around 1.5 and rising to quite a high level on days 700–703 before declining by day 1000.

Next, by looking only at stock 1 (i.e. across row 2), we can describe the movement in its returns over time. When stock 1 has positive returns they tend to stay positive for a while, and when they become negative there is a tendency to remain negative – this means that in reality the stock return is not independent over time (although the latter would be erroneously assumed to be the case in the variance–covariance method).

Now let's think about the correlation *between* the two stock returns. Comparing the returns of stocks 1 and 2, at each point in time (i.e. looking down each column marked 1, 2, 3, ..., 1000), we can see that except for day 3, day 703 and day 1000, the return on stock 1 moves in the same direction as the return on stock 2, so these stock returns are highly positively correlated and would have a high correlation coefficient. So even though we do not directly measure volatilities and correlations, they are there in the historical data. The historical simulation method makes use of this fact, but without assuming that the returns and correlations are constant over time and without imposing a specific distribution (like the normal distribution) when calculating the VaR.

Suppose that today is day 1000 and we currently hold $100m in each stock. We want to forecast the dollar VaR for tomorrow (i.e. day 1001) with a 1% probability (note we have changed from a 5% probability to a 1% probability, purely for expositional purposes). The 1% probability level is also referred to as the '1st percentile'. The HS approach asks the question:

> If I had held my current position of $100m in each stock, what would my profit and loss have looked like on each of the past 1000 days?

To implement the HS approach requires the following steps:

1. Calculate the dollar change in value of your *current* portfolio over each of the last 1000 days. Each of these *separate* 1000 changes in value has occurred with equal probability, since each represents one day out of the 1000 days. But of course, the change in value may be the same on more than one day, and this is evident in the number for the '$-change' in portfolio value in Figure 31.3.
2. Order the daily profits/losses in row 4 from lowest (on the left) to highest (on the right). Some of the lowest figures will be negative, indicating losses.
   This is done in row 5 of Figure 31.3 (we have inserted some figures here and we cannot include all 1000 values).
3. The VaR at a 1% probability level will be the figure in row 5 that is 10th from the left (i.e. 1% of 1000 data points is the 10th data point from the left), so:

   - The dollar VaR using HS (at a 1% probability level) is $6m.

From the above, we can see that when we use the actual historical data to calculate the VaR, we are implicitly incorporating volatilities and correlations each time we calculate the change in the portfolio value. These implicit volatilities and correlations vary over time (e.g. the correlation between the two stock returns in Figure 31.3 is positive on days 1, 2, 700, 701 and 702, but is negative on days 703 and 1000).

We could also produce a histogram for all the values of the dollar change in portfolio value in row 5 of Figure 31.3. Some values occur more than once, which would give a high 'tower' in the histogram. From the histogram we can also obtain a visual picture of any skewness in the daily change in value of the portfolio, and hence we can visually assess any deviations from the normality assumption.

This is done using real data on stock returns in Figure 31.4 for a portfolio of three stocks, with equal amounts of $10,000 held in each stock. These stocks are Bank of America, Boeing and Anheuser Busch. We now measure the VaR at our usual 5% left-tail cut-off point.

In Figure 31.4 you can clearly see the fatter tails (both in the left and right tails) than would be found for the normal distribution. The distribution in both tails is also rather

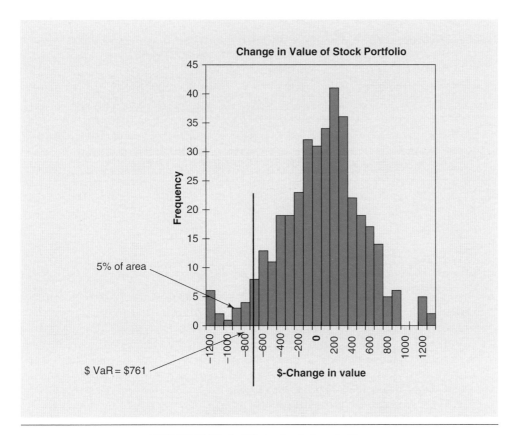

FIGURE 31.4: Historical simulation

irregular – again indicating non-normality. There is also a bit of a 'left skew' (i.e. more large negative returns than positive returns). Because we have constructed the empirical histogram, we do not need to assume normality and the 5% lower-tail cut-off point in Figure 31.4 appears to be around $750. Indeed, if we order all the daily changes in value from lowest to highest, the VaR from the historical simulation method at the 5th percentile is found to be $761.

Using the raw historical data on each of the three stock returns, we have also calculated their standard deviations and the correlation coefficients between each of the returns and calculated the VaR using the variance–covariance method. We find that holding $10,000 in each stock gives a *daily* VaR as follows:

Historical simulation method = $761

Variance–covariance method = $950

The VaR of $761 is 2.54% (= $761/$30,000) of the initial value of your portfolio and $950 is 3.17% of the initial value. So there is some difference between the two estimates of VaR,

	A	B	C	D	E	F	G	H	I	J	K	L	M	N	O	P	Q
1	Excel Spreadsheet : Calculating VaR of Portfolio of 'Spot' Assets (Historic Simulation Approach)																
2																	
3	The Portfolio						Historic Simulation										
4				$-value	weights												
5	Asset 1	Bank of America		10,000	0.3333		Prob. for VaR calculation			0.05		VaR using the historic simulation approach is					
6	Asset 2	Microsoft		10,000	0.3333		Level of Certainty			0.95							
7	Asset 3	Anheuser Busch		10,000	0.3333		Number of observations			999			333.9				
8	Asset 4			0	0		Historic VaR is at position			50							
9	Asset 5			0	0												
10																	
11	Sum			30000	1												
12																	
13																	
14	Date	Prices					Returns					Portfolio	Ascend.	No of	Ascend.	VaR	
15		Asset 1	Asset 2	Asset 3	Asset 4		Asset 1	Asset 2	Asset 3	Asset 4		returns	ordered	obs.	ordered		
16													returns		$'s		
17																	
18	Day 1	40.705	29.35	48.69													
19	Day 2	40.51	29.353	49.2			-0.0048	0.0001	0.0104			0.0019	-0.0346	1	-1038.81		
20	Day 3	40.515	28.89	49.5			0.0001	-0.0159	0.0061			-0.0032	-0.0339	2	-1018.02		
21	Day 4	40.89	28.91	49.6			0.0092	0.0007	0.0020			0.0040	-0.0335	3	-1005.98		
22	Day 5	40.93	26.61	49.77			0.0010	-0.0829	0.0034			-0.0262	-0.0323	4	-969.768		
23	Day 6	36.785	26.91	49.52			-0.1068	0.0112	-0.0050			-0.0335	-0.0316	5	-946.933		
24	Day 7	36.425	27.2	49.2			-0.0098	0.0107	-0.0065			-0.0019	-0.0262	6	-785.012		
25	Day 8	37.18	26.74	48.95			0.0205	-0.0171	-0.0051			-0.0005	-0.0232	7	-697.454		
26	Day 9	37.585	26.12	48.79			0.0108	-0.0235	-0.0033			-0.0053	-0.0207	8	-620.931		
27	Day 10	37.865	26.14	49.26			0.0074	0.0008	0.0096			0.0059	-0.0203	9	-607.894		
28	Day 11	37.995	26.68	49.65			0.0034	0.0204	0.0079			0.0106	-0.0188	10	-564.499		
29																	
30	...	...	...	...	...	...	...	...	...	...	...	...	...	...	...	...	
31																	
32	Day 48	39.625	27.04	52.48			-0.0008	-0.0041	-0.0013			-0.0020	-0.0114	47	-342.751		
33	Day 49	39.625	27.04	52.48			0.0000	0.0000	0.0000			0.0000	-0.0114	48	-342.304		
34	Day 50	39.795	27.21	52.44			0.0043	0.0063	-0.0008			0.0033	-0.0114	49	-341.813		
35	Day 51	40.15	27.46	52.4			0.0089	0.0091	-0.0008			0.0058	-0.0111	50	-333.916	-333.916	
36	Day 52	40.25	27.52	52.33			0.0025	0.0022	-0.0013			0.0011	-0.0111	51	-333.377		
37	Day 53	40.215	27.37	52.68			-0.0009	-0.0055	0.0067			0.0001	-0.0111	52	-331.836		

We calculate the daily returns on the portfolio and the dollar VaR on each day. The values for daily VaR are then ordered from the lowest to the highest. The 5th percentile is then determined, which is the VaR at a 5% significance level. Here, in contrast to the variance–covariance approach, we use the empirical distribution of the returns and we do not assume that daily returns are normally distributed.

Note that the VaR result using historical simulation (= −$333.92) is very similar to the VaR (= −$328), calculated using the variance–covariance approach. This implies that daily portfolio returns are very close to being normally distributed.

which would probably be magnified if we were looking at VaR over a longer horizon than one day.

Why do the two methods of calculating VaR, historical simulation and the variance–covariance approach, give different results? Which is the more accurate? The variance–covariance method assumes that returns are independent (i.e. like a coin flip), that we have accurate forecasts of the standard deviations and correlations and that all returns are normally distributed. The historical simulation method does not assume anything about the distribution of stock returns, but just takes whatever distribution exists in the historical data. It looks from the histogram in Figure 31.4 that the returns are not normally distributed, so we might tend to favour the historical simulation approach. However, we cannot really say which estimate is the more accurate unless we do extensive 'backtesting' and compare the outcomes of the two competing methods.

The HS method can be used to estimate the VaR for any set of assets for which we have a reasonably long series of daily price changes (i.e. returns). So in principle, one of the returns series could be the percentage change in a call or put option, the percentage change in bond prices and the percentage change in the exchange rate. However, accurate estimates of the VaR at the 5th percentile, say, and even more so at the 1st percentile, require a long time series of data, and this is not always available for some assets.

It is precisely because tail events are unusual that we need quite a lot of data for a reliable estimate of the tail. For example, if we are interested in the 1% lower tail, then in our historical data set, this will only occur 1 in every 100 observations. So, to put an extreme case, suppose you only had 100 observations on *daily* returns and 99 of these had a maximum negative value of, say, 1%, but the return on day 1 (i.e. 100 days ago) was *minus* 8%. If you held $100,000 in this stock, your *forecast* of tomorrow's VaR using the HS approach would be 0.08 × $100,000 = $8000. Given the run of actual historical returns, do you really believe that the $8000 is a good estimate of what might happen tomorrow? Only your 'gut feeling' can answer this. The figure of $8000 does seem too high a forecast, given the historical data. Not only that, but the forecast for two days' hence would be around 0.01 × $100,000 = $1000, since the '−8%' would drop out of your moving historical window of 100 days.

So you need quite a lot of data to estimate the 1% tail VaR accurately from historical data. On the other hand, the longer is our historical data set, the more the old data may influence our forecast of *tomorrow's* VaR, relative to the more recent data. Do we really want the forecast of tomorrow's VaR to be heavily influenced by stock returns that happened, say, 1000 days ago (i.e. about three years)?

Of course, to a greater or lesser extent such problems plague almost any method that relies on past data to forecast the future, including the usual variance–covariance VaR method. There are methods to get round this problem of only wanting to use the last 100 days to calculate your forecast for tomorrow's VaR using the HS approach. Bootstrapping repeatedly and randomly re-samples from the past 100 days of historical data, thus increasing the sample size in an artificial way. But because the re-sampling is random, it generates many more data points in the extreme tails (admittedly all based on the actual 100 days of data) and then averages these 'extreme' data points to obtain a new estimate of the VaR (at, say, the 1% cut-off point). This is the bootstrap VaR estimate – for more details see Cuthbertson and Nitzsche (2001b).

31.3 FORECASTING VOLATILITY

It is clear from the above analysis that to calculate daily VaR using the variance – covariance approach we need a forecast of tomorrow's stock-return volatility. Let's look at some possible forecasting schemes. A simple forecasting scheme is to assume that tomorrow's forecast of daily volatility is a **simple moving average (SMA)** of past squared returns R_t^2 over the last 30 days:

$$\sigma_{t+1|t}^2 = (1/n) \sum_{i=0}^{29} R_{t-i}^2 \qquad [11]$$

The subscripts in $\sigma_{t+1|t}$ can be read as 'the forecast for time $t + 1$ (tomorrow) based on information available up to time t (today)'. (Note that we do not subtract the mean return in equation [11] and use the more usual term $(R_{t-i} - \overline{R})^2$ because we have assumed that the daily mean return is zero.)

If today ($= t$) is Monday after the market has closed, then [11] gives a forecast of Tuesday's volatility based on the squared returns from Monday, last Friday, Thursday and so on, for the past 30 trading days. When tomorrow arrives, then on *Tuesday*, we make a new forecast. Now, our forecast for Wednesday includes Tuesday's, Monday's and so on squared returns (and we drop the final day's return from 31 days ago). Hence our forecast is continually updated as we move through time. A problem with the SMA is that it gives equal weight (of 1/30) to all of the past 30 days squared returns, when forecasting *tomorrow's* volatility. It seems more intuitive when forecasting tomorrow, to give relatively greater weight to what has happened in the recent past then in the more distant one. This gives the **exponentially weighted moving average (EWMA)** forecast:

$$\sigma_{t+1|t}^2 = (1 - \lambda) \sum_{i=0}^{\infty} \lambda^i R_{t-i}^2 \qquad [12]$$

where R_t is the daily return on the asset (with mean zero) and λ is a weight lying between 0 and 1 (e.g. $\lambda = 0.94$). The weights λ^i decline exponentially, so this forecasting scheme is known as an EWMA. For example, for $\lambda = 0.94$, the λ^i weights decline as 0.94, 0.88, 0.83, . . . etc. and squared returns that occur further in the past are given less weight in the current forecast for the variance. Actually, equation [12] can be written in a simpler form, as the following *recursion:*

$$\sigma_{t+1|t}^2 = \lambda \sigma_{t|t-1}^2 + (1 - \lambda)R_t^2 \qquad [13]$$

Suppose that you have 250 daily observations on squared returns R_t^2. An arbitrary value for sigma is chosen to start off the recursion in equation [13]. For example, this might be the simple average of the first 29 observations on R_t^2. If we denote this average as $\sigma_{30|29}$, then the forecast can be updated for day 31 using the new value for R_{30}^2:

$$\sigma_{31|30}^2 = \lambda \sigma_{30|29}^2 + (1 - \lambda) R_{30}^2 \qquad [14]$$

The forecast $\sigma_{31|30}^2$ can be updated daily until we get to day 250, namely 'today', at which point we are ready to make a genuine forecast (which can be shown to be independent of our initial guess for the volatility $\sigma_{30|29}$). As additional information on daily returns becomes available, our forecast of the variance (or standard deviation) varies as we move forward through time. It has been found that the EWMA forecasting equation gives better predictions than the SMA.

The above EWMA formula, when applied to daily changes in exchange rates (i.e. FX rates), is shown in Figure 31.5. You can see how the EWMA forecast moves around by quite

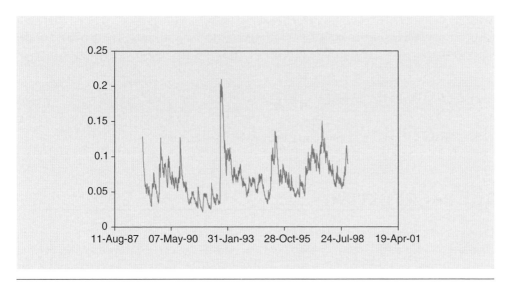

FIGURE 31.5: EWMA forcast of volatility, daily FX returns

substantial amounts, which will directly influence our changing daily forecasts of the VaR of a portfolio of foreign assets.

Banks and financial institutions want to forecast the VaR not only over one day, but also over other horizons such as a week or a month. However, it would be tedious and time consuming (even for a computer) to calculate the many volatilities (not to mention correlations) required for these different horizons. Movements in weekly volatility do not move the same as movements in daily volatility. However, help is at hand. Once the bank has its forecasts of daily volatility, it can scale them up to give a forecast of weekly or monthly volatility, not by statisticians doing additional forecasting using the EWMA formula, but by using the *root-T rule* ($\sqrt{T}$ *rule*)[2]. The standard deviation over T days is:

$$\sigma_T = \sqrt{T}\sigma \qquad\qquad [15]$$

So given our EWMA forecast of tomorrow's daily standard deviation σ, we simply scale it up by $\sqrt{T}$, the number of trading days over which we want to calculate the VaR (e.g. if we want a forecast of the VaR over the next week we use $T = 5$ trading days). For example, if you have a forecast of daily portfolio volatility, $\sigma = 0.02$ (2% per day), then what would be your forecast for volatility over 25 (business) days, and what would be your estimate of VaR over the coming *month* (at a 5% cut-off) if you held a $100m portfolio? Over 25 business days (i.e. approximately one month), the standard deviation increases as the square root of T: $\sigma_{25} = \sqrt{25}\,\sigma = 5\,(0.02) = 0.10$ (10% over 25 days). The VaR estimate for the next 25 days would then be $16.5m ($= $100m $\times$ 1.65 $\times$ 0.10), hence over the *next 25 days* there is only a 5 in 100 chance that you will lose more than $16.5m.

---

[2] The root-T rule assumes that daily returns are independent and identically distributed.

What about forecasts of covariances? Surely these also change over time? They do, and forecasts for covariances use a similar EWMA scheme as for variances. The EWMA for the covariance is:

$$\sigma_{R_1R_2}(t + 1|t) = (1 - \lambda)R_{1t}R_{2t} + \lambda\sigma_{R_1R_2}(t|t - 1) \qquad [16]$$

A detailed discussion can be found in Cuthbertson and Nitzsche (2001b).

31.4 BACKTESTING

Forecasts of daily standard deviations and correlations and hence the daily VaR forecast will change from day to day (even if asset holdings remain unchanged). However, we need to assess whether our estimates of portfolio VaR are accurate. To do so, we can compare our (changing) daily forecast of portfolio $VaR_{t+1|t} = V_{0p}1.65\sigma_p$, with the historical out-turn for the *actual overnight* profit or loss (P/L) on the portfolio. This is done in Figure 31.6.

The rolling-forecast one-day-ahead VaR are the two symmetric solid lines and the actual P/L are the 'stars', assuming that positions in the various assets are unchanged. In other words, the actual P/L figures should reflect the profit/loss *that would have occurred* if the dollar position in each asset had been held for 24 hours (e.g. the market close-to-close positions) and then revalued. The actual P/L must not reflect any position changes due to intra-day trading. If our forecasts of volatilities (and correlations) are adequate, we should observe about 1 in 20 'stars' outside the upper and lower forecast VaR lines. If there are more than 5% of

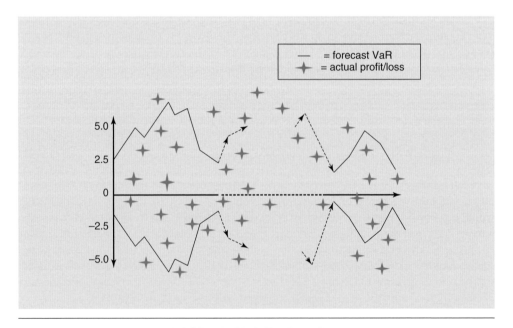

FIGURE 31.6: Backtesting

the stars outside either of these lines, our forecast values for σ and ρ underestimate the true portfolio risk. This testing procedure is known as *backtesting*. In the hypothetical example in Figure 31.6, the actual losses exceed the forecast $VaR_{t+1|t}$ about seven times (out of a total of 100 daily observations). Hence the VaR forecast slightly overstates the potential losses, at the 5th percentile. If the regulator found many more than 7 out of 100 'exceedences', it might require the bank to hold more capital because of the poor performance of its risk model and the chief risk (compliance) officer might also find herself in some trouble.

31.5 CAPITAL ADEQUACY

Financial firms (e.g. securities dealers, market makers, investment banks, pension funds) hold positions in marketable assets and are prone to losses. Prudential considerations imply that capital (i.e. broadly shareholders' funds and loan loss reserves accumulated from past retained profits) should be held as a cushion against potential losses, otherwise the financial institution may become insolvent.

The European Union, the Basle Committee (on Banking Supervision of the Bank for International Settlements, BIS) and the Federal Reserve Board ('the Fed') in the US have agreed what should be held against such risks by most financial institutions.

Basle approach

The Basle capital charge for market risk is based on the VaR of the portfolio: the higher is the forecast portfolio VaR, the higher is the amount of capital you have to hold. But how high? This is determined by specific rules, but with some discretion by the home regulator (e.g. the Financial Services Authority in the UK and often Central Banks in many other countries).

If your VaR model looks a bit 'suspect' (i.e. when backtesting reveals that the VaR model is not forecasting accurately), the home regulator may increase a bank's capital requirements – and you may lose your bonus if you were looking after the in-house risk model. Broadly speaking, the Basle rules stipulate a *minimum* capital charge based on the VaR over a 10-day horizon and measured at the 1% left-tail cut-off (rather than the 5% tail we have used above). The 10-day VaR is calculated using the root-T rule, so the VaR is $\sqrt{10} = 3.16$ times the daily volatility σ_p. Also, the 1% cut-off for the normal distribution is 2.33, so the Basle VaR $= V_0 \, 2.33 \, \sqrt{10} \, \sigma_p$. If the home regulator is not satisfied with the accuracy of the bank's internal risk model, based on backtesting, then it can increase the capital charge above this minimum level because it believes the bank is likely to be subject to greater risk.

31.6 STRESS TESTING

So far our VaR calculations whether using the variance–covariance or historical simulation approach have their difficulties – the former assumes normally distributed returns and the latter requires a long run of past data. Both methods assume in broad terms that an average of recent past data is a good guide to what might happen in the future. Because of these draw-backs, they are often supplemented by stress tests. Stress testing estimates the sensitivity of a portfolio to specific extreme movements in certain key returns. It therefore tells you how much you will lose in a particular state of the world, although it gives no indication of how likely it is that this state of the world will actually occur. The choice of extreme movements may be based on those that occurred in particular crisis periods (e.g. the 1987 stock-market crash, the 1992 crisis when sterling left the ERM, the 1997–98 Russian bond default and the Asian currency crisis). It follows that the implicit volatilities and correlations between asset returns are specific to the crisis periods chosen for the stress tests, but these are likely to be periods when correlations tend to increase dramatically. Alternatively, the financial institu-tion can simply revalue its existing portfolio using whatever returns it thinks 'reasonable and informative' to use. The danger here is that there are too many possible outcomes that bear little or no relation to actual historical events, or that reflect events that have never occurred and are also unlikely to occur. Therefore a lot of judgement is required when undertaking a 'reasonable' simulation.

Clearly, this type of stress testing is best done for relatively simple portfolios, since otherwise the implicit correlations for the chosen scenario may be widely at variance with those in the historical data or even for any conceivable future event. But another danger of stress testing is that a portfolio might actually benefit from extreme movements yet be vulnerable to small movements. For example, the V shape of a long straddle in options indicates large profits if the underlying price moves by a large amount in either direction, but loss of the option pre-mia if the underlying price moves by only a small amount, see Chapter 25.

In general, stress testing has several limitations and the same stress-testing scenario is unlike-ly to be informative for all institutions (portfolios). The choice of inputs for the stress test(s) will depend on the financial institution's assessment of the likely source of the key sensitiv-ities in its own portfolio. For example, a commodities dealer is unlikely to find a stress test of a rise in all interest rates of 300 bp informative, but would base stress tests on movements in spot and derivatives prices of major commodities. One can also usefully turn the scenario approach on its head and ask – given my portfolio, what set of *plausible* scenarios (for inter-est rates, exchange rates, etc.) will yield the worst outcome? Stress testing is therefore a use-ful complement to the usual VaR calculations, but both require considerable judgement in their practical implementation.

SUMMARY

- VaR is the *maximum* dollar amount you *expect* to lose over a specific horizon (e.g. 10 days) with a specific probability (e.g. 5%), assuming that you hold an unchanged portfolio of assets over the period.
- The (dollar) VaR for many assets is easily calculated using the *variance–covariance method*, while VaR calculated using the *historical simulation method* does not require the assumption of normally distributed asset returns.
- Forecasts of variances and covariances (correlations) of returns generally use the *EWMA method*. This is probably better than using a simple moving average.

- We can use the $\sqrt{T}$ *rule* for scaling up daily volatility forecasts in order to forecast VaR over longer horizons of up to one month.
- Banks and regulators check the accuracy of forecasts of VaR by *backtesting*.
- *Stress testing* is used as a complementary procedure to VaR to assess the vulnerability of specific portfolios to extreme movements in asset prices.

EXERCISES

Q1 (a) The mean daily return on AT&T stocks is $\mu = 0$. The standard deviation σ of the return on AT&T is 0.005 (0.5% per day). Daily stock returns are normally distributed. What is the maximum percentage loss you expect on AT&T stocks, 95% of the time (i.e. 19 out of every 20 days)?

  (b) You hold $V_0 = \$115m$ in the stock of AT&T. What is the daily dollar VaR of this position, at 5% probability, and what does this mean?

Q2 Why is the assumption that asset returns are normally distributed so useful when calculating VaR?

Q3 A US investor holds $10m of AT&T shares and has *short sold* $5m of IBM shares. Daily volatilities for AT&T $\sigma_1 = 1.5\%$, and for IBM $\sigma_2 = 1.0\%$, and the correlation between AT&T returns and IBM returns is -0.1. What is the dollar VaR for this portfolio? What is the worst-case VaR?

Q4 You have a portfolio consisting of £10,000 in each of three assets, 1, 2 and 3. You have calculated the daily standard deviations to be 5.0%, 3.0% and 3.6%. The correlation between returns on assets 1 and 2 is 0.962, between assets 1 and 3 is 0.403, and between assets 2 and 3 is 0.610.

  (a) What is the VaR for this portfolio?
  (b) What would be the worst-case VaR if returns on all assets were perfectly positively correlated?
  (c) What is the VaR if £10,000 of asset 2 is short sold?

  This is most easily done in Excel by setting up the formula $VaR_p = (\mathbf{Z}\,\mathbf{C}\,\mathbf{Z}')^{1/2}$.

Q5 Intuitively, why should we want to give more weight to recent movements in returns when forecasting tomorrow's volatility?

Q6 If you have a forecast of daily volatility, $\sigma = 0.01$ (1% per day), then what is your forecast for volatility (variance and/or standard deviation) over 25 (business) days? What assumptions are you making?

Q7 Briefly, what is backtesting in the VaR methodology?

Q8 The regulator for banks (e.g. the FSA in the UK) generally uses a 1% left-tail cut-off (or probability) value for VaR. What do you think the regulator would do if after inspecting your risk-management system in your investment bank, it was found that actual losses exceeded your forecast VaR losses, 10 times out of 175 forecasts?

Q9   Suppose that you have an inventory of 1000 barrels of crude oil that is priced in US dollars, but you are a UK company. The price volatility of your inventory is therefore expressed in sterling (since your operating costs are also in sterling).

The current spot price of oil is $S_{oil} = 70$ $/barrel and the current sterling–US dollar exchange rate is $1.7 per £ ($S_{FX} = 0.5882$ £s per $), the daily volatility of oil prices is 2.0% per day and the daily volatility of the exchange rate is 0.5% per day. Oil prices and the US dollar exchange rate are slightly negatively correlated, so when oil prices rise, one US dollar buys fewer pounds sterling, so that their correlation is -0.1

(a) Intuitively, what determines the VaR?
(b) How would you calculate the VaR in pounds sterling over 25 days (using the variance–covariance method)?
(c) What is the worst-case VaR? Briefly comment on both values for VaR.

Glossary

Abnormal return	The extra return over and above that which is compensation for the riskiness of the investment
Accrued interest	Interest earned on a bond since the last coupon payment
Active portfolio management	Investment strategies which aim to achieve abnormal returns
Adjusted present value	Alternative approach to NPV which takes account of the financial benefits of tax deductibles and certain corporate expenditures
Adverse selection	Economic principle which arises in insurance markets. It describes the problem of pricing insurance products when it is not possible to distinguish between different risk categories of applicants
Agency costs	Costs associated with monitoring contracts
Aggressive stock	Stock whose beta is greater than 1, which means that its return moves more than the market return
Allotment price	Price at which stock is allotted to a successful bidder in a tender offer
American option	Option which may be exercised at any time up to the expiry date
Anomaly	Returns which cannot be explained by known asset pricing models
Arbitrage	An investment strategy that enables a risk-free profit to be made, without using your own funds/capital. Usually involves trading in two (or more) securities
Arbitrage pricing model	Equilibrium asset pricing model which links an asset's return with its sensitivity to economic variables or factors
ARCH/GARCH model	Measures time varying conditional volatility using historical data
Arithmetic Average return	Measure of central tendency, defined as the sum of individual returns divided by the number of returns used
Asian option	Option whose payoff depends on the average price over the life of the option
Ask/Asked (offer) price	The price at which a market maker/dealer offers to sell a security
Asset	General term for anything with economic value
Asset allocation	Decision on how to split your wealth into different asset classes, for instance stocks, bonds and cash

Asymmetric information	Situation where one party has more information than the other party
At-the-money option	An option with a strike price (or the present value of the strike price) equal to the current market price of the underlying security
Auction (gilts)	Sale of new stock at which successful competitive bidders pay the price bid. Non-competitive bidders pay the weighted average price of successful competitive bids
Backwardation	A condition in which the forward/futures price is below the current spot price. Also referred to as selling at a discount. See **Contango**
Bank bill (acceptance credit)	Bank buys a bill of exchange from a corporate (at a discount) and the bank then guarantees future payment to any holder of the bill at maturity
Barbell portfolio	A bond portfolio in which the duration of the individual bonds varies widely
Barrier Option	An option whose final payoff at maturity depends on whether the underlying asset has crossed a predetermined value (the barrier).
Basis	The difference between the spot price of the underlying and the futures price
Basis point (bp)	1/100 of 1% (0.01 percent)
Basis risk	The risk to a hedger associated with variation in the basis over time
Bear market	Market in which prices are falling
Bear spread (with calls)	Describes the payoff profile of selling a call with a low strike price and buying a call with a higher strike price. Both calls will have the same maturity
Bearer bond	Bond for which ownership is determined by possession of the document rather than entry in a register; title is transferred by delivery of the bearer document
Benchmark portfolio	A portfolio which an existing investment is being compared against, with respect to its performance and riskiness
Best execution	Duty of a broker–dealer to provide the lowest available price (when buying stock) or the highest available price (when selling stock) for his customers
Beta	A measure of the responsiveness of a stock's return to changes in the market return – a measure of systematic (market) risk
Bid price	The price a market maker/dealer offers to buy a security
Bid–ask (offer) spread	Difference between the bid and ask (offer) price, see **Bid price, Ask (offer) price**
Bill of exchange	Like a post-dated cheque. The buyer of goods supplies a 'note' promising to pay at a future date. Can be sold in the secondary market for cash, prior to maturity. Used to finance overseas trade

Black–Scholes model	A model for pricing European options on stocks
Bond market	Market where long-term fixed income securities are traded
Bootstrapping	Statistical technique to extract a 'representative' sample from a given data set. The sample is generated by repeated re-sampling of the original observations
BOPM	Binomial option pricing model – in each short period of time only two outcomes for the asset price are possible
Broker	Agents who find best buying and selling prices and also provide IT services, stocks for short-sales and margin finance. Usually are large investment banks
Brownian motion	A specific stochastic process which describes the random path of a variable (e.g. stock price) over small intervals of time
Bubble	Rapid increase in share price which indicates an overvaluation of the company relative to its fundamentals
Bull market	Market in which prices are rising
Bull spread (with calls)	Describes the payoff profile from buying a call with a low strike price and selling a call which has the same maturity but with a high strike price
Bullet portfolio	Bond portfolio which contains bonds where the durations of the individual bonds are close together
Butterfly Spread	Payoff profile engineered by either buying and selling calls or buying and selling puts. This payoff profile will be V-shaped 'with wings'
Call option	A derivative security giving the holder the right (but not the obligation) to buy the underlying security on a specified (expiry) date (European) at a (strike) price agreed at the outset of the contract. An American option can be exercised on the expiry date or at any time before the expiry date
Call premium	Price of a call option
Callable bond	Bond which can be redeemed by the company that issues it, before its maturity date
Calling the mark	The process of calling for margin to be reinstated following a mark-to-market revaluation of a repo transaction
Candlesticks	Method of predicting asset prices based on high–low and open–close prices
Cap	Set of caplets
Capital asset pricing model (CAPM)	An equilibrium model which states that the expected excess return on a stock equals the stock's beta multiplied by the excess return on the market portfolio
Capital market line (CML)	The line which represents expected return and risk (standard deviation) combinations given by mixing risk-free borrowing and lending, with the market portfolio. See **Efficient frontier**

Caplet	Call option, which pays off if the interest rate at expiry exceeds the strike or cap (interest) rate. Caplets can be used for speculating on interest rate rises, or for hedging
Cash flow mapping	Process of converting actual cash flows at different maturities into standardised maturity dates in order to simplify the calculation of 'Value at Risk'
Cash flow matching	Passive bond portfolio strategy which aims to match the actual cash flows of the bond portfolio with the stream of liability payments
Cash settlement	A procedure applicable to certain futures and options contracts wherein a cash transfer is employed at contract settlement rather than the actual delivery of the asset underlying the derivatives contract
Cash-and-carry arbitrage	A (risk-free) arbitrage trading strategy that underlies the carrying charge model of futures prices
Certificate of deposit	A time deposit issued by banks and other financial institutions. It is a bearer denominated money market instrument which is quoted on a yield basis and can be sold in the secondary market
Chaos theory	Attempts to explain the random pattern observable in asset prices and returns by using deterministic non-linear models
Chartist	Technical analyst who bases her forecast of price movements on past price movements. Often implemented using charts or other plots of a price series over time
Cheapest to deliver (CTD)	Refers to the cheapest bond which can be delivered by the short in a T-bond futures contract. The exchange denotes a set of bonds which are eligible for delivery
Clean price	Quoted price of a bond which excludes accrued interest or rebate interest
Clearing house	A firm associated with an options or futures exchange, that guarantees contract performance and otherwise facilitates trading
Closed-end fund	Managed investment company which is listed on the stock exchange. The price of its shares is determined according to demand and supply as well as the underlying value of its assets
Closed-form solution	A mathematical solution of the form $y = f(x, z)$
Closing out	Selling an asset you already hold or buying an asset you have previously shorted (sold)
Closing price	Price of the last trade on a particular day for a specific security
Collar	Combination of a long cap and a long floor
Collateral	The value of any asset held against borrowed funds
Commercial paper	A legal document ('paper') listing the terms on which a loan has been given. Maturity 7-days to 2 years. Active secondary market.
Condor	Options trading strategy which involves buying and selling options with different strike prices
Consol	See **Perpetuity**

Contango	A condition in which the forward price is above either the current or expected future spot price. Also referred to as selling at a premium, see **Backwardation**
Contract	A binding agreement between two parties
Convenience yield	Implicit return from holding the spot commodity, which provides the holder with the ability to supply her regular customers
Conventional 'stocks'	Bonds on which interest payments and principal repayments are fixed. Also known as 'plain vanilla' bonds
Conversion factor	Used to adjust the value of a deliverable Treasury note or Treasury bond in a futures contract
Convertible bond	A bond which gives the holder the right but not the obligation to convert all or part of the bond holding into common stock on specified dates and on specified terms.
Convertible stock	Stock which gives the holder the right but not the obligation to convert all or part of her holding into another stock or stocks, on specified dates and on specified terms
Convexity	Measures the curvature of the price–yield relationship for bonds
Corporation	Form of ownership where the company is owned by its shareholders. In the case of bankruptcy the personal assets of the shareholders cannot be used to pay off any residual debts of the company
Correlation	A measure of the dependence of between two variables. The correlation coefficient lies between $+1$ and -1. Broadly speaking a correlation coefficient of say 0.7 implies that if variable-X increases on any 100 days then variable-Y will also increase on 70 of those days – on the remaining 30 days, there is no association between movements in the two variables
Cost of carry	The cost of holding a spot asset between two time periods – may involve a storage cost, interest cost net of any cash flows accruing to the spot asset and any convenience yield of the spot asset (commodity)
Counterparty	The trader/agent on the other side of a contract
Coupon	Interest paid on a bond, usually in two equal, semi-annual instalments. Sometimes expressed as a cash amount and sometimes as a percentage of the nominal (par) value of the bond – then it is called the coupon *rate*
Coupon stripping	Process which refers to selling the coupons from a bond to various counterparties. This creates a series of zero coupon bonds. The final payment of principal (maturity) on the bond may also be sold separately
Covariance	A measure of the dependence between two variables. A positive covariance implies two variables move in the same direction more than 50% of the time. The value of the covariance depends on the units used to measure the two variables

Covered interest rate parity	Relationship which describes a no arbitrage condition in the foreign exchange market. The interest differential in favour of country-A is equal to the forward discount of country-A's currency
Crack spread	Difference between the spot price of heating oil and the spot price of crude oil. Derivatives are written on the crack spread so that oil refiners can offset risk to their profit margins from changes in these two spot prices
Credit derivatives	A derivative where the payoff depends on a 'credit event' (e.g. credit rating downgrade/upgrade or default).
Credit risk	Describes the general risk that the counterparty will default and not honor the contract, see **Default risk**
Credit risk plus	Methodology proposed by Credit Suisse First Boston to measure credit risk
CreditMetrics™	Methodology proposed by J. P. Morgan to measure changes in credit risk
Cross-hedge	A futures hedge in which the asset underlying the futures contract differs from the asset being hedged
Cross-rate	An exchange rate between two currencies that is implied by their exchange rates with a third currency. For example, dollar-sterling and dollar-euro gives rise to the cross-rate sterling-euro
Cum-dividend	An asset purchased 'cum-dividend' gives the purchaser the right to the next interest (or dividend) payment (see **Ex-dividend**)
Currency swap	In a plain vanilla currency swap two parties agree to exchange two currencies at recurrent intervals based on agreed (fixed) interest rates in the two currencies and on an agreed notional principal amount. The principal amounts in the currency swap are also exchanged at the beginning and end of the swap
Daily price limits	Barriers which indicate the cessation of trading for that day, if those price limits are reached
Day count	Convention about the number of days used for calculating the price of money market instruments. The day count convention determines the use of number of days per month and number of days per year
Day trading	Buying and selling the same securities within the same day. Closing out the positions before the end of the trading day
Dealer	See **Market maker**
Debenture (secured loan stock/bond)	Entitles the holder to specific interest payments and capital repayments. 'Fixed charge' implies payments are backed by specific assets; 'floating charge' implies that future payments are not linked to specific assets of the firm. 'Unsecured loan stock' is debt which is low down the pecking order for receipts (including any available after liquidation)
Debt	Borrowed funds on which cash repayments are required in future periods. Debt holders can place a firm into liquidation

Debt Mangement Office	Runs the computer-based settlement system for UK government (gilt-edged) securities/T-bonds
Default risk	The risk that one counterparty will fail to honour its part or the remaining part of an agreed financial transaction
Defensive stock	Asset with a beta of less than 1. If the market falls the return on this stock would fall by less than the market return
Delivery day	Day when the underlying 'product' has to be delivered and the long position in the contract pays the short (initial seller of the contract) in cash
Delta hedge	To create a hedge (risk-free) position which takes into account the sensitivity of an option's premium to changes in the price of the underlying security on which the option is based
Delta neutral portfolio	A portfolio whose value is not affected by changes in the value of the underlying asset
Deposit insurance	Insured bank deposits. Insurance pays out if the bank goes into liquidation
Derivative security	An asset whose price is dependent, or contingent, upon the price of the underlying asset in the derivative contract
Dirty price	The price of a bond including accrued interest
Discount broker	Firm which offers a limited brokerage service at reduced prices compared to brokers who offer a full range of services
Discount rate (on Treasury bills)	The difference between the redemption (maturity/par) value and the purchase price of a T-bill, expressed as a percentage of the par value of the T-bill
Diversification	A process of adding assets to a portfolio, whose returns have a less than perfect positive correlation with each other – this helps reduce the overall risk (standard deviation) of portfolio returns
Dividend yield	The ratio of the dividend per share to the share price
Dividends	Cash payments made to shareholders of a firm. They can vary over time and are not guaranteed
Duration	A measure of the sensitivity of a bond's price to changes in market rates of interest. The percentage change in the bond price (approximately) equals the duration multiplied by the absolute change in the yield
Dynamic (delta) hedging	A strategy in which the risk of an option's position is offset by continuous trading in the underlying asset or appropriate futures contracts
Economic profit	Method of determining the profitability of a project, proposed by McKinsey. It is defined as the difference between the *return on capital* and the *weighted average cost of capital*, multiplied by the *capital used*
Economic value added (EVA)	Method of measuring and monitoring the performance of divisions within a firm and to compare economic performance across firms

Efficient frontier	Portfolios in which assets are combined so that the overall portfolio standard deviation (risk) is the smallest possible, given the required expected return on the portfolio
Efficient market	A market in which asset prices reflect the 'true', 'intrinsic' or 'fair value' of the asset. The fair value is often determining by calculating the discounted present value of the expected future cash flows accruing to the asset
Efficient set	See **Efficient frontier**
Embedded option	A option which is 'part of' a particular security. For example, a convertible bond has an option to convert the bond into stocks at possible future dates, at a pre-determined price. The possibility to alter/change the production process of a firm if circumstances change is an embedded option – used in real options theory
Equity	Ownership by shareholders in a company
Equity (value)	The share capital in a company = number of shares × current price. The shares themselves are also referred to as stock or equities
Equity market	Any market where shares of companies are traded
Equity premium puzzle	Empirically observed fact that the average return on equity is higher than that predicted by economic models of the risk premium on stocks
Error correction model	Specific type of econometric model which can be used for forecasting. This type of model allows one to distinguish between short run and long run effects
Eurobonds	Bonds sold outside the country of issue and denominated in a foreign currency (e.g. a UK firm issuing bonds denominated in US dollars in New York). Interest is usually paid before tax and they are usually bearer bonds
Eurodollar	A dollar-denominated deposit in a bank located outside the USA
Eurodollar market	Any market where Eurodollar deposits/loans are traded
'Euroland'	Countries in Europe who entered into monetary union by adopting a single currency, the euro
European option	Option which may only be exercised on the expiry date
Excess return	Return on an asset minus the return on the risk-free asset
Excess volatility	The view that asset prices move more than they should if they are determined solely by economic fundamentals
Exchange rate	The price of one currency relative to another currency
Exchange rate overshooting	Type of monetary model which predicts that (because of sticky goods prices, but fully flexible asset prices), the exchange rate overshoots its long run equilibrium value
Exchange rate risk	Uncertainty in the return on a foreign asset caused by fluctuations in the spot exchange rate
Ex-dividend (xd) date	The record date for the payment of coupons/cash flows. The next payment will be made to the person who is the registered holder of the stock on the 'xd date'

Ex-dividend date   Date on which a holder of stock/bond becomes entitled to receive the next cash payment (e.g. dividend/coupon), after which the asset trades 'ex-dividend'

Exercise price   The price at which an option holder may buy or sell the underlying asset, if the option is exercised

Exotic option   Generic term for options with relatively complex payoffs which can be path dependent. Examples of exotic options are Asian options, lookback, barrier and chooser options

Expectations theory   A theory of the term structure of interest rates in which forward rates of interest represent the market's unbiased expectation of future interest rates

Expiry date   Date when an option expires and the underlying asset has to be delivered (if the contract has not been closed out)

Exponential weighted moving average   Statistical method which calculates the variability of a data series, allowing the variability to change over time

Face value   See **Nominal (value)**

Filter rule   Method used by technical analysts to predict price movements based on past price movements in excess of a chosen percentage amount

Financial engineering   The process of designing new financial instruments, especially complex derivative securities. Often describes a combination of different derivative instruments (e.g. calls, puts, futures) to create certain payoff scenarios, see **Synthetic securities**

Financial futures contract   A futures contract written on a financial asset such as a bond, stock, stock index, interest rate or unit of foreign exchange

Financial instrument   An umbrella term used to refer to all types of securities

Flat yield   **= Interest yield = Running yield**. The annual coupon payment on a bond as a percentage of the market price of the bond

Floor   Set of floorlets

Floorlet   Put option whose payoff at expiry is either the difference between the floor (strike) interest rate and the actual interest rate at expiry or zero. Floorlets are used to hedge or speculate against falling interest rates

Foreign exchange market   Market where one currency is exchanged for another currency

Forward contract   An agreement between two parties to exchange 'items' in the future at a price agreed today. For example, a one-year forward contract for oil at a price of $80 per barrel agreed today or exchanging two currencies at a future date but at an exchange rate which is agreed today. Forward contracts usually go to delivery

Forward points   Difference between the forward and spot rate for FX

FRA (forward rate agreement)   The parties involved agree to pay the difference in cash flows between the rate of interest at some point in the future and the rate of interest agreed at the outset of the contract, based on an agreed notional principal amount

FRNs (floating rate notes)	An interest-bearing security with the facility to alter the coupons paid at specified futures dates, based on what interest rates turn out to be at these future dates
Future value	The value at some point in the future of an amount of money invested today
Futures contract	A contract between two parties to trade a specified asset in the future for a known price determined at contract inception. A key difference between a forward and a futures contract is that the latter can be 'reversed' or 'closed out'
Garman–Kohlhagen formula	Valuation formula for European style foreign currency options. Based on the Black–Scholes formula
Gilts, Gilt-edged securities	Sterling, marketable, interest-bearing bonds issued by the United Kingdom Government
Gordon growth model	Economic model to calculate the value of a firm's stock. It assumes that the value of the firm is determined by the level of current dividends, the future dividend growth rate and the discount rate
Greeks	Summary statistics to calculate (the approximate) change in the price of an option, as the variables which determine the option price change by a small amount (e.g. option's delta, gamma, theta, vega)
Haircut	The small commission a broker takes for organising a transaction for a client (e.g. to allow the client to borrow stock for short sales, or to undertake a repo transaction). Also, the difference between the value of collateral and the amount of cash loaned. It should be noted that 'haircut' has several different meanings
Hedge	A transaction in which a trader tries to protect an existing position by taking an offsetting position in another asset. For example, a portfolio of stocks can be hedged by shorting stock index futures contracts
Hedge fund	Actively managed funds which usually use highly leveraged transactions and derivatives in their investment strategies
Hedge ratio	The number of securities-A required to offset any change in the value of existing securities-B. Security-A is often a derivative and security-B the underlying asset in the derivative contract
Herding effect	Many investors following trends in market prices
Historic volatility	The magnitude of historic price fluctuations, often measured by the standard deviation of asset returns, see **Volatility**
Holding period return	The rate of return over a specific period of time – includes capital gains and any cash payments (over the holding period) from the security
Immunisation	Strategy which aims to protect the value of a bond portfolio from changes in yields
Implied volatility	The market's view of the volatility of an asset (e.g. a stock) that is reflected in the current option price. It is derived by solving for the volatility, which makes the market price equal to the theoretical price (e.g. as given by Black–Scholes).

Index linked bond (Treasury Inflation Protected Stock, TIPS)	Bonds on which the interest payments and principal repayment are adjusted to reflect the movements in the retail price index (subject to a lag)
Index tracking	A form of passive portfolio management aiming to replicate the movements of a selected index of securities
Initial margin	A 'good faith deposit' used to guarantee that the parties to a contract honor the terms of the contract. For example, when initially buying or selling a futures contract you must place an initial margin with the clearing house. The margin could be 'safe assets' such as cash or Treasury bills
Interbank market	An informal network of banks that lend and borrow from each other in various currencies, from overnight to one-year
Intercommodity spread	A long and short position in two different futures contracts (i.e. different underlying asset) but with the same delivery date
Inter-dealer broker (IDB)	Firm which obtains price quotes on a no-names basis
Interest rate caps	See **Cap**
Interest rate floor	See **Floor**
Interest rate futures	Futures contracts written on fixed-income securities such as Treasury bills, notes, and bonds. There are also futures written on interest rates
Interest rate parity	see **Covered interest rate parity, Uncovered interest rate parity**
Interest rate swap	Contract which swaps a series of floating rate (variable) interest payments into a series of fixed rate payments (or vice versa)
Interest yield	See **Flat yield**
Internal rate of return (IRR)	The constant rate of return which just allows a project/investment to break even. It is the single discount rate which equates the cost of the investment with the present value of the future cash flows from the investment
In-the-money	A call (put) option where the underlying asset price is greater (less) than (the discounted present value of) the option's strike price
Intracommodity spread	A long and short position in two futures contracts (on the same underlying asset) but with different delivery dates
Intrinsic value (of an option)	For a call (on a stock) this is either the difference between the current stock price and the strike price (when this difference is positive) or otherwise it is zero. For a put this is either the difference between the strike price and the current stock price (when this difference is positive) or otherwise it is zero. The intrinsic value represents the profit which could be earned if the option is exercised immediately. If the intrinsic value is positive the option is said to be **In-the-money**
Investment trust	See **Closed-end funds**
January effect	An empirical anomaly whereby stock returns seem to be higher in January than in other months of the year, even after taking

account of any risk of holding the stocks over the January month.
see **Small firm effect, Weekend effect**

Jensen's alpha — Measures the abnormal return on a stock after taking account of the market risk of the stock, see **Sharpe ratio, Treynor ratio**

Jump diffusion process — A random series for asset prices which experience sudden 'jumps'

Leverage — Increasing both the expected return on an investment strategy and range of possible outcomes. For example, leverage can be achieved by investing borrowed funds, as well as 'own funds' in stocks or by using derivative securities. In corporate finance leverage often applies to increasing the proportion of debt finance relative to equity finance for the firm. Leverage has many different meanings in finance

Limited company — See **Corporation**

Liquidity preference hypothesis — Bonds with long maturities require a higher yield than predicted by the expectations hypothesis and this extra yield (called the term premium) depends only on the term to maturity of the bond and the term premium does not vary over time

Local — A trader on the floor of an exchange who trades on her own account

London Interbank Offer Rate (LIBOR) — The interest rate at which one large highly rated bank will lend funds (in a particular currency) to another highly rated bank

Long position — If you purchase a primary or derivative security then you are said to 'go long'

Margin — Collateral that must be posted to transact in a futures or options contract, in order to insure the clearing house against default risk

Margin call — A request, following the mark-to-market of a position (e.g. in the futures market), for the initial margin to be reinstated

Market maker (Dealer) — A trader who quotes buy–sell prices at which she is willing to trade in specific stated amounts

Market portfolio — Portfolio which results from mean-variance optimisation

Market risk — Risk which cannot be diversified away. Proportion of the asset's total risk which relates to movements in the market return, see **systematic risk**

Market timing — Form of active portfolio management which shifts funds into (out of) the market when the market is predicted to rise (fall)

Mark-to-market — The act of revaluing securities to current market values

Maturity date — Date on which an asset is redeemed. For bonds this involves a cash payment (the principal or maturity value), for a derivative this might involve a cash payment or delivery of the underlying asset

Mean reversion — Process which describes the path of a time series which frequently returns to its long run average value

Mean-variance portfolio	Portfolio optimisation technique which only considers expected returns, variances and covariances of the individual assets
Merger	Agreement by two companies to join together and operate as one company
Mezzanine finance	Hybrid debt often with both debt and equity characteristics. High yield, high risk, often with equity warrants attached. Subordinated debt and junk bonds are counted as mezzanine finance
Mid price	Average of the bid and offer price of an asset
Monetary policy	The use of interest rates or changes in the growth rate of the money supply in order to influence inflation
Money market	The market for borrowing and lending funds with less than one year to maturity
Moral hazard	Economic concept often observed in insurance markets where the likelihood of a claim being made increases after the insurance has been taken out
Mutual fund (Open Ended Fund)	A fund management company that buy/sells a portfolio of shares as investors add/take-out cash from the fund
Naked position	A risky position in an asset
Net present value (NPV)	Present value of 'future positive cash flows less negative cash flows' (e.g. capital or investment costs), see **Adjusted present value**
Nominal (value)	**= Face value = Par value**. The fixed amount in a contract. For example, the final payment on a (plain vanilla) bond or the amount on which interest payments are calculated in an interest rate swap contract
Normal distribution	Bell-shaped, symmetric probability distribution for a continuous random variable. The distribution is fully determined by only two parameters, the population mean and the standard deviation of the underlying random variable
Off balance sheet items	Specific form of financing which is not shown on the liability side of the bank's balance sheet
Open interest	Total number of futures or option contracts (of a specific type) which have not been closed out (or reached expiry/maturity)
Option	Contract which gives the purchaser the right, but not the obligation, to buy (a 'call' option), or to sell (a 'put' option), a specified amount of a commodity or financial asset at a specified price, by or on a specified date
Option premium	The price paid for an option
Options Clearing Corporation (OCC)	The corporation that serves as the clearinghouse for all options traded on US markets except futures options
Ordinary shares	Ordinary shares represent a claim on the profits of a firm. Ordinary shareholders have voting rights and the shareholders are the owners of the firm

Out-of-the-money	A call (put) option where the underlying asset price is below (above) the option's strike price (or present value of the strike price)
Over-the-counter (OTC) instrument	Transaction between two counterparties (often two banks or a bank and a corporate), the details of which are directly negotiated between the issuer and purchaser
P–E ratio (price-earnings ratio)	A company's current share price divided by its earnings per share (measured over some recent historic period)
Par value	See **Nominal value**
Partnership	Form of ownership of a company or organisation where two or more people combine to conduct business
Passive portfolio management	See **Index tracking**
Performance measures	A 'statistic' to measure the performance of a portfolio relative to some benchmark portfolio. Differences in the risk of the different portfolios are usually taken into account
Perpetuity	Fixed-income security which is never redeemed by the issuer and pays coupons for ever
Peso problem	A situation where forecasts appear biased because the sample of data used is not representative of the complete data set. Initially applied to the forward rate of the Mexican peso in the 1970s
Pit	An area on the trading floor of a futures or options exchange where contracts are traded
Plain vanilla swap	A term which describes a basic fixed-for-floating interest rate swap or a simple currency swap
Political risk	Describes the uncertainty in the returns on assets due to policy changes by the government, which would not be in the interests of the investor
Portfolio	A 'basket' of different assets
Portfolio balance model	Model where the exchange rate is determined by the stock of foreign and domestic assets and not just by a single asset, the money supply
Portfolio insurance	A strategy in which a portfolio of stocks and futures contracts mimics the price movements of a portfolio of stocks and a put option. Portfolio insurance is designed to ensure a minimum future value for an equity portfolio
Position limit	The maximum amount held in a particular asset or set of assets. This limit might be set by the individual trader, a broker or the exchange itself (e.g. CBOE)
Position trader	Trader who holds speculative positions over horizons of 1 day to 1 month or even longer
Preference shares	Hybrid instrument which has some characteristics of ordinary shares and some characteristics of debt instruments, see **Ordinary shares**

Present value	Value today of future cash receipts/payments
Primary market	Market where new issues of securities are offered to the public
Principal–agent problem	Describes a conflict of interest which can arise between different agents in or connected with an organisation (e.g. shareholders and directors)
Program trading	The use of computers to assimilate real-time data in order to detect arbitrage opportunities
Project finance	Borrowing where future interest payments depend on the success of a specific project (e.g. hydro-electic plant) rather than on the overall profits of the borrowing firm
PSBR (public sector borrowing requirement) or Budget Deficit	Amount the (UK) government requires to borrow in a year to fund any shortfall of revenue against expenditure
Purchasing power parity	The proposition that prices of traded goods produced in different countries, sell for the same price in a common currency
Pure discount bond	See **Zero coupon bond**
Put	A derivative security giving the buyer the right to sell an underlying asset at a prescribed strike price on or before a specified maturity date
Put premium	Price of a put option
Put–call parity	A pricing relation between puts and calls that follows from arbitrage restrictions
Random walk	A model where the changes in a variable (e.g. stock price, exchange rate) are random and are drawn independently from a normal distribution. This means the (proportionate) *change* in the price is unpredictable and the best predictor of all future values for the *level* of prices is the current price level
Rational expectations	The idea that agents use all relevant information when forecasting a variable and hence do not make systematic forecasting errors
Real option	Term which describes the value of managerial flexibility in deciding what to do in future situations facing the firm. The value of this option should be incorporated in NPV calculations
Rebate interest	Interest due to be paid by the seller of a bond to a purchaser when the bond is purchased without the right to the forthcoming interest payment (i.e. ex-dividend)
Redemption yield	See **Yield to maturity**, YTM. Yield required to equate the purchase price of a bond with the present value of the remaining coupon payments and the maturity value. It is the IRR of the bond
Registration	Process by which ownership of an asset is entered on an official register
Replication portfolio	See **Synthetic securities**
Repo (repurchase agreement)	A form of collateralised borrowing. One party sells securities (e.g. T-bills) to another and at the same time commits to repurchase the securities on a specified future date, or at call, at a specified

	price, which is higher than the initial selling price. The difference between the two prices (expressed as a percentage) is the cost of borrowing in the repo. The securities in the transaction act as collateral
Repo rate	The return earned on a repo transaction expressed as an interest rate (% p.a.)
Retained earnings	Company's earnings which are not distributed to shareholders
Return on capital (ROC)	It is defined as *earnings after depreciation and taxes* divided by *capital used*
Reverse repo	A form of collateralised lending. A reverse repo is a repo transaction as seen from the point of view of the party which initially buys the securities and hence lends money
Rights issue	The sale of stock, often to existing shareholders, to obtain additional finance
Risk	Uncertainty associated with the price or return on assets, see **Systematic risk**, **Unsystematic risk**
Risk averse	A person who will only take part in a gamble in which the expected monetary outcome is positive. For example, if you are willing to pay less than $1 to enter a bet on the toss of a (fair) coin with a $1 payout for 'heads' and a $1 payout for 'tails' then you are risk averse
Risk free rate	The rate of return on an investment which is known with certainty
Risk management	Set of techniques for measuring and controlling risk
Risk neutral valuation	Describes the no arbitrage approach to option pricing where the option price today is a weighted average of the value of the option tomorrow. The weights represent risk neutral probabilities, which implies that price of the underlying asset (e.g. stock) may be assumed to grow at the risk-free rate
Risk neutrality	A situation in which an investor is indifferent between a risky monetary outcome and an equal amount that is certain. A risk neutral investor will take part in a gamble in which the expected monetary outcome is zero. For example, if you are willing to pay $1 to enter a bet on the toss of a (fair) coin with a $1 payout for 'heads' and a $1 payout for 'tails' then you are risk neutral
Risk premium	The additional return (over the risk-free rate) that risk averse investors require to willingly hold speculative assets
RiskGrade™	Methodology proposed by J. P. Morgan to measure the change in risk of a portfolio relative to a 'market' benchmark
RiskMetrics™	Methodology proposed by J. P. Morgan to measure market risk of cash market and derivative assets
Running yield	See **Flat yield**

Scalpers	Name for options or futures traders who buy at the bid and sell at the ask price, before market prices move. They only hold their position for a few minutes
Script issue	Denotes when new shares are given to existing shareholders
Secondary market	Market where securities are traded once they have been issued
Securities and Exchange Commission (SEC)	A Federal agency charged with the regulation of US security and options markets
Security market line	Describes the linear relationship between the expected return on different assets and the riskiness of those assets as measured by their market betas, see **(CAPM)**
Settlement date	The date on which the ownership of an instrument passes from one party to the other
Settlement price	The futures price established at the end of each trading day upon which daily marking-to-market of margin positions is based. The settlement price is usually an average of the last few trades of the day on a particular exchange
Sharpe ratio	= Reward to variability ratio. Risk adjusted measure of portfolio performance – it is the excess return divided by portfolio standard deviation
Short position	Sale of a stock. Often where a market maker (dealer) has sold more of a stock than she actually holds
Short sale (selling)	A transaction in which a security is borrowed (from a broker) and sold in the market, with an obligation to return the borrowed security at a later date. Collateral in the form of margin payments (to the borker) are required
Single index model (SIM)	Linear model which describes the relationship between the (excess) return on an individual stock (or portfolio of stocks) using only one 'variable' (or factor). Using time series data, it is used to estimate the sensitivity of the return to changes in the factor – the coefficient is known as the factor beta
Small firm effect	An empirical anomaly whereby the average stock return of small firms earns a higher return than predicted by its 'market beta'. See **January effect, Weekend effect**
Sole proprietor	Form of ownership where an individual is the owner of a firm and who has unlimited liabilities
Spark spread	Difference between the spot price of electricity and the spot price of natural gas which is used to produce electricity (the two are connected via the heat rate). Derivatives are written on the spark spread so that electricity generating companies can offset risk to their profit margins from changes in these two spot prices
Specific risk (unsystematic risk, diversifiable risk)	The risk of a security that is not attributable to general economic and market conditions. Risk which is specific to the firm, such as strikes, patent disputes, specific regulatory disputes, etc. Risk that can be diversified away

Speculation	Taking risky bets on the future value of an asset
Spot (cash) market	The market for assets that entail immediate (or near immediate) delivery
Spot (cash) price	The current price of an asset traded in the spot market (for immediate delivery)
Spread (yield spread)	Difference between two 'prices'. For example, the difference between a dealer's buying price and selling price for the same asset or the difference between the yields on corporate and government bonds (yield spread)
Spread trading	A trade involving two or more assets, usually involving derivatives, in order to speculate on the direction a spot asset will move (e.g. bull spread) or to benefit from a move in either direction in the underlying spot asset (e.g. straddle)
Static hedge	A strategy in which the value of a (spot) asset is maintained by using a derivatives trade which is held to (near) maturity
Stock index futures	Futures contracts that are written on stock indices (e.g. S&P 500 index). These futures contracts are cash-settled – there is no delivery of the underlying stocks in the index
Stock index option	An option giving the owner the right to buy or sell an entire stock index at the known strike price. These option contracts are cash-settled – there is no delivery of the underlying stocks in the index
Stock split	Refers to the process where the number of stocks held by existing shareholders increases but no additional funds are raised. It implies that the price of the stocks has to fall, since the intrinsic value of the company is unchanged
Straddle	Payoff profile of a call and put with the same strike price. 'V-shaped' or 'inverted V-shaped' payoff profile
Strangle	Option trading strategy which involves the combination of a call and a put with different strike prices. 'Flat bottom' or 'flat top' payoff profile
Strategic asset allocation	Investment strategy based on the long-term prospects for specific sectors or countries
Strike (exercise) price	Price at which the option holder has the right to buy or sell the underlying commodity or financial asset, if the holder chooses to exercise the option
Strips market	This is the secondary market which trades the individual coupons that have been 'stripped' (i.e. legally separated) from a coupon paying bond
Subordinated debt	Ranks behind other bondholder claims if the firm goes bankrupt
Swap dealer	Financial intermediary who provides swaps to counterparties (often corporates)
Swaps	A negotiated agreement between two parties to exchange cash flows at specified future dates according to an agreed schedule. In an interest rate swap the parties involved agree to pay the difference

in cash flows between the rate of interest at specified points in the future and the rate of interest agreed at the outset of the contract, based on an agreed notional principal amount. In an interest rate swap the principal amounts are not exchanged. An interest rate swap is a series of FRAs (See also **Currency swap**)

Swing option Energy option where the rate of consumption must be between a maximum and minimum level – usually with limits on the number of times the holder of the option can change the rate of consumption

Synthetic security 'Engineered' product which replicates the same cash flows as another asset, but uses different financial instruments (e.g. synthetic forward contract using money market assets)

Systematic risk (market risk, undiversifiable risk) The risk of a security that is attributable to changes in the economy in general, which affects all stocks to some degree. Systematic risk cannot be diversified away

Tactical asset allocation Switching funds between assets based on a 'short run' view about the future prospects for the price of these assets

Tail Difference between average price and lowest price accepted at an auction. Usually expressed in terms of the difference in yield

Term repo Repo trades (of maturity greater than 1 day) with a fixed maturity date

Term structure of interest rates The relation between the yield and the time to maturity of bonds of a similar risk class (e.g. all government bonds or all corporate bonds with a particular credit rating)

Tick Units in which minimum price movements are usually recorded and measured

Time value (of an option) The amount by which the option premium exceeds the intrinsic value

Transmission mechanism The process which describes the way the economy (e.g. level of output, inflation) is affected in the long and short run by changes in economic policy

Treasury bill Instrument of up to 12 months maturity, but normally less, issued by governments. It is a discount instrument – its initial selling price is below its maturity (or par or face) value

Treasury bond Debt security issued by a government with a term to maturity in excess of 12 months. Treasury bonds usually have periodic coupon payments payable every 6 months

Treasury note US expression for Treasury bonds with maturity of between 1 and 10 years. Type of Treasury bond

Treynor ratio Risk adjusted measure of portfolio performance. Abnormal return divided by the asset's beta. The abnormal return is measured by alpha and the risk is measured by the market beta

Uncovered interest (rate) parity A risky arbitrage relationship determined by the actions of risk neutral investors. Relationship between interest rates in different countries and the expected change in the exchange rate. Assumes the interest differential in favour of country-A equals the *expected* depreciation of country-A's spot exchange rate

Underlying (asset)	Specific asset on which a derivative contract is based (e.g. commodities, T-bond, equity, equity index)
Unit trusts (UK)	Term for an open-end investment fund in the UK
Unsecured loan stock	Debt which is low down the pecking order for cash receipts (including any funds available after liquidation). If 'convertible' then can be exchanged for equity capital (at a known fixed conversion rate) at the option of the holder
Unsystematic (undiversifiable) risk	See **Specific risk**
Value at risk (VaR)	Maximum expected 'dollar' loss over a specific time horizon at a prespecified probability level
Variance	A measure of the dispersion of a security's return about its expected return; it is the square of the standard deviation. Often taken as a measure of risk or volatility for a security or portfolio
Variation margin	Profits or losses which occur daily, due to marking-to-market of the portfolio
Vega (also known as lambda, kappa and sigma)	A measure of the sensitivity of the call/put premium to small changes in the standard deviation of the returns on the underlying asset (i.e. the volatility of the underlying returns)
Venture capital	Medium term funding provided by banks and wealthy individuals often to high growth technology firms (e.g. Biotechnology, IT and media) to finance the early stages of development. Often the loans are convertible into equity
Volatility	Measure of the variability in asset prices, see **Implied volatility, Historic volatility, variance**
Volatility smile	The relationship between the implied volatility of an option and 'other' variables (e.g. different strike prices, time to maturity)
Warehousing	Denotes the situation where a financial institution carries an open position on its books until a suitable long-term counterparty can be found
Warrant	Instrument which gives the holder the right (but not the obligation) to buy shares directly from the company at a fixed price, at some time(s) in the future. A type of call option
Weather derivative	Derivative where the payoff depends on the weather (e.g. temperature, inches of snowfall, number of frost days)
Weekend effect	Empirical anomaly which describes the fact that shares have lower returns on Mondays than on other days of the week, which is not explained by known risk factors, see **January effect, Small firm effect**
Weighted average cost of capital (WACC)	Overall cost of capital/financing when a mix of debt and equity finance is be used. Calculated on a before and after tax basis

Wiener process	See **Brownian motion**
Writer	The seller of an option contract. The writer of a call or put option has a short position and has to post margin payments with the clearing house
Yield curve	See **Term structure of interest rates**
Yield to maturity	The single interest rate required to equate the purchase price of a stock with the present value of the remaining coupon payments and maturity value. The YTM is the internal rate of return of the bond
Zero coupon bond	A bond which does not pay any coupons. It sells at a discount to its face (par/maturity) value

Internet Sites

Business Newspapers, Magazines and News Channels

Bloomberg	www.bloomberg.com
Business Week	www.businessweek.com
Dow Jones	www.dj.com
Euromoney	www.euromoney.com
Financial Times	www.ft.com
Forbes	www.forbes.com
Hedge Fund Review	www.hedgefundreview.com
Investors Chronicle	www.investorschronicle.co.uk
Reuters	www.reuters.com
The Economist	www.economist.com
Wall Street Journal	www.wsj.com

Global Investment Banks

Bank of America	www.bankofamerica.com
Barclays	www.barcap.com
Citigroup	www.citigroup.com
Deutsche Bank	www.db.com
Goldman Sachs	www2.goldmansachs.com
HSBC	www.hsbc.com
JP Morgan Chase	www.jpmorganchase.com
Lehman Brothers	www.lehman.com
Merrill Lynch	www.ml.com
Mitsubishi UFJ Financial Group	www.mufg.jp/english/
Societe Generale	www.socgen.com
UBS	www.ubs.com

Central Banks

Bank for International Settlements	www.bis.org
Bank of England	www.bankofengland.co.uk
Bank of Japan	www.boj.or.jp/en/
European Central Bank	www.ecb.int
Federal Reserve Board (USA)	www.federalreserve.gov
Federal Reserve Bank of Atlanta	www.frbatlanta.org
Federal Reserve Bank of Boston	www.bos.fed.org
Federal Reserve Bank of Chicago	www.chicagofed.org

Federal Reserve Bank of Cleveland	www.clevelandfed.org
Federal Reserve Bank of Dallas	www.dallasfed.org
Federal Reserve Bank of Kansas City	www.kansascityfed.org
Federal Reserve Bank of Minneapolis	www.minneapolisfed.org
Federal Reserve Bank of New York	www.ny.fed.org
Federal Reserve Bank of Philadelphia	www.philadelphiafed.org
Federal Reserve Bank of Richmond	www.richmondfed.org
Federal Reserve Bank of San Francisco	www.frbsf.org
Federal Reserve Bank of St. Louis	www.stlouisfed.org

Government Financial Institutions

Financial Services Authority	www.fsa.gov.uk
HM Treasury	www.hm-treasury.gov.uk
International Monetary Fund	www.imf.org
US Department of the Treasury	www.ustrea.gov
US Securities and Exchange Commission	www.sec.gov
World Bank	www.worldbank.org

Stock Exchanges

World Federation of Exchanges	www.world-exchanges.org
Gruppe Deutscher Boerse	www.deutsche-boerse.com
Hong Kong Stock Exchange	www.hkex.com.hk
London Stock Exchange	www.londonstockexchange.com
NASDAQ	www.nasdaq.com
NYSE Euronext	www.nyse.com
Shanghai Stock Exchange	www.sse.com.cn/sseportal/en_us/ps/ home.shtml
Tokyo Stock Exchange	www.tse.or.jp/english

Derivative Exchanges

Chicago Board of Trade	www.cbot.com
Chicago Board Options Exchange	www.cboe.com
Chicago Mercantile Exchange	www.cme.com
International Commodities Exchange	www.theice.com
Leipzig Power Exchange	www.lpx.de
London Metal Exchange	www.lme.co.uk
New York Mercantile Exchange	www.enymex.com
Philadelphia Stock Exchange	www.phlx.com

Mutual Funds and Hedge Funds

Fidelity UK	www.fidelity.co.uk
Fidelity US	www.fidelity.com
Investment Management Association	www.investmentuk.org
Morningstar	www.morningstar.com
Mutual Fund Website	www.ici.org/funds/inv/
Hedge Fund Association	www.thehfa.com
Hedge Fund Intelligence	www.hedgefundintelligence.com
Hedge Fund Research	www.hedgefundresearch.com

Credit Ratings Agencies and Risk Management

Fitch	www.fitchratings.com
Moody's	www.moodys.com
RiskGrade	www.riskgrade.com
RiskMetrics	www.riskmetrics.com
Standard & Poor's	www2.standardandpoors.com

Other Useful Websites

British Banker's Association	www.bba.org.uk
CFA Institute	www.cfainstitute.org
Dow Jones Index	www.djindexes.com
Finance Glossary	www.finance-glossary.com
Finance Glossary	www.investorwords.com
Google Finance	www.finance.google.com
KPMG	www.kpmg.co.uk
MSCI Barra	www.mscibarra.com
PriceWaterHouse Cooper	www.pwc.com
PRMIA Professional Risk Manager's International Association	www.prmia.org
Prof. Robert Shiller's website	www.econ.yale.edu/~shiller
Yahoo Finance	www.finance.yahoo.com

References

Ackermann, C., McEnally, R. and Ravenscraft, D. (1999) 'The Performance of Hedge Funds: Risk, Return, and Incentives', *Journal of Finance*, Vol. 54, pp. 833–874.

Agarwal, V. and Naik, N.Y. (2000) 'Multiperiod Performance Persistence Analysis and Hedge Funds Source', *Journal of Financial and Quantitative Analysis*, Vol. 35, pp. 327–342.

Agarwal, V. and Naik, N.Y. (2002) 'Multi-period Performance Persistence Analysis of Hedge Funds', *Journal of Financial and Quantitative Analysis*, Vol. 35, pp. 327–342.

Agarwal, V., Daniel, N.D. and Naik, N.Y. (2006) 'Why is Santa so Kind to Hedge Funds? The December Return Puzzle', SSRN Discussion Paper.

Ali, A., Hwang L-S. and Trombley, M.A. (2003) 'Arbitrage Risk and the Book-to-Market Anomaly' *Journal of Financial Economics,* Vol. 69, pp. 355–373.

Allen, D. and Tan, M. (1999) 'A Test of the Persistence in the Performance of UK Managed Funds', *Journal of Business Finance and Accounting*, Vol. 26, No. 5, pp. 559–593.

Allen, H.L. and Taylor, M.P. (1989) 'Chart Analysis and the Foreign Exchange Market', Bank of England Quarterly Bulletin, Vol. 29, No. 4, pp. 548–551.

Allen, H.L. and Taylor, M.P. (1990) 'Charts, Noise and Fundamentals in the Foreign Exchange Market', *Economic Journal*, Vol. 100, No. 400, pp. 49–59.

Almazan, A., Brown, K.C. Carlson, M. and Chapman, D.A. (2004) 'Why Constrain Your Mutual Fund Manager', *Journal of Financial Economics*, Vol. 73, pp. 289–321.

Ang, A. and Bekaert, G. (2001) 'Stock Return Predictability – Is it There?' Working Paper, Columbia University, New York.

Ardeni, P.G. and Lubian, D. (1991) 'Is There Trend Reversion in Purchasing Power Parity', *European Economic Review*, Vol. 35, No. 5, pp. 1035–1055.

Baks, K.P. (2002) 'On the Performance of Mutual Fund Managers', Working Paper, Emory University.

Barber, B. and Odean, T. (2001) 'Trading is Hazardous to your Wealth: The Common Stock Performance of Individual Investors', *Journal of Finance*, Vol. 55, pp. 773–806.

Barber, B.M., Odean, T. and Zheng, L. (2004) 'Out of Sight, Out of Mind: The Effects of expenses on Mutual Fund Flows', *Journal of Business*, Vol. 78, pp. 2095–2120.

Barberis, N. and Shleifer, A. (2003) 'Style investing'. *Journal of Financial Economics*, Vol. 68, pp. 161–199.

Barberis, N. and Thaler, R.H. (2003) 'A Survey of Behavioural Finance', in *Handbook of the Economics of Finance*, edited by G.M. Constantinidis, M. Harris and R. Stulz, Elsevier Science B.V.

Barberis, N., Ming, H. and Tano, S. (2001) 'Prospect Theory and Asset Prices', *Quarterly Journal of Economics*, Vol. 116, pp. 1–53.

Barclays Capital (1999) *Equity Gilt Study*, London, Barclays Capital.

Barras, L., Scaillet, O. and Wermers, R. (2005) False Discoveries in Mutual Fund Performance: Measuring Luck in Estimated Alphas, FAME Research Paper No.163, University of Geneva.

Benartzi, S. (2001) 'Excessive Extrapolation and the Allocation of 401(k) Accounts to Company Stock', *Journal of Finance*, Vol. 56, No. 5, pp. 1747–1764.

Benartzi, S. and Thaler, R.H. (2001) 'Myopic Loss Aversion and the Equity Premium Puzzle', *Quarterly Journal of Economics*, Vol. CX, No. 1, pp. 73–92.

Bernard, V.L. and Thomas, J. (1989) 'Post-Earnings Announcement Drift: Delayed Price Response or Risk Premium?' *Journal of Accounting Research,* Vol. 27, pp. 1–48.

Bernard, V.L. and Thomas, J. (1990) 'Evidence that Stock Prices do not Fully Reflect the Implications of Current Earnings for Future Earnings', *Journal of Accounting and Economics,* Vol. 13, pp. 305–340.

Bilson, J.F.O. (1981) 'The "Speculative Efficiency" Hypothesis', *Journal of Business*, Vol. 54, pp. 435–451.

Black, F. and Litterman, R. (1992) 'Global Portfolio Optimisation', *Financial Analyst Journal*, Sept./Oct., Vol. 48, No. 5, pp. 28–43.

Black, F. and Scholes, M. (1973) 'The Pricing of Options and Corporate Liabilities', *Journal of Political Economy*, Vol. 81, May/June, pp. 637–659.

Blake, C.A., Elton, E.J. and Gruber, M.J. (1993) 'The Performance of Bond Mutual Funds', *Journal of Business*, Vol. 66, pp. 371–403.

Blake, D. and Timmermann, A. (1998) 'Mutual Fund Performance: Evidence from the UK', *European Finance Review*, Vol. 2, pp. 57–77.

Bodurtha, J., Kim, D. and Lee, C.M. (1993) 'Closed-End Country Funds and US Market Sentiment', *Review of Financial Studies*, Vol. 8, pp. 879–918.

Bollen, N.P.B., and Busse, J.A. (2004) 'Short-Term Persistence in Mutual Fund Performance', *Review of Financial Studies,* Vol. 18, No. 2, pp. 569–597.

Boudoukh, J., Richardson, M. Subrahmanyam, M. and Whitelaw, R.F. (2002) 'State Prices and Strategies for Trading Mutual Funds', *Financial Analyst Journal*, July/August, pp. 53–71.

Bremer, M.A. and Sweeney, R.J. (1991) 'The Reversal of Large Stock Price Decreases', *Journal of Finance*, Vol. 46, No. 2, pp. 747–754.

Britten-Jones, M. (1999) 'The Sampling Error in Estimates of Mean-Variance Efficient Portfolio Weights', *Journal of Finance*, Vol. 52, No. 2, pp. 637–659.

Brock, W., Lakonishak, J. and LeBaron, B. (1992) 'Simple Technical Trading Rules and the Stochastic Properties of Stock Returns', *Journal of Finance*, Vol. 47, No. 5, pp. 1731–1764.

Brown, S.J. and Goetzmann, W.N. (1995) 'Performance Persistence', *Journal of Finance*, Vol. 50, pp. 679–698.

Brown, S.J., Goetzmann, W.N. and Ibbotson, R.G. (1999) 'Offshore Hedge Funds: Survival and Performance 1989–1995', *Journal of Business*, Vol. 72, No. 1, pp. 91–118.

Brown, S.J., Goetzmann, W.N. and Park, J. (2001) 'Careers and Survival Competition and Risk in the Hedge Fund and CTA Industry' *Journal of Finance*, Vol. 56, pp. 1869–1886.

Campbell, J.Y. (2001) 'Forecasting US Equity Returns in the 21st Century', Harvard University, Cambridge, MA, mineo.

Campbell, J.Y. and Shiller, R.J. (1988) 'Stock Prices, Earnings, and Expected Dividends', *Journal of Finance*, Vol. 43, No. 3, pp. 661–676.

Cao and Lerner (2007) 'The Success of Reverse-Leverage Buy-Outs', Harvard Business School Working Paper.

Capocci, D. and Hubner, G. (2004) 'Analysis of Hedge Fund Performance', *Journal of Empirical Finance*, Vol. 11, pp. 55–89.

Carhart, M. (1997) 'On Persistence in Mutual Fund Performance', *Journal of Finance*, Vol. 52, No. 1, pp. 57–82.

Cavaglia, S. and Cuthbertson, K. (1995) 'Industrial Action', *Risk Magazine*, Vol. 8, No. 5, May, pp. 2–4.

Cavaglia, S., Melas, D. and Miyashita, O. (1994) 'Efficiency Across Frontiers', *Risk Magazine*, Vol. 7, No. 10, pp. 56–61.

Chen, H.L, Jegadeesh, N. and Wermers, R. (2000) 'The Value of Active Mutual Fund Management: An Examination of the Stockholdings and Trades of Fund Managers', *Journal of Financial and Quantitative Analysis*, Vol. 35, pp. 343–368.

Cheung, Y.W. and Chinn, M.D. (2001), 'Currency Traders and Exchange Rate Dynamics: A Survey of the US Market', *Journal of International Money and Finance*, Vol. 20, No. 4, pp. 439–471.

Chevalier, J., and Ellison, G. (1999) 'Are Some Mutual Fund Managers Better than Others? Cross-Sectional Patterns in Behavior and Performance', *Journal of Finance*, Vol. 54, pp. 875–899.

Chopra, N., Lakenishok, J. and Ritter, J. (1992) 'Measuring Abnormal Performance: Do Stocks Overreact?' *Journal of Financial Economics*, Vol. 31, pp. 235–268.

Christopherson, J.A., Ferson, W.E. and Glassman, D.A. (1998) 'Conditioning Manager Alphas on Economic Information: Another Look at the Persistence of Performance', *Review of Financial Studies*, Vol. 11, pp. 111–142.

Cochrane, J.H. (2001) 'Asset Pricing'. *Princeton University Press,* Princeton, NJ.

Curcio, R, Goodhart, C.A.E., Guillaume, D. and Payne, R. (1996) 'Do Filter Rules Generate Profits? Conclusions from the Intra-Day Foreign Exchange Market', *FMG Discussion Paper, London School of Economics*.

Cuthbertson, K. and Nitzsche, D. (2001a) *Investments: Spot and Derivatives Markets*, Chicester, 1st edition.

Cuthbertson, K. and Nitzsche, D. (2001b) *Financial Engineering: Derivatives and Risk Management*, John Wiley & Sons, Ltd, Chicester.

Cuthbertson, K. and Nitzsche, D. (2004) *Quantitative Financial Economics*, John Wiley & Sons, Ltd, Chicester, 2nd edition.

Cuthbertson, K., Nitzsche, D. and O'Sullivan, N. (2005) 'Live Now, Pay Later or Pay Now and Live Later', Evidence to the Turner Commission on UK Pension Reform, Pensions Commission, London.

Cuthbertson, K., Nitzsche, D. and O'Sullivan, N. (2008) 'UK Mutual Fund Performance: Skill or Luck', *Journal of Empirical Finance*, forthcoming.

Daniel, K.M., Grinblatt, M., Titman, S. and Wermers, R. (1997) Measuring Mutual Fund Performance With Characteristic Based Benchmarks, *Journal of Finance*, Vol. 52, pp. 1035–1058.

DeBondt, W.F.M. and Thaler, R.H. (1985) 'Does the Stock Market Overreact?', *Journal of Finance*, Vol. 40, No. 3, pp. 793–805.

DeBondt, W.F.M. and Thaler, R.H. (1987) 'Further Evidence on Investors Overreaction and Stock Market Seasonally' *Journal of Finance*, Vol. 42, No. 3, pp. 557–581.

Del Guercio, D. and Tkac, P. (2001) 'Star Power: The Effect of Morningstar Ratings on Mutual Fund Flows', Working Paper, University of Oregon.

DeLong, B.J., Shleifer, A., Summers, L.H. and Waldmann R.J. (1990) 'Positive Feedback Investment Strategies and Destabilizing Rational Speculation', *Journal of Finance*, Vol. 45, No. 2, pp. 379–395.

Dimson, E., Marsh, P. and Staunton, M. (2001) *Triumph of the Optimists*, Princeton University Press, Princeton, N.J.

Dooley, M.P. and Shafer, J.R. (1983) 'Analysis of Short-run Exchange Rate Behavior: March 1973 to November 1981' in *Exchange Rate and Trade Instability: Causes, Consequences and Remedies*, edited by T. Bigman and T. Taya, Harper Business, pp. 43–69.

Dornbusch, R. (1976) 'Expectations and Exchange Rate Dynamic', *Journal of Political Economy*, Vol. 84, No. 6, pp. 1161–1176.

Elton, E.J., Gruber, M.J. and Blake, C.R. (1996) 'The Persistence of Risk Adjusted Mutual Fund Performance', *Journal of Business*, Vol. 69, No.2, pp. 133–157.

Engel, C. and Hamilton, J.D. (1990) 'Long Swings in the Dollar: Are They in the Data and Do Markets Know it', *American Economic Review*, Vol. 80, No. 1, pp. 689–713.

Eun, C.S. and Resnick, B.G. (1997) 'International Equity Investment With Selective Hedging Strategies', *Journal of International Financial Markets, Institutions and Money*, Vol. 7, No. 1, pp. 21–42.

Fama, E.F. and French, K. (1988) 'Dividend Yields and Expected Stock Returns', *Journal of Financial Economics*, Vol. 22, pp. 3–25.

Fama, E.F. and French, K.R. (1996) 'Multifactor Explanations of Asset Pricing Anomalies', *Journal of Finance*, Vol. 47, pp. 426–465.

Fisher, E.O. and Park, J.Y. (1991) 'Testing Purchasing Power Parity Under the Null Hypothesis of Cointegration', *Economic Journal*, Vol. 101, No. 409, pp. 1476–1484.

Fletcher, J. (1997) 'An Examination of UK Unit Trust Performance within the Arbitrage Pricing Framework', *Review of Quantitative Finance and Accounting*, Vol. 8, pp. 91–107.

Fletcher, J. (1999) 'The Evaluation of the Performance of UK American Unit Trusts', *International Review of Economics and Finance*, Vol. 8, No. 4, pp. 455–466.

Fletcher, J. and Forbes, D. (2002) 'An Exploration of the Persistence of UK Unit Trusts Performance', *Journal of Empirical Finance,* Vol. 9, pp. 475–493.

Froot and Dabora (1999) 'How are Stock Prices Affected by the Location of Trade?', *Journal of Financial Economics*, Vol. 53, pp. 189–216.

Frost, P. and Savarino, J. (1988) 'For Better Performance Constrain Portfolio Weights', *Journal of Portfolio Management*, Vol. 14 (Fall), pp. 29–34.

Fung, W. and Hsieh, D.A. (1997) 'Empirical Characteristics of Dynamic Trading Strategies: The case of Hedge Funds', *Review of Financial Studies*, Vol. 10, pp. 275–302.

Fung, W. and Hsieh, D.A. (2004) 'Extracting Portable Alphas From Equity Long-Short Hedge Funds', *Journal of Investment Management*, Vol. 2, No. 4, pp. 1–19.

Fung, W., Hsieh, D.A., Naik, N.Y. and Ramadorai, T. (2006) 'Hedge Funds: Performance, Risk and Capital Formation', Working Paper, Duke University, Durham, N.C.

Genesove, D. and Mayer, C. (2001) 'Loss Aversion and Seller Behavior: Evidence from the Housing Market', *Quarterly Journal of Economics*, Vol. 116, pp. 1233–1260.

Getmansky, M., Lo, A.W. and Makarov, I. (2004) 'An Econometric Model of Serial Correlation and Illiquidity in Hedge Fund Returns', *Journal of Financial Economics*, Vol. 74, pp. 529–609.

Goetzmann, W.N. and Ibbotson, R.G. (1994) 'Do Winners Repeat? Patterns in Mutual Fund Performance', *Journal of Portfolio Management*, Vol. 20, pp. 9–17.

Goodhart, C. and Curcio, R. (1992) 'When Support/Resistance Levels are Broken, Can Profits be Made? Evidence from the Foreign Exchange Market', *Discussion Paper 142.* London School of Economics, Financial Markets Group.

Goodman, S.H. (1979) 'Foreign Exchange Rate Forecasting Techniques: Implications for Business and Policy', *Journal of Finance*, Vol. 34, No. 2, pp. 415–427.

Goodman, S.H. (1980) 'Who's Better than the Toss of a Coin?', *Euromoney*, September, pp. 80–84.

Goyal, A. and Welch, I. (1999) 'The Myth of Predictability: Does the Dividend Yield Forecast the Equity Premium?' UCLA, Working Paper, CA.

Granger, C.W.J and Terasvirta, T. (1993) *Modelling Non-Linear Economic Relationships*, Oxford University Press, Oxford.

Grilli, V. and Kaminsky, G. (1991) 'Nominal Exchange Rate Regimes and the Real Exchange Rate: Evidence from the United States and Great Britain, 1885–1986', *Journal of Monetary Economics*, Vol. 27, No. 2, pp. 191–212.

Grinblatt, M. and Keloharju, M. (2001) 'How Distance, Language, and Culture Influence Stockholdings and Trades', *Journal of Finance*, Vol. 56, pp. 1053–1073.

Grinblatt, M. and Titman, S. (1992) 'The Persistence of Mutual Fund Performance', *Journal of Finance*, Vol. 47, No. 5, pp. 1977–1984.

Gruber, M.J. (1996) 'Another Puzzle: The Growth in Actively Managed Mutual Funds', *Journal of Finance*, Vol. 51, pp. 783–810.

Harvey, C. and Siddique, A. (2000) 'Conditional Skewness in Asset Pricing Tests', *Journal of Finance*, Vol. 55, pp. 1263–1295.

Hendricks, D., Patel, J. and Zeckhauser, R. (1993) 'Hot Hands in Mutual Funds: Short Run Persistence of Performance, 1974–88', *Journal of Finance*, Vol. 48, pp. 93–130.

Hendry, D.F. (1995) *Dynamic Econometrics*, Oxford University Press, Oxford.

Huberman, G. (2001) 'Familiarity Breeds Investments', *Review of Financial Studies*, Vol. 14, pp. 659–680.

Huij, J. and Derwall, J. (2006) '"Hot Hands" in Bond Fund or Persistence in Bond Performance', Working Paper, Erasmus University, February.

Ibbotson Associates (2001) *Stocks, Bonds, Bills and Inflation Yearbook*, Chicago, Ibbotson Associates.

Ibbotson, R.G. and Chen, P. (2005) 'Sources of Hedge Fund Returns: Alphas, Betas and Costs', Yale ICF Working Paper 05-17, Yale University, New Haven, CN.

Ikenberry, D., Lakonishok, J. and Vermaelen, T. (1995) 'Market Underreaction to Open Market Share Repurchases', *Journal of Financial Economics*, Vol. 48, pp. 181–208.

Investment Company Institute (2006) 'Mutual Funds Factbook, Washington DC.

J.P. Morgan (1996) *RiskMetrics, Technical Document*, J.P. Morgan.

Jacqier, C.E., Kane, A. and Marcus, A.J. (2003) 'Geometric or Arithmetic Means: A Reconsideration', *Financial Analysts Journal*, Vol. 59, No. 6, Nov/Dec., 46–53.

Jagannathan, R., Malakhov, A. and Novikov, D. (2006) 'Do Hot Hands Persist Among Hedge Fund Managers ? An Empirical Evaluation', NBER Working Paper No. W12015, National Bureau of Economic Research, Cambridge, MA.

Jain, P. and Wu, J. (2000) 'Truth in Mutual Fund Advertising: Evidence on Future Performance and Fund Flows', *Journal of Finance*, Vol. 55, pp. 937–958.

Jegadeesh, N. and Titman, S. (1993) Returns to Buying Winners and Selling Losers: Implications for Stock Market Efficiency, *Journal of Finance*, Vol. 48, pp. 56–91.

Jegadeesh, N. and Titman, S. (2001) Profitability of Momentum Strategies: Evaluation of Alternative Explanations, *Journal of Finance*, Vol. 56, pp. 699–720.

Jensen, M.C. (1986) 'Agency Costs of Free Cash Flow, Corporate Finance, and Takeovers', *American Economic Review*, Vol. 76, No. 2, pp. 323–332.

Jobson, J.D. and Korkie, B. (1980) 'Estimation for Markowitz Efficient Portfolios', *Journal of American Statistical Association*, September, Vol. 75, pp. 544–554.

Jobson, J.D. and Korkie, B. (1981) 'Putting Markowitz Theory to Work', *Journal of Portfolio Management*, Vol. 7 (Summer), pp. 70–74.

Jorion, P. (2003) 'The Long-term Risks of Global Stock Markets', Graduate School of Management, University of California at Irvine, mimeo.

Jorion, P. and Goetzmann, N.M. (1999) Global Stock Markets in the 20th Century', *Journal of Finance*, Vol. 54, pp. 953–980.

Kaplan and Schoar (2003) 'Private Equity Performance', *NBER WP 9807*, June.

Kat, H. (2003) 'One Hundred and One Things Investors Should Know About Hedge Funds', Working Paper, Cass Business School, London.

Kat, H. and Palaro, H. (2006) 'Hedge Funds; You can Make them Yourself', Working Paper, Cass Business School, London.

Keen, S.M. (1983) Stock Market Efficiency: Theory, Evidence and Implications, Philip Alan, Oxford.

Keim, D.B. and Stambaugh, R.F. (1986) 'Predicting Returns in the Stock and Bond Markets', *Journal of Financial Economics*, Vol. 17, pp. 357–390.

Kellogg, D. and Chames, J.M. (2000) 'Real-Options Valuation for a Biotechnology Company', *Financial Analysts Journal*, Vol. 56, No. 3, pp. 76–84.

Keswani, A. and Stolin, D. (2008) 'Which Money is Smart? Mutual Fund Buys and Sells of Individual and Institutional Investors', *Journal of Finance*, Vol. 63, No. 1 pp. 85–118.

Kosowski, R., Timmermann, A., White, H. and Wermers, R. (2006) 'Can Mutual Fund "Stars" Really Pick Stocks? New Evidence from a Bootstrap Analysis', *Journal of Finance*, LXI, No. 6, pp. 2551–2295.

Lakonishok, J., Shleifer, A. and Vishny, R.W. (1994) 'Contrarian Investment, Extrapolation and Risk', *Journal of Finance*, Vol. 49, No. 5, pp. 1541–1578.

LaPortá, Lakonishok, J., Shleifer, A. and Vishny, R. '(1997) 'Good News for Value Stocks: Further Evidence on Market Efficiency', *Journal of Finance*, Vol. 52, No. 2, pp. 859–874.

Lee, C.M.C., Shleifer, A. and Thaler, R.H. (1990) 'Closed-End Mutual Funds', *Journal of Economic Perspectives*, Vol. 4, No. 4, pp. 153–164.

Lee, C.M.C., Shleifer, A. and Thaler, R.H. (1991) 'Investor Sentiment and the Closed-end Fund Puzzle', *Journal of Finance*, Vol. 46, No. 1, pp. 75–110.

Leger, L. (1997) 'UK Investment Trusts: Performance, Timing and Selectivity', *Applied Economics Letters*, Vol. 4, pp. 207–210.

Lesmond, D.A., Schill, M.J. and Zhou, C. (2004) 'The Illusory Nature of Momentum Profits', *Journal of Financial Economics*, Vol. 71, No. 2, pp. 349–380.

Levich, R.M. (1980) 'Analysing the Accuracy of Foreign Exchange Advisory Services: Theory and Evidence', Chapter 5 in *Exchange Risk and Exposure*, edited by Levich and Wihlborg, Lexington Books.

Levich, R.M. and Thomas, L.R. (1993) 'The Significance of Technical Trading Rule Profits in the Foreign Exchange Market: A Bootstrap Approach', *Journal of International Money and Finance*, Vol. 12, pp. 451–474.

Liang, B. (2000) 'Hedge Funds: The Living and the Dead', *Journal of Financial and Quantitative Analysis*, Vol. 35, pp. 309–326.

Ljungqvist and Richardson (2003) 'The Cash Flow, Return and Risk Characteristics of Private Equity', *NBER WP 9454*, January.

Lo, A. (2001) 'Risk Management for Hedge Fund: Introduction and Overview', *Financial Analyst Journal*, Vol. 57, No. 6, Nov./Dec., pp. 16–33.

Loughran, T. and Ritter, J.R. (1995) 'The New Issues Puzzle', *Journal of Finance*, Vol. 50, pp. 23–51.

Lunde, A., Timmermann, A. and Blake, D. (1999) 'The Hazards of Mutual Fund Underperformance: A Cox Regression Analysis', *Journal of Empirical Finance*, Vol. 6, pp. 121–152.

Lynch, A. and Musto, D. (2003) 'How Investors Interpret Past Fund Returns', *Journal of Finance*, Vol. 58, pp. 2033–2058.

Mahoney, P.G. (2004) 'Manager-Investor Conflicts in Mutual Funds', *Journal of Economic Perspectives*, Vol. 18, pp. 161–182.

Malkiel, B.G. (1977) 'The Valuation of Closed-End Investment-Company Shares', *Journal of Finance*, Vol. 32, No. 3, pp. 847–859.

Malkiel, B.G. (1995) 'Returns from Investing in Equity Mutual Funds 1971 to 1991', *Journal of Finance*, Vol. 50, No. 2, pp. 847–859.

Malkiel, B.G. and Saha, A. (2005) 'Hedge Funds: Risk and Return', *Financial Analyst Journal*, Vol. 61, pp. 80–88.

Mamaysky, H., Spiegel, M. and Zhang, H. (2004) 'Improved Forecasting of Mutual Fund Alphas and Betas', ICF Working Paper 04-23, Yale School of Management.

Michaely, R., Thaler, R.H. and Womack, K.L. (1995) 'Price Reactions to Dividend Initiations and Omissions: Overreaction or Draft?', *Journal of Finance*, Vol. 50, pp. 573–608.

Myers and Majluf (1984) 'Corporate Financing and Investment Decisions When Firms Have Information that Investors Do Not Have', *Journal of Financial Economics*, Vol. 13, No. 2, pp. 187–221.

Naik, N.Y., Kosowski, R. and Teo, M. (2007) 'Do Hedge Funds Deliver Alpha? A Baysian and Bootstrap Analysis', *Journal of Financial Economics*, Vol. 84, No. 1, pp. 229–264.

Neely, C.J. and Weller, P.A. (2003) 'Intraday Technical Trading in the Foreign Exchange Market', *Journal of International Money and Finance*, Vol. 22, pp. 223–237.

Neely, C.J., Weller, P.A. and Dittmar, R. (1997) 'Is Technical Analysis in the Foreign Exchange Market Profitable? A Genetic Programming Approach', *Journal of Financial and Quantitative Analysis*, Vol. 32, pp. 405–426.

Odean, T. (1999) 'Do Investors Trade Too Much?', *American Economic Review*, Vol. 89, pp. 1279–1298.

Osler, C. (2000) 'Support for Resistence: Technical Analysis and Intraday Exchange Rates', *Economic Policy Review (Federal Reserve Bank of New York)*, Vol. 6, No. 2, pp. 53–68.

Pesaran, M.H. and Timmermann, A. (1994) 'Forecasting Stock Returns: An Examination of Stock Market Trading in the Presence of Transaction Costs', *Journal of Forecasting*, Vol. 13, No. 4, pp. 335–367.

Pesaran, M.H. and Timmermann, A. (1995) 'Predictability of Stock Returns: Robustness and Economic Significance', *Journal of Finance*, Vol. 50, No. 4, pp. 1201–1228.

Pesaran, M.H. and Timmermann, A. (2000) 'A Recursive Modelling Approach to Predicting UK Stock Returns' *Economic Journal*, Vol. 110, No. 460, pp. 159–191.

Poterba, J.M. and Summers, L.H. (1988) 'Mean Reversion in Stock Prices: Evidence and Implications', *Journal of Financial Economics*, Vol. 22, pp. 26–59.

Quigley, G. and Sinquefield, R. (1999) 'The Performance of UK Equity Unit Trusts', Report by Dimensional Fund Advisors for Institute for Fiduciary Education.

Quigley, G. and Sinquefield, R.A. (2000) Performance of UK Equity Unit Trusts, *Journal of Asset Management*, Vol. 1, pp. 72–92.

Reinganum, M.R. (1982) 'A Direct Test of Roll's Conjecture on the Firm Size Effect', *Journal of Finance*, Vol. 37, No. 1, pp. 27–35.

Reinganum, M.R. (1983) 'The Anomalous Stock Market Behavior of Small Firms in January: Empirical Tests for Tax-Loss Selling Effects', *Journal of Financial Economics*, Vol. 12, No. 1, pp. 89–104.

Richards, A. (1995) 'Co-movements in Natural Stock Markets Returns: Evidence of Predictability but not Cointegration', *Journal of Monetary Economics*, Vol. 36, pp. 637–654.

Richards, A. (1997) 'Winner-Loser Reversals in National Stock Market Indices: Can They Be Explained?', *Journal of Finance*, Vol. 51, pp. 2129–2144.

Roll, R. (1977) 'A Critique of Asset Pricing Theory's Tests', *Journal of Financial Economics*, Vol. 4, pp. 1073–1103.

Ross, S.A. (1976) 'The Arbitrage Theory of Capital Asset Pricing', *Journal of Economic Theory*, Vol. 13, December, pp. 341–360.

Ross, S.A. and Roll, R. (1995) 'On the Cross-Sectional Relation Between Expected Returns and Betas', *Journal of Finance*, Vol. 50, pp. 185–224.

Schwartz, E.S. and Moon, M. (2000) 'Rational Pricing of Internet Companies', *Financial Analysts Journal*, Vol. 56, No. 3, May/June, pp. 62–75.

Shiller, R. (2006) *Irrational Exuberance*, Princeton University Press, Princeton, N.J., 2nd edition.

Shiller, R.J. (1989) *Market Volatility*, MIT Press, Cambridge, MA.

Shleifer, A. and Summers, L.H. (1990) 'The Noise Trader Approach to Finance', *Journal of Economic Perspectives*, Vol. 4, No. 2, pp. 19–33.

Simons, K. (1999) 'Should U.S. Investors Invest Overseas?', *New England Economic Review*, Nov./Dec., pp. 29–39.

Sirri, E.R. and Tufano, P. (1993) 'Buying and Selling Mutual Funds: Flows, Performance, Fees and Services', *Harvard Business School Working Paper*.

Sirri, E.R. and Tufano, P. (1998) 'Costly Search and Mutual Fund Flows', *Journal of Finance*, Vol. 53, pp. 1589–1622.

Skinner, D. and Sloan, R. (2002) 'Earnings Surprises, Growth Expectations and Stock Returns, or, Don't let an Earnings Torpedo Sink Your Portfolio', *Review of Accounting Studies*, Vol. 7, pp. 289–312.

Solnik, B. (1974) 'Why Not Diversify Internationally?', *Financial Analysts Journal*, Vol. 30, August, pp. 48–54.

Stamburgh, R.F. (1999) 'Predictive Regressions', *Journal of Financial Economics*, Vol. 54, pp. 375–421.

Stulz, R.M. (2007) 'Hedge Funds: Past, Present and Future', Dice Center WP 2007–3, Fisher College of Business, Ohio State University, February.

Sullivan, R., Timmermann, A. and White, H. (2001) 'Dangers of Data Mining: The Case of Calendar Effects in Stock Returns', *Journal of Econometrics*, Vol. 105, No. 1, pp. 249–286.

Taylor, M.P. (1987) 'Covered Interest Parity: A High-Frequency, High Quality Data Survey', *Economica*, Vol. 54, pp. 429–438.

Taylor, M.P. (1989) 'Covered Interest Arbitrage and Market Turbulence', *Economic Journal*, Vol. 99, No. 396, pp. 376–391.

Tremont Asset Flows Report 2nd Quarter, Tremont Capital Management Inc., London.

Trippi, R.R. and Turban, E. (1993) *Neural Networks in Finance and Investing*, Irwin Buor Ridge, IL.

Turner, A. (2006) 'Implementing an Integrated Package of Pension Reforms: The Final Report of the Pensions Commission', The Stationary Office, London.

Volkman, D. and Wohar, M. (1995) 'Determinants of Persistence in Relative Performance of Mutual Funds', *Journal of Financial Research*, Vol. 18, pp. 415–430.

Welch I. (2000) 'Views of Financial Economists on the Equity Risk Premium and Other Issues' *Journal of Business*, Vol. 73, pp. 501–537.

Welch I. (2001) 'The Equity Premium Consensus Forecast Revisited', Working Paper, Yale School of Management.

Wermers, R. (2004), 'Is Money Really "Smart"? New Evidence on the Relation Between Mutual Fund Flows and Performance Persistence', Department of Finance, University of Maryland.

Wilcox, R.T. (2003) 'Bargain Hunting or Star Gazing? Investors' preferences for stock Mutual Funds', *Journal of Business*, Vol. 76, No. 4, pp. 645–663.

WM Company (1999) 'Comparision of Active and Passive Management of Unit Trusts for Virgin Direct Financial Services.

Womack, K.L. (1996), 'Do Brokerage Analysts' Recommendations Have Investment Value?', *Journal of Finance*, Vol. 51, No. 1, pp. 137–167.

Index